JOHN MUIR
HIS LIFE AND LETTERS
AND OTHER WRITINGS

JOHN MUIR
HIS LIFE AND LETTERS
AND OTHER WRITINGS

edited and introduced by Terry Gifford

The Life and Letters of John Muir
Letters Written During a Trip to Scotland
Studies in the Sierra
Essays from ' Picturesque California '
The Proposed Yosemite National Park
Alaska Days with John Muir   Stickeen
Notes on the Pacific Coast Glaciers
The Cruise of the Corwin
Edward Henry Harriman
John Muir as Others Saw Him

BÂTON WICKS · LONDON
THE MOUNTAINEERS · SEATTLE

also in this series
all published under the Diadem imprint:

H.W.TILMAN
THE SEVEN MOUNTAIN-TRAVEL BOOKS

ERIC SHIPTON
THE SIX MOUNTAIN-TRAVEL BOOKS

H.W.TILMAN
THE EIGHT SAILING/MOUNTAIN EXPLORATION BOOKS

ONE STEP IN THE CLOUDS
AN OMNIBUS OF MOUNTAINEERING
NOVELS AND SHORT STORIES

JOHN MUIR
THE EIGHT WILDERNESS-DISCOVERY BOOKS

Published simultaneously in 1996 in Great Britain and the United States by Bâton Wicks Publications, London and The Mountaineers, Seattle.

Introduction © 1996 by Terry Gifford.
The Life and Letters of John Muir © 1924
The Houghton Mifflin Company, Boston,
New York and Chicago.
Letters Written During a Trip to Scotland
and *California Agriculture* © Muir-Hanna Trust,
Holt-Atherton Special Collections, University
of the Pacific Libraries, Stockton, California.
John Muir – Mountaineer © 1993 Sir Edward Peck.
Photographic copyrights and permissions as credited.

All trade enquiries in Great Britain, Europe and the Commonwealth (except Canada) to Bâton Wicks Publications, c/o Cordee, 3a De Montfort Street, Leicester LE1 7HD.

All trade enquiries in the U.S.A. and Canada to The Mountaineers, 1001 SW Klickitat Way, Suite 201, Seattle, WA 98134

British Library Cataloguing in Publication Data
A catalogue record of this books is available at the British Library
ISBN 1-898573-07-7 (U.K.)

United States Library of Congress Catalog Data
A catalogue record for this book is available at the Library of Congress
ISBN 0-89886-463-1 (North America)

CONTENTS

ACKNOWLEDGEMENTS: Terry Gifford suggested this omnibus volume, wrote the introduction, contributed photographs and advised on other editorial matters. Research in the United States was carried out by Mary Metz of The Mountaineers. In addition the following photographers, experts, archivists and libraries are thanked for their help, advice and contributions: Daryl Morrison on behalf of the Muir-Hanna Trust / Holt-Atherton collections / University of the Pacific, Ronald H.Limbaugh, Jill and Larry Giacomino, Patsy Pitts, The National Library of Scotland, Bretton Hall College of Leeds University, Steve and Helen Walker, Brian Suderman of the National Park Service / Alaska, Colin Eastwood of the John Muir Trust, Marge Heath of The Elmer E. Rasmuson Library / University of Alaska Fairbanks, Jeff Reynolds, Alison Reynolds, Tom Prentice, John Beatty, Tom Chatterley, Jim Wickwire, J.H.Czok, W.L.Huber, W.E.Dassonville, Richard Hale, Steve Roper and Sir Edward Peck.

INTRODUCTION

by Terry Gifford

IN JANUARY 1868 the thirty-year old John Muir arrived in Cuba. Here he hoped to recuperate from a fever contracted in Florida before securing onward passage to South America. But no ship was available. Thus it was in the streets of Havana that he made the decision to travel instead to San Francisco and from there trek to the Sierra Nevada range of California. Three months later Muir entered Yosemite Valley for the first time and was captivated. "This Yosemite trip made me hungry for another, far longer, and farther reaching, and I determined to set out again as soon as I had earned a little money, to get near views of the mountains in all their snowy grandeur, and study the wonderful forests, the noblest of their kind I had ever seen."*

Muir's decision to head for the American west was to prove the turning point of his life. He was to explore and study the Sierra Nevada for the next ten years. Here was a magnificent and varied range of mountains with finely sculpted granite peaks and valleys, cloaked with monumental conifer forests and blessed with a constantly changing and invigorating climate.

Muir was quick to recognise the allure of this fabulous mountain range. He was fascinated by the flora and, particularly in the Yosemite, Tuolomne, Hetch Hetchy and Kings Canyon regions, by its dramatic manifestations of geology and glaciological sculpting. With his acute and enquiring sense of observation, he was soon at work writing about his discoveries – initially long anecdotal letters describing his mountain adventures to his friends in the cities, then newspaper articles, scientific papers and finally books. He proved to have a marvellous capacity to convey his wonderment for Nature's works in writing, and his enthusiasm inspired others. Not only did he write, he also spoke, one might say preached. His vivid and charismatic descriptions of what he discovered held his listeners spellbound.

Muir had been an enthusiatic reader of the books of the pioneer Alpine climbers and glaciologists, and he, too, used his verbal and literary skills to inspire others about the fine mountain range on their own doorstep. He was also deeply influenced by the philosophical interpretation of the value of mountains and natural landscapes exemplified in the writings of Thoreau, Emerson and Ruskin. But his communication skills were soon required for more practical political purposes, as Muir and his friends began to realise the threat to the mountains from sectional interests, and the great efforts that would be needed to maintain their wildness and splendour.

* A brief account of these events is in *A Thousand Mile Walk to the Gulf*, Chapter 8.

Muir's books, mainly written in later life or compiled posthumously, are collected in an earlier omnibus.* In this new volume we have concentrated mainly on Muir's letters and essays. *The Life and Letters of John Muir*, which forms its cornerstone, is the first biography of John Muir. It takes the form of selected letters, fragments of Muir's unfinished autobiography and a linking commentary by William Frederic Badè. In this fascinating collection we can see that Muir was in his element as a correspondent to his friends.

What do these eloquent letters tell us about Muir? Much as he complained in later life about the effort of writing of books, he clearly loved to correspond – especially to women – and through his writing he developed a network of sympathetic, often influential, disciples who eventually formed the Sierra Club to protect the interests of wild places. In Britain, The National Trust, and the recently established John Muir Trust are similar organisations. Both bodies acquire land, the latter concentrating on Scotland. (In this respect readers will be interested in the addendum of six letters from Muir's European trip of 1893, during which he returned to Scotland.)

Studies in the Sierra

This essay series forms the second major section of the book. First published in 1874, it is still regarded as one of the most vivid commentaries on the effects of glaciation ever written. It is the *Studies*, perhaps more than any other of his early publications, that made Muir famous. They were the result of an intense period of field work and observation. In them he made a major challenge to the theories of California's professional geologists (geology being an important matter in a state riven by major tectonic faulting). As a precocious amateur geologist he stormed their academic Bastille and won. The *Studies* also have a general relevance to all mountain lovers in looking afresh at their own ranges. In a very populist sense they enrich our knowledge of how mountains are shaped. Muir suggests that the glacial process is akin to a tree of life as he tries to illustrate in words and diagrams his vision of the continuous ebb and flow of the destruction and creation in Nature.

Our addendum to the *Studies* comprises the first three articles Muir ever published (in the *New York Tribune*), together with the historically important [and hitherto unpublished] essay 'California Agriculture', which was prepared for publication in 1890 but apparently rejected. In it Muir describes how irrigation from the rivers draining the Sierra transformed the arid Central Valley of California, bringing prosperity and plenty. It reveals Muir as a practical man, as much concerned with cultivation as with conservation.

Picturesque California

Muir's belief that tourism could be educative, and that public education would lead to the political impulse towards preservation, led to his editing *Picturesque California*, which, in terms of readability, was not altogether

* *John Muir – The Eight Wilderness-Discovery Books* (Diadem/The Mountaineers, 1992)

successful. This was an large illustrated publication but the pictures broke up the text (Muir's chapters being particularly long) to such an extent that it is very difficult to read, although the work of the best artists of the day doubtless did its job in focusing interest on the western wildernesses.

Three of Muir's six essays in the book, those dealing with the Sierra Nevada, are republished to form the third section of this omnibus. The other three appear in *Steep Trails* broken up into ten chapters. Indeed many of Muir's articles and pamphlets were later reshaped for use in his books, but in some cases it is interesting to see them in their original form which was usually crafted for public persuasion or political action. Accordingly, the addendum to the *Picturesque California* selection features the campaigning essays published by *Century* magazine in 1890: *Treasures and Features of the Proposed Yosemite National Park.* These were nicely timed to bring to a head a campaign of lobbying Congress. Two weeks after their publication, President Benjamin Harrison signed a bill to create the first National Park for the protection of wilderness. Thus, though sections of these essays were later recycled in *The Mountains of California,* it was in this form that they had their political impact.

Later Years

Muir was slow to turn to writing books. He completed *The Mountains of California* at the age of fifty-five. His second book appeared nine years later. In the last stressful decade of his life, as he was losing the fight to save the Hetch Hetchy valley from flooding, he completed the manuscripts for four books. So Muir's books are essentially an older man's writing, drawing heavily from the diaries he wrote when he was a young man. By contrast, the vitality of his letters written to friends while in the process of the exciting expeditions of youth, and the elegance of his articles produced under pressure to satisfy newspapers and magazines, provide us with a fresher and more immediate image of Muir. It is significant that his first three published articles were actually compiled from letters to his friends.

It was through his letters and essays that Muir sought to influence people to value the rights of Nature in an age eager to exploit natural resources. Muir was fortunate to be addressing a young and idealistic society. If land had to be made useful to serve the American dream, the extraction of timber and minerals were not the only uses of wilderness. Recreation was a use too, and essential to a pioneering nation. Muir argued that if Yosemite was to be preserved for tourism, its whole wilderness watershed should also be included. This was the reasoning behind the *Treasures and Features* essays.

Alaska Travels

Muir died before he was able to finish the manuscript of *Travels in Alaska,* but he had written about Alaska in earlier essays and books which we have

* Chaps. 3 to 5 and 17 to 23. *Steep Trails* is in *John Muir – The Eight Wilderness-Discovery Books.*

brought together here to complete the Alaska *œuvre*. The report from the 1899 Harriman expedition, *Notes on the Pacific Coast Glaciers*, still manages to convey the "gloriously wild and sublime," just as the entertaining narrative *Stickeen* shows a depth of respect for "all my fellow mortals." *The Cruise of the Corwin* was put together by Badè from letters Muir wrote for the *San Francisco Evening Bulletin*. It combines the tension of a search and rescue expedition with the excitement of exploring a remote and little-known arctic region. Muir's memoir, *Edward Henry Harriman*, may surprise some readers – a conservationist commemorating a railroad magnate? But Muir's faith that the wildernesses being made accessible, would speak to travellers of the need for their preservation, overwhelmed any scepticism he might have had. He did comment about Harriman's wealth – "He has not as much money as I have. I have all I want and Mr Harriman has not" – but Muir's generosity of spirit towards a patron of science gives an insight into his own moral stature. Of course, the best revelation of Muir's character comes from those who shared some epic adventures. Samuel Hall Young's lively account in *Alaska Days with John Muir* is compelling reading for those who always wondered how the solitary sage would respond to a companion in a crisis. When both Young's shoulders were dislocated in a fall, he remembers that Muir's rescue attempt was accompanied by his whistling "The Bluebells of Scotland"! This collection of Alaska material shows how much Muir loved sheer adventure, how much he could not resist going a little further, giving himself a physical (and, of course, scientific) challenge, risking that bit more to explore the frontier he had just missed in California.

How Others Saw Him

Through the recollections of those who knew Muir we can gauge his personal impact on others. After his death his friends in the Sierra Club attempted to convey the nature of his charismatic character in brief memoirs published in several issues of their *Bulletin*. Collected together here as the final section of this book, these memoirs express a deep sense of what Muir stood for. Clearly his contemporaries had no doubts about his stature as a prophet and that reputation persists in the U.S. to this day. In Europe we are only slowly learning the importance of the writings of this great man.

Muir may have been lucky to find such an appealing and dramatically varied landscape in which to develop his ideas, but his lessons are not restricted in their application to the Sierra alone. They have world-wide relevance because *wilderness* really refers to *wildness* in all its forms. "Wildness is a necessity" was the kernel of his message. It could be argued that many areas no longer have any true wildernesses, but through our parks, gardens, and open spaces, preferably uncomplicated by the restrictions of urban living, we show that we understand that the aura of "wildness is a necessity" and its world-wide protection is nothing less than our looking after our home, the planet itself.

THE LIFE AND LETTERS
OF JOHN MUIR

The Life and Letters of John Muir

by William Frederic Badè

First published in two volumes by the Houghton Mifflin Company
(Boston, New York, Chicago, 1924)

PREFACE

TWENTY YEARS after the first companies of forty-niners arrived in California, a unique type of Argonaut landed in San Francisco, crossed the Coast Range and the San Joaquin plain, and, passing through the gold-diggings, went up the Merced until he reached Yosemite valley. Not the gold of California's placers and mines, but the plant gold and beauty of her still unwasted mountains and plains, were the lure that drew and held John Muir. Forty-six years later, in the closing days of fateful 1914, this widely travelled explorer and observer of the world we dwell in faced the greatest of all adventures, dying as bravely and cheerfully as he had lived.

Not only from his large circle of devoted personal friends, but from among the thousands who had been thrilled by his eloquent pen, arose insistent demands for a fuller presentation of the facts of his life than is available in his incomplete autobiography, *The Story of My Boyhood and Youth*, and in his other published works. When the present writer, at the request of Mr. Muir's daughters undertook to edit some of his unpublished journals and to prepare his life and letters, he had no adequate conception of the size and complexity of the task. The amount of the manuscript material to be examined made it vastly more time-consuming than was at first anticipated.

Throughout his life John Muir carried on a prolific and wide-ranging correspondence. His own letters were written by hand, and, with the exception of an occasional preliminary draft, he rarely kept copies. In calendaring the many thousands of letters received from his friends, a systematic effort was made to secure from them and their descendants the originals or copies of Muir's letters for the purposes of this work. The success of this effort was in part thwarted, in part impeded, by the Great War. To the many who responded, the writer expresses his grateful acknowledgments. The Carr series, with some exceptions like the Sequoia letter, was obtained from Mr. George Wharton James, to whose keeping the correspondence had been committed by Mrs. Carr. The preponderance of letters addressed to women correspondents is partly explained by the fact that Muir's men-friends did not preserve his letters as generally as the women. It should be added, also, that several valuable series were lost in the San Francisco earthquake and fire of 1906.

At the time of his death Muir had in preparation a second volume of his autobiography. Though very incomplete, it was found so important that it seemed best to incorporate it in the present work, whose form of presentation and selection of materials had to be accommodated somewhat to make this possible. It is chiefly in the letters, however, that the reader will find revealed the charm of Muir's personality and the spontaneity of his nature enthusiasms.

In conclusion, the writer desires to acknowledge special obligations to William E. Colby for frequent suggestions and assistance in verifying facts, to Elizabeth Gray Potter for working out a valuable and convenient system of arrangement and indexing for the collection of Muiriana, and to his wife, Elizabeth LeBreton Badè, for much practical help and advice.

WILLIAM FREDERIC BADÈ
Berkeley, California
September 23rd, 1923

CONTENTS

MEASURING·A·BIG·TREE·
MARIPOSA·GROVE·

CHAPTER ONE

The Ancestral Background

DELVING one day among miscellaneous papers that had been brought to me from the silent and deserted home of John Muir in the Alhambra Valley, near Martinez, California, I found a sketch of his life which led me to hope that a difficult part of my biographical task had been made easy. Just then my eye caught the laconic comment, "A strange, bold mixture of Muirs!" pencilled across the manuscript in his own familiar flowing hand. Apparently the sketch had been sent to Muir by the admiring author, who, finding himself in need of an ancestry worthy of his subject, had made short shrift of facts to get one. Taking a survey of Muirs available in biographical reference works, he selected as father for John Muir a distinguished Scotch Sanscritist of the same name, gave him as an uncle an equally eminent Scotch Arabist, and for good measure added, as a younger brother, a well-known Scotch chemist. Given the conviction that genius must spring from genius, the would-be biographer had done his best to provide his hero with an adequate pedigree.

But while John Muir's origin was humbler than this invention, the mixture of elements need abate nothing either in strangeness or in boldness. Although unfortunately it is not possible to trace back far the tangled thread of his descent, one feels instinctively that marked ancestral traits and faculties must have gone into the making of a personality so unusual and so fascinating. His name he appears to have taken from his paternal grandfather, a Scotchman by the name of John Muir. Beyond the latter our knowledge of this line of Muirs ceases, and it may be doubted whether a search of Scotch parish records, even, would reveal more than another bare name.

Of this ancestral John Muir we know only that he was a soldier by profession; that he married an English woman by the name of Sarah Higgs; that she bore him two children – Mary and Daniel; that his wife died when the second child was only nine months old; and that he followed her to the grave three months later. The orphaning of Mary and Daniel Muir at so tender an age may account for the fact that the American family tradition of the Muirs has little to report about John Muir, the soldier, and his wife Sarah Higgs Muir, except the tragedy of their untimely deaths. All knowledge of their birthplaces and parentage, tastes, accomplishments, and dispositions is lost in oblivion.

Our detailed knowledge of the family really begins with Daniel Muir, the younger of the two orphans and the only male link in the Muir pedigree at this point. He it was who in due time became the father of John Muir, the naturalist, and to the latter's brief sketch of his father's life, written as an obituary notice, we owe practically all our extant information about the early life of Daniel Muir. The latter was born in Manchester, England, in 1804. His sister Mary Muir was his senior by about eleven years, and when their parents had died she "became a mother to him and brought him up on a farm that belonged to a relative in Lanarkshire, Scotland." From an aged daughter of Mary Muir, Grace Blakley Brown, the writer ascertained the fact that the above-mentioned farm was situated at Crawfordjohn, about thirty-five miles south-east of Glasgow. If it is true, as alleged, that it was one of his mother's people to whom the farm belonged, we are probably not far wrong in supposing that John Muir, the elder, also came from this region, and met Sarah Higgs in Crawfordjohn.

How much importance one may attach to ante-natal influences exerted upon one's forbears by the physical characteristics of a country is a debatable question. "Some of my grandfathers," John Muir once wrote in playful mood to a friend, "must have been born on a muirland, for there is heather in me, and tinctures of bog juices, that send me to Cassiope, and, oozing through all my veins, impel me unhaltingly through endless glacier meadows, seemingly the deeper and danker the better." Did he have in mind some family tradition of a Scotch Highland ancestry? We do not know; but if any of his ancestors came from the country of Lanark there is aptness in the hyperbole. The parish of Crawford consists chiefly of mountains and moors. Coulter Fell, Tinto, Green Louther, Five Cairn Louther, and other summits in the immediate vicinity of Crawfordjohn rise grandly out of the high moorlands that constitute most of the area in the eastern and southern parts of the county. Hard by the village flows Duneaton Water, one of the numerous rushing, songful streams that feed the River Clyde. The highest inhabited land in Scotland is said to lie at Leadhills, on the banks of Glengonner Water, not many miles south of Crawfordjohn.

In any case, it was amid these surroundings, according to John Muir's sketch, that his father "lived the life of a farm servant, growing up a remarkably bright, handsome boy, delighting in athletic games and eager to excel in everything. He was notably fond of music, had a fine voice, and usually took a leading part in the merry song-singing gatherings of the neighbourhood. Having no money to buy a violin, when he was anxious to learn to play that instrument, he made one with his own hands, and ran ten miles to a neighbouring village through mud and rain after dark to get strings for it."

In the course of time his sister Mary married a shepherd-farmer of Crawfordjohn by the name of Hamilton Blakley, whereupon her new home became also that of Daniel Muir. A Scottish peasant's life in a country village, remote from populous centres, must have afforded only narrow opportunities for education and self-improvement. John Muir was accustomed to ascribe the rigidity of his father's prejudices and convictions to the deficient quality of his early education. But it must be admitted that the making of a violin by a boy, who had grown up amid the handicaps of such surroundings, indicates the possession on his part of uncommon native resources of skill and ingenuity. An achievement of this kind suggests the probability that there were other products of his manual craftsmanship, and the remarkable inventive power and "whittling" skill which his son John developed as a young man doubtless were not unconnected with his father's example and ability. "While yet more boy than man," continues the sketch, "he suddenly left home to seek his fortune with only a few shillings in his pocket, but with his head full of romantic schemes for the benefit of his sister and all the world besides. Going to Glasgow and drifting about the great city, friendless and unknown, he was induced to enter the British army, but remained in it only a few years, when he purchased his discharge before he had been engaged in any active service. On leaving the army he married and began business as a merchant in Dunbar, Scotland. Here he remained and prospered for twenty years, establishing an excellent reputation for fair dealing and enterprise. Here, too, his eight children were born, excepting the youngest who was born in Wisconsin." It is strong evidence of his energy and love of adventure that he closed out his business in Dunbar in 1849 and "emigrated to the wilds of America" at the mature age of forty-five years. His original intention was to go to the backwoods of Upper Canada, but he was diverted from this purpose by fellow emigrants who told him that the woods of Canada were so dense and heavy that an excessive amount of labour was required to clear land for agriculture. From Milwaukee he made his way by wagon into the central part of southern Wisconsin, where he bought, cleared, and brought under cultivation, successively, two large farms. They were situated about ten miles from Kingston and were known respectively as the Fountain Lake and the Hickory Hill farms.

[When the second one also was] . . . thoroughly subdued and under cultivation, and his three sons had gone to seek their fortunes elsewhere, he sold it and devoted himself solely to religious work. As an evangelist he went from place to place in Wisconsin, Canada, and Arkansas, distributing books and tracts at his own cost, and preaching the gospel in season and out of season with a firm sustained zeal.

Nor was this period of religious activity restricted to those later years, for throughout almost his whole life as a soldier, merchant, and farmer, as well as evangelist, he was an enthusiastic believer and upholder of the gospel, and it is this burning belief that forms the groundwork of his character and explains its apparent contradictions. He belonged to almost every Protestant denomination in turn, going from one to another, not in search of a better creed, for he was never particular as to the niceties of creeds, but ever in search of a warmer and more active zeal among its members with whom he could contribute his time and money to the spread of the gospel.

Though suffering always under the disadvantage of an imperfect education, he never failed in any important undertaking and never seemed to feel himself overtasked, but by sheer force of will and continuous effort overcame all difficulties that stood in his way. He was successful in business and bestowed much of his earnings on churches and charities.

His life was singularly clean and pure. He never had a single vice excepting, perhaps, the vices of over-industry and over-giving. Good Scripture measure, heaped up, shaken together, and running over, he meted out to all. He loved little children, and beneath a stern face, rigid with principle, he carried a warm and tender heart. He seemed to care not at all what people would think of him. That never was taken into consideration when work was being planned. The Bible was his guide and companion and almost the only book he ever cared to read.

His last years, as he lay broken in body, waiting for rest, were full of calm divine light. Faith in God and charity to all became the end of all his teachings, and he oftentimes spoke of the mistakes he had made in his relation toward his family and neighbours, urging those about him to be on their guard and see to it that love alone was made the guide and rule of every action. . . . His youthful enthusiasm burned on to the end, his mind glowing like a fire beneath all its burden of age and pain, until at length he passed on into the land of light, dying like a summer day in deep peace, surrounded by his children.

On his mother's side John Muir was descended from the old Scottish stock of the Gilderoys whose deeds won a place in the Border lore of Scotland. There is, for instance, the fine old ballad "Gilderoy," but the possibility that its thirteen stanzas may celebrate a member of this branch of the family must remain as remote as it is romantic. In a manuscript copy of the ballad, made for John Muir years ago by a Scotch relative of the Gilroy line, the opening stands run as follows:

> "Gilderoy was a bonnie boy,
> Had roses till his shoon;
> His stockings were of sillken soy,
> Wi' garters hanging doon;
> It was, I ween, a comely sight,
> To see sae trim a boy;
> He was my joy and heart's delight,
> My winsome Gilderoy.

> "Oh! sic twa charming een he had,
> A breath as sweet as rose;
> He never ware a Highland plaid,
> But costly silken clothes.
> He gained the love of ladies gay,
> Nane e'er to him was coy.
> Ah! wae is me! I mourn this day,
> For my dear Gilderoy!" etc.

In Thompson's *Orpheus Caledonius* (1733) the hero of the poem is represented as contemporary with Mary, Queen of Scots. But a later authority, describing this Gilderoy as "the Robin Hood of Scottish minstrelsy," identified him with the leader of a band of freebooters that three centuries ago roamed over the Highlands of Perthshire until both he and his band fell victims to the Stewarts of Atholl in 1638.

According to a Muir family tradition John's maternal great-grandfather, James Gilderoy, had three sons who took respectively the names Gilderoy, Gilroy, and Gilrye. Inquiry of descendants in Scotland has failed to bring to light the first of these. But a James Gilderoy* was resident at Wark in Northumberland, on the Border, in 1765. He is known to have had at least two sons – John and David. The former, born in 1765, took the Gilroy form of the family name and was alternately a professional gardener and a "land agent." David who was born July 15th, 1767, is the "grandfather Gilrye" of Muir's *The Story of My Boyhood and Youth*. Both boys appear to have gradually moved northward along the border, and an old Scotch family Bible, in the possession of a granddaughter of John Gilroy, invests with the importance of an event the arrival of David Gilrye at Dunbar, Scotland, on December 20th, 1794.

David was no longer in the first flush of youth when he settled in Dunbar. He was twenty-seven years old, and in his years of wandering, if we knew something about them, we probably should find no lack of hardship and adventure. Love of gardens and of landscapes, not improbably, gave direction sometimes to his footsteps, for John Muir more than a century later told how his earliest recollections of the country were gained on short walks in company with Grandfather Gilrye, who also loved to take him to Lord Louderdale's gardens. There is something pleasingly suggestive in the picture of seventy-five-year-old David Gilrye leading his three-year-old grandson into the paths that were to bring fame to the one, and rescue from oblivion to the other.

Perhaps it was Margaret Hay who confided to her Bible the date of David's arrival at Dunbar. She had good reason to remember the event, for six months later he led her to the altar and made her his wife. Through Grandmother Gilrye, John Muir thus shared the good Scotch blood of the Hays, a numerous clan, that has produced men and women of distinction both in Europe and in America. A relative of Margaret Hay is said to have suffered martyrdom in the days when the Covenanters were hunted down for their sturdy opposition to "popery and prelacy."

A numerous offspring came to enliven the household of David and Margaret Hay Gilrye – three sons and seven daughters. But death, also, was a tragically persistent visitor. All the sons and three of the daughters died between the ages of seventeen and twenty-six – a fearful toll of life exacted by the white plague. Since two other daughters had died at a tenderer age,

* Also spelled "Gildroy" and "Gilroy" in contemporary documents.

only Margaret, the eldest, and Ann, the seventh of the Gilrye sisters, lived to survive their parents and round out a good old age. The tragedy of such a series of untimely deaths is likely to have had an intensifying influence upon the religious sensibilities of the family. In 1874, when her sister Margaret died at the ripe age of seventy-eight, Ann Gilrye, then the wife of Daniel Muir, described herself as "the last remnant of a numerous family." "My mother," she wrote to her son John, "was just seventy-eight years old when she died, and my father eighty-eight. My parents have mouldered in the dust over twenty years, but Christ is the resurrection and the life, and if we believe in him our souls will never die."

Daniel Muir, coming to Dunbar as a recruiting sergeant, met there his first wife by whom he had one child. She was a woman of some means and enabled him to purchase his release from the army in order to engage in the conduct of a business which she had inherited. Their happiness together was of brief duration, for both she and the child were snatched away by a premature death, leaving him alone.

It seems to have been early in 1833 that Daniel, now a widower with a prospering business, became a familiar caller in the Gilrye family – now also sadly depleted in number. Margaret had been married thirteen years earlier to James Rae and had established her own home. It was Aunt Rae's precious lily garden that later excited the childish admiration of little Johnny Muir and made him wonder whether, when he grew up, he "should ever be rich enough to own anything like so grand." Twenty-year-old Ann and her sixteen-year-old brother David were the only ones left under the parental roof. All the rest were lying side by side in the Dunbar churchyard, whither also the last male scion of the family was to be carried the following year.

On the 28th of November, 1833, Ann Gilrye became the wife of Daniel Muir, and moved across the street into the old house which John Muir has described in his boyhood recollections. A lively brood of children soon came to make their home there. Margaret, Sarah, John, David, Daniel, Mary, and Anna were born there in the given order, Joanna being the only one who was born in Wisconsin. John Muir, third in succession and the eldest boy, was born on the 21st of April, 1838.

The bond of affectionate intimacy which always existed between him and his mother would make a characterisation of her from his pen of more than ordinary interest. But we have to content ourselves with one sentence from a fragmentary autobiographical sketch. "She was a representative Scotch woman," he wrote, "quiet, conservative, of pious, affectionate character, fond of painting and poetry." To this we may add the interesting information, contained in one of his letters, that his mother wrote poetry in her girlhood days.

It is quite apparent from her letters that she shared with him that aesthetic appreciation of nature which is so characteristic an element in his writings. While most of her letters concern home affairs and are full of maternal solicitude for his health and comfort, they are seldom without that additional touch which reveals kinship of soul as well as of blood. Referring to descriptions in one of his early California letters, she writes, "Your enjoyment of the beauties of California is shared by me, as I take much pleasure in reading your accounts."

Underneath the maternal solicitude for his health and safety one may also detect at times the Scotch Covenanter's concern for his spiritual welfare. "Dear John," she writes in 1870, "I hope your health is good – so that you will be able really to enjoy and admire all the vast magnificence with which you are daily surrounded. I know it is far beyond any conception of mine, but we can unite in praising and serving our Heavenly Father who is the maker and supporter of this wonderful world on which we live for a time. But time is short, and we must live forever. I trust we have a good hope, through grace, of spending eternity in mansions of glory everlasting."

The glacial studies with which her son began to busy himself during the seventies must have tried at times her Covenanter faith in so far as it involved a conception of the age and origin of the world different from that which she had learned in her youth. But she continues to write cheerfully about summers and autumns that make rambles in the woods a deepening joy. "The trees and flowers and plants looked more beautiful to me than ever before.... I presume you are quite busy with your studies writing your book. I feel much interested in all that interests you, although in many of your studies you leave me far behind. Yet I rejoice in all your joy, and hopes of future advancement.... You were much talked about and thought about at our last Christmas gathering. Many were the kind wishes and loving thoughts wafted to the valley of Yosemite." Almost to the last year of her life she was accustomed to go to the woods in April in order to gather and send to him with her birthday wishes a few of his favourite Wisconsin spring flowers. These little acts reveal, even more than anything she said, the poetic strain in her blood which kept fresh for her and her eldest boy, until he was nearly sixty and she over eighty, the vernal blossoms they had picked together long ago.

Very different was the attitude which Daniel Muir assumed toward the interests and enthusiasms of his son. Being an extreme literalist as far as the Bible was concerned, he could not look without suspicion upon his scientific studies, because they went "beyond what was written." Whenever he saw an issue arising between his traditional interpretation of the world's origin according to Genesis on the one side, and the facts of geology and glaciation on the other, he was accustomed to say, "Let God be true and every man a liar." John's passion for exploration, and the adventures incidental thereto, he regarded as little less than sinful. That there were different levels of development within the Bible, involving the displacement of earlier and cruder ideas of God and the world by higher and more intelligent ones, never entered his mind. Nor did it ever occur to him, apparently, that the facts of nature are likewise a part of the manuscripts of God, and that he who endeavours to read them accurately may be rendering his fellow men a religious as well as an intellectual service. He sincerely believed that his son was cheating the Almighty in devoting his time to such interests and enjoyments. "You are God's property," he wrote to him once. "You are God's property, soul and body and substance – give those powers up to their owner!" Even the most painstaking naturalist, he maintained, could not discover anything of value in the natural world that the believer did not see at one glance of the eye. These views went hand in hand with a naive credulity that accepted unquestioningly the pious marvels related in the tracts which he was distributing, and of which he kept sending selected ones, with comments, to his son John.

Perhaps the reader will receive a clearer and truer impression of the differing attitudes of his father and mother toward his nature studies if we offer at this point a typical letter of Daniel Muir in which the underscored words are indicated by italics. A note on the envelope, in John's handwriting, says "written after reading the account of my storm night on Shasta."

Portage City, March 19th, 1874

MY VERY DEAR JOHN

Were you as really *happy* as my wish would make you, you would be permanently so in the best sense of the word. I received yours of the third inst. with your slip of paper, but I had read the same thing in *The Wisconsin*, some days before I got yours, and then I *wished* I had not seen it, because it harried up my feelings so with another of your hair-breadth escapes. Had I seen it to be *God's work* you were doing I would have felt the *other* way, but I knew it was not God's work, although you seem to think you are doing God's service. If it had not been for God's boundless mercy you would have been cut off in the midst of your folly. All that you are attempting to show the *Holy Spirit* of God gives the believer to see at one glance of the eye, for according to the tract I send you they can see God's love, power, and glory in everything, and it has the effect of turning away their sight and eyes from the things that are seen and temporal to the things that are not seen and eternal, *according to God's holy word*. It is of no use to look through a glass darkly when we have the *Gospel*, and its *fulfillment*, and when the true practical believer has got the Godhead in fellowship with himself all the time, and reigning in his heart all the time. I know that the world and the church of the world will glory in such as you, but how can they believe which receive honour one of another and seek not the honour that cometh from God only John 5, 44. You cannot warm the heart of the saint of God with your cold icy-topped mountains. O, my dear son come away from them to the spirit of God and His holy word, and He will show our lovely Jesus unto you, who is by His finished work presented to you, without money and price. It will kindle a flame of sacred fire in your heart that will never go out, and then you will go and willingly expend it upon other icy hearts and you will thus be blessed infinitely in tribulation and eternally through Jesus Christ, who is made unto us of God wisdom, righteousness, sanctification, and redemption. I Cor. 1, 30, 31. And the best and soonest way of getting quit of the writing and publishing your book is to burn it, and then it will do no more harm either to you or others. And then, like Paul, look to the cross of Christ and glory in it, and as in the sight of God and in Jesus Christ, my only Lord and Master, I hereby say Amen to it.

I expect, my God willing, to leave Portage City for Hamilton, Toronto, on the last day of this month. I bought a house last October there and without my family, at present, I mean to go in the way of God's providence to spend all my time in His service and wholly by His grace to glorify Him. I shall be glad to hear from you there any time. I will get your letters at the post-office there.

We are all well. Your dear mother sends her love to you.

Your affectionate father in Christ
DANIEL MUIR

The meaning of the last paragraph of the letter will be found in some, disquieting news contained in a letter of Mrs. Daniel Muir, Sr., under date of February 26th, 1872. "We were surprised," she writes, "to hear your father say that he has decided to sell the Hickory Hill farm, and everything he has on it, by auction. So he is at present engaged in putting up bills of sale, the sale to take place on Tuesday, the 5th of March. He says he will not decide on where he will go until the sale is over." The purpose he had in view in coming to this sudden decision is revealed in one of John's letters to his brother David. Daniel Muir's religious fanaticism had in John's view reached a point where it was necessary to ask his brother and his brother-in-law to interfere in the interest of their sisters and their mother.

to David Gilrye Muir

Yosemite Valley, March 1st, 1873

DEAR DAVE

I answer your letter at once because I want to urge you to do what you can in breaking up that wild caprice of father's of going to Bristol and Lord Muller. You and David Galloway are the only reliable common-sense heads in our tribe, and it is important, when the radical welfare of our parents and sisters is at stake, that we should do all that is in our power.

I expected a morbid and semi-fanatical outbreak of this kind as soon as I heard of his breaking free from the wholesome cares of the farm. Yet I hoped that he would find ballast in your town of some Sabbath-school or missionary kind that would save him from any violent crisis like the present. That thick matted sod of Bristol orphans, which is a sort of necessary evil induced by other evils, is all right enough for Muller in England, but all wrong for Muir in America.

The lives of Anna and Joanna, accustomed to the free wild Nature of our woods, if transplanted to artificial fields and dingy towns of England, would wilt and shrivel to mere husks, even if they were not to make their life work amid those pinched and blinking orphans.

Father, in his present feeble-minded condition, is sick and requires the most considerate treatment from all who have access to his thoughts, and his moral disease is by no means contemptible, for it is only those who are endowed with poetic and enthusiastic brains that are subject to it.

Most people who are born into the world remain babies all their lives, their development being arrested like sun-dried seeds. Father is a magnificent baby, who, instead of dozing contentedly like most of his neighbours, suffers growing pains that are ready to usher in the dawn of a higher life.

But to come to our work, can you not induce father to engage in some tract or mission or Sabbath-school enterprise that will satisfy his demands for bodily and spiritual exercise? Can you not find him some thicket of destitution worthy of his benevolence? Can you not convince him that the whole world is full of work for the kind and willing heart? Or, if you cannot urge him to undertake any independent charity, can you not place him in correspondence with some Milwaukee or Chicago society where he would find elbow room for all his importance. An earnest man like father, who also has a little money, is a valuable acquisition to many societies of a philanthropic kind, and I feel sure that if once fairly afloat from this shoal of indolence upon which he now chafes, he would sail calmly the years now remaining to him. At all events, tell mother and the girls, that whether this side the sea or that, they need take no uneasiness concerning bread . . . .

JOHN MUIR

Their efforts were successful. A new home was established in Portage, Wisconsin, and from there Daniel Muir went alone on prolonged evangelistic trips to Canada and parts of the central West. Laid low by old age and a broken limb, he died in Kansas City, at the home of one of his daughters, in 1885. His last years were calm and peaceful as John had foreseen. Eleven years later his wife also followed him into the land of the leal.

Into this parental and ancestral background, sketched in its more significant outlines, was born at Dunbar, Scotland, April 21st, 1838, the subject of this biography. Fleeting glimpses of his earliest childhood reveal Johnny Muir as a vivid, auburn-haired lad with an uncommonly keen and inquiring pair of blue eyes. His boyhood in Scotland extended over only the first eleven years of his life (1838–49), but the fifty and more pages which he devotes to memories of these years in his autobiography reveal the deep impression they made upon his mind. His school education began early before he had completed his third year. But even before that time he had, like his fellow Scotchman Hugh Miller, learned his letters from shop Signs across the street. In this as in other matters Grandfather Gilrye was his earliest teacher and guide.

Scotch pedagogical methods in those days were an uncompromising tyranny. So much is clear from Muir's feeling allusions to the inevitable thrashing, in school and at home, which promptly followed any failure to commit assigned lessons to memory. The learning of a certain number of Bible verses every day was a task which his father superimposed upon the school lessons, and exacted with military precision. "By the time I was eleven years old," wrote the victim of this method, "I had about three-fourths of the Old Testament and all of the New by heart and by sore flesh. I could recite the New Testament from the beginning of Matthew to the end of Revelation without a single stop." Records both written and oral testify to John's phenomenal feats of memory in reciting chapters from the Bible and the poetry of Robert Burns.

Whatever may be thought of the wisdom of this educational method, there can be no doubt that it resulted in forming the boy's literary taste and in giving him a rare training in the use of English undefiled. The dignity and rich quality of his diction, and his arrestingly effective employment of Biblical metaphors disclose the main sources of his literary power in familiarity with the King James Version, the only one available in his boyhood.

The severest kind of pedagogical weather was encountered when he left the old Davel Brae school for the grammar school. Old Mungo Siddons, who presided over the former, seems to have been a man possessed of human sympathies, for he managed to make himself gratefully remembered for the gooseberries and currants, at least, with which he sweetened the closing exercises when vacation days arrived. But Mr. Lyon, the master of the grammar school, was a disciplinarian of the most inflexible kind. "Under him," Muir writes, "we had to get three lessons every day in Latin, three in French, and as many in English, besides spelling, history, arithmetic, and geography. Word lessons in particular, the wouldst-couldst-shouldst-have-loved kind, were kept up, with much warlike thrashing, until I had committed the whole of the French, Latin, and English grammars to memory, and in connection with reading-lessons we were called on to recite parts of them with the rules over and over again, as if all the regular and irregular incomprehensible verb stuff was poetry."

Some of the textbooks he used have survived the accidents of time and travel and furnish illuminating examples of the severe demands that were made upon children in the Dunbar grammar school. One of these is Willymot's *Selections from the Colloquies of Corderius*, which he began to study when he was nine years old, and which would be a severe tax on the wits of most Freshmen of our day. It must have seemed little less than mockery to the pupils that the "Argumentum" of the very first "Colloquium" calls it an *"exemplum ad parvulos blande et comiter in schola tractandos, ne severitate disciplinae absterreantur."* "Kind and gentle treatment of youngsters lest they be frightened away by severity of discipline" – that was no serious concern of schoolmaster Lyon. "Old-fashioned Scotch teachers," wrote Muir in describing his school days, "spent no time in seeking short roads to knowledge, or in trying any of the new-fangled psychological methods so much in vogue nowadays. There was nothing said about making the seats easy or the lessons easy. We were simply driven point-blank against our books like soldiers against the enemy, and sternly ordered 'Up and at 'em. Commit your lessons to memory.' If we failed in any part, however slight, we were whipped; for the grand, simple, all-sufficing Scotch discovery had been made that there was a close connection between the skin and the memory, and that irritating the skin excited the memory to any required degree."

Though John was compelled at this time to store his memory with many things which in his mature judgment were mere "cinders and ashes," the mental discipline at least was a permanent gain. His knowledge of French was sufficient to open for him the treasures of French literature. A considerable section of his library was composed of French works on travel, exploration, and natural science. The Latin he had acquired so drastically from Corderius' *Colloquies* and Turner's *Exercises to the Accidence*, etc., proved useful in botanical and paleontological studies. Besides, the habit, formed early, of committing to memory choice passages from English literature was kept up by him till far into middle life and was commended to his children as a valuable means of education. In a letter to his daughter Wanda, on the occasion of his first visit to Dunbar, forty-four years after he had left his native town, he wrote: "You are now a big girl, almost a woman, and you must mind your lessons and get in a good store of the best words of the best people while your memory is retentive and then you will go through life rich. Ask mother to give you lessons to commit to memory every day, mostly the sayings of Christ in the gospels, and selections from the poets. Find the hymn of praise in *Paradise Lost*, 'These are thy glorious works, Parent of good, Almighty!' and learn it well."

If in these formal elements of John's early education profit and loss were often doubtfully balanced, it was not so with the lessons he learned from Nature. He would have agreed with Henry Adams that life was a series of violent contrasts which gave to life their relative values. Winter and summer, cold and heat, town and country, school and vacation, force and freedom, marked two widely different modes of life and thought. What is more, they all registered their effects in the sum total of what we call education. On the one hand was the wintry, storm-beaten town with its restraint, confinement, and school discipline; on the other, the country with its penetrable hedges, daisied fields, bird-song, and nest hunting expeditions. There, in particular, were skylarks and mavises, the most universally beloved of all the birds of Scotland. John tells how he and his companions used to stand for hours on a broad meadow near Dunbar listening to the singing of the larks; or how they lay on their backs in competitive tests of keensightedness, each trying to outdo the other in keeping a soaring singer in sight.

Among the sublimer aspects of Nature that made an indelible impression upon the boy's mind were those of the stormy North Sea. Answering the letters of some Los Angeles school children in 1904, he tells how the school which they described brought to mind the two schools which he attended when he was a boy in Scotland. "They," he wrote, "were still nearer the sea. One of them stood so near that at high tide on stormy days the waves seemed to be playing tag on our playground wall, running up the sandy shore and perhaps just touching the base of the wall and running back. But sometimes in wild storms the tops of the waves came flying over the wall into the playground, while the finer spray, carried on the wild roaring flood, drenched the schoolhouse itself and washed it fresh and clean. These great roaring storms were glorious sights. But we were taught to pity the poor sailors, for many ships were driven ashore on the stormy coast almost every year, and many sailors drowned. From the highest part of the playground we could see the ships sailing past, and often tried to guess whence they came, where they were bound for, and what they were carrying." The numerous drawings of ships that decorate the fly-leaves of John's schoolbooks may be regarded as tell-tale of what he saw from the windows and the playground of the Davel Brae school.

But there were many other thrilling experiences for the by-hours of a boy like Johnny Muir. He drank in by every pore the sombre wildness of the rugged seashore about his native town, explored the pools among the rocks where shells, seaweeds, eels, and crabs excited his childish wonder when the tide was low, and found adventurous recreation by climbing the craggy headlands. Yet most impressive of all was the roar of North Sea tempests that, mingling sea and sky, hurled mountainous waves against the black headland crowned by the ruins of Dunbar Castle. All this he saw and felt and explored with intense delight.

How ineffaceably these scenes and early experiences engraved themselves upon his memory is revealed by a passage in one of his notebooks. He was a day's journey from the Gulf of Mexico, on his thousand-mile walk through the South, when he suddenly caught a whiff of the sea, borne upon the wind. It was "the first sea-breeze," he writes, "that had touched me in twenty years. I was plodding along with my satchel and plants, leaning wearily forward ... when suddenly I felt the salt air, and before I had time to think, a whole flood of long-dormant associations rolled in upon me. The Firth of Forth, the Bass Rock, Dunbar Castle, and the winds and rocks and hills came upon the wings of that wind, and stood in as clear and sudden light as a landscape flashed upon the view by a blaze of lightning in a dark night."

It is not surprising that John Muir, reflecting upon his Scotch boyhood, should in his later years have learned to regard the natural environment of Dunbar as a source of a valuable part of his early education. The heroic origins of the town are lost in dim traditions that reach back at least a thousand years. Not the least of its romantic associations are represented by such names as Black Agnes of Dunbar, Joanna Beaufort, Earl Bothwell and Mary, Queen of Scots. Just south-east of the town was fought the Battle of Dunbar in which Cromwell won a decisive victory over Leslie. All this, no less than the legends, superstitions, and folklore, which clung like moss about the surviving ruins of other days, could not but exert a strong influence upon the imagination of this active-minded boy.

But the fields and woods exerted by far the strongest attraction upon him. In spite of sure and severe punishments he and his companions regularly managed to slip away into the country to indulge their love of that open "wildness" which, he says, "was ever sounding in our ears. Nature saw to it that besides school lessons and church lessons some of her own lessons should be learned, perhaps with a view to the time when we should be called to wander in wildness to our hearts' content. Oh, the blessed enchantment of those Saturday runaways in the prime of spring! How our young wondering eyes revelled in the sunny, breezy glory of the hills and sky, every particle of us thrilling and tingling with the bees and glad birds and glad streams! Kings may be blessed; we were glorious, we were free, – school cares and scoldings, heart thrashings and flesh thrashings alike, were forgotten in the fullness of Nature's glad wildness. These were my first excursions, – the beginnings of lifelong wanderings."

CHAPTER TWO

Life on a Wisconsin Farm   1849–1860

ONE EVENING in 1849, when John and his younger brother David were studying their next day's lessons at Grandfather Gilrye's fireside, their father brought the information that they would start together for America the next morning. It was wildly exciting news, for it not only meant delivery from the tyranny of schoolmasters, but a life of adventure in a world full of untrodden wildernesses. Their grammar school reader had already kindled their imaginations with stories of American animal life, especially such as had come from the pen of the Scotch ornithologist Alexander Wilson and the American naturalist John James Audubon. News of the recent discovery of gold in California had run like wildfire over Europe and was the talk of the hour also in Dunbar. It is no wonder that the expectations engendered by such tales, together with the prospect of release from bitter school tasks, rendered the two lads "utterly, blindly glorious."

The only bitter strain in all this sweetness was the necessity of parting from Grandfather and Grandmother Gilrye. And yet they hardly realised what it meant to their grandparents to be left alone in their darkening old age, never to see their grandchildren again. The rosy anticipations of childhood left no room for the thought that their beloved grandparents might be near their own time of departure – in their case for "the land of the leal." In three years, as it turned out, both of them were gone. For the time being, however, Grandfather Gilrye exercised some control over the situation by insisting that his daughter and the younger children must not be exposed to the hardships of pioneering in a new country before a comfortable house had been built for their reception. Hence it was decided that only John, David, and Sarah were to accompany their father to America.

In those days large numbers of Scotch emigrants went to the wilds of Upper Canada and Daniel Muir also set out with the intention of joining some Canadian settlement of his compatriots. On shipboard, however, the majority opinion favoured the States, especially Wisconsin and Michigan, where according to common report the forests were less dense and consequently more easily cleared. These advantages were bound to weigh heavily with a man who feared to delay the reunion of his family by the choice of a difficult homestead. Before the end of the voyage he had decided in favour of the western United States, resolving to be guided in his final choice by what he choice by what he might learn on his westward journey. On reaching Buffalo, the reported preeminence of Wisconsin as a wheat-producing State left no further doubt in his mind. From Milwaukee his cumbersome luggage was transported by wagon for a hundred miles over miry roads to the little town of Kingston, where a land-agent helped him to homestead a quarter-section of land amid sunny open woods beside a small lake.* A shanty was hastily erected and the household goods stowed away in it until a more permanent frame house could be built. Before winter came the house was ready for occupancy, and in November, 1849, Mrs. Muir and the rest of the family arrived from Scotland.

The wild nooks about Fountain Lake, and especially the lake itself, at once took a unique place in John's affections. Its beautiful waterlily pads, its bordering meadows full of showy sedges, orchids, and ferns, the great variety of fish, and the abundant population of ducks and muskrats which it harboured, excited his unbounded curiosity and admiration. It was in this lake that he became an expert swimmer, though on one occasion he nearly lost his life through a momentary lack of self-possession, and punished himself for it afterwards in characteristic Scotch fashion by rowing out into the middle of the lake and diving into deep water again and again, shouting, "Take that!" each time as he did it.

The raptures produced in eleven-year-old John by this sudden transplanting from the North Sea coast of Scotland to this lake and the flowery oak-openings of Wisconsin made an ineffaceable impression and even in retrospect taxed to the utmost his powers of description when he was past three-score and ten. "This sudden plash into pure wildness baptism in Nature's warm heart – how utterly happy it made us!" he writes in his boyhood reminiscences: "Nature streaming into us, wooingly teaching her wonderful glowing lessons, so unlike the dismal grammar ashes and cinders so long thrashed into us. Here without knowing it we still were at school; every wild lesson a love lesson, not whipped but charmed into us. Oh, that glorious Wisconsin wilderness! Everything new and pure in the very prime of the spring when Nature's pulses were beating highest and mysteriously keeping time with our own! Young hearts, young leaves, flowers, animals, the winds and the streams and the sparkling lake, all wildly, gladly rejoicing together!"

But it was not to be all joy, this wilderness life. The golden mantle of boyish illusions was soon to be lifted from stern realities. For when the serious work of subduing this wilderness into a farm began, John found frequent occasion to remember the prophecy of Grandfather Gilrye as in boyish exuberance John tried to tell him about all the wonderful things he and David were going to see and do in the new world. "Ah, poor laddies, poor laddies," he said in a trembling voice, "you'll find something else ower the sea forbye gold and sugar, birds' nests and freedom fra lessons and

* The "Fountain Lake" of Muir's memoirs, but now known sometimes as "Muir's Lake," sometimes as "Ennis Lake."

schools. You'll find plenty of hard, hard work.'' Fortunately few forms of work are all toil and drudgery to a gifted lad, and the environment permitted some undesigned good to spring from the iniquity of child labour.

So it happens that the noble part which domestic animals play in the development of an impressionable boy, in this case a future naturalist, is vividly and touchingly reflected in John's recollections of his four-footed fellow labourers on his father's farm. Foremost among them were the oxen which in pioneer days did service on Western farms instead of horses or mules. He shrewdly observes that the experience of working with them enabled him and his brother to know them far better than they should had they been "only trained scientific naturalists.'' To Muir one ox was not like another, mere animated machines which all reacted alike to any given stimulus or situation. For he had seen one ox learn to smash pumpkins with his head while others awkwardly tried to break into them with their teeth. "We soon learned,'' he writes, "that each ox and cow and calf had individual character.''

Later, when the oxen were displaced by horses, he remarked the same difference of sagacity and temperament in them. One was intelligent, affectionate, and teachable, the other balky and dull. Readers of his boyhood memoirs will also recall his sympathetic description of Jack the Indian pony; of its fearlessness, playfulness, and gentleness. The farm was evidently the place where he learned to appreciate what he called the "humanity'' of animals and man's kinship with them. This sympathetic attitude made it easy for Muir to observe evidence of animal intelligence not only in his humble companions-in-labour on the farm, but when he came to study animals in their wild state he was prepared to look there also for differences of intelligence; and not alone between various types of animals, but between individuals of the same species. In other words, to him much the most interesting thing about an animal was its mind and the use to which it put the same. On this point he differed widely with John Burroughs who seemed to become a more and more outspoken champion of the mechanistic theory of animal behaviour which explains the actions of animals in terms of "blind instinct.'' "Blind'' seemed to be coextensive in meaning with "unreasoning,'' thus reducing the actions of all individuals of a given species of animal to the particular brand of instinct characteristic of the species. On one occasion when Burroughs and Muir, meeting at the house of a mutual friend in Berkeley, discussed this issue, Muir in the judgement of those present scored heavily against his opponent. And this was due not to his superior conversational and argumentative powers, but to fact-seasoned conclusions matured amid the observations of a lifetime. It was refreshing and amusing to hear him go after the so-called animal psychologists and behaviourists with their "problem boxes,'' etc., bent on making out, in some cases at least, that animals are nothing but "machines in fur and feathers.'' On the other hand he had no sympathy with the professional observers of wonders who found it profitable not to distinguish between the imagination of the wild and their own wild imaginations.

Now that so competent and well-informed a naturalist as William T. Hornaday has presented the personal observations of a lifetime in his book *The Minds and Manners of Wild Animals*, and has set forth therein a point of view substantially in accord with that of John Muir, we may expect the mechanistic interpreters of animal "behaviour" to vacate the stage for a time. It ought to be added that Muir as early as 1867 confided to his notebook his belief that one of the greatest hindrances to a fruitful study of the intelligence and individual characteristics of animals was the average human beings insufferable self-conceit; that his egotism magnifies his lordship of creation until he is incapable of seeing that animals "are our earth-born companions and fellow mortals." To the fact that the lord-of-creation idea has an abused Biblical origin he attributed the fact that the "fearfully good, the orthodox," are the first "to cry 'heresy' on every one whose sympathies reach out a single hair's breadth beyond the boundary epidermis of our own species. Not content with taking all of earth, they also claim the celestial country as the only ones who possess the kind of souls for whom that imponderable empire was planned." To this same effect is an eloquent passage in *The Story of My Boyhood and Youth* where he touchingly describes the death of his favourite horse Nob, over-driven by his father in going to a church meeting. After remarking that "of the many advantages of farm life for boys one of the greatest is the gaining of a real knowledge of animals as fellow mortals," worthy of respect and love, he adds: "Thus godlike sympathy grows and thrives and spreads far beyond the teachings of churches and schools, where too often the mean, blinding, loveless doctrine is taught that animals have neither mind nor soul, have no rights that we are bound to respect, and were made only for man to be petted, spoiled, slaughtered, or enslaved."

That John Muir survived the relentless severity with which his father held him to adult labour when he was a mere boy probably was due less to his physical vitality than to the buoyancy of his temperament. Called at six in the morning in winter-time, he had to begin the usual chores of feeding horses and cattle, fetching water from the spring at the foot of the hill, bringing in wood and sharpening tools – all before breakfast. Immediately afterwards began the heavier work of the day, such as wood-chopping, fencing, fanning wheat, and various other tasks, indoors and out. The only means of warming the house was the kitchen stove, and even in this he was not allowed to kindle a fire before hastening to the chores. With Spartan fortitude he had to squeeze his chilblained feet into wet socks and soggy boots frozen solid. No wonder that in the memoirs of his boyhood he remembered with regret how great heart-cheering loads of oak and hickory were hauled with misguided industry into waste places to rot instead of being laid up for use in a desperately needed large fireplace. It was a very

unusual boy who amid this senseless aggravation of the natural hardships of
pioneer farm life could find it in his heart "to enjoy the winter beauty – the
wonderful radiance of the snow when it was starry with crystals, and the
dawns and sunsets and white noons, and the cheery, enlivening company of
the brave chickadees and nuthatches."

The summer chores and field labour were different, but not less exacting.
The day began earlier and lasted longer. Among detached jottings under the
heading of "Farm Work" in one of his notebooks I find the following:

> We had to work very hard on the farm in summer, mowing, hoeing, cradling
> wheat, hauling it to the barns, etc. No rest in the shade of trees on the side of
> the fields. When tired we dared not even go to the spring for water in the
> terrible thirst of the muggy dog-days, because the field was in sight of the
> house and we might be seen. . . . We had to make ourselves sick that we
> might lay up something against a sick day, as if we could kill time without
> injuring eternity. The incessant anxiety and strain of some is a well-nigh
> incurable disease. . . . A stitch in time saves nine, so we take a thousand
> stitches today to save nine tomorrow.

John being the eldest boy, the greater part of the hard work of the farm
naturally fell to him. This included the splitting of rails for the zigzag
fences, mostly from trees so knotty and cross-grained that the making of a
hundred rails a day involved the expenditure of much energy and not a little
skill. It was fatiguing work, so much so that his father, after trying rail-
splitting with him for a day or two, left it all to John.

A form of labour which he remembered with special aversion was the
hoeing of corn before the days of cultivators. Under his father's relentless
drive the haying and harvest season bore down hard upon the growing boy.
A natural ambition to excel made him vie with the hired men in mowing and
cradling, and at the age of sixteen John was accustomed to lead the line. He
was no doubt right in thinking that this very severe labour so far exceeded
his strength that it checked his growth. But there was no one in those days
to warn him of the dangers of overwork, least of all his father. The latter's
unnatural severity toward his children made so indelible an impression that
when John recorded the memories of his boyhood he treated with great
frankness an aspect of family life which ordinarily autobiographers veil in
silence. But since he had, as will appear later, a humane purpose in exposing
to public view this aspect of his early home experience, it is clearly a
biographer's duty not to ignore a situation already created, though some
might question the filial propriety of introducing it in the first place.

What John describes as "the old Scotch fashion of whipping for every
act of disobedience or of simple, playful forgetfulness" was continued by
Daniel Muir in the Wisconsin wilderness. Most of the whippings fell upon
John and were "outrageously severe, and utterly barren of fun." But in

telling about the occasion on which he was to receive a beating for having lost his father's ox-whip by tying it to the dog's tail, John makes no concealment of the fact that he was often a wilful and exasperating boy. For when he had escaped a thrashing because David, commanded to find a switch, had brought an unmanageable burr-oak sapling, he engaged in the same sort of mischief the moment his father was out of sight.

But the whippings, however severe, were less serious in their consequences than the excessive grind of work demanded. "Even when sick," writes John, "we were held to our tasks as long as we could stand. Once in harvest-time I had the mumps and was unable to swallow any food except milk, but this was not allowed to make any difference, while I staggered with weakness and sometimes fell headlong among the sheaves. Only once was I allowed to leave the harvest-field when I was stricken down with pneumonia. I lay gasping for weeks, but the Scotch are hard to kill and I pulled through. No physician was called, for father was an enthusiast and always said and believed that God and hard work were by far the best doctors."

Though more excessively industrious than any of his neighbours, Daniel Muir was by no means peculiar in his addictedness to the vice of over-industry. It was a common failing of settlers from England and Scotland, and John Muir doubtless was right in attributing it to their suddenly satisfied land-hunger and the desire to keep their large farms as neat and well tilled as the little garden patches which they had left behind them overseas. But, whatever the cause, there was no doubt about the frenzied manner in which the Muir household was held to the tasks of the farm. To quote John's memoirs again:

We were all made slaves through the vice of over-industry. . . . It often seemed to me that our fierce, over-industrious way of getting the grain from the ground was too closely connected with grave-digging. The staff of life, naturally beautiful, often-times suggested the grave-digger's spade. Men and boys, and in those days even women and girls, were cut down while cutting the wheat. The fat folk grew lean and the lean leaner, while the rosy cheeks brought from Scotland and other cool countries across the sea faded to yellow like the wheat . . . . We were called in the morning at four o'clock and seldom got to bed before nine, making a broiling, seething day seventeen hours long loaded with heavy work, while I was only a small stunted boy; and a few years later my brothers David and Daniel and my older sisters had to endure about as much as I did. In the harvest dog-days and dog-nights and dog-mornings; when we arose from our clammy beds, our cotton shirts clung to our backs as wet with sweat as the bathing-suits of swimmers, and remained so all the long, sweltering days.

The losses sustained by John, both in bodily vigour and in intellectual growth, under the severe farm regime of his father, were the subject of frequent reflection by him in afteryears. "Pondering on the number who have died and crumbled into dust," he writes in one of his journals, "the farmer may say that he is farming the dust of his ancestors and compelling these ancestors to take refuge in turnips and apples.... We might live free, rich, comfortable lives just as well as not. Yet how hard most people work for mere dust and ashes and care, taking no thought of growing in knowledge and grace, never having time to get in sight of their vast ignorance."

This wearing labour of clearing and setting in order the Fountain Lake farm continued uninterruptedly for eight years. By that time it had been fully brought under the plough, fenced and provided with stables for cattle and horses. The original rude burr-oak shanty had been replaced with a more roomy frame house. Its former site on the hill overlooking the lake now is marked only by a depression and by a few stones that may have formed part of the foundation. In 1856 Sarah Muir was married to David M. Galloway, who bought the Fountain Lake farm* from his father-in-law. Thus Sarah succeeded her mother as mistress of the Fountain Lake home, where a warm welcome always awaited John when he returned from his wanderings.

The elder Muir, after relinquishing the farm to his son-in-law, bought half a section of uncleared land about four miles southeast of the original homestead. This new farm was situated twelve and a half miles northeast of Portage and four miles from the Fox River. The summit of a gentle slope covered with an open stand of fine hickory trees was selected as a site for a new house. Its erection in 1857 marked the beginning of another period of hard and exhausting labour. John at this time was nineteen years old and somewhat stunted in his growth, but he prided himself on his physical hardihood and his ability to endure all that was put upon him.

The Hickory Hill house was a simple two-story frame structure, which is still in existence, though veneered with brick and shorn of a lean-to shown in Muir's sketch published in *The Story of My Boyhood and Youth*. It is surrounded by wide-spreading box elders, willows, and apple trees which are said to date from the days of the Muirs. The local tradition is rendered plausible by the age and size of the trees. Especially striking among them is a willow near the well around which by dint of sober necessity the life of the farm revolved. For unlike the first farm, there was on it "no spring or stream or meadow or lake." Yet water was indispensable and to John was assigned the task of finding it.

Long before he struck water by sinking a ninety-foot shaft he had entered into the experience of those "who passing through the valley of weeping make it a well." After the first ten feet he struck a stratum of fine-grained sandstone through which he laboriously chipped his way for eighty feet with

* It has changed ownership several times since then and been subdivided. David Galloway sold it to James White head and he in turn to Samuel Ennis. In 1920 the particular tract on which the Muir house stood was owned by Howard McGwinn.

mason's chisels. Day after day for months he chipped away from dawn until dark. His father, apparently entirely ignorant of the dangers of choke-damp, would lower him by means of a bucket in the morning and draw him up again with the loosened chips at noon. Immediately after the noonday meal he was lowered again and left until night. One morning, as he was putting some left-over chips into the bucket with which he had just been lowered, he began to sway and sink under the effect of carbonic-acid gas that had settled at the bottom of the shaft during the night. His father, alarmed by his silence, and finding that John was not in the bucket when he heard his feeble-voiced request to be taken out, roused him from his stupor sufficiently by his shouted commands to make him get into the bucket. He was unconscious and all but suffocated when he reached the surface. But after a few days of rest and recovery he was lowered again, with some precautions against choke-damp, to chip down another ten feet, when water was struck. That was more than sixty years ago and ever since then the well has furnished an adequate supply of water for the farm. But one shudders to reflect how much of the imperishable wealth of the human spirit might have been sunk forever in that Wisconsin well.

In the month of August, 1858, during the Hickory Hill farm period, there occurred an event which made a deep impression upon John's memory. It was the death of a poor feeble-minded man who on account of his physical frailty, and some engaging social accomplishments, was both pitied and beloved among the neighbours. Many deemed him an entertaining singer of folk-songs and he had a gift of impromptu rhyming. It was generally reported and believed in the neighbourhood that his brother, a blacksmith preacher with whom he was making his home, often beat him and forced him to work beyond his strength, and that one morning he pitched forward and died on a pile of stovewood which he was chopping.

When fifty-five years later Muir was writing the story of his boyhood, the incident was still vivid in his memory and he gave a peculiarly moving account of it such as he only could write when his feelings were deeply stirred. Appearing first in the *Atlantic* it fell under the eye of the blacksmith preacher's son, a boyhood friend of John's of whom he had lost all trace. While no names were given he recognised in the person pilloried by Muir none other than his own father, and wrote John a dignified, friendly letter, pointing out certain mistakes and the fact that it conveyed an erroneous impression concerning his father's character. "I desire in conclusion," said the writer, " to emphasise the respect and admiration I have always entertained for you, beginning with the day we met where the road from your Father's place intersected with what was known as the 'River road,' following the holidays of '63 and '64, when in company we walked twelve miles to Portage and I listened to your conversation, your life and experience at the University to which you were returning. The advice and counsel given caused you to enter into and become a potent factor in my life. Though you did not know it, and have forgotten the circumstances with me it remains an abiding memory and in the years that followed proved a stimulus and incentive to untiring effort. I mention this to assure you that my esteem and faith in you remain unchanged, and that you may also know father was not the blot upon the landscape of that glorious wilderness you believe and have pictured him to be.''

Muir's reply is of unusual interest and biographical value, because it reveals ruling motives of his life and furnishes the reason why he disregarded customary reserve in presenting the disciplinary side of his boyhood training.

Martinez, California, February 13th, 1913

DEAR FRIEND

Your painful letter came to me in my lonely library writing den while hard at work on an Alaska book which should have been written a score of years ago. Seldom, if ever, have I received a letter that has given me so much mingled pleasure and pain – pleasure in hearing from a friend of my boyhood, and learning from you, the best and final authority, that the reports on the use of the Solomonic rod in your father's household, gleaned half a century ago from neighbours, including my sisters, brothers, and brothers-in-law were to say the least, grossly exaggerated; and pain from having been led to write by my lifelong hatred of cruelty that which has given you pain.

I never did intentional injustice to any human being or animal, and I have directed my publishers to cancel all that has so grievously hurt you. For a full understanding of the matter I wish to inform you that the four articles that have appeared in the November, December, January, and February numbers of the *Atlantic* were taken from the manuscript of a book entitled, *My Boyhood and Youth*, being the first volume of my autobiography, soon to be published. I corrected the last of the galley proofs several weeks ago and wrote the publishers that they need not send me the page proofs since their proof-readers were so careful and able. I have not seen any of them, and am unable to tell how far the work has progressed. Possibly part or all of this first volume may be stereotyped, or even printed. If not printed, the unfortunate page will be cut out of the plate at whatever cost.* And at the worst, only a comparatively small first edition may have been printed, and the part that has caused so much trouble will not appear in the ten or twenty following editions I have good reason, as doubtless you know to hate the habit of child-beating, having seen and felt its effects in some of their worst form in my father's house; and all my life I have spoken against the habit in season and out of season. But you make a great mistake in taking what I have written as a judgment or history of your father's character, as I hope to show in another volume. You doubtless know that character is made up of many particulars,

---

* His correspondent disclaimed all desire to have the offending account omitted, so it has been allowed to stand.

and that it is grossly unfair to try the whole general character of any man by one particular, however striking and influential it may be. I was far from doing so in sketching the evil of child-beating from which we both have so bitterly suffered.

When the rod is falling on the flesh of a child, and, what may oftentimes be worse, heartbreaking scolding falling on its tender little heart, it makes the whole family seem far from the Kingdom of Heaven. In all the world I know of nothing more pathetic and deplorable than a broken-hearted child, sobbing itself to sleep after being unjustly punished by a truly pious and conscientious misguided parent. Compare this Solomonic treatment with Christ's. King Solomon has much to answer for in this particular, though I suppose he may in some measure be excused by the trying, irritating size of his family.

Your father, like my own, was, I devoutly believe, a sincere Christian, abounding in noble qualities, preaching the Gospel without money or price while working hard for a living, clearing land, blacksmithing, able for anything, and from youth to death never abating one jot his glorious foundational religious enthusiasm. I revere his memory with that of my father and the New England Puritans – types of the best American pioneers whose unwavering faith in God's eternal righteousness forms the basis of our country's greatness.

Come and see me, and let us become better acquainted after all these eventful years. . . . You must now be nearing three score and ten. I will be seventy-five in a few months, and in the sundown of life we turn fondly back to the friends of the Auld-lang-syne. So I am now doing, and am wishing that you may be assured that I am,

Faithfully your friend
JOHN MUIR

In accordance with a fairly common custom among God-fearing pioneers of earlier days morning and evening family worship was regularly observed in the Muir household. But how easily morning prayers may become a devastating substitute for a day of real religion was apparently exemplified glaringly in both these households. Under such circumstances children often react sharply, not only against the external forms, but also against the substance of religion. The religious convictions of a shallower nature than John Muir's would never have survived the bigotry and rigour of his father's training. The latter, soon after moving to the Hickory Hill farm, conceived the notion of devoting all his time to Bible study, leaving to John and his brother David all the heavy work of the farm. John in the meantime, after much brooding, had evolved the plan of a clock which, when attached to his bed, would set him on his feet at any desired time in the morning. Having thought it out clearly he employed his meagre spare time, and any odd moments he could snatch from work, to carve and whittle this novel clock in wood. To keep it hid from his father he concealed it in a spare bedroom upstairs. One day, however, his father accidentally discovered it and the bad news was promptly conveyed to John by one of his sisters. He had good reason to fear that his father would immediately commit his machine to the fire, for the employment of even his scant spare time upon such tasks was severely disapproved by his father. But nothing happened until some days later when his father introduced the subject at dinner time. "John," he inquired, "what is that thing you are making upstairs?" Meal-times to Daniel Muir were sacramental occasions when no light conversation was permitted, and where every one was expected to cultivate an attitude of mind more befitting the Lord's supper than a family meal. Neither the time nor the subject boded any good for John, so in confusion and despair he replied that he did not know what to call it. But after some heckling John suggested that it might be called "an early-rising machine."

To appreciate the effect of this remark upon the elder Muir we must remind the reader that during the preceding winter John had been getting up at one o'clock to gain time for reading and for the construction of a miniature self-setting sawmill. His father had involuntarily given occasion for this extravagantly early rising, for one evening when ordering John to bed at eight o'clock as usual, as he was lingering a few minutes in the kitchen to read church history, he added conciliatingly that if he was set on reading he might get up in the morning as early as he liked. John rose at one o'clock that very night, feverishly and pathetically elated over the possession of five hours of time that were his own. The cold would not let him read, so during the winter he invested his new "time-wealth" in contriving and making all kinds of mechanical inventions. His workshop was in the cellar underneath his father's bedroom and he must often have disturbed his sleep. But having given his word he stood to it with Scotch fortitude although he remonstrated against the unreasonable use which John was making of the permission granted. It does not seem to have occurred to him that a boy so eager to learn was entitled to some margin of leisure for self improvement during normal working hours.

Such in brief was the background of the occasion on which Daniel Muir broke the sacramental silence of the noonday meal with an inquiry about the strange contrivance John was whittling. To learn that it "might be called an early-rising machine" was almost too much even for his gravity. But he quickly recovered his usual solemnity of face and voice and asked in a stern tone, "Do you not think it very wrong to waste your time on such nonsense?" John meekly replied that he did not think he was doing any wrong. "Well," replied his father, "I assure you I do; and if you were only half as zealous in the study of religion as you are in contriving and whittling these useless, nonsensical things, it would be infinitely better for you. I want you to be like Paul, who said that he desired to know nothing among men but Christ and Him crucified."

Such attempts to set religion at variance with the boy's innocent and commendable desire to develop by his own efforts his manual skill and mechanical ingenuity would have broken the spirit of most lads similarly situated. It is a typical instance of how religiousness, warped out of all semblance to real religion by bigotry and ignorance, may do grievous harm to its victims. But though he experienced a sense of injury and rebellion at the time, he lacked the knowledge and maturity to unravel the complex of fictitious dilemmas which his father propounded. Fortunately, the difficulties thrown in his way only increased his tenacity of purpose and in later years he saw the way out clearly enough. "Strange to say," he wrote in *The Story of My Boyhood and Youth*, "father carefully taught us to consider ourselves very poor worms of the dust, conceived in sin, etc., and devoutly believed that quenching every spark of pride and self-confidence was a sacred duty, without realising that in so doing he might at the same time be quenching everything else."

Luckily, as all his readers know, he escaped the type of reaction which under like circumstances has carried other strong characters into lifelong antagonism to religion. It had no such effect upon John. Indeed, one letter at least, which survives from this period of his boyhood, shows that he did his best to be an Apostle Paul to his own youthful generation, writing long, appealing letters to other boys of the vicinity, urging them to make a "decision for Christ." Their own letters are laden with phrases about the glories of heaven, the shortness and uncertainty of life, the appalling length of eternity, and the importance of being prepared for the fearfully searching inquiries of the day of judgment. Much of this is no doubt a part of the conventional religiousness of the time, fanned into flame seasonally by camp meetings and travelling evangelists. It must, however, be reckoned among the actions and reactions that went into the making of John Muir.

The invention and construction of his first wooden clock was, as we have seen, the outgrowth, in part, of a desire to secure more time for reading. "You say in your letter," writes a friend in March, 1858, "that time to stow wisdom-bins is precious." So it was for a boy who by his own testimony, had to consider himself fortunate if he got five minutes' reading after supper before his father would notice the light and order him to bed. "Night after night,' he writes, "I tried to steal minutes ... and how keenly precious those minutes were, few can nowadays know. Father failed perhaps two or three times in a whole winter to notice my light for nearly ten minutes, magnificent golden blocks of time, long to be remembered like holidays or geological periods."

In this connection the following entry, taken from one of his notebooks, tells more between the lines than in them, being a reflection of the remembered intensity with which the lad pursued his aims. "Many try to make up time," he writes, "by wringing the slumber out of their pores. Not so when I was a boy, springing out of bed at one o'clock in the morning, wide-awake, without the shadow of a yawn, no sleep left in a single fibre of me, burning and bright as a tiger springing on its prey."

John mentions his fifteenth year as the probable time when he began to relish good literature with enthusiasm. Certain it is that about the time of the family's removal to Hickory Hill farm this enthusiasm was a steady flame. One can only guess at the length of the strides he might have made could he have had the advantages of a first-class school. But such an opportunity was not to fall to his lot. Between the time of his departure from Scotland and the year in which he entered the University of Wisconsin he obtained only two months of additional schooling. Where this was received is uncertain, but it probably was in the old Fox River School No. 5 which then stood in a patch of dense forest not far from the first farm. In an undated letter of the fifties, evidently from a schoolmate, the writer expresses the wish that they might meet again ''at the schoolhouse and speak pieces and sing our old 'Press Onward' song as we used to last winter.'' The same correspondent wonders what has become of the teacher, whether he still occasionally thinks of his pupils and the merry times they used to have. ''I wish we might meet him again in the old schoolhouse and hear him call us to order and listen to some of his wonderful speeches.''

Among John's papers of this period is the manuscript of a juvenile poem of some length entitled ''The Old Log Schoolhouse,'' and a memorandum, apparently of the same date as the poem, declares that it was ''written in 1860.'' Since that was the year in which he left home, it is quite possible that it refers to the above-mentioned school. Of more interest than the local colour in these lines of blank verse is the young author's ability to detach himself from his environment and to indulge in seriocomic criticism of its defects and crudities. First comes a word-picture of the school, as follows:

> Old log schoolhouse, warped, and gnarled, and leaky;
> Opening thy crooked ribs and seams and knots
> To rain and snow and all the winds of heaven
> To keep thee sweet and healthy! Many a storm
> Hath played wild music beating on roof and gable,
> Loosely boarded, telling all the weather,
> As if some wondrous instrument thou wert,
> Speaking aloud, through all times and seasons,
> Thy parts of speech so strangely varied, mixing
> With stranger speech within, called English grammar.
> While yet the trunks of which thy walls are built
> Stood on the hills with outspread leaves and branches,
> A shelter, then, thou wert for gladsome birds,
> That made sweet music ring about their nests.
> And still a noisy nest thou art and shelter
> For callow, birdlike children soft and downy,
> Logs woven about them, piled and jointed,
> Crossed like sticks and straws, and roughly plastered
> With clay and mud like nests of mason robins.

An enumeration of what the old school has heard within its walls includes some humorous arithmetic and the hatchet of George Washington that

> Hath hacked small readers voices and the nerves
> Of teachers, in tones strident, rough, and rusty,
> In lessons never-ending, never-mending
> With grammar, too, old schoolhouse, thou hast suffered,
> While Plato, Milton, Shakespeare, have been murdered,
> Torn limb from limb in analytic puzzles
> And wondrous parsing, passing comprehension,
> The poetry and meaning blown to atoms-
> Sad sacrifices in the glorious cause
> Of higher all-embracing education.

"Players, preachers, showmen, singers, sinners" have all taken their-turn in shaking the school's old oaken ribs, but never have its walls rung with stranger sounds than

> Class-meeting converts' speeches; low, tearful,
> Sobbing promises to walk the narrow way
> Henceforward, and prayers for light and strength,
> Conscious of weakness and they know not what.
> Not so the brawny fighting backwoods brother.
> With jaw advanced, and bulging muscles rigid,
> He shouts and stamps and makes thy old logs rattle
> With rough defiance, calling 'Hither come
> Ye men or devils, come all together,
> Ye who would bar the narrow way to heaven.
> Armed for the fight with Christ, my Captain, leading,
> I fear no foe earthborn or from the pit.
> Come on! come on!' as though he were addressing
> Some foe in sight, yet maybe semi-conscious
> The foe was far away, and like to stay far.
>
> Every ism and doxy hath been sounded
> On every key within thy patient walls
> Old schoolhouse; blasts of strong revival,
> Enough to blow thy dovetailed logs asunder,
> While souls were being saved, and pulled, and twisted
> All out of shape, till they no longer fitted
> The frightened bodies that to each belonged.
> Playing at judgment day in lightsome humour,
> Calling, 'Ho! all ye saints that love the Lord,
> Rise up now quickly and take these benches
> On the right side there. And now ye sinners
> Cross over to the left, and stand in row,

> And be ye separate as sheep and goats
> That I may count ye, and get the true statistics
> To give the Master and myself some notion
> How fare these flocks supernal and infernal
> In this section of his backwoods pastures.'
> Then halting suddenly to blow his nose
> And spit, and bite some fresh tobacco,
> He waves his hand and cries, 'Now all be seated,
> And mix up as ye will, but pray remember
> When all your hardened cases come to trial
> In the upper court, I fairly warned ye
> To settle here with me as Heaven's agent, –
> To get a ticket by the gospel route, –
> The only route through our denomination.''

In conclusion the young poet foresees the time when the schoolhouse will have fallen under the doom of ''dust to dust ... perchance to sift and drift in vapour, far and wide o'er hill and dale and grassy plain, to take new forms of beauty.'' And on this passage down the ages ''with Nature'' he bids it a fond farewell.

To the discerning reader these excerpts will reveal at once the fact that he was saturated with the rhythm of Miltonic verse, that he was developing his critical faculty and his sense of word values, and that he had achieved a considerable degree of mental independence in a strongly repressive environment.

These gains had obviously not been accomplished by the only two months of additional schooling which he received between the ages of eleven and twenty-two, for he had during this period been wholly dependent upon his own efforts for his further education. What ways and means did he employ?

In his memoirs Muir has told how in one summer he worked through a higher arithmetic without assistance by using the short intervals of time between the noonday meal and the afternoon start for the fields. Algebra, geometry, and trigonometry were taken up in the same manner. Even the shorthand of that day excited his practical interest. But a broad training in literature and science was more difficult to secure in a backwoods farming community because of the lack of suitable books. Such raw materials of English literature as the neighbourhood afforded were faithfully used by him. Through acquaintanceship and correspondence with boys on neighbouring farms he arranged for the exchange of such books as their homes afforded. Reading became a consuming passion with him, and he seems to have had a marked preference for poetry of which he was accustomed to learn favourite passages by heart, rolling them like sweet morsels under his tongue. Nor were the practical aspects of such study neglected, for in extant correspondence with his young friends they acknowledge the receipt of rhymed letters and poems. Interestingly enough one of the poems was an elegy on the death of an enormous tree whose felling on a neighbouring farm had been described to him by one of his correspondents as a very laborious task.

John has named the age of fifteen as the time when the realm of poetry began to open to him like the dawn of a glorious day, and to the same period of his youthful development he assigns the "great and sudden discovery that the poetry of the Bible, Shakespeare, and Milton" is a source of "inspiring, exhilarating, uplifting pleasure." When the book supply of the neighbourhood was exhausted he had to find other ways of meeting his intellectual wants. Farm products in the backwoods were mostly taken in trade and money was scarce. But by careful saving of pennies and small sums which John secured in one way or another he managed to buy such longed-for books as were not ruled out by the rigid censorship of his all-Bible father. In the course of a few years he was able to count among his treasures "parts of Shakespeare's, Milton's, Cowper's, Henry Kirk White's, Campbell's, and Akenside's works, and quite a number of others seldom read nowadays." Wood's *Natural History*, and the once famous *Ancient History* of the French historian, Charles Rollin, seem also to have made memorable additions to the furniture of his mind.

Included in the slender stock of books accessible to him among the neighbours were the novels of Sir Walter Scott. But these he had to read in secret because his father strictly forbade the reading of novels as a sinful indulgence. The latter was, however, induced to buy Josephus's *Wars of the Jews* and d'Aubigne's *History of the Reformation*, and John vainly did his best to get him to buy Plutarch's *Lives*, until he contrived to circumvent paternal prejudices by suggesting that the old Greek writer might throw valuable light upon the food question. For Daniel Muir had taken up vegetarianism and was seeking to convince his family that the Creator never intended man to eat flesh. It mattered little to John that the old pagan could render no decision on the subject of man's proper diet. The main point, as he says, was that "so at last we gained our glorious Plutarch."

John's father, as indicated in the opening chapter, was a type of the old traditionalist for whom the Bible's authoritativeness was all of one piece and, like many another biblical literalist, he became an easy victim of his own theory. Blinded by his presuppositions, his Bible study plunged him only into deeper mental confusion. John, possessing a thorough knowledge of the Bible himself, was quick to take advantage of the weakness of his father's bibliolatry. After the Plutarch had been secured, he went to the rescue of his mother against his father's vegetarian fad by pointing out that when the Lord commanded the ravens to feed Elijah in hiding by the brook Cherith "the ravens," according to the Scriptures, "brought him bread and flesh in the morning, and bread and flesh in the evening." That ended the discussion. Daniel Muir acknowledged himself mistaken, for the Bible was his final arbiter in everything, and since the ravens were divinely commanded to bring flesh to the prophet it could not be otherwise than legitimate food.

A similar argument ensued when John was caught reading Thomas Dick's *The Christian Philosopher*. This book, by a Scotch contemporary written in a popular and engaging style, was very influential in its time. The aim of the author, in his own words, was "to illustrate the harmony which subsists between the system of nature and the system of revelation, and to show that the manifestations of God in the material universe ought to be blended with our view of the facts and doctrines recorded in the volume of inspiration." John, to his great disappointment, found that the word "Christian" in the title was not sufficient to overcome in his father's mind the suspicions aroused by the word "Philosopher." Timothy, he reminded John, had been advised to avoid "oppositions of science falsely so called," and the Colossians had been warned, "Beware lest any man spoil you through philosophy and vain deceit." John ventured to defend philosophy and science on the ground of their practical usefulness, but his father insisted that the Bible contained all the science and philosophy needed for the conduct of life. "But your spectacles," interposed John, "without which you cannot read the Bible, cannot be made without some knowledge of the science of optics." "Oh !" replied his father, "there will always be plenty of worldly people to make spectacles." Here, again, John found an opportunity to score on his father's literalism by quoting from Jeremiah a passage referring to the time when "all shall know the Lord from the least of them to the greatest of them," "and then," he asked, "who will make the spectacles?" But this time his father refused to acknowledge his discomfiture and ordered him to return the book to its owner. Daniel Muir remained inflexibly hostile to anything that savoured of a "harmony" or compromise between "nature" and "revelation" such as this book offered. John's mind, however, was beginning to trend in precisely that direction, and while for the time being he respected his father's ban of the book, he also records the fact that he "managed to read it later."

An estimate of the influence and importance of the farm period upon Muir's future career would not be complete without considering what he did in his cellar workshop. If the propriety of linking his love of reading with his love of "whittling" were not already sufficiently justified by the practical use to which he put his wooden clock, his own title "Knowledge and Inventions" for chapter seven of *The Story of My Boyhood and Youth* would satisfy the need of further warrant for so doing. By means of the early-rising attachment, which he perfected more and more, his clocks not only measured but created time and opportunity for him, so that knowledge and inventions were jointly furthered by the skill of his hands.

The invention of the self-setting sawmill and the wooden clock was speedily followed by other mechanical contrivances. One of these was a hickory clock shaped like a scythe to symbolise the scythe of Father Time. The handle bore the legend "All flesh is grass," and the pendulum in the form of a bunch of arrows, suggested the flight of time. This clock excited much admiration both at home and among the neighbours. It indicated the days of the week and the month as well as the diurnal time, and was still capably performing its functions fifty years later.

The success of this contrivance encouraged him to invent a still more ambitious clock, one with four dials, like a town clock, designed to be placed on the peak of the barn roof so that it could be read from the fields. But before it was finished his father stopped him, interposing the objection that it would attract too many people to the barn. Neither would he for the same reason allow him to put it in the top of an oak tree near the house where the two-second fourteen-foot pendulum would have had room to swing. He was, therefore, regretfully compelled to lay away the work uncompleted.

Another invention was a large thermometer with a dial on which the expansion and contraction of an iron rod, multiplied about thirty-two thousand times by a series of levers, was indicated by means of a hand operating against a counter-weight. So sensitive was it to variations of temperature that in cold weather the dial hand would move upon the approach of a person. This instrument was regarded as a great wonder by all the neighbours and extant letters show that a Mr. Varnel was seriously thinking of acquiring the right to manufacture it commercially.

While all the world now knows John Muir as a naturalist, his gifts and capacities in that sphere were as yet unrevealed and unrecognised. It was his skill and ingenuity as an inventor that focused the eyes and the interest of his rural friends upon him. They encouraged him to think that he would have no difficulty in securing employment in some machine shop, especially if he took some of his inventions to the Wisconsin State Agricultural Fair. The suggestion appealed to him, and when the Fair was convened in Madison, in the autumn of 1860, he reluctantly prepared to leave the parental roof. The diffident, bashful, home-loving youth, who now stood hesitatingly at the opening of a fateful new chapter of his life, bears little resemblance to the dauntless explorer and world traveller which he was ultimately destined to become.

CHAPTER THREE

As a Questioner at the Tree of Knowledge

WHEN JOHN MUIR left home in September, 1860, the political outlook of the country was far from hopeful. The speeches and debates of Lincoln and Douglas had made clear to the average citizen that some decisive action must soon be taken with respect to slavery; that, as Lincoln had said in 1858, "either the opponents of slavery will arrest the further spread of it, and place it where the public mind shall rest in the belief that it is in course of ultimate extinction; or its advocates will push it forward, till it shall become alike lawful in all the States, old as well as new – North as well as South." In May, 1860, Lincoln was nominated for the Presidency by the Republican National Convention assembled in Chicago, and was elected by an overwhelming popular vote the following November. A few weeks earlier Governor W.H.Gist of South Carolina had written a letter to each of the cotton States inviting their cooperation in case South Carolina should resolve to secede. The replies were favourable, and before Lincoln was inaugurated in March, 1861, at least seven Southern States had adopted ordinances of secession.

Such were conditions in the world beyond Hickory Hill farm when John Muir went forth with scrip and purse to find his fortune. His purse contained nothing but Grandfather Gilrye's farewell gift of a gold sovereign and a few dollars which he had earned by raising grain on a patch of abandoned ground. His scrip was the strangest with which a lad ever went forth from the parental roof – two large clocks whittled out of wood, and a thermometer made out of an old washboard, all tied together in a bundle for convenient transportation on his back. His brother David drove him to Pardeeville, a place he had never seen, though only nine miles distant from his home, and left him with his queer bundle on the station platform. For an account of the sensation which he immediately created with it in the little country town, and afterwards on the train and in Madison, the reader is referred to the vivid closing chapter of *The Story of My Boyhood and Youth*.

Experience promptly disproved his father's prediction that once out in the world he would soon meet with severer taskmasters than he had known in the person of his father. On the contrary, he met with marked kindness wherever he went, a fact which warrants the inference that he possessed engaging personal qualities. As his friends had anticipated, the originality

51

and novelty of Muir's inventions immediately opened all doors for him at the fair of the State Agricultural Society in Madison. Three days before it opened a local newspaper, under the caption of "An Ingenious Whittler," commented on his clocks and predicted that few articles in the exhibit would attract as much attention as these products of Mr. Muir's ingenuity.

During the preceding year the Society had held its meeting and fair at Milwaukee and Lincoln delivered on this occasion an address in which he set forth his conception of industrial education among a free people. In the phrase "free labour" he embodied his idea of contrast with the time when educated people did not value manual skill because they scorned to perform manual labour, regarding it as the lot of the uneducated. This divorce between education and creative toil, he maintained, cannot be approved in a democracy. Curiously enough the Scotch lad who the following year was to come under the notice of the same Agricultural Society through products of his manual skill might almost have stood as a concrete illustration of the following passage in Lincoln's address. "Free labour," he said, "argues that as the Author of man makes every individual with one head and one pair of hands, it was probably intended that heads and hands should cooperate as friends, and that that particular head should direct and control that pair of hands. As each man has one mouth to be fed and one pair of hands to furnish food, it was probably intended that that particular pair of hands should feed that particular mouth, that each head is the natural guardian, director and protector of the hands and mouth inseparably connected with it: and that being so, every head should be cultivated and improved by whatever will add to its capacity for performing its charge. In one word, free labour insists on universal education."

John had found a novel way of making his hands serve his head educationally and vice versa. His exhibition of the educational use to which he had been accustomed to put his clocks by harnessing them to his bed brought him the acquaintanceship of Mrs. Jeanne C. Carr, wife of Professor Ezra Slocum Carr, then Professor of Natural Science and of Chemistry at the University of Wisconsin. She was a native of Vermont, an uncommonly gifted woman, and passionately devoted to the study of plants. The Secretary of the State Agricultural Society, desiring to secure a premium for Muir's inventions, asked Mrs. Carr to report them to the proper committee, since they were not easy to classify under the Society's specifications. She, therefore, accompanied the Secretary to a part of the grounds where John Muir was engaged in exhibiting a practicable cooperative relation between brains and beds. An improvised bedstead, covered with a few blankets, was mysteriously connected with a home-made wooden clock. The latter, when set for a desired rising time, would tilt up the bed and set the sleeper on his feet upon the footboard. To aid him in his demonstrations Muir had secured the enthusiastic assistance of two small boys, one of them the son of James Davie Butler, Professor of Greek in the University of Wisconsin, and the other a son of Mrs. Carr. The lads pretended to be asleep until the contrivance set them on their feet amid the cheers of the spectators who were attracted quite as much by the young inventor's artless and humorously enthusiastic explanations as by the novelty of the mechanism. When some time later Professor Carr reported at home Muir's attendance upon his lectures at the University the two lads, hoping for a course of jack-knife studies, eagerly invited their ingenious friend to their respective homes where he became a frequent and much appreciated guest.

The manner in which Muir became a student at the University of Wisconsin a few months after the close of the fair need not be retold here, since he has done it himself in his published memoirs. The intervening months were spent at Prairie du Chien whither he went at the invitation of a Mr. Wirad who offered him employment in his machine-shop. The opportunity proved a disappointment, though his intercourse with the Pelton family at the Mondell House, where he gave service for his board, became the starting-point of a lifelong friendship, not without profit to the art of letters as will appear later. In short, John was not to win success at a canter. This was impressed upon him even during the first exciting weeks in Madison. A youth whose father had refused to promise assistance in need, and whose paltry hoard of savings was soon spent, had need of all his wits. "A body has an extraordinary amount of longfaced sober scheming and thought to get butter and bread," he writes, in a nostalgic letter to his sister Sarah before the close of the Fair. "Practice economy in all that you do."

"See that all that you do is founded upon Scripture," was the response he got from his father – surely a futile admonition to a penniless, struggling, homesick lad a month after he has left home! "The folks think it funny that you never date your letters, nor write your name at the end," complains his brother David, in allusion to a habit which John was long in outgrowing.

In January 1861, his mother acknowledges a letter from Madison, expresses surprise that he has left Prairie du Chien, and desires to know what he wants to study. She is still further surprised when a month later she learns that he is "batching at the University." She hopes his health, which has not been good lately, will not suffer under the new mode of living. He is having a hard time and she thinks his father will assist him a little, but does not know when. Meanwhile he must not be discouraged but make the best of his circumstances. Two months later his father does send him ten dollars with the admonition to be temperate, to love God more than making machines, and not to forget the poor destitute heathen! John, meanwhile, had no choice but to be temperate, for he occasionally had to cut his expenses for food to fifty cents a week. Daniel Muir's strangely perverted piety was equal to four "protracted meetings" a week and liberal gifts of money to vague and distant causes, while his own son was starving to obtain an education. "Let me know," he wrote, in sending the ten dollars, "when you are in great distress and I will try what I can do." The paternal letters are affectionate in tone at the beginning and the end, but this does not disguise the singular and baffling stolidity with which he holds out to John a doubtful possibility of assistance when his troubles shall have assumed the proportions of really great distress. With religious exhortation he was liberal enough, for practically every letter, from the first line to the last, is a farrago of pious admonition.

When Muir came to the University of Wisconsin there was attached to the institution a preparatory department that served the purpose of a modern accredited high school. John began his studies in this department, but his proficiency and maturity were such that he was admitted to the Freshman class in a few weeks. After a summer of farm work at home he returned to Madison in the autumn of that year, occupying again his old room in North Hall. The expenses of tuition, books, and board, though extremely reasonable when judged by present standards, speedily reduced him to financial straits again, and he decided to earn some money by teaching a country school, a makeshift to which many students resorted, alternating their terms of study with terms of school-teaching. John, however, did not wish to interrupt his studies, so he arranged to carry forward his University studies by night work during the spring term of 1862. A fellow student of the previous year, Harvey Reid, who had to discontinue his University work on account of similar difficulties, applauded his decision to teach. "Not only will it be of benefit to yourself," he wrote, "in giving you a thorough review of the common English branches, but the profession of teaching needs your kindness of heart, depth of principle, and courage in the right, to aid in making the youth of our country what a free people ought to be." The following letter exhibits him in his new role as teacher and "district school philosopher":

to Mr. and Mrs. David M. Galloway

McKeeley's District, Oak Hall, Wisconsin
February 9th, 1862

DEAR SARAH AND DAVID

I got your letter a good long while ago, but I have been so busy I have hardly known where I was. Mother wrote me that you were all pretty well. I am well as usual; the blessings attending district school-teaching do not seem to yield the injurious consequences which I had anticipated. The Monday morning that I commenced I did not know where to look, nor what to say, nor what to do, and I'm sure I looked bashful as any maid. A mud-turtle upside down on a velvet sofa was as much at home. I heard a scholar declare that the teacher didn't seem to know bran, but all moves with regularity and ease now.

I couldn't get my clocks out with me at first, and, as I had not a watch, I set to work and made a clock to keep time until I had an opportunity of getting my other one from Madison. It cost about two hours' work and kept time by water passing in a fine jet through a three cent piece. I have a big wheel set on the wall which tells the different classes when and how long to recite, and a machine, too, for making me a fire in the morning at any hour I please, so that when I go to the old log schoolhouse these cold biting mornings, I find everything warmed and a good fire. I sometimes think of a "fixin'" to box the boys' ears, for at first the cry of "He don't half whip," came loud and angrily from all parts of my parish, and, indeed, I did think it an awful thing to skelp the little chaps, even though so many did give proofs in rich abundance at times of being mischief to the end of the toes. My voice would shake for hours after each hazel application. But now they cause precious little agitation or compunction of soul. My scholars, however, nearly all mean to behave themselves. They are neither good nor bad, certainly not such children as Pollock speaks of, so good and guileless as to seem "made entire of beams of angels' eyes."

Sarah, how would you like to have a new home every five or six days? I often wish I could come home among you all a day or two, but, by the bye, you told Mrs. Parkins that you were coming down some day. I hope you will. The sleighing is good now. Ask for Oak Hall, which is about ten miles from Madison, south, then ask for McKeeley's district, or if you don't wish to come to school I will be in Madison any day you set. You had better come to school, though, and I will give you a lecture. I lecture every Saturday evening on Chemistry or Natural Philosophy, sometimes to sixty or seventy. You know it does not require much sapience to be a district school philosopher. Dave hasn't visited my school, nor I his. But I saw him once, and he said he was infinitely happy among his generous Dutch. He has singing schools, and sabbath schools, and writing schools. I hope Maggie and John are happy, and the wee body. May you all be always blest.   Goodbye.

JOHN MUIR

His term of school-teaching came to an end early in March and a sheaf of letters acknowledging gifts and expressing affectionate appreciation of the training received survive to tell of the deep impression he made upon his pupils. He now devoted his entire time to his university work, improvised a chemical laboratory in his room in North Hall, and continued to indulge his inventive proclivities. Muir's room, in fact, speedily became a show place, a museum, to which both professors and students were accustomed to bring visitors, particularly on Saturdays and Sundays.

One delicate bit of mechanism that especially attracted the attention and admiration of Mrs. Carr was an apparatus for registering the growth of an ascending plant stem during each of the twenty-four hours. The plant he had selected for this purpose was a Madeira Vine (*Boussingaultia baselloides*) which was growing luxuriantly in his sunniest window. A fine needle threaded with the long hair of a woman fellow student made the record upon a paper disk divided into minute spaces with great exactness. One of his wooden clocks applied and controlled the motive power. An invention in lighter vein was what he called his "loafer's chair." It was a wooden chair with a split bottom over which an awkward crosspiece had been nailed in front, apparently to cure the split, but really to make the sitter spread his knees. As soon as the supposed loafer settled down on the chair and leaned back, he pressed a concealed spring which fired a heavily charged old pistol directly under the seat. The leaps of the victims are said to have been worth seeing. These and other contrivances made John's room such a place of wonders to Pat the janitor that for decades afterwards he was accustomed to relate its marvels and point it out to newcomers.

In the autumn of 1916 the writer secured from surviving fellow students at the University of Wisconsin some personal impressions and recollections of John Muir as a student in Madison. Among those consulted were J. G. Taylor, Philip Stein, and Charles E. Vroman, and they all agreed in describing Muir as an extraordinary type of student. The account of Mr. Vroman, who became Muir's room-mate upon entering the University in the spring of 1862, is given as nearly as possible in his own words:

My acquaintance with John Muir began when a tutor, John D. Parkinson, took me in tow and led me to the northeast corner room of North Hall on the first floor. It was my first impression that the tutor was showing me a part of the college museum, for it was a strange-looking place to be the room of a college student. The room was lined with shelves, one above the other, higher than a man could reach. These shelves were filled with retorts, glass tubes, glass jars, botanical and geological specimens, and small mechanical contrivances. On the floor around the sides of the room were a number of machines of larger size whose purposes were not apparent at a glance, but which I came to know later. A young man was busily engaged sawing boards and presently the tutor introduced him as John Muir. I was much younger than he and was entering the preparatory department, but it was the beginning of a close and delightful college friendship. When telling me stories of his early life, or reading Burns, he often dropped into a rich Scotch brogue, although he wrote and spoke English perfectly. The only books which I remember seeing him read were his Bible, the poems of Robert Burns, and his college textbooks. It was a very hard and dreary life which he had been compelled to live on his father's farm, but in spite of all he was the most cheerful, happy-hearted man I ever knew.

Muir boarded himself during his stay at the University, as did other students. His fare was very simple, consisting chiefly of bread and molasses, graham mush, and baked potatoes. Being on good terms with Pat, he had access to the wood furnaces in the basement where he could boil his mush on the coals and bake his potatoes in the hot ashes. For exercise he played wicket, walked, and swam. Muir's course of study, while irregular, corresponded closely to what was then called the modern classical. The last two years of his course were devoted to chemistry and geology. There were no laboratory facilities in the University at that time, so Muir built a chemical laboratory in his own room. He was by common consent regarded as the most proficient chemical student in the college. In disposition Muir was gentle and loving – a high minded Christian gentleman, clean in thought and action. While he was not a very regular attendant at church, he read his Bible regularly, said his morning and evening prayers each day, and led the kind of life which all this implies. He was, however, in no respect austere or lacking in humour, but bubbling over with fun, and a keen participant in frolics and college pranks, especially when Pat the janitor needed to be taken down.

The summer of 1862 Muir spent for the most part at the old Fountain Hill farm with his sister and brother-in-law. The following letter written after his return to Madison reflects the then prevailing uncertainty regarding the continuance of the University. It had no Chancellor at this time and was seriously short of funds. The affairs of the University were administered by the faculty under the chairmanship of Professor John W. Sterling, whose unselfish devotion and unquestioned ability entitled him, in the opinion of the most distinguished alumni, to be made Chancellor. But the strangely myopic regents of this period let him do the work of holding the University together from 1859 to 1867 without even the title of Vice-Chancellor and without extra salary.

On July 2nd, 1862, President Lincoln signed the Morrill Act, which marks one of the greatest advances in the history of American education. By this Act each State was given for educational purposes thirty thousand acres of land for each of its Senators and Representatives in Congress. The conditions attached to the grant were easily fulfilled, but the authorities of the University of Wisconsin allowed four years to elapse before they effected the reorganisation that entitled them to claim the benefit of the Act. Even the prospect of this aid, however, had a heartening effect upon the little group that kept the University alive in hope of better times.

Muir's letter is of interest, too, because it shows that he was training himself in the art of crayon sketching, an art in which he was later to gain great proficiency, and one that proved invaluable to him in the keeping of his exploration journals.

to Mr. and Mrs. David M. Galloway

Madison, Autumn, 1862

DEAR BROTHER AND SISTER

Perhaps you begin to think it long since I wrote last. After leaving the sheaves and thrashing machine, the merry sound of our old bell made me all crazy with joy. I think I love my studies more and more, and instead of the time for dismissing them coming nearer, as one term after another passes, it seems to go farther and farther away.

We live in changing times, and our plans may easily be broken, but if not I shall be seeking knowledge for some years, here or elsewhere.

Our University has reached a crisis in its history, and if not passed successfully, the doors will be closed, when of course I should have to leave Madison for some institution which has not yet been wounded to the death by our war demon.

If John Reid can spare me money I shall not teach this winter, for though it seems an easy way of making a hundred dollars every winter, yet the time for acquiring as much as I desire would in that way be too much prolonged. That money will likely be spent, as the Catholics say, for the benefit of my soul.

Those pictures are framed and I need not tell you that they are prized a good deal. Our tutor takes a great liking to the lake, and wishes it in his room. If more time could be spared for drawing I would send you a picture once or twice in a while, as I know you have a taste for them . . . .

This war seems farther from a close than ever. How strange that a country with so many schools and churches should be desolated by so unsightly a monster. "Leaves have their time to fall," and though indeed there is a kind of melancholy present when they, withered and dead, are plucked from their places and made the sport of the gloomy autumn wind, yet we hardly deplore their fate, because there is nothing unnatural in it. They have done all that their Creator wished them to do, and they should not remain longer in their green vigour. But may the same be said of the slaughtered upon a battle field? If you might be successful you would go far to bring the millennium to get love into those leopards and lambs, would you not?

But goodbye, I wish God's blessing for yourselves and little ones. Come and see me if you can, as possibly I may have to go farther from home.

Give me a letter, each of you, soon.

JOHN MUIR

It was to be expected that a young man of Muir's sensitive nature and rigid religious training would find the Civil War an agonizing problem. Camp Randall, where about seventy thousand men were drilled and mobilized in the course of four years, was situated half a mile west of the University and within full view of the campus. Often he went there to look after the comfort of friends or to bid them farewell.

Fragments of an extensive correspondence show that he became a tender and solicitous religious adviser to numerous enlisted men who craved this service. Among them are former students of the University whose names, apparently, were lost from the alumni records. The fearful toll of life exacted by unsanitary conditions in the military camps weighed heavily upon his mind and probably had something to do with his long-cherished purpose to enter the profession of medicine.

One day in the spring of 1863 his fellow student, M. S. Griswold, accidentally detained him for a moment on the steps of North Hall with questions about a locust blossom that he picked from a branch overhead. It was a fateful moment for Muir. He professed to know nothing about botany, so Mr. Griswold proceeded to tell him about the family relationship of the locust tree, and before the conversation was ended, Muir had caught an entrancing vision of a science new to him. "This fine lesson," he wrote in his memoirs, "charmed me and sent me flying to the woods and meadows in wild enthusiasm. . . . I wandered away at every opportunity, making long excursions round the lakes, gathering specimens and keeping them fresh in a bucket in my room to study at night after my regular class tasks were learned; for my eyes never closed on the plant glory I had seen.'' By such chance occurrences are the destinies of men determined. Had it not been for this new enthusiasm coming into his life he would undoubtedly have entered the medical profession. The following letter is the first to reflect the consequences of his new passion. The ''somewhere much farther away'' refers to incipient plans to enter the Medical School of the University of Michigan.

to Mr. and Mrs. David M. Galloway

Madison, June 1st, 1863

DEAR SARAH AND DAVID

Unless hindered by circumstances not seen now, I shall be at Watson's Thursday, [June] 18th. I am sorry that you have not been able to visit me, as I will not return to Madison, but will go somewhere much farther away, so that you will not be so able to reach me, as now.

I cannot do anything toward analysing your plant, Sarah, without the flower. I mean to be happy for a few days around Fountain Lake in collecting specimens for my herbarium. I returned last Saturday evening from a long ramble of twenty-five miles through marshes, mud, and brushwood with a heavy basketful of flowers, weeds, moss and bush-twigs, having made five or six visits besides, and pressed thirty specimens or more. So you need not cry over my sober face. I am not so feeble, you see.

You would like the study of Botany. It is the most exciting thing in the form of even amusement, much more of study, that I ever knew. Very unlike the grave tangled Greek and Latin, but I will see you soon. Goodbye.

Affectionately yours

J. MUIR

[P.S.] I had almost forgotten, Sarah, to tell you that I was elected judge in one of the debating clubs a short time ago, also President of the Young Men's Christian Association. You say that you expect something great by and by! Am not I great now?

Within a week he withdrew the appointment to be met at Watson's, saying that he was going on a long botanical and geological tour down the Wisconsin River valley and into Iowa. "I am not so well as I was last term," he writes. "I need a rest. Perhaps my tour will do me good, though a three or four hundred mile walk with a load is not, at least in appearance, much of a rest." He went with two companions and an account of the excursion was subsequently communicated to Miss Emily Pelton, then of Prairie du Chien, in a series of letters predated as if they had been written "during the ramble," but actually written six months later, just before he went on a botanical tour into Canada.

to Miss Emily Pelton

Fountain Lake, February 27th, 1864

DEAR FRIEND EMILY

You speak in your last letter of the pleasure which a letter written during the ramble would have given, but it is not yet too late.

"Backward, turn backward, O Time, in your flight!"

Recess in the Bluffs near McGregor, Iowa
July 7th, 1863

DEAR FRIEND EMILY

This evening finds us encamped near McGregor. We have spent a toilsome day, but it has not been without interest. In the morning we were directed to a romantic glen down which a little stream sought a path, turning the mosses to stone as it went, and watering many interesting flowers. "The road that leads to it," said the man, "lies close along the river brink. It is not very far and a log house marks the glen's narrow entrance." We remarked that in following our directions, when we had inquired more particularly about the exact position of the log house after we had proceeded some distance on our way, the person we inquired of gave us some very curious glances which we could not understand. As we proceeded on our way we could not withstand the temptation to climb the bluffs that beetled so majestically overhead, and after many vain attempts we at last found a place where the ascent was practicable. We had to make many a halt for rest, and made as much use of our hands as of our feet, but the splendid view well repaid the toil.

After enjoying the delightful scenery and analysing some specimens which we gathered on our way, we began to wish ourselves down again, as the afternoon was wearing away and we wished to visit the glen before night, but descending was still more difficult, and we several times reached an almost unstoppable velocity. We found the first specimen of Desmodium in this vicinity and several beautiful Labiatae.

After travelling a good way down the river we began to fear that we had already passed the object of our search, but, when the sun's rays were nearly level and we had just emerged from a mass of low leafy trees, we were suddenly struck with the most genuine astonishment at the unique and unexpected sight so full before us. We expected that a log house in such a place would be a faultless specimen of those pioneer establishments with outside chimney, the single window, and door overrun with hop vines or wild honeysuckle, the dooryard alive with poultry and pigs, and the barnyard at hand with its old straw-stack and street of dilapidated stables and sheds, with cows, dirty children, and broken plows sprinkled over all.

But judge, Emily, of our surprise when, upon a piece of ground where the bluffs had curved backward a little from the river, we at once saw the ruinous old house with four gaudily dressed females in an even row in front, with two idle men seated a little to one side looking complacently upon them like a successful merchant upon a stock of newly arrived goods. Not a broken fence, dirty boy, or squealing pig was to be seen, but there on such a background the old decaying logs and the dark majestic hills on which the soft shades of evening were beginning to fall – there, in clothes which had been dipped many times in most glaring dyes, sat the strange four. It was long before I could judge of the character of the establishment, but I saw at once there was something very strange about it, and instinctively fell behind my companion. He was equally ignorant, but boldly marched forward and asked for the glen where fossils were found. This was a subject of which they knew but little. They told us that the path went no further, that the hills were unclimbable, etc. We then took the alarm, gained the summit of the bluffs after an hour's hard labour, built our campfire, congratulated each other on our escape, and spoke much from the first chapter of Proverbs.

You will perhaps soon hear from us again. Truly your friend

J. M.

to Miss Emily Pelton

Camp below the junction of the Wisconsin
with the Mississippi, July 8th, 1863

DEAR FRIEND EMILY

When morning had dawned after our evening log house adventure, we found ourselves upon the brink of one of the highest points overhanging the river. It seemed as though we might almost leap across it. The sun was unclouded, and shone with fine effect upon the fleecy sea of fog contained by its ample banks of bluffs. Later it flowed smoothly away as we gazed and gave us the noble Mississippi in full view.

Breaking the spell which bound us here so long, we leisurely proceeded to explore the pretty glen which we had passed before in the dark. Here we spent some hours of great interest and added some fine plants and fossils to our growing wealth, and soon found ourselves upon the shore of the great river. The genuine calm of a July morning was now master of all. The river flowed on, smooth as a woodland lake, reflecting the full beams of the dreamy light, while not on all the dark foliage which feathered its mountain wall moved a single breeze. We stood harnessed and half asleep with the settled calm, looking wishfully upon the cool waters, when suddenly the thought struck us, "How fine it would be to purchase a boat and sail merrily up the Wisconsin to Portage." We would read and work the oars by turn as our heavy packs would be stowed snugly away beneath the seats, and every few miles we would land at an inviting place and gather new spoils. And so in a few minutes we had our effects packed snugly, as I have described, in a pretty boat, and were joyfully floating on the bosom of the Father of Waters.

But, alas, how vain our large hopes of promised bliss! We reached the mouth of the Wisconsin River and soon our bright faces grow less and less bright till gloomy as a winter's day, as we paddle with all our might, shooting bravely on against the current at the fearful velocity of ten rods per two hours. At last, completely exhausted, we give up, for a moment, in despair and are instantly returned to the Mississippi by the boiling current. But we were not yet beaten, for holding a council of war against the bustling stream, we determined to "Try, try again."

So, landing, we procured a pair of boards, by the necessitous act of self-appropriation, and proceeded to make two pair of oars. They were nearly made before dark. We found a new camping ground and sought repose with hearts again trimmed with fresh hope . . . .

I shall write you again and give you the result of to-day's labour. I wish you would write immediately on receiving this. Address Wauzeka [Wisconsin.] I shall pass near that place in a few days.   Truly your friend

J. MUIR

to Miss Emily Pelton

Farmhouse near Wright's Ferry, July 9th, 1863

DEAR FRIEND EMILY

We started, in good spirits again, this morning, with our long oars manufactured by our hatchet. We applied them to our little boat and soon were again at the mouth of the Wisconsin which came tumbling down rapid and restless as ever. At each pull of the oars our little fairy almost leaps from the water, but we were now in the very midst of the boiling waters. We shoot now to this side, now to that, making very acute angles, and almost capsizing several times. Again we pull harder than ever – again are baffled. We are drenched thoroughly with streaming sweat, but we have strength remaining and have already conquered fifteen or twenty rods. The combat is prolonged amid splashing and boiling, now drifting back, now gaining a few rods, now fast on a sand-bar on this side, now aground on the other, till the victory was again wrenched from us, and, drawing our boat up on a large sand bank we disembarked, laid our packs at our feet, and with uncovered heads, thus addressed the culprit boat, each in turn:

"O Boat, heretic and perverse, why persist in this obstinate and unprofitable determination of opposition to the reasonable demands of thy lords and masters? . . . Shame be thy portion! Thou art small and light as a baby's cradle, but obstinate and unsteerable as Noah's ark. . . . Depart from my service to that of another upon thy parent whom thou seemest to love, and may'st thou serve her better than thou hast served me."

This said, a card was nailed upon a conspicuous place and directed to Mrs. Goodrich*, Dubuque, Iowa, and two three cent stamps placed on it as it was overweight. Then pushing it into the current we watched it a few minutes as it sailed away, now appearing and now lost, as it passed the willows upon the bank. Then we again placed our old companion packs, and soberly

---

* Note by Mrs Emily Pelton Wilson: "A friend he met in our house in Prairie du Chien."

marched away with unequal steps through the tall grass, like good Æneas with his Penates when cast upon Queen Dido's coast.

After a very wearisome walk over wet places and fallen trees we reached the house where I now write. We did not intend to stop here, but only called for our fifth meal, as we had but one yesterday, and we wished to make a fair average. But the old lady of the mansion gave us so good a welcome that we entered and she made us supper. She has invited us to stay all night. She, we had observed from the first, was possessed of a lasting fund of everyday benevolence, and just a few minutes ago she told us her reason. " I have," she said, "a son who was some years in New Mexico. Many times he was refused shelter from storm and compelled to pass long nights in rain and sleet. I was determined that *though I should be occasionally imposed upon* I should never refuse the rites of hospitality *to any*." This, I think, is as noble a sentiment as ever came from mortal lips, and if I live, she shall know some time that I have not forgotten her. My companion, as I write, is listening to the narration of this son's adventures. This is the only place where we have met with a really cordial reception.

Good-bye. You may hear from me again when I reach a convenient point.

Write soon. [JOHN MUIR]

Apparently the trio of young naturalists had difficulty in finding the wherewithal to satisfy their healthy outdoor appetites. The following narrative poem, which accompanied the foregoing letters to Miss Pelton, describes the difficulties they encountered while searching for a breakfast:

IN SEARCH OF A BREAKFAST

Dedicated to the
"Patron of all those luckless brains,
 Which to the wrong side leaning,
Indite much metre with much pains
And little or no meaning."

The early breeze of morning falls
Upon the trembling chamber walls,
The hour of evening, one by one,
Retreat before the joyful sun.
Our heroes' task of resting o'er,
They leave their ever-open door
And yawn, and stretch, and view the sky
With looks and garments much awry;
Then seek, with faltering steps and slow
The bustling stream that winds below,
Where, like wet poultry after rain,

That trim disordered plumes again,
They wash, and lave, and dress their hair,
And for the breakfast search prepare.

All harnessed now, in rambling style,
With bounding glee they march a while;
The gen'rous grass and twigs bestow
Their dewy honours as they go,
Till we might deem the stranger three
All night had drifted in the sea.
Minutely now each sheltered shade,
Soft sedgy pool and waving glade,
Is searched throughout with patient eye,
If stranger plant they might descry.
If such be found, no golden treasure
May bring so much of honest pleasure.
But smoke curls on that mountain brow,
And breakfast is the question now.

The house is gained – with air half bold
Their tale of morning hunger's told;
They ask no bun of prickly taste,
No pie complex with frosty paste,
No fiery mixture striped with candy,
No slimy oysters boiled in brandy,
But bread and milk, at any time
Purchased with a paper dime.
But ah! How marred was breakfast then.
How lost the plans of "mice and men"!
For bread –" I've none," good mother cries,
" Because my risings did not rise.
I've biscuit, but a pair at most,
And as for milk, the cow is lost.
But, three miles farther on your way
You'll come to Dick and Simon Day."

With tardy steps they leave the door
And more a hungered than before,
And slow, the lengthened miles they tread
Which lead to Simon's timber shed.
With growing emphasis they tell
How 'neath a cotton sheet they dwell,
And 'mid the hills all daylight hours
Roam near and far for weeds and flowers.

But growling want still pressing sore
Compels to seek the farmer's door,
And add with deeply serious brow,
How much they feel of hunger now.

But Simon has no bread to spare,
The milk is soured by sultry air.
But Jacob Wise at Fountain well
" Has heaps of cows, and milk to sell."
Then from a fallen log they rise
And gravely steer for Farmer Wise.
Meanwhile the day of sultry June
Approaches fast the hour of noon.
Our heroes, faint and fainter still,
Toil on with braced unfaltering will,
Till on a ridge of thistly ground
The home of Master Wise is found,
And, waxing bold, our starving men
Bestow their tale of want again.
But Jacob with commanding air
Presents on each a Yankee stare,
And slowly, in dull angry tone,
Assures them they "had best be gone."

But stanchly fixed with needful will,
Till fed with milk and bread their fill,
And, wiser grown, they know their task
And kindly divers questions ask:
How long beside this darkened wood
His house and handsome barn have stood?
How old himself and curly dog?
How much had weighed his fattest hog?
How great the price of meadow hay?
How far from here his clearing lay?
These chords so struck resounding well,
With kindling eye he'll warely tell
How first this woodland farm he found
When all was Indian hunting ground.
And coons and herds of fallow deer
Were tame as sheep or broken steer,
And howling wolf and savage yell
Mixed all the echoes up the dell.

Thus poulticed he, inflamed before,

Is calm as Boss, and all her store
Uncreamed, with bread and Sally's pie,
Bestows with kindly beaming eye.
"Nor aught," said he, "will I deny
To honest folks as good as I;
But strolling men of wiley looks,
A peddlin' clothes and dirty books,
Howe'er so larned or big they be
Much comfort ne'er shall get from me."

The following letter, bearing no indication of place or date, probably was written toward the end of July, 1863, shortly before he left Madison to assist his brother-in-law in harvest work on the Fountain Lake farm. If so, it describes, perhaps, the last botanical excursion he made from Madison.

to Mr. and Mrs. David M. Galloway

[Madison, July, 1863]

Since writing last we have been on many a hill, and walked "o'er moors and mosses many o," but the best of all our rambles was one which was completed last Friday. We took the train from here Thursday morning for Kilbourn, a small town on the Wisconsin River towards LaCrosse, rambled all day among the glorious tangled valleys and lofty perpendicular rocks of the famous Dells, stayed over night in Kilbourn, and voyaged to Portage next day upon a raft of our own construction. The thousandth part of what we enjoyed was pleasure beyond telling. At the Dells the river is squeezed between lofty frowning sandstone rocks. The invincible Wisconsin has been fighting for ages for a free passage to the Mississippi, and only this crooked and narrow slit has been granted or gained.

At present all is peace, but the river, though calm, does not appear contented. Only a few foam-bells are seen, but they float with an air of tardy settled sullenness past the black yawning fissures and beetling, threatening rock-brows above. But when winter with its locking ice has yielded to the authoritative looks of the high summer sun, just at the darkest of the year before any flowers are overhead or any of the rock ferns have unrolled their precious bundles, then the war is renewed with the most terrific, roaring, foaming, gnashing fury. Fierce legions come pouring in from many an upland swamp and lake, in irresistible haste, through broken gorge and valley gateways. All in one they rush to battle clad in foam – rise high upon their ever-resisting enemy, and with constant victory year by year gain themselves a wider and straighter way.

Kilbourn station is about two miles below the Dells. We went to the river-side and at once began to find new plants. The banks are rocky and romantic for many miles both above and below the Dells. On going up the river we were delightfully opposed and threatened by a great many semi-gorge ravines running at right angles to the river, too steep to cross at every point and much too long to be avoided if to wish to avoid them were possible. Those ravines are the most perfect, the most heavenly plant conservatories I ever saw. Thousands of happy flowers are there, but ferns and mosses are the favoured ones. No human language will ever describe them. We travelled two miles in eight hours, and such scenery, such sweating, scrambling, climbing, and happy hunting and happy finding of dear plant beings we never before enjoyed.

The last ravine we encountered was the most beautiful and deepest and longest and narrowest. The rocks overhang and bear a perfect selection of trees which hold themselves towards one another from side to side with inimitable grace, forming a flower-veil of indescribable beauty. The light is measured and mellowed. For every flower springs, too, and pools, are there in their places to moisten them. The walls are fringed and painted most divinely with the bright green polypodium and asplenium and mosses and liverworts with grey lichens, and here and there a clump of flowers and little bushes. The floor was barred and banded and sheltered by bossy, shining, moss-clad logs cast in as needed from above. Over all and above all and in all the glorious ferns, tall, perfect, godlike, and here and there amid their fronds a long cylindrical spike of the grand fringed purple orchis.

But who can describe a greenhouse planned and made and planted and tended by the Great Creator himself. Mrs. Davis wished a fernery. Tell her I wish she could see this one and this rock-work. We cannot remove such places to our homes, but they cut themselves keenly into our memories and remain pictured in us forever.

[JOHN MUIR]

Muir had lingered in Madison after the close of the University session, partly to botanize amid its lovely natural surroundings, partly because of his attachment for the place where his eyes had been opened to a greater world of knowledge and of beauty. But the time of departure finally came. "From the top of a hill on the north side of Lake Mendota," he writes in the closing paragraph of *The Story of My Boyhood and Youth*, "I gained a last wistful, lingering view of the beautiful University grounds and buildings where I had spent so many hungry and happy and hopeful days. There with streaming eyes I bade my blessed Alma Mater farewell. But I was only leaving one University for another, the Wisconsin University for the University of the Wilderness."

CHAPTER FOUR

The Sojourn in Canada 1864–1866

WHEN JOHN MUIR left the University of Wisconsin in June, 1863, he had fully resolved to begin the study of medicine at Ann Arbor. There are a number of warmly worded letters of introduction from Madison friends who wished to smooth his way at the University of Michigan. "You will find in him the greatest modesty joined with high moral and religious excellence," wrote one of them to James R. Boise, then Professor of Greek in the latter institution. How far these plans for the definite choice of a profession had progressed is apparent also in the fact that friends addressed letters to him at the Medical School and evinced surprise when they were returned unclaimed. "A draft was being made," he wrote in explanation to one of them, "just when I should have been starting for Ann Arbor, which kept me at home."

Meanwhile his fellow student, James L. High, later a distinguished lawyer in Chicago, wound up his affairs at Madison and made a report in November. "Our class," he wrote, "numbers only five, viz., Wallace, Spooner, Salisbury, Congar, and myself. Leahey has gone into the army, and Lewis is a senior at Union College, New York. So, as you see, we are small in numbers, but we are making a brave fight of it nevertheless. The Societies are doing unusually well this term. Yours numbers about twenty-five members, and ours over forty." Then follows an account of his efforts to collect small loans which Muir had made to fellow students. The society referred to as "yours" was the Athenae Literary and Debating Society of which he was one of the founders.

Returning from his botanical rambles in July, John spent the autumn and winter on the old Fountain Lake farm which, some time in 1856, had passed into the hands of his brother-in-law, David Galloway. "With study and labour I have scarcely been at all sensible of the flight of time since I reached home," he writes at the end of February to his friend Emily Pelton. "In my walks to and from my field work and in occasional rambles I, of course, searched every inch of ground for botanical specimens which, preserved in water, were analysed at night. My task was seldom completed before twelve or one o'clock. I was just thinking today that soon the little anemones would be peering above ground."

But even at this time, when the new sap was barely beginning to swell the buds, the young naturalist was pluming his wings for a long flight. "I have enjoyed the company of my dear relatives very much during this long visit," he adds, "but I shall soon leave them all, and I scarcely think it probable that I shall be blest with so much of home again." As for the study of medicine, he merely remarks that he had "by no means given up all hope of still finding an opportunity to pursue this favourite study some other time." But that time never came. Two days later, on March 1st, 1864, he announces, in a parting note to the same friend, "I am to take the cars in about half an hour. I really do not know where I shall halt. I feel like Milton's Adam and Eve – 'The world was all before them where to choose their place of rest.' "

It would be impossible now to trace any part of the intricate route which finally led him to Meaford, County Grey, Canada West, were it not for one of those fortunate incidents which sometimes occur to gladden the heart of a biographer. In editing Muir's journal and notes written during his "thousand-mile walk to the gulf " the writer began to realise how much easier it would be, at critical points, to follow his wanderings if one had his herbarium specimens with the identification slips, giving date and place of collection. But no part of the herbarium gathered during the sixties seemed to have survived the wanderings of this modern Ulysses.

In looking over some correspondence with Mrs. Julia Merrill Moores, one of his early Indianapolis friends, the writer found reason to suppose that Muir had left for safekeeping at her house some of his belongings when he went South in 1867. Though she had passed on long ago the clue seemed worth following, and a search in Indianapolis proved successful beyond all expectations. For the attic of her son, Charles W. Moores, yielded up large parts of the long forgotten herbarium which Muir had gathered during the years from 1864 to 1867.

Since no letters or notebooks of Muir from the period between March and October, 1864, have been found, the little identification slips, though not precise in giving geographical localities, furnish important clues to his movements. In April he was already wading about in Canadian swamps, and by the month of May he had penetrated northward as far as Simcoe County. On the 18th of that month he started – on a three weeks' ramble through Simcoe and Grey Counties, walking an estimated distance of about three hundred miles through the townships of Guillimbury, Tecumseh, Adjala, Mono, Amaranth, Luther, Arthur, Egremont, Proton, Glenelg, Bentinck, Sullivan, Holland, and Sydenham. "Much of Adjala and Mono," he notes, "is very uneven and somewhat sandy; many fields here are composed of abrupt gravel hillocks; inhabitants are nearly all Irish. Amaranth, Luther, and Arthur abound in extensive Tamarac and Cedar swamps, dotted with beaver meadows. I spent seven and a half hours in one of these solitudes extraordinary. Land and water, life and death, beauty and deformity, seemed here to have disputed empire and all shared equally at last. I shall not soon

forget the chaos of fallen trees in all stages of decay and the tangled branches
of the white cedars through which I had to force my way; nor the feeling
with which I observed the sun wheeling to the West while yet above, beneath,
and around all was silence and the seemingly endless harvest of swamp.
Above all I will not soon forget the kindness shown me by an Irish lady on
my emerging from this shadow of death near her dwelling.''

Of memoranda made on this ramble there survives only the following
additional note:

> It was with no little difficulty that my object in seeking "these wilds traversed
> by few" was explained to the sturdy and hospitable lairds of these remote
> districts. "Botany" was a term they had not heard before in use. What did it
> mean? If told that I was collecting plants, they would desire to know whether
> it was cabbage plants that I sought, and if so, how could I find cabbage
> plants in the bush? Others took me for a government official of some kind,
> or minister, or pedlar.

One day an interesting human discovery is made and recorded thus: "Found
Dunbar people, much to my surprise, far in the dark maple woods; spent a
pleasant day with them in rehearsing Dunbar matters."

During July he was botanising north of Toronto in the Holland River
swamps, and on highlands near Hamilton and Burlington bays. In August he
is again about the shores of Lake Ontario and in the vicinity of Niagara
Falls. A "wolf forest," mentioned on several slips, is doubtless the place on
the southern shore of Lake Ontario where one night he had an adventure
with wolves. That as well as other incidents form the subject of the following
fragmentary autobiographical sketch which fortunately covers this period of
Canadian wanderings in some detail:

> After earning a few dollars working on my brother-in-law's farm near Portage,
> I set off on the first of my long lonely excursions, botanising in glorious
> freedom around the Great Lakes and wandering through innumerable tamarac
> and arbor-vitae swamps, and forests of maple, basswood, ash, elm, balsam,
> fir, pine, spruce, hemlock, rejoicing in their bound wealth and strength and
> beauty, climbing the trees, revelling in their flowers and fruit like bees in
> beds of goldenrods, glorying in the fresh cool beauty and charm of the bog
> and meadow heathworts, grasses, carices, ferns, mosses, liverworts displayed
> in boundless profusion.
>
> The rarest and most beautiful of the flowering plants I discovered on this
> first grand excursion was *Calypso borealis* (the Hider of the North). I had
> been fording streams more and more difficult to cross and wading bogs and
> swamps that seemed more and more extensive and more difficult to force
> one's way through. Entering one of these great tamarac and arbor-vitae
> swamps one morning, holding a general though very crooked course by
> compass, struggling through tangled drooping branches and over and under

broad heaps of fallen trees, I began to fear that I would not be able to reach dry ground before dark, and therefore would have to pass the night in the swamp and began, faint and hungry, to plan a nest of branches on one of the largest trees or windfalls like a monkey's nest, or eagle's, or Indian's in the flooded forests of the Orinoco described by Humboldt.

But when the sun was getting low and everything seemed most bewildering and discouraging, I found beautiful Calypso on the mossy bank of a stream, growing not in the ground but on a bed of yellow mosses in which its small white bulb had found a soft nest and from which its one leaf and one flower sprung. The flower was white and made the impression of the utmost simple purity like a snowflower. No other bloom was near it, for the bog a short distance below the surface was still frozen, and the water was ice cold. It seemed the most spiritual of all the flower people I had ever met. I sat down beside it and fairly cried for joy.

It seems wonderful that so frail and lowly a plant has such power over human hearts. This Calypso meeting happened some forty-five years ago, and it was more memorable and impressive than any of my meetings with human beings excepting, perhaps, Emerson and one or two others. When I was leaving the University, Professor J. D. Butler said, "John, I would like to know what becomes of you, and I wish you would write me, say once a year, so I may keep you in sight." I wrote to the Professor, telling him about this meeting with Calypso, and he sent the letter to an Eastern newspaper [*The Boston Recorder*] with some comments of his own. These, as far as I know, were the first of my words that appeared in print.

How long I sat beside Calypso I don't know. Hunger and weariness vanished, and only after the sun was low in the west I plashed on through the swamp, strong and exhilarated as if never more to feel any mortal care. At length I saw maple woods on a hill and found a log house. I was gladly received. "Where ha ye come fra? The swamp, that awfu' swamp. What were ye doin' there?" etc. "Mony a puir body has been lost in that muckle, cauld, dreary bog and never been found." When I told her I had entered it in search of plants and had been in it all day, she wondered how plants could draw me to these awful places, and said, "It's God's mercy ye ever got out."

Oftentimes I had to sleep without blankets, and sometimes without supper, but usually I had no great difficulty in finding a loaf of bread here and there at the houses of the farmer settlers in the widely scattered clearings. With one of these large backwoods loaves I was able to wander many a long wild fertile mile in the forests and bogs, free as the winds, gathering plants, and glorying in God's abounding inexhaustible spiritual beauty bread. Storms, thunderclouds, winds in the woods – were welcomed as friends.

Only once in these long Canada wanderings was the deep peace of the wilderness savagely broken. It happened in the maple woods about midnight when I was cold and my fire was low. I was awakened by the awfully dismal wolf-howling and got up in haste to replenish the fire. Some of the wolves around me seemed very near, judging by their long-drawn-out howling, while others were replying farther and farther away; but the nearest of all was much nearer than I was aware of, for when I had succeeded in producing a blaze that lighted up the bushes around me, and was in the act of stooping to pick up a branch to add to the blaze, a large grey wolf that had been standing within less than ten feet of me rushed past so startlingly near that I threw the limb at the wolf. This put an end to sleep for that night. I watched and listened and kept up a good far-reaching blaze, which perhaps helped to keep them at bay. Anyhow I saw no more of them, although they continued their howling conversation until near daylight.

I had to stop again and again in all sorts of places when money gave out, accepting work of any kind and at any price, and with a few hard-earned dollars, earned at chopping, clearing, grading, harvesting, going on and on again, thus coming in contact with the people and learning something of their lives.

Among the farmers in the region between Toronto and the Georgian Bay I found not a single American. They were Scotch, English, and Irish, mostly Scotch. Many of them were Highlanders who had been driven from their little farms and garden patches in the glens by the Duke of Sutherland when he cleared his estates of these brave home-loving men to make room for sheep. Most of the old folks, by the time of my visit, had gone to rest in their graves, and the farms they had so laboriously cleared were in the possession of their children, who were living in good brick houses in comparative affluence and ease.

At one of those Highland Scotch farms I stopped for more than a month, working and botanising. The family consisted of the mother, her daughter, and two sons. Here I had a fine interesting time. Mrs. Campbell could hardly have been kinder had I been her own son, and her two big boys,* twenty and twenty-five years of age, were also very kind and fonder of practical jokes than almost anybody I ever met. In the long summer days I used to get up about daylight and take a walk among the interesting plants of a broad marsh through which the Holland River flows. I had not been feeling very well and motherly Mrs. Campbell was somewhat anxious about my health. One morning the boys, finding my bed empty and knowing that I must have gone botanising in the Holland River swamp, and knowing also the anxiety of their mother about my health, put a large bag of carpet rags, that was kept in the garret, in my bed and pulled the blankets over it. When Mrs. Campbell met the boys before breakfast and inquired for John, they with solemn looks replied that "Botany," as they called me, was sick. When she anxiously inquired what ailed me they said they didn't know because they could not get me to speak; they had tried again and again to arouse me but I just lay still without saying a word as if I were dead, though I seemed to be breathing naturally enough. Mrs. Campbell, greatly alarmed, first called me from the foot of the stairs, and, getting no reply, walked half way up and again called,

---

* In a marginal note Muir gives their names as "Alexander and William," with a question sign. In the letter of a correspondent, marked "W.E. Sibley of early Canada botanical days," occurs the following sentence: "I saw D. and A. Campbell and was at their house. They were all quite well and said they intended writing to you." (February 28, 1865.)

"John, John, will you not speak to me?" The continued dead silence corresponded with the boys' cunning story and made her doubly anxious, so she climbed to the bed and shook as she supposed my shoulder, saying, "John, John, will you not speak?" Finally, pulling down the cover, she cried in glad relief, "Oh, those boys again, those boys again!"

Soldiers from the British army occasionally deserted and hid in the woods and swamps. For a certain deserter a considerable reward was offered and the Campbell boys told the officers that they had seen a suspicious character creeping out of the woods and swamps of the Holland River early in the morning, and that they thought he must be getting food from the neighbours and hiding in the swamp. A watch was, therefore, set and when they captured me I had some difflculty in explaining that I was only a botanist.

Here is another of the practical jokes of these irrepressible Highlanders: on frosty moonlight nights in winter when the sleighing was good, many of the young men from the neighbouring village of Bradford took their girls out sleigh-riding. The Campbell boys dressed themselves in white bed sheets and, just before the sleigh-riding began at dusk, they climbed to the roof of a schoolhouse which stood at the crossroads, a mile or so from their farm, and commenced vigorously trying to saw off the chimney with a fence rail. Their reward was in hearing the boys and girls scream and rush back to the village. The people in that neighbourhood were devoted believers in good old-fashioned ghosts.

These boys were capital story-tellers. One of their neighbours had a nose thus described by the elder of the two, "Mr. So-and-so has a big nose. Oh! a very big nose! So big and heavy that it shakes when he walks; and his shaking nose shakes his whole body, and makes the ground shake, and you would think there was an earthquake!"

Farther west were large wooded areas still perfectly wild, on the edges of which homeseekers were laboriously plying their heavy axes, making clearings for fields. At first only a few acres would be slashed down – oak, ash, elm, basswood, maple, etc., of several species. On account of the closeness of the growth these trees were tall and comparatively slender, and the roots formed a net-work that covered the ground so closely that not a single spot was to be found in which a post-hole could be dug without striking roots. These beautiful trees were simply slashed down, falling upon each other and covering the ground many trees deep, cut usually in winter and left to dry.

As soon as the branches were dry enough to burn well, fire was set and they were consumed, leaving only the blackened boles and heavier branches. These were then chopped into manageable lengths of from ten or twelve to fifteen feet, and the neighbours were called to a logging bee. Plenty of whiskey was said to make the work light. The heavier logs were drawn by oxen alongside of each other; the next heavier drawn alongside were rolled up on top of the large ones by means of hand-spikes, the next on top of the second tier, and so on, and the smaller tops and heavy branches were peaked on top of all. A fire was then started on top of these piles which ate its way downward. Soon all the clearing was covered with heavy, deep, glowing fires and the thickest logs after smouldering for days were at last consumed. Next the ashes were leached, boiled down and roasted for potash, which found a market in Europe, and yielded the first saleable crop of the farm.

Next, pains were taken to scrape little hollows between the roots where a few potatoes could be planted, without any reference to placing them in rows. Occasionally separate little pits were made among the roots for a few grains of wheat, which was cut with a sickle and thrashed with flails. Perhaps a sack of grain, for the family bread, could thus be raised from an acre or so.

Gradually the roots nearest the surface decayed and were laboriously chopped and grubbed out, wheat sown and covered with very small strong V-shaped harrows, which bounced about among the stumps. Still larger roots and some of the smallest stumps were grubbed out of the way, and at last the big stumps were laboriously dug out or pulled out with machines worked by oxen. These first small clearings were enlarged from year to year, but a whole lifetime was usually consumed before anything like an ordinary size farm was brought under perfect cultivation and fitted for the use of reaping and sowing machines.

Besides the difficulty of clearing away these dense woods, the first small farms, opening the ground to the light, were subject to late and early frosts, on account of the ground being so covered with humus and leaves that it could absorb but little heat. While surrounded with a dense forest wall the winds could not reach them with heat brought from afar, and the day temperature fell rapidly.

One morning when I was on my way through the woods I came to a little clearing where there was a crop of wheat beginning to head. Frost had fallen on it the night before, and a poor woman was walking along the side of the field weeping, wiping her eyes on her apron, and crying "Oh! the frost, the frost, the weary frost. We'll hae na crop this year and we had nane the last. We'll come to poverty. We'll come to poverty." After a great part of the forest was cleared, the stumps removed, the humus plowed under, and the soil opened to the sunshine and equalising winds these frosts disappeared.

In the spring, when the maple sap began to flow, all the young people had merry, merry times, shared by their elders who remembered their own young days. The sap was boiled in the woods, and when sugaring off at a certain stage it made wax which was cooled in the snow. A big fire was made and the evening spent around it eating maple "wax," and, later on in the "sugaring off," the sugar also. Other amusements were meeting for song singing and general merry-making, but dancing was seldom indulged in, being frowned on by their pious elders.

Most of the settlers were pious and faithfully attended church. All were exceedingly economical on account of the necessity, long continued, of saving while making a living in the wilderness. There was good reason for the scarcity of Americans in that community because of the far greater ease with which a living could be made on the prairies and oak openings of the Middle and Western States.

When I came to the Georgian Bay of Lake Huron, whose waters are so transparent and beautiful, and the forests about its shores with their ferny, mossy dells and deposits of boulder clay, it seemed to be a most favourable place for study, and as I was also at this time out of money again I was eager to stay a considerable time. In a beautiful dell, only a mile or two from the magnificent bay, I fortunately found work in a factory where there was a sawmill and lathes for turning out rake, broom, and fork handles, etc.

During the winter months of his sojourn in this dell near Meaford he had the companionship of his youngest brother, Daniel, who also was seeking employment in Canada at this time. A wee letter, one by two inches in size, dated Meaford, October 23rd, 1864, and addressed in playful mood to his sister Mary, gives an account of the people in this "Hollow" where they found employment. "Our family," he writes, "consists, first of all, of me, a most good man and big boy. Second, Daniel, who is also mostly big and three or four trifles funny. Third, Mr. William Trout, an unmarried boy of thirty summers, who, according to the multiplicity of common prognostications, is going to elect a lady mistress of Trout's Hollow some day. Fourth, Charles Jay, a bird of twenty-five, who is said to coo to a Trout. . . . This Jay and last mentioned Trout are in partnership and are the rulers of the two Scotch heather Muirs." He also mentions Mary and Harriet, two very capable sisters of William Trout, one of them the housekeeper and the other a school-teacher. "We all live happily together," continues the letter. "Occasionally an extra Trout comes upstream or a brother Jay alights at our door, but they are not of our family." The fears of his sister, lest they work too hard, are met by the declaration that they are working neither hard nor long hours; that they "are growing fatter and fatter, and perhaps will soon be as big as Gog and Magog."

Mr. Trout, who was still living in 1916, at my request furnished me with an account of the coming of the Muirs to Meaford. It seems that John and Daniel occasionally travelled independently in their search for work, meeting by arrangement at stated times and places, or, if they had lost connection, found each other again by means of letters from home. One midsummer day in 1864 Daniel appeared in search of work at the Trout sawmill. He remained there six weeks until his brother John had been located through home communications. The two then resumed their botanical journeyings until the approach of winter.

Scenting a possible chance to exercise his inventive genius, John was persuaded that the Hollow might be a good place in which to pass the long Canadian winter. One evening in autumn, 1864, they both arrived at the mill, outlined their plans, and were engaged to assist in building an addition to the rake factory. John's mechanical ability soon proved so advantageous for his employers that they entered into a contract with him to make one thousand dozen rakes and thirty thousand broom handles.

When John Muir made his rake and broom handle contract with us [wrote

Mr. Trout], he also made a proposition to be given the liberty of improving the machinery as he might determine, and that he should receive therefore half the economical results of such improvement during a given period. An arrangement of this kind was entered into, and he began with our self-feeding lathe which I considered a nearly perfect instrument for turning rake, fork, and broom handles and similar articles. By rendering this lathe more completely automatic he nearly doubled the output of broom handles. He placed one handle in position while the other was being turned. It required great activity for him to put away the turned handle and place the new one in position during the turning process. When he could do this eight broom handles were turned in a minute. Corresponding to this lathe I had on the floor immediately above him a machine that would automatically saw from the round log, after it was fully slabbed, eight handles per minute. But setting in the log and the slabbing process occupied about three eighths of the time. This, with keeping saws and place in order, cut the daily output to about twenty-five hundred. John had his difficulties in similar ways and at best could not get ahead of the sawing. It was a delight to see those machines at work. He devised and started the construction of several new automatic machines, to make the different parts of the hand rakes, having previously submitted and discussed them with me.

Daniel returned to Wisconsin after a time, but John continued at Meaford for about a year and a half. During the spring and summer he pursued his favourite study of botany with increasing enthusiasm and industry. Sundays and the long summer evenings were invariably devoted to the plants and the rocks. The lack of a comprehensive manual of the Canadian flora was, of course, a serious disadvantage and many herbarium sheets bear testimony to difficulties he encountered. They also testify to expeditions, made in 1865, of which no other record remains, for here, among numerous specimens from the "garden of J. Lufthorn" and the forests of Owen Sound and Georgian Bay, are trophies from the "Devil's Half Acre, forty miles northeast from Hamilton" and from the vicinity of Niagara Falls.

In Canada, as at the University of Wisconsin, Muir was his own severest taskmaster. His bed, mounted on a cross axle and connected with an alarm clock, was so contrived that it set him on his feet at five o'clock. If he happened to lie in it diagonally he sometimes was thrown out sharply on the floor. "The fall of John's bed," according to Mr. Trout, "was a wake-up signal for every one in the house. If we heard a double shock, caused by a roll-out, we had the signal for a good laugh on John, of which he had further jolly reminders at the breakfast table." His conversational powers already made him a marked member of any company, and he was never loath to engage in a friendly argument at meal time. But a book was always kept within reach for snatches of reading, and his studious habits kept him at work till far into the night.

His young sisters at this time had in him an interesting correspondent.

Apparently they did not give him sufficiently detailed information about home affairs to satisfy his curiosity, for he complains to one of them that, while her letter gave pleasure, "it was not great enough in any of its dimensions, minute enough in its details, or sufficiently knick-knacky in its morals." "Here," he writes, "is a form for a small letter from your locality, though as regards style I by no means commend it to your exact imitation."

Hickory Dale, 1000ft. above the sea,
January 1st, 1865

DEAR JOHN

We are pretty well, but are fast growing weary of the many changes which now seem to be of daily occurrence. We now live in a room made in the upper part of the barn next the orchard.

We reach it by an outside stair. It is hard carrying up the wood and water. Once I slipt and fell with an armful of burr oak firewood and sprained my weeping sinew. The cattle live in the house now – the cows in the cellar, the horses on the first floor, and the sheep upstairs. Nan will not go past the cellar door, but we do the best we can.

The apple trees are dug up and planted upon the cold rocky summit of the observatory where I am sure they will not grow well. The cattle do not stand the severe weather well this winter. They stand drawn together like a dog licking a pot.

Aunt Sally is married, and Lowdy Grahm has the whooping cough. Write soon or sooner.   From your Sis
MARY

P.S. Carrie Muir has enlisted and David is very angry.

There, Mary, you should put some grit and bone of that kind in your letters. I scribble that nonsense only to show you that these small matters which occur in the neighbourhood and which you do not think worthy of note are still of interest to us when so far from home . . . Affectionately
JOHN

To his friend Emily Pelton he writes under date of May 23rd, 1865:

We live in a retired and romantic hollow . . . Our social advantages are, of course, few and, for my part, I do not seek to extend my acquaintance, but work and study and dream in this retirement . . . Our tall, tall forest trees are now all alive, and the ocean of mingled blossoms and leaves waves and curls and rises in rounded swells farther and farther away, like the thick smoke from a factory chimney. Freshness and beauty are everywhere; flowers are born every hour; living sunlight is poured over all, and every thing and creature is glad. Our world is indeed a beautiful one, and I was thinking, on going to church last Sabbath, that I would hardly accept of a free ticket to the moon or to Venus, or any other world, for fear it might not be so good and so fraught with the glory of the Creator as our own. Those miserable hymns, such as

" This world is all a fleeting show
For man's delusion given,"

do not at all correspond with my likings, and I am sure they do not with yours.

The following letter, addressed to three of his sisters, is of interest because it exhibits his love of fun from another angle. The proposed sale of the Hickory Hill farm was not consummated at this time. The Fountain Lake farm, however, to which he had become so deeply attached, was sold about this time by his brother-in-law, David Galloway.

Trout's Hollow, C.W., December 24th, 1865

DEAR SISTERS MARY, ANNA, AND JOANNA

I feel that I owe you a long apology for not replying to your long good letters. I have been exceedingly busy, but this is not a sufficient excuse. My bed sets me upon my feet at five, and I go to bed at eleven, and have to do at least two days' work every day, sometimes three. I sometimes almost forget where I am, what I am doing, or what my name is. I often think of you and wish with all my might that I could see and chat with you. Were it not that I have no time to think, I would grow homesick and die in a day or two. My picture of home is in my room, and when I see it now I feel sorry at the thought of its being sold. Fountain Lake, Oak Grove, Little Valley, Hickory Hill, etc., with all of their long list of associations, pleasant and otherwise, will soon have passed away and been forgotten.

I was glad to hear that Dan was visiting so long with you. I suppose that he told you many a surprising and funny tale of Canada. I think that he can make and enjoy a joke very well indeed. I had a letter from him, and he says that he has plenty of money, clothes, and hope for the future.

I wish you were here. You would find queer things. We have queer trees, queer flowers, queer streams, queer weather, queer customs, and queer people with queer names. One man is called Lake, another Jay, Eagle, Raven, Stirling, Bird. Mr. Jay married Miss Raven a few weeks ago. One day at the table we were speaking about names and Mr. Trout said that "Rose" was a fine name, and I said that Muir was better than Trout, or Jay, or Rose, or Eagle, because that though a Jay or Eagle was a fine bird, and a Trout a good fish, and Rose a fine flower, a Scottish Muir or Moor had fine birds, and fine fishes in its streams, and fine wild roses together with almost every other excellence, but above all "the bonnie bloomin' heather." We may well be proud of our name.

Another story. One Sunday I returned from meeting before the rest and was in the house alone reading one of the "Messengers" mother sent, when a little bird flew into the house and the cat caught it. I chased the cat out of the house, and through the house, till I caught her, to save the bird's life, but she would not let it go, and I choked her and choked her to make her let it go until I choked her to death, though I did not mean to, and they both lay dead upon the floor. I waited to see if she would not receive back one of her nine lives, but to my grief I found that I had taken them all, so I buried her beside some cucumber vines in the garden. When the rest came home I told what had occurred, and Charley Jay, who is as full of wit and jokes as the pond was of cold water one night, said, "Now John is always scolding us about killing spiders and flies but when we are away he chokes the cats," and they kept saying "poor kitty," "poor puss," for weeks afterwards to make me laugh.

I will write you all a long letter some day.

[JOHN MUIR]

The more serious side of his nature and the aspirations he cherished at this time come to expression in a letter which marks the beginning of a long and remarkable correspondence with Mrs. Jeanne C. Carr, whose acquaintance with John Muir, as stated in an earlier chapter, began when he exhibited his wooden clocks at the Wisconsin State Fair in 1860. How much her friendship was to mean to the budding naturalist appears clearly even in the earliest of his letters to her.

From the time of Chancellor John Hiram Lathrop's resignation in July, 1859, to the choice of Paul A. Chadbourne as head of the University of Wisconsin eight years later, Professor John W. Sterling was virtually president. When John Muir failed to return to the University in the autumn of 1864 the faculty, knowing how eager he was to continue his studies, invited him to return as a free student and Professor Sterling was instructed to communicate this decision to him. Whether this invitation was for the autumn of 1864 or 1865 is not entirely clear. Unfortunately the letter never reached him and the opportunity could not be improved. This is the letter of which he writes that he "waited and wearied for it a long time."

Trout's Mills, near Meaford, September 13th, [1865]

DEAR MRS. CARR

Your precious letter with its burden of cheer and good wishes has come to our hollow, and has done for me that work of sympathy and encouragement which I know you kindly wished it to do. It came at a time when much needed, for I am subject to lonesomeness at times. Accept, then, my heartfelt gratitude – would that I could make a better return.

I am sorry over the loss of Professor Sterling's letter, for I waited and wearied for it a long time. I have been keeping up an irregular course of study since leaving Madison, but with no great success. I do not believe that study, especially of the Natural Sciences, is incompatible with ordinary attention to business; still, I seem to be able to do but one thing at a time. Since undertaking, a month or two ago, to invent new machinery for our mill, my mind seems to so bury itself in the work that I am fit for but little else; and then a lifetime is so little a time that we die ere we get ready to live.

I would like to go to college, but then I have to say to myself, "You will die ere you can do anything else." I should like to invent useful machinery, but it comes, "You do not wish to spend your lifetime among machines and you will die ere you can do anything else." I should like to study medicine that I might do my part in lessening human misery, but again it comes, "You will die ere you are ready to be able to do so." How intensely I desire to be a Humboldt! but again the chilling answer is reiterated. Could we but live a *million* of years, then how delightful to spend in perfect contentment so many thousand years in quiet study in college, so many amid the grateful din of machines, so many among human pain, so many thousands in the sweet study of Nature among the dingles and dells of *Scotland*, and all the other less important parts of our world! Then *perhaps* might we, with at least a show of reason, "shuffle off this mortal coil" and look back upon our star with something of satisfaction.

I should be ashamed – if shame might be in the other world – if any of the powers, virtues, essences, etc., should ask me for common knowledge concerning our world which I could not bestow. But away with this *aged* structure and we are back to our handful of hasty years half gone, all of course for the best did we but know all of the Creator's plan concerning us. In our higher state of existence we shall have time and intellect for study. Eternity, with perhaps the whole unlimited creation of God as our field, should satisfy us, and make us patient and trustful, while we pray with the Psalmist, "So teach us to number our days that we may apply our hearts unto wisdom."

I was struck with your remarks about our real home as being a thing of stillness and peace. How little does the outer and noisy world in general know of that "real home" and real inner life! Happy indeed they who have a friend to whom they can unmask the workings of their real life, sure of sympathy and forbearance!

I sent for the book which you recommend. I have just been reading a short sketch of the life of the mother of Lamartine. These are beautiful things you say about the humble life of our Saviour and about the trees gathering in the sunshine.

What you say respecting the littleness of the number who are called to "the pure and deep communion of the beautiful, all-loving Nature," is particularly true of the hard-working, hard drinking, stolid Canadians. In vain is the glorious chart of God in Nature spread out for them. So many acres chopped is their motto, so they grub away amid the smoke of magnificent forest trees, black as demons and material as the soil they move upon. I often think of the Doctor's lecture upon the condition of the different races of men as controlled by physical agencies. Canada, though abounding in the elements of wealth, is too difficult to subdue to permit the first few generations to arrive at any great intellectual development. In my long rambles last summer I did not find a single person who knew anything of botany and but a few who knew the meaning of the word; and wherein lay the charm that could conduct a man, who might as well be gathering mammon, so many miles through these fastnesses to suffer hunger and exhaustion, was with them never to be discovered. Do not these answer well to the person described by the poet in these lines:

> "A primrose by the river's brim,
> A yellow primrose was to him,
> And nothing more."

I thank Dr. Carr for his kind remembrance of me, but still more for the good patience he had with so inapt a scholar. We remember in a peculiar way those who first give us the story of Redeeming Love from the great book of revelation, and I shall not forget the Doctor, who first laid before me the great book of Nature, and though I have taken so little from his hand, he has at least shown me where those mines of priceless knowledge lie and how to reach them. O how frequently, Mrs. Carr, when lonely and wearied, have I wished that like some hungry worm I could creep into that delightful kernel of your house – your library – with its portraits of scientific men, and so bountiful a store of their sheaves amid the blossom and verdure of your little kingdom of plants, luxuriant and happy as though holding their leaves to the open sky of the most flower-loving zone in the world!

That "sweet day" did, as you wished, reach our hollow, and another is with us now. The sky has the haze of autumn and, excepting the aspen, not a tree has motion. Upon our enclosing wall of verdure new tints appear. The gorgeous dyes of autumn are too plainly seen, and the forest seems to have found out that again its leaf must fade. Our stream, too, has less cheerful sound and as it bears its foambells pensively away from the shallow rapids in the rocks it seems to feel that summer is past.

You propose, Mrs. Carr, an exchange of thoughts for which I thank you very sincerely. This will be a means of pleasure and improvement which I could not have hoped ever to have been possessed of, but then here is the difficulty: I feel that I am altogether incapable of properly conducting a correspondence with one so much above me. We are, indeed, as you say, students in the same life school, but in very different classes. I am but an alpha novice in those sciences which you have studied and loved so long. If, however, you are willing in this to adopt the plan that our Saviour endeavoured to beat into the stingy Israelites, viz. to "give, hoping for nothing again," all will be well, and as long as your letters resemble this one before me, which you have just written, in genus, order, cohort, class, province, or kingdom, be assured that by way of reply you shall at least receive an honest "Thank you."

Tell Allie that Mr. Muir thanks him for his pretty flowers and would like to see him, also that I have a story for him which I shall tell some other time. Please remember me to my friends, and now, hoping to receive a letter from you at least *semi-occasionally*, I remain,

Yours with gratitude
JOHN MUIR

Brought up in the strictest tenets of traditional orthodoxy, John Muir's scientific studies gradually forced him to reconstruct the factual basis of his religious beliefs. Darwin's *Origin of Species* had appeared in 1859, and a fierce conflict was raging between champions of the theory of special creation and what now came to be known as the theory of organic evolution. Even at the university he had become aware of the chasm that was opening between the old biblical literalism and the more comprehensive interpretations of religion. A certain prominent clergyman of Madison, who was an advocate of a neighbouring sectarian college, had often assailed what he was pleased to call the atheistic views of certain members of the faculty. Without relaxing his hold on the essentials of his Protestant faith, John Muir's sympathies were unmistakably enlisted on the side of liberalism. He promptly and quite naturally adopted the view that the Bible is not authoritative in the realm of natural science, but that in its explanations of the facts and phenomena of the universe it exhibits the same gradual unfolding of human knowledge which has marked man's progress in other spheres of thought.

It is not easy to trace the steps by which he broke away from the narrow Biblicism of his training, but he would from this period onward have subscribed at any time to the statement of Louis Agassiz that "a physical fact is as sacred as a moral principle." Lyell, who since 1830 had prepared the way for Darwin by showing that the world is very old and the outcome of a long development, excited Muir's enthusiastic interest. Later he became a warm friend of J.D. Hooker and Asa Gray, two of Darwin's earliest supporters.

Nathaniel S. Shaler, who passed through the same period of readjustment as Muir, confessed* that his first contact with natural science in his youth and early manhood had the not uncommon effect of leading him far away from Christianity and that in later years a further insight into the truths of nature had gradually forced him back again to the ground from which he had departed. It is interesting to find that Muir, probably in spite of his upbringing, had no such experience. He saw that the alleged antagonism between natural science and the Bible was due to the accumulated lumber of past generations of faulty Bible teaching. By promptly discarding the crudities of this teaching and adopting a more rational historical interpretation of the Bible he saved his faith both in religion and in science.

In a letter from "The Hollow," written to Mrs. Carr toward the end of January, 1866, we get a glimpse of his mental workings. To the statement that she was writing her letter in the delicious quiet of a Sabbath evening in the country, "with cow bells tinkling instead of steeple chimes, the drone and chirp of myriad insects for choral service, depending for a sermon upon the purple bluffs and flowing river," he responds as follows:

I was interested with the description you gave of your sermon. You speak of

* *The Interpretation of Nature* (1896), Preface, p.iv.

such services like one who appreciates and relishes them. But although the page of Nature is so replete with divine truth it is silent concerning the fall of man and the wonders of Redeeming Love. Might she not have been made to speak as clearly and eloquently of these things as she now does of the character and attributes of God? It may be a bad sympton, but I will confess that I take more intense delight from reading the power and goodness of God from "the things which are made" than from the Bible. The two books harmonise beautifully, and contain enough of divine truth for the study of all eternity. It is so much easier for us to employ our faculties upon these beautiful tangible form than to exercise a simple, humble, living faith such as you so well describe as enabling us to reach out joyfully into the future to expect what is promised as a thing of tomorrow.

On another occasion, in describing to a friend his discovery of *Calypso borealis*, he wrote:

I cannot understand the nature of the curse, "Thorns and thistles shall it bring forth to thee." Is our world indeed the worse for this thistly curse? Are not all plants beautiful, or some way useful? Would not the world suffer by the banishment of a single weed? The curse must be within ourselves.

He was at this time in the full flush of his inventive activity and working hard to complete the contract into which he had entered with his employers.

I have been very busy of late making practical machinery [he writes]. I like my work exceeding well, but would prefer inventions which would require some artistic as well as mechanical skill. I invented and put in operation a few days ago an attachment for a self-acting lathe which has increased its capacity at least one third. We are now using it to turn broom handles, and as these useful articles may now be made cheaper, and as cleanliness is one of the cardinal virtues, I congratulate myself on having done something, like a true philanthropist, for the real good of mankind in general. What say you? I have also invented a machine for making rake teeth, and another for boring for them, and driving them, and still another for making the bows, still another used in making the handles, still another for bending them – so that rakes may now be made nearly as fast again. Farmers will be able to produce grain at a lower rate, and the poor to get more bread to eat. Here is more philanthropy, is it not? I sometimes feel as though I was losing time here, but I am at least receiving my first lessons in practical mechanics and as one of the firm here is a millwright and as I am permitted to make as many machines as I please and to remodel those now in use, the school is a pretty good one.

The thirty thousand broom handles were all turned and stored in every available place about the factory for final seasoning when one stormy night about the first of March, 1866, the building took fire. There was no means of fire control and soon the sawmill and factory with all their laboriously manufactured contents were reduced to a pile of ashes. Since there was no insurance, the owners having lost practically everything, John Muir made as equitable a settlement as possible, taking notes bearing neither interest nor date of payment. He always took pride in the thought that his employers justified his confidence, for every cent was ultimately paid. Leaving some of his books to his Sunday School class of admiring boys, and some of his textbooks on botany to friends whom he had interested in this study, he turned his face toward the States. The motives which influenced him to go to Indianapolis and what he found there are the subject of autobiographical notes which follow in the next chapter.

How warm a place he had made for himself in that Meaford circle of friends we learn from a sheaf of kindly letters that followed him southward on his departure soon after the fire. "Was there ever more freedom of speech, thought, and action felt on earth than in that Hollow?" wrote one of the Trout sisters. "We were all equal; every one did as he chose. Ah me! I hope that the happy days will return; that we may be there again, and that you might be one of our number for at least a short time. The circle would be incomplete without you." "John," wrote another, "you don't know how we missed the little star you used to have in the window for us when we would be coming home after night, and the cheerful fire. And not least, we missed the pleasant welcome you had for us."

But the disaster which led John to resume his wanderings also scattered the members of the Meaford circle far and wide over Canada and the United States. In more than the literal sense he had put a star in the window for many of them, and for several decades grateful letters tell of their progress in the new interests which he had brought into their lives. One of the last to survive was William H. Trout, and with a paragraph from the last letter that Muir wrote to him, in 1912, we conclude the account of his Canadian sojourn:

I am always glad to hear from you. Friends get closer and dearer the farther they travel on life's journey. It is fine to see how youthful your heart remains, and wide and far-reaching your sympathy, with everybody and everything. Such people never grow old. I only regret your being held so long in mechanical bread-winning harness, instead of making enough by middle age and spending the better half of life in studying God's works as I wanted you to do long ago. The marvel is that in the din and rattle of mills you have done so wondrous well. By all means keep on your travels, since you know so well how to reap their benefits. I shall hope to see you when next you come West. And don't wait until the canal year. Delays are more and more dangerous as sundown draws nigh.

CHAPTER FIVE

From Indiana to California 1866–1868

A LITTLE more than a month after the destruction of the mill in Trout's Hollow, John Muir had arrived at Indianapolis, Indiana, for early in May, 1866, he writes from there to his sister Sarah as follows:

I never before felt so *utterly homeless* as now. I do not feel sad, but I cannot find a good boarding place, to say nothing of a home, and so I have not yet unpacked my trunk, and am at any moment as ready to leave this house for a march as were the Israelites while eating the passover. Much as I love the peace and quiet of retirement, I *feel* something within, some restless fires that urge me on in a way very different from my real wishes, and I suppose that I am doomed to live in some of these noisy commercial centres.

Circumstances over which I have had no control almost compel me to abandon the profession of my choice, and to take up the business of an inventor, and now that I am among machines I begin to feel that I have some talent that way, and so I almost think, unless things change soon, I shall turn my whole mind into that channel.

But even at this time, if one may judge from another passage in the same letter, the prospective physician or inventor had not nearly so good a backing in his feelings as the naturalist. "The forest here," he writes, "is almost in full leaf. I have found wild flowers for more than a month now. I gathered a handful about a mile and a half from town this morning before breakfast. When I first entered the woods and stood among the beautiful flowers and trees of God's own garden, so pure and chaste and lovely, I could not help shedding tears of joy."

The considerations that influenced him to go to the capital of Indiana are best told in his autobiographical narrative which is resumed at this point:

Looking over the map I saw that Indianapolis was an important railroad centre, and probably had manufactories of different sorts in which I could find employment, with the advantage of being in the heart of one of the very richest forests of deciduous hard wood trees on the continent. Here I was successful in gaining employment in a carriage material factory, full of circular saws and chucks and eccentric and concentric lathes, etc. I first worked for ten dollars a week, without board of course. The second week my wages were increased to eighteen a week, and later to about twenty-five a week. I greatly enjoyed this mechanical work, began to invent and introduce labour-saving improvements and was so successful that my botanical and geological studies were in danger of being seriously interrupted.

One day a member of the firm asked me, "How long are you going to stay with us?" "Not long," I said. "Just long enough to earn a few hundred dollars, then I am going on with my studies in the woods." He said, "You are doing very well, and if you will stop, we will give you the foremanship of the shop," and held out hopes of a partnership interest in the money-making business. To this I replied that although I liked the inventive work and the earnest rush and roar and whirl of the factory, Nature's attractions were stronger and I must soon get away.

A serious accident hurried me away sooner than I had planned. I had put in a countershaft for a new circular saw and as the belt connecting with the main shaft was new it stretched considerably after running a few hours and had to he shortened. While I was unlacing it, making use of the nail-like end of a file to draw out the stitches, it slipped and pierced my right eye on the edge of the cornea. After the first shock was over I closed my eye, and when I lifted the lid of the injured one the aqueous humour dripped on my hand – the sight gradually failed and in a few minutes came perfect darkness. "My right eye is gone," I murmured, "closed forever on all God's beauty." At first I felt no particular weakness. I walked steadily enough to the house where I was boarding, but in a few hours the shock sent me trembling to bed and very soon by sympathy the other eye became blind, so that I was in total darkness and feared that I would become permanently blind.

When Professor Butler learned that I was in Indianapolis, he sent me a letter of introduction to one of the best families there, and in some way they heard of the accident and came to see me and brought an oculist, who had studied abroad, to examine the pierced eye. He told me that on account of the blunt point of the file having pushed aside the iris, it would never again be perfect, but that if I should chance to lose my left eye, the wounded one, though imperfect, would then be very precious. "You are young and healthy," he said, "and the lost aqueous humour will be restored and the sight also to some extent; and your left eye after the inflammation has gone down and the nerve shock is overcome – you will be able to see about as well as ever, and in two or three months bid your dark room good-bye."

So I was encouraged to believe that the world was still to be left open to me. The lonely dark days of waiting were cheered by friends, many of them little children. After sufficient light could be admitted they patiently read for me, and brought great handfuls of the flowers I liked best.

As soon as I got out into Heaven's light I started on another long excursion, making haste with all my heart to store my mind with the Lord's beauty and thus be ready for any fate, light or dark. And it was from this time that my long continuous wanderings may be said to have fairly commenced. I bade adieu to all my mechanical inventions, determined to devote the rest of my life to the study of the inventions of God. I first went home to Wisconsin, botanising by the way, to take leave of my father and mother, brothers and sisters, all of whom were still living near Portage. I also visited the neighbours I had known as a boy, renewed my acquaintance with them after an absence of several years, and bade each a formal good-bye. When they asked where I was going, I said, "Oh! I don't know – just anywhere in the wilderness southward. I have already had glorious glimpses of the Wisconsin, Iowa, Michigan, Indiana and Canada wildernesses; now I propose to go south and see something of the vegetation of the warm end of the country, and if possible wander far enough into South America to see tropical vegetation in all its palmy glory."

All the neighbours wished me well and advised me to be careful of my health, reminding me that the swamps in the south were full of malaria. I stopped overnight at the home of an old Scotch lady who had long been my friend, and was now particularly motherly in good wishes and advice. I told her that as I was sauntering along the road near sundown I heard a little bird singing, "The day's gone, The day's done." "Weel, John, my dear laddie," she replied, "your day will never be done. There is no end to the kind of studies you are engaged in, and you are sure to go on and on, but I want you to remember the fate of Hugh Miller." She was one of the finest examples I ever knew of a kind, generous, great-hearted Scotchwoman.

After all the good wishes and good-byes were over, and I had visited Fountain Lake and Hickory Hill and my first favourite gardens and ferneries, I took a thousand-mile walk to the Gulf of Mexico from Louisville, across Kentucky, Tennessee, North Carolina, Georgia, and Florida.

At this point Muir's memoirs pass in a few sentences over the entire period between the beginning of this remarkable walk and his arrival in California. His notes on the margin of the manuscript, however, show that he intended to expand this portion of his autobiography considerably, probably by using parts of the journal which he kept during his southward journey in 1867. In the meantime this journal, published separately under the title *A Thousand-Mile Walk to the Gulf*, has become accessible to all interested readers. There are, however, some unpublished passages, crossed out by the author during a revision in later life, that throw light upon the struggle with himself in which he was engaged during his stay in Indianapolis.

Muir's more intimate friends like the Carrs, Butlers, and Merrills had ere this observed in him a strange kind of restlessness, an inward compulsion, which at times caused him to forsake his tools and his occupation for the beauteous ways of those middle western wildernesses that still were pressing close upon the edge of towns. Mrs. Carr, indeed, used to speak of Muir's "good demon" to whose behests he paid heed as did Socrates to his invisible mentor. A letter written to her but two days before he started on his southward journey reveals him under the spell of his good genius. "I wish I knew where I was going," he writes. "Doomed to be 'carried of the spirit into the wilderness,' I suppose. I wish I could be more moderate in my desires, but I cannot, and so there is no rest."

The opening sentences of his journal, also, no less than the cover inscription "John Muir, Earth-planet, Universe," contain significant bits of self-revelation. "Few bodies," he wrote, "are inhabited by so satisfied a soul as to be allowed exemption from extraordinary exertion through a whole life. The sea, the sky, the rivers have their ebbs and floods, and the earth itself throbs and pulses from calms to earthquakes. So also there are tides and floods in the affairs of men, which in some are slight and may be kept within bounds, but in others they overmaster everything." He was one of the "others."

The farewell visit to Fountain Lake and Hickory Hill had a much deeper significance for him than one would infer from the brief reference to it in his memoirs. Twenty-seven years later, in an address on "National Parks and Forest Reservations," delivered at a meeting of the Sierra Club in San Francisco, he related the plans and hopes he had entertained with regard to Fountain Lake:

The preservation of specimen sections of natural flora – bits of pure wildness – was a fond, favourite notion of mine long before I heard of national parks. When my father came from Scotland, he settled in a fine wild region in Wisconsin, beside a small glacier lake bordered with white pond-lilies. And on the north side of the lake, just below our house, there was a carex meadow full of charming flowers – cypripediums, pogonias, calopogons, asters, goldenrods, etc.– and around the margin of the meadow many nooks rich in flowering ferns and heathworts. And when I was about to wander away on my long rambles' I was sorry to leave that precious meadow unprotected; therefore, I said to my brother-in-law, who then owned it, "Sell me the forty acres of lake meadow, and keep it fenced, and never allow cattle or hogs to break into it, and I will gladly pay you whatever you say. I want to keep it untrampled for the sake of its ferns and flowers; and even if I should never see it again, the beauty of its lilies and orchids is so pressed into my mind I shall always enjoy looking back at them in imagination, even across seas and continents, and perhaps after I am dead."

But he regarded my plan as a sentimental dream wholly impracticable. The fence he said would surely be broken down sooner or later, and all the work would be in vain. Eighteen years later I found the deep-water pond lilies in fresh bloom, but the delicate garden-sod of the meadow was broken up and trampled into black mire. On the same Wisconsin farm there was a small flowery, ferny bog that I also tried to save. It was less than half an acre in area, and I said, "Surely you can at least keep for me this little bog." Yes, he would try. And when I had left home, and kept writing about it, he would say in reply, "Let your mind rest, my dear John; the mud hole is safe, and the frogs in it are singing right merrily." But in less than twenty years the beauty of this little glacier-bog also was trampled away.

From a letter to his friend Catherine Merrill, written immediately after his visit to Muir's Lake, or Fountain Lake, as he was later accustomed to call it, we excerpt a more than usually detailed and appreciative description. He had started from Indianapolis about the middle of June, taking with him his young friend Merrill Moores. Eager to see the flora of the Illinois prairies in June, he went to Decatur near the centre of the state and then northward by way of Rockford and Janesville. A week was spent in botanising on the prairie seven miles southwest of Pecatonica, and from there they made their way to his old home in Wisconsin.

We have had our last communion with Muir's Lake [he writes from there on the 12th of August]. It was glassy, calm, and full of shadows in the twilight. I have said farewell to nearly all my friends, too, and will soon leave home once more for I know not where.

You would enjoy a visit to that rocky hill we have spoken of so often, though a mere pimple, I suppose, to the Alps you have enjoyed. The most of Wisconsin is not more than two hundred and fifty or three hundred feet above Lake Michigan, or about one thousand feet above the sea. The Blue Mounds, a few miles west of Madison, are only one thousand six hundred and seventy feet above the sea – the highest land in Wisconsin*. Our Observatory is perhaps one hundred and fifty or one hundred and eighty feet above the plain. It is a broad hill with long sloping sides, and with a great pile of whinstone blocks cast upon the top. It is not quite bare in any part, for its sides are clothed richly in white and black oaks, and the rocky summit has grey cedars and rock ferns. A great many ravines run up against the rocks on every side; these have the Desmodiums and the harebells and many precious ferns and rare peculiar plants of their own. One of these ravines has evidently been scooped out for a fern garden. One hundred and twenty thousand of my favourite Osmundas live there, all regularly planted at equal distances.

The highest point commands a landscape circle of about one thousand square miles, composed of ten or twelve miles of the Fox River, Lake Puckawa and five or six nameless little lakes – marsh and woodland exquisitely arranged and joined – and about two hundred hills, and some prairie. Ah! these are the gardens for me! There is landscape gardening! While we were there, clouds of every texture and size were held above its flowers and moved about as needed, now increasing, now diminishing, lighter and deeper shadow and full sunshine in small and greater pieces, side by side as each portion of the great garden required. A shower, too, was guided over some miles that required watering. The streams and the lakes and dens and rains and clouds in the hand of God weighed and measured myriads of plants daily coming into life, every leaf receiving its daily bread – the infinite work done in calm effortless omnipotence.

But now, Miss Merrill, we must leave our garden, and I am sure I do it with more pain than I should ever feel in leaving all the *jardins des plantes*

* Rib Hill in Marathon county, 1940 feet, is now regarded as the highest point.

in the world, where poor exiled flowers from all countries are mixed and huddled in royal pens.

After a botanical week spent as the guest of his Madison friends, the Butlers and the Carrs, he returned to Indianapolis with the overmastering impulse strong within him, and started from there by rail for Louisville, Kentucky, on the first of September. "I steered through the big city by compass without speaking a word to any one," he wrote in his journal. "Beyond the city I found a road running southward, and after passing a scatterment of suburban cabins and cottages I reached the green woods and spread out my pocket map to rough-hew a plan for my journey."

He was now fairly started on the longest and most adventurous of his many rambles. His general plan was to push southward by the leafiest, wildest, and least trodden ways. This he apparently succeeded in doing, for only about twenty-two towns and cities are mentioned in his journal, a very small number when one considers the distance he covered. He carried with him nothing but a small rubber bag which held a change of underclothing, comb, towel, brush, and three small books – a New Testament, Milton's *Paradise Lost*, and Burns's *Poems*. At night he sought the shelter of farmhouses and country taverns and when this resource failed him he would lie down, as near Elizabethtown, Kentucky, "in the bushes by guess," or enter a schoolhouse and sleep "on the softest-looking of the benches." Indeed, there were stretches in his walk, in the sparsely populated Cumberland mountain region, where he often had "to sleep with the trees in the one great bedroom of the open night."

When he reached Savannah, Georgia, his money was all but gone and the new supply, which he had directed his brother to send thither, either had not arrived or was being withheld by the express agent. He was unable to find work and his impecunious condition did not permit him to live at an inn. It is characteristic of Muir's shrewdness and freedom from ordinary prejudices and superstitions that under these circumstances he sought out the beautiful Bonaventure Cemetery, four miles east of Savannah. There he felt secure from night-prowlers, and his scientific interest was gratified by "one of the most impressive assemblages of animal and plant creatures" he had ever seen. He built himself a shelter of rushes in a thicket of sparkle-berry bushes and lodged there for a week until the money arrived. Meanwhile he had ample time to reflect on the significance of his surroundings, the place of death in the order of nature, and to describe the Tillandsia-draped oaks of Bonaventure. One of the most beautiful passages in all his writings is the account of this graveyard experience published under the title "Camping Among the Tombs" in *A Thousand-Mile Walk to the Gulf.*

The journal of this walk is especially interesting because it shows how his ideas upon certain subjects were maturing at this time. The conception of death which he had inherited with his religious training was bound to yield to a better understanding of Nature's processes. He is convinced now that "on no subject are our ideas more warped and pitiable than on death. Instead of the friendly sympathy, the union of life and death so apparent in Nature, we are taught that death is an accident, a deplorable punishment for the oldest sin, the 'arch-enemy' of life, etc. And upon these primary, never-to-be-questioned dogmas, these time-honoured bones of doctrine, our experiences are founded, tissue after tissue in hideous development, until they form the grimmest body to be found in the whole catalogue of civilized Christian manufactures."

He thinks it especially unfortunate that town children, generation after generation of them, should be steeped in "this morbid death orthodoxy." In the country observation of Nature's on-goings is apt to interpose a corrective, whereas in towns the morbidity of burial customs makes an overpowering impression. "But let a child walk with Nature," he writes, "let him behold the beautiful blendings and communions of death and life, their joyous inseparable unity as taught in woods and meadows, plains and mountains and streams of our blessed star, and they will learn that death is stingless indeed, and has no victory, for it never fights. All is divine harmony."

These excerpts show that he had entirely abandoned the historicity of the early chapters of Genesis as well as the Pauline conception of death based upon them. It was inevitable that the anthropocentric nature philosophy of his day, which held that man was the principal object of creation and that all things existed only for his good, should also fall under his condemnation. In spite of the long letters in which his father urged this theological view of Nature upon him as orthodox Biblical doctrine, he broke away from it radically as contrary to reason and evidence, though without being apparently disturbed in his own strong religious convictions.

The world, we are told [he confides to his journal], was made especially for man – a presumption not supported by all the facts. A numerous class of men are painfully astonished whenever they find anything, living or dead, in all God's universe, which they cannot eat or render in some way what they call useful to themselves. They have precise dogmatic insight of the intentions of the Creator, and it is hardly possible to be guilty of irreverence in speaking of their God any more than of heathen idols. He is regarded as a civilized, law-abiding gentleman in favour either of a republican form of government or of a limited monarchy; believes in the literature and language of England, is a warm supporter of the English constitution and Sunday schools and missionary societies; and is purely a manufactured article as any puppet of a half-penny theatre.

With such views of the Creator it is, of course, not surprising that erroneous views should be entertained of the creation. To such properly trimmed people, the sheep, for example, is an easy problem – food and clothing "for us," eating grass and daisies white by divine appointment for this predestined purpose, on perceiving the demand for wool that would be occasioned by the eating of the apple in the Garden of Eden.

In the same pleasant plan, whales are storehouses of oil for us, to help out the stars in lighting our dark ways until the discovery of the Pennsylvania oil wells. Among plants, hemp, to say nothing of the cereals, is a case of evident destination for ships' rigging, wrapping packages, and hanging the wicked. Cotton is another plain case of clothing. Iron was made for hammers and ploughs, and lead for bullets; all intended for us. And so of other small handfuls of insignificant things.

In satirical mood he then asks these "profound expositors of God's intentions" whether the logic of their reasoning does not indicate also that man is the divinely intended prey of lions, tigers, alligators, and the myriads of noxious insects that plague and destroy him. To say that these maladjustments are "unresolvable difficulties connected with Eden's apple and the devil" is mere evasion. "It never seems to occur to these far-seeing teachers," he writes, "that Nature's object in making animals and plants. might possibly be first of all the happiness of each one of them, not the creation of all for the happiness of one. Why should man value himself as more than a small part of the one great unit of creation? And what creature of all that the Lord has taken the pains to make is not essential to the completeness of that unit – the cosmos? The universe would be incomplete without the smallest transmicroscopic creature that dwells beyond our conceitful eyes and knowledge."

He is convinced that the origin of man is bound up inextricably with the origin of every other creature and that therefore the animal world stands to him in a relation quite different from that which is assigned to it by the religious thought of his day. It arouses his indignation to think that "the fearfully good, the orthodox, of this laborious patchwork of modern civilization cry 'Heresy' on every one whose sympathies reach a single hair's breadth beyond the boundary epidermis of our own species." Nor is he able to accept the "closest researches of clergy" according to whom the world is to be cleansed and renewed by a "universal planetary combustion." Finding that whole kingdoms of creatures have enjoyed existence and returned to dust ere man appeared, he apprehends that human beings also, when they have "played their part in Creation's plan, may disappear without any general burning or extraordinary commotion whatever."

It was the middle of October when Muir reached Florida by a little coastwise steamer, *Sylvan Shore*, then plying between Savannah and Fernandina. The latter town, with its fine harbour, was not only a principal port of entry for marine commerce, but was also the Atlantic terminus of a railroad, opened in 1861, that crossed Florida to Cedar Keys on the Gulf, a distance of one hundred and fifty-five miles. Along this railroad Muir footed his way leisurely across the flowery peninsula, though not without many side excursions into the swamps and pine-barrens wherever new plants beckoned to him. His enthusiasm over the novel flora, even at that time of the year, was unbounded. Several notebook drawings of the palmetto in all stages of growth and maturity testify to his rapture over this new plant acquaintance which, as often under such circumstances, took on a spiritual significance to him. "This palm was indescribably impressive," he writes, "and told me grander things than I ever got from human priest."

It will have occurred to the reader that Muir's habit of sleeping out in the open occasionally when night overtook him, without protection from mosquitoes, was especially dangerous in the South. In the Florida pine barrens where one shelterless night he plashed and groped about until he found a place dry enough to lie down, he observed marked evidences of malaria in the people whom he met. It is not surprising, therefore, that he was taken severely ill soon after he reached Cedar Keys.

In this remote and moribund little town Muir passed one of the most serious crises of his life. Had it not been for a family by the name of Hodgson, who took him into their home and nursed him back to health, he would have filled a nameless grave there soon after his arrival. Mr. Hodgson was the owner of a sawmill which he was operating on a spit of land about two miles from town. Having ascertained that schooners, freighted with lumber, sailed at irregular intervals from Cedar Keys to Galveston, Texas, Muir decided to apply for work at the mill and to await the coming of one of these schooners. His mechanical skill had scarcely secured him the desired employment when he was seized with an attack of fever so violent that he lay unconscious for days.

Exactly half a century after these events my wife and I followed Muir's old trail to Cedar Keys. We had some difficulty even in finding, two miles north of the town, the knoll on which had stood the Hodgson residence in which Muir was nursed back to health, and where he wrote charming descriptions of his surroundings. Amid some picturesque old Tillandsia-draped live-oaks, clearly the same which he had sketched in his journal fifty years earlier, we found evidence of a former habitation – remnants of foundations, of garden-beds bordered by conch shells, all overgrown with cactus and underbrush. From here, during days of convalescence, he sketched Lime Key with its fringe of palmettos and yuccas, and watched the water-birds feeding when the tide went out. The snowy egret was no longer to be seen, but here and there a pelican flapped along on solemn wing; gulls made patches of gleaming white upon the water, and blue herons stalked along the reedy margin of the shore. They settled down at times in the treetops and looked out gravely from umbrageous caves. Seaward, through openings among the trees, one caught glimpses of distant islands – Keys – that floated like giant birds upon the purplish-blue waters, or faded into the opalescent haze, visible only as supports for the plumey palmetto crowns that waved on slender trunks above them.

It was amusing to see how the jaws of the natives dropped under a facial

expanse of blank astonishment whenever I made inquiries about things as
they were in Cedar Keys fifty years ago. The longest memory was that of an
old negro by the name of Jack Cloud, who was introduced as "McLeod."
"You certainly are not a Scotchman," I said; "how do you come by that
name? "Both he and the benchful of black cronies in front of the store
broke into laughter. "No, sah," he said, "my name is Jack Cloud, sah, but
ebberybody done calls me 'McLeod.'" "Were you born here?" "Oh, Lawd,
no; I wuz bawn in Georgia, sah! Aftah de wah, I come down heah to start a
cotton plantation for a man. Dat wuz in 1865. Yes, sah, de railroad wuz
heah, but so delapurdated, it done took a train a week to get heah from
Fernandina. De ties and piles wuz all rotten." He told how all the business
then went over a strait to the neighbouring Key of Atsena Otie where the
first settlement had been begun. He remembered Hodgson's sawmill and had
assisted in dismantling what was left of it many decades ago.

But neither he nor any one else had any recollection of "sharp-visaged"
Captain Parsons and his schooner Island Belle which Muir, in January,
1868, saw threading her way along the tortuous channel that leads into the
harbour of Cedar Keys. Fifty years had swallowed up all memory of him
and his ship; of John Muir and his sojourn; of his friends and their home. In
this unlettered corner of the South, where decay in league with warmth and
sun and rain obliterates the works of man more speedily than anywhere else,
oblivion had swallowed up with equal haste the records of human memories.

Muir still was a convalescent when he boarded the Island Belle and
sailed away to Cuba. For a month he made his home on the vessel, at
anchor in the harbour of Havana, and spent his days botanising on the
outskirts of the city. The captain and the sailors were accustomed to gather
about him when he returned in the evening in order to be entertained with a
recital of the day's adventures and discoveries. He was consumed with a
desire to explore the central mountain range of Cuba through the whole
length of the island and then embark for South America. "My plan," he
writes, "was to go ashore anywhere on the north end of the continent, push
on southward through the wilderness around the headwaters of the Orinoco,
until I reached a tributary of the Amazon, and float down on a raft or skiff
the whole length of the great river to its mouth." It seems strange that such
a trip should ever have entered the dreams of any person, however enthusiastic
and full of daring, particularly under the disadvantages of poor health, of
funds less than a hundred dollars, and of the insalubrity of the Amazon
valley.

His weakened physical condition forced him to admit that the plan to
explore the mountainous wildernesses of Cuba was impossible. After visiting
all the shipping agencies in a vain search for a vessel bound for South
America this rash enterprise was abandoned also, or rather postponed, as he
was accustomed to say. It was then that his mind turned to California,
whose wonders had engaged his fancy for many a year. Upon consulting

Captain Parsons concerning a passage to New York, the latter pointed out to him a trim little fruit schooner loaded with oranges and ready to weigh anchor. With his usual promptness in making decisions he was aboard the little fruiter and bound for New York within twenty-four hours.

Muir's enthusiastic description of this trip in one of the chapters of *A Thousand-Mile Walk to the Gulf* shows that he took almost as much delight in the scenes of the ocean as in those on land. But New York bewildered him by its size, throngs, and noise. By permission of the captain the schooner remained his home while he made arrangements for his passage to Panama. His walks about the city of New York, he says, "extended but little beyond sight of my little schooner home. . . . Often I thought I would like to explore the city if, like a lot of wild hills and valleys, it was clear of inhabitants."

The North American Company at this time had ordered from New York a new steamship for its Pacific Coast traffic. This was the Nebraska, and she had sailed early in January, 1868, on her long maiden voyage around Cape Horn. Muir found that the Santiago de Cuba was scheduled to sail for Aspinwall on the 6th of March, and that her passengers would connect with the northward-bound Nebraska on the Pacific side of the Isthmus of Panama in about ten days. The records show that the Santiago de Cuba, not a large boat, carried on this trip four hundred passengers and five hundred and forty-two tons of freight. So overcrowded was the vessel that many passengers had to sleep on the decks. Nevertheless Muir engaged steerage passage on this boat and made connections with the Nebraska.

Over his experiences on shipboard, both to Panama and from there to California, Muir has drawn the veil of oblivion. He rarely referred to them, even in the circle of his own family, and then only to indicate that they were such as one would have to forget in order to retain one's faith in humanity.

But of the trip across the Isthmus he wrote, "Never shall I forget the glorious flora, especially for the first fifteen or twenty miles along the Chagres River. The riotous exuberance of great forest trees, glowing in purple, red, and yellow flowers, far surpassed anything I had ever seen, especially of flowering trees, either in Florida or Cuba. I gazed from the car platform enchanted. I fairly cried for joy and hoped that sometime I should be able to return and enjoy and study this most glorious of forests to my heart's content."

CHAPTER SIX

Following the Sheep 1868–1869

THE NEBRASKA arrived at San Francisco, March 27th, and Muir lost no time there after he set foot on land. To his friends he was accustomed to relate, with touches of humour, how he met on the street, the morning after debarkation, a man with a kit of carpenter's tools on his shoulders. When he inquired of him "the nearest way out of town to the wild part of the State," the man set down his tools in evident astonishment and asked, "where do you wish to go?" "Anywhere that's wild" was Muir's reply, and he was directed to the Oakland Ferry with the remark that that would be as good a way out of town as any.

On shipboard Muir had made the acquaintanceship of a young Englishman by the name of Chilwell, "a most amusing and faithful companion," who eagerly embraced the opportunity to visit Yosemite Valley with him. In those days the usual route to Yosemite was by river steamer to Stockton, thence by stage to Coulterville or Mariposa, and the remainder of way over the mountains on horseback. But Muir disdained this "orthodox route," for "we had plenty of time," he said, "and proposed drifting leisurely mountain ward by the Santa Clara Valley, Pacheco Pass, and the San Joaquin Valley, and thence to Yosemite by any road that we chanced to find; enjoying the flowers and light; camping out in our blankets wherever overtaken by night and paying very little compliance to roads or times."

In his autobiographical manuscript Muir passes in a few sentences over the first part of this trip, intending according to his pencilled directions to fill in from a description already written. This must refer to the detailed narrative published in *Old and New* in 1872, from which we excerpt the paragraphs descriptive of his walk as far as the top of the Pacheco Pass.

We crossed the bay by the Oakland Ferry and proceeded up the Santa Clara valley to San José. This is one of the most fertile of the many small valleys of the coast; its rich bottoms are filled with wheat-fields, and orchards, and vineyards, and alfalfa meadows.

It was now spring-time, and the weather was the best we ever enjoyed. Larks and streams sang everywhere; the sky was cloudless, and the whole valley was a lake of light. The atmosphere was spicy and exhilarating, my companion acknowledging over his national prejudices that it was the best he ever breathed – more deliciously fragrant than that which streamed over the hawthorn hedges of England. This San Jose sky was not simply pure and bright, and mixed with plenty of well-tempered sunshine, but it possessed a positive flavour, a taste that thrilled throughout every tissue of the body. Every inspiration yielded a well-defined piece of pleasure that awakened thousands of new palates everywhere. Both my companion and myself had lived on common air for nearly thirty years, and never before this discovered that our bodies contained such multitudes of palates, or that this mortal flesh, so little valued by philosophers and teachers, was possessed of so vast a capacity for happiness.

We were new creatures, born again; and truly not until this time were we fairly conscious that we were born at all. Never more, thought I as we strode forward at faster speed, never more shall I sentimentalise about getting free from the flesh, for it is steeped like a sponge in immortal pleasure.

The foothills of the valley are in near view all the way to Gilroy, those of the Monte Diablo range on our left, those of Santa Cruz on our right; they are smooth and flowing, and come down to the bottom levels in curves of most surpassing beauty. They are covered with flowers growing close together in cloud-shaped companies, acres and hillsides in size, white, purple, and yellow, separate, yet blending like the hills upon which they grow....

The Pacheco Pass was scarcely less enchanting than the valley. It resounded with crystal waters, and the loud shouts of thousands of quails. The California quail is a little larger than the Bob White; not quite so plump in form. The male has a tall, slender crest, wider at top than bottom, which he can hold straight up, or droop backward on his neck, or forward over his bill, at pleasure; and, instead of "Bob White," he shouts "pe-check-a," bearing down with a stiff, obstinate emphasis on "check." Through a considerable portion of the pass the road bends and mazes along the groves of a stream, or down in its pebbly bed, leading one now deep in the shadows of dogwoods and alders, then out in the light, through dry chaparral, over green carex meadow banked with violets and ferns, and dry, plantless flood-beds of gravel and sand.

We found ferns in abundance in the pass ... Also in this rich garden pass we gathered many fine grasses and carices, and brilliant penstemons, azure and scarlet, and mints and lilies, and scores of others, strangers to us, but beautiful and pure as ever enjoyed the sun or shade of a mountain home.

At this point Muir's unpublished memoirs resume the thread of the narrative as follows:

At the top of the Pass I obtained my first view of the San Joaquin plain and the glorious Sierra Nevada. Looking down from a height of fifteen hundred feet, there, extending north and south as far as I could see lay a vast level flower garden, smooth and level like a lake of gold – the floweriest part of the world I had yet seen. From the eastern margin of the golden plain arose the white Sierra. At the base ran a belt of gently sloping purplish foothills lightly dotted with oaks, above that a broad dark zone of coniferous forests and above this forest zone arose the lofty mountain peaks, clad in snow. The atmosphere was so clear that although the nearest of the mountain peaks on the axis of the range were at a distance of more than one hundred and fifty miles, they seemed to be at just the right distance to be seen broadly in their relationship to one another, marshalled in glorious ranks and groups, their snowy robes so smooth and bright that it seemed impossible for a man to walk across the open folds without being seen, even at this distance. Perhaps more than three hundred miles of the range was comprehended in this one view.

Descending the pass and wading out into the bed of golden compositae five hundred miles long by forty or fifty wide, I found that the average depth of the vegetation was over knee deep, and the flowers were so crowded together that in walking through the midst of them and over them more than a hundred were pressed down beneath the foot at every step. The yellow of these compositae, both of the ray and disc flowers, is extremely deep and rich and bossy, and exceeds the purple of all the others in superficial quantity forty or fifty times their whole amount. But to an observer who first looks downward, then takes a wider and wider view, the yellow gradually fades, and purple predominates, because nearly all of the purple flowers are taller. In depth, the purple stratum is about ten or twelve inches, the yellow seven or eight, and down in the shade, out of sight, is another stratum of purple, one inch in depth, for the ground forests of mosses are there, with purple stems, and purple cups. The colour beauty of these mosses, at least in the mass, was not made for human eyes, nor for the wild horses that inhabit these plains, nor the antelopes, but perhaps the little creatures enjoy their own beauty, and perhaps the insects that dwell in these forests and climb their shining columns enjoy it. But we know that however faint, and however shaded, no part of it is lost, for all colour is received into the eyes of God.

Crossing this greatest of flower gardens and the San Joaquin River at Hill's Ferry, we followed the Merced River, which I knew drained Yosemite Valley, and ascended the foothills from Snelling by way of Coulterville. We had several accidents and adventures. At the little mining town of Coulterville we bought flour and tea and made inquiries about roads and trails, and the forests we would have to pass through. The storekeeper, an Italian, took kindly pains to tell the pair of wandering wayfarers, new arrived in California, that the winter had been very severe, that in some places the Yosemite trail was still buried in snow eight or ten feet deep, and therefore we would have to wait at least a month before we could possibly get into the great valley, for we would surely get lost should we attempt to go on. As to the forests, the trees, he said, were very large; some of the pines eight or ten feet in diameter.

In reply I told him that it would be delightful to see snow ten feet deep and trees ten feet thick, even if lost, but I never got lost in wild woods. "Well," said he, "go, if you must, but I have warned you; and anyhow you must have a gun, for there are bears in the mountains, but you must not shoot at them unless they come for you and are very, very close up." So at last, at Mr. Chilwell's anxious suggestion, we bought an old army musket, with a few pounds of quail shot and large buckshot, good, as the merchant assured us, for either birds or bears.

Our bill of fare in camps was simple – tea and cakes, the latter made from flour without leaven and toasted on the coals – and of course we shunned hotels in the valley, seldom indulging even in crackers, as being too expensive. Chilwell, being an Englishman, loudly lamented being compelled to live on so light a diet, flour and water, as he expressed it, and hungered for flesh; therefore he made desperate efforts to shoot something to eat, particularly quails and grouse, but he was invariably unsuccessful and declared the gun was worthless. I told him I thought that it was good enough if properly loaded and aimed, though perhaps sighted too high, and promised to show him at the first opportunity how to load and shoot.

Many of the herbaceous plants of the flowing foothills were the same as those of the plain and had already gone to seed and withered. But at a height of one thousand feet or so we found many of the lily family blooming in all their glory, the Calochortus especially, a charming genus like European tulips, but finer, and many species of two new shrubs – especially, Ceanothus and Adenostoma. The oaks, beautiful trees with blue foliage and white bark, forming open groves, gave a fine park effect. Higher, we met the first of the pines, with long grey foliage, large stout cones, and wide-spreading heads like palms. Then yellow pines, growing gradually more abundant as we ascended. At Bower Cave on the north fork of the Merced the streams were fringed with willows and azalea, ferns, flowering dogwood, etc. Here, too, we enjoyed the strange beauty of the Cave in a limestone hill.

At Deer Flat the wagon-road ended in a trail which we traced up the side of the dividing ridge parallel to the Merced and Tuolumne to Crane Flat, lying at a height of six thousand feet, where we found a noble forest of sugar pine, silver fir, libocedrus, Douglas spruce, the first of the noble Sierra forests, the noblest coniferous forests in the world, towering in all their unspoiled beauty and grandeur around a sunny, gently sloping meadow. Here, too, we got into the heavy winter snow – a fine change from the burning foothills and plains.

Some mountaineer had tried to establish a claim to the Flat by building a little cabin of sugar pine shakes, and though we had arrived early in the afternoon I decided to camp here for the night as the trail was buried in the snow which was about six feet deep, and I wanted to examine the topography and plan our course. Chilwell cleared away the snow from the door and floor of the cabin, and made a bed in it of boughs of fernlike silver fir, though I urged the same sort of bed made under the trees on the snow. But he had the house habit.

After camp arrangements were made he reminded me of my promise about the gun, hoping eagerly for improvement of our bill of fare, however slight. Accordingly I loaded the gun, paced off thirty yards from the cabin, or shanty, and told Mr. Chilwell to pin a piece of paper on the wall and see if I could not put shot into it and prove the gun's worth. So he pinned a piece of an envelope on the shanty wall and vanished around the corner, calling out, "Fire away."

I supposed that he had gone some distance back of the cabin, but instead he went inside of it and stood up against the mark that he had himself placed on the wall, and as the shake wall of soft sugar pine was only about half an inch thick, the shot passed through it and into his shoulder. He came rushing out, with his hand on his shoulder, crying in great concern, "You've shot me, you've shot me, Scottie." The weather being cold, he fortunately had on three coats and as many shirts. One of the coats was a heavy English overcoat. I discovered that the shot had passed through all this clothing and into his shoulder, and the embedded pellets had to be picked out with the point of a penknife. I asked him how he could be so foolish as to stand opposite the mark. "Because," he replied, "I never imagined the blank gun would shoot through the side of the 'ouse."

We found our way easily enough over the deep snow, guided by the topography, and discovered the trail on the brow of the valley just as the Bridal Veil came in sight. I didn't know that it was one of the famous falls I had read about, and calling Chilwell's attention to it I said, "See that dainty little fall over there. I should like to camp at the foot of it to see the ferns and lilies that may be there. It looks small from here, only about fifteen or twenty feet, but it may be sixty or seventy." So little did we then know of Yosemite magnitudes!

After spending eight or ten days in visiting the falls and the high points of view around the walls, making sketches, collecting flowers and ferns, etc., we decided to make the return trip by way of Wawona, then owned by Galen Clark, the Yosemite pioneer. The night before the start was made on the return trip we camped near the Bridal Veil Meadows, where, as we lay eating our suppers by the light of the camp-fire, we were visited by a brown bear. We heard him approaching by the heavy crackling of twigs. Chilwell, in alarm, after listening a while, said, "I see it! I see it! It's a bear, a grizzly! Where is the gun? You take the gun and shoot him – you can shoot best." But the gun had only a charge of birdshot in it; therefore, while the bear stood on the opposite side of the fire, at a distance of probably twenty-five or thirty feet, I hastily loaded in a lot of buckshot. The buckshot was too large to chamber and therefore it made a zigzag charge on top of the birdshot charge, the two charges occupying about half of the barrel. Thus armed, the gun held at rest pointed at the bear, we sat hushed and motionless, according to instructions from the man who sold the gun, solemnly waiting and watching, as full of fear as the musket of shot. Finally, after sniffing and whining for his supper what seemed to us a long time, the young inexperienced beast walked off. We were much afraid of his return to attack us. We did not then know that bears never attack sleeping campers, and dreading another visit we kept awake on guard most of the night.

Like the Coulterville trail all the high-lying part of the Mariposa trail was deeply snow-buried, but we found our way without the slightest trouble, steering by the topography in a general way along the brow of the canyon of the south fork of the Merced River, and in a day or two reached Wawona. Here we replenished our little flour sack and Mr. Clark gave us a piece of bear meat.

We then pushed eagerly on up the Wawona ridge through a magnificent sugar pine forest and into the far-famed Mariposa Sequoia Grove. The sun was down when we entered the Grove, but we soon had a good fire and at supper that night we tasted bear meat for the first time. My flesh-hungry companion ate it eagerly, though to me it seemed so rank and oily that I was unable to swallow a single morsel.

After supper we replenished the fire and gazed enchanted at the vividly illumined brown boles of the giants towering about us, while the stars sparkled in wonderful beauty above their huge domed heads. We camped here long uncounted days, wandering about from tree to tree, taking no note of time. The longer we gazed the more we admired not only their colossal size, but their majestic beauty and dignity. Greatest of trees, greatest of living things, their noble domes poised in unchanging repose seemed to belong to the sky, while the great firs and pines about them looked like mere latter-day saplings.

While we camped in the Mariposa Grove, the abundance of bear tracks caused Mr. Chilwell no little alarm, and he proposed that we load the gun properly with buckshot and without any useless birdshot; but there was no means of drawing the charge – it had to be shot off. The recoil was so great that it bruised his shoulder and sent him spinning like a top. Casting down the miserable, kicking, bad luck musket among the Sequoia cones and branches that littered the ground, he stripped and examined his unfortunate shoulder and, in painful indignation and wrath, found it black and blue and more seriously hurt by the bruising recoil blow than it was by the shot at Crane Flat.

When we got down to the hot San Joaquin plain at Snelling the grain fields were nearly ready for the reaper, and we began to inquire for a job to replenish our remaining stock of money which was now very small, though we had not spent much; the grand royal trip of more than a month in the Yosemite region having cost us only about three dollars each. At our last camp, in a bed of cobble-stones on the Merced River bottom, Mr. Chilwell was more and more eagerly hungering for meat. He tried to shoot one of the jack-rabbits cantering around us, but was unable to hit any of them. I told him, when he begged me to take the gun, that I would shoot one for him if he would drive it up to the camp. He ran and shooed and threw cobble-stones without getting any of them up within shooting distance as I took good care to warn the poor beasts by making myself and the gun conspicuous. At last discovering the humour of the thing he shouted: "I say, Scottie, this makes me think of a picture I once saw in Punch – game-keepers driving partridges to be shot by a simpleton Cockney."

Then one of those curious burrowing owls alighted on the top of a fence-post beside us, and I said, "If you are so hungry for flesh why don't you shoot one of those owls?" "Howls," he said in disgust, "are only vermin." I argued that that was mere prejudice and custom, and that if stewed in a pot it would make good soup, and the flesh, too, that he hungered for, might also be found to be fairly good, but that if he didn't care for it, I didn't.

I finally pictured the flavour of the soup so temptingly that with watering lips he consented to try it, and the poor owl was shot. When he came to dress it the pitiful little red carcass seemed so worthless a morsel that he was tempted to throw it away, but I said, "No; now that you have it ready for the pot, boil it and at least enjoy the soup." So it was boiled in the teapot and bravely devoured, though he insisted that he did not like the flavour of either the soup or the meat. He charged me, saying: "Now, Scottie, if you go to England with me to see my folks, after our fortunes are made, don't you tell them as 'ow we 'ad a howl for supper." He was always trying to persuade me to go to England with him.

Next day we got a job in a harvest field at Hopeton and were seated at a table once more. Mr. Chilwell never tired of describing the meanness and misery of so pure a vegetable diet as was ours on the Yosemite trip. "Just think of it," said he, "we lived a whole month on flour and water!" He ate so many hot biscuits at that table, and so much beans and boiled pork, that he was sick for three or four days afterwards, a trick the despised Yosemite diet never played him.

This Yosemite trip only made me hungry for another far longer and farther reaching, and I determined to set out again as soon as I had earned a little money to get near views of the mountains in all their snowy grandeur, and study the wonderful forests, the noblest of their kind I had ever seen – sugar pines eight and nine feet in diameter, with cones nearly two feet long, silver furs more than two hundred feet in height, Douglas spruce and libocedrus, and the kingly Sequoias.

After the harvest was over Mr. Chilwell left me, but I remained with Mr. Egleston several months to break mustang horses; then ran a ferry boat at Merced Falls for travel between Stockton and Mariposa. That same fall I made a lot of money sheep-shearing, and after the shearing was over one of the sheep-men of the neighbourhood, Mr. John Connel, nicknamed Smoky Jack, begged me to take care of one of his bands of sheep, because the then present shepherd was about to quit. He offered thirty dollars a month and board and assured me that it would be a "foin aisy job."

I said that I didn't know anything about sheep, except the shearing of them, didn't know the range, and that his flock would probably be scattered over the plains and lost; but he said he would risk me, that "the sheep would show me the range, and all would go smooth and aisy." At length, considering that, being out every day, a fine opportunity would be offered to watch the growth of the flowery vegetation, and to study the birds and beasts, insects, weather, etc., I dared the job, and sure enough, as my employer said, the sheep soon showed me their range, leading me a wild chase in their search for grass over the dry sunbeaten plains.

Smoky Jack was known far and wide, and I soon learned that he was a queer character. Unmarried, living alone, playing the game of money making, he had already become sheep-rich – the owner of three or four bands as the flocks are called. He had commenced his career as a sheep-man when he was poor, with only a score or two of coarse-wooled ewes, which he herded himself and faithfully followed and improved until they had multiplied into thousands.

He lived mostly on beans. In the morning after his bean breakfast he filled his pockets from the pot with dripping beans for luncheon, which he ate in handfuls as he followed the flock. His overalls and boots soon, of course, became thoroughly saturated, and instead of wearing thin, wore thicker and stouter, and by sitting down to rest from time to time, parts of all the vegetation, leaves, petals, etc., were embedded in them, together with wool fibres, butterfly wings, mica crystals, fragments of nearly everything that part of the world contained – rubbed in, embedded and coarsely stratified, so that these wonderful garments grew to have a rich geological and biological significance, like those of Mr. Delaney's shepherd.

Replying to my inquiry where the sheep were, he directed me to follow the road between French Bar and Snelling four or five miles, and "when you see a cabin on a little hill, that's the place." I found the place, and a queer place it proved to be. The shepherd whom I was to relieve hailed me with delight and within a few minutes of my arrival set off, exulting in his freedom. I begged him to stay until morning and show me the range, but this he refused, saying that it was unnecessary for him to show me the range; all I had to do was simply to let down the corral bars and the starving sheep would soon explain and explore the range.

Left alone, I examined the dismal little hut with dismay. A Dutch oven frying-pan, and a few tin cups lay on the floor; a rickety stool and a bedstead, with a tick made of a wool sack, stuffed with straw and cast-off overalls left by shearers, constituted the furniture. I went outside, looking for a piece of clean ground to lie down on, but no such ground was to be found. Every yard of it was strewn with some sort of sheep camp detritus, bits of shrivelled woolly skin, bacon rinds, bones, horns and skulls mixed with all sorts of mysterious compound unclean rubbish! I therefore had to go back into the shanty and spread my blankets on the dirt floor as the least dangerous part of the establishment.

Next morning, by the time I had fried some pancakes and made a cup of tea, the sunbeams were streaming through the wide vertical seams of the shanty wall, and I made haste to open the corral. The sheep were crowding around the gate, and as soon as it was opened, poured forth like a boisterous uncontrollable flood, and soon the whole flock was so widely outspread and scattered over the plain, it seemed impossible that the mad starving creatures could ever be got together again. I ran around from side to side, headed the leaders off again and again, and did my best to confine the size of the flock to an area of a square mile or so.

About noon, to my delight and surprise, they lay down to rest and allowed me to do the same for an hour or so. Then they again scattered, but not so far nor so wildly, and I was still more surprised about half an hour before sundown, while I was wondering how I could ever get them driven back into the corral, to see them gather of their own accord into long parallel files, cross Dry Creek on the bank of which the corral stood, and pour back into the corral and quietly lie down. This ended my first day of sheep-herding.

After the winter rains had set in, and the grass had grown to a height of three or four inches, herding became easy, for they quietly filled themselves; but at this time, just before the rain, when not a green leaf is to be seen, when the dead summer vegetation is parched and crumpled into dust and fragments of stems, the sheep are always hungry and unmanageable; but when full of green grass the entire flock moves as one mild, bland, contented animal. This year the winter rains did not set in until the middle of December. Then Dry Creek became a full, deep, stately flowing river; every hollow in the hills was flooded, every channel so long dry carried a rushing, gurgling, happy stream.

Being out every day I had the advantage of watching the coming of every species of plant. Mosses and liverworts, no trace of which could be seen when dry and crumpled, now suddenly covered the entire plain with a soft velvet robe of living green. Then, at first one by one, the different species of flowering plants appeared, pushing up with marvellous rapidity and bursting into bloom, until all the ground was covered with golden compositae, interrupted and enriched here and there with charming beds of violets, mints, clover, mariposa tulips, etc.

It was very interesting, too, to watch the awakening and coming to light and life of the many species of ants and other insects after their deathlike sleep during the cold rainy season; and the ground squirrels coming out of their burrows to sun themselves and feed on the fresh vegetation; and to watch the nesting birds and hear them sing – especially the meadow-larks which were in great abundance and sang as if every note was transformed sunshine. Plovers in great numbers and of several species came to feed with snipes and geese and swans.

It was interesting, too, to watch the long-eared hares, or jack-rabbits as they are called, as they cantered over the flowery plain, or confidingly mingled with the flock. Several times I saw inquisitive sheep interviewing the rabbits as they sat erect, even touching noses and indulging apparently in interesting gossip. My dog was fond of chasing the hares, but they bounded along carelessly, and never were so closely pressed as to be compelled to dive into a burrow. They apparently trusted entirely to their speed of foot; but as soon as a golden eagle came in sight they made for the nearest burrow in terrified haste. Then, feeling safe, they would turn around and look out the door to watch the movements of their enemy.

Occasionally I have seen an eagle alight within a yard or two of the door of a burrow into which a hare had been chased, and observed their gestures while the hare and eagle looked each other in the face for an hour at a time, the eagle apparently hoping that the hare might venture forth. When, however, a hare was surprised at any considerable distance from a burrow, the eagle, in swift pursuit, rapidly overtakes it and strikes it down with his elbow, then wheels around, picks it up and carries it to some bare hilltop to feast at leisure.

By the end of May nearly all of the marvellous vegetation of the plains has gone to seed and is so scorched and sun-dried, it crumbles under foot as though it had literally been cast into an oven. Then most of the flocks are driven into the green pastures of the Sierra. A camp is made on the first favourable spot commanding a considerable range, and when it is eaten out the camp is moved to higher and higher pastures in succession, following the upward sweep of grassy, flowery summer towards the summit of the Range.

Ever since I had visited Yosemite the previous year I had longed to get back into the Sierra. When the heavy snows were melting in the spring sunshine, opening the way to the summits of the Range, and I was trying to plan a summer's excursion into their midst, wondering how I could possibly carry food to last a whole summer, Mr. Delaney, a neighbour of Smoky Jack's, noticing my love of plants and seeing some of the drawings I had made in my note-books, urged me to go to the mountains with his flock – not to herd the sheep, for the regular shepherd was to take care of them, but simply to see that the shepherd did his duties. He offered to carry my plant press and blankets, allow me to make his mountain camps my headquarters while I was studying the adjacent mountains, and perfect freedom to pursue my studies, and offering to pay me besides, simply to see that the shepherd did not neglect his flock.

Mr. Delaney was an Irishman who was educated at Maynooth College for a Catholic priest, a striking contrast to his so-called "Smoky" neighbour. He was lean and tall, and I naturally nicknamed him Don Quixote. I told him that I did not think I could be of any practical use to him because I did not know the mountains, knew nothing about the habits of sheep in the mountains, and that I feared that in pushing through brush, fording torrents, and in attacks of bears and wolves, the sheep would be scattered and not half of them ever see the plains again. But he encouraged me by saying that he himself would go to the mountains with the flock, to the first camp, and visit each camp in succession from time to time, bringing letters and fresh provisions, and seeing for himself how his flock was prospering; that the shepherd would do all the herding and that I would be just as free to pursue my studies as if there were no sheep in the question, to sketch and collect plants, and observe the wild animals; but as he could not depend upon his shepherd his fear was that the flock might be neglected, and scattered by bears, and that my services would only be required in cases of accidents of that sort.

I therefore concluded to accept his generous offer. The sheep were counted, the morning the start for the mountains was made, as they passed out of the corral one by one. They numbered two thousand and fifty, and were headed for the mountains. The leaders of the flock had not gone a mile from the home camp before they seemed to understand that they were on their way up to the high green pastures where they had been the year before, and eagerly ran ahead, while Don Quixote, with a rifle on his shoulder, led two pack animals, and the shepherd and an Indian and Chinaman to assist in driving through the foothills, and myself, marched in the rear.

Our first camp after crossing the dusty, brushy foothills, which were scarcely less sunburned than the plains, was made on a tributary of the North

Fork of the Merced River at an elevation of about three thousand feet above the sea. Here there were no extensive grassy meadows, but the hills and hollows and recesses of the mountain divide between the Merced and the Tuolumne waters were richly clothed with grass and lupines, while clover of different species and ceanothus bushes furnished pasture in fair abundance for several weeks, while the many waterfalls on the upper branches of the river, the charming lily gardens at the foot of them, and many new plants and animals to sketch and study, afforded endless work according to my own heart.

The sheep were kept here too long; the pasture within two or three miles of the camp was eaten bare, while we waited day after day, more and more anxiously, for the coming of the Don with provisions, and to assist and direct the moving of the camp to higher fresh pasturage. Our own pasturage was also exhausted. We got out of flour, and strange to say, although we had abundance of mutton and tea and sugar, we began to suffer. After going without bread for about a week it was difficult to swallow mutton, and our stomachs became more and more restless. The shepherd tried to calm his rebellious stomach by chewing great quantities of tobacco and swallowing most of the juice, and by making his tea very strong, using a handful for each cup. Strange that in so fertile a wilderness we should suffer distress for the want of a cracker, or a slice of bread, while the Indians of the neighbourhood sustained their merry, free lives on clover, pine bark, lupines, fern roots, etc., with only now and then a squirrel.

At length the Don came down the long glen, and all our bread woes were ended. He brought with him not only an abundance of provisions, but two men to assist in driving the flock higher. One of these men was an Indian, and I was interested in watching his behaviour while eating, driving, and choosing a place to sleep at night. He kept a separate camp, and how quick his eye was to notice a straggling sheep, and how much better he seemed to understand the intentions and motives of the flock than any of the other assistants.

Our next camp was made on the north side of Yosemite Valley, about a mile back from the top of the wall. Here for six weeks I revelled in the grandeur of Yosemite scenery, sketching from the crown of North Dome, visiting the head of the great Yosemite Fall and making excursions to the eastward to the top of Mount Hoffmann and to Lake Tenaya, enjoying the new plants. The greatest charm of our first camp were the lily gardens, *Lilium pardalinum*, with corollas large enough for babies' bonnets. The species around our Yosemite camp was the mountain lily, *L. parvum*, with from one or two to forty or fifty flowers, the magnificent panicles rising to the height of six or seven feet, or even higher.

The principal tree of the forests at an elevation of eight thousand feet is the magnificent silver fir. The tallest that I measured near camp was no less than two hundred and forty feet in height, while with this grandeur and majesty is combined exquisite beauty of foliage and flower and fruit; the branches like sumptuous fern fronds, arranged in regular whorls round the stem like the leaves of lilies. From this camp I made the acquaintance on the top of Mount

Hoffmann of trees I had not seen before – the beautiful mountain hemlock (*Tsuga Mertensiana*) and most graceful in form of all the California conifers, and the curious dwarf pine *(Pinus albicaulis)* that forms the timberline. To tell the glories of this magnificent camp-ground would require many a volume.

Here, for the first time, the sheep were attacked by bears in the night and scattered. The morning light showed a heap of dead sheep in the corral, killed by suffocation in piling on top of each other and pressing against the wall of the corral, while only two were carried out of the corral and half of the carcasses eaten. The second day after this attack the corral was again visited, another lot of sheep smothered and one carried off and half devoured. Just after we had succeeded in gathering the scattered flock into one again the Don arrived, and immediately ordered the camp moved, saying that the first robber bear and perhaps others, would visit the camp every night, and that no noisy watching, shooting, or building of fires would be of any avail to stop them. Accordingly, next morning the flock was headed toward the high grassy forests north of the Tuolumne meadows which we reached a few days later, where abundance of the best pasturage was found. Here we stayed until the approach of winter warned the Don to turn the flock toward the lowlands. At this camp I had a glorious time climbing, studying, sketching, pressing new plants, etc. But far from satisfied I determined to return next year and as many other years as opportunities offered or were made.

When we arrived at the home ranch the flock was corralled and counted and strange to say, every sheep of the two thousand and fifty was accounted for. A few had been killed for mutton, one was killed by the bite of a rattlesnake, one broke its leg jumping over a rock and had to be killed, one or two were sold to settlers on the way down to the foothills, and so forth, besides those lost by bears. This was a summer of greatest enjoyment of all that I liked best. I climbed the surrounding mountains; made the acquaintance of many new trees, shrubs, and herbaceous plants, the main forest zones, glacier meadows, gardens and endless falls and cascades. There, too, I made the acquaintance of some of the Mono Indians, who visited our camp while on their annual deer hunt. The whole summer was crowded with the noblest pictures and sculptures and monuments of nature's handiwork. I explored the magnificent group of mountains at the head of the Tuolumne River, crossed the range by the Mono Pass, visited Mono Lake and the range of volcanic cones extending from its southern shore, making excursions from camp into all the surrounding region, sketching, writing notes, pressing plants, tracing the works and ways of the ancient glaciers, and revelling in the glorious life and beauty of the unspoiled new-born wilderness. And when at last the snow drove me out of it I determined to return to it again and again as I was able.

Yosemite Valley from Inspiration Point, with El Capitan ((left), Half Dome (centre) and Cathedral Rocks and Bridal Veil Fall (right).

A section of Muir's map of Yosemite Valley (from ''Treasures of The Proposed Yosemite National Park.'')

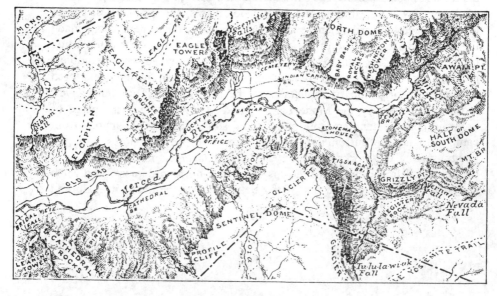

CHAPTER SEVEN

First Yosemite Years 1869–1870

MUIR'S FIRST EXCURSION into the High Sierra ended in September, 1869. What he saw and experienced during that memorable summer is told vividly, and with infectious enthusiasm, in his journal, later published as *My First Summer in the Sierra*. Only one thing there was that marred his joy – the fearful destruction wrought in the forests by the ''hoofed locusts'' which he was set to guard. Though he did not realise it then, the time was coming when his direct observation of the devastating effect of sheeping in the High Sierra was to become an important factor in his campaign to expel the trampling, devouring hordes from the mountains. But the uppermost impression in his mind, when the summer ended, was after all the Edenic loveliness of the regions he had visited. ''I have crossed the Range of Light,'' so runs the concluding sentence of his journal, ''surely the brightest and best of all the Lord has built; and rejoicing in its glory I gladly, gratefully hopefully pray I may see it again.''

The fulfilment of this desire was not to be long delayed, for the means of accomplishment were in his own power. After spending about eight weeks breaking horses for Pat Delaney, building fences, and running a gang-plough over his broad acres below French Bar, he set out on foot for Yosemite by way of Pino Blanco, Coulterville, and Harding's Mill.

Meanwhile his Madison friends, the Carrs, had, during the summer of 1869, removed to California, where Professor Carr had been appointed to a Professorship in the University of California. They had not seen Muir since 1867 and were at this time urging him to pay them a visit in Oakland. ''I thank you most heartily for the very kind invitation you send me,'' he writes from Delaney's ranch near La Grange under date of November 15th, 1869. ''I could enjoy a blink of rest in your new home with a relish that only those can know who have suffered solitary banishment for so many years. But I must return to the mountains – to Yosemite. I am told that the winter storms there will not be easily borne, but I am bewitched, enchanted, and tomorrow I must start for the great temple to listen to the winter songs and sermons preached and sung only there.''

Mrs. Carr, soon after her arrival in California, had visited Yosemite, but to her and Muir's great disappointment the letter which was to call him down from the heights, to meet her in the Valley, failed to reach its destination. Muir at this time was still purposing to go on an exploratory trip to South America, a plan in which Mrs. Carr was warmly abetting him. So fully was his mind made up on this point that in a letter to his brother David he allowed himself only about six months more in California, and the prospect of so early a departure to other lands made him determined to spend these months in the mountains.

The proposed South American journey and the spell which the beauty and grandeur of the Sierra Nevada were weaving about him form the subject of a paragraph in a letter written to his sister Sarah during this same summer while encamped "in a spruce grove near the upper end of Yosemite, two miles from the north wall."

Just think [he writes] of the blessedness of my lot! – have been camped here right in the midst of Yosemite rocks and waters for fifteen days, with nearly all of every day to myself to climb, sketch, write, meditate, and botanise! My foot has pressed no floor but that of the mountains for many a day. I am far from the ways and pursuits of man. I seldom even hear the bleating of our twenty-five hundred sheep. The manifold overwhelming sublimities of the Sierra are all in all. I am with Nature in the grandest, most divine of all her earthly dwelling places ....

A few months will call upon me to decide to what portion of God's glorious star I will next turn. The sweets of home, the smooth waters of civilized life have attractions for me whose power is increased by time and constant rambling, but I am a captive, I am bound. Love of pure unblemished Nature seems to overmaster and blur out of sight all other objects and considerations. I know that I could under ordinary circumstances accumulate wealth and obtain a fair position in society, and I am arrived at an age that requires that I should choose some definite course for life. But I am sure that the mind of no truant schoolboy is more free and disengaged from all the grave plans and purposes and pursuits of ordinary orthodox life than mine. But I wonder what spirit is conjuring up such sober affairs at this time. I only meant to say a word by way of family greeting. Tomorrow I will be among the sublimities of Yosemite and forget that ever a thought of civilization or time-honoured proprieties came among my pathless, lawless thoughts and wanderings.

Few persons at this time had braved the storms and isolation of Yosemite during the winter season. The first to do this was James C. Lamon, a Virginian, who came to California from Texas in 1851 and found his way into Yosemite Valley in 1857. Two years later he planted an orchard opposite Half Dome and in 1862 began to make the Valley his residence both in winter and in summer. In 1864 his example was followed by J. M. Hutchings who brought his wife with him and soon became a sort of *valet de place*. His frame house, situated directly opposite the Yosemite Fall, served also the purpose of a hotel for visitors, and Muir upon his arrival in the Valley naturally sought shelter there. The following letter reflects something of the elation with which he began to explore his new surroundings:

to Mrs. Ezra S. Carr

Yosemite, December 6th, 1869

DEAR FRIEND MRS. CARR

I am feasting in the Lord's mountain house, and what pen may write my blessings! I am going to dwell here all winter magnificently "snow-bound." Just think of the grandeur of a mountain winter in Yosemite! Would that you could enjoy it also!

I read your word of pencil upon the bridge below the Nevada, and I thank you for it most devoutly. No one nor all of the Lord's blessings can enable me to exist without friends, and I know that you are a friend indeed.

There is no snow in the Valley. The ground is covered with the brown and yellow leaves of the oak and maple, and their crisping and rustling make me think of the groves of Madison.

I have been wandering about among the falls and rapids studying the grand instruments of slopes and curves and echoing caves upon which those divine harmonies are played. Only a thin flossy veil sways and bends over Yosemite now, and Pohono, too, is a web of waving mist. New songs are sung, forming parts of the one grand anthem composed and written in "the beginning."

Most of the flowers are dead. Only a few are blooming in summer nooks on the north side rocks. You remember that delightful fernery by the ladders. Well, I discovered a garden meeting of Adiantum far more delicate and luxuriant than those at the ladders. They are in a cove or covelette between the upper and lower Yosemite Falls. They are the most delicate and graceful plant creatures I ever beheld, waving themselves in lines of the most refined of heaven's beauty to the music of the water. The motion of purple dulses in pools left by the tide on the sea coast of Scotland was the only memory that was stirred by these spiritual ferns.

You speak of dying and going to the woods. I am dead, and gone to heaven.

Indian [Tom] comes to the Valley once a month upon snowshoes. He brings the mail, and so I shall hope to hear from you. Address to Yosemite, via Big Oak Flat, care of Mr. Hutchings.

[JOHN MUIR]

A pleasing picture of his employment, his cabin, and the variety of his nature interests during the next two years is drawn in the following passage from unfinished memoirs:

I had the good fortune to obtain employment from Mr. Hutchings in building a sawmill to cut lumber for cottages, that he wished to build in the spring, from the fallen pines which had been blown down in a violent wind-storm a year or two before my arrival. Thus I secured employment for two years, during all of which time I watched the varying aspect of the glorious valley, arrayed in its winter robes; the descent from the heights of the booming, out-bounding avalanches like magnificent waterfalls; the coming and going of the noble storms; the varying songs of the falls; the growth of frost crystals on the rocks and leaves and snow; the sunshine sifting through them in rainbow colours; climbing every Sunday to the top of the walls for views of the mountains in glorious array along the summit of the range, etc.

I boarded with Mr. Hutchings' family, but occupied a cabin that I built for myself near the Hutchings' winter home. This cabin, I think, was the handsomest building in the Valley, and the most useful and convenient for a mountaineer. From the Yosemite Creek, near where it first gathers its beaten waters at the foot of the fall, I dug a small ditch and brought a stream into the cabin, entering at one end and flowing out the other with just current enough to allow it to sing and warble in low, sweet tones, delightful at night while I lay in bed. The floor was made of rough slabs, nicely joined and embedded in the ground. In the spring the common pteris ferns pushed up between the joints of the slabs, two of which, growing slender like climbing ferns on account of the subdued light, I trained on threads up the sides and over my window in front of my writing desk in an ornamental arch. Dainty little tree frogs occasionally climbed the ferns and made fine music in the night, and common frogs came in with the stream and helped to sing with the Hylas and the warbling, tinkling water. My bed was suspended from the rafters and lined with libocedrus plumes, altogether forming a delightful home in the glorious Valley at a cost of only three or four dollars, and I was loath to leave it.

This all too brief account of Muir's earlier Yosemite years we fortunately are able to supplement with the following letters:

to David Gilrye Muir

Yosemite, March 20th, [1870]

DEAR BROTHER DAVID G.

Your last of January 6th reached me here in the rocks two weeks ago. I am very heartily glad to learn that your dear wife and wee ones have escaped from sickness to health. "Ten weeks of fever" – mercy, what intense significance these four words have for me after my Florida experience. We were taught to believe that Providence has special designs to accomplish by the agency of such afflictions. I cannot say that I have the requisite amount of faith to feel the truth of this, but one invariable result of suffering in a love-knit family is to quicken all the powers that develop compact units from clusters of human souls.

I am sitting here in a little shanty made of sugar pine shingles this Sabbath evening. I have not been at church a single time since leaving home. Yet this glorious valley might well be called a church, for every lover of the great Creator who comes within the broad overwhelming influences of the place fails not to worship as he never did before. The glory of the Lord is upon all his works; it is written plainly upon all the fields of every clime, and upon every sky, but here in this place of surpassing glory the Lord has written in capitals. I hope that one day you will see and read with your own eyes.

The only sounds that strike me tonight are the ticking of the clock, the flickering of the fire and the love songs of a host of peaceful frogs that sing out in the meadow up to their throats in slush, and the deep waving roar of the falls like breakers on a rocky coast.

Your description of the sad quiet and deserted loneliness of home made me sorry, and I felt like returning to the old farm to take care of father and mother myself in their old days, but a little reflection served to show that of all the family, my views and habits and disposition make me the most incapable for the task.

You stirred a happy budget of memories in speaking of my work-shop and laboratory. The happiest days and scrap portions of my life were in that old slant-walled garret and among the smooth creeks that trickled among the sedges of Fountain Lake meadow.

In recalling the mechanical achievements of those early days I remember with satisfaction that the least successful one was that horrid guillotine of a thing for slicing off gophers' heads.

. . . I have completed the sawmill here. It works extremely well. If not a "Kirk and a mill" I have at least made a house and a mill here . . . .

to Sarah Muir Galloway

Yosemite Valley, March 24th, 1870

DEAR SISTER

A grand event has occurred in our remote snowbound Valley. Indian Tom has come from the open lower world with the mail . . . .

I wrote you some weeks ago from this place. Tom leaves the Valley to-morrow. I have four letters to write this evening, and it is nearly nine o'clock, so I will not try to write much, but will just say a few things in haste. First of all let me say that though my lot in these years is to wander in foreign lands, my heart is at home. I still feel you all as the chief wealth of my inmost soul and the most necessary elements of my life. What if many a river runs between us. Distance ought not to separate us. Comets that leave their sun for long irregular journeys through the fields of the sky acknowledge as constant and controlling a sympathy with its great centre as the nearer, more civilized stars that travel the more proper roads of steady circles. No one reflection gives me so much comfort as the completeness and unity of our family. An apparently short column of years has made men and women of us all, and as I wrote to Daniel, we stand united like a family clump of trees – may the divine power of family love keep us one. And now do not consider me absent – lost. I have but gone out a little distance to look at the Lord's gardens.

Remember me very warmly to Mrs. Galloway. Tell her that I sympathise very keenly with her in her great affliction. Tell her that my eyes open every day upon the noblest works of God and that I would gladly lend her my own eyes if I could. I think of her very often. I was telling my friend here about her a few nights ago in our little shanty. I do not live "near the Yosemite," but in it – in the very grandest, *warmest* centre of it. I wish you could hear the falls tonight – they speak a most glorious language, and I hear them easily through the thin walls of our cabin.

Of course I am glad to hear from you in this solitude, and I thank you for the daisy and the rose leaf and the old legend. I will tell you all about the Yosemite and many other places when I reach home. The surpassing glory of a place like this explains the beauty of that [which] is written in smaller characters, like that of your Mound hill . . . .

to Mrs. Ezra S. Carr

Yosemite, April 5th, 1870

DEAR MRS. CARR

I wish you were here today, for our rocks are again decked with deep snow. Two days ago a big grey cloud collared Barometer Dome, – the vast looming column of the upper falls was swayed like a shred of loose mist by broken pieces of storm that struck it suddenly, occasionally bending it backwards to the very top of the cliff, making it hang sometimes more than a minute like an inverted bow edged with comets. A cloud upon the Dome and these ever varying rockings and bendings of the falls are sure storm signs, but yesterday's morning sky was clear, and the sun poured the usual quantity of the balmiest spring sunshine into the blue ether of our Valley gulf. But ere long ragged lumps of cloud began to appear all along the Valley rim, coming gradually into closer ranks, and rising higher like rock additions to the walls. From the top of the cloud-banks, fleecy fingers arched out from both sides and met over the middle of the meadows, gradually thickening and blackening until at night big confident snowflakes began to fall.

We thought that the last snow harvest had been withered and reaped long ago by the glowing sun, for the bluebirds and robins sang spring, and so also did the bland unsteady winds, and the brown meadow opposite the house was spotted here and there with blue violets. Carex spikes were shooting up through the dead leaves and the cherry and briar rose were unfolding their leaves; and besides these, spring wrote many a sweet mark and word that I cannot tell, but snow fell all the hours of today in cold winter earnest, and now at evening there rests upon rocks, trees, and weeds, as full and ripe a harvest of snow flowers as I ever beheld in the stormiest, most opaque days of mid-winter.

[Added later :]

April 13th, [1870]

About twelve inches of snow fell in that last snowstorm. It disappeared as suddenly as it came, snatched away hastily almost before it had time to melt, as if a mistake had been made in allowing it to come here at all. A week of spring days, bright in every hour, without a stain or thought of the storm, came in glorious colours, giving still greater pledges of happy life to every living creature of the spring, but a loud energetic snowstorm possessed every hour of yesterday. Every tree and broken weed bloomed yet once more. All summer distinctions were levelled off. All plants and the very rocks and streams were equally polypetalous.

This morning winter had everything in the Valley. The snow drifted about in the frosty wind like meal and the falls were muffled in thick cheeks of frozen spray. Thus do winter and spring leap into the Valley by turns, each remaining long enough to form a small season or climate of its own, or going and coming squarely in a single day. Whitney says that the bottom has fallen out of the rocks here – which I most devoutly disbelieve. Well, the bottom frequently falls out of these winter clouds and climates. It is seldom that any long transition slant exists between dark and bright days in this narrow world of rocks.

I know that you are enchanted with the April loveliness of your new home. You enjoy the most precious kind of sunshine, and by this time flower patches cover the hills about Oakland like coloured clouds. I would like to visit those broad outspread blotches of social flowers that are so characteristic of your hills, but far rather would I see and feel the flowers that are now at Fountain Lake, and the lakes of Madison.

Mrs. Hutchings thought of sending you a bulb of the California lily by mail, but found it too large. She wishes to be remembered to you. Your Squirrel [Florence Hutchings] is very happy. She is a rare creature.

I hope to see you and the Doctor soon in the Valley. I have a great deal to say to you which I will not try to write. Remember me most cordially to the Doctor and to Allie and all the boys. I am much obliged to you for those botanical notes, etc., and I am,   Ever most cordially yours

JOHN MUIR

to David Gilrye Muir

Balmy Sabbath Morning in Yosemite
April 10th, [1870]

DEAR BROTHER

Your geographical, religious and commercial letter was handed me this morning by a little black-eyed witch of a girl [Florence Hutchings], the only one in the Valley. I also received your note of February 8th in due time (that is any time) and I propose to answer them as one, thus accomplishing " twa at a blow''; but I am bewildered by the magnitude and number of the subjects of which they treat. I think that since my pen is perturbed by too big a quantum of levity for Sabbath writing I shall begin with baptism, hoping that my muddy ink and muddy thoughts will settle to the seriousness or anger that naturally belongs to the subject.

I do not like the doctrine of close communion as held by hard-shells, because the whole clumsy structure of the thing rests upon a foundation of coarse-grained dogmatism. Imperious, bolt-upright exclusiveness upon any subject is hateful, but it becomes absolutely hideous and impious in matters of religion, where all men are equally interested. I have no patience at all for the man who complacently wipes his pious lips and waves me away from a simple rite which commemorates the love and sacrifice of Christ, telling me, "Go out from us for you are not of us," and all this not for want of Christian love on my part, or the practice of self-denying virtues in seeking to elevate myself, but simply because in his infallible judgment I am mistaken in the number of quarts of that common liquid we call water which should be made use of in baptism.

I think infant baptism by sprinkling or any other mode is a beautiful and impressive ordinance, and however the Scripture of the thing is interpreted no parent can be doing an unseemly or unchristian act in dedicating a child to God and taking upon him vows to lead his child in the path that all good people believe in. The baptism of an old sinner is apt to do but little good, but the baptism of an infant, in connection with the religious training which is supposed to follow it, is likely to do very much good.

I was baptised three times this morning. 1st (according to the old way of dividing the sermon), in balmy sunshine that penetrated to my very soul, warming all the faculties of spirit, as well as the joints and marrow of the body; 2nd, in the mysterious rays of beauty that emanate from plant corollas; and 3rd, in the spray of the lower Yosemite Falls. My 1st baptism was by immersion, the 2nd by pouring, and the 3rd by sprinkling. Consequently all Baptists are my brethering, and all will allow that I've "got religion."

[JOHN MUIR]

to Mrs. Ezra S. Carr

Yosemite, May 17th, [1870]

DEAR FRIEND MRS. CARR

Our valley is just gushing, throbbing full of open, absorbable beauty, and I feel that I must tell you about it. I am lonely among my enjoyments; the valley is full of visitors, but I have no one to talk to.

The season that is with us now is about what corresponds to full-fledged spring in Wisconsin. The oaks are in full leaf and have shoots long enough to bend over and move in the wind. The good old bracken is waist high already, and almost all the rock ferns have their outermost fronds unrolled.

Spring is in full power and is steadily reaching higher like a shadow, and will soon reach the topmost horizon of rocks. The buds of the poplar opened on the 19th of last month, those of the oaks on the 24th.

May 1st was a fine, hopeful, healthful, cool, bright day, with plenty of the fragrance of new leaves and flowers and of the music of bugs and birds. From the 5th to the 14th was extremely warm, the thermometer averaging about 85° at noon in shade. Craggy banks of cumuli became common about Starr King and the Dome, flowers came in troops, the upper snows melted very fast, raising the falls to their highest pitch of glory. The waters of the Yosemite Fall no longer float softly and downily like hanks of spent rockets, but shoot at once to the bottom with tremendous energy. There is at least ten times the amount of water in the Valley that there was when you were here. In crossing the Valley we had to sail in the boat. The river paid but little attention to its banks, flowing over the meadow in great river-like sheets.

But last Sunday, 15th, was a dark day. The rich streams of heat and light were withheld. The thermometer fell suddenly to 35°; and down among the verdant banks of new leaves, and groves of half-open ferns, and thick settlements of confident flowers came heavy snow in big blinding flakes, coming down with a steady gait and taking their places gracefully upon shrinking leaves and petals as if they were doing exactly right. The whole day was snowy and stormy like a piece of early winter. Snow fell also on the 16th. A good many of the ferns and delicate flowers are killed.

There are about fifty visitors in the Valley at present. When are you and the Doctor coming? Mr. Hutchings has not yet returned from Washington, so I will be here all summer. I have not heard from you since January.

I had a letter the other day from Professor Butler. He has been glancing and twinkling about among the towns of all the states at a most unsubstantial velocity. . . .   Most cordially yours,

                                                                            JOHN MUIR

to Mrs. Ezra S. Carr

                                                        Yosemite, Sunday, May 29th, [1870]

DEAR FRIEND

I received your "apology" two days ago and ran my eyes hastily over it three or four lines at a time to find the place that would say you were coming, but you "fear" that you cannot come at all, and only "hope" that the Doctor may! But I shall continue to look for you, nevertheless. The Chicago party you speak of were here and away again before your letter arrived. All sorts of human stuff is being poured into our Valley this year, and the blank, fleshly apathy with which most of it comes in contact with the rock and water spirits of the place, is most amazing. I do not wonder that the thought of such people being here makes you "mad"; but, after all, Mrs. Carr, they are about harmless. They climb sprawlingly to their saddles like overgrown frogs pulling themselves up a stream bank through the bent sedges, ride up the Valley with about as much emotion as the horses they ride upon – are comfortable when they have "done it all" and long for the safety and flatness of their proper homes.

In your first letter to the Valley you complain of the desecrating influences of the fashionable hordes about to visit here, and say that you mean to come only once more and "into the beyond." I am pretty sure that you are wrong in saying and feeling so, for the tide of visitors will float slowly about the *bottom* of the Valley as a harmless scum collecting in hotel and saloon eddies, leaving the rocks and falls eloquent as ever and instinct with imperishable beauty and greatness; and recollect that the top of the Valley is more than half way to real heaven and the Lord has many mansions in the Sierra equal in power and glory to Yosemite, though not quite so open, and I venture to say that you will yet see the Valley many times both in and out of the body.

I am glad you are going to the Coast Mountains to sleep on Diablo – Angelo – ere this. I am sure that you will be lifted above all the effects of your material work. There is a precious natural charm in sleeping under the open starry sky. You will have a very perfect view of the Joaquin Valley, and the snowy pearly wall of the Sierra Nevada. I lay for weeks last summer upon a bed of pine leaves at the edge of a daisy gentian meadow in full view of Mt. Dana.

Mrs. Hutchings says that the lily bulbs were so far advanced in their growth, when she dug some to send you, that they could not be packed without being broken, but I am going to be here all summer and I know where the grandest plantation of these lilies grows, and I will box up as many of them as you wish, together with as many other Yosemite things as you may ask for, and send it out to you before the pack train makes its last trip. I know the Spirea you speak of – it is abundant all around the top of the Valley and the rocks at Lake Tenaya and reaches almost to the very summit about Mt. Dana. There is also a purple one very abundant on the fringe meadows of Yosemite Creek a mile or two back from the brink of the falls. Of course it will be a source of keen pleasure to me to procure you anything you may desire. I should like to see that grand Agave. I saw some in Cuba, but they did not exceed twenty-five or thirty feet in height.

I have thought of a walk in the wild gardens of Honolulu, and now that you speak of my going there it becomes very probable, as you seem to understand me better than I do myself. I have no square idea about the time I shall get myself away from here. I shall at least stay till you come. I fear that the Agave will be in the spirit world ere that time.

You say that I ought to have such a place as you saw in the gardens of that mile and half of climate. Well, I think those lemon and orange groves would do perhaps to make a living, but for a garden I should not have anything less than a piece of pure nature. I was reading Thoreau's *Maine Woods* a short time ago. As described by him these woods are exactly like those of Canada West. How I long to meet *Linnæa* and *Chiogenes hispidula* once more! I would rather see these two children of the evergreen woods than all the twenty-seven species of palm that Agassiz met on the Amazon.

These summer days "go on" calmly and evenly. Scarce a mark of the frost and snow of the 15th is visible. The bracken are four or five feet high already. The earliest azaleas have opened and the whole crop of buds is ready to burst. The river does not overflow its banks now, but it is exactly brim full.

The thermometer averages about 75° at noon. We have sunshine every morning from a bright blue sky. Ranges of cumuli appear towards the summits with great regularity every day about eleven o'clock, making a splendid background for the South Dome. In a few hours these clouds disappear and give up the sky to sunny evening.

Mr. Hutchings arrived here from Washington a week ago. There are sixty or seventy visitors here at present .... Ever yours most cordially

J. MUIR

When Congress in 1864, by special Act, granted to the State of California the Yosemite Valley, together with a belt of rock and forest a mile in width around the rim, for recreational purposes, no account was taken of the possible claims of such settlers as J. C. Lamon and J. M. Hutchings. These two endeavoured to make good what they regarded as preemption claims to a section of land in the Valley. Their action resulted in prolonged litigations but the issue was finally decided against the claimants both by the supreme Court of the State and the Federal Supreme Court. It was not, however, until 1875 that the Commissioners appointed by the governor found themselves in undisputed control of the Valley. Muir's references to Mr. Hutchings' absences in Washington relate to this matter.

Among Eastern tourists visiting Yosemite Valley in 1870 were Mark Hopkins, then President of Williams College, and Mrs. Robert C. Waterston, the accomplished daughter of Josiah Quincy. "His [Muir's] letters," wrote Mrs. Waterston to a friend, "are poems of great and exquisite beauty – worthy to be written out of a heart whose close communion with nature springs to a perfect love."

Too near to God for doubt or fear,
He shares the eternal calm.

Thérèse Yelverton and her Yosemite novel, in which John Muir and "Squirrel" – Florence Hutchings – were introduced as leading characters, must be reserved for more extended notice in another connection.

to Mrs. Ezra S. Carr

Yosemite, July 29th, [1870]

MY DEAR FRIEND MRS. CARR
I am very, very blessed. The Valley is full of people, but they do not annoy

me. I revolve in pathless places and in higher rocks than *the world* and his ribbony wife can reach. Had I not been blunted by hard work in the mill, and crazed by Sabbath raids among the high places of this heaven, I would have written you long since. I have spent every Sabbath for the last two months in the spirit world, screaming among the peaks and outside meadows like a negro Methodist in revival time, and every intervening clump of week days in trying to fix down and assimilate my shapeless harvests of revealed glory into the spirit and into the common earth of my existence, and I am rich – rich beyond measure, not in rectangular blocks of sifted knowledge, or in thin sheets of beauty hung picture-like about "the walls of memory," but in unselected atmospheres of terrestrial glory diffused evenly throughout my whole substance.

Your Brooksian letters I have read with a great deal of interest. They are so full of the spice and poetry of unmingled Nature, and in many places they express my own present feelings very fully. Quoting from your Forest Glen, "Without anxiety and without expectation all my days come and go *mixed* with such sweetness to every sense," and again, "I don't know anything of time, and but little of space," and "My whole being seemed to open to the sun." All this I do most comprehensively appreciate, and am just beginning to know how fully congenial you are. Would that you could share my mountain enjoyments! In all my wanderings through Nature's beauty, whether it be among the ferns at my cabin door, or in the high meadows and peaks, or amid the spray and music of waterfalls, you are the first to meet me, and I often speak to you as verily present in the flesh.

Last Sabbath I was baptised in the irised foam of the Vernal, and in the divine snow of Nevada, and you were there also and stood in real presence by the sheet of joyous rapids below the bridge.

I am glad to know that McClure and McChesney have told you of our night with upper Yosemite. Oh, what a world is there! I passed, no, I *lived* another night there two weeks ago, entering as far within the veil amid equal glory, together with Mr. Frank Shapleigh of Boston. Mr. Shapleigh is an artist and I like him. He has been here six weeks, and has just left for home. I told him to see you and to show you his paintings. He is acquainted with Charles Sanderson and Mrs. Waterston. Mrs. Waterston left the Valley before your letter reached me, but one morning about sunrise an old lady came to the mill and asked me if I was the man who was so fond of flowers, and we had a very earnest unceremonious chat about the Valley and about "the beyond." She is made of better stuff than most of the people of that heathen town of Boston, and so also is Shapleigh.

Mrs. Yelverton is here and is going to stop a good while. Mrs. Waterston told her to find me, and we are pretty well acquainted now. She told me the other day that she was going to write a Yosemite novel!! and that "Squirrel" and I were going into it. I was glad to find that she knew you. I have not seen Professor LeConte; perhaps he is stopping at one of the other hotels.

Has Mrs. Rapelye or Mr. Colby told you about our camping in the spruce woods on the south rim of the Valley, and of our walk at daybreak to the top of the Sentinel dome to see the sun rise out of the crown peaks of beyond?

About a week ago at daybreak I started up the mountain near Glacier Point to see Pohono in its upper woods and to study the kind of life it lived up there. I had a glorious day, and reached my cabin at daylight, by walking all night. And, oh, what a night among those moon shadows! It was one o'clock a.m. when I reached the top of the Cathedral rocks, a most glorious twenty-four hours of life amid nameless peaks and meadows, and the upper cataracts of Pohono! Mr. Hutchings told me next morning that I had done two or three days' climbing in one and that I was shortening my life; but I had a whole lifetime of enjoyment, and I care but little for the arithmetical length of my days. I can hardly realise that I have not yet seen you here. I thank you for sending me so many friends, but I am waiting for you.

I am going up the mountain soon to see your lily garden at the top of Indian Canyon. "Let the Pacific islands lie." My love to Allie and all your boys and to the Doctor. Tell him that I have been tracing glaciers in all the principal canyons towards the summit.

Ever thine

JOHN MUIR

The meeting of John Muir and Joseph LeConte in August, 1870, was destined to have literary and scientific consequences not foreseen at the time. It appears clearly from the first of the following letters that Muir was already aware of the existence of living glaciers in the Sierra Nevada, a fact not then known to any one else and one which he regarded as having an important bearing upon his theory of Yosemite's origin. Discussion of the broader issues involved we must postpone to the chapter on "Persons and Problems."

to Mrs. Ezra S. Carr

[August 7th, 1870]

[First part of letter missing.] ... Tomorrow we set out for the Lyell Glacier in company with LeConte and his boys. We will be with them four or five days when they will go on Monoward for Tahoe. I mean to set some stakes in a dozen glaciers and gather some arithmetic for clothing my thoughts.

I hope you will not allow old H[utchings] or his picture agent Houseworth to so gobble and bewool poor Agassiz that I will not see him...

I will return to the Valley in about a week, if I don't get overdeep in a crevasse.

Later. Yours of Monday eve has just come. I am glad your boy is so soon to feel mother, home, and its blessings. I hope to meet [John] Torrey, although I will push iceward as before, but may get back in time. I will enjoy Agassiz, and Tyndall even more. I'm sorry for poor [Charles Warren] Stoddard; tell him to come....

Ever yours

JOHN MUIR

to Mrs. Ezra S. Carr

Yosemite, August 20th, [1870]

DEAR FRIEND MRS. CARR

I have just returned from a ten days' ramble* with Professor LeConte and his students in the beyond, and, oh! we have had a most glorious season of terrestrial grace. I do wish I could ramble ten days of equal size in very heaven that I could compare its scenery with that of Bloody Canyon and the Tuolumne Meadows and Lake Tenaya and Mount Dana.

Our first camp after leaving the Valley was at Eagle Point, overlooking the Valley on the north side, from which a much better general view of the Valley and the high crest of the Sierra beyond is obtained than from inspiration Point. Here we watched the long shadows of sunset upon the living map at our feet and in the later darkness half silvered by the moon, went far out of human cares and human civilization.

Our next camp was at Lake Tenaya, one of the countless multitudes of starry gems that make this topmost mountain land to sparkle like a sky. After moonrise LeConte and I walked to the lake shore and climbed upon a big sofa-shaped rock that stood, islet-like, a little way out in the shallow water, and here we found another bounteous throne of earthly grace, and I doubt if John in Patmos saw grander visions than we. And you were remembered there and we cordially wished you with us.

Our next sweet home was upon the velvet gentian meadows of the South Tuolumne. Here we feasted upon soda and burnt ashy cakes and stood an hour in a frigid rain with our limbs bent forward like Lombardy poplars in a gale, but ere sunset the black cloud departed, our spines were straightened at a glowing fire, we forgot the cold and all about half raw mutton and alkaline cakes. The grossest of our earthly coils was shaken off, and ere the last slant sunbeams left the dripping meadow and the spirey mountain peaks we were again in the third alpine heaven and saw and heard things equal in glory to the purest and best of Yosemite itself.

Our next camp was beneath a big grey rock at the foot of Mount Dana. Here we had another rainstorm, which drove us beneath our rock where we lay in complicated confusion, our forty limbs woven into a knotty piece of tissue compact as felt.

Next day we worshipped upon high places on the brown cone of Dana, and returned to our rock. Next day walked among the flowers and cascades of Bloody Canyon, and camped at the lake. Rode next day to the volcanic cone nearest to the lake and bade farewell to the party and climbed to the highest crater in the whole range south of the Mono Lake. Well, I shall not try to tell you anything, as it is unnecessary. Professor LeConte, whose

---

*   Described in Joseph LeConte's privately printed *Journal of Ramblings through the High Sierras of California by the University Excursion Party* (1875). Muir's theory of the glacial origin is mentioned several times in this rare booklet. Reprinted in the *Sierra Club Bulletin*, Vol.III, no. 1 (1900).

company I enjoyed exceedingly, will tell you about our camp meeting on the Tenaya rock.

I will send you a few choice mountain plant children by Mrs. Yelverton. If there is anything in particular that you want, let me know. Mrs. Yelverton will not leave the Valley for some weeks, and you have time to write.

I am ever your friend

JOHN MUIR

The two following letters relate in part to an American colonisation scheme promoted by a Mr. A. D. Piper, of San Francisco, who is said to have received from the Brazilian and Peruvian governments a concession for the navigation of the waters of the upper Amazon, together with a grant of millions of acres on the Purus in the Department of Beni. One of Mrs. Carr's sons joined the expedition and she was anxious to have Muir go also, holding out to him the prospect of a cheap and comfortable passage to the heart of the Andes and the privilege of "locating" three hundred and twenty 'five acres of land anywhere within the grant. Muir was too canny to be inveigled into joining such an expedition. It speedily went to pieces in Brazil, whence Mrs. Carr's son returned seriously broken in health.

to Mrs. Ezra S. Carr

Tuolumne River, two miles below La Grange
November 4th, [1870]

DEAR FRIEND MRS. CARR

Yours of October 2nd reached me a few days since. The Amazon and Andes have been in all my thoughts for many years, and I am sure that I shall meet them some day ere I die, or become settled and civilized and useful. I am obliged to you for all of this information. I have studied many paths and plans for the interior of South America, but none so easy and sure ever appeared as this of your letter.

I thought of landing at Guayaquil and crossing the mountains to the Amazon, float to Para, subsisting on berries and quinine, but to steam along the palmy shores with company and comforts is perhaps more practical, though not so pleasant. Hawthorne says that steam spiritualizes travel, but I think that it squarely degrades and materialises travel. However, flies and fevers have to be considered in this case.

I am glad that Ned has gone. The woods of the Purus will be a grand place for the growth of men. It must be that I am going soon, for you have shown me the way. People say that my wanderings are very many and methodless, but they are all known to you in some way before I think of them. You are a prophet in the concerns of my little outside life, and pray, what says the spirit about my final escape from Yosemite? You saw me at these rock altars years ago, and I think I shall remain among them until you take me away.

I reached this place last month by following the Merced out of the Valley and through all its canyons to the plains above Snelling – a most glorious walk. I intended returning to the Valley ere this, but Mr. Delaney, the man with whom I am stopping at present, would not allow me to leave before I had plowed his field, and so I will not be likely to see Yosemite again before January, when I shall have a grand journey over the snow.

Mrs. Yelverton told me before I started upon my river explorations that she would likely be in Oakland in two weeks, and so I made up a package for you of lily bulbs, cones, ferns, etc., but she wrote me a few days ago that she was still in the Valley.

I find that a portion of my specimens collected in the last two years and left at this place and Hopeton are not very well cared for, and I have concluded to send them to you. I will ship them in a few days by express, and I will be down myself, perhaps, in about a year. If there is anything in these specimens that the Doctor can make use of in his lectures tell him to do so freely, of course.

The purple of these plains and of this whole round sky is very impressively glorious after a year in the deep rocks.

People all throughout this section are beginning to hear of Dr. Carr. He accomplishes a wonderful amount of work. My love to Allie, and to the Doctor, and I am,   Ever most cordially yours

JOHN MUIR

to Mrs. Ezra S. Carr

Near La Grange, California,
December 22nd, [1870]

DEAR MRS. CARR

It is so long since I have heard from you that I begin to think you have sent a letter to Yosemite. I am feeling lonely again, and require a word from you.

Some time ago Mr. Hutchings wrote me saying that he would require my shingle cabin for his sister, and so I am homeless again. I expected to pass the winter there, writing, sketching, etc., and in making exploratory raids back over the mountains in the snow, but Mr. Hutchings' jumping my nest after expressly promising to keep it for me, has broken my pleasant lot of plans, and I am at work making new ones. Were it not that Mr. Hutchings owes me money and that I have a lot of loose notes and outline sketches to work up I should set out for South America at once. As it is, I shall very likely remain where I am for a few months and return to the mountains in the spring. I wish in particular to trace some of the upper Yosemite streams farther and more carefully than I have yet done, and I shall dip yet once more into the fathomless grandeur of the Valley.

I am in comfortable quarters at present, within sight and hearing of the Tuolumne, on a smooth level once the bottom of a shallow lake-like expansion of the river where it leaves the slates.

Evening purple on the mountains seen through an ample gap up the Tuolumne is of terrestrial beauty, the purest and best. The sheet gold of the plain compositae will soon be lighted in the sun days of spring, deepening and glowing yet brighter as it spreads away over the sphered and fluted rock-waves of this old ocean bed. You must not fail to see the April gold of the Joaquin.

I send herewith a letter to Mrs. Yelverton in your care, as you will be likely to know where she is. I have just received a letter which she left for me at Snelling, giving an account* of her fearful perils in the snow. It seems strange to me that I should not have known and felt her anguish in that terrible night, even at this distance. She told me that I ought to wait and guide her out, and I feel a kind of guiltiness in not doing so.

Since writing the above yours of November 19th is received, directed to the "Tuolumne River, etc." You are "glad that I am kindly disposed towards South America, but a year is a long time," etc. But to me a Yosemite year is a very little measure of time, or rather, a measureless and formless mass of time which can in no manner be geometrically or arithmetically dealt with. But, Mrs. Carr, why do you wish to cut me from California and graft me among the groves of the Purus? Please write the reason. This Pacific sunshine is hard to leave. If souls are allowed to go a-rapping and visiting where they please I think that, unbodied, I will be found wallowing in California light.

If the bulbs were lost I will procure some more for you, if you do not send me up the Amazon before next fall.

[JOHN MUIR]

---

* Cf. "Summer with a Countess," by Mary Viola Lawrence in *The Overland Monthly*, November, 1871.

CHAPTER EIGHT

Yosemite, Emerson, and the Sequoias

WHEN THE EARLY winter storms of 1870 stopped Muir's rambles among the peaks he was able to take refuge in his snug den near the foot of the lower Yosemite Fall. Though dispossessed for a time by Mr. Hutchings, as indicated in his December letter from La Grange, he probably passed the greater part of the winter, as well as the following spring and summer, in his attractive sugar pine cabin. There, as the letter of a reminiscent friend reveals, he might of an evening be found under the lamp, beside his cosy fireplace, reading the writings of Alexander von Humboldt, Sir Charles Lyell, John Tyndall, Charles Darwin, and the latest botanical works on trees. Thus the "harvests of revealed glory," gathered on the mountains during the summer months, were further enriched by wide-ranging study during the long winter evenings. "I think of you as far too blessed" writes Mrs. Carr at this time, "to need words from the lower world, and yet I meant to send many and oft repeated greetings to your winter quarters. I think with delight of how the winter home looks, of little brown 'Squirrel' in the glow of the firelight, of the long walks, and readings, and thinkings – the morning tintings of the rocks, the comforting warmth of the pines and firs."

But the approach of the winter of 1871 found him homeless in dead earnest. There is reason for thinking that Muir's employer, Mr. Hutchings, did not look with favour upon the young Scotch man's growing fame and popularity as an interpreter of the Valley. It was a function which he himself had exercised so long that he had come to regard it as peculiarly his own. What could have been more natural under the circumstances than that Hutchings, having no scientific competence to formulate independent ideas on the origin of the Valley, should make a combination of other men's views and preach it to all comers in opposition to Muir? The latter, too, had found the work of a sawmill operator increasingly irksome. In any case, he left the employ of Hutchings during the summer of 1871, and after the close of the tourist season we find him busy removing his chattels from Hutchings' to Black's Hotel, then the newest of the three hostelries in the Valley. Like Leidig's Hotel, still farther down the stream, it was situated on the south bank of the Merced almost opposite Sentinel Rock.

With this habitational background of John Muir in mind, let us resume the thread of his correspondence after his return to Yosemite from La Grange. The first letter, bearing no date, probably was written toward the end of February, or the beginning of March, 1871, for his statement that many storms had swept over the mountains since he returned to the Valley, shows that he had been there for some time.

to Mrs. Ezra S. Carr

[Yosemite, February or March, 1871]

MY DEAR FRIEND MRS. CARR

"The Spirit" has again led me into the wilderness, in opposition to all counter attractions, and I am once more in the glory of Yosemite.

Your very cordial invitation to your home reached me as I was preparing to ascend, and when my whole being was possessed with visions of snowy forests of the pine and spruce, and of mountain spires beyond, pearly and half transparent, reaching into heaven's blue, not purer than themselves.

In company with another young fellow whom I persuaded to walk, I left the plains just as the first gold sheets were being outspread. My first plan was to follow the Tuolumne upward as I had followed the Merced downward, after reaching Hetch Hetchy Valley, which has about the same altitude as Yosemite, and spending a week or so in sketching and exploring its falls and rocks, crossing the high mountains past the west end of the Hoffmann range, and going down into Yosemite by Indian Canyon, passing thus a glorious month with the mountains, with all their snows and crystal brightness, and all the nameless glories of their magnificent winter. But my plan went agley. I lost a week's sleep by the pain of a sore hand, and I became unconfident in my strength when measured against weeks of wading in snow up to the neck. Therefore I reluctantly concluded to push directly for the Valley by Crane's Flat and Tamarack.

Our journey was just a week in length, including one day of rest in the Crane's Flat cabin. Some of our nights were cold, and we were hungry once or twice. We crossed the snow line on the flank of Pilot Peak ridge six or eight miles below Crane's Flat.

From Crane's Flat to the brim of the Valley the snow was about five feet in depth, and as it was not frozen or compacted in any way we of course had a splendid season of wading.

I wish that you could have seen the edge of the snow-cloud which hovered, oh, so soothingly, down to the grand Pilot Peak brows, discharging its heaven-begotten snows with such unmistakable gentleness and moving, perhaps, with conscious love from pine to pine as if bestowing separate and independent blessings upon each. In a few hours we climbed under and into this glorious storm-cloud. What a harvest of crystal flowers, and what wind songs were gathered from the spirey firs and the long fringy arms of the Lambert pine! We could not see far before us in the storm, which lasted until some time in the night, but as I was familiar with the general map of the mountain we had no difficulty in finding our way.

Crane's Flat cabin was buried, and we had to grope about for the door. After making a fire with some cedar rails I went out to watch the coming on of the darkness, which was most impressively sublime. Next morning was every way the purest creation I ever beheld. The little Flat, spot-like in the massive spiring woods, was in splendid vesture of universal white, upon which the grand forest-edge was minutely repeated and covered with a close sheet of snow flowers.

Some mosses grow luxuriantly upon the dead generations of their own species. The common snow flowers belong to the sky and in storms are blown about like ripe petals in an orchard. They settle on the ground – the bottom of the atmospheric sea – like mud or leaves in a lake, and upon this soil, this field of broken sky flowers, grows a luxuriant carpet of crystal vegetation complete and ripe in a single night.

I never before knew that these mountain snow plants were so variable and abundant, forming such bushy clumps and thickets and palmy, ferny groves. Wading waist-deep I had fine opportunities for observing them, but they shrink from human breath – not the only flowers which do so. Evidently not made for man! – neither the flowers composing the snow which came drifting down to us broken and dead, nor the more beautiful crystals which vegetate upon them!

A great many storms have come to the mountains since I passed them, and there can hardly be less than ten feet at the altitude of Tamarack and toward the summit still more.

The weather here is balmy now, and the falls are glorious. Three weeks ago the thermometer at sunrise stood at 12°. I have repaired the mill and dam, and the stream is in no danger of drying up and is more dammed than ever.

To-day has been cloudy and rainy. Tissiack and Starr King are grandly dipped in white cloud. I sent you my plants by express. I am sorry that my Yosemite specimens were not with the others. I left a few notes with Mrs. Yelverton when I left the Valley in the fall. I wish that you would ask her, if you should see her, where she left it, as Mrs. Hutchings does not know....

I have been nearly blind since I crossed the snow. Give my kindest regards to all your homeful, and to my friends. I am

Always yours most cordially J. M.

The following letter is of special interest because it contains a brief description of the "hang-nest" attached to the west-end gable of the sawmill. The included sketch is the only surviving pictorial record both of the mill and of his retreat. The adventure of which he hesitated to tell his sister had already been described in a letter to Mrs. Carr, but follows here more logically the one to his sister. Both are striking revelations of his nature enthusiasms at this time.

to Sarah Muir Galloway

In the Sawmill, Yosemite Valley, April 5th, 1871

DEAR SISTER SARAH
This is one of the most surpassingly glorious of Yosemite days, and I have

suddenly thought to write you. We have rain and storm. The vast column of
the upper Yosemite Falls is swaying with wonderful ever-changing forms of
beauty, and all our mountain walls are wreathed in splendid clouds. In some
places a strip of muffy white cloud reaches almost from the bottom of the
wall to the top, and just across the meadow the summit of a pine-crested
mountain is peering above the clouds like an island in the sky – thus:

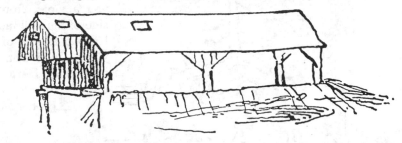

It is hard to write here, as the mill jars so much by the stroke of the saw,
and the rain drips from the roof, and I have to set the log every few minutes.
I am operating this same mill that I made last winter. I like the piney
fragrance of the fresh-sawn boards, and I am in constant view of the grandest
of all the falls. I sleep in the mill for the sake of hearing the murmuring
hush of the water beneath me, and I have a small box-like home fastened
beneath the gable of the mill, looking westward down the Valley, where I
keep my notes, etc. People call it the hang-nest, because it seems unsupported,
thus:

Fortunately, the only people that I dislike are afraid to enter it. The hole
in the roof is to command a view of the glorious South Dome, five thousand
feet high. There is a corresponding skylight on the other side of the roof
which commands a full view of the upper Yosemite Falls, and the window in
the end has a view sweeping down the Valley among the pines and cedars
and silver firs. The window in the mill roof to the right is above my head,
and I have to look at the stars on calm nights.

Two evenings ago I climbed the mountain to the foot of the upper Yosemite
Falls, carrying a piece of bread and a pair of blankets so that I could spend
the night on the rock and enjoy the glorious waters, but I got drenched and
had to go home, reaching the house at two o'clock in the morning. My
wetting was received in a way that I scarcely care to tell. The adventure
nearly cost all. I mean to go tomorrow night, but I will not venture behind
the column again.

Here are the outlines of a grand old pine and gnarly mossy oak that stand a few steps from the mill. You liked the flowers. Well, I will get you a violet from the side of the mill-race, as I go up to shut off the water. Goodnight, with a brother's warmest love.

[JOHN MUIR]

to Mrs. Ezra S. Carr

Midnight, [Yosemite, April 3rd, 1871]

Oh, Mrs. Carr, that you could be here to mingle in this night-noon glory! I am in the upper Yosemite Falls and can hardly calm to write, but from my first baptism hours ago, you have been so present that I must try to fix you a written thought.

In the afternoon I came up the mountain here with a blanket and a piece of bread to spend the night in prayer among the spouts of this fall. But what can I say more than wish again that you might expose your soul to the rays of this heaven?

Silver from the moon illumines this glorious creation which we term "falls," and has laid a magnificent double prismatic bow at its base. The tissue of the fall is delicately filmed on the outside like the substance of spent clouds, and the stars shine dimly through it. In the solid shafted body of the fall is a vast number of passing caves, black and deep, with close white convolving spray for sills and shooting comet sheaves above and down their sides, like lime crystals in a cave. And every atom of the magnificent being, from the thin silvery crest that does not dim the stars to the inner arrowy hardened shafts that strike onward like thunderbolts in sound and energy, all is life and spirit: every bolt and spray feels the hand of God. Oh, the music that is blessing me now! The sun of last week has given the grandest notes of all the yearly anthem. I said that I was going to stop here until morning and pray a whole blessed night with the falls and the moon, but I am too wet and must go down. An hour or two ago I went out somehow on a little seam that extends along the wall behind the falls. I suppose I was in a trance, but I can positively say that I was in the body, for it is sorely battered and wetted. As I was gazing past the thin edge of the fall and away beneath the column to the brow of the rock, some heavy splashes of water struck me, driven hard against the wall. Suddenly I was darkened, down came a section of the outside tissue composed of spent comets. I crouched low, holding my breath, and anchored to some angular flakes of rock, took my baptism with moderately good faith.

When I dared to look up after the swaying column admitted light, I pounced behind a piece of ice and the wall which was wedging tight, and I no longer feared being washed off, and steady moonbeams slanting past the arching meteors gave me confidence to escape to this snug place where McChesney and I slept one night, where I have a fire to dry my socks. This rock shelf, extending behind the falls, is about five hundred feet above the base of the fall on the perpendicular rock face.

How little do we know of ourselves, of our profoundest attractions and repulsions, of our spiritual affinities! How interesting does man become considered in his relations to the spirit of this rock and water! How significant does every atom of our world become amid the influences of those beings unseen, spiritual, angelic mountaineers that so throng these pure mansions of crystal foam and purple granite.

I cannot refrain from speaking to this little bush at my side and to the spray drops that come to my paper and to the individual sands of the slopelet I am sitting upon. Ruskin says that the idea of foulness is essentially connected with what he calls dead unorganised matter. How cordially I disbelieve him tonight, and were he to dwell a while among the powers of these mountains he would forget all dictionary differences betwixt the clean and the unclean, and he would lose all memory and meaning of the diabolical sin-begotten term *foulness*.

Well, I must go down. I am disregarding all of the doctors' physiology in sitting here in this universal moisture. Farewell to you, and to all the beings about us. I shall have a glorious walk down the mountain in this thin white light, over the open brows greyed with Selaginella and through the thick black shadow caves in the live oaks, all stuck full of snowy lances of moonlight.

[JOHN MUIR]

One of the most memorable experiences of John Muir was the coming of Ralph Waldo Emerson to Yosemite Valley, on May 5th, 1871. Muir was thirty three years old and Emerson sixty eight, but the disparity of their years proved no obstacle to the immediate beginning of a warm friendship. The best account of their meeting is contained in a memorandum of after-dinner remarks made by Muir twenty five years later when Harvard University conferred upon him an honorary M.A. degree.

I was fortunate [he said] in meeting some of the choicest of your Harvard men, and at once recognised them as the best of God's nobles. Emerson, Agassiz, Gray – these men influenced me more than any others. Yes, the most of my years were spent on the wild side of the continent, invisible, in the forests and mountains. These men were the first to find me and hail me as a brother. First of all, and greatest of all, came Emerson. I was then living in Yosemite Valley as a convenient and grand vestibule of the Sierra from which I could make excursions into the adjacent mountains. I had not much money and was then running a mill that I had built to saw fallen timber for cottages.

When he came into the Valley I heard the hotel people saying with solemn emphasis, "Emerson is here." I was excited as I had never been excited before, and my heart throbbed as if an angel direct from heaven had alighted on the Sierran rocks. But so great was my awe and reverence, I did not dare to go to him or speak to him. I hovered on the outside of the crowd of people that were pressing forward to be introduced to him and shaking hands with him. Then I heard that in three or four days he was going away, and in the course of sheer desperation I wrote him a note and carried it to his hotel telling him that El Capitan and Tissiack demanded him to stay longer.

The next day he inquired for the writer and was directed to the little sawmill. He came to the mill on horseback attended by Mr. Thayer* and inquired for me. I stepped out and said, "I am Mr. Muir." "Then Mr. Muir must have brought his own letter," said Mr. Thayer, and Emerson said, "Why did you not make yourself known last evening? I should have been very glad to have seen you." Then he dismounted and came into the mill. I had a study attached to the gable of the mill, overhanging the stream, into which I invited him, but it was not easy of access, being reached only by a series of sloping planks roughened by slats like a hen ladder; but he bravely climbed up and I showed him my collection of plants and sketches drawn from the surrounding mountains which seemed to interest him greatly, and he asked many questions, pumping unconscionably.

He came again and again, and I saw him every day while he remained in the valley, and on leaving I was invited to accompany him as far as the Mariposa Grove of Big Trees. I said, "I'll go, Mr. Emerson, if you will promise to camp with me in the Grove. I'll build a glorious campfire, and the great brown boles of the giant Sequoias will be most impressively lighted up, and the night will be glorious." At this he became enthusiastic like a boy, his sweet perennial smile became still deeper and sweeter, and he said, "Yes, yes, we will camp out, camp out"; and so next day we left Yosemite and rode twenty five miles through the Sierra forests, the noblest on the face of the earth, and he kept me talking all the time, but said little himself. The colossal silver firs, Douglas spruce, Libocedrus and sugar pine, the kings and priests of the conifers of the earth, filled him with awe and delight. When we stopped to eat luncheon he called on different members of the party to tell stories or recite poems, etc., and spoke, as he reclined on the carpet of pine needles, of his student days at Harvard. But when in the afternoon we came to the Wawona Tavern....

* James Bradley Thayer, a member of Emerson's party, who, in 1884, published a little volume of reminiscences under the title of *A Western Journey with Mr. Emerson*.

There the memorandum ends, but the continuation is found in his volume *Our National Parks* at the conclusion of the chapter on "The Forests of the Yosemite":

Early in the afternoon, when we reached Clark's Station, I was surprised to see the party dismount And when I asked if we were not going up into the grove to camp they said: "No; it would never do to lie out in the night air. Mr. Emerson might take cold; and you know, Mr. Muir, that would be a dreadful thing." In vain I urged, that only in homes and hotels were colds caught, that nobody ever was known to take cold camping in these woods, that there was not a single cough or sneeze in all the Sierra. Then I pictured the big climate changing, inspiring fire I would make, praised the beauty and fragrance of Sequoia flame, told how the great trees would stand about us transfigured in purple light, while the stars looked between the great domes; ending by urging them to come on and make an immortal Emerson night of it. But the house habit was not to be overcome, nor the strange dread of pure night air, though it is only cooled day air with a little dew in it. So the carpet dust and unknowable reeks were preferred. And to think of this being a Boston choice. Sad commentary on culture and the glorious transcendentalism.

Accustomed to reach whatever place I started for, I was going up the mountain alone to camp, and wait the coming of the party next day. But since Emerson was so soon to vanish, I concluded to stop with him. He hardly spoke a word all evening, yet it was a great pleasure simply to be with him, warming in the light of his face as at a fire. In the morning we rode up the trail through a noble forest of pine and fir into the famous Mariposa Grove, and stayed an hour or two, mostly in ordinary tourist fashion, – looking at the biggest giants, measuring them with a tape line, riding through prostrate fire-bored trunks, etc., though Mr. Emerson was alone occasionally, sauntering about as if under a spell. As we walked through a fine group, he quoted, "There were giants in those days," recognising the antiquity of the race. To commemorate his visit, Mr. Galen Clark, the guardian of the grove, selected the finest of the unnamed trees and requested him to give it a name. He named it Samoset, after the New England sachem, as the best that occurred to him.

The poor bit of measured time was soon spent, and while the saddles were being adjusted I again urged Emerson to stay. "You are yourself a Sequoia," I said. "Stop and get acquainted with your big brethren." But he was past his prime, and was now a child in the hands of his affectionate but sadly civilized friends, who seemed as full of old-fashioned conformity as of bold intellectual independence. It was the afternoon of the day and the afternoon of his life, and his course was now westward down all the mountains into the sunset. The party mounted and rode away in wondrous contentment, apparently, tracing the trail through ceanothus and dogwood bushes, around the bases of the big trees, up the slope of the sequoia basin, and over the divide. I followed to the edge of the grove. Emerson lingered in the rear of the train, and when he reached the top of the ridge, after all the rest of the party were over and out of sight, he turned his horse, took off his hat and waved me a last goodbye. I felt lonely, so sure had I been that Emerson of all men would be the quickest to see the mountains and sing them. Gazing awhile on the spot where he vanished, I sauntered back into the heart of the grove, made a bed of sequoia plumes and ferns by the side of the stream, gathered a store of firewood, and then walked about until sundown. The birds, robins, thrushes, warblers, etc., that had kept out of sight, came about me, now that all was quiet, and made cheer. After sundown I built a great fire, and as usual had it all to myself. And though lonesome for the first time in these forests, I quickly took heart again – the trees had not gone to Boston, nor the birds; and as I sat by the fire, Emerson was still with me in spirit, though I never again saw him in the flesh.

A few days later there occurred a little incident in Oakland which is worth telling, for it reveals through Emerson's appreciativeness the impression which Muir had made upon him. The Carrs, then living in a cottage in Oakland, heard one evening during a dense fog a commotion at their back door. Upon investigation they found Ralph Waldo Emerson standing there, with his cloak wrapped closely about him. He had lost his way in the fog and had come up to the back door in his confusion. Urged to come in, he declined, saying that he must at once follow his wife and daughter who had already gone across the ferry to San Francisco. "But I," he added, "could not go through Oakland without coming up here to thank you for that letter to John Muir."

Though now in the closing decade of his life and growing infirm, Emerson sent him an occasional package of books accompanied with words of good cheer, while Muir wrote him enthusiastic letters, and sent fragrant reminders of his Yosemite surroundings. One of his winter recreations was to climb an Incense Cedar, abloom amid the snows of January, gather some of the golden sprays of staminate blossoms, and mail them to his friends. The delicate attention of such an aromatic gift sent to Emerson drew from him the following letter.

Was it the "incense" quality of this cedar which, combined with some playful allusion in Muir's letter, made the flowers "significant" to the sage of Concord?

from Ralph Waldo Emerson

Concord, 5th February, 1872

MY DEAR MUIR

Here lie your significant cedar flowers on my table, and in another letter; and I will procrastinate no longer. That singular disease of deferring, which kills all my designs, has left a pair of books brought home to send to you months and months ago, still covering their inches on my cabinet, and the letter and letters which should have accompanied, to utter my thanks and lively remembrance, are either unwritten or lost, so I will send this *peccavi*, as a sign of remorse.

I have been far from unthankful – I have everywhere testified to my friends who should also be yours, my happiness in finding you – the right man in the right place – in your mountain tabernacle, and have expected when your guardian angel would pronounce that your probation and sequestration in the solitudes and snows had reached their term, and you were to bring your ripe fruits so rare and precious into waiting society.

I trust you have also had, ere this, your own signals from the upper powers. I know that society in the lump, admired at a distance, shrinks and dissolves, when approached, into impracticable or uninteresting individuals, but always with a reserve of a few unspoiled good men, who really give it its halo in the distance. And there are drawbacks also to solitude, who is a sublime mistress, but an intolerable wife. So I pray you to bring to an early close your absolute contracts with any yet unvisited glaciers or volcanoes, roll up your drawings, herbariums and poems, and come to the Atlantic Coast. Here in Cambridge Dr. Gray is at home, and Agassiz will doubtless be, after a month or two, returned from Terra del Fuego perhaps through San Francisco – or you can come with him. At all events, on your arrival, which I assume as certain, you must find your way to this village, and my house. And when you are tired of our dwarf surroundings, I will show you better people.

With kindest regards   Yours
R. W. EMERSON

[P.S.] I send two volumes of collected essays by book-post.

In an undated fragment of a letter to Mrs. Carr, Muir refers to this letter as follows:

He [Emerson] judges me and my loose drifting voyages as kindly as yourself. The compliments of you two are enough to spoil one, but I fancy that he, like you, considers that I am so mountain-tanned and storm-beaten I may bear it. I owe all of my best friends to you. A prophecy in this letter of Emerson's recalled one of yours sent me when growing at the bottom of a mossy maple hollow in the Canada woods, that I would one day be with you, Doctor, and Priest in Yosemite. Emerson prophesies in similar dialect that I will one day go to him and "better men" in New England, or something to that effect. I feel like objecting in popular slang that I "can't see it." I shall indeed go gladly to the "Atlantic Coast " as he prophesies, but only to see him and the Glacier ghosts of the North. Runkle wants to make a teacher of me, but I have been too long wild, too befogged to burn well in their patent, high-heated, educational furnaces.

Neither Emerson's nor Muir's anticipations were to be realised. "There remained many a forest to wander through," writes Muir, "many a mountain and glacier to cross, before I was to see his Wachusett and Monadnock, Boston and Concord. It was seventeen years after our parting on the Wawona ridge that I stood beside his grave under a pine tree on the hill above Sleepy Hollow. He had gone to higher Sierras, and, as I fancied, was again waving his hand in friendly recognition."

Notes of travel made by Sarah Jane Lippincott in 1871–72, under the pen-name of Grace Greenwood, afford a fleeting contemporary glimpse of John Muir as he appeared at this time to a discerning observer in Yosemite.

Among our visitors in the evening [she writes] was Mr. Muir, the young Scottish mountaineer, student, and enthusiast, who has taken sanctuary in the Yosemite, who stays by the variable Valley with marvellous constancy, who adores her alike in her fast, gay summer life and solemn autumn glories, in her winter cold and stillness, and in the passion of her spring floods and tempests. Not profoundest snows can chill his ardour, not earthquakes can shake his allegiance. Mr. Muir talks with a quiet, quaint humour, and a simple eloquence which are quite delightful. He has a clear blue eye, a firm, free step, and marvellous nerve and endurance. He has the serious air and unconventional ways of a man who has been much with Nature in her grand, solitary places. That tourist is fortunate who can have John Muir for a guide in and about the Valley.

Among the fortunate ones who had in June come to John Muir with a note of introduction from Mrs. Carr was Henry Edwards, by profession an actor, but by avocation an entomologist. "In our lower world Mr. Edwards, who brings you this note," said Mrs. Carr, "is accounted one of Nature's truest and most devoted disciples. You will take pleasure in introducing him to your heavenly bugs and butterflies, and the winged dragons that hover over those hot springs in 'the beyond.' I do not know how long he proposes to sojourn there, but make the most of the time, for he has the keys to the Kingdom."

Mr. Edwards, familiarly known as "Harry" Edwards among his San Francisco friends, was a rather remarkable man. A finished artist in his profession, he was at the same time the gatherer and possessor of what was then regarded as one of the finest private collections of butterflies and beetles in the world. It was to be expected that such an enthusiast would find a kindred spirit in John Muir, who was prevailed upon to collect some high Sierran butterflies for him, with interesting scientific results.

Your kind letter [he wrote to Muir on August 25th, 1871], found me confined to my bed. Today for the first time in nearly two weeks I was sitting for a little while in my butterfly room when our dear friend Mrs. Carr walked in and brought me your box of butterflies. The sight of them has done me good, and I hope in a day or two I will be quite restored. Do not again ever think that you cannot collect, or that what you do find will be valueless. In the small box which you sent me are *four species new to my collection*, and *two* of these are new to science*. I cannot, if I wrote for a week, tell you how interesting they are to me. All the specimens are rare, and are different from those found in the Valley. The two new species are the bright crimson copper one from Cathedral Peak, and one of the small bluish butterflies. There is a pair of greenish yellow ones, very rare and interesting. The species was described from a pair only which were taken by the Geological Survey at the head waters of the Tuolumne River, and strange to say, no others have turned up until you found it now.... It is really very singular that the remove of a few miles from the Yosemite should produce species so very different from those of the Valley itself, and at the same time so characteristic in their forms. It is another of the beautiful fields for thought which your wonderful region opens up, and which render your lovely mountains so enchanting to a worshipper of Nature. I hope you will go on to find your truest and best enjoyment among such scenes, and that in the end your labours may meet the reward they deserve, not from your own self-gratification alone, but from the spontaneous recognition of kindred minds.

This Edwards letter is only one of many that might be quoted to show how profitably Muir was at this time studying the multiformity of his natural environment. In the absence of authoritative treatises on the plants, insects, and wild life of the region he had to send specimens to classifying specialists for identification, or appeal to his friends about San Francisco Bay, particularly J. B. McChesney, to secure the desired information for him. Most of them thought that he was adhering much too closely to his Sierran wildernesses, and even Mrs. Carr laboured to dislodge him from his mountain solitudes and to bring him into what Emerson called "waiting society."

But so intense was his preoccupation with his tasks, so much were they a part of his deepest enjoyments, that her pleadings fell on deaf ears. If anything her remonstrances only served to kindle into flame the poetic fire of his soul. For there was nothing like the provocation of a little aspersion against the worthiness of the objects he was pursuing to bring him to the full stature of his ability as a writer – a vindicator of the objects of his devotion. A letter written under such stimulus is the following:

---

*   There is no further confirmation of this statement in records left by Edwards. But Mr. Frank E. Watson, of the American Museum of Natural History, which now owns the Edwards Collection, calls my attention to the fact that in 1881 the butterfly *Thecla Muiri* was named by Henry Edwards after John Muir. In *Papilio*, vol. 1, p. 54 (1881), Edwards writes, "I have named this exquisite little species after my friend John Muir, so well known for his researches into the geology of the Sierra Nevada, who has frequently added rare and interesting species to my collection."

to Mrs. Ezra S. Carr

Yosemite, December 11th, [1871]

DEAR MRS. CARR

We are snowbound, and your letter of November 1st came two days ago. I sympathise with you for the loss of your brown Japanese, but I am glad to know that you found so much of pure human goodness in the life of your scholar. The whole world is enriched, beautified by a stratum – an atmosphere – of Godlike souls, and it is ignorance alone that banks human love into narrow gutter channels and stagnant pools, making it selfish and impure when it should be boundless as air and light, blending with all the world, keeping sight of our impartial Father who is the fountain sun of all the love that is rayed down to earth.

But glaciers, dear friend – ice is only another form of terrestrial love. I am astonished to hear you speak so unbelievingly of God's glorious crystal glaciers. "They are only pests," and you think them wrong in temperature, and they lived in "horrible times" and you don't care to hear about them "only that they made instruments of Yosemite music." You speak heresy for once, and deserve a dip in Methodist Tophet, or Vesuvius at least.

I have just been sending ice to LeConte and snow to McChesney and I have nothing left but hailstones for you, but I don't know how to send them – to speak them. You confuse me. You have taught me here and encouraged me to read the mountains. Now you will not listen; next summer you will be converted – you will be iced then.

I have been up Nevada to the top of Lyell and found a living glacier, but you don't want that; and I have been in Hetch Hetchy and the canyon above, and I was going to tell you the beauty there; but it is all ice-born beauty, and too cold for you; and I was going to tell about the making of the South Dome, but ice did that too; and about the hundred lakes that I found, but the ice made them, every one; and I had some groves to speak about – groves of surpassing loveliness in *new* pathless Yosemites, but they all grew upon glacial drift – and I have nothing to send but what is frozen or freezable.

You like the music instruments that glaciers made, but no songs were so grand as those of the glaciers themselves, no falls so lofty as those which poured from brows, and chasmed mountains of pure dark ice. Glaciers *made* the mountains and ground corn for all the flowers, and the forests of silver fir, made smooth paths for human feet until the sacred Sierras have become the most approachable of mountains. Glaciers came down from heaven, and they were angels with folded wings, white wings of snowy bloom. Locked hand in hand the little spirits did nobly; the primary mountain waves, unvital granite, were soon carved to beauty. They bared the lordly domes and fashioned the clustering spires; smoothed godlike mountain brows, and shaped lake cups for crystal waters; wove myriads of mazy canyons, and spread them out like lace. They remembered the loudsonged rivers and every tinkling rill. The busy snowflakes saw all the coming flowers, and the grand predestined forests. They said, "We will crack this rock for Cassiope where she may sway her tiny urns. Here we'll smooth a plat for green mosses, and round a bank for bryanthus bells." Thus laboured the willing flake-souls linked in close congregations of ice, breaking rock food for the pines, as a bird crumbles bread for her young, spiced with dust of garnets and zircons and many a nameless gem; and when food was gathered for the forests and all their elected life, when every rock form was finished, every monument raised, the willing messengers, unwearied, unwasted, heard God's "well done" from heaven calling them back to their homes in the sky.

The following was added later on the same sheet:

January 8th, 1872

DEAR FRIEND

We are gloriously snowbound. One storm has filled half of last month, and it is snowing again. Would that you could behold its beauty! I half expected another glacial period, but I will not say anything about ice until you become wiser, though I send you a cascade jubilee which you will relish more than anybody else. I have tried to put it in form for publication, and if you can rasp off the rougher angles and wedge in a few slippery words between bad splices, perhaps it may be sufficiently civilized for *Overland* or *Atlantic*. But I always felt a chill come over my fingers when a calm place in the storm allowed me to think of it. Also I have been sorry for one of our bears, and I think you will sympathise with me. At least I confide my dead friend to your keeping, and you may print what you like. Heavens! if you only had been here in the flood! [JOHN MUIR]

The same note of triumphant apology for his choice of the wilderness instead of the city is found in the following unique letter about the Sequoias. They were deepest in his affections, and under his playful prose-poetry it is not difficult to discover the Muir who in a few years was to arouse the whole nation to the importance of preserving for future generations these greatest and most ancient of all living things. His love for them had in it something personal, and there are those who have overheard him talking to them as to human beings. The original of this letter, written with Sequoia sap, still shines purple after more than half a century. Although it lacks a definite date, internal evidence clearly refers it to his earliest years in Yosemite, perhaps 1870.

to Mrs. Ezra S. Carr

Squirrelville, Sequoia Co. *Nut Time*

DEAR MRS. CARR

Do behold the King in his glory, King Sequoia! Behold! Behold! seems all I can say. Some time ago I left all for Sequoia and have been and am at his feet; fasting and praying for light, for is he not the greatest light in the woods, in the world? Where are such columns of sunshine, tangible, accessible, terrestrialised? Well may I fast, not from bread, but from business, book-making, duty-going, and other trifles, and great is my reward already for the manly, treely sacrifice. What giant truths since coming to Gigantea, what magnificent clusters of Sequoiac *becauses*. From here I cannot recite you one, for you are down a thousand fathoms deep in dark political quagg, not a burr-length less. But I'm in the woods, woods, woods, and they are in *me-ee-ee*. The King tree and I have sworn eternal love – sworn it without swearing, and I've taken the sacrament with Douglas squirrel, drunk Sequoia wine, Sequoia blood, and with its rosy purple drops I am writing this woody gospel letter.

I never before knew the virtue of Sequoia juice. Seen with sunbeams in it, its colour is the most royal of all royal purples. No wonder the Indians instinctively drink it for they know not what. I wish I were so drunk and Sequoical that I could preach the green brown woods to all the juiceless world, descending from this divine wilderness like a John the Baptist, eating Douglas squirrels and wild honey or wild anything, crying, Repent, for the Kingdom of Sequoia is at hand!

There is balm in these leafy Gileads – pungent burrs and living King-juice for all defrauded civilization; for sick grangers and politicians; no need of Salt rivers. Sick or successful, come suck Sequoia and be saved.

Douglas squirrel is so pervaded with rosin and burr juice his flesh can scarce be eaten even by mountaineers. No wonder he is so charged with magnetism! One of the little lions ran across my feet the other day as I lay resting under a fir, and the effect was a thrill like a battery shock. I would eat him no matter how rosiny for the lightning he holds. I wish I could eat wilder things. Think of the grouse with balsam-scented crop stored with spruce buds, the wild sheep full of glacier meadow grass and daisies azure, and the bear burly and brown as Sequoia, eating pine-burrs and wasps' stings and all; then think of the soft lightningless poultice-like pap reeking upon town tables. No wonder cheeks and legs become flabby and fungoid! I wish I were wilder, and so, bless Sequoia, I will be. There is at least a punky spark in my heart and it may blaze in this autumn gold, fanned by the King. Some of my grandfathers must have been born on a muirland for there is heather in me, and tinctures of bog juices, that send me to Cassiope, and oozing through all my veins impel me unhaltingly through endless glacier meadows, seemingly the deeper and danker the better.

See Sequoia aspiring in the upper skies, every summit modelled in fine cycloidal curves as if pressed into unseen moulds, every bole warm in the mellow amber sun. How truly godful in mien! I was talking the other day with a duchess* and was struck with the grand bow with which she bade me

* This may be a playful allusion to Thérèse Yelverton who, still claiming her disputed marriage rights, was supposed to have become a Viscountess when her husband succeeded his father as fourth Viscount of Avonmore in October, 1870.

goodbye and thanked me for the glaciers I gave her, but this forenoon King Sequoia bowed to me down in the grove as I stood gazing, and the high bred gestures of the lady seemed rude by contrast.

There goes Squirrel Douglas, the master spirit of the tree-top. It has just occurred to me how his belly is buffy brown and his back silver grey. Ever since the first Adam of his race saw trees and burrs, his belly has been rubbing upon buff bark, and his back has been combed with silver needles. Would that some of you, wise – terribly wise – social scientists, might discover some method of living as true to nature as the buff people of the woods, running as free as the winds and waters among the burrs and filbert thickets of these leafy, mothery woods.

The sun is set and the star candles are being lighted to show me and Douglas squirrel to bed. Therefore, my Carr, goodnight. You say, "When are you coming down?" Ask the Lord – Lord Sequoia.

[JOHN MUIR]

CHAPTER NINE

Persons and Problems

I

IT SEEMS impossible that any human being can ever have looked upon Yosemite Valley without raising the question of its origin. Its physical features, sculptured in granite, are so extraordinary that they at once stimulate the imagination to go in quest of the efficient cause. Even the Indians are said to have speculated about the Valley's origin in their legends, and the first white men who entered it in 1851, and encamped on the river-bank opposite El Capitan, immediately occupied themselves with the question in their campfire talk. Although the gold rush began in 1849, it was not until the beginning of the sixties that a systematic geological survey of California was begun. Until then the state was, geologically speaking, an unknown land. In the interest of the growing industrial importance of mining this situation called for remedy, and in 1860 the California Legislature passed an Act to create the office of State Geologist, and by a section of the same Act Josiah D. Whitney was appointed to fill the office.

Whitney had the backing of the leading geologists of his day and was a man of such prominence in his field that he was made Professor of Geology at Harvard in 1865. He gathered around him an able staff of assistants, among whom were William H. Brewer, Charles F. Hoffmann, and William M. Gabb. In 1863 Clarence King, also, joined this group as volunteer assistant in geological field-work. During the period from 1860 to 1874 Whitney conducted, with these and other assistants, a topographical, geological, and natural history survey of California, issuing six volumes under the title of *Geological Survey of California* (Cambridge, 1865–70). The first volume, *Geology of California*, published in 1865, brought an intimation of the theory Whitney was going to propound on the subject of Yosemite's origin. "The domes," he wrote, "and such masses as that of Mount Broderick, we conceive to have been formed by the process of upheaval, for we can discover nothing about them which looks like the result of ordinary denudation. The Half Dome seems, beyond a doubt, to have been split asunder in the middle, the lost half having gone down in what may truly be said to have been 'the wreck of matter and the crush of worlds.' " In 1869 he published *The Yosemite Guide-Book* and came to be regarded as the foremost scientific authority on everything pertaining to

Yosemite Valley. In this book he set forth his view of the Valley's origin as follows: "We conceive that, during the process of upheaval of the Sierra, or, possibly, at some time after that had taken place, there was at the Yosemite a subsidence of a limited area, marked by lines of 'fault' or fissures crossing each other somewhat nearly at right angles. In other and more simple language, the bottom of the Valley sank down to an unknown depth, owing to its support being withdrawn from underneath during some of those convulsive movements which must have attended the upheaval of so extensive and elevated a chain."

It only excites wonder now that a geologist of Professor Whitney's standing should have propounded a theory so completely at variance with the evidence. Indeed, members of his own corps pointed out that the floor of the Valley was of one piece with the sides and that there was no evidence of fault lines or of fusion. Although Clarence King had observed enough evidence of glaciation in the Valley to venture the opinion that it had once been filled with ice to the depth of at least a thousand feet, Whitney stoutly asserted that "there is no reason to suppose, or at least no proof, that glaciers have ever occupied the Valley or any portion of it . . . so that this theory [of glacial erosion], based on entire ignorance of the whole subject, may be dropped without wasting any more time upon it." It should be added that Clarence King shared his chief's belief in a cataclysmic origin of the Valley, holding that glaciers only scoured and polished it after it had been formed.*

Whitney's *Yosemite Guide-Book* was published by authority of the California Legislature and the views set forth in it, therefore, had official sanction in the eyes of the public. Its author was the first scientist of standing who had reached a definite conclusion after an examination of the geological evidence and he was little inclined to give serious consideration to any view except his own. It required considerable courage, knowledge, and interpretative ability to go up against such a strongly entrenched and assertive antagonist. But Muir, recognising the subsidence theory as contrary to his reading of the geological record, accepted the challenge. During the very first year of his residence in the Valley (1869–70) he had become convinced that it had not been formed by a cataclysm, but by long, slow, natural processes in which ice played by far the major part. He never lost an opportunity to discuss the question with interested visitors to the Valley and soon became the recognised and finally victorious opponent of the cataclysmic theory. Since there has been some misapprehension among historical geologists

* See original edition of *Mountaineering in the Sierra Nevada*, p.134 (1872). Several writers have mistakenly made Clarence King the originator of the glacial erosion theory as regards Yosemite. He held no such theory. He did not even precede Muir in the publication of his glacial observations in the chapter entitled "Around Yosemite Walls," for that chapter, unlike the others, was not published serially in 1871, but appeared for the first time in the above-mentioned volume in 1872. The dates affixed to the chapters of King's book in the Scribner reprint are misleading, for they do not give the date of publication, but the years in which the observations are supposed to have been made.

as to the time when Muir began to advocate the glacial erosion theory it seems appropriate to introduce some evidence on this point.

In the autumn of 1871 there issued from The Riverside Press, then Hurd and Houghton, a curious novel entitled *Zanita, a Tale of the Yosemite*. Little did the publishers dream that the hero of the tale would one day become one of their most famous authors. Few now remember the writer* of the novel, though she was one of the most noted women of her time, and a warm friend of John Muir. The novel's chief interest lies in the fact that the authoress, coming to Yosemite Valley and taking up her abode there for a season in the spring of 1870, appropriated the inhabitants as characters of her tale, and reported their conversations. The names of Oswald and Placida Naunton are only thin disguises for Mr. and Mrs. J. M. Hutchings; Zanita and Cozy are their daughters, Florence and Gertrude; Methley is James C. Lamon, and Professor Brown seems to play for the most part the role of Professor Josiah D. Whitney, but with occasional admixtures of Professor Joseph LeConte. The hero of the novel is John Muir himself – under the name of Kenmuir. It is the sobriquet by which she addresses him in extant letters, at the same time identifying herself among the characters by signing herself as "Mrs. Brown."

DEAR KENMUIR [she writes in 1871]
The Daughters of Ahwahnee will be out in fall. How you will laugh when you see it. You and Cosa are the best survivors, except the everlasting hills and vales.
                                                                            [T.Y.]

Subsequently, writing from Hong Kong, she complained that the publishers had effaced many passages besides changing the title to *Zanita*. In spite of much exaggeration and unreal sentiment, a student of early Yosemite life will find here more than a historical setting. So much is clear from a reference to the book in one of Muir's letters.

Mrs. Yelverton's book [he writes] I have not yet seen. A friend sent me a copy, but it failed to reach hither. I saw some of the manuscript and have some idea of it. She had a little help from me, the use of my notebooks, etc., some of which, I suppose, she may have worked into her descriptions.
    The Naunton family is the Hutchings family. The name Zanita is a fragment

---

* Thérèse Yelverton, Viscountess Avonmore, 1832-81, authoress and plaintiff in the famous suit of Thelwall vs. Yelverton which the Court of Common Pleas at Dublin, Ireland, decided in her favour. Though on this occasion (1861) the validity of both her Irish and her Scottish marriage to William Charles Yelverton, fourth Viscount Avonmore, was affirmed, the latter finally succeeded in getting a majority of the House of Lords to decide against the marriage (1867). Her maiden name was Maria Teresa Longworth. When her slender fortune had been spent in litigation she supported herself largely by her writings for which she found the materials in wide-ranging travels. Her case was heralded to the entire English-speaking world not only by journalists, but by such plays as Cyrus Redding's *A Wife and not a Wife*, and James Roderick O'Flanagan's novel *Gentle Blood, or The Secret Marriage*.

of the word manzanita, the Spanish name of a very remarkable California shrub. "Zanita" is Floy Hutchings*, a smart and handsome and mischievous Topsy that can scarce be overdrawn.... She is about seven or eight years old. Her sister Cosa, as we call her (I have forgotten what Mrs. Yelverton calls her), is more beautiful far in body and mind, a very precious darling of a child. Mrs. Naunton or Hutchings, was always kind to me, but Mr. Naunton is a very different character in reality, whatever Mrs. Yelverton made of him.

As for Kenmuir, I don't think she knew enough of wild nature to pen him well, but I have often worn shirts, soiled, ragged and buttonless, but with a spray like what I sent you stuck somewhere, or a carex, or chance flower. It is about all the vanity I persistently indulge in, at least in bodily adornments.

There can be little doubt that we have in the pages of this novel a fairly accurate description of Muir's personal appearance in 1870, however distortedly she may have reproduced his views and conversation. While to her mind "his garments had the tatterdemalion style of a Mad Tom," she "soon divined that his refinement was innate, and his education collegiate." "Kenmuir, I decided in my mind, was a gentleman," so runs her naïve comment, revealing her at the same time upon her own lofty perch of assumed gentility. It is of interest to find her noting Muir's "glorious auburn hair," "his open blue eyes of honest questioning," and "his bright intelligent face, shining with a pure and holy enthusiasm." She saw his "lithe figure... skipping over the rough boulders, poising with the balance of an athlete, or skirting a shelf of rock with the cautious activity of a goat, never losing for a moment the rhythmic motion of his flexile form.... His figure was about five feet nine, well knit, and bespoke that active grace which only trained muscles can assume." This new acquaintance, the like of whom, by her own confession, she had never met in all her travels, proved a tempting hero for her tale of Yosemite. Either from lack of skill in portrayal, or because in this case fact was stranger than fiction, the reviewers of *Zanita* were left unconvinced. "One says your character is all 'bosh,'" she writes to Muir, "and only exists in my imagination. I should like to tell him that you had an existence in my heart as well!"

The question of the Valley's origin, always one of the primary interests of Yosemite residents and visitors, is not overlooked by the author of *Zanita*. The appearance of Whitney's *Yosemite Guide-Book* naturally had given new stimulus to discussion, particularly by the authoritative manner in which its author sought to settle the question. The views attributed to Muir in Mrs. Yelverton's reports of these discussions furnish a clue to the early date at which he had reached conclusions opposed to those of Whitney. Among the Valley conversations of 1870, related by her in chapter four, is one in which the alias of Whitney ascribes the formation of the Valley to the falling out

---

* Florence Hutchings was the first white child born in Yosemite Valley (August 23rd 1864). She died in 1881, was buried in the Valley, and Mount Florence was named for her.

of the bottom "in the wreck of creation," whereupon Kenmuir exclaims:

"Good gracious! there never was a 'wreck of creation.' As though the Lord did not know how to navigate. No bottom He made ever fell out by accident. These learned men pretend to talk of a catastrophe happening to the Lord's works, as though it were some poor trumpery machine of their own invention. As it is, it was meant to be.

"Why! I can show the Professor where the mighty cavity has been grooved and wrought out for millions of years. A day and eternity are as one in His mighty workshop. I can take you where you can see for yourself how the glaciers have laboured, and cut and carved, and elaborated, until they have wrought out this royal road."

This novel also indicates that Muir knew at least as early as 1870 that ice had overridden Glacier Point, a fact of some historical interest since the origin of the name is not certainly known, and if any one other than Muir bestowed it he can hardly have grasped the meaning of the evidences of glaciation observed there. One would naturally suppose Clarence King to have been the first to perceive both the fact and the significance of it, but he set the limit of the highest ice-flood far below Glacier Point. But Muir, during the first year of his residence in the Valley, had fathomed the meaning of its glacial phenomena much more completely than he has ever received credit for, and when he propounded a theory of glacial erosion to account for the Valley's origin, he apparently had already correlated the ice-record on Glacier Point. At any rate Mrs. Yelverton, in speaking of Glacier Point as the place where she had first seen Muir, notes the existence there of "traces of ancient glaciers which he said 'are no doubt the instruments the Almighty used in the formation of the Valley.'"

Another, more direct, witness that Muir held the glacial origin theory as early as 1870, and probably earlier, is found in the writings of his friend Joseph LeConte. The latter, for many years Professor of Geology in the University of California, arrived in the State one year later than Muir and made his first visit to Yosemite and the High Sierra with a company of students in the summer of 1870. Muir and LeConte met in Yosemite through the mediation of Mrs. Carr, and Muir, on account of his knowledge of the region north of Yosemite, was invited to accompany the party across the crest of the Sierra to Mono Lake. On the night of the eighth of August the party was encamped on a meadow near what is now called Eagle Peak, and there LeConte made the following entry in his journal:

After dinner, lay down on our blankets, and gazed up through the magnificent tall spruces into the deep blue sky and the gathering masses of white clouds. Mr. Muir gazes and gazes and cannot get his fill. He is a most passionate lover of nature. Plants, and flowers, and forests, and sky, and clouds, and mountains, seem actually to haunt his imagination. He seems to revel in the freedom of this life. I think he would pine away in a city or in conventional life of any kind. He is really not only an intelligent man, as I saw at once, but a man of strong, earnest nature, and thoughtful, closely observing and original mind. I have talked much with him today about the probable manner in which Yosemite was formed. He fully agrees with me that the peculiar cleavage of the rock is a most important point, which must not be left out of account. He further believes that the Valley has been wholly formed by causes still in operation in the Sierra – that the Merced Glacier and the Merced River and its branches . . . have done the whole work.

This reference of LeConte to Muir's glacial observations fully bears out the evidence of Mrs. Yelverton's novel that Muir had as early as 1870 definitely reached the conclusion that Yosemite is not the result of a sudden and exceptional catastrophe, but the product of "causes still in operation," as stated by Professor LeConte. In other words Muir was at this time aware also of the existence of residual glaciers in the High Sierra, for in his letter of August 7th, 1870, he mentions his intention "to set some stakes in a dozen glaciers and gather some arithmetic for clothing my thoughts." A year later (1871) he had verified by actual measurements his belief that what Whitney called snowfields were glaciers, and he had also found one in the Merced group of mountains that was delivering glacial mud, or rock meal, showing that the process of erosion on a small scale was still going on.

LeConte's inference from Muir's conversation, that he believed the ancient Merced Glacier and subsequent Merced River to "have done the whole work" of forming Yosemite Valley, requires some modification, for Muir did assume a certain amount of pre-glacial and post-glacial erosion, as may be seen in certain passages of his *Sierra Studies* [published in book form in 1950]. But it still is far from proved that he was wrong in regarding these particular erosion factors as subordinate. In justice to Muir it must, of course, be remembered that neither he nor any other geologist was at this time reckoning with the work of successive glacial epochs, least of all in Yosemite where the evidence of two glaciations remains speculative and theoretical. These are, at most, but shiftings of the boundaries of the original problem, and in no way detract from the value of Muir's pioneering work.

What concerned Muir most at this time was the ease with which bands of Yosemite pilgrims were captured by Whitney's exceptional creation theory of the Valley's origin, thus coming to regard it as "the latest, most uncompanioned wonder of the earth."

No wonder [said Muir] that a scientist standing on the Valley floor and looking up at its massive walls, has been unable to interpret its history. The magnitude of the characters in which the account of its origin is recorded has prevented him from reading it. "We have interrogated," says the scientist, "all the known valley-producing causes. The torrent has replied, 'It was not I'; the glacier has answered, 'It was not I'; and the august forces that fold and crevasse whole mountain chains disclaim all knowledge of it.''

But, during my few years' acquaintance with it, I have found it not full of chaos, uncompanioned and parentless. I have found it one of many Yosemite valleys, which differ not more than one pine tree differs from another. Attentive study and comparison of these throws a flood of light upon the origin of the Yosemite; uniting her, by birth, with sister valleys distributed through all the principal river-basins of the range.

The scorn with which Whitney and his assistants rejected Muir's theory and observations as those of a "shepherd" had not the slightest discouraging effect upon him, for he knew they had seen but a fraction of the evidence, and that hastily. It only sent him back to his mountain temples for more revealing facts which he wrote and preached to his friends with the zeal of a Hebrew prophet and no apology except that of Amos, "The Lord Jehovah hath spoken; who can but prophesy?" It is the voice of a man with a divine call that is heard in the following letters:

to Catherine Merrill

Yosemite Valley, July 12th, [1871]

DEAR FRIEND

Your sister's note which came with the little plants tells that you are about to escape from the frightful tendencies of a "Christian" school to the smooth shelter of home. I glanced at the regulations, order, etc., in the catalogue which you sent, and the grizzly thorny ranks of cold enslaving "musts" made me shudder as I fancy I should had I looked into a dungeon of the olden times full of rings and thumbscrews and iron chains. You deserve great credit for venturing into such a place. None but an Indiana professor would dare the dangers of such a den of ecclesiastical slave-drivers. I suppose that you were moved to go among those flint Christians by the same motives of philanthropy which urged you amongst other forms of human depravity.

From my page I hold my bosom to our purple rocks and snowy waters and think of the divine repose which enwraps them all together with the tuned flies, and birds, and plants which inhabit them, and I thank God for this tranquil freedom, this glorious mountain Yosemite barbarism.

I have been with you and your apostolic friends these fifteen minutes and I feel a kind of choking and sinking as though I were smothering in nightmare. Come to Yosemite! Change the subject.

Last Sabbath week I read one of the most magnificent of God's own mountain manuscripts. During my rambles of the last two years in the basin of Yosemite Creek north of the Valley, I had gathered many faint hints from what I read as glacial footprints in the rocks worn by the storms and blotting chemistry of ages. Now there is a deep canyon in the top of the Valley wall near the upper Yosemite Falls which has engaged my attention for more than a year, and I could not account for its formation in any other way than by a theory which involved the supposition that a glacier formerly filled the basin of the stream above. Suddenly the big truth came to the birth. I ran up the mountain, 'round to the top of the falls, said my prayers, received baptism in the irised spray and ran northward toward the head of the basin, full of faith, confident that there was a writing for me somewhere on the rock, and I had not drifted four miles before I found all that I had so long sought in a narrow hollow where the ice had been compelled to wedge through under great pressure, thus deeply grooving and hardening the granite and making it less susceptible of decomposition. I continued up the stream to its source in the snows of Mt. Hoffmann, and everywhere discovered strips of meadow and sandy levels formed from the matter of moraine sand and bouldery accumulations of all kinds, smoothed and levelled by overflowing waters.

This dead glacier was about twelve miles in length by about five in breadth – of depth I have as yet no reliable data. Its course was nearly north and south, at right angles to the branches of the summit glaciers which entered Yosemite by the canyons of the Tenaya and Nevada streams. It united with those opposite Hutchings, in the Valley. Perhaps it was not born so early as those of the summits, from the canyons of Nevada and Tenaya. This is intensely interesting to me, and from its semi-philosophic character ought to be so in some degree to any professor. You must write. My love to all. You *must* write. I start tomorrow for the High Sierra about Mt. Dana and over in the Mono basin among the lavas and volcanoes. Will be back in a month.

[JOHN MUIR]

to Mrs. Ezra S. Carr

Yosemite, August 13th, [1871]

DEAR FRIEND

I was so stunned and dazed by your last that I have not been able to write anything. I was sure that you were coming, and you cannot come, and Mr. King, the artist, left me the other day, and I am done with Hutchings, and I am lonely. Well, it must be wait, for although there is no common human reason why I should not see you and civilization in Oakland, I cannot escape from the powers of the mountains. I shall tie some flour and a blanket behind my saddle and return to the Mono region, and try to decide some questions that require undisturbed thought. Then I will stalk about over the summit slates of Dana and Gibbs and Lyell, reading new chapters of glacial manuscript, and more if I can. Then, perhaps, I will follow the Tuolumne down to the Hetch Hetchy Yosemite. Then perhaps follow every Yosemite stream back to its smallest sources in the mountains of the Lyell group and the Cathedral group and the Obelisk and Mt. Hoffmann. This will, perhaps, be my work until the coming of the winter snows, when I will probably find a sheltered rock nook where I can make a nest of leaves and mosses and doze until spring.

I expect to be entirely alone in these mountain walks, and notwithstanding the glorious portion of daily bread which my soul will receive in these fields where only the footprints of God are seen, the gloamin' will be very lonely, but I will cheerfully pay this price of friendship, hunger, and *all* besides.

I suppose you have seen Mr. King, who kindly carried some [butter]flies for Mr. Edwards.* I thought you would easily see him or let him know that you had his specimens. I collected most of them upon Mount Hoffmann, but was so busy in assisting Reilly that I could not do much in butterflies. Hereafter I shall be entirely free.

The purples and yellows begin to come in the green of our groves and the rocks have the autumn haze and the water songs are at their lowest hushings. Young birds are big as old ones, and it is the time of ripe berries, and is it true that those are Bryant's "melancholy days"? I don't know. I will not think, but I will go above these brooding days to the higher brighter mountains....

[JOHN MUIR]

to Mrs. Ezra S. Carr

Yosemite, September 8th, 1871

DEAR FRIEND

I am sorry that King made you uneasy about me. He does not understand me as you do, and you must not heed him so much. He thinks that I am melancholy, and above all that I require polishing. I feel sure that if you were here to see how happy I am, and how ardently I am seeking a knowledge of the rocks you could not call me away, but would gladly let me go with only God and his written rocks to guide me. You would not think of calling me to make machines or a home, or of rubbing me against other minds, or of setting me up for measurement. No, dear friend, you would say, "Keep your mind untrammelled and pure. Go unfrictioned, unmeasured, and God give you the true meaning and interpretation of his mountains."

You know that for the last three years I have been ploddingly making observations about this Valley and the high mountain region to the East of it, drifting broodingly about and taking in every natural lesson that I was fitted to absorb. In particular the great Valley has always kept a place in my mind. How did the Lord make it? What tools did He use? How did He apply them and when? I considered the sky above it and all of its opening canyons, and studied the forces that came in by every door that I saw standing open, but I

---

* Mr. Henry Edwards, actor and entomologist; for a report on this package of butterflies see Chap. 8, pp. 136, 137

could get no light. Then I said, "You are attempting what is not possible for you to accomplish. Yosemite is the *end* of a grand chapter. If you would learn to read it go commence at the beginning." Then I went above to the alphabet valleys of the summits, comparing canyon with canyon with all their varieties of rock structure and cleavage, and the comparative size and slope of the glaciers and waters which they contained. Also the grand congregation of rock creations were present to me, and I studied their forms and sculpture. I soon had a key to every Yosemite rock and perpendicular and sloping wall. The grandeur of these forces and their glorious results overpower me, and inhabit my whole being. Waking or sleeping I have no rest. In dreams I read blurred sheets of glacial writing or follow lines of cleavage or struggle with the difficulties of some extraordinary rock form. Now it is clear that woe is me if I do not drown this tendency toward nervous prostration by constant labour in working up the details of this whole question. I have been down from the upper rocks only three days and am hungry for exercise already.

Professor Runkle,* President of the Massachusetts Institute of Technology, was here last week, and I preached my glacial theory to him for five days, taking him into the canyons of the Valley and up among the grand glacier wombs and pathways of the summit. He was fully convinced of the truth of my readings, and urged me to write out the glacial system of Yosemite and its tributaries for the Boston Academy of Science. I told him that I meant to write my thoughts for my own use and that I would send him the manuscript and if he and his wise scientific brothers thought it of sufficient interest they might publish it.

He is going to send me some instruments, and I mean to go over all the glacier basins carefully, working until driven down by the snow. In winter I can make my drawings and maps and write out notes. So you see that for a year or two I will be very busy.

I have settled with Hutchings and have no dealings with him now. I think that next spring I will have to guide a month or two for pocket money, although I do not like the work. I suppose I might live for one or two seasons without work. I have five hundred dollars here, and I have been sending home money to my sisters and brothers – perhaps about twelve or fifteen hundred, and a man in Canada owes me three or four hundred dollars more which I suppose I could get if I was in need; but you know that the Scotch do not like to spend their last dollar. Some of my friends are badgering me to write for some of the magazines, and I am almost tempted to try it, only I am afraid that this would distract my mind from my main work more than the distasteful and depressing labour of the mill or of guiding. What do you think about it?

Suppose I should give some of the journals my first thoughts about this glacier work as I go along, and afterwards gather them and press them for the Boston wise. Or will it be better to hold my wheesht [Scottish word for

* John Daniel Runkle.

silence] and say it all at a breath? You see how practical I have become, and how fully I have burdened you with my little affairs!

Perhaps you will ask, "What plan are you going to pursue in your work?" Well, here it is – the only book I ever have invented. First, I will describe each glacier with its tributaries separately, then describe the rocks and hills and mountains over which they have flowed or past which they have flowed, endeavouring to prove that all of the various forms which those rocks now have is the necessary result of the ice action in connection with their structure and cleavage, etc. – also the different kinds of canyons and lake basins and meadows which they have made. Then, armed with these data, I will come down to Yosemite, where all of my ice has come, and prove that each dome and brow and wall, and every grace and spire and brother is the necessary result of the delicately balanced blows of well directed and combined glaciers against the parent rocks which contained them, only thinly carved and moulded in some instances by the subsequent action of water, etc.

Libby sent me Tyndall's new book, and I have looked hastily over it. It is an alpine mixture of very pleasant taste, and I wish I could enjoy reading and talking it with you. I expect Mrs. Hutchings will accompany her husband to the East this winter, and there will not be one left with whom I can exchange a thought. Mrs. Hutchings is going to leave me out all the books I want, and Runkle is going to send me Darwin. These, with my notes and maps, will fill my winter hours, if my eyes do not fail. And now that you see my whole position I think that you would not call me to the excitements and distracting novelties of civilization.

This bread question is very troublesome. I will eat anything you think will suit me. Send up either by express to Big Oak Flat or by any other chance, and I will remit the money required in any way you like.

My love to all and more thanks than I can write for your constant kindness.

[J.M.]

to Mrs. Ezra S. Carr

Yosemite, [September or October], 1871

DEAR FRIEND MRS. CARR

I am again upon the bottom meadow of Yosemite, after a most intensely interesting bath among the outer mountains. I have been exploring the upper tributaries of the Cascade and Tamarack streams, and in particular all of the basin of Yosemite Creek. The present basin of every stream which enters the Valley on the north side was formerly filled with ice, which also flowed into the Valley, although the ancient ice basins did not always correspond with the present water basins because glaciers can flow up hill. The *whole* of the north wall of the valley was covered with an unbroken flow of ice, with perhaps the single exception of the crest of Eagle Cliff, and though the book of glaciers gradually dims as we go lower on the range, yet I fully believe that future investigation will show that in the earlier ages of Sierra Nevada ice vast glaciers flowed to the foot of the range east of Yosemite, and also north and south at an elevation of 9000 feet. The glacier basins are almost unchanged, and I believe that ice was the agent by which all of the present rocks received their special forms.

More of this some other day. Would that I could have you here or in any wild place where I can think and speak! Would you not be thoroughly iced? You would not find in me one unglacial thought. Come, and I will tell you how El Capitan and Tissiack were fashioned.

I will most likely live at Black's Hotel this winter in charge of the premises, and before next spring I will have an independent cabin built, with a special Carr corner where you and the Doctor can come and stay all summer. Also, I will have a tent so that we can camp and receive night blessings where we choose, and then I will have horses enough so that we can go to the upper temples also.

I wish you could see Lake Tenaya. It is one of the most perfectly and richly spiritual places in the mountains, and I would like to preempt there. Somehow I should feel like leaving home in going to Hetch Hetchy. Besides, there is room there for many other claims, and soon will fill with coarse homesteads. But as the winter is so severe at Lake Tenaya, very few will care to live there. Hetch Hetchy is about four thousand feet above sea, while Lake Tenaya is eight. I have been living in these mountains in so haunting, hovering, floating a way, that it seems strange to cast any kind of an anchor. All is so equal in glory, so ocean-like, that to choose one place above another is like drawing dividing lines in the sky.

I think I answered your last with respect to remaining here in winter. I can do much of this ice work in the quiet, and the whole subject is purely physical, so that I can get but little from books. All depends upon the goodness of one's eyes. No scientific book in the world can tell me how this Yosemite granite is put together, or how it has been taken down. Patient observation and constant brooding above the rocks, lying upon them for years as the ice did, is the way to arrive at the truths which are graven so lavishly upon them.

Would that I knew what good prayers I could say, or good deeds I could do, so that ravens would bring me bread and venison for the next two years. Then would I get some tough grey clothes, the colour of granite, so no one could see or find me but yourself. Then would I reproduce the ancient ice-rivers, and watch their workings and dwell with them. I go again to my lessons tomorrow morning.

Some snow fell and, bye the bye, I must tell you about it. If poor, good, melancholic Cowper had been here yesterday morning here is just what he would have sung:

> The rocks have been washed, just washed in a shower
> Which winds to their faces conveyed.
> The plentiful cloudlets bemuffled their brows,
> Or lay on their beautiful heads.

> But cold sighed the winds in the fir trees above,
> And down in the pine trees below;
> For the rain that came laving and washing in love
> Was followed, alas, by a snow.

Which, being unmetaphored and prosed into sense, means that yesterday morning a strong southeast wind, cooled among the highest snows of the Sierra, drove back the warm northwest winds from the hot San Joaquin plains and burning foothill woods, and piled up a jagged cloud addition to our Valley walls. Soon those white clouds began to darken and to reach out long filmy edges, which uniting over the Valley made a close dark ceiling. Then came rain, unsteady at first, now a heavy gush, then a sprinkling halt, as if the clouds so long out of practice had forgotten something. But after a half hour of experimental pouring and sprinkling there came an earnest, steady, well-controlled rain. On the mountain the rain soon turned to snow, and some half-melted flakes reached the bottom of the Valley. This morning Starr King and Tissiack and all the upper valley rim is white....

Ever devoutly your friend,

JOHN MUIR

The following letter furnishes a good summary of Muir's glacial studies at the stage which they had reached in 1871. Attention should be called to the fact that in his opening sentence, Muir gives the California State Geological Survey credit for views which its chief had already repudiated, for in his Yosemite Guide Book of 1869 Josiah D. Whitney asserted that he had made an error in the first volume of the Survey when he stated that glaciers had entered the Valley from the head of the Merced.

to Clinton L. Merriam

Yosemite Valley, September 24th, 1871

DEAR MERRIAM

The main trunk glaciers which entered Yosemite by the Tenaya, and Nevada, and South Canyons, have been known to many since the publication of the first volume of the California State Geological Survey; but I am not aware of the existence of any published account of the smaller glaciers, which entered the Valley by the lower side canyons, or indeed that their former existence was known at all.

I have been haunting the rocks of this region for a long time, anxious to spell out some of the great mountain truths which I felt were written here, and ever since the number, and magnitude, and significance of these Yosemite glaciers began to appear, I became eager for knowledge concerning them and am now devoting all my time to their history.

You know my views concerning the formation of Yosemite, that the great Valley itself, together with all of its various domes and sculptured walls, were produced and fashioned by the united labours of the grand combination of glaciers which flowed over and through it, their forces having been rigidly governed and directed by the peculiar physical structure of the granite of which this region is made, and, moreover, that all of the rocks and lakes, and meadows of the whole upper Merced basin owe their specific forms and carving to this same glacial agency.

I left the Valley two weeks ago to explore the main trunk glacier of Yosemite Creek basin, together with its radiating border of tributaries, gathering what data I could read regarding their age, and direction, size, etc., also the kind and amount of work which they had done, but while I was seeking for traces of the western shore of the main stream upon the El Capitan ridge, I discovered that the Yosemite glacier was not the lowest ice stream which flowed to the Valley, but that the Ribbon basin or Virgin's Tears as it is also called, was also the bed of an ancient glacier which flowed nearly south, uniting with the central glaciers of the summits, in the valley below El Capitan.

This Ribbon glacier must have been one of the very smallest of the ice streams which flowed to Yosemite, having been only about four miles in length by three in width. It had some small groove tributaries from the slopes of El Capitan, but most of its ice was derived from a high spur of the Hoffmann group to the north, which runs nearly southwest. Its bed is steep and regular, and it must have flowed with considerable velocity.

I could not find any of the original grooved and polished surfaces of the old bed, but some protected patches may still exist where a boulder of the proper form has settled upon a rounded summit. I found many such preserved patches in the basin of Yosemite creek, one of which is within half a mile of the top of the falls. It has a polished surface of about four square feet, with very distinct striæ and grooves, although the unsheltered rock about it is eroded to the depth of four or five inches.

In as much as this small glacier sloped openly to the sun, and was not very deep, it was one of the first to die, and of course its written pages have been longer exposed to blurring rains and frosts, but notwithstanding the many crumbling blotting storms which have fallen upon the lithographs of this small ice-stream, the great truth of its former existence in this home, written in characters of moraine, and meadow, and fluted slope, is just as clear as when all of its shining newborn rocks gleamed forth the full shadowless poetry of its whole life.

There are a few castle-shaped piles, and crumbling domes upon its east bank, excepting which the basin is now plain and lake-like. But it contains most lovely meadows, interesting in their present flora, and in their glacial history, and noble forests made up mostly of the two silver firs (*Picea amabilis* and *P. grandis*) planted upon moraines which have been spread and levelled by the agency of water.

These rambling researches in the Ribbon basin recalled some observations made by me a year ago in the lower portion of the canyons of the Cascade and Tamarack streams, and I now guessed that careful search would discover abundant glacial manuscript in those basins also. Accordingly on reaching the highest point on the rim of the Ribbon ice, I obtained broad map views of both the Cascade and Tamarack basins, and singled out from their countless adornments many forms of lake, and rock, which seemed to be genuine glacier workmanship, unmarred in any way by the various powers which have come upon them since they were abandoned by their parent ice.

This highest ridge of the Ribbon glacier basin, bounded its ice on the north, and upon its opposite side I saw shining patches, which I ran down to examine. They proved to be polished unchanged fragments of the bottom of another ancient ice stream, which according to the testimony of their striae, had flowed south 40° west. This new glacier proved to be the eastmost tributary of the Cascade. Anxious to know it better, I proceeded west along the Mono trail to Cascade meadows, then turning to the right, entered the mouth of the tributary at the upper end of the meadows. Both of the ridges which formed the banks of the stream are torn and precipitous, evidently the work of ice. I followed up the bed of the tributary to its source, upon the flat west bank of the Yosemite basin, and throughout its whole length there is abundance of polished tablets, and moraines, and various kinds of rock sculpture forming ice testimony as full and indisputable as can be rendered by the most recent glacier pathways of the Alps.

I should gladly have welcomed the grateful toil of exploring the main trunk of this Cascade glacier from its farthest snows upon the Tuolumne divide, to its mouth in the Merced Canyon below Yosemite, but my stock of provisions was too small, and besides I felt that I would most likely have to explore the basin of Tamarack also, and following westward among the older, changed, and covered glacier highways, I might drift as far as the end of Pilot Peak ridge. Therefore turning reluctantly to the easier pages of Yosemite Creek I resolved to leave those lower chapters for future lessons. But before proceeding with Yosemite Creek let me distinctly give here as my opinion that future investigation will discover proofs of the existence in the earlier ages of a Sierra Nevada ice of vast glaciers which flowed to the very foot of the range.

Already it is clear that all of the upper basins were filled with ice, so deep and universal that but few of the ridges were sufficiently high to separate it into individual glaciers. Vast mountains were flowed over, and rounded or moved away like boulders in a river.

Ice flowed into Yosemite by every one of its canyons, and at a comparatively recent period of its history, its north wall, with perhaps the single exception of the crest of Eagle Cliff, was covered with an unbroken stream of ice, the several glaciers having united before coming to the wall.

JOHN MUIR

Fortunately Muir decided not to hold his "wheesht"[Scottish word for silence]. The above letter is an abridgment of an article, entitled "Yosemite Glaciers" that he sent four days later as his "first thoughts" to the *New York Tribune*. After some delay it appeared in that paper, December 5th, 1871, and constitutes the first published statement of the ice erosion theory to account for the origin of Yosemite. It is but just to point out that Muir was not following in any one's footsteps in propounding his theory,[1] for the simple reason that there was no one to be followed, and though he put forward but a small part of his evidence, it proved to be the beginning of the end of Whitney's subsidence theory.

Muir had hardly published his views and discoveries when Professor Samuel Kneeland, of the Massachusetts Institute of Technology, utilised his article, together with letters he had written to President J. D. Runkle, to prepare a paper[2] for the Boston Society of Natural History. Muir did not approve of the use that Kneeland made of his materials, claiming that he gave him "credit for all the smaller sayings and doings and stole the broadest truth to himself." But the paper had the effect of attracting considerable attention to Muir's views and explorations.

Meanwhile Muir was going at his task systematically. The difficulty of correlating his studies without good maps was in large measure surmounted by his ability to sketch accurately and rapidly the physical features of the region under examination. Nothing shows better his industry and the minute care with which he worked than the large number of mountain sketches that date from this period. By means of them he could, when working up his results, call to mind with particularity and vividness the physiography of the country in connection with his notes.

Early in November, 1871, when winter cold was already settling upon the heights, he made his first expedition to Hetch Hetchy, the "Tuolumne Yosemite," as he aptly described it, whose needless destruction and conversion to the domestic uses of San Francisco was to sadden the evening of his life. A hunter by the name of Joseph Screech is said to have discovered the Valley in 1850, a year before Yosemite was entered for the first time by Captain Boling's party. In 1871 its use was claimed by a sheep owner named Smith and consequently was often called Smith's Valley. This man's shepherd and a few Digger Indians were the only occasional inhabitants of the Valley at this time.

---

[1]   William Phipps Blake has been mistakenly credited with being the originator of the theory. In his paper "Sur l'action des anciens glaciers dans la Sierra Nevada de Californie et sur l'origine de la vallée de Yo-Semite," published in the *Comptes Rendus des Seances de l'Academie des Sciences de Paris*, tome 65, 1867, the origin of the Valley is ascribed to sub-glacial erosion by water pouring; from the glaciers above. The precise form of statement is as follows: " On peut en conclure que cette vallée parait due à une érosion sous-glaciaire, due à l'écoulement des eaux provenant de la fonte des glaces supérieures."

[2]   "On the Glaciers of the Yosemite Valley," read at a meeting held February 21, 1872, and published in the *Proceedings* of the Society, Vol. XV, pp. 36-47 (1872). Also republished the same year in Kneeland's book *The Wonders of Yosemite Valley and of California*.

Excerpts from a description of this "last raid of the season" will give the reader an idea of the manner in which he fared on these lonely excursions.

I went alone [he writes], my outfit consisting of a pair of blankets and a quantity of bread and coffee. There is a weird charm in carrying out such a free and pathless plan as I had projected; passing through untrodden forests, from canyon to canyon, from mountain to mountain; constantly coming upon new beauties and new truths. . . . As I drifted over the dome-paved basin of Yosemite Creek . . . sunset found me only three miles back from the brow of El Capitan, near the head of a round smooth gap – the deepest groove in the El Capitan ridge. Here I lay down and thought of the time when the groove in which I rested was being ground away at the bottom of a vast ice-sheet that flowed over all the Sierra like a slow wind. . . . My huge camp fire glowed like a sun. . . . A happy brook sang confidingly, and by its side I made my bed of rich, spicy boughs, elastic and warm. Upon so luxurious a couch, in such a forest, and by such a fire and brook, sleep is gentle and pure. Wildwood sleep is always refreshing; and to those who receive the mountains into their souls, as well as into their sight – living with them clean and free – sleep is a beautiful death, from which we arise every dawn into a new-created world, to begin a new life in a new body.

The second day he suddenly emerged on top of the wall of the main Tuolumne Canyon about two miles above Hetch Hetchy. After describing glowingly the canyon floor four thousand feet below and the sublime wilderness of mountains around and beyond, he indulges in some reflections on the diversity of impression produced upon different persons by such a scene.

To most persons unacquainted with the genius of the Sierra Nevada [he observes], especially to those whose lives have been spent in shadows, the impression produced by such a landscape is dreary and hopeless. Like symbols of a desolate future, the sunburned domes, naves, and peaks, lie dead and barren beneath a thoughtless, motionless sky; weed-like trees darken their grey hollows and wrinkles, with scarcely any cheering effect. To quote from a Boston professor [J. D. Whitney], "The heights are bewildering, the distances overpowering, the stillness oppressive, and the utter barrenness and desolation indescribable." But if you go to the midst of these bleached bones of mountains, and dwell confidingly and waitingly with them, be assured that every death-taint will speedily disappear; the hardest rocks will pulse with life, secrets of divine beauty and love will be revealed to you by lakes, and meadows, and a thousand flowers, and an atmosphere of spirit be felt brooding over all.

He descended into the canyon by what he at first supposed to be a trail laid out by Indians, but soon discovered that it was a bear-path leading to harvests of brown acorns in black oak groves and to thickets of berry-laden manzanita. Muir never went armed on any of these exploratory excursions, his aim being, so far as in him lay, to live at peace with all the inhabitants of the wilds.

The sandy ground [he notes] was covered with bear-tracks; but that gave me no anxiety. because I knew that bears never eat men where berries and acorns abound. Night came in most impressive stillness. My blazing fire illumined the brown columns of my guardian trees, and from between their bulging roots a few withered breckans and golden-rods leaned forward, as if eager to drink the light. Here and there a star glinted through the shadowy foliage overhead, and in front I could see a portion of the mighty canyon walls massed in darkness against the sky; making me feel as if at the bottom of the sea. The near, soothing hush of the river joined faint, broken songs of cascades. I became drowsy, and, on the incense-like breath of my green pillow, I floated away into sleep.

After a careful exploration of the Hetch Hetchy Valley he struck, on his return, straight across the mountains toward Yosemite. November storms often blanket the High Sierra in snow, and he was caught in the edge of a storm on the way back.

During the first night [he writes] a few inches of snow fell, but I slept safely beneath a cedar-log, and pursued my journey next day, charmed with the universal snow-bloom that was upon every tree, bush, and weed, and upon all the ground, in lavish beauty. I reached home the next day, rejoicing in having added to my mountain wealth one more Yosemite Valley.

Thus ended the exploring season of 1871, and in the following letter, written to his mother immediately after the Hetch Hetchy excursion, we get a glimpse of his plans:

to Mrs. Daniel Muir

Yosemite Valley, November 16th, [1871]

DEAR MOTHER

Our high-walled home is quiet now; travel has ceased for the season, and I have returned from my last hard exploratory ramble in the summit mountains. I will remain during the winter at Black's Hotel, taking care of the premises and working up the data which I have garnered during these last months and years concerning the ancient glacial system of this wonderful region. For the last two or three months I have worked incessantly among the most remote and undiscoverable of the deep canyons of this pierced basin, finding many a mountain page glorious with the writing of God and in characters that any earnest eye could read. The few scientific men who have written upon this region tell us that Yosemite Valley is unlike anything else, an exceptional creation, separate in all respects from all other valleys, but such is not true. Yosemite is one of many, one chapter of a great mountain book written by the same pen of ice which the Lord long ago passed over every page of our great Sierra Nevadas. I know how Yosemite and all the other valleys of these magnificent mountains were made and the next year or two of my life will be occupied chiefly in writing their history in a human book – a glorious subject, which God help me preach aright.

I have been sleeping in the rocks and snow, often weary and hungry, sustained by the excitements of my subject and by the Scottish pluck and perseverance which belongs to our family. For the last few days I have been eating and resting and enjoying long warm sleeps beneath a roof, in a warm, rockless, boulderless bed.

In all my lonely journeys among the most distant and difficult pathless, passless mountains, I never wander, am never lost. Providence guides through every danger and takes me to all the truths which I need to learn, and some day I hope to show you my sheaves, my big bound pages of mountain gospel.

I have been busy moving my few chattels from Hutchings' to Black's, about half a mile down the Valley, and I scarce feel at home. Tidings of the great far sweeping fires have reached our hidden home, and I am thankful that your section of towns and farms has been spared. I heard a few weeks ago from David and Joanna and learn that all is well. Wisconsin winter will soon be upon you. May you enjoy its brightness and universal beauty in warm and happy homes.

Our topmost mountains are white with their earliest snow, but the Valley is still bare and brown with rustling leaves of the oak and alder and fronds of the fast fading ferns. Between two and three thousand persons visited the Valley this summer. I am glad they are all gone. I can now think my thoughts and say my prayers in quiet.

Ever devoutly yours in family love
JOHN

II

It was during the winter of 1871–72 that Muir began to write for publication. "In the beginning of my studies I never intended to write a word for the press," he was accustomed to remark to his friends. But in September, 1871, he sent the first of several serial letters to the *New York Tribune*, and it appeared on December 5th, 1871, under the title "Yosemite Glaciers." The second and third, entitled "Yosemite in Winter" and "Yosemite in Spring," appeared January 1st and May 7th, 1872. Extracts from letters written to friends in Boston were read at the February, March, and May meetings of the Boston Society of Natural History by Dr. Samuel Kneeland, and were afterwards published in the *Proceedings* of the Society. In April, 1872, he began a series of contributions to the *Overland Monthly*, whose editorial direction had then passed from Francis Bret Harte to Benjamin P. Avery. This was the magazine upon which John H. Carmany, its publisher, is reputed to have spent thirty thousand dollars – to make Bret Harte famous. Muir's first contribution, placed through the mediation of Mrs. Carr, was "Yosemite Valley in Flood" – a vivid description of a great storm that swept Yosemite for three days during the preceding December. This article, exciting instant and widespread interest, was followed in July by "Twenty Hill Hollow."

Many of his friends at this time were aware of his literary ability through his letters and were urging him to write, but no one had assessed his genius and his literary powers more accurately than his friend Jeanne C. Carr. In an extant fragment of a letter written in March she informs him that she has combined two of his glacial letters, one written to her and the other to Professor LeConte, and that she is sending this combination to Emerson with the request to get it published in the *Atlantic.* "You are not to know anything about it," she writes – "let it take its chances."

"My mind is made up on one point," she continues. "All this fugitiveness is going to be gathered up, lest you should die like Moses in the mountains and God should bury you where 'no man knoweth.' I copied every word of your old Journal. It looks pretty, and reads well. You have only to continue it and make the *Yosemite Year Book,* painting in your inimitable way the march of the seasons there. Try your pen on the humans, too. Get sketches at least. I think it would be a beautiful book. Then you will put your scientific convictions into clear-cut crystalline prose for other uses." To these suggestions the following letter is in part a reaction:

to Mrs. Ezra S. Carr

Yosemite Valley, March 16th, [1872]

DEAR MRS. CARR

Yours of February 26th reached me today, and as I have a chance to send you a hasty line by an Indian who is going to Mariposa I would say that I fear you are giving yourself far too much trouble about those little fragments. If they or any other small pieces that chance to the end of my pen give you and the Doctor any pleasure I am well paid. Very few friends besides will care for them....

You don't understand my reference to Ruskin's "moderation." Don't you remember that he speaks in some of his books about the attributes of Nature, "Repose," "Moderation," etc.? He says many true and beautiful things of Repose, but weak and uninspired things concerning Moderation, telling us most solemnly that Nature is never immoderate! and that if he had the power and the paint he would have "Moderation" brushed in big capitals upon all the doors and lintels of art factories and manufactories of the whole world! etc., etc., as near as I can recollect. The heavy masonry of the Sierra seems immoderate to some.

I am astonished at your copying those dry tattered notes. People speak of writing with one foot in the grave. I wrote most of those winter notes with one foot in bed while stupid with the weariness of Hutchings' logs. I'm not going to die until done with my glaciers. As for that glacier which you propose to construct out of your letter and LeConte's, I cannot see how a balanced unit can be made from such material.

I had a letter from Emerson the other day of which I told you in another letter. He prophesies, in the same dialect that you are accustomed to use, that I shall one day go to the Atlantic Coast. He knows nothing of my present ice work.

I read your Hindu extracts with much interest. I am glad to know, by you and Emerson and others living and dead, that my unconditional surrender to Nature has produced exactly what you have foreseen – that drifting without human charts through light and dark, calm and storm, I have come to so glorious an ocean. But more of this by and by.

As for that idea of Mountain Models, I told Runkle last fall that a model, in plaster of Paris, of a section of the Sierra reaching to the summits, including Yosemite, would do more to convince people of the truth of our glacial theory of the formation of the Valley and of canyons in general than volumes of rocky argument; because magnitudes are so great only very partial views are obtained. He agreed with me and promised to send me a box with plaster for a model three or four feet long, and instruments, barometer, level, etc., but it has not come.

I have material for some outline glacier maps, but as I had no barometer last fall I have no definite depths of canyons or heights. If you think they would be worth presenting to the wise Congress of next summer, I will send them. Emerson told me, hurry done with the mountains. I don't see how he knows I am meddling with them. Have you told him? He says I may go East with Agassiz. I will not be done here for several years.

I am in no hurry. I want to see all the world. I am going to be down about the Golden Gate looking for a mouth to a portion of my ice. I answered two others of yours dated 4th and 8th of February, but the letter is still here. I will risk only this with Lo.   [JOHN MUIR]

During the month of February he had got in touch again with his friend Emily Pelton, of Prairie du Chien days. In 1864, on the way back from his botanical ramble down the Wisconsin River, he had made a detour to pay her a visit, but her uncle, for reasons of his own, had contrived to prevent a meeting by telling him that she was not at home. Years had passed since then, and now her coming to California opened the prospect of a visit to

Yosemite. "You will require no photographs to know me," he writes. "The most sun-tanned and round-shouldered and bashful man of the crowd – if you catch me in a crowd – that's me! ... In all these years since I saw you I have been isolated; somehow I don't mould in with the rest of mankind and have become far more confusedly bashful than when I lived in the Mondell."

He recalls with amusement his odd appearance when he came to Prairie du Chien, and how he rebuked various members of the Mondell circle for irreverence and sins of one kind or another. And then shines forth a characteristic Muir trait – undying loyalty and devotion to his friends. For he adds: "something else I remember, Emily, – your kind words to me the first time I saw you. Kind words are likely to live in any human soil, but planted in the heart of a Scotchman they are absolutely immortal, and whatever Heaven may have in store for you in after years you have at least one friend while John Muir lives."

The subjoined letter to her, though apparently written hurriedly, is significant for its clear-cut and pungent defence of his mode of life and the effect which he believed it to have upon his character. Miss Pelton did not visit the Valley until June, 1873. In her party, which camped in Tenaya Canyon for nine days, were Mrs. Carr, A. Kellogg, botanist of the California Academy of Sciences, William Keith, the artist, and several others. Muir's acquaintanceship with Keith, begun on a previous visit to the Valley, speedily ripened into a devoted and lasting friendship.

The projected excursion with Professor LeConte, mentioned in the same letter, acquires significance in connection with the latter's publication of a paper on "Some Ancient Glaciers of the Sierra," read in September, 1872, before the California Academy of Sciences. In this paper Professor LeConte made the first published announcement of Muir's discovery of living glaciers in the Sierra Nevada. LeConte gave Muir full credit for this discovery, but the freedom with which the latter, in conversation as well as in his letters, poured out the results of his exploratory work before his scientific friends gave point to Mrs. Carr's fear that others, less scrupulous, might obtain the credit and reap the advantage of his glacial discoveries. She therefore urged him, as will appear later, to do his own publishing of his discoveries.

to Emily Pelton

Yosemite Valley, April 2nd, 1872

DEAR FRIEND EMILY

Your broad pages are received. You must never waste letter time in apologies for size. The more vast and prairie-like the better. But now for the business part of your coming. Be sure you let me know within a few days the time of your setting out so that I may be able to keep myself in a findable, discoverable place. I am, as perhaps I told you, engaged in the study of glaciers and mountain structure, etc., and I am often out alone for weeks where you couldn't find me. Moreover, I have a good many friends of every grade who will be here, all of whom have greater or lesser claims on my attention. With Professor LeConte I have made arrangements for a long scientific ramble back in the summits; also with Mrs. Carr. You will readily understand from these engagements and numerous other probabilities of visits, especially from scientific friends who almost always take me *out* of Yosemite, how important it is that I should know very nearly the time of your coming. I would like to have a week of naked, unoccupied time to spend with you and nothing but unavoidable, unescapable engagements will prevent me from having such a week.

If Mr. Knox would bring his team you could camp out, and the expense would be nothing, hardly, and you could make your headquarters at a cabin I am building. This would be much the best mode of travelling and of seeing the Valley. Independence is nowhere sweeter than in Yosemite. People who come here ought to abandon and forget all that is called business and duty, etc.; they should forget their individual existences, should forget they are born. They should as nearly as possible live the life of a particle of dust in the wind, or of a withered leaf in a whirlpool. They should come like thirsty sponges to imbibe without rule. It is blessed to lean fully and trustingly on Nature, to experience, by taking to her a pure heart and unartificial mind, the infinite tenderness and power of her love.

You mention the refining influences of society. Compared with the intense purity and cordiality and beauty of Nature, the most delicate refinements and cultures of civilization are gross barbarisms.

As for the rough vertical animals called men, who occur in and on these mountains like sticks of condensed filth, I am not in *contact* with them; I do not live with them. I live alone, or, rather, with the rocks and flowers and snows and blessed storms; I live in blessed mountain *light*, and love nothing less pure. You'll find me rough as the rocks and about the same colour – granite. But as for loss of pure mindedness that you seem to fear, come and see my teachers; come, see my Mountain Mother, and you will be at rest on that point.

We have had a glorious storm of the kind called earthquake. I've just been writing an account of it for the *New York Tribune* [May 7th, 1872]. It would seem strange that any portion of our perpendicular walls are left unshattered. It is delightful to be trotted and dumpled on our Mother's mountain knee. I hope we will be blessed with some more. The first shock of the morning of [March] 26th, at half-past two o'clock, was the most sublime storm I ever experienced.

Most cordially yours

JOHN MUIR

The above-mentioned earthquake was one of great intensity and made one of the memorable experiences of his life. He sent a description of it to the Boston Society of Natural History and to several friends.

Though I had never enjoyed a storm of this sort [he wrote], the thrilling motion could not be mistaken, and I ran out of my cabin, both glad and frightened, shouting, "A noble earthquake!" feeling sure I was going to learn something. The shocks were so violent and varied, and succeeded one another so closely, that I had to balance myself carefully in walking as if on the deck of a ship among waves, and it seemed impossible that the high cliffs of the valley could escape being shattered. In particular, I feared that the sheer-fronted Sentinel Rock, towering above my cabin, would be shaken down, and I took shelter back of a large yellow pine hoping that it might protect me from at least the smaller outbounding boulders. For a minute or two the shocks became more and more violent – flashing horizontal thrusts mixed with a few twists and battering, explosive, upheaving jolts – as if Nature were wrecking her Yosemite temple, and getting ready to build a better one.

It was on this occasion that he saw Eagle Rock on the south wall give way and fall into the Valley with a tremendous roar.

I saw it falling [writes Muir] in thousands of the great boulders I had so long been studying, pouring to the Valley floor in a free curve luminous with friction, making a terribly sublime spectacle – an arc of glowing passionate fire, fifteen hundred feet span, as true in form and as serene in beauty as a rainbow in the midst of the stupendous roaring rock-storm.

He was thrilled by the phenomenon, for he realised that by a fortunate chance he was enabled to witness the formation of a mountain talus, a process about which he had long been speculating.

Before the great boulders had fairly come to rest he was upon the new-born talus, listening to the grating, groaning noises with which the rocks were gradually settling into their places. His scientific interest in the phenomenon made him so attentive to even its slightest effects that all fear was banished, and he astounded his terrified fellow residents of Yosemite with his enthusiastic recital of his observations. They were ready to flee to the lowlands, leaving the keys of their premises in his hands, while he prepared to resume his glacial studies, armed with fresh clues to the origin of canyon taluses.

to Mrs. Ezra S. Carr

New Sentinel Hotel,
Yosemite Valley, [April, 1872]

Sunday night I was up in the moon among the lumined spray of the upper Falls. The lunar bows were glorious and the music Godful as ever. You will yet mingle amid the forms and voices of this peerless fall.

I wanted to have you spend two or three nights up there in full moon, and planned a small hut for you, but since the boisterous waving of the rocks, the danger seems forbidding, at least for you. We can go up there in the afternoon, spend an hour or two, and return.

I had a grand ramble in the deep snow outside the Valley, and discovered one beautiful truth concerning snow structure, and three concerning the forms of forest trees.

These earthquakes have made me immensely rich. I had long been aware of the life and gentle tenderness of the rocks, and instead of walking upon them as unfeeling surfaces, began to regard them as a transparent sky. Now they have spoken with audible voice and pulsed with common motion. This very instant, just as my pen reached "and" on the third line above, my cabin creaked with a sharp shock and the oil waved in my lamp.

We had several shocks last night. I would like to go somewhere on the west South American coast to study earthquakes. I think I could invent some experimental ...   [Rest of letter lost.]

to Mrs. Ezra S. Carr

New Sentinel Hotel
Yosemite Valley, April 23rd, 1872

DEAR MRS. CARR

Yours of April 9th and 15th, containing Ned's canoe and colonisation adventures came tonight. I feel that you are coming, and I will not hear any words preparatory of consolation for the unsupposable case of your non-appearance.

Come by way of Clark's, and spend a whole day or two in the Sequoias. Thence to Sentinel Dome and Glacier Point. From thence swoop to our meadows and groves *direct* by a trail now in course of construction which will be completed by the time the snow melts. This new trail will be the best in scenery and safety of five which enter the Valley. It leads from Glacier Point down the face of the mountain by an easy grade to a point back of Leidig's hotel, and has over half a dozen Inspiration Points.

I hear that Mr. Paregoy intends building a hotel at Glacier Point. If he does you should halt there for the night after leaving Clark's. If not, then stop at the present "Paregoy's" five or six miles south of the Valley at the Westfall Meadows – built since your visit. You might easily ride from Clark's to the Valley in a day, but a day among the silver firs and another about the glories of the Valley rim and settings is a "sma' request."

The snow is deep this year, and the regular Mariposa trail leading to Glacier Point, etc., will not be open before June. The Mariposa travel of May, and perhaps a week or so of June, will enter the Valley from Clark's by a sort of sneaking trail along the river canyon below the snow, but you must not come that way.

You may also enter the Valley via Little Yosemite and Nevada and Vernal Falls, by a trail constructed last season; also by Indian Canyon on the north side of the Valley by a trail now nearly completed. This last is a noble entrance, but perhaps not equal to the first. Whatever way you come we will travel all of these, up or down, and bear in mind that you must go among the summits in July or August. Bring no friends that will not go to these fountains beyond, or are uncastoffable. Calm thinkers like your Doctor, who first fed me with science, and LeConte are the kind of souls fit for the formation of human clouds adapted to this mountain sky. Nevertheless, I will rejoice beyond measure, though you come as a comet tailed with a whole misty town. Ned is a brave fellow. God bless him unspeakably and feed him with his own South American self.

I shall be most happy to know your Daggetts or anything that you call dear. I have not seen any of my *Tribune* letters, though I have written five or six. Send copy if you can.   Goodnight and love to all.   J. M.

to Miss Catharine Merrill

New Sentinel Hotel
Yosemite Valley, June 9th, 1872

CATHARINE MERRILL
MY DEAR FRIEND
I am very happy to hear your hand language once more, but in some places I am black and blue with your hurricane of scolding.

I |am| glad you so much enjoy your work (not scolding), but am sorry to hear of the languor which clearly speaks of struggles and long continued toil of nerve-exhausting kind. I hope you will not persist in self-sacrifice of so destructive a species. The sea will do you good; bathe in it and bask in sunshine and allow the pure and generous currents of universal uncolleged beauty to blow about your bones and about all the overworked wheels of your mind. I know very well how you toil and toil, striving against lassitude and the cloudy weather of discouraging cares with a brave heart, your efforts toned by the blessedness of doing good; but do not, I pray you, destroy your health. The Lord understands his business and has plenty of tools, and does not require over-exertion of any kind.

I wish you could come here and rest a year in the simple unmingled Love fountains of God. You would then return to your scholars with fresh truth gathered and absorbed from pines and waters and deep singing winds, and you would find that they all sang of fountain Love just as did Jesus Christ and all of pure God manifest in whatever form. You say that good men are "nearer to the heart of God than are woods and fields, rocks and waters" Such distinctions and measurements seem strange to me. Rocks and waters, etc., are words of God and so are men. We all flow from one fountain Soul. All are expressions of one Love. God does not appear, and flow out, only from narrow chinks and round bored wells here and there in favoured races and places, but He flows in grand undivided currents, shoreless and boundless over creeds and forms and all kinds of civilizations and peoples and beasts, saturating all and fountainising all.

You say some other things that I don't believe at all, but I have no room to say them nay; further – I don't stab the old grannies where I wasted so much time, the colleges of all kinds, "Christian" and common, West and Northwest, with their long tails of pretensions. I only said a few words of free sunshine, using the dim old clouds of learning for a background.

My love to Mina and Mrs. Moores and the dear younglings. The falls are in song gush and the light is balmed with summer love. Would I could send some. I shall be sure to keep you an open letter-road so that you can see your Merrill whom you all commit so confidingly to my care. Hoping that you will get strength by the sea and enjoy all the spiritual happiness you deserve.

I am ever cordially   Your friend

JOHN MUIR

to Mrs. Ezra S. Carr

New Sentinel Hotel, Yosemite Valley,
July 6th, [1872]

DEAR MRS. CARR

Yours of Tuesday eve, telling me of our Daggetts and Ned and Merrill Moores, has come. So has the lamp and the book. I have not yet tried the lamp, but it is splendid in shape and shines grand as gold.

The Lyell is just what I wanted. I think that your measure of the Daggetts is exactly right. As good as civilized people can be, they have grown to the top of town culture and have sent out some shoots half-gropingly into the spirit sky.

I am very glad to know that Ned is growing strong. Perhaps we may [see] South America together yet. I hope to see you come to your own of mountain fountains soon. Perhaps Mrs. Hutchings may go with us. You live so fully in my own life that I cannot realise that I have not yet seen you here. A year or two of waiting seems nothing.

Possibly I may be down on your coast this fall or next, for I want to see what relations the coast and coast mountains have to the Sierras. Also I want to go north and south along this range, and then among the basins and ranges eastward. My subject is expanding at a most unfollowable pace. I could write something with data already harvested, but I am not satisfied.

I have just returned from Hetch Hetchy with Mrs. [J. P.] Moore. Of course we had a glory and a fun – the two articles in about parallel columns of equal size. Meadows grassed and lillied head-high, spangled river reaches, and currentless pools, cascades countless and unpaintable in form and whiteness, groves that heaven all the Valley! You were with us in all our joy, and you will come again.

I am a little weary and half incline to truantism from mobs, however blessed, in some unfindable grove. I start in a few minutes for Clouds' Rest with Mr. and Mrs. Moore.

I am ever your friend

J. MUIR

to Mrs. Ezra S. Carr

New Sentinel Hotel, Yosemite Valley,
July 14th, 1872

DEAR MRS. CARR

Yours announcing Dr. [Asa] Gray is received. I have great longing for Gray whom I feel to be a great, progressive, unlimited man like Darwin and Huxley and Tyndall. I will be most glad to meet him. You are unweariable in your kindness to me, and you helm my fate more than all the world beside.

I am approaching a kind of fruiting time in this mountain work, and I want very much to see you. All say "*Write,*" but I don't know how or what; and, besides, I want to see North and South, and the inland basins and the sea-coast, and all the lake basins and the canyons, also the Alps of every country and the continental glaciers of Greenland, before I write the book we have been speaking of. All this will require a dozen years or twenty, and money. The question is, what will I write now, etc.? I have learned the alphabet of ice and mountain structure here, and I think I can read fast in other countries. I would let others write what I have read here, but that they make so damnable a hash of it and ruin so glorious a unit.

I miss the [J. P.] Moores because they were so cordial and kind to me. Mrs. Moore believes in ice and can preach it too. I wish you could bring Whitney and her together and tell me the fight. Mrs. Moore made the most sensible visit to our mountains of all comers I have known. Mr. Moore is a man who thinks and he took to this mountain structure like a pointer to partridges.... Talk to Mrs. Moore about Hetch Hetchy, etc. She knows it all from Hog Ranch to highest sea wave cascades, and higher, yet higher.

I ought not to fun away letter space in speaking to you. Yet I am weary and impractical and fit for nothing serious until I am tuned and toned by a few weeks of calm....

Farewell. I will see you and we will plan work and ease and days of holy mountain rest....

Remember me to Ned and all the boys, and to the Doctor, who ought to come hither with you.   Ever thine

JOHN MUIR

to Sarah Muir Galloway

Yosemite Valley, July 16th, 1872

DEAR SISTER SARAH

Your bundle composed of socks and letters has arrived, for which I am much indebted. I had not seen the *Tribune* letter you sent. I want you to see all I write, good or bad. I may some time write regularly for some journal or other. My scientific friends are clamorous for glaciers, etc.

I have had a great day in meeting Dr. Asa Gray, the first botanist in the world. My Boston friends made him know me before he came, and I expect a grand time with him. While waiting for Gray this afternoon on the mountain-side I climbed the Sentinel Rock, three thousand feet high. Here is an oak sprig from the top.

Merrill Moores came a couple of days ago to spend a few months with me. I am very happy, but have to see too many people for the successful prosecution of my studies.

Full moon lights all the groves and rocks and casts splendid masses of shade on meadow and wall. Visitors jar and noise, but Nature goes grandly and calmly over all confusion like winds over our domes....

I hope to see Agassiz this summer, and if I can get him away into the outside mountains among the old glacier wombs alone, I shall have a glorious time....

J. MUIR

During the latter part of July, Mrs. Carr, in one of her letters, suggested a way in which he might study the Coast Range with her Oakland home as a base.

This is what you are going to do [she writes]. After the harvest time is over, and the last bird plucked (I wish I could see some of your game birds; all that I see are sacred storks and ibises), you will pack up all your duds, ready to leave [Yosemite] two or more years, take your best horse and ride forth some clear September morning. You will live with us, and your horse at Moores near by, whenever you are not exploring the Coast Range. We will have some choice side trips ... You will pass the winter here, and meanwhile ways will open for you to go to South America. You will write up all your settled convictions, and put your cruder reflections in the form of notes and queries, not without scientific worth, and securing to yourself any advantage there may be in priority of observation. So writing, and studying, and visiting, the months will pass swiftly until your Valley home is filled again with colour and song. God will teach you, as He has taught me, that the dear places and the dearer souls are but tents of a night; we must move on and leave them, though it cost heart-breaks. Not those who cling to you, but those who walk apart, yet ever with you, are your true companions.

The proposed plan had for him one fatal defect. It revealed too patent a design to separate him from Yosemite and for this he was not ready. Here follows his reply:

to Mrs. Ezra S. Carr

Yosemite Valley, August 5th, 1872

DEAR MRS. CARR

Your letter telling me to catch my best glacier birds and come to you and the

Coast mountains only makes me the more anxious to see you, and if you cannot come up I will have to come down, if only for a talk. My birds are flying everywhere, into all mountains and plains all climes and times, and some are ducks in the sea, and I scarce know what to do about it. I must see the Coast Ranges and the coast, but I was thinking that a month or so might answer for the present, and then, instead of spending the winter in town, I would hide in Yosemite and write, or I thought I would pack up some meal and dried plums to some deep wind sheltered canyon back among the glaciers of the summits and write there and be ready to catch any whisper of ice and snow in these highest storms.

You anticipate all the bends and falls and rapids and cascades of my mountain life and I know that you say truly about my companions being those who live with me in the same sky, whether in reach of hand or only of spiritual contact, which is the most real contact of all. I am learning to live close to the lives of my friends without ever seeing them. No miles of any measurement can separate your soul from mine.

[Part of the letter missing.]

The Valley is full of sun, but glorious Sierras are piled above the South Dome and Starr King. I mean the bossy cumuli that are daily upheaved at this season, making a cloud period yet grander than the rock-sculpturing, Yosemite making, forest-planting glacial period. Yesterday we had our first midday shower; the pines waved gloriously at its approach, the woodpeckers beat about as if alarmed, but the humming-bird moths thought the cloud shadows belonged to evening and came down to eat among the mints. All the firs and rocks of Starr King were bathily dripped before the Valley was vouchsafed a single drop. After the splendid blessing the afternoon was veiled in calm clouds, and one of intensely beautiful pattern and gorgeously irised was stationed over Eagle Rock at the sunset. Farewell....

As ever... Your friend

JOHN MUIR

Instead of coming down to Oakland he writes to her three weeks later, "My horse and bread, etc., are ready for upward. I returned three days ago from Mounts Lyell, McClure, and Hoffmann. I spent three days on a glacier up there planting stakes, etc. This time I go to the Merced group, one of whose mountains shelters a glacier.... Ink cannot tell the glow that lights me at this moment in turning to the mountains. I feel strong to leap Yosemite walls at a bound. Hotels and human impurity will be far below. I will fuse in spirit skies."

Meanwhile Muir was enlarging the circle of his scientific friends and strengthening the bonds that united him to old ones. Professor Asa Gray had returned to Cambridge, enthusiastic about his Yosemite excursions, and sent Muir a list of live plants he wanted for the Botanic Garden "at the rate of a cigar box full of each." The latter was still nursing disappointment that

Gray had not accompanied him on an excursion into the high mountains north of Yosemite. "If you and Mrs. Gray," he writes, "had only exposed yourselves to the plants and rocks and waters and glaciers of our glorious High Sierra, I would have been content to have you return to your Cambridge classes and to all of the just and proper ding dong of civilization."

Mrs. Carr meanwhile was acting as an intermediary between Muir and Professor Louis Agassiz who was making a brief sojourn in San Francisco, and was then regarded as the leading authority on glaciation. "I sent to Agassiz," she writes, "the [letter] you enclosed. Either that or something from the papers (*New York Tribune* clippings) excited him to say with great warmth, 'Muir is studying to greater purpose and with greater results than any one else has done.' LeConte told me he spoke of your work with enthusiasm."

Among these new friends was also the noted botanist John Torrey, who, writing in September, 1872, from the home of his friend Dr. Engelmann in St. Louis, expressed his great satisfaction over the pleasant and instructive hours he spent with Muir in Yosemite, and gave an interesting account of his visit with Dr. Parry at Empire. It was, as Muir noted on the envelope of Torrey's letter, "his last Yosemite trip," for he died the following March. "That little Botrychium," adds Torrey in reference to a plant Muir had sent him, "looks peculiar and I will report on it when I go home." He never did, and twenty-six years elapsed before any one else found a plant of this genus in the High Sierra.

From the month of October of this same year, 1872, dates the beginning of Muir's devoted friendship with the artist William Keith, who, with a fellow artist by the name of Irwin, came to Yosemite with a letter of introduction from Mrs. Carr. "I commission Mr. Irwin," writes the latter, "to sketch you in your hay-rope suspenders, etc., against the day when you are famous and carry all the letters of the alphabet as a tail to your literary kites. . . . The Agassizes God bless them, go today, taking some of your glacierest letters, and the slip from the *New York Tribune* containing 'A Glacier's Death,' for reading on the way."

And so these letters were lost to the purposes of this biography. But the following one, in which he gives the first full account of his discovery of living glaciers in the Sierra Nevada, has fortunately survived the accidents of time.

to Mrs. Ezra S. Carr

Yosemite Valley, October 8th, 1872

DEAR MRS. CARR

Here we are again, and here is your letter of September 24th. I got down last eve, and boo! was I not weary? Besides pushing through the rough upper half of the great Tuolumne Canyon, have climbed more than twenty-four thousand feet in these ten days! – three times to the top of the glacieret of Mount Hoff[mann] and once to Mounts Lyell and McClure.

Have bagged a quantity of Tuolumne rocks sufficient to build a dozen Yosemites. Strips of cascades longer than ever, lacy or smooth, and white as pressed snow. A glacier basin with ten glassy lakes set all near together like eggs in a nest. Three El Capitans and a couple of Tissiacks. Canyons glorious with yellows and reds of mountain maple and aspen and honeysuckle and ash, and new music immeasurable from strange waters and winds, and glaciers, too, flowing and grinding, alive as any on earth. Shall I pull you out some?

Here is a clean white-skinned glacier from the back of McClure with glassy emerald flesh and singing crystal blood, all bright and pure as a sky, yet handling mud and stone like a navvy, building moraines like a plodding Irishman. Here is a cascade two hundred feet wide, half a mile long, glancing this way and that, filled with bounce and dance and joyous hurrah, yet earnest as a tempest, and singing like angels loose on a frolic from heaven. And here [are] more cascades and more – broad and flat like clouds, and fringed like flowing hair, and falls erect as Pines, and lakes like glowing eyes. And here are visions, too, and dreams, and a splendid set of ghosts, too many for ink and narrow paper....

Professor [Samuel] Kneeland, Secretary of the Massachusetts Institute of Technology, gathered some letters I sent to Runkle and that *Tribune* letter and hashed them into a compost called a paper for the Boston Society of Natural History and gave me credit for all of the smaller sayings and doings, and stole the broadest truth to himself. I have the proof sheets of the paper and will show them to you some time....

As for the living "Glaciers of the Sierra," here is what I have learned concerning them. You will have the first chalice to steal, for I have just concluded my experiments on them for the season and have not yet cast them at any of the great professors or presidents.

One of the yellow days of last October, [1871], when I was among the mountains of the Merced group, following the footprints of the ancient glaciers that once flowed grandly from their ample fountains, reading what I could of their history as written in moraines and canyons and lakes and carved rocks, I came upon a small stream that was carrying mud of a kind I had not before seen. In a calm place where the stream widened I collected some of this mud and observed that it was entirely mineral in composition and fine as flour – like mud from a fine grit grindstone. Before I had time to reason I said, "Glacier mud! – mountain meal!"

Then I observed that this muddy stream issued from a bank of fresh-quarried stones and dirt that was sixty or seventy feet in height. This I at once took to be a moraine. In climbing to the top of it I was struck with the steepness of its slope and with its raw, unsettled, plantless, new-born appearance. The slightest touch started blocks of red and black slate, followed by a rattling train of smaller stones and sand and a cloud of the dry dust of mud, the whole moraine being as free from lichens and weather-stains as if dug from the mountain that very day.

When I had scrambled to the top of the moraine I saw what seemed to be a huge snowbank four or five hundred yards in length by half a mile in width. Embedded in its stained and furrowed surface were stones and dirt like that of which the moraine was built. Dirtstained lines curved across the snowbank from side to side, and when I observed that these curved lines coincided with the curved moraine, and that the stones and dirt were most abundant near the bottom of the bank, I shouted, "A living glacier!" These bent dirt lines show that the ice is flowing in its different parts with unequal velocity, and these embedded stones are journeying down to be built into the moraine, and they gradually become more abundant as they approach the moraine because there the motion is slower.

On traversing my new-found glacier I came to a crevasse down a wide and jagged portion of which I succeeded in making my way, and discovered that my so-called snowbank was clear green ice, and comparing the form of the basin which it occupied with similar adjacent basins that were empty I was led to the opinion that this glacier was several hundred feet in depth.

Then I went to the "snowbanks" of Mounts Lyell and McClure and believed that they also were true glaciers and that a dozen other snowbanks seen from the summit of Mount Lyell, crouching in shadow, were glaciers living as any in the world and busily engaged in completing that vast work of mountain-making accomplished by their giant relatives now dead, which, united and continuous, covered all the range from summit to sea like a sky.

But, although I was myself thus fully satisfied concerning the real nature of these ice masses, I found that my friends* regarded my deductions and statements with distrust. Therefore I determined to collect proofs of the common measured arithmetical kind.

On the 21st of August last, I planted five stakes in the glacier of Mount McClure which is situated east of Yosemite Valley near the summit of the Range. Four of these stakes were extended across the glacier in a straight line, from the east side to a point near the middle of the glacier. The first stake was planted about twenty-five yards from the east bank of the glacier, the second, ninety-four yards, the third, one hundred and fifty-two, and the fourth, two hundred and twenty-five yards. The positions of these stakes were determined by sighting across from bank to bank past a plumb-line made of a stone and a black horsehair.

On observing my stakes on the 6th of October, or in forty-six days after being planted, I found that stake No. 1 had been carried downstream eleven inches, No. 2, eighteen inches, No. 3, thirty-four, No. 4, forty-seven inches. As stake No. 4 was near the middle of the glacier, perhaps it was not far from the point of maximum velocity – forty-seven inches in forty-six days, or one inch per day. Stake No. 5 was planted about midway between the head of the glacier and stake No. 4. Its motion I found to be in forty-six days forty inches.

* An undated fragmentary letter of 1872, addressed to Mrs. Carr, contains the following passage: "I had a good letter from LeConte. He evidently doesn't know what to think of the huge lumps of ice that I sent him. I don't wonder at his cautious withholding of judgment. When my Mountain Mother first told me the tale I could hardly dare to believe either and kept saying, 'What?' like a child half asleep."

Thus these ice masses are seen to possess the true glacial motion. Their surfaces are striped with bent dirt bands. Their surfaces are bulged and undulated by inequalities in the bottom of their basins, causing an upward and downward swedging corresponding to the horizontal swedging as indicated by the curved dirt bands.

The Mount McClure glacier is about one half mile in length and about the same in width at the broadest place. It is crevassed on the southeast corner. The crevasse runs about southeast and northeast and is several hundred yards in length. Its width is nowhere more than one foot.

The Mount Lyell glacier, separate from that of McClure by a narrow crest, is about a mile in width by a mile in length.

I have planted stakes in the glacier of Red Mountain also, but have not yet observed them.

The Sierras adjacent to the Yosemite Valley are composed of slabs of granite set on edge at right angles to the direction of the range, or about N. 30° E., S. 30° W. Also lines of cleavage cross these, running nearly parallel with the main range. Also the granite of this region has a horizontal cleavage or stratification. The first mentioned of these lines have the fullest development, and give direction and character to many valleys and canyons and determine the principal features of many rock forms. No matter how hard and domed and homogeneous the granite may be, it still possesses these lines of cleavage, which require only simple conditions of moisture, time, etc., for their development. But I am not ready to discuss the origin of these planes of cleavage which make this granite so denudable, nor their full significance with regard to mountain structure in general. I will only say here that oftentimes the granite contained between two of these N. 30° E. planes is softer than that outside and has been denuded, leaving vertical walls as determined by the direction of the cleavage, thus giving rise to those narrow slotted canyons called "Devil's slides," "Devil's lanes," "Devil's gateways," etc.

In many places in the higher portions of the Sierra these slotted canyons are filled with "snow," which I thought might prove to be ice – might prove to be living glaciers still engaged in cutting into the mountains like endless saws.

To decide this question on the 23rd of August last, I set two stakes in the narrow slot glacier of Mount Hoffmann, marking their position by sighting across from wall to wall, as I did on the McClure glacier, but on visiting them a month afterwards I found that they had been melted out, and I was unable to decide anything with any considerable degree of accuracy.

On the 4th of October last I stretched a small trout-line across the glacier, fastening both ends in the solid banks, which at this place were only sixteen feet apart. I set a short inflexible stake in the ice so as just to touch the tightly drawn line, by which means I was enabled to measure the flow of the glacier with great exactness.

Examining this stake in twenty-four hours after setting it, I found that it had been carried down about three sixteenths of an inch. At the end of four days I again examined it, and found that the whole downward motion was thirteen sixteenths of an inch, showing that the flow of this glacieret was perfectly regular.

In accounting for these narrow lane canyons so common here, I had always referred them to ice action in connection with special conditions of cleavage, and I was gratified to find that their formation was still going on. This Hoffmann glacieret is about one thousand feet long by fifteen to thirty feet wide, and perhaps about one hundred feet deep in deepest places.

Now, then, Mrs. Carr, I must hasten back to the mountains. I'll go tomorrow.

[JOHN MUIR]

This letter forms the kernel of an article, "Living Glaciers of California," which he published in the *Overland Monthly* of December, 1872. The following January it was reprinted in Silliman's *Journal of Science and Arts*, and so was brought to the attention of a wide circle of scientific men. The blank stubbornness of the prejudices by which Muir was opposed at this time is revealed in the fact that ten years after Muir had published his discovery, and the facts had been confirmed by Professor LeConte and accepted by leading geologists, Professor Whitney asserted in one of his papers, "It may be stated that there are no glaciers at all in the Sierra Nevada. . . . There are certainly none in the higher portions of the Sierra Nevada or Rocky Mountains, these most elevated regions having been sufficiently explored to ascertain that fact." When Israel C. Russell, of the United States Geological Survey, wrote his treatise *Glaciers of North America*, giving Muir full credit for his discovery, he called attention to this curiously dogmatic statement, and to the fact that Clarence King "also rejected Mr. Muir's observations as is shown by several emphatic passages in his report on the exploration of the fortieth parallel."

In the following letter, of which the first part is missing, Muir records some observations regarding the amount of erosion accomplished by water, as compared with ice, since the close of the last glacial epoch. Attention should be called also to Muir's observation that, viewed from mountain tops, the outlines of moraines about Yosemite are marked by fir forests.

to Mrs. Ezra S. Carr

Autumn, [1872]

. . . The bottom portion of the foregoing section, with perpendicular sides is here about two feet in depth and was cut by the water. The Nevada here *never was* more than four or five feet deep, and all of the bank records of all the upper streams say the same thing of the absence of great floods.

The entire region above Yosemite and as far down as the bottom of

Yosemite has scarcely been touched by any other denudation than that of ice. Perhaps all of the post-glacial denudation of every kind would not average an inch in depth for the whole region.

Yosemite and Hetch Hetchy are lake basins filled with sand and the matter of moraines washed from the upper canyons. The Yosemite ice in escaping from the Yosemite basin was compelled to flow upward a considerable height on both sides of the bottom walls of the Valley. The canyon below the Valley is very crooked and very narrow, and the Yosemite glacier flowed across all of its crooks and high above its walls without paying any compliance to it, thus: [drawing]. The light lines show the direction of the ice current.*

In going up any of the principal Yosemite streams, lakes in all stages of decay are found in great abundance regularly becoming younger until we reach the almost countless gems of the summits with scarce an inch of carex upon their shallow sandy borders, and with their bottoms still bright with the polish of ice. Upon the Nevada and its branches there are not fewer than a hundred of these glacial lakes from a mile to a hundred yards in diameter, with countless glistening pondlets not much larger than moons.

All of the grand fir forests about the Valley are planted upon moraines and from any of the mountain tops the shape and extent of the neighbouring moraines may always be surely determined by the firs growing upon them.

Some pines will grow upon shallow sand and crumbling granite, but those luxuriant forests of the silver firs are always upon a generous bed of glacial drift. I discovered a moraine with smooth pebbles upon a shoulder of the South Dome, and upon every part of the Yosemite upper and lower walls.

I am surprised to find that *water* has had so little to do with mountain structure here. Whitney says that there is no proof that glaciers ever flowed in this Valley, yet its walls have not been eroded to the depth of an inch since the ice left it, and glacial action is glaringly apparent many miles below the Valley.

[JOHN MUIR]

In concluding this chapter a few comments are in place on the historical significance of the foregoing series of letters and published communications from the pen of John Muir. One writer, mistaking the facts, has claimed for Clarence King the honour of having been "the first to point out the prominent role which the ice of the glacial epochs must have played in the elaboration of the Yosemite Valley." For two decisive reasons this claim is void. In the first place, King believed that the ice gave nothing to the Valley but a little polishing, and in the next place he did not himself publish anything upon the subject until after William Phipps Blake and John Muir were already in print with their observations. Nor am I able to find that King, when he did

---

* The text of this letter is taken from a typewritten copy of the original which has been lost. Hence it is not possible to reproduce the drawings which was a part of the original letter.

publish, added any important scientific item to what Muir had already said more fully in his *Tribune* article. Since Blake, as previously noted, attributed the erosion of Yosemite to water pouring down from glaciers above the Valley, and not to the abrasion of glaciers themselves, Muir stands out alone as the first one who demonstrated the part that ice played in the making of Yosemite. He, too, was the first one to point out how the glacial action was controlled by the peculiar structure and jointing of the granite. Others who have written upon this feature have in good part only followed in his footsteps.

It would have been interesting if Clarence King and John Muir could have been brought together for a discussion of their theories and observations. But so far as we are able to ascertain they never met personally. From Whitney's report *The Geology of the Sierra Nevada*, Muir knew that King had noted the existence of moraines in Yosemite Valley. But Whitney, in recording the fact, treated King's observations somewhat cavalierly, and four years later stigmatised them as erroneous. Thereafter the decidedly adverse views of his chief probably prevented King from leaving the question of glacial action and the origin of Yosemite open for further investigation. At any rate, six years later King, in his article entitled "The Range," expressly exempts Yosemite from formation by streams and ice, and classifies it as one of those "most impressive passages of the Sierra Valleys that are actual ruptures of the rock; either the engulfment of masses of great size, as Professor Whitney supposes in explanation of the peculiar form of Yosemite, or a splitting asunder in yawning cracks!" The latter was apparently King's own view.

Muir regarded his *Tribune* article in 1871 as only a preliminary statement of his views, continuing meanwhile his study and exploration of the Sierra Nevada, with Yosemite as his base, until 1874. In that year he published, in the *Overland Monthly*, his series of articles under the general title of "Studies in the Sierra."* These articles were a remarkable achievement for the time when they were written and contain the condensed results of five years of careful and detailed field-work. From 1869 to 1874 he had spent the whole of every summer season in the High Sierra, reading, as he put it, "the glacial manuscripts of God." Thereafter these studies were continued intermittently for another five years, so that in 1879 he could say that he had devoted ten years of his life to the interpretation of the Sierra Nevada. Numerous notebooks and sketches attest his industry as well as the minuteness and care with which he went over every part of the region.

* The titles of the individual "Studies"are: 1. "Mountain Sculpture," May, 1874; 2. "Origin of Yosemite Valleys," June, 1874; 3. "Ancient Glaciers and their Pathways," July, 1874; 4. "Glacial Denudation," August, 1874; 5. "Post-Glacial Denudation," November, 1874; 6. "Formation of Soils," December, 1874; 7. "Mountain-Building," January, 1875. Reprinted with the inclusion of Muir's typographical corrections, in the *Sierra Club Bulletin*, Vols. IX-XI (1915-21) [and on pp. 389–481 in this book]. For a convenient summary of Muir's views on Yosemite glaciation the reader is referred to *The Yosemite* (1912) [collected in *John Muir: the Eight Wilderness/Discovery Books*].

When the Sierra Club began to republish Muir's "Studies in the Sierra," the noted geologist E. C. Andrews, of the Geological Survey of Australia, wrote to Secretary William E. Colby:

> John Muir's note on glacial action is very fine indeed. In Muir you had a man in America long ago who explained the action of ice-rivers, and it was really quite unnecessary to have waited until Henry Gannett made his great rediscovery or, rather, belated contribution to glacial studies. John Muir evidently was not understood in his generation, but he will surely come to his own now, and he will become one of the "Immortals" – one who illustrated the force of the passages, "Blessed are the meek, for they shall inherit the earth," and "Blessed are the pure in heart, for they shall see God.". . . Had I had access to the treasure house of knowledge afforded by the Sierra Club's reprint of Muir's notes, I would have written a much better note on "An Excursion to the Yosemite" in 1910, as I would have had a much larger number of valuable facts to draw upon than I had as a result of my limited observations alone.

It is interesting to compare this retrospective tribute with a forward-looking one in a paper read before the Rhode Island Historical Society, in 1872. The writer, John Erastus Lester, met Muir in Yosemite and refers to him as one, "who, Hugh Miller like, is studying the rocks in and around the Valley. . . . He is by himself pursuing a course of geological studies, and is making careful drawings of different parts of the gorge. No doubt he is more thoroughly acquainted with this Valley than any one else. He has been far up the Sierras where glaciers are now in action, ploughing deep depressions in the mountains. He has made a critical examination of the superincumbent rocks, and already has much material upon which to form a correct theory."

Muir did not take up the question as to what the physical contours of the Yosemite region were before the last glacial epoch. In assuming that they were comparatively simple, many competent to form a judgment think he is more likely to have been right than those who speculate about a pre-glacial Yosemite. As for the doctrine of two distinct glaciations of the Sierra Nevada, recently advanced, most students of the question probably will agree with Professor Lawson that this is a theory that "must be subjected to much more critical study before it can be accepted by geologists as an established fact." In evaluating Muir's work it must be borne in mind that he was contending against a theory which eliminated glaciers altogether from the causes that led to the formation of Yosemite. To have injected into his disproof of that theory speculations about a pre-glacial Yosemite would only have weakened, in his days, the penetrative power of his argument.

Now that time has mellowed the issues that once were so hotly debated, and death has removed the actors in the explorers' drama to that bourn whence no traveller returns, we may attempt the task of calmly assessing the originality and importance of the work which these early investigators have severally done. This is not the place to go into details, although we have looked into the work of each of these men with care. But even in the light of the facts presented it will, I think, be conceded without question that Muir was not only the first, but the only one who has presented a reasoned and systematic account of the glaciation of the Sierra Nevada, and who recognised the fact that the origin of Yosemite Valley cannot be separated from the origin of similar Yosemites in the Sierra Nevada. Indeed, the very use of the word "yosemite" in the generic sense was originated by him, and as such contains the essence of his denial of Whitney's and King's assumption that the Valley was of unique cataclysmic origin. In his main contention he was right, and the extent to which his minor conclusions may be modified by advancing geological science is a question quite apart from the credit that belongs to him as the greatest of the pioneer students of the Yosemite problem.

To one who now looks back upon Muir's glacial explorations through his letters, the practical profit of these years of intense preoccupation and activity may seem disproportionately small. But it is all a matter of time and scale and the kind of values for which one is looking. As Sir E. Ray Lankester says in his *Diversions of a Naturalist*, a man's pursuit of science has been sufficiently profitable if "it has given him a new and unassailable outlook on all things both great and small. Science commends itself to us as does Honesty and as does great Art and all fine thought and deed – not as a policy yielding material profits, but because it satisfies man's soul."

Muir's letters show that these deeper satisfactions of the soul were his in full measure during these years. There were those among his friends who again and again in their letters expressed their longing for his peace of mind. "I can see you sitting, reading this," wrote Thérèse Yelverton in 1872, "in some quiet spot in the evening, with all nature as calm and still as your own heart. I used to envy you that, for mine will not be still, but is restless and unquiet." To all such longings he could but say in one form or another, "Camp out among the grass and gentians of glacier meadows, in craggy garden nooks full of Nature's darlings. Climb the mountains and get their good tidings. Nature's peace will flow into you as sunshine flows into trees. The winds will blow their own freshness into you, and the storms their energy, while cares will drop off like autumn leaves."

CHAPTER TEN

Yosemite and Beyond 1872–1873

PERHAPS IT IS natural that so picturesque a personality as John Muir should become a magnet for legends. Several are already afloat in the Valley he loved, and two of them are particularly baseless and absurd. The first is a canard about a sawmill by means of which he is said to have denuded the Valley of trees. It was a tale set afoot during the Hetch Hetchy controversy when his opponents were only too anxious to discredit him in the eyes of the public. The fact that Muir sawed only fallen timber has already been set forth in another connection and requires no further statement. The second concerns the place of his former habitation in the Valley. It owes its origin, no doubt, to the desire of local guides to gratify the curiosity of visitors who wish to see some particular spot that has associations with John Muir.

In a secluded, umbrageous tangle of alders and azaleas, on the spit of land formed by the confluence of Tenaya Creek with the Merced, stands what at first glance looks like the remnants of a log cabin. Examination reveals the fact that there never had been a floor or windows; that it was never more than partly roofed and too low for a man to stand comfortably erect, while the opening which should serve as a door is only three feet high. It is all that remains of the sheep corral of John Lamon, the earliest inhabitant of the Valley. The myth-making faculty of the local guide has glorified it as "Muir's Lost Cabin," and as such it has been pointed out to great numbers of eager sight-seers.

But there is no mystery about the two cabins which Muir erected for himself in Yosemite. The places where they stood are known, although not a vestige of the original structures remains. The first he erected late in 1869 near the lower Yosemite Falls, and the site is now indicated by a bronze plate on a glacial boulder. He left it in the autumn of 1871 to take up his abode at Black's Hotel under the shadow of Sentinel Rock. But during the spring and summer of 1872 he erected for himself a log cabin in a clump of dogwood bushes, near the Royal Arches, on the banks of the Merced. The precise locality is to be sought at the point where the Merced approaches closest to the Royal Arches, and in a bold curve swings southward again across the Valley. In the same neighbourhood Lamon had also built his winter cabin. During the cold season of the year when the south side of the

Valley is wrapped in the frosty shadows of its high walls, the sun shines obliquely against the talus slopes of the north side and generates a grateful warmth. Here, then was Muir's second home in Yosemite Valley – one, however, that he seems to have occupied very little after 1874. The survival of Lamon's old corral in the immediate neighbourhood appears to have led to its identification with this last of Muir's cabins. The following winter letters of 1872 probably were written from there. Asa Gray's visit doubtless had given new stimulus to his study of the Yosemite flora, though in the absence of descriptive botanical handbooks he had great difficulty in determining the species.

to J. B. McChesney

Yosemite, December 10th, 1872

DEAR McCHESNEY

Yours of November 30th is here. Many thanks for the plants, though I am not much wiser. I knew the generic names of the first three. Only two are fully named. I suppose that the specimens I sent were too small and fragmentary to be determined with certainty. If I could only have access to books containing these plants I could easily name them. I have read Tyndall's *Hours of Exercise [in the Alps]*. Tyndall is a true man, with eyes that can see far down into the fountain truths of nature.

I am glad to know that you miss no opportunity in seeking Nature's altars. May she be good to you and feed your soul while you labour amid those Oakland wastes of civilization. I love [the] ocean as I do the mountains – indeed the mountains are an ocean with harder waves than yours.

You must be very happy in communion with so many kindred minds. I hope to know [Charles Warren] Stoddard some day. Tell him that I am going to build a nest and that it will always be open to him. Come next year, all of you. Come to these purest of terrestrial fountains. Come and receive baptism and absolution from civilized sins. You were but sprinkled last year. Come and be immersed! You have never seen our Valley with her jewels on, never seen her flowers of snow.

A few days ago many a flower ripened in the fields of air and they have fallen to us. All the trees and the bushes are flowered beyond summer, bowed down in snow bloom and all the rocks are buried. The day after the "storm" (a most damnable name for the flowering of the clouds) I lay out on the meadow to eat a grand meal of new-made beauty, and about midday I suddenly wanted the outside mountains, and so cast off my coat and ran up towards Glacier Point. I soon was near [the] top, and was very hungry for the view that was so grandly mingled and covered with snow and sky, but the snow was now more than ten feet deep and dusty and light as winter fog. I tried to wallow and swim it, but the slope was so steep that I always fell back and sank out of sight, and I was fully baffled. I had a glorious slide downwards.

Hawthorne speaks of the spirituality of locomotive railroad travel, but this *balmy* slide in the mealy snow out-spiritualised all other motions that I ever made in space.

> Farewell, write again. I am lonely.
>
> [JOHN MUIR]

During the interval between this and the next letter he made a rapid trip to Oakland in order to forward some literary plans in consultation with Mrs. Carr and others. On this occasion he met Edward Rowland Sill. In returning to Yosemite he walked from Turlock via Hopeton and Coulterville. The excursion to Clouds Rest described in his letter to Gray came as the conclusion of this return walk which included a very adventurous first climb through the Tenaya Canyon, and which forms the subject of a long letter to Mrs. Carr, published under the title of "A Geologist's Winter Walk". This very characteristic letter, in which he relates how he punished his "ill behaved bones" for allowing themselves to be demoralised by even a brief sojourn in "civilization," will be found in its completest form in *Steep Trails*. In spite of what Muir characterised as the "angular factiness of his pursuits," Dr. Gray was found to have carefully preserved the following and other Muir letters at the Gray Herbarium in Cambridge.

to Asa Gray

Yosemite Valley, December 18th, 1872

MY DEAR GRAY

I received the last of your notes two days ago, announcing the arrival of the ferns. You speak of three boxes of Primula. I sent seven or eight.

I had some measurements to make about the throat of the South Dome, so yesterday I climbed there, and then ran up to Clouds Rest for your Primulas, and as I stuffed them in big sods into a sack, I said, "Now I wonder what mouthfuls this size will accomplish for the Doctor's primrose hunger." Before filling your sack I witnessed one of the most glorious of our mountain sunsets; not one of the assembled mountains seemed remote – all had ceased their labour of beauty and gathered around their parent sun to receive the evening blessing, and waiting angels could not be more solemnly hushed. The sun himself seemed to have reached a higher life as if he had died and only his soul were glowing with rayless, bodiless *Light*, and as Christ to his disciples, so this departing sun soul said to every precious beast, to every pine and weed, to every stream and mountain, "My peace I give unto you."

I ran home in the moonlight with your sack of roses slung on my shoulder by a buckskin string – down through the junipers, down through the firs, now in black shadow, now in white light, past great South Dome white as the moon, past spirit-like Nevada, past Pywiack, through the groves of

Illilouette and spiry pines of the open valley, star crystals sparkling above, frost crystals beneath, and rays of spirit beaming everywhere.

I reached home a trifle weary, but could have wished so Godful a walk some miles and hours longer, and as I slid your roses off my shoulder I said, "This is one of the big round ripe days that so fatten our lives – so much of sun on one side, so much of moon on the other."

I have a rare chance of getting your plants packed out of the Valley tomorrow, and so have determined to send all together with a few seeds in a box by Wells Fargo Express. The books, both Hutchings' and mine, are along all right. Many thanks. I am hard at work on dead glaciers.

I am very cordially

Your friend

JOHN MUIR

to J. B. McChesney

Yosemite Valley, December 20th, 1872

MY DEAR McCHESNEY

Among all the souls which shine upon my eye up from that dim and distant Oakland none is of purer ray than your own, and living or dying, in this land or in that, I shall never cease to thank God for friends like you.

My excursion down into that befogged jungle of human plants in which you manage to live and love forms a far more notable chapter in my personal history than any of you can comprehend, and now that I am warm again, safe nestled in mountain ether, I seem to have returned to life from a strange and half-remembered death.

Here many a thought comes crowding to my page, but I must hush them back, for they would overcrowd a thousand letters. So drawing a long sigh I must content myself with saying 'thank you' for all your kindness, and leave you to eat the good brown bread of your little hills, and whatsoever of God you can find there, until your angel shall again guide you to the clean fountains of the Sierras.

Remember me to all your family and to Kelsey and any of my friends you chance to see – Miss Brigham, Sill, and all the rest. Kiss your Alice some extra times for me. She is the sweetest flake of childhood I found in all your town, and she comes back to me in form and voice and in touch too, with most living vividness.

Farewell. I am

Ever your friend

JOHN MUIR

One of the gifts that came to his cabin at Christmas time was a beautiful lamp from a friend in Chicago, to whom he addressed the following letter in acknowledgment:

to Mrs. Kate N. Daggett

Yosemite Valley, December 30th, 1872

[Salutation torn off.]

I have just this minute for the first time lighted your elegant lamp, and I send you again most cordial thanks for so precious a gift.

This is the first St. Germain lamp I have seen, and it is certainly the most beautiful of all light fountains. Its forms have been composed by a true artist. Its many curves blend into song with scarce a discordant tone. The trill around the base of the chimney is all that my eye-ear dislikes.

The massive finely moulded foundation glows like an ice-polished dome, and the grateful green of the shade is like that of high glacier lakes. If among the multitude of articles that now enter a human home there be one that deserves to be crowned with beauty above everything else, it is the fountain of light. The poet is the only workman capable of making a candlestick.

It is delightful to observe how steadily God-born beauty is flowing into all the handiwork of man. Nature is insinuating herself into every pore of humanity, and it is oozing out in forms that are constantly becoming less and less impure, and those forms of purer and more direct Godfulness are coming not only from the study cells of the painter and architect and art poets in general recognised as such, but they are flowing from the workshop from the foundry and the forge.

I know little of men, seeing them only afar off and in the lump, but standing as I now do on the mountain-side and contemplating the various hives of industry among civilizations old and new, all looming on my vision, dim in the great sea-divided distances, I have this one big, well-defined faith for humanity as a workman, that the time is coming when every "article of manufacture" will be as purely a work of God as are these mountains and pine trees and bonnie loving flowers.

I only meant to say you another warm thank you, but the fresh dewy beauty of your sunrise lamp conjured and loosened these thoughts and sent them down to my page, as rain and frost loosen and send down trains of rattling rough-angled rocks to Yosemite meadows.

I suppose our dear Mrs. Carr has told you of the eclipse of my life, years ago when my eyes were quenched just at the spring-dawn of summer when the voice of the bluebird began to appear mingled with the first flower-words of Erigenia and Anemone. But though in that terrible darkness I died to light, I lived again, and God who is Light has led me tenderly from light to light to the shoreless ocean of rayless beamless Spirit Light that bathes these holy mountains.

[JOHN MUIR]

The earlier writings of John Ruskin were at this time widely read and discussed both in England and in America, and Muir, also, was a deeply interested reader. But he took exception to the unqualified admiration with which some of his friends accepted Ruskinian ideas. In the following letter we have a brief but searching critique, from his point of view, of the dualism and artificiality of Ruskin's nature philosophy.

to J. B. McChesney

Yosemite Valley, January 10th, 1873

DEAR McCHESNEY

I have just finished a ramble through the handsome gardens of Ruskin that you gave me. Page after page is studded with flowers like a glacier meadow, and most of his chapters of hill and dale make a handsome landscape in spite of his numberless boundaries and human-carved rocks.

Few of our modern writers are so strikingly suggestive as Ruskin. His pungent steel-tempered sentences compel one to think, and his errors and absurdities are so clearly expressed that they do good rather than harm.

Ruskin is great, but not a great man – only a great ready-to-burst bud of a man. He is chained and tethered, not like the stars, by Nature's own laws, but by ropes and chains manufactured in the mills and forges of conventions, and although they are made of good material and are so transparent in places as to be well-nigh invisible, and he roams as if loose over this world and what he takes to be the next, yet after all one never can feel that he is free. His widest world, his highest sky, is enclosed by a hard definite shell making one think of a mouse beneath a huge bellglass, so huge that it does not feel its bounds. The bellglass underneath which Ruskin lives and moves and brandishes his verbal spears is made of the heaviest and most opaque *stuff* in the universe – a thousand times denser than hammered steel.

There are writers of far lesser intellectual development who yet give hints and hopes of indefinite growth – it doth not appear what they *shall* be, but Ruskin leaves us nothing to hope. Among all the possibilities of after-development I can find nothing that will fit him. His very hopes and longing of heaven that he places deep in the immensities and eternities are weighed and measured and branded and they are bounded by surfaces definite as those of a crystal and could be made to order like bricks by Yankee machinery.

But the worst thing I find in his books is his lack of faith in the Scriptures of Nature. Nature, according to Ruskin, is the joint work of God and the devil, and therefore made up of alternate strips and bars of evil and good.

We must not dwell in contact with Nature, he tells us, else we will become blind to her beauty, which is the vulgar gross old heresy that familiarity with God will produce contempt of him. He would have us take beauty as we do roast beef or medicine, at stated times, the intervals to be measured by a London watch instead of inhaling it every moment as we do breath.

Evil, he says, always exists with good and ugliness with beauty, in order to act as foils the one for the other. Beside every mountain angel he sets a mountain devil, that the blackness of the one may be made wholly striking by the whiteness of the other, and that the angel's white may be brightened by the devil's black. Here I want to say so much that I cannot say anything.

Ruskin, with all his well-bred amiability, is an infidel to Nature. You never can feel that there is the slightest *union* betwixt Nature and him. He goes to the Alps and improves and superintends and reports on Nature with the conceit and lofty importance of a factor of a duke's estate.

Kalmia, one of the very dearest of our mountain flowers, a companion of Bryanthus and Cassiope, one of the purest and most outspoken words of love that God has ever uttered on mountain meadow, he calls a type of deceit because when he eats it, it poisons him – is unfit for his stomach – a good English reason for setting it on the devil's half of Nature. But I have lived with and loved Kalmia many a day, and slept with my cheek upon her bonnie purple flowers, and I know that she is not a devil's foil for any plant. She was born and bred in Love Divine and dwells in Love and speaks Love only.

And I know something about "the blasted trunk, and the barren rock, the moaning of the bleak winds, the solemn solitudes of moors and seas, the roar of the black, perilous, merciless whirlpools of the mountain streams;" and they have a language for me, but they declare nothing of wrath or of hell, only Love plain as was ever spoken.

Christianity and mountainanity are streams from the same fountain, and when I read the bogies of Ruskin's "mountain gloom," and mountain evil, and mountain devil, and the unwholesomeness of mountain beauty as everyday breath and bread, then I wish for plenty of words and a preacher's commission.

Farewell. My kindest regards to your parents and wife and younglings. I am

Ever truly thine

JOHN MUIR

to Asa Gray

Yosemite Valley, February 22nd, 1873

DEAR DR. GRAY

Your letter of January 4th arrived just before our trails were snow-blocked. The seeds I sent in a letter envelope are *Libocedrus decurrens.*

As for the express charges on the primula box, I have not got the receipt by me and cannot tell what they amount to, but you must remember that you gave me money sufficient to prepay all such boxes for a year to come.

Did I tell you that our wee primula grows upon the Hoffmann range a few miles west of Mount Hoffmann, and also on the east slope of the Sierra, between Mounts Lyell and Ritter? Next summer I will find a new genus and a half dozen new species for that generous embalming which you propose. Here are a few plants which I wish you would name for me.

Our winter is very glorious. January was a block of solid sun-gold, not of the thin frosty kind, but of a quality that called forth butterflies and tingled the fern coils and filled the noontide with a dreamy hum of insect wings. On the 15th of January I found one big Phacelia in full bloom on the north side of the Valley about one thousand feet above the bottom or five thousand above the sea. Also at the same sunny nook several bushes of *Arctostaphylos glauca* were in full flower, and many other plants were swelling their buds and breathing fragrance, showing that they were full of the thoughts and intentions of spring. Our Laurel was in flower a month ago; so was our winter wheat (*Libocedrus*).

This month up to present date has been profusely filled with snow. About ten feet has fallen on the bottom of the Valley since the 30th of January. Your primulas on Clouds' Rest must be covered to a depth of at least twelve or fifteen feet. I wish you could see our pines in full bloom of soft snow, or waving in storm. They know little of the character of a pine tree who see it only when swaying drowsily in a summer breeze or when balanced motionless and fast asleep in hushed sunshine.

We are grandly snowbound and have all this winter glory of sunlight and storm-shade to ourselves. Our outside doors are locked, and who will disturb us?

I call your attention to the two large yellow and purple plants from the top of Mount Lyell, above all of the pinched and blinking dwarfs that almost justify Darwin's mean ungodly word "struggle". They form a rounded expansion upon the wedge of plant life that slants up into the thin lean sky. They are the noblest plant mountaineers I ever saw, climbing above the glaciers into the frosty azure, and flowering in purple and gold, rich and abundant as ever responded to the thick, creamy sun-gold of the tropics.

Ever very cordially yours

JOHN MUIR

In his reply to this letter, which reflects Muir's watchful interest in the sun-warmed winter cliff gardens above his cabin, Gray reported on the plants Muir had sent for identification. "If you will keep botanising in the High Sierra," he wrote, "you will find curious and new things, no doubt. One such, at least, is in your present collection in letter – the wee mouse-tail *Ivesia*. And the rare species of Lewisia is as good as new, and is so wholly to California. . . . *Ivesia Muirii* is the first fruit – 'the day of small things.' Get a new alpine genus, that I may make a *Muiria glacialis!*" The primula so often referred to is the beautiful alpine red-purple Sierra Primrose (*Primula suffrutescens* Gray).

to Mrs. Ezra S. Carr

Yosemite Valley, March 30th, [1873]

DEAR MRS. CARR

Your two last are received. The package of letters was picked up by a man in the Valley.

There was none for thee. I have Hetch Hetchy about ready. I did not intend that Tenaya ramble ["A Geologist's Winter Walk"] for publication, but you know what is better.

I mean to write and send all kinds of game to you with hides and feathers on, for if I wait until all become one it may be too long. As for LeConte's "Glaciers," they will not hurt mine, but hereafter I will say my thoughts to the public in any kind of words I chance to command, for I am sure they will be better expressed in this way than in any second-hand hash, however able.

Oftentimes when I am free in the wilds I discover some rare beauty in lake or cataract or mountain form, and instantly seek to sketch it with my pencil, but the drawing is always enormously unlike the reality. So also in word sketches of the same beauties that are so living, so loving, so filled with warm God, there is the same infinite shortcoming. The few hard words make but a skeleton, fleshless, heartless, and when you read, the dead bony words rattle in one's teeth. Yet I will not the less endeavour to do my poor best, believing that even these dead bone-heaps called articles will occasionally contain hints to some living souls who know how to find them. I have not received Dr. Stebbins' letter. Give him and all my friends love from me. I sent Harry Edwards the butterflies I had lost. Did he get them?

Farewell, dear, dear spiritual mother. Heaven repay your everlasting love.

JOHN MUIR

to Mrs. Ezra S. Carr

[Yosemite], April 1st, 1873

DEAR MRS. CARR

Yours containing Dr. Stebbins' was received today. Some of our letters come in by Mariposa, some by Coulterville, and some by Oak Flat, causing large delays.

I expect to be able to send this out next Sunday, and with it "Hetch Hetchy," which is about ready, and from this time you will receive about one article a month.

This letter of yours is a very delightful one. I shall look eagerly for the "Rural Homes."

When I know Dr. Stebbins' summer address I will write to him. He is a dear young soul, though an old man. I am "not to write" – therefore, farewell, with love.

I will some time send you

> Big Tuolumne Canyon
> Ascent of Mount Ritter
> Formation of Yosemite Valley
> Other Yosemite Valleys (1, 2, 3, 4, or more)
> The Lake District
> Formation of Lakes
> Transformation of Lakes to Meadows, Wet
> The Glacial Period
> Formation of Simple Canyons to Meadows, Dry
> Formation of Compound Canyons to Sandy
>   Flats, Treeless, or to Sandy Flats, Forested

Description of Each Glacier of Region
Origin of Sierra Forests
Distribution of Forests
A Description of each of the Yosemite Falls,
    and of the Basins from whence derived
Yosemite Shadows, as Related to Groves,
    Meadows and Bends of the River
Avalanches, Earthquakes, Birds, Bears, etc.
    and "mony mae."

[JOHN MUIR]

to Sarah Muir Galloway

Yosemite Valley, September 3rd, 1873

DEAR SISTER SARAH

I have just returned from the longest and hardest trip I have ever made in the mountains, having been gone over five weeks. I am weary, but resting fast; sleepy, but sleeping deep and fast; hungry, but eating much. For two weeks I explored the glaciers of the summits east of here, sleeping among the snowy mountains without blankets and with but little to eat on account of its being so inaccessible. After my icy experiences it seems strange to be down here in so warm and flowery a climate.

I will soon be off again, determined to use all the season in prosecuting my researches – will go next to Kings River a hundred miles south, then to Lake Tahoe and adjacent mountains, and in winter work in Oakland with my pen.

The Scotch are slow, but some day I will have the results of my mountain studies in a form in which you all will be able to read and judge of them. In the mean time I write occasionally for the *Overland Monthly*, but neither these magazine articles nor my first book will form any finished part of the scientific contribution that I hope to make.... The mountains are calling and I must go, and I will work on while I can, studying incessantly.

My love to you all, David and the children and Mrs. Galloway who though shut out from sunshine yet dwells in Light. I will write again when I return from Kings River Canyon. The leaf sent me from China is for Cecelia.

Farewell, with love everlasting

[JOHN MUIR]

The exploratory excursion into the Kings River region, which he had in prospect when he wrote to his sister, forms the subject of several of the following letters. As both the letters and his notebooks show, the trip involved almost incredible physical exertion and endurance on his part. By delaying his start for a day, Muir succeeded in persuading Galen Clark to go along. Unfortunately the latter's duties as Guardian of Yosemite Valley compelled him to leave the party before its objects had been accomplished. In his volume, *The Yosemite*, Muir has paid a warm tribute to Clark both as a man and a mountaineer. After the botanist Dr. A. Kellogg and the artist William Simms left him at Mono, Muir pushed on alone to Lake Tahoe.

to Mrs. Ezra S. Carr

Clark's Station, September 13th, [1873.]

DEAR MRS. CARR

We have just arrived from the Valley, and are now fairly off for the ice in the highest and broadest of the Sierras. Our party consists of the blessed Doctor [A. Kellogg] and Billy Simms, *Artist*, and I am so glad that the Doctor will have company when I am among the summits. We hoped to have secured Clark also, a companion for me among the peaks and snow, but alack, I *must* go alone. Well, I will not complain a word, for I shall be overpaid a thousand, thousand fold. I can give you no measured idea of the time of our reaching Tahoe, but I will write always on coming to stations if such there be in the rocks or sage where letters are written....

Now for God's glorious mountains. I will miss you, yet you will more than half go. It is only now that I feel that I am taking leave of you.

Farewell. Love to all.

[JOHN MUIR]

to Mrs. Ezra S. Carr

Camp on South Fork, San Joaquin, near
divide of San Joaquin and Kings River,
September 27th[?] [1873.]

DEAR MRS. CARR

We have been out nearly two weeks. Clark is going to leave us. Told me five minutes ago. Am a little nervous about it, but will of course push on alone.

We came out through the Mariposa Grove, around the head of the Chiquita Joaquin, across the canyon of the North Fork of San Joaquin, then across the canyon of Middle Fork of San Joaquin, and up the east side of the South Fork one day's journey. Then picked our wild way across the canyon of the South Fork and came up one day's journey on the west side of the canyon; there we made a camp for four days. I was anxious to see the head fountains of this river, and started alone, Clark not feeling able to bear the fatigue involved in such a trip. I set out without blankets for a hard climb; followed the Joaquin to its *glaciers*, and climbed the highest mountain I could find at its head, which was either Mount Humphreys or the mountain next south. This is a noble mountain, considerably higher than any I have before ascended. The map of the Geological Survey gives no detail of this wild region.

I was gone from camp four days; discovered fifteen glaciers, and yosemite valleys "many O." The view from that glorious mountain (13,500 feet high?) is not to be attempted here. Saw over into Owens River valley and all across the fountains of Kings River. I got back to camp last evening. This morning after breakfast Clark said that he ought to be at home attending to business and could not feel justified in being away, and therefore had made up his mind to leave us, going home by way of the valley of the main Joaquin.

We will push over to the Kings River region and attempt to go down between the Middle and North Forks. Thence into the canyon of the South Fork and over the range to Owens Valley, and south to Mount Whitney if the weather holds steady, then for Tahoe, etc. As we are groping through unexplored regions our plans may be considerably modified. I feel a little anxious about the lateness of the season. We may be at Tahoe in three or four weeks.

We had a rough time crossing the Middle Fork of the Joaquin. Browny rolled down over the rocks, not sidewise but end over end. One of the mules rolled boulder-like in a yet more irregular fashion. Billy went forth to sketch while I was among the glaciers, and got lost – was thirty-six hours without food.

I have named a grand *wide-winged* mountain on the head of the Joaquin Mount Emerson. Its head is high above its fellows and wings are white with ice and snow.

This is a dear bonnie morning, the sun rays lovingly to His precious mountain pines. The brown meadows are nightly frosted browner and the yellow aspens are losing their leaves. I wish I could write to you, but hard work near and far presses heavily and I cannot. Nature makes huge demands, yet pays an thousand, thousand fold. As in all the mountains I have seen about the head of Merced and Tuolumne this region is a song of God.

On my way home yesterday afternoon I gathered you these orange leaves from a grove of one of the San Joaquin yosemites. Little thought I that you would receive them so soon.

Remember me to the Doctor and the boys and to Mrs. and Mr. Moore and Keith. Dr. Kellogg wishes to be kindly remembered.   Farewell.

[JOHN MUIR]

to Mrs. Ezra S. Carr

Camp in dear Bonnie Grove where the pines meet
the foothill oaks. About eight or ten miles southeast
from the confluence of the North Fork of Kings
River with the trunk. October 2nd [?] [1873.]

DEAR MRS. CARR

After Clark's departure a week ago we climbed the divide between the South Fork of the San Joaquin and Kings Rivers. I scanned the vast landscape on which the ice had written wondrous things. After a short scientific feast I decided to attempt entering the valley of the west branch of the North Fork, which we did, following the bottom of the valley for about ten miles, then was compelled to ascend the west side of the canyon into the forest. About six miles farther down we made out to re-enter the canyon where there is a yosemite valley, and by hard efforts succeeded in getting out on the opposite side and reaching the divide between the North Fork and the Middle Fork. We then followed the top of the divide nearly to the confluence of the North Fork with the trunk, and crossed the main river yesterday, and are now in the pines again over all the wildest and most impracticable portions of our journey.

In descending the divide to the main Kings River we made a descent of near seven thousand feet, "down derry down" with a vengeance, to the hot pineless foothills. We rose again and it was a most grateful resurrection. Last night I watched the writing of the spiry pines on the sky grey with stars, and if you had been here I would have said, Look! etc.

Last evening when the Doctor and I were bed-building, discussing as usual the goodnesses and badnesses of boughy mountain beds, we were astonished by the appearance of two prospectors coming through the mountain rye. By them I send this note.

Today we will reach some of the Sequoias near Thomas' Mill (*vide* Map of Geological Survey), and in two or three days more will be in the canyon of the South Fork of Kings River. If the weather appears tranquil when we reach the summit of the range I may set out among the glaciers for a few days, but if otherwise I shall push hastily for the Owens River plains, and thence up to Tahoe, etc.

I am working hard and shall not feel easy until I am on the other wise beyond the reach of early snowstorms. Not that I fear snowstorms for myself, but the poor animals would die or suffer.

The Doctor's duster and fly-net are safe, and therefore he is. Billy is in good spirits, apt to teach sketching in and out of season. Remember me to the Doctor and the boys and Moores and Keith, etc.

Ever yours truly

JOHN MUIR

to Mrs. Ezra S. Carr

Independence, October 16th, 1873

DEAR MRS. CARR

All of my season's mountain work is done. I have just come down from Mount Whitney and the newly discovered mountain five miles northwest of Whitney, and now our journey is a simple saunter along the base of the range to Tahoe, where we will arrive about the end of the month, or a few days earlier.

I have seen a good deal more of the high mountain region about the heads of Kings and Kern Rivers than I expected to see in so short and so late a time. Two weeks ago I left the Doctor and Billy in the Kings River yosemite, and set out for Mount Tyndall and adjacent mountains and canyons. I ascended

Tyndall and ran down into the Kern River canyon and climbed some nameless mountains between Tyndall and Whitney, and thus gained a pretty good general idea of the region. After crossing the range by the Kearsage Pass, I again left the Doctor and Billy and pushed southward along the range and northward and up Cottonwood Creek to Mount Whitney; then over to the Kern Canyon again and up to the new "highest" peak which I did not ascend, as there was no one to attend to my horse.

Thus you see I have rambled this highest portion of the Sierra pretty thoroughly, though hastily. I spent a night without fire or food in a very icy wind-storm on one of the spires of the new highest peak, by some called Fisherman's Peak.* That I am already quite recovered from the tremendous exposure proves that I cannot be killed in any such manner. On the day previous I climbed two mountains, making over ten thousand feet of altitude. It seems that this new Fisherman's Peak is causing some stir in the newspapers. If I feel writeful I will send you a sketch of the region for the *Overland*.

I saw no mountains in all this grand region that appeared at all inaccessible to a mountaineer. Give me a summer and a bunch of matches and a sack of meal and I will climb every mountain in the region.

I have passed through Lone Pine and noted the yosemite and local subsidences accomplished by the earthquakes. The bunchy bushy compositae of Owen's Valley are glorious. I got back from Whitney this p.m. How I shall sleep! My life rose wave-like with those lofty granite waves. Now it may wearily float for a time along the smooth flowery plain.

Love to all my friends.

Ever cordially yours

JOHN MUIR

The "stir in the newspapers," alluded to by Muir, was partly at the expense of Clarence King who, in his published account of what he believed to have been the first ascent of Mount Whitney, had described it as a somewhat venturesome undertaking. It now became evident that he had missed Mount Whitney and climbed an easy neighbouring mountain of less elevation. In 1903 Mr. George W. Stewart published in the *Mount Whitney Club Journal* a communication from Muir which is of considerable interest in this connection, not only because it presents the original records of first ascents of Mount Whitney, but also because in it Muir states it to have been his uniform practice never to leave his name on any mountain, rock, or tree. "Reading the accounts of these Whitney climbs [in the above-mentioned journal] recalls to mind," he writes, "my first ascent in October, 1873. Early in the morning of the 25th I left my horse on a meadow a short

* Now called Mount Whitney. An error in the first Geological Survey map, explained by Clarence King in the second edition of his *Mountaineering in the Sierra Nevada,* led to the identification of Sheep Mountain as Mount Whitney.

distance north of the Hockett trail crossing of the summit, and climbed the mountain (now Sheep Mountain), about fourteen thousand feet high, named Mount Whitney on the State Geological Survey map of the region. To the north about eight miles I saw a higher peak and set off to climb it the same day. I reached the summit needles about eleven o'clock that night, and danced most of the time until morning, as the night was bitterly cold and I was in my shirt-sleeves. The stars and the dawn and the sunrise were glorious, but, having had no supper, I was hungry and hastened back to camp, and to Independence, where I left my horse, and set out again for the summit afoot, direct from the east side, going up a canyon opposite Lone Pine. I reached the summit about eight o'clock a.m., October 29th, 1873. In a yeast-powder can I found the following account of first ascents, which I copied into my notebook as follows:

Sept. 19th, 1873. This peak, Mt. Whitney, was this day climbed by Clarence King, U.S. Geologist, and Frank F. Knowles of Tule River. On Sept. 1st, in New York, I first learned that the high peak south of here, which I climbed in 1871, was not Mt. Whitney, and I immediately came here. Clouds and storms prevented me from recognising this in 1871, or I should have come here then.

All honour to those who came here before me.

C. KING

Notice. Gentlemen, the looky finder of this half a dollar is wellkome to it.
CARL RABE Sept. 6th, 1873

"Of course, I replaced these records, as well as Carl Rabe's half a dollar, but did not add my own name. I have never left my name on any mountain, rock, or tree in any wilderness I have explored or passed through, though I have spent ten years in the Sierra alone."

In this Kings-Kern-Tahoe excursion Muir had travelled over a thousand wilderness miles, climbed numerous peaks, and discovered many glaciers and new yosemites. His observations had furnished him with a harvest of new facts to be utilised in the projected series of "Studies in the Sierra" which he had agreed to write for the *Overland Monthly* during the coming winter. His articles on "Hetch Hetchy Valley," and "Explorations in the Great Tuolumne Canyon," had appeared in the same magazine during July and August, lifting him at once to the rank of its foremost contributor. In the second of these articles he had disproved Whitney's statement that the Tuolumne Canyon was "probably inaccessible through its entire length," and that "it certainly cannot be entered from its head." "I have entered the Great Canyon from the north by three different side canyons," wrote Muir, "and have passed through it from end to end ... without encountering any extraordinary difficulties. I am sure that it may be entered at more than fifty different points along the walls by mountaineers of ordinary nerve and skill. At the head it is easily accessible on both sides.''

But Muir, as the reader will have perceived, was a mountaineer of more than ordinary nerve and skill, and one secret of his amazing physical endurance was not in his muscles, but in the spirit which they served. Of this fact he was not wholly unaware when he wrote, ''It is astonishing how high and far we can climb in mountains that we love.'' But he seems to have been conscious, also, of the development, in himself, of a kind of muscle sense referred to in a passage which he wrote during the exploring season of 1873:

The life of a mountaineer is favourable to the development of soul-life as well as limb-life, each receiving abundance of exercise and abundance of food. We little suspect the great capacity that our flesh has for knowledge. Oftentimes in climbing canyon-walls I have come to polished slopes near the heads of precipices that seemed to be too steep to be ventured upon. After scrutinising them, and carefully noting every dint and scratch that might give hope of a foothold, I have decided that they were unsafe. Yet my limbs, possessing a separate sense, would be of a different opinion, after they also had examined the descent, and confidently have set out to cross the condemned slopes against the remonstrances of my other will. My legs sometimes transport me to camp in the darkness, over cliffs and through bogs and forests that are inaccessible to city legs during the day, even when piloted by the mind which owns them.

On the first of November Muir had reached Lake Tahoe and in two weeks he was in Yosemite again. The Yosemite chapter of his life was about to close and it cost him a severe struggle to separate himself from the beloved Valley. But he had engaged himself to bring to paper his mountain studies during the winter, a task that involved at least a temporary sojourn in a place within easy reach of San Francisco. ''I suppose I must go into society this winter,'' he wrote to his sister Sarah on November 14th, 1873. ''I would rather go back in some undiscoverable corner beneath the rafters of an old garret with my notes and books and listen to the winter rapping and blowing on the roof. May start for Oakland in a day or two. Will probably live in Professor Carr's family.''

He departed as the first snowflakes began to whirl over the Valley which thereafter was to know him as a resident no more. When he reached Oakland the Carr household was in deep mourning over the tragic death of the eldest son, so he accepted the offer of a room in the home of his friends Mr. and Mrs. J. B. McChesney, at 1364 Franklin Street.

[THE ORIGINAL VOLUME I ENDED AT THIS POINT]

CHAPTER ELEVEN

On Widening Currents   1873–1875

THE TEN MONTHS' interval of Muir's Oakland sojourn made a complete break in his accustomed activities. It was a storm and stress period to which he refers afterward as "the strange Oakland epoch," and we are left to infer that the strangeness consisted chiefly in the fact that he was housebound by his own choice, to be sure, but nevertheless shut away from the free life of the mountains. It is not surprising, perhaps, that this period is marked by an almost complete stoppage of his correspondence, though he never was more continuously busy with his pen than during these months.

Easily the foremost literary journal of the Pacific Coast at that time was the *Overland Monthly*. It had been founded in 1868, and Bret Harte was the man to whom it owed both its beginning and the fame it achieved under his editorship. The magazine, however, was not a profit-yielding enterprise, for John H. Carmany, its owner, professed to have lost thirty thousand dollars in his endeavour to make it pay. In a sheaf of reminiscences written years afterward, he reveals the double reason why the magazine proved expensive and why so many distinguished names, such as those of Mark Twain, Joaquin Miller, Ambrose Bierce, Edward Roland Sill, Bret Harte, and John Muir, appear on its roll of contributors. "They have reason to remember me," he wrote, "for never have such prices been paid for poems, stories, and articles as I paid to the writers of the old *Overland*."

Bret Harte, balking at a contract designed to correct his dilatory literary habits, left the magazine in 1871, and, after several unsatisfactory attempts to supply his place, Benjamin P. Avery became editor of the *Overland*.

In March, 1874, he wrote a letter acknowledging the first number of Muir's notable series of "Studies in the Sierra," thereby disclosing what the latter had been doing during the winter months. "I am delighted," he tells Muir, "with your very original and clearly written paper on 'Mountain Sculpture' which reveals the law beneath the beauty of mountain and rock forms." This article, accompanied by numerous illustrative line drawings, appeared as the leading contribution in May and was followed in monthly succession by six others, in the order given in an earlier chapter [p.178].

Not many weeks after the receipt of this initial article, Mr. Avery accepted an appointment as Minister to China. "Not ambition or honours," he wrote to Muir, "but the compulsion of broken health made me risk a foreign appointment, and I especially regret that the opportunity to share in the publication of your valuable papers, and to know you most intimately, is to be lost to me." To the deep regret of his friends, Avery died in China the following year. Mr. Carmany, despairing of the *Overland* as a financial venture, let it come to an end in 1875, and Muir, when his current engagements were discharged, formed new literary connections.

There can be no doubt that during the closing years of the magazine, 1874–75, Muir's articles constituted by far the most significant contribution. It was in good measure due to Mrs. Carr that he was finally induced to write his series of "Sierra Studies." She had even suggested suspension of correspondence in order to enable him to accomplish the task.

"You told me I ought to abandon letter writing," he wrote to her on Christmas day, 1872, and I see plainly enough that you are right in this, because my correspondence has gone on increasing year by year and has become far too bulky and miscellaneous in its character, and consumes too much of my time. Therefore I mean to take your advice and allow broad acres of silence to spread between my letters, however much of self-denial may be demanded."

In the same letter, which a strange combination of circumstances has just brought to light again after fifty-two years, he expresses pungently that distaste for the mechanics of writing which undoubtedly accounts in part for the relative smallness of his formal literary output.

Book-making frightens me [he declares], because it demands so much artificialness and retrograding. Somehow, up here in these fountain skies [of Yosemite] I feel like a flake of glass through which light passes, but which, conscious of the inexhaustibleness of its sun fountain, cares not whether its passing light coins itself onto other forms or goes unchanged – neither charcoaled nor diamonded! Moreover, I find that though I have a few thoughts entangled in the fibres of my mind, I possess no words into which I can shape them. You tell me that I must be patient and reach out and grope in lexicon granaries for the words I want. But if some loquacious angel were to touch my lips with literary fire, bestowing every word of Webster, I would scarce thank him for the gift, because most of the words of the English language are made of mud, for muddy purposes, while those invented to contain spiritual matter are doubtful and unfixed in capacity and form, as wind-ridden mist-rags.

These mountain fires that glow in one's blood are free to all, but I cannot find the chemistry that may press them unimpaired into booksellers' bricks. True, with that august instrument, the English language, in the manufacture of which so many brains have been broken, I can proclaim to you that moonshine is glorious, and sunshine more glorious, that winds rage, and waters roar, and that in "terrible times" glaciers guttered the mountains with their hard cold snouts. This is about the limit of what I feel capable of doing for the public – the moiling, squirming, fog-breathing public. But for my few friends I can do more because they already know the mountain harmonies and can catch the tones I gather for them, though written in a few harsh and gravelly sentences.

There was another aspect of writing that Muir found irksome and that was its solitariness. Being a fluent and vivid conversationalist, accustomed to the excitation of eager hearers, he missed the give-and-take of conversation when he sat down with no company but that of his pen. Even the writing of a letter to a friend had something of the conversational about it. But to write between four walls for the "Babylonish mobs" that hived past his window was another matter. Fresh from Cassiope, the heather of the High Sierra, aglow with enthusiasm for the beauty that had burned itself into his soul, he could but wonder and grow indignant at the stolid self-sufficiency of "the metallic, money-clinking crowds," among whom he felt himself as alien as any Hebrew psalmist or prophet by the waters of Babylon.

It is not to be wondered at, therefore, that this first sojourn in the San Francisco Bay region was for Muir a kind of exile under which he evidently chafed a good deal. His human environment was so unblushingly materialistic that, in spite of a few sympathetic friends, it seemed to him well-nigh impossible to obtain a hearing on behalf of Nature from any other standpoint than that of commercial utility. On this point he differed trenchantly with his contemporaries and doubtless engaged in a good many arguments, for his frankness and downright sincerity did not permit him to compromise the supremacy of values which by his own standard far exceeded those of commercialism. It is by reference to such verbal passages of arms that we must explain his allusion in the following letter, to "all the morbidness that has been hooted at me."

The issue was one which, in his own mind, he had settled fundamentally on his thousand mile walk to the Gulf, but which challenged him again at every street corner in Oakland, and he was not the man to retire from combat in such a cause. He was, in fact, an eager and formidable opponent. "No one who did not know Muir in those days," remarked one of his old friends to me, "can have any conception of Muir's brilliance as a conversational antagonist in an argument." The world made especially for the uses of man? "Certainly not," said Muir. "No dogma taught by the present civilization forms so insuperable an obstacle to a right understanding of the relations which human culture sustains to wildness. Every animal, plant, and crystal controverts it in the plainest terms. Yet it is taught from century to century as something ever new and precious, and in the resulting darkness the enormous conceit is allowed to go unchallenged!"

Though grilling in his very blood over this huckster appraisement of nature, Muir laboured hard and continuously with his pen throughout the winter and the following spring and summer. When autumn came he had completed not only his seven "Studies in the Sierra," but had also written a paper entitled "Studies in the Formation of Mountains in the Sierra Nevada" for the American Association for the Advancement of Science, and articles on "Wild Sheep of California" and "Byways of Yosemite Travel." About this time his health had begun to suffer from excessive confinement and irregular diet at restaurants, so, yielding with sudden resolution to an overpowering longing for the mountains, he set out again for Yosemite. The following letter in which his correspondence with Mrs. Carr reaches its highest level and, in a sense, its conclusion, celebrates his escape from an uncongenial environment.

to Mrs. Ezra S. Carr

Yosemite Valley, [September, 1874]

DEAR MRS. CARR

Here again are pine trees, and the wind, and living rock and water! I've met two of my ouzels on one of the pebble ripples of the river where I used to be with them. Most of the meadow gardens are disenchanted and dead, yet I found a few mint spikes and asters and brave, sunful goldenrods and a patch of the tiny Mimulus that has two spots on each lip. The fragrance and the colour and the form, and the whole spiritual expression of goldenrods are hopeful and strength-giving beyond any other flowers that I know. A single spike is sufficient to heal unbelief and melancholy.

On leaving Oakland I was so excited over my escape that, of course, I forgot and left all the accounts I was to collect. No wonder, and no matter. I'm beneath that grand old pine that I have heard so often in storms both at night and in the day. It sings grandly now, every needle sun-thrilled and shining and responding tunefully to the azure wind.

When I left I was in a dreamy exhausted daze. Yet from mere habit or instinct I tried to observe and study. From the car window I watched the gradual transitions from muddy water, spongy tule, marsh and level field as we shot up the San José Valley, and marked as best I could the forms of the stream canyons as they opened to the plain and the outlines of the undulating hillocks and headlands between. Interest increased at every mile, until it seemed unbearable to be thrust so flyingly onward even towards the blessed Sierras. I will study them yet, free from time and wheels. When we turned suddenly and dashed into the narrow mouth of the Livermore pass I was looking out of the right side of the car. The window was closed on account of the cinders and smoke from the locomotive. All at once my eyes clasped a big hard rock not a hundred yards away, every line of which is as strictly and outspokenly glacial as any of the most alphabetic of the high and young Sierra. That one sure glacial word thrilled and overjoyed me more than you will ever believe. Town smokes and shadows had not dimmed my vision, for I had passed this glacial rock twice before without reading its meaning.

As we proceeded, the general glacialness of the range became more and more apparent, until we reached Pleasanton where once there was a grand *mer de glace*. Here the red sun went down in a cloudless glow and I leaned back, happy and weary and possessed with a lifeful of noble problems.

At Lathrop we suppered and changed cars. The last of the daylight had long faded and I sauntered away from the din while the baggage was being transferred. The young moon hung like a sickle above the shorn wheat fields, Ursa Major pictured the northern sky, the Milky Way curved sublimely through the broadcast stars like some grand celestial moraine with planets for boulders, and the whole night shone resplendent, adorned with that calm imperishable beauty which it has worn unchanged from the beginning.

I slept at Turlock and next morning faced the Sierra and set out through the sand afoot. The freedom I felt was exhilarating, and the burning heat and thirst and faintness could not make it less. Before I had walked ten miles I was wearied and footsore, but it was real earnest work and I liked it. Any kind of simple natural destruction is preferable to the numb, dumb, apathetic deaths of a town.

Before I was out of sight of Turlock I found a handful of the glorious *Hemizonia virgata* and a few of the patient, steadfast eriogonums that I learned to love around the slopes of Twenty-Hill Hollow. While I stood with these old dear friends we were joined by a lark, and in a few seconds more Harry Edwards [see p.136–37] came flapping by with spotted wings. Just think of the completeness of that reunion! – Twenty-Hill Hollow, Hemizonia, Eriogonum, Lark, Butterfly, and I, and lavish outflows of genuine Twenty-Hill Hollow sun gold. I threw down my coat and one shirt in the sand, forgetting Hopeton and heedless that the sun was getting hotter every minute. I was wild once more and let my watch warn and point as it pleased.

Heavy wagon loads of wheat had been hauled along the road and the wheels had sunk deep and left smooth bevelled furrows in the sand. Upon the smooth slopes of these sand furrows I soon observed a most beautiful and varied embroidery, evidently tracks of some kind. At first I thought of mice, but soon saw they were too light and delicate for mice. Then a tiny lizard darted into the stubble ahead of me, and I carefully examined the track he made, but it was entirely unlike the fine print embroidery I was studying. However I knew that he might make very different tracks if walking leisurely. Therefore I determined to catch one and experiment. I found out in Florida that lizards, however swift, are shortwinded, so I gave chase and soon captured a tiny grey fellow and carried him to a smooth sand-bed where he could embroider without getting away into grass tufts or holes. He was so wearied that he couldn't skim and was compelled to walk, and I was excited with delight in seeing an exquisitely beautiful strip of embroidery about five-eighths of an inch wide, drawn out in flowing curves behind him as from a loom. The riddle was solved. I knew that mountain boulders moved in music; so also do lizards, and their written music, printed by their feet, moved so swiftly as to be invisible, covers the hot sands with beauty wherever they go.

But my sand embroidery lesson was by no means done. I speedily discovered a yet more delicate pattern on the sands, woven into that of the lizard. I examined the strange combination of bars and dots. No five-toed lizard had printed that music. I watched narrowly down on my knees, following the strange and beautiful pattern along the wheel furrows and out into the stubble. Occasionally the pattern would suddenly end in a shallow pit half an inch across and an eighth of an inch deep. I was fairly puzzled, picked up my bundle, and trudged discontentedly away, but my eyes were hungrily awake and I watched all the ground. At length a grey grasshopper rattled and flew up, and the truth flashed upon me that he was the complementary embroiderer of the lizard. Then followed long careful observation, but I never could see the grasshopper until he jumped, and after he alighted he invariably stood watching me with his legs set ready for another jump in case of danger. Nevertheless I soon made sure that he was my man, for I found that in jumping he made the shallow pits I had observed at the termination of the pattern I was studying. But no matter how patiently I waited he wouldn't *walk* while I was sufficiently near to observe. They are so nearly the colour of sand. I therefore caught one and lifted his wing covers and cut off about half of each wing with my penknife, and carried him to a favourable place on the sand. At first he did nothing but jump and make dimples, but soon became weary and *walked* in common rhythm with all his six legs, and my interest you may guess while I watched the embroidery – the written music laid down in a beautiful ribbon-like strip behind. I glowed with wild joy as if I had found a new glacier – copied specimens of the precious fabric into my notebook, and strode away with my own feet sinking with a dull craunch, craunch, craunch in the hot grey sand, glad to believe that the dark and cloudy vicissitudes of the Oakland period had not dimmed my vision in the least. Surely Mother Nature pitied the poor boy and showed him pictures.

Happen what would, fever, thirst, or sunstroke, my joy for that day was complete. Yet I was to receive still more. A train of curving tracks with a line in the middle next fixed my attention, and almost before I had time to make a guess concerning their author, a small hawk came shooting down vertically out of the sky a few steps ahead of me and picked up something in his talons. After rising thirty or forty feet overhead, he dropped it by the roadside as if to show me what it was. I ran forward and found a little bunchy field mouse and at once suspected him of being embroiderer number three. After an exciting chase through stubble heaps and weed thickets I wearied and captured him without being bitten and turned him free to make his mark in a favourable sand bed. He also embroidered better than he knew, and at once claimed the authorship of the new track work.

I soon learned to distinguish the pretty sparrow track from that of the magpie and lark with their three delicate branches and the straight scratch behind made by the backcurving claw, dragged loosely like a spur of a Mexican vaquero. The cushioned elastic feet of the hare frequently were seen mixed with the pattering scratchy prints of the squirrels. I was now wholly trackful. I fancied I could see the air whirling in dimpled eddies from sparrow and lark wings. Earthquake boulders descending in a song of curves, snowflakes glinting songfully hither and thither. "The water in music the oar forsakes." The air in music the wing forsakes. All things move in music and write it. The mouse lizard, and grasshopper sing together on the Turlock sands, sing with the morning stars.

Scarce had I began to catch the eternal harmonies of Nature when I heard the hearty god-damming din of the mule driver, dust whirled in the sun gold, and I could see the sweltering mules leaning forward, dragging the heavily piled wheat wagons, deep sunk in the sand. My embroidery perished by the mile, but grasshoppers never wearied nor the grey lizards nor the larks, and the coarse confusion of man was speedily healed.

About noon I found a family of grangers feeding, and remembering your admonitions anent my health requested leave to join them. My head ached with fever and sunshine, and I couldn't dare the ancient brown bacon, nor the beans and cakes, but water and splendid buttermilk came in perfect affinity, and made me strong.

Towards evening, after passing through miles of blooming Hemizonia, I reached Hopeton on the edge of the oak fringe of the Merced. Here all were yellow and woebegone with malarious fever. I rested one day, spending the time in examining the remarkably flat water-eroded valley of the Merced and the geological sections which it offers. In going across to the river I had a suggestive time breaking my way through tangles of blackberries and briar-rose and willow. I admire delicate plants that are well prickled and therefore took my scratched face and hands patiently. I bathed in the sacred stream, seeming to catch all its mountain tones while it softly mumbled and rippled over the shallows of brown pebbles. The whole river back to its icy sources seemed to rise in clear vision, with its countless cascades and falls and blooming meadows and gardens. Its pine groves, too, and the winds that play them, all appeared and sounded.

In the cool of the evening I caught Browny and cantered across to the Tuolumne, the whole way being fragrant and golden with Hemizonia. A breeze swept in from your Golden Gate regions over the passes and across the plains, fanning the hot ground and drooping plants and refreshing every beast and tired and weary, plodding man.

It was dark ere I reached my old friend Delaney, but was instantly recognised by my voice, and welcomed in the old good uncivilized way, not to be misunderstood.

All the region adjacent to the Tuolumne River where it sweeps out into the plain after its long eventful journey in the mountains, *is* exceedingly picturesque. Round terraced hills, brown and yellow with grasses and compositæ and adorned with open groves of darkly foliaged live oak are grouped in a most open tranquil manner and laid upon a smooth level base of purple plain, while the river bank is lined with nooks of great beauty and variety in which the river has swept and curled, shifting from side to side, retreating and returning, as determined by floods and the gradual erosion and removal of drift beds formerly laid down. A few miles above here at the village of La Grange the wild river has made some astonishing deposits in its young days, through which it now flows with the manners of stately old age, apparently disclaiming all knowledge of them. But a thousand, thousand boulders gathered from many a moraine, swashed and ground in pot-holes, record their history and tell of white floods of a grandeur not easily conceived. Noble sections nearly a hundred feet deep are laid bare, like a book, by the mining company. Water is drawn from the river several miles above and conducted by ditches and pipes and made to play upon these deposits for the gold they contain. Thus the Tuolumne of today is compelled to unravel and lay bare its own ancient history which is a thousandfold more important than the handfuls of gold sand it chances to contain. I mean to return to these magnificent records in a week or two and turn the gold disease of the La Grangers to account in learning the old story of the Sierra flood period. If these hundred laborious hydraulicers were under my employ they could not do me better service, and all along the Sierra flank thousands of strong arms are working for me, incited by the small golden bait. Who shall say that I am not rich?

Up through the purple foothills to Coulterville, where I met many hearty, shaggy mountaineers glad to see me. Strange to say the *Overland* studies have been read and discussed in the most unlikely places. Some numbers have found their way through the Bloody Canyon pass to Mono.

In the evening Black and I rode together up into the sugar pine forests and on to his old ranch in the moonlight. The grand priest-like pines held their arms above us in blessing. The wind sang songs of welcome. The cool glaciers and the running crystal fountains were in it. I was no longer *on* but *in* the mountains-home again, and my pulses were filled. On and on in white moonlight-spangles on the streams, shadows in rock hollows and briary ravines, tree architecture on the sky more divine than ever stars in their spires, leafy mosaic in meadow and bank. Never had the Sierra seemed so inexhaustible – mile on mile onward in the forest through groves old and young, pine tassels overarching and brushing both cheeks at once. The chirping of crickets only deepened the stillness.

About eight o'clock a strange mass of tones came surging and waving through the pines. "That's the death song," said Black, as he reined up his horse to listen. "Some Indian is dead." Soon two glaring watch-fires shone red through the forest, marking the place of congregation. The fire glare and the wild wailing came with indescribable impressiveness through the still dark woods. I listened eagerly as the weird curves of woe swelled and cadenced, now rising steep like glacial precipices, now swooping low in polished slopes. Falling boulders and rushing streams and wind tones caught from rock and tree were in it. As we at length rode away and the heaviest notes were lost in distance, I wondered that so much of mountain nature should well out from such a source. Miles away we met Indian groups slipping through the shadows on their way to join the death wail.

Farther on, a harsh grunting and growling seemed to come from the opposite bank of a hazelly brook along which we rode. "What? Hush! That's a bear,'' ejaculated Black in a gruff bearish undertone. "Yes," said I, "some rough old bruin is sauntering this fine night, seeking some wayside sheep lost from migrating flocks.'' Of course all night-sounds otherwise unaccountable are accredited to bears. On ascending a sloping hillock less than a mile from the first we heard another grunting bear, but whether or no daylight would transform our bears to pigs may well be counted into the story.

Past Bower Cave and along a narrow winding trail in deep shadow – so dark, had to throw the reins on Browny's neck and trust to his skill, for I could not see the ground and the hillside was steep. A fine, bright tributary of the Merced sang far beneath us as we climbed higher, higher through the hazels and dogwoods that fringed the rough black boles of spruces and pines. We were now nearing the old camping ground of the Pilot Peak region where I learned to know the large nodding lilies (*L. pardalinum*) so abundant along these streams, and the groups of alder-shaded cataracts so characteristic of the North Merced Fork. Moonlight whitened all the long fluted slopes of the opposite bank but we rode in continuous shadow. The rush and gurgle and prolonged *Aaaaaah* of the stream coming up, sifting into the wind, was very solemnly impressive. It was here that you first seemed to join me. I reached up as Browny carried me underneath a big Douglas spruce and plucked one of its long plumy sprays, which brought you from the Oakland dead in a moment. You are more spruce than pine, though I never definitely knew it till now.

Miles and miles of tree scripture along the sky, a bible that will one day be read! The beauty of its letters and sentences have burned me like fire through all these Sierra seasons. Yet I cannot interpret their hidden thoughts. They are terrestrial expressions of the sun, pure as water and snow. Heavens! listen to the wind song! I'm still writing beneath that grand old pine in Black's yard and that other companion, scarcely less noble, back of which I sheltered during the earthquake, is just a few yards beyond. The shadows of their boles lie like charred logs on the grey sand, while half the yard is embroidered with their branches and leaves. There goes a woodpecker with an acorn to drive into its thick bark for winter, and well it may gather its stores, for I can myself detect winter in the wind.

Few nights of my mountain life have been more eventful than that of my ride in the woods from Coulterville, where I made my reunion with the winds and pines. It was eleven o'clock when we reached Black's ranch. I was weary and soon died in sleep. How cool and vital and recreative was the hale young mountain air. On higher, higher up into the holy of holies of the woods! Pure white lustrous clouds overshadowed the massive congregations of silver fir and pine. We entered, and a thousand living arms were waved in solemn blessing. An infinity of mountain life. How complete is the absorption of one's life into the spirit of mountain woods. No one can love or hate an enemy here, for no one can conceive of such a creature as an enemy. Nor can one have any distinctive love of friends. The dearest and best of you all seemed of no special account, mere trifles.

Hazel Green water, famous among mountaineers, distilled from the pores

of an ancient moraine, spiced and toned in a maze of fragrant roots, winter
nor summer warm or cool it! Shadows over shadows keep its fountains ever
cool. Moss and felted leaves guard from spring and autumn frosts, while a
woolly robe of snow protects from the intenser cold of winter. Bears, deer,
birds, and Indians love the water and nuts of Hazel Green alike, while the
pine squirrel reigns supreme and haunts its incomparable groves like a spirit.
Here a grand old glacier swept over from the Tuolumne ice fountains into
the basin of the Merced, leaving the Hazel Green moraine for the food of her
coming trees and fountains of her predestined waters.

Along the Merced divide to the ancient glacial lake-bowl of Crane's Flat
was ever fir or pine more perfect? What groves! What combinations of green
and silver grey and glowing white of glinting sunbeams. Where is leaf or
limb awanting, and is this the upshot of the so-called "mountain glooms"
and mountain storms? If so, is Sierra forestry aught beside an outflow of
Divine Love? These roundbottomed grooves sweeping across the divide, and
down whose sides our horses canter with accelerated speed, are the pathways
of ancient ice-currents, and it is just where these crushing glaciers have
borne down most heavily that the greatest loveliness of grove and forest
appears.

A deep canyon filled with blue air now comes in view on the right. That
is the valley of the Merced, and the highest rocks visible through the trees
belong to the Yosemite Valley. More miles of glorious forest, then out into
free light and down, down, down into the groves and meadows of Yosemite.
Sierra sculpture in its entirety without the same study on the spot. No one of
the rocks seems to call me now, nor any of the distant mountains. Surely this
Merced and Tuolumne chapter of my life is done.

I have been out on the river bank with your letters. How good and wise
they seem to be! You wrote better than you knew. Altogether they form a
precious volume whose sentences are more intimately connected with my
mountain work than any one will ever be able to appreciate. An ouzel came
as I sat reading, alighting in the water with a delicate and graceful glint on
his bosom. How pure is the morning light on the great grey wall, and how
marvellous the subdued lights of the moon! The nights are wholly enchanting.

I will not try [to] tell the Valley. Yet I feel that I am a stranger here. I
have been gathering you a handful of leaves. Show them to dear Keith and
give some to Mrs. McChesney. They are probably the last of Yosemite that I
will ever give you. I will go out in a day or so. Farewell! I seem to be more
really leaving you here than there. Keep these long pages, for they are a kind
of memorandum of my walk after the strange Oakland epoch, and I may
want to copy some of them when I have leisure.

Remember me to my friends. I trust you are not now so sorely overladen.
Good-night. Keep the goldenrod and yarrow. They are auld lang syne.

Ever lovingly yours
JOHN MUIR

To take leave of Yosemite was harder than he anticipated. Days grew into weeks as in leisurely succession he visited his favourite haunts – places to which during the preceding summer he had taken on a camping trip [see p.163] a group of his closest friends, including Emily Pelton and Mrs. Carr. It was on this outing that bears raided the provisions cached by the party during an excursion into the Tuolumne Canyon and Muir saved his companions from hardship by fetching a new supply of food from Yosemite, making the arduous trip of forty miles without pause and in an amazingly short time.

Yosemite Valley, October 7th, 1874

DEAR MRS. CARR

I expected to have been among the foothill drift long ago, but the mountains fairly seized me, and ere I knew I was up the Merced Canyon where we were last year, past Shadow and Merced Lakes and our Soda Springs. I returned last night. Had a glorious storm, and a thousand sacred beauties that seemed yet more and more divine. I camped four nights at Shadow Lake [now called Merced Lake] at the old place in the pine thicket. I have ouzel tales to tell. I was alone and during the whole excursion, or period rather, was in a kind of calm incurable ecstasy. I am hopelessly and forever a mountaineer.

How glorious my studies seem, and how simple. I found out a noble truth concerning the Merced moraines that escaped me hitherto. Civilization and fever and all the morbidness that has been hooted at me have not dimmed my glacial eye, and I care to live only to entice people to look at Nature's loveliness. My own special self is nothing. My feet have recovered their cunning. I feel myself again.

Tell Keith the colours are coming to the groves. I leave Yosemite for over the mountains to Mono and Lake Tahoe. Will be in Tahoe in a week, thence anywhere Shastaward, etc. I think I may be at Brownsville, Yuba County, where I may get a letter from you. I promised to call on Emily Pelton there. Mrs. Black has fairly mothered me. She will be down in a few weeks.

Farewell.

JOHN MUIR

Having worked the Yosemite problem out of his blood he was faced with the question of the next step in his career. Apparently while debating with others the character of the relation which Nature should sustain to man he had found his calling, one in which his glacial studies in Yosemite formed only an incident, though a large one. Hereafter his supreme purpose in life must be "to entice people to look at Nature's loveliness" – understandingly, of course.

In the seventies, before lumber companies, fires, and the fumes from copper smelters had laid a blight upon the Shasta landscapes, the environs of the great mountain were a veritable garden of the Lord. Its famous mineral springs and abundant fish and game, no less than its snowy grandeur, attracted a steady stream of visitors. Clarence King had discovered glaciers on its flanks and many parts of the mountain were still imperfectly explored. The year was waning into late October when Muir, seeking new treasuries of Nature's loveliness, turned his face Shastaward.

In going to Mount Shasta, Muir walked along the main Oregon and California stage road from Redding to Sisson's. Unable to find any one willing to make the ascent of the mountain with him so late in the season, he secured the aid of Jerome Fay, a local resident, to take blankets and a week's supply of food as far as a pack-horse could break through the snow. Selecting a sheltered spot for a camp in the upper edge of the timber belt, he made his adventurous ascent alone from there on the 2nd of November, and returned to his camp before dark. Realising that a storm was brewing, he hastily made a "storm-nest" and snugged himself in with firewood to enjoy the novel sensation of a Shasta storm at an altitude of nine thousand feet. The elements broke loose violently the next morning, and continued for nearly a week, while Muir, his trusty notebook in hand, watched the deposition of snow upon the trees, studied the individual crystals with a lens, observed a squirrel finding her stores under the drifts, and made friends with wild sheep that sought shelter near his camp. He was much disappointed when Mr. Sisson, concerned for his safety, sent two horses through the blinding snowstorm and brought him down on the fifth day from the timber-line to his house. The following letter was written just before he began the first stage of the ascent:

to Mrs. Ezra S. Carr

Sisson's Station, November 1st, 1874

DEAR MRS. CARR
Here is icy Shasta fifteen miles away, yet at the very door. It is all close-wrapt in clean young snow down to the very base — one mass of white from the dense black forest-girdle at an elevation of five or six thousand feet to the very summit. The extent of its individuality is perfectly wonderful. When I first caught sight of it over the braided folds of the Sacramento Valley I was fifty miles away and afoot, alone and weary. Yet all my blood turned to wine, and I have not been weary since.

Stone was to have accompanied me, but has failed of course. The last storm was severe and all the mountaineers shake their heads and say impossible, etc., but you know that I will meet all its icy snows lovingly.

I set out in a few minutes for the edge of the timber-line. Then upwards, if unstormy, in the early morning. If the snow proves to be mealy and loose it is barely possible that I may be unable to urge my way through so many upward miles, as there is no intermediate camping ground. Yet I am feverless and strong now, and can spend two days with their intermediate night in one deliberate unstrained effort.

I am the more eager to ascend to study the mechanical conditions of the fresh snow at so great an elevation; also to obtain clear views of the comparative quantities of lava denudation northward and southward; also general views of the channels of the ancient Shasta glaciers, and many other lesser problems besides – the fountains of the rivers here, and the living glaciers. I would like to remain a week or two, and may have to return next year in summer.

I wrote a short letter* a few days ago which was printed in the *Evening Bulletin*, and I suppose you have seen it. I wonder how you all are faring in your wildernesses, educational, departmental, institutional, etc. Write me a line here in care of Sisson. I think it will reach me on my return from icy Shasta. Love to all – Keith and the boys and the McChesneys. Don't forward any letters from the Oakland office. I want only mountains until my return to civilization.   Farewell.

Ever cordially yours

JOHN MUIR

One of Muir's endearing traits was his genuine fondness for children, who rewarded his sympathy with touching confidence and devotion. The following letter, written to his admiring little chum [see p.186] in the McChesney household, sheds additional light upon his Shasta rambles and the mood, so different from mere adventure-seeking, in which he went questing for knowledge of Nature.

to Alice McChesney

Sisson's Station, Foot of Mount Shasta,
November 8th, 1874

MY DEAR HIGHLAND LASSIE ALICE

It is a stormy day here at the foot of the big snowy Shasta and so I am in Sisson's house where it is cosy and warm. There are four lassies here – one is bonnie, one is bonnier, and one is far bonniest, but I don't know them yet and I am a little lonesome and wish Alice McChesney were here. I can never help thinking that you were a little unkind in sending me off to the mountains without a kiss and you must make that up when I get back.

I was up on the top of Mount Shasta, and it is very high and all deep-buried in snow, and I am tired with the hard climbing and wading and wallowing. When I was coming up here on purpose to climb Mount Shasta people would often say to me, "Where are you going?" and I would say, "To Shasta," and they would say, "Shasta City?" and I would say, "Oh, no, I mean *Mount* Shasta!" Then they would laugh and say, "*Mount Shasta!!* Why man, you can't go on Mount Shasta *now*. You're two months too late.

---

* "Salmon Breeding on the McCloud River," *San Francisco Evening Bulletin*, Oct. 29, 1874.

The snow is ten feet deep on it, and you would be all buried up in the snow, and freeze to death.'' And then I would say, ''But I like snow, and I like frost and ice, and I'm used to climbing and wallowing in it.'' And they would say, ''Oh, that's all right enough to talk about or sing about, but I'm a mountaineer myself, and know all about that Shasta Butte and you just can't go noway and nohow.'' But I did go, because I loved snow and mountains better than they did. Some places I had to creep, and some places to slide, and some places to scramble, but most places I had to climb, climb, climb deep in the frosty snow.

I started at half-past two in the morning, all alone, and it stormed wildly and beautifully before I got back here and they thought that poor, crazy mountain climber must be frozen solid and lost below the drifts, but I found a place at the foot of a low bunch of trees and made a hollow and gathered wood and built a cheery fire and soon was warm; and though the wind and the snow swept wildly past, I was snug-bug-rug, and in three days I came down here. But I liked the storm and wanted to stay longer.

The weather is stormy yet, and most of the robins are getting ready to go away to a warmer place, and so they are gathering into big flocks. I saw them getting their breakfast this morning on cherries. Some hunters are here and so we get plenty of wild venison to eat, and they killed two bears and nailed their skins on the side of the barn to dry. There are lots of both bears and deer on Shasta, and three kinds of squirrels.

Shasta snowflakes are very beautiful, and I saw them finely under my magnifying glass. Here are some bonnie Crataegus leaves I gathered for you. Fare ye well, my lassie. I'm going tomorrow with some hunters to see if I can find out something more about bears or wild sheep.

Give my love to your mother and father and Carrie, and tell your mother to keep my letters until I come back, for I don't want to know anything just now except mountains. But I want your papa to write to me, for I will be up here, hanging about the snowy skirts of Shasta, for one or two or three weeks.

It is a dark, wild night, and the Shasta squirrels are curled up cosily in their nests, and the grouse have feather pantlets on and are all roosting under the broad, shaggy branches of the fir trees. Goodnight, my lassie, and may you nest well and sleep well – as the Shasta squirrels and grouse.

[JOHN MUIR]

During the following weeks he circled the base of the mountain, visited the Black Butte and the foot of the Whitney Glacier, as well as Rhett and Klamath lakes, and gathered into his notebook a rich harvest of observations to be made into magazine articles later. Some of the material, however, he utilised at once in a series of letters to the *Evening Bulletin* of San Francisco.

In explanation of various allusions in some of the following letters to Mrs. Carr, it should be added that she and her husband had in view, and later acquired, a tract of land in what was then the outskirts of Pasadena. Both had been very active in organising the farmers of California into a State Grange in 1873. Two years later Dr. Carr was elected State

Superintendent of Public Instruction, and during his incumbency Mrs. Carr served as deputy Superintendent, discharging most of the routine work of the office in Sacramento, besides lecturing before granges and teachers' institutes throughout the State. There were many quarrelling political factions in California, and the Grangers' movement and the Department of Public Instruction were never far from the centre of the political storms.

to Mrs. Ezra S. Carr

Sisson's Station, December 9th, 1874

DEAR MRS. CARR

Coming in for a sleep and rest I was glad to receive your card. I seem to be more than married to icy Shasta. One yellow, mellow morning six days ago, when Shasta's snows were looming and blooming, I stepped outside the door to gaze, and was instantly drawn up over the meadows, over the forests to the main Shasta glacier in one rushing, cometic whiz, then, swooping to Shasta Valley, whirled off around the base like a satellite of the grand icy sun. I have just completed my first revolution. Length of orbit, one hundred miles; time, one Shasta day.

For two days and a half I had nothing in the way of food, yet suffered nothing, and was finely nerved for the most delicate work of mountaineering, both among crevasses and lava cliffs. Now I am sleeping and *eating*. I found some geological facts that are perfectly glorious, and botanical ones, too.

I wish I could make the public be kind to Keith and his paint.

And so you contemplate vines and oranges among the warm California angels! I wish you would all go a-granging among oranges and bananas and all such blazing red-hot fruits, for you are a species of Hindoo sun fruit yourself. For me, I like better the huckleberries of cool glacial bogs, and acid currants, and benevolent, rosy, beaming apples, and common Indian summer pumpkins.

I wish you could see the holy morning alpenglow of Shasta.

Farewell. I'll be down into grey Oakland some time. I am glad you are essentially independent of those commonplace plotters that have so marred your peace. Eat oranges and hear the larks and wait on the sun.

Ever cordially
JOHN MUIR

to Mrs. Ezra S. Carr

Sisson's Station, December 21st, 1874

DEAR MRS. CARR

I have just returned from a fourth Shasta excursion, and find your [letter] of the 17th. I wish you could have been with me on Shasta's shoulder last eve in the sun-glow. I was over on the head-waters of the McCloud, and what a head! Think of a spring giving rise to a river! I fairly quiver with joyous exultation when I think of it. The infinity of Nature's glory in rock, cloud, and water! As soon as I beheld the McCloud upon its lower course I knew there must be something extraordinary in its alpine fountains, and I shouted, "Oh where, my glorious river, do you come from?" Think of a spring fifty yards wide at the mouth, issuing from the base of a lava bluff with wild songs – not gloomily from a dark cavey mouth, but from a world of ferns and mosses gold and green! I broke my way through chaparral and all kinds of river-bank tangle in eager vigour, utterly unweariable.

The dark blue stream sang solemnly with a deep voice, pooling and boulder-dashing and *aha-a-a-ing* in white flashing rapids, when suddenly I heard water notes I never had heard before. They came from that mysterious spring; and then the Elk forest, and the alpine-glow, and the sunset! Poor pen cannot tell it.

The sun this morning is at work with its blessings as if it had never blessed before. He never wearies of revealing himself on Shasta. But in a few hours I leave this altar and all its – Well, to my Father I say thank you, and go willingly.

I go by stage and rail to Brownsville to see Emily [Pelton] and the rocks there and the Yuba. Then perhaps a few days among the auriferous drifts on the Tuolumne, and then to Oakland and that book, walking across the Coast Range on the way, either through one of the passes or over Mount Diablo. I feel a sort of nervous fear of another period of town dark, but I don't want to be silly about it. The sun glow will all fade out of me, and I will be deathly as Shasta in the dark. But mornings will come, dawnings of some kind, and if not, I have lived more than a common eternity already.

Farewell. Don't overwork – that is not the work your Father wants. I wish you could come a-beeing in the Shasta honey lands. Love to the boys

[JOHN MUIR]

On one of the excursions to which he refers in the preceding letter, Muir accompanied four hunters, three of them Scotchmen,* who were in search of wild sheep. The party went to Sheep Rock, twenty miles north of Sisson's, and from there fifty miles farther to Mount Bremer, then one of the most noted strongholds of wild game in the Shasta region. This expedition afforded Muir a new opportunity to study wild sheep and his observations were charmingly utilised in the little essay "Wild Wool," one of his last contributions to the *Overland* in 1875, republished afterwards in *Steep Trails*.

A week after writing the above letter he was at Knoxville, also known as Brownsville, on the divide between the Yuba and Feather Rivers. It was a mild, but tempestuous, December, and during a gale that sprang up while he

---

* Among these Scots was G. Buchanan Hepburn, of Haddingdonshire, on one of whose letters Muir made the memorandum, "Lord Hepburn, killed in Mexico or Lower California." Twenty years later, during his visit to Scotland, Muir was by chance enabled to communicate the details of the man's unhappy fate to his relatives.

was exploring a valley tributary to the Yuba, he climbed a Douglas spruce in order to be able to enjoy the better the wild music of the storm. The experience afterwards bore fruit in one of his finest descriptions – an article entitled "A Wind Storm in the Forests of the Yuba," which appeared in *Scribner's Monthly* in November, 1878, and later as a chapter in *The Mountains of California*. With the possible exception of his dog story, *Stickeen*, no article drew more enthusiastic comments from readers who felt moved to write their appreciation.

From his earliest youth Muir had derived keen enjoyment from storms, but he had never tried to give a reason for the joy that was in him. The reaction he got from the reading public showed that they regarded his enthusiasm for storms as admirable, but also as singular. The latter was a surprise to Muir, who regarded all the manifestations of Nature as coming within the range of his interest, and saw no reason why men should *fear* storms. Reflecting upon the fact, he reached the conclusion that such fear is due to a wrong attitude toward nature, to imaginary or grossly exaggerated notions of danger, or, in short, to a "lack of faith in the Scriptures of Nature," as, he averred, was the case with Ruskin. As for himself, a great storm was nothing but "a cordial outpouring of Nature's love."

By what he regarded as a fortunate coincidence, he was still on the head waters of the Feather and the Yuba rivers on the date of the memorable Marysville flood, January 19th, 1875. A driving warm rainstorm suddenly melted the heavy snows that filled the drainage basins of these rivers and sent an unprecedented flood down into the lowlands, submerging many homesteads and a good part of Marysville. One can almost sense the haste with which he dashed off the lines of the following letter on the morning of the day of the flood – impatient to heed the call of the storm.

to Mrs. Ezra S. Carr

Brownsville, Yuba County,
January 19th, 1875

MY DEAR MOTHER CARR

Here are some of the dearest and bonniest of our Father's bairns – the little ones that so few care to see. I never saw such enthusiasm in the care and breeding of mosses as Nature manifests among these northern Sierras. I have studied a big fruitful week among the canyons and ridges of the Feather and another among the Yuba rivers, living and dead.

I have seen a dead river – a sight worth going round the world to see. The dead rivers and dead gravels wherein lies the gold form magnificent problems, and I feel wild and unmanageable with the intense interest they excite, but I *will* choke myself off and finish my glacial work and that little book of studies. I have been spending a few fine social days with Emily [Pelton], but now work.

How gloriously it storms! The pines are in ecstasy, and I feel it and must go out to them. I must borrow a big coat and mingle in the storm and make some studies. Farewell.   Love to all.

                                                                                              M.

P.S. How are Ned and Keith? I wish Keith had been with me these Shasta and Feather River days. I have gained a thousandfold more than I hoped. Heaven send you Light and the good blessings of wildness. How the rains plash and roar, and how the pines wave and pray!

Tradition still tells of his return to the Knox House after the storm, dripping and bedraggled; of the pity and solicitude of his friends over his condition, and their surprise when he in turn pitied them for having missed "a storm of exalted beauty and riches." The account of his experience was his final contribution to the *Overland Monthly* in June, 1875, under the title, "A Flood-Storm in the Sierra." Nowhere has he revealed his fervid enjoyment of storms more unreservedly than in this article.* "How terribly downright," he observes, "must be the utterances of storms and earthquakes to those accustomed to the soft hypocrisies of society. Man's control is being extended over the forces of nature, but it is well, at least for the present, that storms can still make themselves heard through our thickest walls. . . . Some were made to think."

There was a new note in his discourses, written and spoken, when he emerged from the forests of the Yuba. Fear and utilitarianism, he was convinced, are a crippling equipment for one who wishes to understand and appreciate the beauty of the world about him. But meanness of soul is even worse. Herded in cities, where the struggle for gain sweeps along with the crowd even the exceptional individual, men rarely come in sight of their better selves. There is more hope for those who live in the country. But instead of listening to the earnest and varied voices of nature, the country resident, also, is too often of the shepherd type who can only hear "baa." "Even the howls and ki-yis of coyotes might be blessings if well heard, but he hears them only through a blur of mutton and wool, and they do him no good."

Despite these abnormalities, Muir insisted, we must live in close contact with nature if we are to keep fresh and clean the fountains of moral sanity. "The world needs the woods and is beginning to come to them," he asserts in his flood-storm article. "But it is not yet ready . . . for storms . . . . Nevertheless the world moves onward, and 'it is coming yet, for a' that,' that the beauty of storms will be as visible as that of calms."

---

* It was incorporated in part only as the chapter on "The River Floods" in The Mountains of California. The omitted portions are important to a student of Muir's personality.

CHAPTER TWELVE

"The World Needs the Woods" 1875–1878

WHEN OUT of doors, Muir was scarcely conscious of the passage of time, so completely was he absorbed, almost physically absorbed, in the natural objects about him. The mountains, the stars, the trees, and sweet-belled Cassiope recked not of time! Why should he? Nor was he at such periods burdened with thoughts of a calling. On the contrary, he rejoiced in his freedom and, like Thoreau, sought by honest labour of any sort only means enough to preserve it intact.

But when he came out of the forests, or down from the mountains, and had to take account, in letters and personal contacts, of the lives, loves, and occupations of relatives and friends, he sometimes was brought up sharply against the fact that he had reached middle age and yet had neither a home nor what most men in those days would have recognised as a profession. Then, as in the following letter, one catches a note of apology for the life he is leading. He can only say, and say it triumphantly, that the course of his bark is controlled by other stars than theirs, that he must be free to live by the laws of his own life.

to Sarah Muir Galloway

Oakland, [February 26th,] 1875

MY DEAR SISTER SARAH

I have just returned from a long train of excursions in the Sierras and find yours and many other letters waiting, all that accumulated for five months. I spent my holidays on the Yuba and Feather rivers exploring. I have, of course, worked hard and enjoyed hard, ascending mountains, crossing canyons, rambling ceaselessly over hill and dale, plain and lava bed.

I thought of you all gathered with your little ones enjoying the sweet and simple pleasures that belong to your lives and loves. I have not yet in all my wanderings found a single person so free as myself. Yet I am bound to my studies, and the laws of my own life. At times I feel as if driven with whips, and ridden upon. When in the woods I sit at times for hours watching birds or squirrels or looking down into the faces of flowers without suffering any feeling of haste. Yet I am swept onward in a general current that bears on irresistibly. When, therefore, I shall be allowed to float homeward, I dinna, dinna ken, but I hope.

The world, as well as the mountains, is good to me, and my studies flow on in a wider and wider current by the incoming of many a noble tributary. Probably if I were living amongst you all you would follow me in my scientific work, but as it is, you will do so imperfectly. However, when I visit you, you will all have to submit to numerous lectures. . . .

Give my love to David and to Mrs. Galloway and all your little ones, and remember me as ever lovingly your brother,

JOHN

On the 28th of April he led a party to the summit of Mount Shasta for the purpose of finding a proper place to locate the monument of the Coast and Geodetic Survey. Two days later he made another ascent with Jerome Fay in order to complete some barometrical observations. While engaged in this task a fierce storm arose, enveloping them, with great suddenness, in inky darkness through which roared a blast of snow and hail. His companion deemed it impossible under the circumstances to regain their camp at timberline, so the two made their way as best they could to the sputtering fumaroles or "Hot Springs" on the summit. The perils of that stormy night, described at some length in *Steep Trails*, were of a much more serious nature than one might infer from the casual reference to the adventure in the following letter.

to Mrs. Ezra S. Carr

1419 Taylor Street, May 4th, 1875

DEAR MRS. CARR

Here I am safe in the arms of Daddy Swett – home again from icy Shasta and richer than ever in dead river gravel and in snowstorms and snow. The upper end of the main Sacramento Valley is entirely covered with ancient river drift and I wandered over many square miles of it. In every pebble I could hear the sounds of running water. The whole deposit is a poem whose many books and chapters form the geological Vedas of our glorious state.

I discovered a new species of hail on the summit of Shasta and experienced one of the most beautiful and most violent snowstorms imaginable. I would have been with you ere this to tell you about it and to give you some lilies and pine tassels that I brought for you and Mrs. McChesney and Ina Coolbrith, but alack! I am battered and scarred like a log that has come down the Tuolumne in flood-time, and I am also lame with frost nipping. Nothing serious, however, and I will be well and better than before in a few days.

I was caught in a violent snowstorm and held upon the summit of the mountain all night in my shirt sleeves. The intense cold and the want of food and sleep made the fire of life smoulder and burn low. Nevertheless in company with another strong mountaineer [Jerome Fay] I broke through six miles of frosty snow down into the timber and reached fire and food and sleep and am better than ever, with all the valuable experiences. Altogether I have had a very instructive and delightful trip.

The Bryanthus you wanted was snow buried, and I was too lame to dig it out for you, but I will probably go back ere long. I'll be over in a few days or so. [JOHN MUIR]

With the approach of summer, Muir returned to the Yosemite and Mount Whitney region, taking with him his friends William Keith, J. B. McChesney, and John Swett. In the letters he wrote from there to the *San Francisco Evening Bulletin* one feels that the forest trees of the Sierra Nevada are getting a deepening hold upon his imagination. "Throughout all this glorious region," he writes, "there is nothing that so constantly interests and challenges the admiration of the traveller as the belts of forest through which he passes."

Of all the trees of the forest the dearest to him was the sugar pine (*Pinus Lambertiana*), and he frequently refers to it as the "King of the pines." "Many a volume," he declares in one of the letters written on this outing, "might be filled with the history of its development from the brown whirling-winged seed-nut to its ripe and Godlike old age; the quantity and range of its individuality, its gestures in storms or while sleeping in summer light, the quality of its sugar and nut, and the glossy fragrant wood"— all are distinctive. But, as his notebooks and some of the following letters show, he now begins to make an intensive study of all the trees of the Pacific Coast, particularly of the redwood. Thus, quite unconsciously, he was in training to become the leading defender of the Sierra forests during critical emergencies that arose in the nineties.

to Mrs. Ezra S. Carr

Yosemite Valley, June 3rd, 1875

DEAR MRS. CARR
Where are you? Lost in conventions, elections, women's rights and fights, and buried beneath many a load of musty granger hay. You always seem inaccessible to me, as if you were in a crowd, and even when I write, my written words seem to be heard by many that I do not like.

I wish some of your predictions given in your last may come true, like the first you made long ago. Yet somehow it seems hardly likely that you will ever be sufficiently free, for your labours multiply from year to year. Yet who knows.

I found poor Lamon's* grave, as you directed. The upper end of the Valley seems fairly silent and empty without him.

---

* James C. Lamon, pioneer settler of Yosemite Valley, who died May 22, 1875. See characterisation of him in Muir's *The Yosemite*.

Keith got fine sketches, and I found new beauties and truths of all kinds. Mack [McChesney] and Swett will tell you all. I send you my buttonhole plume.

Farewell.

JOHN MUIR

to Mrs. Ezra S. Carr

Black's Hotel, Yosemite,
July 31st, 1875

DEAR MRS. CARR

I have just arrived from our long excursion to Mount Whitney, all hale and happy, and find your weary plodding letter, containing things that from this rocky standpoint seem strangely mixed – things celestial and terrestrial, cultivated and wild. Your letters set one a-thinking, and yet somehow they never seem to make those problems of life clear, and I always feel glad that they do not form any part of my work, but that my lessons are simple rocks and waters and plants and humble beasts, all pure and in their places, the Man beast with all his complications being laid upon stronger shoulders.

I did not bring you down any Sedum roots or Cassiope sprays because I had not then received your letter, not that I forgot you as I passed the blessed Sierra heathers, or the primulas, or the pines laden with fragrant, nutty cones. But I am more and more made to feel that my gardens and herbariums and woods are all in their places as they grow, and I know them there, and can find them when I will. Yet I ought to carry their poor dead or dying forms to those who can have no better.

The Valley is lovely, scarce more than a whit the worse for the flower-crushing feet that every summer brings. . . . I am not decided about my summer. I want to go with the Sequoias a month or two into all their homes from north to south, learning what I can of their conditions and prospects, their age, stature, the area they occupy, etc. But John Swett, who is brother now, papa then, orders me home to booking. Bless me, what an awful thing town duty is! I was once free as any pine-playing wind, and feel that I have still a good length of line, but alack! there seems to be a hook or two of civilization in me that I would fain pull out, yet *would not pull out* – O, O, O!

I suppose you are weary of saying book, book, book, and perhaps when you fear me lost in rocks and Mono deserts I will, with Scotch perverseness, do all you ask and more. All this letter is about myself, and why not when I'm the only person in all the wide world that I know anything about – Keith, the cascade, not excepted.

Fare ye well, mother quail, good betide your brood and be they and you saved from the hawks and the big ugly buzzards and cormorants – grangeal, political, right and wrongical, – and I will be   Ever truly

JOHN MUIR

"Only that and nothing more."

to Sarah Muir Galloway

Yosemite Valley, November 2nd, 1875

DEAR SISTER SARAH

Here is your letter with the Dalles in it. I'm glad you have escaped so long from the cows and sewing and baking to God's green wild Dalles and dells, for I know you were young again and that the natural love of beauty you possess had free, fair play. I shall never forget the big happy day I spent there on the rocky, gorgey Wisconsin above Kilbourn City. What lanes full of purple orchids and ferns! *Aspidium fragrans* I found there for the first time, and what hillsides of huckleberries and rare asters and goldenrods. Don't you wish you were wild like me and as free to satisfy your love for whatever is pure and beautiful?

I returned last night from a two and a half months' excursion through the grandest portion of the Sierra Nevada forests. You remember reading of the big trees of Calaveras County, discovered fifteen or twenty years ago. Well, I have been studying the species *(Sequoia gigantea)* and have been all this time wandering amid those giants. They extend in a broken, interrupted belt along the western flank of the range a distance of one hundred and eighty miles. But I will not attempt to describe them here. I have written about them and will send you printed descriptions.

I fancy your little flock is growing fast towards prime. Yet how short seems the time when you occupied your family place on Hickory Hill. Our lives go on and close like a day-morning, noon, night. Yet how full of pure happiness these life days may be and how worthy of the God that plans them and suns them!

The book you speak of is not yet commenced, but I must go into winter quarters at once and go to work. While in the field I can only observe – take in, but give nothing out. The first winter snow is just now falling on Yosemite rocks. The domes are whitened, and ere long avalanches will rush with loud boom and roar, like new-made waterfalls. The November number of *Harper's Monthly* contains "Living Glaciers of California." The illustrations are from my pencil sketches, some of which were made when my fingers were so benumbed with frost I could scarcely hold my pencil.

Give my love to David and the children and Mrs. Galloway, and I will hope yet to see you all. But now, once more, Farewell.

[JOHN MUIR]

In tracing out the main forest belt of the Sierra Nevada, as Muir did during these years, he became appalled by the destructive forces at work therein. No less than five sawmills were found operating in the edge of the Big Tree belt. On account of the size of the trees and the difficulty of felling them, they were blasted down with dynamite, a proceeding that added a new element of criminal waste to the terrible destruction. The noble Fresno grove of Big Trees and the one situated on the north fork of the Kaweah already were fearfully ravaged. The wonderful grove on the north fork of the Kings River still was intact, but a man by the name of Charles Converse had just formed a company to reduce it to cheap lumber in the usual wasteful manner.

Hoping to arouse California legislators to at least the economic importance of checking this destruction he sent to the *Sacramento Record Union* a communication entitled "God's First Temples," with the sub-heading, "How Shall we Preserve our Forests?" It appeared on February 5th, 1876, and while it made little impression upon legislators it made Muir the centre around which conservation sentiment began to crystallise. Few at this time had pointed out, as he did, the practical importance of conserving the forests on account of their relation to climate, soil, and water-flow in the streams. The deadliest enemies of the forests and the public good, he declared, were not the sawmills in spite of their slash fires and wastefulness. That unsavoury distinction belonged to the "sheep-men," as they were called, and Muir's indictment of them in the above mentioned article, based upon careful observation, ran as follows:

Incredible numbers of sheep are driven to the mountain pastures every summer, and in order to make easy paths and to improve the pastures, running fires are set everywhere to burn off the old logs and underbrush. These fires are far more universal and destructive than would be guessed. They sweep through nearly the entire forest belt of the range from one extremity to the other, and in the dry weather, before the coming on of winter storms, are very destructive to all kinds of young trees, and especially to sequoia, whose loose, fibrous bark catches and burns at once. Excepting the Calaveras, I, last summer, examined every sequoia grove in the range, together with the main belt extending across the basins of Kaweah and Tule, and found everywhere the most deplorable waste from this cause. Indians burn off underbrush to facilitate deer-hunting. Campers of all kinds often permit fires to run, so also do mill-men, but the fires of "sheep-men" probably form more than ninety per cent of all destructive fires that sweep the woods. . . . Whether our loose-jointed Government is really able or willing to do anything in the matter remains to be seen. If our law-makers were to discover and enforce any method tending to lessen even in a small degree the destruction going on, they would thus cover a multitude of legislative sins in the eyes of every tree lover. I am satisfied, however, that the question can be intelligently discussed only after a careful survey of our forests has been made, together with studies of the forces now acting upon them.

The concluding suggestion bore fruit years afterward when President Cleveland, in 1896, appointed a commission to report upon the condition of the national forest areas.

to Sarah Muir Galloway

1419 Taylor Street, San Francisco,
April 17th, 1876

DEAR SISTER SARAH

I was glad the other day to have the hard continuous toil of book writing interrupted by the postman handing in your letter. It is full of news, but I can think of little to put in the letter you ask for.

My life these days is like the life of a glacier, one eternal grind, and the top of my head suffers a weariness at times that you know nothing about. I'm glad to see by the hills across the bay, all yellow and purple with buttercups and gilias, that spring is blending fast into summer, and soon I'll throw down my pen, and take up my heels to go mountaineering once more.

My first book is taking shape now, and is mostly written, but still far from complete. I hope to see it in print, rubbed, and scrubbed, and elaborated, some time next year.

Among the unlooked-for burdens fate is loading upon my toil-doomed shoulders, is this literature and lecture tour. I suppose I will be called upon for two more addresses in San Francisco ere I make my annual hegira to the woods. A few weeks ago I lectured at San Jose and Oakland.

I'm glad to hear of the general good health and welfare of our scattered and multiplied family, of Katie's returning health, and Joanna's. Remember me warmly to Mrs. Galloway, tell her I will be in Wisconsin in two or three years, and hope to see her, still surrounded by her many affectionate friends. I was pleasantly surprised to notice the enclosed clipping to-day in the *N.Y. Tribune*. I also read a notice of a book by Professor James Law of Cornell University, whom I used to play with. I met one of his scholars a short time ago. Give my love to David and all your little big ones.

Ever very affectionately yours
JOHN MUIR

to Sarah Muir Galloway

1419 Taylor Street, San Francisco,
January 12th, [1877]

DEAR SISTER SARAH

I received your welcome letter to-day. I was beginning to think you were neglecting me. The sad news of dear old Mrs. Galloway, though not unexpected, makes me feel that I have lost a friend. Few lives are so beautiful and complete as hers, and few could have had the glorious satisfaction, in dying, to know that so few words spoken were other than kind, and so few deeds that did anything more than augment the happiness of others. How many really good people waste, and worse than waste, their short lives in mean bickerings, when they might lovingly, in broad Christian charity, enjoy the glorious privilege of doing plain, simple, everyday good. Mrs. Galloway's character was one of the most beautiful and perfect I ever knew.

How delightful it is for you all to gather on the holidays, and what a grand multitude you must make when you are all mustered. Little did I think when I used to be, and am now, fonder of home and still domestic life than any one of the boys, that I only should be a bachelor and doomed to roam always far outside the family circle. But we are governed more than we know and are driven with whips we know not where. Your pleasures, and the happiness of your lives in general, are far greater than you know, being clustered together, yet independent, and living in one of the most beautiful regions under the sun. Long may you all live to enjoy your blessings and to learn to love one another and make sacrifices for one another's good.

You inquire about [my] books. The others I spoke of are a book of excursions, another on Yosemite and the adjacent mountains, and another "Studies in the Sierra" (scientific). The present volume will be descriptive of the Sierra animals, birds, forests, falls, glaciers, etc., which, if I live, you will see next fall or winter. I have not written enough to compose with much facility, and as I am also very careful and have but a limited vocabulary, I make slow progress. Still, although I never meant to write the results of my explorations, now I have begun I rather enjoy it and the public do me the credit of reading all I write, and paying me for it, which is some satisfaction, and I will not probably fail in my first effort on the book, inasmuch as I always make out to accomplish in some way what I undertake.

I don't write regularly for anything, although I'm said to be a regular correspondent of the [San Francisco] *Evening Bulletin*, and have the privilege of writing for it when I like. *Harper's* have two unpublished illustrated articles of mine, but after they pay for them they keep them as long as they like, sometimes a year or more, before publishing.

Love to David and George, and all your fine lassies, and love, dear Sarah, to yourself.   From your wandering brother

[JOHN MUIR]

The following letter invites comment. Until far into the later years of his life Muir wrote by preference with quills which he cut himself. Over against his bantering remark, that the pen he sends her may be a goose quill after all, should be set the fact that among the mementos preserved by his sister Sarah is a quill-pen wrapped with a cutting from one of John's letters which reads, "Your letter about the first book recalls old happy days on the mountains. The pen you speak of was made of a wing-feather of an eagle, picked up on Mount Hoffmann, back a few miles from Yosemite." The book he wrote with it did not see the light of day, at least in the form which he then gave it, and it is not certain what it contained beyond glowing descriptions of Sierra forests and scenery, and appeals for their preservation. That "the world needs the woods" has now become more than a sentimental conviction with him; the moral and economic aspects of the question begin to emerge strongly. One likes to think it a fact of more than poetic significance that such a book by such a man was written with a quill from an eagle's wing, and that the most patriotic service ever rendered by an American eagle was that of the one who contributed a wing pinion to John Muir for the defence of the western forests.

to Sarah Muir Galloway

San Francisco, April 23rd, 1877

MY DEAR SISTER SARAH

To thee I give and bequeath this old grey quill with which I have written every word of my first book, knowing, as I do, your predilection for curiosities.

I can hardly remember its origin, but I think it is one that I picked up on the mountains, fallen from the wing of a golden eagle; but, possibly, it may be only a pinion feather of some tame old grey goose, and my love of truth compels me to make this unpoetical statement. The book that has grown from its whittled nib is, however, as wild as any that has ever appeared in these tame, civilized days. Perhaps I should have waited until the book was in print, for it is not absolutely certain that it will be accepted by the publishing houses. It has first to be submitted to the tasting critics, but as everything in the way of magazine and newspaper articles that the old pen has ever traced has been accepted and paid for, I reasonably hope I shall have no difficulties in obtaining a publisher. The manuscript has just been sent to New York, and will be reported on in a few weeks. I leave for the mountains of Utah today.

The frayed upper end of the pen was produced by nervous gnawing when some interruption in my logic or rhetoric occurred from stupidity or weariness. I gnawed the upper end to send the thoughts below and out at the other.

Love to all your happy family and to thee and David. The circumstances of my life since I last bade you farewell have wrought many changes in me, but my love for you all has only grown greater from year to year, and whatsoever befalls I shall ever be, Yours affectionately

JOHN MUIR

The statement, in the preceding letter, that he is leaving for the mountains of Utah, the reader familiar with Muir's writings will at once connect with the vivid Utah sketches that have appeared in the volume entitled *Steep Trails*. In the same book are found the two articles on "The San Gabriel Valley " and "The San Gabriel Mountains," which grew out of an excursion he made into southern California soon after his return from Utah.

Mrs. Carr, who in 1877 had suffered the loss of another of her sons, was at this time preparing to carry out her long cherished plan to retire from public life to her new home in the South. With her for a magnet, Carmelita, as she called it, became for a time the literary centre of southern California. There Helen Hunt Jackson wrote the greater part of her novel *Ramona*, and numerous other literary folk, both East and West, made it at one time or another the goal of their pilgrimages. In her spacious garden she indulged to the full her passion for bringing together a great variety of unusual plants, shrubs, and trees, many of them contributed by John Muir. Dr. E. M. Congar, mentioned in one of the following letters, had been a fellow student of Muir at the University of Wisconsin.

to Mrs. Ezra S. Carr

Swett Home, July 23rd, [1877]

DEAR MRS. CARR

I made only a short dash into the dear old Highlands above Yosemite, but all was so full of everything I love, every day seemed a measureless period. I never enjoyed the Tuolumne cataracts so much; coming out of the sun lands, the grey salt deserts of Utah, these wild ice waters sang themselves into my soul more enthusiastically than ever, and the forests' breath was sweeter, and Cassiope fairer than in all my first fresh contacts.

But I am not going to tell it here. I only write now to say that next Saturday I will sail to Los Angeles and spend a few weeks in getting some general views of the adjacent region, then work northward and begin a careful study of the Redwood. I will at least have time this season for the lower portion of the belt, that is for all south of here. If you have any messages, you may have time to write me (I sail at 10 a.m.), or if not, you may direct to Los Angeles. I hope to see Congar, and also the spot you have elected for home. I wish you could be there in your grown, fruitful groves, all rooted and grounded in the fine garden nook that I know you will make. It must be a great consolation, in the midst of the fires you are compassed with, to look forward to a tranquil seclusion in the South of which you are so fond.

John [Swett] says he may not move to Berkeley, and if not I may be here this winter, though I still feel some tendency towards another winter in some mountain den.

It is long indeed since I had anything like a quiet talk with you. You have been going like an avalanche for many a year, and I sometimes fear you will not be able to settle into rest even in the orange groves. I'm glad to know that the Doctor is so well. You must be pained by the shameful attacks made upon your tried friend LaGrange.   Farewell.   Ever cordially yours

JOHN MUIR

to Mrs. Ezra S. Carr

Pico House, Los Angeles,
August 12th 1877

DEAR MRS. CARR

I've seen your sunny Pasadena and the patch called yours. Everything about here pleases me and I felt sorely tempted to take Dr. Congar's advice and invest in an orange patch myself. I feel sure you will be happy here with the Doctor and Allie among so rich a luxuriance of sunny vegetation. How you will dig and dibble in that mellow loam! I cannot think of you standing erect for a single moment, unless it be in looking away out into the dreamy West.

I made a fine shaggy little five days' excursion back in the heart of the San Gabriel Mountains, and then a week of real pleasure with Congar resurrecting the past about Madison. He has a fine little farm, fine little family, and fine cosy home. I felt at home with Congar and at once took possession of his premises and all that in them is. We drove down through the settlements eastward and saw the best orange groves and vineyards, but the mountains I, as usual, met alone. Although so grey and silent and unpromising they are full of wild gardens and ferneries. Lilyries! – some specimens ten feet high with twenty lilies, big enough for bonnets! The main results I will tell you some other time, should you ever have an hour's leisure.

I go north today, by rail to Newhall, thence by stage to Soledad and on to Monterey, where I will take to the woods and feel my way in free study to San Francisco. May reach the City about the middle of next month. . . .

Ever cordially

J. M.

to Mrs. Ezra S. Carr

1419 Taylor Street, San Francisco,
September 3rd, [1877]

DEAR MRS. CARR

I have just been over at Alameda with poor dear old Gibbons.* You have seen him, and I need give no particulars. "The only thing I'm afraid of, John," he said, looking up with his old child face, "is that I shall never be able to climb the Oakland hills again." But he is so healthy and so well cared for, we will be strong to hope that he will. He spoke for an hour with characteristic unselfishness on the injustice done Dr. [Albert] Kellogg in failing to recognise his long-continued devotion to science at the botanical love feast held here the other night. He threatens to write up the whole discreditable affair, and is very anxious to obtain from you a copy of that Gray letter to Kellogg which was not delivered.

I had a glorious ramble in the Santa Cruz woods, and have found out one very interesting and picturesque fact concerning the growth of this Sequoia. I mean to devote many a long week to its study. What the upshot may be I cannot guess, but you know I am never sent empty away.

I made an excursion to the summit of Mt. Hamilton in extraordinary style, accompanied by Allen, Norton, Brawley, and all the lady professors and their friends – a curious contrast to my ordinary *still hunting*. Spent a week at San Jose, enjoyed my visit with Allen very much. Lectured to the faculty on methods of study without undergoing any very great scare.

* W. P. Gibbons, M.D., an able amateur botanist and early member of the California Academy of Sciences.

I believe I wrote you from Los Angeles about my Pasadena week. Have sent a couple of letters to the *Bulletin* from there – not yet published.

I have no inflexible plans as yet for the remaining months of the season, but Yosemite seems to place itself as a most persistent candidate for my winter. I shall soon be in flight to the Sierras, or Oregon.

I seem to give up hope of ever seeing you calm again. Don't grind too hard at these Sacramento mills. Remember me to the Doctor and Allie.

Ever yours cordially

JOHN MUIR

One of the earliest and most distinguished pioneer settlers of California was General John Bidwell, of Chico, at whose extensive and beautiful ranch distinguished travellers and scientists often were hospitably entertained. In 1877, Sir Joseph Hooker and Asa Gray were among the guests of Rancho Chico, when they returned from a botanical trip to Mount Shasta, whither they had gone under the guidance of John Muir. This excursion, of which more later, drew Muir also into the friendly circle of the Bidwell family, and the following letter was written after a prolonged visit at Rancho Chico. "Lize in Jackets," wrote the late Mrs. Annie E. K. Bidwell in kindly transmitting a copy of this letter, "refers to my sister's mule, which, when attacked by yellow jackets whose nests we trod upon, would rise almost perpendicularly, then plunge forward frantically, kicking and twisting her tail with a rapidity that elicited uproarious laughter from Mr. Muir. Each of our riding animals had characteristic movements on this occasion, which Mr. Muir classified with much merriment." Just before his departure, on October 2nd, Muir expressed the wish that he might be able to descend the Sacramento River in a skiff, whereupon General Bidwell had his ranch carpenter hastily construct a kind of boat in which Muir made the trip described in the following letter.

to General John Bidwell, Mrs. Bidwell, and Miss Sallie Kennedy

Sacramento, October 10th, 1877

FRIENDS THREE

The Chico flagship and I are safely arrived in Sacramento, unwrecked, unsnagged, and the whole winding way was one glorious strip of enjoyment. When I bade you good-bye, on the bank I was benumbed and bent down with your lavish kindnesses like one of your vineladen willows. It is seldom that I experience much difficulty in leaving civilization for God's wilds, but I was loath indeed to leave you three that day after our long free ramble in the mountain woods and that five weeks' rest in your cool fruity home. The last I saw of you was Miss Kennedy white among the leaves like a fleck of mist, then sweeping around a bend you were all gone – the old wildness came back, and I began to observe, and enjoy, and be myself again.

My first camp was made on a little oval island some ten or twelve miles down, where a clump of arching willows formed a fine nestlike shelter; and where I spread my quilt on the gravel and opened the box so daintily and thoughtfully stored for my comfort. I began to reflect again on your real goodness to me from first to last, and said, "I'll not forget those Chico three as long as I live."

I placed the two flags at the head of my bed, one on each side, and as the campfire shone upon them the effect was very imposing and patriotic. The night came on full of strange sounds from birds and insects new to me, but the starry sky was clear and came arching over my lowland nest seemingly as bright and familiar with its glorious constellations as when beheld through the thin crisp atmosphere of the mountain-tops.

On the second day the Spoonbill sprang a bad leak from the swelling of the bottom timbers; two of them crumpled out thus [sketch]* at a point where they were badly nailed, and I had to run her ashore for repairs. I turned her upside down on a pebbly bar, took out one of the timbers, whittled it carefully down to the right dimensions, replaced it, and nailed it tight and fast with a stone for a hammer; then calked the new joint, shoved her back into the current) and rechristened her "The Snag-Jumper." She afterwards behaved splendidly in the most trying places, and leaked only at the rate of fifteen tincupfuls per hour.

Her performances in the way of snag-jumping are truly wonderful. Most snags are covered with slimy algae and lean downstream and the sloping bows of the Jumper enabled her to glance gracefully up and over them, when not too high above the water, while her lightness prevented any strain sufficient to crush her bottom. [Sketch of boat.] On one occasion she took a firm slippery snag a little obliquely and was nearly rolled upside down, as a sod is turned by a plough. Then I charged myself to be more careful, and while rowing often looked well ahead for snag ripples – but soon I came to a long glassy reach, and my vigilance not being eternal, my thoughts wandered upstream back to those grand spring fountains on the head of the McCloud and Pitt. Then I tried to picture those hidden tributaries that flow beneath the lava tablelands, and recognised in them a capital illustration of the fact that in their farthest fountains all rivers are lost to mortal eye, that the sources of all are hidden as those of the Nile, and so, also, that in this respect every river of knowledge is a Nile. Thus I was philosophising, rowing with a steady stroke, and as the current was rapid, the Jumper was making fine headway, when with a tremendous bump she reared like "Lize in Jackets," swung around stern downstream, and remained fast on her beam ends, erect like a coffin against a wall. She managed, however, to get out of even this scrape without disaster to herself or to me.

I usually sailed from sunrise to sunset, rowing one third of the time, paddling one third, and drifting the other third in restful comfort, landing

* After Mrs. Bidwell's death, the writer unfortunately was unable to obtain from her relatives the loan of this letter for the reproduction of the two included sketches.

now and then to examine a section of the bank or some bush or tree. Under these conditions the voyage to this port was five days in length. On the morning of the third day I hid my craft in the bank vines and set off cross-lots for the highest of the Marysville Buttes, reached the summit, made my observations, and got back to the river and Jumper by two o'clock. The distance to the nearest foothill of the group is about three miles, but to the base of the southmost and highest butte is six miles, and its elevation is about eighteen hundred feet above its base, or in round numbers two thousand feet above tidewater. The whole group is volcanic, taking sharp basaltic forms near the summit, and with stratified conglomerates of finely polished quartz and metamorphic pebbles tilted against their flanks. There is a sparse growth of live oak and laurel on the southern slopes, the latter predominating, and on the north quite a close tangle of dwarf oak forming a chaparral. I noticed the white mountain spiræa also, and madroa, with a few willows, and three ferns toward the summit. *Pellæa andromedæfolia, Gymnogramma triangularis*, and *Cheilanthes gracillima*; and many a fine flower – penstemons, gilias, and our brave eriogonums of blessed memory. The summit of this highest southmost butte is a coast survey station.

The river is very crooked, becoming more and more so in its lower course, flowing in grand lingering deliberation, now south, now north, east and west with fine un-American indirectness. The upper portion down as far as Colusa is full of rapids, but below this point the current is beautifully calm and lake-like, with innumerable reaches of most surpassing loveliness. How you would have enjoyed it! The bank vines all the way down are of the same species as those that festoon your beautiful Chico Creek (*Vitis californica*), but nowhere do they reach such glorious exuberance of development as with you.

The temperature of the water varies only about two and a half degrees between Chico and Sacramento, a distance by the river of nearly two hundred miles – the upper temperature 64°, the lower 66½°. I found the temperature of the Feather [River] waters at their confluence one degree colder than those of the Sacramento, 65° and 66° respectively, which is a difference in exactly the opposite direction from what I anticipated. All the brown discolouring mud of the lower Sacramento, thus far, is derived from the Feather, and it is curious to observe how completely the two currents keep themselves apart for three or four miles. I never landed to talk to anyone, or ask questions, but was frequently cheered from the bank and challenged by old sailors "Ship ahoy," etc., and while seated in the stern reading a magazine and drifting noiselessly with the current, I overheard a deck hand on one of the steamers say, "Now that's what I call taking it aisy."

I am still at a loss to know what there is in the rig or model of the Jumper that excited such universal curiosity. Even the birds of the river, and the animals that came to drink, though paying little or no heed to the passing steamers with all their plash and outroar, at once fixed their attention on my little flagship, some taking flight with loud screams, others waiting with outstretched necks until I nearly touched them, while others circled overhead. The domestic animals usually dashed up the bank in extravagant haste, one crowding on the heels of the other as if suffering extreme terror. I placed one flag, the smaller, on the highest pinnacle of the Butte, where I trust it may long wave to your memory; the other I have still. Watching the thousand land birds – linnets, orioles, sparrows, flickers, quails, etc. – Nature's darlings, taking their morning baths, was no small part of my enjoyments.

I was greatly interested in the fine bank sections shown to extraordinary advantage at the present low water, because they cast so much light upon the formation of this grand valley, but I cannot tell my results here.

This letter is already far too long, and I will hasten to a close. I will rest here a day or so, and then push off again to the mouth of the river a hundred miles or so farther, chiefly to study the deposition of the sediment at the head of the bay, then push for the mountains. I would row up the San Joaquin, but two weeks or more would be required for the trip, and I fear snow on the mountains.

I am glad to know that you are really interested in science, and I might almost venture another lecture upon you, but in the meantime forbear. Looking backward I see you three in your leafy home, and while I wave my hand, I will only wait to thank you all over and over again for the thousand kind things you have done and said – drives, and grapes, and rest, "a' that and a' that."

And now, once more, farewell.

Ever cordially your friend

JOHN MUIR

During this same summer of 1877, and previous to the experiences narrated in the preceding letter, the great English botanist Sir Joseph Dalton Hooker had accepted an invitation from Dr. F. V. Hayden, then in charge of the United States Geological and Geographical Survey of the Territories, to visit under his conduct the Rocky Mountain region, with the object of contributing to the records of the Survey a report on the botany of the western states. Professor Asa Gray was also of the party. After gathering some special botanical collections in Colorado, New Mexico, and Utah, they came to California and persuaded John Muir, on account of his familiarity with the region, to go with them to Mount Shasta. One September evening, as they were encamped on its flanks in a forest of silver firs, Muir built a big fire, whose glow stimulated an abundant flow of interesting conversation. Gray recounted reminiscences of his collecting tours in the Alleghenies; Hooker told of his travels in the Himalaya and of his work with Tyndall, Huxley, and Darwin. "And of course," notes Muir, "we talked of trees, argued the relationship of varying species, etc.; and I remember that Sir Joseph, who in his long active life had travelled through all the great forests of the world, admitted, in reply to a question of mine, that in grandeur, variety, and beauty, no forest on the globe rivalled the great coniferous forests of my much loved Sierra."

But the most memorable incident of that night on the flanks of Shasta grew out of the mention of *Linnœa borealis* – the charming little evergreen trailer whose name perpetuates the memory of the illustrious Linnaeus. "Muir, why have you not found *linnœa* in California?" said Gray suddenly during a pause in the conversation. "It must be here, or hereabouts, on the northern boundary of the Sierra. I have heard of it, and have specimens from Washington and Oregon all through these northern woods, and you should have found it here." The camp fire sank into heaps of glowing coals, the conversation ceased, and all fell asleep with *Linnœa* uppermost in their minds.

The next morning Gray continued his work alone, while Hooker and Muir made an excursion westward across one of the upper tributaries of the Sacramento. In crossing a small stream, they noticed a green bank carpeted with what Hooker at once recognised as *Linnœa* – the first discovery of the plant within the bounds of California. "It would seem," said Muir, "that Gray had felt its presence the night before on the mountain ten miles away. That was a great night, the like of which was never to be enjoyed by us again, for we soon separated and Gray died."* The impression Muir made upon Hooker is reflected in his letters. In one of them, written twenty-five years after the event, Hooker declares, "My memory of you is very strong and durable, and that of our days in the forests is inextinguishable."

In the following letter to his sister Muir gives some additional details of the Shasta excursion, and makes reference to an exceedingly strenuous exploring trip up the Middle Fork of the Kings River, from which he had just returned.

to Sarah Muir Galloway

Thanksgiving Evening,
at old 1419 Taylor Street
[November 29th, 1877]

MY DEAR SISTER SARAH

I find an unanswered letter of yours dated September 23rd, and though I have been very hungry on the mountains a few weeks ago, and have just been making bountiful amends at a regular turkey thank-feast of the old New England type, I must make an effort to answer it, however incapacitated by "stuffing," for, depend upon it, this Turkish method of thanks does make the simplest kind of literary effort hard; one's brains go heavily along the easiest lines like a laden wagon in a bog.

But I can at least answer your questions. The Professor Gray I was with on Shasta is the writer of the school botanies, the most distinguished botanist in America, and Sir Joseph Hooker is the leading botanist of England. We had a fine rare time together in the Shasta forests, discussing the botanical characters of the grandest coniferous trees in the world, camping out, and enjoying ourselves in pure freedom. Gray is an old friend that I led around Yosemite

* Muir's article on Linnaeus in *Library of the World's Best Literature*, Vol. 16 (1897).

years ago, and with whom I have corresponded for a long time. Sir Joseph I never met before. He is a fine cordial Englishman, President of the Royal Scientific Society, and has charge of the Kew Botanic Gardens. He is a great traveller, but perfectly free from all chilling airs of superiority. He told me a great deal about the Himalayas, the deodar forests there, and the gorgeous rhododendrons that cover their flanks with lavish bloom for miles and miles, and about the cedars of Lebanon that he visited and the distribution of the species in different parts of Syria, and its relation to the deodar so widely extended over the mountains of India. And besides this scientific talk he told many a story and kept the camp in fine lively humour. On taking his leave he gave me a hearty invitation to London, and promised to show me through the famous government gardens at Kew, and all round, etc., etc. When I shall be able to avail myself of this and similar advantages I don't know. I have met a good many of Nature's noblemen one way and another out here, and hope to see some of them at their homes, but my own researches seem to hold me fast to this comparatively solitary life.

Next you speak of my storm night on Shasta. Terrible as it would appear from the account printed, the half was not told, but I will not likely be caught in the same experience again, though as I have said, I have just been very hungry – one meal in four days, coupled with the most difficult, nerve-trying cliff work. This was on Kings River a few weeks ago. Still, strange to say, I did not feel it much, and there seems to be scarce any limit to my endurance.

I am far from being friendless here, and on this particular day I might have eaten a score of prodigious thank dinners if I could have been in as many places at the same time, but the more I learn of the world the happier seems to me the life you live. You speak of your family gatherings, of a week's visit at Mother's and here and there. Make the most of your privileges to trust and love and live in near, unjealous, generous sympathy with one another, for I assure you these are blessings scarce at all recognised in their real divine greatness....

We had a company of fourteen at dinner tonight, and we had what is called a grand time, but these big eating parties never seem to me to pay for the trouble they make, though all seem to enjoy them immensely. A crust by a brookside out on the mountains with God is more to me than all, beyond comparison. Nevertheless these poor legs in their weariness do enjoy a soft bed at times and plenty of nourishment. I had another grand turkey feast a week ago. Coming home here I left my boat at Martinez, thirty miles up the bay, and walked to Oakland across the top of Mount Diablo, and on the way called at my friends, the Strentzels, who have eighty acres of choice orchards and vineyards, where I rested two days, my first rest in six weeks. They pitied my weary looks, and made me eat and sleep, stuffing me with turkey, chicken, beef, fruits, and jellies in the most extravagant manner imaginable, and begged me to stay a month. Last eve dined at a French friend's in the city, and you would have been surprised to see so temperate a Scotchman doing such justice to French dishes. The fact is I've been hungry ever since starving in the mountain canyons.

This evening the guests would ask me how I felt while starving? Why I did not die like other people? How many bears I had seen, and deer, etc.? How deep the snow is now and where the snow line is located, etc.? Then upstairs we chat and sing and play piano, etc., and then I slip off from the company and write this. Now it [is] near midnight, and I must slip from thee also, wishing you and David and all your dear family goodnight.   With love,

[JOHN MUIR]

to General John Bidwell

1419 Taylor Street, San Francisco
December 3rd, 1877

MY DEAR GENERAL

I arrived in my old winter quarters here a week ago, my season's field work done, and I was just sitting down to write to Mrs. Bidwell when your letter of November 29th came in. The tardiness of my Kings River postal is easily explained. I committed it to the care of a mountaineer who was about to descend to the lowlands, and he probably carried it for a month or so in his breeches' pocket in accordance with the well-known business habits of that class of men. And now since you are so kindly interested in my welfare I must give you here a sketch of my explorations since I wrote you from Sacramento.

I left Snag-Jumper at Sacramento in charge of a man whose name I have forgotten. He has boats of his own, and I tied Snag to one of his stakes in a snug out-of-the-way nook above the railroad bridge. I met this pilot a mile up the river on his way home from hunting. He kindly led me into port, and then conducted me in the dark up the Barbary Coast into the town; and on taking leave he volunteered the information that he was always kindly disposed towards strangers but that most people met under such circumstances would have robbed and made away with me, etc. I think, therefore, that leaving Snag in his care will form an interesting experiment on human nature.

I fully intended to sail on down into the bay and up the San Joaquin as far as Millerton, but when I came to examine a map of the river deltas and found that the distance was upwards of three hundred miles, and learned also that the upper San Joaquin was not navigable this dry year even for my craft, and when I also took into consideration the approach of winter and danger of snowstorms on the Kings River summits, I concluded to urge my way into the mountains at once, and leave the San Joaquin studies until my return.

Accordingly I took the steamer to San Francisco, where I remained one day, leaving extra baggage, and getting some changes of clothing. Then went direct by rail to Visalia, thence pushed up the mountains to Hyde's Mill on the Kaweah, where I obtained some flour, which, together with the tea Mrs. Bidwell supplied me with, and that piece of dried beef, and a little sugar, constituted my stock of provisions. From here I crossed the divide, going northward through fine Sequoia woods to Converse's on Kings River. Here I spent two days making some studies on the Big Trees, chiefly with reference to their age. Then I turned eastward and pushed off into the glorious wilderness, following the general direction of the South Fork a few miles back from the brink until I had crossed three tributary canyons from 1500 to 2000 feet deep. In the eastmost and middle one of the three I was delighted to discover some four or five square miles of Sequoia, where I had long guessed the existence of these grand old tree kings.

After this capital discovery I made my way to the bottom of the main South Fork Canyon down a rugged side gorge, having a descent of more than four thousand feet. This was at a point about two miles above the confluence of Boulder Creek. From here I pushed slowly on up the bottom of the canyon, through brush and avalanche boulders, past many a charming fall and garden sacred to nature, and at length reached the grand yosemite at the head, where I stopped two days to make some measurements of the cliffs and cascades. This done, I crossed over the divide to the Middle Fork by a pass 12,200 feet high, and struck the head of a small tributary that conducted me to the head of the main Middle Fork Canyon, which I followed down through its entire length, though it has hitherto been regarded as absolutely inaccessible in its lower reaches. This accomplished, and all my necessary sketches and measurements made, I climbed the canyon wall below the confluence of the Middle and South Forks and came out at Converse's again; then back to Hyde's Mill, Visalia, and thence to Merced City by rail, thence by stage to Snelling, and thence to Hopeton afoot.

Here I built a little unpretentious successor to Snag out of some gnarled, sun-twisted fencing, launched it in the Merced opposite the village, and rowed down into the San Joaquin – thence down the San Joaquin past Stockton and through the tule region into the bay near Martinez. There I abandoned my boat and set off cross lots for Mount Diablo, spent a night on the summit, and walked the next day into Oakland. And here my fine summer's wanderings came to an end. And now I find that this mere skeleton finger board indication of my excursion has filled at least the space of a long letter, while I have told you nothing of my gains. If you were nearer I would take a day or two and come and report, and talk inveterately in and out of season until you would be glad to have me once more in the canyons and silence. But Chico is far, and I can only finish with a catalogue of my new riches, setting them down one after the other like words in a spelling book.

1. Four or five square miles of Sequoias.
2. The ages of twenty-six specimen Sequoias.
3. A fine fact about bears.
4. A sure measurement of the deepest of all the ancient glaciers
      yet traced in the Sierra.
5. Two waterfalls of the first order, and cascades innumerable.
6. *A new Yosemite valley*!!!
7. Grand facts concerning the formation of the central plain of California.
8. A picturesque cluster of facts concerning the river birds and animals.
9. A glorious series of new landscapes, with mountain furniture
      and garniture of the most ravishing grandeur and beauty.

Here, Mrs. Bidwell, is a rose leaf from a wild briar on Mount Diablo whose leaves are more flowery than its petals. Isn't it beautiful? That new Yosemite Valley is located in the heart of the Middle Fork Canyon, the most remote, and inaccessible, and one of the very grandest of all the mountain temples of the range. It is still sacred to Nature, its gardens untrodden, and every nook and rejoicing cataract wears the bloom and glad sun-beauty of primeval wildness – ferns and lilies and grasses over one's head. I saw a flock of five deer in one of its open meadows, and a grizzly bear quietly munching acorns under a tree within a few steps.

The cold was keen and searching the night I spent on the summit by the edge of a glacier lake twenty-two degrees below the freezing point, and a storm wind blowing in fine hearty surges among the shattered cliffs overhead, and, to crown all, snow flowers began to fly a few minutes after midnight, causing me to fold that quilt of yours and fly to avoid a serious snowbound. By daylight I was down in the main Middle Fork in a milder climate and safer position at an elevation of only seventy-five hundred feet. All the summit peaks were quickly clad in close unbroken white.

I was terribly hungry ere I got out of this wild canyon – had less than sufficient for one meal in the last four days, and this, coupled with very hard nerve-trying cliff work was sufficiently exhausting for any mountaineer. Yet strange to say, I did not suffer much. Crystal water, and air, and honey sucked from the scarlet flowers of Zauschneria, about one tenth as much as would suffice for a humming bird, was my last breakfast – a very temperate meal, was it not? – wholly ungross and very nearly spiritual. The last effort before reaching food was a climb up out of the main canyon of five thousand feet. Still I made it in fair time – only a little faint, no giddiness, want of spirit, or incapacity to observe and enjoy, or any nonsense of this kind. How I should have liked to have then tumbled into your care for a day or two !

My sail down the Merced and San Joaquin was about two hundred and fifty miles in length and took two weeks, a far more difficult and less interesting [trip], as far as scenery is concerned, than my memorable first voyage down the Sacramento. Sandbars and gravelly riffles, as well as snags gave me much trouble, and in the Tule wilderness I had to tether my tiny craft to a bunch of rushes and sleep cold in her bottom with the seat for a pillow. I have gotten past most of the weariness but am hungry yet notwithstanding friends have been stuffing me here ever since. I may go hungry through life and into the very grave and beyond unless you effect a cure, and I'm sure I should like to try Rancho Chico – would have tried it ere this were you not so far off.

I slept in your quilt all through the excursion, and brought it here tolerably clean and whole. The flag I left tied to the bush-top in the bottom of the third F Canyon. I have not yet written to Gray, have you? Remember me to your sister, I mean to write to her soon. I must close. With lively remembrances of your rare kindness, I am

Ever very cordially yours

JOHN MUIR

to Dr. and Mrs. John Strentzel, and Miss Strentzel

1419 Taylor Street, San Francisco
December 5th, 1877

FRIENDS THREE

I made a capital little excursion over your Mount Diablo and arrived in good order in San Francisco after that fine rest in your wee white house.

I sauntered on leisurely after bidding you goodbye, enjoying the landscape as it was gradually unrolled in the evening light. One charming bit of picture after another came into view at every turn of the road, and while the sunset fires were burning brightest I had attained an elevation sufficient for a grand comprehensive feast.

I reached the summit a little after dark and selected a sheltered nook in the chaparral to rest for the night and await the coming of the sun. The wind blew a gale, but I did not suffer much from the cold. The night was keen and crisp and the stars shone out with better brilliancy than one could hope for in these lowland atmospheres.

The sunrise was truly glorious. After lingering an hour or so, observing and feasting and making a few notes, I went down to that halfway hotel for breakfast. I was the only guest, while the family numbered four, well attired and intellectual looking persons, who for a time kept up a solemn, quakerish silence which I tried in vain to break up. But at length all four began a hearty, spontaneous discussion upon the art of cat killing, solemnly and decently relating in turn all their experience in this delightful business in bygone time, embracing everything with grave fervour in the whole scale of cat, all the way up from sackfuls of purblind kittens to tigerish Toms. Then I knew that such knowledge was attainable only by intellectual New Englanders.

My walk down the mountain-side across the valleys and through the Oakland hills was very delightful, and I feasted on many a bit of pure picture in purple and gold, Nature's best, and beheld the most ravishingly beautiful sunset on the Bay I ever yet enjoyed in the lowlands.

I shall not soon forget the rest I enjoyed in your pure white bed, or the feast on your fruity table. Seldom have I been so deeply weary, and as for hunger, I've been hungry still in spite of it all, and for aught I see in the signs of the stomach may go hungry on through life and into the grave and beyond.

Heaven forbid a dry year ! May wheat grow !

With lively remembrances of your rare kindness, I am,
Very cordially your friend
JOHN MUIR

The winter and the spring months passed swiftly in the effort to correlate and put into literary form his study of the forests. There were additional "tree days," too, and other visits with the congenial three on the Strentzel ranch. But when the Swetts, with whom he made his home, departed for the summer, taking their little daughter with them, he furloughed himself to the woods again without ceremony. "Helen Swett," he wrote to the Strentzels on May 5th, "left this morning, and the house is in every way most dolefully dull, and I won't stay in it. Will go into the woods, perhaps about Mendocino – will see more trees."

A group of Sequoias, of all ages, in the southern forest of Kaweah.
(from "Treasures of the Proposed Yosemite National Park" – see page 587)

CHAPTER THIRTEEN

Nevada, Alaska, and a Home 1878–1880

DURING THE SUMMER of 1878 the United States Coast and Geodetic Survey made a reconnaissance along the 39th parallel of latitude in order to effect the primary triangulation of Nevada and Utah. The survey party was in charge of Assistant A. F. Rodgers, and was making preparations to set out from Sacramento in June, when Muir returned from a trip to the headwaters of the north and middle forks of the American River. He decided immediately to accept an invitation to join the party, although some of his friends, notably the Strentzels, sought to dissuade him on account of the Indian disturbances which had made Nevada unsafe territory for a number of years. Idaho was then actually in the throes of an Indian war that entailed the destruction and abandonment of the Malheur Reservation across the boundary in Oregon.

But the perils of the situation were in Muir's view outweighed by the exceptional opportunity to explore numerous detached mountain ranges and valleys of Nevada about which little was known at the time. "If an explorer of God's fine wildernesses should wait until every danger be removed," he wrote to Mrs. Strentzel, "then he would wait until the sun set. The war country lies to the north of our line of work, some two or three hundred miles. Some of the Pah Utes have gone north to join the Bannocks, and those left behind are not to be trusted, but we shall be well armed, and they will not dare to attack a party like ours unless they mean to declare war, however gladly they might seize the opportunity of killing a lonely and unknown explorer. In any case we will never be more than two hundred miles from the railroad."

Unfortunately Muir, becoming absorbed the following year in the wonders of Alaska, never found time to reduce his Nevada explorations to writing in the form of well-considered articles. He did, however, write for the *San Francisco Evening Bulletin* a number of sketches during the progress of the expedition, and these, published in *Steep Trails*, can now be supplemented with the following letters to the Strentzels – the only extant series written during that expedition.

Since Muir ultimately married into the Strentzel family, its antecedents are of interest to the reader and may be sketched briefly in this connection. John Strentzel, born in Lublin, Poland, was a participant in the unsuccessful Polish revolution of 1830. To escape the bitter fate of being drafted into the victorious Russian army he fled to Upper Hungary where he obtained a practical knowledge of viticulture, and later was trained as a physician at the University of Buda-Pesth [Budapest]. Coming to the United States in 1840, he joined at Louisville, Kentucky, a party of pioneers known as Peters' Colonisation Company, and went with them to the Trinity River in Texas, where he built a cabin on the present site of the city of Dallas, then a wild Comanche country. When the colony failed and dispersed he removed to Lamar County in the same state, was married at Honeygrove to Louisiana Erwin, a native of Tennessee, and in 1849, with his wife and baby daughter, came across the plains from Texas to California as medical adviser to the Clarkesville "train" of pioneer immigrants. Not long afterwards he settled in the Alhambra Valley* near Martinez, and became one of the earliest and most successful horticulturists of California.

Miss Louie Wanda Strentzel, now arrived at mature womanhood, was not only the pride of the family, but was known widely for the grace with which she dispensed the generous hospitality of the Strentzel household. She had received her education in the Atkins Seminary for Young Ladies at Benicia and, according to her father, was "passionately fond of flowers and music." Among her admiring friends was Mrs. Carr, who at various times had vainly tried to bring about a meeting between Miss Strentzel and Mr. Muir. "You see how I am snubbed in trying to get John Muir to accompany me to your house this week," wrote Mrs. Carr in April, 1875. Mount Shasta was in opposition at the time, and easily won the choice.

But so many roads and interests met at the Strentzel ranch, so many friends had the two in common, that sooner or later an acquaintanceship was bound to result. In 1878 Muir began to be a frequent and fondly expected guest in the Strentzel household, and he was to discover ere long that the most beautiful adventures are not those one deliberately goes to seek.

Meantime, despite the dissuasion of his solicitous friends, he was off to the wildernesses of Nevada. Since the Survey had adopted for triangulation purposes a pentagon whose angles met at Genoa Peak, the party first made its way to the town of the same name in its vicinity, where the first of the following letters was written.

to Dr. and Mrs. John Strentzel

Genoa, Nevada, July 6th, 1878

DEAR STRENTZELS

We rode our horses from Sacramento to this little village via Placerville and Lake Tahoe. The plains and foothills were terribly hot, the upper Sierra along

---

* According to Dr. Strentzel's journal, this was not the original name of the valley. A company of Spanish soldiers, sent to chastise some Indians, was unable to obtain provisions there, and so named it, "Canada de la Hambre," or Valley of Hunger. "Mrs. Strentzel, on arriving here," writes her husband, "was displeased with the name, and remembering Irving's glowing description of the Moorish paradise, decided to re-christen our home Alhambra." Ever since then the valley has borne this modification of the original name.

the south fork of the American River cool and picturesque, and the Lake region almost cold. Spent three delightful days at the Lake – steamed around it, and visited Cascade Lake a mile beyond the western shore of Tahoe.

We are now making up our train ready to push off into the Great Basin. Am well mounted, and with the fine brave old garden desert before me, fear no ill. We will probably reach Austin, Nevada, in about a month. Write to me there, care Captain A. F. Rodgers.

Your fruity hollow wears a most beautiful and benignant aspect from this alkaline standpoint, and so does the memory of your extravagant kindness.

Farewell
JOHN MUIR

to Dr. and Mrs. Strentzel

West Walker River
Near Wellington's Station
July 11th, 1878

DEAR STRENTZELS

We are now fairly free in the sunny basin of the grand old sea that stretched from the Wasatch to the Sierra. There is something perfectly enchanting to me in this young desert with its stranded island ranges. How bravely they rejoice in the flooding sunshine and endure the heat and drought.

All goes well in camp. All the Indians we meet are harmless as sagebushes, though perhaps about as bitter at heart. The river here goes brawling out into the plain after breaking through a range of basaltic lava.

In three days we shall be on top of Mount Grant, the highest peak of the Wassuck Range, to the west of Walker Lake.

I send you some Nevada prunes, or peaches rather. They are very handsome and have a fine wild flavour. The bushes are from three to six feet high, growing among the sage. It is a true *Prunus*. Whether cultivation could ever make it soft enough and big enough for civilized teeth I dinna ken, but guess so. Plant it and see. It will not be ashamed of any pampered "free" or "cling," or even your oranges.

The wild briar roses are in full bloom, sweeter and bonnier far than Louie's best, bonnie though they be.

I can see no post-office ahead nearer than Austin, Nevada, which we may reach in three weeks. The packs are afloat.   Good-morning.

[JOHN MUIR]

to Dr. John Strentzel

Austin, Nevada, August 5th, 1878

DEAR DOCTOR

Your kind note of the 24th was received the other day and your discussion of fruits and the fineness in general of civilized things takes me at some little disadvantage.

From the "Switch" we rode to the old Fort Churchill on the Carson and at the "Upper" lower end of Mason Valley were delighted to find the ancient outlet of Walker Lake down through a very picturesque canyon to its confluence with the Carson. It appears therefore that not only the Humboldt and Carson, but the Walker River also poured its waters into the Great Sink towards the end of the glacial period. From Fort Churchill we pushed eastward between Carson Lake and the Sink. Boo! how hot it was riding in the solemn, silent glare, shadeless, waterless. Here is what the early emigrants called the forty-mile desert, well marked with bones and broken wagons. Strange how the very sunshine may become dreary. How strange a spell this region casts over poor mortals accustomed to shade and coolness and green fertility. Yet there is no real cause, that I could see, for reasonable beings losing their wits and becoming frightened. There are the lovely tender abronias blooming in the fervid sand and sun, and a species of sunflower, and a curious leguminous bush crowded with purple blossoms, and a green saltwort, and four or five species of artemisia, really beautiful, and three or four handsome grasses.

Lizards revelled in the grateful heat and a brave little tamias that carries his tail forward over his back, and here and there a hare. Immense areas, however, are smooth and hard and plantless, reflecting light like water. How eloquently they tell of the period, just gone by, when this region was as remarkable for its lavish abundance of lake water as now for its aridity. The same grand geological story is inscribed on the mountain flanks, old beach lines that seem to have been drawn with a ruler, registering the successive levels at which the grand lake stood, corresponding most significantly with the fluctuations of the glaciers as marked by the terraced lateral moraines and successively higher terminal moraines.

After crossing the Sink we ascended the mountain range that bounds it on the East, eight thousand to ten thousand feet high. How treeless and barren it seemed. Yet how full of small charming gardens, with mints, primroses, briar-roses, penstemons, spiraeas, etc., watered by trickling streams too small to sing audibly. How glorious a view of the Sink from the mountain-top. The colours are ineffably lovely, as if here Nature were doing her very best painting.

But a letter tells little. We next ascended the Augusta Range, crossed the Desetoya and Shoshone ranges, then crossed Reese River valley and ascended the Toyabe Range, eleven thousand feet high. Lovely gardens in all. Discovered here the true *Pinus flexilis* at ten thousand feet. It enters the Sierra in one or two places on the south extremity of the Sierra, east flank. Saw only one rattlesnake. No hostile Indians. Had a visit at my tent yesterday from Captain Bob, one of the Pah Ute plenipotentiaries who lately visited McDowell at San Francisco. Next address for two weeks from this date, Eureka, Nevada.

I'm sure I showed my appreciation of good things. That's a fine suggestion about the grapes. Try me, Doctor, on tame, tame Tokays.

Cordially yours

JOHN MUIR

to Dr. and Mrs. John Strentzel

In camp near Belmont, Nevada
August 28th, 1878

DEAR STRENTZELS

I sent you a note from Austin. Thence we travelled southward down the Big Smoky Valley, crossing and recrossing it between the Toyabe and Toquima Ranges, the dominating summits of which we ascended. Thence still southward towards Death Valley to Lone Mountain; thence northeastward to this little mining town.

From the summit of a huge volcanic table mountain of the Toquima Range I observed a truly glorious spectacle – a dozen "cloud-bursts" falling at once while we were cordially pelted with hail. The falling water cloud-drapery, thunder tones, lightning, and tranquil blue sky windows between made one of the most impressive pictures I ever beheld. One of these cloud-bursts fell upon Austin, another upon Eureka. But still more glorious to me was the big significant fact I found here, fresh, telling glacial phenomena – a whole series. Moraines, *roches moutonnées*, glacial sculptures, and even feeble specimens of glacier meadows and glacier lakes. I also observed less manifest glaciation on several other ranges. I have long guessed that this Great Basin was loaded with ice during the last cold period; but the rocks are as unresisting and the water spouts to which all the ranges have been exposed have not simply obscured the glacial scriptures here, but nearly buried and obliterated them, so that only the skilled observer would detect a single word, and he would probably be called a glaciated monomaniac. Now it is clear that this fiery inland region was icy prior to the lake period.

I have also been so fortunate as to settle that pine species we discussed, and found the nest and young of the Alpine sparrow. What do you think of all this – "'A' that and a' that"? The sun heat has been intense. What a triangle of noses! – Captain Rodgers', Eimbeck's, and mine – mine sore, Eimbeck's sorer, Captain's sorest – scaled and dry as the backs of lizards, and divided into sections all over the surface and turned up on the edges like the surface layers of the desiccated sections of adobe flats.

On Lone Mountain we were *thirsty*. How we thought of the cool singing streams of the Sierra while our blood fevered and boiled and throbbed! Three of us ascended the mountain against my counsel and remonstrances while forty miles from any known water. Two of the three nearly lost their lives. I suffered least, though I suffered as never before, and was the only one strong enough to ascend a sandy canyon to find and fetch the animals after descending the mountain. Then I had to find my two companions. One I found death-like, lying in the hot sand, scarcely conscious and unable to speak above a frightful whisper. I managed, however, to get him on his horse. The other I found in a kind of delirious stupor, voiceless, in the sagebrush. It was a fearfully exciting search, and I forgot my own exhaustion in it, though I never for a moment lost my will and wits, or doubted our ability to endure and escape. We reached water at daybreak of the second day – two days and nights in this fire without water! A lesson has been learned that will last, and we will not suffer so again. Of course we could not eat or sleep all this time, for we could not swallow food and the fever prevented sleep. Tomorrow we set out for the White Pine region.   Cordially yours

J. MUIR

to Mrs. John Strentzel

Belmont, Nevada
August 31st, 1878

DEAR MRS. STRENTZEL

I wrote you a note the other day before receiving your letter of the 14th which reached me this morning. The men are packing up and I have only a moment. We have been engaged so long southward that we may not go to Eureka. If not we will make direct to Hamilton and the box the Doctor so kindly sent I will have forwarded.

The fiery sun is pouring his first beams across the grey Belmont hills, but so long as there is anything like a fair supply of any kind of water to keep my blood thin and flowing, it affects me but little. We are all well again, or nearly so – I quite. Our leader still shows traces of fever. The difference between wet and dry bulb thermometer here is often 40° or more, causing excessive waste from lungs and skin, and, unless water be constantly supplied, one's blood seems to thicken to such an extent that if Shylock should ask, "If you prick him, will he bleed?" I should answer, "I dinna ken." Heavens! if the juicy grapes had come mannalike from the sky that last thirst-night!

Farewell. We go.   Cordially and thankfully yours

JOHN MUIR

[The following note was written, probably the evening of the same day, on the reverse of the letter-sheet.]

The very finest, softest, most ethereal purple hue tinges, permeates, covers, glorifies the mountains and the level. How lovely then, how suggestive of the best heaven, how unlike a desert now! While the little garden, the hurrying moths, the opening flowers, and the cool evening wind that now begins to flow and lave down the grey slopes above, heighten the peacefulness and loveliness of the scene.

to Dr. and Mrs. John Strentzel

Hamilton, Nevada
September 11th, 1878

DEAR STRENTZELS

All goes well in camp save that box of grapes you so kindly sent. I telegraphed for it, on arriving at this place, to be sent by Wells Fargo, but it has not come, and we leave here tomorrow. We had hoped to have been in Eureka by the middle of last month, but the unknown factors so abundant in our work have pushed us so far southward we will not now be likely to go there at all. Nevertheless I have enjoyed your kindness even in this last grape expression of it, but you must not try to send any more, because we will not again be within grape range of railroads until on our way home in October or November. Then, should there be any left, I will manifest for my own good and the edification of civilization a fruit capacity and fervour to be found only in savage camps.

Since our Lone Mountain experience we have not been thirsty. Our course hence is first south for eighty or ninety miles along the western flank of the White Pine Range, then east to the Snake Range near the boundary of the State, etc.

Our address will be Hamilton, Nevada, until the end of this month. Our movements being so uncertain, we prefer to have our mail forwarded to points where we chance to find ourselves. In southern Utah the greater portion of our course will be across deserts.

The roses are past bloom, but I'll send seeds from the first garden I find. Yesterday found on Mount Hamilton the *Pinus aristata* growing on limestone and presenting the most extravagant picturesqueness I have ever met in any climate or species. Glacial traces, too, of great interest. This is the famous White Pine mining region, now nearly dead. Twenty-eight thousand mining claims were located in the district, which is six miles by twelve. Now only fifteen are worked, and of these only one, the Eberhardt, gives much hope or money. Both Hamilton and Treasure City are silent now, but Nature goes on gloriously.   Cordially yours

                                                    JOHN MUIR

                              to Dr. John Strentzel

                                        Ward, Nevada, Saturday Morning
                                                September 28th, 1878

DEAR DOCTOR

Your kind letter of the 8th ultimo reached me yesterday, having been forwarded from Hamilton. This is a little three-year-old mining town where we are making a few days' halt to transact some business and rest the weary animals. We arrived late, when it was too dark to set the tents, and we recklessly camped in a corral on a breezy hilltop. I have a great horror of sleeping upon any trodden ground near human settlements, not to say ammoniacal pens, but the Captain had his blankets spread alongside the wagon, and I dared the worst and lay down beside him. A wild equinoctial gale roared and tumbled down the mountain-side all through the night, sifting the dry fragrant snuff about our eyes and ears, notwithstanding all our care in tucking and rolling our ample blankets. The situation was not exactly distressing, but most absurdly and d—dly ludicrous. Our camp traps, basins, bowls, bags, went speeding wildly past in screeching rumbling discord with the earnest wind-tones. A heavy mill-frame was blown down, but we suffered no great damage, most of our runaway gear having been found in fence corners. But how terribly we stood in need of deodorisers! – not dealkalizers, as you suggest.

Next morning we rented a couple of rooms in town where we now are and washed, rubbed, dusted, and combed ourselves back again into countenance. Half an hour ago, after reading your letter a second time, I tumbled out my pine tails, tassels, and burrs, and was down on my knees on the floor making a selection for you according to your wishes and was casting about as to the chances of finding a suitable box, when the Captain, returning from the post-office, handed me your richly laden grape box, and now the grapes are out and the burrs are in. Now this was a coincidence worth noting, was it not? – better than most people's special providences. The fruit was in perfect condition, every individual spheroid of them all fresh and bright and as tightly bent as drums with their stored-up sun-juices. The big bunch is hung up for the benefit of eyes, most of the others have already vanished, causing, as they fled, a series of the finest sensuous nerve-waves imaginable.

The weather is now much cooler – the nights almost bracingly cold – and all goes well, not a thirst trace left. We were weather-bound a week in a canyon of the Golden Gate Range, not by storms, but by soft, balmy, hazy Indian summer, in which the mountain aspens ripened to flaming yellow, while the sky was too opaque for observations upon the distant peaks.

Since leaving Hamilton, have obtained more glacial facts of great interest, very telling in the history of the Great Basin. Also many charming additions to the thousand, thousand pictures of Nature's mountain beauty. I understand perfectly your criticism on the blind pursuit of every scientific pebble, wasting a life in microscopic examinations of every grain of wheat in a field, but I am not so doing. The history of this vast wonderland is scarce at all known, and no amount of study in other fields will develop it to the light. As to that special thirst affair, I was in no way responsible I was fully awake to the danger, but I was not in a position to prevent it.

Our work goes on hopefully towards a satisfactory termination. Will soon be in Utah. All the mountains yet to be climbed have been seen from other summits save two on the Wasatch, viz. Mount Nebo and a peak back of Beaver. Our next object will be Wheeler's Peak, forty miles east of here.

The fir I send you is remarkably like the Sierra *grandis*, but much smaller, seldom attaining a greater height than fifty feet. In going east from the Sierra it was first met on the Hot Creek Range, and afterwards on all the higher ranges thus far. It also occurs on the Wasatch and Oquirrh Mountains. Of the two pines, that with the larger cones is called "White Pine" by the settlers. It was first met on Cory's Peak west of Walker Lake, and afterwards on all the mountains thus far that reached an elevation of ten thousand feet or more. This, I have no doubt, is the species so rare on the Sierra, and which I found on the eastern slope opposite the head of Owens Valley. Two years ago I saw it on the Wasatch above Salt Lake. I mean to send specimens to Gray and Hooker, as they doubtless observed it on the Rocky Mountains. The other species is the *aristata* of the southern portion of the Sierra above the Kern and Kings Rivers. Is but little known, though exceedingly interesting. First met on the Hot Creek Range, and more abundantly on the White Pine Mountains – called Fox-Tail Pine by the miners, on account of its long bushy tassels. It is by far the most picturesque of all pines, and those of these basin ranges far surpass those of the Sierra in extravagant and unusual beauty of the picturesque kind. These three species and the Fremont or nut pine and junipers are the only coniferous trees I have thus far met in the State. Possibly the Yellow Pine (*ponderosa*) may be found on the Snake Range. I observed it last year on the Wasatch, together with one Abies. Of course that small portion of Nevada which extends into the Sierra about Lake Tahoe is not considered in this connection, for it is naturally a portion of California.

Cordially yours

JOHN MUIR

Upon his return from the mountains of Nevada Muir found that sickness had invaded the family of John Swett, with whom he had made his home for the last three years, and it became necessary for him to find new lodgings. In a letter addressed to Mrs. John Bidwell, under date of February 17th, 1879, he writes: "I have settled for the winter at 920 Valencia Street [San Francisco], with my friend Mr. [Isaac] Upham, of Payot, Upham and Company, Booksellers; am comfortable, but not very fruitful thus far – reading more than writing." This remained his temporary abode until his marriage and removal to Martinez the following year. The famous wooden clock shared also this last removal and continued its service as a faithful timepiece for many years to come.

to Dr. and Mrs. John Strentzel

920 Valencia Street, San Francisco

January 28th, 1879

DEAR FRIENDS

The vast soul-stirring work of flitting is at length done and well done. Myself, wooden clock, and notebooks are once more planted for the winter out here on the outermost ragged edge of this howling metropolis of dwelling boxes.

And now, well what now? Nothing but work, book-making, brick-making, the transformation of raw bush sugar and mountain meal into magazine cookies and snaps. And though the spectacled critics who ken everything in wise ignorance say "well done, sir, well done," I always feel that there is something not quite honourable in thus dealing with God's wild gold – the sugar and meal, I mean.

Yesterday I began to try to cook a mess of bees, but have not yet succeeded in making the ink run sweet. The blessed brownies winna buzz in this temperature, and what can a body do about it? Maybe ignorance is the deil that is spoiling the – the – the broth – the nectar, and perhaps I ought to go out and gather some more Melissa and thyme and white sage for the pot.

The streets here are barren and beeless and ineffably muddy and mean-looking. How people can keep hold of the conceptions of New Jerusalem and immortality of souls with so much mud and gutter, is to me admirably strange. A Eucalyptus bush on every other corner, standing tied to a painted stick, and a geranium sprout in a pot on every tenth window sill may help heavenward a little, but how little amid so muckle down-dragging mud!

This much for despondency; per contra, the grass and grain is growing, and man will be fed, and the nations will be glad, etc., and the sun rises every day.

Helen [Swett] is well out of danger, and is very nearly her own sweet amiable engaging little self again, and I can see her at least once a week.

I'm living with Mr. Upham and am comfortable as possible. Summer will soon be again.

When you come to the city visit me, and see how bravely I endure; so touching a lesson of resignation to metropolitan evils and goods should not be lightly missed.   Hoping all goes well with you, I am,

Cordially your friend

JOHN MUIR

Frequently, in letters to friends, Muir complains that in town he is unable to compel the right mood for the production of readable articles. "As yet I have accomplished very nearly nothing," he writes some weeks after the above letter; he had only " reviewed a little book, and written a first sketch of our bee pastures! . . . How astoundingly empty and dry – box-like! – is our brain in a house built on one of those precious 'lots' one hears so much about!"

The fact is that Muir's personal letters, like his conversation, flowed smoothly and easily; but when he sat down to write an article, his critical faculty was called into play, and his thoughts, to employ his own simile, began to labour like a laden wagon in a bog. There was a consequent loss of that spontaneity which made him such a fascinating talker. "John polishes his articles until an ordinary man slips on them," remarked his friend and neighbour John Swett when he wished to underline his own sense of the difference between Muir's spoken and written words. Such was the brilliance of his conversation during the decades of his greatest power that the fame of it still lingers as a literary tradition in California. Organisations and individuals vied with each other to secure his attendance at public and private gatherings, convinced that the announcement "John Muir will be there" would assure the success of any meeting. It was with this thought in mind that the manager of a great Sunday-School convention, scheduled to meet in Yosemite in June, 1879, offered him a hundred dollars just to come and talk.

It seems a pity that in his earlier years no one thought of having his vivid recitals of observations and adventures recorded by a stenographer and then placed before him for revision. By direction of the late E. H. Harriman,

Muir's boyhood memoirs were taken down from his conversation at Pelican Lodge to be subsequently revised for publication. Though he often entirely rewrote the conversational first draft, the possession of the raw material in typed form acted as a stimulus to literary production, and enabled him to bring to completion what otherwise might have been lost to the world.

But, however much he chafed and groaned under the necessity of meeting his contracts for articles, the remarkable series which he wrote during the late seventies for *Harper's Magazine* and *Scribner's Monthly* are conclusive demonstrations of his power. Among them was "The Humming-Bird of the California Waterfalls" which loaded his mail with letters from near and far, and evoked admiration from the foremost writers of the time. Though Muir was not without self-esteem, the flood of praise that descended upon him gave him more embarrassment than gratification, especially when his sisters desired to know the identity of this or that lady who had dedicated a poem to him.

Scarcely anyone knew at this time that there was a lady not far from San Francisco who, though not writing poems, was playing rival to the bee pastures of his articles, and that when, during the spring of 1879, he disappeared occasionally from the Upham household on Valencia Street, he could have been found, and not alone, in the Strentzel orchards at Martinez. "Everyone," writes John to Miss Strentzel in April – "everyone, according to the eternal unfitness of civilized things, has been seeking me and calling on me while I was away. John Swett, on his second failure to find me, left word with Mr. Upham that he was coming to Martinez some time to see me during the summer vacation! The other day I chanced to find in my pocket that slippery, fuzzy mesh you wear round your neck." The feminine world probably will recognise in the last sentence a characteristically masculine description of a kind of head-covering fashionable in those days and known as a "fascinator."

The same letter contains evidence that the orchards did not let him forget them when he returned to San Francisco, for after reporting that he had finished "Snow Banners" and was at work upon "Floods," he breaks off in the middle of a sentence to exclaim "Boo!!! aren't they lovely!!! The bushel of bloom, I mean. Just came this moment. Never was so blankly puzzled in making a guess before lifting the lid. An orchard in a band-box!!! Who wad ha thocht it? A swarm of bees and fifty humming-birds would have made the thing complete."

Early in the year Muir had carefully laid his plans for a new exploration trip, this time into the Puget Sound region. There doubtless was something in the circumstances and uncertainties of this new venture that brought to culmination his friendship with Miss Strentzel, for they became engaged on the eve of his departure, though for months no one outside of the family knew anything about it, so closely was the secret kept. Even to Mrs. Carr, who had ardently hoped for this outcome, he merely wrote: "I'm going home – going to my summer in the snow and ice and forests of the north coast. Will sail tomorrow at noon on the Dakota for Victoria and Olympia. Will then push inland and alongland. May visit Alaska.''

He did, as it turned out, travel to Alaska that summer, and the first literary fruitage of this trip took the form of eleven letters to the *San Francisco Evening Bulletin*. Written on the spot, they preserve the freshness of his first impressions, and were read with breathless interest by an ever-enlarging circle of readers. Toward the close of his life these vivid sketches were utilised, together with his journals, in writing the first part of his *Travels in Alaska*. It was at Fort Wrangell that he met the Reverend S. Hall Young, then stationed as a missionary among the Thlinkit Indians. Mr. Young later accompanied him on various canoe and land expeditions, particularly the one up Glacier Bay, that resulted in the discovery of a number of stupendous glaciers, the largest of which was afterwards to receive the name of Muir. In his book, *Alaska Days with John Muir*, Mr. Young has given a most readable and vivid account of their experiences together, and the interested reader will wish to compare, among other things, the author's own account of his thrilling rescue from certain death on the precipices of Glenora Peak with Muir's modest description of the heroic part he played in the adventure.

It is Young also who relates how Muir, by his daring and original ways of inquiring into Nature's every mood, came to be regarded by the Indians as a mysterious being whose motives were beyond all conjecture. A notable instance was the occasion on which, one wild, stormy night, he left the shelter of Young's house and slid out into the inky darkness and wind-driven sheets of rain. At two o'clock in the morning a rain-soaked group of Indians hammered at the missionary's door, and begged him to pray. ''We scare. All Stickeen scare,'' they said, for some wakeful ones had seen a red glow on top of a neighbouring mountain and the mysterious, portentous phenomenon had immediately been communicated to the whole frightened tribe. ''We want you play [pray] God; plenty play,'' they said.

The reader will not find it difficult to imagine what had happened, for Muir was the unconscious cause of their alarm. He had made his way through the drenching blast to the top of a forested hill. There he had contrived to start ''a fire, a big one, to see as well as to hear how the storm and trees were behaving.'' At midnight his fire, sheltered from the village by the brow of the hill, was shedding its glow upon the low-flying storm-clouds, striking terror to the hearts of the Indians, who thought they saw something that ''waved in the air like the wings of a spirit.'' And while they were imploring the prayers of the missionary for their safety, Muir, according to his own account, was sitting under a bark shelter in front of his fire, with ''nothing to do but look and listen and join the trees in their hymns and prayers.''

Meanwhile Muir's *Bulletin* letters had greatly enlarged its circulation and were being copied all over the country, to the great delight of the editor, Sam Williams, who had long been a warm friend of Muir. The latter's descriptions reflected the boundless enthusiasm which these newfound wildernesses of Alaska aroused in him. In the Sierra Nevada his task was to reconstruct imaginatively, from vestiges of vanished glaciers, the picture of their prime during the ice period; but here he saw actually at work the stupendous landscape-making glaciers of Alaska, and in their action he found verified the conclusions of his *Studies in the Sierra*. No wonder he tarried in the North months beyond the time he had set for his return. "Every summer," he wrote to Miss Strentzel from Fort Wrangell in October – "every summer my gains from God's wilds grow greater. This last seems the greatest of all. For the first few weeks I was so feverishly excited with the boundless exuberance of the woods and the wilderness, of great ice floods, and the manifest scriptures of the ice-sheet that modelled the lovely archipelagoes along the coast, that I could hardly settle down to the steady labour required in making any sort of Truth one's own. But I'm working now, and feel unable to leave the field. Had a most glorious time of it among the Stickeen glaciers, which in some shape or other will reach you."

Upon landing in Portland on his return in January, he was persuaded to give several public lectures and to make an observation trip up the Columbia River. At his lodgings in San Francisco there had gathered meanwhile an immense accumulation of letters, and among them one that bridged the memories of a dozen eventful years. It was from Katharine Merrill Graydon, one of the three little Samaritans who used to visit him after the accidental injury to one of his eyes in an Indianapolis wagon factory. "The three children you knew best," said the writer, "the ones who long ago in the dark room delighted to read to you and bring you flowers, are now men and women. Merrill is a young lawyer with all sorts of aspirations. Janet is at home, a young lady of leisure. Your 'little friend Katie' is teacher in a fashionable boarding-school, which I know is not much of a recommendation to a man who turns his eyes away from all flowers but the wild rose and the sweet-briar." The main occasion of the letter was to introduce Professor David Starr Jordan and Mr. Charles Gilbert, who were going to the Pacific Coast. "I send this," continued the writer, "with a little quaking of the heart. What if you should ask, 'Who is Kate Graydon?' Still I have faith that even ten or twelve years have not obliterated the pleasant little friendship formed one summer so long ago. The remembrance on my part was wonderfully quickened one morning nearly two years ago when Professor Jordan read to our class the sweetest, brightest, most musical article on the Water Ouzel from *Scribner's*. The writer, he said, was John Muir. The way my acquaintance of long ago developed into friendship, and the way I proudly said I knew you, would have made you laugh."

This letter brought the following response:

to Miss Katharine Merrill Graydon

920 Valencia Street, San Francisco
February 5th, 1880

MY DEAR KATIE, MISS KATE GRAYDON,
Professor of Greek and English Literature,

MY DEAR, FRAIL, WEE, BASHFUL LASSIE AND DEAR MADAM
I was delighted with your bright charming letter introducing your friends
Professor [David Starr] Jordan and Charles Gilbert. I have not yet met either
of the gentlemen. They are at Santa Barbara, but expect to be here in April,
when I hope to see them and like them for your sake, and Janet's, and their
own worth.

Some time ago I learned that you were teaching Greek, and of all the
strange things in this changeful world, this seemed the strangest, and the
most difficult to get packed quietly down into my awkward mind. Therefore
I will have to get you to excuse the confusion I fell into at the beginning of
my letter. I mean to come to you in a year or two, or any time soon, to see
you all in your new developments. The sweet blooming underbrush of boys
and girls – Moores, Merrills, Graydons, etc. – was very refreshing and
pleasant to me all my Indiana days, and now that you have all grown up into
trees, strong and thrifty, waving your outreaching branches in God's Light, I
am sure I shall love you all. Going to Indianapolis is one of the brightest of
my hopes. It seems but yesterday since I left you all. And indeed, in very
truth, all these years have been to me one unbroken day, one continuous
walk in one grand garden.

I'm glad you like my wee dear ouzel. He is one of the most complete of
God's small darlings. I found him in Alaska a month or two ago. I made a
long canoe trip of seven hundred miles from Fort Wrangell northward,
exploring the glaciers and icy fiords of the coast and inland channels with
one white man and four Indians. And on the way back to Wrangell, while
exploring one of the deep fiords with lofty walls like those of Yosemite
Valley, and with its waters crowded with immense bergs discharged from the
noble glaciers, I found a single specimen of his blessed tribe. We had camped
on the shore of the fiord among huge icebergs that had been stranded at high
tide, and next morning made haste to get away, fearing that we would be
frozen in for the winter; and while pushing our canoe through the bergs,
admiring and fearing the grand beauty of the icy wilderness, my blessed
favourite came out from the shore to see me, flew once round the boat, gave
one cheery note of welcome, while seeming to say, "You need not fear this
ice and frost, for you see I am here," then flew back to the shore and
alighted on the edge of a big white berg, not so far away but that I could see
him doing his happy manners.

In this one summer in the white Northland I have seen perhaps ten times
as many glaciers as there are in all Switzerland. But I cannot hope to tell you
about them now, or hardly indeed at any time, for the best things and

thoughts one gets from Nature we dare not tell. I will be so happy to see you again, not to renew my acquaintance, for that has not been for a moment interrupted, but to know you better in your new growth.

Ever your friend
JOHN MUIR

Years afterwards Dr. Jordan, as he notes in his autobiography, *The Days of a Man*, took the opportunity to bestow the name Ouzel Basin on the old glacier channel "near which John Muir sketched his unrivalled biography of a water ouzel."

Anyone who has heard the February merriment of Western meadowlarks in the Alhambra Valley must know that winter gets but a slight foothold there, for it tilts toward the sun, and is in full radiance of blossom and song during March and April. John Muir and Louie Wanda Strentzel chose the fourteenth of the latter flower month for their wedding day and were ready to share their secret with their friends. "Visited the immortals Brown and 'Swett," confesses John to his fiancee in one of his notes, and the announcement was followed immediately by shoals of congratulatory letters. The one from Mrs. John Swett, in whose home he had spent so many happy days, is not only fairly indicative of the common opinion, but draws some lines of Muir's character that make it worthy of a place here.

to Louie Wanda Strentzel

San Francisco, April 8th, 1880

MY DEAR MISS STRENTZEL
When Mr. Muir made his appearance the other night I thought he had a sheepish twinkle in his eye, but ascribed it to a guilty consciousness that he had been up to Martinez again and a fear of being rallied about it. Judge then of the sensation when he exploded his bombshell! At first laughing incredulity – it was April. We were on our guard against being taken in, but the mention of Dr. Dwinell's name and a date settled it, and I have hunted up a pen to write you a letter of congratulation. For John and I are jubilant over the match. It gratifies completely our sense of fitness, for you both have a fair foundation of the essentials of good health, good looks, good temper, etc. Then you both have culture, and to crown all you have "prospects" and he has talent and distinction.

But I hope you are good at a hair-splitting argument. You will need to be to hold your own with him. Five times today has he vanquished me. Not that I admitted it to him – no, never! He not only excels in argument, but always takes the highest ground – is always on the right side. He told Colonel Boyce the other night that his position was that of champion for a mean, brutal policy. It was with regard to Indian extermination, and that he (Boyce) would be ashamed to carry it with one Indian in personal conflict. I thought the Colonel would be mad, but they walked off arm in arm. Further, he is so truthful that he not only will never embellish sketch or word-picture by any imaginary addition, but even retains every unsightly feature lest his picture should not be true.

There, I have said all I can in his favour, and as an offset I must tell you that I have been trying all day to soften his hard heart of an old animosity and he won't yield an inch. It is sometimes impossible to please him. . . .

With hearty regard, I am

Yours very truly

MARY LOUISE SWETT

The occasion of the following letter was one from Miss Graydon in which she rallied him on her sudden discovery of how much sympathy she had wasted on him because she had imagined him without friends or companions except glaciers and icebergs, and without even a mother to wear out her anxious heart about him. "I heard," she wrote, "that your mother was still living and that you had not been near her for twelve years. And then, while I supposed you had not a lady friend in the world, I heard you were the centre of an adoring circle of ladies in San Francisco. If you heard anyone laugh about that time, it was I. See if I ever waste my sympathy on you again!"

to Miss Katharine Merrill Graydon

1419 Taylor Street, San Francisco

April 12th, 1880

MY DEAR GIRL, WOMAN, KATIE AND MISS KATE

Your letter of March 28th has reached me, telling how much loving sympathy I am to have because I have a mother and because of the story of my adoring circle of lady friends. Well, what is to become of me when I tell you that I am to marry one of those friends the day after tomorrow? What sympathy will be left the villain who has a mother and a wife also, and even a home and a circle, etc., and twice as muckle as a' that? But now, even now, Katie, don't, don't withdraw your sympathy. You know that I never did demand pity for the storm-beatings and rock-beds and the hunger and loneliness of all these years since you were a frail wee lass, for I have been very happy and strong through it all – the happiest man I ever saw; but, nevertheless, I want to hold on to and love all my friends, for they are the most precious of all my riches.

I hope to see you all this year or next, and no amount of marrying will diminish the enjoyment of meeting you again. And some of you will no doubt come to this side of the Continent, and then how happy I will be to welcome you to a warm little home in the Contra Costa hills near the bay.

I have been out of town for a week or two, and have not seen much of Professor Jordan and Mr. Gilbert. They are very busy about the fishes, crabs, clams, oysters, etc. Have called at his hotel two or three times, and have had some good Moores and Merrill talks, but nothing short of a good long excursion in the free wilderness would ever mix us as much as you seem to want.

Now, my brave teacher lassie, good luck to you. Heaven bless you, and believe me,   Ever truly your friend

JOHN MUIR

It was fitting, perhaps, that one who loved Nature in her wildest moods, should have his wedding day distinguished by a roaring rainstorm through which he drove Dr. I. E. Dwinell, the officiating clergyman, back to the Martinez station in a manner described by the latter as ''like the rush of a torrent down the canyon.'' Both relatives and friends, to judge by their letters, were so completely surprised by the happy event that it proved ''a nine days' wonder.'' The social stir occasioned by the wedding was, however, far from gratifying to Mr. Muir, who had to summon all his courage to prevent his besetting bashfulness from driving him to the seclusion of the nearest canyon.

But lest the reader imagine that Muir's home was henceforward to be on the beaten crossways of annoying crowds, let me hasten to add that the old Strentzel home, which the bride's parents vacated for their daughter, was a more than ordinarily secluded and quiet place. Cascades of ivy and roses fell over the corners of the wide verandas, and the slope upon which the house stood had an air of leaning upon its elbows and looking tranquilly down across hill-girt orchards to the blue waters of Carquinez Straits. There, a mile away, at the entrance of the valley, nestled the little town of Martinez, but scarcely a whisper of its activities might be heard above the contented hum of Alhambra bees. It was an ideal place for a honeymoon and there we leave the happy pair.

CHAPTER FOURTEEN

The Second Alaska Trip and the Search
for the Jeannette 1880–1882

I

AFTER HIS MARRIAGE Muir rented from his father-in-law a part of the Strentzel ranch, and then proceeded with great thoroughness to master the art of horticulture, for which he possessed natural and perhaps inherited aptitude. But when July came, the homing instinct for the wilderness again grew strong within him. He doubtless had an understanding with his wife that he was to continue during the next summer the unfinished explorations of 1879. The lure of "something lost behind the ranges" was in his case a glacier, as Mr. Young reports in his *Alaska Days with John Muir*. The more immediate occasion of his departure was a letter from his friend Thomas Magee, of San Francisco, urging him to join him on a trip to southeastern Alaska. The two had travelled together before, and he acted at once upon the suggestion, leaving for the North on July 30th.

to Mrs. Muir

Off Cape Flattery, Monday,
August 2nd, 1880, 10 a.m.

MY DEAR WIFE

All goes well. In a few hours we will be in Victoria. The voyage thus far has been singularly calm and uneventful. Leaving you is the only event that has marred the trip and it is marred sorely, but I shall make haste to you and reach you ere you have the time to grieve and weary. If you will only be calm and cheery all will be better for my short spell of ice-work.

The sea has been very smooth, nevertheless Mr. Magee has been very sick. Now he is better. As for me I have made no sign, though I have had some headache and heartache. We are now past the Flattery Rocks, where we were so roughly storm-tossed last winter, and Neah Bay, where we remained thirty-six hours. How placid it seems now – the water black and grey with reflections from the cloudy sky, fur seals popping their heads up here and there, ducks and gulls dotting the small waves, and Indian fishing-boats towards the shore, each with a small glaring red flag flying from the masthead.

Behind the group of white houses nestled in the deepest bend of the bay rise rounded, ice-swept hills, with mountains beyond them folding in and in, in beautiful braids, and all densely forested. We are so near the shore that with the mate's glasses I can readily make out some of the species of the trees. The forest is in the main scarce at all different from those of the Alaskan coast. Now the Cape Lighthouse is out of sight and we are fairly into the strait. Vancouver Island is on [the] left in fine clear view, with forests densely packed in every hollow and over every hill and mountain. How beautiful it is! How deep and shadowy its canyons, how eloquently it tells the story of its sculpture during the Age of Ice! How perfectly virgin it is! Ships loaded with Nanaimo coal and Puget Sound coal and lumber, a half dozen of them, are about us, beating their way down the strait, and here and there a pilot boat to represent civilization, but not one scar on the virgin shore, nor the smoke of a hut or camp.

I have just been speaking with a man who has spent a good deal of time on the island. He says that so impenetrable is the underbrush, his party could seldom make more than two miles a day though assisted by eight Indians. Only the shores are known.

Now the wind is beginning to freshen and the small waves are tipped with white, milk white, caps, almost the only ones we have seen since leaving San Francisco. The Captain and first officer have been very attentive to us, giving us the use of their rooms and books, etc., besides answering all our questions anent the sea and ships.

We shall reach Victoria about two or three o'clock. The California will not sail before tomorrow sometime, so that we shall have plenty [of] time to get the charts and odds and ends we need before leaving. Mr. Magee will undoubtedly go on to Wrangell, but will not be likely to stop over.

Ten minutes past two by your clock

We are just rounding the Esquimalt Lighthouse, and in a few minutes more will be tied up at the wharf. Quite a lively breeze is blowing from the island, and the strait is ruffled with small shining wavelets glowing in the distance like silver. Hereabouts many lofty moutonnéed rock-bosses rise above the forests, bare of trees, but brown looking from the mosses that cover them. Since entering the strait, the heavy swell up and down, up and down, has vanished and all the sick have got well and are out in full force, gazing at the harbour with the excitement one always feels after a voyage, whether the future offers much brightness or not.

The new Captain of the California is said to be good and careful, and the pilot and purser I know well, so that we will feel at home during the rest of our trip as we have thus far; and as for the main objects, all Nature is unchangeable, loves us all, and grants gracious welcome to every honest votary.

I hope you do not feel that I am away at all. Any real separation is not possible. I have been alone, as far as [concerns] the isolation that distance makes, so much of my lifetime that separation seems more natural than absolute contact, which seems too good and indulgent to be true.

Her Majesty's ironclad Triumph is lying close alongside. How huge she seems and impertinently strong and defiant, with a background of honest green woods! Jagged-toothed wolves and wildcats harmonise smoothly enough, but engines for the destruction of human beings are only devilish, though they carry preachers and prayers and open up views of sad, scant tears. Now we are making fast. "Make fast that line there, make fast," "let go there," "give way."

We will go on to Victoria this afternoon, taking our baggage with us, and stay there until setting out on the California. The ride of three miles through the woods and round the glacial bosses is very fine. This you would enjoy. I shall look for the roses. Will mail this at once, and write again before leaving this grand old ice-ribbed island.

And now, my dear Louie, keep a good heart and do the bits of work I requested you to do, and the days in Alaska will go away fast enough and I will be with you again as if I had been gone but one day.

Ever your affectionate husband
JOHN MUIR

to Mrs. Muir

Victoria, B.C. August 3rd, 1880, 3.45 p.m.

DEAR LOUIE

The Vancouver roses are out of bloom hereabouts but I may possibly find some near Nanaimo. I mailed you a letter yesterday which you will probably receive with this.

Arriving at Esquimalt we hired a carriage driven by a sad-eyed and sad-lipped negro to take us with all our baggage to Victoria, some three miles distant. The horses were also of melancholic aspect, lean and clipper-built in general, but the way they made the fire fly from the glacial gravel would have made Saint Jose and his jet beef-sides hide in the dust. By dint of much blunt praise of his team he put them to their wiry spring-steel metal and we passed everything on the road with a whirr – cab, cart, carriage, and carryall. We put up at the Driard House and had a square, or cubical, meal. Put on a metallic countenance to the landlord on account of the money and experience we carried, nearly scared him out of his dignity and made him give us good rooms.

At 6.45 p.m. the California arrived, and we went aboard and had a chat with Hughes, the purser. He at once inquired whether I had *anyone* with me, meaning you, as Vanderbilt had given our news. Learned that the California would not sail until this evening and made up our minds to take a drive out in the highways and byways adjacent to the town. While strolling about the streets last evening I felt a singular interest in the Thlinkit Indians I met and something like a missionary spirit came over me. Poor fellows, I wish I could serve them.

There is good eating, but poor sleeping here. My bed was but little like our own at home. Met Major Morris, the Treasury agent, this morning. He is going up with us. He is, you remember, the writer of that book on Alaska that I brought with me.

About nine o'clock we got a horse and buggy at the livery stable and began our devious drive by going back to the Dakota to call on First Officer Griffith and give him a box of weeds for his kind deeds. Then took any road that offered out into the green leafy country. How beautiful it is, every road banked high and embowered in dense, fresh, green, tall ferns six to eight feet high close to the wheels, then spiraea, two or three species, wild rose bushes, madroño, hazel, hawthorn, then a host of young Douglas spruces and silver firs with here and there a yew with its red berries and dark foliage, and a maple or two, then the tall firs and spruces forming the forest primeval. We came to a good many fields of grain, but all of them small as compared with the number of the houses. The oats and barley are just about ripe. We saw little orchards, too; a good many pears, little red-brown fellows, six hatfuls per tree, and the queerest little sprinkling of little red and yellow cherries just beginning to ripen. Many of the cottage homes about town are as lovely as a cottage may be, embowered in honeysuckle and green gardens and bits of lawn and orchard and grand oaks with lovely outlooks. The day has been delightful. How you would have enjoyed it – all three of you.

Our baggage is already aboard and the hour draws nigh. I must go. I shall write you again from Nanaimo.

Goodbye again, my love. Keep a strong heart and speedily will fly the hours that bring me back to thee. Love to mother and father. Farewell.

Ever your affectionate husband
JOHN MUIR

to Mrs. Muir

On Board the California
10 a.m., August 4th, 1880

DEAR LOUIE

We are still lying alongside the wharf at Victoria. It seems a leak was discovered in one of the water tanks that had to be mended, and the result was that we could not get off on the seven o'clock tide last night.

Victoria seems a dry, dignified, half-idle town, supported in great part by government fees. Every erect, or more than erect, backleaning, man has an office, and carries himself with that peculiar aplomb that all the Hail Britannia people are so noted for. The wharf and harbour stir is very mild. The steamer Princess Louise lies alongside ours, getting ready for the trip to New Westminster on [the] Fraser River. The Hudson's Bay Company's steamer Otter, a queer old tubby craft, left for the North last night. A few sloops, plungers, and boats are crawling about the harbour or lying at anchor, doing or dreaming a business nobody knows. Yonder comes an Indian canoe with its one unique sail calling up memories, many, of my last winter's rambles among the icebergs. The water is ruffled with a slight breeze, scarce enough for small white-caps. Though clearer than the waters of most harbours, it is not without the ordinary drift of old bottles, straw, and defunct domestic animals. How rotten the piles of the wharf are, and how they smell, even in this cool climate!

They are taking hundreds of barrels of molasses aboard – for what purpose? To delight the Alaska younglings with 'lasses bread and smear their happy chubby cheeks, or to make cookies and gingerbread? No, whiskey, Indian whiskey! It will be bought by Indians, nine tenths of it and more; they will give their hard earned money for it, and their hard-caught furs, and take it far away along many a glacial channel and inlet, and make it into crazing poison. Onions, too, many a ton, are coming aboard to boil and fry and raise a watery cry.

Alone on the wharf, I see a lone stranger dressed in shabby black. He has a kind of unnerved, drooping look, his shoulders coming together and his toes and his knees and the two ends of his vertebral column, something like a withering leaf in hot sunshine. Poor fellow, he looks at our ship as if he wanted to go again to the mines to try his luck. And here come two Indian women and a little girl trotting after them. They seem as if they were coming aboard, but turn aside at the edge of the wharf and descend rickety stairs to their canoe, tied to a pile beneath the wharf. Now they reappear with change of toilet, and the little girl is carrying a bundle, something to eat or sell or sit on.

Yonder comes a typical John Bull, grand in size and style, carmine in countenance, abdominous and showing a fine tight curve from chin to knee, when seen in profile, yet benevolent withal and reliable, confidence-begetting. And here just landed opposite our ship is a pile of hundreds of bears' skins, black and brown, from Alaska, brought here by the Otter, a few deer skins too, and wildcat and wolverine. The Hudson's Bay Company men are about them, showing their ownership.

Ten minutes to twelve o'clock

"Let go that line there," etc., tells that we are about to move. Our steamer swings slowly round and heads for Nanaimo. How beautiful the shores are! How glacial, yet how leafy! The day becomes calmer, and brighter, and everybody seems happy. Our fellow passengers are Major Morris and wife, whom I met last year, Judge Deady, a young Englishman, and [a] dreamy, silent old grey man like a minister.

8 p.m. We are entering Nanaimo Harbour.

to Mrs. Muir

> Departure Bay (a few miles from
> Nanaimo) 9 a.m., August 5th, 1880

DEAR LOUIE

We are coaling here, and what a rumble they are making! The shores here are very imposing, a bevelled bluff, topped with giant cedar, spruce, and fir and maple with varying green; here and there a small madrono too, which here is near its northern limit.

We went ashore last eve at Nanaimo for a stroll, Magee and I, and we happened to meet Mr. Morrison, a man that I knew at Fort Wrangell, who told me particulars of the sad Indian war in which Toyatte was killed. He was present and gave very graphic descriptions.

We sailed hither at daylight this morning, and will probably get away, the Captain tells me, about eleven o'clock, and then no halt until we reach Wrangell, which is distant from here about sixty hours.

I hardly know, my lassie, what I've been writing, nothing, I fear, but very small odds and ends, and yet these may at least keep you from wearying for an hour, and the letters, poor though they be, shall yet tell my love, and that will redeem them. I mail this here, the other two were mailed in Victoria, my next from Wrangell.

Heaven bless you, my love, and mother and father. I trust that you are caring for yourself and us all by keeping cheery and strong, and avoiding the bad practice of the stair-dance. Once more, my love, farewell, I must close in haste. Farewell.

Ever your affectionate husband
JOHN MUIR

Missionary S. Hall Young was standing on the wharf at Fort Wrangell on the 8th of August, watching the California coming in, when to his great joy he spied John Muir standing on the deck and waving his greetings. Springing nimbly ashore, Muir at once fired at him the question, "When can you be ready?" In response to Young's expostulations over his haste, and his failure to bring his wife, he exclaimed: "Man, have you forgotten? Don't you know we lost a glacier last fall? Do you think I could sleep soundly in my bed this winter with that hanging on my conscience? My wife could not come, so I have come alone and you've got to go with me to find the lost. Get your canoe and crew and let us be off."

to Mrs. Muir

Sitka on board the California, August 10th, 1880,
10.30 p.m. of your time.

MY OWN DEAR LOUIE

I'm now about as far from you as I will be this year – only this wee sail to the North and then to thee, my lassie. And I'm not away at all, you know, for only they who do not love may ever be apart. There is no true separation for those whose hearts and souls are together. So much for love and philosophy. And now I must trace you my way since leaving Nanaimo.

We sailed smoothly through the thousand evergreen isles, and arrived at Fort Wrangell at 4.30 a.m. on the 8th. Left Wrangell at noon of the same day and arrived here on the 9th at 6 a.m. Spent the day in friendly greetings and saunterings. Found Mr. Vanderbilt and his wife and Johnnie and, not every way least, though last, little Annie, who is grown in stature and grace and beauty since last I kissed her.

Today Mr. Vanderbilt kindly took myself and Mr. Magee and three other fellow passengers on an excursion on his steamer up Peril Strait, about fifty miles. (You can find it on one of the charts that I forgot to bring.) We returned to the California about half-past nine, completing my way thus far.

And now for my future plans. The California sails tomorrow afternoon some time for Fort Wrangell, and I mean to return on her and from there set out on my canoe trip. I do not expect to be detained at Wrangell, inasmuch as I saw Mr. [S. Hall] Young, who promised to have a canoe and crew ready. I mean to keep close along the mainland, exploring the deep inlets in turn, at least as far north as the Taku, then push across to Cross Sound and follow the northern shore, examining the glaciers that crowd into the deep inlet that puts back northward from near the south extremity of the Sound, where I was last year. Thence I mean to return eastward along the southern shore of the Sound to Chatham Strait, turn southward down the west shore of the Strait to Peril Strait, and follow this strait to Sitka, where I shall take the California. Possibly, however, I may, should I not be pushed for time, return to Wrangell. Mr. Magee will, I think, go with me, though very unwilling to do so....

August 11th, at noon

I have just returned from a visit to the Jamestown. The Commander, Beardslee, paid me a visit here last evening, and invited me aboard his ship. Had a pleasant chat, and an invitation to make the Jamestown my home while here.

I also found my friend Koshoto, the Chief of the Hoonas, the man who, I told you, had entertained Mr. Young and me so well last year on Cross Sound, and who made so good a speech. He is here trading, and seemed greatly pleased to learn that I was going to pay him another visit; said that meeting me was like meeting his own brother who was dead, his heart felt good, etc....

I have been learning all about the death of the brave and good old Toyatte. I think that Dr. Corliss, one of the Wrangell missionaries, made a mistake in reference to the seizure of some whiskey, which caused the beginning of the trouble.

This is a bright, soft, balmy day. How you would enjoy it! You must come here some day when you are strong enough.... Everybody inquires first on seeing me, "Have you brought your wife?" and then, "Have you a photograph?" and then pass condemnation for coming alone! ...

The mail is about to close, and I must write to mother.

Affectionately your husband
JOHN MUIR

How eagerly I shall look for news when I reach Fort Wrangell next month!

to Mrs. Muir

Residence of Mr. Young, Fort Wrangell
11.45 a.m., August 14th, 1880

DEAR LOUIE

I am back in my old quarters, and how familiar it all seems! – the lovely water, the islands, the Indians with their baskets and blankets and berries, the jet ravens prying and flying here and there, and the bland, dreamy, hushed air drooping and brooding kindly over all. I miss Toyatte so much. I have just been over the battleground with Mr. Young, and have seen the spot where he fell.

Instead of coming here direct from Sitka we called at Klawak on Prince of Wales Island for freight, – canned salmon, oil, furs, etc., – which detained us a day. We arrived here last evening at half-past ten. Klawak is a fishing and trading station located in a most charmingly beautiful bay, and while lying there, the evening before last, we witnessed a glorious auroral display which lasted more than three hours. First we noticed long white lance-shaped streamers shooting up from a dark cloud-like mass near the horizon, then a well-defined arch, the corona, almost black, with a luminous edge appeared, and from it, radiating like spokes from a hub, the streamers kept shooting with a quick glancing motion, and remaining drawn on the dark sky, distinct, and white, as fine lines drawn on a blackboard. And when half the horizon was adorned with these silky fibrous lances of light reaching to and converging at the zenith, broad flapping folds and waves of the same white auroral light came surging on from the corona with astonishing energy and quickness, the folds and waves spending themselves near the zenith like waves on a smooth sloping sand-beach. But throughout the greater portion of their courses the motion was more like that of sheet lightning, or waves made in broad folds of muslin when rapidly shaken; then in a few minutes those delicate billows of light rolled up among the silken streamers, would vanish, leaving the more lasting streamers with the stars shining through them; then some of the seemingly permanent streamers would vanish also, and appear again in vivid white, like rockets shooting with widening base, their glowing shafts reflected in the calm water of the bay among the stars.

It was all so rare and so beautiful and exciting to us that we gazed and shouted like children at a show, and in the middle of it all, after I was left alone on deck at about half-past eleven, the whole sky was suddenly illumined by the largest meteor I ever saw. I remained on deck until after midnight, watching. The corona became crimson and slightly flushed the bases of the streamers, then one by one the shining pillars of the glorious structure were taken down, the foundation arch became irregular and broke up, and all that was left was only a faint structureless glow along the northern horizon, like the beginning of the dawn of a clear frosty day. The only sounds were the occasional shouts of the Indians, and the impressive roar of a waterfall.

Mr. Young and I have just concluded a bargain with the Indians, Lot and his friend, to take us in his canoe for a month or six weeks, at the rate of sixty dollars per month. Our company will be those two Indians, and Mr. Young and myself, also an Indian boy that Mr. Young is to take to his parents at Chilkat, and possibly Colonel Crittenden as far as Holkham Bay. . . .

You will notice, dear, that I have changed the plan I formerly sent you in this, that I go on to the Chilkat for Mr. Young's sake, and farther; now that Mr. Magee is out of the trip, I shall not feel the necessity I previously felt of getting back to Sitka or Wrangell in time for the next steamer, though it is barely possible that I shall. Do not look for me, however, as it is likely I shall have my hands full for two months. Tomorrow is Sunday, so we shall not get away before Monday, the 16th. How hard it is to wait so long for a letter from you! I shall not get a word until I return. I am trying to trust that you will be patient and happy, and have that work done that we talked of.

Every one of my old acquaintances seems cordially glad to see me. I have not yet seen Shakes, the Chief, though I shall ere we leave. He is now one of the principal church members, while Kadachan has been getting drunk in the old style, and is likely, Mr. Young tells me, to be turned out of the church altogether. John, our last year's interpreter, is up in the Cassiar mines. Mrs. McFarlane, Miss Dunbar, and the Youngs are all uncommonly anxious to know you and are greatly disappointed in not seeing you here, or at least getting a peep at your picture. "Why could she not have come up and stayed with us while you were about your ice business?" they ask in disappointed tone of voice.

Now, my dear wife, the California will soon be sailing southward, and I must again bid you goodbye. I must go, but you, my dear, will go with me all the way. How gladly when my work is done will I go back to thee! With love to mother and father, and hoping that God will bless and keep you all, I am ever in heart and soul the same,   JOHN MUIR

6 p.m. I have just dashed off a short *Bulletin* letter.

The events that followed are graphically narrated in Part II of *Travels in Alaska*. Eight days after his arrival at Fort Wrangell, Muir and Mr. Young got started with their party, which consisted of the two Stickeen Indians – Lot Tyeen and Hunter Joe – and a half-breed named Smart Billy. There was also Mr. Young's dog Stickeen, whom Mr. Muir at first accepted rather grudgingly as a supercharge of the already crowded canoe, but who later won his admiration and became the subject of one of the noblest dog stories in English literature.

The course of the expedition led through Wrangell Narrows between Mitkof and Kupreanof Islands, up Frederick Sound past Cape Fanshaw and across Port Houghton, and then up Stephens Passage to the entrance of Holkham Bay, also called Sumdum. Fourteen and a half hours up the Endicott Arm of this bay, which Muir was the first white man to explore, he found the glacier he had suspected there – a stream of ice three quarters of a mile wide and eight or nine hundred feet deep, discharging bergs with sounds of thunder. He had scarcely finished a sketch of it when he observed another glacial canyon on the west side of the fiord and, directing his crew to pull around a glaciated promontory, they came into full view of a second glacier, still pouring its ice into a branch of the fiord. Muir gave the first of these glaciers the name Young in honour of his companion, who complains that some later chart-maker substituted the name Dawes, thus committing the larceny of stealing his glacier.

In retracing their course, after some days spent in exploring the head of the fiord, they struck a side-arm through which the water was rushing with great force. Threading the narrow entrance, they found themselves in what Muir described as a new Yosemite in the making. He called it Yosemite Bay, and has furnished a charming description of its flora, fauna, and physical characteristics in his *Travels in Alaska*.

On August 21st, Young being detained by missionary duties, Muir set out alone with the Indians to explore what is now known as the Tracy Arm of Holkham Bay. The second day he found another kingly glacier hidden within the benmost bore of the fiord. "There is your lost friend," said the Indians, laughing, and as the thunder of its detaching bergs reached their ears, they added, "He says, Sagh-a-ya?" (How do you do?)

After leaving Taku Inlet, Muir laid his course north through Stephens Passage and around the end of Admiralty Island, where a camp was made only with difficulty. The next morning he crossed the Lynn Canal with his boat and crew and pitched camp, after a voyage of twenty miles, on the west end of Farewell Island, now Pyramid Island. Early the following day they turned Point Wimbledon, crept along the lofty north wall of Cross Sound, and entered Taylor Bay. During a part of this trip, the canoe was exposed to a storm and swells rolling in past Cape Spencer from the open ocean. It was an undertaking that called for courage, skill, and hardihood of no mean order.

At the head of Taylor Bay, Muir found a great glacier consisting of three branches whose combined fronts had an extent of about eight miles. Camp was made near one of these fronts in the evening of August 29th. Early the following morning, Muir became aware that "a wild storm was blowing and calling," and before any one was astir he was off – too eager to stop for breakfast – into the rain-laden gale, and out upon the glacier. It was one of the great, inspired days of his life, immortalised in the story of *Stickeen*, the brave little dog* that had become his inseparable companion.

---

*   Muir received so many letters inquiring about the dog's antecedents that he asked Mr. Young in 1897 to tell him what he knew of Stickeen's earlier history. Some readers may be interested in his reply which was as follows: "Mrs. Young got him as a present from Mr. H —, that Irish sinner who lived in a cottage up the beach towards the Presbyterian Mission in Sitka."

Muir's time was growing short, so he hastened on with his party the next day into Glacier Bay where, among other great glaciers, he had discovered the previous autumn the one that now bears his name. Several days were spent there most happily, exploring and observing glacial action, and then the canoe was turned Sitka-ward by way of Icy, Chatham, and Peril Straits, arriving in time to enable him to catch there the monthly mail steamer to Portland. Thus ended the Alaska trip of 1880.

II

"After all, have you not found there is some happiness in this world outside of glaciers, and other glories of nature?" The friend who put this question to John Muir, in a letter full of pleasantries and congratulations, had just received from him a jubilant note announcing the arrival of a baby daughter on March 27th. His fondness of children now had scope for indulgence at home, and he became a most devoted husband and father.

But for the time being he was to be deprived of this new domestic joy. For when he received an invitation to accompany the United States Revenue steamer Corwin on an Arctic relief expedition in search of DeLong and the Jeannette, it was decided in family council that so unusual an opportunity to explore the northern parts of Alaska and Siberia must not be neglected. His preparations had to be made in great haste while the citizens of Oakland were giving a banquet in honour of Captain C. L. Hooper and the officers of the Corwin at the Galinda Hotel in Oakland on April 29th. Fortunately, the Captain was an old friend whom he had known in Alaska and to whom he could entrust the purchase of the necessary polar garments from the natives in Bering Straits.

The Corwin sailed from San Francisco on May 4th, 1881, and the following series of letters was written to his wife during the cruise. They supplement at many points the more formal account of his experiences published in The Cruise of the Corwin. One of the objectives of the expedition was Wrangell Land in the Arctic Ocean, north of the Siberian coast, because it had been the expressed intention of Commander DeLong to reach the North Pole by travelling along its eastern coast, leaving cairns at intervals of twenty-five miles. It was not known at this time that Wrangell Land did not extend toward the Pole, but was an island of comparatively small extent. It was found later, by the log of the Jeannette, that the vessel had drifted, within sight of the island, directly across the meridians between which it lies. While the Corwin was still searching for her and her crew, the Jeannette was crushed in the ice and sank on June 12th, 1881, in the Arctic Ocean, one hundred and fifty miles north of the New Siberian Islands.

Meanwhile Captain Hooper succeeded in penetrating, with the Corwin, the ice barrier that surrounded Wrangell Land. So far as known, the first human beings that ever stood upon the shores of this mysterious island were in Captain Hooper's landing party, August 12th, 1881, and John Muir was of the number. The earliest news of the event, and of the fact that DeLong had not succeeded in touching either Herald Island or Wrangell Land, reached the world at large in a letter from Muir published in the *San Francisco Evening Bulletin*, September 29th, 1881.

Since the greater part of the first two letters, written to his wife at sea and while approaching Unalaska, was quoted in the writer's introduction to *The Cruise of the Corwin*, they are omitted here for the sake of brevity.

to Mrs. Muir

Monday, 4 p.m., May 16th, [1881]

DEAR LOUIE

Since writing this forenoon, we reached the mouth of the strait that separates Unalaska Island from the next to the eastward, against a strong headwind and through rough snow squalls, when the Captain told me that he thought he would not venture through the Strait today, because the swift floodtide setting through the Strait against the wind was surely raising a dangerously rough sea, but rather seek an anchorage somewhere in the lee of the bluffs, and wait the fall of the wind. As he approached the mouth of the Strait, however, he changed his mind and determined to try it.

When the vessel began to pitch heavily and the hatches and skylights were closed, I knew that we were in the Strait, and made haste to get on my overcoat and get up into the pilot house to enjoy the view of the waves. The view proved to be far wilder and more exciting than I expected. Indeed, I never before saw water in so hearty a storm of hissing, blinding foam. It was all one leaping, clashing, roaring mass of white, mingling with the air by means of the long hissing streamers dragged from the wavetops, and the biting scud. Our little vessel, swept onward by the flood pouring into Bering's Sea and by her machinery, was being buffeted by the head-gale and the huge, white, over-combing waves that made her reel and tremble, though she stood it bravely and obeyed the helm as if in calm water. After proceeding about five or six miles into the heart of this grand uproar, it seemed to grow yet wilder and began to bid defiance to any farther headway against it. At length, when we had nearly lost our boats and [were] in danger of having our decks swept, we turned and fled for refuge before the gale. The giant waves, exulting in their strength, seemed to be chasing us and threatening to swallow us at a gulp, but we finally made our escape, and were perhaps in no great danger farther than the risk of losing our boats and having the decks swept.

After going back about ten miles, we discovered a good anchorage in fifteen fathoms of water in the lee of a great bluff of lava about two thousand feet high, and here we ride in comfort while the blast drives past overhead. If we do not get off tomorrow, I will go ashore and see what I can learn.

Have learned already since the snow ceased falling that all the region hereabouts has been glaciated just like that thousand miles to the eastward. All the sculpture shows this clearly.

How pleasant it seems to be able to walk once more without holding on and to have your plate lie still on the table!

It is clearing up. The mountains are seen in groups rising back of one another, all pure white. The sailors are catching codfish. There are two waterfalls opposite our harbour.

Goodnight to all. Oh, if I could touch my baby and thee!

This has been a very grand day – snow, waves, wind, mountains!

[JOHN MUIR]

to Mrs. Muir

Unalaska Harbour
Tuesday, May 17th, 1881

DEAR LOUIE

The gale having abated early this morning, we left our anchorage on the south side of the island and steamed round into the Strait to try it again after our last evening's defeat, and this time we were successful, after a hard contest with the tide, which flows here at a speed of ten miles an hour.

The clouds lifted and the sun shone out early this morning, revealing a host of mountains nobly sculptured and grouped and robed in spotless white. Turn which way you would, the mountains were seen towering into the dark sky, some of them with streamers of mealy snow wavering in the wind, a truly glorious sight. The most interesting feature to me was the fine, clear, telling, glacial advertisement displayed everywhere in the trends of the numerous inlets and bays and valleys and ridges, in the peculiar shell-shaped névé amphitheatres and in the rounded valley bottoms and forms of the peaks and the cliff fronts facing the sea. No clearer glacial inscriptions are to be found in any mountain range, though I had been led to believe that these islands were all volcanic upheavals, scarce at all changed since their emergence from the waves, but on the contrary I have already discovered that the amount of glacial degradation has been so great as to cut the peninsula into islands. I have already been repaid for the pains of the journey.

My health is improving every day in this bracing cold, and you will hardly recognise me when I return. The summer will soon pass, and we hope to be back to our homes by October or November. . . . This is a beautiful harbour, white mountains shutting it in all around – white nearly to the water's edge. . . .

I will write again ere we leave, and then you will not hear again, probably, until near the middle of June, when we expect to meet the St. Paul belonging to the Alaska Commercial Company at St. Michael. Then I will write and you may receive my letter a month or two later.

Goodbye until tomorrow.

[JOHN MUIR]

to Mrs. Muir

Unalaska, Wednesday, May 18th, 1881

DEAR LOUIE

The Storm-King of the North is again up and doing, rolling white, combing waves through the jagged straits between this marvellous chain of islands, circling them about with beaten, updashing foam, and piling yet more and more snow on the clustering cloud-wrapped peaks. But we are safe and snug in this landlocked haven enjoying the distant storm-roar of wave and wind. I have just been on deck; it is snowing still and the deep bass of the gale is sounding on through the mountains. How weird and wild and fascinating all this hearty work of the storm is to me. I feel a strange love of it all, as I gaze shivering up the dim white slopes as through a veil darkly, becoming fainter and fainter as the flakes thicken and at length hide all the land.

Last evening I went ashore with the Captain, and saw the chief men of the place and the one white woman, and a good many of the Aleuts. We were kindly and cordially entertained by the agent of the Alaska Commercial Company, Mr. Greenbaum, and while seated in his "elegant" parlour could hardly realise that we were in so remote and cold and silent a wilderness.

As we were seated at our ease discussing Alaskan and Polar affairs, a knock came to the door, and a tall, hoary, majestic old man slowly entered, whom I at once took for the Russian priest, but to whom I was introduced as Dr. Holman. He shook hands with me very heartily and said, "Mr. Muir, I am glad to see you. I had the pleasure of knowing you in San Francisco." Then I recognised him as the dignified old gentleman that I first met three or four years ago at the home of the Smiths at San Rafael, and we had a pleasant evening together. He has been in the employ of the Alaska Commercial Company here for a year, caring for the health of the Company's Aleuts. His own health has been suffering the meanwhile, and today I sent him half a dozen bottles of the Doctor's wine to revive him. This notable liberality under the circumstances was caused, first, by his having advised me years ago to take good care of my steps on the mountains; second, to get married; third, for his pictures, drawn for me, of the bliss of having children; fourth, for the sake of our mutual friends; fifth, for his good looks and bad health; and half-dozenth, because fifteen or twenty years ago on a dark night, while seeking one of his patients in the Contra Costa hills, he called at the house of Doctor Strentzel for directions and was invited in and got a glass of good wine. A half-dozen bottles for a half-dozen reasons! "That's consistent, isn't it?" I mean to give a bottle to a friend of the Captain who is stationed at St. Michael, and save one bottle for our first contact with the polar ice-pack, and one with which to celebrate the hour of our return to home, friends, wives, bairns.

We had fresh-baked stuffed codfish for breakfast, of which I ate heartily, stuffing and all, though the latter was grey and soft and much burdened with minced onions, and then I held out my plate for a spoonful of opaque, oleaginous gravy! This last paragraph is for grandmother as a manifestation of heroic, all-enduring, all-engulfing health.

We have not yet commenced to coal, so that we will not get off for the North before Sunday. There is a schooner here that will sail for Shoalwater Bay, Oregon, in a few days, and by it I will send four or five letters. The three or four more that I intend writing ere we leave this port I will give to the agent of the Company here to be forwarded by the next opportunity in case the first batch should be lost. Then others will be sent from St. Michael by the Company's steamer, and still others from the Seal Islands and from points where we fall in with any vessel homeward bound.

Goodnight to all. I am multiplying letters in case some be lost. A thousand kisses to my child. This is the fifth letter from Unalaska. Will write two more to be sent by other vessels.   [JOHN MUIR]

to Mrs. Muir

Sunday afternoon, May 22nd, 1881

DEAR LOUIE

We left Unalaska this morning at four o'clock and are now in Bering Sea on our way to St. George and St. Paul Islands. . . Next Tuesday or Wednesday we expect to come in sight of the ice, but hope to find open water, along the west shore, that will enable us to get through the Strait to Cape Serdze or thereabouts. In a month or so we expect to be at St. Michael, where we will have a chance to send more letters and still later by whalers.

You will, therefore, have no very long period of darkness, though on my side I fear I shall have to wait a long time for a single word, and it is only by trusting in you to be cheerful and busy for the sake of your health and for the sake of our little love and all of us that I can have any peace and rest throughout this trip, however long or short. Now you must be sure to sleep early to make up for waking during the night, and occupy all the day with light work and cheerful thoughts, and never brood and dream of trouble, and I will come back with the knowledge that I need and a fresh supply of the wilderness in my health. I am already quite well and eat with savage appetite whatsoever is brought within reach.

This morning I devoured half of a salmon trout eighteen inches long, a slice of ham, half a plateful of potatoes, two biscuits, and four or five slices of bread, with coffee and something else that I have forgotten, but which was certainly buried in me and lost. For lunch, two platefuls of soup, a heap of fat compound onion hash, two pieces of toast, and three or four slices of bread, with potatoes, and a big sweet cake, and now at three o'clock I am very hungry – a hunger that no amount of wave tossing will abate. Furthermore, I look forward to fat seals fried and boiled, and to walrus steaks and stews, and doughnuts fried in train oil, and to all kinds of bears and fishy fowls with eager longing. There! Is that enough, grandmother? All my table whims are rapidly passing into the sere and yellow leaf and falling off.

I promise to comfort and sustain you beyond your highest aspirations when I return and fall three times a day on your table like a wolf on the fold. You know those slippery yellow custards – well, I eat those also!

You must not forget Sam Williams.* And now, my love, goodnight. I hope you are feeling strong-hearted. I wish I could write anything, sense or nonsense, to cheer you up and brighten the outlook into the North. I will try to say one more line or two when we reach the Islands tomorrow.

Love to all. Kiss Annie for me.

[JOHN MUIR]

to Mrs. Muir

Plover Bay, Siberia June 16th, 1881

MY BELOVED WIFE

We leave this harbour tomorrow morning at six o'clock, for St. Michael, and the northward. The Corwin is in perfect condition, and since the season promises to be a favourable one, we hope to find the Jeannette and get home this fall. I have not yet seen the American shore, but hope to see it very thoroughly, as everything seems to work towards my objects. That the Asiatic and American continents were one a very short geological time ago is already clear to me, though I shall probably obtain much more available proof than I now have. This is a grand fact. While the crystal glaciers were creating Yosemite Valley, a thousand were uniting here to make Bering Strait and Bering Sea. The south side of the Aleutian chain of islands was the boundary of the continent and the ocean.

Since the Tom Pope came into the harbour, I have written five *Bulletin* letters which are for you mostly, and therefore I need the less to write any detailed narrative of the cruise. She will sail at the same hour as we do, and her Captain, Mr. Millard, who has been many times in the Arctic both here and on the Greenland side, has promised to make you a visit, and will be able to give you much information.

If I could only get a line, one word, from you to know that you were all well, I would be content to await the end of the voyage with patience and fortitude. But, my dear, it's terrible at times to have to endure for so long a dark silence. We will not be likely to get a word before September. No doubt you have already received the six or seven letters that I sent from Unalaska, and St. Paul, also the two or three *Bulletin* letters from Unalaska. Write [W.C.] Bartlett or the office for a dozen copies of each, and save them for me.

We are drifting in the harbour among cakes of ice about the size of the orchard, but they can do us no harm. The great mountains forming the walls are covered yet with snow, except on a few bare spots near their bases, and

* Editor of the *San Francisco Evening Bulletin*.

there is not a single tree. Scarce a hint of any spring or summer have I seen since leaving San Francisco and the orchard. I hope you will see Mr. Millard. You must keep Annie Wanda downstairs or she may fall; and now, my wife and child, daughter and mother, I must bid good-bye. Heaven bless you all! Send copies of my *Bulletin* letters to my mother, and put this letter with my papers and notebooks. You will get many other letters now that the whalers are returning.

My heart aches, not to go home ere I have done my work, but just to know that you are well.

> Your affectionate husband
> JOHN MUIR

to Mrs. Muir

St. Michael, Alaska, June 21st, 1881

Sunshine, dear Louie, sunshine all the day, ripe and mellow sunshine, like that which feeds the fruits and vines! It came to us just [three] days ago when we were approaching this little old-fashioned trading post at the mouth of the Yukon River....

On the day of our arrival from Plover Bay, a little steamer came into the harbour from the Upper Yukon, towing three large boats loaded with traders, Indians, and furs – all the furs they had gathered during the winter. We went across to the storeroom of the Company to see them. A queer lot they were, whites and Indians, as they unloaded their furs. It was worth while to look at the furs too – big bundles of bear skins brown and black, wolf, fox, beaver, marten, ermine, moose, wolverine, wildcat – many of them with claws spread and hair on end as if still alive and fighting for their lives. Some of the Indian chiefs, the wildest animals of all, and the more notable of the traders, not at all wild save in dress, but rather gentle and refined in manners, like village parsons. They held us in long interesting talks and gave us some valuable information concerning the broad wilds of the Yukon.

Yesterday I took a long walk of twelve or fourteen miles over the tundra to a volcanic cone and back, leaving the ship about twelve in the forenoon and getting back at half-past eight. I found a great number of flowers in full bloom, and birds of many species building their nests, and a capital view of the surrounding country from the rim of an old crater, altogether making a delightful day, though a very wearisome one on account of the difficult walking.

The ground back of St. Michael stretches away in broad brown levels of boggy tundra promising fine walking, but proving about as tedious and exhausting as possible. The spongy covering [is] roughened with tussocks of grass and sedge and creeping heathworts and willows, among which the foot staggers about and sinks and squints, seeking rest and finding none, until far down between the rocking tussocks. This covering is composed of a plush of mosses, chiefly sphagnum, about eight inches or a foot deep, resting on ice that never melts, while about half of the surface of the moss is covered with white, yellow, red, and grey lichens, and the other half is planted more or less with grasses, sedges, heathworts, and creeping willows, and a flowering plant here and there such as primula and purple-spiked *Pedicularis*. Out in this grand solitude – solitary as far as man is concerned – we met a great many of the Arctic grouse, ptarmigan, cackling and screaming at our approach like old laying hens; also plovers, snipes, curlews, sandpipers, loons in ponds, and ducks and geese, and finches and wrens about the crater and rocks at its base....

And now goodbye again, and love to all, wife, darling baby Anna, grandmother, and grandfather.

[JOHN MUIR]

to Mrs. Muir

Between Plover Bay and St. Lawrence Island,
July 2nd, 1881

MY BELOVED WIFE

After leaving St. Michael, on the twenty second of June ... we went again into the Arctic Ocean to Tapkan, twelve miles northwest of Cape Serdze, to seek the search party that we left on the edge of the ice-pack opposite Koliuchin Island, and were so fortunate as to find them there, having gone as far as the condition of the ice seemed to them safe, and after they had reached the fountain-head of all the stories we had heard concerning the lost whaler Vigilance and determined them to be in the main true. At Cape Wankarem they found three Chukchis who said that last year when the ice was just beginning to grow, and when the sun did not rise, they were out seal-hunting three or four miles from shore when they saw a broken ship in the drift ice, which they boarded and found some dead men in the cabin and a good many articles of one sort and another which they took home and which they showed to our party. This evidence reveals the fate of at least one of the ships we are seeking.

Our party, when they saw us, came out to the edge of the ice, which extended about three miles from shore, and after a good deal of difficulty reached the steamer. The north wind was blowing hard, sending huge black swells and combing waves against the jagged, grinding edge of the pack with terrible uproar, making it impossible for us to reach them with a boat. We succeeded, however, in throwing a line to them, which they made fast to a skin boat that they had pushed over the ice from the shore, and, getting into it, they were dragged over the stormy edge of ice waves and water waves and soon got safely aboard, leaving the tent, provisions, dogs, and sleds at the Indian village, to be picked up some other time.

Then we sailed southward again to take our interpreter Chukchi Joe to his home, which we reached two hours ago. Now we are steering for St. Michael again, intending to land for a few hours on the north side of St. Lawrence Island on the way. At St. Michael we shall write our letters, which will be carried to San Francisco by the Alaska Commercial Company's steamer St. Paul, take on more provisions, and then sail north again along the American shore, spending some time in Kotzebue Sound, perhaps exploring some of the rivers that flow into it, and then push on around Point Barrow and out into the ocean northward as we can, our movements being always determined by the position and movements of the ice-pack.

Before making a final effort in August or September to reach Wrangell Land in search of traces of the Jeannette, we will return yet once more to St. Michael for coal and provisions which we have stored there in case we should be compelled to pass a winter north of Bering Strait. The season, however, is so favourable that we have sanguine hopes of finding an open way to Wrangell Land and returning to our homes in October. The Jeannette has not been seen, nor any of her crew, on the Asiatic coast as far west as Cape Yaken, and I have no hopes of the vessel ever escaping from the ice; but her crew, in case they saved their provisions, may yet be alive, though it is strange that they did not come over the ice in the spring. Possibly they may have reached the American coast. If so, they will be found this summer. Our vessel is in perfect condition, and our Captain is very cautious and will not take any considerable chances of being caught in the North pack.

How long it seems since I left home, and yet according to the almanac it will not be two months until the day after tomorrow! I have seen so much and gone so far, and the nightless days are so strangely joined, it seems more than a year. And yet how short a time is the busy month at home among the fruit and the work! My wee lass will be big and bright now, and by the time I can get her again in my arms she will be afraid of my beard. I have a great quantity of ivory dolls and toys – ducks, bears, seals, walruses, etc. – for her to play with, and some soft white furs to make a little robe for her carriage. But it is a sore, hard thing to be out of sight of her so long, and of thee, Lassie, but still sorer and harder not to hear. Perhaps not one word until I reach San Francisco! You, however, will hear often....

This is a lovely, cool, clear, bright day, and the mountains along the coast of Asia stand in glorious array, telling the grand old story of their birth beneath the sculpturing ice of the glacial period. But the snow still lingers here and there down to the water's edge, and a little beyond the mouth of Bering Strait the vast, mysterious ice-field of the North stretches away beneath a dark, stormy sky for thousands of miles. I landed on East Cape yesterday and found unmistakable evidence of the passage over it of a rigid ice-sheet from the North, a fact which is exceedingly telling here....

My health is so good now that I never notice it. I climbed a mountain at East Cape yesterday, about three thousand feet high, a mile through snow knee-deep, and never felt fatigue, my cheeks tingling in the north wind.... I have a great quantity of material in my notebooks already, lots of sketches [of] glaciers, mountains, Indians, Indian towns, etc. So you may be sure I have been busy, and if I could only hear a word now and then from that home in the California hills I would be the happiest and patientest man in all Hyperborea.

I am alone in the cabin; the engine is grinding away, making the lamp that is never lighted now rattle, and the joints creak everywhere, and the good Corwin is gliding swiftly over smooth blue water about half way to St. Lawrence Island. And now I must to bed! But before I go I reach my arms towards you, and pray God to keep you all. Goodnight.

[JOHN MUIR]

to Mrs. Muir

St. Michael, July 4th, 1881

DEAR LOUIE

We arrived here this afternoon at three o'clock and intend to stay about three days, taking in coal and provisions, and then to push off to the North. We intend to spend nearly a month along the American shore, perhaps as far north as Point Barrow, before we attempt to go out into the Arctic Ocean among the ice, for it is in August and September that the ice is most open. Then, if, as we hope from the favourableness of the season, we succeed in reaching Wrangell Land to search for traces of the Jeannette, or should find any sure tidings of her, we will be back in sunny, iceless California about the end of October, in grape-time. Otherwise we will probably return to St. Michael and take on a fresh supply of coal and nine months' provisions, and go north again prepared to winter in case we should get caught in the north of Bering Strait.

A few miles to the north of Plover Bay some thirteen or fourteen canoe-loads of natives came out to trade; more than a hundred of them were aboard at once, making a very lively picture. When we proceeded on our way, they allowed us to tow them for a mile or two in order to take advantage of the northerly current in going back to their village. They were dragged along, five or six canoes on each side, making the Corwin look like a mother field-mouse with a big family hanging to her teats, one of the first country sights that filled me with astonishment when a boy.

In coming here I had very fine views of St. Lawrence Island from the north side, showing the trend of the ice-sheet very plainly, much to my delight. The middle of the island is crowded with volcanic cones, mostly post-glacial, and therefore regular in form and but little wasted, and I counted upwards of fifty from one point of view. Just in front of this volcanic portion on the coast there is a dead Esquimo village where we landed and found that every soul of the population had died two years ago of starvation. More than two hundred skeletons were seen lying about like rubbish, in one hut thirty, most of them in bed. Mr. E. W. Nelson, a zealous collector for the Smithsonian Institution, gathered about one hundred skulls as specimens, throwing them together in heaps to take on board, just as when a boy in Wisconsin I used to gather pumpkins in the fall after the corn was shocked. The boxfuls on deck looked just about as unlike a cargo of cherries as possible, but I will not oppress you with grim details.

Some of the men brought off guns, axes, spears, etc., from the abandoned huts, and I found a little box of child's playthings which might please Anna Wanda, but which, I suppose, you will not let into the house. Well, I have lots of others that I bought, and when last here I engaged an Indian to make her a little fur suit, which I hope is ready so that I can send it down by the St. Paul. I hope it may fit her. I wish she were old enough to read the stories that I should like to write her. Love to all. Goodnight.

Ever yours
JOHN MUIR

to Mrs. Muir

St. Michael, July 9th, 1881

MY DEAR WIFE

We did not get away last evening, as we expected, on account of the change in plans – as to taking all our winter stores on board, instead of leaving them until another visit in September. It is barely possible we might get caught off Point Barrow or on Wrangell [Land] by movements in the ice-pack that never can be anticipated. Therefore we will be more comfortable with abundance of bread about us. In the matter of coal, there is a mine on the north coast where some can be obtained in case of need, and also plenty of driftwood.

Our cruise, notwithstanding we have already made two trips into a portion of the Arctic usually blocked most of the summer, we consider is just really beginning. For we have not yet made any attempt to get to the packed region about Herald Island and Wrangell Land. Perhaps not once in twenty years would it be possible to get a ship alongside the shores of Wrangell Land, although its southern point is about nine degrees south of points attained on the eastern side of the continent. To find the ocean ice thirty or forty feet thick away from its mysterious shores seems to be about as hopeless as to find a mountain glacier out of its canyon. Still, this has been so remarkably open and mild a winter, and so many north gales have been blowing this spring, [gales] calculated to break up the huge packs and grind the cakes and blocks against one another, that we have sanguine hopes of accomplishing all that we are expected to do and get home by the end of October. If I can see as much of the American coast as I have of the Asiatic, I will be satisfied, and should the weather be as favourable I certainly shall....

We may, possibly, be home ere you receive any more [letters]. If not, think of me, dear, as happily at work with no other pain than the pain of separation from you and my wee lass. I have many times been weighing chances as to whether you have sent letters by the Mary-and-Helen, now called the "Rodgers," which was to sail about the middle of June. She is a slow sailer, and has to go far out of her course by Petropavlovskii, the capital of Kamchatka, for dogs, and will not be through the Strait before the end of the season nearly. Yet a letter by her is my only hope for hearing from you this season.

How warm and bland the weather is here, 60° in the shade, and how fine a crop of grass and flowers is growing up along the shores and back on the spongy tundra! The Captain says I can have a few hours on shore this afternoon. I mean to go across the bay three miles to a part of the tundra I have not yet seen. I shall at least find a lot of new flowers and see some of the birds. Once more, goodbye. I send Anna's parka by the St. Paul. Give my love to Sam Williams. You must not forget him.

[JOHN MUIR]

A month and three days after the date of the preceding letter the Corwin succeeded in making a landing on Wrangell Land. From some unpublished notes of Muir under the heading "Our New Arctic Territory" we excerpt the following account of the event:

Next morning [August 12th] the fog lifted, and we were delighted to see that though there was now about eight miles of ice separating us from the shore, it was less closely packed, and the Corwin made her way through it without great difficulty until within two miles of the shore, where the craggy berg-blocks were found to be extremely hard and wedged closely together. But a patch of open water near the beach, now plainly in sight, encouraged a continuance of the struggle, and with a full head of steam on, the barrier was forced. By 10 o'clock a.m. our little ship was riding at anchor less than a cable's length from the beach, opposite the mouth of a river.

This landing point proved to be in latitude 71° 4', longitude 177° 40' 30" W., near the East Cape. After taking formal possession of the country, one party examined the level beach about the mouth of the river, and the left bank for a mile or two, and a hillside that slopes gently down to the river, while another party of officers, after building a cairn, depositing records in it, and setting the flag on a conspicuous point of the bluff facing the ocean, proceeded northwestward along the brow of the short bluff to a marked headland, a distance of three or four miles, searching attentively for traces of the Jeannette expedition and of any native inhabitants that might chance to be in the country. Then all were hurriedly recalled and a way was forced to open water through ten miles of drift ice which began to close upon us.

to Mrs. Muir

Point Barrow, August 16th, 1881

MY BELOVED WIFE

Heaven only knows my joy this night in hearing that you were well. Old as the letter is and great as the number of days and nights that have passed since your love was written, it yet seems as if I had once more been upstairs and held you and Wanda in my arms. Ah, you little know the long icy days, so strangely nightless, that I have longed and longed for one word from you. The dangers, great as they were, while groping and grinding among the vast immeasurable ice-fields about that mysterious Wrangell Land would have seemed as nothing before I knew you. But most of the special dangers are past, and I have grand news for you, my love, for we have succeeded in landing on that strange ice-girt country and our work is nearly all done and I am coming home by the middle of October. No thought of wintering now and attempting to cross the frozen ocean from Siberia. We will take no more risks. All is well with our stanch little ship. She is scarce at all injured by the pounding and grinding she has undergone, and sailing home seems nothing more than crossing San Francisco Bay. We have added a large territory [Wrangell Land] to the domain of the United States and amassed a grand lot of knowledge of one sort and another.

Now we sail from here tomorrow for Cape Lisburne, or, if stormy, to Plover Bay, to coal and repair our rudder, which is a little weak. Thence we will go again around the margin of the main polar pack about Wrangell Land, but not into it, and possibly discover a clear way to land upon it again and obtain more of its geography; then leave the Arctic about the 10th of September, call at St. Michael, at Unalaska, and then straight home.

I shall not write at length now, as this is to go down by the Legal Tender, which sails in a few days and expects to reach San Francisco by the 20th of September, but we may reach home nearly as soon as she. I have to dash off a letter for the *Bulletin* tonight, though I ought to go to bed. Not a word of it is yet written.

We came poking and feeling our way along this icy shore a few hours ago through the fog, little thinking that a letter from you was just ahead. Then the fog lifted, and we saw four whalers at anchor and a strange vessel. When the Captain of the Belvidere shouted, "Letters for you, Captain, by the Legal Tender," which was the strange vessel, our hearts leaped, and a boat was speedily sent alongside. I got the letter package and handed them round, and yours, love, was the very last in the package, and I dreaded there was none. The Rodgers had not yet been heard from. One of the whale ships was caught here and crushed in the ice and sank in twenty minutes a month ago.

Goodbye, love. I shall soon be home. Love to all. My wee lass-love – she seems already in my arms. Not in dreams this time! From father and husband and lover.

JOHN MUIR

Muir's collection of plants, gathered in the Arctic lands touched by the Corwin, was naturally of uncommon interest to botanists. Asa Gray returned from a European trip in November, and in response to an inquiry from Muir at once wrote him to send on his Arctic plants for determination. Those from Herald Island and Wrangell Land, represented by a duplicate set in the Gray Herbarium at Harvard, are still the only collections known to science from those regions. In determining the plants, Gray found among them a new species of erigeron, and in reporting it to the American Academy of Arts and Sciences named it *Erigeron Muirii* in honour of its discoverer. Muir found it in July at Cape Thompson on the Arctic shore of Alaska.*

This cruise in the Arctic Ocean, as it turned out, was to be the last of his big expeditions for some time. Domestic cares and joys, and the development of the fruit ranch, absorbed his attention more and more. The old freedom was gone, but the following paragraph, from a letter written to Mrs. John Bidwell, of Rancho Chico, on January 2nd, 1882, suggests that he had found a satisfying substitute for the independence of earlier years:

I have been anxious to run up to Chico in the old free way to tell you about the majestic icy facts that I found last summer in the Lord's Arctic palaces, but, as you can readily guess, it is not now so easy a matter to wing hither and thither like a bird, for here is a wife and a baby and a home, together with the old press of field studies and literary work, which I by no means intend to lose sight of even in the bright bewitching smiles of my wee bonnie lassie. Speaking of brightness, I have been busy, for a week or two just past, letting more light into the house by means of dormer windows, and in making two more open brick fireplaces. Dormer-windows, open wood-fires, and perfectly happy babies make any home glow with warm sunny brightness and bring out the best that there is in us.

---

* A complete list of his various collections and of his glacial observations will be found in the appendix to *The Cruise of the Corwin* (1917).

CHAPTER FIFTEEN

Winning a Competence 1881–1891

THERE WAS an interval of ten years during which Mr. Muir devoted himself with great energy and success to the development of the Alhambra fruit ranch. According to a fictitious story, still encountered in some quarters, he was penniless at the time of his marriage. On the contrary, he had several thousand dollars at interest and, according to a fragment of uncompleted memoirs, was receiving from one hundred to two hundred and fifty dollars for each of his magazine articles. "After my first article," he wrote, "I was greatly surprised to find that everything else I offered was accepted and paid for. That I could earn money simply with written words seemed very strange."

In the same memoirs Muir generalises as follows on the decade between 1881 and 1891:

About a year before starting on the Arctic expedition I was married to Louie Strentzel, and for ten years I was engaged in fruit-raising in the Alhambra Valley, near Martinez, clearing land, planting vineyards and orchards, and selling the fruit, until I had more money than I thought I would ever need for my family or for all expenses of travel and study, however far or however long continued. But this farm work never seriously interrupted my studies. Every spring when the snow on the mountains had melted, until the approach of winter, my explorations were pushed farther and farther. Only in the early autumn, when the table grapes were gathered, and in winter and early spring, when the vineyards and orchards were pruned and cultivated, was my personal supervision given to the work. After these ten years I sold part of the farm and leased the balance, so as to devote the rest of my life, as carefree as possible, to travel and study. Thus, in 1891, I was again free from the farm and all bread winning cares.

In the extant correspondence of the early eighties one gets only indirect and fugitive hints of Muir's activities. Worthy of notice is the fact that during July, 1884, he took his wife to the Yosemite Valley, and their joint letters to the grandparents and the little daughter, left at home, afford amusing glimpses of a husband who has never played courier to a wife and of a wife who mistakes trout for catfish and suspects a bear behind every bush. It should be added that in Mrs. Muir's letters there is a note of concern for her husband's health, which had begun to suffer under the exacting cares of the ranch. "I am anxious about John," she writes. "The journey was hard for him, and he looks thin and pale and tired. He must not leave the mountains until he is well and strong again."

The arrival, in 1886, of a second daughter, believed to have been of frail health during her infant years, brought an increase of parental cares and anchored the family to the ranch more closely than ever. Mrs. Muir was naturally disinclined to travel, and both of them were full of misgivings regarding anything that might imperil the safety of the children. Under the circumstances Muir became more and more absorbed in the management of the ranch and care for his own.

Meanwhile time was working changes in the Wisconsin family circle from which John had gone out in 1867. Nearly eighteen years had gone by since he had seen his father and mother, brothers and sisters. His brother-in-law David Galloway died suddenly in September, 1884, his father and mother were growing infirm, the wife of his brother David was smitten with an incurable malady, and death was thinning the ranks of the friends of his youth. In view of these circumstances he began to feel more and more strongly the desire to revisit the scenes and friends of his boyhood. "I mean to see you all some time this happy new year [1885]," he wrote to his brother David at the close of December. "Seeing you after so long a journey in earth's wildest wildernesses will make [the experience] indeed new to me. I could not come now without leaving the ranch to go to wreck, a score of workmen without a head, and no head to be found, though I have looked long for a foreman. Next spring after the grapes are pruned and sulphured, etc., and the cherry crop sold, I mean to pay off all but a half-dozen or so and leave things to take their course for a month or two. Can't you send me some good steady fellow to learn this fruit business and take some of the personal supervision off my shoulders? Such a person could be sure of a job as long as he liked."

It seems worth while to record, in this connection, an incident of dramatic and pathetic interest which occurred during the summer of 1885, just before Muir made his first return trip to his old Wisconsin home. Helen Hunt Jackson had come to San Francisco in June after months of illness, caused, as she thought, by defective sanitation in a Los Angeles boarding-house. Having recently been appointed Special Commissioner to inquire into the conditions surrounding the Mission Indians of California, she gave herself with devotion and ability to the righting of their wrongs. Among her particular friends was Mrs. Carr, at whose suburban Pasadena home, "Carmelita," she had written a part of her Indian story *Ramona*. It was quite natural, therefore, that she should apply to John Muir for help in planning a convalescent's itinerary in the mountains. "I know with the certainty of instinct," she wrote, "that nothing except three months out of doors night and day will get this poison out of my veins. The doctors say that in six weeks I may be strong enough to be laid on a bed in a wagon and drawn about."

It is easy to imagine the surprise and amusement of Muir when he read her statement of the conditions and equipment required for her comfort. She wished to be among trees where it was moist and cool, being unable to endure heat. She wanted to keep moving, but the altitudinal range must not exceed four thousand feet, and, above all, she must not get beyond easy reach of express and post offices. Her outfit was to consist of eight horses, an ambulance, two camp-wagons for tents, and a phaeton buggy. The attendants were to comprise four servants, a maid, and a doctor.

"Now do you know any good itinerary she inquired," for such a cumbrous caravan as this? How you would scorn such lumbering methods! I am too ill to wish any other. I shall do this as a gamester throws his last card!" In conclusion she stated that she had always cherished the hope of seeing him some time. "I believe," she adds, "I know every word you have written. I never wished myself a man but once. That was when I read how it seemed to be rocked in the top of a pine tree in a gale!"

Muir's reply to this request, according to the draft of a letter found among his papers, was as follows:

to Helen Hunt Jackson

Martinez, June 16th, 1885

MY DEAR MRS. JACKSON
Your letter of June 8th has shown me how sick you are, but also that your good angel is guiding you to the mountains, and therefore I feel sure that you will soon be well again.

When I came to California from the swamps of Florida, full of malarial poison, I crawled up the mountains over the snow into the blessed woods about Yosemite Valley, and the exquisite pleasure of convalescence and exuberant rebound to perfect health that came to me at once seem still as fresh and vivid after all these years as if enjoyed but yesterday.

The conditions you lay down for your itinerary seem to me desperately forbidding. No path accessible to your compound congregation can be traced across the range, maintaining anything like an elevation of four thousand feet, to say nothing of coolness and moisture, while along the range the topography is still less compliant to your plans. When I was tracing the Sequoia belt from the Calaveras to the Kern River I was compelled to make a descent of nine thousand feet in one continuous swoop in crossing the Kings River Valley, while the ups and downs from ridge to ridge throughout the whole course averaged nearly five thousand feet.

No considerable portion of the middle and southern Sierra is cool and moist at four thousand feet during late summer, for there you are only on the open margin of the main forest zone, which is sifted during the day by the dry warm winds that blow across the San Joaquin plains and foothills, though the night winds from the summit of the range make the nights delightfully cool and refreshing.

The northern Sierra is considerably cooler and moister at the same heights. From the end of the Oregon Railroad beyond Redding you might work up by a gentle grade of fifty miles or so to Strawberry Valley where the elevation is four thousand feet. There is abundance of everything, civilized as well as wild, and from thence circle away all summer around Mount Shasta where the circumference is about one hundred miles, and only a small portion of your way would lie much above or below the required elevation, and only the north side, in Shasta Valley, would you find rather dry and warm, perhaps, while you would reach an express station at every round or a good messenger could find you in a day from the station at any point in your orbit. And think how glorious a centre you would have! – so glorious and inspiring that I would gladly revolve there, weary, afoot, and alone for all eternity.

The Kings River yosemite would be a delightful summer den for you, abounding in the best the mountains have to give. Its elevation is about five thousand feet, length nine miles, and it is reached by way of Visalia and Hyde's Mills among the Sequoias of the Kaweah, but not quite accessible to your wheels and pans, I fear. Have you considered the redwood region of the Coast Range about Mendocino? There you would find coolness, moist air, and spicy woods at a moderate elevation.

If an elevation of six thousand feet were considered admissible, I would advise your going on direct to Truckee by rail, rather than to Dutch Flat, where the climate may be found too dry and hot. From Truckee by easy stages to Tahoe City and thence around the Lake and over the Lake all summer. This, as you must know, is a delightful region cool and moist and leafy, with abundance of food and express stations, etc.

What an outfit you are to have – terrible as an army with banners! I scarce dare think of it. What will my poor Douglas squirrels say at the sight? They used to frisk across my feet, but I had only two feet, which seemed too many for the topography in some places, while you have a hundred, besides wooden spokes and spooks. Under ordinary circumstances they would probably frighten the maid and stare the doctor out of countenance, but every tail will be turned in haste and hidden at the bottom of the deepest knot-holes. And what shuffling and haste there will be in the chaparral when the bears are getting away! Even the winds might hold their breath, I fancy, "pause and die," and the great pines groan aghast at the oncoming of so many shining cans and carriages and strange colours.

But go to the mountains where and how you will, you soon will be free from the effects of this confusion, and God's sky will bend down about you as if made for you alone, and the pines will spread their healing arms above you and bless you and make you well again, and so delight the heart of

JOHN MUIR

"If nothing else comes of my camping air-castle," she wrote from 1600 Taylor Street, San Francisco, two days after receiving Muir's answer, "I have at least one pleasure from it – your kind and delightful letter. I have read it so many times I half know it. I wish Mrs. Carr were here that I might triumph over her. She wrote me that I might as well ask one of the angels of heaven as John Muir, 'so entirely out of his line' was the thing I proposed to do. I knew better, however, and I was right. You are the only man in California who could tell me just what I needed to know about ranges of climate, dryness, heat, etc., also roads.''

But the author of *Ramona* was never to have an opportunity to play her last card, for she was beyond even the healing of the mountains if she could have reached them. Indeed, one detects a presentiment of her doom in the closing lines of her letter to the man who had fired her imagination with his contagious faith in the restorative powers of nature. ''If you could see me,'' she writes, ''you would only wonder that I have courage to even dream of such an expedition. I am not at all sure it is not of the madness which the gods are said to send on those whom they wish to destroy. They tell me Martinez is only twenty miles away: do you never come into town? The regret I should weakly feel at having you see the 'remains' (ghastly but inimitable word) of me would, I think, be small in comparison with the pleasure I should feel in seeing you. I am much too weak to see strangers – but it is long since you were a stranger.'' Whether the state of his own health had permitted him to call on ''H. H.,'' as she was known among her friends, before he started East, in August, to see his parents, is not clear. Certain it is that by a singular coincidence he was ringing her door bell almost at the moment when the brave spirit of this noble friend of the Indians was taking flight. ''Mrs. Jackson may have gone away somewhere,'' he remarked in writing to his wife the next day: ''could get no response to my ringing – blinds down.''

The immediate occasion of his decision to go East is best told in some further pages from unpublished memoirs under the title of ''Mysterious Things.'' Though Muir's boyhood was passed in communities where spooks, and ghosts, and clairvoyance were firmly believed in, he was as a man singularly free from faith in superstitions of this kind. But there were several occasions when he acted upon sudden and mysterious impulses for which he knew no explanation, and which he contents himself simply to record. One of these relates to the final illness and death of his father and is told as follows:

In the year 1885, when father was living with his youngest daughter in Kansas City, another daughter, who was there on a visit, wrote me that father was not feeling as well as usual on account of not being able to take sufficient exercise. Eight or ten years before this, when he was about seventy years of age, he fell on an icy pavement and broke his leg at the hip joint, a difficult break to heal at any time, but in old age particularly so. The bone never knitted, and he had to go on crutches the balance of his life.

One morning, a month or two after receiving this word from my sister, I suddenly laid down my pen and said to my wife: ''I am going East, because somehow I feel this morning that if I don't go now I won't see father again." At this time I had not seen him for eighteen years. Accordingly I went on East, but, instead of going direct to Kansas City, I first went to Portage, where one of my brothers and my mother were living.

As soon as I arrived in Portage, I asked mother whether she thought she was able to take the journey to Kansas City to see father, for I felt pretty sure that if she didn't go now she wouldn't see him again alive. I said the same to my brother David. "Come on, David: if you don't go to see father now, I think you will never see him again." He seemed greatly surprised and said: "What has put that in your head? Although he is compelled to go around on crutches, he is, so far as I have heard, in ordinary health." I told him that I had no definite news, but somehow felt that we should all make haste to cheer and comfort him and bid him a last good-bye. For this purpose I had come to gather our scattered family together. Mother, whose health had long been very frail, said she felt it would be impossible for her to stand the journey. David spoke of his business, but I bought him a railway ticket and compelled him to go.

On the way out to Kansas City I stopped at Lincoln, Nebraska, where my other brother, Daniel, a practicing physician, was living. I said, "Dan, come on to Kansas City and see father." "Why?" he asked. "Because if you don't see him now, you never will see him again. I think father will leave us in a few days." "What makes you think so?" said he; "I have not heard anything in particular." I said, "Well, I just kind of feel it. I have no reason." "I cannot very well leave my patients, and I don't see any necessity for the journey." I said, "Surely you can turn over your patients to some brother physician. You will not probably have to be away more than four or five days, or a week, until after the funeral." He said, "You seem to talk as though you knew everything about it." I said, "I don't know anything about it, but I have that feeling – that presentiment, if you like – nothing more." I then bought him a ticket and said, "Now let's go: we have no time to lose." Then I sent the same word to two sisters living in Kearney and Crete, Nebraska, who arrived about as soon as we did.

Thus seven of the eight in our family assembled around father for the first time in more than twenty years. Father showed no sign of any particular illness, but simply was confined to his bed and spent his time reading the Bible. We had three or four precious days with him before the last farewell. He died just after we had had time to renew our acquaintance with him and make him a cheering, comforting visit. And after the last sad rites were over, we all scattered again to our widely separated homes.

The reader who recalls, from the opening chapters of this work, the paternal severity which embittered for John Muir the memory of the youthful years he spent on the farm, will be interested in a few additional details of this meeting of father and son after eighteen years. In spite of the causes which had estranged them so long ago, John had never withheld his admiration for the nobler traits of his father's character, and he apparently cherished the hope that some day he might be able to sit down quietly with him and talk it all out. It seemed futile to do this so long as the old man was actively engaged in evangelistic work, which shut out from calm consideration anything that seemed to him to have been or to be an embarrassment of his calling. Now that he was laid low, John deemed that the proper time had arrived, but for this purpose he had come too late.

"Father is very feeble and helpless," he wrote to his wife from the aged man's bedside. "He does not know me, and I am very sorry. He looks at me and takes my hand and says, 'Is this my dear John?' and then sinks away on the pillow, exhausted, without being able to understand the answer. This morning when I went to see him and was talking broad Scotch to him, hoping to stir some of the old memories of Scotland before we came here, he said, 'I don't know much aboot it noo,' and then added, 'You're a Scotchman, aren't you?' When I would repeat that I was his son John that went to California long ago and came back to see him, he would start and raise his head a little and gaze fixedly at me and say, 'Oh, yes, my dear wanderer,' and then lose all memory again.... I'm sorry I could not have been here two or three months earlier, though I suppose all may be as well, as it is."

A few months earlier, when Daniel Muir was still in full possession of his faculties, he had particularly mentioned to his daughter Joanna some of the cruel things he had said and done to his "poor wandering son John." This wanderer, crossing the mountains and the plains in response to a mysterious summons, had gathered the scattered members of the former Fountain Lake home to his dying father's bedside, and, as the following letter shows, was keeping solitary vigil there, when the hour of dissolution came.

to Mrs. Muir

803 Wabash Avenue, Kansas City,
Missouri, October 6th, 1885

DEAR LOUIE

You will know ere this that the end has come and father is at rest. He passed away in a full summer day evening peace, and with that peace beautifully expressed, and remaining on his countenance as he lies now, pure and clean like snow, on the bed that has borne him so long.

Last evening David and I made everybody go to bed and arranged with each other to keep watch through the night, promising the girls to give warning in time should the end draw near while they slept. David retired in an adjoining room at ten o'clock, while I watched alone, he to be called to take my place at two or three in the morning, should no marked change take place before that time.

About eleven o'clock his breathing became calm and slow, and his arms, which had been moved in a restless way at times, at length were folded on his breast. About twelve o'clock his breathing was still calmer, and slower, and his brow and lips were slightly cold and his eyes grew dim. At twelve-fifteen I called David and we decided to call up the girls, Mary, Anna, and Joanna, but they were so worn out with watching that we delayed a few minutes longer, and it was not until about one minute before the last breath that all were gathered together to kiss our weary affectionate father a last goodbye, as he passed away into the better land of light.

Few lives that I know were more restless and eventful than his – few more toilsome and full of enthusiastic endeavour onward towards light and truth and eternal love through the midst of the devils of terrestrial strife and darkness and faithless misunderstanding that well-nigh overpowered him at times and made bitter burdens for us all to bear.

But his last years as he lay broken in body and silent were full of calm divine light, and he often times spoke to Joanna of the cruel mistakes he had made in his relations towards his children, and spoke particularly of me, wondering how I had borne my burdens so well and patiently, and warned Joanna to be watchful to govern her children by love alone....

Seven of the eight children will surely be present [at the funeral]. We have also sent telegrams to mother and Sarah, though I fear neither will be able to endure the fatigues of the journey. . . . In case they should try to be present, David or I would meet them at Chicago. Then the entire family would be gathered once more, and how gladly we would bring that about, for in all our devious ways and wanderings we have loved one another.

In any case, we soon will be scattered again, and again gathered together. In a few days the snow will be falling on father's grave and one by one we will join him in his last rest, all our separating wanderings done forever.

Love to all, Wanda, Grandma, and Grandpa. Ever yours, Louie

JOHN MUIR

to Mrs. Muir

Portage City, Wisconsin,
September 10th, 1885

DEAR LOUIE

I have just returned from a visit to the old people and old places about our first home in America, ten or twelve miles to the north of this place, and am glad to hear from you at last. Your two letters dated August 23rd and 28th and the Doctor's of September 1st have just been received, one of them having been forwarded from the Yellowstone, making altogether four letters from home besides Wanda's neat little notes which read and look equally well whichever side is uppermost. Now I feel better, for I had begun to despair of hearing from you at all, and the weeks since leaving home, having been crowded with novel scenes and events, seemed about as long as years.

As for the old freedom I used to enjoy in the wilderness, that, like youth and its enthusiasms, is evidently a thing of the past, though I feel that I could still do some good scientific work if the necessary leisure could be secured. Your letters and the Doctor's cheer and reassure me, as I felt that I was staying away too long and leaving my burdens for others to carry who had enough of their own, and though you encourage me to prolong my stay and reap all the benefit I can in the way of health and pleasure and knowledge, I cannot shut my eyes to the fact that the main vintage will soon be on and require my presence, to say nothing of your uncertain state of health. Therefore I mean to begin the return journey next Saturday morning by way of Chicago and Kansas City....

Still another of your letters has just arrived, dated August 31st, by which I learn that Wanda is quite well and grandma getting stronger, while you are not well as you should be. I have tried to get you conscious of the necessity of the utmost care of your health – especially at present – and again remind you of it.

The Yellowstone period was, as you say, far too short, and it required bitter resolution to leave all. The trip, however, as a whole has been far from fruitless in any direction. I have gained telling glimpses of the Continent from the car windows, and have seen most of the old friends and neighbours of boyhood times, who without exception were almost oppressively kind, while a two weeks' visit with mother and the family is a great satisfaction to us all, however much we might wish it extended....

I saw nearly all of the old neighbours, the young folk, of course, grown out of memory and unrecognisable; but most of the old I found but little changed by the eighteen years since last I saw them, and the warmth of my welcome was in most instances excruciating. William Duncan, the old Scotch stone-mason who loaned me books when I was little and always declared that "Johnnie Moor will mak a name for himsel some day," I found hale and hearty, eighty-one years of age, and not a grey hair in his curly, bushy locks – erect, firm of step, voice firm with a clear calm ring to it, memory as good as ever apparently, and his interest in all the current news of the world as fresh and as far-reaching. I stopped overnight with [him] and talked till midnight.

We were four days in making the round and had to make desperate efforts to get away. We climbed the Observatory that used to be the great cloud-capped mountain of our child's imagination, but it dwindled now to a mere hill two hundred and fifty feet high, half the height of that vineyard hill opposite the house. The porphyry outcrop on the summit is very hard, and I was greatly interested in finding it grooved and polished by the ice-sheet. I began to get an appetite and feel quite well. Tell Wanda I'll write her a letter soon. Everybody out in the country seemed disappointed, not seeing you also.

Love to all.   Ever yours

JOHN MUIR

Early in 1887 a letter from Janet Moores, one of the children who had visited Muir in his dark-room in Indianapolis many years ago, brought him news that she had arrived in Oakland. She was the daughter of his friend Mrs. Julia Merrill Moores, and a sister of Merrill Moores, who spent a season with John in Yosemite and in 1915 was elected a member of Congress from Indiana.

to Miss Janet Douglass Moores

Martinez, California,
February 23rd, 1887

MY DEAR FRIEND JANET

Have you really turned into a woman, and have you really come to California, the land of the sun, and Yosemite and a' that, through the whirl of all these years! Seas between us braid hae roared, my lassie, sin' the auld lang syne, and many a storm has roared over broad mountains and plains since last we parted. Yet, however, we are but little changed in all that signifies, saved from many dangers that we know, and from many more that we never shall know – kept alive and well by a thousand, thousand miracles!

Twenty years! How long and how short a time that seems today! How many times the seas have ebbed and flowed with their white breaking waves around the edges of the continents and islands in this score of years, how many times the sky has been light and dark, and the ground between us been shining with rain, and sun, and snow: and how many times the flowers have bloomed, but for a' that and a' that you seem just the same to me, and time and space and events hide you less than the thinnest veil. Marvellous indeed is the permanence of the impressions of those sunrise days, more enduring than granite mountains. Through all the landscapes I have looked into, with all their wealth of forests, rivers, lakes, and glaciers, and happy living faces, your face, Janet, is still seen as clear and keenly outlined as on the day I went away on my long walk.

Aye, the auld lang syne is indeed young. Time seems of no avail to make us old except in mere outer aspects. Today you appear the same little fairy girl, following me in my walks with short steps as best you can, stopping now and then to gather buttercups, and anemones, and erigenias, sometimes taking my hand in climbing over a fallen tree, threading your way through tall grasses and ferns, and pushing through very small spaces in thickets of underbrush. Surely you must remember those holiday walks, and also your coming into my dark room with light when I was blind! And what light has filled me since that time, I am sure you will be glad to know – the richest sun-gold flooding these California valleys, the spiritual alpenglow steeping the high peaks, silver light on the sea, the white glancing sunspangles on rivers and lakes, light on the myriad stars of the snow, light sifting through the angles of sun-beaten icebergs, light in glacier caves, irised spray wafting from white waterfalls, and the light of calm starry nights beheld from mountain-tops dipping deep into the clear air. Aye, my lassie, it is a blessed thing to go free in the light of this beautiful world, to see God playing upon everything, as a man would play on an instrument, His fingers upon the lightning and torrent, on every wave of sea and sky, and every living thing, making all together sing and shine in sweet accord, the one love-harmony of the Universe. But what need to write so far and wide, now you are so near, and when I shall so soon see you face to face?

I only meant to tell you that you were not forgotten. You think I may not know you at first sight, nor will you be likely to recognise me. Every exper-ience is recorded on our faces in characters of some sort, I suppose, and if at all telling, my face should be quite pictur-esque and marked enough to be readily known by anybody looking for me: but when I look in the glass, I see but little more than the marks of rough weather and fasting. Most people would see only a lot of hair, and two eyes, or one and a half, in the middle of it, like a hillside with small open spots, mostly overgrown with shaggy chaparral, as this portrait will show. Wanda, peeping past my elbow, asks,

A SELF PORTRAIT
Drawing in the letter of February 23rd, 1887
to Miss Janet Douglass Moores

"Is that you, Papa?" and then goes on to say that it is just like me, only the hair is not curly enough; also that the little ice and island sketches are just lovely, and that I must draw a lot just like them for her. I think that you will surely like her. She remarked the other day that she was well worth seeing now, having got a new gown or something that pleased her. She is six years old.

The ranch and the pasture hills hereabouts are not very interesting at this time of year. In bloom-time, now approaching, the orchards look gay and Dolly Vardenish, and the home garden does the best it can with rose bushes and so on, all good in a food and shelter way, but about as far from the forests and gardens of God's wilderness as bran-dolls are from children. I should like to show you my wild lily and Cassiope and Bryanthus gardens, and homes not made with hands, with their daisy carpets and woods and streams and other fine furniture, and singers, not in cages; but legs and ankles are immensely important on such visits. Unfortunately most girls are like flowers that have to stand and take what comes, or at best ride on iron rails around and away from what is worth seeing; then they are still something like flowers – flowers in pots carried by express.

I advised you not to come last Friday because the weather was broken, and the telephone was broken, and the roads were muddy, but the weather will soon shine again, and then you and Mary can come, with more comfort and safety. Remember me to Mary, and believe me,

Ever truly your friend
JOHN MUIR

Muir's literary unproductiveness during the eighties began to excite comment among his friends if one may judge by several surviving letters in which they inquire whether he has forsaken literature. His wife, also, was eager to have him continue to write, and it was, perhaps, due to this gentle pressure from several quarters that he accepted in 1887 a proposal from the J.Dewing Company to edit and contribute to an elaborately illustrated work entitled *Picturesque California*. As usual with such works, it was issued in parts, sold by subscription, and while it bears the publication date of 1888, it was not finished until a year or two later.

As some of the following letters show, Muir found it a hard grind to supply a steady stream of copy to the publishers and to supervise his corps of workmen on the ranch at the same time. "I am all nerve-shaken and lean as a crow – loaded with care, work, and worry," he wrote to his brother David after a serious illness of his daughter Helen in August, 1887. "The care and worry will soon wear away, I hope, but the work seems rather to increase. There certainly is more than enough of it to keep me out of mischief forever. Besides the ranch I have undertaken a big literary job, an illustrated work on California and Alaska. I have already written and sent in the two first numbers and the illustrations, I think, are nearly ready."

The prosecution of this task involved various trips, and on some of them he was accompanied by his friend William Keith, the artist. Perhaps the longest was the one on which they started together early in July, 1888, travelling north as far as Vancouver and making many halts and side excursions, both going and coming. Muir was by no means a well man when he left home, but in a train letter to his wife he expressed confidence that he would "be well at Shasta beneath a pine tree." The excursion took him to Mount Hood, Mount Rainier, Snoqualmie and Spokane Falls, and Victoria, up the Columbia, and to many places of minor interest in the Puget Sound region. In spite of his persistent indisposition he made the ascent of Mount Rainier. "Did not mean to climb it," he wrote to his wife, "but got excited and soon was on top."

It did not escape the keen eyes of his devoted wife that the work of the ranch was in no small measure responsible for the failure of his health. "A ranch that needs and takes the sacrifice of a noble life," she wrote to her husband on this trip, "ought to be flung away beyond all reach and power for harm. . . . The Alaska book and the Yosemite book, dear John, must be written, and you need to be your own self, well and strong, to make them worthy of you. There is nothing that has a right to be considered beside this except the welfare of our children."

Muir's health, however, improved during the following winter and summer, notwithstanding the fact that the completion of *Picturesque California* kept him under tension all the time. By taking refuge from the tasks of the ranch at a hotel in San Francisco, during periods of intensive application, he learned to escape at least the strain of conflicting responsibilities. But even so he had to admit at times that he was "hard at work on the vineyards and orchards while the publishers of *Picturesque California* are screaming for copy." In letters written to his wife, during periods of seclusion in San Francisco, Muir was accustomed to quote choice passages for comment and approval. The fact is of interest because it reveals that he had in her a stimulating and appreciative helper.

to Mrs. Muir

Grand Hotel, San Francisco,
July 4th, 1889

DEAR LOUIE

I'm pegging away and have invented a few good lines since coming here, but it is a hard subject and goes slow. However, I'll get it done somehow and sometime. It was cold here last evening and I had to put on everything in my satchel at once....

Last evening an innocent-looking *Examiner* reporter sent up his card, and I, really innocent, told the boy to let him come up. He began to speak of the Muir Glacier, but quickly changed the subject to horned toads, snakes, and Gila monsters. I asked him what made him change the subject so badly and what there was about the Muir Glacier to suggest such reprobate reptiles. He said snakes were his specialty and wanted to know if I had seen many, etc. I talked carelessly for a few minutes, and judge of my surprise in seeing this villainous article. "John Muir says they kill hogs and eat rabbits, but don't eat hogs because too big, etc." What poetry! It's so perfectly ridiculous, I have at least had a good laugh out of it. "The toughness of the skin makes a difference," etc. – should think it would!

The air has been sulphurous all day and noisy as a battlefield. Heard some band music, but kept my room and saw not the procession.

Hope your finger is not going to be seriously sore and that the babies are well. I feel nervous about them after reading about those geological snakes of John Muir....

My room is better than the last, and I might at length feel at home with my Puget Sound scenery had I not seen and had nerves shaken with those Gila monsters. I hope I'll survive, though the *Examiner* makes me say, "If the poison gets into them it takes no time at all to kill them" (the hogs), and my skin is not as thick. Remember me to Grandma, Grandpa, and the babies, and tell them not the sad story of the snakes of Fresno.

Ever yours
JOHN MUIR

to Mrs. Muir

Grand Hotel, San Francisco,
July 5th, 1889

DEAR LOUIE

Here are more snakes that I found in the *Call* this morning! The curly, crooked things have fairly gained the papers and bid fair to crawl through them all, leaving a track never, I fear, to be obliterated. The *Chronicle's* turn will come next, I fancy, and others will follow. I suppose I ought to write a good post-glacial snake history for the *Bulletin*, for just see how much better this lady's snakes are than mine in the *Examiner*! "The biggest snake that ever waved a warning rattle" – almost poetry compared with "John Muir says they don't eat sheep." "Wriggling and rattling aborigines!" I'm ashamed of my ramshackle *Examiner* prose. The Indians "tree the game" and "hang up his snakeship" "beautifully cured" in "sweet fields arrayed in living green," "and very beautiful they are," etc., etc., etc. Oh, dear, how scrawny and lean and mean my snake composition seems! Worse in its brutal simplicity than Johnnie's composition about "A Owl." Well, it must be borne.

I'm pegging away. Saw Upham today. Dr. Vincent is at the Palace. Haven't called on him; too busy. Love to all. Don't tell anybody about my poor snakes.   Kiss the babies.

J. M.

to Mrs. Muir

Grand Hotel, July 6th, 1889

Oh, dear Louie, here are more of "them snakes" – "whirled and whizzed like a wheel," "big as my thigh, and head like my fist," all of them, you see, better and bigger than John Muir's.

And when, oh, when, is that fatal interview to end? How many more idiotic articles are to grow out of it? "Muir's Strange Story," "Elephants' bones are sticking in the Yukon River, says geologist John Muir"! "Bering Straits maybe bridged because Bering Sea is shallow!" Oh! Oh! if the *Examiner* would only examine its logic!!! Anyhow, I shall take fine cautious care that the critter will not examine me again.

Oh, dear Louie, here's more, and were these letters not accompanied by the documentary evidence, you might almost think that these reptiles were bred and born in alcohol! "The Parson and the Snakes!" Think of that for Sunday reading! What is to become of this nation and the *Examiner* ?

It's Johnson, too. Who would have thought it? And think of Longfellow's daughter being signed to such an article!

Well, I'm pegging away, but very slowly. Have got to the thirtieth page. Enough in four days for five minutes' reading. And yet I work hard, but the confounded subject has got so many arms and branches, and I am so cruelly severe on myself as to quality and honesty of work, that I can't go fast. I just get tired in the head and lose all power of criticism until I rest awhile.

It's very noisy here, but I don't notice it. I sleep well, and eat well, and my queer throat feeling has nearly vanished. The weather is very cool. Have to put my overcoat on the bed to reinforce the moderate cover. . . . Good night.   Love to babies and all.

J. M.

to Mrs. Muir

Grand Hotel, San Francisco,
July 11th, 1889

DEAR LOUIE

I was very glad to get your letter today, for somehow I was getting anxious about you all as if, instead of a week, I had been gone a year and had nothing but lonesome silence all the time.

You must see, surely, that I am getting literary, for I have just finished writing for the day and it is half-past twelve. Last evening I went to bed at this time and got up at six and have written twenty pages today, and feel proud that now I begin to see the end of this article that has so long been a black, growling cloud in my sky. Some of the twenty pages were pretty good, too, I think. I'll copy a little bit for you to judge. Of course, you say, "go to bed." Well, never mind a little writing more or less, for I'm literary now, and the fountains flow. Speaking of climate here, I say:

> The Sound region has a fine, fresh, clean climate, well washed, both winter and summer with copious rains, and swept with winds and clouds from the mountains and the sea. Every hidden nook in the depths of the woods is searched and refreshed, leaving no stagnant air. Beaver-meadows, lake-basins, and low, willowy bogs are kept wholesome and sweet, etc.

Again:

> The outer sea margin is sublimely drenched and dashed with ocean brine, the spicy scud sweeping far inland in times of storm over the bending woods, the giant trees waving and chanting in hearty accord, as if surely enjoying it all.

Here's another bit: [Quotes from what is now the concluding paragraph of Chapter Seventeen in *Steep Trails*, beginning "The most charming days here are days of perfect calm," etc.].

Well, I may be dull tomorrow, and then too, I have to pay a visit to that charming, entertaining, interesting [dentist] "critter" of files and picks, called Cutlar. So much, I suppose, for cold wind in my jaw.   Goodnight.

Love to all,
J. M.

to Mrs. Muir

Grand Hotel, San Francisco
July 12th, 1889

DEAR LOUIE

Twelve and a half o'clock again, so that this letter should be dated the 13th. Was at the dentist's an hour and a half. . . . Still, have done pretty well, seventeen pages now, eighty-six altogether. Dewing is telegraphing like mad from New York for Muir's manuscript. He will get it ere long. Most of the day's work was prosy, except the last page just now written. Here it is. Speaking of masts sent from Puget Sound, I write:

Thus these trees, stripped of their leaves and branches, are raised again, transplanted and set firmly erect, given roots of iron, bare cross-poles for limbs, and a new foliage of flapping canvas, and then sent to sea, where they go merrily bowing and waving, meeting the same winds that rocked them when they stood at home in the woods. After standing in one place all their lives, they now, like sightseeing tourists, go round the world, meeting many a relative from the old home forest, some, like themselves, arrayed in broad canvas foliage, others planted close to shore, head downward in the mud, holding wharf platforms aloft to receive the wares of all nations.

Imaginative enough, but I don't know what I'll think of it in the sober morning. I see by the papers that [John] Swett is out of school, for which I am at once glad, sorry, and indignant, if not more. Love to all. Goodnight.

J. M.

to Mrs. Muir

Grand Hotel, San Francisco,
July 14th, 1889

DEAR LOUIE

It is late, but I will write very fast a part of today's composition. Here is a bit you will like:

The upper Snoqualmie Fall is about seventy five feet high, with bouncing rapids at head and foot, set in a romantic dell thatched with dripping mosses and ferns and embowered in dense evergreens and blooming bushes. The road to it leads through majestic woods with ferns ten feet long beneath the trees, and across a gravelly plain disforested by fire many years ago, where orange lilies abound and bright shiny mats of kinnikinick sprinkled with scarlet berries. From a place called "Hunt's," at the end of the wagon road, a trail leads through fresh dripping woods never dry – Merten, Menzies, and Douglas spruces and maple and Thuja. The ground is covered with the best moss-work of the moist cool woods of the north, made up chiefly of the various species of hypnum, with *Marchantia jungermannia*, etc., in broad sheets and bosses where never a dust particle floated, and where all the flowers, fresh with mist and spray, are wetter than water-lilies.

In the pool at the foot of the fall there is good trout-fishing, and when I was there I saw some bright beauties taken. Never did angler stand in a spot more romantic, but strange it seemed that anyone could give attention to hooking in a place so surpassingly lovely to look at – the enthusiastic rush and song of the fall; the venerable trees overhead leaning forward over the brink like listeners eager to catch every word of their white refreshing waters; the delicate maidenhairs and aspleniums, with fronds outspread, gathering the rainbow spray, and the myriads of hooded mosses, every cup fresh and shining.

Here's another kind – starting for Mount Rainier:

The guide was well mounted, Keith had bones to ride, and so had small queer Joe, the camp boy, and I. The rest of the party travelled afoot. The distance to the mountain from Yelm in a straight line is about fifty miles. But by the Mule-and-Yellow-Jacket trail, that we had to follow, it is one hundred miles. For, notwithstanding a part of the trail runs in the air where the wasps work hardest, it is far from being an air-line as commonly understood.

At the Soda Springs near Rainier:

Springs here and there bubble up from the margin of a level marsh, both hot and cold, and likely to tell in some way on all kinds of ailments. At least so we were assured by our kind buxom hostess, who advised us to drink without ceasing from all in turn because "every one of 'em had medicine in it and [was] therefore sure to do good!" All our party were sick, perhaps from indulging too freely in "canned goods" of uncertain age. But whatever the poison might have been, these waters failed to wash it away though we applied them freely and faithfully internally and externally, and almost eternally as one of the party said.

Next morning all who had come through the ordeal of yellow-jackets, ancient meats, and medicinal waters with sufficient strength, resumed the journey to Paradise Valley and Camp of the Clouds, and, strange to say, only two of the party were left behind in bed too sick to walk or ride. Fortunately at this distressing crisis, by the free application of remedies ordinary and extraordinary, such as brandy, paregoric, pain-killer, and Doctor somebody-or-other's Golden Vegetable Wonder, they were both wonderfully relieved and joined us at the Cloud Camp next day, etc., etc..

The dentist is still hovering like an angel or something over me. The writing will be finished to-morrow if all goes well. But punctuation and revision will take some time, and as there is now enough to fill two numbers, I suppose it will have to be cut down a little.

Guess I'll get home Thursday, but will try for Wednesday. Hoping all are well, I go to slumber.   With loving wishes for all

[JOHN MUIR]

to James Davie Butler

Martinez, September 1st, 1889

MY DEAR OLD FRIEND PROFESSOR BUTLER

You are not forgotten, but I am stupidly busy, too much so to be able to make good use of odd hours in writing. All the year I have from fifteen to forty men to look after on the ranch, besides the selling of the fruit, and the editing of *Picturesque California*, and the writing of half of the work or more. This fall I have to contribute some articles to the *Century* magazine, so you will easily see that I am laden.

It is delightful to see you in your letters with your family and books and glorious surroundings. Every region of the world that has been recently glaciated is pure and wholesome and abounds in fine scenery, and such a region is your northern lake country. How gladly I would cross the mountains to join you all for a summer if I could get away! But much of my old freedom is now lost, though I run away right or wrong at times. Last summer I spent a few months in Washington Territory studying the grand forests of Puget Sound. I then climbed to the summit of Mount Rainier, about fifteen thousand feet high, over many miles of wildly shattered and crevassed glaciers. Some twenty glaciers flow down the flanks of this grand icy cone, most of them reaching the forests ere they melt and give place to roaring turbid torrents. This summer I made yet another visit to my old Yosemite home, and out over the mountains at the head of the Tuolumne River. I was accompanied by one of the editors of the *Century*, and had a delightful time. When we were passing the head of the Vernal Falls I told our thin, subtle, spiritual story to the editor.

In a year or two I hope to find a capable foreman to look after this ranch work, with its hundreds of tons of grapes, pears, cherries, etc., and find time for book-writing and old-time wanderings in the wilderness. I hope also to see you ere we part at the end of the day.

You want my manner of life. Well, in short, I get up about six o'clock and attend to the farm work, go to bed about nine and read until midnight. When I have a literary task I leave home, shut myself up in a room in a San Francisco hotel, go out only for meals, and peg away awkwardly and laboriously until the wee sma' hours or thereabouts, working long and hard and accomplishing little. During meals at home my little girls make me tell stories, many of them very long, continued from day to day for a month or two....

Will you be likely to come again to our side of the continent? How I should enjoy your visit! To think of little Henry an alderman! I am glad that you are all well and all together. Greek and ozone holds you in health....

With love to Mrs. Butler and Henry, James, the girls, and thee, old friend, I am ever   Your friend

JOHN MUIR

The event of greatest ultimate significance in the year 1889 was the meeting of Muir with Robert Underwood Johnson, the *Century* editor mentioned in the preceding letter. Muir had been a contributor to the magazine ever since 1878, when it still bore the name of *Scribner's Monthly*, and therefore he was one of the men with whom Mr. Johnson made contact upon his arrival in San Francisco. Muir knew personally many of the early California pioneers and so was in a position to give valuable advice in organising for the *Century* a series of articles under the general title of "Gold-Hunters." This accomplished, it was arranged that Muir was to take Mr. Johnson into the Yosemite Valley and the High Sierra. Beside a camp-fire in the Tuolumne Meadows, Mr. Johnson suggested to Muir that he initiate a project for the establishment of the Yosemite National Park.* In order to further the movement it was agreed that he contribute a series of articles to the *Century*, setting forth the beauties of the region. Armed with these articles and the public sentiment created by them, Johnson proposed to go before the House Committee on Public Lands to urge the establishment of a national park along the boundaries to be outlined by Muir.

Our country has cause for endless congratulation that the plan was carried out with ability and success. In August and September, 1890, appeared Muir's articles "The Treasures of Yosemite" and "Features of the Proposed Yosemite National Park," both of which aroused strong public support for the project. A bill introduced in Congress by General William Vandever embodied the limits of the park as proposed by Mr. Muir, and on October 1st, 1890, the Yosemite National Park became an accomplished fact. The following letters relate to the beginning and consummation of his far-sighted beneficial project.

to Mrs. Muir

Yosemite Valley, California,
June 3rd, 1889

DEAR LOUIE

We arrived here about one o'clock after a fine glorious ride through the forests; not much dust, not very hot. The entire trip very delightful and restful and exhilarating. Johnson was charming all the way. I looked out as we passed Martinez about eleven o'clock, and it seemed strange I should ever go past that renowned town. I thought of you all as sleeping and safe. Whatever more of travel I am to do must be done soon, as it grows ever harder to leave my nest and young.

The foothills and all the woods of the Valley are flowery far beyond what I could have looked for, and the sugar pines seemed nobler than ever. Indeed, all seems so new I fancy I could take up the study of these mountain glories with fresh enthusiasm as if I were getting into a sort of second youth, or

---

* For a very readable account of this eventful incident see Robert Underwood Johnson's *Remembered Yesterdays* (1923).

dotage, or something of that sort. Governor W– was in our party, big, burly, and somewhat childishly jolly; also some other jolly fellows and fellowesses.

Saw Hill and his fine studio. He has one large Yosemite – very fine, but did not like it so well as the one you saw. He has another Yosemite about the size of the Glacier that I fancy you would all like. It is sold for five hundred dollars, but he would paint another if you wished.

Everybody is good to us. Frank Pixley is here and Ben Truman that wrote about Tropical California. I find old Galen Clark also. He looks well, and is earning a living by carrying passengers about the Valley. Leidig's and Black's old hotels are torn down, so that only Bernards' and the new Stoneman House are left. This last is quite grand; still it has a silly look amid surroundings so massive and sublime. McAuley and the immortal twins still flounder and flourish in the ethereal sky of Glacier Point.

I mean to hire Indians, horses, or something and make a trip to the Lake Tenaya region or Big [Tuolumne] Meadows and Tuolumne Canyon. But how much we will be able to accomplish will depend upon the snow, the legs, and the resolution of the *Century*. Give my love to everybody at the two houses and kiss and keep the precious babies for me as for thee.

Will probably be home in about a week.   Ever thine

                                                                        J. M.

to Robert Underwood Johnson

Martinez, March 4th, 1890

DEAR MR. JOHNSON

... The love of Nature among Californians is desperately moderate; consuming enthusiasm almost wholly unknown. Long ago I gave up the floor of Yosemite as a garden, and looked only to the rough taluses and inaccessible or hidden benches and recesses of the walls. All the flowers are wall-flowers now, not only in Yosemite, but to a great extent throughout the length and breadth of the Sierra. Still, the Sierra flora is not yet beyond redemption, and much may be done by the movement you are making.

As to the management, it should, I think, be taken wholly out of the Governor's hands. The office changes too often and must always be more or less mixed with politics in its bearing upon appointments for the Valley. A commission consisting of the President of the University, the President of the State Board of Agriculture, and the President of the Mechanics Institute would, I think, be a vast improvement on the present commission. Perhaps one of the commissioners should be an army officer. Such changes would not be likely, as far as I can see, to provoke any formidable opposition on the part of Californians in general. Taking back the Valley on the part of the Government would probably be a troublesome job.... Everybody to whom I have spoken on the subject sees the necessity of a change, however, in the management, and would favour such a commission as I have suggested. For my part, I should rather see the Valley in the hands of the Federal

Government. But how glorious a storm of growls and howls would rend our sunny skies, bursting forth from every paper in the state, at the outrage of the *Century* Editor snatching with unholy hands, etc., the diadem from California's brow! Then where, oh, where would be the "supineness" of which you speak? These Californians now sleeping in apathy, caring only for what "pays," would then blaze up as did the Devil when touched by Ithuriel's spear. A man may not appreciate his wife, but let her daddie try to take her back!

... As to the extension of the grant, the more we can get into it the better. It should at least comprehend all the basins of the streams that pour into the Valley. No great opposition would be encountered in gaining this much, as few interests of an antagonistic character are involved. On the Upper Merced waters there are no mines or settlements of any sort, though some few land claims have been established. These could be easily extinguished by purchase. All the basins draining into Yosemite are really a part of the Valley, as their streams are a part of the Merced. Cut off from its branches, Yosemite is only a stump. However gnarly and picturesque, no tree that is beheaded looks well. But like ants creeping in the furrows of the bark, few of all the visitors to the Valley see more than the stump, and but little of that. To preserve the Valley and leave all its related rocks, waters, forests to fire and sheep and lumbermen is like keeping the grand hall of entrance of a palace for royalty, while all the other apartments from cellar to dome are given up to the common or uncommon use of industry – butcher-shops, vegetable-stalls, liquor-saloons, lumber-yards, etc.

But even the one main hall has a hog-pen in the middle of the floor, and the whole concern seems hopeless as far as destruction and desecration can go. Some of that stink, I'm afraid, has got into the pores of the rocks even. Perhaps it was the oncoming shadow of this desecration that caused the great flood and earthquake – "Nature sighing through all her works giving sign of woe that all was lost." Still something may be done after all. I have indicated the boundary line on the map in dotted line as proposed above. A yet greater extension I have marked on the same map, extending north and south between Lat. 38° and 37° 30' and from the axis of the range westward about thirty-six or forty miles. This would include three groves of Big Trees, the Tuolumne Canyon, Tuolumne Meadows, and Hetch Hetchy Valley. So large an extension would, of course, meet more opposition. Its boundary lines would not be nearly so natural, while to the westward many claims would be encountered; a few also about Mounts Dana and Warren, where mines have been opened.

Come on out here and take another look at the Canyon. The earthquake taluses are all smooth now and the chaparral is buried, while the river still tosses its crystal arches aloft and the ouzel sings. We would be sure to see some fine avalanches. Come on. I'll go if you will, leaving ranch, reservations, Congress bills, *Century* articles, and all other terrestrial cares and particles.

In the meantime I am,   Cordially yours

JOHN MUIR

to Robert Underwood Johnson

Martinez, April 19th, 1890

MY DEAR MR. JOHNSON

I hope you have not been put to trouble by the delay of that manuscript. I have been interrupted a thousand times, while writing, by coughs, grippe, business, etc. I suppose you will have to divide the article. I shall write a sketch of the Tuolumne Canyon and Kings River yosemite, also the charming yosemite of the Middle Fork of Kings River, all of which may, I think, be got into one article of ten thousand words or twenty. If you want more than is contained in the manuscript sent you on the peaks and glaciers to the east of Yosemite, let me know and I will try to give what is wanted with the Tuolumne Canyon.

The Yosemite *Century* leaven is working finely, even thus far, throughout California. I enclose a few clippings. The *Bulletin* printed the whole of Mack's *Times* letter on our honest Governor. [Charles Howard] Shinn says that the *Overland* is going out into the battle henceforth in full armour. The *Evening Post* editorial, which I received last night and have just read, is a good one and I will try to have it reprinted. . . .

Mr. Olmsted's paper was, I thought, a little soft in some places, but all the more telling, I suppose, in some directions. Kate, like fate, has been going for the Governor, and I fancy he must be dead or at least paralysed ere this.

How fares the Bill Vandever? I hope you gained all the basin. If you have, then a thousand trees and flowers will rise up and call you blessed, besides the other mountain people and the usual "unborn generations," etc.

In the meantime for what you have already done I send you a reasonable number of Yosemite thanks, and remain,

Very truly your friend
JOHN MUIR

to Mr. and Mrs. John Bidwell

Martinez, California, April 19th, 1890

DEAR MRS. BIDWELL AND GENERAL

I've been thinking of you every day since dear Parry* died. It seems as if all the good flower people, at once great and good, have died now that Parry has gone – Torrey, Gray, Kellogg, and Parry. Plenty more botanists left, but none we have like these. Men more amiable apart from their intellectual power I

---

*   Charles C. Parry, 1823–90. Explored and collected on the Mexican boundary, in the Rocky Mountains, and in California. The other botanists mentioned are John Torrey, 1796–1873; Asa Gray, 1810–88; and Albert Kellogg, who died in 1887.

never knew, so perfectly clean and pure they were – pure as lilies, yet tough and unyielding in mental fibre as live-oaks. Oh, dear, it makes me feel lonesome, though many lovely souls remain. Never shall I forget the charming evenings I spent with Torrey in Yosemite, and with Gray, after the day's rambles were over and they told stories of their lives, Torrey fondly telling all about Gray, Gray about Torrey, all in one summer; and then, too, they told me about Parry for the first time. And then how fine and how fruitful that trip to Shasta with you! Happy days, not to come again! Then more than a week with Parry around Lake Tahoe in a boat; had him all to myself – precious memories. It seems easy to die when such souls go before. And blessed it is to feel that they have indeed gone before to meet us in turn when our own day is done.

The Scotch have a proverb, "The evenin' brings a' hame." And so, however separated, far or near, the evening of life brings all together at the last. Lovely souls embalmed in a thousand flowers, embalmed in the hearts of their friends, never for a moment does death seem to have had anything to do with them. They seem near, and are near, and as if in bodily sight I wave my hand to them in loving recognition.   Ever yours

JOHN MUIR

to Robert Underwood Johnson

Martinez, May 8th, 1890

MY DEAR MR. JOHNSON

. . . As I have urged over and over again, the Yosemite Reservation ought to include all the Yosemite fountains. They all lie in a compact mass of mountains that are glorious scenery, easily accessible from the grand Yosemite centre, and are not valuable for any other use than the use of beauty. No other interests would suffer by this extension of the boundary. Only the summit peaks along the axis of the range are possibly gold-bearing, and not a single valuable mine has yet been discovered in them. Most of the basin is a mass of solid granite that will never be available for agriculture, while its forests ought to be preserved. The Big Tuolumne Meadows should also be included, since it forms the central camping ground for the High Sierra adjacent to the Valley. The Tuolumne Canyon is so closely related to the Yosemite region it should also be included, but whether it is or not will not matter much, since it lies in rugged rocky security, as one of Nature's own reservations.

As to the lower boundary, it should, I think, be extended so far as to include the Big Tree groves below the Valley, thus bringing under Government protection a section of the forest containing specimens of all the principal trees of the Sierra, and which, if left unprotected, will vanish like snow in summer. Some private claims will have to be bought, but the cost will not be great.

Yours truly

JOHN MUIR

While travelling about with Keith in the Northwest during July, 1888, gathering materials for *Picturesque California*, Muir was one day watching at Victoria the departure of steamers for northern ports. Instantly he heard the call of the "red gods" of Alaska and began to long for the old adventurous days in the northern wildernesses. "Though it is now ten years since my last visit here," he wrote to his wife in the evening, "Alaska comes back into near view, and if a steamer were to start now it would be hard indeed to keep myself from going aboard. I must spend one year more there at the least. The work I am now doing seems much less interesting and important.... Only by going alone in silence, without baggage, can one truly get into the heart of the wilderness. All other travel is mere dust and hotels and baggage and chatter."

The longed-for opportunity came two years later. During the winter of 1890 he had suffered an attack of the grippe which brought on a severe bronchial cough. He tried to wear it out at his desk, but it grew steadily worse. He then, as he used to relate with a twinkle in his eye, decided upon the novel experiment of trying to wear it out by going to Alaska and exploring the upper tributaries of the Muir Glacier. In the following letter we get a glimpse of him after two weeks of active exploration around Glacier Bay.

to Mrs. Muir

Glacier Bay – Camp near eastern end of
Ice Wall, July 7th, [1890]

DEAR LOUIE

The steamer Queen is in sight pushing up Muir Inlet through a grand crowd of bergs on which a clear sun is shining. I hope to get a letter from you to hear how you and the little ones and older ones are.

I have had a good instructive and exciting time since last I wrote you by the Elder a week ago. The weather has been fine and I have climbed two mountains that gave grand general views of the immense mountain fountains of the glacier and also of the noble St. Elias Range along the coast mountains, La Perouse, Crillon, Lituya, and Fairweather. Have got some telling facts on the forest question that has so puzzled me these many years, etc., etc. Have also been making preliminary observations on the motion of the glacier. Loomis and I get on well, and the Reid* and Cushing party camped beside us are fine company and energetic workers. They are making a map of the Muir Glacier and Inlet, and intend to make careful and elaborate measurements of its rate of motion, size, etc. They are well supplied with instruments and will no doubt do good work.

I have yet to make a trip round Glacier Bay, to the edge of the forest and over the glacier as far as I can. Probably Reid and Cushing and their companions will go with me. If this weather holds, I shall not encounter serious trouble. Anyhow, I shall do the best I can. I mean to sew the bear

*   Professor Harry Fielding Reid.

skin into a bag, also a blanket and a canvas sheet for the outside. Then, like one of Wanda's caterpillars, I can lie warm on the ice when night overtakes me, or storms rather, for here there is now no night. My cough has gone and my appetite has come, and I feel much better than when I left home. Love to each and all.

If I have time before the steamer leaves I will write to my dear Wanda and Helen. The crowd of visitors are gazing at the grand blue crystal wall, tinged with sunshine.   Ever thine

J. M.

The crowning experience of this Alaska trip was the sled-trip which he made across the upper reaches of the Muir Glacier between the 11th and the 21st of July. Setting out from his little cabin on the terminal moraine, Muir pushed back on the east side of the glacier toward Howling Valley, fifteen miles to the northward, examined and sketched some of the lesser tributaries, then turned to the westward and crossed the glacier near the confluence of the main tributaries, and thence made his way down the west side to the front. No one was willing to share this adventure with him so he faced it, as usual, alone.

Chapter Eighteen of *Travels in Alaska* gives, in journal form, an account of Muir's experiences and observations on this trip. To this may be added his description of two incidents as related in fragments of unpublished memoirs:

In the course of this trip I encountered few adventures worth mention apart from the common dangers encountered in crossing crevasses. Large timber wolves were common around Howling Valley, feeding apparently on the wild goats of the adjacent mountains.

One evening before sundown I camped on the glacier about a mile above the head of the valley, and, sitting on my sled enjoying the wild scenery, I scanned the grassy mountain on the west side above the timber-line through my field glasses, expecting to see a good many wild goats in pastures so fine and wild. I discovered only two or three at the foot of a precipitous bluff, and as they appeared perfectly motionless, and were not lying down, I thought they must be held there by attacking wolves. Next morning, looking again, I found the goats still standing there in front of the cliff, and while eating my breakfast, preparatory to continuing my journey, I heard the dismal long drawn out howl of a wolf, soon answered by another and another at greater distances and at short intervals coming nearer and nearer, indicating that they had discovered me and were coming down the mountain to observe me more closely, or perhaps to attack me, for I was told by my Indians while exploring in 1879 and 1880 that these wolves attack either in summer or winter, whether particularly hungry or not; and that no Indian hunter ever ventured far into the woods alone, declaring that wolves were much more dangerous than bears. The nearest wolf had evidently got down to the margin of the glacier, and although I had not yet been able to catch sight of any of them, I made haste to a large square boulder on the ice and sheltered myself from attack from behind, in the same manner as the hunted goats. I had no firearms, but thought I could make a good fight with my Alpine ice axe. This, however, was only a threatened attack, and I went on my journey, though keeping a careful watch to see whether I was followed.

At noon, reaching the confluence of the most easterly of the great tributaries and observing that the ice to the westward was closely crevassed, I concluded to spend the rest of the day in ascending what is now called Snow Dome, a mountain about three thousand feet high, to scan the whole width of the glacier and choose the route that promised the fewest difficulties. The day was clear and I took the bearings of what seemed to be the best route and recorded them in my notebook so that in case I should be stopped by a blinding snowstorm, or impassable labyrinth of crevasses, I might be able to retrace my way by compass.

In descending the mountain to my sled camp on the ice I tried to shorten the way by sliding down a smooth steep fluting groove nicely lined with snow; but in looking carefully I discovered a bluish spot a few hundred feet below the head, which I feared indicated ice beneath the immediate surface of the snow; but inasmuch as there were no heavy boulders at the foot of the slope, but only a talus of small pieces an inch or two in diameter, derived from disintegrating metamorphic slates, lying at as steep an angle as they could rest, I felt confident that even if I should lose control of myself and be shot swiftly into them, there would be no risk of broken bones. I decided to encounter the adventure. Down I glided in a smooth comfortable swish until I struck the blue spot. There I suddenly lost control of myself and went rolling and bouncing like a boulder until stopped by plashing into the loose gravelly delta.

As soon as I found my legs and senses I was startled by a wild, piercing, exulting, demoniac yell, as if a pursuing assassin long on my trail were screaming: "I've got you at last." I first imagined that the wretch might be an Indian, but could not believe that Indians, who are afraid of glaciers, could be tempted to venture so far into the icy solitude. The mystery was quickly solved when a raven descended like a thunderbolt from the sky and alighted on a jag of a rock within twenty or thirty feet of me. While soaring invisible in the sky, I presume that he had been watching me all day, and at the same time keeping an outlook for wild goats, which were sometimes driven over the cliffs by the wolves. Anyhow, no sooner had I fallen, though not a wing had been seen in all the clear mountain sky, than I had been seen by these black hunters who now were eagerly looking me over and seemed sure of a meal. The explanation was complete, and as they eyed me with a hungry longing stare I simply called to them: "Not yet!"

Sequoia domes looming into view above the firs and sugar pines
(from ''Treasures of the Proposed Yosemite National Park'' – see page 679)

CHAPTER SIXTEEN

Trees and Travel   1891–1897

THE SUDDEN DEATH of Dr. Strentzel on the last of October, 1890, brought in its train a change of residence for the Muir family. At the time of his marriage, Muir had first rented and later purchased from his father-in-law the upper part of the Alhambra ranch. Dr. Strentzel thereupon left the old home to his daughter, and removed to the lower half of the ranch, where he and his wife built and occupied a large new frame house on a sightly hilltop. Since Mrs. Strentzel, after her husband's death, needed the care of her daughter, the Muirs left the upper ranch home, in which they had lived for ten years, and moved to the more spacious, but on the whole less comfortable, house which thereafter became known as the Muir residence.

At the beginning of his father-in-law's illness, Muir was on the point of starting on a trip up the Kings River Canyon in order to secure additional material for a *Century* article. The project, naturally, had to be abandoned. "It is now snowy and late," he wrote to Mr. Johnson in November, "I fear I shall not be able to get into the canyons this season. I think, however, that I can write the article from my old notes. I made three trips through the Kings River Canyon, and one through the wild Middle Fork Canyon with its charming Yosemite." The deeper purpose of this article was to serve as a starter for another national park. It means that two weeks after the successful issue of the campaign for the creation of the Yosemite National Park, Muir, ably assisted by Mr. R. U. Johnson, began to advocate the enlargement of the Sequoia National Park so as to embrace the Kings River region and the Kaweah and Tule Sequoia groves. John W. Noble was then Secretary of the Interior (1889–93), and it is fair to say that, measured by the magnitude of benefits conferred upon the country, no more useful incumbent has ever filled that office. He at once declared himself ready to withdraw the region from entry if Muir would delimit upon Land Office maps the territory that should go into a park.

"I am going to San Francisco this morning," Muir wrote to Johnson on May 13, 1891, "and will get the best map I can and will draw the boundaries of the proposed new park.... This map I shall send you tomorrow." During the same month he made another trip up the canyon of the Kings River, particularly the South Fork, and afterwards wrote for the *Century* [Nov, 1891] an unusually telling description of it under the title of "A Rival of the Yosemite." "This region," he said in concluding the article, "contains no mines of consequence; it is too high and too rocky for agriculture, and even the lumber industry need suffer no unreasonable restriction. Let our law-givers then make haste, before it is too late, to save this surpassingly glorious region for the recreation and well-being of humanity, and the world will rise up and call them blessed.''

Advance sheets of the article, placed in the hands of Secretary Noble, moved him to bring Muir's proposal to the immediate attention of Congress with the recommendation of "favourable consideration and action." But over thirty years have passed since then, and Muir's dream of good still awaits realisation at the hands of our law-givers. The Roosevelt Sequoia National Park bill, now before Congress, is substantially Muir's original proposal and fittingly recognises the invaluable service which Theodore Roosevelt rendered to the cause of forests and parks, partly in cooperation with Muir, as shown in a succeeding chapter. This bill should be speedily passed, over the paltering objections of adventurers who place their private farthing schemes above the immeasurable public benefit of a national playground that not only rivals the already overcrowded Yosemite in beauty and spaciousness, but is, in the words of Muir, "a veritable song of God."

Muir had now reached the stage in his career when he had not only the desire, but also the power, to translate his nature enthusiasms into social service. Increasing numbers of progressive citizens, both East and West, were looking to him for leadership when corrupt or incompetent custodians of the public domain needed to be brought to the bar of public opinion. And there was much of this work to be done by a man who was not afraid to stand up under fire. Muir's courageous and outspoken criticism of the mismanagement of Yosemite Valley by the State Commissioners aroused demands in Washington for an investigation of the abuses and a recession of the Valley to the Federal Government as part of the Yosemite National Park.

Since there was likelihood of a stiff battle over this and other matters, Muir's friends, particularly Mr. R. U. Johnson, urged him to get behind him a supporting organisation on the Pacific Coast through which men of kindred aims could present a united front. This led to the formal organisation of the Sierra Club on the 4th of June, 1892. It declared its purpose to be a double one: first, "to explore, enjoy, and render accessible the mountain regions of the Pacific Coast, [and] to publish authentic information concerning them"; and, second, "to enlist the support and cooperation of the people and government in preserving the forests and other natural features of the Sierra Nevada Mountains." The Club, in short, was formed with two sets of aims, and it gathered into its membership on the one hand persons who were primarily lovers of mountains and mountaineering, and on the other hand those whose first interest was to conserve the forests and other natural features for future generations. In no single individual were both these interests better represented than in the person of Muir, who became the first president of the Club, and held the office continuously until his death twenty-two years later. Among the men who deserve to be remembered in connection with the organisation and early conservation activities of the Club were Warren Olney, Sr., and Professors Joseph LeConte, J. H. Senger, William Dallam Armes, and Cornelius Beach Bradley.

One of the first important services of the Club was its successful opposition to the so called "Caminetti Bill," a loosely drawn measure introduced into Congress in 1892 with the object of altering the boundaries of the Yosemite National Park in such a way as to eliminate about three hundred alleged mining claims, and other large areas desired by stockmen and lumbermen. The bill underwent various modifications, and finally, in 1894, it was proposed to authorise the Secretary of the Interior to make the alterations. Muir's public interviews and the organised resistance of the Club, fortunately, repelled this contemplated raid upon the new park; for watchful guardians of the public domain regarded it as of ill omen that Secretary Hoke Smith, who had succeeded John W. Noble in 1893, reported that he had no objection to interpose to the bill's passage.

It should be recorded to the lasting honour of President Harrison and the Honourable John W. Noble that they established the first forest reserves under an Act of Congress* passed March 3rd, 1891. It was the first real recognition of the practical value of forests in conserving water-flow at the sources of rivers. The Boone and Crockett Club on April 8th, 1891, made it the occasion of a special vote of thanks addressed to the President and Secretary Noble on the ground that "this society recognises in these actions the most important steps taken in recent years for the preservation of our forests." Though not so recognised at the time, it was a happy augury for the future that the resolution was inspired, signed, and transmitted by Theodore Roosevelt.

Among the few surviving Muir letters of the early nineties is the following one to his Indianapolis friend Mrs. Graydon, who had expressed a hope that, if he returned to her home city during the current year, she might be able to arrange for a social evening with the poet James Whitcomb Riley.

to Mrs. Mary Merrill Graydon

Martinez, February 28th, 1893

MY DEAR MRS. GRAYDON

I am glad to hear from you once more. You say you thought on account of long silence we might be dead, but the worst that could be fairly said is "not dead but sleeping" – hardly even this, for, however silent, sound friendship never sleeps, no matter how seldom paper letters fly between.

My heart aches about Janet – one of the sad, sad, sore cases that no human wisdom can explain. We can only look on the other side through tears and grief and pain and see that pleasure surpasses the pain, good the

---

* The authorisation of the President to make forest reservations is contained in a clause inserted in the Sundry Civil Bill of that year. The credit of it belongs to Edward A. Bowers whose name deserves to be held in remembrance for other noble services to the cause of forest conservation.

evil, and that, after all, Divine love is the sublime boss of the universe.

The children greatly enjoy the [James Whitcomb] Riley book you so kindly sent. I saw Mr. Riley for a moment at the close of one of his lectures in San Francisco, but I had to awkwardly introduce myself, and he evidently couldn't think who I was. Professor [David Starr] Jordan, who happened to be standing near, though I had not seen him, surprised me by saying, "Mr. Riley, this man is the author of the Muir Glacier." I invited Mr. Riley to make us a visit at the ranch, but his engagements, I suppose, prevented even had he cared to accept, and so I failed to see him save in his lecture.

I remember my visit to your home with pure pleasure, and shall not forget the kindness you bestowed, as shown in so many ways. As to coming again this year, I thank you for the invitation, but the way is not open so far as I can see just now.

I think with Mr. Jackson that Henry Riley* shows one of the good sides of human nature in so vividly remembering the little I did for him so long ago. I send by mail with this letter one of the volumes of *Picturesque California* for him in your care, as I do not know his address. Merrill Moores knows him, and he can give him notice to call for the book. It contains one of my articles on Washington, and you are at liberty to open and read it if you wish.

Katie [Graydon] I have not seen since she went to Oakland, though only two hours away. But I know she is busy and happy through letters and friends. I mean to try to pass a night at McChesney's, and see her and find out all about her works and ways. The children and all of us remember her stay with us as a great blessing.

Remember me to the Hendricks family, good and wholesome as sunshine, to the venerable Mr. Jackson, and all the grand Merrill family, your girls in particular, with every one of whom I fell in love, and believe me, noisy or silent.   Ever your friend

                                                        JOHN MUIR

Muir had long cherished the intention of returning to Scotland in order to compare his boyhood memories of the dingles and dells of his native land with what he described, before the California period of his life, as "all the other less important parts of our world." In the spring of 1893 he proceeded to carry out the plan. The well remembered charms of the old landscapes were still there, but he was to find that his standards of comparison had been changed by the Sierra Nevada. On the way East he paid a visit to his mother in Wisconsin, lingered some days at the Chicago World's Fair, and then made his first acquaintance with the social and literary life of New York and Boston. The following letters give some hint of the rich harvest of lasting friendships which he reaped during his eastern sojourn.

* One of his fellow workmen in the wagon factory Indianapolis, 1866–67. "Your name is a household word with us," wrote Mr. Riley in acknowledging Muir's gift. "The world has travelled on at a great rate in the twenty-five years since you and I made wheels together, and you, I am proud to say, have travelled with it."

to Mrs. Muir

3420 Michigan Avenue, Chicago
May 29th, 1893, 9 a.m.

DEAR LOUIE

I leave for New York this evening at five o'clock and arrive there to-morrow evening at seven, when I expect to find a letter from you in care of Johnson at the *Century* Editorial Rooms. The Sellers' beautiful home has been made heartily my own, and they have left nothing undone they could think of that would in any way add to my enjoyment. Under their guidance I have been at the [World's] Fair every day, and have seen the best of it, though months would be required to see it all.

You know I called it a "cosmopolitan rat's nest*," containing much rubbish and commonplace stuff as well as things novel and precious. Well, now that I have seen it, it seems just such a rat's nest still, and what, do you think, was the first thing I saw when I entered the nearest of the huge buildings? A high rat's nest in a glass case about eight feet square, with stuffed wood rats looking out from the mass of sticks and leaves, etc., natural as life! So you see, as usual, I am "always right."

I most enjoyed the art galleries. There are about eighteen acres of paintings by every nation under the sun, and I *wandered* and *gazed* until I was ready to fall down with utter exhaustion. The Art Gallery of the California building is quite small and of little significance, not more than a dozen or two of paintings all told: four by Keith, not his best, and four by Hill, not his best, and a few others of no special character by others, except a good small one by Yelland. But the National Galleries are perfectly overwhelming in grandeur and bulk and variety, and years would be required to make even the most meagre curiosity of a criticism.

The outside view of the buildings is grand and also beautiful. For the best architects have done their best in building them, while Frederick Law Olmsted laid out the grounds. Last night the buildings and terraces and fountains along the canals were illuminated by tens of thousands of electric lights arranged along miles of lines of gables, domes, and cornices, with glorious effect. It was all fairyland on a colossal scale and would have made the Queen of Sheba and poor Solomon in all their glory feel sick with helpless envy. I wished a hundred times that you and the children and Grandma could have seen it all, and only the feeling that Helen would have been made sick with excitement prevented me from sending for you.

I hope Helen is well and then all will be well. I have worked at my article at odd times now and then, but it still remains to be finished at the *Century* rooms. Tell the children I'll write them from New York tomorrow or next day.   Love to all.   Goodbye.   Ever yours

JOHN MUIR

* Refers to the wood rat or pack rat (*Neotoma*) which builds large mound-like nests and "packs" into them all kinds of amusing odds and ends.

to Mrs. Muir

The Thorndike, Boston, Massachusetts
June 12th, 1893

DEAR LOUIE

I have been so crowded and overladen with enjoyments lately that I have lost trace of time and have so much to tell you I scarce know where and how to begin. When I reached New York I called on Johnson, and told him I meant to shut myself up in a room and finish my articles and then go with Keith to Europe. But he paid no attention to either my hurry or Keith's, and quietly ordered me around and took possession of me.

New York, June 13th

DEAR LOUIE

I was suddenly interrupted by a whole lot of new people, visits, dinners, champagne, etc., and have just got back to New York by a night boat by way of Fall River. So I begin again. Perhaps this is the 13th, Tuesday, for I lose all track of time.

First I was introduced to all the *Century* people, with their friends also as they came in. Dined with Johnson first. Mrs. J. is a bright, keen, accomplished woman....

Saw Burroughs the second day. He had been at a Walt Whitman Club the night before, and had made a speech, eaten a big dinner, and had a headache. So he seemed tired, and gave no sign of his fine qualities. I chatted an hour with him and tried to make him go to Europe with me. The *Century* men offered him five hundred dollars for some articles on our trip as an inducement, but he answered today by letter that he could not go, he must be free when he went, that he would above all things like to go with me, etc., but circumstances would not allow it. The "circumstances" barring the way are his wife. I can hardly say I have seen him at all.

Dined another day with [Richard Watson] Gilder. He is charming every way, and has a charming home and family.... I also dined in grand style at Mr. Pinchot's, whose son is studying forestry. The home is at Gramercy Park, New York. Here and at many other places I had to tell the story of the minister's dog. Everybody seems to think it wonderful for the views it gives of the terrible crevasses of the glaciers as well as for the recognition of danger and the fear and joy of the dog. I must have told it at least twelve times at the request of Johnson or others who had previously heard it. I told Johnson I meant to write it out for *St. Nicholas*, but he says it is too good for "*St. Nick*," and he wants it for the *Century* as a separate article. When I am telling it at the dinner-tables, it is curious to see how eagerly the liveried servants listen from behind screens, half-closed doors, etc.

Almost every day in town here I have been called out to lunch and dinner at the clubs and soon have a crowd of notables about me. I had no idea I was so

well known, considering how little I have written. The trip up the Hudson was
delightful. Went as far as West Point, to Castle Crags, the residence of the
[Henry Fairfield] Osborns. Charming drives in the green flowery woods, and,
strange to say, all the views are familiar, for the landscapes are all freshly
glacial. Not a line in any of the scenery that is not a glacial line. The same is
true of all the region hereabouts. I found glacial scoring on the rocks of
Central Park even.

Last Wednesday evening Johnson and I started for Boston, and we got
back this morning, making the trip both ways in the night to economise
time. After looking at the famous buildings, parks, monuments, etc., we took
the train for Concord, wandered through the famous Emerson village, dined
with Emerson's son, visited the Concord Bridge, where the first blood of the
Revolution was shed, and where "the shot was fired heard round the world."
Went through lovely, ferny, flowery woods and meadows to the hill cemetery
and laid flowers on Thoreau's and Emerson's graves. I think it is the most
beautiful graveyard I ever saw. It is on a hill perhaps one hundred and fifty
feet high in the woods of pine, oak, beech, maple, etc., and all the ground is
flowery. Thoreau lies with his father, mother, and brother not far from
Emerson and Hawthorne. Emerson lies between two white pine trees, one at
his head, the other at [his] feet, and instead of a mere tombstone or monument
there is a mass of white quartz rugged and angular, wholly uncut, just as it
was blasted from the ledge. I don't know where it was obtained. There is not
a single letter or word on this grand natural monument. It seems to have
been dropped there by a glacier, and the soil he sleeps in is glacial drift
almost wholly unchanged since first this country saw the light at the close of
the glacial period. There are many other graves here, though it is not one of
the old cemeteries. Not one of them is raised above ground. Sweet kindly
Mother Earth has taken them back to her bosom' whence they came. I did not
imagine I would be so moved at sight of the resting places of these grand
men as I found I was, and I could not help thinking how glad I would be to
feel sure that I would also rest here. But I suppose it cannot be, for Mother
will be in Portage. . . .

After leaving Thoreau and Emerson, we walked through the woods to
Walden Pond. It is a beautiful lake about half a mile long, fairly embosomed
like a bright dark eye in wooded hills of smooth moraine gravel and sand,
and with a rich leafy undergrowth of huckleberry, willow, and young oak
bushes, etc., and grass and flowers in rich variety. No wonder Thoreau lived
here two years. I could have enjoyed living here two hundred years or two
thousand. It is only about one and a half or two miles from Concord, a mere
saunter, and how people should regard Thoreau as a hermit on account of his
little delightful stay here I cannot guess.

We visited also Emerson's home and were shown through the house. It is
just as he left it, his study, books, chair, bed, etc., and all the paintings and
engravings gathered in his foreign travels. Also saw Thoreau's village
residence and Hawthorne's old manse and other home near Emerson's. At
six o'clock we got back from Walden to young Emerson's father-in-law's

place in Concord and dined with the family and Edward Waldo Emerson. The latter is very like his father – rather tall, slender, and with his father's sweet perennial smile. Nothing could be more cordial and loving than his reception of me. When we called at the house, one of the interesting old colonial ones, he was not in, and we were received by his father-in-law, a college mate of Thoreau, who knew Thoreau all his life. The old man was sitting on the porch when we called. Johnson introduced himself, and asked if this was Judge Keyes, etc. The old gentleman kept his seat and seemed, I thought, a little cold and careless in his manner. But when Johnson said, "This is Mr. Muir," he jumped up and said excitedly, "John Muir! Is this John Muir?" and seized me as if I were a long-lost son. He declared he had known me always, and that my name was a household word. Then he took us into the house, gave us refreshments, cider, etc., introduced us to his wife, a charming old fashioned lady, who also took me for a son. Then we were guided about the town and shown all the famous homes and places. But I must hurry on or I will be making a book of it.

We went back to Boston that night on a late train, though they wanted to keep us, and next day went to Professor Sargent's grand place, where we had a perfectly wonderful time for several days. This is the finest mansion and grounds I ever saw. The house is about two hundred feet long with immense verandas trimmed with huge flowers and vines, standing in the midst of fifty acres of lawns, groves, wild woods of pine, hemlock, maple, beech, hickory, etc., and all kinds of underbrush and wild flowers and cultivated flowers – acres of rhododendrons twelve feet high in full bloom, and a pond covered with lilies, etc., all the ground waving, hill and dale, and clad in the full summer dress of the region, trimmed with exquisite taste.

The servants are in livery, and everything is fine about the house and in it, but Mr. and Mrs. Sargent are the most cordial and unaffected people imaginable, and in a few minutes I was at my ease and at home, sauntering where I liked, doing what I liked, and making the house my own. Here we had grand dinners, formal and informal, and here I told my dog story, I don't know how often, and described glaciers and their works. Here, the last day, I dined with Dana, of the New York *Sun*, and Styles, of the *Forest and Stream*, Parsons, the Superintendent of Central Park, and Matthews, Mayor of Boston. Yesterday the Mayor came with carriages and drove us through the public parks and the most interesting streets of Boston, and he and Mr. and Mrs. Sargent drove to the station and saw us off. While making Sargent's our headquarters, Mr. Johnson took me to Cambridge, where we saw the classic old shades of learning, found Royce, who guided us, saw Porter, and the historian Parkman, etc., etc. We called at Eliot's house, but he was away.

We also went to the seaside at Manchester, forty miles or so from Boston, to visit Mrs.[James T.] Fields, a charming old lady, and how good a time! Sarah Orne Jewett was there, and all was delightful. Here, of course, Johnson made me tell that dog story as if that were the main result of glacial action and all my studies, but I got in a good deal of ice-work better than this, and never had better listeners.

Judge Howland, whom I met in Yosemite with a party who had a special car, came in since I began this letter to invite me to a dinner tomorrow evening with a lot of his friends. I must get that article done and set the day of sailing for Europe, or I won't get away at all. This makes three dinners ahead already. I fear the tail of my article will be of another colour from the body. Johnson has been most devoted to me ever since I arrived, and I can't make him stop. I think I told you the *Century* wants to publish my book. They also want me to write articles from Europe.

Must stop. Love to all. How glad I was to get Wanda's long good letter this morning, dated June 2nd! All letters in Johnson's care will find me wherever I go, here or in Europe.   [JOHN MUIR]

to Mrs. Muir

Dunbar, Scotland, July 6th, 1893

DEAR LOUIE

I left Liverpool Monday morning, reached Edinburgh early the same day, went to a hotel, and then went to the old book-publisher David Douglas, to whom Johnson had given me a letter. He is a very solemn-looking, dignified old Scotchman of the old school, an intimate friend and crony of John Brown, who wrote *Rab and His Friends*, knew Hugh Miller, Walter Scott, and indeed all the literary men, and was the publisher of Dean Ramsay's *Reminiscences of Scottish Life and Character*, etc. He had heard of me through my writings, and, after he knew who I was, burst forth into the warmest cordiality and became a perfect gushing fountain of fun, humour, and stories of the old Scotch writers. Tuesday morning he took me in hand, and led me over Edinburgh, took me to all the famous places celebrated in Scott's novels, went around the Calton Hill and the Castle, into the old churches so full of associations, to Queen Mary's Palace Museum, and I don't know how many other places.

In the evening I dined with him, and had a glorious time. He showed me his literary treasures and curiosities, told endless anecdotes of John Brown, Walter Scott, Hugh Miller, etc., while I, of course, told my icy tales until very late – or early – the most wonderful night as far as humanity is concerned I ever had in the world. Yesterday forenoon he took me out for another walk and filled me with more wonders. His kindness and warmth of heart, once his confidence is gained, are boundless. From feeling lonely and a stranger in my own native land, he brought me back into quick and living contact with it, and now I am a Scotchman and at home again.

In the afternoon I took the train for Dunbar and in an hour was in my own old town. There was no carriage from the Lorne Hotel that used to be our home, so I took the one from the St. George, which I remember well as Cossar's Inn that I passed every day on my way to school. But I'm going to the Lorne, if for nothing else [than] to take a look at that dormer window I climbed in my nightgown, to see what kind of an adventure it really was.

I sauntered down the street and went into a store on which I saw the sign Melville, and soon found that the proprietor was an old playmate of mine, and he was, of course, delighted to see me. He had been reading my articles, and said he had taken great pride in tracing my progress through the far-off wildernesses. Then I went to William Comb, mother's old friend, who was greatly surprised, no doubt, to see that I had changed in forty years. "And this is Johnnie Muir! Bless me, when I saw ye last ye were naething but a small mischievous lad." He is very deaf, unfortunately, and was very busy. I am to see him again today.

Next I went in search of Mrs. Lunam, my cousin, and found her and her daughter in a very pretty home half a mile from town. They were very cordial, and are determined to get me away from the hotel. I spent the evening there talking family affairs, auld lang syne, glaciers, wild gardens, adventures, etc., till after eleven, then returned to the hotel.

Here are a few flowers that I picked on the Castle hill on my walk with Douglas, for Helen and Wanda. I pray Heaven in the midst of my pleasure that you are all well. Edinburgh is, apart from its glorious historical associations, far the most beautiful town I ever saw. I cannot conceive how it could be more beautiful. In the very heart of it rises the great Castle hill, glacier-sculptured and wild like a bit of Alaska in the midst of the most beautiful architecture to be found in the world. I wish you could see it, and you will when the babies grow up. . . .

Goodbye.

to Helen Muir

Dunbar, Scotland, July 12th, 1893

HELLO, MIDGE, MY SWEET HELEN

Are you all right? I'm in Scotland now, where I used to live when I was a little boy, and I saw the places where I used to play and the house I used to live in. I remember it pretty well, and the school where the teacher used to whip me so much, though I tried to be good all the time and learn my lessons. The round tower on the hill in the picture at the beginning of the letter is one of the places I used to play at on Saturdays when there was no school.

Here is a little sprig of heather a man gave me yesterday and another for Wanda. The heather is just beginning to come into bloom. I have not seen any of it growing yet, and I don't know where the man found it. But I'm going pretty soon up the mountains, and then I'll find lots of it, and won't it be lovely, miles and miles of it, covering whole mountains and making them look purple. I think I must camp out in the heather.

I'm going to come home just as soon as I get back from Switzerland, about the time the grapes are ripe, I expect. I wish I could see you, my little love.

Your papa
JOHN MUIR

to Mrs. Muir

Dunbar, Scotland, July 12th, 1893

DEAR LOUIE

I have been here nearly a week and have seen most of my old haunts and playgrounds, and more than I expected of my boy playmates. Of course it is all very interesting, and I have enjoyed it more than I anticipated. Dunbar is an interesting place to anybody, beautifully located on a plateau above the sea and with a background of beautiful hills and dales, green fields in the very highest state of cultivation, and many belts and blocks of woods so arranged as to appear natural. I have had a good many rides and walks into the country among the fine farms and towns and old castles, and had long talks with people who listen with wonder to the stories of California and far Alaska.

I suppose, of course, you have received my Edinburgh letter telling the fine time with David Douglas. I mean to leave here next Monday for the Highlands, and then go to Norway and Switzerland.

I am stopping with my cousin, who, with her daughter, lives in a handsome cottage just outside of town. They are very cordial and take me to all the best places and people, and pet me in grand style, but I must on and away or my vacation time will be past ere I leave Scotland.

At Haddington I visited Jeanie Welch Carlyle's grave in the old abbey. Here are two daisies, or gowans, that grew beside it.

I was on a visit yesterday to a farmer's family three miles from town – friends of the Lunams. This was a fine specimen of the gentleman-farmers' places and people in this, the best part of Scotland. How fine the grounds are, and the buildings and the people! . . .

I begin to think I shall not see Keith again until I get back, except by accident, for I have no time to hunt him up; but anyhow I am not so lonesome as I was and with David Douglas's assistance will make out to find my way to fair advantage.

The weather here reminds me of Alaska, cool and rather damp. Nothing can surpass the exquisite fineness and wealth of the farm crops, while the modulation of the ground stretching away from the rocky, foamy coast to the green Lammermoor Hills is charming. Among other famous places I visited the old castle of the Bride of Lammermoor and the field of the battle of Dunbar. Besides, I find fine glacial studies everywhere.

I fondly hope you are all well while I am cut off from news. Ever yours

JOHN MUIR

to Wanda Muir

Dunbar, Scotland, July 13th, 1893

DEAR WANDA

It is about ten o'clock in the forenoon here, but no doubt you are still asleep, for it is about midnight at Martinez, and sometimes when it is today here it is yesterday in California on account of being on opposite sides of the round world. But one's thoughts travel fast, and I seem to be in California whenever I think of you and Helen. I suppose you are busy with your lessons and peaches, peaches especially. You are now a big girl, almost a woman, and you must mind your lessons and get in a good store of the best words of the best people while your memory is retentive, and then you will go through the world rich.

Ask mother to give you lessons to commit to memory every day. Mostly the sayings of Christ in the gospels and selections from the poets. Find the hymn of praise in *Paradise Lost* – "These are thy glorious works, Parent of Good, Almighty," and learn it well.

Last evening, after writing to Helen, I took a walk with Maggie Lunam along the shore on the rocks where I played when a boy. The waves made a grand show breaking in sheets and sheaves of foam, and grand songs, the same old songs they sang to me in my childhood, and I seemed a boy again and all the long eventful years in America were forgotten while I was filled with that glorious ocean psalm.

Tell Maggie I'm going today to see Miss Jaffry, the minister's daughter who went to school with us. And tell mamma that the girl Agnes Purns, that could outrun me, married a minister and is now a widow living near Prestonpans. I may see her. Goodbye, dear. Give my love to grandma and everybody.   Your loving father
                                                            JOHN MUIR

                              to Mrs. Muir

                                        Station Hotel, Oban, July 22nd, 1893
DEAR LOUIE
I stayed about ten days at Dunbar, thinking I should not slight my old home and cousins. I found an extra cousin in Dunbar, Jane Mather, that I had not before heard of, and she is one to be proud of, as are the Lunams. I also found a few of the old schoolmates, now grey old men, older-looking, I think, and greyer than I, though I have led so hard a life. I went with Maggie Lunam to the old school house where I was so industriously thrashed half a century ago. The present teacher, Mr. Dick, got the school two years after I left, and has held it ever since. He had been reading the *Century*, and was greatly interested. I dined with him and at table one of the guests said, "Mr. Dick, don't you wish you had the immortal glory of having whipped John Muir?"

I made many short trips into the country, along the shores, about the old castle, etc. Then I went back to Edinburgh, and then to Dumfries, Burns's country for some years, where I found another cousin, Susan Gilroy, with whom I had a good time. Then I went through Glasgow to Stirling, where I had a charming walk about the castle and saw the famous battlefield, Bruce's and Wallace's monuments, and glacial action.

This morning I left Stirling and went to Callander, thence to Inversnaid by coach and boat, by the Trossachs and Loch Katrine, thence through Loch

Lomond and the mountains to a railroad and on to this charming Oban. I have just arrived this day on Lochs Katrine and Lomond, and the drives through the passes and over the mountains made famous by Scott in *The Lady of the Lake* will be long remembered – "Ower the muir amang the heather."

The heather is just coming into bloom and it is glorious. Wish I could camp in it a month. All the scenery is interesting, but nothing like Alaska or California in grandeur. Tomorrow I'm going back to Edinburgh and next morning intend to start for Norway, where I will write.

Possibly I may not be able to catch the boat, but guess I will. Thence I'll return to Edinburgh and then go to Switzerland. Love to all. Dear Wanda and Helen, here is some bell heather for you.　　　　　Ever yours

J. M.

Euston Hotel, London, September 1st, 1893

DEAR LOUIE

Yesterday I went to the home of Sir Joseph Hooker at Sunningdale with him and his family.... Now I am done with London and shall take the morning express to Edinburgh tomorrow, go thence to the Highlands and see the heather in full bloom, visit some friends, and go back to Dunbar for a day....

I have been at so many places and have seen so much that is new, the time seems immensely long since I left you. Sir Joseph and his lady were very cordial. They have a charming country residence, far wilder and more retired than ours, though within twenty-five miles of London. We had a long delightful talk last evening on science and scientific men, and this forenoon and afternoon long walks and talks through the grounds and over the adjacent hills. Altogether this has been far the most interesting day I have had since leaving home. I never knew before that Sir Joseph had accompanied Ross in his famous Antarctic expedition as naturalist. He showed me a large number of sketches he made of the great icecap, etc., and gave me many facts concerning that little known end of the world entirely new to me. Long talks, too, about Huxley, Tyndall, Darwin, Sir Charles Lyell, Asa Gray, etc. My, what a time we had! I never before knew either that he had received the Copley Medal, the highest scientific honour in the world.

I hope to hear from you again before sailing, as I shall order my mail forwarded from London the last thing. I feel that my trip is now all but done, though I have a good many people to see and small things to do, ere I leave. The hills in full heather bloom, however, is not a small thing.

Much love

JOHN MUIR

to Helen Muir

Killarney, Ireland, September 7th, 1893

MY OWN DEAR HELEN

After papa left London he went to the top of Scotland to a place called Thurso, where a queer Scotch geologist [Robert Dick] once lived; hundreds of miles thereabouts were covered with heather in full bloom. Then I went to Inverness and down the canal to Oban again. Then to Glasgow and then to Ireland to see the beautiful bogs and lakes and Macgillicuddy's Reeks. Now I must make haste tomorrow back towards Scotland and get ready to sail to New York on the big ship Campania, which leaves Liverpool on the sixteenth day of this month, and then I'll soon see darling Helen again. Papa is tired travelling so much, and wishes he was home again, though he has seen many beautiful and wonderful places, and learned a good deal about glaciers and mountains and things. It is very late, and I must go to bed. Kiss everybody for me, my sweet darling, and soon I'll be home.

[JOHN MUIR]

to James and Hardy Hay
and all the glorious company about them, young and old.

Cunard Royal Mail Steamship Campania
September 16th, 1893

DEAR COUSINS

I am now fairly aff and awa' from the old home to the new, from friends to friends, and soon the braid sea will again roar between us; but be assured, however far I go in sunny California or icy Alaska, I shall never cease to love and admire you, and I hope that now and then you will think of your lonely kinsman, whether in my bright home in the Golden State or plodding after God's glorious glaciers in the storm-beaten mountains of the North.

Among all the memories that I carry away with me this eventful summer none stand out in so divine a light as the friends I have found among my own kith and kin: Hays, Mathers, Lunams, Gilroys. In particular I have enjoyed and admired the days spent with the Lunams and you Hays. Happy, Godful homes; again and again while with you I repeated to myself those lines of Burns: "From scenes like these old Scotia's grandeur springs, that makes her loved at home, revered abroad."

Don't forget me and if in this changing world you or yours need anything in it that I can give, be sure to call on

Your loving and admiring cousin
JOHN MUIR

from George W. Cable

Dryads Green
Northampton, Massachusetts
December 18th, 1893

MY DEAR MR. MUIR

I am only now really settled down at home for a stay of a few weeks. I wanted to have sent to you long ago the book I mail now and which you kindly consented to accept from me – Lanier's *Poems*. There are in Lanier such wonderful odours of pine, and hay, and salt sands and cedar, and corn, and such whisperings of Eolian strains and every outdoor sound – think you would have had great joy in one another's personal acquaintance.

And this makes me think how much I have in yours. Your face and voice, your true, rich words, are close to my senses now as I write, and I cry hungrily for more. The snow is on us everywhere now, and as I look across the white, crusted waste I see such mellowness of yellow sunlight and long blue and purple shadows that I want some adequate manly partnership to help me reap the rapture of such beauty. In one place a stretch of yellow grass standing above the snow or blown clear of it glows golden in the slant light. The heavens are blue as my love's eyes and the elms are black lace against their infinite distance.

Last night I walked across the frozen white under a moonlight and starlight that made the way seem through the wastes of a stellar universe and not along the surface of one poor planet.

Write and tell me, I pray you, what those big brothers of yours, the mountains, have been saying to you of late. It will compensate in part, but only in part, for the absence of your spoken words.

Yours truly
G. W. CABLE

to Robert Underwood Johnson

Martinez, April 3rd, 1894

MY DEAR MR. JOHNSON

The book, begotten Heaven knows when, is finished and out of me, therefore hurrah, etc., and thanks to you, very friend, for benevolent prodding. Six of the sixteen chapters are new, and the others are nearly so, for I have worked hard on every one of them, leaning them against each other, adding lots of new stuff, and killing adjectives and adverbs of redundant growth the verys, *intenses, gloriouses, ands,* and *buts,* by the score. I feel sure the little alpine thing will not disappoint you. Anyhow I've done the best I could. Read the opening chapter when you have time. In it I have ventured to drop into the poetry that I like, but have taken good care to place it between bluffs and buttresses of bald, glacial, geological facts.

Mrs. Muir keeps asking me whether it is possible to get Johnson to come out here this summer. She seems to regard you as a Polish brother. Why, I'll be hanged if I know. I always thought you too cosmically good to be of any clannish nation. By the way, during these last months of abnormal cerebral activity I have written another article for the *Century* which I'll send you soon.

JOHN MUIR

The book mentioned in the preceding letter was his *Mountains of California,* which appeared in the autumn of 1894 from the press of the *Century* Company. "I take pleasure in sending you with this a copy of my first book," he wrote to his old friend Mrs. Carr. "You will say that I should have written it long ago; but I begrudged the time of my young mountain-climbing days." To a Scotch cousin, Margaret Hay Lunam, he characterised it as one in which he had tried to describe and explain what a traveller would see for himself if he were to come to California and go over the mountain ranges and through the forests as he had done.

The warmth of appreciation with which the book was received by the most thoughtful men and women of his time did much to stimulate him to further literary effort. His friend Charles S. Sargent, director of the Arnold Arboretum, then at work upon his great work *The Silva of North America*, wrote as follows: "I am reading your Sierra book and I want to tell you that I have never read descriptions of trees that so picture them to the mind as yours do. No fellow who was at once a poet, naturalist, and keen observer has to my knowledge ever written about trees before, and I believe you are the man who ought to have written a silva of North America. Your book is one of the great productions of its kind and I congratulate you on it."

Equally enthusiastic was the great English botanist J. D. Hooker. "I have just finished the last page of your delightful volume," he wrote from his home at Sunningdale, "and can therefore thank you with a full heart. I do not know when I have read anything that I have enjoyed more. It has brought California back to my memory with redoubled interest, and with more than redoubled knowledge. Above all it has recalled half-forgotten scientific facts, geology, geography, and vegetation that I used to see when in California and which I have often tried to formulate in vain. Most especially this refers to glacial features and to the conifers; and recalling them has recalled the scenes and surroundings in which I first heard them."

The acclaim of the book by reviewers was so enthusiastic that the first edition was soon exhausted. It was his intention to bring out at once another volume devoted to the Yosemite Valley in particular. With this task he busied himself in 1895, revisiting during the summer his old haunts at the headwaters of the Tuolumne and passing once more alone through the canyon to Hetch-Hetchy Valley. As in the old days he carried no blanket and a minimum of provisions, so that he had only a handful of crackers and a pinch of tea left when he reached Hetch-Hetchy. "The bears were very numerous," he wrote to his wife on August 17th, "this being berry time in the canyon. But they gave no trouble, as I knew they wouldn't. Only in tangled underbrush I had to shout a good deal to avoid coming suddenly on them." Having no food when he reached Hetch-Hetchy, he set out to cover the twenty miles from there to Crocker's on foot, but had gone only a few miles when he met on the trail two strangers and two well-laden pack-animals. The leader, T. P. Lukens, asked his name, and then told him that he had come expressly to meet John Muir in the hope that he might go back with him into Hetch-Hetchy. "On the banks of the beautiful river beneath a Kellogg oak" the bonds of a new mountain friendship were sealed while beautiful days rolled by unnoticed. "I am fairly settled at home again," he

1 John Muir at the age of twenty-five. *Photo:* © *Muir-Hanna Trust,*
Holt-Atherton Special Collections, University of the Pacific

2 (this page) A view of Half Dome and Clouds Rest from Glacier Point.

3 (below) Looking up Tenaya Canyon from Half Dome's summit to the snow-covered High Sierra watershed peaks in the distance. Both photos show the moutonnée character of the heavily glaciated mid-height peaks that Muir discussed in *Studies in the Sierra. Photos: Bâton Wicks archive and John Beatty*

4, 5, 6 Views of the Muir Glacier in 1971 (above) and 1899, and (inset) Muir with John Burroughs during the 1899 Harriman expedition. *Photos: National Park Service and Rasmuson Library, University of Alaska*

7, 8, 9, 10 Muir in old age
(above left); during a Kings
Canyon trip 1902 (above);
at Martinez in 1913 with
Mrs Herbert W. Gleason and
Mr and Mrs Edward T. Parsons
(left); with a group of artists and
explorers: Charles Keeler, Muir,
William Keith, Francis Fisher
Brown and John Burroughs
(seated). *Photos: © Muir-
Hanna Trust (top right) and
archive photos*

11   Mt. Whitney seen from
the base of Mt. Barnard
to the north-west.
Photo: J.H. Czok

12   John Muir bivouacing
at Big Arroyo Camp in
Kern Canyon, 1908.
Photo: W.L. Huber

wrote to his aged mother on his return, ''and the six weeks of mountaineering of this summer in my old haunts are over, and now live only in memory and notebooks like all the other weeks in the Sierra. But how much I enjoyed this excursion, or indeed any excursion in the wilderness, I am not able to tell. I must have been born a mountaineer and the climbs and 'scootchers' of boyhood days about the old Dunbar Castle and on the roof of our house made fair beginnings. I suppose old age will put an end to scrambling in rocks and ice, but I can still climb as well as ever. I am trying to write another book, but that is harder than mountaineering.''

During the spring of the following year, Mr. Johnson saw some article on Muir which moved him to ask whether he had ever been offered a professorship at Harvard, and whether Professor Louis Agassiz had declared him to be ''the only living man who understood glacial action in the formation of scenery.''

to Robert Underwood Johnson

Martinez, May 3rd, 1895

MY DEAR MR. JOHNSON
To both your questions the answer is, No. I hate this personal rubbish, and I have always sheltered myself as best I could in the thickest shade I could find, celebrating only the glory of God as I saw it in nature.

The foundations for the insignificant stories you mention are, as far as I know, about as follows. More than twenty years ago Professor Runkle was in Yosemite, and I took him into the adjacent wilderness and, of course, night and day preached to him the gospel of glaciers. When he went away he urged me to go with him, saying that the Institute of Technology in Boston was the right place for me, that I could have the choice of several professorships there, and every facility for fitting myself for the duties required, etc., etc.

Then came Emerson and more preaching. He said, Don't tarry too long in the woods. Listen for the word of your guardian angel. You are needed by the young men in our colleges. Solitude is a sublime mistress, but an intolerable wife. When Heaven gives the sign, leave the mountains, come to my house and live with me until you are tired of me and then I will show you to better people.

Then came Gray and more fine rambles and sermons. He said, When you get ready, come to *Harvard.* You have good and able and enthusiastic friends there and we will gladly push you ahead, etc., etc. So much for *Ha-a-a-rvard* But you must surely know that I never for a moment thought of leaving God's big show for a mere profship, call who may.

The Agassiz sayings you refer to are more nearly true than the college ones. Yosemite was my home when Agassiz was in San Francisco, and I never saw him. When he was there I wrote him a long icy letter, telling what glorious things I had to show him and urging him to come to the mountains.

The reply to this letter was written by Mrs. Agassiz, in which she told me that, when Agassiz read my letter, he said excitedly, "Here is the first man I have ever found who has any adequate conception of glacial action." Also that he told her to say in reply to my invitation that if he should accept it now he could not spend more than six weeks with me at most. That he would rather go home now, but next year he would come and spend all summer with me. But, as you know, he went home to die.

Shortly afterward I came down out of my haunts to Oakland and there met Joseph LeConte, whom I had led to the Lyell Glacier a few months before Agassiz's arrival. He (LeConte) told me that, in the course of a conversation with Agassiz on the geology of the Sierra, he told him that a young man by the name of Muir studying up there perhaps knew more about the glaciation of the Sierra than any one else. To which Agassiz replied warmly, and bringing his fist down on the table, "He knows all about it." Now there! You've got it all, and what a mess of mere J. M. you've made me write. Don't you go and publish it. Burn it.

Ever cordially yours
JOHN MUIR

[P.S.] What of the summer day now dawning? Remember you have a turn at the helm. How are you going to steer? How fares Tesla and the auroral lightning? Shall we go to icy Alaska or to the peaks and streets and taluses of the Sierra? That was a good strong word you said for the vanishing forests.

to Robert Underwood Johnson

Martinez, September 12th, 1895

MY DEAR MR. JOHNSON

I have just got home from a six weeks' ramble in the Yosemite and Yosemite National Park. For three years the soldiers have kept the sheepmen and sheep out of the park, and I looked sharply at the ground to learn the value of the military influence on the small and great flora. On the sloping portions of the forest floor, where the soil was loose and friable, the vegetation has not yet recovered from the dibbling and destructive action of the sheep feet and teeth. But where a tough sod on meadows was spread, the grasses and blue gentians and erigerons are again blooming in all their wild glory.

The sheepmen are more than matched by the few troopers in this magnificent park, and the wilderness rejoices in fresh verdure and bloom. Only the Yosemite itself in the middle of the grand park is downtrodden, frowsy, and like an abandoned backwoods pasture. No part of the Merced and Tuolumne wilderness is so dusty, downtrodden, abandoned, and pathetic as the Yosemite. It looks ten times worse now than when you saw it seven years ago. Most of the level meadow floor of the Valley is fenced with barbed and unbarbed wire and about three hundred head of horses are turned loose every night to feed and trample the flora out of existence. I told the hotel and horsemen that they were doing all they could to prevent lovers of wild beauties from visiting the Valley, and that soon all *tourist travel* would cease. This year only twelve hundred regular tourists visited the Valley, while two thousand campers came in and remained a week or two. . . .

I have little hope for Yosemite. As long as the management is in the hands of eight politicians appointed by the ever-changing Governor of California, there is but little hope. I never saw the Yosemite so frowsy, scrawny, and downtrodden as last August, and the horsemen began to inquire, "Has the Yosemite begun to play out?". . .

Ever yours

JOHN MUIR

At the June Commencement in 1896, Harvard bestowed upon Muir an honorary M.A. degree,* The offer of the honour came just as he was deciding, moved by a strange presentiment of her impending death, to pay another visit to his mother. Among Muir's papers, evidently intended for his autobiography, I find the following description of the incident under the heading of "Mysterious Things":

As in the case of father's death, while seated at work in my library in California in the spring of 1896, I was suddenly possessed with the idea that I ought to go back to Portage, Wisconsin, to see my mother once more, as she was not likely to live long, though I had not heard that she was failing. I had not sent word that I was coming. Two of her daughters were living with her at the time, and, when one of them happened to see me walking up to the house through the garden, she came running out, saying, "John, God must have sent you, because mother is very sick." I was with her about a week before she died, and managed to get my brother Daniel, the doctor, to come down from Nebraska to be with her. He insisted that he knew my mother's case very well, and didn't think that there was the slightest necessity for his coming. I told him I thought he would never see her again if he didn't come, and he would always regret neglecting this last duty to mother, and finally succeeded in getting him to come. But brother David and my two eldest sisters, who had since father's death moved to California, were not present.

The following letter gives a brief summary of his Eastern experiences up to the time when he joined the Forestry Commission in Chicago. It should be added that Muir went along unofficially at the invitation of C. S. Sargent, the Chairman of the Commission. Of the epochal work of this Commission and Muir's relation to it, more later.

* President Eliot's salutation, spoken in Latin, was as follows: "Johannem Muir, locorum incognitorum exploratorem insignem; fluminum qui sunt in Alaska serratisque montibus conglaciatorum studiosum; diligentem silvarum et rerum agrestium ferarumque indagatorem, artium magistrium."

to Helen Muir

S.W. Cor. LaSalle and Washington Streets,
Chicago, July 3rd, 1896

MY DEAR LITTLE HELEN

I have enjoyed your sweet, bright, illustrated letters ever and ever so much; both the words and the pictures made me see everything at home as if I was there myself – the peaches, and the purring pussies, and the blue herons flying about, and all the people working and walking about and talking and guessing on the weather.

So many things have happened since I left home, and I have seen so many people and places and have travelled so fast and far, I have lost the measure of time, and it seems more than a year since I left home. Oh, dear! how tired I have been and excited and swirly! Sometimes my head felt so benumbed, I hardly knew where I was. And yet everything done seems to have been done for the best, and I believe God has been guiding us. . . .

I went to New York and then up the Hudson a hundred miles to see John Burroughs and Professor Osborn, to escape being sunstruck and choked in the horrid weather of the streets; and then, refreshed, I got back to New York and started for Boston and Cambridge and got through the Harvard business all right and caught a fast train . . . back to Portage in time for the funeral. Then I stopped three or four days to settle all the business and write to Scotland, and comfort Sarah and Annie and Mary; then I ran down a half-day to Madison, and went to Milwaukee and stayed a night with William Trout, with whom I used to live in a famous hollow in the Canada woods thirty years ago. Next day I went to Indianapolis and saw everybody there and stopped with them one night. Then came here last night and stopped with [A. H.] Sellers. I am now in his office awaiting the arrival of the Forestry Commission, with whom I expect to start West tonight at half-past ten o'clock. It is now about noon. I feel that this is the end of the strange lot of events I have been talking about, for when I reach the Rocky Mountains I'll feel at home. I saw a wonderful lot of squirrels at Osborn's, and Mrs. Osborn wants you and Wanda and Mamma to visit her and stay a long time.

Goodbye, darling, and give my love to Wanda and Mamma and Grandma and Maggie. Go over and comfort Maggie and tell Mamma to write to poor Sarah. Tell Mamma I spent a long evening with [Nicola] Tesla and I found him quite a wonderful and interesting fellow.   [JOHN MUIR]

to Wanda Muir

Hot Springs, South Dakota, July 5th, 1896

MY DEAR WANDA

I am now fairly on my way West again, and a thousand miles nearer you than I was a few days ago. We got here this morning, after a long ride from

Chicago. By *we* I mean Professors Sargent, Brewer, Hague, and General Abbot – all interesting wise men and grand company. It was dreadfully hot the day we left Chicago, but it rained before morning of the 4th, and so that day was dustless and cool, and the ride across Iowa was delightful. That State is very fertile and beautiful. The cornfields and wheatfields are boundless, or appear so as we skim through them on the cars, and all are rich and bountiful-looking. Flowers in bloom line the roads, and tall grasses and bushes. The surface of the ground is rolling, with hills beyond hills, many of them crowned with trees. I never before knew that Iowa was so beautiful and inexhaustibly rich.

Nebraska is monotonously level like a green grassy sea – no hills or mountains in sight for hundreds of miles. Here, too, are cornfields without end and full of promise this year, after three years of famine from drought.

South Dakota, by the way we came, is dry and desert-like until you get into the Black Hills. The latter get their name from the dark colour they have in the distance from the pine forests that cover them. The pine of these woods is the ponderosa or yellow pine, the same as the one that grows in the Sierra, Oregon, Washington, Nevada, Utah, Colorado, Montana, Idaho, Wyoming, and all the West in general. No other pine in the world has so wide a range or is so hardy at all heights and under all circumstances and conditions of climate and soil. This is near its eastern limit, and here it is interesting to find that many plants of the Atlantic and Pacific slopes meet and grow well together....

[JOHN MUIR]

to Helen and Wanda Muir

Sylvan Lake Hotel,
Custer, South Dakota, July 6th, 1896

HELLO, MIDGE! HELLO, WANDA!
My!! if you could only come here when I call you how wonderful you would think this hollow in the rocky Black Hills is! It is wonderful even to me after seeing so many wild mountains – curious rocks rising alone or in clusters, grey and jagged and rounded in the midst of a forest of pines and spruces and poplars and birches, with a little lake in the middle and carpet of meadow gay with flowers. It is in the heart of the famous Black Hills where the Indians and Whites quarrelled and fought so much. The whites wanted the gold in the rocks, and the Indians wanted the game – the deer and elk that used to abound here. As a grand deer pasture this was said to have been the best in America, and no wonder the Indians wanted to keep it, for wherever the white man goes the game vanishes.

We came here this forenoon from Hot Springs, fifty miles by rail and twelve by wagon. And most of the way was through woods fairly carpeted with beautiful flowers. A lovely red lily, *Lilium Pennsylvanicum*, was common, two kinds of spiræa and a beautiful wild rose in full bloom, anemones, calochortus, larkspur, etc., etc., far beyond time to tell. But I must not fail to mention linnæa. How sweet the air is! I would like to stop a long time and have you and Mamma with me. What walks we would have!

We leave tonight for Edgemont. Here are some mica flakes and a bit of spiræa I picked up in a walk with Professor Sargent.

Goodbye, my babes. Sometime I must bring you here. I send love and hope you are well.

JOHN MUIR

The following letter expresses Muir's stand in the matter of the recession of Yosemite Valley by the State of California to the Federal Government. The mismanagement of the Valley under ever-changing political appointees of the various Governors had become a national scandal, and Muir was determined that, in spite of some objectors, the Sierra Club should have an opportunity to express itself on the issue. The bill for recession was reported favourably in the California Assembly in February, but it encountered so much pettifogging and politically inspired opposition that it was not actually passed until 1905.

to Warren Olney, Sr.

Martinez, January 18th, 1897

MY DEAR OLNEY

I think with you that a resolution like the one you offered the other day should be thoroughly studied and discussed before final action is taken and a close approximation made to unanimity, if possible. Still, I don't see that one or two objectors should have the right to kill all action of the Club in this or any other matter rightly belonging to it. Professor Davidson's objection is also held by Professor LeConte, or was, but how they can consistently sing praise to the Federal Government in the management of the National Parks, and at the same time regard the same management of Yosemite as degrading to the State, I can't see. For my part, I'm proud of California and prouder of Uncle Sam, for the U.S. is all of California and more. And as to our Secretary's objection, it seemed to me merely political, and if the Sierra Club is to be run by politicians, the sooner mountaineers get out of it the better. Fortunately, the matter is not of first importance, but now it has been raised, I shall insist on getting it squarely before the Club. I had given up the question as a bad job, but so many of our members have urged it lately I now regard its discussion as a duty of the Club.

JOHN MUIR

CHAPTER SEVENTEEN

Unto the Last

I

1897–1905

THOUGH LITTLE evidence of the fact appears in extant letters, the year 1897 was one of great importance in Muir's career. So significant, indeed, was his work in defending the recommendations of the National Forest Commission of 1896[1] that we must reserve fuller discussion of it for a chapter on Muir's service to the nation. With the exception of his story of the dog Stickeen and a vivid description of an Alaska trip, appearing respectively in the August and September numbers of the *Century*, nearly the entire output of his pen that year was devoted to the saving of the thirteen forest reservations proclaimed by President Cleveland on the basis of the Forest Commission's report.

During the month of August he joined Professor C. S. Sargent and Mr. William M. Canby on an expedition to study forest trees in the Rocky Mountains and in Alaska. To this and other matters allusion is made in the following excerpt from a November letter to Professor Henry Fairfield Osborn.

I spent a short time [he writes] in the Rocky Mountain forests between Banff and Glacier with Professor Sargent and Mr. Canby, and then we went to Alaska, mostly by the same route you travelled. We were on the Queen and had your state-rooms. The weather was not so fine as during your trip. The glorious colour we so enjoyed on the upper deck was wanting, but the views of the noble peaks of the Fairweather Range were sublime. They were perfectly clear, and loomed in the azure, ice-laden and white, like very gods. Canby and Sargent were lost in admiration as if they had got into a perfectly new world, and so they had, old travellers though they are.

I've been writing about the forests, mostly, doing what little I can to save them. *Harper's Weekly*[2] and the *Atlantic Monthly* have published something; the latter published an article ["American Forests"] last August. I sent another two weeks ago and am pegging away on three others for the same magazine on the national parks – Yellowstone, Yosemite, and Sequoia – and

---

1 This service was specially recognised in 1897 by the University of Wisconsin, his *alma mater*, in the bestowall of an LL.D. degree.

2 "Forest Reservations and National Parks," June 5th, 1897.

I want this winter to try some more Alaska. But I make slow, hard work of it
– slow and hard as glaciers. . . . When are you coming again to our wild side
of the continent and how goes your big book? I suppose it will be about as
huge as Sargent's *Silva*.

One of the pleasant by-products of Muir's spirited defence of the reservations
was the beginning of a warm friendship with the late Walter Hines Page,
then editor of the *Atlantic*. The latter, like Robert Underwood Johnson,
stimulated his literary productiveness and was largely responsible for his
final choice of Houghton, Mifflin & Company as his publishers. Some years
later, in 1905, Mr. and Mrs. Page paid a visit to Muir at his home in the
Alhambra Valley. The articles contributed to the *Atlantic* during the nineties
were in 1901 brought out in book form under the title of *Our National
Parks*.

Apropos of Muir's apologetic references to the fact that he found writing
a slow, hard task, Page remarked: "I thank God that you do not write in
glib, acrobatic fashion: anybody can do that. Half the people in the world
are doing it all the time, to my infinite regret and confusion. . . . The two
books on the Parks and on Alaska will not need any special season's sales,
nor other accidental circumstances: they'll be Literature! "On another
occasion, in October, 1897, Page writes: "Mr. John Burroughs has been
spending a little while with me, and he talks about nothing else so earnestly
as about you and your work. He declares in the most emphatic fashion that
it will be a misfortune too great to estimate if you do not write up all those
bags of notes which you have gathered. He encourages me, to put it in his
own words, to 'keep firing at him, keep firing at him'."

In February, 1898, Professor Sargent wrote Muir that he was in urgent
need of the flowers of the red fir to be used for an illustrative plate in his
Silva. The following letter is in part a report on Muir's first futile effort to
secure them. Ten days later, above Deer Park in the Tahoe region, he
succeeded in finding and collecting specimens of both pistillate and staminate
flowers, which up to that time, according to Sargent, "did not exist in any
herbarium in this country or in Europe."

to Charles Sprague Sargent

Martinez, June 7th, 1898

MY DEAR PROFESSOR SARGENT

Yesterday I returned from a week's trip to Shasta and the Scott Mountains
for [*Abies*] *magnifica* flowers, but am again in bad luck. I searched the
woods, wallowing through the snow nearly to the upper limit of the fir belt,
but saw no flowers or buds that promised anything except on a few trees. I
cut down six on Shasta and two on Scott Mountains west of Sissons. On one
of the Shasta trees I found the staminate flowers just emerging from the

scales, but not a single pistillate flower. I send the staminate, though hardly worth while. Last year's crop of cones was nearly all frost-killed and most of the leaf buds also, so there is little chance for flowers thereabouts this year.

Sonne writes that the Truckee Lumber Company is to begin cutting Magnifica in the Washoe Range ten miles east of Truckee on the 8th or 10th of this month, and he promises to be promptly on hand among the fresh-felled trees to get the flowers, while Miss Eastwood starts this evening for the Sierra summit above Truckee, and I have a friend in Yosemite watching the trees around the rim of the Valley, so we can hardly fail to get good flowers even in so bad a year as this is.

I have got through the first reading of your Pine volume.[1] It is bravely, sturdily, handsomely done. Grand old Ponderosa you have set forth in magnificent style, describing its many forms and allowing species-makers to name as many as they like, while showing their inseparable characters. But you should have mentioned the thick, scaly, uninflammable bark with which, like a wandering warrior of King Arthur's time, it is clad, as accounting in great part for its wide distribution and endurance of extremes of climate. You seem to rank it above the sugar pine. But in youth and age, clothed with beauty and majesty, Lambertiana is easily King of all the world-wide realm of pines, while Ponderosa is the noble, unconquerable mailed knight without fear and without reproach.

By brave and mighty Proteus-Muggins[2] you have also done well, though you might have praised him a little more loudly for hearty endurance under manifold hardships, defying the salt blasts of the sea from Alaska to the California Golden Gate, and the frosts and fires of the Rocky Mountains – growing patiently in mossy bogs and on craggy mountain-tops – crouching low on glacier granite pavements, holding on by narrow cleavage joints, or waving tall and slender and graceful in flowery garden spots sheltered from every wind among columbines and lilies, etc. A line or two of sound sturdy Mother Earth poetry such as you ventured to give Ponderosa in no wise weakens or blurs the necessarily dry, stubbed, scientific description, and I'm sure Muggins deserves it. However, I'm not going fault-finding. It's a grand volume – a kingly Lambertiana job; and on many a mountain trees now seedlings will be giants and will wave their shining tassels two hundred feet in the sky ere another pine book will be made. So you may well sing your nunc dimittis, and so, in sooth, may I, since you have engraved my name on the head of it.

That Alleghany trip you so kindly offer is mighty tempting. It has stirred up wild lover's longings to renew my acquaintance with old forest friends and gain new ones under such incomparable auspices. I'm just dying to see

1 Volume XI of Sargent's *Silva*, devoted to the Coniferae. The author's dedication reads, "To John Muir, lover and interpreter of nature, who best has told the story of the Sierra forests, this eleventh volume of *The Silva of North America* is gratefully dedicated."

2 Probably *Pinus contorta* of the *Silva*, one of its variants being the Murray or Tamarac Pine of the High Sierra.

basswood and shell-bark and liriodendron once more. When could you start, and when would you have me meet you? I think I might get away from here about the middle of July and go around by the Great Northern and lakes, stopping a few days on old familiar ground about the shores of Georgian Bay. I want to avoid cities and dinners as much as possible and travel light and free. If tree-lovers could only grow bark and bread on their bodies, how fine it would be, making even handbags useless!

Ever yours

JOHN MUIR

[P.S.] While trying to avoid people as much as possible and seeing only you and trees, I should, if I make this Eastern trip, want to call on Mrs. Asa Gray, for I heartily love and admire Gray, and in my mind his memory fades not at all.

The projected trip into the Alleghanies with Sargent and Canby was undertaken during September and October when the Southern forests were in their autumn glory. Muir had entered into the plan with great eagerness. "I don't want to die," he wrote to Sargent in June, "without once more saluting the grand, godly, round-headed trees of the east side of America that I first learned to love and beneath which I used to weep for joy when nobody knew me." The task of mapping a route was assigned by Sargent to Mr. Canby on account of his special acquaintance with the region. "Dear old streak o' lightning on ice," the latter wrote to Muir in July, "I was delighted to hear from the glacial period once more and to know that you were going to make your escape from Purgatory and emerge into the heavenly forests of the Alleghanies. . . . Have you seen the Luray Caverns or the Natural Bridge? If not, do you care to? I should like to have you look from the summit of Salt Pond Mountain in Virginia and the Roan in North Carolina."

For a month or more the three of them roamed through the Southern forests, Muir being especially charmed by the regions about Cranberry, Cloudland, and Grandfather Mountain, in North Carolina. From Roan Mountain to Lenoir, about seventy-five miles, they drove in a carriage – in Muir's judgment "the finest drive of its kind in America." In Tennessee, Georgia, and Alabama he crossed at various times his old trail of 1867.

On his return to Boston, he "spent a night at Page's home and visited Mrs. Gray and talked over old botanic times." On the first of November he is at "Four Brook Farm," R. W. Gilder's country-place at Tyringham in the Berkshire Hills, whence he writes to his daughter Wanda: "Tell mamma that I have enjoyed Mr. and Mrs. Gilder ever so much. On the way here, on the car, I was introduced to Joseph Choate, the great lawyer, and on Sunday Mr. Gilder and I drove over to his fine residence at Stockbridge to dinner, and I had a long talk with him about forests as well as glaciers. Today we all go back to New York. This evening I dine with Johnson, and tomorrow I go up the Hudson to the Osborns'."

to Helen Muir

"Wing-and-Wing", Garrisons-on-Hudson,
November 4th, 1898

MY DARLING HELEN

This is a fine calm thoughtful morning, bracing and sparkling, just the least touch of hoar-frost, quickly melting where the sunbeams, streaming through between the trees, fall in yellow plashes and lances on the lawns. Every now and then a red or yellow leaf comes swirling down, though there is not the slightest breeze. Most of the hickories are leafless now, but the big buds on the ends of the twigs are full of baby leaves and flowers that are already planning and thinking about next summer. Many of the maples, too, and the dogwoods are showing leafless branches; but many along the sheltered ravines are still rejoicing in all their glory of colour, and look like gigantic goldenrods. God's forests, my dear, are among the grandest of terrestrial things that you may look forward to. I have not heard from Professor Sargent since he left New York a week ago, and so I don't know whether he is ready to go to Florida, but I'll hear soon, and then I'll know nearly the time I'll get home. Anyhow, it won't be long.

I am enjoying a fine rest. I have "the blue room" in this charming home, and it has the daintiest linen and embroidery I ever saw. The bed is so soft and fine I like to lie awake to enjoy it, instead of sleeping. A servant brings in a cup of coffee before I rise. This morning when I was sipping coffee in bed, a red squirrel looked in the window at me from a branch of a big tulip-tree, and seemed to be saying as he watched me. "Oh, John Muir! camping, tramping, tree-climbing scrambler! Churr, churr! why have you left us? Chip churr, who would have thought it?"

Five days after the date of the above letter he writes to his wife: "Dear Lassie – It is settled that I go on a short visit to Florida with Sargent. . . . I leave here [Wing-and-Wing] tomorrow for New York, dine with Tesla and others, and then meet Sargent at Wilmington, Wednesday. I've had a fine rest in this charming home and feel ready for Florida, which is now cool and healthy. I'm glad to see the South again and may write about it."

The trip to Florida, replete with colour and incident, is too full of particularity for recital here. A halt in Savannah, Georgia, stirred up old memories, for "here," he writes in a letter to his wife, "is where I spent a hungry, weary, yet happy week camping in Bonaventure graveyard thirty-one years ago. Many changes, I'm told, have been made in its groves and avenues of late, and how many in my life!"

A dramatic occurrence was the finding at Archer of Mrs. Hodgson, who had nursed him back to health on his thousand-mile walk to the Gulf. The incident is told in the following excerpt from a letter to his wife under date of November 21st, 1898:

The day before yesterday we stopped at Palatka on the famous St. Johns River, where I saw the most magnificent magnolias, some four feet in diameter and one hundred feet high, also the largest and most beautiful hickories and oaks. From there we went to Cedar Keys. Of course I inquired for the Hodgsons, at whose house I lay sick so long. Mr. Hodgson died long ago, also the eldest son, with whom I used to go boating, but Mrs. Hodgson and the rest of the family, two boys and three girls, are alive and well, and I saw them all today, except one of the boys. I found them at Archer, where I stopped four hours on my way from Cedar Keys. Mrs. Hodgson and the two eldest girls remembered me well. The house was pointed out to me, and I found the good old lady who nursed me in the garden. I asked her if she knew me. She answered no, and asked my name. I said Muir. "*John* Muir?" she almost screamed. "*My* California John Muir? My California John?" I said, "Why, yes, I promised to come back and visit you in about twenty-five years, and though a little late I've come." I stopped to dinner and we talked over old times in grand style, you may be sure.

The following letter, full of good-natured badinage and new plans for travel, was written soon after his return home in December:

to Charles Sprague Sargent

Martinez, December 28th, 1898

MY DEAR PROFESSOR SARGENT

I'm glad you're miserable about not going to Mexico, for it shows that your heartwood is still honest and loving towards the grand trees down there, though football games and Connecticut turkey momentarily got the better of you. The grand Taxodiums were object enough for the trip, and I came pretty near making it alone – would certainly have done it had I not felt childishly lonesome and woe-begone after you left me. No wonder I looked like an inland coot to friend Mellichamp. But what would that sharp observer have said to the Canby huckleberry party gyrating lost in the Delaware woods, and splashing along the edge of the marshy bay "froggin' and crabbin' " with devout scientific solemnity! ! !

Mellichamp I liked ever so much, and blessed old Mohr more than ever. For these good men and many, many trees I have to thank you, and I do over and over again as the main blessings of the passing year. And I have to thank you also for Gray's writings – Essays, etc. – which I have read with great interest. More than ever I want to see Japan and eastern Asia. I wonder if Canby could be converted to sufficient sanity to go with us on that glorious dendrological trip.... Confound his Yankee savings bank! He has done more than enough in that line. It will soon be dark. Soon our good botanical pegs will be straightened in a box and planted, and it behooves us as reasonable naturalists to keep them tramping and twinkling in the woods as long as possible....

Wishing you and family and *Silva* happy New Year, I am, Ever yours

JOHN MUIR

There were not a few among Muir's literary friends, men like Walter Hines Page and Richard Watson Gilder, who as early as 1898 began to urge him to write his autobiography. "I thank you for your kind suggestions about *Recollections of a Naturalist*," he replies to Gilder in March, 1899. "Possibly I may try something of the sort some of these days, though my life on the whole has been level and uneventful, and therefore hard to make a book of that many would read. I am not anxious to tell what I have done but what Nature has done – an infinitely more important story."

In April, 1899, he accepted an invitation to join the Harriman Alaska Expedition. During the cruise a warm friendship sprang up between him and Mr. Harriman, who came to value highly not only his personal qualities, but also his sturdy independence. It was some years afterward, while he was the guest of Mr. Harriman at Pelican Lodge on Klamath Lake, that Muir was persuaded to dictate his memoirs to Mr. Harriman's private secretary. We owe it to the use of this expedient that Muir was enabled to complete at least a part of his autobiography before he passed on. The little book written by Muir in appreciation of Mr. Harriman after his death* sprang from memories of many kindnesses, and unheralded occasions too, when Mr. Harriman's influence turned the scales in favour of some important conservation measure dear to Muir's heart. Both held in warm regard Captain P. A. Doran, of the Elder, which in 1899 carried the expeditionary party. "I am deeply touched at your letter of the second just received," wrote Mr. Harriman to Muir on August 8th, 1907, shortly after a tragedy of the sea in which Captain Doran perished. "We all grieved much over poor Doran. I had grown to look upon him as a real friend and knew him to be a true man. I am glad to have shared his friendship with you. I am fortunate in having many friends and am indeed proud to count you among the best. My troubles are not to be considered with yours and some others, for they are only passing and will be eventually cleared up and understood even by the 'some' to whom you refer. The responsibilities weigh most when such misfortunes occur as the loss of the poor passenger who passed on with brave Doran."

to Charles Sprague Sargent

Martinez, April 30th, 1899

MY DEAR PROFESSOR SARGENT

You are no doubt right about the little Tahoe reservation – a scheme full of special personalities, pushed through by a lot of lawyers, etc., but the more we get the better anyhow. It is a natural park, and because of its beauty and accessibility is visited more than any other part of the Sierra except Yosemite.

All I know of the Rainier and Olympic reservations has come through the newspapers. The Olympic will surely be attacked again and again for its timber, but the interests of Seattle and Tacoma will probably save Rainier. I

---

* *Edward Henry Harriman* by John Muir. 1916.

expect to find out something about them soon, as I am going north from Seattle to Cook Inlet and Kodiak for a couple of months with a "scientific party." . . . This section of the coast is the only one I have not seen, and I'm glad of the chance.

Good luck to you. I wish I were going to those leafy woods instead of icy Alaska. Be good to the trees, you tough, sturdy pair. Don't frighten the much-enduring Cratæguses and make them drop their spurs, and don't tell them quite eternally that you are from Boston and the Delaware Huckleberry Peninsula.

My love to Canby – keep his frisks within bounds. Remember me to the Biltmore friends and blessed Mohr and Mellichamp. And remember me also to the Messrs. Hickory and Oak, and, oh, the magnolias in bloom! Heavens, how they glow and shine and invite a fellow! Goodbye. I'll hope to see you in August.

Ever yours
JOHN MUIR

to Walter Hines Page

[Martinez, California, May, 1899]

MY DEAR PAGE

I send the article on Yosemite Park today by registered mail. It is short, but perhaps long enough for this sort of stuff. I have three other articles on camping in the park, and on the trees and shrubs, gardens, etc., and on Sequoia Park, blocked out and more than half written. I wanted to complete these and get the book put together and off my hands this summer, and, now that I have all the material well in hand and on the move, I hate to leave it.

I start tomorrow on a two months' trip with Harriman's Alaska Expedition. John Burroughs and Professor [W. H.] Brewer and a whole lot of good naturalists are going. But I would not have gone, however tempting, were it not to visit the only part of the coast I have not seen and one of the scenes that I would have to visit sometime anyhow. This has been a barren year, and I am all the less willing to go, though the auspices are so good. I lost half the winter in a confounded fight with sheep and cattlemen and politicians on behalf of the forests. During the other half I was benumbed and interrupted by sickness in the family, while in word works, even at the best, as you know, I'm slow as a glacier. You'll get these papers, however, sometime, and they will be hammered into a book – if I live long enough.

I was very glad to get your letter, as it showed you were well enough to be at work again.   With best wishes, I am,   Faithfully yours

J. M.

to Mrs. Muir

Victoria, June 1st, 1899

DEAR LOUIE

We sail from here in about two hours, and I have just time to say another goodbye. The ship is furnished in fine style, and I find we are going just where I want to go – Yakutat, Prince William Sound, Cook Inlet, etc. I am on the Executive Committee, and of course have something to say as to routes, time to be spent at each point, etc. The company is very harmonious for scientists. Yesterday I tramped over Seattle with John Burroughs. At Portland the Mazamas were very demonstrative and kind. I hope you are all busy with the hay. Helen will keep it well tumbled and tramped with Keenie's help. I am making pleasant acquaintances. Give my love to Maggie.

Goodbye.   Ever your affectionate husband

JOHN MUIR

to Wanda and Helen Muir

Fort Wrangell, June 5th, [1899] 7 a.m.

How are you all? We arrived here last evening. This is a lovely morning – water like glass. Looks like home. The flowers are in bloom, so are the forests. We leave in an hour for Juneau. The mountains are pure white. Went to church at Metlakatla, heard Duncan preach, and the Indians sing; Had fine ramble in the woods with Burroughs. He is ashore looking and listening for birds. The song sparrow, a little dun, speckledy muggins, sings best. Most of the passengers are looking at totem poles.

Have letters for me at Seattle. No use trying to forward them up here, as we don't know where we will touch on the way down home.

I hope you are all well and not too lonesome. Take good care of Stickeen and Tom. We landed at four places on the way up here. I was glad to see the woods in those new places.   Love to all. Ever your loving papa

J. M.

to Louie, Wanda, and Helen

Juneau, June 6th, [1899] 9 a.m.

Cold rainy day. We stop here only a few minutes, and I have only time to scribble love to my darlings. The green mountains rise into the grey cloudy sky four thousand feet, rich in trees and grass and flowers and wild goats.

We are all well and happy. Yesterday was bright and the mountains all the way up from Wrangell were passed in review, opening their snowy, icy recesses, and closing them, like turning over the leaves of a grand picture book. Everybody gazed at the grand glaciers and peaks, and we saw icebergs floating past for the first time on the trip.

We landed on two points on the way up and had rambles in the woods, and the naturalists set traps and caught five white-footed mice. We were in the woods I wandered in twenty years ago, and I had many questions to answer. Heaven bless you. We go next to Douglas Mine, then to Skagway, then to Glacier Bay.   Goodbye

JOHN MUIR

to Mrs. Muir and daughters

Sitka, Alaska, June 10th, 1899

DEAR LOUIE, WANDA, AND HELEN

I wrote two days ago, and I suppose you will get this at the same time as the other. We had the Governor at dinner and a society affair afterward that looked queer in the wilderness. This eve we are to have a reception at the Governor's, and tomorrow we sail for Yakutat Bay, thence to Prince William Sound, Cook Inlet, etc. We were at the Hot Springs yesterday, fifteen miles from here amid lovely scenery.

The Topeka arrived last eve, and sails in an hour or so. I met Professor Moses and his wife on the wharf and then some Berkeley people besides; then the Raymond agent who introduced a lot of people, to whom I lectured in the street. The thing was like a revival meeting. The weather is wondrous fine, and all goes well. I regret not having [had] a letter forwarded here, as I long for a word of your welfare. Heaven keep you, darlings. Ever yours

JOHN MUIR

Sitka, June 14th, 1899

DEAR LOUIE AND BAIRNS

We are just entering Sitka Harbour after a delightful sail down Peril Straits, and a perfectly glorious time in Glacier Bay – five days of the most splendid weather I ever saw in Alaska. I was out three days with Gilbert and Palache revisiting the glaciers of the upper end of the Bay. Great changes have taken place. The Pacific Glacier has melted back four miles and changed into three separate glaciers, each discharging bergs in grand style. One of them, unnamed and unexplored, I named last evening, in a lecture they made me give in the social hall, the Harriman Glacier, which was received with hearty cheers. After the lecture Mr. Harriman came to me and thanked me for the great honour I had done him. It is a very beautiful glacier, the front discharging bergs like the Muir – about three quarters of a mile wide on the sea wall.

Everybody was delighted with Glacier Bay and the grand Muir Glacier, watching the beautiful bergs born in thunder, parties scattered out in every direction in rowboats and steam and naphtha launches on every sort of quest. John Burroughs and Charlie Keeler climbed the mountain on the east side of Muir Glacier, three thousand feet, and obtained a grand view far back over the mountain to the glorious Fairweather Range. I tried hard to get out of lecturing, but was compelled to do it. All seemed pleased. Lectures every night. The company all good-natured and harmonious. Our next stop will be Yakutat.

I'm all sunburned by three bright days among the bergs. I often wish you could have been with us. You will see it all some day. Heaven bless you. Remember me to Maggie.   Goodbye

[JOHN MUIR]

to Mrs. Muir

Off Prince William Sound, June 24th, 1899

DEAR LOUIE AND DARLINGS

We are just approaching Prince William Sound – the place above all others I have long wished to see. The snow and ice-laden mountains loom grandly in crowded ranks above the dark, heaving sea, and I can already trace the courses of some of the largest of the glaciers. It is 2 p.m., and in three or four hours we shall be at Orca, near the mouth of the bay, where I will mail this note.

We had a glorious view of the mountains and glaciers in sailing up the coast along the Fairweather Range from Sitka to Yakutat Bay. In Yakutat and Disenchantment Bays we spent four days, and I saw their three great glaciers discharging bergs and hundreds of others to best advantage. Also the loveliest flower gardens. Here are a few of the most beautiful of the rubuses. This charming plant covers acres like a carpet. One of the islands we landed on, in front of the largest thundering glacier, was so flower-covered that I could smell the fragrance from the boat among the bergs half a mile away.

I'm getting strong fast, and can walk and climb about as well as ever, and eat everything with prodigious appetite.

I hope to have a good view of the grand glaciers here, though some of the party are eager to push on to Cook Inlet. I think I'll have a chance to mail another letter ere we leave the Sound.

Love to all

J. M.

to Wanda Muir

Unalaska, July 8th, 1899

MY DEAR WANDA AND HELEN AND MAMMA

We arrived here this cloudy rainy, foggy morning after a glorious sail from Sand Harbour on Unga Island, one of the Shumagin group, all the way along the volcano-dotted coast of the Alaska Peninsula and Unimak Island. The volcanoes are about as thick as haycocks on our alfalfa field in a wet year, and the highest of them are smoking and steaming in grand style. Shishaldin is the handsomest volcanic cone I

ever saw and it looked
like this last evening.

I'll show you a
better sketch in my
notebook when I
get home. About

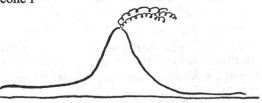

nine thousand feet high, snow and ice on its slopes, hot and bare at the top. A few miles from Shishaldin there is a wild rugged old giant of a volcano that blew or burst its own head off a few years ago, and covered the sea with ashes and cinders and killed fish and raised a tidal wave that lashed the shores of San Francisco and even Martinez.

There is a ship, the Loreclo, that is to sail in an hour, so I'm in a hurry, as usual. We are going to the Seal Islands and St. Lawrence Island from here, and a point or two on the Siberian coast – then home. We are taking on coal, and will leave in three or four hours. I hope fondly that you are all well. I'll soon be back, my darlings. God bless you.   Goodbye

[JOHN MUIR]

To the "Big Four": the Misses Mary and Cornelia Harriman, and the Misses Elizabeth Averell and Dorothea Draper, who with Carol and Roland [Harriman], the "Little Two," kept us all young on the never-to-be-forgotten H.A.E.*

[Martinez] August 30th, 1899

DEAR GIRLS

I received your kind compound letter from the railroad washout with great pleasure, for it showed, as I fondly thought, that no wreck, washout, or crevasse of any sort will be likely to break or wash out the memories of our grand trip, or abate the friendliness that sprung up on the Elder among the wild scenery of Alaska during these last two memorable months. No doubt every one of the favoured happy band feels, as I do, that this was the grandest trip of his life. To me it was peculiarly grateful and interesting because nearly all my life I have wandered and studied alone. On the Elder, I found not only the fields I liked best to study, but a hotel, a club, and a home, together with a floating University in which I enjoyed the instruction and companionship of a lot of the best fellows imaginable, culled and arranged like a well-balanced bouquet, or like a band of glaciers flowing smoothly together, each in its own channel, or perhaps at times like a lot of round boulders merrily swirling and chafing against each other in a glacier pothole.

And what a glorious trip it was for you girls, flying like birds from wilderness to wilderness, the wildest and brightest of America, tasting almost every science under the sun, with fine breezy exercise, scrambles over mossy logs and rocks in the spruce forests, walks on the crystal prairies of the glaciers, on the flowery boggy tundras, in the luxuriant wild gardens of Kodiak and the islands of Bering Sea, and plashing boat rides in the piping bracing winds, all the while your eyes filled with magnificent scenery – the Alexander Archipelago with its thousand forested islands and calm mirror waters, Glacier Bay, Fairweather Mountains, Yakutat and Enchantment Bays, the St. Elias Alps and glaciers and the glorious Prince William Sound, Cook Inlet, and the Aleutian Peninsula with its flowery, icy, smoky volcanoes, the

*   Harriman Alaska Expedition.

blooming banks and braes and mountains of Unalaska, and Bering Sea with its seals and Innuits, whales and whalers, etc., etc., etc.

It is not easy to stop writing under the exhilaration of such an excursion, so much pure wildness with so much fine company. It is a pity so rare a company should have to be broken, never to be assembled again. But many, no doubt, *will* meet again. On your side of the continent perhaps half the number may be got together. Already I have had two trips with Merriam to the Sierra Sequoias and Coast Redwoods, during which you may be sure the H.A.E. was enjoyed over again. A few days after I got home, Captain Doran paid me a visit, most of which was spent in a hearty review of the trip. And last week Gannett came up and spent a couple of days, during which we went over all our enjoyments, science and fun, mountain ranges, glaciers, etc., discussing everything from earth sculpture to Cassiope and rhododendron gardens – from Welsh rarebit and jam and cracker feasts to Nunatak. I hope to have visits from Professor Gilbert and poet Charlie ere long, and Earlybird Ritter, and possibly I may see a whole lot more in the East this coming winter or next. Anyhow, remember me to all the Harrimans and Averells and every one of the party you chance to meet. Just to think of them!! Ridgway with wonderful bird eyes, all the birds of America in them; Funny Fisher ever flashing out wit; Perpendicular E., erect and majestic as a Thlinket totem pole; Old-sea-beach G., hunting upheavals, downheavals, sideheavals, and hanging valleys; the Artists revelling in colour beauty like bees in flower-beds; Ama-a-merst tripping along shore like a sprightly sandpiper, pecking kelp-bearded boulders for a meal of fossil molluscs; Genius Kincaid among his beetles and butterflies and "red-tailed bumble-bees that sting awful hard"; Innuit Dall smoking and musing; flowery Trelease and Coville; and Seaweed Saunders; our grand big-game Doctor, and how many more! Blessed Brewer of a thousand speeches and stories and merry ha-has, and Genial John Burroughs, who growled at and scowled at good Bering Sea and me, but never at thee. I feel pretty sure that he is now all right at his beloved Slabsides and I have a good mind to tell his whole Bering story in his own sort of good-natured, gnarly, snarly, jungle, jangle rhyme.

There! But how unconscionably long the thing is! I must stop short. Remember your penitential promises. Kill as few of your fellow beings as possible and pursue some branch of natural history at least far enough to see Nature's harmony. Don't forget me. God bless you.   Goodbye.

Ever your friend

JOHN MUIR

to Julia Merrill Moores

July 25th, 1900

MY DEAR FRIENDS

I scarce need say that I have been with you and mourned with you every day since your blessed sister was called away, and wished I could do something to help and comfort you. Before your letter came, I had already commenced to write the memorial words you ask for, and I'll send them soon.

Her beautiful, noble, helpful life on earth was complete, and had she lived a thousand years she would still have been mourned, the more the longer she stayed. Death is as natural as life, sorrow as joy. Through pain and death come all our blessings, life and immortality.

However clear our faith and hope and love, we must suffer – but with glorious compensation. While death separates, it unites, and the sense of loneliness grows less and less as we become accustomed to the new light, communing with those who have gone on ahead in spirit, and feeling their influence as if again present in the flesh. Your own experience tells you this, however. The Source of all Good turns even sorrow and seeming separation to our advantage, makes us better, drawing us closer together in love, enlarging, strengthening, brightening our views of the spirit world and our hopes of immortal union. Blessed it is to know and feel, even at this cost, that neither distance nor death can truly separate those who love.

My friends, whether living or dead, have always been with me in my so-called lonely wanderings, so kind and wonderful are God's compensations. Few, dear friends, have greater cause for sorrow, or greater cause for joy, than you have. Your sister lives in a thousand hearts, and her influence, pure as sunshine and dew, can never be lost. . . .

Read again and again those blessed words, ever old, ever new: "Who redeemeth thy life from destruction; who crowneth thee with loving kindness and tender mercy," who pities you "like as a father pitieth his children, for He knoweth our frame, He knoweth that we are dust. Man's days are as grass, as a flower of the field the wind passeth over it and it is gone, but the mercy of the Lord is from everlasting to everlasting."

In His strength we must live on, work on, doing the good that comes to heart and hand, looking forward to meeting in that City which the streams of the River of Life make glad.

Ever your loving friend   J. M.

to Walter Hines Page

Martinez, June 12th, 1900

MY DEAR MR. PAGE

I sent by mail today manuscript of ice article for the Harriman book, the receipt of which please acknowledge, and as it is short I hope you will read it, not for wandering words and sentences out of plumb, but for the ice of it. Coming as you do from the unglacial South, it may "fill a long-felt want." And before you settle down too hopelessly far in book business take a trip to our western Iceland. Go to Glacier Bay and Yakutat and Prince William Sound and get some pure wildness into your inky life. Neglect not this glacial advice and glacial salvation this hot weather, and believe me

Faithfully yours
JOHN MUIR

Very many letters of appreciation were written to Muir by persons who were strangers to him, except in spirit. One such came during the autumn of 1900 from an American woman resident in Yokohama. "More than twenty years ago," said the writer, "when I was at my mountain home in Siskiyou County, California, I read a short sketch of your own, in which you pictured your sense of delight in listening to the wind, with its many voices, sweeping through the pines. That article made a lifelong impression on me, and shaped an inner perception for the wonders of Nature which has gladdened my entire life since.... It has always seemed that I must some time thank you."

to Mrs. Richard Swain

Martinez, California, October 21st, 1900

MRS. RICHARD SWAIN

That you have so long remembered that sketch of the wind-storm in the forest of the Yuba gives me pleasure and encouragement in the midst of this hard life work, for to me it is hard, far harder than tree or mountain climbing. When I began my wanderings in God's wilds, I never dreamed of writing a word for publication, and since beginning literary work it has never seemed possible that much good to others could come of it. Written descriptions of fire or bread are of but little use to the cold or starving. Descriptive writing amounts to little more than "Hurrah here's something! Come!"

When my friends urged me to begin, saying, "We cannot all go to the woods and mountains; you are free and love wildness; go and bring it to us," I used to reply that it was not possible to see and enjoy for others any more than to eat for them or warm for them. Nature's tables are spread and fires burning. You must go warm yourselves and eat. But letters like yours which occasionally come to me show that even nature writing is not altogether useless.

Some time I hope to see Japan's mountains and forests. The flora of Japan and Manchuria is among the richest and most interesting on the globe.

With best wishes, I am

Very truly yours

[JOHN MUIR]

to Katherine Merrill Graydon

Martinez, October 22nd, 1900

MY DEAR MISS GRAYDON

... Of course you know you have my sympathy in your loneliness – loneliness not of miles, but of loss – the departure from earth of your great-aunt Kate, the pole-star and lodestone of your life and of how many other lives. What she was to me and what I thought of her I have written and sent to your Aunt Julia for a memorial book* her many friends are preparing. A rare beloved

---

* *The Man Shakespeare, and Other Essays* by Catherine Merrill (Bowen-Merrill Company, 1902)

soul sent of God, all her long life a pure blessing. Her work is done; and she has gone to the Better Land, and now you must get used to seeing her there and hold on to her as your guide as before. ...

Wanda, as you know, is going to school, and expects soon to enter the University. She is a faithful, steady scholar, not in the least odd or brilliant, but earnest and unstoppable as an avalanche. She comes home every Friday or Saturday by the new railway that crosses the vineyards near the house. Muir Station is just above the Reid house. What sort of a scholar Helen will be I don't know. She is very happy and strong. My sister Sarah is now with us, making four Muirs here, just half the family. ...

Ever your friend.   [JOHN MUIR]

to Dr. C. Hart Merriam

Martinez, October 23rd, 1900

MY DEAR DR. MERRIAM

I am very glad to get your kind letter bringing back our big little Sierra trip through the midst of so many blessed chipmunks and trees. Many thanks for your care and kindness about the photographs and for the pile of interesting bird and beast Bulletins. No.3[1] contains lots of masterly work and might be expanded into a grand book. This you should do, adding and modifying in accordance with the knowledge you have gathered during the last ten years. But alas! Here you are pegging and puttering with the concerns of others as if in length of life you expect to rival Sequoia. That stream and fountain[2] article, which like Tennyson's brook threatened to "go on forever," is at last done, and I am now among the Big Tree parks. Not the man with the hoe, but the poor toiler with the pen, deserves mile-long commiseration in prose and rhyme.

Give my kindest regards to Mrs. and Mr. Bailey, and tell them I'll go guide with them to Yosemite whenever they like unless I should happen to be hopelessly tied up in some way. With pleasant recollections from Mrs. Muir and the girls, I am,   Very truly yours

JOHN MUIR

to Mrs. Henry Fairfield Osborn

Martinez, November 18th, 1900

MY DEAR MRS. OSBORN

Nothing could be kinder than your invitation to Wing-and-Wing, and how gladly we would accept, you know. But grim Duty, like Bunyan's Apollyon, is now "straddling across the whole breadth of the way," crying "No." ...

---

1   *North American Fauna*, No.3 – Results of a Biological Survey of San Francisco Mountains and the Desert of the Little Colorado, Arizona, by C. Hart Merriam, September, 1900.

2   *Fountains and Streams of the Yosemite National Park*, Atlantic, April, 1901.

I am at work on the last of a series of park and forest articles to be collected and published in book form by Houghton, Mifflin & Company and which I hope to get off my hands soon. But there is endless work in sight ahead – Sierra and Alaska things to follow as fast as my slow, sadly interrupted pen can be spurred to go.

Yes, I know it is two years since I enjoyed the dainty chickaree room you so kindly call mine. Last summer as you know I was in Alaska. This year I was in the Sierra, going up by way of Lake Tahoe and down by Yosemite Valley, crossing the range four times along the headwaters of the Truckee, Carson, Mokelumne, Stanislaus, Calaveras, Walker, Tuolumne and Merced Rivers, revisiting old haunts, examining forests, and learning what I could about birds and mammals with Dr. Merriam and his sister and Mr Bailey – keen naturalists with infinite appetite for voles, marmots, squirrels, chipmunks, etc. We had a delightful time, of course, and in Yosemite I remembered your hoped-for visit to the grand Valley and wished you were with us. I'm sorry I missed Sir Michael Foster. Though prevented now, I hope ere long to see Wing-and-Wing in autumn glory. In the mean time and always

I am ever your friend

JOHN MUIR

to Walter Hines Page

Martinez, California, January 10th, 1902

Big thanks, my dear Page, for your great letter. The strength and shove and hearty ringing inspiration of it is enough to make the very trees and rocks write. The Park book, the publishers tell me, is successful. To you and Sargent it owes its existence; for before I got your urgent and encouraging letters I never dreamed of writing such a book. As to plans for others, I am now at work on :

1. A small one, *Yosemite and Other Yosemites*, which Johnson has been trying to get me to write a long time and which I hope to get off my hands this year. I'll first offer it to the *Century* Company, hoping they will bring it out in good shape, give it a good push toward readers and offer fair compensation....

2. The California tree and shrub book was suggested by Merriam last summer, but I have already written so fully on forest trees and their underbrush I'm not sure that I can make another useful book about them. Possibly a handy volume, with short telling descriptions and illustrations of each species, enabling the ordinary observer to know them at sight, might be welcomed. This if undertaken will probably be done season after next, and you shall have the first sight of it.

3. Next should come a mountaineering book – all about walking, climbing, and camping, with a lot of illustrative excursions.

4. Alaska – glaciers, forests, mountains, travels, etc.

5. A book of studies – the action of landscape-making forces, earth sculpture,

distribution of plants and animals, etc. My main real book in which I'll have to ask my readers to cerebrate. Still I hope it may be made readable to a good many.

6. Possibly my autobiography which for ten years or more all sorts of people have been begging me to write. My life, however, has been so smooth and regular and reasonable, so free from blundering exciting adventures, the story seems hardly worth while in the midst of so much that is infinitely more important. Still, if I should live long enough I may be tempted to try it. For I begin to see that such a book would offer fair opportunities here and there to say a good word for God.

The Harriman Alaska book is superb and I gladly congratulate you on the job. In none of the reviews I have seen does Dr. Merriam get half the credit due him as editor.

Hearty thanks for the two Mowbray volumes. I've read them every word. The more of such nature books the better. Good luck to you. May your shop grow like a sequoia and may I meet you with all your family on this side the continent amid its best beauty.   Ever faithfully yours

JOHN MUIR

to Dr. C. Hart Merriam

[January, 1902]

MY DEAR DR. MERRIAM

I send these clippings to give a few hints as to the sheep and forests. Please return them. If you have a file of *The Forester* handy, you might turn to the February and July numbers of 1898, and the one of June, 1900, for solemn discussions of the "proper regulation" of sheep grazing.

With the patronage of the business in the hands of the Western politician, the so-called proper regulation of sheep grazing by the Forestry Department is as hopelessly vain as would be laws and regulations for the proper management of ocean currents and earthquakes.

The politicians, in the interest of wealthy mine, mill, sheep, and cattle owners, of course nominate superintendents and supervisors of reservations supposed to be harmlessly blind to their stealings. Only from the Military Department, free from political spoils poison, has any real good worth mention been gained for forests, and so, as far as I can see, it will be, no matter how well the Forestry Department may be organised, until the supervisors, superintendents, and rangers are brought under Civil Service Reform. Ever yours

JOHN MUIR

to Charles Sprague Sargent

Martinez, September 10th, 1902

MY DEAR SARGENT

What are you so wildly "quitting" about? I've faithfully answered all your letters, and as far as I know you are yourself the supreme quitter – Quitter gigantea – quitting Mexico, quitting a too trusting companion in swamps and sand dunes of Florida, etc., etc. Better quit quitting, though since giving the world so noble a book you must, I suppose, be allowed to do as you like until time and Siberia effect a cure.

I am and have been up to the eyes in work, insignificant though it be. Last spring had to describe the Colorado Grand Canyon – the toughest job I ever tackled, strenuous enough to disturb the equanimity of even a Boston man. Then I had to rush off to the Sierra with [the Sierra] Club outing. Then had to explore Kern River Canyon, etc. Now I'm at work on a little Yosemite book. Most of the material for it has been published already, but a new chapter or two will have to be written. Then there is the *Silva* review, the most formidable job of all, which all along I've been hoping some abler, better equipped fellow would take off my hands. Can't you at least give me some helpful suggestions as to the right size, shape, and composition of this review?

Of course I want to take that big tree trip with you next season, and yet I should hate mortally to leave either of these tasks unfinished. Glorious congratulations on the ending of your noble book!

Ever faithfully yours

JOHN MUIR

to Mrs. Anna R. Dickey

Martinez, October 12th, 1902

DEAR MRS. DICKEY

I was glad to get your letter. It so vividly recalled our memorable ramble, merry and nobly elevating, and solemn in the solemn aboriginal woods and gardens of the great mountains – commonplace, sublime, and divine. I seemed to hear your voice in your letter, and see you gliding, drifting, scrambling along the trails with all the gay good company, or seated around our many camp-fires in the great illuminated groves, etc., etc. – altogether a good trip in which everybody was a happy scholar at the feet of Nature, and all learned something direct from earth and sky, bird and beast, trees, flowers, and chanting winds and waters; hints, suggestions, little-great lessons of God's infinite power and glory and goodness. No wonder your youth is renewed and Donald goes to his studies right heartily.

To talk plants to those who love them must ever be easy and delightful. By the way, that little fairy, airy, white-flowered plant which covers sandy dry ground on the mountains like a mist, which I told you was a near relative to Eriogonum, but whose name I could never recall, is *Oxytheca spergulina*. There is another rather common species in the region we travelled but this is the finest and most abundant.

I'm glad you found the mountain hemlock, the loveliest of conifers. You will find it described in both my books. It is abundant in Kings River Canyon, but not beside the trails. The "heather" you mention is no doubt Bryanthus or Cassiope. Next year you and Donald should make collections of at least the most interesting plants. A plant press, tell Donald, is lighter and better than a gun. So is a camera, and good photographs of trees and shrubs are much to be desired.

I have heard from all the girls. Their enthusiasm is still fresh, and they are already planning and plotting for next year's outing in the Yosemite, Tuolumne, and Mono regions. . . . Gannett stayed two days with us, and is now, I suppose at home. I was hoping you might have a day or two for a visit to our little valley. Next time you come to the city try to stop off at "Muir Station" on the Santa Fé. We are only an hour and a half from the city. I should greatly enjoy a visit at your Ojai home, as you well know, but when fate and work will let me I dinna ken. . . . Give my sincere regard to Donald.

Ever faithfully yours
JOHN MUIR

to Robert Underwood Johnson

Martinez, September 15th, 1902

DEAR MR. JOHNSON

On my return from the Kern region I heard loud but vague rumours of the discovery of a giant sequoia in Converse Basin on Kings River, one hundred and fifty-three feet in circumference and fifty feet in diameter, to which I paid no attention, having heard hundreds of such "biggest-tree-in-the-world" rumours before. But at Fresno I met a surveyor who assured me that he had himself measured the tree and found it to be one hundred and fifty-three feet in circumference six feet above ground. So of course I went back up the mountains to see and measure for myself, carrying a steel tapeline.

At one foot above ground it is 108 feet in circumference
At four feet above ground it is 97 feet, 6 inches in circumference
At six feet above ground it is 93 feet in circumference

One of the largest and finest every way of living sequoias that have been measured. But none can say it is certainly *the largest*. The immensely larger dead one that I discovered twenty-seven years ago stands within a few miles of this new wonder, and I think I have in my notebooks measurements of living specimens as large as the new tree, or larger. I have a photo of the tree and can get others, I think, from a photographer who has a studio in Converse Basin. I'll write a few pages on Big Trees in general if you like; also touching on the horrible destruction of the Kings River groves now going on fiercely about the mills.

As to the discovery of a region grander than Yosemite by the Kelly brothers in the Kings Canyon, it is nearly all pure bosh. I explored the Canyon long ago. It is very deep, but has no El Capitan or anything like it.

Ever yours faithfully
JOHN MUIR

to Henry Fairfield Osborn

Martinez, July 16th, 1904

DEAR MR. OSBORN

In the big talus of letters, books, pamphlets, etc., accumulated on my desk during more than a year's absence, I found your Boone and Crockett address* and have heartily enjoyed it. It is an admirable plea for our poor horizontal fellow-mortals, so fast passing away in ruthless starvation and slaughter. Never before has the need for places of refuge and protection been greater. Fortunately, at the last hour, with utter extinction in sight! the Government has begun to act under pressure of public opinion, however slight. Therefore your address is timely and should be widely published. I have often written on the subject, but mostly with non-effect. The murder business and sport by saint and sinner alike has been pushed ruthlessly, merrily on, until at last protective measures are being called for, partly, I suppose, because the pleasure of killing is in danger of being lost from there being little or nothing left to kill, and partly, let us hope, from a dim glimmering recognition of the rights of animals and their kinship to ourselves.

How long it seems since my last visit to Wing-and-Wing, and how far we have been! I got home a few weeks ago from a trip more than a year long. I went with Professor Sargent and his son Robeson through Europe visiting the principal parks, gardens, art galleries, etc. From Berlin we went to St. Petersburg, thence to the Crimea, by Moscow, the Caucasus, across by Dariel Pass from Tiflis, and back to Moscow. Thence across Siberia, Manchuria, etc., to Japan and Shanghai.

At Shanghai left the Sargents and set out on a grand trip alone and free to India, Egypt, Ceylon, Australia, New Zealand. Thence by way of Port Darwin, Timor, through the Malay Archipelago to Manila. Thence to Hong Kong again and Japan and home by Honolulu. Had perfectly glorious times in India, Australia, and New Zealand. The flora of Australia and New Zealand is so novel and exciting I had to begin botanical studies over again, working night and day with endless enthusiasm. And what wondrous beasts and birds, too, are there!

Do write and let me know how you all are. Remember me with kindest regards to Mrs. Osborn and the children and believe me ever

Faithfully yours

JOHN MUIR

---

* "Preservation of the Wild Animals of North America," *Forest and Stream*, April 16th, 1904 (pp. 312-313).

II
1905–1914

The closing period of Muir's life began with a great triumph and a bitter sorrow – both in the same year. His hour of triumph came with the successful issue of a seventeen-year campaign to rescue his beloved Yosemite Valley from the hands of spoilers. His chief helpers were Mr. Johnson in the East and Mr. William E. Colby in the West. The latter had, under the auspices of the Sierra Club, organised and conducted for many years summer outings of large parties of Club members into the High Sierra. These outings, by their simple and healthful camping methods, by their easy mobility amid hundreds of miles of superb mountain scenery, and by the deep love of unspoiled nature which they awakened in thousands of hearts, not only achieved a national reputation, but trained battalions of eager defenders of our national playgrounds. No one was more rejoiced by the growing success of the outings than John Muir, and the evenings when he spoke at the High Sierra camp-fires are treasured memories in many hearts.

When the battle for the recession of the Yosemite Valley grew keen during January and February, 1905, Mr. Muir and Mr. Colby went to Sacramento in order to counteract by their personal presence the propaganda of falsehoods which an interested opposition was industriously spreading. The bill passed by a safe majority and the first of the two following letters celebrates the event; the second relates to the later acceptance of the Valley by Congress, to be administered thereafter as an integral part of the Yosemite National Park.

On the heels of this achievement came a devastating bereavement the death of his wife. Earlier in the year his daughter Helen had been taken seriously ill, and when she became convalescent she had to be removed to the dry air of Arizona. While there with her, a telegram called him back to the bedside of his wife, in whose case a long-standing illness had suddenly become serious. She died on the sixth of August, 1905, and thereafter the old house on the hill was a shelter and a place of work from time to time, but never a home again. "Get out among the mountains and the trees, friend, as soon as you can," wrote Theodore Roosevelt. "They will do more for you than either man or woman could." But anxiety over the health of his daughter Helen bound him to the Arizona desert for varying periods of time. There he discovered remnants of a wonderful petrified forest, which he studied with great eagerness. He urged that it be preserved as a national monument, and it was set aside by Theodore Roosevelt in 1906 under the name of the Petrified Forest National Monument.

These years of grief and anxiety proved comparatively barren in literary work. But part of the time he probably was engaged upon a revised and enlarged edition of his *Mountains of California*, which appeared in 1911 with an affectionate dedication to the memory of his wife. In some notes, written during 1908, for his autobiography, Muir alludes to this period of stress with a pathetic foreboding that he might not live long enough to gather a matured literary harvest from his numerous notebooks.

The letters of the closing years of his life show an increasing sense of urgency regarding the unwritten books mentioned in his letter to Walter Hines Page, and he applied himself to literary work too unremittingly for the requirements of his health. Much of his writing during this period was done at the home of Mr. and Mrs. J. D. Hooker in Los Angeles and at the summer home of Mr. and Mrs. Henry Fairfield Osborn at Garrison's-on-the-Hudson. The last long journey, in which he realised the dreams of a lifetime, was undertaken during the summer of 1911. It was the trip to South America, to the Amazon the goal which he had in view when he set out on his thousand-mile walk to the Gulf in 1867. His chief object was to see the araucaria forests of Brazil. This accomplished, he went from South America to South Africa in order to see the Baobab tree in its native habitat.

During these few later years of domestic troubles and anxieties [he wrote in 1911] but little writing or studying of any sort has been possible. But these, fortunately, are now beginning to abate, and I hope that something worth while may still be accomplished before the coming of life's night. I have written but three* books as yet, and a number of scientific and popular articles in magazines, newspapers, etc. In the beginning of my studies I never intended to write a word for the press. In my life of lonely wanderings I was pushed and pulled on and on through everything by unwavering never-ending love of God's earth plans and works, and eternal, immortal, all-embracing Beauty; and when importuned to "write, write, write, and give your treasures to the world," I have always said that I could not stop field work until too old to climb mountains; but now, at the age of seventy, I begin to see that if any of the material collected in notebooks, already sufficient for a dozen volumes, is to be arranged and published by me, I must make haste.

to Robert Underwood Johnson

Martinez, February 24th, [1905]

Dear Mr. Johnson

I wish I could have seen you last night when you received my news of the Yosemite victory, which for so many years, as commanding general, you have bravely and incessantly fought for.

---

* *Mountains of California, Our National Parks,* and *My First Summer in the Sierra.*

About two years ago public opinion, which had long been on our side, began to rise into effective action. On the way to Yosemite [in 1903] both the President and our Governor* were won to our side, and since then the movement was like Yosemite avalanches. But though almost everybody was with us, so active was the opposition of those pecuniarily and politically interested, we might have failed to get the bill through the Senate but for the help of Mr. H – , though, of course, his name or his company were never in sight through all the fight. About the beginning of January I wrote to Mr. H – . He promptly telegraphed a favourable reply.

Wish you could have heard the oratory of the opposition – fluffy, nebulous, shrieking, howling, threatening like sand-storms and dust whirlwinds in the desert. Sometime I hope to tell you all about it.

I am now an experienced lobbyist; my political education is complete. Have attended Legislature, made speeches, explained, exhorted, persuaded every mother's son of the legislators, newspaper reporters, and everybody else who would listen to me. And now that the fight is finished and my education as a politician and lobbyist is finished, I am almost finished myself.

Now, ho! for righteous management. . . . Of course you'll have a long editorial in the *Century*.

Faithfully yours
[JOHN MUIR]

to Robert Underwood Johnson

Adamana, Arizona, July 16th, 1906

Yes, my dear Johnson, sound the loud timbrel and let every Yosemite tree and stream rejoice!

You may be sure I knew when the big bill passed. Getting Congress to accept the Valley brought on, strange to say, a desperate fight both in the House and Senate. Sometime I'll tell you all the story. You don't know how accomplished a lobbyist I've become under your guidance. The fight you planned by that famous Tuolumne camp-fire seventeen years ago is at last fairly, gloriously won, every enemy down derry down.

Write a good, long, strong, heart-warming letter to Colby. He is the only one of all the Club who stood by me in downright effective fighting.

I congratulate you on your successful management of Vesuvius, as Gilder says, and safe return with yourself and family in all its farspreading branches in good health. Helen is now much better. Wanda was married last month, and I am absorbed in these enchanted carboniferous forests. Come and let me guide you through them and the great Canyon.

Ever yours
MUIR

---

*   President Theodore Roosevelt and Governor George C. Pardee.

*to Francis Fisher Browne**

325 West Adams Street,
Los Angeles, California
June 1st, 1910

MY DEAR MR. BROWNE

Good luck and congratulations on the *Dial's* thirtieth anniversary, and so Scottishly and well I learned to know you two summers ago, with blessed John Burroughs & Co., that I seem to have known you always.

I was surprised to get a long letter from Miss Barrus written at Seattle, and in writing to Mr. Burroughs later I proposed to him that he follow to this side of the continent and build a new Slabsides "where rolls the Oregon," and write more bird and bee books instead of his new-fangled Catskill Silurian and Devonian geology on which he at present seems to have gane gite, clean gite, having apparently forgotten that there is a single bird or bee in the sky. I also proposed that in his ripe, mellow, autumnal age he go with me to the basin of the Amazon for new ideas, and also to South Africa and Madagascar, where he might see something that would bring his early bird and bee days to mind.

I have been hidden down here in Los Angeles for a month or two and have managed to get off a little book to Houghton Mifflin, which they propose to bring out as soon as possible. It is entitled *My First Summer in the Sierra*. I also have another book nearly ready, made up of a lot of animal stories for boys, drawn from my experiences as a boy in Scotland and in the wild oak openings of Wisconsin. I have also rewritten the autobiographical notes dictated at Harriman's Pelican Lodge on Klamath Lake two years ago, but that seems to be an endless job, and, if completed at all, will require many a year. Next month I mean to try to bring together a lot of Yosemite material into a handbook for travellers, which ought to have been written long ago.

So you see I am fairly busy, and precious few trips will I be able to make this summer, although I took Professor Osborn and family into the Yosemite for a few days, and Mr. Hooker and his party on a short trip to the Grand Canyon.

Are you coming West this year? It would be delightful to see you once more.

I often think of the misery of Mr. Burroughs and his physician, caused by our revels in Burns' poems, reciting verse about in the resonant board chamber whose walls transmitted every one of the blessed words to the sleepy and unwilling ears of John. Fun to us, but death and broken slumbers to Oom John!

With all best wishes, my dear Browne, and many warmly cherished memories, I am

Ever faithfully your friend
JOHN MUIR

---

*   Editor of *The Dial* from 1880 to his death in 1913. A tribute by Muir under the title "Browne the Beloved" appeared in *The Dial* during June, 1913.

to Henry Fairfield Osborn

325 West Adams Street,
Los Angeles, California,
June 1st, 1910

MY DEAR MR. OSBORN

Many thanks for the copy you sent me of your long good manly letter to Mr. Robert J. Collier on the Hetch-Hetchy Yosemite Park. As I suppose you have seen by the newspapers, San Francisco will have until May 1st, 1911, to show cause why Hetch-Hetchy Valley should not be eliminated from the permit which the Government has given the city to develop a water supply in Yosemite Park. Meantime the municipality is to have detailed surveys made of the Lake Eleanor watershed, of the Hetch-Hetchy, and other available sources, and furnish such data and information as may be directed by the board of army engineers appointed by the President to act in an advisory capacity with Secretary Ballinger. Mr Ballinger said to the San Francisco proponents of the damming scheme, ''I want to know, what is necessary so far as the Hetch-Hetchy is concerned.'' He also said, ''What this Government wants to know and the American people want to know is whether it is a matter of absolute necessity for the people of San Francisco to have this water supply. Otherwise it belongs to the people for the purpose of a national park for which it has been set aside.'' Ballinger suggested that the Lake Eleanor plans should be submitted to the engineers at once so that they could have them as a basis for ascertaining if the full development of that watershed is contemplated, and to make a report of its data to the engineers as its preparation proceeded so that they may be kept in immediate touch with what is being done. Of the outcome of this thorough examination of the scheme there can be no doubt, and it must surely put the question at rest for all time, at least as far as our great park is concerned, and perhaps all the other national parks.

I have been hidden down here in Los Angeles a month or two working hard on books. Two or three weeks ago I sent the manuscript of a small book to Houghton Mifflin Company, who expect to bring it out as soon as possible. It is entitled *My First Summer in the Sierra*, written from notes made forty-one years ago. I have also nearly ready a lot of animal stories for a boys' book, drawn chiefly from my experiences as a boy in Scotland and in the wild oak openings of Wisconsin. I have also rewritten a lot of autobiographical notes dictated at Mr. Harriman's Pelican Lodge on Klamath Lake two years ago. Next month I hope to bring together a lot of Yosemite sketches for a sort of travellers' guidebook, which ought to have been written many years ago.

So you see, what with furnishing illustrations, reading proof, and getting this Yosemite guidebook off my hands, it will not be likely that I can find time for even a short visit to New York this summer. Possibly, however, I may be able to get away a few weeks in the autumn. Nothing, as you well know, would be more delightful than a visit to your blessed Garrison's-on-the-Hudson, and I am sure to make it some time ere long, unless my usual good luck should fail me utterly.

With warmest regards to Mrs. Osborn and Josephine and all the family, I am, my dear Mr. Osborn,

Ever faithfully your friend

JOHN MUIR

to Mrs. J. D. Hooker

Martinez, September 15th, 1910

DEAR MRS. HOOKER

Be of good cheer, make the best of whatever befalls; keep as near to headquarters as you may, and you will surely triumph over the ills of life, its frets and cares, with all other vermin of either earth or sky.

I'm ashamed to have enjoyed my visit so much. A lone good soul can still work miracles, charm an outlandish, crooked, zigzag flat into a lofty inspiring Olympus.

Do you know these fine verses of Thoreau?

> "I will not doubt for evermore,
>   Nor falter from a steadfast faith,
> For though the system be turned o'er,
>   God takes not back the word which once he saith.

> "I will, then, trust the love untold
>   Which not my worth nor want has bought,
> Which wooed me young and wooes me old,
>   And to this evening hath me brought."

Ever your friend

JOHN MUIR

to Mrs. J. D. Hooker

Martinez, December 17th, 1910

DEAR MRS. HOOKER

I'm glad you're at work on a book, for as far as I know, however high or low Fortune's winds may blow o'er life's solemn main, there is nothing so saving as good hearty work. From a letter just received from the Lark I learn the good news that Mr. Hooker is also hard at work with his pen.

As for myself, I've been reading old musty dusty Yosemite notes until I'm tired and blinky blind, trying to arrange them in something like lateral, medial, and terminal moraines on my den floor. I never imagined I had accumulated so vast a number. The long trains and embankments and heaped-up piles are truly appalling. I thought that in a quiet day or two I might select all that would be required for a guidebook; but the stuff seems enough for a score of big jungle books, and it's very hard, I find, to steer through it on anything like a steady course in reasonable time. Therefore, I'm beginning to see that I'll have to pick out only a moderate-sized bagful for the book and abandon the bulk of it to waste away like a snowbank or grow into other forms as time and chance may determine.

So, after all, I may be able to fly south in a few days and alight in your fine canyon garret. Anyhow, with good will and good wishes, to you all, I am   Ever faithfully, affectionately
                                                            JOHN MUIR

to Mrs. J. D. Hooker

[June 26th, 1911]
. . . I went to New Haven Tuesday morning, the 20th, was warmly welcomed and entertained by Professor Phelps and taken to the ball game in the afternoon. Though at first a little nervous, especially about the approaching honourary degree ceremony, I quickly caught the glow of the Yale enthusiasm. Never before have I seen or heard anything just like it. The alumni, assembled in classes from all the country, were arrayed in wildly coloured uniforms, and the way they rejoiced and made merry, capered and danced, sang and yelled, marched and ran, doubled, quadrupled, octupled is utterly indescribable; autumn leaves in whirlwinds are staid and dignified in comparison.

Then came memorable Wednesday when we donned our radiant academic robes and marched to the great hall where the degrees were conferred, shining like crow blackbirds. I was given perhaps the best seat on the platform, and when my name was called I arose with a grand air, shook my massive academic plumes into finest fluting folds, as became the occasion, stepped forward in awful majesty and stood rigid and solemn like an ancient sequoia while the orator poured praise on the honoured wanderer's head – and in this heroic attitude I think I had better leave him. Here is what the orator said. Pass it on to Helen at Daggett.
                              My love to all who love you.
                                    Faithfully, affectionately
                                                            JOHN MUIR

to John Burroughs

                                          Garrison, N.Y. July 14th, 1911
DEAR JOHN BURROUGHS
When I was on the train passing your place I threw you a hearty salute across the river, but I don't suppose that you heard or felt it. I would have

been with you long ago if I had not been loaded down with odds and ends of duties, book-making, book-selling at Boston, Yosemite and Park affairs at Washington, and making arrangements for getting off to South America, etc., etc. I have never worked harder in my life, although I have not very much to show for it. I have got a volume of my autobiography finished. Houghton Mifflin are to bring it out. They want to bring it out immediately, but I would like to have at least part of it run through some suitable magazine, and thus gain ten or twenty times more readers than would be likely to see it in a book.

I have been working for the last month or more on the Yosemite book, trying to finish it before leaving for the Amazon, but I am not suffering in a monstrous city. I am on the top of as green a hill as I have seen in all the State, with hermit thrushes, woodchucks, and warm hearts, something like those about yourself.

I am at a place that I suppose you know well, Professor Osborn's summer residence at Garrison's, opposite West Point. After Mrs. Harriman left for Arden I went down to the *Century* Editorial Rooms, where I was offered every facility for writing in Gilder's room, and tried to secure a boarding-place near Union Square, but the first day was so hot that it made my head swim, and I hastily made preparations for this comfortable home up on the hill here, where I will remain until perhaps the 15th of August, when I expect to sail.

Nothing would be more delightful than to go from one beautiful place to another and from one friend to another, but it is utterly impossible to visit a hundredth part of the friends who are begging me to go and see them and at the same time get any work done. I am now shut up in a magnificent room pegging away at that book, and working as hard as I ever did in my life. I do not know what has got into me, making so many books all at once. It is not natural. . . .

With all good wishes to your big and happy family, I am ever

Faithfully your friend
JOHN MUIR

to Mrs. Henry Fairfield Osborn

Para, Brazil, August 29th, 1911

DEAR MRS. OSBORN

Here at last is The River and thanks to your and Mrs. Harriman's loving care I'm well and strong for all South American work in sight that looks like mine.

Arrived here last eve – after a pleasant voyage – a long charming slide all the way to the equator between beautiful water and beautiful sky.

Approaching Para, had a glorious view of fifty miles or so of forest on the right bank of the river. This alone is noble compensation for my long desired and waited-for Amazon journey, even should I see no more.

And it's delightful to contemplate your cool restful mountain trip which is really a part of this equator trip. The more I see of our goodly Godly star, the more plainly comes to sight and mind the truth that it is all one like a face, every feature radiating beauty on the others.

I expect to start up the river to Manaos in a day or two on the Dennis. Will write again on my return before going south – and will hope to get a letter from you and Mr. Osborn, who must be enjoying his well-earned rest. How often I've wished him with me. I often think of you and Josephine among the Avalanche Lake clintonias and linnaeas. And that lovely boy at Castle Rock. Virginia played benevolent mother delightfully and sent me off rejoicing.

My love to each and all; ever, dear friend and friends,

Faithfully, gratefully

JOHN MUIR

to Mrs. J. D. Hooker

Para, Brazil, September 19th, 1911

. . . Of course you need absolute rest. Lie down among the pines for a while, then get to plain, pure, white love-work with Marian, to help humanity and other mortals and the Lord – heal the sick, cheer the sorrowful, break the jaws of the wicked, etc. But this Amazon delta sermon is growing too long. How glad I am that Marian was not with me, on account of yellow fever and the most rapidly deadly of the malarial kinds so prevalent up the river.

Nevertheless, I've had a most glorious time on this trip, dreamed of nearly half a century – have seen more than a thousand miles of the noblest of Earth's streams, and gained far more telling views of the wonderful forests than I ever hoped for. The Amazon, as you know, is immensely broad, but for hundreds of miles the steamer ran so close to the bossy leafy banks I could almost touch the out-reaching branches – fancy how I stared and sketched.

I was a week at Manaos on the Rio Negro tributary, wandered in the wonderful woods, got acquainted with the best of the citizens through Mr. Sanford, a graduate of Yale, was dined and guided and guarded and befriended in the most wonderful way, and had a grand telling time in general. I have no end of fine things for you in the way of new beauty. The only fevers I have had so far are burning enthusiasms, but there's no space for them in letters.

Here, however, is something that I must tell right now. Away up in that wild Manaos region in the very heart of the vast Amazon basin I found a little case of books in a lonely house. Glancing over the titles, none attracted me except a soiled volume at the end of one of the shelves, the blurred title of which I was unable to read, so I opened the glass door, opened the book, and out of it like magic jumped Katharine and Marian Hooker, apparently in the very flesh. The book, needless to say, was *Wayfarers in Italy*. The joy-shock I must not try to tell in detail, for medical Marian might call the whole story an equatorial fever dream.

Dear, dear friend, again goodbye. Rest in God's peace.

Affectionately

JOHN MUIR

to Mrs. J. D. Hooker

Pyramides Hotel, Montevideo,
December 6th, 1911

MY DEAR FRIEND

Your letter of October 4th from San Francisco was forwarded from Para to Buenos Aires and received there at the American Consulate. Your and Marian's letter, dated August 7th, were received at Para, not having been quite in time to reach me before I sailed, but forwarded by Mrs. Osborn. I can't think how I could have failed to acknowledge them. I have them and others with me, and they have been read times numberless when I was feeling lonely on my strange wanderings in all sorts of places.

But I'm now done with this glorious continent, at least for the present, as far as hard journeys along rivers, across mountains and tablelands, and through strange forests are concerned. I've seen all I sought for, and far, far, far more. From Para I sailed to Rio de Janeiro and at the first eager gaze into its wonderful harbour saw that it was a glacier bay, as unchanged by weathering as any in Alaska, every rock in it and about it a glacial monument, though within 23° of the equator, and feathered with palms instead of spruces, while every mountain and bay all the way down the coast to the Rio Grande do Sul corroborates the strange icy story. From Rio I sailed to Santos, and thence struck inland and wandered most joyfully a thousand miles or so, mostly in the State of Parana, through millions of acres of the ancient tree I was so anxious to find, *Araucaria Brasiliensis*. Just think of the glow of my joy in these noble aboriginal forests – the face of every tree marked with the inherited experiences of millions of years. From Paranagua I sailed for Buenos Aires; crossed the Andes to Santiago, Chile; thence south four or five hundred miles; thence straight to the snow-line, and found a glorious forest of *Araucaria imbricata*, the strangest of the strange genus.

The day after tomorrow, December 8th, I intend to sail for Tenerife on way to South Africa; then home some way or other. But I can give no address until I reach New York. I'm so glad your health is restored, and, now that you are free to obey your heart and have your brother's help and Marian's cosmic energy, your good-doing can have no end. I'm glad you are not going to sell the Los Angeles garret and garden. Why, I hardly know. Perhaps because I'm weary and lonesome, with a long hot journey ahead, and I feel as if I were again bidding you all goodbye. I think you may send me a word or two to Cape Town, care of the American Consul. It would not be lost, for it would follow me.

It's perfectly marvellous how kind hundreds of people have been to this
wanderer, and the new beauty stored up is far beyond telling. Give my love
to Marian, Maude, and Ellie and all who love you. I wish you would write a
line now and then to darling Helen. She has a little bungalow of her own
now at 233 Formosa Avenue, Hollywood, California.

It's growing late, and I've miserable packing to do. Goodnight. And once
more, dear, dear friend, goodbye.

JOHN MUIR

to Mr. and Mrs. Henry Fairfield Osborn

near Zanzibar, January 31st, 1912

DEAR FRIENDS

What a lot of wild water has been roaring between us since those blessed
Castle Rock days! But, roll and roar as it might, you have never been out of
heart-sight.

How often I've wished you with me on the best of my wanderings so full
of good things guided by wonderful luck, or shall I reverently, thankfully say
Providence? Anyhow, it seems that I've had the most fruitful time of my life
on this pair of hot continents. But I must not try to write my gains, for they
are utterly unletterable both in size and kind. I'll tell what I can when I see
you, probably in three months or less. From Cape Town I went north to the
Zambesi baobab forests and Victoria Falls, and thence down through a glacial
wonderland to Beira, where I caught this steamer, and am on my way to
Mombasa and the Nyanza Lake region. From Mombasa I intend starting
homeward via Suez and Naples and New York, fondly hoping to find you
well. In the meantime I'm sending lots of wireless, tireless love messages to
each and every Osborn, for I am   Ever faithfully yours

JOHN MUIR

to Mrs. Anna R. Dickey

Martinez May 1st, 1912

DEAR CHEERY, EXHILARATING MRS. DICKEY

Your fine lost letter has reached me at last. I found it in the big talus-heap
awaiting me here.

The bright, shining, faithful, hopeful way you bear your crushing burdens
is purely divine, out of darkness cheering everybody else with noble godlike
sympathy. I'm so glad you have a home with the birds in the evergreen oaks
– the feathered folk singing for you and every leaf shining, reflecting God's
love. Donald, too, is so brave and happy. With youth on his side and joyful
work, he is sure to grow stronger and under every disadvantage do more as a
naturalist than thousands of others with every resource of health and wealth
and special training.

I'm in my old library den, the house desolate, nobody living in it save a hungry mouse or two.... [I hold] dearly cherished memories about it and the fine garden grounds full of trees and bushes and flowers that my wife and father-in-law and I planted – fine things from every land.

But there's no good bread hereabouts and no housekeeper, so I may never be able to make it a home, fated, perhaps, to wander until sundown. Anyhow, I've had a glorious life, and I'll never have the heart to complain. The roses now are overrunning all bounds in glory of full bloom, and the Lebanon and Himalaya cedars, and the palms and Australian trees and shrubs, and the oaks on the valley hills seem happier and more exuberant than ever.

The Chelan trip would be according to my own heart, but whether or no I can go I dinna ken. Only lots of hard pen work seems certain. Anywhere, anyhow, with love to Donald, I am

Ever faithfully, affectionately yours
JOHN MUIR

to William E. Colby and
Mr. and Mrs. Edward T. Parsons

1525 Formosa Avenue,
Hollywood, California
June 24th, 1912

DEAR MR. COLBY AND MR. AND MRS. PARSONS

I thank you very much for your kind wishes to give me a pleasant Kern River trip, and am very sorry that work has been so unmercifully piled upon me that I find it impossible to escape from it, so I must just stay and work.

I heartily congratulate you and all your merry mountaineers on the magnificent trip that lies before you. As you know, I have seen something of nearly all the mountain-chains of the world, and have experienced their varied climates and attractions of forests and rivers, lakes and meadows, etc. In fact, I have seen a little of all the high places and low places of the continents, but no mountain-range seems to me so kind, so beautiful, or so fine in its sculpture as the Sierra Nevada. If you were as free as the winds are and the light to choose a campground in any part of the globe, I could not direct you to a single place for your outing that, all things considered, is so attractive, so exhilarating and uplifting in every way as just the trip that you are now making. You are far happier than you know. Good luck to you all, and I shall hope to see you all on your return – boys and girls, with the sparkle and exhilaration of the mountains still in your eyes. With love and countless fondly cherished memories,

Ever faithfully yours
JOHN MUIR

[P.S.] Of course, in all your camp-fire preaching and praying you will never forget Hetch-Hetchy.

to Howard Palmer

Martinez, California
December 12th, 1912

Mr. Howard Palmer
Secretary American Alpine Club
New London, Connecticutt.

DEAR SIR

At the National Parks conference in Yosemite Valley last October, called by the Honourable Secretary of the Interior, comparatively little of importance was considered. The great question was, "Shall automobiles be allowed to enter Yosemite?" It overshadowed all others, and a prodigious lot of gaseous commercial eloquence was spent upon it by auto-club delegates from near and far.

The principal objection urged against the puffing machines was that on the steep Yosemite grades they would cause serious accidents. The machine men roared in reply that far fewer park-going people would be killed or wounded by the auto-way than by the old prehistoric wagon-way. All signs indicate automobile victory, and doubtless, under certain precautionary restrictions, these useful, progressive, blunt-nosed mechanical beetles will hereafter be allowed to puff their way into all the parks and mingle their gas-breath with the breath of the pines and waterfalls, and, from the mountaineer's standpoint, with but little harm or good.

In getting ready for the Canal-celebration visitors the need of opening the Valley gates as wide as possible was duly considered, and the repair of roads and trails, hotel and camp building, the supply of cars and stages and arrangements in general for getting the hoped-for crowds safely into the Valley and out again. But the Yosemite Park was lost sight of, as if its thousand square miles of wonderful mountains, canyons, glaciers, forests, and songful falling rivers had no existence.

In the development of the Park a road is needed from the valley along the upper canyon of the Merced, across to the head of Tuolumne Meadows, down the great Tuolumne Canyon to Hetch-Hetchy valley, and thence back to Yosemite by the Big Oak Flat road. Good walkers can go anywhere in these hospitable mountains without artificial ways. But most visitors have to be rolled on wheels with blankets and kitchen arrangements.

Of course the few mountaineers present got in a word now and then on the need of park protection from commercial invasion like that now threatening Hetch-Hetchy. In particular the Secretary of the American Civic Association and the Sierra Club spoke on the highest value of wild parks as places of recreation, Nature's cathedrals, where all may gain inspiration and strength and get nearer to God.

The great need of a landscape gardener to lay out the roads and direct the work of thinning out the heavy undergrowth was also urged.

With all good New Year wishes, I am

Faithfully yours

JOHN MUIR

to Asa K. McIlhaney

Martinez, California,,

January 10th, 1913

Mr. Asa K. McIlhaney
Bath, Pennsylvania.

DEAR SIR

I thank you for your fine letter, but in reply I can't tell which of all God's trees I like best, though I should write a big book trying to. Sightseers often ask me which is best, the Grand Canyon of Arizona or Yosemite. I always reply that I know a show better than either of them – both of them.

Anglo-Saxon folk have inherited love for oaks and heathers. Of all I know of the world's two hundred and fifty oaks perhaps I like best the *macrocarpa, chrysolepis, lobata, Virginiana, agrifolia,* and *Michauxii.* Of the little heather folk my favourite is Cassiope; of the trees of the family, the Menzies arbutus, one of the world's great trees. The hickory is a favourite genus – I like them all, the pecan the best. Of flower trees, magnolia and liriodendron and the wonderful baobab; of conifers, *Sequoia gigantea,* the noblest of the whole noble race, and sugar pine, king of pines, and silver firs, especially *magnifica.* The grand larch forests of the upper Missouri and of Manchuria and the glorious deodars of the Himalaya, araucarias of Brazil and Chile and Australia. The wonderful eucalyptus, two hundred species, the New Zealand metrosideros and agathis. The magnificent eriodendron of the Amazon and the palm and tree fern and tree grass forests, and in our own country the delightful linden and oxydendron and maples and so on, without end. I may as well stop here as anywhere.

Wishing you a happy New Year and good times in God's woods,

Faithfully yours

JOHN MUIR

to Miss M. Merrill

Martinez, California,

May 31st, 1913

DEAR MINA MERRILL

I am more delighted with your letter than I can tell – to see your handwriting once more and know that you still love me. For through all life's wanderings you have held a warm place in my heart, and I have never ceased to thank

God for giving me the blessed Merrill family as lifelong friends. As to the Scotch way of bringing up children, to which you refer, I think it is often too severe or even cruel. And as I hate cruelty, I called attention to it in the boyhood book while at the same time pointing out the value of sound religious training with steady work and restraint.

I'm now at work on an Alaska book, and as soon as it is off my hands I mean to continue the autobiography from leaving the University to botanical excursions in the northern woods, around Indianapolis, and thence to Florida, Cuba, and California. This will be volume number two.

It is now seven years since my beloved wife vanished in the land of the leal. Both of my girls are happily married and have homes and children of their own. Wanda has three lively boys, Helen has two and is living at Daggett, California. Wanda is living on the ranch in the old adobe, while I am alone in my library den in the big house on the hill where you and sister Kate found me on your memorable visit long ago.

As the shadows lengthen in life's afternoon, we cling all the more fondly to the friends of our youth. And it is with the warmest gratitude that I recall the kindness of all your family when I was lying in darkness. That Heaven may ever bless you, dear Mina, is the heart prayer of your –

Affectionate friend

JOHN MUIR

to Mrs. Henry Fairfield Osborn

Martinez, July 3rd, 1913

DEAR MRS. OSBORN

Warm thanks, thanks, thanks for your July invitation to blessed Castle Rock. How it goes to my heart all of you must know, but wae's me! I see no way of escape from the work piled on me here – the gatherings of half a century of wilderness wanderings to be sorted and sifted into something like clear, useful form. Never mind – for, anywhere, everywhere in immortal soul sympathy, I'm always with my friends, let time and the seas and continents spread their years and miles as they may.

Ever gratefully, faithfully

JOHN MUIR

to Henry Fairfield Osborn

Martinez, July 15th, 1913

DEAR FRIEND OSBORN

I had no thought of your leaving your own great work and many-fold duties to go before the House Committee on the everlasting Hetch-Hetchy fight, but only to write to members of Congress you might know, especially to President Wilson, a Princeton man. This is the twenty-third year of almost continual battle for preservation of Yosemite National Park, sadly interrupting my natural work. Our enemies now seem to be having most everything their own wicked way, working beneath obscuring tariff and bank clouds, spending millions of the people's money for selfish ends. Think of three or four ambitious, shifty traders and politicians calling themselves "The City of San Francisco," bargaining with the United States for half of the Yosemite Park like Yankee horse-traders, as if the grandest of all our mountain playgrounds, full of God's best gifts, the joy and admiration of the world, were of no more account than any of the long list of tinker tariff articles.

Where are you going this summer? Wish I could go with you. The pleasure of my long lovely Garrison-Hudson Castle Rock days grows only the clearer and dearer as the years flow by.

My love to you, dear friend, and to all who love you.

Ever gratefully, affectionately
JOHN MUIR

to Mr. and Mrs. Henry Fairfield Osborn

Martinez, January 4th, 1914

DEAR FRIENDS OSBORNS

With all my heart I wish you a happy New Year. How hard you have fought in the good fight to save the Tuolumne Yosemite I well know. The battle has lasted twelve years, from Pinchot and Company to President Wilson, and the wrong has prevailed over the best aroused sentiment of the whole country.

That a lane lined with lies could be forced through the middle of the U.S. Congress is truly wonderful even in these confused political days – a devil's masterpiece of log-rolling road-making. But the approval of such a job by scholarly, virtuous, Princeton Wilson is the greatest wonder of all! Fortunately wrong cannot last; soon or late it must fall back home to Hades, while some compensating good must surely follow.

With the new year to new work right gladly we will go – you to your studies of God's langsyne people in their magnificent Wyoming-Idaho mausoleums, I to crystal ice.

So devoutly prays your grateful admiring friend

JOHN MUIR

to Andrew Carnegie

Martinez, California, January 22nd, 1914

Many thanks, dear Mr. Carnegie, for your admirable "Apprenticeship." To how many fine godly men and women has our stormy, craggy, glacier-sculptured little Scotland given birth, influencing for good every country under the sun! Our immortal poet while yet a boy wished that for poor auld Scotland's sake he might "sing a sang at least." And what a song you have sung with your ringing, clanging hammers and furnace fires, blowing and flaming like volcanoes – a truly wonderful Caledonian performance. But far more wonderful is your coming forth out of that tremendous titanic iron and dollar work with a heart in sympathy with all humanity.

Like John Wesley, who took the world for his parish, you are teaching and preaching over all the world in your own Scotch way, with heroic benevolence putting to use the mine and mill wealth won from the iron hills. What wonderful burdens you have carried all your long life, and seemingly so easily and naturally, going right ahead on your course, steady as a star! How strong you must be and happy in doing so much good, in being able to illustrate so nobly the national character founded on God's immutable righteousness that makes Scotland loved at home, revered abroad! Everybody blessed with a drop of Scotch blood must be proud of you and bid you godspeed.   Your devoted admirer

                                                                                JOHN MUIR

                              to Dr. C. Hart Merriam

                                                              Martinez, California,
                                                              February 11th, 1914

DEAR DR. MERRIAM

I was very glad to hear from you once more last month, for, as you say, I haven't heard from you for an age. I fully intended to grope my way to Lagunitas in the fall before last, but it is such ancient history that I have only very dim recollections of the difficulty that hindered me from making the trip. I hope, however, to have better luck next spring for I am really anxious to see you all once more.

I congratulate Dorothy on her engagement to marry Henry Abbot. If he is at all like his blessed old grandfather he must prove a glorious prize in life's lottery. I have been intimately acquainted with General Abbot ever since we camped together for months on the Forestry Commission, towards the end of President Cleveland's second administration.

Wanda, her husband, and three boys are quite well, living on the ranch here, in the old adobe, while I am living alone in the big house on the hill.

After living a year or two in Los Angeles, Helen with her two fine boys and her husband returned to the alfalfa ranch on the edge of the Mojave Desert near Daggett, on the Santa Fé Railway. They are all in fine health and will be glad to get word from you.

Our winter here has been one of the stormiest and foggiest I have ever experienced, and unfortunately I caught the grippe. The last two weeks, however, the weather has been quite bright and sunny and I hope soon to be as well as ever and get to work again.

That a few ruthless ambitious politicians should have been able to run a tunnel lined with all sorts of untruthful bewildering statements through both houses of Congress for Hetch-Hetchy is wonderful, but that the President should have signed the Raker Bill is most wonderful of all. As you say, it is a monumental mistake, but it is more, it is a monumental crime.

I have not heard a word yet from the Baileys. Hoping that they are well and looking forward with pleasure to seeing you all soon in California, I am as ever   Faithfully yours

                                                                JOHN MUIR

Despite his hopeful allusion to the grippe which he had caught early in the winter of 1914, the disease made farther and farther inroads upon his vitality. Yet he worked away steadily at the task of completing his Alaska book. During the closing months he had the aid of Mrs. Marion Randall Parsons, at whose home the transcription of his Alaska journals had been begun in November, 1912. Unfortunately the Hetch-Hetchy conspiracy became acute again, and the book, barely begun, had to be laid aside that he might save, if possible, his beloved "Tuolumne Yosemite." "We may lose this particular fight," he wrote to William E. Colby, "but truth and right must prevail at last. Anyhow we must be true to ourselves and the Lord."

This particular battle, indeed, was lost because the park invaders had finally got into office a Secretary of the Interior who had previously been on San Francisco's payroll as an attorney to promote the desired Hetch-Hetchy legislation; also, because various other politicians of easy convictions on such fundamental questions of public policy as this had been won over to a concerted drive to accomplish the "grab" during a special summer session when no effective representation of opposing organisations could be secured. So flagrant was the performance in every aspect of it that Senator John D. Works of California afterwards introduced in the Senate a bill to repeal the Hetch-Hetchy legislation and in his vigorous remarks accompanying the same set forth the points on which he justified his action. But the fate of the Valley was sealed.

John Muir turned sadly but courageously to his notebooks and memories of the great glacier-ploughed wilderness of Alaska. Shortly before Christmas, 1914, he set his house in order as if he had a presentiment that he was leaving it for the last time, and went to pay a holiday visit to the home of his younger daughter at Daggett. Upon his arrival there he was smitten with pneumonia and was rushed to a hospital in Los Angeles, where all his wanderings ended on Christmas Eve. Spread about him on the bed, when the end came, were manuscript sheets of his last book – *Travels in Alaska* – to which he was bravely struggling to give the last touches before the coming of "the long sleep."

CHAPTER EIGHTEEN

His Public Service

"The last rays of the setting sun are shining into our window at the Palace Hotel and perhaps it is the last sunset we shall ever see in this city of the Golden Gate. I could not think of leaving the Pacific Coast without saying goodbye to you who so much love all the world about here. California, you may say, has made you, and you in return have made California, and you are both richer for having made each other." The concluding sentence of this parting message of former travel companions, sent to John Muir in 1879 when he was exploring the glaciers of Alaska, has grown truer each succeeding decade since then.

Intimately as his name was already identified with the natural beauty of California in 1879, the service which Muir was ultimately to render to the nation was only beginning at that time. Then there was only one national park, that of the Yellowstone, and no national forest reserves at all. Amid such a wealth of beautiful forests and wildernesses as our nation then possessed it required a very uncommon lover of nature and of humanity to advocate provision against a day of need. But that friend of generations unborn arose in the person of John Muir. Before he or any one had ever heard of national parks the idea of preserving some sections of our natural flora in their unspoiled wildness arose spontaneously in his mind.

It was a lovely carex meadow beside Fountain Lake, on his father's first Wisconsin farm, that gave him the germinal idea of a park in which plant societies were to be protected in their natural state. During the middle sixties, as he was about to leave his boyhood home forever, he found unbearable the thought of leaving this precious meadow unprotected, and offered to purchase it from his brother-in-law on condition that cattle and hogs be kept securely fenced out. Early correspondence shows that he pressed the matter repeatedly, but his relative treated the request as a sentimental dream, and ultimately the meadow was trampled out of existence. More than thirty years later, at a notable meeting of the Sierra Club in 1895, he for the first time made public this natural park dream of his boyhood. It was the national park idea in miniature, and the proposal was made before even the Yellowstone National Park had been established.

This was the type of man who during the decade 1879 – 1889 wrote for *Scribner's Monthly* and the *Century Magazine* a series of articles the like of which had never been written on American forests and scenery. Such were Muir's articles entitled "In the Heart of the California Alps," "Wild Sheep of the Sierra," "Coniferous Forests of the Sierra Nevada," and "Bee-Pastures of California." There was also the volume, edited by him, entitled *Picturesque California*, with numerous articles by himself. The remarkably large correspondence which came to him as a result of this literary activity shows how deep was its educative effect upon the public mind.

Then came the eventful summer of 1889, during which he took Robert Underwood Johnson, one of the editors of the *Century*, camping about Yosemite and on the Tuolumne Meadows, where, as Muir says, he showed him how uncountable sheep had eaten and trampled out of existence the wonderful flower gardens of the seventies. We have elsewhere shown how the two then and there determined to make a move for the establishment of what is now the Yosemite National Park, and to make its area sufficiently comprehensive to include all the headwaters of the Merced and the Tuolumne. This was during President Harrison's administration, and, fortunately for the project, John W.Noble, a faithful and far-sighted servant of the American people, was then Secretary of the Interior.

One may imagine with what fervour Muir threw himself into that campaign. The series of articles on the Yosemite region which he now wrote for the *Century* are among the best things he has ever done. Public-spirited men all over the country rallied to the support of the National Park movement, and on the first of October, 1890, the Yosemite National Park bill went through Congress, though bitterly contested by all kinds of selfishness and pettifoggery. A troop of cavalry immediately came to guard the new park; the "hoofed locusts" were expelled, and the flowers and undergrowth gradually returned to the meadows and forests.

The following year (1891) Congress passed an act empowering the President to create forest reserves. This was the initial step toward a rational forest conservation policy, and President Harrison was the first to establish forest reserves – to the extent of somewhat more than thirteen million acres. We cannot stop to go into the opening phases of this new movement, but the measure in which the country is indebted to John Muir also for this public benefit may be gathered from letters of introduction to scientists abroad which influential friends gave to Muir in 1893 when he was contemplating extensive travels in Europe. "It gives me great pleasure," wrote one of them, "to introduce to you Mr. John Muir, whose successful struggle for the reservation of about one-half of the western side of the Sierra Nevada has made him so well known to the friends of the forest in this country."

During his struggle for the forest reservations and for the establishment of the Yosemite National Park Muir had the effective cooperation of a considerable body of public-spirited citizens of California, who in 1892 were organised into the Sierra Club, in part, at least, for the purpose of assisting in creating public sentiment and in making it effective. During its long and

Right: The map that John Muir and Robert Johnson used to illustrate proposals to transform the state-run Yosemite Valley area (inner box) into a much larger National Park. The map was published as part of Muir's articles on "The Proposed Yosemite National Park" (see page 679) in Johnson's magazine "Century" in 1890 and was also submitted to the Committee on Public Lands a few weeks before the critical debate in Congress. This brought to a climax the campaign to preserve the valleys and upper alpine slopes of the western Sierra from commercial exploitation. As a result the Yosemite, Sequoia and Kings Canyon National Parks were established, the former covering an even larger area than that proposed here.

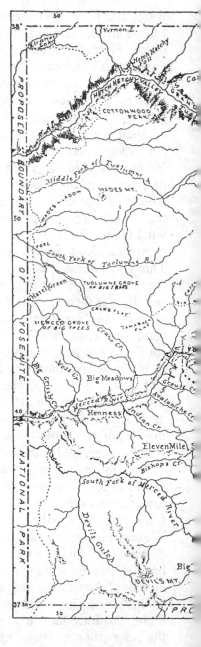

distinguished public service this organisation never swerved from one of its main purposes, "to enlist the support and cooperation of the people and the government in preserving the forests and other features of the Sierra Nevada Mountains," and when that thrilling volume of Muir's, *My First Summer in the Sierra*, appeared in 1911, it was found to be dedicated "To the Sierra Club of California, Faithful Defender of the People's Playgrounds."

The assistance of this Club proved invaluable when Muir's greatest opportunity for public service came in 1896. It was then that our Federal Government began to realise at last the imperative necessity of doing something at once to check the appalling waste of our forest resources. Among the causes which led up to this development of conscience was the report of Edward A. Bowers, Inspector of the Public Land Service. He estimated the value of timber stolen from the public lands during six years in the eighties at thirty-seven million dollars. To this had to be added the vastly greater loss annually inflicted upon the public domain by sheepmen and prospectors, who regularly set fire to the forests in autumn, the former to secure open pasturage for their flocks, the latter to lay bare the outcrops of mineral-bearing rocks. But the most consequential awakening of the public mind followed the appearance of Muir's *Mountains of California* in 1894. All readers of it knew immediately

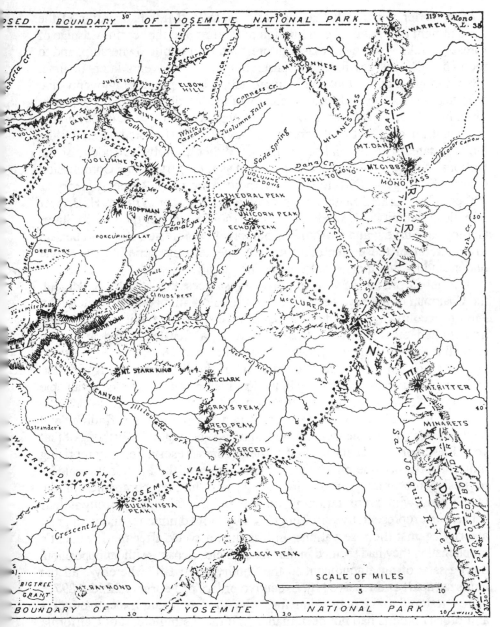

that the trees had found a defender whose knowledge, enthusiasm, and gift of expression made his pen more powerful than a regiment of swords. Here at last was a man who had no axes to grind by the measures he advocated and thousands of new conservation recruits heard the call and enlisted under his leadership. One remarkable thing about the numerous appreciative letters he received is the variety of persons, high and low, from whom they came.

The reader will recall that, as early as 1876, Muir had proposed the appointment of a national commission to inquire into the fearful wastage of forests, to take a survey of existing forest lands in public ownership, and to recommend measures for their conservation. Twenty years later, in June, 1896, Congress at last took the required action by appropriating twenty-five thousand dollars "to enable the Secretary of the Interior to meet the expenses of an investigation and report by the National Academy of Sciences on the inauguration of a national forestry policy for the forested lands of the United States." In pursuance of this act Wolcott Gibbs, President of the National Academy of Sciences, appointed as members of this Commission Charles S. Sargent, Director of the Arnold Arboretum; General Henry L. Abbot, of the United States Engineer Corps; Professor William H. Brewer of Yale University; Alexander Agassiz; Arnold Hague of the United States Geological Survey; and Gifford Pinchot, practical forester. It should be said to the credit of these men that they all accepted this appointment on the understanding that they were to serve without pay.

It is not surprising, in view of the circumstances, that Charles S. Sargent, the Chairman of the newly appointed Commission, immediately invited John Muir to accompany the party on a tour of investigation, and it was fortunate, as it turned out afterwards, that he went as a free-lance and not as an official member of the party. During the summer of 1896, this Commission visited nearly all of the great forest areas of the West and the Northwest, and letters written to him later by individual members testify to the invaluable character of Muir's personal contribution to its work.

A report, made early in 1897, embodied the preliminary findings and recommendations of the Commission, and on Washington's Birthday of that year President Cleveland created thirteen forest reservations, comprising more than twenty-one million acres. This action of the President created a rogues' panic among the mining, stock, and lumber companies of the Northwest, who were fattening on the public domain. Through their subservient representatives in Congress they moved unitedly and with great alacrity against the reservations. In less than a week after the President's proclamation they had secured in the United States Senate, without opposition, the passage of an amendment to the Sundry Civil Bill whereby "all the lands set apart and reserved by Executive orders of February 22nd, 1897," were "restored to the public domain ... the same as if said Executive orders and proclamations had not been made." To the lasting credit of California let it be said that the California reservations were expressly exempted from the provisions of this nullifying amendment at the request of the California Senators, Perkins and White, behind whom was the public sentiment of the State, enlightened by John Muir and many like-minded friends.

The great battle between the public interest and selfish special interests, or between "landscape righteousness and the devil," as Muir used to say, was now joined for a fight to the finish. The general public as yet knew little about the value of forests as conservers and regulators of water-flow in streams. They knew even less about their effect upon rainfall, climate, and public welfare, and the day when forest reserves would be needed to meet the failing timber supply seemed far, far off.

But there is nothing like a great conflict between public and private interests to create an atmosphere in which enlightening discussion can do its work, and no-one knew this better than John Muir. "This forest battle," he wrote, "is part of the eternal conflict between right and wrong. . . . The sooner it is stirred up and debated before the people the better, for thus the light will be let into it." When travelling with the Forestry Commission he had on one occasion seen an apparently well-behaved horse suddenly take a fit of bucking, kicking, and biting that made every one run for safety. Its strange actions were a mystery until a yellow jacket emerged from its ear!

Muir seized the occurrence for an explanation of the sudden and insanely violent outcry against forest reservations. "One man," he said, "with a thousand-dollar yellow jacket in his ear will make more bewildering noise and do more effective kicking and fighting on certain public measures than a million working men minding their own business, and whose cash interests are not visibly involved. But as soon as the light comes the awakened million creates a public opinion that overcomes wrong however cunningly veiled."

He was not mistaken, as we shall see, though for a time wrong seemed triumphant. The amendment nullifying the forest reservations died through lack of President Cleveland's signature. But in the extra session, which followed the inauguration of President McKinley, a bill was passed in June, 1897, that restored to the public domain, until March 1st, 1898, all the forest reservations created by Cleveland, excepting those of California. This interval, of course, was used shamelessly by all greedy forest-grabbers, while Congress was holding the door open! Emboldened by success, certain lumbermen even tried to secure Congressional authority to cut the wonderful sequoia grove in the General Grant National Park.

But John Muir's Scotch fighting blood was up now. Besides, his friends, East and West, were calling for the aid of his eagle's quill to enlighten the citizens of our country on the issues involved in the conflict. "No man in the world can place the forests' claim before them so clearly and forcibly as your own dear self," wrote his friend Charles Sprague Sargent, Chairman of the Commission now under fire. "No one knows so well as you the value of our forests – that their use for lumber is but a small part of the value." He proposed that Muir write syndicate letters for the public press. "There is no one in the United States," he wrote, "who can do this in such a telling way as you can, and in writing these letters you will perform a patriotic service."

Meanwhile the public press was becoming interested in the issue. To a request from the editor of *Harper's Weekly* Muir responded with an article entitled "Forest Reservations and National Parks," which appeared opportunely in June, 1897. The late Walter Hines Page, then editor of the

Atlantic Monthly, opened to him its pages for the telling contribution entitled "The American Forests." In both these articles Muir's style rose to the impassioned oratory of a Hebrew prophet arraigning wickedness in high places, and preaching the sacred duty of so using the country we live in that we may not leave it ravished by greed and ruined by ignorance, but may pass it on to future generations undiminished in richness and beauty.

Unsparingly he exposed to public scorn the methods by which the government was being defrauded. One typical illustration must suffice. "It was the practice of one lumber company," he writes, "to hire the entire crew of every vessel which might happen to touch at any port in the redwood belt, to enter one hundred and sixty acres each and immediately deed the land to the company, in consideration of the company's paying all expenses and giving the jolly sailors fifty dollars apiece for their trouble."

This was the type of undesirable citizens who, through their representatives in Congress, raised the hue and cry that poor settlers looking for homesteads, were being driven into more hopeless poverty by the forest reservations – a piece of sophistry through which Muir's trenchant language cut like a Damascus blade:

The outcries we hear against forest reservations [he wrote] come mostly from thieves who are wealthy and steal timber by wholesale. They have so long been allowed to steal and destroy in peace that any impediment to forest robbery is denounced as a cruel and irreligious interference with "vested rights," likely to endanger the repose of all ungodly welfare. Gold, gold, gold! How strong a voice that metal has! . . . Even in Congress, a sizable chunk of gold, carefully concealed will outtalk and outfight all the nation on a subject like forestry . . . in which the money interests of only a few are conspicuously involved. Under these circumstances the bawling, blethering oratorical stuff drowns the voice of God himself. . . . Honest citizens see that only the rights of the government are being trampled, not those of the settlers. Merely what belongs to all alike is reserved, and every acre that is left should be held together under the federal government as a basis for a general policy of administration for the public good. The people will not always be deceived by selfish opposition, whether from lumber and mining corporations or from sheepmen and prospectors, however cunningly brought forward underneath fables of gold.

He concluded this article with a remarkable peroration which no tree-lover could read without feeling, like the audiences that heard the philippics of Demosthenes, that something must be done immediately.

Any fool [he wrote] can destroy trees. They cannot run away; and if they could, they would still be destroyed – chased and hunted down as long as fun or a dollar could be got out of their bark hides, branching horns, or magnificent bole backbones. Few that fell trees plant them; nor would planting avail much towards getting back anything like the noble primeval forests. During a man's life only saplings can be grown, in the place of the old trees – tens of centuries old – that have been destroyed. It took more than three thousand years to make some of the trees in these Western woods – trees that are still standing in perfect strength and beauty, waving and singing in the mighty forests of the Sierra. Through all the wonderful, eventful centuries since Christ's time – and long before that – God has cared for these trees, saved them from drought, disease, avalanches, and a thousand straining, levelling tempests and floods; but He cannot save them from fools – only Uncle Sam can do that.

The period of nine months during which the Cleveland reservations had been suspended came to an end on the first of March, 1898. Enemies of the reservation policy again started a move in the Senate to annul them all. "In the excitement and din of this confounded [Spanish-American] War, the silent trees stand a poor show for justice," wrote Muir to his friend C. S. Sargent, who was sounding the alarm. Meanwhile Muir was conducting a surprisingly active campaign by post and telegraph, and through the Sierra Club. At last his efforts began to take effect and his confidence in the power of light to conquer darkness was justified. "You have evidently put in some good work," wrote Sargent, who was keeping closely in touch with the situation. "On Saturday all the members of the Public Lands Committee of the House agreed to oppose the Senate amendment wiping out the reservations." A large surviving correspondence shows how he continued to keep a strong hand on the helm. On the eighth of July the same friend, who was more than doing his own part, wrote, "Thank Heaven! the forest reservations are safe ... for another year."As subsequent events have shown, they have been safe ever since. One gets directly at the cause of this gratifying result in a sentence from a letter of John F. Lacey, who was then Chairman of the Public Lands Committee of the House. In discussing the conflicting testimony of those who were urging various policies of concession toward cattle and sheep men in the administration of the reserves he said, "Mr. Muir's judgment will probably be better than that of any one of them."

We have been able to indicate only in the briefest possible manner the decisive part that Muir played in the establishment and defence of the thirty-nine million acres of forest reserves made during the Harrison and Cleveland administrations. But even this bare glimpse of the inside history of that great struggle reveals the magnitude of the service John Muir rendered the nation in those critical times.

There were not lacking those who charged him with being an advocate of conservatism without use. But this criticism came from interested persons – abusers, not legitimate users – and is wholly false.

The United States Government [he said] has always been proud of the welcome it has extended to good men of every nation seeking freedom and homes and bread. Let them be welcomed still as nature welcomes them, to the woods as well as the prairies and plains.... The ground will be glad to feed them, and the pines will come down from the mountains for their homes as willingly as the cedars came from Lebanon for Solomon's temple. Nor will the woods be the worse for this use, or their benign influences be diminished any more than the sun is diminished by shining. Mere destroyers, however, tree-killers, spreading death and confusion in the fairest groves and gardens ever planted, let the government hasten to cast them out and make an end of them. For it must be told again and again, and be burningly borne in mind, that just now, while protective measures are being deliberated languidly, destruction and use are speeding on faster and farther every day. The axe and saw are insanely busy, chips are flying thick as snowflakes, and every summer thousands of acres of priceless forests, with their underbrush, soil, springs, climate, scenery, and religion, are vanishing away in clouds of smoke, while, except in the national parks, not one forest guard is employed.

Stripped of metaphor, this moving appeal of John Muir to Uncle Sam was an appeal to the intelligence of the American people, and they did not disappoint his faith in their competence to deal justly and farsightedly with this problem. Great as was the achievement of rescuing in eight years more than thirty-nine million acres of forest from deliberate destruction by sheeping, lumbering, and burning, it was only an earnest of what awakened public opinion was prepared to do when it should find the right representative to carry it into force. That event occurred when Theodore Roosevelt came to the Presidency of the United States, and it is the writer's privilege to supply a bit of unwritten history on the manner in which Muir's informed enthusiasm and Roosevelt's courage and love of action were brought into cooperation for the country's good. In March, 1903, Dr. Chester Rowell, a Senator of the California Legislature, wrote to Muir confidentially as follows: "From private advices from Washington I learn that President Roosevelt is desirous of taking a trip into the High Sierra during his visit to California, and has expressed a wish to go with you practically alone.... If he attempts anything of the kind, he wishes it to be entirely unknown, carried out with great secrecy so that the crowds will not follow or annoy him, and he suggested that he could foot it and rough it with you or anybody else."

John Muir had already engaged passage for Europe in order to visit, with Professor Sargent, the forests of Japan, Russia, and Manchuria, and felt constrained to decline. But upon the urgent solicitation of President Benjamin Ide Wheeler, and following the receipt of a friendly letter from President Roosevelt, he postponed his sailing date, writing to Professor Sargent, "An influential man from Washington wants to make a trip into the Sierra with me, and I might be able to *do some forest good* in freely talking around the campfire."

By arrangement Muir joined the President at Raymond on Friday, the fifteenth of May, and at the Mariposa Big Trees the two inexorably separated themselves from the company and disappeared in the woods until the following Monday. Needless to say this was not what the disappointed politicians would have chosen, but their chagrin fortunately was as dust in the balance against the good of the forests.

In spite of efforts to keep secret the President's proposed trip to Yosemite, he had been met at Raymond by a big crowd. Emerging from his car in rough camp costume, he said: "Ladies and Gentlemen: I did not realise that I was to meet you today, still less to address an audience like this! I had only come prepared to go into Yosemite with John Muir, so I must ask you to excuse my costume." This statement was met by the audience with cries of "It is all right!" And it was all right. For three glorious days Theodore Roosevelt and John Muir were off together in Yosemite woods and on Yosemite trails. Just how much was planned by them, in those days together, for the future welfare of this nation we probably never shall fully know, for death has sealed the closed accounts of both. But I am fortunately able to throw some light upon the attendant circumstances and results of the trip.

While I was in correspondence with Theodore Roosevelt in 1916 over a book I had published on the Old Testament, he wrote, "Isn't there some chance of your getting to this side of the continent before you write your book on Muir? Then you'll come out here to Sagamore Hill; and I'll tell you all about the trip, and give you one very amusing instance of his quaint and most unworldly forgetfulness."

In November of the same year it was my privilege to go for a memorable visit to Sagamore Hill, and while Colonel Roosevelt and I were pacing briskly back and forth in his library, over lion skins and other trophies, he told about the trip with John Muir, and the impression which his deep solicitude over the destruction of our great forests and scenery had made upon his mind. Roosevelt had shown himself a friend of the forests before this camping trip with Muir, but he came away with a greatly quickened conviction that vigorous action must be taken speedily, ere it should be too late. Muir's accounts of the wanton forest-destruction he had witnessed, and the frauds that had been perpetrated against the government in the acquisition of redwood forests, were not without effect upon Roosevelt's statesmanship, as we shall see. Nor must we, in assessing the near and distant public benefits of this trip, overlook the fact that it was the beginning of a lifelong friendship between these two men. By a strange fatality Muir's own letter accounts of what occurred on the trip went from hand to hand until they were lost. There survives a passage in a letter to his wife in which he writes: "I had a perfectly glorious time with the President and the mountains. I never before had a more interesting, hearty, and manly companion." To his friend Merriam he wrote: "Camping with the President was a memorable experience. I fairly fell in love with him." Roosevelt, John Muir, the Big

Trees, and the lofty summits that make our "Range of Light"! – who could think of an association of men and objects more elementally great and more fittingly allied for the public good? In a stenographically reported address delivered by Roosevelt at Sacramento immediately after his return from the mountains, we have a hint of what the communion of these two greatest outdoor men of our time was going to mean for the good of the country.

> I have just come from a four days' rest in Yosemite [he said], and I wish to say a word to you here in the capital city of California about certain of your great natural resources, your forests and your water supply coming from the streams that find their sources among the forests of the mountains. . . . No small part of the prosperity of California in the hotter and drier agricultural regions depends upon the preservation of her water supply; and the water supply cannot be preserved unless the forests are preserved. As regards some of the trees, I want them preserved because they are the only things of their kind in the world. Lying out at night under those giant sequoias was lying in a temple built by no hand of man, a temple grander than any human architect could by any possibility build, and I hope for the preservation of the groves of giant trees simply because it would be a shame to our civilization to let them disappear. They are monuments in themselves.
>
> I ask for the preservation of other forests on grounds of wise and far-sighted economic policy. I do not ask that lumbering be stopped . . . only that the forests be so used that not only shall we here, this generation, get the benefit for the next few years, but that our children and our children's children shall get the benefit. In California I am impressed by how great the State is, but I am even more impressed by the immensely greater greatness that lies in the future, and I ask that your marvellous natural resources be handed on unimpaired to your posterity. We are not building this country of ours for a day. It is to last through the ages.

Let us now recall Muir's modest excuse for postponing a world tour in order to go alone into the mountains with Theodore Roosevelt – that he "might be able to do some forest good in freely talking around the camp-fire." It was in the glow of those camp-fires that Muir's enlightened enthusiasm and Roosevelt's courage were fused into action for the public good. The magnitude of the result was astonishing and one for which this country can never be sufficiently grateful. When Roosevelt came to the White House in 1901, the total National Forest area amounted to 46,153,119 acres, and we have already seen what a battle it cost Muir and his friends to prevent enemies in Congress from securing the annulment of Cleveland's twenty-five million acres of forest reserves. When he left the White House, in the spring of 1909, he had set aside more than one hundred and forty-eight million acres of additional National Forests – more than three times as much as Harrison, Cleveland, and McKinley combined! Similarly the number of National Parks was doubled during his administration.

But the Monuments and Antiquities Act, passed by Congress during Roosevelt's administration, gave him a new, unique opportunity. During the last three years of his presidency he created by proclamation sixteen National Monuments. Among them was the Grand Canyon of the Colorado with an area of 806,400 acres. Efforts had been made, ever since the days of Benjamin Harrison, to have the Grand Canyon set aside as a national park, but selfish opposition always carried the day. Sargent and Johnson and Page had repeatedly appealed to Muir to write a description of the Canyon. "It is absolutely necessary," wrote Page in 1898, "that this great region as well as the Yosemite should be described by you, else you will not do the task that God sent you to do." When in 1902 his masterly description did appear, it led to renewed, but equally futile, efforts to have this wonder of earth sculpture included among our national playgrounds. Then Muir passed on to Roosevelt the suggestion that he proclaim the Canyon a national monument. A monument underground was a new idea, but there was in it nothing inconsistent with the Monuments and Antiquities Act, and so Roosevelt, with his characteristic dash, in January, 1908, declared the whole eight hundred thousand acres of the Canyon a National Monument and the whole nation smiled and applauded. Subsequently Congress, somewhat grudgingly, changed its status to that of a national park, thus realising the purpose for which Roosevelt's proclamation reserved it at the critical time.

The share of John Muir in the splendid achievements of these Rooseveltian years would be difficult to determine precisely, for his part was that of inspiration and advice – elements as imponderable as sunlight, but as all-pervasively powerful between friends as the pull of gravity across stellar spaces. And fast friends they remained to the end, as is shown by the letters that passed between them. Neither of them could feel or act again as if they had not talked "forest good" together beside Yosemite campfires. "I wish I could see you in person," wrote Roosevelt in 1907 at the end of a letter about national park matters. "I wish I could see you in person; and how I do wish I were again with you camping out under those great sequoias, or in the snow under the silver firs!"

In 1908 occurred an event that threw a deep shadow of care and worry and heart-breaking work across the last six years of Muir's life – years that otherwise would have gone into books which perforce have been left forever unwritten. We refer to the granting of a permit by James R. Garfield, then Secretary of the Interior, to the city of San Francisco to invade the Yosemite National Park in order to convert the beautiful Hetch-Hetchy Valley into a reservoir. In Muir's opinion it was the greatest breach of sound conservation principles in a whole century of improvidence, and in the dark and devious manner of its final accomplishment a good many things still wait to be brought to light. The following letter to Theodore Roosevelt, then serving his second term in the White House, is a frank presentation of the issues involved.

to Theodore Roosevelt

[Martinez, California, April 21st, 1908]

DEAR MR. PRESIDENT

I am anxious that the Yosemite National Park may be saved from all sorts of commercialism and marks of man's work other than the roads, hotels, etc., required to make its wonders and blessings available. For as far as I have seen there is not in all the wonderful Sierra, or indeed in the world, another so grand and wonderful and useful a block of Nature's mountain handiwork.

There is now under consideration, as doubtless you well know, an application of San Francisco supervisors for the use of the Hetch-Hetchy Valley and Lake Eleanor as storage reservoirs for a city water supply. This application should, I think, be denied, especially the Hetch-Hetchy part, for this Valley, as you will see by the inclosed description, is a counterpart of Yosemite, and one of the most sublime and beautiful and important features of the Park, and to dam and submerge it would be hardly less destructive and deplorable in its effect on the Park in general than would be the damming of Yosemite itself. For its falls and groves and delightful camp-grounds are surpassed or equalled only in Yosemite, and furthermore it is the hall of entrance to the grand Tuolumne Canyon, which opens a wonderful way to the magnificent Tuolumne Meadows, the focus of pleasure travel in the Park and the grand central camp-ground. If Hetch-Hetchy should be submerged, as proposed, to a depth of one hundred and seventy-five feet, not only would the Meadows be made utterly inaccessible along the Tuolumne, but this glorious canyon way to the High Sierra would be blocked.

I am heartily in favour of a Sierra or even a Tuolumne water supply for San Francisco, but all the water required can be obtained from sources outside the Park, leaving the twin valleys, Hetch-Hetchy and Yosemite, to the use they were intended for when the Park was established. For every argument advanced for making one into a reservoir would apply with equal force to the other, excepting the cost of the required dam.

The few promoters of the present scheme are not unknown around the boundaries of the Park, for some of them have been trying to break through for years. However able they may be as capitalists, engineers, lawyers, or even philanthropists, none of the statements they have made descriptive of Hetch-Hetchy dammed or undammed is true. But they all show forth the proud sort of confidence that comes of a good, sound, substantial irrefragable ignorance.

For example, the capitalist Mr. James D. Phelan says, "There are a thousand places in the Sierra equally as beautiful as Hetch-Hetchy: it is inaccessible nine months of the year, and is an unlivable place the other three months because of mosquitoes." On the contrary, there is not another of its kind in all the Park excepting Yosemite. It is accessible all the year, and is not more mosquitoful than Yosemite. "The conversion of Hetch-

Hetchy into a reservoir will simply mean a lake instead of a meadow." But Hetch-Hetchy is not a meadow: it is a Yosemite Valley .... These sacred mountain temples are the holiest ground that the heart of man has consecrated, and it behooves us all faithfully to do our part in seeing that our wild mountain parks are passed on unspoiled to those who come after us, for they are national properties in which every man has a right and interest.

I pray therefore that the people of California be granted time to be heard before this reservoir question is decided, for I believe that as soon as light is cast upon it, nine tenths or more of even the citizens of San Francisco would be opposed to it. And what the public opinion of the world would be may be guessed by the case of the Niagara Falls.

Faithfully and devotedly yours
JOHN MUIR

[P.S.]   Oh for a tranquil camp hour with you like those beneath the sequoias in memorable 1903!

Muir did not know at the time, and it was a discouraging shock to discover the fact, that Chief Forester Gifford Pinchot had on May 28th, 1906, written a letter to a San Francisco city official not only suggesting, but urging, that San Francisco "make provision for a water supply from the Yosemite National Park." In the work of accomplishing this scheme, he declared, "I will stand ready to render any assistance in my power." Six months later he wrote again to the same official, saying: "I cannot, of course, attempt to forecast the action of the new Secretary of the Interior [Mr. Garfield] on the San Francisco watershed question, but my advice to you is to assume that his attitude will be favourable, and to make the necessary preparations to set the case before him. I had supposed from an item in the paper that the city had definitely given up the Lake Eleanor plan and had purchased one of the other systems."

It was not surprising that his forecast of an action, which he already stood pledged to further with any means in his power, although he knew other sources to be available, proved correct. Neither Mr. Pinchot nor Mr. Garfield had so much as seen the Valley, and the language of the latter's permit shows that his decision was reached on partisan misrepresentations of its character which were later disproved in public hearings when the San Francisco authorities, unable to proceed with the revocable Garfield permit, applied to Congress for a confirmation of it through an exchange of lands. To take one of the two greatest wonders of the Yosemite National Park and hand it over, as the New York *Independent* justly observed, "without even the excuse of a real necessity, to the nearest hungry municipality that asks for it, is nothing less than conservation buried and staked to the ground. Such guardianship of our national resources would make every national park the backyard annex of a neighbouring city."

Muir's letter to Roosevelt showed him that his official advisers were thinking more of political favour than of the integrity of the people's playground; that, in short, a mistake had been made; and he wrote Muir that he would endeavour to have the project confined to Lake Eleanor. But his administration came to an end without definite steps taken in the matter one way or another. President Taft, however, and Secretary Ballinger directed the city and county of San Francisco, in 1910, "to show why the Hetch-Hetchy Valley should not be eliminated from the Garfield permit." President Taft also directed the War Department to appoint an Advisory Board of Army Engineers to assist the Secretary of the Interior in passing upon the matters submitted to the Interior Department under the order to show cause.

In March, 1911, Secretary Ballinger was succeeded by Walter L. Fisher, during whose official term the city authorities requested and obtained five separate continuances, apparently in the hope that a change of administration would give them the desired political pull at Washington. Meantime the Advisory Board of Army Engineers reported: "The Board is of the opinion that there are several sources of water supply that could be obtained and used by the City of San Francisco and adjacent communities to supplement the nearby supplies as the necessity develops. From any one of these sources the water is sufficient in quantity and is, or can be made suitable in quality, while the engineering difficulties are not insurmountable. The determining factor is principally one of cost."

Under policies of National Park protection now generally acknowledged to be binding upon those who are charged to administer them for the public good, the finding of the army engineers should have made it impossible to destroy the Hetch-Hetchy Valley for a mere commercial difference in the cost of securing a supply of water from any one of several other adequate sources. But, as Muir states in one of his letters, "the wrong prevailed over the best aroused sentiment of the entire country."

The compensating good which he felt sure would arise, even out of this tragic sacrifice, must be sought in the consolidation of public sentiment against any possible repetition of such a raid. In this determined public sentiment, aroused by Muir's leadership in the long fight, his spirit still is watching over the people's playgrounds.

ADDENDUM

Letters Written During a Trip to Scotland and Europe, 1893

Editor's Note: In addition to the letters on Muir's European trip selected by William Badè (pp.313–318), further unpublished letters from the Holt-Atherton collection have been selected as a brief record of Muir's travels and his observations on the effects of glaciation in the Highlands, the Lake District, Norway and Switzerland.

to Helen and Wanda Muir

Steamship Chevalier,
Near Oban, July [23rd],1893.

HELLO HELEN AND WANDA

My two darling babies, I am on a steamboat sailing down through the midst of beautiful islands along the coast of Scotland on my way to Glasgow and Edinburgh. You can see the brown heather on the hills and the sheep scattered about like white dots. It is all beautiful hereabouts like the coast of Alaska, only there are very few trees. All the hills and mountains are green and brown, with grass and bushes and heather. The heather where it is thickest makes the brownish patches. The heather is a good deal like Cassiope, a small shrub tufty and dense and makes delightful fragrant beds for Highlanders and all lovers of fresh, flowery, breezy wildness. I have not yet climbed the Scotch hills to find out much about heather. I have seen two species, the bell and the common kind. It seldom grows higher than a foot or so, two feet at most. It is very hardy though so lovely, and will endure any amount of trampling, nibbling and burning. The sheep eat it, and heather mutton may well be the best.

O how I would like to camp out on these shaggy hills, but I must make haste to get back to my babies. I have to go to Norway a week or two and then to Switzerland, and the time flies fast. The steamer shakes so much with the machinery I can hardly write.

It is a cloudy day and showery at times, but the sun just now is streaming its mellow light through shifting openings and making many a bright golden patch on the green brown hills, and the water sparkles and glints and shines like silver.

I must go in haste. We change steamers here. Ever, my darlings,

Your loving father,
JOHN MUIR

to Helen Muir

North of Scotland & Orkney & Shetland
Steam Navigation Co. "St Sunniva,"
August 1st, 1893.

MY DEAR HELEN

Norway is out of sight and we are near Bonnie Scotland again. I see the green hills and the high rocks along the shore and the white waves fringing them like pretty lace. We are near a queer old Scotch town called Aberdeen and soon we will land there, and then we will go to Leith near Edinburgh. We will get to Leith tonight, and the long sail over the beautiful water will be done. Everybody says we have had a lovely time in Norway.

Good morning, Midge. I am in Edinburgh now, and in a few minutes I will be going on the cars to Wordsworth's country in England. Then to London and Basle, Switzerland. I fondly hope you and Wanda and Mama and Grandma are well. I have not heard from you since leaving New York, and it seems a long time. I suppose your letters are all in London at the London, Paris, and American Bank Limited, which is the best address. Tell Mama to address letters there, and I will have them forwarded wherever I may be. It is raining today, but I have a good waterproof.

Here are a few more Naradale and Romsdale flowers and love to all. I'll be home, my darlings. Heaven bless you.   Goodbye,

J.M.

to William Keith

Hotel Metropole, London,
August 8th, 1893.

DEAR WILLIE

Wandering Willie, where in all this confused world of streets, cars, hotel, stations, etc., are you? I got to Liverpool July 1st by the Etruria, and feeling sure you were off to Spain gave up all hope in my infantile loneliness of finding [you]. Most of the time since then I couldn't even find myself, and yet on the whole I've had a sort of good time. I went to Edinburgh and there David Douglas, a publisher to whom I had a letter, took pity on me and looked after me. Then I went to Dunbar and found a cousin of the old home and the school where I was thrashed. Thence back to Edinburgh, thence to Dumfries, thence to Stirling and through the Trossachs to Oban, to Leith, and thence to Norway. Had a glorious glacial and other times there. Thence back to Edinburgh and thence to Windermere, Grassmere [Grasmere], etc., a charming region – to London – arrived here yesterday. Tomorrow I start for Switzerland. Then perhaps a little more of the north of Scotland and home. I heard from home today. All well. Expect to get back to Edinburgh by the end of the month, perhaps, and home by the end of October.

I hope you and Mrs.K. had a good time, but your Scotch or Swedenborgian conscience must have been sore at times. My address till the end of this month is London, Paris, and American Bank Limited. Later it will be David Douglas, 10 Castle Street, Edinburgh.

Hoping to meet in S. F., I am,

Yours,

J. MUIR

to Mrs Muir

Hotel Metropole, London,
August 8th, 1893.

DEAR LOUIE

Wanda has so often mentioned some trouble about your eyes and Grandma's that I feel distressed about it. At first I thought it was only some cold, but the cause seems to be in something more serious, since it lasts so long. Do try to take better care of your health. Above all, don't worry about things. I feel lonesome whenever I set out on a new journey like this one to London or Switzerland, but I soon gain friends and feel better as soon as I can talk to people. Even after riding only an hour or two in a car the people I have spoken to shake hands with me at parting, saying "I'm glad, sir, I have met you. I'm truly obliged to you for your information, and I wish you a safe and happy journey." On the trip of twelve days to Norway almost everybody on the ship thanked me for what I told them about the scenery, the shaping of the mountains, etc., and there was a grand hearty shaking of hands and invitations to their homes when we were parting. Although the Scotch and English are so reserved and slow to make new friends, I do believe I could spend all the balance of my life in visits at the homes of these same conservative people.

I learned so much in my own special studies in Norway. It was all like a language that with painstaking industry I had learned elsewhere. This alone was well worth the time and cost of the summer's trip. The trips in Scotland were also telling in a glacial way, and I find myself able to get hold of the general main facts in the history of all the lands I have seen in a very short time.

The trip to the English Lake District was perfectly delightful in every way. Such lovely glacier lakes – the shores curving in and out, fringed with charming woods, green islands here and there, and mountains and hills all green and bosky all around, flowers from lilies to heather in glorious abundance and beautiful cottages and mansions all steeped in fine associations. The hotels even are picturesque and charming, and I never before saw a place where I was so anxious to have you with me to enjoy it. Surely after spending so much of your life, worried with drought and weeds and hired

you should get one good look at the world and the best it can show. This I
look forward to when the babies grow big. Here are some leaves I picked for
you from the branches leaning over Wordsworth's grave.

With love to Grandma and everybody, I am,

Ever yours,

JOHN MUIR

to Mrs Margaret Hay Lunam and daughter*

Hotel Metropole, London,.
August 8th, 1893

DEAR COUSINS TWO
I feel woefully lost here, and yet I've had a good time in many ways since I left you.
I went to Dumfries without getting much lost, and found Susan. I fell in love with
her and would have stayed with her an extravagant and unreasonable time had it not
been for the illness of Mrs. McKie. So I left her next day after my arrival, showing
in this great and praiseworthy self denial. Then I went to Stirling, and through the
Trossachs to Oban; thence to Edinburgh by Glasgow, and next morning sailed from
Leith to Norway: thence back to Edinburgh; thence to Windermere, Grasmere, etc.
and thence to this grand and glorious, lonely wilderness, London. The Highland trip
was very fine, but the Norway one was truly glorious, and besides the pure pleasure
I gained many grand glacial facts bearing on earth sculpture and earth beauty.

Windermere was lovely, charming aside from its Wordsworthian associations,
and I gained glacial facts there too into the bargain. All these beautiful and famous
lakes are Glacier lakes, and every line in the noble landscapes there are glacial lines.
What a pity it is that Wordsworth, with all his fine feeling for nature, died without
any knowledge of the glacial gospel.

I got here last night and I start tomorrow morning for Switzerland. I expect to go
to Dover, Brussels, Basle, Lucerne, Interlaken, Grindelwald, Lauterbrunnen,
Lausanne, Zermatt, Martingny, Chamounix, Geneva, Berne, etc., etc. and hope to
get back about the end of this month: then go to the north of Scotland again, and
perhaps to Elgin, Melrose, etc; spend a few days at Liverpool and get off for home
about the last week of September. Write me Care of David Douglas, Esq., 10 Castle
St., Edinburgh, before I get back from Switzerland, letting me know when you will
be in Dunbar, for if you are not there I will not go back. In case you don't get back
in time I hope you can meet me elsewhere and have Maggie go to the Hays with me.

Ever cordially yours,

JOHN MUIR

[P.S.] My love to Cousin Mather.

---

* Badè notes that the original of this letter is in the possession of Miss Margaret Rae [Hay?] Lunam,
Dunbar, Scotland.

to Wanda Muir

Hotel Belvedere, Switzerland,
August 25th, 1893.

Dear Wanda

I began a letter to you in Italy but was interrupted before I had got far and so I begin again from here. I think I wrote to Mama and Helen from Chamonix, which I suppose you know, is in France. From there I went through grand scenery to Geneva – a beautiful town on a beautiful lake surrounded with vineyards and charming homes. Thence I went to Neufchatel, another beautiful and quaint old town on the shore of a lovely lake more than twenty miles long. Here the great and famous Louis Agassiz was once a professor before he went to America. Next day I went across the famous Jura Mountains through many wild gorges and tunnels to Basle, a big town on the famous river Rhine. Thence to Zurick [Zürich], the most beautiful, I think, of all the towns of Switzerland, and the Lake of Zurick is also more beautiful than I can tell – such lovely pale blue glacier water – such picturesque shores – such grand icy mountains in the distance. From Zurick next day I went to a queer ancient place more than five hundred years old, some of it about a thousand, called Chur or Coire. The way to it was so beautiful and wonderful that if I should try to tell you about [it] more than a hundred pages would be needed. A good deal of the scenery was like Yosemite Valley. The Rhine runs through most of it – that is, one of the upper glacier tributaries of the Rhine.

Next day from Chur I went over the mountains in a kind of stage called a diligence to Chivianno [Chiavenna] in Italy by the wildest pass and wildest road I ever saw – especially the road – such wonderful feats of engineering – hundreds of loops and spirals cut in the solid granite and arched ways built solidly of lime and hewn stone. Part of this road ran from seven or eight miles through the Via Mala and part down the wall of a wild Yosemite valley. The pass is called the Splügen – strange that such places have never been described. I could spend a lifetime writing about what I [have] seen in these few weeks. My what vineyards I saw up among the rough rocks, and what a queer town is Chivianno, and what lots of queer muggins of boys and girls, black-eyed and barefooted. And how hot and tired I was at night when I got down over all the wild loops and folds of the road, past all the pretty waterfalls, and the grand mountains and the glaciers, and through all the miles and miles of chestnut woods. Chivianno is at the bottom of a deep valley like Yosemite. I looked out of my window before going to bed and above a great rock 3000 feet high I saw the three stars of the handle of the big dipper, and four cottages shining white high up [on] the rock looked like the rest of the constellation. Next day I rode thirty miles more to see the famous Lake Como, said to be the most beautiful of all the Italian lakes, and oftentimes spoken of by geologists as being very wonderful on account of its surface being about a thousand feet above the sea and its bottom about a thousand feet below it, but I saw nothing strange in this, for the level of the sea has no necessary relationship with the bottoms of lakes such as these. It is simply a grand glacier lake – but I fear this sort of thing you will not understand. Well, I sailed on this lovely mountain lake from a place called Colico to another queer and beautiful old Italian town called Managgio. Then back to Chivianno, and wasn't I tired again, though my cough is much better. When I turned back yesterday from Managgio I then commenced my journey home. Today I came here in diligence from Chivianno, another wonderful day's ride through chestnut groves, vineyards, wild forests of larch and spruce, grand mountains, and O dear! I don't know all what, but I'm sleepy and tired and it is late and I ought to be in bed, for I have to get up tomorrow morning about 4 o'clock to take the stage for a place called Davos or Dorf over another pass, etc., Then I'll try to get to Lake Constance and the falls of the Rhine at Schaffhausen, and then to Basle and straight back to London. Then a day or two in Scotland. Ho! for America and Martinez. And now, Wanda, if ever you mean to travel hereabouts, learn to speak French. My! what a mess I make of it. Even the dogs don't understand it as I speak it and refuse to wag their tails to my "bon chien, bon chien." Not one person in ten thousand understands English, and when I try chinook or pidgin English it does no good. I must go to bed. Goodnight, goodnight, goodnight. Love to you my dear Wanda – to you all. Many kisses for Helen. Tell Mama I'll write in a day or two.

[JOHN MUIR]

[P.S.] The Engadine Valley 6000 feet above the sea, with a row of glaciers poking their blunt cold blue noses down over the walls on either side, and a row of lovely green and blue lakes along the bottom, beautiful flowery meadows about their shores dotted with queer castles, chateaux, and cottages, dark forests of spruce and larch between the meadows and glaciers – sharp jaggedy peaks above the glaciers, and a lovely blue sky over all. Some Engadine flowers I picked tonight. I hope I'll get letters at London. It seems so long since I saw or heard you. Hello, Midge, I'm throwing you lots of kisses across the mountains and sea.

STUDIES IN THE SIERRA
and other essays

Studies in the
Sierra

and other essays

''Studies in the Sierra'' were first published (in serial form) in 1874–75
in the *Overland Monthly*, San Francisco
and republished in the *Sierra Club Bulletin*, Vols IX–X1 (1915–21).

CONTENTS

A reconstruction of Yosemite Valley before and after glaciation. The upper end of the valley would have been deepened by 600 metres and the lower end by 200 metres. This hollow would have been filled by a lake that steadily silted up to form a fertile valley bed.

CHAPTER ONE

Mountain Sculpture

IN THE BEGINNING of the long glacial winter, the lofty Sierra seems to have consisted of one vast undulated wave, in which a thousand separate mountains, with their domes and spires, their innumerable canyons and lake basins, lay concealed. In the development of these, the Master Builder chose for a tool, not the earthquake nor lightning to rend and split asunder, not the stormy torrent nor eroding rain, but the tender snowflowers, noiselessly falling through unnumbered seasons, the offspring of the sun and sea. If we should attempt to restore the range to its pre-glacial unsculptured condition, its network of profound canyons would have to be filled up, together with all its lake and meadow basins; and every rock and peak, however lofty, would have to be buried again beneath the fragments which the glaciers have broken off and carried away. Careful study of the phenomena presented warrants the belief that the unglaciated condition of the range was comparatively simple; yet the double summits about the head of Kern River and Lake Tahoe, and the outlying spurs of Hoffmann and Merced, would appear to indicate the primary existence of considerable depressions and elevations. Even these great features, however, may be otherwise accounted for.

All classes of glacial phenomena are displayed in the Sierra on the grandest scale, furnishing unmistakable proof of the universality of the ice-sheet beneath whose heavy folds all her sublime landscapes were moulded. Her ice winter is now nearly ended, and her flanks are clothed with warm forests; but in high latitudes, north and south, and in many lofty mountains, it still prevails with variable severity. Greenland and the lands near the South Pole are undergoing glaciation of the most comprehensive kind, and present noble illustrations of the physical and climatic conditions under which the Sierra lay when all the sublime pages of her history were sealed up. The lofty Himalaya, the Alps, and the mountains of Norway are more open, their glacial covering having separated into distinct glaciers that flow down their valleys like rivers, illustrating a similar glacial condition in the Sierra, when all her valleys and canyons formed channels for separate ice-rivers. These have but recently vanished, and when we trace their retiring footsteps back to their fountains among the high summits, we discover small residual glaciers in considerable numbers, lingering beneath cool shadows, silently completing the sculpture of the summit peaks.

The transition from one to the other of these different glacial conditions was gradual and shadow-like. When the great cycle of icy years was nearly accomplished, the glacial mantle began to shrink along the bottom; domes and crests rose like islets above its white surface, long dividing ridges began to appear, and distinct glacier rivers flowed between. These gradually became feeble and torpid. Frost-enduring carices and hardy pines pushed upward along every moraine and sun-warmed slope, closing steadily upon the retreating glaciers, which, like shreds of summer clouds, at length disappeared from the young and sunny landscapes.

We can easily understand that an ice-sheet hundreds or thousands of feet in thickness, slipping heavily down the flanks of a mountain chain, will wear its surface unequally, according to the varying hardness and compactness of its rocks; but these are not the only elements productive of inequalities. Glaciers do not only wear and grind rocks by slipping over them, as a tool wears the stone upon which it is whetted; they also crush and break, carrying away vast quantities of rock, not only in the form of mud and sand, but of splinters and blocks, from a few inches to forty or fifty feet in diameter.

The whole mass of the Sierra, as far as our observation has reached, is built up of brick-like blocks, whose forms and dimensions are determined chiefly by the degree of development of elected *planes of cleavage*, which individualise them, and make them separable from one another while yet forming undisturbed parts of the mountain. The force which binds these blocks together is not everywhere equal; therefore, when they are subjected to the strain of glaciers, they are torn apart in an irregular and indeterminate manner, giving rise to endless variety of rock forms.

The granite in some portions of the range is crumbling like meal by the decomposition of its feldspar throughout the mass, but the greater portion has suffered scarcely any disintegration since the close of the glacial period. These harder areas display three series of cleavage or separating planes, two nearly vertical, the other horizontal, which, when fully developed, divide the rock into nearly regular parallelopipeds. The effects of this separable structure upon the glacial erodibility of rocks will be at once appreciated. In order that we may know how mountain chains are taken apart, it is important that we first learn how they are put together; and now that we have ascertained the fact that the Sierra, instead of bang a huge wrinkle of the earth's crust without any determinate structure, is built up of regularly formed stones like a work of art, we have made a great advance in our mountain studies; we may now understand the Scripture: "He hath builded the mountains," as not merely a figurative but a literal expression.

In order that we may obtain some adequate estimate of the geological value of this cleavage factor in the production of canyons, rock forms, and separate mountains, with their varied sculpture, wc must endeavour to find out its range, variations, and what forces are favourable to its development; what are the effects of its suppression in one place, and development in another; what are the effects of the unequal development of the several series. In the prosecution of these inquiries, we soon discover that the middle region of the west flank is most favourable for our purposes, because the lower is covered to a great extent with soil, and the upper, consisting of sharp peaks, is so shattered, or rather has *all* the various planes so fully developed, we are unable to study them in their simple, uncombined conditions. But the middle region, while it has all its cleavage phenomena on the largest scale both of magnitude and specialisation, is also simple and less obscured by forests and surface weathering, and affords the deepest, as well as widest naked sections, the former in Yosemite canyons, the latter in flat basins like those of Yosemite Creek, Lake Tenaya, and upper Tuolumne Valley, wherein broad areas of glacier-polished granite are spread out, as clean and unblurred as new maps.

I should have stated that the three series of cutting planes mentioned above are not the only ones existing in these rocks, but we will consider them first, because they are most marked in their modes of development, and have come most prominently into play in the formation of those unrivalled canyons and rocks which have made the Sierra famous. In studying their direction and range, we find that they extend along the west flank from latitude 36° to 40° at least, and from the summit to the soil-covered foot-hills, and in all probability further observation would show *that they are co-extensive with the length and breadth of the chain.* We measured the direction of the strike of hundreds, belonging to the two vertical series, many of which run unbrokenly for miles in a tolerably uniform course, the better developed ones nearly at right angles to the axis of the range, the other parallel with it. Canyon sections show that they cleave the granite

Fig. 1 Homogenous domes (A,B,C,D) and cleavage planes (with Muir's original notation).

vertically to a depth of 5000 feet without betraying any tendency to give out. The horizontal series appear also to be universal. In some places these divisional planes are extended within a few inches of each other, while in others only one conspicuous seam is visible in a breadth of bare rock half a mile in extent. Again, many large domes occur that exhibit none of these planes, and appear to be as entirely homogeneous in structure as leaden balls. Thus, let Fig.1 represent a horizontal section of the range; A, B, C, D, cones and conoides where none of the cleavage planes appear. The question

here arises, are these domed portions cleavageless, or do they possess the
same cleavage as the surrounding rock, in an undeveloped or latent condition?
Careful observation proves the latter proposition to be the true one, for on
the warm and moist surfaces of some of the older domes we detect the
appearance of incipient planes running parallel with the others, and in general
wherever any rock apparently homogeneous in structure is acted upon by
the spray of a waterfall, its cleavage planes will appear. We may conclude,
therefore, that however numerous the areas may be which seem solid and
equal in structure, they are still traversed in definite directions by invisible

Fig. 2 Parallelopipedal blocks at the foot of a dome at the head of Yosemite Fall.

Fig. 3 Closely jointed granite tower
on Mount Hoffman.

Fig. 4 The steeply dipping cleavage
planes of the Three Brothers.

Fig. 5   The relationship of cleavage planes to roof shape and
gable-end forms in Tuolumne Canyon

cutting planes, which render them separable when the conditions required
for their development have been supplied.

Fig. 2 represents the side of a dome at the head of Yosemite Fall, with
parallelopipedal blocks developed along its base. The development of the
brick structure is probably due to spray blown back from the brow of the fan
in storms. It is to the development of these brick-making planes by long-
continued atmospheric action, that the picturesque ruins so frequently met
with on lofty summits are due. Where only one of the cutting vertical series
has been developed in a granitic region otherwise strong in its physical
structure, and a sufficient amount of glacial force exerted in a favourable
direction has been concentrated upon it, its rocks have been broken up in
flakes and slabs, and those majestic mural precipices produced which constitute
so sublime a part of the Yosemitic scenery of the Sierra. Fig. 3 represents a
granite tower on the crest of Mount Hoffmann, composed of jointed blocks.

Another series of cutting planes which pass diagonally through those we
have been considering, give rise to pyramidal and roof-shaped forms. This
diagonal cleavage is found in its fullest development in the metamorphic
slate of the summit, producing the sharp-pointed peaks for which the summit
region is noted. To it is also due the huge gables which are found in
Yosemite and Tuolumne canyons, such as the Three Brothers, and the
pointed rock adjoining the Royal Arches. Fig. 4 represents the highest of the
Three Brothers, Yosemite Valley, illustrating *diagonal cleavage in Granite*;
and Fig. 5 is a gable on the south wall of the big Tuolumne Canyon. It will

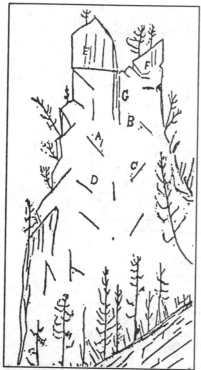

Fig. 6 Diagonal and rectangular cleavage planes and resultant rock form near El Capitan.

be at once perceived that the forms contained in Fig. 6 (a rock situated near the small side canyon which separates El Capitan and the Three Brothers, in Yosemite Valley), have resulted from the partial development of both diagonal and rectangular cleavage joints. At A, B, C, D incipient diagonal planes are beginning to appear on the otherwise solid front. Some of the planes which have separated the two summit blocks, E and F, may be seen at G.

The greatest check to the free play and controlling power of these divisional planes is the occurrence, in immense numbers and size, of domes, cones, and round wave-ridges, together with an innumerable brood of modified forms and combinations. The curved cleavage which measures and determines these rounded forms, may be designated *the dome cleavage*, inasmuch as the dome is apparently the most perfect typical form of the group.

Domes of close-grained silicious granite are admirably calculated to withstand the action of atmospheric and mechanical forces. No other rock form can compare with it in strength; no other offered so unflinching a resistance to the tremendous pressure of the glaciers. A dam of noble domes extends across the head of Yosemite Valley, from Mount Starr King to North Dome, which was effectually broken through by the combined force of the Hoffmann and Tenaya glaciers; but the great south Lyell glacier, which entered the valley between Starr King and Half Dome, was unable to force the mighty barrier, and the approach of the long summer which terminated the glacial epoch, found it still mazing and swedging compliantly among the strong unflinching bosses, just as the winds are compelled to do at the present time.

The Starr King group of domes (Fig. 7) is perhaps the most interesting of the Merced basin. The beautiful conoid, Starr King, the loftiest and most perfect of the group, was one of the first to emerge from the glacial sea, and ere its new-born brightness was marred by storms, dispersed light like a crystal island over the snowy expanse in which it stood alone. The moraine at the base is planted with a very equal growth of manzanita.

There appear to be no positive limits to the extent of dome structure in the granites of the Sierra, when considered in all its numerous modifications.

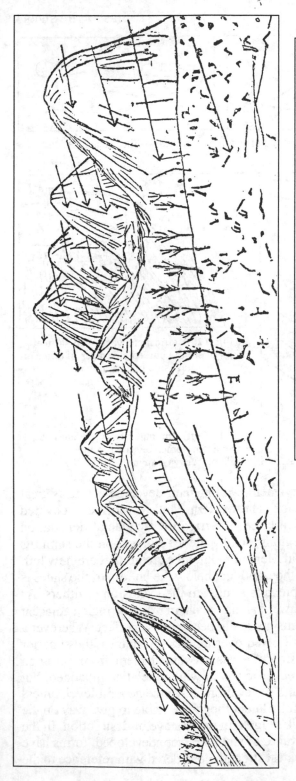

Fig. 7   The Starr King group of domes –
arrows indicate the direction of the flow of ice

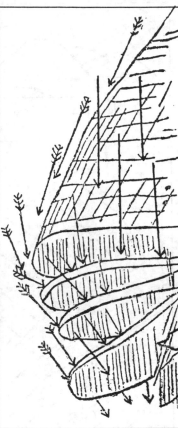

Fig. 8   A rock dome with vertical cleavage
planes and down-slope removal of fractured
rock by ice (seen in Tuolomne Canyon).

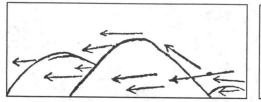

Figs 9 and 10   Ice movement and shaping of domes without cleavages.

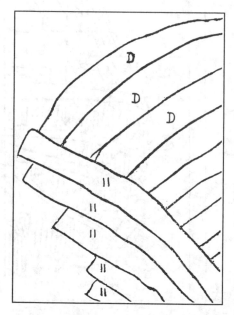

Fig. 12   Vertical cleavages (30–40 feet high) overlying curved cleavages of dome on east side of El Capitan.

Fig. 11 (left)   Internal cleavage planes of adjacent domes revealed in the walls of Tenaya Canyon.

Rudimentary domes exist everywhere, waiting their development, to as great a depth as observation can reach. The western flank was formerly covered with slates, which have evidently been carried off by glacial denudation from the middle and upper regions; small patches existing on the summits and spurs of the Hoffmann and Merced mountains are all that are now left. When a depth of two or three thousand feet below the bottom of the slates is reached, the dome structure prevails almost to the exclusion of others. As we proceed southward or northward along the chain from the region adjacent to Yosemite Valley, dome forms gradually become less perfect. Wherever a broad sheet of glacier ice has flowed over a region of domes, the superior strength of their concentric structure has prevented them from being so extensively denuded as the weaker forms in which they lie embedded; but after thus obtaining a considerable elevation above the general level, unless their cleavage planes were wholly latent they were liable to give way on the lower side, producing forms like Fig. 8, in every stage of destruction. In the case of rocks wherein no cleavages of any kind were developed, forms have resulted which express the greatest strength considered with reference to the weight and direction of the glacier that overflowed them. Their most common form is given in Fig. 9. Some of their cross-sections are approximately given in Fig. 10. But few examples are to be found where cleavage and irregularity of hardness do not come in to complicate the problem, in the production of that variety of which nature is so fond.

We have already seen that domes offer no absolute barrier to the passage of vertical and horizontal cleavage planes; but it is also true that domes cut one another. Fig. 11 is a section obtained near the head of a remarkably deep and crooked gorge in the Tenaya Canyon, four miles above Mirror Lake. The broken edges of the concentric layers of a dome, marked "II", present themselves on the overleaning wall of the gorge, and upon the buried dome whose section thus appears another dome is resting, furnishing conclusive evidence that a series of concentric shells which form a dome may be cut by another series of the same kind giving rise to domes within domes and domes upon domes.

Fig. 12 represents bricks, thirty or forty feet in height, placed directly upon a smooth, well-curved dome, which dome, in turn, is borne upon or rather stands out from a yet larger dome-curved surface forming a portion of the east side of El Capitan rock, near the top.

The Tuolumne middle region presents a sublime assemblage of glacier-born rocks, of which a general view may be obtained from the summit of Mount Hoffmann. These were overswept by the wide outlets of the great Tuolumne *mer de glace*. The Tuolumne Canyon outlet flowed across the edges of the best developed or north 35° east vertical cleavage planes, which gave rise to an extraordinary number of rocks, like Fig. 8, with their split and fractured faces invariably turned downstream, and round abraded sides up against the ice-current.

This glaciated landscape is unrivalled in general effect, combining as it does so many elements of sublimity. The summit mountains, majestic monuments of glacial force, rise grandly along the azure sky. The brown Tuolumne meadow, level as a floor, is spread in front, and on either side a broad swath of sombre pines, interrupted with many small meadow openings, around the edges of which the forest presses in smooth close lines. On the level bottom of the *mer de glace*, mountains once stood, which have been broken and swept away during the ice-winter like loose stones from a pavement. Where the deep glacial flood began to break down into the region of domes, a vast number of rock forms are seen on which their glacial history is written in lines of noble simplicity.

No attribute of this glacial landscape is more remarkable than the map-like distinctness of its varied features. The directions and magnitudes of the main ice-currents, with their numerous subordinate streams, together with the history of their fluctuations and final death, are eloquently expressed in the specific rocks, hills, meadows, and valleys over which they flowed red. No commercial highway of the sea, edged with buoys and lamps, or of the land, with fences and guide-boards, is so unmistakably marked as these long-abandoned highways of the dead glaciers.

If, from some outlook still more comprehensive, the attentive observer contemplates the wide flank of the Sierra, furrowed with canyons, dimpled with lake basins, and waved with ridges and domes, he will quickly perceive that its present architectural surface is not the one upon which the first snows of the glacial winter fell, because, with the simple exceptions of the jagged summit-peaks from whose *névé* fountains the glaciers descended, there exists over all the broad flank of the range not one weak rock form. All that remain to roughen and undulate the surface are strong domes, or ridge-waves, or crests, with pavement-like levels or solid-walled canyons between. All the rest have been broken up and swept away by the glaciers. Some apparent exceptions to this general truth will present themselves, but these will gradually disappear in the light of patient investigation. The observer will learn that near the summit ice-fountains there are absolutely no exceptions, even in appearance, and that it is only when he follows down in the paths of the glaciers, and thus comes among rocks which were longer left bare by them in their gradual recession, that he begins to find instances of rocks at once weak in structure and strong in form.

The regular transition from strong to weak rocks will indicate that the greater weakness of those farther removed from the summits, is due to some force or forces which acted upon them subsequently to the time they were sustaining the wear and tear of the glaciers. The causes of this afterweakness are various. First we may note the most apparent – the slow decomposition of the mass of the rock by the atmosphere, under favourable conditions of heat and moisture. Some varieties of granite crumbled rapidly by the decomposition of their feldspar throughout the mass. Rocks traversed by feldspathic veins, that are otherwise strong, fall apart on the decomposition of the veins, into a heap of loose blocks. Frost also, combined with moisture, produces a wasted, shattered appearance. But far the most general and influential cause of the feeble condition of old rocks, which formerly withstood

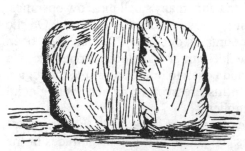

Fig. 13 Decomposition of a granite block along a felspar rich vein.

the terrible ordeal of glacial action, is the subsequent development of one or several of their cleavage planes. For example, here is (Fig. 13) a boulder of hard metamorphic slate, which, after withstanding many a crush and blow in its winter history, until its angles were worn and battered, at length, on the recession of the glacier to which it belonged, came to rest on a smooth hard pavement, so level that it could not have rolled or fallen to its present position. Yet it is now split in two, having fallen apart by its own weight, on the ripening of one of its cleavage planes, just as the valves of seeds ripen, open, and fall.

Fig. 14 is a profile view of a rock 200 yards from the head of the Yosemite Fall, which is now weak and ready to fall apart by the development of the vertical north 35° east cleavage planes, the edges of which are seen in front; yet it is certain that this rock was once subjected to the strain of the oversweeping Yosemite basin glacier, when on its way to join the main trunk Yosemite glacier in the valley.

Fig. 14 The decomposition of granite along cleavage planes since the retreat of the ice

Fig. 15   Elongated long diameter of ruinous and crumbling dome indicates
shaping by oversweeping ice current.

Fig. 15 is a ruinous dome-top on the divide between Yosemite Creek basin and cascade. The beginner in such studies would not perceive that it had been overswept; yet hard portions near the base show clear evidence of glacial action, and, though ruinous and crumbling, it will at once appear to the educated eye that its longer diameter is exactly in the direction of the oversweeping ice-current, as indicated in the figure by the arrows. Rock masses, hundreds or even thousands of feet in height, abound in the channels of the ancient glaciers, which illustrate this argument by presenting examples in every stage of decay, the most decayed always occurring just where they have been longest exposed to disintegrating and general weathering agents.

The record of ice phenomena, as sculptured, scratched, and worn upon the mountain surfaces, is like any other writing, faint and blurred according to the length of time and hard usage to which it has been exposed. It is plain, therefore, that the present sculptured condition of the Sierra is due to the action of ice and the variously developed cleavage planes and concentric seams which its rocks contain. The architect may build his structures out of any kind of stone, without their forms betraying the physical characters of the stone employed; but in Sierra architecture, *the style always proclaims the nature of the rock.*

In walking the sublime canyon streets of the Sierra, when we see an arch spanning the pine groves, we know that there is the section of a glacier-broken dome; where a gable presents itself, we recognise the split end of a ridge, with diagonal cleavage planes developed atop, and these again cut by a vertical plane in front. If a sheer precipice springs from the level turf thousands of feet into the sky, there we know the rock is very hard, and has but one of its vertical cutting planes developed. If domes and cones appear, there we know the concentric structure predominates. No matter how abundant the glacial force, *a vertical precipice can not be produced unless its cleavage be vertical,* nor a dome without dome structure in the rock acted upon. Therefore, when we say that the glacial ice-sheet and separate glaciers *moulded* the mountains, we must remember that their moulding power upon *hard granite possessing a strong physical structure* is comparatively slight. In such hard, strongly built granite regions, *glaciers do not so much mould and shape,* as *disinter forms already conceived and ripe.* The harder the rock, and the better its specialised cleavage planes are developed, the greater will be the degree of controlling power possessed by it over its own forms, as compared with that of the disinterring glacier; and the softer the rock and more generally developed its cleavage planes, the less able will it be to resist ice action and maintain its own forms. In general, *the grain of a rock* determines its surface forms; yet it would matter but little what the grain might be – straight, curved, or knotty – if the excavating and sculpturing tool were sharp, because in that case it would cut without reference to the grain. Every carpenter knows that only a dull tool will follow the grain of wood. Such a tool is the glacier, gliding with tremendous pressure past splitting precipices and smooth swelling domes, flexible as the wind, yet hard-tempered as steel. Mighty as its effects appear to us, it has only developed the predestined forms of mountain beauty which were ready and waiting to receive the baptism of light.

CHAPTER TWO

The Origin of Yosemite Valleys

ALL THE VALLEYS and canyons of the western flank of the Sierra, between 36° and 39° north latitude, naturally classify themselves under two genera, each containing two species. One genus comprehends all the slate valleys, the other all that are built of granite. The latter is far the more important, both on account of the greater extent of its geographical range and the grandeur and simplicity of its phenomena. All the valleys of both genera are valleys of erosion. Their chief distinguishing characteristics may be seen in the following descriptions:

SLATE VALLEYS

1. Cross-sections, V-shaped, or somewhat rounded at bottom, walls *irregular in structure*, shattered and weak in appearance, because of the development of slaty cleavage planes and joints, which also prevent the formation of plane-faced precipices. Bottom showing the naked bedrock, or covered by rocky debris, and sloping in the direction of the trend. Nearly all of the foothill valleys belong to this species. Some of the older specimens are smoothly covered with soil, but *meadows and lakes are always wanting.*
2. More or less widened, *branching at the head.* Bottom, with meadows, or groves, or lakelets, or all together. Sections and walls about as in No.1. Fine examples of this species occur on the headwaters of the San Joaquin.

GRANITE VALLEYS

1. Cross-sections narrowly or widely V-shaped. Walls seldom interrupted by side canyons, magnificently simple in structure and general surface character, and presenting plane precipices in great abundance. Bottom sloping in the direction of the trend, mostly bare, or covered with unstratified glacial and avalanche boulders. Groves and meadows wanting.
2. *Branching at head, with bevelled and heavily abraded lips at foot.* Bottom *level*, meadowed, laked, or groved. Walls usually very high, often interrupted by side canyons. Sections as in No. 1. To this species belongs the far-famed Yosemite whose origin we will now discuss.

We will henceforth make use of the word Yosemite both as a specific and geographical term.

Yosemite Valley is on the main Merced, in the middle region of the range. It is about seven miles long from east to west with an average width at bottom of a little more than half a mile, and at the top of a mile and a half. The elevation of the bottom above sea level is about 4,000 feet. The average height of the walls is about 3,000 feet, made up of a series of sublime rock forms, varying greatly in size and structure, partially separated from one another by small side canyons. These immense wall-rocks, ranged picturesquely together, do not stand in line. Some advance their sublime fronts far out into the open valley, others recede. A few are nearly vertical, but far the greater number are inclined at angles ranging from twenty to seventy degrees. The meadows and sandy flats outspread between support a luxuriant growth of sedges and ferns, interrupted with thickets of azalea, willow and briar-rose. The warmer sloping ground along the base of the walls is planted with noble pines and oaks, while countless alpine flowers fringe the deep and dark side canyons, through which glad streams descend in falls and cascades, on their way from the high fountains to join the river. The life-giving Merced flows down the valley with a slow, stately current, curving hither and thither through garden and grove, bright and pure as the snow of its fountains. Such is Yosemite, the noblest of Sierra temples, everywhere expressing the working of Divine harmonious law, yet so little understood that it has been regarded as "an exceptional creation," or rather *exceptional destruction* accomplished by violent and mysterious forces. The argument advanced to support this view is substantially as follows: It is too wide for a water-eroded valley, too irregular for a fissure valley, and too angular and local for a primary valley originating in a fold of the mountain surface during the process of upheaval; therefore, a portion of the mountain bottom must have suddenly fallen out, letting the super-incumbent domes and peaks fall rumbling into the abyss, like coal into the bunker of a ship. This violent hypothesis, which furnishes a kind of Tophet for the reception of bad mountains, commends itself to the favour of many, by seeming to account for the remarkable sheerness and angularity of the walls, and by its marvellousness and obscurity, calling for no investigation, but rather discouraging it. Because we cannot observe the bedrock to ascertain whether or not it is fractured, this engulfment hypothesis seems to rest safely under cover of darkness, yet a film of lake gravel and a meadow blanket are its only concealments, and, by comparison with exposed sections in other Yosemites where the sheer walls unite with the solid, unfissured bottom, even these are in effect removed. It becomes manifest, by a slight attention to facts, that the hypothetical subsidence must have been limited to the valley proper, because both at the head and foot we find the solid bedrock.

The breaking down of only one small portion of the mountain floor, leaving all adjacent to it undisturbed, would necessarily give rise to a very strongly marked line of demarcation, but no such line appears; on the contrary, the unchanged walls are continued indefinitely, up and down the river canyon, and lose their distinguishing characteristics in a gradual manner easily accounted for by changes in the structure of the rocks and lack of concentration of the glacial energy expended upon them. That there is comparatively so small a quantity of debris at the foot of Yosemite walls is advanced as an argument in favour of subsidence, on the grounds that the valley is very old, and that a vast quantity of debris must, therefore, have fallen from the walls by atmospheric agencies, and that the hypothetical "abyss" was exactly required to furnish storage for it. But the Yosemite Valley is not very old. It is very young, and no vast quantity of debris has ever fallen from its walls. Therefore, no abyss was required for its accommodation.

If, in accordance with the hypothesis, Yosemite is the only valley furnished with an abyss for the reception of debris, then we might expect to find all abyssless valleys choked up with the great quantity assumed to have fallen; but, on the contrary, we find their debris in the same condition as in Yosemite, and not more abundant. Indeed, in some portions of valleys as deep and sheer as Yosemite there is absolutely no talus, and that there never has been any is proved by both walls and bottom being *solid and ice-polished.* Many examples illustrative of this truth may be seen in the great Tuolumne and Kings River valleys.

Where the granite of Yosemite walls is intersected with feldspathic veins, as in the lowest of the Three Brothers and rocks near Cathedral Spires, large masses are loosened, from time to time, by the action of the atmosphere, and hurled to the bottom with such violence as to shake the whole valley; but the aggregate quantity which has been thus weathered off, so far from being sufficient to fill any great abyss, *forms but a small part of the debris slopes actually found on the surface,* all the larger angular taluses having been formed simultaneously by severe earthquake shocks that occurred three or four hundred years ago, as shown by their forms and the trees growing upon them. The attentive observer will perceive that *wherever a large talus occurs, the wall immediately above it presents a scarred and shattered surface* whose area is always proportional to the size of the talus, but *where there is no talus the wall is invariably moutonnée or striated,* showing that it is young and has suffered little change since it came to light at the close of the glacial period. On the 23rd of March, 1872, I was so fortunate as to witness the sudden formation of one of these interesting taluses by the precipitation of the Yosemite Eagle Rock by the first heavy shock of the Inyo earthquake, whereby their local character and simultaneity of formation was fully accounted for. This *new earthquake* gave rise to the formation of many *new taluses* throughout the adjacent valleys, corresponding in every particular with the older and larger ones whose history we have been considering.

As to the important question, What part may water have played in the formation of Sierra valleys we observe that, as far as Yosemite is concerned, the five large streams which flow through it are universally engaged in the work of *filling it up.* The granite of the region under consideration is but slightly susceptible of water denudation. Throughout the greater portion of the main upper Merced valley the river has not eroded its channel to a depth exceeding three feet since it first began to flow at the close of the glacial epoch, although acting under every advantage of concentration and quick descent. The highest flood-mark the young river has yet recorded upon the clean glacial tablets of its banks is only seven or eight feet above the present level, at ordinary stages. Nevertheless, the aggregate annual quantity that formerly passed down these canyon valleys was undoubtedly far greater than passes at the present time, because on the gradual recession of the glaciers at the close of the period, the supply would necessarily be more constant, from their melting all through the seasons. The evidence, however, is incontestable, which shows that the highest floods of Sierra rivers in the upper and middle regions of the range never much exceeded those of the present time.

Five immense glaciers from five to fifteen hundred feet in depth poured their icy floods into Yosemite, uniting to form one huge trunk, moved down through the valley with irresistible and never-ceasing energy, crushing and breaking up its strongest rocks, and scattering them in moraines far and near. Many, while admitting the possibility of ice having been the great agent in the production of Yosemite valleys, conjecture that earthquake fissures, or cracks from cooling or upheaval of the earth's crust, were required to enable the glaciers to make a beginning and to guide them in the work. We have already shown [in the earlier chapter on mountain sculpture] that cleavage planes and joints exist in a latent or developed condition in all the granite of the region, and that these exert immense influence on its glacial erodibility. During five years' observation in the Sierra, I have failed to discover a single fissure of any kind, although extensive areas of clean-swept glacial pavements afford ample opportunity for their detection, did they exist. Deep slots, with regular walls appearing as if sawed, or mortised, frequently occur. These are formed by the disintegration of soft seams a few inches or feet in thickness, contained between walls of stronger granite. Such is the character of the so-called fissure said to exist in a hard portion of the south wall of Yosemite, opposite the Three Brothers, so frequently quoted in speculations upon the valley's origin.

The greatest effects of earthquakes on the valley we have already noticed in avalanche taluses, which were formed by the precipitation of weak headlands, that fell like ripe fruit. The greatest obstacle in the way of reading the history of Yosemite valleys is not its complexity or obscurity, but simply the *magnitude of the characters* in which it is written. It would require years of enthusiastic study to master the English alphabet if it were carved upon the flank of the Sierra in letters sixty or seventy miles long, their bases set in the foothills, their tops leaning back among the glaciers and shattered peaks of the summit, often veiled with forests and thickets, and their continuity often broken by cross-gorges and hills. So also the sculptured alphabet canyons of the Sierra are magnificently simple, yet demand years of laborious research for their apprehension. A thousand blurred fragments must be conned and brooded over with studious care, and kept vital and formative on the edges, ready to knit like broken living bones, while a final judgment is being bravely withheld until the entire series of phenomena has been weighed and referred to an all-unifying, all-explaining law. To one who can leisurely contemplate Yosemite from some commanding outlook, it offers, as a whole, a far more natural combination of features than is at all apparent in partial views obtained from the bottom. Its stupendous domes and battlements blend together and manifest delicate compliance to law, for the mind is then in some measure emancipated from the repressive and enslaving effects of their separate magnitudes, and gradually rises to a comprehension of their unity and of the poised harmony of their general relations.

Nature is not so poor as to possess only one of anything, nor throughout her varied realms has she ever been known to offer an exceptional creation, whether of mountain or valley. When, therefore, we explore the adjacent Sierra, we are not astonished to find that there are many Yosemite valleys identical in general characters, each presenting on a varying scale the same species of mural precipices, level meadows, and lofty waterfalls. The laws which preside over their distribution are as constant and apparent as those governing the distribution of forest trees. They occur only in the middle region of the chain, where the declivity is considerable and where the granite is Yosemitic in its internal structure. The position of each valley upon the Yosemitic zone indicates a marked and inseparable relation to the ancient glaciers, which, when fully deciphered, amounts to cause and effect. So constant and obvious is this connection between the various Yosemites and the névé amphitheatres which fountained the ancient ice-rivers, that an observer, inexperienced in these phenomena, might easily anticipate the position and size of any Yosemite by a study of the glacial fountains above it, or the position and size of the fountains by a study of their complementary Yosemite. *All Yosemites occur at the junction of two or more glacial canyons.* Thus the greater and lesser Yosemites of the Merced, Hetch Hetchy, and those of the upper Tuolumne, those of Kings River, and the San Joaquin, all occur immediately below the confluences of their ancient glaciers. If, in following down the canyon channel of the Merced Glacier, from its origin in the *névé* amphitheatres of the Lyell group, we should find that its sudden expansion and deepening at Yosemite occurs without a corresponding union of glacial tributary canyons, and without any similar expansion elsewhere, then we might well be driven to the doctrine of special marvels. But this emphatic deepening and widening becomes harmonious when we observe smaller Yosemites occurring at intervals all the way down, across the Yosemitic zone, *wherever a tributary canyon unites with the trunk*, until, on reaching Yosemite, where the enlargement is greatest, we find the number

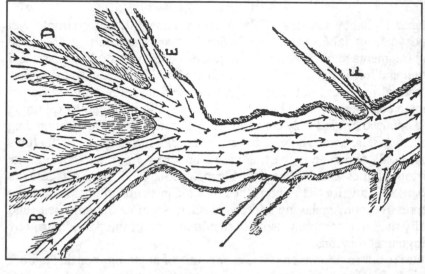

Fig. 3 – Merced Yosemite glaciers. (A, Yosemite
Creek; B, Hoffmann; C, Tenaya; D, South Lyell;
E, Illilouette; F, Pohono)

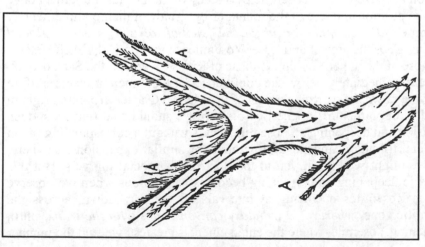

Fig. 2 – Kings River Yosemite
(B B B B, Glaciers)

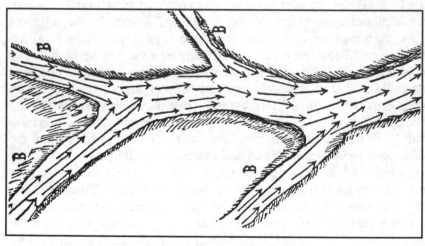

Fig. 1 – Tuolumne Yosemite
(A A A, Glaciers)

of confluent glacier-canyons is also greatest, as may be observed by reference to Fig. 1. Still further, the aggregate areas of their cross-sections is approximately equal to the area of the cross-sections of the several resulting Yosemites, just as the cross-section of a tree trunk is about equal to the sum of the sections of its branches. *Furthermore, the trend of Yosemite valleys is always a direct resultant of the sizes, directions, and declivities of their confluent canyons,* modified by peculiarities of structure in their rocks. Now, all the canyons mentioned above are the abandoned channels of glaciers; therefore, these Yosemites and their glaciers are inseparably related. Instead of being local in character, or formed by obscure and lawless forces, *these valleys are the only great sculpture phenomena whose existence and exact positions we may confidently anticipate.*

THE DEPTH OF YOSEMITE

Much stress has been laid on the mere uncompared arithmetical depth of Yosemite, but this is a character of no consequence to the consideration of its origin. The greatest Merced Yosemite is 3,000 feet deep; the Tuolumne, 2,000; another, 1,000; but what geologist would be so unphilosophical as to decide against the identity of their origin from difference in depth only. One pine tree is 100 feet high, lean and crooked, from repressing winds and the poverty of the soil which nourished it; while another, more fortunate in the conditions of its life, is 200 feet high, erect and vigorous. So, also, one Yosemite is 3,000 feet deep because of the favourable structure of its rocks and the depth and number of ice rivers that excavated it; another is half as deep, because of the strength of its rocks, or the scantiness of the glacial force exerted upon it. What would be thought of a botanist who should announce that our gigantic *Sequoia* was not a tree at all, offering as a reason that it was too large for a tree, and, in describing it, should confine himself to some particularly knotty portion of the trunk? In Yosemite there is an evergreen oak double the size of ordinary oaks of the region, whose trunk is craggy and angular as the valley itself, and coloured like the granite boulders on which it is growing. At a little distance this trunk would scarcely be recognised as part of a tree, until viewed in relation to its branches, leaves and fruit. It is an admirable type of the craggy Merced canyon-tree, whose angular Yosemite does not appear as a natural portion thereof until viewed in its relation to its wide-spreading branches, with their fruit and foliage of meadow and lake.

We present a ground-plan of three Yosemite valleys, showing the positions of their principal glaciers, and the relation of their trends and areas to them. The large arrows in Figs. 1, 2, 3 show the positions and directions of movement of the main confluent glaciers concerned in the erosion of three Yosemites. With regard to the number of their main glaciers, the Tuolumne Yosemite may be called a Yosemite of the *third* power; the Kings River Yosemite, of the fourth power; and the Merced Yosemite, of the fifth power.

The granite in which each of these three Yosemites is excavated is of the same general quality; therefore, the differences of width, depth, and trend observed, are due almost entirely to the number, magnitude, declivity and mode of combination of the glacial system of each. The similarity of their ground-plans is obvious from a single glance at the figures; their cross-sections are no less similar. One of the most characteristic from each of the valleys under consideration is shown in Figs. 4, 5 and 6, drawn on the same scale.

The perpendicularity of Yosemite walls is apt to be greatly over-estimated. If the slopes of the Merced Yosemite walls were to be carefully measured with a clinometer at intervals of say 100 yards, it would be found that the average angle they make with the horizon is less than 50°, as shown in Fig. 7. It is not possible that the bottom could drop out of a valley thus shaped, no matter how great the upheaval, or downheaval, or sideheaval.

Having shown that Yosemite, so-called is not unique in its ground-plan or cross-sections, we will now consider some of the most remarkable of its rock forms. The beautiful San Joaquin Dome in the canyon of the San Joaquin, near the confluence of the south fork, looking south (Fig. 9), shows a remarkable resemblance to the Yosemite Half Dome, as see from Tenaya Canyon (Fig. 8). They are similarly situated with reference to the glaciers

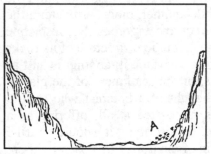

Fig. 4   Section across the Hetch Hetchy
Valley, or lower Tuolumne Yosemite

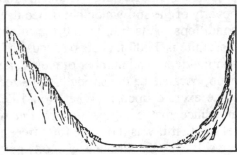

Fig. 5   Section across the
Kings River Yosemite

Fig. 6   Section across Merced
Yosemite

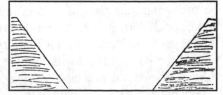

Fig. 7   Idealised section across
Merced Yosemite

that denuded them, Half Dome having been assailed by the combined Tenaya and Hoffman glaciers on the one side, and by the South Lyell or Merced Glacier on the other; the San Joaquin Dome, by the combined glaciers of the middle and north forks, on one side, and by the glaciers of the south fork on

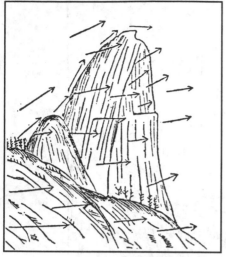

Fig. 8   Yosemite Half Dome   Fig. 9   San Joaquin Dome

the other. The split dome of Kings River Yosemite is a worthy counterpart of the great Half Dome of the Merced Yosemite. They occur at about the same elevation, and are similarly situated with reference to the ancient glacial currents, which first overswept them and then glided heavily by on either side, breaking them up in chips and slabs, until fashioned and sculptured to their present condition. The Half Dome is usually regarded as being the most mysterious and unique rock form in the valley, or, indeed, in the world, yet when closely approached and studied, its history becomes plain.

From A to B, Fig. 10, the height is about 1,800 feet; from A to the base, 3,000. The upper portion is almost absolutely plain and vertical, the lower is inclined at an angle with the horizon of about 37°. The observer may ascend from the south side to the shoulder of the dome at D, and descend along the face toward A H. In the notch at F a section of the dome may be seen, showing that it is there made up of immense slabs set on edge. These evidently have been produced by the development of cleavage planes, which, cutting the dome perpendicularly, have determined the plane of its face, which is the most striking characteristic of the rock. Along the front toward A H may be seen the stumps of slabs which have been successively split off the face. At H may be seen the edges of residual fragments of the same slabs. At the summit we perceive the cut edges of the concentric layers which have given the curved dome outline, B B. At D, a small gable appears, which has been produced by the development of diagonal cleavage planes which have been cut in front by vertical planes. After the passage of the main Tenaya Glacier in the direction of the arrows, small glacierets seem to have flowed down in front, eroding shallow groove channels in the direction of greatest declivity; and even before the total recession of the main glacier a wing-shaped ice-slope probably leaned back in the shadow, and with slow action

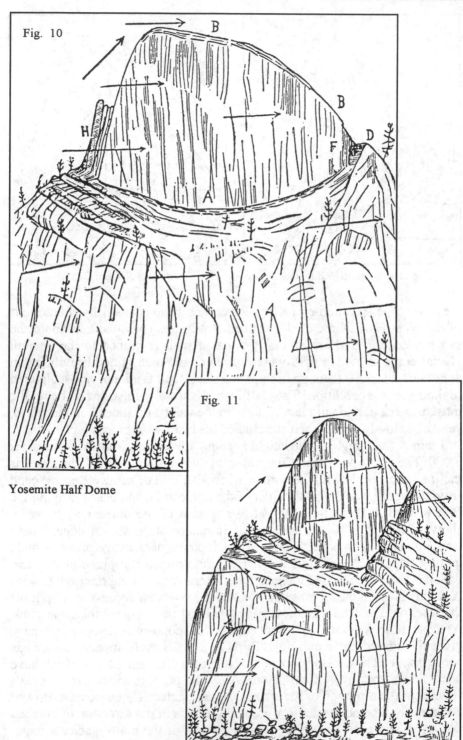

Fig. 10

Yosemite Half Dome

Fig. 11

Fig. 12   Yosemite Half Dome.

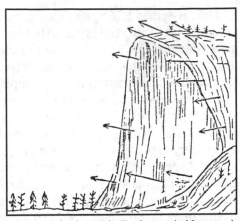

Fig. 14   El Capitan, Big Tuolumne (mid canyon).

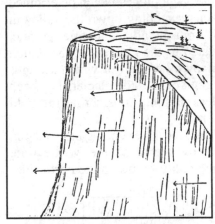

Fig. 14   El Capitan of Yosemite.

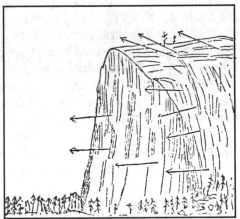

Fig. 15   El Capitan, Big Tuolumne (canyon head).

eroded the upper portion of the dome. All the rocks forming the south walls of deep Yosemite canyons exhibit more or less of this light after-sculpture, effected in the shade after the north sun-beaten rocks were finished.

The south side of the dome has been heavily *moutonnée* by the Lyell Glacier, but is, nevertheless, nearly as vertical as the north split side. The main body of the rock corresponds in form and attitude with every other rock similarly situated with reference to ice rivers, and to elevation above sea level, the special split dome-top being, as we have seen, a result of special structure in the granite out of which it was formed. Numerous examples of this interesting species of rock may be culled from the various Yosemites, illustrating every essential character on a gradually changing scale.

Fig. 12 is a view of the back or south side of Half Dome, Yosemite, showing its *moutonnée* condition; Fig. 13 represents El Capitan of Yosemite, situated on the north side of the valley; Fig. 14, El Capitan of Big Tuolumne Canyon, near the middle, situated on the north side; Fig. 15, El Capitan of Big Tuolumne Canyon, near the head, situated on the north side.

The far-famed El Capitan rock presents a sheer cleaved front, over three thousand feet high, and is scarcely less impressive than the great dome. We have collected fine specimens of this clearly defined rock form from all the principal Yosemites of the region. Nevertheless, it also has been considered exceptional. Their origin is easily explained. They are simply *split ends of ridges which have been broken through by glaciers* [i.e. truncated spurs].

For their perfect development the granite must be strong, and have some of its vertical cleavage planes well developed, nearly to the exclusion of all the others, especially of those belonging to the diagonal and horizontal series. A powerful trunk glacier must sweep past in front nearly in the direction of its cutting planes, with small glaciers, tributary to the first, one on each side of the ridge out of which the Capitan is to be made. This arrangement is illustrated in Fig.16, where A represents a horizontal section of a Capitan rock, exposing edges of the cleavage planes which determined the character of its face; B, the main glacier sweeping down the valley in front; and C C, the tributaries isolating it from the adjacent softer granite. The three Capitans figured stand thus related to the glaciers of the region where they are found. I have met with many others, all of which are thus situated, though in some instances one or both of the side glaciers had been wanting, leaving the resulting Capitan less perfect, considering the bold advancing Yosemite Capitan as a typical form.

When the principal surface features of the Sierra were being blocked out, the main ice-sheet was continuous and moved in a southerly direction, therefore the most perfect Capitans are invariably found on the north sides

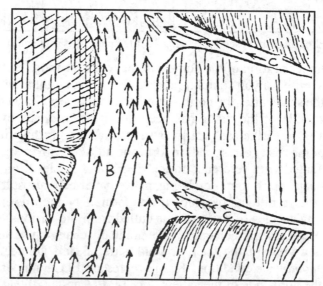

Fig. 16 Idealised Capitan (truncated spur) and valleys showing
the relationship of cleavage planes to vertical side valleys

 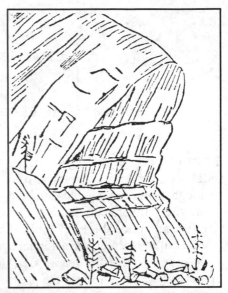

Figs. 17 and 18   North fork of San Joaquin River Canyon – the relationship of
overhanging 'leaning fronts' to steeply dipping cleavage planes.

of valleys trending east and west. The reason will be readily perceived by
referring to Fig. 8 of Chapter One [showing Capitans as *roches moutonnées*].

To illustrate still further how fully the split fronts of rocks facing deep
canyons have the angles at which they stand measured by their cleavage
planes, we give two examples (Figs. 17 and 18) of leaning fronts from the
canyon of the north fork of the San Joaquin River. Sentinel and Cathedral
rocks also are found in other glacial canyons, and in every instance their
forms, magnitudes, and positions are obviously the necessary results of the
internal structure and general mechanical characters of the rocks out of
which they were made, and of the glacial energy that has been brought to
bear on them. The abundance, therefore, of lofty angular rocks, instead of
rendering Yosemite unique, is the characteristic which unites it most intimately
with all the other similarly situated valleys in the range.

CHAPTER THREE

Ancient Glaciers and Their Pathways

THOUGH the gigantic glaciers of the Sierra are dead, their history is indelibly recorded in characters of rock, mountain, canyon, and forest; and, although other hieroglyphics are being incessantly engraved over these, "line upon line," the glacial characters are so enormously emphasised that they rise free and unconfused in sublime relief, through every after inscription, whether of the torrent, the avalanche, or the restless heaving atmosphere.

In order to give the reader definite conceptions of the magnitude and branches. We have seen (in the previous chapter) that Yosemite received the simultaneous thrust of the Yosemite Creek, Hoffmann, Tenaya, South Lyell, and Illilouette glaciers. These welded themselves together into one huge trunk, which swept down through the valley, receiving small affluents in its course from Pohono, Sentinel, and Indian canyons, and those on both sides of El Capitan Rock. At this period most of the upper portions of the walls of the valley were bare; but during its earliest history, the wide mouths of these several glaciers formed an almost uninterrupted covering of ice. All the ancient glaciers of the Sierra fluctuated in depth and width, and in degree of individuality, down to the latest glacial days. It must, therefore, be distinctly borne in mind that the following sketches of these upper Merced glaciers relate only to their separate condition, and to that phase of their separate condition which they presented toward the close of the period when Yosemite and its branches were works nearly accomplished.

YOSEMITE CREEK GLACIER

The broad, many-fountained glacier to which the basin of Yosemite Creek belonged, was about fourteen miles in length by four in width, and in many places was not less than a thousand feet in depth. Its principal tributaries issued from lofty amphitheatres laid well back among the northern spurs of the Hoffmann range. These at first pursued a westerly course; then, uniting with each other and absorbing a series of small affluents from the Tuolumne divide, the trunk thus formed swept round to the south in a magnificent curve, and poured its ice into Yosemite in cascades two miles wide. This broad glacier formed a kind of wrinkled ice cloud. As it grew older, it became more regular and river like; encircling peaks overshadowed its upper fountains, rock islets rose at intervals among its shallowing currents, and its bright sculptured banks, nowhere overflowed, extended in massive simplicity all the way to its mouth. As the ice-winter drew near a close, the main trunk, becoming torpid, at length wholly disappeared in the sun, and a waiting multitude of plants and animals entered the new valley to inhabit the mansions prepared for them. In the meantime the chief tributaries, creeping slowly back into the shelter of their fountain shadows, continued to live and work independently, spreading moraine soil for gardens, scooping basins for lakelets, and leisurely completing the sculpture of their fountains. These also have at last vanished, and the whole basin is now full of light. Forests flourish luxuriantly over all its broad moraines, lakes and meadows nestle among its domes, and a thousand flowery gardens are outspread along its streams.

HOFFMANN GLACIER

The short, swift-flowing Hoffmann Glacier offered a striking contrast to the Yosemite Creek, in the energy and directness of its movements, and the general tone and tendencies of its life. The erosive energy of the latter was diffused over a succession of low boulderlike domes. Hoffmann Glacier, on the contrary, moved straight to its mark, making a descent of 5,000 feet in about five miles, steadily deepening and contracting its current, and finally thrusting itself against the upper portion of Yosemite in the form of a wedge of solid ice, six miles in length by four in width. The concentrated action of this energetic glacier, combined with that of the Tenaya, accomplished the greater portion of the work of the disinterment and sculpture of the great Half Dome, North Dome, and the adjacent rocks. Its fountains, ranged along the southern slopes of the main Hoffmann ridge, gave birth to a series of flat, wing-shaped tributaries, separated from one another by picturesque walls built of massive blocks, bedded and jointed like masonry. The story of its death is not unlike that of the Yosemite Creek, though the declivity of its channel and equal exposure to sun heat prevented any considerable portion from passing through a torpid condition. It was first burned off on its lower course; then, creeping slowly back, lingered a while at the base of its mountains to finish their sculpture, and encircle them with a zone of moraine soil for gardens and forests. The grey slopes of Mount Hoffmann are singularly barren in aspect, yet the traveller who is so fortunate as to ascend them will find himself in the very loveliest gardens of the Sierra. The lower banks and slopes of the basin are plushed with chaparral rich in berries and bloom – a favourite resort for bears; while the middle region is planted with the most superb forest of silver-fir I ever beheld. Nowhere are the cold footsteps of ice more warmly covered with light and life.

TENAYA GLACIER

The rugged, strong-limbed Tenaya Glacier was about twelve miles long, and from half a mile to two and a half miles wide. Its depth varied from near 500 to 2,000 feet, according as its current was outspread in many channels or compressed in one. Instead of drawing its supplies directly from the summit fountains, it formed one of the principal outlets of the Tuolumne *mer de glace* issuing at once from this noble source, a full-grown glacier two miles wide and more than a thousand feet deep. It flowed in a general southwesterly direction, entering Yosemite at the head, between Half and North Domes. In setting out on its life-work it moved slowly, spending its strength in ascending the Tuolumne divide, and in eroding a series of parallel sub-channels leading over into the broad, shallow basin of Lake Tenaya. Hence, after uniting its main current, which had been partially separated in crossing the divide, and receiving a swift-flowing affluent from the fountains of Cathedral Peak, it set forth again with renewed vigour, pouring its massive floods over the southwestern rim of the basin in a series of splendid cascades; then, crushing heavily against the ridge of Clouds Rest, curved toward the west, quickened its pace, focalised its wavering currents, and bore down upon Yosemite with its whole concentrated energy. Toward the end of the ice-period, and while the upper tributaries of its Hoffmann companion continued to grind rock-meal for coming forests, the whole body of Tenaya became torpid, withering simultaneously from end to end, instead of dying gradually from the foot upward. Its upper portion separated into long parallel strips extending between the Tenaya basin and Tuolumne *mer de glace*. These, together with the shallow ice-clouds of the lake basin, melted rapidly, exposing broad areas of rolling rock-waves and glossy pavements, on whose channelless surface water ran everywhere wild and free. There are no very extensive morainal accumulations of any sort in the basin. The largest occur on the divide, near the Big Tuolumne Meadows, and on the sloping ground northwest of Lake Tenaya.*

For a distance of six miles from its mouth the pathway of this noble glacier is a simple trough from 2,000 to 3,000 feet deep, countersunk in the solid granite, with sides inclined at angles with the horizon of from thirty to fifty degrees. Above this its grand simplicity is interrupted by huge *moutonnéed* ridges extending in the general direction of its length over into the basin of Lake Tenaya. Passing these, and crossing the bright glacial pavements that border the lake, we find another series of ridges, from 500 to 1,200 feet in height, extending over the divide to the ancient Tuolumne ice-fountain. Their bare *moutonnéed* forms and polished surfaces indicate that they were overswept, existing at first as mere boulders beneath the mighty glacier that flowed in one unbroken current between Cathedral Peak and the southeast shoulder of the Hoffmann range.

---

* Because the main trunk died almost simultaneously throughout its whole extent, we, of course, find no terminal moraines curved across its channels; nor, since its banks were in most places too steeply inclined for their disposition, do we find much of the two laterals. One of the first Tenaya glacierets was developed in the shadow of Yosemite Half Dome. Others were formed along the bases of Coliseum Peak, and the long, precipitous walls extending from near Lake Tenaya to the Big Tuolumne Meadows. The latter, on account of the uniformity and continuity of their protecting shadows, formed moraines of considerable length and regularity, that are liable to be mistaken for portions of the left lateral moraine of the main glacier.

Portion of the left bank of the channel of the South Lyell Glacier, near the
mouth of the Cathedral tributary.

NEVADA OR SOUTH LYELL GLACIER

The South Lyell Glacier was less influential than the last, but longer and
more symmetrical, and the only one of the Merced system whose sources
extended directly to the main summits on the axis of the chain. Its numerous
ice-wombs, now mostly barren, range side by side in three distinct series at
an elevation above sea-level of from 10,000 to 12,000 feet. The first series
on the right side of the basin extends from the Matterhorn to Cathedral Peak
in a northwesterly direction a distance of about twelve miles. The second
series extends in the same direction along the left side of the basin in the
summits of the Merced group, and is about six miles in length. The third is
about nine miles long, and extends along the head of the basin in a direction
at right angles to that of the others, and unites with them at their southeastern
extremities. The three ranges of summits in which these fountains are laid,
and the long continuous ridge of Clouds Rest, enclose a rectangular basin
leaving an outlet near the southwest corner opposite its principal névé
fountains, situated in the dark jagged peaks of the Lyell group. The main
central trunk, lavishly fed by these numerous fountains, was from 1,000 to
1,400 feet in depth, from three-fourths of a mile to a mile and a half in
width. and about fifteen miles in length. It first flowed in a northwesterly
direction for a few miles then curving toward the left, pursued a westerly
course, and poured its shattered cascading currents down into Yosemite
between Half Dome and Mount Starr King.

Could we have visited Yosemite toward the close of the glacial period,
we should have found its ice-cascades vastly more glorious than their tiny
water representatives of the present hour. One of the most sublime of these
was formed by that portion of the South Lyell current which descended the
broad, rounded shoulder of Half Dome. The whole glacier resembled an oak

with a gnarled swelling base and wide-spreading branches. Its banks, a few miles above Yosemite, were adorned with groups of picturesque rocks of every conceivable form and mode of combination, among which glided swift descending affluents, mottled with black slates from the summits, and grey granite blocks from ridges and headlands. One of the most interesting facts relating to the early history of this glacier is, that the lofty cathedral spur forming the northeast boundary of its basin was broken through and overflowed by deep ice currents from the Tuolumne region. The scored and polished gaps eroded by them in their passage across the summit of the spur, trend with admirable steadiness in a northeasterly and southwesterly direction; a fact of great importance, considered in its bearings upon questions relating to the universal ice-sheet. *Traces of a similar overflow from the northeast occur on the edges of the basins of all the Yosemite glaciers.*

The principal moraines of the basin occur in short, irregular sections scattered along the sides of the valleys, or spread in rough beds in level portions of their bottoms, without manifesting subordination to any system whatever. This fragmentary condition is due to interruptions caused by portions of the sides of the valleys being too precipitous for moraine matter to rest upon and to breakings and down-washings of torrents and avalanches of winter snow. The obscurity resulting from these causes is further augmented by forests and underbrush, making a patient study of details indispensable to the recognition of their unity and simple grandeur. The south lateral moraine of the lower portion of the trunk may be traced about five miles, from the mouth of the north tributary of Mount Clark to the canyon of Illilouette, though simplicity of structure has in most places been prevented by the nature of the ground and by the action of a narrow margin glacier which descended against it with variable pressure from cool, shadowy slopes above. The corresponding section of the right lateral, extending from the mouth of Cathedral tributary to Half Dome, is far more perfect in structure, because of the evenness of the ground, and because the ice-wing which curved against Clouds Rest and descended against it was fully exposed to the sun, and was, therefore, melted long before the main trunk, allowing the latter to complete the formation of this section of its moraine undisturbed. Some conception of its size and general character may be obtained by following the Clouds Rest and Yosemite trail, which crosses it obliquely, leading past several cross-sections made by small streams. A few slate boulders from the Lyell group may be seen, but the main mass of the moraine is composed of ordinary granite and porphyry, the latter having been derived from Feldspar and Cathedral valleys.

The elevation of the top of the moraine near Cathedral tributary is about 8,100 feet; near Half Dome, 7,600. It rests upon the side of the valley at angles varying from fifteen to twenty-five degrees, and in many places is straight and uniform as a railroad embankment. The greatest depth of the glacier between Clouds Rest and Mount Starr King, measuring from the highest points of its lateral moraines, was 1,300 feet. The recurrence of ridges and terraces on its sides indicate oscillations in the level of the glacier, probably caused by clusters of cooler or snowier seasons which no doubt diversified the great glacial winter, just as clusters of sunny or stormy days occasion fluctuations in the level of the streams and prevent monotony in our annual winters. When the depth of the South Lyell Glacier diminished to about 500 feet, it became torpid, on account of the retardation caused by the roughness and crookedness of its channel. But though it henceforth made no farther advance of its whole length, it possessed feeble vitality – in small sections, of exceptional slope or depth, maintaining a squirming and swedging motion, while it lay dying like a wounded serpent. The numerous fountain wombs continued fruitful long after the lower valleys were developed and vitalised with sun-heat. These gave rise to an imposing series of short residual glaciers, extending around three sides of the quadrangle basin, a distance of twenty-four miles. Most of them have but recently succumbed to the demands of the changing seasons, dying in turn, as determined by elevation, size, and exposure. A few still linger in the loftiest and most comprehensive shadows, actively engaged upon the last hieroglyphics which will complete the history of the South Lyell Glacier, forming one of the noblest and most symmetrical sheets of ice manuscripts in the whole Sierra.

ILLILOUETTE

The broad, shallow glacier that inhabited the basin of Illilouette more resembled a lake than a river, being nearly half as wide as it was long. Its greatest length was about ten miles, and its depth perhaps nowhere much exceeded 700 feet. Its chief fountains were ranged along the western side of the Merced spur at an elevation of about 10,000 feet. These gave birth to magnificent affluents, flowing in a westerly direction for several miles, in full independence, and uniting near the centre of the basin. The principal trunk curved northward, grinding heavily against the lofty wall forming its left bank, and finally poured its ice into Yosemite by the South Canyon between Glacier Point and Mount Starr King. All the phenomena relating to glacial action in this basin are remarkably simple and orderly, on account of the sheltered positions occupied by its principal fountains with reference to the unifying effects of ice currents from the main summits of the chain. A fine general view, displaying the principal moraines sweeping out into the middle of the basin from Black, Red, Gray, and Clark mountains may be obtained from the eastern base of the cone of Starr King. The right lateral of the tributary which took its rise between Red and Black mountains is a magnificent piece of ice work. Near the upper end, where it is joined to the shoulder of Red Mountain, it is 250 feet in height, and displays three well-marked terraces. From the first to the second of these, the vertical descent is eighty-five feet, and inclination of the surface fifteen degrees; from the second to the third, ninety-five feet, and inclination twenty-five degrees; and from the third to the bottom of the channel, seventy feet, made at an angle of nineteen degrees. The smoothness of the uppermost terrace shows that it is considerably more ancient than the others, many of the blocks of which it was composed having crumbled to sand.

A few miles farther down, the moraine has an average slope in front of about twenty seven degrees, and an elevation above the bottom of the channel of six hundred and sixty six feet. More than half of the side of the channel from the top is covered with moraine matter, and overgrown with a dense growth of chaparral, composed of manzanita, cherry, and castanopsis. Blocks of rose-coloured granite, many of them very large, occur at intervals all the way from the western base of Mount Clark to Starr King, indicating exactly the course pursued by the ice when the north divide of the basin was overflowed, Mount Clark being the only source whence they could possibly have been derived.

Near the middle of the basin, just where the regular moraines flatten out and disappear, there is outspread a smooth gravel slope, planted with the olive-green *Arctostaphylos glauca* so as to appear in the distance as a delightful meadow. Sections cut by streams show it to be composed of the same material as the moraines, but finer and more water-worn. The main channel, which is narrow at this point, appears to have been dammed up with ice and terminal moraines, thus giving rise to a central lake at the bottom of which moraine matter was re-ground and subsequently spread and levelled by the impetuous action of its out breaking waters. The southern boundary of the basin is a strikingly perfect wall, extending sheer and unbroken from Black Mountain* to Buena Vista Peak, casting a long, cool shadow all through the summer for the protection of fountain snow. The northern rim presents a beautiful succession of smooth undulations, rising here and there to a dome, their pale grey sides dotted with junipers and silver-leafed pines, and separated by dark, feathery base-fringes of fir.

The ice-ploughs of Illilouette, ranged side by side in orderly gangs, have furrowed its rocks with admirable uniformity, producing irrigating channels for a brood of wild streams, and abundance of deep, rich soils, adapted to every requirement of garden and grove. No other section of the Yosemite uplands is in so high a state of glacial cultivation. Its clustering domes, sheer walls, and lofty towering peaks, however majestic in themselves, are only border adornment, submissively subordinate to their sublime garden centre. The basins of Yosemite Creek, Tenaya, and South Lyell are pages of sculptured rocks embellished with gardens. The Illiouette basin is one grand garden embellished with rocks.

Nature manifests her love for the number five in her glaciers, as well as in the petals of the flowers which she plants in their pathways. These five Yosemite glaciers we have been sketching are as directly related to one another, and for as definite an object, as are the organs of a plant. After

---

* This mountain occurs next south of Red Mountain, and must not be confounded with the Black Mountain six miles farther south.

uniting in the valley, and expending the down-thrusting power with which they were endowed by virtue of the declivity of their channels, the trunk flowed *up out of* the valley without yielding much compliance to the crooked and comparatively small river canyon extending in a general westerly direction from the foot of the main valley. In effecting its exit a considerable ascent was made, traces of which are to be seen in the upward slope of the worn, rounded extremities of the valley walls. Down this glacier-constructed grade descend both the Coulterville and Mariposa trails; and we might further observe in this connection that, because the ice sheet near the period of transition to distinct glaciers flowed southerly, the south lips of all Yosemites trending east and west, other conditions being equal, are more heavily eroded, making the construction of trails on that side easier. The first trail, therefore, that was made into Yosemite, was of course made down over the south lip. The only trail entering the Tuolumne Yosemite descends the south lip, and so also does the only trail leading into the Kings River Yosemite. A large majority of deer and bear and Indian trails likewise descend the south lips of Yosemites. So extensively are the movements of men and animals controlled by the previous movements of certain snow-crystals combined as glaciers.

The direction pursued by the Yosemite trunk, after escaping from the valley, is unmistakably indicated by its immense lateral moraines extending from its lips in a west-southwesterly direction. The right moraine was disturbed by the large tributary of Cascade Creek, and is extremely complicated in structure. The left is simple until it comes under the influence of tributaries from the southeast, and both are further obscured by forests which flourish upon their mixed soil, and by the washing of rains and melting snows, and the weathering of their boulders, making a smooth, sandy, unmorainelike surface. It is, therefore, the less to be wondered at that the nature of these moraines, which represent so important a part of the chips hewn from the valley in the course of its formation, should not have

been sooner recognised. *Similarly situated moraines extend from the lips of every Yosemite* wherever the ground admits of their deposition and retention. In Hetch-Hetchy and other smaller and younger Yosemites of the upper Merced, the ascending *striae* which measure the angle of ascent made by the bottom of their glaciers in their outflow are still clearly visible.

Fig. 1 is the horizontal section of the end of a Yosemite valley, showing the ordinary boat-shaped edge, and lateral moraines (M M) extending from the lips. The moraines and arrows indicate the course pursued by the outflowing ice.

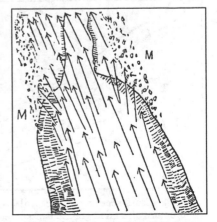

Fig. 1 Lateral moraines (M M) at lower end of a Yosemite valley indicating the direction of flow of ice.

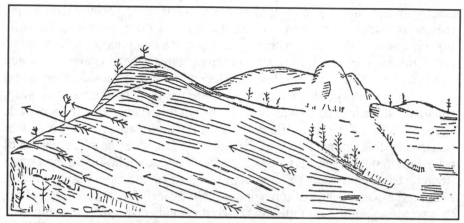

Fig. 2 Moraines and striae on the upper Merced indicate upward flow of ice.

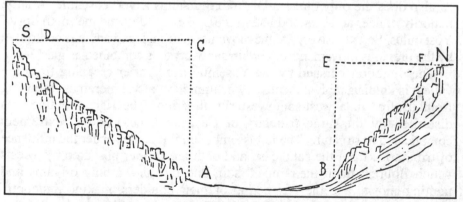

Fig. 3   Drift-covered floor (A B) of Yosemite Valley – assumed top masks stumps of granite slabs and columns of similar structure to the valley sides. Conclusion is that the valley has been eroded and is not as a result of down-folding.

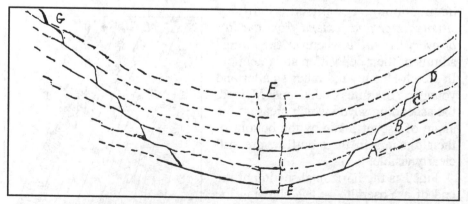

Fig. 4   Cross-section of lower Illilouette valley showing granite folds removed by ice (structure of eroded granite is assumed to reflect that of the valley sides). Erosion by water alone would have resulted in a much narrower valley (E F).

Fig. 2 represents the right lip of Yosemite, situated on the upper Merced below the confluence of Cathedral tributary. The whole lip is polished and striated. The arrows indicate the direction of the *striae*, which measure the angle of ascent made by the outflowing ice.

In the presentation of these studies, we have proceeded thus far with the assumption that all the valleys of the region are valleys of erosion, and that glaciers were the principal eroding agents; because the intelligible discussion of these propositions requires some knowledge of the physiognomy and general configuration of the region, as well as of the history of its ancient glaciers. Our space is here available only for very brief outlines of a portion of the argument, which will be gradually developed in subsequent articles.

That fossils were created as they occur in the rocks, is an ancient doctrine, now so little believed that geologists are spared the pains of proving that nature ever deals in fragmentary creations of any sort. All of our valleys are clearly fragmentary in some degree. Fig. 3 is a section across Yosemite Valley from Indian Canyon, which displays the stumps of slabs and columns of which the granite is here composed. Now the complements of these broken rocks must have occupied all, or part, or more than all of the two portions of the valley, A C D and B E F. The bottom, A B, is covered with drift, but we may assume that if it were laid bare we would find it made up of the ends of slabs and columns like the sides, which filled the space A C E B; because in all valleys where the bottom is naked, the broken stumps *do* appear showing that this valley was not formed by a fold in the mountain surface, or by a splitting asunder, or by subsidence, but by a breaking up and translation of rocks which occupied its place; or, in other words, by erosion.

Fig. 4 is a section across the lower portion of the valley of Illilouette south of Mount Starr King. In this case the bottom is naked, and the dotted reconstructed portions of the huge granite folds A B C have evidently been eroded.* Even the smoothly curved trough of two rock waves which afford sections like Fig. 5 cannot be regarded as a valley originating in a fold of the surface, for we have shown in the first paper of this series that domes or extended waves, with a concentric structure like A C, may exist as concretionary or crystalline masses beneath the surface of granite possessing an entirely different structure or no determinate structure whatever, as in B.

EVIDENCE OF FORMATION OF VALLEYS BY ICE

The chief valley-eroding agents are water and ice. Each has been vaguely considered the more influential by different observers, although the phenomena to which they give rise are immensely different. These workmen are known by their chips, and only glacier chips form moraines which correspond in kind and quantity to the size of the valleys and condition of their surfaces Also their structure unfolds the secret of their origin. The constant and

---

* Water never erodes a wide U-shaped valley in granite, but always a narrow gorge like E F, in Fig.4.

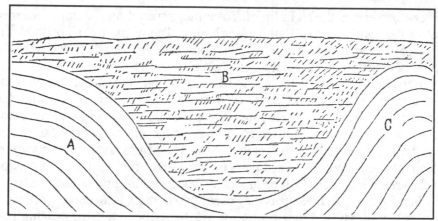

Fig. 5 Cross-section of a hypothetical valley where the structure of the granite originally occupying the trough may not reflect the structure of the valley sides.

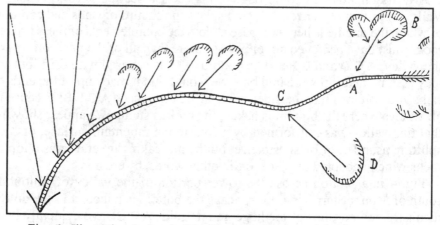

Fig. 6 Illustrating the bend of the Upper Tuolumne Valley where tributary glaciers have determined the course of the main valley.

inseparable relations of trend, size, and form which these Sierra valleys sustain to the ice-fountains in which they all head, as well as their grooved and broken sides, proclaim the eroding force to be ice. We have shown in the second chapter that the trend of Yosemite valleys is always a direct resultant of the forces of their ancient glaciers, modified by obvious peculiarities of physical structure of their rocks. The same is true of all valleys in this region. We give one example, the upper Tuolumne Valley, which is about eight miles long, and from 2,000 to 3,000 feet deep, and trends in a generally northerly direction. If we go to its head on the base of Mount Lyell, and follow it down, we find that after trending steadily about two miles it makes a bend of a few degrees to the *left* (A, Fig. 6). Looking for the cause we perceive a depression on the *opposite* or right wall; ascending to it, we find the depression to be the mouth of a tributary valley which lead to a crater-shaped ice fountain (B) which gave rise to the tributary glacier that, in thrusting itself into the valley trunk, caused the bend we are studying. After maintaining the new trend thus acquired for a distance of about a mile and a half, the huge valley swerves lithely to the *right* at C. Looking for the cause, we find another tributary ice-grooved valley coming in on the left, which like the first conducts back to an ice-womb (D) which gave birth to a glacier that in uniting with the trunk pushed it aside as far as its force, modified by the direction, smoothness, and declivity of its channel, enabled it to do. Below this, the noble valley is again pushed round in a curve to the *left* by a series of small tributaries which, of course, enter on the *right*, and with each change in trend there is always a corresponding change in width or depth, or in both. *No valley changes its direction without becoming larger.* On nearing the Big Meadows it is swept entirely round to the west by huge glaciers, represented by the large arrows, which descended from the flanks of Mounts Dana, Gibbs, Ord, and others to the south. For thirty miles farther, we find everywhere displayed the same delicate yielding to glacial law, showing that, throughout the whole period of its formation, the huge granite valley was lithe as a serpent, and winced tenderly to the touch of every tributary. So simple and sublime is the dynamics of the ancient glaciers.

Every valley in the region gives understandable evidence of having been equally obedient and sensitive to glacial force, and to no other. The erosive energy of ice is almost universally underrated, because we know so little about it. Water is our constant companion, but we cannot dwell with ice. Water is far more human than ice, and also far more outspoken. If glaciers, like roaring torrents, were endowed with voices commensurate with their strength, we would be slow to question any ascription of power that has yet been bestowed upon them. With reference to size, we have seen that the greater the ice-fountains the greater the resulting valleys; but no such direct and simple proportion exists between areas drained by water streams and the valleys in which they flow. Thus, the basin of Tenaya is *not one-fourth the size* of the South Lyell, although *its canyon is much larger.* Indeed, many canyons have no streams at all, whose topographical circumstances are also such as demonstrate the impossibility of their ever having had any. This state of things could not exist if the water streams which succeeded the glaciers could follow in their tracks, but the mode and extent of the compliance which glaciers yield to the topography of a mountainside, is very different from that yielded by water streams; both follow the lines of greatest declivity but the former in a far more general way. Thus, the greater portion of the ice current which eroded Tenaya Canyon flowed over the divide from the Tuolumne region, *making an ascent of over 500 feet.* Water streams of course, could not follow; hence the dry channels, and the disparity, to which we have called attention, between Tenaya Canyon and its basin.

Anyone who has attentively observed the habits and gestures of the upper Sierra streams, could not fail to perceive that they are young, and but little acquainted with the mountains; rushing wildly down steep inclines, whirling in pools, sleeping in lakes, often halting with an embarrassed air and turning back, groping their way as best they can, moving most lightly just where the glaciers bore down most heavily. With glaciers as a key the secrets of every valley are unlocked. Streams of ice explain all the phenomena; streams of water do not explain any; neither do subsidences, fissures, or pressure plications.

We have shown in the previous paper that *post-glacial streams have not eroded the 500,000th part of the upper Merced canyons.* The deepest water gorges with which we are acquainted are between the upper and lower Yosemite Falls, and in the Tenaya Canyon about four miles above Mirror Lake. These are from twenty to a hundred feet deep, and are easily distinguished from ice-eroded gorges by their narrowness and the ruggedness of their washed and pot-holed sides.

The gorge of Niagara River, below the falls, is perhaps the grandest known example of a valley eroded by water in compact rock; yet, comparing equal lengths, the glacier-eroded valley of Yosemite is a hundred times as large, reckoning the average width of the former 900 feet, and depth 200. But the erosion of Yosemite valley, besides being a hundred times greater, was accomplished in hard granite, while the Niagara was in shales and limestones. Moreover, Niagara canyon, as it now exists, expresses nearly the whole amount of erosion effected by the river; but the present Yosemite is by no means an adequate expression of the whole quantity of glacial erosion effected there since the beginning of the glacial epoch, or even from that point in the period when its principal features began to be developed, because the walls were being cut down on the top simultaneously with the deepening of its bottom. We may fairly ascribe the formation of the Niagara gorge to its river, because we find it at the upper end engaged in the work of its further extension toward Lake Erie; and for the same reason we may regard glaciers as the workmen that excavated Yosemite, for at the heads of some of its branches we find small glaciers engaged in the same kind of excavation. Merced canyons may be compared to mortises in the ends of which we still find the chisels that cut them, though now rusted and worn out. If Niagara River should vanish, or be represented only by a small brook, the evidence of the erosion of its gorge would still remain in a thousand water-worn monuments upon its walls. Nor, since Yosemite glaciers have been burned off by the sun, is the proof less conclusive that in their greater extension they excavated Yosemite, for, both in shape and sculpture, *every Yosemite rock is a glacial monument.*

When we walk the pathways of Yosemite glaciers and contemplate their separate works – the mountains they have shaped, the canyons they have furrowed, the rocks they have worn, and broken, and scattered in moraines – on reaching Yosemite, instead of being overwhelmed as at first with its uncompared magnitude, we ask, *Is this all?* wondering that so mighty a concentration of energy did not find yet grander expression.

CHAPTER FOUR

Glacial Denudation

GLACIAL DENUDATION is one of the noblest and simplest manifestations of sun-power. Ocean water is lifted in vapour, crystallised into snow, and sown broadcast upon the mountains. Thaw and frost, combined with the pressure of its own weight, change it to ice, which, although in appearance about as hard and inflexible as glass, immediately begins to flow back toward the sea whence it came, and at a rate of motion about equal to that of the hour-hand of a watch.

This arrangement is illustrated in Fig. 1, wherein a wheel, constructed of water, vapour, snow, and ice, and as irregular in shape as in motion, is being sun-whirled against a mountainside with a mechanical wearing action like that of an ordinary grindstone.

In north Greenland, Nova Zembla, the arctic regions of southeastern Alaska and Norway, the snow supply and general climatic conditions are such that their glaciers discharge directly into the sea, and so perhaps did all first-class glaciers when in their prime; but now the world is so warm, and the snow-crop so scanty, most glaciers melt long before reaching the ocean.

Fig. 1   The cycle of water-vapour (O), snow and ice (G)
and mechanical grinding of mountainside by ice.

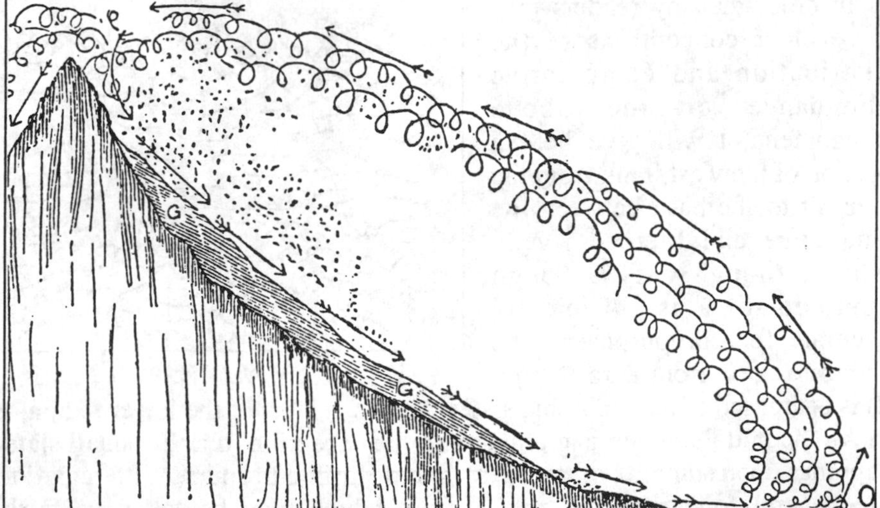

Schlagenweit tells us those of Switzerland melt on the average at an elevation of about 7,400 feet above sea-level; the Himalaya glacier, in which the Ganges takes its rise, does not descend below 12,914 feet;* while those of our Sierra melt at an average elevation of about 11,000 feet. In its progress down a mountain-side *a glacier follows the directions of greatest declivity*, a law subject to the very important modifications in its general application. Subordinate ranges many hundred feet in height are frequently overswept smoothly and gracefully without any visible manifestations of power. Thus, the Tenaya outlet of the ancient Tuolumne *mer de glace* glided over the Merced divide, which is more than 500 feet high, impelled by the force of that portion of the glacier which was descending the higher slopes of Mounts Dana, Gibbs, and others, at a distance of ten miles.

The deeper and broader the glacier, the greater the horizontal distance over which the impelling force may be transmitted. No matter how much the courses of glaciers are obstructed by inequalities of surface, such as ridges and canyons, if they are deep enough and wide enough, and the *general* declivity be sufficient, they will flow smoothly over them all just as calm water-streams flow over the stones and wrinkles of their channels.

THE PRESENT SIERRA AND GLACIAL ACTION

The most obvious glacial phenomena presented in the Sierra are: first, polished, striated, scratched, and grooved surfaces, produced by the glaciers slipping over and past the rocks in their pathways. Secondly, moraines, or accumulations of mud, dust, sand, gravel, and blocks of various dimensions, deposited by the glaciers in their progress, in certain specific methods. Thirdly, sculpture in general, as seen in canyons, lake-basins, hills, ridges, and separate rocks, whose forms, trends, distribution, etc., are the peculiar offspring of glaciers.

In order that my readers may have clear conceptions of the distribution and comparative abundance of the above phenomena, I will give here a section of the west flank from the summit to the base between the Tuolumne and Merced rivers, which, though only a rough approximation, is sufficiently accurate for our purposes. The summit region from D to C (Fig.

Fig. 2

2) is composed of metamorphic slates, so also is most of the lower region, B to A. The middle region is granite, with the exception of a few small slate-cappings upon summits of the Merced and Hoffmann spurs. With regard to the general topography of the section, which may be taken as fairly

* According to Captain Hodgson.

characteristic of the greater portion of the range, the summit forms are *sharp and angular*, because they have, been *down*-flowed; all the middle and lower regions comprising the bulk of the range have *rounded forms*, because they have been *over*flowed. In the summit region all the glacial phenomena mentioned above are found in a fresh condition simply on account of their youthfulness and the strong, indestructible character of the granite. Scores of small glaciers still exist on the summit peaks where we can watch their actions. But the middle region is the most interesting, because, though older, it contains all the phenomena, on a far grander scale, on account of the superior physical structure of granite for the reception of enduring glacial history.

Notwithstanding the grandeur of the canyons and moraines of this region, with their glorious adornments, stretching in sublime simplicity delicately compliant to glacial law, and the endless variety of picturesque rocks rising in beautiful groups out of the dark forests, by far the most striking of all the ice phenomena presented to the ordinary observer are the polished surfaces, the beauty and mechanical excellence of which no words will describe. They occur in large irregular patches many acres in extent in the summit and upper half of the middle regions, bright and stainless as the untrodden sky. They reflect the sunbeams like glass, and though they have been subject to the corroding influences of the storms of countless thousands of years, to frosts, rains, dews, yet are they in many places unblurred, undimmed, as if finished but yesterday. The attention of the mountaineer is seldom arrested by moraines however conspicuously regular and artificial in form, or by canyons however deep, or rocks however noble, but he stoops and rubs his hand admiringly on these shining surfaces, and tries hard to account for their mysterious smoothness. He has beheld the summit snows descending in booming avalanches, but he concludes that these cannot be the work of snow, because he finds it far beyond the reach of avalanches; neither can water be the agent, he says, for he finds it on the tops of the loftiest domes. Only the winds seem capable of following and flowing in the paths indicated by the scratches and grooves, and some observers have actually ascribed the phenomenon to this cause. Even horses and dogs gaze wonderingly at the strange brightness of the ground, and smell it, and place their feet upon it cautiously; only the wild mountain sheep seems to move wholly at ease upon these glistening pavements.

This polish is produced by glaciers slipping with enormous pressure over hard, close-grained slates or granite. The fine striations, so small as to be scarcely visible, are evidently caused by grains of sand embedded in the the ice; the scratches and smaller grooves, by stones with sharp graving edges. Scratches are therefore most abundant and roughest in the region of metamorphic slates, which break up by the force of the overflowing currents into blocks with hard cutting angles, and gradually disappear where these graving tools have been pushed so far as to have had their edges worn off.

The most extensive areas of polished surfaces are found in the upper half of the middle region, *where the granite is most solid in structure and contains the greatest quantity of silex*. They are always brighter, and extend farther down from the axis of the range, on the *north sides* of canyons that trend in a westerly direction than on the south sides; because, when wetted by corroding rains and snows, they are sooner dried, the north sides receiving sunshine, while the south walls are mostly in shadow and remain longer wet, and of course their glaciated surfaces become corroded sooner. The lowest patches are found at elevations of from 3,000 to 5,000 feet above the sea, and thirty to forty miles below the summits, on the sunniest and most enduring portions of vertical walls, protected from the drip and friction of water and snow by the form of the walls above them, and on hard swelling bosses on the bottom of wide canyons, protected and kept dry by broad boulders with overhanging eaves.

MORAINES

In the summit region we may watch the process of the formation of moraines of every kind among the small glaciers still lingering there. The material of which they are composed has been so recently quarried from the adjacent mountains that they are still plantless, and have a raw, unsettled appearance, as if newly dumped, like the stone and gravel of railroad embankments. The moraines belonging to the ancient glaciers are covered with forests, and extend with a greater or less degree of regularity down across the middle zone, as we have seen in Chapter Three. Glacial rock forms occur throughout this region also, in marvellous richness, variety, and magnitude, composing all that is most special in Sierra scenery. So also do canyons, ridges and sculpture phenomena in general, descriptions of whose scenic beauties and separate points of scientific interest would require volumes. In the lower regions the polished surfaces, as far as my observations have reached, are wholly wanting. So also are moraines, though the material which once composed them is found scattered, washed, crumbled, and reformed, over and over again, along riversides and over every flat and filled-up lake-basin, but so changed in position, form of deposit, and mechanical condition, that unless we begin with the undisturbed moraines of the summit region and trace them carefully to where they become more and more obscure, we would be inclined to question the glacial character of these ancient deposits.

The canyons themselves, the valleys, ridges, and the large rock masses are the most unalterable and indestructible glacial phenomena under consideration, *for their general forms, trends, and geographical position are specifically glacial*. Yet even these are so considerably obscured by post-glacial erosion, and by a growth of forests, underbrush, and weeds, that only the patient and educated eye will be able to recognise them beneath so many veils.

The ice-sheet of the glacial period, like an immense sponge, wiped the Sierra bare of all pre-glacial surface inscriptions, and wrote its own history upon the ample page. We may read the letter-pages of friends when written over and over, if we are intimately acquainted with their handwriting, and under the same conditions we may read Nature's writings on the stone pages of the mountains. Glacial history upon the summit of the Sierra page is clear, and the farther we descend, the more we find its inscriptions crossed and recrossed with the records of other agents. Dews have dimmed it, torrents have scrawled it here and there, and the earthquake and avalanche have covered and erased many a delicate line. Groves and meadows, forests and fields, darken and confuse its more enduring characters along the bottom, until only the laborious student can decipher even the most emphasised passages of the original manuscript.

METHODS OF GLACIAL DENUDATION

All geologists recognise the fact that glaciers wear away the rocks over which they move, but great vagueness prevails as to the size of fragments, their abundance, and the way in which glacial energy expends itself in detaching and carrying them away. And, if possible, still greater vagueness prevails as to the forms of the rocks and valleys resulting from erosion. This is not to be wondered at when we consider how recently glacial history has been studied, and how profound the silence and darkness under which glaciers prosecute their works.

In this article I can do little more for my readers than indicate methods of study, and results which may be obtained by those who desire to study the phenomena for themselves. In the first place, we may go to the glaciers themselves and learn what we can of their weight, motions, and general activities* – how they detach, transport, and accumulate rocks from various sources. Secondly, we may follow in the tracks of the ancient glaciers, and study their denuding power from the forms of their channels and from the fragments composing the moraines and the condition of the surfaces from which they were derived, and whether these fragments were rubbed off, split off, or broken off.

The waters which rush out from beneath all glaciers are turbid, and if we follow them to their resting-places in pools we shall find them depositing fine mud, which, when rubbed between the thumb and finger, is smooth as flour. This mud is ground off from the bed of the glacier by a smooth, slipping motion accompanied with immense pressure, giving rise to the polished surfaces we have already noticed. These mud particles are the smallest chips which glaciers make in the degradation of mountains.

Toward the end of the summer, when the winter snows are melted, particles of dust and sand are seen scattered over the surfaces of the Sierra glaciers in considerable quantities, together with angular masses of rock derived from the shattered storm-beaten cliffs that tower above their heads.

---

* Here I would refer my readers to the excellent elementary works of Agassiz, Tyndall and Forbes.

The separation of these masses, which vary greatly in size, is due only in part to the action of the glacier, although they all are borne down like drift on the surface of a river and deposited together in moraines. The winds scatter down most of the sand and dust. Some of the larger fragments are set free by the action of frost, rains, and general weathering agencies; while considerable quantities are borne down in avalanches of snow, and hurled down by the shocks of earthquakes. Yet the glacier performs an important part in the production of these superficial effects, by undermining the cliffs whence the fragments fall. During my Sierra explorations in the summers of 1872 and 1873, almost every glacier I visited offered illustrations of the special action of earthquakes in this connection, the earthquake of March, 1872, having just finished shaking the region with considerable violence, leaving the rocks which it hurled upon the ice fresh and nearly unchanged in position.

But in all moraines we find stones, which, from their shape and composition, and the finish of their surfaces, we know were not thus derived from the summit peaks overtopping the glaciers, but from the rocks past which and *over* which they flowed. I have seen the north Mount Ritter Glacier and many of the glaciers of Alaska in the act of grinding the side of their channels, and breaking off fragments and rounding their angles by crushing and rolling them between the wall and ice. In all the pathways of the ancient glaciers, also, there remain noble illustrations of the power of ice, not only in wearing away the sides of their channels in the form of mud, but in breaking them up into huge blocks. Explorers into the upper portion of the middle granite region will frequently come upon blocks of great size and regularity of form, possessing some character of colour or composition which enables them to follow back on their trail and discover the rock or mountain-side from which they were torn. The size of the blocks, their abundance along the line of dispersal, and the probable rate of motion of the glacier which quarried and transported them, form data by which some approximation to the rate of this sort of denudation may be reached. Fig. 3 is a rock about two miles west of Lake Tenaya, with a train of boulders derived from it. The boulders are scattered along a level ridge, where they have not been disturbed in any appreciable degree since they came to rest toward the close of the glacial period. An examination of the rock proves conclusively that not only were these blocks – many of which are twelve feet in

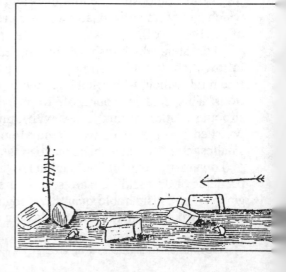

diameter – derived from it, but that they were *torn off its side* by the direct mechanical action of the glacier that swept over and past it. For had they simply fallen upon the surface of the glacier from above, then the rock would present a crumbling, ruinous condition – which it does not – and a talus of similar blocks would have accumulated at its base after there was no glacier to remove them as they fell; but no such talus exists, the rock remaining compact, as if it had scarcely felt the touch of a single storm. Yet, what countless seasons of weathering, combined with earthquake violence, could not accomplish, was done by the Tenaya Glacier, as it swept *past* on its way to Yosemite.

A still more striking and instructive example of side-rock erosion may be found about a mile north of Lake Tenaya. Here the glaciated pavements are more perfectly preserved than elsewhere in the Merced basin. Upon them I found a train of granite blocks, which attracted my attention from their isolated position, and the uniformity of their mechanical characters. Their angles were unworn, indicating that their source could not be far off. It proved to be on the *side* of one of the lofty elongated ridges stretching toward the Big Tuolumne Meadows. They had been quarried from the *base* of the ridge, which is ice-polished and undecayed to the summit. The reason that only this particular portion of the ridge afforded blocks of this kind, and so abundantly as to be readily traceable, is that the cleavage planes here separated the rock into parallelopipeds which sloped forward obliquely into the side of the glacier, which was thus enabled to grasp them and strip them off, just as the spikelets of an ear of wheat are stripped off by running the fingers down from the top toward the base. An instance where the structure has an exactly opposite effect upon the erodibility of the side of a rock is

Fig. 3 (below) Rock two miles west of Lake Tenaya, with a train of boulders derived from it.

given in Fig. 4, where the cleavage planes separate it into slabs which overlap each other with reference to the direction of the glacier's motion, like the shingles of a roof. Portions of the sides of rocks or canyon walls whose structure is of the latter character always project, because of the greater resistance they have been able to offer to the action of the past-flowing glacier, while those portions whose structure is similar to that of the former example always recede.

Fig 4   Landform resists erosion when cleavage planes create slabs like roof shingles.

Fig. 5 is a profile view of a past-flowed glacier rock, about 1,500 feet high, forming part of the north wall of Little Yosemite Valley near the head. Its grooved, polished, and fractured surface bears witness in unmistakable terms to the enormous pressure it has sustained from that portion of the great South Lyell Glacier which forced its way down through the valley, and to the quantity, and size, and kind of fragments which have been removed from it as a necessary result of this action. The dotted lines give an approximate reconstruction of the block as far as to the outside layer at A. Between A and B the broken ends of concentric layers, of which the whole rock seems to be built, give some idea of the immense size of some of the chips. The reason for the greater steepness of the front from A to B than from B to C will be perceived at a glance; and, since the cleavage planes and other controlling elements in its structure are evidently the same throughout the greater portion of its mass as those which determined its present condition, if the glacial winter had continued longer its more characteristic features would probably have remained essentially the same until the rock was nearly destroyed.

Fig. 5   Distinct slope angles of Little Yosemite determined by angle of dip of cleavage planes.

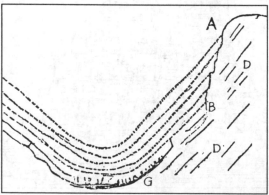

The section given in Fig. 6 is also taken from the north side of the same valley. It is inclined at an angle of about twenty-two degrees, and therefore has been more flowed *over* than flowed *past*. The whole surface, excepting the vertical portion at A, which is forty feet high, is polished and striated. The arrows indicate the direction of the striae. At A a few incipient cleavage planes are beginning to appear, which show the sizes of some of the chips which the glacier would have broken or split off had it continued longer at work. The whole of the missing layer which covered the rock at B, was evidently detached and carried off in this way. The abrupt trans-

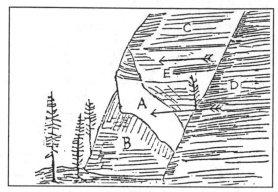

Fig. 6 Lack of striae and polished surface at B indicates detachment and plucking of block of granite by ice.

sition from the polished surface to the split angular front at A, shows in a most unequivocal manner that glaciers erode rocks in at least two very different modes – first, by grinding them into mud; second, by breaking and splitting them into blocks, whose sizes are measured by the divisional planes they possess and the intensity and direction of application of the force brought to bear upon them. That these methods prevail in the denudation of *over*flowed as well as *past*-flowed rocks, is shown by the condition of every canyon of the region. For if mud particles only were detached, then all the bottoms would be smooth grooves, interrupted only by flowing undulations; but, instead of this condition, we find that every canyon bottom abounds in steps sheer-fronted and angular, and some of them hundreds of feet in height, though ordinarily from one to ten or twelve feet. These step-fronts in most cases measure the size of the chips of erosion as to depth. Many of these interesting ice-chips may be seen in their tracks removed to great distances or only a few feet, when the melting of the glaciers at the close of the period put a stop to their farther progress, leaving them as lessons of the simplest kind.

Fig. 7 Polished surfaces, Yosemite Creek basin.

Fig. 7, taken from the Hoffmann fork of Yosemite Creek basin, shows the character of some of these steps. This one is fifteen feet high at the highest place, and the surface, both at top and bottom, is ice-polished, indicating that no disturbing force has interfered with the phenomena since the termination of the glacial period.

Fig. 8   Application of ice force and consequent erosion pattern on a dome.

Fig. 8 is a dome on the upper San Joaquin, the top of which is about 7,700 feet above sea-level. The arrow indicates the direction of application of the ice-force, which is seen to coincide with the position of remaining fragments of layers, the complements of which have been eroded away. Similar fragments occur *on the stricken side of all domes whose structure and position were favourable for their formation and preservation.*

Fig. 9 is a fragmentary dome situated on the south side of the Mono

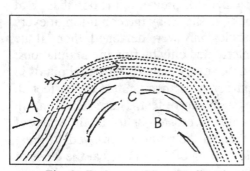

Fig. 9   Dome near Mono Trail.

trail, near the base of Mount Hoffmann. Remnants of concentric shells of granite from five to ten feet thick are seen on the up-stream side at A, where it received the thrust of the Hoffmann Glacier, when on its way to join the Tenaya, above Mirror Lake. The edges of unremoved layers are visible at B and C. This rock is an admirable illustration of the manner in which a broad deep glacier *clasps* and denudes a dome. When we narrowly inspect it, and trace the striae, we perceive that it has been eroded at once in front, back and sides, and none of the fragments thus removed are to be found around its base. Here I would direct special attention to the fact that it is on the upper side of this rock at A *just where the pressure was greatest, that the erosion has been least,* because there the layers were pressed against one another, instead of away from one another, as on the sides and back, and could not, therefore be so easily broken up.

These simple observations we have been making plainly indicate that the Sierra, from summit to base, was covered by a sheet of crawling ice, as it is now covered by the atmosphere. Its crushing currents slid over the highest domes, as well as along the deepest canyons, wearing, breaking, and degrading every portion of the surface, however resisting. The question, therefore, arises: What is the quantity of this degradation? As far as its limit is concerned it is clear that, inasmuch as glaciers cannot move without in some way and at some rate lowering the surfaces they are in contact with, a mountain range *may* be denuded until the declivity becomes so slight that the glaciers come to rest, or are melted, as was the case with those concerned in the degradation of the Sierra. However slow the rate of wear, given a sufficient length of time, and any thickness of rock, whether a foot or hundreds of thousands of feet, will be removed. No student pretends to give an arithmetical expression to the glacial epoch, though it is universally admitted that it extended through thousands or millions of years. Nevertheless, geologists are found who can neither give Nature time enough for her larger operations, or for the erosion of a mere canyon furrow, without resorting to sensational cataclysms for an explanation of the phenomena.

If the Sierra were built of one kind of rock, homogeneous in structure throughout its sections, then perhaps we would be unable to produce any plain evidence relative to the amount of denudation effected; but, fortunately for the geologist, this is not the case. The summits of the range in the section under special consideration are capped with slates; so are several peaks of outlying spurs, as those of the Merced and Hoffmann, and all the base is slate-covered. The circumstances connected with their occurrence in these localities and absence in others, furnish proof little short of demonstration that they once covered all the range, and, from their known thickness in the places where they occur, we may approximate to the quantity removed where they are less abundant or wanting. Moreover, we have seen in Study No. III [Chapter 3] that the physical structure of granite is such that we may know whether or not its forms are broken. The opposite sides of valley walls exhibiting similar fragmentary sections often demonstrate that the valleys were formed by the removal of an amount of rock equal in depth to that of the valleys.

Fig. 10 is an ideal section across the range from base to summit. That slates covered the whole granitic region between B and D is shown by the fact that slates cap the summits of spurs in the denuded gap where they are

Fig. 10   Ideal section across the range from base to summit. Slate capped summits (C) are evidence are evidence of removal of slate and exposed granite between D and B.

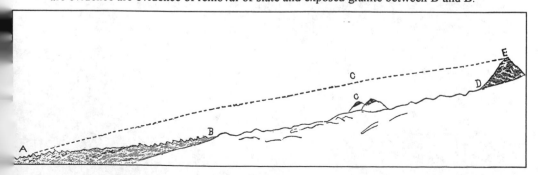

sufficiently high, as at C. Also, where the granite comes in contact with the slates, and for a considerable depth beneath the line of contact, it partakes, in a greater or less degree, of the physical structure of slates, enabling us to determine the fact that in many places slates *have* covered the granite where none are now visible for miles, and also furnishing data by which to approximate the depth at which these surfaces lie beneath the original summit of the granite. Phenomena relating to this portion of the argument abound in the upper basins of the tributary streams of the Tuolumne and Merced; for their presentation, however, in detail, we have no space in these brief outlines.

If, therefore, we would restore this section of the range to its unglaciated condition, we would have, first, to fill up all the valleys and canyons. Secondly, all the granite domes and peaks would have to be buried until the surface reached the level of the line of contact with the slates. Thirdly, in the yet grander restoration of the missing portions of both granite and slates up the line between the summit slates and those of the base, as indicated in Fig. 10 by the dotted line, the maximum thickness of the restored rocks in the middle region would not be less than a mile and a half, and average a mile. But, because the summit peaks are only *sharp residual fragments*, and the foothills *rounded residual fragments*, when all the intervening region is restored up to the dotted line in the figure, we still have only partially reconstructed the range, for the summits may have towered many thousands of feet above their present heights. And when we consider that residual glaciers are still engaged in lowering the summits which are already worn to mere blades and pinnacles, it will not seem improbable that the whole quantity of glacial denudation in the middle region of the western flank of the Sierra considerably exceeds a mile in average depth. So great was the amount of chipping required to bring out the present architecture of the Sierra.

CHAPTER FIVE

Post-Glacial Denudation

WHEN NATURE lifted the ice-sheet from the mountains she may well be said not to have turned a new leaf, but to have made a new one of the old. Throughout the unnumbered seasons of the glacial epoch the range lay buried, crushed, and sunless. In the stupendous denudation to which it was then subjected, all its pre-glacial features disappeared. Plants, animals, and landscapes were wiped from its flanks like drawings from a blackboard, and the vast page left smooth and clean, to be re-pictured with young life and the varied and beautiful inscriptions of water, snow, and the atmosphere.

The variability in hardness, structure, and mineralogical composition of the rocks forming the present surface of the range has given rise to irregularities in the amount of post-glacial denudation effected in different portions, and these irregularities have been greatly multiplied and augmented by differences in the kind and intensity of the denuding forces, and in the length of time that different portions of the range have been exposed to their action. The summits have received more snow, the foothills more rain, while the middle region has been variably acted upon by both of these agents. Again, different portions are denuded in a greater or less degree according to their relations to level. The bottoms of trunk valleys are swept by powerful rivers, the branches by creeks and rills, while the intervening plateaus and ridges are acted upon only by thin feeble currents, silent and nearly invisible. Again some portions of the range are subjected every winter to the scouring action of avalanches, while others are entirely beyond the range of such action. But the most influential of the general causes that have conspired to produce irregularity in the quantity of post-glacial denudation is the difference in the length of time during which different portions of the range have been subjected to denuding agents. The ice-sheet melted from the base of the range tens of thousands of years ere it melted from the upper regions. We find, accordingly, that the foothill region is heavily weathered and blurred, while the summit, excepting the peaks, and a considerable the middle region remain fresh and shining as if they had never suffered from the touch of a single storm.

Perhaps the least known among the more outspoken agents of mountain degradation are those currents of eroding rock called avalanches. Those of the Sierra are of all sizes, from a few sand grains or crystals worked loose by the weather and launched to the bottoms of cliffs, to those immense earthquake avalanches that thunder headlong down amid fire and smoke and dust, with a violence that shakes entire mountains. Many avalanche-producing causes, such as moisture, temperature, winds, and earthquakes are exceedingly variable in the scope and intensity of their action. During the dry, equable summers of the middle region, atmospheric disintegration goes silently on, and many a huge mass is made ready to be advantageously acted upon by the first winds and rains of winter. Inclined surfaces are then moistened and made slippery, decomposed joints washed out, frost-wedges driven in, and the grand avalanche storm begins. But though these stone-storms occur only in winter, the attentive mountaineer may have the pleasure of witnessing small avalanches in every month of the year. The first warning of the bounding free of a simple avalanche is usually a dull muffled rumble, succeeded by a ponderous crunching sound; then perhaps a single huge block weighing a hundred tons or more may be seen wallowing down the face of a cliff, followed by a train of smaller stones, which are gradually left behind on account of the greater relative resistance they encounter as compared with their weight. The eye may therefore follow the large block undisturbed, noting its awkward, lumbering gestures as it gropes its way through the air in its first wild journey, and how it is made to revolve like a star upon its axis by striking on projecting portions of the walls while it pursues the grand smooth curves of general descent. Where it strikes a projecting boss it gives forth an intense gasping sound, which, coming through the darkness of a storm-night, is indescribably impressive; and when at length it plunges into the valley, the ground trembles as if shaken by an earthquake.

On the 12th of March, 1873, I witnessed a magnificent avalanche in Yosemite Valley from the base of the second of the Three Brothers. A massive stream of blocks bounded from ledge to ledge and plunged into the talus below with a display of energy inexpressibly wild and exciting. Fine grey foam-dust boiled and swirled along its path, and gradually rose above the top of the cliff, appearing as a dusky cloud on the calm sky. Unmistakable traces of similar avalanches are visible here, probably caused by the decomposition of the feldspathic veins with which the granite is interlaced.

Earthquakes, though not of frequent occurrence in the Sierra, are powerful causes of avalanches. Many a lofty tower and impending brow stood firm through the storms of the first post-glacial seasons. Torrents swept their bases, and winds and snows slipped glancingly down their polished sides, without much greater erosive effect than the passage of cloud-shadows. But at length the new-born mountains were shaken by an earthquake-storm, and thousands of avalanches from canyon walls and mountain sides fell in one simultaneous crash. The records of this first post-glacial earthquake present themselves in every canyon and around the bases of every mountain summit that I have visited; and it is a fact of great geological interest that to it alone more than nine-tenths of all the cliff taluses which form so strikingly a characteristic of canyon scenery are due. The largest of these earthquake taluses are from 500 to 1,000 feet in height, and are timbered with spruce, pine, and live-oak over their entire surfaces, showing that they have not been disturbed since their formation, either by denudation or accessions of fresh material.

The earthquake which destroyed the village of Lone Pine, in March, 1872, shook the Sierra with considerable violence, giving rise to many new taluses, the formation of one of which I was so fortunate as to witness.

The denuding action of avalanches is not unlike that of water-torrents. They are frequently seen descending the summit peaks, flowing in regular channels, the surfaces of which they erode by striking off large chips and blocks, as well as by wearing off sand and dust.

A considerable amount of grinding also goes on in the body of the avalanche itself, reducing the size of the masses, and preparing them for the action of other agents. Some avalanches hurl their detritus directly into the beds of streams, thus bringing it under the influence of running water, by which a portion of it is carried into the ocean.

The range of rock avalanches, however produced, is restricted within comparatively narrow bounds. The shattered peaks are constant fountains, but the more powerful mountain-shaking avalanches are confined to the edges of deep canyons in a zone twelve or fifteen miles wide, and gradually merge into land-slips along their lower limits.

Large rock avalanches pour freely through the air from a height of hundreds or thousands of feet, and on striking the bottom of the valley are dashed into a kind of coarse stone foam. Or, they make the descent in several leaps, or rumble over jagged inclines in the form of cascades. But in any case they constitute currents of loose-flowing fragments. Landslips, on the contrary, slip in one mass, and, unless sheer cliffs lie in their paths, may come to rest right-side up and undivided. There is also a marked difference in their geographical distribution, landslips being restricted to deeply eroded banks and hillsides of the lower half of the range, beginning just where rock avalanches cease. Again, the material of land-slips is chiefly fine soil and decomposing boulders, while that of rock avalanches is mostly of unweathered angular blocks.

Let Figure 1 represent a section across a valley in which moraine matter, A, is deposited upon the inclined bedrock, B B B. Now, strong young moraine material deposited in this way, in a kind of rude masonry, always rests, or is capable of resting, at a much steeper angle than the same material after it has grown old and rotten.

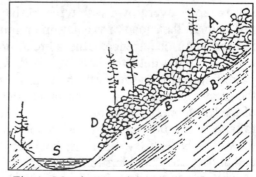

Fig. 1   Moraine material on inclined bedrock.

If a poultice of acid mud be applied to a strong boulder, it will not be much affected in an hour or day, but if kept on for a few thousands or tens of thousands of years, it will at length soften and crumble. Now, Nature thus patiently poultices the boulders of the moraine banks under consideration. For many years subsequent to the close of the ice period very little acid for this purpose was available, but as vegetation increased and decayed, acids became more plentiful, and boulder decomposition went on at an accelerated rate, until a degree of weakness was induced that caused the sheerest portions of the deposits, as A B D (Fig. 1), to give way, perhaps when jarred by an earthquake, or when burdened with snow or rain, or partially undermined by the action of a stream.

It appears, therefore, that the main cause of the first post-glacial land-slips is old age. They undoubtedly made their first appearance in moraine banks at the foot of the range, and gradually extended upward to where we now find them, at a rate of progress measured by that of the recession of the ice-sheet, and by the durability of moraines and the effectiveness of the corroding forces brought into action upon them. In those portions of the Sierra where the morainal deposits are tolerably uniform in kind and exposure, the upper limits of the landslip are seen to stretch along the range with as great constancy of altitude as that of the snowline.

The above-described species of land-slip is followed up the range by another of greater size, just as the different forest trees follow one another in compliance with conditions of soil and climate. After the *sheer end* of the deposit (A B D, Fig. 1) has slipped, the *whole mass* may finally slip on the bedrock by the further decomposition, not only of the deposit itself, but of the bed-rock on which it rests. Bedrocks are usually more or less uneven. Now, it is plain that when the inequalities B B B crumble by erosion, the mass of the deposit will not be so well supported; moreover, the weight of the mass will continue to increase as its material is more thoroughly pulverised, because a greater quantity of moisture will be required to saturate it. Thus it appears that the support of moraine deposits diminishes, just as the necessity for greater support increases, until a slip is brought on.

Slips of this species are often of great extent, the surface comprising several acres overgrown with trees, perhaps moving slowly and coming to rest with all their load of vegetation uninjured, leaving only a yawning rent to mark their occurrence. Others break up into a muddy disorderly flood, moving rapidly until the bottom of the wall is reached. Landslides occur more frequently on the north than on the south sides of ridges, because of the greater abundance of weight-producing and decomposing moisture. One of the commonest effects of landslips is the damming of streams, giving rise to large accumulations of water, which speedily burst the dams and deluge the valleys beneath, sweeping the finer detritus before them to great distances, and at first carry boulders tons in weight.

The quantity of denudation accomplished by the Sierra landslips of both species is very small. Like rock-falls, they erode the surface they slip upon in a mechanical way, and also bring down material to lower levels, where it may be more advantageously exposed to the denuding action of other agents, and open scars whereby rain-torrents are enabled to erode gullies; but the sum of the areas thus affected bears an exceedingly small proportion to the whole surface of the range.

The part which snow avalanches play in the degradation of mountains is simpler than that of free falling or cascading rocks, or either species of landslip; these snow avalanches being external and distinct agents. Their range, however, is as restricted as that of either of the others, and like them they only carry their detritus a short distance and leave it in heaps at the foot of cliffs and steep inclines. There are three well-marked and distinct species of snow avalanche in the upper half of the Sierra, differing widely in structure, geographical distribution, and in the extent and importance of the geological changes they effect. The simplest and commonest species is formed of fresh mealy snow, and occurs during and a short time after every heavy snow-fall wherever the mountain slopes are inclined at suitable angles. This species is of frequent occurrence throughout all the steep-flanked mountains of the summit of the range, where it reaches perfection, and is also common throughout the greater portion of the middle region. Avalanches are the feeders of the glaciers, pouring down their dry mealy snow into the womb-amphitheatres, where it is changed to névé and ice. Unless distributed by storm-winds, they cascade down the jagged heights in regular channels, and glide gracefully out over the glacier slopes in beautiful curves; which action gives rise in summer to a most interesting and comprehensive system of snow-sculpture. The detritus discharged upon the surface of the glaciers forms a kind of stonedrift which is floated into moraines like the straws and chips of rivers.

Few of the defrauded toilers of the plain know the magnificent exhilaration of the boom and rush and outbounding energy of great snow avalanches. While the storms that breed them are in progress, the thronging flakes darken the air at noonday. Their muffled voices reverberate through the gloomy canyons, but we try in vain to catch a glimpse of their noble forms until rifts appear in the clouds, and the storm ceases. Then in cliff-walled valleys like Yosemite we may witness the descent of half a dozen or more snow avalanches within a few hours.

The denuding power of this species of avalanche is not great, because the looseness of the masses allows them to roll and slip upon themselves. Some portions of their channels, however, present a roughly scoured appearance, caused by rocky detritus borne forward in the under portion of the current. The avalanche is, of course, collected in a heap at the foot of the cliff, and on melting, leaves the detritus to accumulate from year to year. These taluses present striking contrasts to those of rock avalanches caused by the first great pre-glacial earthquake. The latter are grey in colour, with a covering of slow-growing lichens, and support extensive groves of pine, spruce, and live-oak; while the former, receiving additions from year to year, are kept in a raw formative state, neither trees nor lichens being allowed time to grow, and it is a fact of great geological significance that no one of the Yosemite snow avalanches, although they have undoubtedly flowed in their present channels since the close of the glacial period, has yet accumulated so much débris as some of the larger earthquake avalanches which were formed in a few seconds.

The next species of avalanche in natural order is the annual one, composed of heavy crystalline snows which have been subjected to numerous alternations of frost and thaw. Their development requires a shadowed mountain side 9,000 or 10,000 feet high, inclined at such an angle that loose fresh snow will lodge and remain upon it, and bear repeated accessions throughout the winter without moving; but which, after the spring thaws set in, and the mountain side thus becomes slippery, and the nether surface of the snow becomes icy, will then give way.

One of the most accessible of the fountains of annual avalanches is the northern slope of Clouds Rest, above the head of the Yosemite Valley. Here I have witnessed the descent of three within half an hour. They have a vertical descent of nearly a mile on a smooth granite surface. Fine examples of this species of avalanche may also be observed upon the north side of the dividing ridge between the basins of Ribbon and Cascade creeks, and in some portions of the upper Nevada Canyon. Their denuding power is much greater than that of the first species, on account of their greater weight and compactness. Where their pathways are not broken by precipices, they descend all or part of their courses with a hard snout kept close down on the surface of the rock, and because the middle of the snout is stronger, the detritus heaps are curved after the manner of terminal moraines. These detritus heaps also show an irregularly corrugated and concentric structure. An examination of the avalanche pathways shows conclusively that the annual accretions of detritus, scraped from their surfaces, are wholly insufficient to account for the several large concentric deposits. But when, after the detritus of many years has been accumulated by avalanches of ordinary magnitude, a combination of causes, such as rain, temperature, and abundant snow-fall, gives rise to an avalanche of extraordinary size, its superior momentum will carry it beyond the limits attained by its predecessors, and sweep forward the accumulations of many years concentric with others of like magnitude into a single mass. A succession of these irregularities will obviously produce results corresponding in every particular with the observed phenomena.

What we may call century avalanches, as distinguished from annual, are conceived and nourished on cool mountain sides 10,000 or 12,000 feet in height, where the snow falling from winter to winter will not slip, and where the exposure and temperature are such that it will not always melt off in summer. Snow accumulated under these conditions may linger without seeming to greatly change for years, until some slowly organised group of causes, such as temperature, abundance of snow, condition of snow, or the mere occurrence of an earthquake, launches the grand mass. In swooping down the mountain flanks they usually strip off the forest trees in their way, as well as the soil on which they were growing.

Some of these avalanche pathways are 200 yards wide and extend from the upper limit of the tree-line to the bottom of the valleys. They are all well "blazed" on both sides by descending trunks, many of which carry sharp stones clutched in their up-torn roots. The height of these "blazes" on the trees bordering the avalanche gap measures the depth of the avalanche at the sides, while in rare instances some noble silver-fir is found standing out in the channel, the only tree sufficiently strong to withstand the mighty onset; the scars upon which, or its broken branches, recording the depth of the current. The ages of the trees show that some of these colossal avalanches occur only once in a century, or at still wider intervals. These avalanches are by far the most powerful of the three species, although from the rarity of their occurrence and the narrowness of the zone in which they find climatic conditions suited to their development, the sum of the denudation accomplished by them is less than that of either of the others.

We have seen that water in the condition of rain, dew, vapour, and melting snow, combined with air, acts with more or less efficiency in corroding the whole mountain surface, thus preparing it for the more obviously mechanical action of winds, rivers, and avalanches. Running water is usually regarded as the most influential of all denuding agents. Those regions of the globe first laid bare by the melting of the ice-sheet present no unchanged glaciated surfaces from which, measuring down, we may estimate the amount of post-glacial denudation. The streams of these old eroded countries are said by the poets to "go on forever," and the conceptions of some geologists concerning them are scarcely less vague.

Beginning at the foot of the Sierra glaciers, and following the torrents that rush out from beneath them down the valleys, we find that the rocks over which they flow are weathered gradually, and increasingly, the farther we descend; showing that the streams in coming into existence grew like trees from the foot of the range upward, gradually ramifying higher and wider as the ice-sheet was withdrawn – some of the topmost branchlets being still in process of formation.

Rivers are usually regarded as irregular branching strips of running water, shaped somewhat like a tree stripped of its leaves. As far as more striking features and effects are concerned, the comparison is a good one; for in tracing rivers to their fountains we observe that as their branches divide and redivide, they speedily become silent and inconspicuous, and apparently channelless; yet it is a mistake to suppose that streams really terminate where they become too small to sing out audibly, or erode distinct channels. When we stoop down and closely examine any portion of a mountain surface during the progress of a rain-storm, we perceive minute water-twigs that continue to bifurcate until like netted veins of leaves the innumerable currentlets disappear in a broad universal sheet.

It would appear, therefore, that rivers more nearly resemble certain gigantic *algae* with naked stalks, and branches webbed into a flat *thallus*. The long unbranched stalks run through the dry foothills; the webbed branches frequently overspread the whole surface of the snowy and rainy alpine and middle regions, as well as every moraine, bog, and névé bank. The gently gliding rain-*thallus* fills up small pits as lakelets and carries away minute specks of dust and mica. Larger sand-grains are overflowed without being moved unless the surface be steeply inclined, while the rough grains of quartz, hornblende, and feldspar, into which granite crumbles, form obstacles around which it passes in curves. Where the currentlets concentrate into small rills, these larger chips and crystals are rolled over and over, or swept forward partly suspended, just as dust and sand grains are by the wind.

The transporting power of steeply inclined torrents is far greater than is commonly supposed. Stones weighing several tons are swept down steep canyon gorges and spread in rugged deltas at their mouths, as if they had been floated and stranded like blocks of wood. The denudation of gorges by the friction of the boulders thus urged gratingly along their channels is often quite marked.

Strong torrents also denude their channels by the removal of blocks made separable from the solid bedrock by the development of cleavage planes. Instructive examples of this species of denudation may be studied in the gorges between the upper and lower Yosemite falls and the Tenaya Canyon, four miles above Mirror Lake. This is the most rapid mode of torrent denudation I have yet observed, but its range is narrowly restricted, and its general denuding effects inappreciable.

Water-streams also denude mountains by dissolving them and carrying them away in solution, but the infinite slowness of this action on hard porphyritic granite is strikingly exemplified by the fact that in the upper portion of the middle region granite ice-planed pavements have been flowed upon incessantly since they were laid bare on the breaking up of the glacial winter without being either decomposed, dissolved, or mechanically eroded to the depth of the one-hundredth part of an inch.

Wind-blown dust, mica flakes, sand, and crumbling chips are being incessantly moved to lower levels wherever wind or water flows. But even in the largest mountain rivers the movement of large boulders is comparatively a rare occurrence. When one lies down on a river-bank opposite a boulder-spread incline and listens patiently for a day or two, a dull thumping sound may occasionally be heard from the shifting of a boulder, but in ordinary times few streams do much boulder work; all the more easily moved blocks having been adjusted and readjusted during freshets, when the current was many times more powerful. All the channels of Sierra streams are subjected to the test action of at least one freshet per season, on the melting of the winter snow, when all weakly constructed dams and drift-heaps are broken up and re-formed.

It is a fact of great geological interest that only that portion of the general detritus of post-glacial denudation – that is, in the form of mud, sand, fine gravel, and matter held in solution – has ever at any time been carried entirely out of the range into the plains or ocean. In the canyon of the Tuolumne River, we find that the chain of lake basins which stretch along the bottom from the base of Mount Lyell to the Hetch-Hetchy Valley are filled with detritus, through the midst of which the river flows; but the washed boulders, which form a large portion of this detritus, instead of being constantly pushed forward from basin to basin, lie still for centuries at a time, as is strikingly demonstrated by an undisturbed growth of immense sugar-pines and firs inhabiting the river-banks. But the presence of these trees upon water-washed boulders only shows that no displacement has been effected among them for a few centuries. They still must have been swept forward and outspread in some grand flood prior to the planting of these trees. But even this grand old flood of glacial streams, whose magnificent traces occur everywhere on both flanks of the range, *did not remove a single boulder from the higher to the lower Sierra in that section of the range drained by the Tuolumne and Merced, much less into the ocean,* because the lower portion of the Hetch-Hetchy basin, situated about half-way down the western flank, *is still in process of filling up,* and as yet contains only sand and mud to as great a depth as observation can reach in river sections. The river flows slowly through this alluvial deposit and out of the basin *over a lip of solid bedrock, showing that not a single high Sierra boulder ever passed it since the close of the glacial period;* and the same evidence is still more strikingly exhibited in similarly situated basins in the Merced Valley.

Frost plays a very inferior part in Sierra degradation. The lower half of the range is almost entirely exempt from its disruptive effects, while the upper half is warmly snow-mantled throughout the winter months. At high elevations of from ten to twelve thousand feet, sharp frosts occur in the months of October and November, before much snow has fallen; and where shallow water-currents flow over rocks traversed by open divisional joints, the freezing that ensues forces the blocks apart and produces a ruinous appearance, without effecting much absolute displacement. The blocks thus loosened are, of course, liable to be moved by flood currents. This action, however, is so limited in range, that the general average result is inappreciable.

Atmospheric weathering has, after all, done more to blur and degrade the glacial features of the Sierra than all other agents combined, because of the universality of its scope. No mountain escapes its decomposing and mechanical effects. The bases of mountains are mostly denuded by streams of water, their summits by streams of air. The winds that sweep the jagged peaks assume magnificent proportions, and effect changes of considerable importance. The smaller particles of disintegration are rolled or shoved to lower levels just as they are by water currents, or they are caught up bodily in strong, passionate gusts, and hurled against trees or higher portions of the surface. The manner in which exposed tree trunks are thus wind-carved and boulders polished will give some conception of the force with which this agent moves.

Where boulders of a form fitted to shed off snow and rain have settled protectingly upon a polished and striated surface, then the protected portion will, by the erosion and removal of the unprotected surface around it, finally come to form a pedestal for the stone which saved it. Figure 2 shows where a boulder, B, has settled upon and protected from erosion a portion of the original glaciated surface until the pedestal, A, has been formed, the height of which is of course the exact measure of the whole quantity of post-glacial denudation at that point. These boulder pedestals, furnishing so admirable a means of gauging atmospheric erosion, occur throughout the middle granitic region in considerable numbers: some with their protecting boulders still poised in place, others naked, their boulders having rolled off on account of the stool having been eroded until too small for them to balance upon. It is because of this simple action that all very old, deeply weathered ridges and slopes are boulderless, Nature having thus leisurely rolled them off, giving each a whirling impulse as it fell from its pedestal once in hundreds or thousands of years.

Fig. 2 Post-glacial weathering can be assessed by the height of a pedestal beneath a deposited boulder.

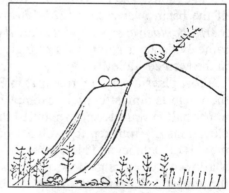

Fig. 3 Poised boulders on *roches moutonnées* indicate minimal post-glacial denudation.

Moutonnéed rock forms shaped like Figure 3 are abundant in the middle granitic region. They frequently wear a single pine, jauntily windslanted, like a feather in a cap, and a single large boulder, poised by the receding ice-sheet, that often produces an impression of having been thus placed artificially, exciting the curiosity of the most apathetic mountaineer. Their occurrence always shows that the surfaces they are resting upon are not yet deeply eroded.

Ice-planed veins of quartz and feldspar are frequently weathered into relief by the superior resistance they offer to erosion, but they seldom attain a greater height than three or four inches ere they become weather-cracked and lose their glacial polish, thus becoming useless as means of gauging denudation. Ice-burnished feldspar crystals are brought into relief in the same manner to the height of about an inch, and are available to this extent in determining denudation over large areas in the upper portion of the middle region.

This brief survey of the various forces incessantly or occasionally at work wasting the Sierra surface would at first lead us to suppose that the sum total of the denudation must be enormous; but, on the contrary, so indestructible are the Sierra rocks, and so brief has been the period through which they have been exposed to these agents, that the general result is found to be comparatively insignificant. The unaltered polished areas constituting so considerable a portion of the upper and middle regions have not been denuded the one-hundredth part of an inch. Farther down measuring tablets abound bearing the signature of the ice. The amount of torrential and avalanchial denudation is also certainly estimated within narrow limits by measuring down from the unchanged glaciated surfaces lining their banks. Farther down the range, where the polished surfaces disappear, we may still reach a fair approximation by the height of pot-holes drilled into the walls of gorges, and by the forms of the bottoms of the valleys containing these gorges, and by the shape and condition of the general features.

Summing up these results, we find that the average quantity of post-glacial denudation in the upper half of the range, embracing a zone twenty five or thirty miles wide, probably does not exceed a depth of three inches.

That of the lower half has evidently been much greater – probably several feet – but certainly not so much as radically to alter any of its main features. In that portion of the range where the depth of glacial denudation exceeds a mile, that of post-glacial denudation is less than a foot.

From its warm base to its cold summit, the physiognomy of the Sierra is still strictly glacial. Rivers have only traced shallow wrinkles, avalanches have made scars, and winds and rains have blurred it, but the change, as a whole, is not greater than that effected on a human countenance by a single year of exposure to common alpine storms.

CHAPTER SIX

Formation of Soils

NATURE HAS ploughed the Sierra flanks more than a mile deep through lava, slate, and granite, thus giving rise to a most lavish abundance of fruitful soils. The various methods of detachment of soil-fragments from the solid rocks have been already considered in the foregoing studies on glacial and post-glacial denudation. It now remains to study the formation of the variously eroded fragments into beds available for the uses of vegetable life.

If all the soils that now mantle the Sierra flanks were spread out in one sheet of uniform thickness, it would measure only a few feet in depth, and its entire removal would not appreciably affect the configuration of any portion of the range. The largest beds rarely exceed a hundred feet in average thickness, and a very considerable proportion of the whole surface is naked. But we have seen that glaciers alone have ground the west flank of the range into soil to a depth of more than a mile, without taking into account the work of other soil-producing agents, such as rains, avalanches , torrents, earthquakes, etc. It appears, therefore, that not the one-thousandth part of the whole quantity of soil eroded from the range since the beginning of the glacial epoch is now left upon its flanks.

The cause of this comparative scantiness of the Sierra soil-beds will be readily apprehended when we reflect that the glacier, which is the chief soil-producing agent, no sooner detaches a soil-fragment than it begins to carry it away. During the long glacial winter, soil-material was poured from the range as from a fountain, borne outward by the mighty currents of the ice-sheet to be deposited in its terminal moraines. The only one of these ancient ice-sheet moraines which has retained its principal characteristics unaltered down to the present time is that magnificent belt of soil upon which all the majestic forests of the Sierra are growing. It stretches along the west flank of the range like a smooth-flowing ribbon, waving compliantly up and down over a thousand hills and hollows, at an elevation of from four to seven thousand feet above the level of the sea. In some places it is more than a hundred feet deep and twenty miles wide, but it is irregular as a sun-wasted snow-wreath both in width and in depth, on account of the configuration of the surface upon which it rests, and the varying thickness and declivity of the ice-sheet at the period of its deposition. The long weathering and the multitude of storm-washings to which it has been subjected have made its outlines still more indefinite and variable. Furthermore, its continuity is interrupted at intervals of fifteen or twenty miles by the river canyons which cross it nearly at right angles. For, at the period of the deposition of the main soil-belt as a terminal moraine of the ice-sheet, long finger-like glaciers extended down every one of these canyons, thus effectually preventing the continuance of the main terminal moraine across the canyon channels.

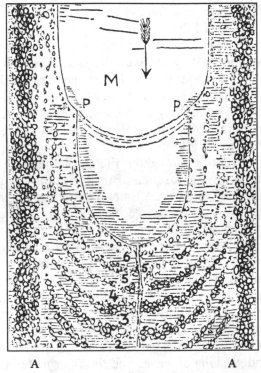

Fig. 1   Recessional moraine belts (raw material of productive forests and meadow bearing soils).

The method of the deposition of broad belts of terminal-moraine soil will be made plain by reference to Figure 1, which represents a deposit of this kind lying at the foot of Moraine Lake, made by the Bloody Canyon glacier in its recess toward the period of its extinction. A A are the main lateral moraines extending from the jaws of the canyon out into the Mono Plain; 1, 2, 3, 4, 5, 6 are concentric belts of terminal-moraine soil deposited by the glacier in its retreat.

These soil-belts or furrows are twenty or thirty yards apart. After belt number 1 was laid down, the glacier evidently withdrew at a faster rate, until a change of climate as regards heat or cold, or the occurrence of a cluster of snowier years, checked its backward motion sufficiently to afford it time to deposit belt number 2, and so on; the speed of the dying glacier's retreat being increased and diminished in rhythmic alternations of frost and thaw, sunshine and snow, all of which found beautiful and enduring expression in its ridged moraines. The promontories P P are portions of a terminal soil-belt, part of which is covered by the lake.

Similar fields of corrugated moraine matter occur farther down, marking lingering and fluctuating periods in the recession of the glacier similar to the series we have been studying. Now, it is evident that if, instead of thus dying a lingering death, the glacier had melted suddenly while it extended into the Mono plain, these wide soil-fields could not have been made. Neither could the grand soil-belt of the western flank have existed: the ice-sheet had melted in one immense thaw while it extended as a seamless mantle over all the western flank. Fortunately for Sierra vegetation and the life dependent upon it, this was not the case; instead of disappearing suddenly, like a sun-stricken cloud, it withdrew from the base of the great soil-belt upward, in that magnificently deliberate way so characteristic of nature – adding belt to belt in beautiful order over lofty plateaus and rolling hills and valleys, wherever soil could be made to lie.

Winds and rains, acting throughout the ample centuries, smooth rough glacial soils like harrows and rollers. But this culture is carried on at an infinitely slow rate, as we measure time. Comparing the several moraine-fields of Bloody Canyon, we observe that the ridged concentric structure (Fig. 1) becomes gradually less distinct the farther we proceed out into the plain, just as the plow-ridges in a farmer's field become less distinct the more they are harrowed. Now, the difference in time between the deposition of contiguous moraine-fields in Bloody Canyon is probably thousands of years, yet the difference as regards smoothness and freshness of aspect corresponding to this difference in time is in some instances scarcely discernible. In the field represented in Figure 1 these levelling operations may be studied to excellent advantage. The furrows between the several ridges are leisurely filled up by the inblowing and washing of leaves and the finer material of the adjacent ridges. As the weathering of the surface boulders goes on, the crumbling material which falls from them collects about their bases, thus tending to bury them, and produce that smoothness of surface which characterises all the more ancient moraine-fields of the Sierra. The great forest soil-belt of the west flank has not been hitherto recognised as a moraine at all, because not only is it so immensely extended that general views of it cannot be easily obtained, but it has been weathered until the greater portion of its surface presents as smooth an appearance as a farmer's wheat-field

It may be urged against the morainal origin of the forest belt that its sections exposed by freshet streams present a quite different appearance from similar sections of more recent moraine-beds unmistakably such but careful inspection shows the same gradual transition from the boulder roughness of the one to the crumbled earthiness of the other that we have already traced between the superficial roughness and smoothness of moraines according to age.

Under certain conditions moraine boulders decompose more rapidly beneath than upon the surface. Almost every section of the forest belt presents specimens in every stage of decay, and, because those that are water-rounded and polished are more enduring than others, they occur in comparatively greater abundance as the soil becomes more ancient. The position of the soil-belt is given in the ideal cross-section of the range (Fig. 2). *Its upper limit; nearly coincides with the edge of a comparatively level bench,* A B, *extending back to the summit peaks.* Upon this lofty, gently inclined bed the waning ice-sheet lay nearly motionless, shallowing simultaneously across its whole breadth, and finally broke up into distinct ice-streams which occupied the present river canyons. These have left their lateral moraines in the form of long branching ridges of soil, several miles apart, extending from the summit ice-wombs down to the main soil-belt, into which they blend and disappear. But if the ice-sheet had maintained its continuity to the very end of the glacial epoch, soil would evidently have been laid down in one continuous bed all the way back to the summit, because under these conditions every portion of the surface in succession would have been loaded with terminal moraine-belts pressed one against the other like plow-ridges. Under the conditions which prevailed toward the close of the great winter, the

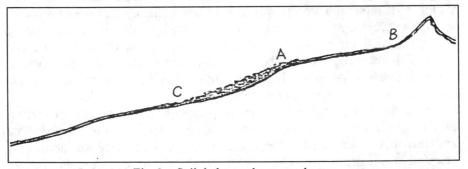

Fig. 2   Soil belts on the upper slopes.

seperate glaciers as well as the ice-sheet shallowed, becoming torpid, and died away simultaneously throughout all this upper region; no terminal moraines are therefore to be met until we reach those of the small residual glaciers which took shelter in the loftiest and coolest shadows of the summit peaks. Nor will this state of things be wondered at, when we consider how slight the difference in elevation, and consequently in climate, between the upper and lower limits (A and B, Fig. 2) of this bare alpine bench, as compared with that of the slope (C A) beneath it, upon which the soilbelt lies.

The effect of shadows in determining the formation, size, and distribution of glacial soil-beds must not be overlooked. When the seasons grew warm and the long crooked glaciers were driven from the sun-beaten summit bench, thousands of small residual glaciers, from half a mile to two or three miles in length, lingered on through many a century in the shelter of frosty shadows. Accordingly, we find the moraines of these hiding glaciers in the highest and coolest recesses, shaped and measured with strict reference to their adjacent shadows. A considerable number of these interesting shadow-moraines are still in process of formation, presenting a raw and rubbish-like appearance, as if the boulders, mud, and sand of which they are composed had been newly mined from the mountain's flank, and dumped loosely from a car. Ancient shadow-moraines, delightfully gardened and forested, occur in all deep Yosemitic canyons trending in an east and west direction; but their first forms are so heavily obscured by thousands of years of weathering that their shadow-glacial origin would scarcely be suspected.

In addition to these broad zones and fields and regularly deposited moraine ridges, glacial soil occurs in isolated strips and patches upon the wildest and most unlikely places – aloft on jutting crags, and along narrow horizontal benches ranged one above another, on sheer-fronted precipices, wherever the strong and gentle glaciers could get a boulder to lie. To these inaccessible soil-beds companies of pines and alp-loving flowers have found their way, and formed themselves into waving fringes and rosettes, whose beauty is strikingly relieved upon the massive ice-sculpted walls.

Nothing in the history of glacial soil-beds seems more remarkable than their durability in the forms in which they were first laid down. The wild violence of mountain storms would lead one to fancy that every moraine would be swept from plateau and ridge in less than a dozen seasons, yet we find those of the upper half of the range scarcely altered by the tear and wear of thousands of years. Those of the lower half are far more ancient, and their material has evidently been shifted and re-formed until their original characteristics are almost entirely lost.

These fresh glacier-formed soils are subject to modifications of various kinds. After the coarse, unbolted moraine soils derived from granite, slate and lava have been well watered and snow-pressed, they are admirably adapted for the ordinary food and anchorage of coniferous trees, but further manipulation is required to fit them for special grove and garden purposes. The first and most general action to which they are subjected is that of slow atmospheric decomposition, which mellows and smooths them for the reception of blooming robes of under-shrubs and grasses, and up to a certain point augments their capacity for the support of pines and firs. Streams of rain and melting snow rank next in importance as modifiers of glacial soils. Powerful torrents waste and change the most compact beds with great rapidity, but the work done by small rain-currents and low-voiced brooks is very much less than is vaguely supposed. The brook which drains the south flank of the Clouds Rest ridge above Yosemite Valley, in making its way southward to join the Nevada Creek, is deflected to the west by the right lateral moraine of the ancient Nevada glacier, and compelled to creep and feel its way along the outside of the moraine as far as to where it is caught between the moraine and an escarpment which advances from the Clouds Rest crest. When halted here, it spread into a pool, and rose until it was able to effect its escape over escape over the lowest portion of the barrier. Now, this stream, which in ordinary stages is about five feet wide and a foot deep, seems to have flowed unfailingly in one channel throughout all the long post-glacial centuries, but the only erosion the moraine has suffered is the removal of sand, mud, and some of the smaller boulders, while the large stones, jammed into a kind of wall, are merely polished by the friction of the stream, and bid fair to last tens of thousands of years. The permanence of soils depends more upon their position and mechanical structure than upon their composition. Coarse porous moraine matter permits rains and melting snows to percolate unimpeded, while muddy and impermeable beds are washed and wasted on the surface.

Snow avalanches more resemble glaciers in their methods of soil formation and distribution than any other of the post-glacial agents. The century avalanche sweeps down all the trees that chance to stand in its path, together with soils of every kind, mixing all together without reference to the size of their component fragments. Most of the uprooted trees are deposited in lateral windrows, heads downward, piled upon each other, and tucked snugly in alongside the clearing; while a few are carried down into the valley on the snout of the avalanche, and deposited with stones and leaves, and burs, in a kind of terminal moraine.

The soil accumulations of annual avalanches are still more moraine-like in form, and frequently attain a depth of from forty to fifty feet. They are composed of mud, sand, coarse granules, and rough angular blocks, avalanched from the mountain side, and sometimes water-washed pebbles also, derived from the channels of streams.

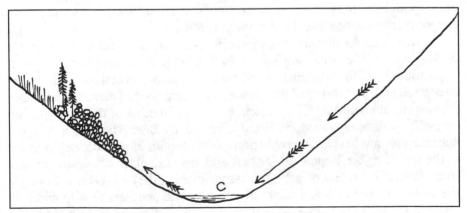

Fig. 3   River detritus pushed up the slope of Tenaya Creek by avalanche action.

Thus, the largest of the Clouds Rest avalanches, in rushing down their magnificent pathway of nearly a mile in vertical depth, on their arrival at the Tenaya Creek (Fig. 3) dash across its channel and up the opposite bank to a height of more than a hundred feet, pushing all the pebbles and boulders of the stream up with them. Spring freshets bring down a fresh supply of pebbles and boulders from year to year, which the avalanches patiently add to their moraine, until in a few thousand years these washed pebbles form a considerable proportion of the mass. Trees over a hundred years old occur upon the upper portions of some of these avalanche-beds, showing that no avalanche of sufficient power to disturb them had occurred since they began to grow. The lower portions of these beds are, on the contrary, in a raw formative condition, and about as plantless as the shining boulder-beds in the bottoms of rivers.

Again, stone avalanches have their share in depositing soil. The observer among beetling Yosemitic cliffs occasionally sees a single boulder eight or ten feet in diameter whizzing down the sky like a comet with a tail of dust two thousand feet long. When these huge soil-grains strike among other boulders at the end of their course, they make a sound deeper and heavier than thunder; the ground trembles, and stone-spray is whirled and spattered like water-spray at the foot of a fall.

The crushed and pounded soil-beds to which avalanches of this kind give rise seem excellently well adapted to the growth of forest trees, but few of them are sufficiently matured to be available, and the trees that venture upon them are in constant danger of their lives. These unplanted beds occur most commonly at the base of cliffs intersected by feldspathic veins, the decomposition of which causes the downfall of additional material from year to year. On the contrary, the rougher and far more important soil-beds resulting from earthquake avalanches are formed almost instantaneously, without being subsequently augmented in any appreciable degree for centuries. The trees, therefore, and various shrubs and flowers which find them tolerable or congenial dwelling-places soon take possession of them, and soothe their rugged features with a mantle of waving verdure.

At first thought no one would suppose that in a tumultuous pellmell down-crash of rifted rocks any specialisation could be accomplished in their deposition. Both the suddenness and the violence of the action would seem to preclude the possibility of the formation of any deposit more orderly than a battered rubbish-heap. Every atom, however, whether of the slow glacier or swift avalanche, is inspired and directed by law. The larger blocks, because they are heavier in proportion to the amount of surface they present to the impeding air, bound out farther; and, because obstructions of surface irregularities have less effect upon larger blocks, they also *roll* farther on the bottom of the valley. The small granules and sand-grains slip and roll close to the cliff, and come to rest on the top of the talus, while the main mass of the talus is perfectly graduated between these extremes. Besides this graduation accomplished in a vertical and forward direction, beautiful sections are frequently made in a horizontal and lateral direction, as illustrated in Figure 4. A B is a kind of natural trough or spout near the base of the cliff, directed obliquely downward, into which a portion of the avalanche-stream, F, falls, and is spouted to the left of its original course. Because the larger boulders composing the spouted portion of the current move faster, their momentum carries them farther toward H, giving rise to the talus E, while the finer material is deposited at D. Again, the blocks sufficiently large to bound out beyond the deflecting spout from the rough talus C, while the smallest fragments of all – namely, the fine dust derived from chafing – float out far beyond, and settle in thin films silently as dew.

In portions of canyon walls where diagonal cleavage is developed, inclines such as A B (Fig. 5) are common. If two boulders in falling from the heights above should strike glancingly at A, the greater mass or more favourable form of boulder B might cause it to bound sufficiently far to reach the second incline, which would carry it toward D; while the smaller boulder, C, falling short, might fall under the guidance of a third incline, and be shed off toward E, the two boulders finally coming to rest a hundred yards or more apart. By these means the most delicate decompositions of stone-torrents are effected, the various resulting soils being delivered at different shoots and spouts, like the bran, shorts, and fine flour of a gristmill. The ages of the oldest trees growing upon these soils furnish data by which some approximation to the time of their formation may be made.

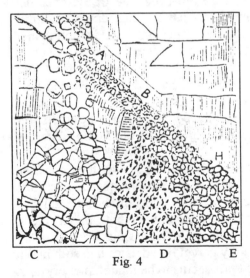

C   D   E

Fig. 4

Falling patterns of different sizes of talus.

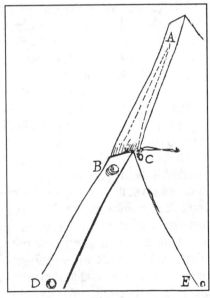

Fig. 5

The first post-glacial earthquake sufficiently severe to produce large avalanches occurred at least three centuries ago, and no other of equal power has occurred since. By this earthquake alone, thousands of acres of noble soil-beds were suddenly and simultaneously deposited throughout all the deep canyons of the range. Though thus hurled into existence at a single effort, they are the most changeless and indestructible soil formations in the

Sierra. Excepting those which were launched directly into the channels of rivers, scarcely one of their wedged and locked boulders has been moved since the day of their creation. In striking contrast with these terrible demonstrations of mechanical energy, made in the deposition of earthquake soils, is the silent and motionless transformation of solid granite into loose fine soil-beds by oozing water and the tranquil play of the atmosphere. Beds eight or ten feet deep occur on Mounts Watkins and El Capitan, on the edge of the Yosemite Valley where the decomposition had been effected so calmly that the physical structure presents no conspicuous change; the quartz, mica, and hornblende retaining the same relative positions as when solid, yet so perfectly disintegrated that, like sand, it may be cut into with a spade. But these unmoved beds created on the spot are of relatively small extent, and as yet play an insignificant part in the support of Sierra vegetation. The main body of the smaller soil-fragments, weathered loose by the atmosphere, are transported and redeposited by winds and rains. Magnificent wind-rivers sweep the high Sierra, carrying large quantities of sand, dust, and mica flakes, besides larger fragments in the form of rough grains. These are distributed in smooth undulating fields and patches, adapted to the wants of the dwarf *Pinus albicaulis* and many of the most precious of Sierra shrubs and flowers. Many of the smaller alpine wind-beds are exceedingly beautiful, nestling in the lee of rough beaten rocks, their edges waved and embroidered, and their surfaces delicately dinted and ruffled like the garden-plats of children. During the post-glacial eruptions of the volcanoes of the Mono basin, winds distributed showers of cinders and ashes upon all the soil-beds of the adjacent Sierra. Hundreds of square miles of area are thus sprinkled on the upper basins of the San Joaquin, Merced, and Tuolumne rivers; the copiousness of the cinder-showers increasing the nearer the Mono volcanoes are approached as a centre.

The numerous domes and castellated rocks distributed over the ridges and divides of the middle region abound in garnet, tourmaline, quartz, mica, and feldspar crystals, which, as the mass of the rocks decompose, are set free and fall in minute avalanches, and gradually accumulate until they come to form belts of crystalline soil. In some instances, the various crystals occur only here and there, sprinkled in the grey gravel like daisies in a sod; but in others, half or more of the encircling talus seems to be made up of crystals, tilted at all angles, and laid open to the sun. And whether in the mild flush of morning or evening, or in the dazzling white of high noon, they manifest themselves as the most exquisitely beautiful of all the soil-beds in the range.

In the hollows and levels we find soil-beds that have been compounded and laid down by streams of water. But these may be regarded as little more than reformations of glacial deposits; for the quantity of soil material eroded from solid rock by post-glacial agents is as yet hardly appreciable. Water-beds present a wide range of variability both in size and structure. Some of the smallest, each sustaining a tuft or two of grass, have scarcely a larger area than the flower-plat; while others are miles in extent, and support luxuriant groves of pine trees two hundred feet in height. Some are composed of mud and sand-grains. others of ponderous boulders, according to the power of the depositing current and the character of the material that chanced to lie in its way.

Glaciers are admirably calculated for the general distribution of soils in consequence of their rigidity and independence of minor inequalities of surface. Streams of water, on the contrary, are fitted only for special work. Glaciers give soil to high and low places almost alike; water-currents are dispensers of special blessings, constantly tending to make the ridges poorer and the valleys richer. Glaciers mingle all kinds of materials together, mud particles and rock blocks a hundred feet in diameter; water, whether in oozing currents or passionate torrents, constantly discriminates both with regard to size and shape of material, and acts as a series of sieves for its separation and transportation.

Glacial mud is the finest mountain meal ground for any purpose, and its transportation into the still water of lakes, where it is deposited in layers of clay, was the first work that the young post-glacial streams of the Sierra were called upon to do. Upon the clay-beds thus created avalanches frequently pile tangled masses of tree-trunks, mingled with burs and leaves and rocky detritus scraped from the mountain side. Other layers of mud are deposited in turn, together with freshet-washings of sand and gravel This goes on for centuries from season to season, until at length the basin is filled and gradually becomes drier. At first, the soil is fit only for sedges and willows, then for grasses and pine-trees. This, with minor local modifications, is the mode of creation of the so-called flat and meadow soil so abundantly distributed over all parts of the range.

Genuine bogs in this period of Sierra history occur only in shallow alpine basins, where the climate is sufficiently cool for the growth of sphagnum, and where the surrounding topographical conditions are such that they are safe, even in the most copious rains and thaws, from the action of flood-currents capable of carrying stones and sand, but where the water supply is nevertheless sufficiently constant and abundant for the growth of sphagnum and a few other plants equally fond of cold water. These dying from year to year – ever dying beneath and living above – gradually give rise to those rich spongy peat-soils that are the grateful abodes of so many of the most delightful of alpine plants.

Beds of sloping bog-soil, that seem to hang like ribbons on cool mountain sides, are originated by the fall of trees in the paths of small creeks and rills, in the same climates with level bogs. The interlaced trunks and branches obstruct the feeble streams and dissipate them into oozing webs and stagnant pools. Sphagnum speedily discovers and takes possession of them, absorbing every pool and driblet into its spongy stems, and at length covers the muddy ground and every log and branch with its rich rounded bosses.

Here the attentive observer is sure to ask the question – are the fallen trees more abundant in bogs than elsewhere in the surrounding forest? – and if so, then, why? We *do* find the fallen trees in far greater abundance in sloping bogs, and the cause is clearly explained by young illustrative bogs in process of formation. In the first place, a few chance trees decay and fall in such a manner as to dam the stream and flood the roots of other trees. Every tree so flooded dies, decays, and falls. Thus, the so called chance-falling of a few causes the fall of many, which form a network, in the meshes of which the entangled moisture is distributed with a considerable degree of uniformity, causing the resulting bog to be evenly inclined, instead of being cast into a succession of irregular terraces, one for each damming log.

Black flat meadow deposits, largely composed of humus, are formed in lake basins that have reached the last stage of filling up. The black vegetable matter is derived from rushes and sedges decaying in shallow water for long periods. It is not essential that these beds be constantly covered with water during their deposition, but only that they be subject to frequent inundations and remain sufficiently moist through the driest seasons for the growth of sedges. They must, moreover, be exempt from the action of overflowing flood-currents strong enough to move gravel and sand. But no matter how advantageous may be the situation of these humus beds, their edges are incessantly encroached upon, making their final burial beneath drier mineral formations inevitable. This obliterating action is going on at an accelerated rate on account of the increasing quantity of transportable material rain-streams find in their way. For thousands of years subsequent to the close of the ice-winter, a large proportion of the Sierra presented a bare, polished surface, and the streams that flowed over it came down into the meadows about as empty-handed as if their courses had lain over clean glass. But when at length the glacial hard-finish was weathered off, disintegration went on at a greatly accelerated speed, and every stream found all the carrying work it could do.

Bogs die also, in accordance with beautiful laws. Their lower limit constantly rises as the range grows older. The snow-line is not a more trustworthy exponent of the climate than the bog line is of the age of the regions where it occurs, dating from the end of the ice epoch.

Besides bogs, meadows, and sandy flats, water constructs soil beds with washed pebbles, cobblestones, and large boulders. The former class of beds are made deliberately by tranquil currents, the latter by freshets, caused by the melting of the winter snow, severe rain-storms, and by floods of exceptional power, produced by rare combinations of causes, which in the Sierra occur only once in hundreds of years. So vast is the difference between the transporting power of rivers in their ordinary everyday condition and the same rivers in loud-booming flood, that no definite gradation exists between their level silt-beds and rugged boulder deltas. The ordinary power of Sierra streams to transport the material of boulder soils is very much overestimated. Throughout the greater portion of their channels they cannot, in ordinary stages of water, move pebbles with which a child might play; while in the sublime energy of flood they toss forward boulders tons in weight without any apparent effort. The roughly imbricated flood-beds so commonly found at the mouths of narrow gorges and valleys are the highest expressions of torrential energy with which I am acquainted. At some time before the occurrence of the grand soil-producing earthquake, thousands of magnificent boulder-beds were simultaneously hurried into existence by one noble flood. These ancient boulder and cobble beds are distributed throughout the deep valleys and basins of the range between latitude 39° and 36° 30'; how much farther I am unable to say. They are now mostly overgrown with groves of oak and pine, and have as yet suffered very little change. Their distinguishing characteristics are, therefore, easily readable, and show that the sublime outburst of mechanical energy developed in their creation was rivalled only in the instantaneous deposition of the grand earthquake beds.

Notwithstanding the many august implements employed as modifiers and reformers of soils, the glacier is the only great producer. Had the ice-sheet melted suddenly, leaving the flanks of the Sierra soil less, her farfamed forests would have had no existence. Numerous groves and thickets would undoubtedly have established themselves on lake and avalanche beds, and many a fair flower and shrub would have found food and a dwelling-place in weathered nooks and crevices. Yet the range, as a whole, would seem comparatively naked. The tattered alpine fringe of the Sierra forest, composed of *Pinus flexilis* and *Pinus aristate*, oftentimes ascends stormy mountain flanks above the upper limit of moraines, upon lean, crumbling rock but when they have the opportunity, these little alpine pines show that they know well the difference between rich, mealy moraines and their ordinary meagre fare. The yellow pine is also a hardy rock-climber, and can live on wind and snow, but it assembles in forests and attains noble dimensions only upon nutritious moraines: while the sugar pine and the two silver firs, which form so important a part of the grand forest belt, can scarcely maintain life upon bald rocks in any form, and reach full development only in the best moraine beds, no matter what the elevation may be. The mass of the Sierra forests indicates the extent and position of the moraine-beds far more accurately than it does lines of climate. No matter how advantageous the conditions of temperature and moisture, forests cannot exist without soil, and Sierra soils have been laid down upon the solid rock. Accordingly, we find luxuriant forests two hundred feet high terminated abruptly by bald glacier-polished pavements.

Man also is dependent upon the bounty of the ice for the broad fields of fertile soil upon which his wheat and apples grow. The wide plains extending along the base of the range on both sides are mostly reformations of morainal detritus variously sorted and intermixed. The valleys of the Owens, Walker, and Carson rivers have younger soils than those of the Sacramento and San Joaquin – that is, those of the former valleys are of more recent origins, and are less changed by post-glacial washings and decomposition. All the soil-beds remaining upon the Sierra flanks, when comprehended in one view, appear like clouds in a sky half-clear; the main belt extending along the middle, with long branching mountains above it, a web of washed patches beneath, and with specialised meadow and garden flecks everywhere.

When, after the melting of the winter snow, we walk the dry channel of a stream that we love, its beds of pebbles, dams of boulders, its poolbasins and potholes and cascade inclines, suggest all its familiar forms and voices, as if it were present in the full gush of spring. In like manner the various Sierra soil-beds vividly bring before the mind the noble implements employed by nature in their creation. The meadow recalls the still lake, the boulder delta, the grey booming torrent, the rugged talus, the majestic avalanche, and the moraine reveals the mighty glaciers silently spreading soil upon a thousand mountains. Nor in all these involved operations may we detect the faintest note of disorder; every soil-atom seems to yield enthusiastic obedience to law – boulders and mud-grains moving to music as harmoniously as the far-whirling planets.

CHAPTER SEVEN

Mountain-Building

THIS STUDY of mountain-building refers particularly to that portion of the range embraced between latitudes 36° 30' and 39'. It is about 200 miles long, sixty wide, and attains an elevation along its axis of from 8,000 to nearly 15,000 feet above the level of the sea. The individual mountains that are distributed over this vast area, whether the lofty and precipitous alps of the summit, the more beautiful and highly specialised domes and mounts dotted over the undulating flanks, or the huge bosses and angles projecting horizontally from the sides of canyons and valleys, have all been sculptured and brought into relief during the glacial epoch by the direct mechanical action of the ice-sheet, with the individual glaciers into which it afterward separated. Our way to a general understanding of all this has been made clear by previous studies of valley formations – studies of the physical characters of the rocks out of which the mountains under consideration have been made, and of the widely contrasted methods and quantities of glacial and post-glacial denudation.

Notwithstanding the accessibility and imposing grandeur of the summit alps, they remain almost wholly unexplored. A few nervous raids have been made among them from random points adjacent to trails, and some of the more easily accessible, such as Mounts Dana, Lyell, Tyndall, and Whitney, have been ascended, while the vast wilderness of mountains in whose fastnesses the chief tributaries of the San Joaquin and Kings rivers take their rise, have been beheld and mapped from a distance, without any attempt at detail. Their echoes are never stirred even by the hunter's rifle, for there is no game to tempt either Indian or white man as far as the frosty lakes and meadows that lie at their bases, while their avalanche-swept and crevassed glaciers, their labyrinths of yawning gulfs and crumbling precipices, offer dangers that only powerful motive will induce anyone to face.

The view southward from the colossal summit of Mount Humphreys is indescribably sublime. Innumerable grey peaks crowd loftily into the keen azure, infinitely adorned with light and shade; lakes glow in lavish abundance around their bases; torrents whiten their denuded gorges; while many a glacier and bank of fountain névé leans back in their dark recesses. Awe-inspiring, however, as these vast mountain assemblies are, and incomprehensible as they may at first seem, their origin and the principal facts of their individual histories are problems easily solved by the patient student.

Beginning with pinnacles, which are the smallest of the summit mountainets: no geologist will claim that these were formed by special upheavals, nor that the little chasms which separated them were formed by special subsidences or rivings asunder of the rock; because many of these chasms are as wide at the bottom as at the top, and scarcely exceed a foot in depth; and many may be formed artificially by simply removing a few blocks that have been loosened.

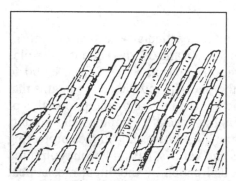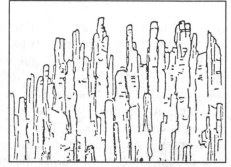

Figs. 1 and 2   Pinnacle forms and dimensions are determined by the orientation of cleavage planes.

The Sierra pinnacles are from less than a foot to nearly a thousand feet in height, and in all the cases that have come under my observation their forms and dimensions have been determined, not by cataclysmic fissures, but by the gradual development of orderly joints and cleavage planes, which gave rise to leaning forms where the divisional planes are inclined, as in Figure 1, or to vertical where the planes are vertical, as in Figure 2. Magnificent crests tipped with leaning pinnacles adorn the jagged flanks of Mount Ritter, and majestic examples of vertical pinnacle architecture abound among the lofty mountain cathedrals on the heads of Kings and Kern rivers. The minarets to the south of Mount Ritter are an imposing series of partially separate pinnacles about 700 feet in height, set upon the main axis of the range. Glaciers are still grinding their eastern bases, illustrating in the plainest manner the blocking out of these imposing features from the solid. The formation of small peaklets that roughen the flanks of large peaks may in like manner be shown to depend, not upon any up-thrusting or down-thrusting forces, but upon the orderly erosion and transportation of the material that occupied the intervening notches and gorges.

The same arguments we have been applying to peaklets and pinnacles are found to be entirely applicable to the main mountain peaks; for careful detailed studies demonstrate that as pinnacles are separated by eroded chasms, and peaklets by notches and gorges, so the main peaks are separated by larger chasms, notches, gorges, valleys, and wide ice-womb amphitheatres. When across hollows we examine continuous sides of mountains, we perceive that the same mechanical structure is continued across intervening spaces of every kind, showing that there has been a removal of the material that once filled them – the occurrence of large veins oftentimes rendering this portion of the argument exceedingly conclusive, as in two peaks of the Lyell group (Fig. 3), where the wide veins, N N, are continued across the valley from peak to peak. We frequently find rows of pinnacles set upon a base, the cleavage of which does not admit of pinnacle formation, and in an analogous way we find immense slate mountains, like Dana and Gibbs, resting upon a plain granite pavement, as if they had been formed elsewhere, transported and set down in their present positions, like huge erratic boulders. It appears, therefore, that the loftiest mountains as well as peaklets and pinnacles of the summit region are residual masses of the once solid wave of the whole range, and that all that would be required to unbuild and obliterate these imposing structures would simply be the filling

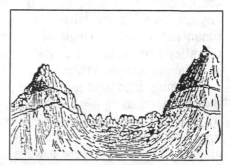

Fig. 3   Mechanical structure of two peaks in the Lyell group is continued across the intervening valley.

up of the labyrinth of intervening chasms, gorges, canyons, etc., which divide them, by the restoration of rocks that have disappeared. Here the important question comes up. What has become of the missing material, not the millionth part of which is now to be seen? It has not been engulfed, because the bottoms of all the dividing valleys and basins are unmistakably solid. It must, therefore, have been carried away; and because we find portions of it scattered far and near in moraines, easily recognised by peculiarities of mineralogical composition, we infer that glaciers were the transporting agents. That glaciers have brought out the summit peaks from the solid with all their imposing architecture, simply by the formation of the valleys and basins in which they flowed, is a very important proposition, and well deserves careful attention.

We have already shown, in Studies 3 and 4, that all the valleys of the region under consideration, from the minute striae and scratches of the polished surface less than a hundredth part of an inch in depth, to the Yosemitic gorges half a mile or more in depth, were all eroded by glaciers, and that post-glacial streams, whether small glancing brooklets or impetuous torrents, had not yet lived long enough to fairly make their mark, no matter how unbounded their eroding powers may be still, it may be conjectured that preglacial rivers furrowed the range long ere a glacier was born, and that when at length the ice-winter came on with its great skyfuls of snow, the young glaciers crept into these river channels, overflowing their banks, and deepening, widening, grooving, and polishing them without destroying their identity. For the destruction of this conjecture it is only necessary to observe that the trends of the present valleys are strictly glacial, and glacial trends are extremely different from water trends; pre-glacial rivers could not, therefore, have exercised any appreciable influence upon their formation.

Neither can we suppose fissures to have wielded any determining influence, there being no conceivable coincidence between the zigzag and apparently accidental trends of fissures and the exceedingly specific trends of ice-currents. The same argument holds good against primary foldings of the crust, dislocations, etc. Finally, if these valleys had been hewn or dug out by any pre-glacial agent whatever, traces of such agent would be visible on mountain masses which glaciers have not yet segregated; but no such traces of valley beginnings are anywhere manifest. The heads of valleys extend back into mountain masses just as far as glaciers have gone and no farther.

Granting, then, that the greater part of the erosion and transportation of the material missing from between the mountains of the summit was effected by glaciers, it yet remains to be considered what agent or agents shaped the upper portions of these mountains, which bear no traces of glacial action, and which probably were always, as they now are, above the reach of glaciers. Even here we find the glacier to be indirectly the most influential agent, constantly eroding backward, thus undermining their bases, and enabling gravity to drag down large masses, and giving greater effectiveness to the winter avalanches that sweep and furrow their sides. All the summit peaks present a crumblimg, ruinous, unfinished aspect. Yet they have suffered very little change since the close of the glacial period, for if denudation had been extensively carried on, their separating pits and gorges would be choked with debris; but on the contrary, we find only a mere sprinkling of post-glacial detritus and that the streams could not have carried much of this away is conclusively shown by the fact that the small lake-bowls through which they flow have not been filled up.

In order that we may obtain clear conceptions concerning the methods of glacial mountain-building, we will now take up the formation of a few specially illustrative groups and peaks, without, however, entering into the detail which the importance of the subject deserves.

The Lyell group lies due east from Yosemite Valley, at a distance of about sixteen miles in a straight course. Large tributaries of the Merced, Rush, Tuolumne, and San Joaquin rivers take their rise amid its ice and snow. Its geographical importance is further augmented by its having been a centre of dispersal for some of the largest and most influential of the ancient glaciers. The traveller who undertakes the ascent of Mount Lyell, the dominating mountain of the group, will readily perceive that, although its summit is 13,200 feet above the level of the sea, all that individually pertains to it is a small residual fragment less than a thousand feet high, whose existence is owing to slight advantages of physical structure and position with reference to the heads of ancient glaciers, which prevented its being eroded and carried away as rapidly as the common mountain mass circumjacent to it.

Glacier wombs are rounded in a horizontal direction at the head, for the same reason that they are at the bottom; this being the form that offers greatest resistance to glacial erosion. The semicircular outline thus determined is maintained by the glaciers in eroding their way backward into the mountain masses against which they head; and where these curved basins have been continued quite through the axis of the chain or spur, separate mountains have been produced, the degree of whose individuality depends upon the extent and variation of this erosion. Thus, let A B (Fig. 4) represent a section of a portion of the summit of a mountain chain, and C D E F G H, etc., the wombs of glaciers dead or active, then the residual masses 1 2 3 will be the so-called mountains.

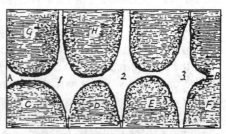

Fig. 4 The shapes of the separate mountains (1 2 3) are determined by the erosion of the glacial wombs (cirques).

It may well excite surprise that snow collected in these fountain-wombs should pass so rapidly through the névé condition, and begin to erode at the very head; that this, however, was the case is shown by unmistakable traces of that erosion upon the sides and heads as well as bottoms of wombs now empty. The The change of climate which broke up the glacial winter would obviously favour the earlier transformation of snow into eroding ice, and thus produce the present conditions as necessary consequences.

The geological effects of shadows in prolonging the existence and in guiding and intensifying the action of portions of glaciers are manifested in moraines, lake-basins, and the difference in form and sculpture between the north and south sides of mountains and valleys. Thus, the attentive observer will perceive that the architecture of deep valleys trending in a northerly and southerly direction, as Yosemite, abounds in small towers, crests, and shallow flutings on the shadowy south side, while the sun-beaten portions of the north walls are comparatively plain. The finer sculpture of the south walls is directly owing to the action of *small shadow-glacierettes* – which lingered long after the disappearance of the main glaciers that filled the valleys from wall to wall.

Every mountaineer and Indian knows that high mountains are more easily ascended on the south than on the north side. Thus, the Hoffmann spur may be ascended almost anywhere from the south on horseback, while it breaks off in sheer precipices on the north. There is not a mountain peak in the range which does not bear witness in sculpture and general form to this glacial-shadow action, which in many portions of the summit may still be observed in operation. But it is only to the effects of shadows in the segregation of mountain masses that I would now direct special attention. Figure 5 is a map of the Merced range adjacent to Yosemite Valley, with a portion of the ridge which unites it to the main axis. The arrows indicate the direction of extension of the deep glacial amphitheatres, and it will be at once seen that they all point in a southerly direction beneath the protection of shadows cast by the peaks and ridges. Again, it will be seen that because the Merced spur (S P) trends in a northerly direction, its western slopes are in shadow in the forenoon, its eastern in the afternoon, consequently it has a series of glacial wombs on *both* sides; but because the ridge (P G) trends in an easterly direction, its southern slopes are scarcely at all in shadow, consequently deep glacial wombs occur *only* upon the *northerly* slopes. Still further, because the Merced spur (S P) trends several degrees west of north, its eastern slopes are longer in shadow than the western, consequently the ice-wombs of the former are deeper and their headwalls are sheerer; and in general, because the main axis of the Sierra has a northwesterly direction, the summit peaks are more precipitous on the eastern than on the western sides.

In the case of ice-wombs on the north side of a mountain equally shadowed on the east and west, it will be found that such wombs, other conditions being equal, curve back in a direction a little to the west of south, because forenoon sunshine is not so strong as afternoon sunshine. The same admirable obedience to shadows* is conspicuous in all parts of the summits of the range. Now, glaciers are the only eroders that are thus governed by shadows.

Figure 6 illustrates the mode in which the heads (H H) of tributaries of the Tuolumne and Merced glaciers have eroded and segregated the mountain mass (L M) into two mountains – namely, Lyell and McClure – by moving backward until they met at C, leaving only the thin crest as it now exists.

Mount Ritter lies a few miles to the south of Lyell, and is readily accessible to good mountaineers by way of the Mono plains. The student of mountain-building will find it a kind of textbook, abounding in wonderfully clear and beautiful illustrations of the principles of Sierra architecture we have been studying. Upon the north flank a small active glacier may still be seen at work blocking out and separating a peak from the main mass, and its whole surface is covered with clearly cut inscriptions of frost, the storm-wind, and the avalanche. Though not the very loftiest, Ritter is to me far the noblest mountain of the chain. All its neighbours stand well back, enabling it to give full expression to its commanding individuality; while living glaciers, rushing torrents, bright-eyed lakes, gentian meadows; flecks of lily and anemone, shaggy thickets and groves, and polleny zones of sun-filled *compositae*, combine to irradiate its massive features, and make it as beautiful as noble.

The Merced spur (see Fig. 5), lying about ten miles to the southeast of Yosemite Valley and about the game distance from the main axis, presents a finely individualised range of peaks, 11,500 to 12,000 feet high, hewn from the solid. The authors of this beautiful piece of sculpture were two series of tributaries belonging to the glaciers of the Nevada and Illilouette.

* For further illustrations of the above observations on shadows, refer to Gardiner and Hoffmann's map of the Sierra adjacent to Yosemite Valley, or, still better, the mountains themselves.

Fig. 6 (right) The thin ridge crest
between Mounts Lyell and McClure
created by backward glacial action.

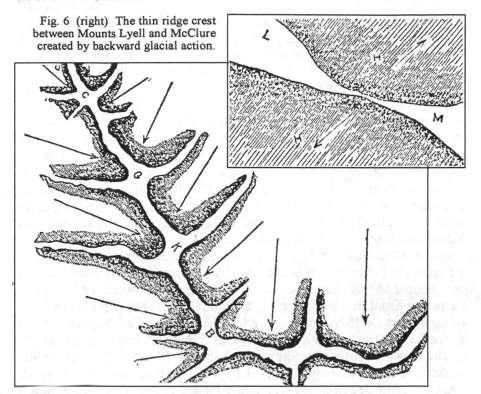

Fig. 5   The finely sculpted peaks of the Merced spur – arrows indicate the
backward erosion of the glacial wombs.

The truly magnificent group of nameless granite mountains stretching in a
broad swath from the base of Mount Humphreys forty miles southward, is far
the largest and loftiest of the range. But when we leisurely penetrate its wild
recesses, we speedily perceive that, although abounding in peaks 14,000 feet
high, these, individually considered, are mere pyramids, 1,000 to 2,000 feet in
height, crowded together upon a common base, and united by jagged columns
that swoop in irregular curves from shoulder to shoulder. That all this
imposing multitude of mountains was chiselled from one grand pre-glacial
mass is everywhere proclaimed in terms understandable by mere children.

Mount Whitney lies a few miles to the south of this group, and is
undoubtedly the highest peak of the chain, but, geologically or even scenically
considered, it possesses no special importance. When beheld either from the
north or south, it presents the form of a helmet, or, more exactly, that of the
Scotch cap called the "Glengarry." The flattish summit curves gently toward
the valley of the Kern on the west, but falls abruptly toward Owens River
Valley on the east, in a sheer precipice near 2,000 feet deep. Its north and
southeast sides are scarcely less precipitous, but these gradually yield to
accessible slopes, round from southwest to northwest. Although highest of
all the peaks, Mount Whitney is far surpassed in colossal grandeur and

general impressiveness of physiognomy, not only by Mount Ritter, but by Mounts Dana, Humphreys, Emerson, and many others that are nameless. A few meadowless lakes shine around its base, but it possesses no glaciers, and, toward the end of summer, very little snow on its north side, and none at all on the south. Viewed from Owens Valley, in the vicinity of Lone Pine, it appears as one of many minute peaklets that adorn the massive uplift of the range like a cornice. Toward the close of the glacial epoch, the grey porphyritic summit of what is now Mount Whitney peered a few feet above a zone of névé that fed glaciers which descended into the valleys of the Owens and Kern rivers. These, eroding gradually deeper, brought all that specially belongs to Mount Whitney into relief. Instead of a vast upheaval, it is merely a remnant of the common mass of the range, which, from relative conditions of structure and position, has suffered a little less degradation than the portions circumjacent to it.

Regarded as measures of mountain-building forces, the results of erosion are negative rather than positive, expressing more directly what has *not* been done than what *has* been done. The difference between the peaks and the passes is not that the former are elevations, the latter depressions; both are depressions, differing only in degree. The abasement of the peaks having been effected at a slower rate, they were, of course, left behind as elevations.

The transition from the spiky, angular summit mountains to those of the flanks with their smoothly undulated outlines is exceedingly well marked; weak towers, pinnacles, and crumbling, jagged crests at once disappear,* leaving only hard, knotty domes and ridge-waves as geological illustrations, on the grandest scale, of the survival of the strongest.

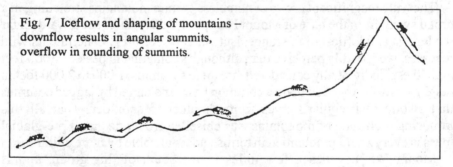

Fig. 7   Iceflow and shaping of mountains –
downflow results in angular summits,
overflow in rounding of summits.

Figure 7 illustrates, by a section, the general cause of the angularity of summit mountains, and curvedness of those of the flanks: the former having been *down*-flowed, the latter *over*flowed. As we descend from the alpine summits on the smooth pathways of the ancient ice-currents, noting where they have successively denuded the various rocks – first the slates, then the slaty-structured granites, then the curved granites – we detect a constant

---

*   For exceptions to this general law, real or apparent, see Chapter 1.

growth of specialisation and ascent into higher forms. Angular masses, cut by cleavage planes begin to be comprehended in flowing curves. These masses, in turn, become more highly organised, giving rise by the most gradual approaches to that magnificent dome scenery for which the Sierra is unrivalled. In the more strongly specialised granite regions, the features, and, indeed, the very existence, of overflowed mountains are in great part due neither to ice, water, nor any eroding agent whatsoever, but to building forces – crystalline, perhaps – which put them together and bestowed all that is more special in their architectural physiognomy, while they yet lay buried in the common fountain mass of the range.

The same silent and invisible mountain-builders performed a considerable amount of work upon the down-flowed mountains of the summit, but these were so weakly put together that the heavy hand of the glacier shaped and moulded, without yielding much compliance to their undeveloped forms. Had the unsculptured mass of the range been every way homogeneous, glacial denudation would still have produced summit mountains, differing not essentially from those we now find, but the rich profusion of flank mountains and mountainets, so marvellously individualised, would have had no existence, as the whole surface would evidently have been planed down into barren uniformity.

Thus the want of individuality which we have been observing among the summit mountains is obviously due to the comparatively uniform structure and erodibility of the rocks out of which they have been developed; their forms in consequence being greatly dependent upon the developing glaciers; whereas the strongly structured and specialised flank mountains, while accepting the ice-currents as developers, still defended themselves from their destructive and form-bestowing effects.

The wonderful adaptability of ice to the development of buried mountains, possessing so wide a range of form and magnitude, seems as perfect as if the result of direct plan and forethought. Granite crystallizes into landscapes; snow crystallizes above them to bring their beauty to the light. The grain of no mountain oak is more gnarled and interfolded than that of Sierra granite, and the ice-sheet of the glacial period is the only universal mountain eroder that works with reference to the grain. Here it smooths a pavement by slipping flatly over it, removing inequalities like a carpenter's plane; again it *makes* inequalities, gliding mouldingly over and around knotty dome-clusters, groping out every weak spot, sparing the strong, crushing the feeble, and following lines of predestined beauty obediently as the wind.

Rocks are brought into horizontal relief on the sides of valleys wherever superior strength of structure or advantageousness of position admits of such development, just as they are elsewhere in a vertical direction. Some of these prejections are of a magnitude that well deserves the name of *horizontal mountain*. That the variability of resistance of the rocks themselves accounts for the variety of these horizontal features is shown by the prevalence of this law. *Where the uniformity of glacial pressure has not been disturbed by the entrance of tributaries, we find that where valleys are narrowest their walls are strongest; where widest, weakest.*

In the case of valleys with sloping walls, their salient features will be mostly developed in an oblique direction; but neither horizontal nor oblique mountainets or mountains can ever reach as great dimensions as the vertical, because the retreating curves formed in weaker portions of valley walls are less eroded the deeper they become, on account of receiving less and less pressure, while the alternating salient curves are more heavily pressed and eroded the farther they project into the past-squeezing glacier; thus tending to check irregularity of surface beyond a certain limit, which limit is measured by the resistance offered by the rocks to the glacial energy brought to bear upon them. So intense is this energy in the case of large steeply inclined glaciers, that many salient bosses are broken off on the lower or downstream side with a fracture like that produced by blasting. These fractures occur in all deep Yosemitic canyons, forming the highest expressions of the intensity of glacial force I have observed.

The same tendency toward maintaining evenness of surface obtains to some extent in vertical erosion also; as when hard masses rise abruptly from a comparatively level area exposed to the full sweep of the overpassing current. If vertical cleavage be developed in such rocks, *moutonnéed* forms will be produced with a split face turned away from the direction of the flow, as shown in Figure 8, Study No. I [Chapter One]. These forms, measuring from a few inches to a thousand feet or more in height, abound in hard granitic regions. If no cleavage be developed, then long ovals will be formed, with their greater diameters extended in the direction of the current. The general tendency, however, in vertical erosion is to make the valleys deeper and ridges relatively higher, the ice-currents being constantly attracted to the valleys, causing erosion to go on at an accelerated rate, and drawn away from the resisting ridges until they emerge from the ice-sheet and cease to be eroded; the law here applicable being, "to him that hath shall be given."

Thus it appears that, no matter how the preglacial mass of the range came into existence, all the separate mountains distributed over its surface between latitude 36° 30' and 39°, whether the lofty alps of the summit, or richly sculptured dome-clusters of the flank, or the burnished bosses and mountainets projecting from the sides of valleys – all owe their development to the ice-sheet of the great winter and the separate glaciers into which it afterward separated. In all this sublime fulfilment there was no upbuilding, but a universal razing and dismantling, and of this every mountain and valley is the record and monument.

ADDENDUM

"Yosemite Glaciers" was first published on December 5th, 1871
in the *New York [Weekly] Tribune*

"Yosemite in Winter" was first published on January 1st, 1872
under the title "In the Yo-semite: Holidays Among the Rocks"
in the *New York [Weekly] Tribune*

"California Agriculture", hitherto un-published, was written in 1890,
the original manuscript being held in the John Muir Papers, Holt-Atherton Library, University of the
Pacific, Stockton, California, and on the microfilm "The John Muir Papers – 1858–1957" available
from Chadwyck-Healey (Cambridge, England, 1986), held by the National Library of Scotland.

Note: The copies of "Yosemite in Winter" and "California Agriculture" obtained for this
book contained ambiguities because of damaged microfilm, unclear text and corrections.

I

Yosemite Glaciers

The Ice Streams of the Great Valley.
Their Progress and Present Condition – Scenes among the Glacier Beds.

YOSEMITE VALLEY September 28th, 1871. Two years ago, when picking flowers in the mountains back of Yosemite Valley, I found a book. It was blotted and storm-beaten; all of its outer pages were mealy and crumbly, the paper seemed to dissolve like the snow beneath which it had been buried; but many of the inner pages were well preserved, and though all were more or less stained and torn, whole chapters were easily readable. In this condition is the great open book of Yosemite glaciers today; its granite pages have been torn and blurred by the same storms that wasted the castaway book. The grand central chapters of the Hoffman, and Tenaya, and Nevada glaciers are stained and corroded by the frosts and rains, yet, nevertheless, they contain scarce one unreadable page; but the outer chapters of the Pohono, and the Illilouette, and the Yosemite Creek, and Ribbon, and Cascade glaciers, are all dimmed and caten away on the bottom, though the tops of their pages have not been so long exposed, and still proclaim in splendid characters the glorious actions of their departed ice. The glacier which filled the basin of the Yosemite Creek was the fourth ice-stream that flowed to Yosemite Valley. It was about fifteen miles in length by five in breadth at the middle of the main stream, and many places was not less than 1,000 feet in depth. It united with the central glaciers in the valley by a mouth reaching from the east side of El Capitan to Yosemite Point, east of the falls. Its western rim was rayed with short tributaries, and on the north its divide from the Tuolumne glacier was deeply grooved; but few if any of its ridges were here high enough to separate the descending ice into distinct tributaries. The main central trunk flowed nearly south, and, at a distance of about 10 miles, separated into three nearly equal branches, which were turned abruptly to the east.

BRANCH BASINS

Those branch basins are laid among the highest spurs of the Hoffman range, and abound in small, bright lakes, set in the solid granite without the usual terminal moraine dam. The structure of those dividing spurs is exactly similar, all three appearing as if ruins of one mountain, or rather as perfect units hewn from one mountain rock during long ages of glacial activity. As their north sides are precipitous, and as they extend east and west, they were enabled to shelter and keep alive their hiding glaciers long after the death of the main trunk. Their basins are still dazzling bright, and their lakes have as yet accumulated but narrow rings of border meadow, because their feeding streams have had but little time to carry the sand of which they are made. The east bank of the main stream, all the way from the three forks to the mouth, is a continuous, regular wall, which also forms the west bank of the Indian Canyon glacier-basin. The tributaries of the west side of the main basin touched the east tributaries of the cascade, and the great Tuolumne glacier from Mount Dana, the mightiest ice-river of this whole region, flowed past on the north. The declivity of the tributaries was great, especially those which flowed from the spurs of the Hoffman on the Tuolumne divide, but the main stream was rather level, and in approaching Yosemite was compelled to make a considerable ascent back of Eagle Cliff. To the concentrated currents of the central glaciers, and to the levelness and width of mouth of this one, we in a great measure owe the present height of the Yosemite Falls. Yosemite Creek lives the most tranquil life of all the large streams that leap into the valley, the others occupying the canyons of narrower and, consequently, of deeper glaciers, while yet far from the valley, abound in loud falls and snowy cascades, but Yosemite Creek flows straight on through smooth meadows and hollows, with only two or three gentle cascades, and now and then a row of soothing, rumbling rapids, biding its time, and hoarding up the best music and poetry of its life for the one anthem at Yosemite, as planned by the ice.

YOSEMITE VALLEY

When a bird's-eye view of Yosemite Basin is obtained from any of its upper domes, it is seen to possess a great number of dense patches of black forest, planted in abrupt contact with bare grey rocks. Those forest plots mark the number and the size of all the entire and fragmentary moraines of the basin, as the latter eroding agents have not yet had sufficient time to form a soil fit for the vigorous life of large trees.

Wherever a deep-wombed tributary was laid against a narrow ridge, and was also shielded from the sun by compassing rock-shadows, there we invariably find more small terminal moraines, because when such tributaries were melted off from the trunk they retired to those upper strongholds of shade, and lived and worked in full independence, and the moraines which they built are left entire because the water-collecting basins behind are too small to make streams large enough to wash them away; but in the basins of exposed tributaries there are no terminal moraines, because their glaciers died with the trunk. Medial and lateral moraines are common upon all the outside slopes, some of them nearly perfect in form; but down in the main basin there is not left one unaltered moraine of any kind, immense floods having washed down and levelled them into harder meadows for the present stream, and into sandy flower beds and fields for forests.

GLACIER HISTORY

Such was Yosemite glacier, and such is its basin, the magnificent work of its hands. There is sublimity in the life of a glacier. Water rivers work openly, and so the rains and the gentle dews, and the great sea also grasping all the world: and even the universal ocean of breath, though invisible, yet speaks aloud in a thousand voices, and proclaims its modes of working and its power: but glaciers work apart from men, exerting their tremendous energies in silence and darkness, outspread, spirit-like, brooding above predestined rocks unknown to light, unborn, working on unwearied through unmeasured times, unhalting as the stars, until at length, their creations complete, their mountains brought forth, homes made for the meadows and the lakes, and fields for waiting forests, earnest, calm as when they came as crystals from the sky, they depart.

The great valley itself, together with all its domes and walls, was brought forth and fashioned by a grand combination of glaciers, acting in certain directions against granite of peculiar physical structure. All of the rocks and mountains and lakes and meadows of the whole upper Merced basin received their specific forms and carvings almost entirely from this same agency of ice.

I have been drifting about among the rocks of this region for several years, anxious to spell out some of the mountain truths which are written here; and since the number, and magnitude, and significance of these ice-rivers began to appear, I have become anxious for more exact knowledge regarding them; with this object, supplying myself with blankets and bread, I climbed out of the Yosemite by Indian Canyon, and am now searching the upper rocks and moraines for readable glacier manuscript.

I meant to begin by exploring the main trunk glacier of Yosemite Creek, together with all of its rim tributaries one by one, gathering what data I could find regarding their depth, direction of flow, the kind and amount of work which each had done, etc., but when I was upon the El Capitan Mountain, seeking for the western shore of the main stream, I discovered that the Yosemite Creek glacier was not the lowest [most western] ice stream which flowed to the valley, but that the Ribbon Stream basin west of El Capitan had also been occupied by a glacier, which flowed nearly south, and united with the main central glaciers of the summits in the valley below El Capitan.

RIBBON STREAM BASIN

I spent two days in this new basin. It must have been one of the smallest ice streams that entered the valley, being only about four miles in length by three in width. It received some small tributaries from the slopes of El Capitan ridge, which flowed south 35° west; but most of the ice was derived from a spur of the Hoffman group, running nearly southwest. The slope of its bed is steep and pretty regular, and it must have flowed with considerable velocity. I have not thus far discovered any of the original striated surfaces, though possibly some patches may still exist somewhere in the basin upon hard plates of quartz, or where a boulder of protecting form has settled upon a rounded surface. I found many such patches in the basin of Yosemite Glacier; some within a mile of the top of the falls – about two feet square in extent of surface, very perfect in polish, and its striae distinct, although the surrounding unprotected rock is disintegrated to a depth of at least four inches. As this small glacier sloped fully with unsheltered bosom to the sun, it was one of the first to die, and of course its tablets have been longer exposed to blurring rains and dews, and all eroding agents; but notwithstanding the countless blotting, crumbling storms which have fallen upon the historic lithographs of its surface, the great truth of its former existence printed in characters of moraine and meadow and valley groove, is still as clear as when every one of its pebbles and new-born rocks gleamed forth the full sun-shadowed poetry of its whole life. With the exception of a few castled piles and broken domes upon its east banks, its basin is rather smooth and lake-like, but it has charming meadows, most interesting in their present flora and glacier history, and noble forest of the two silver firs (*Picea Amabilis* and *P. grandis*)* planted upon moraines spread out and levelled by overflowing waters.

These researches in the basin of the Ribbon Creek recalled some observations made by me some time ago in the lower portions of the basins of the Cascade and Tamarac streams, and I now thought it probable that careful search would discover abundant traces of glacial action in those basins also. Accordingly, on reaching the highest northern slope of the Ribbon, I obtained comprehensive views of both the Cascade and Tamarac basins, and amid their countless adornments could note many forms of lake and rock which appeared as genuine glacial characters unmarred and unaltered. Running down the bare slope of an icy-looking canyon, in less than half an hour I came upon a large patch of the old glacier bed, polished and striated, with the direction of the flow of the long dead glacier clearly written – South 40° West. This proved to be the lowest, eastern-most tributary of the Cascade glacier. I proceeded westward as far as the Cascade meadows on the Mono trail, then turning to the right, entered the mouth of the tributary at the head of the meadows. Here there is a well-defined terminal moraine, and the ends of both ridges which formed the banks of the ice are broken and precipitous, giving evidence of great pressure. I followed up this tributary to its source on the west bank of the Yosemite glacier about two miles north of the Mono trail, and throughout its entire length there is abundance of polished tablets with moraines, rock sculpture, etc., giving glacier testimony as clear and indisputable as can be found in the most recent glacier pathways of the Alps.

---

*   The silver fir is not found in Southern California. These trees were probably the red fir (*Abies magnifica*) and white fir (*Abies concolor*).

VANISHED GLACIERS

I would gladly have explored the main trunk of this beautiful basin, from the highest snows upon the divide of the Tuolumne, to its mouth in the Merced Canyon below Yosemite, but alas! I had not sufficient bread, besides I felt sure that I should also have to explore the Tamarac basin, and, following westward among the fainter, most changed, and covered glacier pathways, I might probably be called as far as the end of the Pilot Peak Ridge. Therefore, I concluded to leave those lower chapters for future lessons, and go on with the easier Yosemite pages which I had already begun.

But before taking leave of those lower streams let me distinctly state, that in my opinion future investigation will uncover proofs of the existence in the earlier ages of Sierra Nevada ice, of vast glaciers which flowed to the very foot of the range.* Already it is clear that all of the upper basins were filled with ice so deep and universal that but few of the highest crests and ridges were sufficiently great to separate it into individual glaciers, many of the highest mountains having been flowed over and rounded like the boulders in a river. Glaciers poured into Yosemite by every one of its canyons, and at a comparatively recent period of its history its northern wall, with perhaps the single exception of the crest of Eagle Cliff, was covered by one unbroken flow of ice, the several glaciers having united before they reached the wall .

September 30th – Last evening I was camped in a small round glacier meadow, at the head of the easternmost tributary of the cascade. The meadow was velvet with grass, and circled with the most beautiful of all the coniferae, the Williamson spruce. I built a great fire, and the daisies of the sod rayed as if conscious of a sun. As I lay on my back, feeling the presence of the trees-gleaming upon the dark, and gushing with life – coming closer and closer about me, and saw the small round sky coming down with its stars to dome my trees, I said, ''Never was mountain mansion more beautiful, more spiritual; never was moral wanderer more blessedly homed.'' When the sun rose, my charmed walls were taken down, the trees returned to the common fund of the forest, and my little sky fused back into the measureless blue. I was left upon common ground to follow my glacial labour.

YOSEMITE RIVER BASINS

I followed the main Yosemite River northward, passing around the head of the second Yosemite tributary, which flowed about north-east until bent southward by the main current. About noon I came to the basin of the third ice tributary of the west rim, a place of domes which had long engaged my attention, and as I was anxious to study their structure, and the various moraines, etc., of the little glacier which had issued from their midst, I

---

* Muir made an error here as the western foothills of the Sierra Nevada display no evidence of glacial activity.

camped here near the foot of two of the most beautiful of the domes, in a
sheltered hollow, the womb of the glacier. At the foot of these two domes
are two lakes exactly alike in size and history, beautiful as any I ever
beheld; first there is the crystal water centre, then a yellowish fringe of
Carex, which has lone arching leaves which dip to the water; then a bevelled
bossy border of yellow of Sphagnum moss, exactly marking the limits of the
lake; further back is a narrow zone of dryer meadow, smooth and purple
with grasses which grow in soft plushy sods, interrupted here and there by
clumpy gatherings of blueberry bushes. The purple Kalmia grows here also,
and the splendidly flowered Phyllodoce; but these are small, and weave into
the sod, spreading low in the grasses and glowing with them. Besides these
flowering shrubs, the meadow is lightly sprinkled with daisies, and
dodecatheons and white violets, most lovely meadows divinely adjusted to
most lovely lakes.

    In the afternoon I followed down the bed of the tributary to its junction
with the main glacier; then, turning to the right, crossed the mouths of the
first two tributaries which I had passed in the morning; then, bearing east,
examined a cross section of the main trunk, and reached camp by following
up the north bank of the tributary. Between the three tributaries above-
mentioned are well-defined medial moraines, having been preserved from
levelling floods by their position on the higher slopes, with but small water-
collecting basins behind them. Down by their junctions, where they were
swept round by the main stream, is a large, level field of moraine matter,
which, like all the drift-fields of this basin, is planted with heavy forests,
composed mainly of a pine and fir (*Pinus contorta*, and *Picea amabilis*).
This forest is now on fire. I wanted to pass through it, but feared the falling
trees. As I stood watching the flapping flames and estimating chances, a tall
blazing pine crashed across the gap which I wished to pass, and in a few
minutes two more fell. This stirred a broken thought about special
providences, and caused me to go around out of danger. *Pinus contorta* is
very susceptible to fire, as it grows very close, in grovey thickets, and
usually every tree is trickled and beaded with gum. The summit forests are
almost entirely composed of this pine.*

DEER IN THE VALLEY

Emerging from this wooded moraine I found a great quantity of loose
separate boulders upon a polished hilltop, which had formed a part of the
bottom of the main ice stream. They were a extraordinary size, some large
as houses, and I started northward to seek the mountain from which they
had been torn. I had gone but a little way when I discovered a deer quietly
feeding upon a narrow strip of green meadow about sixty or seventy yards
ahead of me. As the wind blew gently toward it, I thought the opportunity

---

*   A reference to the lodgepole pine – the eastern larch, or tamarak, does not grow in California.

good for testing the truth of hunters' accounts of the deer's wonderful keenness of scent, and stood quite still, and as the deer continued to feed tranquilly, only casting round his head occasionally to drive away the flies, I began to think his nose was no better than my own, when suddenly, as if pierced by a bullet, he sprang up into the air and galloped confusedly without turning to look; but in a few seconds, as if doubtful of the direction of the danger, he came bounding back, caught a glimpse of me, and ran off a second time in a settled direction.

The Yosemite basin is a favourite summer home of the deer. The leguminous vines and juicy grasses of the great moraines supply savoury food, while the many high hidings of the Hoffman Mountain, accessible by narrow passes, afford favourite shelter. Grizzly and brown bears also love Yosemite Creek. Berries of the dwarf manzanita, and acorns of the dwarf live-oak are abundant upon the dry hilltops; and these with some plants and the larvae of black ants are the favourite food of bears if varied occasionally by a stolen sheep or a shepherd. The gorges of the Tuolumne Canyon, on the north end of the basin, are their principal hiding places of this region. Higher in the range their food is not plentiful and lower they are molested by man.

On returning to camp I passed three of the domes of the north bank, and was struck by the exact similarity of their structure, the same concentric layers, with a perpendicular cleavage, but less perfectly developed and more irregular. This little dome tributary, about 2½ miles long by 1½ wide, must have been one of the most beautiful of the basin: all of its upper circling rim is adorned with domes, some half-born, sunk in the parent rock, some broken and torn up on the sides by the ice, and a few nearly perfect, from their greater strength of structure or more favourable position. The two lakes above described are the only ones of the tributary basin, both domes and lakes handiwork of the glacier.

A GLACIER'S DEATH

In the waning days of this mountain ice, when the main river began to shallow and break like a summer cloud, its crests and domes rising higher and higher, and island rocks coming to light far out in the main current, then many a tributary died, and this one, cut off from its trunk, moved slowly back amid the gurgling and gushing of its bleeding rills, until, crouching in the shadows of this half-mile hollow, it lived a feeble separate life. Here its days come and go, and the hiding glacier lives and works. It brings boulders and sand and fine dust polishings from its sheltering domes and canyons, building up a terminal moraine, which forms a dam for the waters which issue from it; and beneath, working in the dark, it scoops a shallow lake basin. Again the glacier retires, crouching under cooler shadows, and a cluster of steady years enables the dying glacier to make yet another moraine dam like the first; and, where the granite begins to rise in curves to form the upper dam, it scoops another lake. Its last work is done, and it dies. The twin lakes are full of pure, green water, and floating masses of snow and broken ice. The domes, perfect in sculpture, gleam in new-born purity, lakes and domes reflecting each other bright as the ice which made them. God's seasons circle on, glad brooks born of the snow and the rain sing in the rocks, and carry sand to the naked lakes, and, in the fullness of time, comes many a chosen plant; first a lowly carex with dark brown spikes, then taller sedges and rushes, fixing a shallow soil, and now come many grasses, and daisies, and blooming shrubs, until lake and meadow growing throughout the season like a flower in summer, develop to the perfect beauty of today.

How softly comes night to the mountains. Shadows grow upon all the landscape; only the Hoffman Peaks are open to the sun. Down in this hollow it is twilight, and my two domes, more impressive, than in a broad day, seem to approach me. They are not vast and over-spiritual, like Yosemite Tissiack, but comprehensible and companionable, and susceptible of human affinities. The darkness grows, and all of their finer sculpture dims. Now the great arches and deep curves sink also, and the whole structure is massed in black against the starry sky.

I have set fire to two pine logs, and the neighbouring trees are coming to my charmed circle of light. The two-leaved pine, with sprays and tassels innumerable, the silver fir, with magnificent fronded whorls of shining boughs, and the graceful nodding spruce, dripping with cones, and seeming yet more spiritual in this campfire light. Grandly do my logs give back their light, slow gleaned from the suns of a hundred summers, garnered beautifully away in dotted cells and in beads of amber gum; and, together with this outgust of light, seems to flow all the other riches of their life, and their living companions are looking down as if to witness their perfect and beautiful death. But I am weary and must rest. Goodnight to my two logs and two lakes, and to my two domes high and black on the sky, with a cluster of stars between.

Yosemite in Winter

Wild Weather – A Picturesque Christmas Dinner –
Idyllic Amusements – Poetic Storms – A Paradise of Clouds.

YOSEMITE VALLEY, January 1st, 1872. Winter has taken Yosemite, and we are snowbound. The latest leaves are shaken from the oaks and alders; the snow-laden pines, with drooping boughs, look like barbed arrows aimed at the sky, and the fern-tangles and meadows are spread with a smooth cloth of snow. Our latest visitor fled two weeks ago. He came via Mariposa, and was safely conducted over the mountain snows by Galen Clark, the well-known pioneer and guardian of the Valley. The total number of visitors to the valley in 1870 was near 1,700, which was about 600 more than on any previous year. This season, about 2,150 entered the valley. As soon as bipeds left Yosemite, bears came in; not to grunt flattery to the falls, but to dine upon ridden-to-death horses. One burly old chief was killed at Nevada Falls by a party of Mono Indians. He was a brown or cinnamon bear, the prevailing species of the region.

Another of the same kind was seen down the valley on the meadow of the Bridal Veil, and another on the Mariposa trail, near the hermitage, and the smooth sand which rims Mirror Lake is grandly printed with their matchless paws. These bears are our grandest game, noblest expressions of mountain power. They deserve a Yosemite home, and the Sierras require them to companion their rocks and domes, and to blend in with their brown sequoias and cedars, and tangles of chaparral. Our winter population – not including the bears – totals twenty-six, employed as follows. Making lumber, ten; making a trail, two; feeding poultry, two; building fences, one; rebuilding a house, one; women, two; children, six; and a pair of Digger Indians with no visible means of support. All of our landlords except one, have disappeared, and doubtless are engaged in concert with stage and railroad companies, with next year's problems of travel, sorting their labyrinth of tolls and trails – their webs for the flies of '72. The 20th of November first brought us signs of winter. Broad, fibrous arcs of white cloud, spanned the valley from wall to wall; grand, island-like masses, bred among the upper domes and brows, wavered doubtfully up and down, some of them suddenly devoured by a swoop of thirsty wind; others, waxing to grand proportions; drifted loosely and heavily about like bergs in a calm sea, or jammed and wedged themselves among spiry crests, or, drawing themselves out like woollen rolls, muffled the highest brows sometimes leaving bare summits cut off from the walls with pine tops atop, that seemed to float loose as the clouds. Tissiack was compassed by a soft, furry cloud, upon which her dome seemed to repose clear and warm in yellow light. At the end of these transition days, the whole company of valley clouds were marshalled for storm; they fused close, and blended, until every seam and bay of blue sky was shut, and our temple, throughout all of its cells and halls, was smoothly full. Rain and snow fell steadily for three days, beginning November 24th, giving about four feet of snow to the valley rim. The snow line descended to the bottom of the valley on the night of November 25th, but after-rains prevented any considerable accumulation.

Then the rocks began to fall. During our equable rainless summers, atmospheric disintegration goes on with the greatest gentleness, and scare a rock is cast down, but the first rains find many a huge mass ripe for change, and after-slopes made slippery, seams washed out, and water-wedges driven. Constant thunder proclaims the magnitude of accomplished work. We ran repeatedly from the house to hear the larger masses journeying down with a tread that shook the valley.

This three days' chapter of rain was underscored by a seam of sunshine half a day in width, beneath which darkness began to gather for a chapter of snow; heavy cloud-masses rolled down the black-washed walls, circling cathedral rocks and domes, and hiding off all the upper brows and peaks. Thin strips of sunshine slid through momentary seams that were quickly blinded out. The darkness deepened for hours, until every separating shade and line were dimmed to equal black, and all the bright air of our gulf was sponged up, and fastened windless and pulseless in universal cloud. "It's bound to snow," said a mountaineer to me, as he gazed into the heavy gloom, "bound to snow when it gathers cloud material gradual as this. We'll have a regular old-fashioned storm afore long." Scarce had he delivered himself of this meteorological prophecy, ere the beginning flakes appeared, journeying tranquilly down with waving, slow-circling gestures, easy and confident as if long familiar with the paths of sky. Before dark they accomplished a most glorious work of gentle, noiseless beauty. Twelve inches of snow fell during the night and when morning opened our temple, there was more of beauty than pen can tell – from meadow to summit, from wall to wall, every tree and bush, and sculptured rock was muffled and dazzled in downy, unbroken, undrifted snow. Transparent film-clouds hung in the open azure or draped the walls, the grey granite showing dimly through their fairy veil. This after-storm gauze is formed when vapour is made by sun-rays upon exposed portions of the wet walls, which is of higher temperature than the air with which it drifts into contact.

One day usually is sufficient to dry the warmest portions of the wall and to lave and mix the air until it is about equal in temperature to the rocks which contain it – then that reeky storm-tissue disappears. After every heavy snow-fall, numerous avalanches are born upon all of the slopes and canyons of suitable steepness. In general appearance they resemble waterfalls of the highest free-falling kind, being like them, close, opaque, white in colour, and composed of companies of comets shooting downward with unequal velocity, amid a casing atmosphere of whirling dust. They are most numerous about the slopes of Glacier Point and Tissiack, but by far the grandest avalanches of this Yosemite region are those of Clouds Rest, on the north side, up Tenaya Canyon. The highest Clouds Rest avalanches have a clear, unbroken course of not less than 5,000 feet, and they frequently wipe down great quantities of granite, pushing it a considerable distance up the opposite slope of the canyon. The avalanches of the Summit Mountains often-times descend below the thick zone of pines that grow upon their bases, cutting straight gaps, without leaving a single tree.

The latter half of December was one vast snow-storm, stained and washed by torrents of rain. We have had only one mail in two months, and if our everlasting mountains are to have such everlasting storms, you may not receive this before June or July. The average temperature of last month at Black's on the south side the valley, was at sunrise, 33° Fahrenheit; at noon, 39°; maximum morning temperature, 41°; minimum morning temperature, +13°; maximum noon temperature, 55°; minimum noon temperature, 34°; 21 inches of rain and 41 inches of snow fell during the month up to December 25th. The morning temperature of the sunny, eclipsed side of the valley does not differ much from the south side, but the noon temperature of the north side in clear weather is often as much as 20° higher. Also owing to the difference in height and angle of the various parts of the valley walls and to the irregular form of the bottom of the valley, both north and south sides have a number of well-marked climates. The delta of Indian Canyon is the warmest portion of the valley, both in winter and summer.

[The year drew to a close in] ...Yosemite and we slid smoothly over the astronomical edge of '71; Santa Claus came with very little ado, gave trinkets to our half-dozen younglings, and dropped crusted cakes into bachelors' cabins; but upon the whole our holidays were sorry, unhilarious, whiskified affairs. A grand intercampal Christmas dinner was devised on a scale and style becoming our peerless valley; heaps of solemn substantials were to be lightened and broidered with cookies, and backed by countless cakes, blocky and big as boulders, and a craggy trough-shaped pie was planned for the heart and soul of the feast. It was to have formed a rough model of Yosemite, with domes and brows of "duff" and falls of guttering gravy.

"South Dome be mine," cried one, "softened with sauce of Pohono."

"I'll eat Royal Arches," cried another, "salted with Bachelor's Tears."

"And I'll choose Riverbank Meadow, plummed with avalanche boulders. And some purple granite for me, cut smooth from the cliffs of El Capitan."etc. etc. – all very well conceived but, alas, like all other ladyless feasts, it was a failure. In my last [letter] I gave you a list of our inhabitants, together with their various employments; now you may peep at our social life, quarrels, amusements, etc. Of course you will guess that in our glorious home we gather on the meadow when our work is done, to feast on the moonlit rocks or dark pines spiring up in the stars, and to drink song from the falls like water, and breathe the deep spirit-hush of the winter. But, alas – no! We only quarrel and gossip, and [drink] whisky! And, to show you how much our rocks and quarrels correspond in magnitude, I will give you our last in detail, which is, perhaps, one of average size.

At the close of this last visiting season each hotel-keeper found among his remaining provisions a living mutton, and it was desirable that these three sheep should be kept over winter in the valley to be in readiness for the first pilgrim customers of '72. Now, in winters of ordinary severity, sheep can care for themselves with but little attention from the shepherd, and at first our sheep seemed to have promise of a mild winter. They had rich, sunny days with noontimes dreamily warm. They nibbled the willow bushes on the meadows and silver lupines beneath the pines, and gathered bunch grass and later erigonums up on the rugged debris, but a month ago, when heavy snow fell, they had to be cared for, and trouble began. The three shepherds were equally concerned in the three sheep, and bickerings arose about turns in hunting them up; also about the depth of snow which rendered hunting them up necessary, Black's shepherd holding, with characteristic obstinacy, that in light storms the sheep were better let alone to nibble a living from chaparral in the lee of big rocks. Also, it was proposed that when they were driven up, instead of outraging their gregarious instincts by compelling each to eat his bog sedges in solitude, they should be kept together and "boarded round" from barn to barn. But this union could not be effected, because the three sheep were not equal in size, and moreover, Mr Black's hay was cut on the Bridal Veil Meadow, while Mr L's was cut on the Bachelor's Tears, and it was argued that one tun of Bachelor's Tears hay was worth two tuns of Bridal Veil, because the Bachelor's Tears was sweet, while the Bridal Veil article was boggy and sour. Black's shepherd denied all this, affirming that Bridal Veil carex was as good as Bachelor's Tears carex, or Virgin's Tears carex, or any other in the valley, salt or sour. The geographical position of H's meadow midway between the Veil and Tears, determined the quality of its carex as medium. These bickerings increased in acrimony, and as Black's shepherd was Scotch, L's Dutch, and H's Yankee, there was grave danger of a war of the races. But by brain-racking diplomacy, and a profusion of bloodless blixen, our pastoral sky was cleared, and now all goes heartily well, and each sheep eats its own sedge in its own barn, tended by its own shepherd. All this beneath Tutocahnula and the domes. Ruskin who deals in the relationships of men and mountains, may find some difficult problems here. In striking contrast with these diminutive wranglings are the broad, loving harmonies of our whisky soirées of which about seven are held weekly.

Each of the two bars now open has its own particular friends and patrons, but neither between dealers nor patrons does there exist the faintest trace of opposition or jealousy. This dealer A gathers up his patrons and repairs to the whisky of B which, together with cards, and bear stories, and shooting scrapes of early days, are freely discussed. Next evening B gathers his patrons and repairs to the whisky of A. The two whiskies are about a mile apart, and between them a nocturnal see-saw of admirable fidelity is maintained, although the two whiskies are not of the same species, one being "bushhead" and the other "golden" pronounced with a long lazy emphasis on the 'o'.

More shingle houses are being built, one of which is to be a saloon. At the present rate of progress, flimsy buildings will soon bedraggle the valley from end to end, making it appear like the raw pine towns of a new railroad. Also the meadows are being fenced up, with trees living and dead chopped down and the divine banks and thickets of the briar-rose and azalea are being trampled and cleared away under the name of d----d chaparral, and all destroyable natural beauty in general is fast fading before the armed presence of vulgar mercenary "improvement". But happily, by far the great portion of Yosemite is unimprovable. Her trees and flowers will melt like snow, but her domes and falls are everlasting. I have said that one-half of last month was filled with storm, but the first gift of December weather was a ripe cluster of golden days filling up all the other half. Days and nights glowed past in equal splendour, and not until the afternoon of the 16th was there any sign of coming storm. On the night of the 17th we had a light rain, which changed to snow, and in the morning about ten inches remained unmelted on the meadows. On the night of the 18th rain fell in torrents, but with a temperature of 34°, and the snowline remained high above the meadows. But some time after eleven o clock the temperature was suddenly raised by a south wind to 42° carrying the snow line up to the tops of the valley and far beyond out on the upper basins, perhaps to the very summit of the range, and morning saw Yosemite in the grandeur of flood. Torrents of warm rain were washing the walls, and melting the snow of the surrounding mountains, and the liberated meltings joined with the rains, sang jubilee in glorious congregations of cascades and falls. On both sides [of] the Sentinel foamed a splendid cascade, and over on Three Brothers, half concealed by the pines, I could see fragments of an uncountable company of snowy falls and cascades of every form and voice, and I ran for the open meadows to see the whole circumference of living rocks at once. The meadow between Blacks and Hutchings was full of green lakes, edged and islanded with floating snow, but after fording many a young torrent, I succeeded in groping along the debris to a wadeable meadow between Hutchings and Laymans, in the open midst of the most glorious assemblage of waterfalls ever laid bare to mortal eyes. Between Blacks and Hutchings, there were ten majestic cascades and falls; around Glacier Point, six; on the shoulder of South Dome, facing the main valley, three; on South Dome, facing Mirror Lake, eight; between Mt. Watkins and Washington Column, ten; between Arch Falls and Three Brothers, nineteen – fifty-six newborn falls occupying this upper end of the valley, beside countless host of silvery arteries gleaming everywhere,. In the whole valley there must have been nearly a hundred.

And be it remembered that those falls were not mere momentary transient gushes, but noble-mannered waters, shooting from an average height of near three thousand feet – the very smallest with notes audible at a distance of several miles. From this meadow standpoint only one fall is normally seen, but on this jubilee day there were forty, all perfect and distinct.

The Upper Yosemite Fall is queen of all these mountain waters yet in the first half day of this jubilee her voice was scarcely heard and her manners betrayed no warmth of sympathy with the gushing enthusiasm that encompassed her. She sang her everyday song in everyday dress, but about three o clock in the afternoon I suddenly heard an overwhelming crashing and booming mixed with heavy gaspings and rocky explosions. I ran from the house thinking that a rock avalanche had started, but quickly discovered that all this outbreak of overmastering sounds came from Yosemite Fall. The great flood wave gathered from many a glacier canyon of the Hoffman mountains had just arrived, sweeping logs and ice before it and plunging over the tremendous verge, at once blended in crowning grandeur with the universal anthem storm.

On November 28th came one of the most picturesque snow storms I have ever seen. It was a tranquil day in Yosemite. About midday a close-grained cloud grew in the middle of the valley, blurring the sun; but rocks and trees continued to caste shadow. In a few hours the cloud-ceiling deepened and gave birth to a rank down-growth of silky streamers. These cloud-weeds were most luxuriant about the Cathedral Rocks, completely hiding all their summits. Then heavier masses, hairy outside with a dark nucleus, appeared, and foundered almost to the ground. Toward night all cloud and rock distinctions were blended out, rock after rock disappeared, El Capitan, the Domes and the Sentinel, and all the brows about Yosemite Falls were wiped out, and the whole valley was filled with equal, seamless gloom. There was no wind and every rock and tree and grass blade had a hushed, expectant air. The fullness of time arrived, and down came the big flakes in tufted companies of full grown flowers. Not jostling and rustling like autumn leaves or blossom showers of an orchard whose castaway flakes are hushed into any hollow for a grave, but they journeyed down with gestures of confident life, alighting upon predestined places on rock and leaf, like flocks of linnets or showers of summer flies. Steady, exhaustless, innumerable. The trees, and bushes, and dead brown grass were flowered far beyond summer, bowed down in blossom, and all the rocks were buried. Every peak and dome, every niche and tablet had their share of snow. And blessed are the eyes that beheld morning open the glory of that one dead storm. In vain did I search for some special separate mass of beauty on which to rest my gaze. No island appeared throughout the whole gulf of the beauty. The glorious crystal sediment was everywhere. From wall to wall of our beautiful temple, from meadow to sky was one finished unit of beauty, one star of equal ray, one glowing sun, weighed in the celestial balances and found perfect.

III

Yosemite in Spring
The Reign of the Earthquake – The Beauties of the Falls – The Time for Tourists

YOSEMITE VALLEY, May 7th, 1872. The salons of our State Capitol have disbanded – disintegrated from the awful majesty of Senate and House to common men, who have betaken themselves to their taverns and ranches without giving us one Yosemite law, save our paltry one-thousand dollar appropriation for salary of Guardian. A great deal of chatter took place at different times during the Session, about smooth mountain highways and solid appropriations for the settlement of "claims", but the several Bills, after being tossed from House to Senate, from Senate to committees, were nibbled to death, and we are left to providence for another year, roadless and moneyless, with only a thousand dollar drop of legislation for the burning thirst of our rights and wrongs. There be some who would shed the salt tear for unmitigated soreness of our Sierra Eden woes, not for the distracting uncertainties of private claimants, which are deplorable enough, but for our rugged unapproachableness and improvement discouragements. To such mourners these earthquake storms may seem sympathetic – Yosemite sighing through all her works, giving signs of woe that all is lost. But the billed laws of Sacramento, and paper compulsions and prohibitions of our managing commissioners, do us little harm or good. Human sparrows of improvement will not ruffle El Capitan, and he needs no legal props; he can stand alone. The Falls will manage their harmonies well enough and the birds will sing, and meadows grow green notwithstanding any quantity of the hush or buzz of Sacramento flies. Xerxes made laws for the sea; we make laws for the mountains – make "Commissioners to manage Yosemite Valley," as we'll make Commissioners for the management of the moon.

This Yosemite portion of the Sierra Nevada mountains still yields supple compliance to the time and rhyme of earthquakes, and most of our one-score-and-ten inhabitants are over-satisfied with their uncountable abundance, and at every new burst of shock-waves, and subterranean thunders, declare that it is "full time them goings on down there were lettin' up," for though founded on a rock, some of us consider our houses insecure, and fear they sink fast by our native shore. Since the severe opening shocks of March 26th, the valley has not been calm for a single day. About the middle of April the earthquakes and rumblings became so gentle that they were found only buy those who sought for them, and it was general believed among us that our rocking domes were about to return to trustworthy solidity and fixedness, but a few days ago they were all atremble again.

THE MANNERS OF THE EARTHQUAKE

Since March 26th, we have enjoyed, on the average, about a dozen shocks per day; most of those consisted of a few moderate horizontal thrusts or jars, kept up for fifteen or twenty seconds, with rarely a mingling of twisting motions and blows from underneath. They have occurred at all hours of the night and day, and in all kinds of weather, snow, rain, or sun. There was no preceding murkiness of sky observable, nor extraordinary quietude, and however bird and beast may read foretelling signs of upper storms, they seem ignorant as man of those below. While the varied stream of life flows confidingly on, and our mountains repose in blue sky or storm, smooth, rumbling sounds are heard from below, which are followed by gentle or swift shattering oscillations, mostly from north to south, or parallel with the range. The regularity of these initial oscillations is disturbed by similar less intense oscillations, from east to west, perhaps finishing up by a sudden twisting or upjolting. As soon as the mountains are let alone, they undulate gently back to rest with smooth, slow motion, like the calming waters of a lake. Earthquakes have provoked lively discussions concerning the formation of the valley, and most believe beyond, or rather behind, the regions of doubt that Yosemite is an earthquake crack produced by a hard crack of an earthquake. A severe earthquake storm occurred in Yosemite Valley two or three hundred years ago. Unmistakeable history of this storm is written in huge avalanche slopes a thousand-fold greater than those of the present storm, but corresponding with them in minutest particulars of structure. There is evidence of the simultaneous formation of the different portions of the same slopes, and also the simultaneous occurrence of all the principal slopes on both sides of the valley. A fair approximation to the period of the formation of these slopes may be possible by ascertaining the age of the oldest trees grown upon them because their first generation of forest has not yet passed away. But the severity of the earthquake, which made these slopes cannot be correctly measured by the size of the slopes. We have all become philosophers, deep thinkers. Instead of wasting breath when we meet on the green of meadows or brightness of the sky, we salute by great shakes, solemnly comparing numbers and intensities. What care we for the surface of things. Our thoughts go far below to the underground country where roll the strange thunders, and the waves to which our mountains are a liquid ocean and a sky. Half believing, we paint hypothetic landscapes of the earth beneath, volcanic fountains, lakes, and seas of molten rock fed by a thousand glowing rivers. Amazons of gurgling, rippling fire flowing in bevelled valleys, or deep Yosemite canyons, with a glare of red falls and cascades, with which our upper valley, in all its glory, will not compare.

THE WATERFALLS

These forty days of earthquake ague have made no visible alteration to the health of the valley. Now is the birth-time of leaves; the pines are retassled, and the oaks are sprayed with young purple. Spring is fully committed. Ferns are a foot high, willows are letting fly drifts of ripe seeds. Balm of Gilead poplars, after weeks of caution, have launched their buds full of red and leaves of tender glossy yellow. Cherries, honeysuckles, violets, bluettes, buttercups, larkspurs, gillias, are full of bloom of leaf and flower. Plant-odour fills the valley in light floating clouds and mists; it covers the ground and trees, the chaparral and tabled rocks, coming in small flakes from the impartial stow. Standing on the smooth, plushed meadows, bossed here and there with willows, and browned along the edge with dead ferns, the yellow spray of white-stemmed poplars is seen against the purple of oaks and the high green groves of pine, back of which rise purple and grey-rock walls fringed with glossy green live-oak, spotted with the yellow and orange of mistletoe. The scents and sounds and forms of Yosemite spring-time are as exquisitely compounded as her colours. The weather is warm. The noonday temperature is about 65° Fahr. in the shade; night temperature, about 45°; and the abundant snows of our compassing mountains are freely melted into flooded streams. Beside the five principal falls of the valley – Pohono, Illouette, Vernal, Nevada and Yosemite – there are at present fed from the universal snows a large number of smaller cascades and falls, which come down on steps from a few feet to thousands of feet in height. The best known of these are the Big and Little Sentinel, Cascades,

Yosemite Falls

the Batchelor's Tears, and the Virgin's Tears – magnificent weepers both of them. El Capitan is softened with a most graceful little stream that steals confidingly over his massive brow in a clear fall of more than a thousand feet. Seen at the right time the whole breadth of this fall is irised almost from top to bottom. But of all the white outgush of Yosemite waters, the Upper Yosemite Fall is the greatest. It is on the north side of the valley and about 1,600ft in height. Its waters gather from a basin filled with domes, which reaches back to the edge of the main Tuolomne River canyon, a distance in a straight line of ten to twelve miles. The size of Yosemite Creek, near the brink of the valley, in the months of May and June, in a snow season like the present, is where the current runs at the rate of three miles an hour, about twenty-five feet in width and four feet in depth. Those who have not visited this fall can have little conception of the forms and sounds that water can develop when, after being churned and foamed, it is launched free in air and left for 1,600 feet to its own devices. Few persons see this fall at a distance of less than a mile, and very little intimation is granted at so uncordial a distance of its surprising glory. It is easily approached on the east side by a climb up the rocks to an altitude of 1,200 feet.

Seen from up the valley near Lamon's, at about 8 a.m., a cross-section five or six hundred feet in length is most gorgeously irised throughout – not as a motionless arc, but as a living portion of the fall with ordinary forms and motions of shooting rockets and whirling sprays of endless variety of texture transformed to the substance of rainbow melted and flowing. At this Upper Yosemite Fall, and also at the Middle Yosemite Fall, magnificent lunar bows may be found for half a dozen nights in the months of April, May, June, and sometimes July. If the weather continues sunful, the falls will speedily attain to highest development. May and June are usually branded best for visits to the region; but those who behold the legions of Yosemites that are encamped around and beyond Yosemite so-called, should come any time from the end of June to the end of October. The Spring visiting campaign has just been opened by half a dozen skirmishing parties, who reached the valley by forced marches, mostly from Mariposa; but all three of the war trails will soon be opened, although Tamarac and Crane Flat, on the Big Oak Flat and the Coulterville roads are still deeply snow-clad. Tourists will find no difficulty procuring bread and smiles – bread at three dollars a day, smiles free – both articles in abundance, and excellent in quality.

IV

California Agriculture

WHEN ONE comes out of the mountains, to the lowlands everything seems novel, the great dome of the sky, the smooth plain, the fields, horses, oxen, dogs etc., are noticed as if never seen before, and even one's fellow-beings are regarded with something of the same keenness and freshness of conception that we bring to the study of a new species of wild animal. Once after making a long three months excursion from Yosemite along the Sequoia belt I suddenly found myself in the great California Valley among grangers. Most of my mountaineering has been done on foot and alone (in clear independence), carrying no blankets and only a minimum of bread, lying down by any lake or streamside wherever overtaken by weariness and night. But on this trip I had been persuaded to take a little brown mule with me to carry a pair of blankets and a better supply of bread. The owner of the animal, who had frequently noticed my weary exhausted look when I came in from the High Sierra to replenish my bread-sack, assured me that this wonderful mule could go anywhere that a man could go. But tough and sinewy as he was and accomplished as a rock-climber, many a time in the course of that eventful journey, while he was wedged fast in the rocks or struggling out of sight in a wilderness of chaparral, I wished myself once more wholly free with only my own way to make (and find), notwithstanding the cold nights and hunger that would follow. After many adventures, having completed my studies for the year, I descended from the rough region about the head-waters of the south fork of the Tule River to the Central Valley of California near Tulare Lake, and thence made my way back to Yosemite Valley just before the winter snowstorms set in. On my way down the mountains from beneath the shadows of the grand Sequoia forests to the sunny plains, the first people I met were a company of lumbermen, fragrant rosiny fellows, redolent of pine-gum and balsam. The faces of the older specimens were furrowed like the bark of the logs they were rolling and about as brown. A little of everything in the woods was sticking to them and their trousers, instead of wearing thin, were evidently growing thicker and stronger with age, gaining concentric rings of rosin and sawdust like the annual wood rings of trees.

Further down, following a wagon road that led from the mills, I met a long string of dusty teamsters that were hauling lumber from the pines to the plains. These formed two well-marked varieties whose distinguishing characteristics were chiefly derived from the animals they drove, equine and bovine, both of which, dragging over the sun-beaten hills beneath clouds of dust, recalled the scripture, "Dust thou art," so completely were they covered and filled with it.

Among the Douglas oaks in the lower foothills I discovered what is called a queer genius, a Rocky Mountain adventurer living alone in a little log cabin, whose free wild life with its enjoyments and battles was patent in every line and sign of his weather-beaten countenance. Near the cabin of this mountaineer, on the bank of a small stream I found the camp of two bear hunters, who seemed to live and move and have their being in bears. I noticed a large pile of five-gallon tin cans near the camp-fire that had been used for kerosene, and on inquiring what they were going to do with so many, they said they were for holding bears' grease, which they could sell at a good price. They had spent the summer, they told me, prospecting in Arizona for gold, and getting back to California "dead broke" they had taken up the business of bear-hunting for a living. It paid pretty well they told me, better than farming, besides leaving them free and yielding pleasurable excitement. They had already killed I forget how many. The bears at this late autumn season come down out of the pine woods to the open foothills to feast on the acorns of the Douglas oak, and thus expose themselves to comparatively easy and profitable hunting. These hunters seemed to be carrying on their bear business as regularly and industriously as any other butchers. Setting out from camp early in the morning they scanned the hills carefully from commanding points with field-glasses, and seldom failed, they said, to kill any bear they discovered feeding under the oaks, provided they saw it before the bear saw then. Besides the grease, they said they could sell the skins, and most of the meat also, which they claimed was as good as beef.

Leaving these wild hunters I wandered out on the smooth Tulare plain and next encountered a group of gentle grangers, who were fairly radiant with joy, as if fortune had been bestowing extraordinary favours on them that very day. Every face was dissolved into one big deep smile and challenged congratulation like home-bound prospectors who had "struck it rich." In no part of California had I ever before seen a happy farmer. They always seemed to me to be afflicted with a sort of dull apathetic dry rot, which made this jubilant group appear all the more remarkable. Inquiring how they were getting along, they seemed so eager to tell all their good luck that their words came forth in a hasty choking rush and rumble like boulders from a narrow-throated gorge in a flood. "Look! Look!" they shouted, "at these green fields of ours, green even now at this dried up time of year. The rich ground can't rest and just keeps on giving us crop after crop faster than we can haul them away. Look at that broom-corn over there, how tall and rank it is, close as a canebrake, broom enough on it to sweep all California and that Indian corn grown after a buster of a wheat crop, stalks twelve feet high and ears so far up you can't touch them on tiptoe. And look at the big maps of alfalfa mowed heaven knows how many times or how many tons to the acre – our hogs are all fat, you see and the cattle are fat, the land and everything fat, I tell you, sir, we have found it out. We want no better thing, no bigger bonanza.

"For the last twenty years we have been playing at farming here like we were playing at cards, hoping for wet seasons and just steadily drying up like scaly horned toads, keeping on a-speculating and gambling on the clouds and the rain, scouring over thousand-acre patches with sunburned gang plooughs and mustangs, putting in crop after crop, year after year, and them crops, most of 'em, are in yet; for if we got back our seed it was as much as a bargain.

"But just at the last when we were dried out, dead broke, gone to the dogs, we had just enough of last gasp and kick left in us to see that all we wanted was a water ditch. So we got together in the desperation of hunger and made one, and you see what's happened. We're just drying and dying, some of us said one day, and water's what we want, and there's water a plenty in Kings River and fall enough to bring it to Mussel Slough, and so we all fell to and made the ditch, and all our farms and everybody and everything is now plumb happy and flourishing. I tell you water is King in California! That's our town over there, Grangeville, with schoolhouse, church, jail, and all in it. And it never would have been built, not a hint or hut or house of it, if it hadn't been for the water ditch. Water down here means everything in the world."

In the blocking out of the mountains by glaciers, and in their after sculpture by torrents and avalanches immense quantities of detritus have been carried to the plains; and it was in tracing these mountain chips that I was led into the Grangeville fields.

But to return to this wonder-working irrigation ditch, the first I had seen, I found that it was three feet deep, twenty-five feet wide on the bottom, and that the water flowed in it for the first time in April of this same year. It appears therefore that this notable agricultural revival was accomplished in six months, a fact that seems incredible on passing over the grey, arid plain ground out of which these green fields were made. In the application of the water it was found that the soil became evenly saturated for a distance of two hundred yards or more from the sides of the branch ditches, making the overflowing of the fields unnecessary. But so simple a method is not applicable everywhere. The soil of the Grangeville fields and a considerable portion of the plain between them and the foothills is composed of a sandy loam deposited by the Kings River floods layer over layer in nearly level sheets like the leaves of a book. But the greater portion of the lands of the great Central Valley of California are put together in a different way from those of the river deltas, and in irrigating most of them the water must be spread out in a sheet over the whole surface.

With reference to irrigation, all the lands of the Central Valley in general may be regarded as belonging to two distinct classes. The first, all that are being degraded by atmospheric weathering, the second, all that are being elevated by deposition of fresh layers of soil by rains and floods. The so-called hog-wallow lands belong to the first, all the river bottoms to the second, each with various soils requiring different methods of irrigation. But California farmers are now awakening from their long sleep and a knowledge of their advantages and how best to use them is being acquired. Many experiments are being made and problems connected with the management of all kinds of soil and crops worked out with an enthusiasm strikingly in contrast with former inaction.

In the early days, when the gold mines began to fail, drifting adventurers would ask one another "What are you going to do this winter?" One would say "I'm going to hunt for a living – shoot ducks and geese for the San Francisco market, or deer in the coast range." Another would cautiously choose wood-chopping as a "dead sure thing" so as to have money to go prospecting in the mountains after the melting of the winter snow. Another would say "I'm going down to the plains to lass (lasso) a lot of mustangs and go to farming. Smith made a thousand dollars at it last year and if he can farm I can. The Arkansas boys on the Stanislaus are going to furnish the seed and take a chance with me."

With a vast area of unclaimed, unsurveyed government land before him he would choose a place near some creek or river where water was easily obtained, build a box cabin, hitch his kicking mustangs to a Stockton gang plough and sweep around fifty or five hundred unmeasured acres, ploughing in the seed two or three inches deep without harrowing. The natural vegetation being made up mostly of annuals, there is no tough sod to contend with as in the old west of the Mississippi Valley. For weeks or months the work goes on in solitude commencing with the first rain of the season, when the ground is strewn with the dead leaves and stems of last year's growth. Soon the ground becomes bright with young leaves, and perhaps before the last furrows were drawn the farmer would be wading knee deep in purple and yellow broom. Of all wild farming this was the wildest. Should the season's rainfall be abundant, say from fifteen to twenty inches and well distributed, the yield of wheat would be perhaps from five to fifteen bushels per acre. But in the case of a dry year with only four or five inches of rain the venture would be a failure, leaving the farmer nothing but the pleasure of gambling for his pains. Turning his animals loose to shift for themselves and perhaps selling his cabin to some sheepman, he would leave his so-called farm, a mere cloud-like scar on the bosom of the great level valley and set out in quest of new adventures.

A thousand-acre wheat-field is considered small in the Central Valley of California. Ten and even twenty thousand-acre fields along which to draw a single furrow would be a good day's work, and may still be found on the large Spanish grants. But fortunately farming on so colossal a scale even with improved implements and good cultivation seldom pays, and therefore the big grants are being subdivided into comparatively small lots and sold to true husbandmen. In many portions of the Valley when the ground is thoroughly stirred to a depth of eight or ten inches fair crops may usually be raised without irrigation, but with water in abundance applied when needed, two or three crops a year of double yield may be obtained. The snow fountains of the Sierra Nevada are placed just where they may do the most good and are sufficient to water every rod of the Valley and call forth crops of every clime in unsurpassed abundance. The orange, fig, olive, etc., grow beside the cereals, vegetables, and the acid apples and berries of temperate regions. Perhaps nowhere else in the world may soil and climate be found where the good things of both the north and the south grow together in such benevolent profusion. Comparatively few as yet have settled in this grand garden valley, though even now it has the largest wine and raisin vineyards in the world, and the largest wheat-fields. But the time must surely come when ten millions of happy people shall dwell in this one Great Californian valley enjoying the best things earth has to give, as free from want as if in heaven.

The price of land around the Grangeville canal nearly quadrupled the first year. It is now worth about from thirty to a hundred dollars per acre; and the first irrigating company offered water shares to the settlers at prime cost. The price charged for the irrigation of fields belonging to outsiders was a dollar and a half per acre per year. To farmers coming from the rainlands of the east it must seem hard to have to buy both land and water as if the first comers had taken possession of the clouds. Nevertheless everybody seems satisfied with the conditions of the new agriculture on trial, declaring they would rather have a water ditch of their own than a rain cloud of their own as being more reliable and manageable. From year to year irrigation ditches are being made, though the question of water rights is beset with troublesome difficulties. Some of the most important canals are owned by stock companies from whom small farmers have difficulty in obtaining shares. But notwithstanding a' that and a' that irriguous revivals are breaking forth over all the thirsty valley, cheerless shanties, sifted through and through by dry winds, are being replaced by cottages embowered in trees and lovingly embroidered with flowers; and contentment, perhaps the rarest of the virtues in California, is beginning to grow.

On the East side of the Sierra, the Great Basin, part of which lies within the bounds of California, stretches eastward 400 miles to the Wasatch Mountains in Utah. To the farmer it seems one vast desert of sage, salt and sand hopelessly irredeemable. For though it has gardens and grain fields generously productive, these compared with the broad arid stretches of valley and plain and bare mountain ranges, as seen in general views, are mere specks lying inconspicuously here and there thirty or forty miles apart. Only on its eastern and western margins, along the base of the snowy Sierra and

Wasatch Mountains perennial streams of considerable volume available for irrigation abound. The Owens, Walker, Carson, and Truckee rivers flow into it from the Sierra; the Bear, Jordan, Spanish Fork and many smaller streams on the east.

Only the Utah streams have been put to any great use by the Mormons. Travelling along the base of the range we find the size of the settlements measured by the size of the streams flowing into them – so many families for so much water. So consistent and obvious is this relationship the fields, dwellings, churches, cattle, people, etc seem to have been washed down from the heights like boulder deltas. Well may the Mormon farmers sing "From the hills cometh our strength." On the many subordinate mountain ranges of the basin there is no lasting snow and therefore no large streams.

In leafy regions blessed with copious rains we are accustomed to measure the productive capacity of the soil by its natural vegetation. But this rule is inapplicable here, for notwithstanding its savage nakedness, scarce at all veiled by a sparse growth of sage and brush and linosyris, the desert soil of the Great Basin is as rich in the elements that in moist regions rise and ripen into food as that of any State in the Union. The rocks of the numerous mountain ranges have been thoroughly crushed and ground by the ancient glaciers, vitalised by the sun, and are sifted and outspread in lake basins by powerful torrents that attended the breaking up of the Glacial Period, as if in every way Nature had been carefully preparing the land for the husbandman. Soil, climate, topographical conditions – all are favourable; only water is wanting. The present rainfall is wholly inadequate for agriculture even if it were advantageously distributed over the lowlands, while most of it is poured out on the heights in sudden and violent thunder showers called "cloudbursts", the boisterous waters of which are fruitlessly swallowed up in sandy gulches and deltas a few minutes after they fall.

The principal mountain chains of the interior of the Great Basin receive a good deal of snow during winter, but no great masses are stored up as fountains for perennial streams capable of irrigating considerable areas. Most of it is melted before the end of May and absorbed by moraines and gravelly taluses which send forth small rills that slip quietly down the upper canyons through narrow strips of flowery verdure, most of them sinking and evaporating long before they reach the base of their fountain ranges. Perhaps not one in ten of the whole number flows out into the open plains and not a single drop of even the largest rivers of the basin reaches the ocean. Only a few of the interior streams are large enough to irrigate more than one farm of moderate size. It upon these small outflowing rills that most of the ranches of the State of Nevada are located, lying countersunk beneath the general level just where the mountains meet the plains at an average elevation of about 5000 feet above sea level. All the cereals and garden vegetables thrive here and yield bountiful crops. Fruit, however, has been grown only on a few specially favoured spots as yet.

Another class of ranches are found sparsely distributed along the lowest portions of the plains or valleys where the ground is kept moist by springs or narrow threads of moving water called rivers, fed by some one or more of the most vigorous of the mountain rills that have succeeded in making their escape from the mountain canyons. These are mostly devoted to the growth of wild hay, though in some the natural grasses and sedges have been mixed with timothy and alfalfa, and where the soil is not strongly impregnated with salts some grain is raised. Reese River Valley, White River Valley, and Big Smoky Valley offer fair illustrations of this kind of agriculture. Compared with the foothill ranches these are considerably larger and less inconspicuous as they lie in the wide unshadowed levels of the plains – wavy-edged flecks of green in a wilderness of grey.

Still another class of ranches in the Great Basin is restricted to eastern California and that part of Nevada that lies within reach of the Sierra rivers of the east flank mentioned above. In the valleys through which they flow are found by far the most extensive hay and grain fields of the entire basin excepting perhaps those of the valley of the Jordan. Irrigating streams are led off right and left through innumerable channels and the dusty sleeping ground starts at once into fruitful action and pours forth its wealth without stint. But notwithstanding the many porous fields thus fertilised a considerable portion of the waters of all these rivers continue to reach their old deathbeds in the desert – Owens, Walker, Carson, Pyramid and Winnamuca lakes – showing that in these valleys there still is room for coming farmers. But in Middle and Eastern Nevada and Western Utah every rill that I have seen during three years of exploration at all available for irrigation has been put to use. It appears therefore that under present conditions the limit of agricultural development in these regions has been reached or at least approached, a result caused not alone by natural restrictions as to the area susceptible of development but by the extraordinary stimulus furnished by the mines to agricultural effort. The gathering of gold and silver, barley, vegetables and hay, has gone on together. Most of the mid-valley bogs and meadows, and foothill rills capable of irrigating from five to fifty acres were claimed more than 30 years ago. A majority of these pioneer settlers are plodding Dutchmen living content in the back lanes of Nature, but the high price of farm products tempted a good many of the keen Yankee prospectors made wise in California, to bind themselves down to this sure kind of mining. The wildest of wild hay made chiefly of carices and rushes used to sell at from two hundred to three hundred dollars a ton on the ranches. The same kind of hay is still worth from ten to twenty dollars per ton, according to distance from mines and railways. With rich mine markets the Nevada hermit farmers can make more money by loose ragged methods than the same class of farmers in any other State I have seen, while the savage isolation in which they live seems grateful to them. Even in those instances where the advent of neighbours brings no disputes concerning water rights and pasture ranges they seem to prefer solitude, most of them having been elected from adventurous Californians, the pioneers of pioneers. By them the passing stranger is welcomed, supplied with the best his home affords and in the evening around the fireside, while he smokes his pipe very little encouragement is required to bring forth the story of his life – hunting, mining, fighting in the early Indian times. Only the few who are married hope to return to civilization to educate their children and the ease with which money is made renders the fulfilment of these hopes comparatively sure.

After dwelling so long on the farms of this dry old wonderland my readers may be led to fancy them of more importance as compared with the wild, arid deserts, than they really are. Making your way along any of the wide grey valleys that stretch from north to south seldom will your eye be interrupted by a single mark of civilization or cultivation. The smooth lake-like valleys sweep on indefinitely growing more and more dim and hazy in the glowing sunshine, while a mountain range from eight to ten thousand feet high bounds the view on either hand. There is no singing water, no green sod, no leafy nook to rest in. Mountain and valley seem alike naked in the glare of the downpouring sunshine, and though perhaps travelling a wellworn road to some mining-camp, and supplied with repeated instructions, you scarce hope to find any human habitation, so vast and impressive and deadly is the solitude. But after riding some thirty or forty miles, and while the red sun may be sinking behind a range of mirage-distorted mountains you come suddenly on signs of life. Clumps of willow indicate water, and water indicates a farm. Approaching you discover what may be a patch of barley on the bottom of a flood-bed, broken perhaps and rendered ragged edged and indistinct by boulder piles and the fringing willows of the stream. At length the bounds of the farm became clear, a dirt-roofed cabin comes to view littered with sun-cracked implements and girdled with patches of potatoes, cabbages and alfalfa. The immense expanse of mountain-girt valleys on the edges of which these hidden ranches lie makes even the largest of them seem comic in size. The smallest however are not insignificant in a pecuniary view. On the east side of the Toiyabe Range I discovered a jolly Irishman whose income from a foothill ranch reinforced by a sheep range on the adjacent mountains was from seven to nine thousand dollars a year. His irrigating brook is about four feet wide, eight inches deep with a current of about two miles an hour.

On the California side of the Sierra, grain will not ripen much higher than 4000 feet above the sea. The valleys of Nevada and Western Utah lie at a height of about from 4000 to 5000 feet, and both wheat and barley ripen wherever water may be had up to 7000 feet. The harvest, of course, is later as the elevation increases. In the valleys of the Carson and Walker rivers about 4300 feet above the sea the grain harvest is about a month later than in the Central Valley of California. In Reese River Valley at a height of

6000 feet it commences about the end of August. Winter wheat ripens somewhat earlier, while occasionally one finds a patch of barley in some cool canyon a thousand feet higher that will not mature before the middle of September.

Unlike California, Nevada will probably be richer for many years in gold and silver than in grain and fruits. Utah farmers hope to change the climate of their territory by prayer and point to the recent rise in the waters of the Great Salt Lake as a beginning of moister times. But Nevada's only hope in the way of any considerable increase in agriculture is from artesian wells. The cleft and porous character of the mountain rocks dipping at every angle, and the presence of springs bursting forth at a few places in the valleys far from the mountain sources, indicate accumulations of water from rains and melting snows that have escaped evaporation, and which may in many places now barren, be brought to the surface in flowing wells. Experiments have been tried on a small scale with encouraging success, but what is now wanted is the boring of a few trial wells of large size out in the 'main valleys. The encouragement that successful experiments of this kind would give to farm-seekers forms, it seems to me, an object well worth the attention of the Government.

The grand California valley seems to lack nothing desirable that is not within easy reach. Opening to the sea on one side, and with the great white roof of the Sierra, 450 miles long, looming above it on the other and sending down a magnificent row of rivers – the Kern, Tule, Kaweah, Kings, San Joaquin, Fresno, Merced, Tuolumne, Stanislaus, Calaveras, Cosumnes, Mokelumne, American Feather and Sacramento – with all this wealth of water and soil joined with a benevolent climate and sublime scenery, Californians have only to see to it that the forests on which the regular and manageable flow of the rivers depend are preserved, that storage reservoirs are made at the foot of the Range and all the bounty of the mountains may be put to use. Then will theirs be the most foodful and beautiful of all the lowland valleys of like extent in the world.

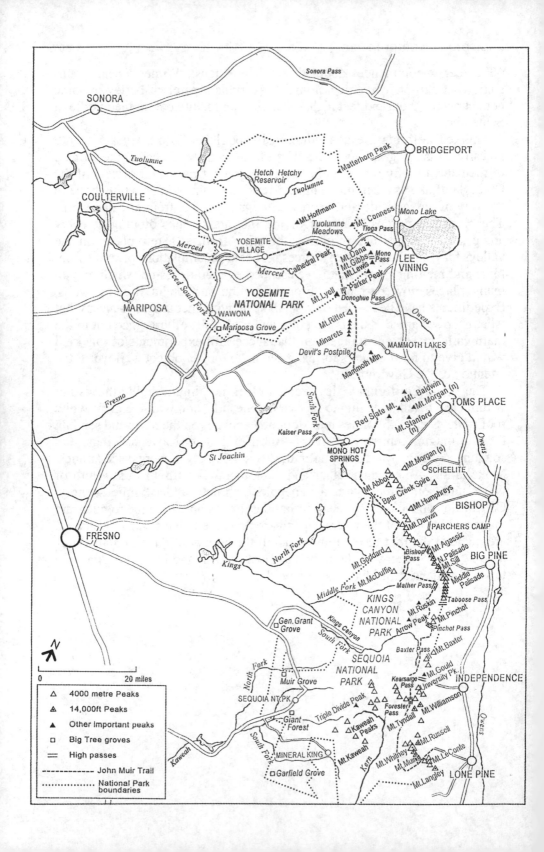

ESSAYS FROM
PICTURESQUE CALIFORNIA
and
THE TREASURES AND FEATURES
OF THE PROPOSED
YOSEMITE NATIONAL PARK

Essays from

Picturesque California

and "Treasures and Features of the
Proposed Yosemite National Park"

First published in two volumes comprising twenty-six chapters (edited by Muir, who wrote six of the chapters) by J. Dewing and Company (San Francisco, 1888–90)

Republished as a single facsimile edition (entitled *West of the Rocky Mountains*) by Running Press (Philadephia, 1976)

''The Treasure of Yosemite'' was first published in *Century* magazine in August, 1890

''Features of the Proposed Yosemite National Park'' was published in *Century* magazine in September, 1890

CONTENTS

The above are Muir's chapters from *Picturesque California,* the full contents of which are:
1. Peaks and Glaciers of the High Sierra (Muir); 2. The Passes of the High Sierra (Muir); 3. A Glimpse of Monterey (J.R.Fitch); 4. The Yosemite Valley (Muir); 5. Totokonulu (poem) (J.Vance Cheney); 6. A Visit to the Lick Observatory (Edward S. Holden); 7. About the Bay of San Francisco (W.C.Bartlett); 8. Game Regions of the Upper Sacramento (Joaquin Miller); 9. The Heart of Southern California (Jeanne C. Carr); 10. Mount Shasta (Muir); 11. Southernmost California (T.S.Van Dyke); 12. North of the Golden Gate (Kate Field); 13. Early California Mining and the Argonauts (Joaquin Miller); 14. The Santa Clara Valley and Santa Cruz Mountains (George Hamlin Fitch); 15. The San Joaquin Valley (Joaquin Miller); 16. The Foothill Region of the Northern Coast Range (Charles Howard Shinn); 17. The New City by the Great Sea – San Francisco (Joaquin Miller); 18. On the Height (poem) (J.Vance Cheney); 19. The Sacramento Valley (John P.Irish); 20. The Tule Region (Charles Howard Shinn); 21. Monterey to Ventura (William L.Ogle); 22. The Plain of Oaks (Albert E.Gray); 23. The Land of the Redwoods (Shinn); 24. Washington and the Puget Sound (Muir); 25. The Basin of the Columbia River (Muir); 26. The Canadian Rockies (Ernest Ingersoll)

EDITOR'S NOTE

Picturesque California marks Muir's graduation from essayist to editor and bookmaker. The six essays he contributed to the book describe the great mountain wildernesses of California, Oregon and Washington. These fill up two thirds of the book, the other twenty contributions being shorter pieces dealing, for the most part, with the towns, sights and industries of the area.

The two-volume book gave Muir, by then already aged fifty, an opportunity to weave together material from previous newspaper and magazine articles into a series of flowing, informative and engaging chapters. As the general editor Muir also took on the role of selecting and inspiring the contributing authors. To Jeanne Carr he wrote that, ''what a bright appreciative traveller would like to see and hear is what is wanted'', and when her manuscript turned out to read ''too much like the preface of some Professor's big book'', Muir advised her to ''look at landscapes as the sun looks at them.''

Muir's three Sierra essays, reprinted here in a conventional narrative layout, show the quality of his descriptive writing and what he was trying to achieve. His essays on 'Mount Shasta', 'Washington and the Puget Sound' and 'The Basin of the Columbia River' were later broken up into smaller chapters by Badè, and used in *Steep Trails*. In its original form Muir's writing in *Picturesque California* seems to have been less influencial than his magazine articles and his later books and, as a result, may not have been given the critical attention it deserved. One reason for this may be that the publisher (possibly in consultation with Muir) used the text as a foil to fit around what Muir called ''firm illustrations by the best artists''. Indeed one of the strengths of this large-format book is its plethora of magnificent illustrations – wood engravings, etchings, photographs and monochrome renditions of the monumental landscape paintings of William Keith, Julian Rix and others. The inappropriate positioning of many of these illustrations suggests that Muir was not closely involved with the final stages of the layout. Nevertheless, as a pictorial record of the scenic spendour of the western United States, it works well, but as a vehicle for serious reading it less satisfactory. Muir's own copies bristle with his pencilled corrections.

Muir clearly hoped that this combination of words and pictures would capture the imagination of readers: that entertainment could lead to education, that pride in American landscape could lead to protection, that an appreciation of the 'picturesque' could lead to political action by the voting public. His comments at the end of chapter two – that "Americans are little aware as yet of the grandeur of their own land" and in the Yosemite chapter where he notes there is "at least a beginning of our return to nature [by tourists who are] travelling to better purpose than they know", give a clear indication of why he associated himself with this popular travelogue.

CHAPTER ONE

The Peaks and Glaciers of the High Sierra

LOOKING ACROSS the broad, level plain of the Sacramento and San Joaquin from the summit of the Coast Range opposite San Francisco, after the sky has been washed by the winter rains, the lofty Sierra may be seen throughout nearly its whole extent, stretching in simple grandeur along the edge of the plain, like an immense wall, four hundred miles long and two and a half miles high, coloured in four horizontal bands; the lowest rose-purple of exquisite beauty of tone, the next higher dark purple, the next blue, and the highest pearl-white – all delicately interblending with each other and with the pale luminous sky and the golden yellow of the plain, and varying in tone with the time of day and the advance of the season.

The thousand landscapes of the Sierra are thus beheld in one view, massed into one sublime picture, and such is the marvellous purity of the atmosphere it seems as near and clear as a painting hung on a parlour wall. But nothing can you see or hear of all the happy life it holds, or of its lakes and meadows and lavish abundance of white falling water. The majestic range with all its treasures hidden stretches still and silent as the sunshine that covers it.

The rose-purple zone rising smoothly out of the yellow plain is the torrid foothill region, comprehending far the greater portion of the gold-bearing rocks of the range, and the towns mills, and ditches of the miners – a waving stretch of comparatively low, rounded hills and ridges, cut into sections by the main river canyons, roughened here and there with outcropping masses of red and grey slates, and rocky gold gulches rugged and riddled; the whole faintly shaded by a sparse growth of oaks, and patches of scrubby ceanothus and manzanita chaparral. Specks of cultivation are scattered from end to end of the zone in fertile flats and hollows far apart – rose embowered cottages, small glossy orange groves, vineyards and orchards,and sweet-scented hay fields, mostly out of sight, and making scarce any appreciable mark on the landscape in wide general views; a paradise of flowers and bees and bland purple skies during the spring months – dusty, sunbeaten, parched and bare all the rest of the year. The dark-purple and blue zones are the region of the giant pines and sequoia and silver-firs, forming the noblest coniferous forests on the face of the globe. They are everywhere vocal with running water and drenched with delightful sunshine.

Miles of tangled bushes are blooming beneath them, and lily gardens, and meadows, and damp ferny glens in endless variety of colour and richness, compelling the admiration of every beholder. Sweeping on over the ridges and valleys they extend a continuous belt from end to end of the range, only slightly interrupted at intervals of fifteen and twenty miles by tremendous canyons 3,000 to 5,000 feet in depth.   Into these main river-canyons innumerable side-canyons and gorges open, occupied by bouncing, dancing, rejoicing cascades, making haste to join the rivers, which, grey with foam, are beating their way with resistless energy to the lowlands and the sea. All these waters sounding together give glorious animation to the onlooking forests, and to the stern, rocky grandeur of the canyon-walls.   There too, almost directly opposite our point of view, is the far-famed Yosemite Valley and to right and left on the same zone many other valleys of the same type, some of them, though but little known as yet, not a whit less interesting, either in regard to the sublimity of their architecture, or the grandeur and beauty of their falling waters.

Above the upper edge of the silver-fir zone, the forest is maintained by smaller pines and spruces, that sweep on higher around lakes and meadows, and over smooth waves of outspread moraines, until, dwarfed and storm-bent, the utmost limit of tree growth is reached at a height of from 10,000 to 12,000 feet. While far above the bravest climbers of them all, rises the lofty, snow-laden, icy Sierra, composed of a vast wilderness of peaks, and crests, and splintered spires, swept by torrents and avalanches, and separated by deep gorges and notches and wide amphitheatres, the treasuries of the snow and fountain-heads of the rivers, holding in their dark mysterious recesses all that is left of the grand system of glaciers that once covered the entire range. During many years of faithful explorations in the Sierra, sixty-five glaciers have been discovered and studied, and it is not likely that many more will be found. Over two-thirds of the entire number lie between Lat. 36° 30' and 39°, sheltered from the wasting sunshine on the northern slopes of the highest peaks, where the snowfall on which they depend is most concentrated and abundant.

Nothing was known of the existence of active glaciers in the Sierra until October, 1871, when I made the discovery of Black Mountain Glacier and measured its movements. It lies near the head of a wide shadowy basin between Red and Black Mountains, two of the dominating summits of the Merced Group. This group consists of the highest portion of a spur that straggles out from the main axis of the chain near Mount Ritter, in the direction of Yosemite Valley. Its western slopes are drained by Illilouette Creek, a tributary of the Merced, which pours its waters into Yosemite in a fine fall bearing the same name as the stream.

No excursion can be made into the Sierra that may not prove an enduring blessing. Notwithstanding the great height of the summits, and the ice and the snow, and the gorges and canyons and sheer giddy precipices, no mountain chain on the globe is more kindly and approachable. Visions of ineffable beauty and harmony, health and exhilaration of body and soul, and grand foundation lessons in Nature's eternal love are the sure reward of every earnest looker in this glorious wilderness.

The Yosemite Valley is a fine hall of entrance to one of the highest and most interesting portions of the Sierra at the head of the Merced, Tuolumne, San Joaquin, and Owens rivers. The necessary outfit may be procured here, in the way of pack animals, provisions, etc., and trails lead from the valley towards Mounts Dana, Lyell, and Ritter, and the Mono Pass; and also into the lower portion of the Illilouette Basin.

W. KEITH

Glacier between
Mounts Ritter and Lyell.

Going to the Black Mountain Glacier, only a few days' provision is required, and a pair of blankets, if you are not accustomed to sleeping by a camp-fire without them.

Leaving the valley by the trail leading past the Vernal and Nevada falls, you cross the lower end of Little Yosemite Valley, and climb the Starr King Ridge, from which you obtain a fine general view of the Illilouette Basin, with its grand array of peaks and domes and dark spirey forests – all on a grand scale of magnitude, yet keenly fine in finish and beauty. Forming one of the most interesting of the basins that lie round about Yosemite Valley, they pour their tribute of songful water into it, swelling the anthems ever sounding there.

The glacier is not visible from this standpoint, but the two mountains between which it lies make a faithful mark, and you can hardly go wrong, however inexperienced in mountain ways.

Going down into the heart of the basin, through beds of zauchneria, and manzanita chaparral, where the bears love to feed, you follow the main stream past a series of cascades and falls until you find yourself between the two lateral moraines that come sweeping down in curves from the shoulders of Red and Black mountains. These henceforth will be your guide, for they belonged to the grand old glacier, of which Black Mountain Glacier is a remnant, one that has endured until now the change of climate which has transformed a wilderness of ice and snow into a wilderness of warm exuberant life. Pushing on over this glacial highway you pass lake after lake set in solid basins of granite, and many a well-watered meadow where the deer with their young love to hide; now clanking over smooth shining rock where not a leaf tries to grow, now wading plushy bogs knee deep in yellow and purple sphagnum, or brushing through luxuriant garden patches among larkspurs eight feet high and lilies with thirty flowers on a single stalk. The lateral moraines bounding the view on either side are like artificial embankments, and are covered with a superb growth of silver-firs and pines, many specimens attaining a height of 200 feet or more.

But this garden and forest luxuriance is soon left behind. The trees are dwarfed, the gardens become exclusively alpine, patches of the heath-like bryanthus and cassiope begin to appear, and arctic willows pressed into flat close carpets by the weight of the winter snow. The lakes, which a few miles down the valley are so deeply embedded in the tall woods, or embroidered with flowery meadows, have here, at an elevation of 10,000 feet above sea level, only thin mats of carex, leaving bare glaciated rock bosses around more than half their shores. Yet amid all this alpine suppression, the sturdy brown-barked mountain pine is seen tossing his storm-beaten branches on edges and buttresses of Red Mountain, some specimens over a hundred feet high and twenty-four feet in circumference, seemingly as fresh and vigorous as if made wholly of sunshine and snow. If you have walked well and have not lingered among the beauties of the way, evening will be coming on as you enter the grand fountain amphitheatre in which the glacier lies. It is about a mile wide in the middle, and rather less than two miles long. Crumbling spurs and battlements of Red Mountain bound it on the north, the sombre rudely sculptured precipices of Black Mountain on the south, and a hacked and splintered col curves around from mountain to mountain at the head, shutting it in on the east.

You will find a good campground on the brink of a glacier lake, where a thicket of Williamson spruce affords shelter from the night wind, and wood for your fire.

As the night advances the mighty rocks looming darkly about you seem to come nearer, and the starry sky stretches across from wall to wall, fitting closely down into all the spiky irregularities of the summits in most impressive grandeur. Then, as you lie by your fireside, gazing into this strange weird beauty, you fall into the clear, death-like sleep that comes to the tired mountaineer.

In the early morning the mountain voices are hushed, the night wind dies away, and scarce a leaf stirs in the groves. The birds that dwell here, and the marmots, are still crouching in their nests. The stream, cascading from pool to pool, seems alone to be awake and doing. But the spirit of the opening, blooming day calls to action. The sunbeams stream gloriously through jagged openings of the eastern wall, glancing on ice-burnished pavements, and lighting the mirror surface of the lake, while every sunward rock and pinnacle burns white on the edges like melting iron in a furnace.

Passing round the northern shore of the lake, and tracing the stream that feeds it back into its upper recesses, you are led past a chain of small lakes set on bare granite benches and connected by cascades and falls. Here the scenery becomes more rigidly arctic. The last dwarf pine is left far below, and the streams are bordered with icicles. The sun now with increasing warmth loosens rock masses on shattered portions of the wall that come bounding down gullies and couloirs in dusty, spattering avalanches, echoing wildly from crag to crag. The main lateral moraines, that stretch so formally from the huge jaws of the amphitheatre into the middle of the basin, are continued along the upper walls in straggling masses wherever the declivity is sufficiently low to allow loose material to rest, while separate stones, thousands of tons in weight, are lying stranded here and there out in the middle of the channel. Here too you may observe well characterised frontal moraines ranged in regular order along the south wall of Black Mountain, the shape and size of each corresponding with the daily shadows cast by the wall above them.

Tracing the main stream back to the last of its chain of lakelets, you may notice that the stones on the bottom are covered with a deposit of fine grey mud, that has been ground from the rocks in the bed of the glacier and transported by its draining stream, which is seen issuing from the base of a raw, fresh looking moraine still in process of formation. Not a plant or weather-stain is visible on its rough unsettled surface. It is from 60 to more than 100 feet in height and plunges down in front at an angle of 38°, which is the steepest at which this form of moraine material will lie. Climbing it is therefore no easy undertaking. The slightest touch loosens ponderous blocks that go rumbling to the bottom, followed by a train of smaller stones and sand.

Cautiously picking your way, you at length gain the top, and there outspread in full view is the little giant glacier swooping down from the sombre precipices of Black Mountain in a finely graduated curve, fluent in all its lines, yet seemingly as rugged and immovable as the mountain against which it is leaning. The blue compact ice appears on all the lower portions of the glacier sprinkled with dirt and stones embedded in its surface. Higher, the ice disappears beneath coarsely granulated snow. The face is still further characterised by dirt bands and the outcropping edges of blue veins, that sweep across from side to side in beautiful concentric curves, showing the laminated structure of the mass; and at the head of the glacier where the névé joins the mountain it is traversed by a huge yawning bergschrund, in some places twelve to fourteen feet in width, and bridged at intervals by the remains of snow avalanches. Creeping along the lower edge holding on with benumbed fingers, clear sections are displayed where the bedded and ribbon structure of glaciers are beautifully illustrated. The surface snow, though everywhere sprinkled with stones shot down from the cliffs, is in some places almost pure white, gradually becoming crystalline, and changing to porous whitish ice of varying shades, and this again changing at a depth of 20 or 30 feet to blue, some of the ribbon-like bands of which are nearly pure and solid, and blend with the paler bands in the most gradual and exquisite manner imaginable, reminding one of the way that colour bands come together in the rainbow.

Should you wish to descend into the weird ice-world of the 'schrund, you may find a way or make a way, by cutting steps with an axe. Its chambered hollows are hung with a multitude of clustered icicles, amidst which thin subdued light pulses and shimmers with ineffable loveliness. Water drips and tinkles among the icicles overhead, and from far below there come strange solemn murmurs from currents that are feeling their way in the darkness among veins and fissures on the bottom. Ice creations of this kind are perfectly enchanting, notwithstanding one feels strangely out of place in their cold fountain beauty. Dripping and shivering you are glad to seek the sunshine, though it is hard to turn away from the delicious music of the water, and the still more delicious beauty of the light in the crystal chambers. Coming again to the surface you may see stones of every size setting out on their downward journey with infinite deliberation, to be built into the terminal moraine. And now the noonday warmth gives birth to a network of sweet-voiced rills that run gracefully down the glacier, curling and swirling in their shining channels, and cutting clear sections in which the structure of the ice is beautifully revealed, their quick, gliding, glancing movements contrasting widely with the invisible flow of the glacier itself on whose back they are all riding. The series of frontal moraines noted further down, forming so striking a picture of the landscape, correspond in every particular with those of this active glacier; and the cause of their distribution with reference to shadows, is now plainly unfolded. When those climatic changes came on that broke up the main glacier that once filled the amphitheatre from wall to wall, a series of residual glaciers was left in the cliff shadows, under whose protection they lingered until the terminal moraines under consideration were formed. But as the seasons became yet warmer, or the snow supply less abundant, they wasted and vanished in succession, all excepting the one we have just seen; and the causes of its longer life are manifest in the greater extent of snow in its more perfect shelter from the action of the sun. How much longer this little glacier will last to enrich the landscape will of course depend upon climate and the changes slowly effected in the form and exposure of its basin.

But now these same shadows reaching quite across the main basin and up the slopes of Red Mountain, mark the time for returning to camp, and also hint the ascent of the mountain next day, from whose summit glorious views are to be seen far down over the darkening woods, and north and south over the basins of Nevada Creek, and San Joaquin, with their shining lakes and lace of silvery streams, and eastward to the snowy Sierras, marshalled along the sky near enough to be intensely impressive. This ascent will occupy most of your third day, and on the fourth, sweeping around the southern boundary of the Illilouette Basin, and over the Glacier Point Ridge, you may reach your headquarters in Yosemite by way of the Glacier Point trail, thus completing one of the most telling trips one can make into the icy Yosemite fountains.

The glaciers lying at the head of the Tuolumne and North fork of the San Joaquin may also be reached from Yosemite, as well as many of the most interesting of the mountains, Mounts Dana, Lyell, Ritter, and Mammoth Mountain – the Mono Pass also, and Mono Lake and volcanoes on the eastern flank of the range. For this grand general excursion into the heart of the High Sierra, good legs and nerves are required, and great caution, and a free number of weeks. Then you may feel reasonably safe among the loose crags of the peaks and crevasses of the glaciers, and return to the lowlands and its cares, rich forever in mountain wealth beyond your most extravagant expectations.

The best time to go to the High Sierra is about the end of September, when the leaf colours are ripe, and the snow is in great part melted from the glaciers, revealing the crevasses that are hidden earlier in the season. Setting out with a pack-animal by the way of Vernal and Nevada falls at the lower end of Little Yosemite Valley, you will strike the old Mariposa and Mono Trail, which will lead you along the base of Clouds Rest, past Cathedral Peak, and down through beautiful forests into the Big Tuolumne Meadows. There, leaving the trail which crosses the meadows and makes direct for the head of the Mono Pass, you turn to the right and follow on up the meadow to its head near the base of Mount Lyell, where a central camp should be established, from which short excursions may be made under comfortable auspices to the adjacent peaks and glaciers.

Throughout the journey to the central camp you will be delighted with the intense azure of the sky, the fine purplish-grey tones of the granite, the reds and browns of dry meadows and the translucent purple and crimson of huckleberry bogs, the flaming yellow of aspen groves, the silvery flashing of the streams in their rocky channels, and the bright green and blue of the glacier lakes. But the general expression of the scenery is savage and bewildering to the lover of the picturesque. Threading the forests from ridge to ridge, and scanning the landscapes from every outlook, foregrounds, middle-grounds, backgrounds, sublime in magnitude, yet seem all alike – bare rock waves, woods, groves, diminutive flecks of meadow and strips of shining water, pictures without lines of beginning or ending.

Cathedral Peak, grandly sculptured, a temple hewn from the living rock, of noble proportions and profusely spired, is the first peak that concentrates the attention. Then come the Tuolumne Meadows, a wide roomy stretch lying at a height of about 8,500 feet above the sea, smooth and lawn-like, with the noble forms of Mounts Dana and Gibbs in the distance, and curiously sculptured peaks on either side. But it is only towards evening of the second day from the valley, that in approaching the upper end of the meadows you gain a view of a truly beautiful and well-balanced picture. It is composed of one lofty group of snow-laden peaks, of which Mount Lyell is the centre, with pine-fringed, granite bosses braided around its base, the whole surging free into the sky from the head of a magnificent valley, whose lofty walls are bevelled away on both sides so as to embrace it all without admitting anything not strictly belonging to it.

The foreground is now aflame with autumn colours, brown, and purple, and gold, ripe and luminous in the mellow sunshine, contrasting brightly with the deep cobalt-blue of the sky, and the black and grey, and pure spiritual white of the rocks and glaciers. Down through the heart of the picture the young Tuolumne River is seen pouring from its crystal fountains, now resting in glassy pools as if changing back again into ice, now leaping in white cascades as if turning to snow, gliding right and left between granite bosses, then sweeping on through the smooth meadow levels of the valley, swaying pensively from side to side, with calm, stately gestures, past dipping sedges and willows, and around groves of arrowy pine; and throughout its whole eventful course, flowing however fast or slow, singing loud or low, ever filling the landscape with delightful animation, and manifesting the granduer of its sources in every movement and tone.

The excursion to the top of Mount Lyell, 13,000 feet high, will take you through the midst of this alpine grandeur, and one day is all the time required. From your camp on the bank of the river you bear off up the right wall of the canyon and on direct to the glacier, keeping towards its western margin, so as to reach the west side of the extreme summit of the mountain where the ascent is least dangerous. The surface of the glacier is shattered with crevasses in some places; these, however, are easily avoided, but the sharp wave-like blades of granular snow covering a great part of the upper slopes during most of the season are exceedingly fatiguing, and are likely to stop any but the most determined climbers willing to stagger, stumble, and wriggle onward against every difficulty. The view from the summit overlooks the wilderness of peaks towards Mount Ritter, with their bright array of snow, and ice, and lakes; and northward Mount Dana, Castle Peak, Mammoth Mountain, and many others; westward, sweeping sheets of meadow, and heaving swells of ice-polished granite, and dark lines of forest and shadowy canyons towards Yosemite; while to eastward the view fades dimly among the sunbeaten deserts and ranges of the Great Basin. These grand mountain scriptures laid impressively open will make all your labour light, and you will return to camp braced and strengthened for yet grander things to come.

The excursion to Mount Ritter will take about three days from the Tuolumne Camp, some provision therefore will have to be carried, but no one will chafe under slight inconveniences while seeking so noble a mark. Ritter is king of all the giant summits hereabouts. Its height is about 13,300 feet, and it is guarded by steeply inclined glaciers, and canyons and gorges of tremendous depth and ruggedness, rendering it comparatively inaccessible. But difficulties of this kind only exhilarate the mountaineer.

Setting out from the Tuolumne, carrying bread, and an axe to cut steps in the glaciers, you go about a mile down the valley to the foot of a cascade that beats its way through a rugged gorge in the canyon wall from a height of about 900 feet, and pours its foaming waters into the river. Along the edge of this cascade you will find a charming way to the summit. Thence you cross the axis of the range and make your way southward along the eastern flank to the northern slopes of Ritter, conforming to the topography as best you can, for to push on directly through the peaks along the summit is impossible.

Climbing along the dashing border of the cascade, bathed from time to time in waftings of irised spray, you are not likely to feel much weariness, and all too soon you find yourself beyond its highest fountains. Climbing higher, new beauty comes streaming on the sight – autumn-painted meadows, late-blooming goldenrods, peaks of rare architecture, bright crystal lakes, and glimpses of the forested lowlands seen far in the west.

Over the divide the Mono Desert comes full into view, lying dreaming silent in thick purple light – a desert of heavy sun-glare, beheld from a foreground of ice-burnished granite. Here the mountain waters separate, flowing east to vanish in the volcanic sands and dry sky of the Great Basin, west to pass through the Golden Gate to the sea.

Passing a little way down over the summit until an elevation of about ten thousand feet is reached, you then push on southward dealing instinctively with every obstacle as it presents itself. Massive spurs, alternating with deep gorges and canyons, plunge abruptly from the shoulders of the snowy peaks and plant their feet in the warm desert. These are everywhere marked with characteristic sculptures of the ancient glaciers that swept over this entire region like one vast ice-wind, and the polished surfaces produced by the ponderous flood are still so perfectly preserved that in many places you will find them about as trying to the eyes as sheets of snow. But even on the barest of these ice pavements, in sheltered hollows countersunk beneath the general surface into which a few rods of well-ground moraine chips have been dumped, there are groves of spruce and pine thirty to forty feet high, trimmed around the edges with willow and huckleberry bushes; and sometimes still further with an outer ring of grasses bright with lupines, larkspurs, and showy columbines. All the streams, too, and the pools at this elevation, are furnished with little gardens, which, though making scarce any show at a distance, constitute charming surprises to the appreciative mountaineer in their midst. In these bits of leafiness a few birds find grateful homes, and having no acquaintance with man they fear no ill and flock curiously around the stranger, almost allowing themselves to be taken in hand. In so wild and so beautiful a region your first day will be spent, every sight and sound novel and inspiring, and leading you far from yourself. Wearied with enjoyment and the crossing of many canyons you will be glad to camp while yet far from Mount Ritter. With the approach of evening long, blue, spiky-edged shadows creep out over the snowfields, while a rosy glow, at first scarce discernible, gradually deepens, suffusing every peak and flushing the glaciers and the harsh crags above them. This is the alpenglow, the most impressive of all the terrestrial manifestations of God. At the touch of this divine light the mountains seem to kindle to a rapt religious consciousness, and stand hushed like worshippers waiting to be blessed. Then suddenly comes darkness and the stars.

On my first visit to Ritter I found a good campground on the rim of a glacier basin about 11,000 feet above the sea. A small lake nestles in the bottom of it, from which I got water for my tea, and a storm-beaten thicket nearby furnished abundance of firewood. Sombre peaks, hacked and shattered, circle half way round the horizon, wearing a most solemn aspect in the gloaming, and a waterfall chanted in deep base tones across the lake on its way down from the foot of a glacier. The fall and the lake and the glacier are almost equally bare, while the pines anchored in the fissures of the rocks are so dwarfed and shorn by storm-winds you may walk over the tops of them as if on a shaggy rug. The scene was one of the most desolate in tone I ever beheld. But the darkest scriptures of the mountains are illumined with bright passages of Nature's eternal love and they never fail to manifest themselves when one is alone. I made my bed in a nook of the pine thicket where the branches were pressed and crinkled overhead like a roof, and bent down on the sides. These are the best bed-chambers the Sierra affords, snug as squirrel-nests, well-ventilated, full of spicy odours, and with plenty of wind-played needles to sing one asleep. I little expected company in such a place, but creeping in through a low opening I found five or six small birds nestling among the tassels. The night wind begins to blow soon after dark, at first only a gentle breathing, but increasing toward midnight to a gale in strength, that fell on my leafy roof in rugged surges like a cascade, while the waterfall sang in chorus, filling the old ice-fountain with its solemn roar, and seeming to increase in power as the night advanced – fit voice for such a landscape. How glorious a greeting the sun gives the mountains! To behold this alone is worth the pains of any excursion a thousand times over. The highest peaks burn like islands in a sea of liquid shade. Then the lower peaks and spires catch the glow, and the long lances of light streaming through many a notch and pass, fall thick on the frosty meadows. The whole mountain world awakes. Frozen rills begin to flow. The marmots come out of their nests beneath the boulders and climb sunny rocks to bask. The lakes seen from every ridge-top shimmer with white spangles like the glossy needles of the low tasselled pines. The rocks, too, seem responsive to the vital sun-heat, rock-crystals and snow-crystals throbbing alike. Thrilled and exhilarated one strides onward in the crisp bracing air as if never more to feel fatigue, limbs moving without effort, every sense unfolding and alert like the thawing flowers to take part in the new day harmony.

All along your course thus far, excepting while crossing the canyons, the landscapes are open and expansive. On your left the purple plains of Mono repose dreamy and warm. On your right and in front, the near Alps spring keenly into the thin sky with more and more impressive sublimity.

But these larger views are at length lost. Rugged spurs and moraines and huge projecting buttresses begin to shut you in, until arriving at the summit of the dividing ridge between the head waters of Rush Creek and the northmost tributaries of the San Joaquin, a picture of pure wildness is disclosed, far surpassing every other you have yet seen.

There, immediately in front, looms the majestic mass of Mt. Ritter, with a glacier swooping down its face nearly to your feet, then curving, westward and pouring its frozen flood into a blue-green lake whose shores are bound with precipices of crystalline snow, while a deep chasm drawn between the divide and the glacier separates the sublime picture from everything else. Only the one huge mountain in sight, the one glacier, and one lake; the whole veiled with one blue shadow – rock, ice, and water, without a single leaf. After gazing spell-bound you begin instinctively to scrutinize every notch and gorge and weathered buttress of the mountain with reference to making the ascent. The entire front above the glacier appears as one tremendous precipice, slightly receding at the top and bristling with comparatively short spires and pinnacles set above one another in formidable array. Massive lichen-stained battlements stand forward, here and there hacked at the top with angular notches and separated by frosty gullies and recesses that have been veiled in shadow ever since their creation, while to right and left, far as the eye can reach, are huge crumbling buttresses offering no invitation to the climber. The head of the glacier sends up a few fingerlike branches through couloirs, but these are too steep and short to be available, and numerous narrow-throated gullies down which stones and snow are avalanched seem hopelessly steep, besides being interrupted by vertical cliffs past which no side way is visible. The whole is rendered still more terribly forbidding by the chill shadow, and the gloomy blackness of the rocks, and the dead silence relieved only by the murmur of small rills among the crevasses of the glacier, and ever and anon the rattling report of falling stones. Nevertheless the mountain may be climbed from this side, but only tried mountaineers should think of making the attempt.

Near the eastern extremity of the glacier you may discover the mouth of an avalanche gully, whose general course lies oblique to the plane of the front, and the metamorphic slates of which the mountain is built are cut by cleavage planes in such a way that they weather off in angular blocks, giving rise to irregular steps that greatly facilitate climbing on the steepest places. Thus you make your way into a wilderness of crumbling spires aud battlements built together in bewildering combinations, and glazed in many places with a thin coating of ice, which must be removed from your steps; while so steep is the entire ascent one would inevitably fall to the glacier in case a single slip should be made.

Towards the summit the face of the mountain is still more savagely hacked and torn. It is a maze of yawning chasms and gullies, in the angles of which rise beetling crags and piles of detached boulders, made ready, apparently, to be launched below. The climbing is, however, less dangerous here, and after hours of strained, nerve-trying climbing, you at length stand on the topmost crag, out of the shadow in the blessed light. How truly glorious the landscape circled this noble summit! Giant mountains, innumerable valleys, glaciers, and meadows, rivers and lakes, with the dark blue sky bent tenderly over them all.

Looking southward along the axis of the range, the eye is first caught by a row of exceedingly sharp and slender spires, which rise openly to a height of about a thousand feet from a series of short glaciers that lean back against their bases, their fantastic sculpture and the unrelieved sharpness with which they spring out of the ice rendering them peculiarly wild and striking. These are the Minarets. Beyond them you behold the highest mountains of the range, their snowy summits crowded together in lavish abundance, peak beyond peak, aspiring higher, and higher as they sweep on southward, until the culminating point is reached in Mount Whitney near the head of the Kern River, at an elevation of nearly 15,000 feet above the level of the sea.

Westward the general flank of the range is seen flowing grandly away in smooth undulations, a sea of grey granite waves, dotted with lakes and meadows, and fluted with stupendous canyons that grow steadily deeper as they recede in the distance.

Below this grey region lie the dark forests, broken here and there by upswelling ridges and domes; and yet beyond is a yellow, hazy belt marking the broad plain of the San Joaquin, bounded on its farther side by the blue mountains of the coast. Turning now to the northward, there in the immediate foreground is the Sierra Crown, with Cathedral Peak a few degrees to the left, the grey, massive form of Mammoth Mountain to the right, 13,000 feet high, and Mounts Ord, Gibbs, Dana, Conness, Tower Peak, Castle Peak, and Silver Mountain, stretching away in the distance, with a host of noble companions that are as yet nameless.

To the eastward the whole region seems a land of pure desolation covered with beautiful light. The hot volcanic basin of Mono, with its lake fourteen miles long, Owens Valley, and the wide table land at its head dotted with craters, and the Inyo Mountains; these are spread map-like beneath you, with many of the short ranges of the Great Basin passing and overlapping each other and fading on the glowing horizon.

At a distance of less than 3,000 feet below the summit you see the tributaries of the San Joaquin and Owens Rivers bursting forth from their sure fountains of ice, while a little to the north of here are found the highest affluents of the Tuolumne and Merced. Thus the fountain heads of four of the principal rivers of California are seen to lie within a radius of four or five miles.

Lakes, the eyes of the wilderness, are seen gleaming in every direction – round, or square, or oval like very mirrors; others narrow and sinuous, drawn close about the peaks like silver girdles; the highest reflecting only rock and snow and sky. But neither these nor the glaciers, nor yet the brown bits of meadow and moorland that occur here and there, are large enough to make any marked impression upon the mighty host of peaks. The eye roves around the vast expanse rejoicing in so grand a freedom, yet returns again and again to the fountain mountains. Perhaps some one of the multitude excites special attention, some gigantic castle with turret and battlement, or gothic cathedral more lavishly spired than any ever chiselled by art. But generally, when looking for the first time from an all-embracing standpoint like this, the inexperienced observer is oppressed by the incomprehensible grandeur of the peaks crowded about him, and it is only after they have been studied long and lovingly that their far-reaching harmonies begin to appear. Then penetrate the wilderness where you may, the main telling features to which all the topography is subordinate are quickly perceived, and the most chaotic alp-clusters stand revealed and regularly fashioned and grouped in accordance with law, eloquent monuments of the ancient glaciers that brought them into relief. The grand canyons likewise are recognised as the necessary results of causes following one another in melodious sequence – Nature's poems carved on tables of stone, the simplest and most emphatic of her glacial compositions.

Had we been here to look during the glacial period we would have found a wrinkled ocean of ice continuous as that now covering North Greenland and the lands about the South Pole, filling every valley and canyon, flowing deep above every ridge, leaving only the tops of the peaks rising darkly above the rock-encumbered waves, like foam-streaked islets in the midst of a stormy sea – these islets the only hints of the glorious landscapes now lying warm and fruitful beneath the sun. Now all the work of creation seems done. In the deep, brooding silence all appears motionless. But in the midst of this outer steadfastness we know there is incessant motion. Ever and anon avalanches are falling from yonder peaks. These cliff-bound glaciers seemingly wedged fast and immovable, are flowing like water and grinding the rocks beneath them. The lakes are lapping their granite shores, and wearing them away, and every one of these young rivers is fretting the air into music, and carrying the mountains to the plains. Here are the roots of the life of the lowlands with all their wealth of vineyard and grove, and here more simply than elsewhere is the eternal flux of nature manifested.

But in the thick of these fine lessons you must remember that the sun is wheeling far to the west, and you have many a weary and nerve-trying step to make ere you can reach the timber-line where you may lie warm through the night. But with keen caution and instinct and the guidance of your guardian angel you may pass every danger in safety, and in another delightful day win your way back again to your camp to rest on the beautiful Tuolumne River.

The Mount Lyell Group from Tuolumne River

CHAPTER TWO

The Passes of the High Sierra

THE ROADS that Nature has opened through the heart of the High Sierra are hard to travel. So the sedate plodder of the lowlands would say, whether accustomed to trace the level furrows of fields, or the paved streets of cities. But as people oftentimes build better than they know, so also do they walk and climb and wander better than they know, and so it comes, that urged onward by a mysterious love of wild beauty and adventure, we find ourselves far from the beaten ways of life, toiling through these rugged mountain passes without thinking of a reason for embracing with such ungovernable enthusiasm so much stern privation and hardship.

"Try not the pass" may sound in our ears, but despite the solemn warning, come from whom it may, the passes will be tried until the end of time, in the face of every danger of rock, avalanche, and blinding storm. And whatever the immediate motive may be that starts us on our travels – wild landscapes, or adventures, or mere love of gain, the passes themselves will in the end be found better than anything to which they directly lead; calling every faculty into vigorous action, rousing from soul-wasting apathy and ease, and opening windows into the best regions of both earth and heaven.

The glaciers were the pass makers of the Sierra, and by them the ways of all mountaineers have been determined. A short geological time before the coming on of that winter of winters, called "The Glacial Period," a vast deluge of molten rocks poured from many a chasm and crater on the flanks and summit of the range, obliterating every distinction of peak and pass throughout its northern portions, filling the lake basins, flooding ridge and valley alike, and effacing nearly every feature of the pre-glacial landscapes.

Then, after these all-destroying fire-floods ceased to flow, but while the great volcanic cones built up along the axis of the range, still burned and smoked, the whole Sierra passed under the domain of ice and snow. Over the bald, featureless, fire-blackened mountains glaciers crawled, covering them all from summit to base with a mantle of ice; and thus with infinite deliberation the work was begun of sculpturing the range anew. Those mighty agents of erosion, halting never through unnumbered centuries, ground and crushed the flinty lavas and granites beneath their crystal folds. Particle by particle, chip by chip, block by block the work went on, wasting and building, until in the fullness of time the mountains were born again, the passes and the summits between them, ridges and canyons, and all the main features of the range coming to the light nearly as we behold them today.

Looking into the passes near the summits, they seem singularly gloomy and bare, like raw quarries of dead, unfertilised stone – gashes in the cold rock-bones of the mountains above the region of life, empty as when they first emerged from beneath the folds of the ice-mantle. Faint indeed are the marks of any kind of life, and at first sight they may not be seen at all. Nevertheless birds sing and flowers bloom in the highest of them all, and in no part of the range, north or south, is there any break in the chain of life, however much it may be wasted and turned aside by snow and ice, and flawless granite.

Pass through the Minarets

Compared with the well-known passes of Switzerland, those of the south half of the Sierra are somewhat higher, but they contain less ice and snow, and enjoy a better summer climate, making them, upon the whole, more open and approachable. A carriage-road has been constructed through the Sonora Pass, the summit of which is 10,150 feet above the level of the sea – 878 feet higher than the highest carriage-pass in Switzerland – the Stelvio Pass.

In a distance of 140 miles between lat. 36° degrees 20' and 38° degrees the lowest pass I have yet discovered exceeds 9,000 feet, and the average height of all above sea-level is perhaps not far from 11,000 feet.

Substantial carriage-roads lead through the Carson and Johnson Passes near the head of Lake Tahoe, over which immense quantities of freight were hauled from California to the mining regions of Nevada prior to the construction of the Central Pacific Railroad through the Donner Pass. Miles of mules and ponderous wagons might then be seen slowly crawling beneath a cloud of dust through the majestic forest aisles, the drivers shouting in every language, and making a din and disorder strangely out of keeping with the solemn grandeur of the mountains about them.

To the northward of the memorable Donner Pass, 7,056 feet in height, a number of lower passes occur, through whose rugged defiles long emigrant trains, with footsore cattle and sun-cracked wagons a hundred times mended, wearily toiled during the early years of the Gold Period. Coming from far, through a thousand dangers, making a way over trackless wastes, the snowy Sierra at length loomed in sight, to them the eastern wall of the Land of Gold. And as they gazed through the tremulous haze of the desert, with what joy must they have descried the gateway through which they were so soon to pass to the better land of all their golden hopes and dreams!

Between the Sonora Pass and the southern extremity of the High Sierra, a distance of a 160 miles, there is not a single carriage-road conducting from one side of the range to the other, and only five passes with trails of the roughest description. These are barely practicable for animals, a pass in this region meaning simply any notch with its connecting canyon and ridges through which one may, by the exercise of unlimited patience, make out to lead a surefooted mule or mustang, one that can not only step well among loose stones, but also jump well down rugged stairways, and slide with limbs firmly braced down smooth inclines of rock and snow.

Only three of the five may be said to be in use – the Kearsarge, Mono, and Virginia Creek passes – the tracks leading through the others being only obscure Indian trails not graded in the least, and scarce at all traceable by white men. Much of the way lies over solid pavements where the unshod ponies of the Indians leave no appreciable sign, and across loose taluses where only a slight displacement is visible here and there, and through thickets of weeds and bushes, leaving marks that only skilled mountaineers can follow, while a general knowledge of the topography must be looked to as the main guide.

One of these Indian trails leads through a nameless pass between the head waters of the south and middle forks of the San Joaquin, another between the north and middle forks of the same river, to the south of the Minarets, this last being about 9,000 feet high, and the lowest of the five.

The Kearsarge is the highest. It crosses the summit of the range near the head of the south fork of Kings River, about eight miles to the north of Mount Tyndall, through the midst of the grandest scenery. The highest point on the trail is upward of 12,000 feet above the sea. Nevertheless it is one of the safest of the five, and is travelled every summer from July to October or November by hunters, prospectors, and stock-owners, and also to some extent by enterprising pleasure-seekers. For besides the surpassing grandeur of the scenery about the summit, the trail in ascending the western flank of the range leads through a forest of the giant Sequoias, and through the magnificent Kings River Valley, that rivals Yosemite in the varied beauty and grandeur of its granite masonry and falling waters. This, as far as I know, is probably the highest travelled pass on the American continent.

The South Wall of Kings River Canyon

The Mono Pass lies to the east of Yosemite Valley, at the head of one of the tributaries of the South Fork of the Tuolumne, and is the best known of all the High Sierra passes. A rough trail, invisible mostly, was made through it about the time of the Mono and Aurora gold excitements, in the year 1858, and it has been in use ever since by mountaineers of every description. Though more than a thousand feet lower than the Kearsarge it is scarcely inferior in sublimity of rock-scenery, while in snowy, loud-sounding water it far surpasses the Kearsarge.

The Virginia Creek Pass, situated a few miles to the northward, at the head of the southmost tributary of Walker River, is somewhat lower, but less travelled than the Mono. It is used chiefly by "Sheep-men" who drive their flocks through it on the way to Nevada, and roaming bands of Pah Ute Indians, who may be seen occasionally in long straggling files, strangely attired, making their way to the hunting grounds of the western slope, or returning laden with game of startling variety.

These are all the travelled passes of the high portion of the range of which I have any knowledge. But leaving wheels and pack-animals out of the question, the free mountaineer, carrying only a little light dry food strapped firmly on his shoulders, and an axe for ice-work, can make his way across the Sierra almost everywhere, and at any time of year when the weather is calm. To him nearly every notch between the peaks is a pass, though much patient step-cutting is in some cases required up and down steeply inclined glaciers and ice-walls, and cautious scrambling over precipices that at first sight appear hopelessly inaccessible to the inexperienced lowlander. All the passes make their steepest ascents on the east flank of the range, where the average rise is nearly a thousand feet to the mile, while on the west it is about two hundred feet. Another marked difference between the east and west portions of the passes is that the former begin between high moraine embankments at the very foot of the range, and follow the canyons, while the latter can hardly be said to begin until an elevation of from seven to ten thousand feet or more is reached by following the ridges, the canyons on the west slope being accessible only to the birds and the roaring falling rivers. Approaching the range from the grey levels of Mono and Owens Valley the steep short passes are in full view between the peaks, their feet in hot sand, their heads in snow, the courses of the more direct being disclosed nearly all the way from top to bottom. But from the west side one sees nothing of the pass sought for until nearing the summit, after spending days in threading the forests on the main dividing ridges between the canyons of the rivers, most of the way even the highest peaks being hidden.

The more rugged and inaccessible the general character of the topography of any particular region, the more surely will the trails of white men, Indians, bears, deer, wild sheep, etc., converge into the best passes. The Indians of the west slope venture cautiously across the range in settled weather to attend dances and obtain loads of pine-nuts and the larvae of a small fly that breeds in Mono and Owens lakes, while the desert Indians cross to the west for acorns and to hunt, fight, etc. The women carry the heavy burdens with marvellous endurance over the sharpest stones barefooted, while the men stride on erect a little in advance, stooping occasionally to pile up stepping-stones for them against steep rock-fronts, just as they would prepare the way in difficult places for their ponies. Sometimes, delaying their journeys until too late in the season, they are overtaken by heavy snowstorms and perish miserably, not all their skill in mountain-craft being sufficient to save them under the fierce onsets of the most violent of autumn storms when caught unprepared. Bears evince great sagacity as mountaineers, but they seldom cross the range. I have several times tracked them through the Mono Pass, but only in late years, after cattle and sheep had passed that way, when they doubtless were following to feed on the stragglers and those that had fallen over the precipices. Even the wild sheep, the best mountaineers of all, choose regular passes in crossing the summits on their way to their summer or winter pastures. Deer seldom cross over from one side of the range to the other. I have never seen the Mule-deer of the Great Basin west of the summit, and rarely the Black-tailed species on the eastern slopes, notwithstanding many of the latter ascend the range nearly to the head of the canyons among the peaks every summer to hide and feed in the wild gardens, and bring forth their young.

Having thus indicated in a general way the height, geographical position, and leading features of the main passes, we will now endeavour to see the Mono Pass more in detail, since it may, I think, be regarded as a good example of the higher passes accessible to the ordinary traveller in search of exhilarating scenery and adventure. The greater portion of it is formed by Bloody Canyon, which heads on the summit of the range, and extends in a general east-northeasterly direction to the edge of the Mono Plain. Long before its discovery by the whites, this wonderful canyon was known as a pass by the Indians of the neighbourhood, as is shown by their many old trails leading into it from every direction. But little have they marked the grand canyon itself, hardly more than the birds have in flying through its shadows. No stone tells a word of wild foray or raid. Storm-winds and avalanches keep it swept fresh and clean.

The first white men that forced a way through its sombre depths with pack-animals were companies of eager adventurous miners, men who would build a trail down the throat of the darkest inferno on their way to gold. The name Bloody Canyon may have been derived from the red colour of the metamorphic slates in which it is in great part eroded, or more probably from the blood stains made by the unfortunate animals that were compelled to slide and shuffle awkwardly over the rough cutting edges of the rocks, in which case it is too well named, for I have never known mules or horses, however sure-footed, to make their way either up or down the canyon, without leaving a trail more or less marked with blood. Occasionally one is killed outright by falling over some precipice like a boulder. But such instances are less common than the appearance of the place would lead one to expect, the more experienced, when driven loose, picking their way with wonderful sagacity.

During the exciting times that followed the discovery of gold near Mono Lake it frequently became a matter of considerable pecuniary importance to force a way through the canyon with pack trains early in the spring, while it was yet heavily choked with winter snow. Then, though the way was smooth, it was steep and slippery, and the footing of the animals giving way, they sometimes rolled over sidewise with their loads, or end over end, compelling the use of ropes in sliding them down the steepest slopes where it was impossible to walk.

A good bridle-path leads from Yosemite through the Big Tuolumne Meadows to the head of the canyon. Here the scenery shows a sudden and startling condensation. Mountains red, black, and grey rise close at hand on the right, white in the shadows with banks of enduring snow. On the left swells the huge red mass of Mt. Gibbs, while in front the eye wanders down the tremendous gorge, and out on the warm plain of Mono, where the lake is seen in its setting of grey light like a burnished disc of metal, volcanic cones to the south of it, and the smooth mountain ranges of Nevada beyond fading in the purple distance.

Entering the mountain gateway the sombre rocks seem to come close about us, as if conscious of our presence. Happily the ouzel and old familiar robin are here to sing us welcome, and azure daisies beaming with sympathy, enabling us to feel something of Nature's love even here, beneath the gaze of her coldest rocks. The peculiar impressiveness of the huge rocks is enhanced by the quiet aspect of the wide Alpine meadows through which the trail meanders just before entering the narrow pass. The forests in which they lie, and the mountain-tops rising beyond them, seem hushed and

Bloody Canyon – Mono Trail

tranquil. Yielding to their soothing influences, we saunter on among flowers and bees scarce conscious of any definite thought; then suddenly we find ourselves in the huge, dark jaws of the canyon, closeted with nature in one of her wildest strongholds.

After the first bewildering impression begins to wear off, and we become reassured by the glad birds and flowers, a chain of small lakes is seen, extending from the very summit of the pass, linked together by a silvery stream, that seems to lead the way and invite us on. Those near the summit are set in bleak rough rock-bowls, scantily fringed with sedges. Winter storms drive snow through the canyon in blinding drifts, and avalanches shoot from the heights rushing and booming like waterfalls. Then are these sparkling tarns filled and buried leaving no sign of their existence. In June and July they begin to blink and thaw out like sleepy eyes; sedges thrust up their short brown spikes about their shores, the daisies bloom in turn, and the most profoundly snow-buried of them all is at length warmed and dressed as if winter were only the dream of a night. Red Lake is the lowest of the chain and also the largest. It seems rather dull and forbidding, at first sight, lying motionless in its deep, dark bed, seldom stirred during the day by any wind strong enough to make a wave.

The canyon wall rises sheer from the water's edge on the south, but on the opposite side there is sufficient space and sunshine for a fine garden. Daisies star the sod about the margin of it, and the centre is lighted with tall lilies, castilleias, larkspurs and columbines, while leafy willows make a fine protecting hedge; the whole forming a joyful outburst of warm, rosy plant-life keenly emphasised by the raw, flinty baldness of the onlooking cliffs.

After resting in the lake the happy stream sets forth again on its travels warbling and trilling like an ouzel, ever delightfully confiding, no matter how rough the way; leaping, gliding, hither, thither, foaming or clear, and displaying the beauty of its virgin wildness at every bound.

One of its most beautiful developments is the Diamond Cascade, situated a short distance below Red Lake. The crisp water is first dashed into coarse granular spray that sheds off the light in quick flashing lances, mixed farther down with loose dusty foam; then it is divided into a diamond pattern by tracing the diagonal cleavage joints that intersect the face of the precipice over which it pours. Viewed in front, it resembles a wide sheet of embroidery of definite pattern, with an outer covering of fine mist, the whole varying with the temperature and the volume of water. Scarce a flower may be seen along its snowy border. A few bent pines look on from a distance, and small fringes of cassiope and rock-ferns grow in fissures near the head, but these are so lowly and undemonstrative only the attentive observer will be likely to notice them.

A little below the Diamond Cascade, on the north wall of the canyon, there is a long, narrow fall about two thousand feet in height that makes a fine, telling show of itself in contrast with the dull, red rocks over which it hangs. A ragged talus curves up against the cliff in front of it, overgrown with a tangle of snow-pressed willows, in which it disappears with many a surge, and swirl, and plashing leap, and finally wins its way, still grey with foam, to a confluence with the main canyon stream.

Below this point the climate is no longer arctic. Butterflies become more abundant, grasses with showy purple panicles wave above your shoulders, and the deep summery drone of the bumble-bee thickens the air. *Pinus Albicaulis*, the tree mountaineer that climbs highest and braves the coldest blasts, is found in dwarfed, wind-bent clumps throughout the upper half of the canyon, gradually becoming more erect, until it is joined by the two-leafed pine, which again is succeeded by the taller yellow and mountain pines. These, with the burly juniper and trembling aspen, rapidly grow larger as they descend into the richer sunshine, forming groves that block the view; or they stand more apart in picturesque groups here and there, making beautiful and obvious harmony with each other, and with the rocks. Blooming underbrush also becomes abundant, – azalea, spirea, and dogwood weaving rich fringes for the stream, and shaggy rugs for the stern unflinching rock-bosses, adding beauty to their strength, and fragrance to the winds and the breath of the waterfalls. Through this blessed wilderness the canyon stream roams free, without any restraining channel, stirring the bushes like a rustling breeze, throbbing and wavering in wide swirls and zigzags, now in the sunshine, now in the shade; dancing, falling, flashing from side to side beneath the lofty walls in weariless exuberance of energy.

A glorious milky way of cascades is thus developed whose individual beauties might well call forth volumes of description. Bower Cascade is among the smallest, yet it is perhaps the most beautiful of them all. It is situated in the lower region of the pass where the sunshine begins to mellow between the cold and warm climates. Here the glad stream, grown strong with tribute gathered from many a snowy fountain, sings richer strains, and becomes more human and lovable at every step. Now you may see the rose and homely yarrow by its side, and bits of meadow with clover, and bees. At the head of a low-browed rock, luxuriant cornel and willow bushes arch over from side to side, embowering the stream with their leafy branches; and waving plumes, kept in motion by the current, make a graceful fringe in front.

From so fine a bower as this, after all its dashing among bare rocks on the heights, the stream leaps out into the light in a fluted curve, thick-sown with sparkling crystals, and falls into a pool among brown boulders, out of which it creeps grey with foam, and disappears beneath a roof of verdure like that from which it came. Hence to the foot of the canyon the metamorphic slates give place to granite, whose nobler sculpture calls forth corresponding expressions of beauty from the stream in passing over it – bright trills of rapids, booming notes of falls, and the solemn hushing tones of smooth gliding sheets, all chanting and blending in pure wild harmony. And when at length its impetuous alpine life is done, it slips through a meadow at the foot of the canyon, and rests in Moraine Lake. This lake, about a mile long, lying between massive moraines piled up centuries ago by the grand old canyon glacier, is the last of the beautiful beds of the stream. Tall silver firs wave soothingly about its shores, and the breath of flowers, borne by the winds from the mountains, drifts over it like incense. Henceforth the stream, now grow stately and tranquil, glides through meadows full of gentians, and groves of rustling aspen, to its confluence with Rush Creek, with which it flows across the desert and falls into the Dead Sea.

At Moraine Lake the canyon terminates, although apparently continued by two lateral moraines of imposing dimensions and regularity of structure. They extend out into the plain about five miles, with a height, toward their upper ends, of nearly three hundred feet. Their cool, shady sides are evenly forested with silver-firs, while the sides facing the sun are planted with showy flowers, a square rod containing five to six profusely flowered eriogonums of several species, about the same number of bahias and linosyris, and a few poppies, phloxes, gilias and grasses, each species planted trimly apart with bare soil between as if cultivated artificially.

My first visit to Bloody Canyon was made in the summer of 1869, under circumstances well calculated to heighten the impressions that are the peculiar offspring of mountains. I came from the blooming tangles of Florida, and waded out into the plant-gold of the great Central plain of California while its unrivalled flora was as yet untrodden. Never before had I beheld congregations of social flowers half so extensive, or half so glorious. Golden compositae covered all the ground from the Coast Range to the Sierra like a

Two lateral moraines of Bloody Canyon Glacier
with Moraine Lake in the foreground.

stratum of denser sunshine, in which I revelled for weeks, then gave myself up to be borne forward on the crest of the summer plant-wave that sweeps annually up the Sierra flank, and spends itself on its snowy summits. At the Big Tuolumne Meadows I remained more than a month, sketching, botanising, and climbing among the surrounding mountains ere the fame of Bloody Canyon had reached me.

The mountaineer with whom I camped was one of those remarkable men so frequently found in California, the bold angles of whose character have been brought into relief by the grinding effects of the gold-period, like the features of glacier landscapes. But at this late day my friend's activities had subsided, and his craving for rest had caused him to become a gentle shepherd, and literally to lie down with a lamb, on the smoothest meadows he could find. Recognising my Scotch Highland instincts, he threw out some hints about Bloody Canyon, and advised me to explore it. "I have never seen it myself," he said, "for I never was so unfortunate as to pass that way; but I have heard many a strange story about it; and I warrant you will find it wild enough."

Next day I made up a package of bread, tied my notebook to my belt, and strode away in the bracing air, every nerve and muscle tingling with eager indefinite hope, and ready to give welcome to all the wilderness might offer. The plushy lawns starred with blue gentians and daisies soothed my morning haste, and made me linger; they were all so fresh, so sweet, so peaceful.

Climbing higher, as the day passed away, I traced the paths of the ancient glaciers over many a shining pavement, and marked the lanes in the upper forests that told the power of the winter avalanches. Still higher, I noted the gradual dwarfing of the pines in compliance with climate, and on the summit discovered creeping mats of the arctic willow, low as the lowliest grasses; and patches of dwarf vaccinium, with its round pink bells sprinkled over the sod as if they had fallen from the sky like hail; while in every direction the landscape stretched sublimely away in fresh wildness, a manuscript written by the hand of Nature alone.

At length, entering the gate of the pass, the huge rocks began to close around me in all their mysterious impressiveness; and as I gazed awe-stricken down the shadowy gulf, a drove of grey, hairy creatures came suddenly into view, lumbering towards me with a kind of boneless wallowing motion like bears. However, grim and startling as they appeared, they proved to be nothing more formidable than Mono Indians dressed in a loose, shapeless way in the skins of sage rabbits sewed together into square robes. Both the men and women begged persistently for whiskey and tobacco, and seemed so accustomed to denials, that it was impossible to convince them that I had none to give. Excepting the names of these two luxuries, they spoke no English, but I afterwards learned that they were on their way to Yosemite Valley to feast awhile on fish and flour, and procure a load of acorns to carry back through the pass to their huts on the shore of Mono Lake.

A good countenance may now and then be discovered among the Monos, but these, the first specimens I have seen, were mostly ugly, or altogether hideous. The dirt on their faces was fairly stratified in the hollows, and seemed so ancient and undisturbed as almost to possess a geological significance. The older faces were, moreover, strangely blurred and divided into sections by furrows that looked like some of the cleavage joints of rocks, suggesting exposure in a castaway condition for ages. They seemed to have no right place in the landscape, and I was glad to see them fading down the pass out of sight.

Then came evening, and the sombre cliffs were inspired with the ineffable beauty of the alpenglow. A solemn calm fell upon every feature of the scene. All the lower depths of the canyon were in the gloaming shadow, and one by one the mighty rock fronts forming the walls grew dim and vanished in the thickening darkness. Soon the night-wind began to flow and pour in torrents among the jagged peaks, mingling its strange tones with those of the waterfalls sounding far below. And as I lay by my camp-fire in a little hollow near one of the upper lakes listening to the wild sounds, the great full moon looked down over the verge of the canyon wall, her face seemingly filled with intense concern, and apparently so near as to produce a startling effect, as if she had entered one's bedroom, forsaking all the world besides to concentrate on me alone.

The night was full of strange weird sounds, and I gladly welcomed the morning. Breakfast was soon done, and I set forth in the exhilarating freshness of the new day, rejoicing in the abundance of pure wildness so closely pressed about me. The stupendous rock walls, like two separate mountain ranges, stood forward in the thin, bright light, hacked and scarred by centuries of storms, while down in the bottom of the canyon, grooved and polished bosses heaved and glistened like swelling sea-waves, telling a grand old story of the ancient glacier that once poured its crushing floods above them.

Here for the first time I met the Artic daisies in all their perfection of pure spirituality – gentle mountaineers, face to face with the frosty sky, kept safe and warm, by a thousand miracles. I leaped lightly from rock to rock, glorying in the eternal freshness and sufficiency of nature, and in the rugged tenderness with which she nurtures her mountain darlings in the very homes and fountains of storms.

Fresh beauty appeared at every step, delicate rock-ferns, and tufts of the fairest flowers. Now another lake came to view, now a waterfall. Never fell light in brighter spangles, never fell water in whiter foam. I seemed to float through the canyon enchanted, feeling nothing of its roughness, and was out in the glaring Mono levels ere I was aware.

Looking back from the shore of Moraine Lake, my morning ramble seemed all a dream. There curved Bloody Canyon, a mere glacier furrow two thousand and three thousand feet deep, with *moutonnée* rocks advancing from the sides, and braided together in the middle like rounded, swelling muscles. Here the lilies were higher than my head, and the sunshine was warm enough for palms. Yet the snow around the Arctic willows on the summit was plainly visible, only a few miles away, and between lay narrow specimen belts of all the principal climates of the globe.

About five miles below the foot of Moraine Lake, where the lateral moraines terminate in the plain, there was a field of wild rye, growing in magnificent waving bunches six to eight feet high, and bearing heads from six to twelve inches long. Indian women were gathering the grain in baskets, bending down large handfuls of the ears, beating them with sticks, and fanning out the rye in the wind. They formed striking and picturesque groups as one caught glimpses of them here and there in winding lanes and openings with splendid tufts arching overhead, while their incessant chat and laughter proclaimed their careless joy.

I found the so-called Mono Desert, like the rye-field, in a high state of natural cultivation with the wild rose and the delicate pink-flowered abronia; and innumerable erigerons, gilias, phloxes, poppies and bush-compositae, growing not only along stream-banks, but out in the hot sand and ashes in openings among the sage-brush, and even in the craters of the highest volcanoes, cheering the grey wilderness with their rosy bloom, and literally giving beauty for ashes.

Beyond the moraines the trail turns to the left toward Mono Lake, now in sight around the spurs of the mountains, and touches its western shore at a distance from the foot of the pass of about six miles. Skirting the lake, you make your way over low bluffs and moraine piles, and through many a tangle of snow-crinkled aspens and berry bushes, growing on the banks of fine, dashing streams that come from the snows of the summits.

Here are the favourite camping grounds of the Indians, littered with piles of pine-burrs from which the seeds have been beaten. Many of their fragile willow huts are broken and abandoned; others arch airily over family groups that are seen lying at ease, pictures of thoughtless contentment, their wild, animal eyes glowering at you as you pass, their black shocks of hair perchance bedecked with red castileias and their bent, bulky stomachs filled with no white man knows what. Some of these mountain streams pouring into the lake have deep and swift currents at the fording places, and their channels are so roughly paved with boulders that crossing them at the time of high water is rather dangerous. That Mono Lake should have no outlet, while so many perennial streams flow into it, seems strange at first sight, before the immense waste by evaporation in so dry an atmosphere is recognised. Most of its shores being low, any considerable rise of its waters greatly enlarges its area, followed of course by a corresponding increase of evaporation, which tends towards constancy of level within comparatively narrow limit. Nevertheless, on the flanks of the mountains, drawn in well-marked lines, you may see several ancient beaches that mark the successive levels at which the lake stood toward the close of the glacial period, the highest more than six hundred feet above the present level. Then, under a climate as marked by coolness and excessive moisture as the present by devouring drought, the dimensions of the lake must have been vastly greater. Indeed, a study of the whole plateau region, named by Fremont "the Great Basin," extending from the Sierra to the Wahsatch mountains, a distance of 400 miles, shows that it was covered by inland seas of fresh water that were only partially separated by the innumerable hills and mountain ranges of the region, which then existed as islands, forming an archipelago of unrivalled grandeur.

The lake water is as clear as the snow-streams that feed it, but intensely acrid and nauseating from the excessive quantities of salts accumulated by evaporation beneath a burning sun. Of course no fish can live in it, but large flocks of geese, ducks, and swans come from beyond the mountains at certain seasons, and gulls also in great numbers, to breed on a group of volcanic islands that rise near the centre of the lake, thus making the dead, bitter sea lively and cheerful while they stay. The eggs of the gulls used to be gathered for food by the Indians, who floated to the islands on rafts made of willows; but since the occurrence of a great storm on the lake a few years ago, that overtook them on their way back from the islands, they have not ventured from the shore. Their rafts were broken up and many were drowned. This disaster, which some still living have good cause to remember, together with certain superstitious fears concerning evil spirits supposed to dwell in the lake and rule its waves, make them content with the safer and far more important product of the shores, chief of which is the larvae of a small fly that breeds in the slimy froth in the shallows. When the worms are ripe,

Native american hunter/gathers – Indians packing
acorns from Yosemite to Mono Lake (right) and
others collecting roots and berries

andthe waves have collected them and driven them up the beach in rich oily windrows, then old and young make haste to the curious harvest, and gather he living grain in baskets and buckets of every description. After being washed and dried in the sun it is stored for winter. Raw or cooked, it is regarded as a fine luxury, and delicious dressing for other kinds of food – acorn-mush, clover-salad, grass-seed-pudding, etc. So important is this small worm to the neighbouring tribes, it forms a subject of dispute about as complicated and perennial as the Newfoundland cod. After waging worm-wars until everybody is weary and hungry, the belligerents mark off boundary lines, assigning stated sections of the shores to each tribe, where the harvest may be gathered in peace until fresh quarrels have time to grow. Tribes too feeble to establish rights must needs procure their worm supply from their more fortunate neighbours, giving nuts, acorns or ponies in exchange.

This "diet of worms" is further enriched by a large, fat caterpillar, a species of silk-worm found on the yellow pines to the south of the lake; and as they also gather the seeds of this pine, they get a double crop from it – meat and bread from the same tree.

Forbidding as this grey, ashy wilderness is to the dweller in green fields, to the red man it is a paradise full of all the good things of life. A Yosemite Indian with whom I was acquainted while living in the valley, went over the mountains to Mono every year on a pleasure trip, and when I asked what could induce him to go to so poor a country when, as a hotel servant, he enjoyed all the white man's good things in abundance, he replied, that Mono

had better things to eat than anything to be found in the hotel – plenty deer, plenty wild sheep, plenty antelope, plenty worm, plenty berry, plenty sage-hen, plenty rabbit – drawing a picture of royal abundance that from his point of view surpassed everything else the world had to offer.

A sail on the lake develops many a fine picture – the natives along the curving shores seen against so grand a mountain background; water birds stirring the glassy surface into white dancing spangles; the islands, black, pink and grey, rising into a cloud of white wings of gulls; volcanoes dotting the hazy plain; and, grandest of all overshadowing all, the mighty barrier wall of the Sierra, heaving into the sky from the water's edge, and stretching away to north and south with its marvellous wealth of peaks and crests and deep-cutting notches keenly defined, or fading away in the soft purple distance; cumulus clouds swelling over all in huge mountain bosses of pearl, building a mountain range of cloud upon a range of rock, the one as firmly sculptured, and as grand and showy and substantial as the other.

The magnificent cluster of volcanoes to the south of the lake may easily be visited from the foot of Bloody Canyon, the distance being only about six miles. The highest of the group rises about 2,700 feet above the lake. They are all post-glacial in age, having been erupted from what was once the bottom of the south end of the lake, through stratified glacial drift. During their numerous periods of activity they have scattered showers of ashes and cinders over all the adjacent plains and mountains within a radius of twenty to thirty miles.

Nowhere within the bounds of our wonder-filled land are the antagonistic forces of fire and ice brought more closely and contrastingly together. So striking are the volcanic phenomena, we seem to be among the very hearths and firesides of nature. Then turning to the mountains while standing in drifting ashes, we behold huge moraines issuing from the cool jaws of the great canyons, marking the pathways of glaciers that crawled down the mountain sides laden with debris and pushed their frozen floods into the deep waters of the lake in thundering icebergs, as they are now descending into the inland waters of Alaska, not a single Arctic character being wanting, where now the traveller is blinded in a glare of tropical light.

Americans are little aware as yet of the grandeur of their own land, as is too often manifested by going on foreign excursions, while the wonders of our unrivalled plains and mountains are left unseen. We have Laplands and Labradors of our own, and streams from glacier-caves – rivers of mercy sacred as the Himalaya-born Ganges. We have our Shasta Vesuvius also, and bay, with its Golden Gate, beautiful as the Bay of Naples. And here among our inland plains are African Saharas, dead seas, and deserts, dotted with oases, where congregate the travellers, coming in long caravans – the trader with his goods and gold, and the Indian with his weapons – the Bedouin of the California desert.

CHAPTER 3

The Yosemite Valley

THE FAR-FAMED Yosemite Valley lies well back on the western slope of the Sierra, about a hundred and fifty miles to the eastward of San Francisco. It is about seven miles long, from half a mile to a mile wide, and nearly a mile deep, carved in the solid granite flank of the range. Its majestic walls are sculptured into a bewildering variety of forms – domes and gables, towers and battlements, and sheer massive cliffs, separated by grooves and furrows and deep, shadowy canyons, and adorned with evergreen trees. The bottom is level and park-like, finely diversified with meadows and groves, and bright, sunny gardens; the River of Mercy [Merced], clear as crystal, sweeping in tranquil beauty through the midst, while the whole valley resounds with the music of its unrivalled waterfalls.

It is a place compactly filled with wild mountain beauty and grandeur – floods of sunshine, floods of snowy water, beautiful trees of many species, thickets of flowering shrubs, beds of flowers of every colour, from the blue and white violets on the meadows, to the crimson pillars of the snow-flowers glowing among the brown needles beneath the firs. Ferns and mosses find grateful homes in a thousand moist nooks among the rocks, humming-birds are seen glinting about among the showy flowers, small singers enliven the under-brush, and wide-winged hawks and eagles float in the calm depths between the mighty walls; squirrels in the trees, bears in the canyons; all find peaceful homes, beautiful life of every form, things frail and fleeting and types of enduring strength meeting and blending, as if into this grand mountain mansion nature had gathered her choicest treasures, whether great or small.

Three good carriage roads enter the valley by way of Big Oak Flat, Coulterville, and Raymond, the greater part of the journey from San Francisco being made by rail. Each of the three roads, according to the measurements of rival agents, is the shortest, least dusty, and leads through the finest scenery. No one, however, possesses any great advantage over the others. All are dusty and, to most people, monotonous throughout their lower courses in the foothills, and all necessarily pass through belts of the noblest coniferous trees to be found in the world so that a journey to Yosemite by any possible route, even with Yosemite left out, would still be worth the exertion it costs a thousand times over.

In May, when the travel to Yosemite begins, the snow is still deep in the upper forest through which the roads pass, but the foothill region is already

547

dry and forbidding. The whole country, soil, plants, and sky seems kiln dried, most of the vegetation crumbles to dust beneath the foot, the ground is cracked, and the sky is hot, withered, dim, and desolate though glowing, and we gaze through the white, hazy glare towards the snowy mountains and streams of cold eager longing, but not one is in sight. Lizards glide about on the burning rocks, enjoying a constitution that no drought can dry, and small ants in amazing numbers seem to be going everywhere in haste, their tiny sparks of life only burning the brighter with the sun-fire however intense. Rattlesnakes lie coiled in out-of-the-way places, and are seldom seen. The noisy magpies, jays, and ravens gather beneath the best shade trees on the ground, with wings drooped and bills wide open, scarce a sound coming from any one of them during the midday hours. These curious groups, friends in distress, are frequently joined by the large buzzard, or California condor as it is sometimes called, while the quail also seeks the shade about the tepid alkaline water-holes in the channels of the larger streams, now nearly dry. Rabbits scurry from shade to shade beneath the ceanothus bushes, and the long-eared hare may be seen now and then as he canters gracefully across the wider openings where there is a sparse growth of oaks. The nights are about as dry as the days, dewless and calm, but a thousand voices proclaim the abundance of life, notwithstanding the desolating effects of the fierce drought. Birds, crickets, hylas, etc., make a pleasant stir in the darkness, and coyotes, the small despised dogs of the wilderness, looking like rusty bunches of hair, bark in chorus, filling the air with their keen, lancing notes, and making it hot and peppery, as if filled with exploding fire crackers. On the upper edge of this torrid foothill region the curious Sabine pine is found, the first of the mountain conifers met by the traveller in ascending the range. Nobody at first sight would take it to be a pine or conifer of any kind, it is so loose and

widespread in habit, and its foliage is so thin and grey. The sunbeams sift through even the leafiest trees with scarce any interruption, and the weary, heated traveller finds but little protection in their shade. It grows only on the dry foothills, seeming to enjoy the most ardent sunshine like a palm, springing up here and there singly or in scattered groups among scrubby white-oaks and thickets of ceanothus and manzanita.

The generous crop of sweet, nutritious nuts it yields renders it a favourite with the Indians and bears. Indians gathering the ripe nuts make a striking picture. The men climb the trees and beat off the magnificent cones with sticks, while the squaws gather them in heaps, and roast them until the scales open and allow the hard-shelled seeds to be beaten out. Then, in the cool evenings, men, women, and children, smeared with resin, form circles around their campfires on the bank of some stream, and lie in easy independence, cracking nuts, and laughing and chatting as heedless of the future as bears and squirrels.

Fifteen to twenty miles farther on, at the height of from 2,000 to 3,000 feet above the sea, you reach the lower edge of the main forest belt, composed of the gigantic sugar-pine, yellow pine, incense-cedar, Douglas spruce, silver-fir, and sequoia. However dense and sombre the woods may appear in general views, neither on the rocky heights or down in leafiest hollows will you see any crowded growth to remind you of the dark malarial selvas of the Amazon and Orinoco with their boundless contiguity of shade, nor of the monotonous uniformity of the Deodar forests of the Himalaya, or of the pine woods of the Atlantic States. These giant conifers wave in the open sunshine, rising above one another on the mountain benches in most imposing array, each species giving forth the utmost expression of its own peculiar beauty and grandeur with inexhaustible variety and harmony. All the different species stand more or less apart in groves or small irregular groups, through which the roads meander, making delightful ways along sunny colonnades and across openings that have a smooth surface strewn with brown needles and cones. Now you cross a wild garden, now a ferny, willowy stream, and ever and anon you emerge from all the groves and gardens upon some granite pavement or high bare ridge commanding glorious views above the waving sea of evergreens far and near.

The sugar-pine surpasses all the other pines in the world, not only in size, but also in kingly majesty and beauty. It towers sublimely from every ridge and canyon of the range at an elevation of from three to seven thousand feet above the sea, attaining most perfect development at a height of about five thousand feet. Full-grown specimens are commonly about two hundred and twenty feet high, and from six to eight feet in diameter near the ground, though some grand old patriarch is occasionally met that has enjoyed five or six centuries of storms and attained a thickness of ten or even twelve feet, living on undecayed, sweet and sound in every fibre. The trunk is a smooth, round delicately tapered shaft, mostly without limbs to a height of one hundred feet. At the top of this magnificent bole the long, curved branches sweep gracefully outward and downward, sometimes forming a palm-like crown sixty feet in diameter, or even more, around the rim of which the magnificent cones are hung. When ripe, in September and October, the cones are commonly from fifteen to eighteen inches long, and three in diameter, green, shaded with purple on their sunward sides, but changing to a warm, yellowish brown after the seeds are discharged. Then their diameter is nearly doubled by the spreading of the scales, and they remain pendant on the ends of the branches, producing a fine ornamental effect all winter. The wood is fine-grained, fragrant, and is considered the most valuable of all the Sierra pine.

From the heartwood, where wounds have been made, the sugar, from which the common name is derived, exudes in crisp, candy-like masses. When fresh, it is white and delicious, but inasmuch as most of the wounds on which it is found have been made by fire, the exuding sap is stained on the charred surface, and the hardened sugar becomes brown. The Indians are fond of it, but because of its laxative properties only small quantities may be eaten.

The most constant companion of this species is the yellow-pine, and a worthy companion it is. The Douglas spruce, libacedrus, sequoia, and the silver-firs are also more or less associated with it, but on many deep-soiled mountain sides, about five thousand feet above the sea, it forms the bulk of the forest. The majestic crowns approaching each other in bold curves make a lofty canopy through which the tempered sunbeams pour, silvering the needles, and gilding the boles and flowery ground into a scene of enchantment. On the warmest slopes the chamoebatia, a small shrub belonging to the rose family, is spread in a continuous growth like a carpet, brightened in the spring with the crimson *sarcodes*, or snow plant, and the wild rose. On the northern slopes the boles are more slender, and the ground is mostly occupied by an under-brush of hazel, ceanothus, and flowering dogwood, but never so dense as to prevent the traveller from sauntering where he will.

The yellow or silver-pine (*P. ponderosa*) ranks second among the Sierra pines as a lumber tree, and almost rivals the sugar-pine in size and nobleness of port. Seen in winter laden with snow, or in summer when its brown staminate clusters hang thick among the shimmering needles, and its large purple cones are ripening in the mellow light, it forms a magnificent spectacle. But it is during cloudless wind-storms that these colossal pines are most impressively beautiful. Then they bow like willows, their leaves streaming forward all in one direction, and when the sun shines on them at the required angle they glow as if every needle were burnished silver. The fall of sunlight on the royal crown of a palm as it breaks upon the glossy leaves in long lance-like rays, is a truly glorious spectacle, like a mountain stream breaking upon boulders. But still more impressively beautiful is the fall of the light on these lofty silver-pines; it seems beaten to the finest dust, and is shed off in myriads of minute, glinting sparkles that hide all the green foliage and make one glowing mass of white radiance.

The famous big tree, *sequoia gigantea*, extends from the well-known Calaveras Grove to the head of Deer Creek, near the big bend of Kern River, a distance of nearly two hundred miles, at an elevation of about five to eight thousand feet above the sea. From the Calaveras to the south fork of Kings River it occurs only in small, isolated groves among the pines and firs, and is so sparsely and irregularly distributed that this portion of the belt is not easily traced. Two gaps nearly forty miles wide occur in it between the Calaveras and Tuolumne groves, and between those of the Fresno and Kings rivers. From Kings River the belt extends across the broad, rugged basins of the Kaweah and Tule rivers to its southern limit on the head of Deer Creek, interrupted only by deep, rocky canyons, the width of this portion of the belt being from three to nearly eight miles, and the length seventy miles.

In the northern groves few young trees or saplings are found promising to take the places of the failing old ones, giving rise to the notion that the species is doomed to speedy extinction, as being only an expiring remnant of an ancient flora once far more widely distributed. But careful study has shown that the Big Tree has never formed a greater part of these post-glacial forests than it does at the present time, however widely it may have been distributed in the pre-glacial forests.

To the southward of Kings River no tree in the woods appears to be more firmly established in accordance with climate and soil. For many miles they occupy the surface almost exclusively, growing vigorously over all kinds of ground – on rocky ledges, along water-courses, and on moraines and avalanche detritus, coarse or fine, while a multitude of thrifty seedlings and saplings, and middle-aged trees are growing up about the old giants, ready to take their places and maintain the race in all its grandeur. But, unfortunately, fire and the axe are already busy on many of the more accessible portions of the belt, spreading sure destruction, and unless protective measures be speedily adopted and applied, in a few decades all that may be left of this noblest of trees will be a few hacked and scarred monuments.

There is something wonderfully telling and impressive about sequoia, even when beheld at a distance of several miles. Its dense foliage and smoothly rounded outlines enable us to recognise it in any company, and when one of the oldest patriarchs attains full stature on some commanding ridge it seems the very god of the woods. Full-grown specimens are about fifteen and twenty feet in diameter, measured above the swelling base, and about two hundred and fifty feet high. Trees twenty-five feet in diameter are not rare, and one is now and then found thirty feet in diameter, but very rarely any larger. The grandest specimen that I have measured is a stump about ninety feet high, which is thirty-five feet, eight inches in diameter, measured inside the bark, above the bulging base. The wood is dull purplish red in colour, easily worked, and very enduring; lasting, even when exposed to the weather, for hundreds of years. Fortunate old trees that have passed their three thousandth birthday, without injury from lightning, present a mound-like summit of warm, yellow-green foliage, and their colossal shafts are of a beautiful brown colour, exquisitely tapered, and branchless to a height of a hundred and fifty feet. Younger trees have darker, bluish foliage, and shoot up with tops comparatively sharp.

The Calaveras Grove is the northmost, and was discovered first of all. It may be visited by tourists to the valley by way of Milton, Murphy's Camp, and Big Oak Flat, though it is not on any of the roads leading directly to Yosemite. The flowery leafiness of this grove is one of its most charming characteristics. Lilies, violets, and trientales cover the ground along the bottom of the glen, and carpets of the blooming chamoebatia are outspread where the light falls free, forming a beautiful ground of colour for the brown sequoia trunks; while rubus, dogwood, hazel, maple, and several species of ceanothus make a shaggy underbrush in the cooler shadows.

Most of the larger trees have been slightly disfigured by names carved and painted on marble tablets and countersunk into the bark, and two have been killed; one of them by removing the bark in sections to be set up in the London exposition, the other felled because somebody wanted to dance upon the stump, and the noble monarch now lies a mass of ruins. With these exceptions, the grove has been well preserved, that is, let alone, the underbrush and smaller plants in particular retaining their primitive wildness unimpaired.

Travellers to the valley, by way of Big Oak Flat, pass through the small Tuolumne Grove of Big Trees on the dividing ridge between the waters of the Tuolomne and Merced rivers. Those who take the Raymond route may visit the Mariposa and Fresno groves, by stopping over a day at Clark's Station. While those who choose the Coulterville route will pass through the Big Tree Grove of the Merced. These groves on the different routes are not equally interesting to most people, but all contain giants that are worthy representatives of their race. The traveller, however, who would see *sequoia gigantea* in all its glory, must visit the forests of the Kaweah and Tule rivers.

From the Big Tree groves the roads conduct for a few hours through forests of sugar-pine and silver-fir which become yet more beautiful and interesting as you advance. Then, looking and admiring as best you can while being rapidly whirled onward through dust in a coach drawn by six horses, Yosemite Valley comes suddenly into view, and in an hour you are down the nerve-trying grade – out of the shadows from the noblest forest trees in the world, into the midst of the grandest rocks and waterfalls. Riding up the valley through stately groves, and around the margin of emerald meadows, the lofty walls on either hand looming into the sky with their marvellous wealth of architectural forms, bathed in the purple light of evening, and beating time to the tones of the falls, the whole seems a work of enchantment.

The Grizzly Giant –
thirty-three feet in diameter

The first object to catch the eye on entering the valley is the Bridal Veil Fall, 900 feet in height – a soft, delicate-looking thing of beauty, as seen at a distance of a mile or two, pouring its snowy folds and irised spray with the utmost gentleness, while the wind sways it from side to side like a downy cloud. But on a near approach it manifests the speed and wild ungovernable energy of an avalanche.

On the other side of the valley, almost immediately opposite the Bridal Veil, there is another fine fall, considerably wider at times when the snow is melting, and more than a thousand feet in height from the brow of the cliff where it first leaps free into the air to the head of a rocky talus, where it strikes and is broken up into ragged cascades. It is called the Ribbon Fall or Virgin's Tears. During the spring floods it is a magnificent object, but the suffocating blasts of spray that fill the recess in the wall which it occupies prevent a near approach. In autumn however, when its feeble current falls in a shower it may then pass for tears with the sentimental onlooker fresh from a visit to the Bridal Veil. Just beyond these two falls are the grand outstanding masses of the Cathedral and El Capitan rocks, 2,700 and 3,300 feet in height, the latter making a most imposing display of sheer, enduring, unflinching granite, by many regarded as the most sublime feature of the valley. Then the Three Brothers present themselves – a vast mountain building of three gables, the highest 4,000 feet above the valley floor. On the south side, opposite the Brothers, the Sentinel Rock, 3,000 feet high, stands forward in bold relief like some special monument, gracefully adorned with a beautiful cascade on either side and fringed at its base with spruce and pine.

The general masses of the walls between the more prominent rocks thus far mentioned, are sculptured into a great variety of architectural forms, impossible to describe separately, each fitted to its place in this grand harmony.

Beyond the Three Brothers the Yosemite Fall is at length seen in one grand view throughout its entire length, pouring its floods of snowy rejoicing waters from a height of 2,600 feet down to the groves and green meadows of the valley, bathing the mighty cliffs with clouds of spray, and making them tremble with its deep, massy thunder-tones.

At the head of the valley, now clearly revealed, stands the Half Dome, the loftiest, most sublime and the most beautiful of all the rocks that guard this glorious temple. From a broad, sloping base planted on the level floor of the valley, it rises to a height of 4,750 feet in graceful flowing folds finely sculptured and poised in calm, deliberate majesty. Here the main valley sends out three branches, forming the Tenaya, Merced, and Illilouette canyons. Tracing the Tenaya Canyon from the valley up Tenaya Creek, you have the Half Dome on the right, and the Royal Arches, Washington Column, and the North Dome on the left. Half a mile beyond Washington Column you come to Mirror Lake, lying imbedded in beautiful trees at the foot of Half Dome. A mile beyond the lake the picturesque Tenaya Fall is seen gleaming through the rich leafy forest that fills this portion of the canyon, and to the left of the fall are the Dome Cascades, about a thousand feet in height, filling the canyon with their deep booming roar.

Just above the Tenaya Fall, on the left side, rises the grand projecting mass of Mt. Watkins, with a sheer front of solid granite like El Capitan, and on the right, the lofty wave-like ridge of Clouds Rest, a mile in height.

A little farther up the canyon, you come to the Tenaya Cascades, 700 feet in vertical descent gliding in a showy plume-like ribbon down a smooth incline of bare granite. Above the cascades you pass a succession of less showy cascades and falls, and many small filled-up lake-basins, with charming lily gardens, and groves of pine and silver-fir, set in the midst of waving folds of shining glacier-planed granite and rocks of every form, until, at a distance of about ten miles from the valley, the canyon opens into the beautiful basin of Lake Tenaya, and the noble Cathedral Peak, with its many spires on the east, towers above it.

The Illilouette Canyon, through which the beautiful Illilouette basin is drained, is about two miles long. From different standpoints in its rough, boulder-choked bottom, a series of most telling and strangely varied views of the head of the valley may be obtained. The Illilouctte Fall, near the head of the canyon, is one of the most interesting in the valley. It is nearly 600 feet high, but is seldom visited on account of the roughness of the way leading to it over the rocks. The canyon of the main middle branch of the river extends back to the axis of the range in the Lyell Group, and contains so many waterfalls, cascades of every kind, lakes, and beautiful valleys with walls that are sculptured like those of Yosemite, that nothing like a complete description of it can be given here.

About a mile up the canyon from the main valley, along the margin of wild dashing rapids charmingly embowered, you come to the beautiful Vernal Fall, 400 feet in height. At the head of the fall lies the small Emerald Pool, and a mile beyond, the snowy Nevada Fall is seen, which, next to the Yosemite, is the grandest of all. It is about 600 feet in height, and on account of its waters being so tossed and beaten before reaching the brink of the precipice it is intensely white; while all the way down to the head of the Vernal Fall the river forms a continuous chain of cascades and rapids, hardly less interesting to most travellers than the falls. The majestic rock called, from its shape, the Liberty Cap, rises close alongside the Nevada, adding greatly to the grandeur of the view.

Tracing the river back from the head of the fall, you pass through the Little Yosemite Valley. It resembles the main Yosemite, though formed on a smaller scale. Then you find a long train of booming, dancing cascades, alternating with rapids and lakes and short, tranquil reaches, and a grand variety of smaller Yosemite valleys, garden patches and forests in hollows, here and there, where soil has been accumulated, until at length the icy fountains of the river are reached among the alpine peaks of the summit.

The Yosemite Valley was discovered in 1851, by Captain Boling, who then, with two Indians as guides, led a company of soldiers into it from Mariposa to punish a band of marauding Indians who occupied the valley as their home and stronghold.

The regular Yosemite pleasure travel began in 1856, and has gradually increased until the present time. Considering the remoteness of many of the fountains of this current of travel, its flow has been remarkably constant. The regular tourist, ever in motion, is one of the most characteristic productions of the present century; and however frivolous and inappreciative the poorer specimens may appear, viewed comprehensively they are a hopeful and significant sign of the times, indicating at least a beginning of our return to nature; for going to the mountains is going home. Perhaps nowhere else along the channels of pleasure travel may so striking and interesting a variety of people be found together as in this comparatively wild and remote Yosemite. Men, women, and children of every creed and colour come here from every country under the sun; farmers, men of business, lawyers, doctors, and divines; scientists seeking causes, wealthy and elegant loafers trying to escape from themselves, the titled and obscure, all in some measure seeing and loving wild beauty, and travelling to better purpose than they know, borne onward by currents that they cannot understand, like ships at sea.

Arriving in the valley most parties keep together and fall into the hands of the local guides by whom they are led hastily from point to point along the beaten trails. Others separate more or less and follow their own ways. These are mostly members of Alpine Clubs, sturdy Englishmen and Germans, with now and then a cannie Scotchman, all anxious to improve their opportunities to the utmost. Besides rambling at will into odd corners of the valley, they climb about the canyons, and around the tops of the walls; or push out bravely over the adjacent mountains, radiating far into the High Sierra among the ice and snow. They thread the mazes of the glorious forests, and trace the wild young streams in their courses down from the glaciers through grandly sculptured canyons, past garden hollows and lake basins, and down glossy inclines, sharing in all their exhilarating rush and roar.

Gentle, contemplative grandmothers, and a few fine-grained specimens of fewer years, spend most of their time sauntering along the banks of the river, and sitting in the shade of the trees; admiring sky and cliff, and falling water, in a quiet way, enriching their lives far more than their neighbours who keep themselves in perpetual motion, following each other along dusty trails, painfully "doing" the valley by rule.

Little children are, of course, the most delightfully natural of all the visitors, flashing around the hotel verandahs, or out beneath the trees, glowing in rainbow-hued ruffles and ribbons like butterflies and scarlet tanagers. They consider the lilies and birds and bees, nor are they altogether unconscious of the glorious sublimities about them; for one may see them at times gazing silently with upturned faces at the mighty cliffs, and at the white water

The Illilouette Falls
from the painting by Thomas Hill

pouring out of the sky, their pure, natural wonderment offering a refreshing contrast to the mean complacency and blindness of the finished tourist, who has seen all, knows all, and is engulfed in eternal apathetic tranquillity.

The Yosemite Fall is partially separated into an upper and lower fall, with a series of smaller falls and cascades between them, but when viewed in front they appear as one, only slightly interrupted by striking on what seems to be a narrow ledge. First there is a sheer descent of about 1,600 feet; then a succession of cascades and smaller falls nearly a third of a mile long, and making altogether a descent of 600 feet; then a final sheer fall of about 400 feet is made to the bottom of the valley. So grandly does this magnificent fall display itself from the floor of the valley few visitors take the trouble to climb the wall to gain nearer views, unable to realise how vastly more impressive it becomes when closely approached, instead of being seen at a distance of from one to two miles.

The views developed in a walk up the zigzags of the trail leading to the upper fall are as varied and impressive and almost as extensive, as those on the well-known Glacier Point Trail. One rises as if on wings. The groves, meadows, fern-flats, and reaches of the river at once gain new interest, as if never seen before, and all become new over and over again as we go higher from point to point; the foreground also changes every few rods in the most surprising manner, although the bench on the face of the wall over which the trail passes is very monotonous and commonplace in appearance as seen from the bottom of the valley. Up we climb with glad exhilaration, through shaggy fringes of laurel and ceanothus, and glossy-leaved manzanita and live oak from shadow to shadow across bars of sunshine, the leafy openings making charming frames for the valley pictures beheld through them, and for the glimpses of the high alps that appear in the distance. The higher we go, the farther we seem to be from the summit of the vast carved wall up which we are creeping. Here we pass a huge projecting buttress whose grooved and rounded surface tells a wonderful story of the time when the valley now filled with sunshine was filled with ice, when a grand old glacier, flowing river-like from its many fountains on the snow-laden summits of the range, swept through the valley with its crushing, grinding floods, wearing its way ever deeper, and fashioning these sublime cliffs to the varied forms of beauty they now possess. Here a white, battered gully marks the pathway of an avalanche of rocks, now we cross the channel of an avalanche of snow. Farther on we come to a small stream clinging to the face of the cliff in lace-like strips, or leaping from ledge to ledge, too small and feeble to be called a fall, trickling, dripping, slipping, oozing, a pathless wanderer from the upland meadows, seeking a way century after century to the depths of the valley without having worn any appreciable channel. Constant dropping has not worn away these stones. Every morning, after a cool night, evaporation being checked, it gathers strength and sings like a bird, but as the day advances, and the sun strikes its thin currents outspread on the heated precipices, most of its waters vanish long ere the bottom of the valley is reached. Many a fine, hanging garden aloft on these breezy inaccessible heights owe to it their freshness and fullness of beauty; ferneries in shady nooks, filled with adiantum, woodwardia, woodsia, aspidium, pellæa, and cheilanthes; rosetted and tufted and ranged in lines, daintily overlapping, thatching the stupendous cliffs with softest beauty, the delicate fronds seeming to float on the warm, moist air, without any connection with rock or stream. And coloured plants, too, in abundance, wherever they can find a place to cling to; the showy cardinal mimulus, lilies and mints, and glowing cushions of the golden bahia, together with sedges and grasses growing in tufts, and the butterflies and bees and all the small, happy creatures that belong to them.

After the highest point on the lower division of the trail is gained it conducts along a level terrace on the face of the wall, around a shoulder, and into the deep recess occupied by the great Upper Yosemite Fall, the noblest display of falling water to be found in the valley, or, perhaps, in the world. When it first comes in sight, it seems almost within reach of one's hand, so great is its volume and velocity, yet it is still nearly a third of a mile away, and appears to recede as we advance. The sculpture of the walls about it is on a scale of grandeur, according nobly with the fall, plain and massive, though elaborately finished, like all the other cliffs about the valley.

In the afternoon an immense shadow is cast athwart the plateau in front of the fall, and far over the fields of chaparral that clothe the slopes and benches of the wall to the eastward, creeping upward upon the fall until it is wholly overcast, the contrast between the shaded and illuminated sections being very striking in near views.

Under this shadow, during the cool centuries immediately following the breaking up of the Glacial Period, dwelt a small residual glacier, one of the few that lingered on this sun-beaten side of the valley after the main trunk glacier had vanished. It sent down a long winding current through the narrow canyon on the west side of the fall, and must have formed a striking feature of the ancient scenery of the valley; the lofty fall of ice and fall of water side by side, yet separate and distinct.

The coolness of the afternoon shadow and the abundant dewy moisture from the spray of the fall make a fine climate for ferns and grasses on the plateau, and for the beautiful azalia, which grows here in profusion and blooms in September, long after the warmer thickets down the valley have withered and gone to seed. Even close to the fall, and behind it at the base of the cliff, a few venturesome plants may be found, undisturbed by the rock-shaking torrent.

The basin at the foot of the fall into which the current directly pours when it is not swayed by the wind is about ten feet deep, and fifteen to twenty feet in diameter. That it is not much deeper is surprising, when the great height and force of the fall is considered. But the rock where the water strikes probably suffers much less erosion than it would were the descent

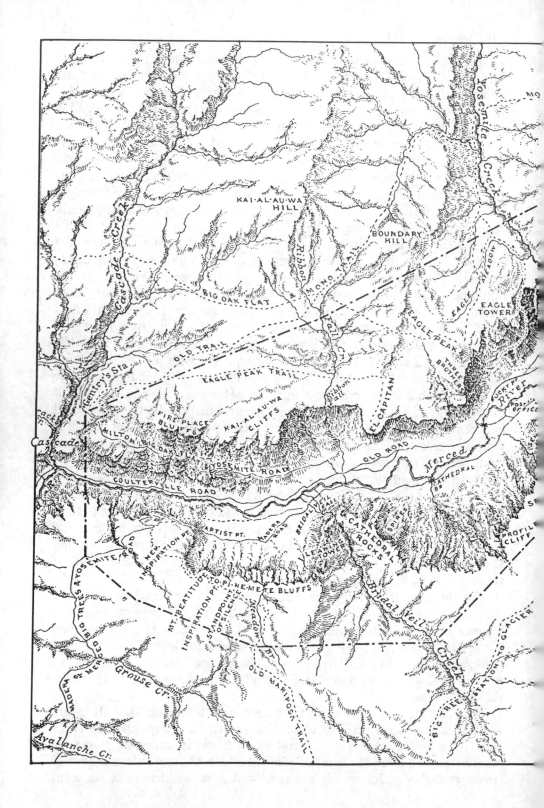

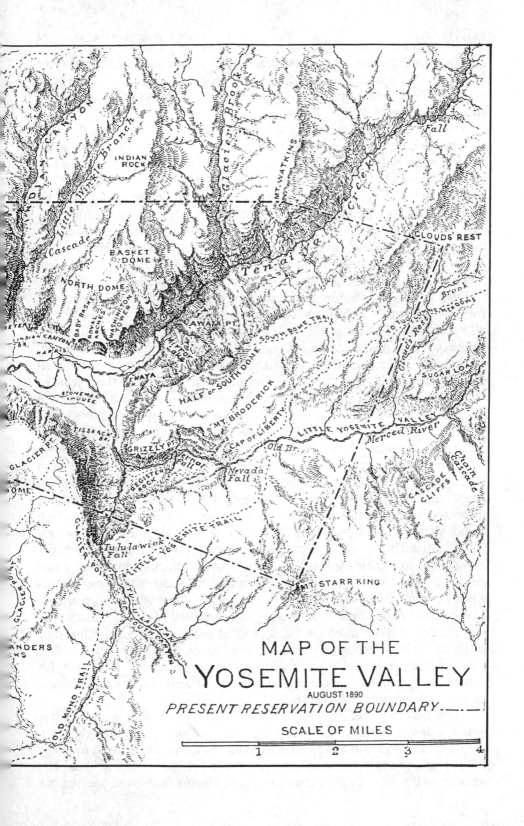

MAP OF THE
YOSEMITE VALLEY
AUGUST 1890
PRESENT RESERVATION BOUNDARY —·—

SCALE OF MILES

less than half as great, since the current is outspread, and much of its force is spent ere it reaches the bottom; being received on the air as upon an elastic cushion, and borne outward and dissipated over a surface more than fifty yards wide.

This surface, easily examined when the water is low, is intensely clean and fresh-looking. It is the raw, quick flesh of the mountain wholly untouched by the weather. In summer droughts, when the snowfall of the preceding winter has been light, the fall is reduced to a mere shower of separate drops without any obscuring spray. Then we may safely go to the back of the fall and view the crystal shower from beneath, which, when the sun is shining, is extremely beautiful, each drop wavering and pulsing as it makes its way through the air, and flashing off jets of coloured light of ravishing beauty. But all this is invisible from the bottom of the valley, like a thousand other interesting things. One must labour for beauty as for bread here as elsewhere.

During the time of spring floods the best near view of the fall is obtained from a ledge on the east side above the blinding spray, at a height of about 400 feet from the base of the fall. A climb of about 1,400 feet from the valley has to be made, and there is no trail, but to anyone fond of climbing, and who is at all stirred by a love of adventure, this will make the ascent all the more delightful. The ledge runs out back of the fall on the sheer front of the cliff, so that the fall may be approached as closely as we wish. When the afternoon sunshine is streaming through the thronging masses of down-rushing waters the marvellous firmness and variety of their forms are beautifully revealed. The whole fall is a majestic column of foaming, snowy water, ever wasting, ever renewed. At the top it seems to burst forth from some grand, throbbing heart of the mountain in irregular pulses, comet-like spurts succeeding one another in sublime rhythm. Now and then one mighty throb sends forth a mass into the free air far beyond the others, which rushes alone to the bottom of the fall with long, streaming, tail-like, combed silk, illumined by the sun, while the others, descending in clusters, gradually mingle and lose their identity. They rush past with amazing velocity and display of power, though apparently drowsy and deliberate in their movements when observed from the bottom of the valley at a distance of a mile or two. The heads of these comet-like masses are composed of nearly solid water, and are dense white in colour, like pressed snow, from the friction they suffer in rushing through the air, the portion worn off forming the tail, between the white lustrous threads and films of which, faint, greyish pencillings appear, while the outer, finer sprays of waste water-dust, whirling in sunny eddies, are pearl grey throughout.

At the bottom of the fall there is but little distinction of form visible. It is mostly a driving, boiling, upswirling mass of scud and spray, through which the light sifts in grey and purple tones, while at times, when the sun strikes at the required angle, the whole is changed to brilliant rainbow hues. The middle portion of the fall is the most openly beautiful; lower, the various forms into which the waters are wrought are more closely and voluminously veiled, while higher, towards the head, the current is more simple and compact. But even at the bottom, in the boiling clouds of spray, there is no confusion, while the rainbow light makes all divine, adding glorious beauty and peace to glorious power. The Upper Yosemite Fall has far the richest, as well as the most powerful voice of all the falls of the valley, its tones varying from the sharp hiss and rustle of the wind in the glossy leaves of the live oaks and the soft, sifting, hushing tones of the pines, to the loudest rush and roar of storm-winds and thunder among the crags of the summit peaks. The low bass, booming, reverberating tones, heard under favourable circumstances five or six miles away, are formed by the dashing and exploding of heavy masses of water and air upon two projecting ledges on the cliff, 400 and 600 feet above the base of the fall. The torrent of massive comets is continuous at time of high water, while the explosive, booming, notes are wildly intermittent, because, unless influenced by the wind, most of the heavier masses shoot out from the face of the precipice, and pass the ledges upon which at other times they are wrecked. Occasionally the whole fall is swayed away from the front of the cliff, then suddenly clashed flat against it, or vibrated from side to side like a pendulum, giving rise to endless variety of forms and sounds.

Once during a violent wind-storm, while I watched the fall from the shelter of a pine-tree, the whole ponderous column was suddenly arrested in its descent at a point about midway between the base and top, and was neither blown upward or turned aside, but simply held stationary in mid-air as if gravitation below that point had ceased to act. Thus it remained for more than a minute, resting in the arms of the stormwind, the usual quantity of water meanwhile coming over the brow of the cliff and accumulating in the air as if falling upon an invisible floor, swedging and widening. Then, as if commanded to go on, scores of arrowy water-comets shot forth from the base of the suspended fountain, and the grand anthem of the fall once more began to sound. After bathing so long in the spray of the fall it is natural to look above and beyond it and say: "Where does all this chanting water come from?" This is easily learned by going and seeing.

The Yosemite Creek is the most tranquil of all the larger streams that pour over the valley walls. The others, while yet a good way back from the verge of the valley, abound in loud-voiced falls and cascades or rushing rapids, but Yosemite Creek, as if husbanding its resources, after the descent of its main tributaries from the snowy heights of the Hoffman Range, flows quietly on through strips of level meadow and smooth hollows and flats, with only a few small cascades, showing nothing in all its course to suggest the grandeur of its unrivalled falls in the valley.

Its wide and shallow basin is so crowded with domes it seems paved with them. Some castellated piles adorn its western rim, while the great Tuolumne Canyon sweeps past it on the north, and the cool, shadow-covered precipices of the Hoffman Range bound it on the east and northeast. During winter and spring most of the waters of the basin are derived directly from snow, but in summer only two or three, and in the drier seasons only one of its many streams draws its source from perennial fountains of snow and ice. Then the main dependence of the many tributaries are moraines of the ancient glaciers, in which a part of the melting snows and rains are absorbed.

Issuing from their moraine fountains, each shining thread of water at once begins to sing, running gladly onward, over boulders, over rock-stairs, over dams of fallen trees; now groping in shadows, now gliding free in the light on glacier-planed pavements, not a leaf on their borders; diving under willows, fingering their red roots and low-dipping branches, then absorbed in green bogs; out again among mosaics of leaf, shadows and light, whirling in pools giddy and ruffled, then restful and calm, not a foambell in sight; whispering low, solemn in gestures as full grown rivers, slowly meandering through green velvet meadows, banks embossed with bryanthus and yet finer cassiope, white and blue violets blending with white and blue daisies in smooth, silky sods of the Alpine agrostis; out again on bare granite, flowing over gravel and sand mixed with mica and garnets and white crystal quartz, making tiny falls and cascades in rapid succession, until at length all the bright, rejoicing choir meet together to form the main stream which flows calmly down to its fate in the valley, sweeping over the tremendous verge beneath a mantle of diamond spray. Amid the varied foams and fine ground mists of the mountain streams that are ever rising from a thousand waterfalls, there is an affluence and variety of rainbows scarce at all known to the careworn visitor from the lowlands. Both day and night, winter and summer, this divine light may be seen wherever water is falling in spray and foam, a silent interpreter of the heart-peace of nature, amid the wildest displays of her power. In the bright spring mornings the black-walled recess at the foot of the Lower Yosemite Fall is lavishly filled with irised spray, which does not simply span the dashing foam, but the foam itself, the whole mass of it, seems to be coloured, and drifts and wavers, mingling with the foliage of the adjacent trees, without suggesting any relationship to the ordinary rainbow. This is perhaps the largest and most reservoir-like accumulation of iris colour to be found in the valley.

The lunar rainbows, or spraybows, are grandly developed in the spray of the Upper Fall. Their colours are as distinct as those of the sun, and as regularly and obviously banded, though less vivid. They may be seen any night when there is plenty of moonlight and spray.

Even the secondary bow is at times distinctly visible. The best point from which to observe them is on the upper ledge, 400 feet above the base of the fall on the east side. For some time after moonrise the arc is about 400 to 500 feet span, set upright, one end planted in the spray at the bottom, the other in the edge of the fall, creeping lower, of course, and becoming less upright as the moon rises higher. This grand arc of colour, glowing with such invincible peacefulness and mild shapely beauty in so weird and dark a chamber of shadows, and amid the rush and roar and tumultuous dashing of this thunder-voiced fall, is one of the most impressive sights offered in all this wonder-filled valley.

Smaller bows may be seen in the gorge on the plateau between the upper and lower falls. Once toward midnight, after spending a few hours with the wild beauty of the upper fall, I sauntered along the edge of the gorge, looking in here and there, wherever the footing felt safe, to see what I could learn of the night aspects of the smaller falls that dwell there. And down in an exceedingly black, pit-like portion of the gorge, at the foot of the highest of the intermediate falls, while the moonbeams were pouring into it through a narrow opening, I saw a well-defined spraybow, beautifully distinct in colours, spanning across from side to side of the pit.

In the pool at the foot of the fall pure white foam waves were constantly springing up into the moonshine, beneath the beautiful bow, like a band of dancing ghosts.

The leaping waves so foamy white, amid rocks and shadows so weird and black, and the mystic circle of coloured light, made a scene in the general gloom of the night marvellously vivid and wild. Another marvellous night scene, but not a safe one, is a view of the full moon through the edge of the Upper Fall, from the narrow ledge that extends back of it, 400 feet above its base. But the ledge is less than a foot wide on the face of the wall at one place, and though considerably wider behind the fall, it is rounded on the edge by the action of the water, and the fall is liable to be swayed against it even in calm nights; therefore one is in danger of being washed off. My own experiences one night back of the fall, when it was booming in all its glory, were such that I shall never venture there again. But the effect was enchanting; wild music above, beneath, around. The moon appeared to be in the very midst of the rushing waters and struggling to keep her place, on account of the ever-varying density and forms of the masses through which she was seen; now darkened by a rush of opaque comets, now flashing out through openings of gaudy tissue, suffering a rushing succession of eclipses that lasted but a moment – a rare astronomical phenomenon, a transit of a thousand comets across the disc of the moon.

A very telling excursion may be made to Glacier Point and Sentinel Dome, thence across the Illilouette and Little Yosemite Valley, and return to the valley past the Nevada and Vernal falls. On the trail leading up the craggy wall to Glacier Point, the main rocks and falls of the valley are seen in striking positions and combinations, developing marvellously grand and beautiful effects as you climb from point to point. At an elevation of about 500 feet, a wide sweeping view down the valley is obtained past the Sentinel, and between Cathedral Rock and El Capitan. At 1,500 feet the wide upper end of the valley comes in sight, bounded by the great Half Dome, that looms sublimely into the azure, overshadowing every other feature of the landscape.

From Glacier Point you look down over the edge of a sheer wall 3,000 feet high, upon soft green meadows and innumerable spires of the yellow pine, with the bright ribbon of the river curving through their midst. On the opposite side of the valley a fine general view is presented of the Royal Arches, North Dome, Indian Canyon, and Eagle Cliff; with Mt. Hoffman and the dome-paved basin of Yosemite Creek in the distance. To the eastward, Clouds Rest is seen beyond the Half Dome, and Mt. Starr King girdled with silver firs, the deeply sculptured peaks of the Merced Group, and about Mt. Lyell on the axis of the range, and broad swaths of forests growing on ancient moraines, while the Nevada, Vernal, and Yosemite falls, in full view, are as distinctly heard as if one were standing in their spray.

Here the attentive observer will not fail to perceive that all this glorious landscape is new, lately brought to light from beneath the universal ice-sheet of the Glacial Period, and that the loftiest domes have been overswept by it as boulders are overswept by a flood. Hence the most resisting parts of the landscape are the highest. Every dome, ridge, and mountain in the fore and middle grounds are seen to have rounded outlines, while those of the summit peaks are sharp, the former having been *over*flowed by the heavy grinding folds of the ice-sheet, while the latter were *down*flowed, thus grinding them into sharp peaks and crests. Here you see the tributary valleys or canyons of the main Yosemite Valley branching far and wide into the fountains of perpetual ice and snow. Adown these wide polished valleys once poured the ancient glaciers that united here to form the main Yosemite Glacier that eroded the valley out of the solid [rock], wearing its channel gradually deeper, crawling on, unhalting, unresting, throughout the countless centuries of the Ice Period.

The distant views from the summit of Sentinel Dome are still more extensive and telling, and many charming Alpine plants – phlox, telinum, eriogonæ, rock-ferns, etc. are found there.

On the way to Little Yosemite a view of the Illilouette Fall may be obtained from its head, though it is much inferior to the view obtained at the foot of the fall by scrambling up its rocky canyon from the valley. The fall in general appearance most resembles the Nevada. Before coming to the brink of the precipice its waters are severely dashed and tossed by steps and jutting angles on the bottom and sides of its channel, therefore it is a very white and finely textured fall. When in full play it is columnar and richly fluted from the partial division of its waters on the roughened lip of the precipice. It is not nearly so grand a fall as the Upper Yosemite, so symmetrical as the Vernal, or so nobly simple as the Bridal Veil; nor does it present so overwhelming an outgush of snowy magnificence as the Nevada, but in the richness and exquisite fineness of texture of its flowing folds it surpasses them all. After crossing the Illilouette Valley the trail descends into the Little Yosemite near the lower end, and thence down past the Nevada and Vernal falls to the main valley. But before returning, a visit should be made through the Little Yosemite. It is about four miles long, half a mile wide, and its walls are from 1,500 to 2,500 feet in height, bold and sheer and sculptured in true Yosemite style. And, since its rocks have not been so long exposed to post-glacial weathering, they are less blurred than those of the lower valley, large areas of the wall surfaces showing a beautiful glacial polishing that reflect the sunshine like glass.

The bottom of the valley is flat and covered with showy gardens, meadows, rose and azalia thickets, and beautiful groves of silver-fir and pine; while the river, charmingly embowered, flows through the midst of them, softly gliding over smooth, shining sands in peaceful, restful beauty. At the head of the valley there is a showy cascade where the river flows over a bar of granite so moderately inclined that one may enjoy a climb close alongside the glad dancing flood, with but little danger of being washed away.

This used to be a favourite hunting ground of the Indians, where they found abundance of game – mountain quail, grouse, deer, and the cinnamon bear – gathered together as if enclosed in a high-walled park with gates easily guarded. But the noisy, destructive methods of tourist sportsmen have driven most of the game away.

As the river approaches the Nevada Fall after its tranquil flow through the valley levels, its channel is roughened with projecting rock-ribs and elbows, the object of which seems to be to fret the stream into foam and fit it for its grand display. And with what eager enthusiasm it accepts its fate, dashing on side angles, surging against round, bossy knobs, swirling in pot-holes, upglancing in shallow, curved basins, then bounding out over the brink and down the grand descent, more air than water, glowing like a sun-beaten cloud. Into the heart of it all any one with good nerve and good conscience may gaze from the end of a granite slab that juts out over the giddy precipice and is brushed by the flood as it bounds over the brink.

Blinding drifts of scud and spray prevent a near approach from below until autumn. Then, its thunder hushed, the fall shrinks to a whispering web of embroidery clinging to the face of the cliff, more interesting and beautiful to most observers than the passionate flood-fall of spring.

The view down the canyon is one of the most wonderful about the valley – the river, gathering its shattered waters, rushing in wild exultation down the Emerald Pool and over the Vernal Fall; the sublime walls on either hand, with the stupendous mass of the Glacier Point Ridge blocking the view in front, forming an immense three sided, hopper-shaped basin 3,000 feet deep, resounding with the roar of winds and waters, as if it were some grand mill in which the mountains were being ground to dust. A short distance above the head of the fall the river gives off a small part of its waters, which, descending a narrow canyon to the north of the fall, along the base of the Liberty Cap, forms a beautiful cascade, and finally joins the main stream again a few yards below the fall. Sometime ago the officer in charge of the valley seemed to regard the cascades as so much waste water, inasmuch as they employed an enterprising and ingenious gentleman to "fix the falls," as he said, by building a dam across the cascade stream where it leaves the river, so as to make all the water tumble and sing together. No great damage was done, however, by this dam or any other improvement. Mending the Yosemite waterfalls would seem to be about the last branch of industry that even unsentimental Yankees seeking new outlets for enterprise would be likely to engage in. As well whitewash the storm-stained face of El Capitan or gild the domes.

The Vernal Fall is a general favourite among the visitors to the valley, doubtless because it is better seen and heard than any of the others, on account of its being more accessible. A good stairway leads up the cliffs alongside of it, and the open level plateau over the edge of which it enables one to saunter in safety close to its brow and watch its falling waters as they gradually change from green to purplish grey and white, until broken into spray at the bottom. It is the most staid and orderly of all the great falls, and never shows any marked originality of form or behaviour. After resting in Emerald Pool, the river glides calmly over the smooth lip of a perfectly plain and sheer precipice, and descends in a regular sheet about 80 feet wide, striking upon a rough talus with a steady, continuous roar that is but little influenced by the winds that sweep the cliffs. Thus it offers in every way a striking contrast to the impetuous Nevada, which so crowds and hurries its chafed and twisted waters over the verge, which seemingly are glad to escape, as they plunge free in the air, while their deep, booming tones go sounding far out over the listening landscape.

From the foot of the Vernal the river descends to its confluence with the Illilouette Creek in a tumultuous rush and roar of cascades, and emerges from its shadowy, boulder-choked canyon in a beautiful reach of rapids, stately spaces forming a wall on either side; while the flowering dogwood, rubus nutkanus, azalea, and tall, plumy ferns, well watered and cool, make beautiful borders. Through the open, sunny levels of the meadows it flows with a clear, foamless current, swelled by its Tenaya and Yosemite Creek tributaries, keeping calm and transparent until nearly opposite the Bridal Veil Fall, where it breaks into grey rapids in crossing a moraine dam. In taking leave of the valley, the river makes another magnificent stretch of cascades and rapids on its way down its lower canyon, a fine view of which may be had from the Coulterville road that runs across the bottom of a rough talus close alongside the massy surging flood, and past the beautiful Cascade Fall.

Climbing the great Half Dome is fine Yosemite exercise. With the exception of a few minor spires and pinnacles, the Dome is the only rock about the valley that is strictly inaccessible without artificial means, and its inaccessibility is expressed in very severe and simple terms. But longing eyes were nonetheless fixed on its noble brow, until at length, in the year

Right: The difficult ascent of Half Dome

1875, George Anderson, an indomitable Scotchman, succeeded in making a way to the summit. The side facing the Tenaya Canyon is an absolutely vertical precipice from the summit to a depth of about 1,600 feet, and on the opposite side it is nearly vertical for about as great a depth. The southwest side presents a very steep and finely drawn curve from the top down a thousand feet or more, while on the northeast where it is united with the Clouds Rest Ridge, one may easily reach the Saddle, within 700 feet of the summit, where it rises in a smooth, graceful curve a few degrees too steep for unaided climbing.

A year or two before Anderson gained the summit, John Conway, a resident of the valley, and his son, excellent mountaineers, attempted to reach the top from the Saddle by climbing barefooted up the grand curve with a rope which they fastened at irregular intervals by means of eye-bolts driven into joints of the rock. But, finding that the upper portion of the curve would require laborious drilling, they abandoned the attempt, glad to escape from the dangerous position they had reached, some 300 feet above the Saddle.

Anderson began with Conway's old rope, which had been left in place, and resolutely drilled his way to the top inserting eye-bolts five to six feet apart, and making his rope fast to each in succession, resting his feet on the last bolt while he drilled a hole for the next above. Occasionally some irregularity in the curve or slight foothold, would enable him to climb a few feet without the rope, which he would pass and begin drilling again, and thus the whole work was accomplished in less than a week. Notwithstanding the enthusiastic eagerness of tourists to reach the crown of the Dome, the views of the valley from this lofty standpoint are far less striking than from many other points comparatively low, chiefly on account of the foreshortening effect produced by looking down from so great a height. The North Dome is dwarfed almost beyond recognition, the grand sculpture of the Royal Arches may not be noticed at all, and the whole range of the walls on both sides seem comparatively low and sunken, especially when the valley is flooded with noonday sunshine; while the Dome itself, the most sublime feature of all general views of Yosemite, is beneath one's feet. Little Yosemite Valley is well seen, but a better view of it may be obtained from the base of the Starr King cone. The summit landscapes, however, toward Mounts Ritter, Lyell, and Dana, are very effective and grand. My first view from the top of the Dome, in November, after the first winter snow had fallen on the mountains, was truly glorious. A massive cloud of pure pearl lustre was arched across the valley, from wall to wall, one end resting on the grand abutment of El Capitan, the other on Cathedral Rock, apparently as fixed and calm as the brown meadow and groves in the shadow beneath it. Then, as I stood on the tremendous verge overlooking Mirror Lake, a flock of smaller clouds, white as snow came swiftly from the north, trailing over the dark forests and, arriving on the brink of the valley, descended with imposing gestures through Indian Canyon and over the Arches and North Dome. On they came with stately deliberation, nearer, nearer, gathering and massing beneath my feet, and filling the Tenaya abyss. Then the sun shone free, painting them with rainbow colours and making them burn on the edges with glorious brightness. It was one of those brooding, changeful days that come just between the Indian summer and winter, when the leaf colours begin to grow dim and the clouds come and go, moving about among the cliffs like living creatures; now hovering aloft in the tranquil sky, now caressing rugged rock-brows with infinite gentleness, or, wandering afar over the tops of the forests, touch the spires of fir and pine with their soft silken fringes as if telling the coming of the snow. Now and then the valley appeared all bright and cloudless, with its crystal river wavering and shimmering through meadow and grove, while to the eastward the white peaks rose in glorious array keenly outlined on the dark blue sky; then the clouds would gather again, wreathing the Dome and making a darkness like night.

On the crown of the Dome, notwithstanding its severely bare appearance, there are four clumps of pines representing three species; *Pinus albicaulis, P. contorta,* and *P. ponderosa,* var. *Jeffreyi,* all three repressed and storm-beaten. The alpine spiraea grows there also, and blooms freely with potentilla, ivesia, erigeron, solidago, pentstemon, eriogonum, and four or five species of grasses and sedges, like those of other granite summits of the same elevation.

When the all-embracing ice-mantle of the Glacial Period began to grow thin and form separate glaciers that flowed like rivers in the canyons, Half Dome was probably the first of the Yosemite rocks to emerge from the ice, burnished and glowing like a crystal. Centuries of storms have passed over it since first it came to light, but it still remains a telling monument of the glaciers that brought it into relief from the general mass of the range. Its flinty surface, scarcely at all wasted, is covered with glacial inscriptions from base to crown, and the meaning of these is the reward of all who devoutly study them.

The quick, smart visitor to the valley who buys his ticket early, determined to take the water-falls by the forelock, when their streaming manes are whitest, and when the flooded meadows are covered with mirrors, can have but dim conceptions of the beauties of the peaceful yellow autumn when these same Yosemite waters flow gently and calm in the thick golden haze of the Indian summer. The river then forms a series of pools united by gentle trickling currents that glide softly over brown pebbles and sand with scarce an audible murmur. In and out, in bay and promontory, their shore lines curve, giving to each pool the appearance of lake, with banks embossed with briar and azalea, sedge and grass; and above these, in all their glory of autumn colours, a mingled growth of alder and willow, dogwood, and balm of Gilead. Mellow sunshine overhead, mellow shadows beneath, flecked with dashes of free-falling light, the yellow sunbeams falling on the ripe leaves, streaming through their countless thousands of windows, makes an atmosphere of marvellous beauty over each glassy pool, the surface stirred gently in spots by bands of whirling water-beetles, or startled trout glancing from shelter to shelter beneath fallen trees or some overhanging portion of the bank. The falls, too, are quiet; no wind stirs; the whole valley floor is a finely blended mosaic of ripe, painted leaves, all in bloom every morning with crystals of hoar frost. Even the rocks seem strangely mellow and soft, as if they too had ripened, all their flinty strength hidden and held in abeyance.

In December comes the snow, or perhaps in November. The clouds descending clasp the mountain from base to summit. Then follows an interval of brooding stillness. Small flakes or single crystals at length appear, glinting gently in zigzags and spirals in the dull grey sky. As the storm progresses the thronging flakes darken the air, and soon the rush and roar, and deep muffled booming of avalanches are heard; but we try in vain to catch a glimpse of their noble currents until rifts occur in the clouds and the storm ceases. Then, standing in the middle of the valley, we may witness the descent of several of the largest size within a few minutes or hours, according to the abundance and condition of the snow on the heights. When the mass first slips on the upper slopes of the mountain a dull, rumbling sound is heard, which increases with heavy deliberation, seeming to come nearer and nearer with appalling intensity of tone. Presently the grand flood is seen rushing with wild, outbounding energy over some precipitous portion of its channel, long, back-trailing streamers fringing the main body of the current like the spray and whirling folds of mist about a waterfall. Now it is partly hidden behind fringes of live-oak, now in full view, leaping from bench to bench, spreading and narrowing and throwing out long fringes of rockets airily draped with convolving gossamer tissue of snow-dust.

Compared with waterfalls, these snow-falls have none of the keen, kissing, clashing sounds so common in some portions of the currents of waterfalls, but the loud, booming thunder-tones, the pearly whiteness of the mass, with lovely grey tones in the half shadows, the arching leaps over precipices, the narrowing in gorges, the expansions into lace-like sheets upon smooth inclines, and the final dashing into upswirling clouds of spray at the bottom are the same in both.

In winter the thin outer folds and whirling spray of the great Yosemite Fall are frozen while passing through the air freely exposed, and are deposited around the base of the fall in the form of a hollow, truncated cone, which sometimes attains a height of more than 400 feet.

In the building of this cone, part of the frozen spray falls directly to its place in the form of minute particles like the dust of wind-beaten snow, but a considerable portion is frozen upon the face of the cliff along the edges of the fall, and attains a thickness of a foot or more during the night. When the sun strikes this ice-coating on the cliff it is cracked off in large masses and built into the walls of the cone, while in windy, frosty weather, when the fall is swayed from side to side, the whole surface is drenched, binding the whole mass of loose blocks and dust firmly together. While in process of formation the surface is smooth, and pure white, the outlines finely drawn, the whole presenting the appearance of a beautiful crystal hill wreathed with clouds of irised spray, with the fall descending into the heart of it with a tremendous roar, as if pouring down the throat of a crater. In spring, however, while wasting and breaking up, it is strewn with leaves, pine branches, stones, sand, etc., that have been carried over the fall, making it look like a heap of wasting avalanche detritus.

After being engulfed and churned in the stormy interior of the cone, the waters of the fall issue from arched openings at the base seemingly chafed and weary and glad to escape; while belching spray, spouted up out of the throat of the cone past the sides of the descending waters, is wafted away in irised drifts over the evergreen bushes and trees, making a most enchanting show when the sun is shining; the wet pines, warmly green, drenched with billows of rainbow dust, waving with noble gestures, as if devoutly bowing their acknowledgments of the marvellous blessing.

During wind-storms, when the fall is blown aslant, one may look down the throat of the cone from the ledge above. The mouth is then seen to be an irregular oval about 100 and 200 feet in diameter, with heavy, uneven, forbidding lips, white and glowing in contrast with the gloomy depth of the abyss.

Once I scaled the side of the cone and held my ear close down upon it while it sounded like a huge, bellowing, exploding drum; but falling ice from the wall, and choking drifts of spray, when the wind wavered, prevented my reaching the summit.

The best general view of the fall, and the ice-cone, and their grand surroundings, may be obtained without danger from a standpoint about 200 yards from the base of the cone. On bright days in March or February, when the sunshine is streaming into the grand amphitheatre at the most favourable angle, the view from here is truly glorious. Out of the blue sky into the white crater the vast torrent pours, irised spray rising and falling steeping everything in rainbow colours – grey cliffs, wet black rock, the white hill of ice, trees, brush-fringes, and the surging, roaring torrents escaping down the gorge in front, glorifying all, and proclaiming the triumph of Peace and eternal invincible Harmony.

The summit peaks of the Sierra decorated with snow-banners was the most sublime winter phenomenon I ever witnessed, far surpassing the most imposing effects of the water-falls, floods, or avalanches.

Early one winter morning I was awakened by the fall of pine cones on the roof of my cabin. A noble storm-wind from the north filled the valley with its sea-like roar, arousing the pines to magnificent activity, swaying the most steadfast giants of them all like supple reeds, plucking off branches and plumes and strewing them on the clean smooth snow. The sky was garish white, without clouds, the strange glare being produced no doubt by fine snow dust diffused through the air. The wild swirling and bending of the pine-trees, the dazzling light, the roar of the wind sweeping around the grand domes and headlands and eddying in many a rugged canyon and hollow, made altogether a most exciting picture; but afar on the summits of the range the storm was expressing itself in yet grander terms.

The Upper Yosemite Fall was torn into gauzy strips and blown horizontally along the face of the cliff leaving the ice-cone dry.

While making my way to the top of the overlooking ledge on the east side of it to seize so favourable an opportunity of studying the structure of the cone, the peaks of the Merced Group appeared over the shoulder of the Half Dome, each waving a resplendent banner in the blue sky, as regular in form, and as firm and fine in texture as if made of silk. Each banner was at first curved upward from the narrow point of attachment, then continued in long, drawn out, lustrous sheets for a length of at least 3,000 feet, judging from the known height of the mountains and their distances apart.

Eager to gain a general view, I pushed my way up through the snow by Indian Canyon to a commanding ridge beyond the walls, about 8,000 feet in height, where the most glorious storm-view that I had ever beheld awaited me. Every alpine peak along the axis of the range as far as the view extended had its banner, from 2,000 to 600 feet in length, streaming out horizontally, free, and unconfused, slender at the point of attachment, then widening gradually as it extended from the peak until it was a thousand to fifteen hundred feet in breadth, each waving with a visible motion in the sun glow, and clearly outlined on the dark blue sky without a single cloud to mar their simple grandeur.

The tremendous currents of the north wind were sweeping the northern curves of the mountain peaks just as the glaciers they once nourished were swept down, a supply of wind-driven, wind-ground, mealy, frosty snow being incessantly spouted upward over the peaks in a close concentrated current, owing to the peculiar sculpture of their north sides. Thus, ever-wasting, ever-renewed, these glorious banners, a mile long, waved in the gale, constant in form, and apparently as definite and substantial as a silken streamer at a masthead.

The vast depth of the valley, and the sheerness of its walls and westerly trend, causes a great difference between the climates of the north and south sides, more so than exists between many countries hundreds of miles apart, because the south wall is constantly in shadow during the winter months, while the north is bathed in sunshine every clear day, which falls vertically or nearly so on a great portion of the bevelled rocks, making mellow spring weather on one side of the valley, while winter rules the other.

Far up the northern cliffs, even where they seem perpendicular, many a sheltered nook may be found, closely embraced by warm, sunny rock-bosses, in which flowers bloom every month of the year. Butterflies too swarm in these high winter gardens, and may be seen any day except when storms are in progress, and for a few days after they have ceased. In January, near the head of the Lower Yosemite Fall, I found the ant-lions lying in wait in their warm sand-cups, rock-ferns being unrolled, club-mosses covered with fresh growing points, the flowers of the laurel nearly open, and the honeysuckle vines abounding there were rosetted with bright, young leaves, every plant telling of the spring and tingling with vital sunshine. All the winter birds resort to the warm shelters of the north side, and make out to pass the short days in comfort, seldom suffering when the snow is deepest.

Even on the shadow side of the valley the frost is never severe. The average temperature on 24 days in January at 9 a.m. and 3 p.m. was 32°F. minimum 22°, maximum 40°. Another specimen of January weather gave three days rainy, three cloudy, two snowy, and ten clear sunshine.

The winter birds sweeten these shadowy days with their hopeful chatter and song. They are not many, but a cheerier set never sang in snow. First and best of all is the water-ouzel, a dainty, dusky little bird about the size of a robin, that sings a sweet fluty song all winter – all summer – in storm and calm sunshine and shade – haunting the wild rapids and water-falls with marvellous constancy, building his nest in the cleft of a rock bathed in spray. He is not web-footed, yet he dives fearlessly into foaming rapids, seeming to take the greater delight the more boisterous the stream, cheerful and calm as any linnet in a grove. All his gestures as he flits about amid the loud uproar of the falls bespeak the utmost simplicity and confidence – bird and stream one and inseparable. What a pair, yet well related. A yet finer bloom than the foambell in eddying pool is this little bird. Like some delicate flower growing on a tree of rugged strength, the little ouzel grows on the booming stream, showing savage power changed to terms of sweetest love, plain and easily understood to human hearts. We may miss the meaning of the loud resounding torrent, but the flute-like voice of this little bird – only love is in it. A few robins, belated on their way down from the upper meadows, linger in the valley and make out to spend the winter in comparative comfort, feeding on the mistletoe berries that grow on the oaks. In the depths of the mountain forests, in the severest solitudes, they seem as much at home as in the old apple orchards about the busy habitations of man. They ascend the Sierra as the snow melts, following the green footsteps of Spring, until in July or August the highest glacier meadows are reached on the summit of the range. Then, after the short summer is over, and their work in sweetening and cheering these lofty wilds is done, they gradually make their way down again in concord with the weather, keeping ahead of the snow, lingering here and there to feast on huckleberries and frost-nipped wild cherries growing on the upper slopes. Thence down to the vineyards and orchards of the lowlands to spend the winter, and about the Bay of San Francisco, and along the coast; entering the gardens of the great towns as well as parks and fields, where the blessed wanderers are too often slaughtered for food – surely a poor use for so fine a musical instrument: better make stove-wood of pianos to feed the kitchen fire.

The kingfisher winters in the valley, and the golden-winged woodpecker, likewise the species that lay up large stores of acorns in the bark of trees; wrens also; with a few brown and grey finches, and flocks of the arctic blue-bird, which make lively pictures among the snow-laden mistleberries. About six species of ducks are found among the winter birds, as the river is never wholly frozen over. Among these are the mallard and beautiful wood duck, though now less abundant than formerly on account of being so often shot at.

Flocks of wandering geese usually visit the valley in March or April, driven down by hunger, or weariness, or stress of weather while on their way across the range. They come in by the river canyon, but oftentimes are sorely bewildered in trying to get out again. I have frequently seen them try to fly over the walls until tired out and compelled to re-alight. They would rise from the meadow or river, wheel around in a spiral until a height of 400 feet or thereabouts was reached, then form their ranks and fly straight toward the wall as if resolved to fly over it. But Yosemite magnitudes seem to be as deceptive to geese as to men, for they would suddenly find themselves in danger of dashing against the face of the cliff, much nearer the bottom than the top. Then turning in confusion, they would try again and again until ex-hausted. I have occasionally observed large flocks on their travels crossing the summits of the range at a height not less than 14,000 feet above the level of the sea, and even in so rare an atmosphere as this they seemed to be sustaining themselves without extra effort. Strong, however, as they are of wind and wing, they cannot fly over Yosemite walls, starting from the bottom.

Eagles hunt all winter along the northern cliffs and down the river canyon, and there are always plenty of owls for echoes.

Toward the end of March carex sprouts on the warmer portions of the meadows are about an inch high, the aments of the alders along the banks of the river are nearly ripe, the libocedrus is sowing its pollen, willows put forth their silky catkins, and a multitude of happy insects and swelling buds proclaim the promise of spring.

Wild strawberries are ripe in May; the early flowers are in bloom; the birds are busy in the groves, and frogs in the shallow meadow pools.

In June and July the Yosemite summer is in all its glory. It is the prime time of plant-bloom and water-bloom, and the lofty domes and battlements are then bathed in divine purple light.

August is the season of ripe nuts and berries – raspberries, blackberries, thimbleberries, gooseberries, shadberries, blackcurrants, puckery choke cherries, pine-nuts, etc., offering a royal feast to squirrels, bears, Indians, and birds of every feather. All the common orchard fruits as well as the cereal, grow well in the valley, and have been successfully cultivated there for many years by the old pioneer, Lamon, the first of all the Yosemite settlers who cordially and unreservedly adopted the valley as home. In the spring of 1859 he loaded an old horse with fruit-trees and a scant supply of provisions, and made his way into the valley from Mariposa, built himself a cabin beneath the shadow of the great Half Dome, cleared a fertile spot on the left bank of Tenaya Creek, and planted an orchard and garden; toiling faithfully as he was able, under hardships and discouragements not easily appreciated now that the valley has been opened to the world. His friends assured him that his trees would never bear fruit in that deep valley surrounded by snowy mountains, that he could raise nothing, sell nothing, and eventually starve. But year after year he held on undaunted, clearing and stirring the virgin soil, planting and pruning; remaining alone winter and summer with marvellous constancy. He was surprised to find the weather so sunful and kindly. When storms were blowing he lay snug in his cabin, pushing out now and then to keep the snow from his door and to listen to the thunder of the avalanches.

Late in the autumn, while Lamon thus lived alone, three Indians, who were hunting deer on the headwaters of the Bridal Veil Creek, killed a man by the name of Gould, who was on his way from Mono to Mariposa, and hid the body in a dense part of the forest beneath leaves and bark. The division of the spoils – gun, blankets, and money – brought on a quarrel, and one of the Indians confessed the murder. Lamon being the only white man known to be in the Yosemite region, it was feared that he was the victim, and two men were immediately sent into the valley to seek him. This was in January, and the appearance of the two weary messengers coming up the valley in midwinter was a grand surprise. After learning their errand, he assured his friends that nowhere else had he ever felt so safe or so happy as in his lonely Yosemite home.

After the fame of Yosemite had spread far and wide, and he had acquired sufficient means to enjoy a long afternoon of life in easy affluence, he died. He was a fine, erect, whole-souled man more than six feet high. No stranger to hunger and weariness, he was quick to feel for others, and many there be, myself among the number, who knew his simple kindness that gained expression in a thousand small deeds. A block of Yosemite granite, chiselled and lettered, marks his grave, and some of his fruit trees still live, but his finest monument is in the hearts of his friends. He sleeps in a beautiful spot among trees and flowers near the foot of the Yosemite Fall, and every crystal pressing on his coffin vibrates in harmony with its sublime music.

Before the Sierra was explored, Yosemite was generally regarded as a solitary, unrelated wonder. But many other valleys like it have been discovered, which occupy the same relative positions on the flank of the range, were formed by the same forces in the same kind of granite, and have similar

Lamon's Cabin

waterfalls, sculpture, and vegetation. One of these, called "Hetch Hetchy" by the Indians, lies in a north-westerly direction from Yosemite, at a distance of about eighteen miles, and is easily accessible by a trail that leaves the Big Oak Flat road at Bronson Meadows, a few miles below Crane Flat.

As the Merced River flows through Yosemite, so does the Tuolumne through Hetch Hetchy. The bottom of Yosemite is about 4,000 feet above the level of the sea, the bottom of Hetch Hetchy is about 3,800 feet, and in both the walls are of grey granite, and rise precipitously from a level bottom, with but little debris along their bases.

Standing boldly out from the south wall, near the lower end of the valley, is the rock Kolàna, considerably over 2,000 feet in height, and seeming still to bid defiance to the mighty glacier that once pressed over and around it. This is the most strikingly picturesque rock in the valley, forming the outermost of a group that corresponds with the Cathedral group of Yosemite. Facing Kolàna, on the opposite side of the valley, there is a rock 1,800 feet in height which presents a sheer massive front like El Capitan, and over its brow flows a stream that makes, without exception, the most graceful fall I have ever seen. Tuccoolala it is called by the Indians. From the brow of the cliff it leaps clear and free for a thousand feet, then breaks up into a ragged foaming sheet of cascades among the boulders of an earthquake talus. Towards the end of summer it shrinks and vanishes, since its fountain streams do not reach back to the lasting snows of the summits.

Kolàna Rock, Hetch-Hetchy Valley

When I last saw it in June, 1872, it was indescribably beautiful. The only fall that I know of with which it may fairly be compared is the Yosemite Bridal Veil, but it excels even that fall in floating, swaying gracefulness, and tender repose. For if we attentively observe the Bridal Veil, even toward the end of summer when the wind blows aside the fine outer folds of spray, dense, comet-shaped masses may be seen shooting with tremendous energy, revealing the stern fixedness of purpose with which its waters seek the new world below. But from the top of the cliff all the way down the snowy form of the Hetch Hetchy Veil is in perfect repose, like a plume of white cloud becalmed in the depths of the sky. Moreover, the Bridal Veil inhabits a shadow-haunted recess, inaccessible to the main wind-currents of the valley, and has to depend for its principal wind gestures upon broken waves and whirlpools of air that oftentimes compel it to rock and bend in a somewhat fitful, teasing manner; but the Hetch Hetchy Veil, floating free in the open valley, is ever ready to offer graceful compliance to the demands and suggestions of calm or storm. Looking across the valley on a bright, calm day about the beginning of June, the view is surpassingly glorious. The Hetch Hetchy El Capitan is seen rising out of a dense growth of shining live oaks, glowing with sun-gold from its green grovy base to its brow in the blue air. At intervals along its dizzy edge a few venturesome pines are seen looking wistfully outward, and before its sunny face, immediately in front of you, Tuccoolala waves her silvery scarf, gloriously embroidered, and burning with white sun-fire in every fibre. In approaching the brink of the precipice her waters flow fast but confidingly, and at their first arching leap into the air a little eagerness appears, but this eagerness is speedily hushed in divine repose, and their tranquil progress to the base of the cliff is like that of downy feathers in a still room. The various tissues into which her waters are woven, now that they are illumined by the streaming sunshine, are brought out with marvellous distinctness. They sift and float down the face of that grand grey rock in so leisurely and unconfused a manner, and with such exquisite gentleness, that you may examine their texture and patterns as you would a piece of embroidery held in the hand. Near the bottom the width of the fall has increased from 25 to about 100 feet. Here it is composed of yet finer tissue, more air than water, yet still without a trace of disorder. Air, water, and sunlight are woven into a cloth that spirits might wear.

On the same side of the valley thunders the great Hetch Hetchy Fall, called Wapama by the Indians. It is about 1,800 feet high, and is so near Tuccoolala that both are in full view from one standpoint. Seen immediately in front it appears nearly vertical, but viewed in profile from farther up the valley it is seen to be considerably inclined. Its location is similar to that of the Yosemite Fall, but its volume of water is much greater.

No two falls could be more unlike to make one perfect whole, like rock and cloud, sea and shore. Tuccoolala speaks low, like a summer breeze in the pines; Wapama, in downright thunder, descending with the weight and energy of an avalanche in its deep rocky gorge. Tuccoolala whispers, he dwells in peace; Wapama is the thunder of his chariot wheels in power.

This noble pair are the principal falls of the valley. A few other small streams come over the walls with bird-like song, leaping from crag to crag too small to be much noticed in company so imposing, though essential to the grand, general harmony. That portion of the north wall immediately above Wapama corresponds both in outline and details of sculpture with the same relative portion of the Yosemite wall. In Yosemite the steep face of the cliff is terraced with two conspicuous benches fringed with live-oak. Two benches, similarly situated, and fringed in the same way, occur on the same relative portion of the Hetch Hetchy wall, and on no other.

The floor of the valley is about three miles long, and from a fourth to half a mile wide. The lower portion is mostly level meadow, with the trees confined to the sides, and separated partially from the sandy, park-like upper portion by a low bar of glacier-polished granite, across which the river breaks in swift-gliding rapids. The principal tree of the valley is the great yellow-pine, attaining here a height of 200 feet. They occupy the dry sandy levels, growing well apart in small groves or singly, thus allowing each tree to be seen in all its beauty. The common pteris grows beneath them in rough green sheets, tufted here and there by ceanothus and manzanita, and brightened with mariposa tulips and golden-rods. Near the walls, on the earthquake taluses that occur in many places, the pines give place to the mountain live oak, which forms the shadiest and most extensive groves of the valley. Their glossy foliage, densely crowded at the top, forms a beautiful ceiling, containing a few irregular openings for the admission of sunbeams, while the bare grey trunks and branches, gnarled and twisted, are exceedingly picturesque. This sturdy oak, so well calculated for a mountaineer, not only covers the angular boulder slopes, but climbs along fissures, and up steep side-canyons, to the top of the walls and far beyond, dwarfing as it goes from a tree 30 to 40 feet high and 4 to 6 feet in diameter near the ground to a small shrub no thicker than one's finger.

The sugar-pine, sabine-pine, and two-leafed pine, also the Douglas spruce, incense-cedar, and the two silver-firs, grow here and there in the cool side-canyons and scattered among the yellow pines, while on the warmest spots fine groves of the black-oak occur, whose acorns form so important a part of the food of Indians and bears. Bees and hummingbirds find rich pasturage flowers – mints, clover, honeysuckle, lilies, orchids, etc.

On a stream that comes in from the northeast at the head of the valley there is a series of charming cascades that give glad animation to the glorious wilderness, broad plumes like that between the Vernal and Nevada of Yosemite, half sliding, half leaping down smooth open folds of the granite covered with crisp, clashing spray, into which the sunbeams pour with glorious effect. Others shoot edgewise through a deep narrow gorge chafing and laving beneath rainbow mists in endless variety of form and tone.

Following the river from the head of the valley, you enter the great Tuolumne Canyon. It is 20 miles long, 2,000–4,000 feet deep, and may be regarded as a Yosemite Valley from end to end, abounding in glorious cascades, falls, and rocks of sublime architecture. To the lover of pure wildness, a saunter up this mountain street is a grand indulgence, however rough the sidewalks and pavements which extend along the cool, rushing river.

The new Kings River Yosemite is larger, and in some respects more interesting, than either the Hetch Hetchy or the Yosemite of the Merced. It is situated on the south fork of Kings River, about 80 miles from Yosemite in a straight line, and 40 miles from Visalia, the nearest point on the Southern Pacific railroad. It is about nine miles long, half a mile wide at the bottom, and 5,000 feet above the level of the sea. The walls are quite as precipitous as those of Yosemite, 3,000 to 4,000 feet high, and sculptured in the same grand style so characteristic of all the valleys of this kind in the Sierra. As to water-falls, those of the new Yosemite are less striking in form and in the songs they sing, although the whole quantity of water pouring into the valley is greater, and comes from higher sources. The descent of the Kings Valley waters is made mostly in long, dashing cascades, and falls of moderate height, that are far less showy in general views than those of Yosemite.

My last visit to this magnificent valley was made with a small party in July, 1875, when the beauty of its wildness was still complete. We set out from Yosemite,

Fall on the South Fork
of Kings River.

Sentinel Rock or Half Dome,
South Fork, Kings River.

pushing our way through the wilderness, past Clark's Station, through the Mariposa grove of big trees, and the luxuriant forests of upper Fresno, down to the dappled plain of the San Joaquin. Thence, skirting the margin of the foot hills, we crossed the stately current of Kings River near Centreville, and facing eastward, climbed again into the sugar-pine woods, and on through the grand Sequoia forests of the Kaweah. Here we heard the sound of axes, and soon came upon a group of men busily engaged in preparing a section of one of the big trees they had felled for the Centennial Exhibition. This tree was 25 feet in diameter at the base, and so fine was the taper of the trunk it still measured 10 feet in diameter at a height of 200 feet from the ground. According to the testimony of the annual wood-rings, it was upwards of 2,000 years of age.

Out of this solemn ancient forest we climbed yet higher into the cool realms of the Alpine pines, until at length we caught a long sweeping view of the glorious Yosemite we were so eagerly seeking. The trail by which we descended to the bottom of the valley enters at the lower or west end, zigzagging in a wild, independent fashion over the south lip of the valley, and corresponding both in position and direction with the old Mariposa trail of Yosemite, and like it, affording a series of grand views up the valley, over the groves and meadows between the massive granite walls. So fully were these views Yosemitic in all their leading features it was hard to realise that we were not entering the old Yosemite by Inspiration Point.

In about two hours after beginning the descent we found ourselves among the sugar-pine groves at the lower end of the valley; and never did pines seem more noble and religious in gesture and tone.

The sun, pouring down mellow gold, seemed to be shining only for them, and the wind gave them voice; but the gestures of their outstretched arms appeared wholly independent of the wind, and impressed one with a solemn awe that overbore all our knowledge of causes, and brought us into the condition of being newly arrived from some other world. The ground was strewn with leaves and cones, making a fine surface for shadows; many a wide even bar from tapering trunk and column, and rich mosaic from leaf and branch; while ever and anon we came to small forest openings wholly filled with sunshine like lakes of light.

We made our first camp on the river bank, a mile or two up the valley, on the margin of a small circular meadow that was one of the most perfect flower gardens I have ever discovered in the Sierra. The trampling mules, whom I would gladly have kept out, fairly disappeared beneath the broad over-arching ferns that encircled it. The meadow was filled with lilies and orchids, larkspurs and columbines, daisies and asters and sun-loving golden-rods, violets and roses and purple geraniums, with a hundred others in prime of bloom, but whose names few would care to read, though all would enjoy fresh, wild beauty. One of the lilies that I measured was six feet long, and had eleven open flowers, five of them in their prime. The wind rocked this splendid panicle above the heads of the geraniums and briar-roses, forming a spectacle of pure beauty, exquisitely poised and harmonised in all its parts.

It was as if nature had fingered every leaf and petal that very day, readjusting every curving line and touching the colours of every corolla; and so, she had for not a leaf was misbent, and every plant was so placed with reference to every other, that the whole garden had seemingly been arranged like one tasteful bouquet. Here we lived a fine, unmeasured hour, considering the lilies, every individual flower radiating beauty as real and appreciable as sunbeams. Many other wild gardens occur along the river bank, and in many a cool side dell where streams enter, but neither at this time nor on my first visit to the valley were any discovered so perfect as this one. Toward the upper end of the valley there is quite an extensive meadow stretching across from wall to wall. The river borders are made up chiefly of alder, poplar, and willow, with pines and silver-fir where the banks are dry, and the common fringe of underbrush and flowers, all combined with reference to the best beauty and the wants of the broad crystal river.

The first two miles of the walls, beginning at the lower end of the valley, are bevelled off at the top, and are so broken and soil-besprinkled that they support quite a growth of trees and shaggy bushes; but farther up, the granite speedily assumes Yosemitic forms and dimensions, rising in stupendous cliffs, abrupt and sheer, from the level flats and meadows. On the north wall there is a rock like the El Capitan, and just above it a group like the Three Brothers. Further up, on the same side, there is an Indian Canyon, and North Dome, and Washington Column. On the south wall counterparts of the Cathedral and Sentinel Rocks occur in regular order, bearing the same relations to each other that they do in the old Yosemite. Our journey up the valley was perfectly enchanting, every bend of river presenting reaches of surpassing beauty, the sunbeams streaming through the border groves, or falling in broad masses upon white rapids or deep, calm pools. Here and there a dead pine, that had been swept down in flood-time, reached out over the current, its mosses and lichens contrasting with the crystal sheen of the water, and its gnarled roots forming shadowy caves for speckled trout, where the current eddies slowly, and protecting sedges and willows dip their leaves. Amid these varied and everchanging river views the appreciative artist may find studies for a lifetime. The deeply sculptured walls presented more and more exciting views, calling forth enthusiastic admiration. Bold, sheer brows, standing forth in a full blaze of light; deep, shadow-filled side canyons and gorges, inhabited by wild cascades, groups of gothic gables, glacier-polished domes coming in sight in ever changing combinations and with different foregrounds. Yet no rock in the valley equals El Capitan, or the great Half Dome; but, on the other hand, from no part of the Yosemite walls could a section five miles in length be selected equal in beauty and grandeur to five miles of the middle portion of the south wall of the new valley.

We camped for the night at the base of the new Washington Column, where ferns and lilies reached to our heads, the lavish exuberance of the vegetation about us contrasting with the bare, massive fronts of the walls. The summer day died in purple and gold, and we lay watching the fading sunshine and growing shadows among the heights. Each member of the party made his own bed, like birds building nests. Mine was made of overlapping fern fronds, with a few mint spikes in the pillow, combining luxurious softness and fragrance, and making the down beds of palaces and palace hotels seem poor and vulgar.

The full moon rose just after the night darkness was fairly established. Down the valley one rock after another caught the silvery glow, and stood out from the dusky shadows in long, imposing ranks like weird spirits, while the thickets and groves along the river were masses of solid darkness. The sky bloomed with stars like a meadow with flowers. It was too surpassingly beautiful a night for sleep, and we gazed long into the heart of the solemn, silent grandeur ere the weariness of enjoyment closed our eyes.

Next morning we continued on up the valley in the sunshine, following the north bank of the valley to where it forks at the head. The glacier-polished rocks glowed in the slant sunbeams in many places as if made of burnished metal. All the glacial phenomena of the new valley – the polished surfaces, *roches moutonnées*, and moraines are fresher, and therefore less changed, than those of the old. It is evidently a somewhat younger valley, a fact easily explained by its relations to the fountains of the ancient glaciers lying above it among the loftiest summits of the range. Like the old valley, this is a favourite resort of Indians because it produces acorns, and its waters abound in trout. They, doubtless, have names for all the principal rocks and cascades, and many grotesque and ornamental legends relating to them, though as yet I have not learned any of them.

This valley is already beginning to attract tourists from all parts of the world, and its fame may yet equal that of the old. It is quite accessible, the greater part of the distance from the railroad being by a good wagon-road, and all the necessary supplies may be obtained at Visalia. A good mountain trail conducts out of the valley at the head along the edge of the cascading river, and across the range by the Kearsarge Pass to Owens Valley, which we followed, and reached Independence on the east side of the Sierra in two days. From here we set out for the summit of Mt. Whitney. Then turning northward, we skirted the eastern flank of the range until we reached the Mono region. Thence crossing the range by the Bloody Canyon Pass, we entered the Yosemite Valley from above. Thus through the grand old forests, from mountain to mountain, from Yosemite to Yosemite we drifted free, making a round trip without wheels or tickets, that for grandeur and general interest cannot be surpassed in all the Sierra, or perhaps in any other mountain range in the world.

ADDENDUM

The Sentinel, Yosemite Valley
From the painting by Julian Rix

Treasures and Features of the Proposed Yosemite National Park

I

The Treasures of the Yosemite

THE YOSEMITE VALLEY, in the heart of the Sierra Nevada, is a noble mark for the traveller, whether tourist, botanist, geologist, or lover of wilderness pure and simple. But those who are free may find the journey a long one; not because of the miles, for they are not so many – only about two hundred and fifty from San Francisco, and passed over by rail and carriage road in a day or two – but the way is so beautiful that one is beguiled at every step, and the great golden days and weeks and months go by uncounted. How vividly my own first journey to Yosemite comes to mind, though made more than a score of years ago. I set out afoot from Oakland, on the bay of San Francisco. in April. It was the bloom-time of the year over all the lowlands and ranges of the coast; the landscape was fairly drenched with sunshine, the larks were singing, and the hills were so covered with flowers that they seemed to be painted. Slow indeed was my progress through these glorious gardens, the first of the California flora I had seen Cattle and cultivation were making few scars as yet, and I wandered enchanted in long, wavering curves, aware now and then that Yosemite lay to the eastward, and that, some time, I should find it.

One shining morning, at the head of the Pacheco Pass, a landscape was displayed that after all my wanderings still appears as the most divinely beautiful and sublime I have ever beheld. There at my feet lay the great central plain of California, level as a lake, thirty or forty miles wide, four hundred long, one rich furred bed of golden Compositae. And along the eastern shore of this lake of gold rose the mighty Sierra, miles in height, massive, tranquil grandeur, so gloriously coloured and so radiant that it seemed not clothed with light, but wholly composed of it, like the wall of some celestial city. Along the top, and extending a good way down, was a rich pearl-grey belt of snow; then a belt of blue and dark purple, marking the extension of the forests; and stretching along the base of the range a broad belt of rose-purple, where lay the miners' gold and the open foothill gardens – all the colours smoothly blending, making a wall of light clear as crystal and ineffably fine, yet firm as adamant. Then it seemed to me the Sierra should be called, not the Nevada or Snowy Range, but the Range of Light. And after ten years in the midst of it, rejoicing and wondering, seeing the glorious floods of light that fill it – the sunbursts of morning among the mountain-peaks, the broad noonday radiance on the crystal rocks, the flush of the alpenglow, and the thousand dashing waterfalls with their marvellous abundance of irised spray – it still seems to me a range of light. But no terrestrial beauty may endure forever. The glory of wildness has already departed from the great central plain. Its bloom is shed, and so in part is the bloom of the mountains. In Yosemite even under the protection of the Government, all that is perishable is vanishing apace.

The Sierra is about 500 miles long, 70 miles wide, and from 7000 to nearly 15,000 feet high. In general views no mark of man is visible upon it, nor anything to suggest the wonderful depth and grandeur of its sculpture. None of its magnificent forest-crowned ridges seems to rise much above the general level to publish its wealth. No great valley or river is seen, or group of well-marked features of any kind standing out as distinct pictures. Even the summit peaks, marshalled in glorious array so high in the sky, seem comparatively smooth and featureless. Nevertheless the whole range is furrowed with canyons to a depth of from 2,000 to 5,000 feet, in which once flowed majestic glaciers, and in which now flow and sing the bright Sierra rivers.

Though of such stupendous depth, these canyons are not raw, gloomy, jagged-walled gorges, savage and inaccessible. With rough passages here and there, they are mostly smooth, open pathways conducting to the fountains of the summit; mountain streets full of life and light, graded and sculptured by the ancient glaciers, and presenting throughout all their courses a rich variety of novel and attractive scenery – the most attractive that has yet been discovered in the mountain ranges of the world. In many places, especially in the middle region of the western flank, the main canyons widen into spacious valleys or parks of charming beauty, level and flowery and diversified like landscape gardens with meadows and groves and thickets of blooming bushes, while the lofty walls, infinitely varied in form, are fringed with ferns, flowering plants shrubs of many species, and tall evergreens and oaks which find anchorage on a thousand narrow steps and benches, the whole enlivened and made glorious with rejoicing streams that come dancing and foaming over the sunny brows of the cliffs, and through side canyons in falls of every conceivable form, to join the shining river that flows in tranquil beauty down the middle of each one of them.

The most famous and accessible of these canyon valleys, and also the one that presents their most striking and sublime features on the grandest scale, is the Yosemite, situated on the upper waters of the Merced at an elevation of 4,000 feet above the level of the sea It is about seven miles long, half a mile to a mile wide, and nearly a mile deep, and is carved in the solid granite flank of the range. The walls of the valley are made up of rocks, mountains in size, partly separated from each other by side canyons and gorges; and they are so sheer in front, and so compactly and harmoniously built together on a level floor, that the place comprehensively seen, looks like some immense hall or temple lighted from above.

But no temple made with hands can compare with Yosemite. Every rock in its walls seems to glow with life. Some lean back in majestic repose; others, absolutely sheer or nearly so for thousands of feet, advance beyond their companions in thoughtful attitudes, giving welcome to storms and calms alike, seemingly conscious, yet heedless of everything going on about them. Awful in stern, immovable majesty, how softly these mountain rocks are adorned and how fine and reassuring the company they keep – their feet set in groves and gay emerald meadows, their brows in the thin blue sky, a thousand flowers leaning confidingly against their adamantine bosses, bathed in floods of booming water, floods of light, while snow, clouds, winds, avalanches, shine and sing and wreathe about them as the years go by. Birds, bees, butterflies, and myriads of nameless wings stir the air into music and give glad animation. Down through the midst flows the crystal Merced – river of mercy – peacefully gliding, reflecting lilies and trees and the onlooking rocks, things frail and fleeting and types of endurance meeting here and blending in countless forms, as if into this one mountain mansion Nature had gathered her choicest treasures, whether great or small, to draw her lovers into close and confiding communion with her.

Sauntering towards Yosemite up the foothills, richer and wilder become the forests and streams. At an elevation of 6,000 feet above the level of the sea the silver firs are 200 feet high, with branches whorled around the colossal shafts in regular order, and every branch beautifully pinnate like a fern leaf. The Douglas spruce and the yellow and sugar pines here reach their highest developments of beauty and grandeur, and the rich, brown-barked libocedrus with warm, yellow-green plumes. The majestic sequoia, too, is here the king of conifers, ''the noblest of a noble race.'' All these colossal trees are as wonderful in the fineness of their beauty and proportions as in stature, growing together, an assemblage of conifers surpassing all that have yet been discovered in the forests of the world. Here, indeed, is the tree-lover's paradise, the woods, dry and wholesome, letting in the light in shimmering masses, half sunshine, half shade, the air indescribably spicy and exhilarating, plushy fir boughs for beds, and cascades to sing us asleep as we gaze through the trees to the stars.

On the highest ridges passed over on our way to Yosemite the lovely silver fir (*Abies amabilis*) forms the bulk of the woods, pressing forward in glorious array to the very brink of the walls on both sides and far beyond to a height of from 8,000 to 9,000 feet above the level of the sea. Thus it appears that Yosemite, presenting such stupendous faces of bare granite, is nevertheless embedded in magnificent forests. All the main species of pine, fir, spruce, and libocedrus are also found in the valley itself. But there are no "big trees" (*Sequoia gigantea*) in the valley or about the rim of it. The nearest are about ten miles beyond the boundary wall of the grant, on small tributaries of the Merced and Tuolumne. The sequoia belt extends along the western flank of the range, from the well known Calaveras Grove on the north to the head of Deer Creek on the south, a distance of about two hundred miles, at an elevation of from about 5,000 to 8,000 feet above sea level. From the Calaveras to the south fork of Kings River the species occurs only in small isolated groves or patches so sparsely distributed along the belt that two of the gaps that occur are nearly forty miles wide, one of them between the Stanislaus and Tuolumne groves, the other between those of the Fresno and Kings River. Hence southward, instead of forming small sequestered groups among the other conifers, the big trees sweep majestically across the broad, rugged basins of the Kaweah and Tule in noble forests a distance of nearly seventy miles, with a width of from three to ten miles, the continuity of this portion of the belt being interrupted only by deep canyons.

The Fresno, the largest of the northern groves, occupies an area of three or four square miles, and is situated a short distance to the southward of the famous Mariposa Grove. Along the bevelled rim of the canyon of the south fork of Kings River there is a stately forest of sequoia about six miles long and two miles wide. This is the northernmost assemblage of big trees that may fairly be called a forest. Descending the precipitous divide between Kings River and the Kaweah one enters the grand forests that form the main continuous portion of the belt. Advancing southward the trees become more and more irrepressibly exuberant, heaving their massive crowns into the sky from every ridge, and waving onward in graceful compliance with the complicated topography. The finest of the Kaweah portion of the belt is on the broad ridge between Marble Creek and the middle fork, and extends from the granite headlands overlooking the hot plains back to within a few miles of the cool glacial fountains. The extreme upper limit of the belt is reached between the middle and south forks of the Kaweah, at an elevation of 8,400 feet. But the finest block of sequoia in the entire belt is on the north fork of the Tule River. In the northern groups there are comparatively few young trees or saplings. But here for every old, storm-stricken giant there is one or more in all the glory of prime, and for each of these there are many young trees and crowds of eager, hopeful saplings growing heartily everywhere – on moraines, rocky ledges, along watercourses, and in the deep, moist alluvium of meadows, seemingly in hot pursuit of eternal life.

Though the area occupied by the species increases so much from north to south, there is no marked increase in the size of the trees. A height of two hundred and seventy-five feet and a diameter of twenty is perhaps about the average for full-grown trees; specimens twenty-five feet in diameter are not rare, and a good many are nearly three hundred feet high. The largest I have yet met in the course of my explorations is a majestic old monument in the new Kings River forest. It is thirty-five feet and eight inches in diameter inside the bark four feet from the ground, and a plank of solid wood the whole width of the tree might be hewn from it without the slightest decay.

Under the most favourable conditions these giants live five or six thousand years, though few of even the larger specimens are more than half as old. The sequoia seems to be entirely exempt from the diseases that afflict and kill other conifers – mildew, dry rot, or any other kind of rot. I never saw a sick sequoia, or one that seemed to be dying of old age. Unless destroyed by man, they live on indefinitely until burned, smashed by lightning, or cast down by the giving way of the ground on which they stand.

These king trees, all that there are of their kind in the world, are surely worth saving, whether for beauty, science, or bald use. But as yet only the isolated Mariposa Grove has been reserved as a park for public use and pleasure. Were the importance of our forests at all understood by the people in general, even from an economic standpoint their preservation would call forth the most watchful attention of the Government. At present, however, every kind of destruction is moving on with accelerated speed. Fifteen years ago I found five mills located on or near the lower margin of the main sequoia belt, all of which were cutting big tree lumber. How many more have been built since that time I am unable to say, but most of the Fresno group are doomed to feed the large mills established near them, and a company with ample means is about ready for work on the magnificent forests of Kings River. In these mill operations waste far exceeds use. For after the young, manageable trees have been cut, blasted, and sawed, the woods are fired to clear the ground of limbs and refuse, and of course the seedlings and saplings, and many of the unmanageable giants, are destroyed, leaving but little more than black, charred monuments. These mill ravages, however, are small as yet compared with the comprehensive destruction caused by "sheep men." Incredible numbers of sheep are driven to the mountain pastures every summer, and desolation follows them. Every garden within reach is trampled, the shrubs are stripped of leaves as if devoured by locusts, and the woods are burned to improve the pasturage. The entire belt of forests is thus swept by fire, from one end of the range to the other; and, with the exception of the resinous *Pinus contorta*, the sequoia suffers most of all. Steps are now being taken towards the creation of a national park about the Yosemite, and great is the need, not only for the sake of the adjacent forests, but for the valley itself. For the branching canyons and valleys of the basins of the streams that pour into Yosemite are as closely related to it as are the fingers to the palm of the hand – as the branches, foliage, and flowers of a tree to the trunk. Therefore, very naturally, all the fountain region above Yosemite, with its peaks, canyons, snow fields, glaciers, forests, and streams, should be included in the park to make it an harmonious unit instead of a fragment, great though the fragment be; while to the westward, below the valley, the boundary might be extended with great advantage far enough to comprehend the Fresno, Mariposa, Merced, and Tuolumne groves of big trees, three of which are on roads leading to the valley, while all of them are in the midst of conifers scarcely less interesting than the colossal brown giants themselves.

From the heights on the margin of these glorious forests we at length gain our first general view of the valley – a view that breaks suddenly upon us in all its glory far and wide and deep; a new revelation in landscape affairs that goes far to make the weakest and meanest spectator rich and significant evermore.

Along the curves and zigzags of the road, all the way down to the bottom, the valley is in sight with ever-changing views, and the eye ranges far up over the green grovy floor between the mighty walls, bits of the river gleaming here and there, while as we draw nearer we begin to hear the song of the waters. Gazing at random, perhaps the first object to gain concentrated attention will be the Bridal Veil, a beautiful waterfall on our right. Its brow, where it first leaps free from the rock, is about nine hundred feet above us; and as it sways and sings in the wind, with gauzy, sun-sifted spray half falling, half floating, it seems infinitely gentle and fine; but the hymn it sings tells the solemn power that is hidden beneath the soft clothing it wears.

On the other side of the valley, opposite the Veil, there is another magnificent fall, called the Ribbon Fall, or Virgin's Tears. The "tears" fall from a height of about 3,000 feet, and are most extravagantly copious when the snow is melting, coming hissing and roaring with force enough to drive a mile of mills, suggesting the "weeping skies" of cyclones and hurricanes.

Just beyond this glorious flood the El Capitan rock is seen through the pine groves pressing forward beyond the general line of the wall in most imposing grandeur. It is 3,300 feet high, a plain, severely simple, glacier - sculptured face of granite, the end of one of the most compact and enduring of the mountain ridges, standing there in supreme height and breadth, a type of permanence.

Across the valley from here, above the Bridal Veil, are the picturesque Cathedral Rocks, nearly 2,700 feet high, making a noble display of fine yet massive sculpture. They are closely related to El Capitan, having been hewn from the same mountain ridge by the Yosemite glacier when the valley was in process of formation.

Beyond El Capitan the next in succession of the most striking features of the north wall are the Three Brothers, an immense mountain mass with three gables fronting the valley one above the other, the topmost nearly 4,000 feet high. They were named for three brothers captured here during the Indian war, sons of Tenaya, the old Yosemite chief.

On the south wall opposite the Brothers towers the Sentinel Rock to a height of more than 3,000 feet, a telling monument of the icy past.

Sauntering up the valley through meadow and grove, in the company of these majestic rocks, which seem to follow as we advance gazing, admiring, looking for new wonders ahead where all about us is wonderful, the thunder of the Yosemite Fall is heard, and when we arrive in front of the Sentinel it is revealed in all its glory from base to summit, half a mile in height, and seeming to gush direct from the sky. But even this fall, perhaps the most wonderful in the world, cannot at first control our attention, for now the wide upper portion of the valley is displayed to view, with the North Dome, Royal Arches, and Washington Column on our left; Glacier Point Rock, with its magnificent sculpture, on the right; and in the middle Tissiack or Half Dome, the most beautiful and most sublime of all the mountain rocks about the valley. It rises in serene majesty from the fertile level into the sky to a height of 4,750 feet.

Here the valley divides into three branches, the Tenaya, Nevada, and Illilouette canyons and valleys, extending back into the fountains of the High Sierra, with scenery every way worthy the relation they bear to Yosemite.

In the south branch, a mile or two from the main valley, is the Illilouette Fall, 600 feet high, one of the most beautiful of all the Yosemite choir, but to most people inaccessible as yet on account of its rough, boulder-choked canyon. Its principal fountains of ice and snow lie in the beautiful and interesting mountains of the Merced group, while its broad, open basin in general is noted for the beauty of its lakes and extensive forests.

Going up the north branch of the valley, we pass between the North Dome and the Half Dome, and in less than an hour come to Mirror Lake, the Dome Cascades, and Tenaya Fall, each interesting in its own way. Beyond the fall, on the north side of the canyon, is the sublime El Capitan-like rock called Mount Watkins; on the south the vast granite wave of Clouds Rest, a mile in height; and between them the fine Tenaya Cascade with silvery plumes outspread on smooth, glacier-polished folds of granite, making a vertical descent in all of about 700 feet.

Just beyond the Dome Cascades, on the shoulder of Mount Watkins, there is an old trail once used by the Indians on their way across the range to Mono, but in the canyon above this point there is no trail of any sort. Between Mount Watkins and Clouds Rest the canyon is accessible only to mountaineers, and it is so dangerous in some places that I hesitate to advise even good climbers anxious to test their nerve and skill to pass through it. Beyond the Cascades no great difficulty will be encountered. A succession of charming lily gardens and meadows occur in filled up lake basins among the rock-waves in the bottom of the canyon, and everywhere the surface of the granite has a smooth-wiped appearance, and in many places, reflecting the sunbeams, shines like glass – phenomena due to glacial action, the canyon having been the channel of one of the main tributaries of the ancient Yosemite glacier.

Ten miles above the valley we come to the beautiful Tenaya Lake, and

here the canyon terminates. A mile or two above the lake stands the grand
Sierra Cathedral, a building of one stone, hewn from the living rock, with
sides, roof, gable, spire, and ornamental pinnacles, fashioned and finished
symmetrically like a work of art, and set on a well-graded plateau about
9,000 feet high, as if nature in making so fine a house had also been careful
that it should be finely seen. From every direction its peculiar form and
graceful beauty of expression never fail to charm. Its height from the floor
to the ridge of the roof is about 2,500 feet, and among the pinnacles that
adorn the front glorious views may be gained of the upper basins of the
Merced and Tuolumne.

Passing on each side of the Cathedral we descend into the delightful
Tuolumne Valley, from which excursions may be made to Mount Dana,
Mono Lake, Mount Lyell, to the many curious peaks that rise above the
meadows on the south, and to the Big Tuolumne Canyon with its glorious
abundance of rocks and falling, gliding, tossing water. For all these the
spacious meadows near the Soda Springs form a delightful centre.

Returning now to Yosemite, and ascending the middle or Nevada branch
of the valley, which is occupied by the main Merced River, we come within a
few miles to the Vernal and Nevada falls, 400 and 600 feet high, and set in
the midst of most novel and sublime rock-work. Above these, tracing the
river, we are led into the Little Yosemite, a valley like the great Yosemite in
form, sculpture, and vegetation. It is about three miles long, with walls 1,500
to 2,000 feet high, cascades coming over them, and the river flowing through
the meadows and groves of the level bottom in tranquil crystal reaches.

Beyond this there are four other little Yosemites in the main canyon,
making a series of five in all, the highest situated a few miles below the base
of Mount Lyell, at an elevation of about 7,800 feet above the sea. To
describe these, with all their wealth of Yosemite furniture, and the wilderness
of lofty peaks above them, the home of the avalanche and treasury of the
fountain snow, would take us far beyond the bounds of a magazine article.
We cannot here consider the formation of these mountain landscapes – how
the crystal rocks with crystal snow were brought to the light, making beauty
whose influence is so mysterious on everybody who sees it; the blooming of
the clouds; the fall of the snow; the flight of the avalanches; the invisible
march of the grinding glaciers; the innumerable forms of the falling streams.

Of the small glacier lakes so characteristic of these upper regions, there
are no fewer than sixty-seven in the basin of the main middle branch,
besides countless smaller pools, all their waters crisp and living and looking
out on beautiful skies. In the basin of the Illilouette there are sixteen, in the
Tenaya and its branches thirteen, in the Yosemite Creek basin fourteen, and
in the Pohono or Bridal Veil one, making a grand total of a hundred and
eleven lakes whose waters come to sing at Yosemite. So glorious is the
background of the great valley, so harmonious its relations to its wide
spreading fountains. On each side also the same harmony prevails. Climbing

out of the valley by the subordinate canyons, we find the ground rising from the brink of the walls – on the south side to the fountains of Pohono or Bridal Veil Creek, the basin of which is noted for the extent and beauty of its meadows and its superb forests of silver fir; on the north side through the basin of the Yosemite Creek to the dividing ridge along the Tuolumne Canyon and the fountains of the Hoffman spur.

In general views the Yosemite Creek basin seems to be paved with domes and smooth whaleback masses of granite in every stage of development – some showing only their crowns; others rising high and free above the girdling forests, singly or in groups. Others again are developed only on one side, forming bold outstanding bosses usually well fringed with shrubs and trees, and presenting the polished shining surfaces given them by the glacier that brought them into relief. On the upper portion of the basin broad moraine beds have been deposited, and on these fine, thrifty forests are growing. Lakes and meadows and small spongy bogs may be found hiding here and there among the domes, in the woods, or back in the fountain recesses of Mount Hoffman, while a thousand gardens are planted along the banks of the streams. All the wide, fan-shaped upper portion of the basin is covered with a network of small rills that go cheerily on their way to their grand fall in the valley, now flowing on smooth pavements in sheets thin as glass, now diving under willows and laving their red roots, oozing through bogs, making tiny falls and cascades, whirling and dancing, calming again, gliding through bits of smooth glacier meadows with sod of Alpine agrostis mixed with blue and white violets and daisies, breaking, tossing among rough boulders and fallen trees, flowing together until, all united, they go to their fate with stately, tranquil air like a full-grown river.

At the crossing of the Mono trail, about two miles above the head of the Yosemite Fall the stream is nearly forty feet wide, and when the snow is melting rapidly in the spring about four feet deep, with a current of two and a half miles an hour. This is about the volume of water that forms the fall in May and June when there has been much snow the preceding winter; but it varies greatly from month to month. The snow rapidly vanishes from the open portion of the basin, which faces southward, and only a few of the tributaries reach back to perennial snow and ice fountains in the shadowy amphitheatres on the northern slopes of Mount Hoffman. The total descent made by the stream from its highest sources to its confluence with the Merced in the valley is about 6,000 feet, while the distance is only about ten miles, an average fall of 600 feet per mile. The last mile of its course lies between the sides of sunken domes and swelling folds of the granite that are clustered and pressed together like a mass of bossy cumulus clouds. Through this shining way Yosemite Creek goes to its fate, swaying and swirling with easy, graceful gestures and singing the last of its mountain songs before it reaches the dizzy edge of Yosemite to fall 2,600 feet into another world, where climate, vegetation, inhabitants, all are different. Emerging from this last canyon the stream glides, in flat, lace-like folds, down a smooth incline into a small pool where it seems to rest and compose itself before making the grand plunge. Then calmly, as if leaving a lake, it slips over the polished lip of the pool down another incline and out over the brow of the precipice in a magnificent curve thick sown with rainbow spray.

In tracing the stream for the first time, getting acquainted with the life it lived in the mountains, I was eager to reach the extreme verge to see how it behaves in flowing so far through the air; but after enjoying this view and getting safely away I have never advised anyone to follow my steps. The last incline down which the stream journeys so gracefully is so steep and smooth one must slip cautiously forward on hands and feet alongside the rushing water, which so near one's head is very exciting. But to gain a perfect view one must go yet farther, over a curving brow to a slight shelf on the extreme brink. This shelf, formed by the flaking off of a fold of the granite, is about three inches wide, just wide enough for a safe rest for one's heels. To me it seemed nerve-trying to slip to this narrow foothold and poise on the edge of such a precipice so close to the confusing whirl of the waters; and after casting longing glances over the shining brow of the fall and listening to its sublime psalm, I concluded not to attempt to go nearer, but did, nevertheless, against reasonable judgment. Noticing some tufts of artemisia in a cleft of rock, I filled my mouth with the leaves, hoping their bitter taste might help to keep caution keen and prevent giddiness; then I reached the little ledge, got my heels well set, and worked side-wise twenty or thirty feet to a point close to the out-plunging current. Here the view is perfectly free down into the heart of the bright irised throng of comet-like streams into which the whole ponderous volume of the fall separates a little below the brow. So glorious a display of pure wildness, acting at close range while one is cut off from all the world beside, is terribly impressive.

About forty yards to the eastward of the Yosemite Fall on a fissured portion of the edge of the cliff a less nerve-trying view may be obtained, extending all the way down to the bottom from a point about two hundred feet below the brow of the fall, where the current, striking a narrow ledge, bounds out in the characteristic comet-shaped masses. Seen from here towards noon, in the spring, the rainbow on its brow seems to be broken up and mingled with the rushing comets until all the fall is stained with iris colours, leaving no white water visible. This is the best of the safe views from above, the huge steadfast rocks, the flying waters, and the rainbow light forming one of the most glorious pictures conceivable.

The Yosemite Fall is separated into an upper and a lower fall with a series of falls and cascades between them, but when viewed in front from the bottom of the valley they all appear as one.

The Nevada Fall usually is ranked next to the Yosemite in general interest among the five main falls of the valley. Coming through the Little Yosemite in tranquil reaches, charmingly embowered, the river is first broken into rapids on a moraine boulder bar that crosses the lower end of the valley. Thence it pursues its way to the head of the fall in a very rough channel, cut in the solid granite, dashing on side angles, heaving in heavy, surging masses against bossy knobs, and swirling and swashing in potholes without a moment's rest. Thus, already chafed and dashed to foam, over-folded and twisted, it plunges over the brink of the precipice as if glad to escape into the open air. But before it reaches the bottom it is pulverized yet finer by impinging upon a sloping portion of the cliff about half way down, thus making it the whitest of all the falls of the valley, and altogether one of the most wonderful in the world.

On the north side, close to the head of the fall, a slab of granite projects over the brink, forming a fine point for a view over the throng of streamers and wild plunging thunderbolts; and through the broad drifts of spray we see the river far below gathering its spent waters and rushing on again down the canyon in glad exultation into Emerald Pool, where at length it grows calm and gets rest for what still lies before it. All the features of the view correspond with the waters. The glacier-sculptured walls of the canyon on either hand, with the sublime mass of the Glacier Point Ridge in front, form a huge triangular, pit-like basin, which, filled with the roar of the falling river, seems as if it might be the hopper of one of the mills of the gods in which the mountains were being ground to dust.

The Vernal, famous for its rainbows, is a staid, orderly, easy-going fall, proper and exact in every movement, with scarce a hint of the passionate enthusiasm of the Yosemite or the Nevada. Nevertheless it is a favourite with most visitors, doubtless because it is better seen than any other. A good stairway ascends the cliff beside it, and the level plateau at the head enables one to saunter safely along the edge of the stream as it comes from Emerald Pool and to watch its waters, calmly bending over the brow of the precipice, in a sheet 80 feet wide and changing from green to purplish grey and white until dashed on the rough boulder talus below. Thence issuing from beneath the clouds of the out-wafting spray we can see the adventurous stream, still unspent, beating its way down the rugged canyon in grey continuous cascades, dear to the ousel, until it sweeps around the shoulder of the Half Dome on its approach to the head of the main valley.

The Illilouette in general appearance most resembles the Nevada. The volume of water is less than half as great, but it is about the same height (600 feet), and its waters receive the same kind of preliminary tossing in a rocky, irregular channel. Therefore it is a very white and fine-grained fall. When it is in full spring time bloom it is partly divided by rocks that roughen the lip of the precipice, but this division amounts only to a kind of fluting and grooving of the column, which has a beautiful effect. It is not nearly so grand a fall as the upper Yosemite, or so symmetrical as the Vernal, or so airily graceful and simple as the Bridal Veil, nor does it ever display so tremendous an outgush of snowy magnificence as the Nevada;

but in the exquisite fineness and richness of texture of its flowing folds it surpasses them all.

One of the finest things I ever saw in Yosemite or elsewhere I found on the brow of this beautiful fall. It was in the Indian summer, when the leaf colours were ripe and the great cliffs and domes were transfigured in the hazy golden air. I had wandered up the rugged talus-dammed canyon of the Illilouette, admiring the wonderful views to be had there of the great Half Dome and the Liberty Cap, the foliage of the maples, dogwoods, rubus tangles, etc., the late goldenrods and asters, and the extreme purity of the water, which in motionless pools on this stream is almost perfectly invisible. The voice of the fall was now low, and the grand flood had waned to floating gauze and thin-broidered folds of linked and arrowy lace-work. When I reached the fall slant sunbeams were glinting across the head of it, leaving all the rest in shallow; and on the illumined brow a group of yellow spangles were playing, of singular form and beauty, flashing up and dancing in large flame-shaped masses, wavering at times, then steadying, rising and falling in accord with the shifting forms of the water. But the colour changed not at all. Nothing in clouds or flowers, on bird-wings or the lips of shells, could rival it in fineness. It was the most divinely beautiful mass of yellow light I ever beheld – one of nature's precious sights that come to us but once in a lifetime.

For about a mile above Mirror Lake the canyon is level and well planted with fir, spruce, and libocedrus, forming a remarkably fine grove, at the head of which is the Tenaya Fall. Though seldom seen or described, this is, I think, the most picturesque fall in the valley. For a considerable distance above it Tenaya Creek comes rushing down, white and foamy, over a flat pavement inclined at an angle of about eighteen degrees. In time of high water this sheet of bright rapids is nearly seventy feet wide, and is varied in a very striking way by three parallel furrows that extend in the direction of the flow. These furrows, worn by the action of the stream upon cleavage joints, vary in width, are slightly sinuous, and have large boulders firmly wedged in them here and there in narrow places, giving rise, of course, to a complicated series of wild dashes, doublings, and arching bounds in the swift torrent.

Just before it reaches the sheer precipice of the fall the current is divided, the left division making a vertical fall of about eighty feet in a romantic leafy nook, while the other forms a rugged cascade.

Lunar rainbows or spray bows also abound; their colours as distinct as those of the sun, and as obviously banded, though less vivid. Fine specimens may be found any night at the foot of the upper Yosemite Fall, glowing gloriously amid the gloomy shadows of the canyon whenever there is plenty of moonlight and spray, silent interpreters of the heart-peace of nature in the stormy darkness. Even the secondary bow is at times distinctly visible.

The best point from which to observe them is on Fern Ledge. For some time after moonrise the arc has a span of about five hundred feet, and is set upright; one end planted in the boiling spray at the bottom, the other in the edge of the fall, creeping lower, of course, and becoming less upright as the moon rises higher. This grand arc of colour, glowing in mild, shapely beauty in so weird and huge a chamber of night shadows, and amid the rush and roar and tumultuous dashing of this thunder-voiced fall, is one of the most impressive and most cheering of all the blessed evangels of the mountains.

A wild scene, but not a safe one, is made by the moon as it appears through the edge of the Yosemite Fall when one is behind it. Once after enjoying the night-song of the waters, and watching the formation of the coloured bow as the moon came round the domes and sent her beams into the wild uproar, I ventured out on the narrow bench that extends back of the fall from Fern Ledge and began to admire the dim-veiled grandeur of the view. I could see the fine gauzy threads of the outer tissue by having the light in front; and wishing to look at the moon through the meshes of some of the denser portions of the fall I ventured to creep farther behind it while it was gently wind-swayed, without taking sufficient thought about the consequences of its swaying back to its natural position after the wind pressure should be removed. The effect was enchanting. Fine, savage music sounded above, beneath, around me; while the moon, apparently in the very midst of the rushing waters, seemed to be struggling to keep her place, on account of the ever varying form and density of the water masses through which she was seen, now darkened by a rush of thick-headed comets, now flashing out through openings between them.

I was in fairyland, between the dark wall and the wild throng of illumined waters, but suffered sudden disenchantment; for, like the witch scene in Alloway Kirk, "in an instant all was dark." Down came a dash of spent comets, thin and harmless-looking in the distance, but desperately solid and stony in striking one's shoulders. It seemed like a mixture of choking spray and gravel. Instinctively dropping on my knees, I laid hold of an angle of the rock, rolled myself together with my face pressed against my breast, and in this attitude submitted as best I could to my thundering baptism. The heavier masses seemed to strike like cobblestones, and there was a confused noise of many waters about my ears – hissing, gurgling, clashing sounds that were not heard as music. The situation was easily realised. How fast one's thoughts burn at such times! I was weighing the chances of escape. Would the column be swayed a few inches away from the wall, or would it come yet closer? The fall was in flood, and not so lightly would its ponderous mass be swayed. My fate seemed to depend on a breath of the "idle wind." It was moved gently forward, the pounding ceased, and I once more revisited the glimpses of the moon. But fearing I might be caught at a disadvantage in making too hasty a retreat, I moved only a few feet along the bench to where a block of ice lay. Between the ice and the wall I wedged myself, and lay face downwards until the steadiness of the light gave encouragement to get away. Somewhat nerve-shaken, drenched, and benumbed, I made out to build a fire, warmed myself; ran home to avoid taking cold, reached my cabin before daylight, got an hour or two of sleep, and awoke sane and comfortable, better, not worse, for my wild bath in moonlit spray.

Owing to the westerly trend of the valley and its vast depth there is a great difference between the climates of the north and south sides – greater than between many countries far apart; for the south wall is in shadow during the winter months, while the north is bathed in sunshine every clear day. Thus there is mild spring weather on one side of the valley while winter rules the other. Far up the north-side cliffs many a nook may be found closely embraced by sun-beaten rock-bosses in which flowers bloom every month of the year. Even butterflies may be seen in these high winter gardens except when storms are falling and a few days after they have ceased. Near the head of the lower Yosemite Fall in January I found the ant lions lying in wait in their warm sand cups, rock ferns being unrolled, club mosses covered with fresh growing points, the flowers of the laurel nearly open, and the honeysuckle rosetted with bright young leaves; every plant seemed to be thinking about summer and to be stirred with good vital sunshine. Even on the shadow side of the valley the frost is never very sharp. The lowest temperature I ever observed during four winters was +7°F. The first twenty-four days of January had an average temperature at 9 a.m. of 32°, minimum 22°; at 3 p.m. the average was 40° 30', the minimum 32°.

Throughout the winter months the spray of the upper Yosemite Fall is frozen while falling thinly exposed and is deposited around the base of the fall in the form of a hollow truncated cone, which sometimes reaches a height of five hundred feet or more, into the heart of which the whole volume of the fall descends with a tremendous roar as if pouring down the throat of a crater. In the building of this ice-cone, part of the frozen spray falls directly to its place, but a considerable portion is first frozen upon the race of the cliff on both sides of the fall, and attains a thickness of a foot or more during the night. When the sun strikes this ice-coating it is expanded and cracked off in masses weighing from a few pounds to several tons, and is built into the walls of the cone; while in windy, frosty weather, when the fall is swayed from side to side, the cone is well drenched, and the loose ice-masses and dust are all firmly frozen together. The thundering, reverberating reports of the falling ice-masses are like those of heavy cannon. They usually occur at intervals of a few minutes, and are the most strikingly characteristic of the winter sounds of the valley, and constant accompaniments of the best sunshine. While this stormy building is in progress the surface of the cone is smooth and pure white, the whole presenting the appearance of a beautiful crystal hill wreathed with folds of spray which are oftentimes irised. But when it is wasting and breaking up in the spring its surface is strewn with leaves, pine branches, stones, sand, etc., that have been brought over the fall, making it look like a heap of avalanche detritus.

After being engulfed and churned in the stormy interior of the crater the waters of the fall issue from arched openings at the base seemingly scourged and weary and glad to escape, while belching spray, spouted up out of the throat past the descending current, is wafted away in irised drifts to the rocks and groves.

Anxious to learn what I could about the structure of this curious ice-hill, I tried to climb it, carrying an axe to cut footsteps. Before I had reached the base of it I was met by a current of spray and wind that made breathing difficult. I pushed on backward, however, and soon gained the slope of the hill, where by creeping close to the surface most of the blast was avoided. Thus I made my way nearly to the summit, halting at times to peer up through the wild whirls of spray, or to listen to the sublime thunder beneath me, the whole hill sounding as if it were a huge, bellowing, exploding drum. I hoped that by waiting until the fall was blown aslant I should be able to climb to the lip of the crater and get a view of the interior; but a suffocating blast, half air, half water, followed by the fall of an enormous mass of ice from the wall, quickly discouraged me. The whole cone was jarred by the blow, and I was afraid its side might fall in. Some fragments of the mass sped past me dangerously near; so I beat a hasty retreat, chilled and drenched, and laid myself on a sunny rock in a safe place to dry.

The Bridal Veil, upper Yosemite, and the Tu-ee-u-la-la of Hetch Hetchy (the next canyon to the north), on account of their height and exposure, are greatly influenced by winds. The common summer winds that come up the river canyon from the plains are never very strong, partly on account of the roughness of the way they have to travel. But the north winds of winter do some very wild work, worrying the falls and the forests, and hanging snow banners, a mile long, on the peaks of the summit of the range. One morning I was awakened by the pelting of pine cones on the roof of my cabin, and found, on going out, that the north wind had taken possession of the valley, filling it with a sea-like roar, and, arousing the pines to magnificent action, made them bow like supple willows. The valley had been visited a short time before by a succession of most beautiful snowstorms, and the floor, and the cliffs, and all the region round about were lavishly laden with winter jewellery. Rocks, trees, the sandy flats and the meadows, all were in bloom, and the air was filled with a dust of shining petals. The gale increased all day, and branches and tassels and empty burs of the silver pine covered the snow, while the falls were being twisted and torn and tossed about as if they were mere wisps of floating mist. In the morning the great ponderous column of the upper Yosemite fall, increased in volume by the melting of the snow during a warm spell, was caught by a tremendous blast, bent upwards, torn to shreds, and driven back over the brow of the cliff whence it came, as if denied admission to the valley. This kind of work would be kept up for ten or fifteen minutes, then a partial lull in the storm would allow the vast torrent to arrange its tattered skirts, and come back again to sing on in its accustomed course. Amid all this rocking and bending and baffling of the waters they were lighted by a steady glare of sunlight, strangely white from spicules of snow crystals. The lower fall, though less exposed, was yet violently swirled and torn and thrashed about in its narrow canyon, and at times appeared as one resplendent mass of iris colours from top to bottom, as if a hundred rainbows had been doubled up into a mass four or five hundred feet in diameter. In the afternoon, while I watched the upper fall from the shelter of a pine tree, it was suddenly arrested in its descent at a point about half way down, and was neither blown upward nor driven aside, but was simply held stationary in mid air, as if gravitation below that point in the path of its descent had ceased to act. The ponderous flood, weighing hundreds of tons, was sustained hovering, hesitating, like a bunch of thistledown, while I counted 190. All this time the ordinary amount of water was coming over the cliff and accumulating in the air, swedging and widening and forming an irregular cone 700 feet high tapering to the top of the wall, the whole standing still, resting on the invisible arm of the north wind. At length, as if commanded to go on again, scores of arrowy comets shot forth from the bottom of the suspended mass as if escaping from separate outlets.

The brow of El Capitan was decked with long streamers of snow-like hair, Clouds Rest was enveloped in drifting gossamer films, and the Half Dome loomed up in the garish light like some majestic living creature clad in the same gauzy, wind-woven drapery, upward currents meeting overhead sometimes making it smoke like a volcano.

Glorious as are these rocks and waters when jumbled in storm winds, or chanting rejoicing in everyday dress, there is a glory that excelleth, when rare conditions of weather meet to make every valley, hollow, gorge, and canyon sing with flood waters. Only once have I seen Yosemite in full bloom of flood during all the years I have lived there. In 1871 the early winter weather was delightful; the days all sunshine, the nights clear and serene, calling forth fine crops of frost crystals for the withered ferns and grasses, the most luxuriant growths of hoar-frost imaginable. In the afternoon of December 16th, when I was sauntering on the meadows, I noticed a massive crimson cloud growing in solitary grandeur above Cathedral Rocks, its form scarcely less striking than its colour. It had a picturesque, bulging base like an old sequoia, a smooth, tapering stem, and a bossy, down-curling crown like a mushroom; all its parts coloured alike, making one mass of translucent crimson. Wondering what the meaning of that lonely red cloud might be, I was up betimes next morning looking at the weather, but all seemed tranquil as yet. Towards noon grey clouds began to grow which had a close, curly grain like bird's-eye maple, and late at night rain fell, which soon changed to snow; next morning about ten inches lay on the meadows, and it was still falling in a fine, cordial storm.

During the night of the 18th a torrent of rain fell on the snow, but as the temperature was 34°, the snow line was only a few hundred feet above the bottom of the valley, and to get out of the rainstorm into the snowstorm one had only to climb a little above the tops of the pines. The streams, therefore, instead of being increased in volume, were diminished by the storm, because the snow sponged up part of their waters and choked the smaller tributaries. But about midnight the temperature suddenly rose to 42°, carrying the snow line far beyond the valley, over the upper basins perhaps to the summit of the range, and next morning Yosemite was rejoicing in a glorious flood. The warm, copious rain falling on the snow was at first absorbed and held back, and so also was that portion of the snow that the rain melted, and all that was melted by the warm wind, until the whole mass of snow was saturated and became sludgy, and at length slipped and rushed simultaneously from a thousand slopes into the channels in wild extravagance, heaping and swelling flood over flood, and plunging into the valley in one stupendous avalanche.

Awakened by the roar, I looked out and at once recognised the extraordinary character of the storm. The rain was still pouring in torrents, and the wind, blowing a gale, was working in passionate accord with the 'flood. The section of the north wall visible from my cabin was covered with a network of falls – new visitors that seemed strangely out of place. Eager to get into the midst of the show, I snatched a piece of bread for breakfast and ran out. The mountain waters, suddenly liberated, seemed to be holding a grand jubilee. The two Sentinel cascades rivalled the great falls at ordinary stages, and across the valley by the Three Brothers I caught glimpses of more falls than I could readily count; while the whole valley throbbed and trembled, and was filled with an awful, massive, solemn, sea-like roar. After looking about me bewildered for a few moments I tried to reach the upper meadows, where the valley is widest, that I might be able to see the walls on both sides, and thus gain general views. But the meadows were flooded, forming an almost continuous lake dotted with blue sludgy islands, while innumerable streams roared like lions across my path and were sweeping forward rocks and logs with tremendous energy over ground where tiny gilias had been growing but a short time before. Climbing into the talus slopes, w here these savage torrents were broken among earthquake boulders, I succeeded in crossing them, and forced my way up the valley to Hutchings' Bridge, where I crossed the river and waded to the middle of the upper meadow. Here most of the new falls were in sight, probably the most glorious assemblage of waterfalls ever displayed from any one standpoint in the world. On that portion of the south wall between Hutchings' and the Sentinel there were ten falls plunging and booming from a height of nearly 3,000 feet, the smallest of which might have been heard miles away. In the neighbourhood of Glacier Point there were six; between the Three Brothers and Yosemite Fall, nine; between Yosemite and Royal Arch Falls, ten; from Washington Column to Mount Watkins, ten; on the slopes of Half Dome, facing Mirror Lake, eight; on the shoulder of Half Dome, facing the valley, three – fifty-six new falls occupying the upper end of the valley, besides a countless host of silvery threads gleaming everywhere. In all the valley there must have been upward of a hundred. As if celebrating some great event, falls and cascades came thronging in Yosemite costume from every groove and canyon far and near.

All summer visitors will remember the comet forms of the Yosemite Fall and the laces of the Bridal Veil and Nevada. In the falls of this winter jubilee the lace forms predominated, but there was no lack of thunder-toned comets. The lower portion of one of the Sentinel cascades was composed of two main white shafts, the space between them filled in with chained and beaded gauze of intricate pattern, through the singing threads of which the purplish-grey rock could be dimly seen. The series above Glacier Point was still more complicated in structure, displaying every form that one would imagine water might be dashed and combed and woven into. Those on the north wall between Washington Column and the Royal Arch Fall were so nearly related that they formed an almost continuous sheet, and these again were but slightly separated from those about Indian Canyon. The group about the Three Brothers and El Capitan, owing to the topography and' cleavage of the cliffs back of them, were more broken and irregular. The Tissiack cascades were comparatively small, yet sufficient to give that noblest of mountain rocks a glorious voice. In the midst of all this rejoicing the Yosemite Fall was scarce heard until about three o'clock in the afternoon. Then I was startled by a sudden thundering crash as if a rock avalanche had come to join the chorus. This was the flood wave of Yosemite Creek, which had just arrived, delayed by the distance it had to travel, and by the choking snows of its widespread fountains. Now, with volume tenfold increased beyond its springtime fullness, it took its place as leader of the glorious choir. No idle, silent water was to be found anywhere; all sang loud or low in divine harmony.

And the winds sang too, playing on every pine, leaf, and rock, surging against the huge brows and domes and outstanding battlements, deflected hither and thither, broken into a thousand cascading currents that whirled in the hollow. And these again, reacting on the clouds, eroded immense cavernous spaces in their grey depths, sweeping forward the resulting detritus in ragged trains like the moraines of glaciers. These cloud movements in turn published the work of the winds, giving them a visible body, and enabling us to trace their wild career. As if endowed with independent motion, some detached cloud would rise hastily upon some errand to the very top of the wall in a single effort, examining the faces of the cliffs, and then perhaps as suddenly descend to sweep imposingly along the meadows, trailing draggled fringes through the pines, fondling their waving spires with infinite gentleness, or, gliding behind a grove or a single tree, bring it into striking relief, while all bowed and waved in solemn rhythm. Sometimes as they drooped and condensed, or thinned to, misty gauze, half the valley would be veiled at once, leaving here and there some lofty headland cut off from all visible connection with the walls, looming alone, dim, spectral, as if belonging to the sky – visitors, like the new falls, come to take part in the festival. Thus for two days and nights in measureless extravagance the storm went on, and mostly without spectators, at least of a terrestrial kind. I saw nobody out – bird, bear, squirrel, or man.

Tourists had vanished months before, and the hotel people and labourers were out of sight, careful about getting cold and wet, and satisfied with views from doors and windows. The bears, I suppose, were in their boulder dens in the canyons, the squirrels in their knot-hole nests, the grouse in close fir groves, and the small singers in the chaparral. Strange to say, I did not see even the water-ousel, though he must have greatly enjoyed the storm.

This was the most sublime waterfall flood I ever saw – clouds, winds, rocks, waters, throbbing together as one. And then to contemplate what was going on simultaneously with all this in other mountain temples: the Big Tuolumne Canyon – how the white waters were singing there, and the winds, and how the clouds were marching. In Hetch Hetchy Valley also, and the great Kings River Yosemite, and in all the other canyons and valleys of the Sierra from Shasta to the southernmost fountains of the Kern – five hundred miles of flooded waterfalls chanting together. What a psalm was that!

II

Features of the Proposed Yosemite National Park

THE UPPER Tuolumne Valley is the widest, smoothest, most serenely spacious, and in every way the most delightful summer pleasure park in all the high Sierra. And since it is connected with Yosemite by two good trails, and with the levels of civilization by a broad, well graded carriage-road that passes between Yosemite and Mount Hoffman, it is also the most accessible. It lies in the heart of the high Sierra at a height of from 8,500 to 9,000 feet above the level of the sea, at a distance of less than ten miles from the northeastern boundary of the Yosemite reservation. It is bounded on the southwest by the grey, jagged, picturesque Cathedral range, which extends in a southeasterly direction from Cathedral Peak to Mount Lyell and Mount Ritter, the culminating peaks of the grand mass of icy mountains that form the "crown of the Sierra"; on the northeast, by a similar range or spur, the highest peak of which is Mount Conness; on the east, by the smooth, majestic masses of Mount Dana, Mount Gibbs, Mount Ord, and others, nameless as yet, on the axis of the main range; and on the west by a heaving, billowy mass of glacier-polished rocks, over which the towering masses of Mount Hoffman are seen. Down through the open sunny levels of the valley flows the bright Tuolumne River, fresh from many a glacial fountain in the wild recesses of the peaks, the highest of which are the glaciers that lie on the north sides of Mount Lyell and Mount McClure.

Along the river is a series of beautiful glacier meadows stretching, with but little interruption, from the lower end of the valley to its head, a distance of about twelve miles. These form charming sauntering grounds from which the glorious mountains may be enjoyed as they look down in divine serenity over the majestic swaths of forest that clothe their bases. Narrow strips of pine woods cross the meadow-carpet from side to side, and it is somewhat roughened here and there by groves, moraine boulders, and dead trees brought down from the heights by avalanches; but for miles and miles it is so smooth and level that a hundred horsemen may ride abreast over it.

The main lower portion of the meadow is about four miles long and from a quarter to half a mile wide; but the width of the valley is, on an average, about eight miles. Tracing the river we find that it forks a mile above the Soda Springs, which are situated on the north bank opposite the point where the Cathedral trail comes in – the main fork turning southward to Mount Lyell, the other eastward to Mount Dana and Mount Gibbs. Along both forks strips of meadow extend almost to their heads. The most beautiful portions of the meadows are spread over lake basins, which have been filled up by deposits from the river. A few of these river-lakes still exist, but they are now shallow and are rapidly approaching extinction. The sod in most places is exceedingly fine and silky and free from rough weeds and bushes; while charming flowers abound, especially gentians, dwarf daisies, ivesias, and the pink bells of dwarf vaccinium. On the banks of the river and its tributaries Cassiope and Bryanthus may be found where the sod curls over in bosses, and about piles of boulders. The principal grass of these meadows is a delicate Calamagrostis with very slender leaves, and when it is in flower the ground seems to be covered with a faint purple mist, the stems of the spikelets being so fine that they are almost invisible, and offer no appreciable resistance in walking through them. Along the edges of the meadows beneath the pines and throughout the greater part of the valley tall ribbon-leaved grasses grow in abundance, chiefly Bromus, Triticum, and Agrostis.

In October the nights are frosty, and then the meadows at sunrise, when every leaf is laden with crystals, are a fine sight. The days are warm and calm, and bees and butterflies continue to waver and hum about the late blooming flowers until the coming of the snow, usually late in November. Storm then follows storm in close succession, burying the meadows to a depth of from ten to twenty feet, while magnificent avalanches descend through the forests from the laden heights, depositing huge piles of snow mixed with uprooted trees and boulders. In the open sunshine the snow lasts until June, but the new season's vegetation is not generally in bloom until late in July. Perhaps the best time to visit this valley is in August. The snow is then melted from the woods, and the meadows are dry and warm, while the weather is mostly sunshine, reviving and exhilarating in quality; and the few clouds that rise and the showers they yield are only enough for freshness, fragrance, and beauty.

The groves about the Soda Springs are favourite camping-grounds on account of the pleasant tasting, ice-cold water of the springs, charged with carbonic acid, and because of the fine views of the mountains across the meadow – the Glacier Monument, Cathedral Peak, Cathedral Spires, Unicorn Peak, and their many nameless companions rising in grand beauty above a noble swath of forest that is growing on the left lateral moraine of the ancient Tuolumne Glacier, which, broad and deep and far reaching, exerted vast influence on the scenery of this portion of the Sierra. But there are fine camping-grounds all along the meadows, and one may move from grove to grove every day all summer enjoying a fresh home and finding enough to satisfy every roving desire for change.

There are four capital excursions to be made from here – to the summits of Mounts Dana and Lyell; to Mono Lake and the volcanoes; through Bloody Canyon; and to the great Tuolumne Canyon as far as the foot of the main cascades. All of these are glorious, and sure to be crowded with joyful and exciting experiences; but perhaps none of them will be remembered with keener delight than the days spent in sauntering in the broad velvet lawns by the river, sharing the pure air and light with the trees and mountains, and gaining something of the peace of nature in the majestic solitude.

The excursion to the top of Mount Dana is a very easy one; for though the mountain is 13,000 feet high, the ascent from the west side is so gentle and smooth that one may ride a mule to the very summit. Across many a busy stream, from meadow to meadow, lies your flowery way, the views all sublime; and they are seldom hidden by irregular foregrounds. As you gradually ascend, new mountains come into sight, enriching the landscape; peak rising above peak with its individual architecture, and its masses of fountain snow in endless variety of position and light and shade. Now your attention is turned to the moraines sweeping in beautiful curves from the hollows and canyons of the mountains, regular in form as railroad embankments, or to the glossy waves and pavements of granite rising here and there from the flowery sod, polished a thousand years ago and still shining. Towards the base of the mountain you note the dwarfing of the trees, until at a height of about 11,000 feet you find patches of the tough white-barked pine pressed so flat by the ten or twenty feet of snow piled upon them every winter for centuries that you may walk over them as if walking on a shaggy rug. And, if curious about such things, you may discover specimens of this hardy mountaineer of a tree, not more than four feet high and about as many inches in diameter at the ground, that are from two hundred to four hundred years old, and are still holding on bravely to life, making the most of their short summers, shaking their tasselled needles in the breeze right cheerily, drinking the thin sunshine, and maturing their fine purple cones as if they meant to live forever. The general view from the summit is one of the most extensive and sublime to be found in all the range. To the eastward you gaze far out over the hot desert plains and mountains of the "Great Basin," range beyond range extending with soft outlines blue and purple in the distance. More than six thousand feet below you lies Lake Mono, overshadowed by the mountain on which you stand. It is ten miles in diameter from north to south and fourteen from east to west, but appears nearly circular, lying bare in the treeless desert like a disk of burnished metal, though at times it is swept by storm-foam. To the south of the lake there is a range of pale-grey volcanoes, now extinct, and though the highest of them rise nearly two thousand feet above the lake, you can look down into their well-defined circular, cup-like craters, from which, a comparatively short time ago, ashes and cinders were showered over the surrounding plains and glacier-laden mountains.

To the westward the landscape is made up of grey glaciated rocks and ridges, separated by a labyrinth of canyons and darkened with lines and broad fields of forest, while small lakes and meadows dot the foreground. Northward and southward the jagged peaks and towers that are marshalled along the axis of the range are seen in all their glory, crowded together in some places like trees in groves, making landscapes of wild, extravagant, bewildering magnificence, yet calm and silent as the scenery of the sky.

Some eight glaciers are in sight. One of these is the Dana Glacier on the northeast side of the mountain, lying at the foot of a precipice about a thousand feet high, with a lovely pale-green lake in the general basin a little below the glacier. This is one of the many small shrunken remnants of the vast glacial system of the Sierra that once filled all the hollows and valleys of the mountains and covered all the lower ridges below the immediate summit fountains, flowing to right and left away from the axis of the range, lavishly fed by the snows of the glacial period.

In the excursion to Mount Lyell the immediate base of the mountain is easily reached on horseback by following the meadows along the river. Turning to the southward above the forks of the river you enter the Lyell branch of the valley, which is narrow enough and deep enough to be called a canyon. It is about eight miles long and from 2,000 to 3,000 feet deep. The flat meadow bottom is from about 300 to 200 yards wide, with gently curved margins about 50 yards wide, from which rise the simple massive walls of grey granite at an angle of about thirty-three degrees, mostly timbered with a light growth of pine and streaked in many places with avalanche channels. Towards the upper end of the canyon the grand Sierra crown comes into sight, forming a sublime and finely balanced picture, framed by the massive canyon walls. In the foreground you have the purple meadow fringed with willows; in the middle distance, huge swelling bosses of granite that form the base of the general mass of the mountain, with fringing lines of dark woods marking the lower curves, but smoothly snow-clad except in the autumn.

13 The view south-east from Mt. Hoffmann, across Tenaya Lake, to Mt. Lyell and Mt. Ritter and their satellite peaks. *Photo: Terry Gifford*

14 (left) The Vernal Fall with the Merced in spate. *Photo: Jeff Reynolds*

15, 16 (right) Muir's home and study (inset) at Martinez, California. *Photos: Terry Gifford*

17 (below) Glaciated rock domes around Tenaya Lake seen from the road to Tuolumne. *Photo: Tom Prentice*

18, 19 (above and far right) The monumental Sequoias of Mariposa Grove.
Photos: Terry Gifford and Jeff Reynolds

20, 21 Knarled and wind-blasted conifers that eke out an existence on the rock slabs above Olmsted Point (right) on the Tioga Pass Road, and on the approach to Half Dome (left).
Photos: Tom Chatterley

and the Third Needle the prominent tops to the left. *Photo: Jeff Reynolds*

23 (below left) Above Mirror Lake on the Mount Whitney trail from Whitney Portal. *Photo: Tom Chatterley*

24 (below right) Looking east along the South Fork of Kings Canyon from near Yucca Point. *Photo: Jeff Reynolds*

25   Mount Shasta (4317m/14,162ft). *Photo: Jeff Reynolds*

26   An aerial view down Johns Hopkins Inlet in Glacier Bay – looking west to the peaks of the Fairweather Range. *Photo: Jim Wickwire*

There is a good camping-ground on the east side of the river about a mile above. A fine cascade comes down over the canyon wall in telling style and makes fine camp music. At one place near the top careful climbing is necessary, but it is not so dangerous or difficult as to deter any climber of ordinary strength and skill, while the views from the summit are glorious. To the northward are Mammoth Mountain, Mounts Gibbs, Dana, Warren, Conness, and many others, unnumbered and unnamed; to the southeast the indescribably wild and jagged range of Mount Ritter and the Minarets; southwestward stretches the dividing ridge between the North Fork of the San Joaquin and the Merced, uniting with the Obelisk or Merced group of peaks that form the main fountains of the Illilouette branch of the Merced River; and to the northwestward extends the Cathedral spur. All these spurs, like distinct ranges, meet at your feet. Therefore you look over them mostly in the direction of their extension, and their peaks seem to be massed and crowded together in bewildering combinations; while immense amphitheatres, canyons and subordinate masses, with their wealth of lakes, glaciers, and snow-fields, maze and cluster between them. In making the ascent in June or October the glacier is easily crossed, for then its snow mantle is smooth or mostly melted off. But in midsummer the climbing is exceedingly tedious, because the snow is then weathered into curious and beautiful blades, sharp and slender, and set on edge in a leaning position. They lean towards the head of the glacier, and extend across from side to side in regular order in a direction at right angles to the direction of greatest declivity, the distance between the crests being about two or three feet, and the depth of the troughs between them about three feet. No more interesting problem is ever presented to the mountaineer than a walk over a glacier thus sculptured and adorned.

The Lyell Glacier is about a mile wide and less than a mile long, but presents, nevertheless, all the more characteristic features of large, river-like glaciers – moraines, earth-bands, blue-veins, crevasses, etc., while the streams that issue from it are turbid with rock-mud, showing its grinding action on its bed. And it is all the more interesting since it is the highest and most enduring remnant of the great Tuolumne Glacier, whose traces are still distinct fifty miles away, and whose influence on the landscape was so profound. The McClure Glacier, once a tributary of the Lyell, is much smaller. Eighteen years ago I set a series of stakes in it to determine its rate of motion, which towards the end of summer, in the middle of the glacier, I found to be a little over an inch in twenty-four hours.

The trip to Mono from the Soda Springs can be made in a day, but Bloody Canyon will be found rough for animals. The scenery of the canyon, however, is wild and rich, and many days may profitably be spent around the shores of the lake and out on its islands and about the volcanoes.

In making the trip down the Big Tuolumne Canyon animals may be led as far as a small, grassy, forested lake basin that lies below the crossing of hunter, in 1850, a year before the discovery of the great Merced Yosemite. It lies in a northwesterly direction from Yosemite, at a distance of about twenty miles, and is easily accessible to mounted travellers by a trail that leaves the Big Oak Flat road at Bronson's Meadows, a few miles below Crane Flat. But by far the best way to it for those who have useful limbs is across the divide direct from Yosemite. Leaving the valley by Indian Canyon or Fall Canyon, you cross the dome-paved basin of Yosemite Creek, then bear to the left around the head fountains of the South Fork of the Tuolumne to the summit of the Big Tuolumne Canyon, a few miles above the head of Hetch Hetchy. Here you will find a glorious view. Immediately beneath you, at a depth of more than 4,000 feet, you see a beautiful ribbon of level ground, with a silver thread in the middle of it, and green or yellow according to the time of year. That ribbon is a strip of meadow, and the silver thread is the main Tuolumne River. The opposite wall of the canyon rises in precipices, steep and angular, or with rounded brows like those of Yosemite, and from this wall as a base extends a fine wilderness of mountains, rising dome above dome, ridge above ridge, to a group of snowy peaks on the summit of the range. Of all this sublime congregation of mountains Castle Peak is king: robed with snow and light, dipping unnumbered points and spires into the thin blue sky, it maintains amid noble companions a perfect and commanding individuality.

You will not encounter much difficulty in getting down into the canyon, for bear trails may readily be found leading from the upper feeding-grounds to the berry gardens and acorn orchards of Hetch Hetchy, and when you reach the river you have only to saunter by its side a mile or two down the canyon before you find yourself in the open valley. Looking about you, you cannot fail to discover that you are in a Yosemite valley. As the Merced flows through Yosemite, so does the Tuolumne through Hetch Hetchy. The bottom of Yosemite is about 4,000 feet above sea level, the bottom of Hetch Hetchy is about 3,000 feet, and in both, the walls are of grey granite and rise abruptly in precipices from a level bottom, with but little debris along their bases. Furthermore it was a home and stronghold of the Tuolumne Indians, as Ahwahne was of the grizzlies. Standing boldly forward from the south wall near the lower end of the valley is the rock Kolana, the outermost of a picturesque group corresponding to the Cathedral Rocks of Yosemite, and about the same height. Facing Kolana on the north side of the valley is a rock about 1,800 feet in height, which presents a bare, sheer front like El Capitan, and over its massive brow flows a stream that makes the most graceful fall I have ever seen. Its Indian name is Tu ee-u-la-la, and no other, so far as I have heard, has yet been given it. From the brow of the cliff it makes a free descent of a thousand feet and then breaks up into a ragged, foaming web of cascades among the boulders of an earthquake talus. Towards the end of summer it vanishes, because its head streams do not reach back to the lasting snows of the summits of the range, but in May and June it is the Virginia Creek trail. And from this point any one accustomed to walk on earthquake boulders, carpeted with canyon chaparral, can easily go down the canyon as far as the big cascades and return to camp in one day. Many, however, are not able to do this, and it is far better to go leisurely, prepared to camp anywhere, and enjoy the marvellous grandeur of the place.

The canyon begins near the lower end of the meadows and extends to the Hetch Hetchy Valley, a distance of about eighteen miles, though it will seem much longer to any one who scrambles through it. It is from 1,200 to about 5,000 feet deep, and is comparatively narrow, but there are several fine, roomy, park-like openings in it, and throughout its whole extent Yosemite features are displayed on a grand scale – domes, El Capitan rocks, gables, Sentinels, Royal Arches, glacier points, Cathedral Spires, etc. There is even a Half Dome among its wealth of rock forms, though less sublime and beautiful than the Yosemite Half Dome. It also contains falls and cascades innumerable. The sheer falls, except when the snow is melting in early spring are quite small in volume as compared with those of Yosemite and Hetch Hetchy; but many of them are very beautiful, and in any other country would be regarded as great wonders. But it is the cascades or sloping falls on the main river that are the crowning glory of the canyon, and these in volume, extent, and variety surpass those of any other canyon in the Sierra. The most showy and interesting of the cascades are mostly in the upper part of the canyon, above the point where Cathedral Creek and Hoffman Creek enter. For miles the river is one wild, exulting on-rushing mass of snowy purple bloom, spreading over glacial waves of granite without any definite channel, and through avalanche taluses, gliding in silver plumes; dashing and foaming through huge boulder-dams, leaping high into the air in glorious wheel-like whirls, tossing from side to side, doubling, glinting, singing in glorious exuberance of mountain energy.

Everyone who is anything of a mountaineer should go on through the entire length of the canyon, coming out by Hetch Hetchy. There is not a dull step all the way. With wide variations it is a Yosemite Valley from end to end.

THE HETCH HETCHY VALLEY

Most people who visit Yosemite are apt to regard it as an exceptional creation, the only valley of its kind in the world. But nothing in Nature stands alone. She is not so poor as to have only one of anything. The explorer in the Sierra and elsewhere finds many Yosemites, that differ not more than one tree differs from another of the same species. They occupy the same relative positions on the mountain flanks, were formed by the same forces in the same kind of granite, and have similar sculpture, waterfalls, and vegetation. The Hetch Hetchy Valley has long been known as the Tuolumne Yosemite. It is said to have been discovered by Joseph Screech, a indescribably lovely. The only fall that I know with which it may fairly be compared is the Bridal Veil, but it excels even that fall in peaceful, floating, swaying gracefulness. For when we attentively observe the Bridal Veil, even towards the middle of summer when its waters begin to fail, we may discover, when the winds blow aside the outer folds of spray, dense comet-shaped masses shooting through the air with terrible energy; but from the top of the cliff, where the Hetch Hetchy veil first floats free, all the way to the bottom it is in perfect repose. Again, the Bridal Veil is in a shadow-haunted nook inaccessible to the main wind currents of the valley, and has to depend for many of its gestures on irregular, teasing side currents and whirls, while Tu-ee-u-la-la, being fully exposed on the open cliff, is sun-drenched all day, and is ever ready to yield graceful compliance to every wind that blows. Most people unacquainted with the behaviour of mountain streams fancy that when they escape the bounds of their rocky channels and launch into the air they at once lose all self-control and tumble in confusion. On the contrary, on no part of their travels do they manifest more calm self-possession. Imagine yourself in Hetch Hetchy. It is a sunny day in June, the pines sway dreamily, and you are shoulder deep in grass and flowers. Looking across the valley through beautiful open groves you see a bare granite wall 1,800 feet high rising abruptly out of the green and yellow vegetation and glowing with sunshine, and in front of it the fall, waving like a downy scarf, silver bright, burning with white sun-fire in every fibre. In coming forward to the edge of the tremendous precipice and taking flight a little hasty eagerness appears, but this is speedily hushed in divine repose. Now observe the marvellous distinctness and delicacy of the various kinds of sun-filled tissue into which the waters are woven. They fly and float and drowse down the face of that grand grey rock in so leisurely and unconfused a manner that you may examine their texture and pattern as you would a piece of embroidery held in the hand. It is a flood of singing air, water and sunlight woven into cloth that spirits might wear.

The great Hetch Hetchy Fall, called Wapama by the Tuolumnes, is on the same side of the valley as the Veil, and so near it that both may be seen in one view. It is about 1,800 feet in height, and seems to be nearly vertical when one is standing in front of it, though it is considerably inclined. Its location is similar to that of the Yosemite Fall, but the volume of water is much greater. No two falls could be more unlike than Wapama and Tu-ee-u-la-la, the one thundering and beating in a shadowy gorge, the other chanting in deep, low tones, and with no other shadows about it than those of its own waters, pale-grey mostly, and violet and pink delicately graded. One whispers, "He dwells in peace," the other is the thunder of his chariot wheels in power. This noble pair are the main falls of the valley, though there are many small ones essential to the perfection of the general harmony.

The wall above Wapáma corresponds, both in outlines and in details of sculpture, with the same relative portion of the Yosemite wall. Near the

Yosemite Fall the cliff has two conspicuous benches extending in a horizontal direction 500 and 1,500 feet above the valley. Two benches similarly situated, and timbered in the same way, occur on the same relative position on the Hetch Hetchy wall, and on no other portion. The upper end of Yosemite is closed by the great Half Dome, and the upper end of Hetch Hetchy is closed in the same way by a mountain rock. Both occupy angles formed by the confluence of two large glaciers that have long since vanished. In front of this head rock the river forks like the Merced in Yosemite. The right fork as you ascend is the main Tuolumne, which takes its rise in a glacier on the north side of Mount Lyell and flows through the Big Canyon. I have not traced the left fork to its highest source, but, judging from the general trend of the ridges, it must be near Castle Peak. Upon this left or North Fork there is a remarkably interesting series of cascades, five in number, ranged along a picturesque gorge, on the edges of which we may saunter safely and gain fine views of the dancing spray below. The first is a wide-spreading fan of white, crystal-covered water, half leaping half sliding over a steep polished pavement, at the foot of which it rests and sets forth clear and shining on its final flow to the main river. A short distance above the head of this cascade you discover the second, which is as impressively wild and beautiful as the first, and makes you sing with it as though you were a part of it. It is framed in deep rock walls that are coloured yellow and red with lichens, and fringed on the jagged edges by live-oaks and sabine pines, and at the bottom in damp nooks you may see ferns, lilies, and azaleas.

Three or four hundred yards higher you come to the third of the choir, the largest of the five. It is formed of three smaller ones inseparably combined, which sing divinely, and make spray of the best quality for rainbows. A short distance beyond this the gorge comes to an end, and the bare stream, without any definite channel, spreads out in a thin, silvery sheet about 150 feet wide. Its waters are, throughout almost its whole extent, drawn out in overlapping folds of lace, thick sown with diamond jets and sparks that give an exceedingly rich appearance. Still advancing, you hear a deep muffled booming, and you push eagerly on through flowery thickets until the last of the five appears through the foliage. The precipice down which it thunders is fretted with projecting knobs, forming polished keys upon which the wild waters play.

The bottom of the valley is divided by a low, glacier-polished bar of granite, the lower portion being mostly meadow land, the upper dry and sandy, and planted with fine Kellogg oaks, which frequently attain a diameter of six or seven feet. On the talus slopes the pines give place to the mountain live-oak, which forms the shadiest groves in the valley and the greatest in extent. Their glossy foliage, warm yellow green and closely pressed, makes a kind of ceiling, supported by bare grey trunks and branches gnarled and picturesque. A few specimens of the sugar pine and tamarack pine are found in the valley, also the two silver firs. The Douglas spruce and the libocedrus

attain noble dimensions in certain favourable spots, and a few specimens of
the interesting *Torreya Californica* may be found on the south side. The
briar-rose occurs in large patches, with tall, spiky mints and arching grasses.
On the meadows lilies, larkspurs, and lupines of several species are abundant,
and in some places reach above one's head. Rockferns of rare beauty fringe
and rosette the walls from top to bottom – *Pellœa densa, P. mucronata* and
P. Bridgesii, Cheilanthes gracillima, Allosorus, etc. Adiantum pedatum
occurs in a few mossy corners that get spray from the falls. *Woodwardia
radicans* and *Asplenium felix-foemina* are the tallest ferns of the valley –
six feet high, some of them. The whole valley was a charming garden when
I last saw it, and the huts of the Indians and a lone cabin were the only
improvements.

As will be seen by the map, I have thus briefly touched upon a number of
the chief features of a region which it is proposed to reserve out of the
public domain for the use and recreation of the people. A bill has already
been introduced in Congress by Mr. Vandever creating a national park
about the reservation which the State now holds in trust for the people. It is
very desirable that the new reservation should at least extend to the limits
indicated by the map, and the bill cannot too quickly become a law. Unless
reserved or protected the whole region will soon or late be devastated by
lumbermen and sheepmen, and so of course be made unfit for use as a
pleasure ground. Already it is with great difficulty that campers, even in the
most remote parts of the proposed reservation and in those difficult of
access, can find grass enough to keep their animals from starving; the
ground is already being gnawed and trampled into a desert condition, and
when the region shall be stripped of its forests the ruin will be complete.
Even the Yosemite will then suffer in the disturbance effected on the watershed, the clear streams becoming muddy and much less regular in their
flow. It is also devoutly to be hoped that the Hetch Hetchy will escape such
ravages of man as one sees in Yosemite. Axe and plow, hogs and horses,
have long been and are still busy in Yosemite's gardens and groves. All that
is accessible and destructible is being rapidly destroyed – more rapidly than
in any other Yosemite in the Sierra, though this is the only one that is under
the special protection of the Government. And by far the greater part of this
destruction of the fineness of wildness is of a kind that can claim no right
relationship with that which necessarily follows use.

THE DISCOVERY OF GLACIER BAY

incorporating

ALASKA DAYS WITH JOHN MUIR

STICKEEN

NOTES ON THE PACIFIC COAST GLACIERS

The Discovery of Glacier Bay

incorporating

ALASKA DAYS WITH JOHN MUIR
by Samuel Hall Young

STICKEEN

NOTES ON THE
PACIFIC COAST GLACIERS

First published by Fleming H. Revell Company,
(New York, Chicago, London and Edinburgh 1915)

CONTENTS

Note: Muir's original account 'The Discovery of Glacier Bay (1879)', which might naturally form an introduction to this section, is reproduced, with a few minor changes, in *Travels in Alaska* (see *John Muir – The Eight Wilderness-Discovery Books*, pp. 785–973).

ALASKA DAYS WITH JOHN MUIR

The blue-veined glacier, cold of heart and pale,
Warmed, at his gaze, to amethystene blush,
And murmured deep, fond undertones of love.

Samuel Hall Young

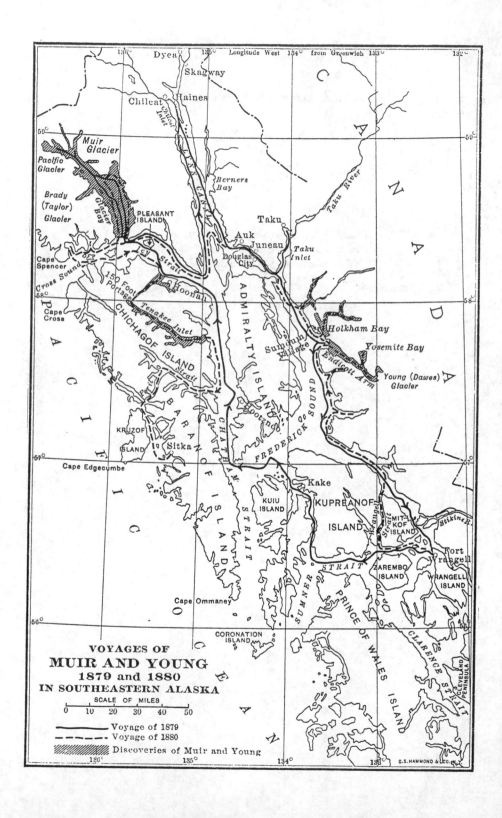

Dyea
Skagway
Chilcat Haines
Chilcat Inlet
Muir Glacier
Pacific Glacier
Berners Bay
Brady (Taylor) Glacier
Glacier Bay
PLEASANT ISLAND
Taku
Taku River
Auk
Juneau
Taku Inlet
Cape Spencer
Cross Sound
150 Foot Portage
Ice Strait
Hoonah
Douglas City
Cape Cross
Tenakee Inlet
CHICHAGOF ISLAND
ADMIRALTY ISLAND
Holkham Bay
Yosemite Bay
Sumdum
Endicott Arm
Young (Dawes) Glacier
Peril Strait
BARANOF
KRUZOF ISLAND
Sitka
Hootsnahoo
CHATHAM STRAIT
FREDERICK SOUND
Cape Edgecumbe
ISLAND
Kake
KUIU ISLAND
KUPREANOF ISLAND
Wrangell
MIT-KOF ISLAND
Stikine R.
Fort Wrangell
Cape Ommaney
SUMNER STRAIT
ZAREMBO ISLAND
WRANGELL ISLAND
CORONATION ISLAND
PRINCE OF WALES ISLAND
CLARENCE STR.
CLEVELAND PENINSULA

PACIFIC OCEAN

C A N A D A

Longitude West from Greenwich

VOYAGES OF
MUIR AND YOUNG
1879 and 1880
IN SOUTHEASTERN ALASKA

SCALE OF MILES
0 10 20 30 40 50

——————— Voyage of 1879
– – – – – – Voyage of 1880
▨▨▨▨ Discoveries of Muir and Young

C.S. HAMMOND & CO.

I

Alaska Days with John Muir
by Samuel Hall Young

CONTENTS

CHAPTER ONE

The Mountain

IN THE SUMMER of 1879 I was stationed at Fort Wrangell in southeastern Alaska, whence I had come the year before, a green young student fresh from college and seminary – very green and very fresh – to do what I could towards establishing the white man's civilization among the Thlinget Indians. I had very many things to learn and many more to unlearn.

Thither came by the monthly mail steamboat in July to aid and counsel me in my work three men of national reputation – Dr. Henry Kendall of New York; Dr. Aaron L. Lindsley of Portland, Oregon, and Dr. Sheldon Jackson of Denver and the West. Their wives accompanied them and they were to spend a month with us.

Standing a little apart from them as the steamboat drew to the dock, his peering blue eyes already eagerly scanning the islands and mountains, was a lean, sinewy man of forty, with waving, reddish-brown hair and beard, and shoulders slightly stooped. He wore a Scotch cap and a long, grey tweed ulster, which I have always since associated with him, and which seemed the same garment, unsoiled and unchanged, that he wore later on his northern trips. He was introduced as Professor Muir, the Naturalist. A hearty grip of the hand, and we seemed to coalesce at once in a friendship which, to me at least, has been one of the very best things I have known in a life full of blessings. From the first he was the strongest and most attractive of these four fine personalities to me, and I began to recognise him as my Master who was to lead me into enchanting regions of beauty and mystery, which without his aid must forever have remained unseen by the eyes of my soul. I sat at his feet; and at the feet of his spirit I still sit, a student, absorbed, surrendered, as this "priest of Nature's inmost shrine" unfolds to me the secrets of his "mountains of God."

Minor excursions culminated in the chartering of the little steamer Cassiar, on which our party, augmented by two or three friends, steamed between the tremendous glaciers and through the columned canyons of the swift Stickeen River through the narrow strip of Alaska's cup-handle to Glenora, in British Columbia, one hundred and fifty miles from the river's mouth. Our captain was Nat. Lane, a grandson of the famous Senator Joseph Lane of Oregon. Stocky, broad-shouldered, muscular, given somewhat to strange oaths and strong liquids, and eying askance our group as we struck the bargain, he was withal a genial, good-natured man, and a splendid river pilot.

Dropping down from Telegraph Creek (so named because it was a principal station of the great projected trans-American and trans-Siberian line of the Western Union, that bubble pricked by Cyrus Field's cable), we tied up at Glenora about noon of a cloudless day.

"Amuse yourselves," said Captain Lane at lunch. "Here we stay till two o'clock to-morrow morning. This gale, blowing from the sea, makes safe steering through the canyon impossible, unless we take the morning's calm."

I saw Muir's eyes light up with a peculiar meaning as he glanced quickly at me across the table. He knew the leading strings I was in; how those well-meaning D.D.s and their motherly wives thought they had a special mission to suppress all my self-destructive proclivities toward dangerous adventure, and especially to protect me from "that wild Muir" and his hare-brained schemes of mountain climbing.

"Where is it?" I asked, as we met behind the pilot house a moment later.

He pointed to a little group of jagged peaks rising right up from where we stood – a pulpit in the centre of a vast rotunda of magnificent mountains. "One of the finest viewpoints in the world," he said.

"How far to the highest point?"

"About ten miles."

"How high?"

"Seven or eight thousand feet."

That was enough. I caught the D.D.s with guile. There were Stickeen Indians there catching salmon, and among them Chief Shakes, who our interpreter said was "The youngest but the headest Chief of all." Last night's palaver had whetted the appetites of both sides for more. On the part of the Indians, a talk with these "Great White Chiefs from Washington" offered unlimited possibilities for material favour; and to the good divines the "simple faith and childlike docility" of these children of the forest were a constant delight. And then how well their high-flown compliments and flowery metaphors would sound in article and speech to the wondering East! So I sent Stickeen Johnny, the interpreter, to call the natives to another *hyou wawa* (big talk) and, note-book in hand, the doctors "went gayly to the fray." I set the speeches a-going, and then slipped out to join the impatient Muir.

"Take off your coat," he commanded, "and here's your supper."

Pocketing two hardtacks apiece we were off, keeping in shelter of house and bush till out of sight of the council-house and the flower picking ladies. Then we broke out. What a matchless climate! What sweet, lung-filling air! Sunshine that had no weakness in it – as if we were springing plants. Our sinews like steel springs, muscles like India rubber, feet soled with iron to grip the rocks. Ten miles? Eight thousand feet? Why, I felt equal to forty miles and the Matterhorn!

"Eh, mon!" said Muir, lapsing into the broad Scotch he was so fond of using when enjoying himself, "ye'll see the sicht o' yer life the day. Ye'll get that'll be o' mair use till ye than a' the gowd o' Cassiar."

From the first, it was a hard climb. Fallen timber at the mountain's foot covered with thick brush swallowed us up and plucked us back. Beyond, on the steeper slopes, grew dwarf evergreens, five or six feet high – the same fir that towers a hundred feet with a diameter of three or four on the river banks, but here stunted by icy mountain winds. The curious blasting of the branches on the side next to the mountain gave them the appearance of long-armed, humpbacked, hairy gnomes, bristling with anger, stretching forbidding arms downwards to bar our passage to their sacred heights. Sometimes an inviting vista through the branches would lure us in, when it would narrow, and at its upper angle we would find a solid phalanx of these grumpy dwarfs. Then we had to attack boldly, scrambling over the obstinate, elastic arms and against the clusters of stiff needles, till we gained the upper side and found another green slope.

Muir led, of course, picking with sure instinct the easiest way. Three hours of steady work brought us suddenly beyond the timber-line, and the real joy of the day began. Nowhere else have I seen anything approaching the luxuriance and variety of delicate blossoms shown by these high, mountain pastures of the North. "You scarce could see the grass for flowers." Everything that was marvellous in form, fair in colour, or sweet in fragrance seemed to be represented there, from daisies and campanulas to Muir's favourite, the cassiope, with its exquisite little pink-white bells shaped like lilies-of-the-valley and its subtle perfume. Muir at once went wild when we reached this fairyland. From cluster to cluster of flowers he ran, falling on his knees, babbling in unknown tongues, prattling a curious mixture of scientific lingo and baby talk, worshipping his little blue-and-pink goddesses.

"Ah! my blue-eyed darlin', little did I think to see you here. How did you stray away from Shasta?"

"Well, well! Who'd 'a' thought that you'd have left that niche in the Merced mountains to come here!"

"And who might you be, now, with your wonder look? Is it possible that you can be (two Latin polysyllables)? You're lost, my dear; you belong in Tennessee."

"Ah! I thought I'd find you, my homely little sweetheart," and so on unceasingly.

So absorbed was he in this amatory botany that he seemed to forget my existence. While I, as glad as he, tagged along, running up and down with him, asking now and then a question, learning something of plant life, but far more of that spiritual insight into Nature's lore which is granted only to those who love and woo her in her great outdoor palaces. But how I anathematised my short-sighted foolishness for having as a student at old Wooster shirked botany for the "more important" studies of language and metaphysics. For here was a man whose natural science had a thorough technical basis, while the super-structure was built of "lively stones," and was itself a living temple of love!

With all his boyish enthusiasm, Muir was a most painstaking student; and any unsolved question lay upon his mind like a personal grievance until it was settled to his full understanding. One plant after another, with its sand-covered roots, went into his pockets, his handkerchief and the "full" of his shirt, until he was bulbing and sprouting all over, and could carry no more. He was taking them to the boat to analyze and compare at leisure. Then he began to requisition my receptacles. I stood it while he stuffed my pockets, but rebelled when he tried to poke the prickly, scratchy things inside my shirt. I had not yet attained that sublime indifference to physical comfort, that Nirvana of passivity, that Muir had found.

Hours had passed in this entrancing work and we were progressing upwards but slowly. We were on the southeastern slope of the mountain, and the sun was still staring at us from a cloudless sky. Suddenly we were in the shadow as we worked around a spur of rock. Muir looked up, startled. Then he jammed home his last handful of plants, and hastened up to where I stood.

"Man!" he said, "I was forgetting. We'll have to hurry now or we'll miss it, we'll miss it."

"Miss what?" I asked.

"The jewel of the day," he answered; "the sight of the sunset from the top."

Then Muir began to *slide* up that mountain. I had been with mountain climbers before, but never one like him. A deer-lope over the smoother slopes, a sure instinct for the easiest way into a rocky fortress, an instant and unerring attack, a serpent-glide up the steep; eye, hand and foot all connected dynamically; with no appearance of weight to his body – as though he had Stockton's negative gravity machine strapped on his back.

Fifteen years of enthusiastic study among the Sierras had given him the same pre-eminence over the ordinary climber as the Big Horn of the Rockies shows over the Cotswold. It was only by exerting myself to the limit of my strength that I was able to keep near him. His example was at the same time my inspiration and despair. I longed for him to stop and rest, but would not have suggested it for the world. I would at least be game, and furnish no hint as to how tired I was, no matter how chokingly my heart thumped. Muir's spirit was in me, and my "chief end," just then, was to win that peak with him. The impending calamity of being beaten by the sun was not to be contemplated without horror. The loss of a fortune would be as nothing to that!

We were now beyond the flower garden of the gods, in a land of rocks and cliffs, with patches of short grass, caribou moss and lichens between. Along a narrowing arm of the mountain, a deep canyon flumed a rushing torrent of icy water from a small glacier on our right. Then came moraine matter, rounded pebbles and boulders, and beyond them the glacier. Once a giant, it is nothing but a baby now, but the ice is still blue and clear, and the crevasses many and deep. And that day it had to be crossed, which was a ticklish task. A misstep or slip might land us at once fairly into the heart of the glacier, there to be preserved in cold storage for the wonderment of future generations. But glaciers were Muir's special pets, his intimate companions, with whom he held sweet communion. Their voices were plain language to his ears, their work, as God's landscape gardeners, of the wisest and best that Nature could offer.

No Swiss guide was ever wiser in the habits of glaciers than Muir, or proved to be a better pilot across their deathly crevasses. Half a mile of careful walking and jumping and we were on the ground again, at the base of the great cliff of metamorphic slate that crowned the summit. Muir's aneroid barometer showed a height of about seven thousand feet, and the wall of rock towered threateningly above us, leaning out in places, a thousand feet or so above the glacier. But the earth-fires that had melted and heaved it, the ice mass that chiselled and shaped it, the wind and rain that corroded and crumbled it, had left plenty of bricks out of that battlement, had covered its face with knobs and horns, had ploughed ledges and cleaved fissures and fastened crags and pinnacles upon it, so that, while its surface was full of mantraps and blind ways, the human spider might still find some hold for his claws.

The shadows were dark upon us, but the lofty, icy peaks of the main range still lay bathed in the golden rays of the setting sun. There was no time to be lost. A quick glance to the right and left, and Muir, who had steered his course wisely across the glacier, attacked the cliff, simply saying, "We must climb cautiously here."

Now came the most wonderful display of his mountain-craft. Had I been alone at the feet of these crags I should have said, "it can't be done," and have turned back down the mountain. But Muir was my "control," as the Spiritists say, and I never thought of doing anything else but following him. He thought he could climb up there and that settled it. He would do what he thought he could. And such climbing! There was never an instant when both feet and hands were not in play, and often elbows, knees, thighs, upper arms, and even chin must grip and hold. Clambering up a steep slope, crawling under an overhanging rock, spreading out like a flying squirrel and edging along an inch wide projection while fingers clasped knobs above the head, bending about sharp angles, pulling up smooth rock faces by sheer strength of arm and chinning over the edge, leaping fissures, sliding flat around a dangerous rock-breast, testing crumbly spurs before risking his weight, always going up, up, no hesitation, no pause – that was Muir! My task was the lighter one; he did the head-work, I had but to imitate. The thin fragment of projecting slate that stood the weight of his one hundred and fifty pounds would surely sustain my hundred and thirty. As far as possible I did as he did, took his hand-holds, and stepped in his steps.

But I was handicapped in a way that Muir was ignorant of, and I would not tell him for fear of his veto upon my climbing. My legs were all right – hard and sinewy; my body light and supple, my wind good, my nerves steady (heights did not make me dizzy); but my arms – there lay the trouble. Ten years before I had been fond of breaking colts – till the colts broke me. On successive summers in West Virginia, two colts had fallen with me and dislocated first my left shoulder, then my right. Since that both arms had been out of joint more than once. My left was especially weak. It would not sustain my weight, and I had to favour it constantly. Now and again, as I pulled myself up some difficult reach I could feel the head of the humerus move from its socket.

Muir climbed so fast that his movements were almost like flying, legs and arms moving with perfect precision and unfailing judgment. I must keep close behind him or I would fail to see his points of vantage. But the pace was a killing one for me. As we neared the summit my strength began to fail, my breath to come in gasps, my muscles to twitch. The overwhelming fear of losing sight of my guide, of being left behind and failing to see that sunset, grew upon me, and I hurled myself blindly at every fresh obstacle, determined to keep up. At length we climbed upon a little shelf, a foot or two wide, that corkscrewed to the left. Here we paused a moment to take breath and look around us. We had ascended the cliff some nine hundred and fifty feet from the glacier, and were within forty or fifty feet of the top.

Among the much-prized gifts of this good world one of the very richest was given to me in that hour. It is securely locked in the safe of my memory and nobody can rob me of it – an imperishable treasure. Standing out on the rounded neck of the cliff and facing the southwest, we could see on three sides of us. The view was much the finest of all my experience. We seemed to stand on a high rostrum in the centre of the greatest amphitheatre in the world. The sky was cloudless, the level sun flooding all the landscape with golden light. From the base of the mountain on which we stood stretched the rolling upland. Striking boldly across our front was the deep valley of the Stickeen, a line of foliage, light green cottonwoods and darker alders, sprinkled with black fir and spruce, through which the river gleamed with a silvery sheen, now spreading wide among its islands, now foaming white through narrow canyons. Beyond, among the undulating hills, was a marvellous array of lakes. There must have been thirty or forty of them, from the pond of an acre to the wide sheet two or three miles across. The strangely elongated and rounded hills had the appearance of giants in bed, wrapped in many-coloured blankets, while the lakes were their deep, blue eyes, lashed with dark evergreens, gazing steadfastly heavenward. Look long at these recumbent forms and you will see the heaving of their breasts.

The whole landscape was alert, expectant of glory. Around this great camp of prostrate Cyclops there stood an unbroken semi-circle of mighty peaks in solemn grandeur, some hoary-headed, some with locks of brown, but all wearing white glacier collars. The taller peaks seemed almost sharp enough to be the helmets and spears of watchful sentinels. And the colours! Great stretches of crimson fireweed, acres and acres of them, smaller patches of dark blue lupins, and hills of shaded yellow, red, and brown, the many-shaded green of the woods, the amethyst and purple of the far horizon – who can tell it? We did not stand there more than two or three minutes, but the whole wonderful scene is deeply etched on the tablet of my memory, a photogravure never to be effaced.

CHAPTER TWO

The Rescue

MUIR WAS the first to awake from his trance. Like Schiller's king in *The Diver*, "Nothing could slake his wild thirst of desire."

"The sunset," he cried; "we must have the whole horizon."

Then he started running along the ledge like a mountain goat, working to get around the vertical cliff above us to find an ascent on the other side. He was soon out of sight, although I followed as fast as I could. I heard him shout something, but could not make out his words. I know now he was warning me of a dangerous place. Then I came to a sharp-cut fissure which lay cross my path – a gash in the rock, as if one of the Cyclops had struck with his axe. It sloped very steeply for some twelve feet below, opening on the face of the precipice above the glacier, and was filled to within about four feet of the surface with flat, slaty gravel. It was only four or five feet across, and I could easily have leaped it had I not been so tired. But a rock the size of my head projected from the slippery stream of gravel. In my haste to overtake Muir I did not stop to make sure this stone was part of the cliff, but stepped with springing force upon it to cross the fissure. Instantly the stone melted away beneath my feet, and I shot with it down towards the precipice. With my peril sharp upon me I cried out as I whirled on my face, and struck out both hands to grasp the rock on either side.

Falling forward hard, my hands struck the walls of the chasm, my arms were twisted behind me, and instantly both shoulders were dislocated. With my paralysed arms flopping helplessly above my head, I slid swiftly down the narrow chasm. Instinctively I flattened down on the sliding gravel, digging my chin and toes into it to check my descent; but not until my feet hung out over the edge of the cliff did I feel that I had stopped. Even then I dared not breathe or stir, so precarious was my hold on that treacherous shale. Every moment I seemed to be slipping inch by inch to the point when all would give way and I would go whirling down to the glacier.

After the first wild moment of panic when I felt myself falling, I do not remember any sense of fear. But I know what it is to have a thousand thoughts flash through the brain in a single instant – an anguished thought of my young wife at Wrangell, with her imminent motherhood; an indignant thought of the insurance companies that refused me policies on my life; a thought of wonder as to what would become of my poor flocks of Indians among the islands; recollections of events far and near in time, important and trivial; but each thought printed upon my memory by the instantaneous photography of deadly peril. I had no hope of escape at all. The gravel was rattling past me and piling up against my head. The jar of a little rock, and all would be over. The situation was too desperate for actual fear. Dull wonder as to how long I would be in the air, and the hope that death would be instant – that was all. Then came the wish that Muir would come before I fell, and take a message to my wife.

Suddenly I heard his voice right above me. "My God!" he cried. Then he added, "Grab that rock, man, just by your right hand."

I gurgled from my throat, not daring to inflate my lungs, "My arms are out."

There was a pause. Then his voice rang again, cheery, confident, unexcited, "Hold fast; I'm going to get you out of this. I can't get to you on this side; the rock is sheer. I'll have to leave you now and cross the rift high up and come down to you on the other side by which we came. Keep cool."

Then I heard him going away, whistling "The Blue Bells of Scotland," singing snatches of Scotch songs, calling to me, his voice now receding, as the rocks intervened, then sounding louder as he came out on the face of the cliff. But in me hope surged at full tide. I entertained no more thoughts of last messages. I did not see how he could possibly do it, but he was John Muir, and I had seen his wonderful rockwork. So I determined not to fall and made myself as flat and heavy as possible, not daring to twitch a muscle or wink an eyelid, for I still felt myself slipping, slipping down the greasy slate. And now a new peril threatened. A chill ran through me of cold and nervousness, and I slid an inch. I suppressed the growing shivers with all my will. I would keep perfectly quiet till Muir came back. The sickening pain in my shoulders increased till it was torture, and I could not ease it.

It seemed like hours, but it was really only about ten minutes before he got back to me. By that time I hung so far over the edge of the precipice that it seemed impossible that I could last another second.

Now I heard Muir's voice, low and steady, close to me, and it seemed a little below.

"Hold steady," he said. "I'll have to swing you out over the cliff."

Then I felt a careful hand on my back, fumbling with the waistband of my pants, my vest and shirt, gathering all in a firm grip. I could see only with one eye and that looked upon but a foot or two of gravel on the other side.

"Now!" he said, and I slid out of the cleft with a rattling shower of stones and gravel. My head swung down, my impotent arms dangling, and I stared straight at the glacier, a thousand feet below. Then my feet came against the cliff.

"Work downwards with your feet."

I obeyed. He drew me close to him by crooking his arm and as my head came up past his level he caught me by my collar with his teeth! My feet struck the little two-inch shelf on which he was standing, and I could see Muir, flattened against the face of the rock and facing it, his right hand stretched up and clasping a little spur, his left holding me with an iron grip, his head bent sideways, as my weight drew it. I felt as alert and cool as he.

"I've got to let go of you," he hissed through his clenched teeth. "I need both hands here. Climb upward with your feet."

How he did it, I know not. The miracle grows as I ponder it. The wall was almost perpendicular and smooth. My weight on his jaws dragged him outwards. And yet, holding me by his teeth as a panther her cub and clinging like a squirrel to a tree, he climbed with me straight up ten or twelve feet, with only the help of my iron-shod feet scrambling on the rock. It was utterly impossible, yet he did it!

When he landed me on the little shelf along which we had come, my nerve gave way and I trembled all over. I sank down exhausted, Muir only less tired, but supporting me.

The sun had set; the air was icy cold and we had no coats. We would soon chill through. Muir's task of rescue had only begun and no time was to be lost. In a minute he was up again, examining my shoulders. The right one had an upward dislocation, the ball of the humerus resting on the process of the scapula, the rim of the cup. I told him how, and he soon snapped the bone into its socket. But the left was a harder proposition. The luxation was downward and forward, and the strong, nervous reaction of the muscles had pulled the head of the bone deep into my armpit. There was no room to work on that narrow ledge. All that could be done was to make a rude sling with one of my suspenders and our handkerchiefs, so as to both support the elbow and keep the arm from swinging.

Then came the task to get down that terrible wall to the glacier, by the only practicable way down the mountain that Muir, after a careful search, could find. Again I am at loss to know how he accomplished it. For an unencumbered man to descend it in the deepening dusk was a most difficult task; but to get a tottery, nerve-shaken, pain-wracked cripple down was a feat of positive wonder. My right arm, though in place, was almost helpless. I could only move my forearm; the muscles of the upper part simply refusing to obey my will. Muir would let himself down to a lower shelf, brace himself, and I would get my right hand against him, crawl my fingers over his shoulder until the arm hung in front of him, and falling against him, would be eased down to his standing ground. Sometimes he would pack me a short distance on his back. Again, taking me by the wrist, he would swing me down to a lower shelf, before descending himself. My right shoulder came out three times that night, and had to be reset.

It was dark when we reached the base; there was no moon and it was very cold. The glacier provided an operating table, and I lay on the ice for an hour while Muir, having slit the sleeve of my shirt to the collar, tugged and twisted at my left arm in a vain attempt to set it. But the ball was too deep in its false socket, and all his pulling only bruised and made it swell. So he had to do up the arm again, and tie it tight to my body. It must have been near midnight when we left the foot of the cliff and started down the mountain. We had ten hard miles to go, and no supper, for the hardtack had disappeared ere we were halfway up the mountain. Muir dared not take me across the glacier in the dark; I was too weak to jump the crevasses. So we skirted it and came, after a mile, to the head of a great slide of gravel, the fine moraine matter of the receding glacier. Muir sat down on the gravel; I sat against him with my feet on either side and my arm over his shoulder. Then he began to hitch and kick, and presently we were sliding at great speed in a cloud of dust. A full half-mile we flew, and were almost buried when we reached the bottom of the slide. It was the easiest part of our trip.

Now we found ourselves in the canyon, down which tumbled the glacial stream, and far beneath the ridge along which we had ascended. The sides of the canyon were sheer cliffs.

"We'll try it," said Muir. "Sometimes these canyons are passable."

But the way grew rougher as we descended. The rapids became falls and we often had to retrace our steps to find a way around them. After we reached the timber-line, some four miles from the summit, the going was still harder, for we had a thicket of alders and willows to fight. Here Muir offered to make a fire and leave me while he went forward for assistance, but I refused. "No," I said, "I'm going to make it to the boat."

All that night this man of steel and lightning worked, never resting a minute, doing the work of three men, helping me along the slopes, easing me down the rocks, pulling me up cliffs, dashing water on me when I grew faint with the pain; and always cheery, full of talk and anecdote, cracking jokes with me, infusing me with his own indomitable spirit. He was eyes, hands, feet, and heart to me – my caretaker, in whom I trusted absolutely. My eyes brim with tears even now when I think of his utter self-abandon as he ministered to my infirmities.

About four o'clock in the morning we came to a fall that we could not compass, sheer a hundred feet or more. So we had to attack the steep walls of the canyon. After a hard struggle we were on the mountain ridges again, traversing the flower pastures, creeping through openings in the brush, scrambling over the dwarf fir, then down through the fallen timber. It was half-past seven o'clock when we descended the last slope and found the path to Glenora. Here we met a straggling party of whites and Indians just starting out to search the mountain for us.

As I was coming wearily up the teetering gang-plank, feeling as if I couldn't keep up another minute, Dr. Kendall stepped upon its end, barring my passage, bent his bushy white brows upon me from his six feet of height, and began to scold:

"See here, young man; give an account of yourself. Do you know you've kept us waiting – "

Just then Captain Lane jumped forward to help me, digging the old Doctor of Divinity with his elbow in the stomach and nearly knocking him off the boat.

"Oh, hell!" he roared. "Can't you see the man's hurt?"

Mrs. Kendall was a very tall, thin, severe-looking old lady, with face lined with grief by the loss of her children. She never smiled. She had not gone to bed at all that night, but walked the deck and would not let her husband or the others sleep. Soon after daylight she began to lash the men with the whip of her tongue for their "cowardice and inhumanity" in not starting at once to search for me.

"Mr. Young is undoubtedly lying mangled at the foot of a cliff, or else one of those terrible bears has wounded him; and you are lolling around here instead of starting to his rescue. For shame!"

When they objected that they did not know where we had gone, she snapped: "Go everywhere until you find him."

Her fierce energy started the men we met. When I came on board she at once took charge and issued her orders, which everybody jumped to obey. She had blankets spread on the floor of the cabin and laid me on them. She obtained some whisky from the captain, some water, porridge and coffee from the steward. She was sitting on the floor with my head in her lap, feeding me coffee with a spoon, when Dr. Kendall came in and began on me again:

"Suppose you had fallen down that precipice, what would your poor wife have done? What would have become of your Indians and your new church?"

Then Mrs. Kendall turned and thrust her spoon like a sword at him. "Henry Kendall," she blazed, "shut right up and leave this room. Have you no sense? Go instantly, I say!" And the good Doctor went.

My recollections of that day are not very clear. The shoulder was in a bad condition – swollen, bruised, very painful. I had to be strengthened with food and rest, and Muir called from his sleep of exhaustion, so that with four other men he could pull and twist that poor arm of mine for an hour. They got it into its socket, but scarcely had Muir got to sleep again before the strong, nervous twitching of the shoulder dislocated it a second time and seemingly placed it in a worse condition than before. Captain Lane was now summoned, and with Muir to direct, they worked for two or three hours. Whisky was poured down my throat to relax my stubborn, pain-convulsed muscles. Then they went at it with two men pulling at the towel knotted about my wrist, two others pulling against them, foot braced to foot, Muir manipulating my shoulder with his sinewy hands, and the stocky Captain, strong and compact as a bear, with his heel against the yarn ball in my armpit, takes me by the elbow and says, "I'll set it or pull the arm off!"

Well, he almost does the latter. I am conscious of a frightful strain, a spasm of anguish in my side as his heel slips from the ball and kicks in two of my ribs, a snap as the head of the bone slips into the cup – then kindly oblivion.

I was awakened about five o'clock in the afternoon by the return of the whole party from an excursion to the Great Glacier at the Boundary Line. Muir, fresh and enthusiastic as ever, had been the pilot across the moraine and upon the great ice mountain; and I, wrapped like a mummy in linen strips, was able to join in his laughter as he told of the big D.D.'s heroics, when, in the middle of an acre of alder brush, he asked indignantly, in response to the hurry-up calls: "Do you think I'm going to leave my wife in this forest?"

One overpowering regret – one only – abides in my heart as I think back upon that golden day with John Muir. He could, and did, go back to Glenora on the return trip of the Cassiar, ascend the mountain again, see the sunset from its top, make charming sketches, stay all night and see the sunrise, filling his cup of joy so full that he could pour out entrancing descriptions for days. While I – well, with entreating arms about one's neck and pleading, tearful eyes looking into one's own, what could one do but promise to climb no more? But my lifelong lamentation over a treasure forever lost, is this: "I never saw the sunset from that peak."

CHAPTER THREE

The Voyage

THE SUMMER and fall of 1879 Muir always referred to as the most interesting period of his adventurous life. From about July 10th to November 20th he was in southeastern Alaska. Very little of this time did he spend indoors. Until steamboat navigation of the Stickeen River was closed by the forming ice, he made frequent trips to the Great Glacier – thirty miles up the river, to the Hot Springs, the Mud Glacier and the interior lakes, ranges, forests and flower pastures. Always upon his return (for my house was his home the most of that time) he would be full to intoxication of what he had seen, and dinners would grow cold and lamps burn out while he held us entranced with his impassioned stories. Although his books are all masterpieces of lucid and glowing English, Muir was one of those rare souls who talk better than they write; and he made the trees, the animals, and especially the glaciers, live before us. Somehow a glacier never seemed cold when John Muir was talking about it.

On September 19th a little stranger whose expected advent was keeping me at home arrived in the person of our first-born daughter. For two or three weeks preceding and following this event Muir was busy writing his summer notes and finishing his pencil sketches, and also studying the flora of the islands. It was a season of constant rains when the *saanah*, the southeast rain-wind, blew a gale. But these stormy days and nights, which kept ordinary people indoors, always lured him out into the woods or up the mountains.

One wild night, dark as Erebus, the rain dashing in sheets and the wind blowing a hurricane, Muir came from his room into ours about ten o'clock with his long, grey overcoat and his Scotch cap on.

"Where now?" I asked.

"Oh, to the top of the mountain," he replied. "It is a rare chance to study this fine storm."

My expostulations were in vain. He rejected with scorn the proffered lantern: "It would spoil the effect." I retired at my usual time, for I had long since learned not to worry about Muir. At two o'clock in the morning there came a hammering at the front door. I opened it and there stood a group of our Indians, rain-soaked and trembling – Chief Tow-a-att, Moses, Aaron, Matthew, Thomas.

"Why, men," I cried, "what's wrong? What brings you here?"

"We want you play (pray)," answered Matthew.

I brought them into the house, and, putting on my clothes and lighting the lamp, I set about to find out the trouble. It was not easy. They were greatly excited and frightened.

"We scare. All Stickeen scare; plenty cly. We want you play God; plenty play."

By dint of much questioning I gathered at last that the whole tribe were frightened by a mysterious light waving and flickering from the top of the little mountain that overlooked Wrangell; and they wished me to pray to the white man's God and avert dire calamity.

"Some miner has camped there," I ventured.

An eager chorus protested; it was not like the light of a camp-fire in the least; it waved in the air like the wings of a spirit. Besides, there was no gold on the top of a hill like that; and no human being would be so foolish as to camp up there on such a night, when there were plenty of comfortable houses at the foot of the hill. It was a spirit, a malignant spirit.

Suddenly the true explanation flashed into my brain, and I shocked my Indians by bursting into a roar of laughter. In imagination I could see him so plainly – John Muir, wet but happy, feeding his fire with spruce sticks, studying and enjoying the storm! But I explained to my natives, who ever afterwards eyed Muir askance, as a mysterious being whose ways and motives were beyond all conjecture.

"Why does this strange man go into the wet woods and up the mountains on stormy nights?" they asked.

"Why does he wander alone on barren peaks or on dangerous ice-mountains? There is no gold up there and he never takes a gun with him or a pick. *Icta mamook* – what make? Why – why?"

The first week in October saw the culmination of plans long and eagerly discussed. Almost the whole of the Alexandrian Archipelago, that great group of eleven hundred wooded islands that forms the southeastern cup-handle of Alaska, was at that time a *terra incognita*. The only seaman's chart of the region in existence was that made by the great English navigator, Vancouver, in 1807. It was a wonderful chart, considering what an absurd little sailing vessel he had in which to explore those intricate waters with their treacherous winds and tides.

But Vancouver's chart was hastily made, after all, in a land of fog and rain and snow. He had not the modern surveyor's instruments, boats or other helps. And, besides, this region was changing more rapidly than, perhaps, any other part of the globe. Volcanic islands were being born out of the depths of the ocean; landslides were filling up channels between the islands; tides and rivers were opening new passages and closing old ones; and, more than all, those mightiest tools of the great Engineer, the glaciers, were furrowing valleys, dumping millions of tons of silt into the sea, forming islands, promontories and isthmuses, and by their recession letting the sea into deep and long fiords, forming great bays, inlets and passages, many of which did not exist in Vancouver's time. In certain localities the living glacier stream was breaking off bergs so fast that the resultant bays were lengthening a mile or more each year. Where Vancouver saw only a great crystal wall across the sea, we were to paddle for days up a long and sinuous fiord; and where he saw one glacier, we were to find a dozen.

My mission in the proposed voyage of discovery was to locate and visit the tribes and villages of Thlingets to the north and west of Wrangell, to take their census, confer with their chiefs and report upon their condition, with a view to establishing schools and churches among them. The most of these tribes had never had a visit from a missionary, and I felt the eager zeal of an Eliot or a Martin at the prospect of telling them for the first time the Good News. Muir's mission was to find and study the forests, mountains and glaciers. I also was eager to see these and learn about them, and Muir was glad to study the natives with me – so our plans fitted into each other well.

"We are going to write some history, my boy," Muir would say to me. "Think of the honour! We have been chosen to put some interesting people and some of Nature's grandest scenes on the page of human record and on the map. Hurry! We are daily losing the most important news of all the world."

In many respects we were most congenial companions. We both loved the same poets and could repeat, verse about, many poems of Tennyson, Keats, Shelley and Burns. He took with him a volume of Thoreau, and I one of Emerson, and we enjoyed them together. I had my printed Bible with me, and he had his in his head – the result of a Scotch father's discipline. Our studies supplemented each other and our tastes were similar. We had both lived clean lives and our conversation together was sweet and high, while we both had a sense of humour and a large fund of stories.

But Muir's knowledge of Nature and his insight into her plans and methods were so far beyond mine that, while I was organiser and commander of the expedition, he was my teacher and guide into the inner recesses and meanings of the islands, bays and mountains we explored together.

Our ship for this voyage of discovery, while not so large as Vancouver's, was much more shapely and manageable – a *kladushu etlan* (six fathom) red-cedar canoe. It belonged to our captain, old Chief Tow-a-att, a chief who had lately embraced Christianity with his whole heart – one of the simplest, most faithful, dignified and brave souls I ever knew. He fully expected to meet a martyr's death among his heathen enemies of the northern islands; yet he did not shrink from the voyage on that account.

His crew numbered three. First in importance was Kadishan, also a chief of the Stickeens, chosen because of his powers of oratory, his kinship with Chief Shathitch of the Chilcat tribe, and his friendly relations with other chiefs. He was a born courtier, learned in Indian lore, songs and customs, and able to instruct me in the proper Thlinget etiquette to suit all occasions. The other two were sturdy young men – Stickeen John, our interpreter, and Sitka Charley. They were to act as cooks, camp-makers, oarsmen, hunters and general utility men.

We stowed our baggage, which was not burdensome, in one end of the canoe, taking a simple store of provisions – flour, beans, bacon, sugar, salt and a little dried fruit. We were to depend upon our guns, fishhooks, spears and clamsticks for other diet. As a preliminary to our palaver with the natives we followed the old Hudson Bay custom, then firmly established in the North. We took materials for a *potlatch*, – leaf tobacco, rice and sugar. Our Indian crew laid in their own stock of provisions, chiefly dried salmon and seal grease, while our table was to be separate, set out with the white man's viands.

We did not get off without trouble. Kadishan's mother, who looked but little older than himself, strongly objected to my taking her son on so perilous a voyage and so late in the fall, and when her scoldings and entreaties did not avail she said: "If anything happens to my son, I will take your baby as mine in payment."

One sunny October day we set our prow to the unknown northwest. Our hearts beat high with anticipation. Every passage between the islands was a corridor leading into a new and more enchanting room of Nature's great gallery. The lapping waves whispered enticing secrets, while the seabirds screaming over head and the eagles shrilling from the sky promised wonderful adventures.

The voyage naturally divides itself into the human interest and the study of Nature; yet the two constantly blended throughout the whole voyage. I can only select a few instances from that trip of six weeks whose every hour was new and strange.

Our captain, taciturn and self-reliant, commanded Muir's admiration from the first. His paddle was sure in the stern, his knowledge of the wind and tide unfailing. Whenever we landed the crew would begin to dispute concerning the best place to make camp. But old Tow-a-att, with the mast in his hand, would march straight as an arrow to the likeliest spot of all, stick down his mast as a tent-pole and begin to set up the tent, the others invariably acquiescing in his decision as the best possible choice.

At our first meal Muir's sense of humour cost us one third of a roll of butter. We invited our captain to take dinner with us. I got out the bread and other viands, and set the two pound roll of butter beside the bread and placed both by Tow-a-att. He glanced at the roll of butter and at the three who were to eat, measured with his eye one third of the roll, cut it off with his hunting knife and began to cut it into squares and eat it with great gusto. I was about to interfere and show him the use we made of butter, but Muir stopped me with a wink. The old chief calmly devoured his third of the roll, and rubbing his stomach with great satisfaction pronounced it "*hyas klosh* (very good) glease."

Of necessity we had chosen the rainiest season of the year in that dampest climate of North America, where there are two hundred and twenty-five rainy days out of the three hundred and sixty-five. During our voyage it did not rain every day, but the periods of sunshine were so rare as to make us hail them with joyous acclamation.

We steered our course due westward for forty miles, then through a sinuous, island-studded passage called Rocky Strait, stopping one day to lay in a supply of venison before sailing on to the village of the Kake Indians. My habit throughout the voyage, when coming to a native town, was to find where the head chief lived, feed him with rice and regale him with tobacco, and then induce him to call all his chiefs and head men together for a council. When they were all assembled I would give small presents of tobacco to each, and then open the floodgate of talk, proclaiming my mission and telling them in simplest terms the Great New Story. Muir would generally follow me, unfolding in turn some of the wonders of God's handiwork and the beauty of clean, pure living; and then in turn, beginning with the head chief, each Indian would make his speech. We were received with joy everywhere, and if there was suspicion at first old Tow-a-att's tearful pleadings and Kadishan's oratory speedily brought about peace and unity.

These palavers often lasted a whole day and far into the night, and usually ended with our being feasted in turn by the chief in whose house we had held the council. I took the census of each village, getting the heads of the families to count their relatives with the aid of beans – the large brown beans representing men, the large white ones, women, and the small Boston beans, children. In this manner the first census of southeastern Alaska was taken.

Before starting on the voyage, we heard that there was a Harvard graduate, bearing an honoured New England name, living among the Kake Indians on Kouyou Island. On arriving at the chief town of that tribe we inquired for the white man and were told that he was camping with the family of a sub-chief at the mouth of a salmon stream. We set off to find him. As we neared the shore we saw a circular group of natives around a fire on the beach, sitting on their heels in the stoical Indian way. We landed and came up to them. Not one of them deigned to rise or show any excitement at our coming. The eight or nine men who formed the group were all dressed in coloured four dollar blankets, with the exception of one, who had on a ragged fragment of a filthy, two-dollar, Hudson Bay blanket. The back of this man was towards us, and after speaking to the chief, Muir and I crossed to the other side of the fire, and saw his face. It was the white man, and the ragged blanket was all the clothing he had upon him! An effort to open conversation with him proved futile. He answered only with grunts and mumbled monosyllables. Thus the most filthy, degraded, hopelessly lost savage that we found in this whole voyage was a college graduate of great New England stock!

"Lift a stone to mountain height and let it fall," said Muir, "and it will sink the deeper into the mud."

At Angoon, one of the towns of the Hootz-noo tribe, occurred an incident of another type. We found this village hilariously drunk. There was a very stringent prohibition law over Alaska at that time, which absolutely forbade the importation of any spirituous liquors into the Territory. But the law was deficient in one vital respect – it did not prohibit the importation of molasses; and a soldier during the military occupancy of the Territory had instructed the natives in the art of making rum. The method was simple. A five-gallon oil can was taken and partly filled with molasses as a base; into that alcohol was placed (if it were obtainable), dried apples, berries, potatoes, flour, anything that would rot and ferment; then, to give it the proper tang, ginger, cayenne pepper and mustard were added. This mixture was then set in a warm place to ferment. Another oil can was cut up into long strips, the solder melted out and used to make a pipe, with two or three turns through cool water, forming the worm, and the still. Talk about your forty-rod whiskey – I have seen this "hooch," as it was called because these same Hootz-noo natives first made it, kill at more than forty rods, for it generally made the natives *fighting* drunk.

Through the large company of screaming, dancing and singing natives we made our way to the chief's house. By some miracle this majestic-looking savage was sober. Perhaps he felt it incumbent upon him as host not to partake himself of the luxuries with which he regaled his guests. He took us hospitably into his great community house of split cedar planks with carved totem poles for corner posts, and called his young men to take care of our canoe and to bring wood for a fire that he might feast us. The wife of this chief was one of the finest looking Indian women I have ever met – tall, straight, lithe and dignified. But, crawling about on the floor on all fours, was the most piteous travesty of the human form I have ever seen. It was an idiot boy, sixteen years of age. He had neither the comeliness of a beast nor the intellect of a man. His name was *Hootz-too* (Bear Heart), and indeed all his motions were those of a bear rather than of a human being. Crossing the floor with the swinging gait of a bear, he would crouch back on his haunches and resume his constant occupation of sucking his wrist, into which he had thus formed a livid hole. When disturbed at this horrid task he would strike with the claw-like fingers of the other hand, snarling and grunting. Yet the beautiful chieftainess was his mother, and she *loved* him. For sixteen years she had cared for this monster, feeding him with her choicest food, putting him to sleep always in her arms, taking him with her and guarding him day and night. When, a short time before our visit, the medicine men, accusing him of causing the illness of some of the head men of the village, proclaimed him a witch, and the whole tribe came to take and torture him to death, she fought them like a lioness, not counting her own life dear unto her, and saved her boy.

When I said to her thoughtlessly, "Oh, would you not be relieved at the death of this poor idiot boy?" she saw in my words a threat, and I shall never forget the pathetic, hunted look with which she said:

"Oh, no, it must not be; he shall not die. Is he not my son, *uh-yeetkutsku* (my dear little son)?"

If our voyage had yielded me nothing but this wonderful instance of mother-love, I should have counted myself richly repaid.

One more human story before I come to Muir's part. It was during the latter half of the voyage, and after our discovery of Glacier Bay. The climax of the trip, so far as the missionary interests were concerned, was our visit to the Chilcat and Chilcoot natives on Lynn Canal, the most northern tribes of the Alexandrian Archipelago. Here reigned the proudest and worst old savage of Alaska, Chief Shathitch. His wealth was very great in Indian treasures, and he was reputed to have cached away in different places several houses full of blankets, guns, boxes of beads, ancient carved pipes, spears, knives and other valued heirlooms. He was said to have stored away over one hundred of the elegant Chilcat blankets woven by hand from the hair of the mountain goat. His tribe was rich and unscrupulous. Its members were the middle-men between the whites and the Indians of the Interior. They did not allow these Indians to come to the coast, but took over the mountains articles purchased from the whites – guns, ammunition, blankets, knives and so forth – and bartered them for furs. It was said that they claimed to be the manufacturers of these wares and so charged for them what prices they pleased. They had these Indians of the Interior in a bondage of fear, and would not allow them to trade directly with the white men. Thus they carried out literally the story told of Hudson Bay traffic – piling beaver skins to the height of a ten dollar Hudson Bay musket as the *price* of the musket. They were the most quarrelsome and warlike of the tribes of Alaska, and their villages were full of slaves procured by forays upon the coasts of Vancouver Island, Puget Sound, and as far south as the mouth of the Columbia River. I was eager to visit these large and untaught tribes, and establish a mission among them.

About the first of November we came in sight of the long, low-built village of Yin-des-tuk-ki. As we paddled up the winding channel of the Chilcat River we saw great excitement in the town. We had hoisted the American flag, as was our custom, and had put on our best apparel for the occasion. When we got within long musket-shot of the village we saw the native men come rushing from their houses with their guns in their hands and mass in front of the largest house upon the beach. Then we were greeted by what seemed rather too warm a reception – a shower of bullets falling unpleasantly around us. Instinctively Muir and I ceased to paddle, but Tow-a-att commanded, "*Ut-ha, ut ha!* – pull, pull!" and slowly, amid the dropping bullets, we zigzagged our way up the channel towards the village. As we drew near the shore line of runners extended down the beach to us, keeping within shouting distance of each other. Then came the questions like bullets – "*Gusuwa-eh?* – Who are you? Whence do you come? What is your business here?" And Stickeen John shouted back the reply: "A great preacher-chief and a great ice-chief have come to bring you a good message."

The answer was shouted back along the line, and then returned a message of greeting and welcome. We were to be the guests of the chief of Yin-des-tuk-ki, old Don-na-wuk (Silver Eye), so called because he was in the habit of wearing on all state occasions a huge pair of silver-bowed spectacles

which a Russian officer had given him. He confessed he could not see
through them, but thought they lent dignity to his countenance. We paddled
slowly up to the village, and Muir and I, watching with interest, saw the
warriors all disappear. As our prow touched the sand, however, here they
came, forty or fifty of them, without their guns this time, but charging down
upon us with war-cries, *"Hoo-hooh, hoo-hooh,"* as if they were going to
take us prisoners. Dashing into the water they ranged themselves along each
side of the canoe; then lifting up our canoe with us in it they rushed with
excited cries up the bank to the chief's house and set us down at his door. It
was the Thlinget way of paying us honour as great guests.

Then we were solemnly ushered into the presence of Don-na-wuk. His
house was large, covering about fifty by sixty feet of ground. The interior
was built in the usual fashion of a chief's house – carved corner posts, a
square of gravel in the centre of the room for the fire surrounded by great
hewn cedar planks set on edge; a platform of some six feet in width running
clear around the room; then other planks on edge and a high platform, where
the chieftain's household goods were stowed and where the family took their
repose. A brisk fire was burning in the middle of the room; and after a short
palaver, with gifts of tobacco and rice to the chief, it was announced that he
would pay us the distinguished honour of feasting us first.

It was a never-to-be-forgotten banquet. We were seated on the lower
platform with our feet towards the fire, and before Muir and me were placed
huge washbowls of blue Hudson Bay ware. Before each of our native
attendants was placed a great carved wooden trough, holding about as much
as the washbowls. We had learned enough of Indian etiquette to know that
at each course our respective vessels were to be filled full of food, and we
were expected to carry off what we could not devour. It was indeed a "feast
of fat things." The first course was what, for the Indian, takes the place of
bread among the whites – dried salmon. It was served, a whole wash-
bowlful for each of us, with a dressing of seal-grease. Muir and I adroitly
manoeuvred so as to get our salmon and seal-grease served separately; for
our stomachs had not been sufficiently trained to endure that rancid grease.
This course finished, what was left was dumped into receptacles in our
canoe and guarded from the dogs by young men especially appointed for
that purpose. Our washbowls were cleansed and the second course brought
on. This consisted of the back fat of the deer, great, long hunks of it, served
with a gravy of seal grease. The third course was little Russian potatoes
about the size of walnuts, dished out to us, a wash-bowlful, with a dressing
of seal grease. The final course was the only berry then in season, the long
fleshy apple of the wild rose mellowed with frost, served to us in the usual
quantity with the invariable sauce of seal grease.

"Mon, mon!" said Muir aside to me, "I'm fashed we'll be floppin'
aboot i' the sea, whiles, wi' flippers an' forked tails."

When we had partaken of as much of this feast of fat things as our civilized stomachs would stand, it was suddenly announced that we were about to receive a visit from the great chief of the Chilcats and the Chilcoots, old Chief Shathitch (Hard-to-Kill). In order to properly receive His Majesty, Muir and I and our two chiefs were each given a whole bale of Hudson Bay blankets for a couch. Shathitch made us wait a long time, doubtless to impress us with his dignity as supreme chief.

The heat of the fire after the wind and cold of the day made us very drowsy. We fought off sleep, however, and at last in came stalking the biggest chief of all Alaska, clothed in his robe of state, which was an elegant chinchilla blanket; and upon its yellow surface, as the chief slowly turned about to show us what was written thereon, we were astonished to see printed in black letters these words, ''To Chief Shathitch, from his friend, William H. Seward!'' We learned afterwards that Seward, in his voyage of investigation, had penetrated to this far-off town, had been received in royal state by the old chief and on his return to the States had sent back this token of his appreciation of the chief's hospitality. Whether Seward was regaled with viands similar to those offered to us, history does not relate.

To me the inspiring part of that voyage came next day, when I preached from early morning until midnight, only occasionally relieved by Muir and by the responsive speeches of the natives.

''More, more; tell us more,'' they would cry. ''It is a good talk; we never heard this story before.'' And when I would inquire, ''Of what do you wish me now to talk?'' they would always say, ''Tell us more of the Man from Heaven who died for us.''

Runners had been sent to the Chilcoot village on the eastern arm of Lynn Canal, and twenty-five miles up the Chilcat River to Shathitch's town of Klukwan; and as the day wore away the crowd of Indians had increased so greatly that there was no room for them in the large house. I heard a scrambling upon the roof, and looking up I saw a row of black heads around the great smoke-hole in the centre of the roof. After a little a ripping, tearing sound came from the sides of the building. They were prying off the planks in order that those outside might hear. When my voice faltered with long talking Tow-a-att and Kadishan took up the story, telling what they had learned of the white man's religion; or Muir told the eager natives wonderful things about what the great one God, whose name is Love, was doing for them. The all day meeting was only interrupted for an hour or two in the afternoon, when we walked with the chiefs across the narrow isthmus between Pyramid Harbour and the eastern arm of Lynn Canal, and I selected the harbour, farm and town site now occupied by Haines mission and town and Fort William H. Seward. This was the beginning of the large missions of Haines and Klukwan.

CHAPTER FOUR

The Discovery

THE NATURE-STUDY part of the voyage was woven in with the missionary trip as intimately as warp with woof. No island, rock, forest, mountain or glacier which we passed, near or far, was neglected. We went so at our own sweet will, without any set time or schedule, that we were constantly finding objects and points of surprise and interest. When we landed, the algae, which sometimes filled the little harbours, the limpets and lichens of the rocks, the fucus pods that snapped beneath our feet, the grasses of the beach, the moss and shrubbery among the trees, and, more than all, the majestic forests, claimed attention and study. Muir was one of the most expert foresters this country has ever produced. He was never at a loss. The luxuriant vegetation of this wet coast filled him with admiration, and he never took a walk from camp but he had a whole volume of things to tell me, and he was constantly bringing in trophies of which he was prouder than any hunter of his antlers. Now it was a bunch of ferns as high as his head; now a cluster of minute and wonderfully beautiful moss blossoms; now a curious fungus growth; now a spruce branch heavy with cones; and again he would call me into the forest to see a strange and grotesque moss formation on a dead stump, looking like a tree standing upon its head. Thus, although his objective was the glaciers, his thorough knowledge of botany and his interest in that study made every camp just the place he wished to be. He always claimed that there was more of pure ethics and even of moral evil and good to be learned in the wilderness than from any book or in any abode of man. He was fond of quoting Wordsworth's stanza:

> "One impulse from a vernal wood
> Will teach you more of man,
> Of moral evil and of good,
> Than all the sages can."

Muir was a devout theist. The Fatherhood of God and the Unity of God, the immanence of God in Nature and His management of all the affairs of the universe, was his constantly reiterated belief. He saw design in many things which the ordinary naturalist overlooks, such as the symmetry of an island, the balancing branches of a tree, the harmony of colours in a group of flowers, the completion of a fully rounded landscape. In his view, the Creator of it all saw every beautiful and sublime thing from every viewpoint, and had thus formed it, not merely for His own delight, but for the delectation and instruction of His human children.

"Look at that, now," he would say, when, on turning a point, a wonderful vista of island-studded sea between mountains, with one of Alaska's matchless sunsets at the end, would wheel into sight. "Why, it looks as if these giants of God's great army had just now marched into their stations; every one placed just right, just right! What landscape gardening! What a scheme of things! And to think that He should plan to bring us feckless creatures here at the right moment, and then flash such glories at us! Man, we're not worthy of such honour!"

Thus Muir was always discovering to me things which I would never have seen myself and opening up to me new avenues of knowledge, delight and adoration. There was something so intimate in his theism that it purified, elevated and broadened mine, even when I could not agree with him. His constant exclamation when a fine landscape would burst upon our view, or a shaft of light would pierce the clouds and glorify a mountain, was, "Praise God from whom all blessings flow!"

Two or three great adventures stand out prominently in this wonderful voyage of discovery. Two weeks from home brought us to Icy Straits and the homes of the Hoonah tribe. Here the knowledge of the way on the part of our crew ended. We put into the large Hoonah village on Chichagof Island. After the usual preaching and census-taking, we took aboard a sub-chief of the Hoonahs, who was a noted seal hunter and, therefore, able to guide us among the ice-floes of the mysterious Glacier Bay of which we had heard. Vancouver's chart gave us no intimation of any inlet whatever; but the natives told of vast masses of floating ice, of a constant noise of thunder when they crashed from the glaciers into the sea; and also of fearsome bays and passages full of evil spirits which made them very perilous to navigate.

In one bay there was said to be a giant devil-fish with arms as long as a tree, lurking in malignant patience, awaiting the passage that way of an unwary canoe, when up would flash those terrible arms with their thousand suckers and, seizing their prey, would drag down the men to the bottom of the sea, there to be mangled and devoured by the horrid beak. Another deep fiord was the abode of *Koosta-kah*, the Otterman, the mischievous Puck of Indian lore, who was waiting for voyagers to land and camp, when he would seize their sleeping forms and transport them a dozen miles in a moment, or cradle them on the tops of the highest trees. Again there was a most rapacious and ferocious killer whale in a piece of swift water, whose delight it was to take into his great, tooth-rimmed jaws whole canoes with their crews of men, mangling them and gulping them down as a single mouthful. Many were these stories of fear told us at the Hoonah village the night before we started to explore the icy bay, and our credulous Stickeens gave us rather broad hints that it was time to turn back.

"There are no natives up in that region; there is nothing to hunt; there is no gold there; why do you persist in this *cultus coly* (aimless journey)? You are likely to meet death and nothing else if you go into that dangerous region."

All these stories made us the more eager to explore the wonders beyond, and we hastened away from Hoonah with our guide aboard. A day's sail brought us to a little, heavily wooded island near the mouth of Glacier Bay. This we named Pleasant Island.

As we broke camp in the morning our guide said: "We must take on board a supply of dry wood here, as there is none beyond."

Leaving this last green island we steered northwest into the great bay, the country of ice and bare rocks. Muir's excitement was increasing every moment, and as the majestic arena opened before us and the Muir, Geicke, Pacific and other great glaciers (all nameless as yet) began to appear, he could hardly contain himself. He was impatient of any delay, and was constantly calling to the crew to redouble their efforts and get close to these wonders. Now the marks of recent glaciation showed plainly. Here was a conical island of grey granite, whose rounded top and symmetrical shoulders were worn smooth as a Scotch monument by grinding glaciers. Here was a great mountain slashed sheer across its face, showing sharp edge and flat surface as if a slab of mountain size had been sawed from it. Yonder again loomed a granite range whose huge breasts were rounded and polished by the resistless sweep of that great ice mass which Vancouver saw filling the bay.

Soon the icebergs were charging down upon us with the receding tide and dressing up in compact phalanx when the tide arose. First would come the advance guard of smaller bergs, with here and there a house-like mass of cobalt blue with streaks of white and deeper recesses of ultramarine; here we passed an eight-sided, solid figure of bottle-green ice; there towered an antlered formation like the horns of a stag. Now we must use all caution and give the larger icebergs a wide berth. They are treacherous creatures, these icebergs. You may be paddling along by a peaceful looking berg, sleeping on the water as mild and harmless as a lamb; when suddenly he will take a notion to turn over, and up under your canoe will come a spear of ice, impaling it and lifting it and its occupants skyward; then, turning over, down will go canoe and men to the depths.

Our progress up the sixty miles of Glacier Bay was very slow. Three nights we camped on the bare granite rock before we reached the limit of the bay. All vegetation had disappeared; hardly a bunch of grass was seen. The only signs of former life were the sodden and splintered spruce and fir stumps that projected here and there from the bases of huge gravel heaps, the moraine matter of the mighty ice mass that had engulfed them. They told the story of great forests which had once covered this whole region, until the great sea of ice of the second glacial period overwhelmed and ground them down, and buried them deep under its moraine matter. When we landed there were no level spots on which to pitch our tent and no sandy beaches or gravel beds in which to sink our tent-poles. I learned from Muir the gentle art of sleeping on a rock, curled like a squirrel around a boulder.

We passed by Muir Glacier on the other side of the bay, seeking to attain the extreme end of the great fiord. We estimated the distance by the tide and our rate of rowing, tracing the shore-line and islands as we went along and getting the points of the compass from our little pocket instrument.

Rain was falling almost constantly during the week we spent in Glacier Bay. Now and then the clouds would lift, showing the twin peaks of La Perouse and the majestic summits of Mts. Fairweather and Crillon. These mighty summits, twelve thousand, fifteen thousand and sixteen thousand feet high, respectively, pierced the sky directly above us; sometimes they seemed to be hanging over us threateningly. Only once did the sky completely clear; and then was preached to us the wonderful Sermon of Glacier Bay.

Early that morning we quitted our camp on a barren rock, steering towards Mt. Fairweather. A night of sleepless discomfort had ushered in a bleak grey morning. Our Indians were sullen and silent, their scowling looks resenting our relentless purpose to attain to the head of the bay. The air was damp and raw, chilling us to the marrow. The forbidding granite mountains, showing here and there through the fog, seemed suddenly to push out threatening fists and shoulders at us. All night long the ice-guns had bombarded us from four or five directions, when the great masses of ice from living glaciers toppled into the sea, crashing and grinding with the noise of thunder. The granite walls hurled back the sound in reiterated peals, multiplying its volume a hundredfold.

There was no love apparent on that bleak, grey morning – power was there in appalling force. Visions of those evergreen forests that had once clung trustingly to these mountain walls, but had been swept, one and all, by the relentless forces of the ice and buried deep under mountains of moraine matter, but added to the present desolation. We could not enjoy; we could only endure. Death from overturning icebergs, from charging tides, from mountain avalanche, threatened us.

Suddenly I heard Muir catch his breath with a fervent ejaculation "God, Almighty!" he said. Following his gaze towards Mt. Crillon, I saw the summit highest of all crowned with glory indeed. It was not sunlight; there was no appearance of shining; it was as if the Great Artist with one sweep of His brush had laid upon the king-peak of all a crown of the most brilliant of all colours – as if a pigment, perfectly made and thickly spread, too delicate for crimson, too intense for pink, had leaped in a moment upon the mountain top; "An awful rose of dawn." The summit nearest heaven had caught a glimpse of its glory! It was a rose blooming in ice-fields, a love-song in the midst of a stern epic, a drop from the heart of Christ upon the icy desolation and barren affections of a sin-frozen world. It warmed and thrilled us in an instant. We who had been dull and apathetic a moment before, shivering in our wet blankets, were glowing and exultant now. Even the Indians ceased their paddling, gazing with faces of awe upon the wonder. Now, as we watched that kingly peak, we saw the colour leap to one and another and another of the snowy summits around it. The monarch had a whole family of royal princes about him to share his glory. Their radiant heads, ruby crowned, were above the clouds, which seemed to form their silken garments.

As we looked in ecstatic silence we saw the light creep down the mountains. It was changing now. The glowing crimson was suffused with soft, creamy light. If it was less divine, it was more warmly human. Heaven was coming down to man. The dark recesses of the mountains began to lighten. They stood forth as at the word of command from the Master of all; and as the changing mellow light moved downward that wonderful colosseum appeared clearly with its battlements and peaks and columns, until the whole majestic landscape was revealed.

Now we saw the design and purpose of it all. Now the text of this great sermon was emblazoned across the landscape – "*God is Love*"; and we understood that these relentless forces that had pushed the molten mountains heavenward, cooled them into granite peaks, covered them with snow and ice, dumped the moraine matter into the sea, filling up the sea, preparing the world for stronger and better race of men (who knows ?), were all a part of that great "All things" that "work together for good."

Our minds cleared with the landscape; our courage rose; our Indians dipped their paddles silently, steering without fear amidst the dangerous masses of ice. But there was no profanity in Muir's exclamation, "We have met with God!" A lifelong devoutness of gratitude filled us, to think that we were guided into this most wonderful room of God's great gallery, on perhaps the only day in the year when the skies were cleared and the sunrise, the atmospheric conditions and the point of view all prepared for the matchless spectacle. The discomforts of the voyage, the toil, the cold and rain of the past weeks were a small price to pay for one glimpse of its surpassing loveliness. Again and again Muir would break out, after a long silence of blissful memory, with exclamations:

"We saw it; we saw it! He sent us to His most glorious exhibition. Praise God, from whom all blessings flow!"

Two or three inspiring days followed. Muir must climb the most accessible of the mountains. My weak shoulders forbade me to ascend more than two or three thousand feet, but Muir went more than twice as high. Upon two or three of the glaciers he climbed, although the speed of these icy streams was so great and their "frozen cataracts" were so frequent, that it was difficult to ascend them.

I began to understand Muir's whole new theory, which theory made Tyndall pronounce him the greatest authority on glacial action the world had seen. He pointed out to me the mechanical laws that governed those slow-moving, resistless streams; how they carved their own valleys; how the lower valley and glacier were often the resultant in size and velocity of the two or three glaciers that now formed the branches of the main glaciers; how the harder strata of rock resisted and turned the masses of ice; how the steely ploughshares were often inserted into softer leads and a whole mountain split apart as by a wedge.

Muir would explore all day long, often rising hours before daylight and disappearing among the mountains, not coming to camp until after night had fallen. Again and again the Indians said that he was lost; but I had no fears for him. When he would return to camp he was so full of his discoveries and of the new facts garnered that he would talk until long into the night, almost forgetting to eat.

Returning down the bay, we passed the largest glacier of all, which was to bear Muir's name. It was then fully a mile and a half in width, and the perpendicular face of it towered from four to seven hundred feet above the surface of the water. The ice masses were breaking off so fast that we were forced to put off far from the face of the glacier. The great waves threatened constantly to dash us against the sharp points of the icebergs. We wished to land and scale the glacier from the eastern side. We rowed our canoe about half a mile from he edge of the glacier, but, attempting to land, were forced hastily to put off again. A great wave, formed by the masses of ice breaking off into the water, threatened to dash our loaded canoe against the boulders on the beach. Rowing further away, we tried it again and again, with the same result. As soon as we neared the shore another huge wave would threaten destruction. We were fully a mile and a half from the edge of the glacier before we found it safe to land.

Muir spent a whole day alone on the glacier, walking over twenty miles across what he called the glacial lake between two mountains. A cold, penetrating, mist-like rain was falling, and dark clouds swept up the bay and clung about the shoulders of the mountains. When night approached and Muir had not returned, I set the Indians to digging out from the bases of the gravel hills the frazzled stumps and logs that remained of the buried forests.

These were full of resin and burned brightly. I made a great fire and cooked a good supper of venison, beans, biscuit and coffee. When itchy darkness gathered, and still Muir did not come, Tow-a-att made some torches of fat spruce, and taking with him Charley, laden with more wood, he went up the beach a mile and a half, climbed the base of the mountain and kindled a beacon which flashed its cheering rays far over the glacier.

Muir came stumbling into camp with these two Indians a little before midnight, very tired but very happy. "Ah!" he sighed, "I'm glad to be in camp. The glacier almost got me this time. If it had not been for the beacon and old Tow-a-att, I might have had to spend the night on the ice. The crevasses were so many and so bewildering in their mazy, crisscross windings that

I was actually going farther into the glacier when I caught the flash of light.''

I brought him to the tent and placed the hot viands before him. He attacked them ravenously, but presently was talking again:

''Man, man; you ought to have been with me. You'll never make up what you have lost to-day. I've been wandering through a thousand rooms of God's crystal temple. I've been a thousand feet down in the crevasses, with matchless domes and sculptured figures and carved ice work all about me. Solomon's marble and ivory palaces were nothing to it. Such purity, such colour, such delicate beauty! I was tempted to stay there and feast my soul, and softly freeze, until I would become part of the glacier. What a great death that would be!''

Again and again I would have to remind Muir that he was eating his supper, but it was more than an hour before I could get him to finish the meal, and two or three hours longer before he stopped talking and went to sleep. I wish I had taken down his descriptions. What splendid reading they would make!

But scurries of snow warned us that winter was coming, and, much to the relief of our natives, we turned the prow of our canoe towards Chatham Strait again. Landing our Hoonah guide at his village, we took our route northward again up Lynn Canal. The beautiful Davison Glacier with its great snowy fan drew our gaze and excited our admiration for two days; then the visit to the Chilcats and the return trip commenced. Bowling down the canal before a strong north wind, we entered Stevens Passage, and visited the two villages of the Auk Indians, a squalid, miserable tribe. We camped at the site of what is now Juneau, the capital of Alaska, and no dream of the millions of gold that were to be taken from those mountains disturbed us. If we had known, I do not think that we would have halted a day or staked a claim. Our treasures were richer than gold and securely laid up in the vaults of our memories.

An excursion into Taku Bay, that miniature of Glacier Bay, with its then three living glaciers; a visit to two villages of the Taku Indians; past Ft. Snettisham, up whose arms we pushed, mapping them; then to Sumdum. Here the two arms of Holkham Bay, filled with ice, enticed us to exploration, but the constant rains of the fall had made the ice of the glaciers more viscid and the glacier streams more rapid; hence the vast array of icebergs charging down upon us like an army, spreading out in loose formation and then gathering into a barrier when the tide turned, made exploration to the end of the bay impossible. Muir would not give up his quest of the mother glacier until the Indians frankly refused to go any further; and old Tow-a-att called our interpreter, Johnny, as for a counsel of state, and carefully set forth to Muir that if he persisted in his purpose of pushing forward up the bay he would have the blood of the whole party on his hands.

Said the old chief: ''My life is of no account, and it does not matter whether I live or die; but you shall not sacrifice the life of my minister.'' I laughed at Muir's discomfiture and gave the word to retreat. This one defeat of a victorious expedition so weighed upon Muir's mind that it brought him back from the California coast next year and from the arms of his bride to discover and climb upon that glacier.

On down now through Prince Frederick Sound, past the beautiful Norris Glacier, then into Le Conte Bay with its living glacier and icebergs, across the Stickeen flats, and so joyfully home again, Muir to take the November steamboat back to his sunland.

I have made many voyages in that great Alexandrian Archipelago since, travelling by canoe over fifteen thousand miles – not one of them a dull one – through its intricate passages; but none compared, in the number and intensity of its thrills, in the variety and excitement of its incidents and in its lasting impressions of beauty and grandeur, with this first voyage when we groped our way northward with only Vancouver's old chart as our guide.

CHAPTER FIVE

The Lost Glacier

JOHN MUIR was married in the spring of 1880 to Miss Strentzel, the daughter of a Polish physician who had come out in the great stampede of 1849 to California, but had found his gold in oranges, lemons and apricots on a great fruit ranch at Martinez, California. A brief letter from Muir told of his marriage, with just one note in it, the depth of joy and peace of which I could fathom, knowing him so well. Then no word of him until the monthly mail boat came in September. As I stood on the wharf with the rest of the Wrangell population, as was the custom of our isolation, watching the boat come in, I was overjoyed to see John Muir on deck, in that same old, long, grey ulster and Scotch cap. He waved and shouted at me before the boat touched the wharf.

Springing ashore he said, "When can you be ready?"

"Aren't you a little fast?" I replied. "What does this mean? Where's your wife?"

"Man," he exclaimed, "have you forgotten? Don't you know we lost a glacier last fall? Do you think I could sleep soundly in my bed this winter with that hanging on my conscience? My wife could not come, so I have come alone and you've got to go with me to find the lost. Get your canoe and crew and let us be off."

The ten months since Muir had left me had not been spent in idleness at

Wrangell. I had made two long voyages of discovery and missionary work on my own account, one in the spring, of four hundred fifty miles around Prince of Wales Island, visiting the five towns of Hydah Indians and the three villages of the Hanega tribe of Thlingets. Another in the summer down the coast to the Cape Fox and Tongass tribes of Thlingets, and across Dixon entrance to Ft. Simpson, where there was a mission among the Tsimpheans, and on fifteen miles further to the famous mission of Father Duncan at Metlakahtla. I had written accounts of these trips to Muir; but for him the greatest interest was in the glaciers and mountains of the mainland.

Our preparations were soon made. Alas! we could not have our noble old captain, Tow-a-att, this time. On January 10th, 1880, the darkest day of my life, this ''noblest Roman of them all'' fell dead at my feet with a bullet through his forehead, shot by a member of that same Hootz-noo tribe where he had preached the gospel of peace so simply and eloquently a few months before. The Hootz-noos, maddened by the fiery liquor that bore their name, came to Wrangell, and a preliminary skirmish led to an attack at daylight of that winter day upon the Stickeen village. Old Tow-a-att had stood for peace, and rather than have any bloodshed had offered all his blankets as a peace offering, although in no physical fear himself; but when the Hootz-noos, encouraged by the seeming cowardice of the Stickeens, broke into their houses, and the Christianized tribe, provoked beyond endurance, came out with their guns, Tow-a-att came forth armed only with his old carved spear, the emblem of his position as chief, to see if he could not call his tribe back again. At my instance, as I stood with my hand on his shoulder, he lifted up his voice to recall his people to their houses, when, in an instant, the volley commenced on both sides, and this Christian man, one of the simplest and grandest souls I ever knew, fell dead at my feet, and the tribe was tumbled back into barbarism; and the white man, who had taught the Indians the art of making rum, and the white man's government, which had afforded no safeguard against such scenes, were responsible.

Muir mourned with me the fate of this old chief; but another of my men, Lot Tyeen, was ready with a swift canoe. Joe, his son-in-law, and Billy Dickinson, a half-breed boy of seventeen who acted as interpreter, formed the crew. When we were about to embark I suddenly thought of my little dog Stickeen and made the resolve to take him along. My wife and Muir both protested and I almost yielded to their persuasion. I shudder now to think what the world would have lost had their arguments prevailed! That little, long-haired, brisk, beautiful, but very independent dog, in co-ordination with Muir's genius, was to give to the world one of its greatest dog-classics. Muir's story *Stickeen* ranks with *Rab and His Friends, Bob, Son of Battle*, and far above *The Call of the Wild*. Indeed, in subtle analysis of dog character, as well as beauty of description, I think it outranks all of them. All over the world men, women and children are reading with laughter, thrills and tears this exquisite little story.

I have told Muir that in his book he did not do justice to my puppy's beauty. I think that he was the handsomest dog I have ever known. His markings were very much like those of an American Shepherd dog – black, white and tan; although he was not half the size of one; but his hair was so silky and so long, his tail so heavily fringed and beautifully curved, his eyes so deep and expressive and his shape so perfect in its graceful contours, that I have never seen another dog quite like him; otherwise Muir's description of him is perfect.

When Stickeen was only a round ball of silky fur as big as one's fist, he was given as a wedding present to my bride, two years before this voyage. I carried him in my overcoat pocket to and from the steamer as we sailed from Sitka to Wrangell. Soon after we arrived a solemn delegation of Stickeen Indians came to call on the bride; but as soon as they saw the puppy they were solemn no longer. His gravely humorous antics were irresistible. It was Moses who named him Stickeen after their tribe – an exceptional honour. Thereafter the whole tribe adopted and protected him, and woe to the Indian dog which molested him. Once when I was passing the house of this same Lot Tyeen, one of his large hunting dogs dashed out at Stickeen and began to worry him. Lot rescued the little fellow, delivered him to me and walked into his house. Soon he came out with his gun, and before I knew what he was about he had shot the offending Indian dog – a valuable hunting animal.

Stickeen lacked the obtrusively affectionate manner of many of his species, did not like to be fussed over, would even growl when our babies enmeshed their hands in his long hair; and yet, to a degree I have never known in another dog, he attracted the attention of everybody and won all hearts.

As instances: Dr. Kendall, "The Grand Old Man" of our Church, during his visit of 1879 used to break away from solemn counsels with the other D.D.s and the carpenters to run after and shout at Stickeen. And Mrs. McFarland, the Mother of Protestant missions in Alaska, often begged us to give her the dog; and, when later he was stolen from her care by an unscrupulous tourist and so forever lost to us, she could hardly afterwards speak of him without tears.

Stickeen was a born aristocrat, dainty and scrupulously clean. From puppyhood he never cared to play with the Indian dogs, and I was often amused to see the dignified but decided way in which he repulsed all attempts at familiarity on the part of the Indian children. He admitted to his friendship only a few of the natives, choosing those who had adopted the white man's dress and mode of living, and were devoid of the rank native odours. His likes and dislikes were very strong and always evident from the moment of his meeting with a stranger. There was something almost uncanny about the accuracy of his judgment when "sizing up" a man.

It was Stickeen himself who really decided the question whether we should take him with us on this trip. He listened to the discussion, pro and con, as he stood with me on the wharf, turning his sharp, expressive eyes and sensitive ears up to me or down to Muir in the canoe. When the argument seemed to be going against the dog he suddenly turned, deliberately walked down the gangplank to the canoe, picked his steps carefully to the bow, where my seat with Muir was arranged, and curled himself down on my coat. The discussion ended abruptly in a general laugh, and Stickeen went along.

Then the acute little fellow set about, in the wisest possible way, to conquer Muir. He was not obtrusive, never "butted in"; never offended by a too affectionate tongue. He listened silently to discussions on his merits, those first days; but when Muir's comparisons of the brilliant dogs of his acquaintance with Stickeen grew too "odious" Stickeen would rise, yawn openly and retire to a distance, not slinkingly, but with tail up, and lie down again out of earshot of such calumnies. When we landed after a day's journey Stickeen was always the first ashore, exploring for field mice and squirrels; but when we would start to the woods, the mountains or the glaciers the dog would join us, coming mysteriously from the forest. When our paths separated, Stickeen, looking to me for permission, would follow Muir, trotting at first behind him, but gradually ranging alongside.

After a few days Muir changed his tone, saying, "There's more in that wee beastie than I thought"; and before a week passed Stickeen's victory was complete; he slept at Muir's feet, went with him on all his rambles; and even among dangerous crevasses or far up the steep slopes of granite mountains the little dog's splendid tail would be seen ahead of Muir, waving cheery signals to his new-found human companion.

Our canoe was light and easily propelled. Our outfit was very simple, for this was to be a quick voyage and there were not to be so many missionary visits this time. It was principally a voyage of discovery; we were in search of the glacier that we had lost. Perched in the high stern sat our captain, Lot Tyeen, massive and capable, handling his broad steering paddle with power and skill. In front of him Joe and Billy pulled oars, Joe, a strong young man, our cook, hunter and best oarsman; Billy, a lad of seventeen, our interpreter and Joe's assistant. Towards the bow, just behind the mast, sat Muir and I, each with a paddle in his hands. Stickeen slumbered at our feet or gazed into our faces when our conversation interested him. When we began to discuss a landing place he would climb the high bow and brace himself on the top of the beak, an animated figure-head, ready to jump into the water when we were about to camp.

Our route was different from that of '79. Now we struck through Wrangell Narrows, that tortuous and narrow passage between Mitkof and Kupreanof Islands, past Norris Glacier with its far-flung shaft of ice appearing above the forests as if suspended in air; past the bold Pt. Windham with its bluff of three thousand feet frowning upon the waters of Prince Frederick Sound; across Port Houghton, whose deep fiord had no ice in it and, therefore, was not worthy of an extended visit. We made all haste, for Muir was, as the Indians said, "always hungry for ice," and this was more especially his expedition. He was the commander now, as I had been the year before. He had set for himself the limit of a month and must return by the October boat. Often we ran until late at night against the protests of our Indians, whose life of infinite leisure was not accustomed to such rude interruption. They could not understand Muir at all, nor in the least comprehend his object in visiting icy bays where there was no chance of finding gold and nothing to hunt.

The vision rises before me, as my mind harks back to this second trip of seven hundred miles, of cold, rainy nights, when, urged by Muir to make one more point, the natives passed the last favourable camping place and we blindly groped for hours in pitchy darkness, trying to find a friendly beach. The intensely phosphorescent water flashed about us, the only relief to the inky blackness of the night. Occasionally a salmon or a big halibut, disturbed by our canoe, went streaming like a meteor through the water, throwing off coruscations of light. As we neared the shore, the waves breaking upon the rocks furnished us the only illumination. Sometimes their black tops with waving seaweed, surrounded by phosphorescent breakers, would have the appearance of mouths set with gleaming teeth rushing at us out of the dark as if to devour us. Then would come the landing on a sandy beach, the march through the seaweed up to the wet woods, a fusillade of exploding fucus pods accompanying us as if the outraged fairies were bombarding us with tiny guns. Then would ensue a tedious groping with the lantern for a camping place and for some dry, fat spruce wood from which to coax a fire; then the big camp-fire, the bean-pot and coffee-pot, the cheerful song and story, and the deep, dreamless sleep that only the weary voyager or hunter can know.

Four or five days sufficed to bring us to our first objective – Sumdum or Holkham Bay, with its three wonderful arms. Here we were to find the lost glacier. This deep fiord has two great prongs. Neither of them figured in Vancouver's chart, and so far as records go we were the first to enter and follow to its end the longest of these, Endicott Arm. We entered the bay at night, caught again by the darkness, and groped our way uncertainly. We probably would have spent most of the night trying to find a landing place had not the gleam of a fire greeted us, flashing through the trees, disappearing as an island intervened, and again opening up with its fair ray as we pushed on. An hour's steady paddling brought us to the camp of some Cassiar miners – my friends. They were here at the foot of a glacier stream, from the bed of which they had been sluicing gold. Just now they were in hard luck, as the constant rains had swelled the glacial stream, burst through their wingdams, swept away their sluice-boxes and destroyed the work of the summer. Strong men of the wilderness as they were, they were not discouraged, but were discussing plans for prospecting new places and trying it again here next summer. Hot coffee and fried venison emphasised their welcome, and we in return could give them a little news from the outside world, from which they had been shut off completely for months.

Muir called us before daylight the next morning. He had been up since two or three o'clock, "studying the night effects," he said, listening to the roaring and crunching of the charging ice as it came out of Endicott Arm, spreading out like the skirmish line of an army and grinding against the rocky point just below us. He had even attempted a moonlight climb up the sloping face of a high promontory with Stickeen as his companion, but was unable to get to the top, owing to the smoothness of the granite rock. It was newly glaciated – this whole region – and the hard rubbing ice-tools had polished the granite like a monument. A hasty meal and we were off.

"We'll find it this time," said Muir.

A miner crawled out of his blankets and came to see us start. "If it's scenery you're after," he said, "ten miles up the bay there's the nicest canyon you ever saw. It has no name that I know of, but it is sure some scenery."

The long, straight fiord stretched southeast into the heart of the granite range, its funnel shape producing tremendous tides. When the tide was ebbing that charging phalanx of ice was irresistible, storming down the canyon with race-horse speed; no canoe could stem that current. We waited until the turn, then getting inside the outer fleet of icebergs we paddled up with the floodtide. Mile after mile we raced past those smooth mountain shoulders; higher and higher they towered, and the ice, closing in upon us, threatened a trap. The only way to navigate safely that dangerous fiord was to keep ahead of the charging ice. As we came up towards the end of the bay the narrowing walls of the fiord compressed the ice until it crowded dangerously around us. Our captain, Lot, had taken the precaution to put a false bow and stern on his canoe, cunningly fashioned out of curved branches of trees and hollowed with his hand-adz to fit the ends of the canoe. These were lashed to the bow and stern by thongs of deer sinew. They were needed. It was like penetrating an arctic ice-floe. Sometimes we would have to skirt the granite rock and with our poles shove out the ice-cakes to secure a passage. It was fully thirty miles to the head of the bay, but we made it in half a day, so strong was the current of the rising tide.

I shall never forget the view that burst upon us as we rounded the last point. The face of the glacier where it discharged its icebergs was very narrow in comparison with the giants of Glacier Bay, but the ice cliff was higher than even the face of Muir Glacier. The narrow canyon of hard granite had compressed the ice of the great glacier until it had the appearance of a frozen torrent broken into innumerable crevasses, the great masses of ice tumbling over one another and bulging out for a few moments before they came crashing and splashing down into the deep water of the bay. The fiord was simply a cleft in high mountains, and the depth of the water could only be conjectured. It must have been hundreds of feet, perhaps thousands, from the surface of the water to the bottom of that fissure. Smooth, polished, shining breasts of bright grey granite crowded above the glacier on every side, seeming to overhang the ice and the bay. Struggling clumps of evergreens clung to the mountain sides below the glacier, and up, away up, dizzily to the sky towered the walls of the canyon. Hundreds of other Alaskan glaciers excel this in masses of ice and in grandeur of front, but none that I have seen condense beauty and grandeur to finer results.

"What a plucky little giant!" was Muir's exclamation as we stood on a rock-mound in front of this glacier. "To think of his shouldering his way through the mountain range like this! Samson, pushing down the pillars of the temple at Gaza, was nothing to this fellow. Hear him roar and laugh!"

Without consulting me Muir named this "Young Glacier," and right proud was I to see that name on the charts for the next ten years or more, for we mapped Endicott Arm and the other arm of Sumdum Bay as we had Glacier Bay; but later maps have a different name. Some ambitious young ensign on a surveying vessel, perhaps, stole my glacier, and later charts give it the name of Dawes. I have not found in the Alaskan statute books any penalty attached to the crime of stealing a glacier, but certainly it ought to be ranked as a felony of the first magnitude, the grandest of grand larcenies.

A couple of days and nights spent in the vicinity of Young Glacier were a period of unmixed pleasure. Muir spent all of these days and part of the nights climbing the pinnacled mountains to this and that viewpoint, crossing the deep, narrow and dangerous glacier five thousand feet above the level of the sea, exploring its tributaries and their side canyons, making sketches in his notebook for future elaboration. Stickeen by this time constantly followed Muir, exciting my jealousy by his plainly expressed preference. Because of my bad shoulder the higher and steeper ascents of this very rugged region were impossible to me, and I must content myself with two thousand feet and even lesser climbs. My favourite perch was on the summit of a sugar-loaf rock which formed the point of a promontory jutting into the bay directly in front of my glacier, and distant from its face less than a quarter of a mile. It was a granite fragment which had evidently been broken off from the mountain; indeed, there was a niche five thousand feet above into which it would exactly fit. The sturdy evergreens struggled halfway up its sides, but the top was bare.

On this splendid pillar I spent many hours. Generally I could see Muir, fortunate in having sound arms and legs, scaling the high rock-faces, now coming out on a jutting spur, now spread like a spider against the mountain wall. Here he would be botanising in a patch of green that relieved the grey of the granite, there he was dodging in and out of the blue crevasses of the upper glacial falls. Darting before him or creeping behind was a little black speck which I made out to be Stickeen, climbing steeps up which a fox would hardly venture. Occasionally I would see him dancing about at the base of a cliff too steep for him, up which Muir was climbing, and his piercing howls of protest at being left behind would come echoing down to me.

But chiefly I was engrossed in the great drama which was being acted before me by the glacier itself. It was the battle of gravity with flinty hardness and strong cohesion. The stage setting was perfect; the great hall formed by encircling mountains; the side curtains of dark-green forest, fold on fold; the grey and brown top-curtains of the mountain heights stretching clear across the glacier, relieved by vivid moss and flower patches of yellow, magenta, violet and crimson. But the face of the glacier was so high and rugged and the ice so pure that it showed a variety of blue and purple tints I have never seen surpassed – baby-blue, sky-blue, sapphire, turquoise, cobalt, indigo, peacock, ultra-marine, shading at the top into lilac and amethyst. The base of the glacier face, next to the dark-green water of the bay, resembled a great mass of vitriol, while the top, where it wept out of the canyon, had the curves and tints and delicate lines of the iris.

But the glacier front was not still; in form and colour it was changing every minute. The descent was so steep that the glacial rapids above the bay must have flowed forward eighty or a hundred feet a day. The ice cliff, towering a thousand feet over the water, would present a slight incline from the perpendicular inwards toward the canyon, the face being white from powdered ice, the result of the grinding descent of the ice masses. Here and there would be little cascades of this fine ice spraying out as they fell, with glints of prismatic colours when the sunlight struck them. As I gazed I could see the whole upper part of the cliff slowly moving forward until the ice-face was vertical. Then, foot by foot it would be pushed out until the upper edge overhung the water. Now the outer part, denuded of the ice powder, would present a face of delicate blue with darker shades where the mountain peaks cast their shadows. Suddenly from top to bottom of the ice cliff two deep lines of prussian blue appeared. They were crevasses made by the ice current flowing more rapidly in the centre of the stream. Fascinated, I watched this great pyramid of blue-veined onyx lean forward until it became a tower of Pisa, with fragments falling thick and fast from its upper apex and from the cliffs out of which it had been split. Breathless and anxious, I awaited the final catastrophe, and its long delay became almost a greater strain than I could bear. I jumped up and down and waved my arms and shouted at the glacier to "hurry up".

Suddenly the climax came in a surprising way. The great tower of crystal shot up into the air two hundred feet or more, impelled by the pressure of a hundred fathoms of water, and then, toppling over, came crashing into the water with a roar as of rending mountains. Its weight of thousands of tons, falling from such a height, splashed great sheets of water high into the air, and a rainbow of wondrous brilliance flashed and vanished. A mighty wave swept majestically down the bay, rocking the massive bergs like corks, and, breaking against my granite pillar, tossed its spray half way up to my lofty perch. Muir's shout of applause and Stickeen's sharp bark came faintly to my ears when the deep rumbling of the newly formed icebergs had subsided.

That night I waited supper long for Muir. It was a good supper – a mulligan stew of mallard duck, with biscuits and coffee. Stickeen romped into camp about ten o'clock and his new master soon followed.

"Ah!" sighed Muir between sips of coffee, "what a Lord's mercy it is that we lost this glacier last fall, when we were pressed for time, to find it again in these glorious days that have flashed out of the mists for our special delectation. This has been a day of days. I have found four new varieties of moss, and have learned many new and wonderful facts about world-shaping. And then, the wonder and glory! Why, all the values of beauty and sublimity – form, colour, motion and sound – have been present today at their very best. My friend, we are the richest men in all the world tonight."

Charging down the canyon with the charging ice on our return, we kept to the right-hand shore, on the watch for the mouth of the canyon of "some scenery." We had not been able to discover it from the other side as we ascended the fiord. We were almost swept past the mouth of it by the force of the current. Paddling into an eddy, we were suddenly halted as if by a strong hand pushed against the bow, for the current was flowing like a cataract out of the narrow mouth of this side canyon. A rocky shelf afforded us a landing place. We hastily unloaded the canoe and pulled it up upon the beach out of reach of the floating ice, and there we had to wait until the next morning before we could penetrate the depths of this great canyon.

We shot through the mouth of the canyon at dangerous speed. Indeed, we could not do otherwise; we were helpless in the grasp of the torrent. At certain stages the surging tide forms an actual fall, for the entrance is so narrow that the water heaps up and pours over. We took the beginning of the flood tide, and so escaped that danger; but our speed must have been, at the narrows, twenty miles an hour. Then, suddenly, the bay widened out, the water ceased to swirl and boil and the current became gentle.

When we could lay aside our paddles and look up, one of the most glorious views of the whole world "smote us in the face," and Muir's chant arose, "Praise God from whom all blessings flow."

Before entering this bay I had expressed a wish to see Yosemite Valley. Now Muir said: "There is your Yosemite; only this one is on much the grander scale. Yonder towers El Capitan, grown to twice his natural size; there are the Sentinel, and the majestic Dome; and see all the falls. Those three have some resemblance to Yosemite Falls, Nevada and Bridalveil; but the mountain breasts from which they leap are much higher than in Yosemite, and the sheer drop much greater. And there are so many more of these and they fall into the sea. We'll call this Yosemite Bay – a bigger Yosemite, as Alaska is bigger than California."

Two very beautiful glaciers lay at the head of this canyon. They did not descend to the water, but the narrow strip of moraine matter without vegetation upon it between the glaciers and the bay showed that it had not been long since they were glaciers of the first class, sending out a stream of icebergs to join those from the Young Glacier. These glaciers stretched away miles and miles, like two great antennae, from the head of the bay to the top of the mountain range. But the most striking features of this scene were the wonderfully rounded and polished granite breasts of these great heights. In one stretch of about a mile on either side of the narrow bay parallel mouldings, like massive cornices of grey granite, five or six thousand feet high, overhung the water. These had been fluted and rounded and polished by the glacier stream, until they seemed like the upper walls and Corinthian capitals of a great temple. The power of the ice stream could be seen in the striated shoulders of these cliffs. What awful force that tool of steel-like ice must have possessed, driven by millions of tons of weight, to mould and shape and scoop out these flinty rock faces, as the carpenter's forming plane flutes a board!

When we were half-way up this wonderful bay the sun burst through a rift of cloud. "Look, look!" exclaimed Muir. "Nature is turning on the coloured lights in her great show house."

Instantly this severe, bare hall of polished rock was transformed into a fairy palace. A score of cascades, the most of them invisible before, leapt into view, falling from the dizzy mountain heights and spraying into misty veils as they descended; and from all of them flashed rainbows of marvellous distinctness and brilliance, waving and dancing – a very riot of colour. The tinkling water falling into the bay waked a thousand echoes, weird, musical and sweet, a riot of sound. It was an enchanted palace, and we left it with reluctance, remaining only six hours and going out at the turn of the flood tide to escape the dangerous rapids. Had there not been so many things to see beyond, and so little time in which to see them, I doubt if Muir would have quit Yosemite Bay for days.

CHAPTER SIX

The Dog and the Man

THERE IS NO TIME to tell of all the bays we explored; of Holkham Bay, Port Snettisham, Tahkou Harbour; all of which we rudely put on the map, or at least extended the arms beyond what was previously known. Through Gastineau Channel, now famous for some of the greatest quartz mines and mills in the world, we pushed, camping on the site of what is now Juneau, the capital city of Alaska.

An interesting bit of history is to be recorded here. Pushing across the flats at the head of the bay at high tide the next morning (for the narrow, grass-covered flat between Gastineau Channel and Stevens Passage can only be crossed with canoes at flood tide), we met two old gold prospectors whom I had frequently seen at Wrangell – Joe Harris and Joe Juneau. Exchanging greetings and news, they told us they were out from Sitka on a leisurely hunting and prospecting trip. Asking us about our last camping place, Harris said to Juneau, "Suppose we camp there and try the gravel of that creek."

These men found placer gold and rock "float" at our camp and made quite a clean-up that fall, returning to Sitka with a "gold-poke" sufficiently plethoric to start a stampede to the new diggings. Both placer and quartz locations were made and a brisk "camp" was built the next summer. This town was first called Harrisburg for one of the prospectors, and afterwards Juneau for the other. The great Treadwell gold quartz mine was located three miles from Juneau in 1881, and others subsequently. The territorial capital was later removed from Sitka to Juneau, and the city has grown in size and importance, until it is one of the great mining and commercial centres of the Northwest.

Through Stevens Passage we paddled, stopping to preach to the Auk Indians; then down Chatham Strait and into Icy Strait, where the crystal masses of Muir and Pacific glaciers flashed a greeting from afar. We needed no Hoonah guide this time, and it was well we did not, for both Hoonah villages were deserted. The inhabitants had gone to their hunting, fishing or berry-picking grounds.

At Pleasant Island we loaded, as on the previous trip, with dry wood for our voyage into Glacier Bay. We were not to attempt the head of the bay this time, but to confine our exploration to Muir Glacier, which we had only touched upon the previous fall. Pleasant Island was the scene of one of Stickeen's many escapades. The little island fairly teemed with big field mice and pine squirrels, and Stickeen went wild. We could hear his shrill bark, now here, now there, from all parts of the island. When we were ready to leave the next morning he was not to be seen. We got aboard as usual, thinking that he would follow. A quarter of a mile's paddling and still no little black head could be discovered in our wake. Muir, who was becoming very much attached to the little dog, was plainly worried.

"Row back," he said.

So we rowed back and called, but no Stickeen. Around the next point we rowed and whistled; still no Stickeen. At last, discouraged, I gave the signal to move off. So we rounded the curving shore and pushed towards Glacier Bay. At the far point of the island, a mile from our camping place, we suddenly discovered Stickeen away out in the water, paddling calmly and confidently towards our canoe. How he had ever got there I cannot imagine. I think he must have been taking a long swim out on the bay for the mere pleasure of it. Muir always insisted that he had listened to our discussion of the route to be taken, and, with an uncanny intuition that approached clairvoyance, knew just where to head us off.

When we took him aboard he went through his usual performance, making his way, the whole length of the canoe, until he got under Muir's legs, before shaking himself. No protests or discipline availed, for Muir's kicks always failed of their pretended mark. To the end of his acquaintance with Muir, he always chose the vicinity of Muir's legs as the place to shake himself after a swim.

At Muir Glacier we spent a week this time, making long trips up the mountains that overlooked the glacier and across its surface. On one occasion Muir, with the little dog at his heels, crossed entirely in a diagonal direction the great glacial lake, a trip of some thirty miles, starting before daylight in the morning and not appearing at camp until long after dark. Muir always carried several handkerchiefs in his pockets, but this time he returned without any, having used them all up making moccasins for Stickeen, whose feet were cut and bleeding from the sharp honeycomb ice of the glacial surface. This mass of ice is so vast and so comparatively still that it has but few crevasses, and Muir's day for traversing it was a perfect one – warm and sunny.

Another day he and I climbed the mountain that overlooked it and skirted the mighty ice-field for some distance, then walked across the face of the glacier just back of the rapids, keeping away from the deep crevasses. We drove a straight line of stakes across the glacial stream and visited them each day to watch the deflection and curves of the stakes, and thus arrive at some conception of the rate at which the ice mass was moving. In some parts of the glacial stream this ice current flowed as fast as fifty or sixty feet a day, and we could understand the constant breaking off and leaping up and smashing down of the ice and the formation of that great mass of bergs.

Shortly before we left Muir Glacier, I saw Muir furiously angry for the first and last time in my acquaintance with him. We had noticed day after day, whenever the mists admitted a view of the mountain slopes, bands of mountain goats looking like little white mice against the green of the high pastures. I said to Joe, the hunter, one morning: "Go up and get us a kid. It will be a great addition to our larder."

He took my breech-loading rifle and went. In the afternoon he returned with a fine young buck on his shoulders. While we were examining it he said:

"I picked the fattest and most tender of those that I killed."

"What!" I exclaimed, "did you kill more than this one?"

He put up both hands with fingers extended and then one finger:

"*Tatlum-pe-ict* (eleven)," he replied.

Muir's face flushed red, and with an exclamation that was as near to an oath as he ever came, he started for Joe. Luckily for that Indian he saw Muir and fled like a deer up the rocks, and would not come down until he was assured that he would not be hurt. I shared Muir's indignation and would have enjoyed seeing him administer the richly deserved thrashing.

Muir had a strong aversion to taking the life of any animal; although he would eat meat when prepared, he never killed a wild animal; even the rattlesnakes he did not molest during his rambles in California. Often his softness of heart was a source of some annoyance and a great deal of astonishment to our natives; for he would take pleasure in rocking the canoe when they were trying to get a bead on a flock of ducks or a deer standing on the shore.

On leaving the mouth of Glacier Bay we spent a week or more exploring the inlets and glaciers to the west. These days were rainy and cold. We groped blindly into unknown, unmapped, fog-hidden fiords and bayous, exploring them to their ends and often making excursions to the glaciers above them.

The climax of the trip, however, was the last glacier we visited, Taylor Glacier, the scene of Muir's great adventure with Stickeen. We reached this fine glacier in the afternoon of a very stormy day. We were approaching the open Pacific, and the saanah, the southeast rain-wind, was howling through the narrow entrance into Cross Sound. For twenty miles we had been facing strong head winds and tidal waves as we crept around rocky points and along the bases of dizzy cliffs and glacier-scored rock-shoulders. We were drenched to the skin; indeed, our clothing and blankets had been soaking wet for days. For two hours before we turned the point into the cosy harbour in front of the glacier we had been exerting every ounce of our strength; Lot in the stern wielding his big steering paddle, now on this side, now on that, grunting with each mighty stroke, calling encouragement to his crew, "*Ut-ha, ut-ha! hlitsin! hlitsin-tin!* (pull, pull, strong, with strength!)"; Joe and Billy rising from their seats with every stroke and throwing their whole weight and force savagely into their oars; Muir and I in the bow bent forward with heads down, butting into the slashing rain, paddling for dear life; Stickeen, the only idle one, looking over the side of the boat as though searching the channel and then around at us as if he would like to help. All except the dog were exhausted when we turned into the sheltered cove.

While the men pitched the tents and made camp Muir and I walked through the thick grass to the front of the large glacier, which front stretched from a high, perpendicular rock wall about three miles to a narrow promontory of moraine boulders next to the ocean.

"Now, here is something new," exclaimed Muir, as we stood close to the edge of the ice. "This glacier is the great exception. All the others of this region are receding; this has been coming forward. See the mighty plough share and its furrow!"

For the icy mass was heaving up the ground clear across its front, and, on the side where we stood, had evidently found a softer stratum under a forest-covered hill, and inserted its shovel point under the hill, heaved it upon the ice, cracking the rocks into a thousand fragments; and was carrying the whole hill upon its back towards the sea. The large trees were leaning at all angles, some of them submerged, splintered and ground by the crystal torrent, some of the shattered trunks sticking out of the ice. It was one of the most tremendous examples of glacial power I have ever seen.

"I must climb this glacier tomorrow," said Muir. "I shall have a great day of it; I wish you could come along."

I sighed, not with resignation, but with a grief that was akin to despair. The condition of my shoulders was such that it would be madness to attempt to join Muir on his longer and more perilous climbs. I should only spoil his day and endanger his life as well as my own.

That night I baked a good batch of camp bread, boiled a fresh kettle of beans and roasted a leg of venison ready for Muir's breakfast, fixed the coffee-pot and prepared dry kindling for the fire. I knew he would be up and off at daybreak, perhaps long before.

"Wake me up," I admonished him, "or at least take time to make hot coffee before you start." For the wind was rising and the rain pouring, and I knew how imperative the call of such a morning as was promised would be to him. To traverse a great, new, living, rapidly moving glacier would be high joy; but to have a tremendous storm added to this would simply drive Muir wild with desire to be himself a part of the great drama played on the glacier-stage.

Several times during the night I was awakened by the flapping of the tent, the shrieking of the wind in the spruce-tops and the thundering of the ocean surf on the outer barrier of rocks. The tremulous howling of a persistent wolf across the bay soothed me to sleep again, and I did not wake when Muir arose. As I had feared, he was in too big a hurry to take time for breakfast, but pocketed a small cake of camp bread and hastened out into the storm-swept woods. I was aroused, however, by the controversy between him and Stickeen outside of the tent. The little dog, who always slept with one eye and ear alert for Muir's movements, had, as usual, quietly left his warm nest and followed his adopted master. Muir was scolding and expostulating with him as if he were a boy. I chuckled to myself at the futility of Muir's efforts; Stickeen would now, as always, do just as he pleased – and he would please to go along.

Although I was forced to stay at the camp, this stormy day was a most interesting one to me. There was an old Hoonah chief camped at the mouth of the little river which flowed from under Taylor Glacier. He had with him his three wives and a little company of children and grandchildren. The many salmon weirs and summer houses at this point showed that it had been at one time a very important fishing place.

But the advancing glacier had played havoc with the chief's salmon stream. The icy mass had been for several years travelling towards the sea at the rate of at least a mile every year. There were still silver hordes of fine red salmon swimming in the sea outside of the river's mouth. But the stream 'was now so short that the most of these salmon swam a little ways into the mouth of the river and then out into the salt water again, bewildered and circling about, doubtless wondering what had become of their parent stream.

The old chief came to our camp early, followed by his squaws bearing gifts of salmon, porpoise meat, clams and crabs; and at his command two of the girls of his family picked me a basketful of delicious wild strawberries. He sat motionless by my fire all the forenoon, smoking my leaf tobacco and pondering deeply. After the noon meal, which I shared with him, he called Billy, my interpreter, and asked for a big talk.

With all ceremony I made preparations, gave more presents of leaf tobacco and hardtack and composed myself for the palaver. After the usual preliminaries, in which he told me at great length what a great man I was, how like a father to all the people, comparing me to sun, moon, stars and all other great things; I broke in upon his stream of compliments and asked what he wanted.

Recalled to earth he said: "I wish you to pray to your God."

"For what do you wish me to pray?" I asked.

The old man raised his blanketed form to its full height and waved his hand with a magnificent gesture towards the glacier. "Do you see that great ice mountain?"

"Yes."

"Once," he said, "I had the finest salmon stream upon the coast." Pointing to a point of rock five or six miles beyond the mouth of the glacier he continued: "Once the salmon stream extended far beyond that point of rock. There was a great fall there and a deep pool below it, and here for years great schools of king salmon came crowding up to the foot of that fall. To spear them or net them was very easy; they were the fattest and best salmon among all these islands. My household had abundance of meat for the winter's need. But the cruel spirit of that glacier grew angry with me, I know not why, and drove the ice mountain down towards the sea and spoiled my salmon stream. A year or two more and it will be blotted out entirely. I have done my best. I have prayed to my gods. Last spring I sacrificed two of my slaves, members of my household, my best slaves, a strong man and his wife, to the spirit of that glacier to make the ice mountain stop; but it comes on, and now I want you to pray to *your* God, the God of the white man, to see if He will make the glacier stop!''

I wish I could describe the pathetic earnestness of this old Indian, the simplicity with which he told of the sacrifice of his slaves and the eager look with which he awaited my answer. When I exclaimed in horror at his deed of blood he was astonished; he could not understand.

"Why, they were *my* slaves," he said, "and the man suggested it himself. He was glad to go to death to help his chief."

A few years after this our missionary at Hoonah had the pleasure of baptising this old chief into the Christian faith. He had put away his slaves and his plural wives, had surrendered the implements of his old superstition, and as a child embraced the new gospel of peace and love. He could not get rid of his superstition about the glacier, however, and about eight years afterwards, visiting at Wrangell, he told me as an item of news which he expected would greatly please me that, doubtless as a result of my prayers, Taylor Glacier was receding again and the salmon beginning to come into that stream.

At intervals during this eventful day I went to the face of the glacier and even climbed the disintegrating hill that was riding on the glacier's ploughshare, in an effort to see the bold wanderers; but the jagged ice peaks of the high glacial rapids blocked my vision, and the rain driving passionately in horizontal sheets shut out the mountains and the upper plateau of ice. I could see that it was snowing on the glacier, and imagined the weariness and peril of dog and man exposed to the storm in that dangerous region. I could only hope that Muir had not ventured to face the wind on the glacier, but had contented himself with tracing its eastern side, and was somewhere in the woods bordering it, beside a big fire, studying storm and glacier in comparative safety.

When the shadows of evening were added to those of the storm I had my men gather materials for a big bonfire, and kindle it well out on the flat, where it could be seen from mountain and glacier. I placed dry clothing and blankets in the fly tent facing the camp-fire, and got ready the best supper at my command: clam chowder, fried porpoise, bacon and beans, "savoury meat" made of mountain kid with potatoes, onions, rice and curry, camp biscuit and coffee, with dessert of wild strawberries and condensed milk.

It grew pitch-dark before seven, and it was after ten when the dear wanderers staggered into camp out of the dripping forest. Stickeen did not bounce in ahead with a bark, as was his custom, but crept silently to his piece of blanket and curled down, too tired to shake himself. Billy and I laid hands on Muir without a word, and in a trice he was stripped of his wet garments, rubbed dry, clothed in dry underwear, wrapped in a blanket and set down on a bed of spruce twigs with a plate of hot chowder before him. When the chowder disappeared the other hot dishes followed in quick succession, without a question asked or a word uttered. Lot kept the fire blazing just right, Joe kept the victuals hot and baked fresh bread, while Billy and I waited on Muir.

Not till he came to the coffee and strawberries did Muir break the silence. "Yon's a brave doggie," he said. Stickeen, who could not yet be induced to eat, responded by a glance of one eye and a feeble pounding of the blanket with his heavy tail.

Then Muir began to talk, and little by little, between sips of coffee, the story of the day was unfolded. Soon memories crowded for utterance and I listened till midnight, entranced by a succession of vivid descriptions the like of which I have never heard before or since. The fierce music and grandeur of the storm, the expanse of ice with its bewildering crevasses, its mysterious contortions, its solemn voices were made to live before me.

When Muir described his marooning on the narrow island of ice surrounded by fathomless crevasses, with a knife-edged sliver curving deeply "like the cable of a suspension bridge" diagonally across it as the only means of escape, I shuddered at his peril. I held my breath as he told of the terrible risks he ran as he cut his steps down the wall of ice to the bridge's end, knocked off the sharp edge of the sliver, hitched across inch by inch and climbed the still more difficult ascent on the other side. But when he told of Stickeen's cries of despair at being left on the other side of the crevasse, of his heroic determination at last to do or die, of his careful progress across the sliver as he braced himself against the gusts and dug his little claws into the ice, and of his passionate revulsion to the heights of exultation when, intoxicated by his escape, he became a living whirlwind of joy, flashing about in mad gyrations, shouting and screaming "Saved! saved!" my tears streamed down my face. Before the close of the story Stickeen arose, stepped slowly across to Muir and crouched down with his head on Muir's foot, gazing into his face and murmuring soft canine words of adoration to his god.

Not until 1897, seventeen years after the event, did Muir give to the public his story of Stickeen. How many times he had written and rewritten it I know not. He told me at the time of its first publication that he had been thinking of the story all of these years and jotting down paragraphs and sentences as they occurred to him. He was never satisfied with a sentence until it balanced well. He had the keenest sense of melody, as well as of harmony, in his sentence structure, and this great dog story of his is a remarkable instance of the growth to perfection of the great production of a great master.

The wonderful power of endurance of this man, whom Theodore Roosevelt has well called a "perfectly natural man," is instanced by the fact that, although he was gone about seventeen hours on this day of his adventure with Stickeen, with only a bite of bread to eat, and never rested a minute of that time, but was battling with the storm all day and often racing at full speed across the glacier, yet he got up at daylight the next morning, breakfasted with me and was gone all day again, with Stickeen at his heels, climbing a high mountain to get a view of the snow fountains and upper reaches of the glacier; and when he returned after nightfall he worked for two or three hours at his notes and sketches.

The latter part of this voyage was hurried. Muir had a wife waiting for him at home and he had promised to stay in Alaska only one month. He had dallied so long with his icy loves, the glaciers, that we were obliged to make all haste to Sitka, where he expected to take the return steamer. To miss that would condemn him to Alaska and absence from his wife for another month. Through a continually pouring rain we sailed by the then deserted town of Hoonah, ascended with the rising tide a long, narrow, shallow inlet, dragged our canoe a hundred yards over a little hill and then descended with the receding tide another long, narrow passage down to Chatham Strait; and so on to the mouth of Peril Strait which divided Baranof from Chichagof Island.

On the other side of Chatham Strait, opposite the mouth of Peril, we visited again Angoon, the village of the Hootz-noos. From this town the painted and drunken warriors had come the winter before and attacked the Stickeens, killing old Tow-a-att, Moses and another of our Christian Indians. The trouble was not settled yet, and although the two tribes had exchanged some pledges and promised to fight no more, I feared a fresh outbreak, and so thought it wise to pay another visit to the Hootz-noos. As we approached Angoon, however, I heard the war-drums beating with their peculiar cadence, "tum-tum" – a beat off – "tum-tum, tum-tum." As we came up to the beach I saw what was seemingly the whole tribe dancing their war-dances, arrayed in their war-paint with their fantastic war gear on. So earnestly engaged were they in their dance that they at first paid no attention whatever to me. My heart sank into my boots. "They are going back to Wrangell to attack the Stickeens," I thought, "and there will be another bloody war."

Driving our canoe ashore, we hurried up to the head chief of the Hootz-noos, who was alternately haranguing his people and directing the dances.

"Anatlask," I called, "what does this mean? You are going on the warpath. Tell me what you are about. Are you going back to Stickeen?"

He looked at me vacantly a little while, and then a grin spread from ear to ear. It was the same chief in whose house I had seen the idiot boy a year before.

"Come with me," he said.

He led us into his house and across the room to where in state, surrounded by all kinds of chieftain's gear, Chilcat blankets, totemic carvings and paintings, chieftain's hats and cunningly woven baskets, there lay the body of a stalwart young man wrapped in a button-embroidered blanket. The chief silently removed the blanket from the face of the dead. The skull was completely crushed on one side as by a heavy blow. Then the story came out.

The hootz, or big brown bear of that country, is as large and savage as the grizzly bear of the Rockies. At certain seasons he is, as the natives say, *"quonsum sollex"* (always mad). The natives seldom attack these bears, confining their attention to the more timid and easily killed black bears. But this young man with a companion, hunting on Baranof Island across the Strait, found himself suddenly confronted by an enormous hootz. The young man rashly shot him with his musket, wounding him sufficiently to make him furious. The tremendous brute hurled his thousand pounds of ferocity at the hunter, and one little tap of that huge paw crushed his skull like an egg-shell. His companion brought his body home; and now the whole tribe had formally declared war on that bear, and all this dancing and painting and drumming was in preparation for a war party, composed of all the men, dogs and guns in the town. They were going on the warpath to get that bear. Greatly relieved, I gave them my blessing and sped them on their way.

We had been rowing all night before this incident, and all the next night we sailed up the tortuous Peril Strait, going upward with the flood, one man steering while the other slept, to the meeting place of the waters; then down with the receding tide through the islands, and so on to Sitka. Here we met a warm reception from the missionaries, and also from the captain and officers of the old man-of-war Jamestown, afterwards used as a school ship for the navy in the harbour of San Francisco.

Alaska at that time had no vestige of civil government, no means of punishing crime, no civil officers except the customs collectors, no magistrate or police – everyone was a law to himself. The only sign of authority was this cumbersome sailing vessel with its marines and sailors. It could not move out of Sitka harbour without first sending by the monthly mail steamer to San Francisco for a tug to come and tow it through these intricate channels to the sea where the sails could be spread. Of course, it was not of much use to this vast territory. The officers of the Jamestown were supposed to be doing some surveying, but, lacking the means of travel, what they did amounted to very little.

They were interested at once in our account of the discovery of Glacier Bay and of the other unmapped bays and inlets that we had entered. At their request, from Muir's notes and our estimate of distances by our rate of sailing, and of directions from observations of our little compass, we drew a rough map of Glacier Bay. This was sent on to Washington by these officers and published by the Navy Department. For six or seven years it was the only sailing chart of Glacier Bay, and two or three steamers were wrecked, groping their way in these uncharted passages, before surveying vessels began to make accurate maps. So from its beginning has Uncle Sam neglected this greatest and richest of all his possessions.

Our little company separated at Sitka. Stickeen and our Indian crew were the first to leave, embarking for a return trip to Wrangell by canoe. Stickeen had stuck close to Muir, following him everywhere, crouching at his feet where he sat, sleeping in his room at night. When the time came for him to leave Muir explained the matter to him fully, talking to and reasoning with him as if he were human. Billy led him aboard the canoe by a dog-chain, and the last Muir saw of him he was standing on the stern of the canoe, howling a sad farewell.

Muir sailed south on the monthly mail steamer; while I took passage on a trading steamer for another missionary trip among the northern tribes.

So ended my canoe voyages with John Muir. Their memory is fresh and sweet as ever. The flowing stream of years has not washed away nor dimmed the impressions of those great days we spent together. Nearly all of them were cold, wet and uncomfortable, if one were merely an animal, to be depressed or enlivened by physical conditions. But of these so-called "hardships" Muir made nothing, and I caught his spirit; therefore, the beauty, the glory, the wonder and the thrills of those weeks of exploration are with me yet and shall endure – a rustless, inexhaustible treasure.

CHAPTER SEVEN

The Man in Perspective

THE FRIENDSHIP between John Muir and myself was of that fine sort which grows and deepens with absence almost as well as with companionship. Occasional letters passed from one to the other. When I felt like writing to Muir I obeyed the impulse without asking whether I "owed" him a letter, and he followed the same rule – or rather lack of rule. Sometimes answers to these letters came quickly; sometimes they were long delayed, so long that they were not answers at all. When I sent him "news of his mountains and glaciers" that contained items really novel to him his replies were immediate and enthusiastic. When he had found in his great outdoor museum some peculiar treasure he talked over his find with me by letter.

Muir's letters were never commonplace and sometimes they were long and rich. I preserved them all; and when, a few years ago, an Alaska steamboat sank to the bottom of the Yukon, carrying with it my library and all my literary possessions, the loss of these letters from my friend caused me more sorrow than the loss of almost any other of my many priceless treasures.

The summer of 1881, the year following that of our second canoe voyage, Muir went, as scientific and literary expert, with the U. S. revenue cutter *Rogers*, which was sent by the Government into the Arctic Ocean in search of the ill-fated De Long exploring party. His published articles written on the revenue cutter were of great interest; but in his more intimate letters to me there was a note of disappointment.

"There have been no mountains to climb," he wrote, "although I have had entrancing long-distance views of many. I have not had a chance to visit any glaciers. There were no trees in those arctic regions, and but few flowers. Of God's process of modelling the world I saw but little – nothing for days but that limitless, relentless ice-pack. I was confined within the narrow prison of the ship; I had no freedom, I went at the will of other men; not of my own. It was very different from those glorious canoe voyages with you in your beautiful, fruitful wilderness."

A very brief visit at Muir's home near Martinez, California, in the spring of 1883 found him at what he frankly said was very distasteful work – managing a large fruit ranch. He was doing the work well and making his orchards pay large dividends; but his heart was in the hills and woods. Eagerly he questioned me of my travels and of the "progress" of the

Our paths did not converge again for nine years; but I was to have, after all, a few more Alaska days with John Muir. The itch of the wanderlust in my feet had become a wearisome, nervous ache, increasing with the years, and the call of the wild more imperative, until the fierce yearning for the North was at times more than I could bear.

The first of the great northward gold stampedes – that of 1897 to the Klondyke in Northwestern Canada on the borders of Alaska – afforded me the opportunity for which I was longing to return to the land of my heart. The latter part of August saw me on *The Queen*, the largest of that great fleet of passenger boats that were traversing the thousand miles of wonder and beauty between Seattle and Skagway. These steamboats were all laden with gold seekers and their goods. Seattle sprang into prominence and wealth, doubling her population in a few months. From every community in the United States, from all Canada and from many lands across the oceans came that strange mob of lawyers, doctors, clerks, merchants, farmers, mechanics, engineers, reporters, sharpers – all gold-struck – all mad with excitement – all rushing pell-mell into a thousand new and hard experiences.

As I stood on the upper deck of the vessel, watching the strange scene on the dock, who should come up the gang-plank but John Muir, wearing the same old grey ulster and Scotch cap! It was the last place in the world I would have looked for him. But he was not stampeding to the Klondyke. His being there at that time was really an accident. In company with two other eminent "tree-men" he had been spending the summer in the study of the forests of Canada and the three were "climaxing," as they said, in the forests of Alaska.

Five pleasurable days we had together on board *The Queen*. Muir was vastly amused by the motley crowd of excited men, their various outfits, their queer equipment, their ridiculous notions of camping and life in the wilderness. "A nest of ants," he called them, "taken to a strange country and stirred up with a stick."

As our steamboat touched at Port Townsend, Muir received a long telegram from a San Francisco newspaper, offering him a large sum if he would go over the mountains and down the Yukon to the Klondyke, and write them letters about conditions there. He brought the telegram to me, laughing heartily at the absurdity of anybody making him such a proposition.

"Do they think I'm daft," he asked, "like a' the lave o' thae puir bodies? When I go into that wild it will not be in a crowd like this or on such a sordid mission. Ah! my old friend, they'll be spoiling our grand Alaska."

He offered to secure for me the reporter's job tendered to him. I refused, urging my lack of training for such work and my more important and responsible position.

"Why, that same paper has a host of reporters on the way to the Klondyke now," I said. "There is —— " (naming a noted poet and author of the Coast). "He must be halfway down to Dawson by this time."

glaciers and woods of Alaska. Beyond a few short mountain trips he had seen nothing for two years of his beloved wilds.

Passionately he voiced his discontent: "I am losing the precious days. I am degenerating into a machine for making money. I am learning nothing in this trivial world of men. I must break away and get out into the mountains to learn the news."

In 1888 the ten years' limit which I had set for service in Alaska expired. The educational necessities of my children and the feeling that was growing upon me like a smothering cloud that if I remained much longer among the Indians I would lose all power to talk or write good English, drove me from the Northwest to find a temporary home in Southern California.

I had not notified Muir of my coming, but suddenly appeared in his orchard at Martinez one day in early summer. It was cherry-picking time and he was out among his trees superintending a large force of workmen. He saw me as soon as I discovered him, and dropping the basket he was carrying came running to greet me with both hands outstretched.

"Ah! my friend," he cried, "I have been longing mightily for you. You have come to take me on a canoe trip to the countries beyond – to Lituya and Yakutat bays and Prince William Sound; have you not? My weariness of this hum-drum, work-a-day life has grown so heavy it is like to crush me. I'm ready to break away and go with you whenever you say."

"No," I replied, "I am leaving Alaska."

"Man, man!" protested Muir, "how can you do it? You'll never carry out such a notion as that in the world. Your heart will cry every day for the North like a lost child; and in your sleep the snow-banners of your white peaks will beckon to you.

"Why, look at me," he said, "and take warning. I'm a horrible example. I, who have breathed the mountain air – who have really lived a life of freedom – condemned to penal servitude with these miserable little bald-heads!" (holding up a bunch of cherries). "Boxing them up; putting them in prison! And for money! Man! I'm like to die of the shame of it.

"And then you're not safe a day in this sordid world of money-grubbing men. I came near dying a mean, civilized death, the other day. A Chinaman emptied a bucket of phosphorus over me and almost burned me up. How different that would have been from a nice white death in a glacier crevasse!

"Gin it were na for my bairnies I'd rin awa' frae a' this tribble an' hale ye back north wi' me."

So Muir would run on, now in English, now in broad Scotch; but through all his raillery there ran a note of longing for the wilderness. "I want to see what is going on," he said. "So many great events are happening, and I'm not there to see them. I'm learning nothing here that will do me any good."

I spent the night with him, and we talked till long after midnight, sailing anew our voyages of enchantment. He had just completed his work of editing *Picturesque California* and gave me a set of the beautiful volumes.

" —— doesn't count," replied Muir, "for the patent reason that everybody knows he can't tell the truth. The poor fellow is not to blame for it. He was just made that way. Everybody will read with delight his wonderful tales of the trail, but nobody will believe him. We all know him too well."

Muir contracted a hard cold the first night out from Seattle. The hot, close stateroom and a cold blast through the narrow window were the cause. A distressing cough racked his whole frame. When he refused to go to a physician who was on the boat I brought the doctor to him. After the usual examination the physician asked, "What do you generally do for a cold?"

"Oh," said Muir, "I shiver it away."

"Explain yourself," said the puzzled doctor.

"We-ll," drawled Muir, "two or three years ago I camped by the Muir Glacier for a week. I had caught just such a cold as this from the same cause – a stuffy stateroom. So I made me a little sled out of spruce boughs, put a blanket and some sea biscuit on it and set out up the glacier. I got into a labyrinth of crevasses and a driving snowstorm, and had to spend the night on the ice ten miles from land. I sat on the sled all night or thrashed about it, and had a dickens of a time; I shivered so hard I shook the sled to pieces. When morning came my cold was all gone. That is my prescription, Doctor. You are welcome to use it in your practice."

"Well," laughed the doctor, "if I had such patients as you in such a country as this I might try your heroic remedy, but I am afraid it would hardly serve in general practice."

Muir and I made the most of these few days together, and walked the decks till late each night, for he had much to tell me. He had at last written his story of Stickeen; and was working on books treating of the Big Trees, the National Parks and the glaciers of Alaska.

At Wrangell, as we went ashore, we were greeted by joyful exclamations from the little company of old Stickeen Indians we found on the dock. That sharp intaking of the breath which is the Thlinget's note of surprise and delight, and the words *Nuknate Ankow ka Glate Ankow* (Priest Chief and Ice Chief) passed along the line. Death had made many gaps in the old circle of friends, both white and native, but the welcome from those who remained warmed our hearts.

From Wrangell northward the steamboat followed the route of our canoe voyage of 1880 through Wrangell Narrows into Prince Frederick Sound, past Norris Glacier and Holkham Bay into Stevens Passage, past Taku Bay to Juneau and on to Lynn Canal – then on the track of our voyage of 1879 up to Haines and beyond fifteen miles to that new, chaotic camp in the woods called Skagway.

The two or three days which it took *The Queen* to discharge her load of passengers and cargo of their outfits were spent by Muir and his scientific companions in roaming the forests and mountains about Skagway and examining the flora of that region. They kept mostly off the trail of the struggling, straggling army of *Cheechakoes* (newcomers) who were blunderingly trying to get their goods and themselves across the rugged, jagged mountains on their way to the promised land of gold; but Muir found time to spend some hours with me in my camp under a hemlock, where he ate again of my cooking over a campfire. "You are going on a strange journey this time, my friend," he admonished me. "I don't envy you. You'll have a hard time keeping your heart light and simple in the midst of this crowd of madmen. Instead of the music of the wind among the spruce-tops and the tinkling of the waterfalls, your ears will be filled with the oaths and groans of these poor, deluded, self-burdened men. Keep close to Nature's heart, yourself; and break clear away, once in a while, and climb a mountain or spend a week in the woods. Wash your spirit clean from the earthstains of this sordid, gold-seeking crowd in God's pure air. It will help you in your efforts to bring to these men something better than gold. Don't lose your freedom and your love of the Earth as God made it."

In 1899 it was my good fortune to have one more Alaska day with John Muir at Skagway. After a year in the Klondyke I had spent the winter of 1898–99 in the Eastern States arousing the Christian public to the needs of this newly discovered Empire of the North; and was returning with other ministers to interior and western Alaska. The White Pass Railroad was completed only to the summit; and it was a laborious task, requiring a month of very hard work, to get our goods from Skagway over the thirty miles of mountains to Lake Bennett, where we could load them on our open boat for the voyage of two thousand miles down the Yukon.

While I was engaged in this task there came to Skagway the steamship *George W. Elder*, carrying one of the most remarkable companies of scientific men ever gathered together in one expedition. Mr. Harriman, the great railroad magnate, had chartered the steamer, and had invited as his guests many men of world reputation in various branches of natural science. Among them were John Burroughs, Drs. Merriam and Dahl of the Smithsonian Institute, and, not least, John Muir. Indeed he was called the Nestor of the expedition and his advice followed as that of no other.

The enticing proposition was made me by Muir, and backed by Mr. Harriman's personal invitation, that I should join this distinguished company, share Muir's stateroom and spend the summer cruising along the southern and western coasts of Alaska. However, the new mining camps were calling with a still more imperative voice, and I had to turn my back to the Coast and face the great, sun-bathed Interior. But what a joy and inspiration it would have been to climb Muir, Geicke and Taylor glaciers again with Muir, note the rapid progress God was making in His work of landscape gardening by means of these great tools, make at last our deferred visits to Lituya and Yakutat bays and the fine glaciers of Prince William's Sound, and renew my studies of this good world under my great Master.

A letter from Muir about his summer's cruise, written in November,

1899, reached me at home in June, 1900; for those of us who had reached that bleak, exposed northwestern coast and wintered there did not get any mail for six months. We were fifteen hundred miles from a post-office.

In his letter Muir wrote: ''The voyage was a grand one, and I saw much that was new to me and packed full of interest and instruction. But, do you know, I longed to break away from the steamboat and its splendid company, get a dugout canoe and a crew of Indians, and, with you as my companion, poke into the nooks and crannies of the mountains and glaciers which we could not reach from the steamer. What great days we have had together, you and I!''

This day at Skagway, in 1899 was the last of my Alaska days with John Muir, except as I bring them back and live them over in my thoughts. How often in my long voyages, by canoe or steamer, among the thousand islands of southeastern Alaska, the intricate channels of Prince William's Sound, the great rivers and multitudinous lakes of the Interior, and the treeless, windswept coasts of Bering Sea and the Arctic Ocean; or in my tramps in the summer over the mountains and plains of Alaska, or in the winter with my dogs over the frozen wilderness fighting the great battle with the fierce cold or spellbound under the magic of the Aurora – how often have I longed for the presence of Muir to heighten my enjoyment by his higher ecstasy, or reveal to me what I was too dull to see or understand. I have had inspiring companions, and my life has been blessed by many friendships inestimably precious and rich; but for me the world has produced but one John Muir; and to no other man do I feel that I owe so much; for I was blind and he made me see!

Only once since 1899 did I meet him, and then but for an hour at his temporary home in Los Angeles in 1910. He was putting the finishing touches on his rich volume, *The Story of My Boyhood and Youth*. I submitted for his review and correction the article which forms the first two chapters of this book. With that nice regard for absolute verity which always characterised him he pointed out two or three passages in which his recollection clashed with mine, and I at once made the changes he suggested.

Muir never grew old. After he was sixty years of age (as men count age) some of his most daring feats of mountain climbing and some of his longest journeys into the wilds were undertaken. When he was past seventy he was still tramping and camping in the forests and among the hills. When he was seventy-three he made long trips to South America and Africa, and to the very end he was exploring, studying, working and enjoying.

All his writings exult with the spirit of immortal youth. There is in his books an intimate companionship with the trees, the mountains, the flowers and the animals, that is altogether fine. Surely no such books of mountains and forests were ever written as his *Mountains of California, My First Summer in the Sierra, The Yosemite* and *Our National Parks*. His brooks and trees are the abode of dryads and hamadryads – they live and talk.

And when he writes of the animals he has met in his rambles, without any attempt to put into their characters anything that does not belong to them, without "manufacturing his data," he somehow manages to do much more than introduce them to you; he makes you their intimate and admiring friends, as he was. His ouzel bobs you a cheery good morning and sprays you with its "ripple of song"; his Douglas squirrel scolds and swears at you with rough good nature; and his big-horn gazes at you with frank and friendly eyes and challenges you to follow to its splendid heights, not as a hunter but as a companion. You love them all, as Muir did.

As an instance of this power in his writings, when I returned from the Klondyke in 1898 the story of Stickeen had been published in a magazine a few months before. I met in New York a daughter of the great Field family, who when a child had heard me tell of Muir's exploit in rescuing me from the mountain top, and who had shouted with delight when I told of our sliding down the mountain in the moraine gravel. She asked me eagerly if I was the Mr. Young mentioned in Muir's story. When I said that I was she called to her companions and introduced me as the Owner of Stickeen; and I was content to have as my claim to an earthly immortality my ownership of an immortalised dog.

I cannot think of John Muir as dead, or as much changed from the man with whom I canoed and camped. He was too much a part of nature – too natural – to be separated from his mountains, trees and glaciers. Somewhere, I am sure, he is making other explorations, solving other natural problems, using that brilliant, inventive genius to good effect and some time again I shall hear him unfold anew, with still clearer insight and more eloquent words, fresh secrets of his "mountains of God."

The Thlingets have a Happy Hunting Ground in the Spirit Land for dogs as well as for men; and Muir used to contend that they were right – that the so-called lower animals have as much right to a Heaven as humans. I wonder if he has found a still more beautiful – a glorified – Stickeen; and if the little fellow still follows and frisks about him as in those great, old days. I like to think so; and when I too cross the Great Divide – and it can't be long now – I shall look eagerly for them both to be my companions in fresh adventures. In the meantime I am lonely for them and think of them often, and say, with *The Harvester*, "What a dog! – and what a MAN!!"

STICKEEN

First published in book form by the Houghton Mifflin Company
(Boston, New York, Chicago, 1909)

II

Stickeen

The Story of a Dog

IN THE SUMMER of 1880 I set out from Fort Wrangel in a canoe to continue the exploration of the icy region of south-eastern Alaska, begun in the fall of 1879. After the necessary provisions, blankets, etc. had been collected and stowed away, and my Indian crew were in their places ready to start, while a crowd of their relatives and friends on the wharf were bidding them goodbye and good-luck, my companion, the Rev. S. H. Young, for whom we were waiting, at last came aboard, followed by a little black dog, that immediately made himself at home by curling up in a hollow among the baggage. I like dogs, but this one seemed so small and worthless that I objected to his going, and asked the missionary why he was taking him.

"Such a little helpless creature will only be in the way," I said; "you had better pass him up to the Indian boys on the wharf, to be taken home to play with the children. This trip is not likely to be good for toy-dogs. The poor silly thing will be in rain and snow for weeks or months, and will require care like a baby."

But his master assured me that he would be no trouble at all; that he was a perfect wonder of a dog, could endure cold and hunger like a bear, swim like a seal, and was wondrous wise and cunning, etc., making out a list of virtues to show he might be the most interesting member of the party.

Nobody could hope to unravel the lines of his ancestry. In all the wonderfully mixed and varied dog-tribe I never saw any creature very much like him, though in some of his sly, soft, gliding motions and gestures he brought the fox to mind. He was short-legged and bunchy-bodied, and his hair, though smooth, was long and silky and slightly waved, so that when the wind was at his back it ruffled, making him look shaggy. At first sight his only noticeable feature was his fine tail, which was about as airy and shady as a squirrel's, and was carried curling forward almost to his nose. On closer inspection you might notice his thin sensitive ears, and sharp eyes with cunning tan-spots above them. Mr. Young told me that when the little fellow was a pup about the size of a woodrat he was presented to his wife by an Irish prospector at Sitka, and that on his arrival at Fort Wrangel he was adopted with enthusiasm by the Stickeen Indians as a sort of new good-luck totem, was named "Stickeen" for the tribe, and became a universal favourite, petted, protected, and admired wherever he went, and regarded as a mysterious fountain of wisdom.

On our trip he soon proved himself a queer character – odd, concealed, independent, keeping invincibly quiet, and doing many little puzzling things that piqued my curiosity. As we sailed week after week through the long intricate channels and inlets among the innumerable islands and mountains of the coast, he spent most of the dull days in sluggish ease, motionless, and apparently as unobserving as if in deep sleep. But I discovered that somehow he always knew what was going on. When the Indians were about to shoot at ducks or seals, or when anything along the shore was exciting our attention, he would rest his chin on the edge of the canoe and calmly look out like a dreamy-eyed tourist. And when he heard us talking about making a landing, he immediately roused himself to see what sort of a place we were coming to, and made ready to jump overboard and swim ashore as soon as the canoe reached the beach. Then, with a vigourous shake to get rid of the brine in his hair, he ran into the woods to hunt small game. But though always the first out of the canoe, he was always the last to get into it. When we were ready to start he could never be found, and refused to come to our call. We soon found out, however, that though we could not see him at such times, he saw us, and from the cover of the briars and huckleberry bushes in the fringe of the woods was watching the canoe with wary eye. For as soon as we were fairly off he came trotting down the beach, plunged into the surf, and swam after us, knowing well that we would cease rowing and take him in. When the contrary little vagabond came alongside, he was lifted by the neck, held at arms length a moment to drip, and dropped aboard. We tried to cure him of this trick by compelling him to swim a long way, as if we had a mind to abandon him; but this did no good: the longer the swim the better he seemed to like it.

Though capable of great idleness, he never failed to be ready for all sorts of adventures and excursions. One pitch-dark rainy night we landed about ten o'clock at the mouth of a salmon stream when the water was phosphorescent. The salmon were running, and the myriad fins of the unrushing multitude were churning all the stream into a silvery glow, wonderfully beautiful and impressive in the ebon darkness. To get a good view of the show I set out with one of the Indians and sailed up through the midst of it to the foot of a rapid about half a mile from camp, where the swift current dashing over rocks made the luminous glow most glorious. Happening to look back down the stream, while the Indian was catching a few of the struggling fish, I saw a long spreading fan of light like the tail of a comet, which we thought must be made by some big strange animal that was pursuing us. On it came with its magnificent train, until we imagined we could see the monster's head and eyes; but it was only Stickeen, who, finding I had left the camp, came swimming after me to see what was up.

When we camped early, the best hunter of the crew usually went to the woods for a deer, and Stickeen was sure to be at his heels, provided I had not gone out. For, strange to say, though I never carried a gun, he always followed me, forsaking the hunter and even his master to share my wanderings. The days that were too stormy for sailing I spent in the woods, or on the adjacent mountains, wherever my studies called me; and Stickeen always insisted on going with me, however wild the weather, gliding like a fox through dripping huckleberry bushes and thorny tangles of panax and rubus, scarce stirring their rain-laden leaves; wading and wallowing through snow, swimming icy streams, skipping over logs and rocks and the crevasses of glaciers with the patience and endurance of a determined mountaineer, never tiring or getting discouraged. Once he followed me over a glacier the surface of which was so crusty and rough that it cut his feet until every step was marked with blood; but he trotted on with Indian fortitude until I noticed his red track, and, taking pity on him, made him a set of moccasins out of a handkerchief. However great his troubles he never asked help or made any complaint, as if, like a philosopher, he had learned that without hard work and suffering there could be no pleasure worth having. Yet none of us was able to make out what Stickeen was really good for. He seemed to meet danger and hardships without anything like reason, insisted on having his own way, never obeyed an order, and the hunter could never set him on anything, or make him fetch the birds he shot. His equanimity was so steady it seemed due to want of feeling; ordinary storms were pleasures to him as for mere rain, he flourished in it like a vegetable.

No matter what advances you might make, scarce a glance or a tail-wag would you get for your pains. But though he was apparently as cold as a glacier and about as impervious to fun, I tried hard to make his acquaintance, guessing there must be something worth while hidden beneath so much courage, endurance, and love of wild-weathery adventure. No superannuated mastiff or bulldog grown old in office surpassed this fluffy midget in stoic dignity. He sometimes reminded me of a small, squat, unshakable desert cactus. For he never displayed a single trace of the, merry, tricksy, elfish fun of the terriers and collies that we all know, nor of their touching affection and devotion. Like children, most small dogs beg to be loved and allowed to love; but Stickeen seemed a very Diogenes, asking only to be let alone: a true child of the wilderness, holding the even tenor of his hidden life with the silence and serenity of nature. His strength of character lay in his eyes. They looked as old as the hills, and as young, and as wild. I never tired of looking into them: it was like looking into a landscape; but they were small and rather deepset, and had no explaining lines around them to give out particulars. I was accustomed to look into the faces of plants and animals, and I watched the little sphinx more and more keenly as an interesting study. But there is no estimating the wit and wisdom concealed and latent in our lower fellow mortals until made manifest by profound experiences; for it is through suffering that dogs as well as saints are developed and made perfect.

After exploring the Sumdum and Tahkoo fiords and their glaciers, we sailed through Stephen's Passage into Lynn Canal and thence through Icy

Strait into Cross Sound, searching for unexplored inlets leading toward the great fountain ice-fields of the Fairweather Range. Here, while the tide was in our favour, we were accompanied by a fleet of icebergs drifting out to the ocean from Glacier Bay. Slowly we paddled around Vancouver's Point, Wimbledon, our frail canoe tossed like a feather on the massive heaving swells coming in past Cape Spenser. For miles the sound is bounded by precipitous mural cliffs, which, lashed with wave-spray and their heads hidden in clouds, looked terribly threatening and stern. Had our canoe been crushed or upset we could have made no landing here, for the cliffs, as high as those of Yosemite, sink sheer into deep water. Eagerly we scanned the wall on the north side for the first sign of an opening fiord or harbour, all of us anxious except Stickeen, who dozed in peace or gazed dreamily at the tremendous precipices when he heard us talking about them. At length we made the joyful discovery of the mouth of the inlet now called "Taylor Bay," and about five o'clock reached the head of it and encamped in a spruce grove near the front of a large glacier.

While camp was being made, Joe the hunter climbed the mountain wall on the east side of the fiord in pursuit of wild goats, while Mr. Young and I went to the glacier. We found that it is separated from the waters of the inlet by a tide-washed moraine, and extends, an abrupt barrier, all the way across from wall to wall of the inlet, a distance of about three miles. But our most interesting discovery was that it had recently advanced, though again slightly receding. A portion of the terminal moraine had been plowed up and shoved forward, uprooting and overwhelming the woods on the east side. Many of the trees were down and buried, or nearly so, others were leaning away from the ice-cliffs, ready to fall, and some stood erect, with the bottom of the ice plough still beneath their roots and its lofty crystal spires towering high above their tops. The spectacle presented by these century-old trees standing close beside a spiry wall of ice, with their branches almost touching it, was most novel and striking. And when I climbed around the front, and a little way up the west side of the glacier, I found that it had swelled and increased in height and width in accordance with its advance, and carried away the outer ranks of trees on its bank.

On our way back to camp after these first observations I planned a far-and-wide excursion for the morrow. I awoke early, called not only by the glacier, which had been on my mind all night, but by a grand flood-storm. The wind was blowing a gale from the north and the rain was flying with the clouds in a wide passionate horizontal flood, as if it were all passing over the country instead of falling on it. The main perennial streams were booming high above their banks, and hundreds of new ones, roaring like the sea, almost covered the lofty grey walls of the inlet with white cascades and falls. I had intended making a cup of coffee and getting something like a breakfast before starting, but when I heard the storm and looked out I made haste to join it; for many of Nature's finest lessons are to be found in her storms, and if careful to keep in right relations with them, we may go safely abroad with them, rejoicing in the grandeur and beauty of their works and ways, and chanting with the old Norsemen. "The blast of the tempest aids our oars, the hurricane is our servant and drives us whither we wish to go." So, omitting breakfast, I put a piece of bread in my pocket and hurried away.

Mr. Young and the Indians were asleep, and so, I hoped, was Stickeen; but I had not gone a dozen rods before he left his bed in the tent and came boring through the blast after me. That a man should welcome storms for their exhilarating music and motion, and go forth to see God making landscapes, is reasonable enough; but what fascination could there be in such tremendous weather for a dog? Surely nothing akin to human enthusiasm for scenery or geology. Anyhow, on he came, breakfastless, through the choking blast. I stopped and did my best to turn him back. "Now don't," I said, shouting to make myself heard in the storm, "now don't Stickeen. What has got into your queer noddle now? You must be daft. This wild day has nothing for you. There is no game abroad, nothing but weather. Go back to camp and keep warm, get a good breakfast with your master, and be sensible for once. I can't carry you all day or feed you, and this storm will kill you."

But Nature, it seems, was at the bottom of the affair, and she gains her ends with dogs as well as with men, making us do as she likes, shoving and pulling us along her ways, however rough, all but killing us at times in getting her lessons driven hard home. After I had stopped again and again, shouting good warning advice, I saw that he was not to be shaken off; as well might the earth try to shake off the moon. I had once led his master into trouble, when he fell on one of the topmost jags of a mountain and dislocated his arm; now the turn of his humble companion was coming. The pitiful little wanderer just stood there in the wind, drenched and blinking, saying doggedly, "Where thou goest I will go." So at last I told him to come on if he must, and gave him a piece of the bread I had in my pocket; then we struggled on together, and thus began the most memorable of all my wild days.

The level flood, driving hard in our faces, thrashed and washed us wildly until we got into the shelter of a grove on the east side of the glacier near the front, where we stopped awhile for breath and to listen and look out. The exploration of the glacier was my main object, but the wind was too high to allow excursions over its open surface, where one might be dangerously shoved while balancing for a jump on the brink of a crevasse. In the mean time the storm was a fine study. Here the end of the glacier, descending an abrupt swell of resisting rock about five hundred feet high, leans forward and falls in ice cascades. And as the storm came down the glacier from the north, Stickeen and I were beneath the main current of the blast, while favourably located to see and hear it. What a psalm the storm was singing, and how fresh the smell of the washed earth and leaves and how sweet the still small voices of the storm! Detached wafts and swirls were coming through the woods, with music from the leaves and branches and furrowed boles, and even from the splintered rocks and ice-crags overhead, many of the tones soft and low and flute-like, as if each leaf and tree, crag and spire were a tuned reed.

A broad torrent, draining the side of the glacier, now swollen by scores of new streams from the mountains, was rolling boulders along its rocky channel, with thudding, bumping, muffled sounds, rushing towards the bay with tremendous energy, as if in haste to get out of the mountains; the waters above and beneath calling to each other, and all to the ocean, their home.

Looking southward from our shelter, we had this great torrent and the forested mountain wall above it on our left, the spiry ice-crags on our right, and smooth grey gloom ahead. I tried to draw the marvellous scene in my notebook, but the rain blurred the page in spite of all my pains to shelter it, and the sketch was almost worthless. When the wind began to abate, I traced the east side of the glacier. All the trees standing on the edge of the woods were barked and bruised, showing high-ice mark in a very telling way, while tens of thousands of those that had stood for centuries on the bank of the glacier farther out lay crushed and being crushed. In many places I could see down fifty feet or so beneath the margin of the glacier-mill, where trunks from one to two feet in diameter were being ground to pulp against outstanding rock-ribs and bosses of the bank. About three miles above the front of the glacier I climbed to the surface of it by means of axe-steps made easy for Stickeen. As far as the eye could reach, the level, or nearly level, glacier stretched away indefinitely beneath the grey sky, a seemingly boundless prairie of ice. The rain continued, and grew colder, which I did not mind, but a dim snowy look in the drooping clouds made me hesitate about venturing far from land. No trace of the west shore was visible, and in case the clouds should settle and give snow, or the wind again become violent, I feared getting caught in a tangle of crevasses. Snow-crystals, the flowers of the mountain clouds, are frail, beautiful things, but terrible when flying on storm-winds in darkening, benumbing swarms or when welded together into glaciers full of deadly crevasses. Watching the weather, I sauntered about on the crystal sea. For a mile or two out I found the ice remarkably safe. The marginal crevasses were mostly narrow, while the few wider ones were easily avoided by passing around them, and the clouds began to open here and there.

Thus encouraged, I at last pushed out for the other side; for Nature can make us do anything she likes. At first we made rapid progress, and the sky was not very threatening, while I took bearings occasionally with a pocket compass to enable me to find my way back more surely in case the storm should become blinding; but the structure lines of the glacier were my main guide. Toward the west side we came to a closely crevassed section in which we had to make long, narrow tacks and doublings, tracing the edges of tremendous transverse and longitudinal crevasses, many of which were from twenty to thirty feet wide, and perhaps a thousand feet deep – beautiful and awful. In working a way through them I was severely cautious, but Stickeen came on as unhesitating as the flying clouds. The widest crevasse that I could jump he would leap without so much as halting to take a look at it. The weather was now making quick changes, scattering bits of dazzling brightness through the wintry gloom; at rare intervals, when the sun broke forth wholly free, the glacier was seen from shore to shore with a bright array of encompassing mountains partly revealed, wearing the clouds as garments, while the prairie bloomed and sparkled with irised light from myriads of washed crystals. Then suddenly all the glorious show would be darkened and blotted out.

Stickeen seemed to care for none of these things, bright or dark, nor for the crevasses, wells, moulins, or swift flashing streams into which he might fall. The little adventurer was only about two years old, yet nothing seemed novel to him, nothing daunted him. He showed neither caution nor curiosity, wonder nor fear, but bravely trotted on as if glaciers were playgrounds. His stout, muffled body seemed all one skipping muscle, and it was truly wonderful to see how swiftly and to all appearance heedlessly he flashed across nerve-trying chasms six or eight feet wide. His courage was so unwavering that it seemed to be due to dullness of perception, as if he were only blindly bold; and I kept warning him to be careful. For we had been close companions on so many wilderness trips that I had formed the habit of talking to him as if he were a boy and understood every word.

We gained the west shore in about three hours; the width of the glacier here being about seven miles. Then I pushed northward in order to see as far back as possible into the fountains of the Fairweather Mountains, in case the clouds should rise. The walking was easy along the margin of the forest, which, of course, like that on the other side, had been invaded and crushed by the swollen, overflowing glacier. In an hour or so, after passing a massive headland, we came suddenly on a branch of the glacier, which, in the form of a magnificent ice-cascade two miles wide, was pouring over the rim of the main basin in a westerly direction, its surface broken into wave-shaped blades and shattered blocks, suggesting the wildest updashing, heaving, plunging motion of a great river cataract. Tracing it down three or four miles, I found that it discharged into a lake, filling it with icebergs.

I would gladly have followed the lake outlet to tide-water, but the day was already far spent, and the threatening sky called for haste on the return trip to get off the ice before dark. I decided therefore to go no farther and, after taking a general view of the wonderful region, turned back, hoping to see it again under more favourable auspices. We made good speed up the canyon of the great ice-torrent, and out on the main glacier until we had left the west shore about two miles behind us. Here we got into a difficult network of crevasses, the gathering clouds began to drop misty fringes, and soon the dreaded snow came flying thick and fast. I now began to feel anxious about finding a way in the blurring storm. Stickeen showed no trace of fear. He was still the same silent, able little hero. I noticed, however, that after the storm-darkness came on he kept close up behind me. The snow urged us to make still greater haste, but at the same time hid our way. I pushed on as best I could, jumping innumerable crevasses, and for every hundred rods or so of direct advance travelling a mile in doubling up and down in the turmoil of chasms and dislocated iceblocks. After an hour or two of this work we came to a series of longitudinal crevasses of appalling width, and almost straight and regular in trend, like immense furrows. These I traced with firm nerve, excited and strengthened by the danger, making wide jumps, poising cautiously on their dizzy edges after cutting hollows for my feet before making the spring, to avoid possible slipping or any uncertainty on the farther sides, where only one trial is granted – exercise at once frightful and inspiring. Stickeen followed seemingly without effort.

Many a mile we thus travelled, mostly up and down, making but little real headway in crossing, running instead of walking most of the time as the danger of being compelled to spend the night on the glacier became threatening. Stickeen seemed able for anything. Doubtless we could have weathered the storm for one night, dancing on a flat spot to keep from freezing, and I faced the threat without feeling anything like despair; but we were hungry and wet, and the wind from the mountains was still thick with snow and bitterly cold, so of course that night would have seemed a very long one. I could not see far enough through the blurring snow to judge in which general direction the least dangerous route lay, while the few dim, momentary glimpses I caught of mountains through rifts in the flying clouds were far from encouraging either as weather signs or as guides. I had simply to grope my way from crevasse to crevasse, holding a general direction by the ice-structure, which was not to be seen everywhere, and partly by the wind. Again and again I was put to my mettle, but Stickeen followed easily, his nerve apparently growing more unflinching as the danger increased. So it always is with mountaineers when hard beset. Running hard and jumping, holding every minute of the remaining daylight, poor as it was, precious, we doggedly persevered and tried to hope that every difficult crevasse we overcame would prove to be the last of its kind. But on the contrary, as we advanced they became more deadly trying.

At length our way was barred by a very wide and straight crevasse, which I traced rapidly northward a mile or so without finding a crossing or hope of one; then down the glacier about as far, to where it united with another uncrossable crevasse. In all this distance of perhaps two miles there was only one place where I could possibly jump it, but the width of this jump was the utmost I dared attempt, while the danger of slipping on the farther side was so great that I was loath to try it. Furthermore, the side I was on was about a foot higher than the other, and even with this advantage the crevasse seemed dangerously wide. One is liable to underestimate the width of crevasses where the magnitudes in general are great. I therefore stared at this one mighty keenly, estimating its width and the shape of the edge on the farther side, until I thought that I could jump it if necessary, but that in case I should be compelled to jump back from the lower side I might fail. Now, a cautious mountaineer seldom takes a step on unknown ground which seems at all dangerous that he cannot retrace in case he should be stopped by unseen obstacles ahead. This is the rule of mountaineers who live long, and, though in haste, I compelled myself to sit down and calmly deliberate before I broke it.

Retracing my devious path in imagination as if it were drawn on a chart, I saw that I was recrossing the glacier a mile or two farther up stream than the course pursued in the morning, and that I was now entangled in a section I had not before seen. Should I risk this dangerous jump, or try to regain the woods on the west shore, make a fire, and have only hunger to endure while waiting for a new day? I had already crossed so broad a stretch of dangerous ice that I saw it would be difficult to get back to the woods through the storm, before dark, and the attempt would most likely result in a dismal nightdance on the glacier; while just beyond the present barrier the surface seemed more promising, and the east shore was now perhaps about as near as the west. I was therefore eager to go on. But this wide jump was a dreadful obstacle.

At length, because of the dangers already behind me, I determined to venture against those that might be ahead, jumped and landed well, but with so little to spare that I more than ever dreaded being compelled to take that jump back from the lower side. Stickeen followed, making nothing of it, and we ran eagerly forward, hoping we were leaving all our troubles behind. But within the distance of a few hundred yards we were stopped by the widest crevasse yet encountered. Of course I made haste to explore it, hoping all might yet be remedied by finding a bridge or a way around either end. About three-fourths of a mile upstream I found that it united with the one we had just crossed, as I feared it would. Then, tracing it down, I found it joined the same crevasse at the lower end also, maintaining throughout its whole course a width of forty to fifty feet. Thus to my dismay I discovered that we were on a narrow island about two miles long, with two barely possible ways of escape: one back by the way we came, the other ahead by an almost inaccessible sliver-bridge that crossed the great crevasse from near the middle of it!

After this nerve-trying discovery I ran back to the sliver-bridge and cautiously examined it. Crevasses, caused by strains from variations in the rate of motion of different parts of the glacier and convexities in the channel, are mere cracks when they first open, so narrow as hardly to admit the blade of a pocket-knife, and gradually widen according to the extent of the strain and the depth of the glacier. Now some of these cracks are interrupted, like the cracks in wood, and in opening, the strip of ice between overlapping ends is dragged out, and may maintain a continuous connection between the sides, just as the two sides of a slivered crack in wood that is being split are connected. Some crevasses remain open for months or even years, and by the melting of their sides continue to increase in width long after the opening strain has ceased; while the sliver-bridges, level on top at first and perfectly safe, are at length melted to thin, vertical, knife-edged blades, the upper portion being most exposed to the weather; and since the exposure is greatest in the middle, they at length curve downward like the cables of suspension bridges. This one was evidently very old, for it had been weathered and wasted until it was the most dangerous and inaccessible that ever lay in my way. The width of the crevasse was here about fifty feet, and the sliver crossing diagonally was about seventy feet long; its thin knife-edge near the middle was depressed twenty-five or thirty feet below the level of the glacier, and the upcurving ends were attached to the sides eight or ten feet below the brink. Getting down the nearly vertical wall to the end of the sliver and up the other side were the main difficulties, and they seemed all but insurmountable. Of the many perils encountered in my years of wandering on mountains and glaciers none seemed so plain and stern and merciless as this. And it was presented when we were wet to the skin and hungry, the sky dark with quick driving snow, and the night near. But we were forced to face it. It was a tremendous necessity.

Beginning, not immediately above the sunken end of the bridge, but a little to one side, I cut a deep hollow on the brink for my knees to rest in. Then, leaning over, with my short-handled axe I cut a step sixteen or eighteen inches below, which on account of the sheerness of the wall was necessarily shallow. That step, however, was well made; its floor sloped slightly inward and formed a good hold for my heels. Then, slipping cautiously upon it, and crouching as low as possible, with my left side toward the wall, I steadied myself against the wind with my left hand in a slight notch, while with the right I cut other similar steps and notches in succession, guarding against losing balance by glinting of the axe, or by wind-gusts, for life and death were in every stroke and in the niceness of finish of every foothold.

After the end of the bridge was reached I chipped it down until I had made a level platform six or eight inches wide, and it was a trying thing to poise on this little slippery platform while bending over to get safely astride of the sliver. Crossing was then comparatively easy by chipping off the sharp edge with short, careful strokes, and hitching forward an inch or two at a time, keeping my balance with my knees pressed against the sides. The tremendous abyss on either hand I studiously ignored. To me the edge of that blue sliver was then all the world. But the most trying part of the adventure, after working my way across inch by inch and chipping another small platform, was to rise from the safe position astride and to cut a step-ladder in the nearly vertical face of the wall, – chipping, climbing, holding on with feet and fingers in mere notches. At such times one's whole body is eye, and common skill and fortitude are replaced by power beyond our call or knowledge. Never before had I been so long under deadly strain. How I got up that cliff I never could tell. The thing seemed to have been done by somebody else. I never have held death in contempt, though in the course of my explorations I have oftentimes felt that to meet one's fate on a noble mountain, or in the heart of a glacier, would be blessed as compared with death from disease, or from some shabby lowland accident. But the best death, quick and crystal-pure, set so glaringly open before us, is hard enough to face, even though we feel gratefully sure that we have already had happiness enough for a dozen lives.

But poor Stickeen, the wee, hairy, sleekit beastie, think of him! When I had decided to dare the bridge, and while I was on my knees chipping a hollow on the rounded brow above it, he came behind me, pushed his head past my shoulder, looked down and across, scanned the sliver and its approaches with his mysterious eyes, then looked me in the face with a startled air of surprise and concern, and began to mutter and whine; saying as plainly as if speaking with words, "Surely, you are not going into that awful place." This was the first time I had seen him gaze deliberately into a crevasse, or into my face with an eager, speaking, troubled look. That he should have recognised and appreciated the danger at the first glance showed wonderful sagacity. Never before had the daring midget seemed to know that ice was slippery or that there was any such thing as danger anywhere. His looks and tones of voice when he began to complain and speak his fears were so human that I unconsciously talked to him in sympathy as I would to a frightened boy, and in trying to calm his fears perhaps in some measure moderated my own. "Hush your fears, my boy," I said, "we will get across safe, though it is not going to be easy. No right way is easy in this rough world. We must risk our lives to save them. At the worst we can only slip, and then how grand a grave we will have, and by and by our nice bones will do good in the terminal moraine."

But my sermon was far from reassuring him: he began to cry, and after taking another piercing look at the tremendous gulf, ran away in desperate excitement, seeking some other crossing. By the time he got back, baffled of course, I had made a step or two. I dared not look back, but he made himself heard; and when he saw that I was certainly bent on crossing he cried aloud in despair. The danger was enough to daunt anybody, but it seems wonderful that he should have been able to weigh and appreciate it so justly. No mountaineer could have seen it more quickly or judged it more wisely, discriminating between real and apparent peril.

When I gained the other side, he screamed louder than ever, and after running back and forth in vain search for a way of escape, he would return to the brink of the crevasse above the bridge, moaning and wailing as if in the bitterness of death. Could this be the silent, philosophic Stickeen? I shouted encouragement, telling him the bridge was not so bad as it looked, that I had left it flat and safe for his feet, and he could walk it easily. But he was afraid to try. Strange so small an animal should be capable of such big, wise fears. I called again and again in a reassuring tone to come on and fear nothing; that he could come if he would only try. He would hush for a moment, look down again at the bridge, and shout his unshakable conviction that he could never, never come that way; then lie back in despair, as if howling, "O-o-oh! what a place! No-o-o, I can never go-o-o down there!" His natural composure and courage had vanished utterly in a tumultuous storm of fear. Had the danger been less, his distress would have seemed ridiculous. But in this dismal, merciless abyss lay the shadow of death, and his heartrending cries might well have called Heaven to his help. Perhaps they did. So hidden before, he was now transparent, and one could see the workings of his heart and mind like the movements of a clock out of its case. His voice and gestures, hopes and fears, were so perfectly human that none could mistake them; while he seemed to understand every word of mine. I was troubled at the thought of having to leave him out all night, and of the danger of not finding him in the morning. It seemed impossible to get him to venture. To compel him to try through fear of being abandoned, I started off as if leaving him to his fate, and disappeared back of a hummock; but this did no good; he only lay down and moaned in utter hopeless misery. So, after hiding a few minutes, I went back to the brink of the crevasse and in a severe tone of voice shouted across to him that now I must certainly leave him, I could wait no longer, and that, if he would not come, all I could promise was that I would return to seek him next day. I warned him that if he went back to the woods the wolves would kill him, and finished by urging him once more by words and gestures to come on, come on.

He knew very well what I meant, and at last, with the courage of despair, hushed and breathless, he crouched down on the brink in the hollow I had made for my knees, pressed his body against the ice as if trying to get the advantage of the friction of every hair, gazed into the first step, put his little feet together and slid them slowly, slowly over the edge and down into it, bunching all four in it and almost standing on his head. Then, without lifting his feet, as well as I could see through the snow, he slowly worked them over the edge of the step and down into the next and the next in succession in the same way, and gained the end of the bridge. Then, lifting his feet with the regularity and slowness of the vibrations of a second's pendulum, as if counting and measuring *one-two-three*, holding himself steady against the gusty wind, and giving separate attention to each little step, he gained the foot of the cliff, while I was on my knees leaning over to give him a lift should he succeed in getting within reach of my arm. Here he halted in dead silence, and it was here I feared he might fail, for dogs are poor climbers. I had no cord. If I had had one, I would have dropped a noose over his head and hauled him up. But while I was thinking whether an available cord might be made out of clothing, he was looking keenly into the series of notched steps and finger-holds I had made, as if counting them, and fixing the position of each one of them in his mind. Then suddenly up he came in a springy rush, hooking his paws into the steps and notches so quickly that I could not see how it was done, and whizzed past my head, safe at last !

And now came a scene! "Well done, well done, little boy! Brave boy!" I cried, trying to catch and caress him; but he would not be caught. Never before or since have I seen anything like so passionate a revulsion from the depths of despair to exultant, triumphant, uncontrollable joy. He flashed and darted hither and thither as if fairly demented, screaming and shouting, swirling round and round in giddy loops and circles like a leaf in a whirlwind, lying down, and rolling over and over, sidewise and heels over head, and pouring forth a tumultuous flood of hysterical cries and sobs and gasping mutterings. When I ran up to him to shake him, fearing he might die of joy, he flashed off two or three hundred yards, his feet in a mist of motion; then, turning suddenly, came back in a wild rush and launched himself at my face, almost knocking me down, all the time screeching and screaming and shouting as if saying, "Saved! saved! saved!" Then away again, dropping suddenly at times with his feet in the air, trembling and fairly sobbing. Such passionate emotion was enough to kill him. Moses' stately song of triumph after escaping the Egyptians and the Red Sea was nothing to it. Who could have guessed the capacity of the dull, enduring little fellow for all that most stirs this mortal frame? Nobody could have helped crying with him !

But there is nothing like work for toning down excessive fear or joy. So I ran ahead, calling him in as gruff a voice as I could command to come on and stop his nonsense, for we had far to go and it would soon be dark. Neither of us feared another trial like this. Heaven would surely count one enough for a lifetime. The ice ahead was gashèd by thousands of crevasses, but they were common ones. The joy of deliverance burned in us like fire, and we ran without fatigue, every muscle with immense rebound glorying in its strength. Stickeen flew across everything in his way, and not till dark did he settle into his normal fox-like trot. At last the cloudy mountains came in sight, and we soon felt the solid rock beneath our feet, and were safe. Then came weakness. Danger had vanished, and so had our strength. We tottered down the lateral moraine in the dark, over boulders and tree trunks, through the bushes and devil club thickets of the grove where we had sheltered ourselves in the morning, and across the level mud-slope of the terminal moraine. We reached camp about ten o'clock, and found a big fire and a big supper. A party of Hoona Indians had visited Mr. Young, bringing a gift of porpoise meat and wild strawberries, and Hunter Joe had brought in a wild goat. But we lay down, too tired to eat much, and soon fell into a troubled sleep. The man who said, "The harder the toil, the sweeter the rest," never was profoundly tired. Stickeen kept springing up and muttering in his sleep, no doubt dreaming that he was still on the brink of the crevasse; and so did I, that night and many others long afterward, when I was overtired.

Thereafter Stickeen was a changed dog. During the rest of the trip, instead of holding aloof, he always lay by my side, tried to keep me constantly in sight, and would hardly accept a morsel of food, however tempting, from any hand but mine. At night, when all was quiet about the camp-fire, he would come to me and rest his head on my knee with a look of devotion as if I were his god. And often as he caught my eye he seemed to be trying to say, ''Wasn't that an awful time we had together on the glacier?''

Nothing in after years has dimmed that Alaska storm-day. As I write it all comes rushing and roaring to mind as if I were again in the heart of it. Again I see the grey flying clouds with their rain-floods and snow, the ice-cliffs towering above the shrinking forest, the majestic ice cascade, the vast glacier outspread before its white mountain fountains, and in the heart of it the tremendous crevasse – emblem of the valley of the shadow of death – low clouds trailing over it, the snow falling into it; and on its brink I see little Stickeen, and I hear his cries for help and his shouts of joy. I have known many dogs, and many a story I could tell of their wisdom and devotion; but to none do I owe so much as to Stickeen. At first the least promising and least known of my dog-friends, he suddenly became the best known of them all. Our storm-battle for life brought him to light, and through him as through a window I have ever since been looking with deeper sympathy into all my fellow mortals.

None of Stickeen's friends knows what finally became of him. After my work for the season was done I departed for California, and I never saw the dear little fellow again. In reply to anxious inquiries his master wrote me that in the summer of 1883 he was stolen by a tourist at Fort Wrangel and taken away on a steamer. His fate is wrapped in mystery. Doubtless he has left this world – crossed the last crevasse – gone to another. But he will not be forgotten. To me Stickeen is immortal.

NOTES ON THE
PACIFIC COAST GLACIERS

First published in *The Harriman Alaska Expedition* Vol. I 1901

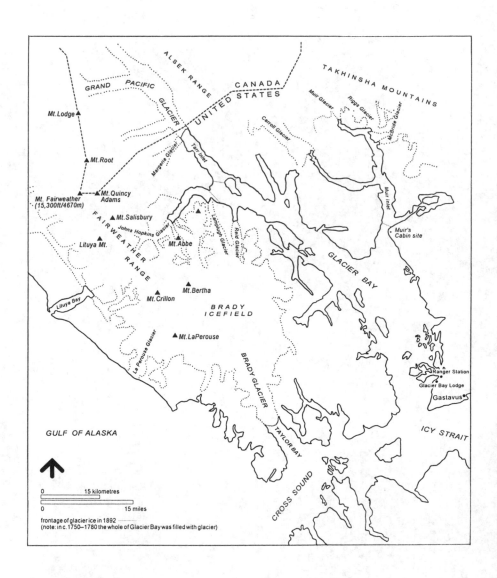

III

Notes on the
Pacific Coast Glaciers

THE GLACIERS that load the mountains of the Pacific Coast form a belt about two thousand miles long, of which the south half is mostly narrow and broken, the north continuous and broad.

On the Sierra Nevada of California between latitudes 36° 30' and 39° there are sixty-five small glaciers, distributed singly or in groups of three or four on the northern slopes of the highest peaks at an elevation of 11,000 to 12,000 feet above the sea. These slow-flowing, ragged-edged, residual masses, few of which are more than a mile in length or width, are all that is left of the great glaciers which once covered the Range. More than two-thirds of their number lie between latitudes 37° and 38° and form the highest fountains of the San Joaquin, Tuolumne, Merced, and Owens rivers. Mt. Shasta, near the northern boundary of the state, still supports a few shrinking remnants, the largest of which is about two and a half miles long and descends to within 9,000 feet of the level of the sea, the lowest point reached by any glacier in California. Northward along the Cascade Range through Oregon and Washington, groups of larger residual glaciers still exist on all the highest mountains – The Three Sisters, Mounts Jefferson, Hood, St.Helens, Adams, Rainier, Baker and others. From Mount Rainier, the highest of this series of volcanic cones, eight glaciers five to ten miles long radiate, descending to within 3,000 or 4,000 feet of the sea level. On through British Columbia and southeastern Alaska the broad, lofty mountains along the coast are usually laden with ice. The upper branches of nearly all the canyons are occupied by glaciers, which increase in size gradually and descend lower until the region which is highest and snowiest, between latitudes 56° and 61° is reached, where a considerable number discharge fleets of icebergs into the sea. This is the Iceland of Alaska, the region of greatest glacial abundance on the west side of the continent. It is about 500 miles long, 100 broad, and probably includes nine tenths of the ice on the coast. To the north of latitude 61° the glaciers diminish in size and number to about latitude 62° 30' or 63°. Beyond this all the way up to the north end of the continent few if any glaciers now exist, the ground being comparatively low and the snowfall light.

In the iciest region the smaller glaciers, a mile or two to ten or fifteen miles in length, once tributary to large ones, now fill all the subordinate canyons and upper hollows of the mountains in countless thousands.

Of the great glaciers of the second class, flowing down nearly to the sea but not entering it, there are about a hundred, distributed along the coast from the mouth of the Stikine River to Cook Inlet and thence southwestward along the Alaska Peninsula, pouring their majestic crystal floods from far-reaching fountains in the recesses of the peaks, and sweeping down through the forests to the shores of the fiords or of the ocean. The expanded fan-shaped ends of many of them are from two to four miles wide, and all are separated from tide water by mud and gravel flats or terminal moraines – the waste from melting and evaporation equalling or exceeding the supply. The best known of this class are the Baird and Patterson, at the head of fiords opening into Prince Frederick Sound, and the Auk, Eagle, and Davidson glaciers, seen from Lynn Canal; but the largest front the ocean along the Fairweather and St.Elias ranges. The Malaspina Glacier is the largest of all, being about twenty miles long and sixty-five or seventy wide, a vast plateau of ice at the base of the St.Elias Mountains, separated from the sea by a girdle of forested moraines five or six miles wide, except at Icy Cape, where it presents magnificent bluffs of pure ice undermined by the waves. The broad outspread Miles Glacier, near the mouth of Copper River; the Yakutat, the Grand Plateau, Crillon, La Perouse, and many others are of the same type though less extensive. La Perouse, like the Malaspina at Icy Cape, presents to the open ocean grand ice bluffs, which are washed and undermined to some extent at high tide by the waves that occasionally detach berg-like fragments. These fragments are mostly small, however, and are speedily broken up and melted.

Of complete glaciers of the first class flowing out into deep ocean water and, of course, discharging bergs, I have seen twenty-eight and there are at least three others, making thirty-one altogether, while several promising fiords in Prince William Sound remain unexplored. At the head of the LeConte Fiord, in latitude 56° 50', there is one; about a degree farther north, at the heads of branches of Holkam Bay, there are four; in Taku Inlet there is one; in Glacier Bay there are nine; in Lituya Bay two; in Disenchantment Bay three; and in Prince William Sound eleven. All the fiords into which these glaciers of the first class flow are encumbered, some of them jammed and crowded, with bergs of every conceivable form, which by the most active of the glaciers are given off at intervals of a few minutes with loud thundering roaring that may be heard five or six miles, proclaiming the restless work and motion of these mighty crystal rivers, so widely contrasting with the deathlike stillness and silence of the second-class decadent glaciers, though they also, except at their decaying ends are ceaselessly flowing and grinding, making soil, and completing the sculpture of their basins. As compared with the immense icebergs which adorn and guard the shores of Greenland and the Antarctic Continent those discharged by the Alaska glaciers are small. The very largest I have seen did not exceed a thousand feet in length, few of them three or four hundred feet. And, so far as I have observed, only from Glacier Bay, where the greatest number of bergs are born, do any of them escape to the open ocean. Nearly all are drifted back and forth by wind and tide in the long island-blocked channels until melted.

The southmost of the glaciers which flow into arms of the sea is the Le Conte. It occupies a narrow, forested, picturesque fiord about ten miles north of the mouth of the Stikine River, in latitude 56° 50', called Hutli or Thunder Bay by the Indians, from the noise made by the rising and falling bergs.

Holkam or Sum Dum Bay, the next icy inlet to the northwestward, is one of the most interesting of all the Alaska fiords, but the bergs in it are usually far too closely packed to allow a passage for vessels of any size; often times it is difficult to reach its glaciers even in the smallest canoes. About five miles from the mouth the bay divides into two main arms, about twenty and twenty-five miles long, in the farthest recesses of which its four glaciers are hidden. A hundred or more glaciers of the second and third class may be seen along the walls, and about as many snowy cataracts, which with the plunging bergs keep all the fiord in a roar. The scenery in both of the long arms and their side branches is of the wildest description, especially in their upper reaches, where the granite walls, streaked with waterfalls, rise in sheer, massive precipices, like those of Yosemite Valley, to a height of 3,000 and even over 4,000 feet.

The Taku Inlet, usually accessible to the tourist steamers, is about eighteen miles long, and drains many glaciers, great and small. Sailing up the middle of it one may still count some forty-five, descending from a group of high mountains at the head and making a grand display of their crystal wealth. Three of them reach the level of the sea; only one, however, the beautiful Taku Glacier, now discharges bergs. It comes sweeping forward in majestic curves and pours its countless roaring, plunging ice masses into a western branch of the Inlet, next the one occupied by the Taku River. Thus we have here in one view, flowing into the sea side by side, a river of ice and a river of water, both abounding in cascades and rapids, yet infinitely different in their rate of motion and in the songs they sing – a rare object lesson, worth coming far to learn.

Glacier Bay, about fifty miles long, with many deep, high-walled branches, is the iciest of all the inlets which fringe the coast. Both to the north and south of it the great tide-water glaciers are generally less active, less lavishly snow-fed, and of course give birth to fewer bergs; while, as we have seen, the decadent second-class glaciers, with no ice to spare for bergs, reach their greatest size at the base of the St. Elias Range.

Of the nine berg-bearing glaciers in Glacier Bay the Muir is the largest, the main trunk below the confluence of the principal tributaries being about twenty-five miles wide, while the area of its basin can hardly be less than a thousand square miles.

The most active of the three Disenchantment Bay glaciers is the Hubbard, a truly noble glacier. It has two main tributaries pouring majestic floods into the broad, widely crevassed trunk, and it furnishes most of the bergs which fill the upper end of the bay from shore to shore.

The grandest and most active of the ten Prince William Sound glaciers visited by the Harriman Expedition, so far as I saw them, are the Columbia, Harvard, and Yale, though the Barry, Serpentine, Harriman and Surprise –

the last three discovered by the expedition – are also superb and imposing; while the cascading glaciers in Port Wells Fiord named for Wellesley, Vassar, Bryn Mawr, Smith, and Radcliffe colleges are the finest and wildest of their kind, looking, as they come bounding down a smooth mountain side through the midst of lush flowery gardens and goat pastures, like tremendous leaping, dancing cataracts in prime of flood.

None of the glaciers south of Icy Strait were visited by the expedition, though telling glimpses of them were obtained in the bright weather as we sailed through the enchanting Alexander Archipelago, the icy canyons opening and closing as we advanced and showing their wealth like the quickly turned leaves of a picture-book. In Glacier Bay we remained nearly a week, so that we were able to note the changes which had taken place since my first visit in the fall of 1879. I then sailed around the bay, exploring all its branches and sketching the glaciers which occupied them, sailing up to their discharging fronts and landing on those which were not rendered inaccessible by the freezing together of their crowded bergs. Then there were only six berg-discharging glaciers in the bay; now there are nine, the three new ones being formed by one of the tributaries of the Hugh Miller and two of the Grand Pacific, separated from the main glaciers and rendered independent by the recession of the trunks beyond their points of confluence. The Hugh Miller and Muir have receded about two miles in the last twenty years, the Grand Pacific about four, and the Geikie, Rendu and Carrol perhaps from seven to ten miles. By the recession of the Grand Pacific and corresponding extension of Reid Inlet an island two-and-a-half or three miles long, and over a thousand feet high, has been added to the landscape. Only the end of this island was visible in 1879. New islands have been born in some of the other fiords also, and some still enveloped in the glaciers show only their heads as they bide their time to take their places in the young landscape. Here, then, we have the work of glacial earth-sculpture going on before our eyes, teaching lessons so plain that he who runs may read. Evidently all the glaciers hereabouts were no great time ago united, and with the multitude of glaciers which loaded the mountains to the south, once formed a grand continuous ice-sheet that flowed over all the island region of the coast and extended at least as far down as the Strait of Juan de Fuca. All the islands of the Alexander Archipelago, great and small, as well as the headlands and promontories of the mainland, have a smooth, over-rubbed appearance, generally free from angles except where modified by the after-action of local glaciers, and they all have the form of greatest strength with reference to their physical structure and the action of an oversweeping ice sheet.

The network of so called canals, passages, straits, channels, sounds, fiords and so on, between the islands manifest in their forms and trends and general characteristics the same subordination to the grinding action of a continuous ice-sheet, being simply the portions of the margin of the continent eroded below the sea level and therefore covered with the ocean waters, which flowed into them as the ice was melted out. And, as we have seen, this action is still going on and new islands and new channels are being added to the famous archipelago. The steamer trip to the fronts of the glaciers of Glacier Bay is now from two to eight or ten miles longer than it was only twenty years ago. That the domain of the sea is being extended over the land by the wearing away of its shores is well known, but in this region the coast rocks have been so short a time exposed to wave action that the more resistant of them are as yet scarcely at all wasted. Even as far south as Victoria the superficial glacial scoring and polish may still be seen on the hardest of the harbour rocks below the tide line. The extension hereabouts of the sea by its own action in post-glacial time is probably less than a millionth part as much as that effected by recent glacial action.

On our way up the coast to Yakutat the majestic Fairweather Mountains we had so often admired from the Glacier Bay side were buried in clouds, but the broad outspread lower portions of the glaciers were clearly displayed beneath the clouds up to an elevation of about 2,000 feet. All of them are cut off from the sea by enormous moraine deposits, except a mile or two of the front of La Perouse Glacier which presents a bold crystal wall to the waves at high tide. Not a single iceberg was seen. That there should be no discharge from the sea side of the Fairweather Range and so lavish a discharge from the other is not so surprising, however, when we consider that the area of the western slope and its snowfields is far less extensive, while at the same time the waste from the sea winds and from sunshine, on account of the direction of the trend of the Range, is greater. A landing was made near the west end of the La Perouse ice-wall to examine a forest, part of which had been overwhelmed by an advance of the glacier; another part was falling by the undermining action of a glacial stream. Some of the Taylor Bay and Prince William Sound forests have been destroyed in the same way, whether simultaneously or not I am unable to say. When I visited the Brady Glacier in the summer of 1880 I found thousands of trees, many of them more than a century old, which had been uprooted and crushed like weeds before the flow, showing that this glacier, instead of receding, had risen higher and advanced its front beyond the position where it stood when Vancouver explored the bay in 1794. The trees lining the banks were barked and scarred, very effectively blazing a high ice-mark for miles. The surface of the glacier had already fallen fifteen or twenty feet below its highest flood-level, though the front had receded but little; its huge ice-cliffs on the east end were still towering portentously above the spruces that stood a few feet in front of them. The buried forests of Glacier Bay record still greater and more impressive changes in the recession and advance of grand ice floods and water floods.

In our northward journey dark clouds hid the mountains until we reached Yakutat. Then the heavens opened and St.Elias, gloriously arrayed, bade us welcome, while the heaving, plunging bergs roared and thundered.

Here we spent immortal days, studying, gazing, sailing the blue waters, climbing the hills and glaciers and warm, flowery islands, considering the abounding life – everybody naturally enthusiastic and busy and happy to the heart. The scenery about the head of Disenchantment Bay is gloriously wild and sublime – majestic mountains and glaciers, barren moraines, bloom-covered islands amid icy, swirling waters, enlivened by screaming gulls, hair seals, and roaring bergs. On the other hand, the beauty of the southern extension of the bay is tranquil and restful and perfectly enchanting. Its shores, especially on the east side, are flowery and finely sculptured, and the mountains, of moderate height, are charmingly combined and reflected in the quiet waters. A comparatively short time ago it was a fresh-water lake about 150 feet above the tide – until it was lowered and opened to the sea by the retreat of the Hubbard Glacier. The front of the great Hubbard Glacier is about five miles wide, and bergs are discharged from the west half of it. The other half has receded from the bay and is covered with moraines, sparsely planted here and there with epilobium and dwarf willows, where a multitude of gulls breed. The Turner Glacier, a short distance to the west of the Hubbard, is much smaller and sends off but few bergs. The Nunatak Glacier discharges still fewer, and at the present rate of waste will soon die away into the second class, like its neighbour, the Hidden Glacier.

For an hour or two before we left Yakutat we enjoyed glorious views of Malaspina's crystal prairie, and of St.Elias and his noble compeers, then down came clouds and fog, leaving only a dim little circle of water about us. But just as we entered the famous Prince William Sound, that I had so long hoped to see, the sky cleared, disclosing to the westward one of the richest, most glorious mountain landscapes I ever beheld – peak over peak dipping deep in the sky, a thousand of them, icy and shining, rising higher, higher, beyond and yet beyond one another, burning bright in the afternoon light, purple cloud-bars above them, purple shadows in the hollows, and great breadths of sun-spangled, ice-dotted waters in front. The nightless days circled away while we gazed and studied, sailing among the islands, exploring the long fiords, climbing moraines and glaciers and hills clad in blooming heather – grandeur and beauty in a thousand forms awaiting us at every turn in this bright and spacious wonderland. But that first broad, far-reaching view in celestial light was the best of all.

The most important discovery made here is the magnificent new inlet, rightly named the Harriman Fiord. It is full of glaciers of every description, waterfalls, gardens and grand old forests – nature's best and choicest alpine treasures purely wild – a place after my own heart. Here we camped in the only pure forest of mountain hemlock I ever saw, the most beautiful of evergreens, growing at sea-level, some of the trees over three feet in diameter and nearly a hundred feet high. This is the same species (*Tsuga mertensianga Sarg.*) which grows on the High Sierra of California near the timber line.

Every feature of Prince William Sound shows that it was once filled by a grand glacier; but, with the exception of its complicated network of fiords, it has long been open to the sea – probably a thousand years or more. On the north shore I found a Sitka spruce 380 years old, and the ruins on the forest floor bear witness to several generations of these trees. And on the shore of the Harriman Fiord, well up toward the head, where the ice must have lingered long after the main central glacier had vanished, I counted 325 annual rings on a hemlock stump only nine inches in diameter.

From this glorious sound we sailed to Cook Inlet, from which most of the great glaciers that once loaded its mountains have vanished, thence to flowery, grassy Kadiak and Unalaska, gaining splendid general views of the wonderful chain of volcanoes extending along the west shore of Cook Inlet, the Alaska Peninsula, and the Aleutian Islands. Several of the great white cones were sending up plumes of smoke or steam 200 or 300 feet high and sending down broad glaciers nearly to the shore line.

After leaving Unalaska and entering Bering Sea not a glacier of any sort was seen, though the traces of ancient ones are not rare, especially in the fiords and low mountain ranges. Plover Bay on the Siberian Coast, in which the Expedition made a short stay, and which I explored in 1881, is a well characterised glacier fiord. Its walls rise to an average height of about 2,000 feet and present a severely desolate and bedraggled appearance, owing to the crumbling condition of the rocks, which in most places are being rapidly disintegrated, loading the slopes with loose detritus wherever the angle is low enough to allow it to rest. But on the most resisting portions I discovered rounded glaciated surfaces, grooved, scratched and polished, from near the sea-level up to a height of a thousand feet or more.

And in high, spacious cirques I found well formed unwasted moraines made up of concentric masses shoved together, indicating that the glaciers to which they belonged receded with changes of level and rate of decadence in accordance with conditions of snowfall, temperature and so on, like those of lower latitudes. When the main glacier which filled the fiord was in its prime it was about thirty miles long and five to six wide, with five main tributaries, which, as the trunk melted, became separate glaciers, and these melting in turn left many smaller tributaries ranging from less than a mile to several miles in length. These, also, as far as I have seen, have vanished, though possibly some wasting remnants may still exist in the snowiest recesses of the mountains.

From Port Clarence we turned back, homeward bound and Heaven-favoured, for all the mountains between Prince William Sound and Cross Sound, veiled in clouds on the way up, were now revealed to us in all their glory. The sky was pure azure, the sea calm, and the mountains in their robes of ice and light towered in awful majesty.

In passing the Malaspina Glacier we ran in for a nearer view of the ice bluffs at Icy Cape, then skirted the moraine- and forest-covered border, gaining glorious views of the immense ice-field and its tributaries pouring in from their sublime sun-beaten fountains.

The sail down the coast from St.Elias along the magnificent Fairweather Range, when every mountain stood transfigured in divine light, was the crowning grace and glory of the trip and must be immortal in the remembrance of every soul of us.

THE CRUISE OF THE CORWIN

The Cruise of the Corwin

First published by the Houghton Mifflin Company
(Boston, New York, Chicago, 1917).

CONTENTS

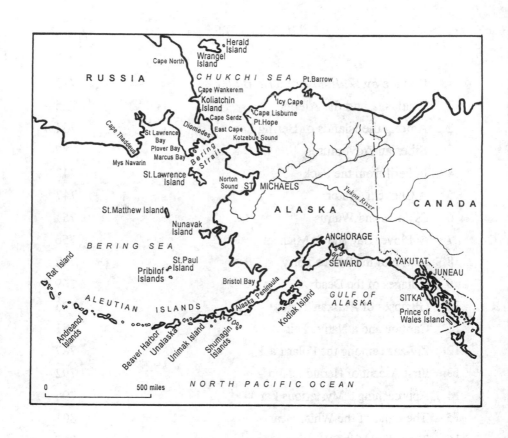

PREFACE

ONE OF THE poignant tragedies of north polar exploration, that of the *Jeannette*, still lingers in the memory of persons now living, though a generation has since passed away. John Muir, who joined the first search expedition dispatched from San Francisco, had already achieved distinction by his glacial studies in the Sierra Nevada and in Alaska. The Corwin expedition afforded him a coveted opportunity to cruise among the islands of Bering Sea and the Arctic Ocean, and to visit the frost-bitten shores of northeastern Siberia and northwestern Alaska. So enticing was the lure of this new adventure, so eager was he to study the evidence of glaciation in the Far North, that he said a reluctant goodbye to his young wife and fared forth upon the deep. "You remember," he wrote to her from the Siberian coast, "that I told you long ago how eager I was to get upon those islands in the middle of the Bering Sea and Strait to read the ice record there."

The events which led up to this memorable cruise of the Corwin in 1881 had their origin in the widespread interest which north polar exploration was exciting at this time all over the world. In 1877 Lieutenant George W. De Long, an American naval officer, was searching among the northern ports of England for a whaling vessel adapted to the requirements of Arctic exploration. De Long had commanded the Juniata which was sent out for the relief of the Polaris, and through this experience had grown enthusiastic over his own plans for reaching the North Pole.

The whaling industry was at that time a very profitable one, and few owners of whalers and sealers were willing to part with their vessels. Though Sir Allen Young's steam yacht Pandora, which De Long finally selected, had already made two Arctic voyages, she appears to have been chosen more because she was available than because of her superior fitness for ice navigation. In any case she was purchased by James Gordon Bennett, patron of the proposed expedition, was fitted out at Deptford, England, and renamed the Jeannette. Though the new name evaded the suggestion of a box of evils, she proved to be one for those who sailed in her. Commander De Long himself brought her around Cape Horn to San Francisco. In the month of July, 1879, she sailed from that port for Bering Strait and the Arctic Ocean – never to return. Crushed in the ice, she sank, June 12th, 1881, in the Arctic Ocean, one hundred and fifty miles north of the New Siberian Islands.

The retreat southward across the ice-floes was one of great peril. Only thirteen out of thirty-four men ultimately reached civilization and safety. De Long himself, and ten of the men with him, died of starvation and exposure on the delta of the Lena River, where two of the Jeannette's storm-beaten cutters landed in the middle of September, 1881. One of them, commanded by Chief Engineer Melville, reached a Russian village on one of the eastern mouths of the Lena River. He promptly organised a search party, recovering the ship's records in November, 1881, and the bodies of his unfortunate shipmates the following spring.

When the North Pacific whaling fleet returned from Arctic waters in the autumn of 1879, two ships, the Mount Wollaston and the Vigilant, were reported missing. They had been last seen in October in the same general region, near Herald Island, where the Jeannette had entered the polar ice. The Mount Wollaston was commanded by Captain Nye, of New Bedford, Massachusetts, one of the keenest and bravest men that ever sailed the frigid seas. He it was who at a conference of whaling captains, called by De Long in San Francisco before the departure of his expedition, hesitated to give an opinion on the practicability of De Long's plans. But when urged for an expression of his views, he said, "Put her [the Jeannette] into the ice and let her drift, and you may get through, or you may go to the devil, and the chances are about equal."

In the service of the United States Treasury Department there was at this time a staunch little steamer called the Corwin. Built at Abina, Oregon, she was constructed throughout of the finest Oregon fir, fastened with copper, galvanised iron, and locust-tree nails. She had a draught of nearly eleven feet, twenty-four feet beam, and was one hundred and thirty-seven feet long between perpendiculars. The ordinary duties of the captain of such a revenue steamer involved primarily the enforcement of federal laws for the protection of governmental interests on the Fur Seal Islands and the sea-otter hunting grounds of Alaska. But the supposed plight of the Jeannette and the unknown fate of two whalers caught in the ice were soon to increase the Corwin's duties, and call her into regions where her sturdy sailing qualities were to prove of the utmost importance.

In the spring of 1880 the Corwin, in command of Captain Calvin L. Hooper, was ordered into North Alaskan waters in pursuance of her regular duties. But Captain Hooper had also been directed to make all possible inquiries for the missing whalers and the Jeannette. He returned with no tidings of the lost, but with reports of starvation and death among the Eskimos of St. Lawrence Island on account of an uncommonly severe and stormy winter in the Arctic regions. He entertained no hope for the lost whalers, but thought De Long and his party might be safe.

A general demand for relief expeditions now arose. Petitions poured into Congress, and the American Geographical Society addressed a forcible appeal to President Garfield. When the Corwin was sent to Alaskan waters again in 1881 it was with the following specific instructions to Captain Hooper:

No information having been received concerning the whalers Mount Wollaston and Vigilant, you will bear in mind the instructions for your cruise of last year, and it is hoped you may bring back some tidings of the missing vessels. You will also make careful inquiries in the Arctic regarding the progress and whereabouts of the steamer Jeannette, engaged in making explorations under command of Lieutenant-Commander De Long, U. S. N., and will, if practicable, communicate with and extend any needed assistance to that vessel.... You will in your season's cruise touch at such places as may be practicable on the mainland or islands where there are settlements of natives, and examine into and report upon their condition.

A letter written to his mother from Dutch Harbour, Unalaska, gives Muir's own account of his purpose in joining the expedition.

I wrote you from San Francisco [he says] that I had suddenly made up my mind to avail myself of the opportunity offered to visit the Arctic region on the steamer Thomas Corwin sent to seek the Jeannette and the missing whalers that were lost in the ice two years ago off Point Barrow....

I have been interested for a long time in the glaciation of the Pacific Coast, and I felt that I must make a trip of this sort to the Far North some time, and no better chance could in any probability offer. I am acquainted with our captain, and have every comfort the ship can afford, and every facility to pursue my studies.

We mean to proceed from here past the seal islands St. Paul and St. George, then northward along the Siberian coast to about Cape Serdze, where a sledge party with dogs will be sent out to search the North Siberian coast, while the steamer the meanwhile will cross to the American shore and call at St. Michael, Kotzebue Sound, and other places, [where we shall have the opportunity of] making short journeys inland. Then, as the ice melts and breaks up, we will probably push eastward around Point Barrow, then return to the Siberian side to pick up our land party, then endeavour to push through the ice to the mysterious unexplored Wrangell Land. We hope to return to San Francisco by October or November, but may possibly be compelled to winter in the Arctic somewhere.

De Long, in a letter to his wife, had written that his plan was to "proceed north by the eastern coast of Wrangell Land," touching first at Herald Island to build a cairn and leave news of the Jeannette's progress. Believing that Wrangell Land extended northward toward the Pole, he proposed to leave similar records along its eastern coast, under cairns, at intervals of twenty-five miles. These known intentions of De Long show why it was one of the foremost objects of the Corwin expedition to reach what Muir called "the mysterious unexplored Wrangell Land."

How keenly Muir appreciated the possibilities of science and adventure in the exploration of this unknown Arctic land may be seen in the fourteenth chapter of this volume. Up to this time nothing was actually known about Wrangell Land except its existence. The first European who reported its discovery was Captain Kellett of H.M.S. Herald. He saw it in 1849 when he discovered Herald Island, which was named after his vessel. By right of discovery Kellett's name should have been given to Wrangell Land, and upon British Admiralty charts it was very properly indicated as "Kellett Land."

The name Wrangell Land, it seems, became associated with the island through a report of Captain Thomas Long, of the whaling bark Nile. In 1867 he reported that he had

> sailed to the eastward along the land during the fifteenth and part of the sixteenth [of August], and in some places approached it as near as fifteen miles. I have named this northern land Wrangell Land [he says] as an appropriate tribute to the memory of a man who spent three consecutive years north of latitude 68° and demonstrated the problem of this open polar sea forty-five years ago, although others of much later date have endeavoured to claim the merit of this discovery. The west cape of this land I have named Cape Thomas, after the man who first reported the land from the masthead of my ship, and the southeastern cape I have named after the largest island in this group [Hawaii].*

Captain Long apparently was unaware of the fact that the island already bore the name of Kellett by right of discovery eighteen years earlier. But since Baron Wrangell had made such a brave and determined search for this "problematical land of the North," as he referred to it in his final report, there is a certain poetic justice in applying his name to what he only sought, but never found.

While Captain Hooper, in his report of 1880, had expressed the conviction that Wrangell Land was an island, the first demonstration of its insularity was made by Commander De Long, who had practically staked the success of his expedition on the belief that it was a country of large extent northward, and suitable for winter quarters. But before his vessel was crushed in the ice it drifted, within sight of Wrangell Land, directly across the meridians between which it lies. This fatal drift of the Jeannette not only furnished conclusive disproof of the theory that Wrangell Land might be part of a continent stretching across the north polar regions, but proved it to be an island of limited extent. It is an inaccuracy, therefore, when the United States Hydrographer's report for 1882 sets the establishment of this fact down to the credit of the Rodgers expedition.

So far as known, the first human beings that ever stood upon the shores

---

* Quoted from a letter by Captain Long published in the *Honolulu Commercial Advertiser*, November 1867. The same paper contains a letter from Captain George W. Raynor, of the ship Reindeer, giving additional geograhic details.

of this island were in Captain Hooper's landing party, August 12th, 1881, and John Muir was of the number. The earliest news of the event, and of the fact that De Long had not succeeded in touching either Herald Island or Wrangell Land, reached the world at large in a letter from Muir published in the *San Francisco Evening Bulletin,* September 29th, 1881. But the complete record of Muir's observations, together with some of the sketches contained in his journals, is now given to the public for the first time.

A second Jeannette relief expedition, already mentioned as that of the Rodgers, was sent out under the direction of the Secretary of the Navy. It succeeded in reaching Wrangell Land two weeks after the Corwin. In order to make our geographical and scientific knowledge of this remote island as complete in this volume as possible, we deem it desirable to include a brief account of what was achieved during the cruise of the Rodgers.

This vessel, a stout and comparatively new whaler, known before its re-baptism as the Mary and Helen, was placed in command of Lieutenant, now Rear Admiral, Robert M. Berry. He discovered on the southern shore of Wrangell Land a snug little harbour where he kept the Rodgers at anchor for nineteen days while two search parties, in whaleboats, going in opposite directions, explored the coast for possible survivors of the missing whalers and for cairns left by the crew of the Jeannette. These search parties nearly circumnavigated the island without finding anything except Captain Hooper's cairn, and Commander Berry, in his report to the Secretary of the Navy, said, "I believe it impossible that any of the missing parties ever landed here."

The principal gain of this exploration was a running survey of the coast and a general determination of the size of the island. In other respects the harvest of scientific facts gathered on Wrangell Land by the Rodgers was meagre, if one may judge by W. H. Gilder's *Ice Pack and Tundra.* Unfortunately, the act which carried the appropriation for the expedition provided that the vessel selected "be wholly manned by volunteers from the Navy." This fact seems to have prevented the taking of men trained in the natural sciences, like John Muir or E. W. Nelson. Nineteen days on Wrangell Land would have enabled them to obtain a large amount of interesting information about its flora, fauna, avifauna, and geology.

Commander Berry, taking charge of an exploring party, penetrated twenty miles into the interior of the island and ascended a conspicuous mountain whose height, by barometric measurement, was found to be twenty-five hundred feet. He reported that he "could see from its summit the sea in all directions, except between S.S.W. by W. per compass. The day was very clear, and no land except Herald Island was visible from this height. There was no ice in sight to the southward." A letter of inquiry addressed to Rear Admiral Berry by the editor brought a courteous reply, stating that he did not know of any photographs or sketches, made by members of the Rodgers expedition, which would show the coast or interior topography of the island; that "the vegetation was scant, consisting of a few Arctic plants, a little moss, etc;'' that "polar bears, walrus, and seal were quite common upon or near the island,'' and that the provisional map which accompanied his report to the Secretary of the Navy in 1881 is the only one available.

From our reproduction of this map, and from the report of the Rodgers, it will be seen that practically the whole interior of the island still awaits exploration. Estimates of its size vary between twenty-eight and forty miles as to width, and between sixty-five and seventy-five as to length. Striking an average, one might say that it contains about twenty-five hundred square miles of territory. The distance across Long Strait from the nearest point on the Siberian coast is about eighty-five or ninety miles, and Herald Island lies about thirty miles east of Wrangell Land.

In 1914 the Karluk, Steffánsson's flagship of the Canadian Arctic Expedition, was crushed in the ice, and sank not far from the place where the Jeannette was lost. Under the able leadership of Captain Robert A. Bartlett the members of the expedition made their way to Wrangell Land, where they remained encamped while Captain Bartlett, with an Eskimo, crossed Long's Strait to Siberia over the ice. Thence he made his way to St. Michael, Alaska, and enlisted aid for the Karluk survivors. Their rescue was effected successfully, and, so far as we are able to discover, these members of the Canadian Arctic Expedition are the only human beings that have been on Wrangell Land since the visit of the Corwin and the Rodgers in 1881.

We venture to mention, in this connection, a few facts which call for consideration in the interest of a historical and consistent geographical nomenclature. The United States Geographic Board has done much to bring order out of the chaos of Alaskan names, and its decisions are available in Baker's *Geographic Dictionary of Alaska*, which has been followed in the editing of this volume. There is a "Wrangell Island" in southeastern Alaska, well known to readers of Muir's *Travels in Alaska*, hence it occasions needless confusion to call Wrangell Land by the same name, as even recent Hydrographic Office charts continue to do, besides misspelling the name. The retention of the term "land" for an island is supported by abundant precedent, especially in the Arctic regions.

The altitude of the mountain ascended by Commander Berry had already been determined with remarkable accuracy by Captain Long in 1867. He described it as having "the appearance of an extinct volcano," and it is shown on his sketch of Wrangell Land, reproduced on the map accompanying Nourse's *American Explorations in the Ice Zones*. Captain Hooper, in his report of the cruise of the Corwin, declares that the peak had been appropriately named for Long, and adds, "Singular as it may appear, this name to which Captain Long was justly entitled has, notwithstanding our pretended custom of adhering to original names, been set aside on a recent issue of American charts." It is some compensation, however, that the wide stretch of water between the North Siberian coast and Wrangell Land is now known as Long Strait.

Captain Hooper and his party, being the first to set foot upon Wrangell Land, exercised the privilege of taking possession of it in the name of the United States. In order to avoid the confusion of the two names, Kellett and Wrangell, which it already bore, Captain Hooper named it New Columbia. This name, which was set aside by the Hydrographic Office, he says

> was suggested by the name which had been given to the islands farther west, New Siberia. It is probable that the name Wrangell Land will continue in use upon American charts, but its justice, in view of all the facts, is not so apparent. In my opinion the adoption by us of the name Kellett Land given by the English would be appropriate, and avoid the confusion which is sure to follow in consequence of its having two names.
>
> Headlands and other geographical features of the island were named by us, but as the names which were applied to features actually discovered by the Corwin and heretofore unnamed have been ignored, it is possible that a desire to do honour to the memory of Wrangell is not the only consideration. To avoid the complications which would result from duplicating geographical names, I have dropped all bestowed by the Corwin and adopted *the more recent ones* applied by the Hydrographic Office. I have also adopted the plan of the island [from surveys of the Rodgers] as shown on the small chart accompanying Hydrographic Notice No. 84, although the trend of the coast and the geographical position of the mouth of the river where we first planted the flag do not agree with the result of the observations and triangulations made by the Corwin.

Now that Captain Hooper and nearly all the men who had a share in these explorations of the early eighties have passed on, it is proper that the basic facts as well as conflicting judgments should be set down here for the just consideration of geographers. Both from Muir's vivid narrative of the Corwin's penetration to the shores of Wrangell Land, and from Captain Hooper's admirable report published in 1884 as Senate Executive Document No. 201, the reader will conclude that the Captain of the Corwin had a better right to be remembered in connection with the geographical features of the island than most of the persons whose names have been attached to them by the Hydrographic Office.

Whether Wrangell Land became United States territory when Hooper formally raised our flag over it is a question. The editor is unable to discover any treaty between Russia and the United States which would debar possession by the latter. But questions involving rights of territorial discovery have not, so far as we know, been raised between the two governments.

Muir's opportunity to join the Corwin apparently arose out of his acquaintanceship with Captain Hooper, and when the invitation came he had little time to prepare for the cruise. A letter to his wife affords a glimpse of his surroundings and plans when the Corwin was approaching Unalaska:

send my glasses and barometer and coat. We will procure furs as we proceed
north, so as to be ready in case we should be compelled to winter in the
Arctic regions. It is remarkably cold even here, and dark and blue and
forbidding every way, though it is fine weather for health.

I was just thinking this morning of our warm sunny home . . . and of the
red cherries down the hill, and the hundreds of blunt-billed finches, every
one of them with red bills soaked in cherry juice. Not much fruit juice
beneath this sky!

During the cruise Muir kept a daily record of his experiences and
observations. He also wrote a series of letters to the *San Francisco Evening
Bulletin* in which he turned to account the contents of his journal. Comparison
of the letters with the journal shows that his note-books contain a large
amount of interesting literary and scientific material which has not been
utilised in the *Bulletin* letters. To publish both would involve too much
duplication. It has seemed best, therefore, to make the letters the foundation
of the volume and to insert the additional matter from the journal wherever
it belongs chronologically in the epistolary record. Most of the letters have
thus grown far beyond their original size.

The performance of this task has often been trying and time-consuming,
especially when it became the editor's duty to avoid repetition, or overlapping,
by selecting what seemed to be the more comprehensive, the more finished,
or the more vivid form of statement. But this method of solving the difficulty
has the advantage, for the reader, of unifying in the present volume practically
the whole of Muir's literary and scientific work during the cruise of the
Corwin. Sometimes, as in chapters eleven and twelve, all the material is new
and has been derived exclusively from the journal. The style of the latter
may generally be recognised by its telegraphic conciseness.

During his studies in the Sierra Nevada Muir had acquired skill, speed,
and accuracy in sketching the features of a landscape. This ability he turned
to good account during the cruise of the Corwin, for one of his journals is
filled with a variety of sketches which prove to be remarkably faithful
pictures in cases where it has been possible to compare them with
photographs.

Since Muir's primary object in joining the Corwin expedition was to look
for evidence of glaciation in the Arctic and subarctic regions, we have
deemed it desirable to include in this volume the article in which he gathered
up the results of his glacial studies and discoveries. It was published in
1884, with Captain C. L. Hooper's report, as Senate Executive Document
No. 204 of the Forty-eighth Congress.

Both the Hooper report and the article on glaciation were elaborately
illustrated from Muir's pencil sketches, though the fact that they were Muir's
is nowhere stated. "The 'Glacier Article' arrived on the sixth," wrote
Captain Hooper to Muir under date of February 7th, 1884, "and was sent

All goes well on our little ship [he writes] and not all the tossing of the waves, and the snow and hail on the deck, and being out of sight of land so long, can make me surely feel that I am not now with you all as ever, so sudden was my departure, and so long have I been accustomed in the old lonely life to feel the influence of loved ones as if present in the flesh, while yet far.... There are but three of us in the cabin, the Captain, the Surgeon, and myself, and only the same three at table, so that there is no crowding ....

Should we be successful in reaching Wrangell Land we would very likely be compelled to winter on it, exploring while the weather permitted. In case we are unsuccessful in reaching Wrangell Land, we may get caught farther west and be able to reach it by dog-sledges in winter while the pack is frozen. Or we may have to winter on the Siberian coast, etc., etc., according to the many variable known and unknown circumstances of the case. Of course if De Long is found we will return at once. If not, a persistent effort will be made to force a way to that mysterious ice-girt Wrangell Land, since it was to it that De Long was directing his efforts when last heard from. We will be cautious, however, and we hope to be back to our homes this fall. Do not allow this outline of Captain Hooper's plan to get into print at present.

From another letter written the following day we quote this breezy bit of description:

How cold it is this morning! How it blows and snows! It is not "the wolf's long howl on Unalaska's shore," as Campbell has it, but the wind's long howl. A more sustained, prolonged, screeching, raving howl I never before heard. But the little Corwin rides on through it in calm strength, rising and falling amid the foam-streaked waves like a loon. The cabin boy, Henry, told me this morning [May 16th] early that land was in sight. So I got up at six o'clock – nine of your time – and went up into the pilot-house to see it. Two jagged black masses were visible, with hints of snow mountains back of them, but mostly hidden beneath a snow-storm.

After breakfast we were within two miles of the shore. Huge snow-peaks, grandly ice-sculptured, loomed far into the stormy sky for a few moments in tolerably clear relief; then the onrush of snowflakes, sweeping out into the dark levels of the sea, would hide it all and fill our eyes, while we puckered our brows and tried to gaze into the face of it all.

We have to proceed in the dimness and confusion of the storm with great caution, stopping frequently to take soundings, so it will probably be one or two o'clock before we reach the harbour of Unalaska on the other side of the island. I tried an hour ago to make a sketch of the mountains along the shore for you, to be sent with this letter, but my fingers got too cold to hold the pencil, and the snow filled my eyes, and so dimmed the outlines of the rocks that I could not trace them.

Down here in the cabin it is warm and summerish, and when the Captain and Doctor are on deck I have it all to myself .... I am glad you thought to on its way rejoicing the same day. The Honourable Secretary [of the Treasury] assures me that he will see that the whole is printed without delay. Please accept my thanks for the article, which is very interesting. The sketches are very fine and will prove a valuable addition to the report. That of the large glacier from Mount Fairweather is particularly fine.''

The article on glaciation should have been published a year earlier, in the same volume with the ''Botanical Notes.'' But for some reason Muir was misinformed, and an apologetic letter to him from Major E. W. Clark, then Chief of the United States Revenue Marine, hints at a petty intrigue as the cause. ''I regret very much,'' he writes, ''that I had not myself corresponded with you regarding your contribution to the Arctic report. Your article on glaciation would have been exactly the thing and would have admitted of very effective illustration. I feel well assured that you were purposely misinformed regarding the report, and could readily explain the reason to you in a personal interview. There has been much anxious inquiry for your notes on glaciation.'' It was the writer of this letter after whom Captain Hooper named the river at whose mouth the Corwin anchored on Wrangell Land. This fact has been recorded by Professor Joseph Everett Nourse, U. S. N., in his work *American Explorations in the Ice Zones*. He states that through the courtesy of Major Clark he had access to the unpublished official report of the cruise of the Corwin. Since the river in question appears without a name upon the chart of Wrangell Land, we must suppose it to be one of the names which Captain Hooper complains the Hydrographic Office ignored.

Besides the illustrative drawings which accompany Muir's article on glaciation in the Far North, his note-books contain numerous interesting sketches of geological and topographical features of Arctic landscapes. They show with what tireless industry and pains he worked at his task. This is the first publication of the general conclusions of his Arctic studies, supported in detail by the records of his journal. In its present form the article follows a revised copy found among Muir's papers.

Muir's report on the flora of Herald Island and Wrangell Land still remains, after thirty-six years, the only one ever made on the vegetation of these remote Arctic regions. It has seemed best, therefore, to include also his article entitled ''Botanical Notes' as an appendix to this volume. It was first published in 1883 as a part of Treasury Department Document No. 429. Strangely enough, the letter of transmittal from the Secretary of the Treasury refers to it as ''the observations on glaciation in the Arctic Ocean and the Alaska region made by John Muir.''

The author never saw printer's proof after he sent the manuscript, and the number of typographical errors made in the technical parts of his article must have established a new record, for they mount into hundreds. Knowing that Muir had sent a duplicate set of his Arctic plant collection to Dr. Asa Gray for final scientific determination, the editor went to the Gray Herbarium of Harvard University, in order to make the necessary corrections and verifications. Fortunately the writer found there not only the original plants, but also Muir's letters to Asa Gray. "I returned a week ago," wrote Muir under date of October 31st, 1881, "from the polar region around Wrangell Land and Herald Island, and brought a few plants from there which I wish you would name as soon as convenient, as I have to write a report on the flora for the expedition. I had a fine icy time, and gathered a lot of exceedingly interesting facts concerning the formation of the Bering Sea and the Arctic Ocean, and the configuration of the shores of Siberia and Alaska. Also concerning the forests that used to grow there, etc., which I hope some day to discuss with you."

The editor has made no attempt to reduce the genus and species names to modern synonymy. As in the case of Muir's *A Thousand-Mile Walk to the Gulf*, it has seemed best to offer the original determinations, making the necessary corrections by reference to the *Index Kewensis*, and, in the case of the ferns, to Christensen's *Index Filicum*. Since Muir's lists did not follow any particular order of classification we have adopted the order of families laid down in the last edition of Gray's *Manual of Botany*.

Special interest attaches to the fact that Muir found on the Arctic shore of Alaska, near Cape Thompson, a species of Erigeron new to science. It is an asteraceous plant with showy, daisy-like flowers. In reporting this find to the American Academy of Arts and Sciences, Asa Gray described it as "the most interesting and apparently the only new species of an extensive and truly valuable collection made by Mr. Muir in a recent searching cruise which he accompanied, and which extended to Wrangel Island [Wrangell Land]. The plant seems to have been abundant, for it occurs in the collection under three numbers."

Gray promptly named it *Erigeron Muirii* in honour of its finder, thus redeeming for the second time a promise made ten years earlier when he wrote to Muir, "Pray, find a new genus, or at least a new species, that I may have the satisfaction of embalming your name, not in glacier ice, but in spicy wild perfume."

WILLIAM FREDERIC BADÈ
1917

CHAPTER ONE

Unalaska and the Aleuts

UNALASKA, May 18th, 1881. The Storm King of the North is abroad today, working with a fine, hearty enthusiasm, rolling a multitude of white combing waves through the rocky jagged straits between this marvellous chain of islands, circling them about with beaten foam, and heaping a lavish abundance of snow on their lofty, cloud-wrapped mountains. The deep bass of the gale, sounding on through the rugged, ice-sculptured peaks and gorges, is delightful music to our ears, now that we are safely sheltered in a land-locked harbour.

The steamer Thomas Corwin arrived here about noon today, after a prosperous run of thirteen days from San Francisco, intending to take on coal and additional supplies of every kind for her long cruise in the Arctic in search of the Jeannette and the missing whalers. Nothing especially noteworthy occurred on the voyage. The weather was remarkably cold for this season of the year, the average temperature for the first day or two being about, 55° F., falling gradually to 35° as we approached Unalaska, accompanied by blustering squalls of snow and hail, suggestive of much higher latitudes than this.

On the morning of the fifteenth we met a gale from the northeast, against which the Corwin forced her way with easy strength, rising and falling on the foam-streaked waves as lightly as a duck. We first sighted land on the morning of the seventeenth, near the southeast extremity of Unalaska Island. Two black outstanding masses of jagged lava were visible, with the bases of snowy peaks back of them, while all the highlands were buried beneath storm clouds. After we had approached within three or four miles of the shore, a ragged opening in the clouds disclosed a closely packed cluster of peaks, laden with snow, looming far into the stormy sky for a few moments in tolerably clear relief, then fading again in the gloom of the clouds and fresh squalls of blinding snow and hail. The fall of the snowflakes among the dark, heaving waves and curling breakers was a most impressive sight.

Groping cautiously along the coast, we at length entered the Akutan Pass. A heavy flood tide was setting through it against the northeast gale, which raised a heavy sea. The waves reared as if about to fall backward, while the wind tore off their white curling tops and carried them away in the form of grey scud. Never before have I seen the sea in so hearty and exhilarating a motion. It was all one white, howling, rampant, runaway

725

mass of foam from side to side. We feared getting our decks swept. Caught, therefore, as we were between the tide and the gale, we turned to seek shelter and wait better times.

We found good anchorage in the lee of a red lava bluff near Cook's Harbour, a few miles to the westward of the mouth of the Pass. The sailors got out their cod-lines, and in a few minutes a dozen fine cod were flapping on the deck. They proved to be excellent fish, eaten fresh. But whether they are as good as the renowned Newfoundland article I cannot judge, as I never have tasted fresh cod. The storm sounding on over the mountains made fine music while we lay safely at anchor, and we enjoyed it all the more because we were in a wild, nameless place that we had ourselves discovered.

The next morning, the gale having abated somewhat, we entered the strait. Wind and tide were flowing in company, but they were against us, and so strong was the latter that we could not stem it, and were compelled to fall back until it was near the turn. The Aleutian chain extends across from continent to continent like an imperfect dam between the Pacific and Bering Sea, and through the gaps between the islands the tide rushes with tremendous speed and uproar. When the tide was favourable, we weighed anchor and passed through the strait and around Kalekta Point into this magnificent harbour[1] without further difficulty.

The harbour of Unalaska is excellent, land-locked, and has a good holding bottom. By virtue of its geographical position it is likely to remain for a long time the business centre of western Alaska. The town[2] is situated on a washed and outspread terminal moraine at the mouth of one of the main glaciers that united here to excavate the harbour. Just above the village there is a glacial lake only a few feet above tide, and a considerable area of level ground about it where the cattle belonging to the town find abundance of fine grass.

Early in the forenoon the clouds had lifted and the sun had come out, revealing a host of noble mountains, grandly sculptured and composed, and robed in spotless white, some of the highest adorned with streamers of mealy snow wavering in the wind – a truly glorious spectacle. To me the features of greatest interest in this imposing show were the glacial advertisements everywhere displayed in clear, telling characters – the trends of the numerous inlets and canyons pointing back into the ancient ice-fountains among the peaks, the sculpture of the peaks themselves and their general outlines, and the shorn faces of the cliffs fronting the sea. No clearer and more unmistakable glacial inscriptions are to be found upon any portion of the mountain ranges of the Pacific Coast.

---

[1]   Dutch Harbour, on the eastern side of Amaknck Island in Unalaska Bay.

[2]   The chief town of Unalaska Island, the most important of the Aleutians, is Iliuliuk. It was founded by Sovovief during the decade between 1760 and 1770 and its Aleut name, according to one interpretation, means "harmony," according to another, "the curved beach." The name Unalaska is often applied loosely to the town as well as the island.

It seems to be guessed in a general way by most observers who have made brief visits to this region that all the islands of the Aleutian chain are clearly volcanic upheavals, scarce at all changed since the period of their emergence from the sea. This is an impression made, no doubt, by the volcanic character of the rocks of which they are composed, and by the numerous extinct and active volcanoes occurring here and there along the summits of the highest masses. But it is plain that the amount of glacial denudation which these ancient lavas have undergone is very great; so great that now every feature presented, with the exception of the few recent craters, is glacial.

The glaciers, that a short time ago covered all the islands, have sculptured the comparatively featureless rock masses into separate mountain peaks, and perhaps into separate islands. Certainly they have done this in some cases. All the inlets or fiords, also, that I have seen are simply the channels of the larger of those old ice rivers that flowed into the sea and eroded their beds beneath its level. The size and the trend of every one of these fiords correspond invariably with the size and the trend of the glacier basin at its head, while not a single fiord or canyon may be found that does not conduct back to mountain fountains whence the eroding glacier drew its sources. The Alaska Peninsula, before the coming on of the glacial period, may have comprehended the whole of the Aleutian chain, its present condition being mostly due to the down grinding action of ice. Frost and fire have worked hand in hand to produce the grand effects presented in this majestic crescent of islands .

UNALASKA, May 21st, 1881.   The Aleutian chain of islands is one of the most remarkable and interesting to be found on the globe. It sweeps in a regular curve a thousand miles long from the'end of the Alaska Peninsula towards Kamchatka and nearly unites the American and Asiatic continents. A very short geological time ago, just before the coming on of the glacial period, this connection of the continents was probably complete, inasmuch as the entire chain is simply a degraded portion of the North American coast mountains, with its foothills and connecting ridges between the summit peaks a few feet under water. These submerged ridges form the passes between the islands as they exist today, while it is evident that this segregating degradation has been effected by the majestic down-grinding glaciers that lately loaded all the chain. Only a few wasting remnants of these glaciers are now in existence, lingering in the highest, snowiest fountains on the largest of the islands.

The mountains are from three thousand to nine thousand feet high, many of them capped with perpetual snow, and rendered yet more imposing by volcanoes emitting smoke and ashes – the feeble manifestations of upbuilding volcanic force that was active long before the beginning of the great ice winter. To the traveller from the south, approaching any portion of the chain during the winter or spring months, the view presented is exceedingly desolate and forbidding. The snow comes down to the water's edge, the solid winter-white being interrupted only by black outstanding bluffs with faces too sheer for snow to lie upon, and by the backs of clustering rocks and long rugged reefs beaten and overswept by heavy breakers rolling in from the Pacific Ocean or Bering Sea, while for ten or eleven months in the year all the mountains are wrapped in gloomy, ragged storm-clouds.

Nevertheless, there is no lack of warm, eager life even here. The stormy shores swarm with fishes – cod, halibut, herring, salmon trout, etc.; also with whales, seals, and many species of water birds, while the sea-otter, the most valuable of the fur-bearing animals, finds its favourite home about the outlying wave-washed reefs. The only land animals occurring in considerable numbers are, as far as I have been able to learn, three or four species of foxes, which are distributed from one end of the chain to the other, with the Arctic grouse, the raven, snowbirds, wrens, and a few finches. There are no deer, wild sheep, goats, bears, or wolves, though all of these are abundant on the mainland in the same latitude.

In two short excursions that I made to the top of a mountain, about two thousand feet high, back of the settlement here, and to a grassy island in the harbour, I found the snow in some places well tracked by foxes and grouse, and saw six species of birds, mostly solitary or in twos and threes. The vegetation near the level of the sea and on bare windswept ridges, up to a height of a thousand feet or more, is remarkably close and luxuriant, covering every foot of the ground.

First there is a dense plush of mosses and lichens from six inches to a foot in depth. Out of the moss mantle and over it there grow five or six species of good nutritious grasses, the tallest shoulder-high; also three species of vaccinium, cranberry, empetrum, the delightful linnaea in extensive patches, the beautiful purple-flowered bryanthus, a pyrola, two species of dwarf willow, three of lycopodium, two saxifrages, a lupine, wild pea, archangelica, geranium, anemone, draba, bearberry, and the little goldthread coptis, besides two ferns and a few withered specimens that I could not make out.

The anemone, draba, and bearberry are already in bloom; the willows are beginning to show the ends of their silky catkins, and a good many green leaves are springing up in sheltered places near the level of the sea. At a height of four or five hundred feet, however, winter still holds sway, with scarce a memory of the rich and beautiful bloom of the summer time. How beautiful these mountains must be when all are in bloom, with the bland summer sunshine on them, the butterflies and bees among them, and the deep glacial fiords calm and full of reflections! The tall grasses, with their showy purple panicles in flower, waving in the wind over all the lower mountain slopes, with a growth heavy enough for the scythe, must then be a beautiful sight, and so must the broad patches of heathworts with their multitude of pink bells, and the tall lupines and ferns along the banks of the streams.

There is not a tree of any kind on the islands excepting a few spruces brought from Sitka and planted by the Russians some fifty years ago. They are still alive, but have made very little growth – a circumstance no doubt due to the climate. But in what respect it differs from the climate of southeastern Alaska, lying both north and south of this latitude, where forests flourish exuberantly in all kinds of exposures, on rich alluvium or on bare rocks, I am unable to say. The only wood I noticed, and all that is said to exist on any of the islands, is small patches of willow, with stems an inch thick, and of several species of woody-stemmed heathworts; this the native Aleuts gather for fuel, together with small quantities of driftwood cast on the shores by the winds and currents.

Grass of good quality for stock is abundant on all the larger islands, and cattle thrive and grow fat during the summer wherever they have been tried. But the wetness of the summer months will always prevent hay from being made in any considerable quantity and make stock-raising on anything like a large scale impossible.

The agricultural possibilities of the islands are also very limited. Oats and barley head out but never fully mature, and if they did, it would be very difficult to get them dry enough for the granary. Potatoes, lettuce, cabbage, turnips, beets, etc., do well in spots that are well drained and have a southern exposure.

According to the census taken last year, the inhabitants of these islands number 2451. Of this population 82 are whites, 479 creoles, and 1890 Aleuts. The Aleuts are far more civilized and Christianised than any other tribe of Alaska Indians. From a third to one half of the men and women read and write. Their occupation is the hunting of the sea-otter for the Alaska Commercial Company.

A good hunter makes from four hundred to eight hundred dollars per annum. In this pursuit they go hundreds of miles in their frail skin-covered canoes, which are so light that they may easily be carried under one's arm. Earning so much money, they are able to support themselves with many comforts beyond the reach of most of the labouring classes of Europe. Nevertheless, with all their advantages, they are fading away like other Indians. The deaths exceed the births in nearly every one of their villages, and it is only a question of time when they will vanish from the face of the earth.

On the way back to the ship I sauntered through the town. It contains about one hundred buildings, half of them frame, built by the Alaska Commercial and Western Fur and Trading Companies. Aleutian huts are called "barabaras." They are built of turf on a frame of wood; some of them have floors, and are divided into many rooms, very small ones. The smells are horrible to clean nostrils, and the air is foul and dead beyond endurance. Some of the bedrooms are not much larger than coffins. The floors are below the surface of the ground two or three feet, and the doors are at the end away from the direction of the prevailing wind. There are one or two small windows of glass or bladder, and a small pipe surmounts a very small Russian stove in which the stems of empetrum are burned.

In most of the huts that I entered I found a Yankee clock, a few pictures, and ordinary cheap crockery and furniture; accordions, also, as they are fond of music. All such bits of furniture and finery of foreign manufacture contrast meanly with their old fashioned kind. Altogether, in dress and home gear, they are so meanly mixed, savage and civilized, that they make a most pathetic impression. The moisture rained down upon them every other day keeps the walls and the roof green, even flowery, and as perfectly fresh as the sod before it was built into a hut. Goats, once introduced by the Russians, make these hut tops their favourite play and pasture grounds, much to the annoyance of their occupants. In one of these huts I saw for the first time arrowheads manufactured out of bottle glass. The edges are chipped by hard pressure with a bit of deer horn.

As the Tlingit Indians of the Alexander Archipelago make their own whiskey, so these Aleuts make their own beer, an intoxicating drink, which, if possible, is more abominable and destructive than hootchenoo. It is called "kvass," and was introduced by the Russians, though the Aleutian kvass is only a coarse imitation of the Russian article, as the Indian hootchenoo is of whiskey. In its manufacture they put a quantity of sugar and flour, or molasses and flour, with a few dried apples, in a cask, fill it up with water, and leave it to ferment. Then they make haste to drink it while it is yet thick and acrid, and capable of making them howling drunk. It also creates a fiery thirst for alcohol, which is supplied by traders whenever they get a chance. This renders the misery of the Aleuts complete.

There are about two thousand of them scattered along the chain of islands, living in small villages. Nearly all the men are hunters of the fur seal, the most expert making five hundred dollars or more per season. After paying old debts contracted with the Companies, they invest the remainder in trinkets, in clothing not so good as their own furs, and in beer, and go at once into hoggish dissipation, hair-pulling, wife-beating, etc. In a few years their health becomes impaired, they become less successful in hunting, their children are neglected and die, and they go to ruin generally. When they toss in their kayaks among surf-beaten rocks where their prey dwells, their business requires steady nerve. But all the proceeds are spent for what is worse than useless. The best hunters have been furnished with frame cottages by the Companies. These cottages have a neat appearance outside, but are very foul inside. Rare exceptions are those in which one finds scrubbed floors or flowers in pots on window-sills and mantels.

We called at the house of the priest of the Greek Church, and were received with fine civility, ushered into a room which for fineness of taste in furniture and fixtures might well challenge the very best in San Francisco or New York. The wallpaper, the ceiling, the floor, the pictures of Yosemite and the Czar on the walls, the flowers in the window, the books on the tables, the window curtains white and gauzy, tied with pink ribbon, the rugs, and odds and ends, all proclaimed exquisite taste of a kind that could not possibly originate anywhere except in the man himself or his wife. This room would have made a keen impression upon me wherever found, and is, I am sure, not dependent upon the squalor of most other homes here, nor upon the wildness and remoteness of Unalaska, for the interest it excites. He spoke only Russian, so that I had but little conversation with him, as I had to speak through our interpreter. We smoked and smiled and gestured and looked at his beautiful home.

Bishop Nestor, who has charge of the Alaskan diocese, is said to be a charming and most venerable man. He now resides in San Francisco, but is having a house built in Unalaska. He is empowered to build and support, at the expense of the home church, a certain number of parish churches. Two out of seven of these are located among the Aleuts – at Unalaska and Belkofski. The other Aleutian villages which have churches, and nearly all have, build and support them at their own expense. The Russian Church claims about eleven thousand members in all Alaska. About one half of these are Aleuts, one thousand creoles, and the rest Indians of Nushagak, Yukon, and Kenai missions, over which the Church exercises but a feeble control. Shamanism with slight variations extends over all Siberia and Alaska and, indeed, all America.

CHAPTER TWO

Among the Islands of Bering Sea

ST. PAUL, ALASKA, May 23rd, 1881. About four o'clock yesterday morning the Corwin left Unalaska, and arrived at St Paul shortly after noon today, the distance being about one hundred and ninety miles. This is the metropolis of the Fur Seal Islands, situated on the island of St.Paul – a handsome village of sixty-four neat frame cottages, with a large church, schoolhouse, and priest's residence and a population of nearly three hundred Aleuts and from twelve to twenty whites. It is interesting to find here an isolated group of Alaskan natives wholly under white influence and control, and who have in great part abandoned their own pursuits, clothing and mode of life in general, and adopted that of the whites. They are all employed by the Alaska Commercial Company as butchers, to kill and flay the hundred thousand seals that they take annually here and at the neighbouring island of St. George. Their bloody work lasts about two months, when they earn tfrom three hundred to six hundred dollars apiece, being paid forty cents per skin.

The Company supplies them with a school, medical attendance, and comfortable dwellings, and looks after their welfare in general, its own interest being involved. They even have a bank, and are encouraged to save their money, which many of them do, having accounts of from two hundred to three thousand dollars. Fortunately, the Aleuts of St. Paul and St. George are pretty effectively guarded against whiskey, and to some extent against kvass also. Only limited quantities of sugar and other kvass material are sold to them. Nevertheless, one of their number told one of our officers today that he had a bank account of eight hundred dollars and would give it all for five bottles of whiskey; and an agent of the Company gave it as his opinion that there were not six perfectly sober Aleuts on the whole island today.

The number of fur seals that resort to these two islands, St. Paul and St. George, during the breeding season, is estimated at from three to four million, and there seems to be no falling off in numbers since the Alaska Commercial Company began operations here. Only young males are killed by the Company, but many of both sexes are taken far from here among the' Aleutian Islands and around the shores of Vancouver Island and the outermost of the Alexander Archipelago.

No one knows certainly whence they come or whither they go. But inasmuch as they make their appearance every year about the shores of the Aleutian Islands shortly after their disappearance from St. Paul and St. George, and then later to the southward, toward the coast of British Columbia, it is supposed that they are the same animals, and that they thus make journeys every year of a thousand miles or more, and return to their birthplaces like shoals of salmon. They begin to appear on the breeding-grounds about the first of June. These are old males, who at once take up their stations on high ground a short distance from the shore, and keep possession of their places while they await the coming of the pregnant females who arrive about a month later, accompanied by the younger members of the community. At the height of the season the ground is closely covered with them, and they seldom go back into the water or take any food until the young are well grown and all are ready to leave the islands in the fall.

In addition to the one hundred thousand taken here, the Company obtains about forty thousand by purchase from the Russians at Bering and Copper Islands, and from Indians and traders at different points south as far as Oregon. These skins are said to be worth fifteen dollars apiece in the London market, to which they are all sent. The government revenue derived from the one hundred thousand killed each year is $317,000. Next in importance among the fur animals of Alaska is the sea-otter, of which about six thousand a year are taken, worth from eighty dollars to one hundred dollars apiece.

The Aleuts obtain from thirty to fifty dollars in goods or money, an alternative not due to the fact that the goods are sold for their money value, but to the fact that the traders sooner or later receive back whatever money they pay out instead of goods. Unlimited competition would, of course, run the price much higher, as, for example, it has done in southeastern Alaska. Here the only competition lies between the Western Fur and Trading Company and the Alaska Commercial Company. The latter gets most of them. Each company seeks the goodwill of the best hunters by every means in its power, by taking them to the hunting grounds in schooners, by advancing provisions and all sorts of supplies, by building cottages for them, and supplying them with the services of a physician and medicine free. Only Indians are allowed by law to take furs, and whites married to Indian women. This law has induced some fifteen white men to marry Indians for the privilege of taking sea-otter. They have settled at Unga Island, one of the Shumagin group, where there is a village of some hundred and eighty-five Indians.

Seen from the sea, all the Pribilof Islands – St. Paul, St. George, and Otter Island – appear as mere rocks, naked and desolate fragments of lava, wasted into bluffs where they touch the sea, and shorn off on top by the ice-sheet. The grey surfaces are roughened here and there by what, at a distance, seem to be degraded volcanic cones. Nevertheless, they are exceedingly interesting, not only because of the marvellous abundance of life about them – seals, water birds, and fishes – but because they tell so grand a story concerning the ice-sheet that swept over them all from the north.

STEAMER CORWIN, TAPKAN, SIBERIA, May 31st, 1881.
On the twenty-fourth of this month, a bleak, snowy day, we enjoyed our first view of the northern ocean ice at a distance of only a few hours from the Pribilof Islands in latitude 58°. This is not far from its southern limit, though strong north winds no doubt carry wasting fragments somewhat farther. It always reaches lower on the American side. Norton Sound is seldom clear before the middle or end of June. Here the ice occurs in ragged, berg-like masses from a foot to a hundred feet in breadth, and with the highest point not more than ten or twelve feet above the water. Its colour is bluish white, looking much like coarse, granular snow, with pale blue stratified bases under water.

We ran past one flat cake on which lay a small white seal which kept its place, though we were within fifteen or twenty feet of it. Guns were then brought into the pilot-house and loaded. In a few minutes another seal was discovered riding leisurely on its ice raft and shot. The engine was stopped, the boat lowered, and a sailor stepped on the ice and threw the heedless fellow into the boat. It seemed to pay scarce any attention to the steamer, and, when wounded by the first ball that was fired, it did not even then seek to escape, which surprised me since those among the fiords north of Wrangell and Sitka are so shy that my Indians, as we glided toward them in a canoe, seldom were successful in getting a shot. The seal was nearly white – a smooth oval bullet without an angle anywhere, large, prominent, humanlike eyes, and long whiskers. It seemed cruel to kill it, and most wonderful to us, as we shivered in our overcoats, that it could live happily enough to grow fat and keep full of warm red blood with water at 32° F for its pasture field, and wet sludge for its bed.

In half an hour we descried another, a large one, which we also shot as it lay at ease on a large cake against which the waves were beating. Like the other two, it waited until we were within easy range, and allowed itself to be shot without the slightest effort to escape. This one proved to be a fine specimen of the saddleback species, *Histriophoca fasciata*, still somewhat rare in collections, and eagerly sought for. It derives its name from the saddlelike bands of brown across the back. This specimen weighed about two hundred pounds. The skins of both were saved, and the next morning we had some of the flesh of the small one for breakfast. The meat proved to be excellent, dark red, and very tender with a taste like that of good venison.

We were steering direct for St. Matthew Island, noted for the great numbers of polar bears that haunt its shores. But as we proceeded, the ice became more and more abundant, and at length it was seen ahead in a solid pack. Then we had to abandon our plan of landing on the island, and steered eastward around the edge of the pack across the mouth of Anadir Gulf.

On the twenty-seventh we sighted the Siberian coast to the north of the Gulf, snow-clad mountains appearing in clear outline at a distance of about seventy miles. Even thus far the traces of glacial action were easily recognised in the peculiar sculpture of the peaks, which here is as unmistakably marked as it is on the summits of the Sierra. Strange that this has not before attracted the attention of observers. The highest of the peaks seems to be perhaps four thousand feet above the sea. I hope I may yet have the chance to ascend them.

On the morning of the twenty-eighth we came to anchor near an Eskimo village at the northwest end of St. Lawrence Island. It was blowing and snowing at the time, and the poor storm-beaten row of huts seemed inexpressibly dreary through the drift. Nevertheless, out of them came a crowd of jolly, well-fed people, dragging their skin canoes, which they shoved over the rim of stranded ice that extended along the shore, and soon they were alongside the steamer, offering ivory, furs, sealskin boots, etc., for tobacco and ammunition.

There was much inquiry for beads, molasses, and most of all for rum and rifles, though they willingly parted with anything they had for tobacco and calico. After they had procured a certain quantity of these articles, however, nothing but rifles, cartridges, and rum would induce them to trade. But according to American law, these are not permitted to be sold. There seems to be no good reason why common rifles* should be prohibited, inasmuch as they would more surely and easily gain a living by their use, while they are

---

* By a "common rifle" Muir probably meant a single-shot or muzzle loading rifle. He changed his mind on this subject when he became aware of the excessive slaughter of caribou, or wild reindeer, committed by natives with repeating rifles.

peaceable and can hardly be induced to fight without very great provocation.

As to the alcohol, no restriction can possibly be too stringent. To the Eskimo it is misery and oftentimes quick death. Two years ago the inhabitants of several villages on this island died of starvation caused by abundance of rum, which rendered them careless about the laying up of ordinary supplies of food for the winter. Then an unusually severe season followed, bringing famine, and, after eating their dogs, they lay down and died in their huts. Last year Captain Hooper found them where they had died, hardly changed. Probably they are still lying in their rags. They numbered several hundreds.

When the people from this village came aboard today they said ours was the first ship of the season, and they were greatly delighted, running over the ship like children. We gave them lead, powder and caps, tobacco, etc. for ivory, arctic shoes, and reindeer parkas, in case we should need them for a winter in the ice, ordinary boots and woollen clothing being wholly inadequate. These are the first Eskimos that I have seen. They impress me as being taller and less distinct as a race than I had been led to suppose. They do not greatly differ from the Tlingits of southeastern Alaska; have Mongolian features well marked, seem to have less brain than the Tlingits, longer faces, and are more simple and childlike in behaviour and disposition. They never quarrel much among themselves or with their neighbours, contrasting greatly in this respect with the Tlingits or Koluschans.

It was interesting to see how keenly and quickly they felt a joke, and winced when exposed to ridicule. Some of the women are nearly white. They show much taste in the manufacture of their clothing, and make everything durable. With their reindeer trousers, sack, shirt, and sealskin shoes they bid defiance to the most extreme cold. Their sack, made from the intestine of the sea lion, while exceedingly light, is waterproof. Some of their parkas are made of the breast skins of ducks, but in no case do they wear blankets. When they can procure calico or drilling they wear overshirts of this material, which gives them a very shabby and dirty look. Why they should want such flimsy and useless material I cannot guess. Dressed in their roomy furs, tied at the waist, they seem better-dressed than any other Indians I have seen. The trousers of the men are made of seal skin, with the fur outside. Those of the women are of deerskin and are extremely baggy. The legs, where gathered and tied below the knee, measure about two feet in diameter.

The chief of this village is a large man, five feet ten inches or six feet tall, with a very long flat face and abruptly tapering forehead, small, bright, cunning eyes, and childishly good-natured and wide awake to everything curious. Always searching for something to laugh at, they are ready to stop short in the middle of most important bargainings to get hold of some bit of fun. Then their big faces would fall calm with ludicrous suddenness, either from being empty or from some business requiring attention. There was less apparent squalor and misery among them than among any other Indians I have seen.

It is a curious fact that they cut off their hair close to the scalp, all save a narrow rim around the base, much like the Chinese without the queue. The hair in colour and coarseness is exactly like that of the Chinese; in a general way they resemble them also in their clothes. Their heads seem insensible to cold, for they bare them to the storms, and seem to enjoy it when the snow falls on their skulls. There is a hood, however, attached to most parkas, which is drawn up over the head in very severe weather.

Their mode of smoking is peculiar. The pipe is made of brass or copper, often curiously inlaid with lead, and the bowl is very small, not over a quarter of an inch in diameter inside, and with a flaring cup-like rim to prevent loss when it is being filled. only a small pinch of finely pulverised tobacco is required to fill it. The Eskimo smoker lights it with a match, or flint and steel, and without removing the pipe from his mouth, sucks in the smoke and inhales it, inflating his lungs to the utmost and holding it a second or two, expels it, coughs, and puts his pipe and little bag of tobacco away, the whole smoke not lasting one minute. From the time he commences he holds his breath until it is finished. The more acrid and pungent the tobacco the better. If it does not compel them to cough and gasp it is not considered good. In buying any considerable quantity they try it before completing the bargain. This method of smoking is said to be practised among all the Eskimos and also the Chukchis of Siberia.

In buying whisky or rum from the traders it is said that they select one of their number to test its strength. The trader gives nearly pure alcohol, so that the lucky tester becomes drunk at once, which satisfies them. Then the keg that is purchased is found to be well watered and intoxication goes on slowly and feebly, much to their disgust and surprise.

CHAPTER THREE

Siberian Adventures

[STEAMER CORWIN, TAPKAN, SIBERIA, May 31st, 1881]   After inquiring about the movements of the ice and the whaling fleet, we weighed anchor and steered for Plover Bay on the coast of Siberia, taking several of the natives with us. They had a few poles for the frame of a boat and skins to cover it, and for food a piece of walrus flesh which they ate raw. This, with a gun and a few odds and ends, was all their property, yet they seemed more confident of their ability to earn a living than most whites on their farms.

The afternoon was clear and the mountains about Plover Bay showed themselves in bold relief, quite imposing and Yosemitic in sculpture and composition. There was so much ice at the mouth of the bay, which is a glacial fiord, that we could not enter. In the edge of the pack we spoke the whaler Rainbow, and delivered the Arctic mail. Then we proceeded a short distance northward, put into Marcus Bay, and anchored in front of a small Chukchi settlement. A boatful of natives came aboard and told a story "important if true," concerning the destruction of the lost whaler Vigilant and the death of her crew. Three Chukchi seal hunters, they said while out on the ice last November, near Cape Serdzekamen, discovered the ship in the pack, her masts broken off by the ice, and the crew dead on the deck and in the cabin. They had brought off a bag of money and such articles as they could carry away, some of which had been shown to other natives, and the story had travelled from one settlement to another thus far down the coast.

All this was told with an air of perfect good faith, and they seemed themselves to believe what they were telling. We had heard substantially the same story at St. Lawrence Island. But knowing the ability of these people for manufacturing tales of this sort, we listened with many grains of allowance, though of course determined to investigate further.

Here we began to inquire for dogs, and were successful in hiring a team of six, and their owner to drive them. The owner is called "Chukchi Joe," and since he can speak a little English he is also to act in the capacity of interpreter, his language being the same as that spoken by the natives of the north Siberian coast. While we were trying to hire him, one of his companions kept reiterating that there was no use in sending out people to look for the crews of those ships, for they were all dead. Joe also said that it was no use going, and that he was afraid to venture so far for fear he would never get back. The snow, he objected, was too soft at this time of year, and many rivers hard to cross were in the way, and he did not like to leave his family.

But after we had promised to pay him well, whether our lost friends were found or not, he consented to go, and when he went ashore to get ready we went with him.

The settlement consisted of only two habitations with twenty five or thirty persons, located back three quarters of a mile from the coast. On reaching home Joe quickly vanished. His hut was about twenty-five feet in diameter, and was made of poles bent down at the top, where they all met to form a hemisphere. This frame was covered with skins of seal, sea-lion, and walrus, chiefly the latter.... Since much of the flesh on which the Chukchis subsist is eaten raw, only very small fires are made, and the huts are cold. The ground inside of this one was wet and muddy as a California corral in the rainy season, and seemed almost as large. But around the sides of this cold, squalid shell, little more than a wind-break and partial shelter from rain and snow, there were a number of very snug, clean, luxurious bedrooms, whose sides, ceiling, and floor were made of fur; they were lighted by means of a pan of whale-oil with a bit of moss for a wick. After being out all day hunting in the stormy weather, or on ice-packs or frozen tundras, the Chukchi withdraws into this furry sanctum, takes off all his clothing, and spreads his wearied limbs in luxurious ease, sleeping perfectly nude in the severest weather.

After introducing ourselves and shaking hands with a few of the most dignified of the old men, we looked about the strange domicile. Dogs, children, men, women, and utensils; spears, guns, whale-lances, etc., were stuck about the rafters and hanging on the supporting posts. We looked into one of the fur bedrooms, about six by seven, and found Joe enjoying a bath ere putting on his fine clothes to set out with us. Soon he emerged clad in a blue cloth army coat with brass buttons and shoulder straps and army cap! I scarcely knew him.

In the meantime Captain H[ooper] was off taking a drive over the snow with a dog-team and sled. When he returned Joe was having a farewell talk with his wife, who seemed very anxious about his safety and long absence. His little boy, too, about a year and a half old, had been told that his father was going away and he seemed to understand somewhat, as he kept holding him by the legs and trying to talk to him while looking up in his face. When we started away from the house he kissed his boy and bade him goodbye. The little fellow in his funny bags of fur toddled after him until caught and carried back by some of the women who were looking on. Joe's wife came aboard for a final farewell. After taking him aside and talking with him, the tears running down her cheeks, she left the vessel and went back with some others who had come to trade deerskins, while we sailed away. One touch of nature makes all the world kin, and here were many touches among the wild Chukchis.

We next proceeded to St. Lawrence Bay in search of furs and more dogs, and came to anchor at the mouth of the bay, opposite a small Chukchi settlement of two huts, at half-past one in the afternoon, May 29th. This bay, like all I have seen along this coast, is of glacial formation, conducting back into glacial fountains in a range of peaks of moderate height. The wind was blowing hard from the south and snow was falling. The natives, however, came off at once to trade. Here we met the voluble Jaroochah, who sat gravely on the sloppy deck in the sludge, and told the story of the wrecked Vigilant in a loud, vehement, growling, roaring voice and with frantic gestures. He assured us over and over again that there was no use in going to seek any of the crew, for they were all dead and the ship with her broken masts had drifted away again to the north with the ice-pack. When told that we would certainly seek them whether dead or alive, he explained that the snow and ice were too soft for sleds at this time of year. Seeing that we were still unconvinced, he doubtless regarded us as foolish and incorrigible white trash.

We went ashore to fetch some dogs they offered to sell, but they changed their minds and refused to sell at any price, nor were they willing to barter deerskins that we needed for the trip and for winter clothing in case we should be caught in the ice and compelled to pass a winter in the Arctic. We presented them with a bucket of hardtack which no one of the party touched until the old orator gave orders to his son to divide it. This he did by counting it out on the deck, laying down one biscuit for each person and then adding one to each until all was exhausted, piling them on each other like a money-changer counting out coins. The mannerly reserve and unhasting dignity of all these natives when food is set before them is very striking as compared with the ravenous, snatching haste of the hungry poor among the whites. Even the children look wistfully at the heap of bread, without touching it until invited, and then eat very slowly as if not hungry at all. Nor do they ever need to be told to wait. Even when a year of famine occurs from any cause, they endure it with fortitude such as would be sought for in vain among the civilized, and after braving the most intense cold of these dreary ice-bound coasts in search of food, if unsuccessful, they wrap themselves in their furs and die quietly as if only going to sleep. This they did by hundreds two years ago on St. Lawrence Island.

Finding that we could not buy anything that we wanted here, savage eloquence being the only article offered, we sailed for the Diomedes. Here we found the natives eager to trade away everything they had. We bought a lot of furs and nineteen dogs, paying a sack of flour for each dog. This Arctic cattle market was in every way lively and picturesque, and ended satisfactorily to all the parties concerned. The scene of barter as each Eskimo, pitching alongside in his skin boat, hoisted the howling wolves aboard and thence to the upper deck in front of the pilot-house, was a rare one .

The villages are perched on the steep rocky slopes of mountains which drop at once sheer into deep water, one mountain per island.* No margin is left for a village along the shore, so, like the seabirds that breed here and fly about in countless multitudes darkening the water, the rocks, and the air, the natives had to perch their huts on the cliffs, dragging boats and everything up and down very steep trails. The huts are mostly built of stone with skin

---

* Muir noted in his journal that "Fairway Rock near the East Diomede is a similar smaller island, on which the granite rock is glaciated."

roofs. They look like mere stoneheaps, black dots on the snow at a distance, with whalebone posts set up and framed at the top to lay their canoes beyond the dogs that would otherwise eat them. The dreariest towns I ever beheld – the tops of the islands in gloomy storm-clouds; snow to the water's edge, and blocks of rugged ice for a fringe; then the black water dashing against the ice; the grey sleety sky, the screaming water birds, the howling wind, and the blue gathering sludge!

We now pushed on through the strait and into the Arctic Ocean without encountering any ice, and passed Cape Serdzekamen this afternoon [May 31st]. The weather has been calm and tolerably clear for the last twenty-four hours, enabling us to see the coast now and then. It showed hills of moderate height, rising here and there to mountains.

About twelve miles northwest from Cape Serdzekamen we observed a marked bluff where the shore ice seemed narrower than elsewhere, and we approached, intending to examine it with reference to landing the party here. When we were within a mile of it we saw a group of natives signalling us to land by waving something over their heads. The Captain, Joe, and myself got on the ice from the boat, and began to scramble over it toward the bluff, but found the ice very rough and made slow progress. The pack is made up of a crushed mass of blocks and pinnacles tilted at every angle up to a height of from ten to thirty feet, and it seemed to become rougher and more impassable as we advanced.

Fortunately we discovered a group of natives a quarter of a mile or so to the westward, coming toward the ship, when we returned to our boat that was lying at the edge of the ice, and went around to meet them. After shaking hands with the most imposing of the group of eight, we directed Joe to tell them the object we had in coming, and to inquire whether two of their number would go with our sledge party to assist in driving the teams. One of them, a strapping fellow over six feet tall, said that he had a wife and four boys and two girls to hunt seals for, and therefore could not go. As Joe interpreted him in whaler English, he was "already hungry like hell." Another said that the journey was too long for *him*, that our friends were not along the coast, else he would certainly have heard about them, and therefore the journey would be vain. We urged that we were going to seek them whether they were to be found or not, and that if they would go with us we would leave more food for their families than they could get for them by hunting.

Two of the number at length consented to go, after being assured that we would pay them well, whether the journey proved successful or otherwise. Then we intimated that we would like to visit their village, which seemed to please them; for they started at once to guide us over the hummocky ice to where they had left their dog-teams and sleds. It was a rough scramble at best, and even the natives slipped at times and hesitated cautiously in choosing a way, while we, encumbered with overcoats and not so well shod, kept sinking with awkward glints and slumps into hopper-shaped hollows and chasms filled with snow. One of them kindly gave me his balancing-stick.

Beyond the roughest portion of the hummock region we found the dogs, nearly a hundred of them, with eleven sleds, making, as they lay at their ease, an imposing picture among the white ice. Three of the teams were straightened out and one of them given in charge of Joe, who is an adept at driving, while the Captain and I were taken on behind the drivers of the other two; and away we sped over the frozen ceiling of the sea, two rows of tails ahead.

The distance to the village, called "Tapkan" by the natives, was about three miles, the first mile very rough and apparently hopelessly inaccessible to sleds. But the wolfish dogs and drivers seemed to regard it all as a regular turnpike, and jogged merrily on, up one side of a tilted block or slab and down the other with a sudden pitch and plunge, swishing round sideways on squinted cakes, and through pools of water and sludge in blue, craggy hollows, on and on, this way and that, with never a halt, the dogs keeping up a steady jog trot, and the leader simply looking over his shoulder occasionally for directions in the worst places. The driver admonished them with loud calls of "Hoora! Hoora! Shedack! Shedack! Knock! Knock!" but seldom struck them. He had to hold himself in constant readiness to jump off and hold the sled while guiding it around sharp angles and across the high cutting ridges. My sled was not upset at all, and the Captain's only twice .

Part of our way was across the mouth of a bay on smooth ice that had not been subjected to the mashing, upheaving strain of the ocean ice, and over this we glided rapidly. My Chukchi driver, now that he had no care about the upsetting of the sled, frequently turned with a smile and did his best to entertain me, though he did not understand a word of English. It was a rare, strange ride for us, yet accomplished with such everyday commonplace confidence, that it seemed at the time as if this might be the only mode of land travel in the world.

Some teams were just arriving from the village as we were going to it. When we met, the dogs passed each other to right or left as they were told by their drivers, who kept flourishing a whip and jingling some iron rings that were tied loosely to one end of a short stick that had an iron goad in the other, and of which the dogs knew the use all too well. They are as steady as oxen, each keeping its trace-line tight, and showing no inclination to shirk – utterly unlike the illustrations I had seen, in which all are represented as running at a wild gallop with mouths wide open.

The village is built on a sand-bar pushed up by the ice on the west side of a narrow bay. I counted twenty huts in all. When we drove up, the women and children, and a few old men who had not been tempted to make the journey to the ship, came out to meet us. Captain Hooper went to the house belonging to his driver, I to the one belonging to mine; afterwards we joined and visited in company. We were kindly received and shown to good seats on reindeer skins. All of them smiled good-naturedly when we shook hands with them, and tried to repeat our salutations. When we discussed our proposed land journey the women eagerly joined and the children listened attentively.

We inquired about the Vega, knowing that she had wintered hereabouts.

At first they said they knew nothing about her; that no ship had wintered here two years ago. Then, as if suddenly remembering, one of them said a three-masted ship, a steamer like the Corwin, had stopped one season in the ice at a point a few miles east of the village, and had gone away when it melted in the summer. A woman, who had been listening, then went to a box, and after turning it over, showed us a spoon, fork, and pocket compass of Russian manufacture, which she said the captain had given them.

The huts here are like those already described, only they are dry because of the porous character of the ground. Three or four families live in one, each having a private polog of deerskins, of which there are several thicknesses on the floor. We were shown into one – the snuggest storm nest imaginable, and perfectly clean. The common hut is far otherwise; dogs mingle with the food, hair is everywhere, and strangely persistent smells that defy even the Arctic frosts. The children seemed in fair ratio with the adults. When a child is to be nursed the mother merely pulls out one of her arms from the roomy sleeve of her parka and pushes it down until the breast is exposed. The breasts are pendulous and cylindrical, like those of the Tlingits.

The dishes used in domestic affairs are of wood, and in the smallest of these the puppies, after licking them, were often noticed to lie down. They seemed made specially for them, so well did they fit. Dogs were eagerly licking the large kettles, also, in which seal meat had been boiled. They seemed to be favoured in these establishments like the pigs in Irish huts. Spears, lances, guns, and nets were fastened about the timbers of the roof and sides, but little food of any kind was visible. A pot was swinging over a small fire of driftwood when we entered one of the huts, and an old dame was stirring it occasionally, and roasting seal liver on the coals beneath it. On leaving we were each presented with a pair of fur mittens.

At the last moment, when we were ready to return to the ship, one of the men we had engaged to go with the land party changed his mind and concluded to stay at home. The other stuck to his engagement, though evidently feeling sore about leaving his family. His little boy cried bitterly when he learned that his father was going away, and refused all the offers made by the women to comfort him. After we had sped away over the ice, half a mile from the village, we could still hear his screams. Just as the ship was about to weigh anchor, the second man again offered to go with us, but Joe said to the Captain, ''More better not take that fellow, he too much talk.''

The group of lookers-on congregated on the edge of the ice was very picturesque seen from the vessel as we moved away. The Chukchis are taller and more resolute-looking people than the Eskimos of the opposite coast, but both are Mongols and nearly alike in dress and mode of life, as well as in religion.

The weather is promising this evening. No portion of the polar pack is in sight, and we mean to push on westward as far as we can with safety.

CHAPTER FOUR

In Peril from the Pack

STEAMER CORWIN, NEAR THE EDGE OF THE SHORE ICE, OPPOSITE KOLIUCHIN ISLAND, 6 p.m., June 2nd, 1881. After leaving Tapkan, twelve miles northwest of Cape Serdzekamen, on the evening of the last day of May, we steamed along the coast to the westward, tracing the edge of the shore-ice, which seemed to be from three to six miles wide. The weather was tranquil, though rather thick at times, and the water was like glass and as smooth as a mill-pond. About half-past five yesterday afternoon we reached the end of the open lead that we had been following, one hundred and thirty miles west of Cape Serdzekamen, latitude 68° 28' N., longitude 175° 10' W., having thus early in the season gained a point farther west than the Corwin was able to reach at any time last year.

At this point the firm coast ice united with the great polar pack, and, as there was danger of its drifting south at any time and cutting us off, we made haste to the eastward, keeping as far off shore as possible, that we might be able to watch the movements of the pack. About seven o'clock last evening, the weather becoming thick, the engine was stopped and the vessel was allowed to proceed slowly under sail.

Shortly after one o'clock this morning I was awakened by unusual sounds on deck, and after listening for a few minutes, concluded that we must be entangled in the edge of the pack and were unshipping the rudder for fear it might be carried away. Going on deck, I was surprised to see the broken rudder being hoisted, for I had not been awakened by the blow. The oak shaft was broken completely off, and also all three of the pintles. It seems that about midnight, owing to the fog and snow, we got into a field of heavy masses of ice on the edge of the main pack, which, on account of a north wind that had commenced to blow, was now moving slowly southward, and while backing out of it, a moderate bump that chanced to take the rudder at the greatest disadvantage broke it off without any appreciable strain.

The situation was sufficiently grave and exciting – dark weather, the wind from the north and freshening every minute, and the vast polar pack pushing steadily shoreward. It was a cold, bleak, stormy morning, with a close, sweeping fall of snow, that encumbered the deck and ropes and nearly blinded one when compelled to look to windward. Our twenty-five dogs made an effective addition to the general uproar, howling as only Eskimo dogs can. They were in the way, of course, and were heartily kicked hither and thither. The necessary orders, however, were being promptly given and obeyed. As soon as the broken rudder was secured on deck, four long spars were nailed and lashed firmly together, fastened astern and weighted to keep them in place at the right depth in the water. This made a capital jury-rudder. It was worked by ropes attached on either side and to the steam windlass. The whole was brought into complete working order in a few hours, nearly everybody rendering service, notwithstanding the blinding storm and peril, as if jury-rudder making under just these circumstances were an everyday employment. Then, finding everything worked well, we made our escape from the closing ice and set out for Plover Bay to repair the damage.

About four in the afternoon, as the clouds lifted, we sighted Koliuchin Island, which our two Chukchi natives hailed with joyful, beaming eyes. They evidently were uneasy because of the accident, and on account of being so long out of sight of land – a state of mind easily explained by the dangers attending their mode of life among the ice. In front of the island the ice seemed to be two or three miles wide and lavishly roughened with jammed, angular hummocks. Captain Hooper was now very anxious to get his sledge party landed. Everything was ready to be put on shore as soon as a safe landing-place should be discovered. The two Chukchis were in the pilot-house gazing wistfully at the gloomy snow-covered island as it loomed up in the grey, stormy sky with its jagged reach of ice in the foreground beaten by the waves.

The Captain directed Chukchi Joe, the interpreter, to ask his companion, the dog driver, who was familiar with the condition of the ice on this part of the coast, whether this was a good point on which to land. His answer, as interpreted by Joe, was: "He says it's good; it's pretty good, he says." "Then get ready, Mr. Herring, for your journey," ordered the Captain. "Here, Quartermaster, get the provisions on deck." "Lower the boats there." "Joe, harness the dogs."

In a few minutes all was in readiness and in the boats. The party is composed of First Lieutenant Herring, in charge; Third Lieutenant Reynolds, a sailor* and the two Chukchis. They have twenty-five dogs, four sleds, a light skin boat to cross rivers and any open water they may find in their way, and two months' provisions. They were directed to search the coast as far to the westward as possible for the crew of the Jeannette or any tidings concerning the fate of the expedition; to interview the natives they met; to explore the prominent portions of the coast for cairns and signals of any kind, and to return to Tapkan, where we would meet them, while in the mean time we propose to cruise wherever, under existing conditions, we can best carry out the objects of the expedition.

The party and all their equipments were carried from the vessel to the ice in three boats, roped together at intervals of twenty five or thirty feet, the

* Coxswain Gessler

lifeboat leading with the party, clothing, provisions, etc. Then came the dinghy, loaded nearly to the water's edge with the dogs, and one man to thrash them and keep some sort of order while they worried each other and raised an outrageous noise, on account of their uncomfortable, tumbled together condition. And last, the skin boat, flying-light, with only the sleds aboard and one man to steer, the whole making a very extraordinary show.

Soon after the boats had left, while we were still watching the tossing fleet from the pilot-house and scanning the shore with reference to a landing-place, we noticed three dark objects on top of a hummock near the edge of the ice, and just back of them and to one side on a flat portion of the ice, a group of black dots. These proved to be three natives with their dog teams. They were out hunting seals, and had descried the ship with their sharp eyes and now came forward to gaze. This was a glad discovery to us, and no doubt still more so to the party leaving the ship, as they were now sure of the passable state of the ice, and would have guides with local knowledge to conduct them to the land. When the dogs got upon the ice, their native heath, they rolled and raced about in exuberant sport. The rough pack was home sweet home to them, though a more forbidding combination of sky, rough water, ice, and driving snow could hardly be imagined by the sunny civilized south.

After all were safely landed and our boats had returned, we went on our way, while the land party, busied about their sled packing and dogs, gradually faded in the snowy gloom. All seems well this evening; no ice is in sight to the northward, and the jury-rudder is working extremely well.

[STEAMER CORWIN, EN ROUTE SOUTHWARD TO PLOVER BAY.] June 3rd. Snowing nearly all day. Cleared towards four in the afternoon. Spoke the Helen Mar; had taken five whales; another had already nine. Seven other whalers in sight, all of them save two smoking like steamers. They are trying out their abundant blubber; in danger of being blubber-logged. Saw an Indian canoe leaving the Helen Mar as we approached; probably had been trading, the sea being smooth.

Had a good view of the two Diomedes; the western one is very distinctly glaciated, nearly all of the summit being comprehended in one beautiful ice-fountain, giving it a crater-like form. The residual glacial action, however, has been light, comparatively, here. No deep canyons putting back into the mountains, most of which are low. It is interesting, however, to see undoubted traces both of general and local glaciation thus far north, where the ground is in general rather low. Came up to the ice-pack about ten in the evening, so turned back and lay to.

June 4th. Calm, bland, foggy water, glassy and still as a millpond. Cleared so that one could see a mile ahead at ten o'clock, and we got under. Sun nearly clear for the first day since coming into the Arctic. Mild, too, for it is 45° F. at noon; even seemed hot. The clouds lifted from the mountains, showing their bases and slopes up to a thousand feet; summits capped. East Cape in fine view; high headland still streaked with snow nearly to the base, summit white at close range. All the coast for at least two hundred miles west of East Cape shows distinct glaciation, both general and local. Many glacier fountains well characterised. Indian village off here. Were boarded by three canoe loads of Indian seal hunters from East Cape village. They traded ivory and shoes, called "susy" by their interpreter. We were anxious to tell them about our sledge party and inquired of one who spoke a few words of English whether any of their number could speak good English. He seemed to think us very unreasonable, and said, "Me speak good." Got a female eider duck; very fat. In one of the canoes there was a very large seal, weighing perhaps four hundred pounds.

This has been by far the most beautiful and gentle of our Arctic days, the water perfectly glassy and with no swell, mirroring the sky, which shows a few blue cloudless spots, white as satin near the horizon, of beautiful luster, trying to the eyes. More whalers in sight. Gulls skimming the glassy level. Innumerable multitudes of eider ducks, the snowy shore, and all the highest mountains cloud-capped – a rare picture and perfectly tranquil and peaceful! God's love is manifest in the landscape as in a face. How unlike yesterday! In the evening a long approach to sunset, a red sky mingling with brown and white of the ice-blink. Growing colder towards midnight. There is no night at all now; only a partial gloaming; never, even in cloudy midnights, too dark to read. So for more than a week. Ice in sight, but hope to pass it by running a few miles to shore. Are now, at half-past eleven in the evening, beyond St. Lawrence Bay. Hope to get into Plover Bay tomorrow morning at six o'clock.

CHAPTER FIVE

A Chukchi Orator

STEAMER CORWIN, ST. LAWRENCE BAY, SIBERIA, June 6th, 1881. Yesterday morning at half-past one o'clock, when we were within twenty-five miles of Plover Bay, where we hoped to be able to repair our rudder, we found that the ice-pack was crowding us closer and closer inshore, and that in our partly disabled condition it would not be safe to proceed farther. Accordingly we turned back and put into St. Lawrence Bay, to await some favourable movement in the ice.

We dropped anchor at half-past seven in the morning opposite a small Chukchi settlement. In a few hours the wind began to blow fresh from the north, steadily increasing in force, until at eight in the evening it was blowing a gale, and we were glad that we were in a good harbour instead of being out at sea, slashing and tumbling about with a broken rudder among the wind-driven ice. It also rained and snowed most of the afternoon, the blue and grey sleet mingling in grand uproar with the white scud swept from the crests of the waves, making about as stormy and gloomy an atmosphere as I ever had the fortune to breathe. Now and then the clouds broke and lifted their ragged edges high enough to allow the mountains along the sides and around the head of the bay to be dimly seen, not so dimly, however, as to hide the traces of the heavy glaciation to which they have been subjected. This long bay, as shown by its trends, its relation to the ice-fountains at its head and the sculpture of its walls, is a glacial fiord that only a short time ago was the channel of a glacier that poured a deep and broad flood into Bering Sea, in company with a thousand others north and south along the Siberian coast. The more I see of this region the more I am inclined to believe that all of Bering Sea and Strait is a glacial excavation.

In a party of natives that came aboard soon after we had dropped anchor, we discovered the remarkable Chukchi orator, Jaroochah, whose acquaintance we made at the settlement on the other side of the bay, during our first visit, and who had so vividly depicted the condition of the lost whaler *Vigilant*. Today, after taking up a favourable position in the pilot-house, he far surpassed his previous efforts, pouring forth Chukchi in overwhelming torrents, utterly oblivious of the presence of his rival, the howling gale.

During a sudden pause in the midst of his volcanic eloquence he inquired whether we had rum to trade for walrus ivory, whereupon we explained, in total abstinence phrase, that rum was very bad stuff for Chukchis, and by way of illustration related its sad effects upon the Eskimo natives of St. Lawrence Island. Nearly all the natives we have thus far met admitted very readily that whiskey was not good for them. But Jaroochah was not to be so easily silenced, for he at once began an anti-temperance argument in saloon-and-moderate-drinker style, explaining with vehement gestures that some whiskey was good, some bad; that he sometimes drank five cupfuls of the good article in quick succession, the effect of which was greatly to augment his happiness, while out of a small bottle of the bad one, a small glass made him sick. And as for whiskey or rum causing people to die, he knew, he said, that was a lie, for he had drunk much himself, and he had a brother who had enjoyed a great deal of whiskey on board of whalers for many years, and that though now a grey old man he was still alive and happy.

This speech was warmly applauded by his listening companions, indicating a public opinion that offers but little hope of success for the efforts of temperance societies among the Chukchis. Captain Hooper, the surgeon, and myself undertook to sketch the orator, who, when he had gravely examined our efforts, laughed boisterously at one of them, which, in truth, was a slanderous caricature of even *his* countenance, villainous as it was.

In trading his ivory for supplies of some sort, other than alcohol, he tried to extract some trifling article above what had been agreed on, when the trader threatened to have nothing further to do with him on account of the trouble he was making. This set the old chief on his dignity, and he made haste to declare that he was a good and honourable man, and that in case the trade was stopped he would give back all he had received and go home, leaving his ivory on the deck heedless of what became of it. The woman of the party, perhaps eighteen years of age, merry and good-looking, went among the sailors and danced, sang, and joked with them.

The gale increased in violence up to noon today, when it began to abate slightly, and this evening it is still blowing hard. The Corwin commenced to drag her anchor shortly after midnight, when another that was kept in readiness was let go with plenty of chain, which held, so that we rode out the gale in safety. The whalers Francis Palmer and Hidalgo came into the bay last evening from Bering Strait and anchored near us. This morning the Hidalgo had vanished, having probably parted her cable.

Last evening a second party of natives came aboard, having made their way around the head of the bay or over the ice. Both parties remained on board all night as they were unable to reach the shore in their light skin boats against the wind. Being curious to see how they were enduring the cold, I went on deck early. They seemed scarcely to feel it at all, for I found most of them lying on the deck amid the sludge and sleeping soundly in the clothes they wore during the day. Three of them were sleeping on the broken rudder, swept by the icy wind and sprinkled with snow and fragments of ice that were falling from the rigging, their heads and necks being nearly bare.

I inquired why their reindeer parkas were made without hoods, while those of the Eskimos of St. Lawrence Island had them; observing that they seemed far more comfortable in stormy weather, because they kept the head and neck warm and dry. They replied that they had to hunt hard and look quick all about them for a living, therefore it was necessary to keep their heads free; while the St. Lawrence Eskimos were lazy, and could indulge in effeminate habits. They gave the same reason for cutting off most of the hair close to the scalps, while the women wear the hair long.

One of their number was very dirty, and Captain Hooper, who is becoming interested in glacial studies, declared that he had discovered two terminal moraines in his ears. When asked why he did not wash himself, our interpreter replied, "Because he is an old fellow, and it is too much work to wash." This was given with an air of having explained the matter beyond further question. Considering the necessities of the lives they lead, most of these people seem remarkably clean and well-dressed and well-behaved.

The old orator poured forth his noisy eloquence late and early, like a perennial mountain spring, some of his deep chest tones sounding in the storm like the roar of a lion. He rolled his wolfish eyes and tossed his brown skinny limbs in a frantic storm of gestures, now suddenly foreshortening himself to less than half his height, then shooting aloft with jack-in-the-box rapidity, while his people looked on and listened, apparently half in fear, half in admiration. We directed the interpreter to tell him that we thought him a good man, and were, therefore, concerned lest some accident might befall him from so much hard speaking. The Chukchis, as well as the Eskimos we have seen, are keenly sensitive to ridicule, and this suggestion disconcerted him for a moment and made a sudden pause. However, he quickly recovered and got under way again, like a wave withdrawing on a shelving shore, only to advance and break again with gathered force.

The chief man of the second party from the other side of the bay is owner of a herd of reindeer, which he said were now feeding among the mountains at a distance of one sleep – a day's journey – from the head of a bay to the south of here. He readily indicated the position on a map that we spread before him, and offered to take us to see them on a sled drawn by reindeer, and to sell us as many skins and as much meat as we cared to buy. When we asked how many reindeer he had, all who heard the question laughed at the idea of counting so many. "They cover a big mountain," he said proudly, "and nobody can count them." He brought a lot of ivory to trade for tobacco, but said nothing about it until the afternoon. Then he signified his readiness for business after awakening from a sound sleep on the wet icy deck.

Shortly after we had breakfasted, the reindeer chief having intimated that he and his friends were hungry, the Captain ordered a large pot of tea, with hardtack, sugar, and molasses, to be served to them in the pilot-house. They ate with dignified deliberation, showing no unseemly haste, but eating rather like people accustomed to abundance. Jaroochah, who could hardly stem his eloquence even while eating, was particular about having his son invited in to share the meal; also, two boys about eight years old, giving as a reason, "they are little ones." We also called in a young woman, perhaps about eighteen years old, but none of the men present seemed to care whether she shared with them or not, and when we inquired the cause of this neglect, telling them that white men always served the ladies first, Jaroochah said that while girls were "little fellows" their parents looked after them, but when they grew big they went away from their parents with "some other fellow," and were of no more use to them and could look out for themselves.

Those who were not invited to this meal did not seem to mind it much, for they had brought with them plenty of what the whalers call "black skin" – the skin of the right whale – which is about an inch thick, and usually has from half an inch to an inch of blubber attached. This I saw them eating raw with hearty relish, snow and sludge the only sauce, cutting off angular blocks of it with butcher knives, while one end of the tough black rubberlike mass was being held in the left hand, the other between their teeth. Long practice enables them to cut off mouthfuls in this way without cutting their lips, although they saw their long knives back and forth, close to their faces, as if playing the violin. They get the whale skin from the whalers, excepting the little they procure themselves. They hunt the whale now with lances and gear of every kind bought from the whalers, and sometimes succeed in killing a good many. They eat the carcass, and save the bone to trade to the whalers, who are eager to get it.

After the old orator left the steamer, the reindeer man accused him of being "a bad fellow, like a dog." He evidently was afraid that we were being fooled by his overwhelming eloquence into believing that he was a great man, while the precious truth to be impressed upon us was that he, the reindeer man, whose herd covers a big mountain, was the true chief. I asked his son, who speaks a little English, why he did not make a trip to San Francisco, to see the white man's big town. He replied, as many a civilized man does under similar circumstances, that he had a little boy, too little to be left, and too little to leave home, but that soon he would be a big fellow, so high, indicating the hoped-for stature with his hand, then he would go to San Francisco on some whale-ship, to see where all the big ships and good whiskey came from.

These [Chukchis] also had heard the story of the Vigilant. The reindeer man's son is going with us to Plover Bay to look after some of his father's debtors. He has been supplying them with tobacco and other goods on credit, and he thought it time they were paying up. His little boy, he told us, was sick – had a hot, sore head that throbbed, showing with his hand how it beat in aching pulses, and asked for medicine, which the surgeon gave him with necessary directions, greatly to his relief of mind, it seemed.

Around the shore opposite our anchorage the ground is rather low, where the ancient glacier that filled the bay swept over in smooth curves, breaking off near the shore, an abrupt wall from seventy to a hundred feet high. Against this wall the prevailing north winds have piled heavy drifts of snow that curve over the bluff at the top and slope out over the fixed ice along the shore from the base. The gale has been loosening and driving out past the vessel, without doing us any harm, large masses of the ice, capped with the edge of the drift. One large piece drifted close past the steamer and immediately in front of a large skin canoe capable of carrying thirty men. The canoe, which was tied to the stem of the ship, we thought was doomed to be carried away. The owners looked wistfully over the stern, watching her fate, while the sailors seemed glad of the bit of excitement caused by the hope of an accident that would cost them nothing. Greatly to our surprise, however, when the berg, rough and craggy, ten or twelve feet high, struck her bow, she climbed up over the top of it, and, dipping on the other side, glided down with a graceful, launching swoop into the water, like a living thing, wholly uninjured. The sealskin buffer, fixed in front and inflated like a bladder, no doubt greatly facilitated her rise. She was tied by a line of walrus hide.

Now that the wind is abating, we hope to get away from here to-morrow morning, and expect to find most of the ice that stopped our progress yesterday broken up and driven southward far enough to enable us to reach Plover Bay without further difficulty.

CHAPTER SIX

Eskimos and Walrus

STEAMER CORWIN, PLOVER BAY, June 15th, 1881. We left our anchorage in St. Lawrence Bay at four in the morning, June 7th, and steered once more for Plover Bay. The norther that had been blowing so long gave place to a light southerly breeze, and a gentle dusting of snow was falling. In the afternoon the sea became smooth and glassy as a mountain lake, and the clouds lifted, gradually unveiling the Siberian coast up to the tops of the mountains. First the black bluffs, standing close to the water, came in sight; then the white slopes, and then one summit after another until a continuous range forty or fifty miles long could be seen from one point of view, forming a very beautiful landscape. Smooth, dull, dark water in the foreground;

next, a broad belt of ice mostly white like snow, with numerous masses of blue and black shade among its jagged, uplifted blocks. Then a strip of comparatively low shore, black and grey; and back of that the pure white mountains. With only here and there dark spots, where the rock faces are too steep for snow to lie upon. Sharp peaks were seen, fluted by avalanches; glacier wombs, delicate in curve and outline as shells; rounded, overswept brows and domes, and long, withdrawing valleys leading back into the highest alpine groups, whence flowed noble glaciers in imposing ranks into what is now Bering Sea.

We had hoped the gale had broken and driven away the floe that barred our way on the fifth [of June], but while yet thirty miles from the entrance of the bay we were again stopped by an immense field of heavy ice that stretched from the shore southeastward as far as the eye could reach. We pushed slowly into the edge of it a few miles, looking for some opening, but the man in the crow's nest reported it all solid ahead and no water in sight. We thereupon steamed out and steered across to St. Lawrence Island to bide our time.

While sailing amid the loose blocks of ice that form the edge of the pack, we saw a walrus, and soon afterward a second one with its young. The Captain shot and killed the mother from the pilot house, and the dinghy was lowered to tow it alongside. The eyes of our Indian passengers sparkled with delight in expectation of good meat after enduring poor fare aboard the ship. After floating for eight or ten minutes she sank to the bottom and was lost – a sad fate and a luckless deed.

It was pitiful to see the young one swimming around its dying mother, heeding neither the ship nor the boat. They are said to be very affectionate and bold in the defence of one another against every enemy whatever. We have as yet seen but few, though in some places they are found in countless thousands. Many vessels are exclusively employed in killing them on the eastern Greenland coast, and along some portions of the coast of Asia. Here also, the whalers, when they have poor success in whaling, devote themselves to walrus hunting, both for the oil they yield and for the valuable ivory. The latter is worth from forty to seventy cents per pound in San Francisco, and a pair of large tusks weighs from eight to ten pounds.

Along all the coasts, both of Asia and of America, the natives hunt and kill this animal, which to them is hardly less important for food and other uses than the seals. A large walrus is said to weigh from one to two tons. Its tough hide is used for cordage, and to cover canoes. The flesh is excellent, while the ivory formerly was employed for spear heads and other uses, and is now an important article of trade for guns, ammunition, calico, bread, flour, molasses, etc. The natives now kill a good many whales, having obtained lances and harpoons from the whites. Bone, in good years, is more important than the ivory, and furs are traded, also, in considerable quantity. By all these means they obtain more of the white man's goods than is well used. They probably were better off before they were possessed of a single civilized blessing – so many are the evils accompanying them!

Our Chukchi passenger does not appear to entertain a very good opinion of the St. Lawrence natives. He advised the Captain to keep a close watch of those he allowed to come aboard. We asked him today the Chukchi name of ice, which he gave as "eigleegle." When we said that another of his people called it "tingting," he replied that that was the way poor common people spoke the word, but that rich people, the upper aristocratic class to which he belonged, called it "eigleegle." His father, being a rich man, had three wives; most of his tribe, he said, have only one.

At nine o'clock in the evening we were still more than an hour's run from St. Lawrence Island, though according to reckoning we should have reached the northeast end of the island at eight o'clock. We had been carried north about sixteen miles, since leaving St. Lawrence Bay, by the current setting through the Strait. The water, having been driven south by the north gale, was pouring north with greater velocity than ordinary. The sky was a mass of dark, grainless cloud, banded slightly near the northwest horizon; one band, a degree in breadth above the sun, was deep indigo, with a few short streaks of orange and red. We have not seen a star since leaving San Francisco, and have seen the sun perfectly cloudless only once! We came to anchor near the northwest end of the island about midnight.

The next day, the eighth of June, was calm and mild. A canoe with ten men and women came alongside this morning, just arrived from Plover Bay, on their way home. They made signs of weariness, having pulled hard against this heavy current. The distance is fifty miles. It is not easy to understand how they manage to find their way in thick weather, when it is difficult enough for seamen with charts and compass.

In trying to account for the observed similarity between the peoples of the opposite shores of Asia and America, and the faunas and floras, scientists have long been combating a difficulty that does not exist save in their own minds. They have suggested that canoes and ships from both shores either were wrecked and drifted from one to the other, or that natives crossed on the ice which every year fills Bering Strait. As today, so from time immemorial canoes have crossed for trade or mere pleasure, steering by the swell of the sea when out of sight of land. As to crossing on the ice, the natives tell me that they frequently go with their dog-sleds from the Siberian side to the Diomedes, those halfway houses along the route, but seldom or never from the Diomedes to the American side, on account of the movements of the ice. But, though both means of communication, assumed to account for distribution as it is found to exist today, were left out, land communication in any case undoubtedly existed, just previous to the glacial period, as far south as the Aleutian Islands, and northward beyond the mouth of the Strait.

While groping in the dense fogs that hang over this region, sailors find their way at times by the flight of the innumerable sea birds that come and go from the sea to the shore. The direction, at least, of the land is indicated, which is very important in the case of small islands. How the birds find their way is a mystery.

This canoe alongside was "two sleeps" in making the passage. Time, I suppose, is reckoned by sleeps during summer, as there is no night and only one day. They at once began to trade eagerly, seeming to fear that they would be left unvisited, now that the whalers have all gone to the Arctic. In the forenoon, after the natives had left, we took advantage of the calm weather to go in search of the wrecked Lolita, which went ashore last fall a few miles to the north of here. On the way we passed through a good deal of ice in flat cakes that had been formed in a deep still bay, sheltered from floating ice which jams and packs it. This ice did not seem to be more than two or three feet thick, possibly the depth to which it froze last winter less the amount melted and evaporated since spring commenced.

Walruses, in groups numbering from two to fifty, were lying on cakes of ice. They were too shy, however, to be approached within shooting range, though many attempts were made. Some of the animals were as bulky, apparently, as oxen. They would awaken at the sound of the vessel crunching through the loose ice, lift their heads and rear as high as possible, then drop or plunge into the water. The ponderous fellows took headers in large groups; twenty pairs of flippers sometimes were in the air at once. They can stay under water five or six minutes, then come up to blow. If they are near the ship they dive again instantly, going down like porpoises, always exposing a large curving mass of their body while dropping their heads, and, lastly, their flippers are stretched aloft for an instant. Sometimes they show fight, make combined attacks on boats, and defend one another bravely. The cakes on which they congregate are of course very dirty, and show to a great distance. Since they soon sink when killed in the water, they are hunted mostly on the ice, and, when it is rough and hummocky are easily approached.

We were not successful in finding the Lolita, so we steamed back to our anchorage in the lee of a high bluff near the Eskimo village. Soon three or four canoes came alongside, loaded with furs, ivory, and whalebone. Molasses, which they carry away in bladders and seal skins, is with them a favourite article of trade. Mixed with flour and blocks of "black skin," it is esteemed, by Eskimo palates, a dish fit for the gods. A group of listeners laughed heartily when I described a mixture that I thought would be to their taste. They smacked their lips, and shouted "yes! yes!" One brought as a present to our Chukchi, the reindeer man's son, a chunk of "black skin" that, in colour and odour, seemed to be more than a year old. He no doubt judged that our Chukchi, if not starving was at least faring poorly on civilized trash.

A study of the different Eskimo faces, while important trades were pending, was very interesting. They are better behaved than white men, not half so greedy, shameless, or dishonest. I made a few sketches of marked faces.

One, who received a fathom of calico more than was agreed upon, seemed extravagantly delighted and grateful. He was lost in admiration of the Captain, whose hand he shook heartily.

We continued at anchor here the following day, June 9th. It was snowing and the decks were sloppy. Several canoe loads of Eskimos came aboard, and there was a brisk trade in furs, mostly reindeer hides and parkas for winter use; also fox [skins] and some whale bone and walrus ivory. Flour and molasses were the articles most in demand. Some of the women, heedless of the weather, brought their boys, girls, and babies. One little thing, that the proud mother held up for our admiration, smiled delightfully, exposing her two precious new teeth. No happier baby could be found in warm parlours, where loving attendants anticipate every want and the looms of the world afford their best in the way of soft fabrics. She looked gaily out at the strange colours about her from her bit of a fur bag, and when she fell asleep, her mother laid her upon three oars that were set side by side across the canoe. The snowflakes fell on her face, yet she slept soundly for hours while I watched her, and she never cried. All the youngsters had to be furnished with a little bread which both fathers and mothers begged for them, saying, "He little fellow, little fellow."

Four walrus heads were brought aboard and the ivory sold, while the natives, men and women, sat down to dine on them with butcher-knives. They cut off the flesh and ate it raw, apparently with good relish. As usual, each mouthful was cut off while held between the teeth. To our surprise they never cut themselves. They seemed to enjoy selecting tidbits from different parts of the head, turning it over frequently and examining pieces here and there, like a family leisurely finishing the wrecked hull of a last day's dinner turkey.

These people interest me greatly, and it is worth coming far to know them, however slightly. The smile, or, rather, broad grin of that Eskimo baby went directly to my heart, and I shall remember it as long as I live. When its features had subsided into perfect repose, the laugh gone from its dark eyes, and the lips closed over its two teeth, I could make its sweet smile bloom out again as often as I nodded and chirruped to it. Heaven bless it! Some of the boys, too, lads from eight to twelve years of age, were well-behaved, bashful, and usually laughed and turned away their faces when looked at. But there was a response in their eyes which made you feel that they are your very brothers.

CHAPTER SEVEN

At Plover Bay and St. Michael

STEAMER CORWIN, PLOVER BAY, June 15th, 1881. A little before four o'clock the next morning, June 10th, I was awakened by the officer of the deck coming into the cabin and reporting that the weather was densely foggy, and that ice in large masses was crowding down upon us, which meant "The Philistines be upon thee, Samson!" Shortly afterward, the first mass struck the ship and made her tremble in every joint; then another and another, in quick succession, while the anchor was being hurriedly raised. The situation in which we suddenly found ourselves was quite serious. The ice, had it been like that about the ship of the Ancient Mariner, "here and there and all around," would have raised but little apprehension. But it was only on one side of us, while a rocky beach was close by on the other, and against this beach in our disabled condition the ice was steadily driving us. Whether backing or going ahead in so crowded a bit of water, the result for some time was only so many shoves toward shore.

At length a block of small size, twenty or thirty feet in diameter, drifted in between the Corwin and the shore, and by steaming against it and striking it on the land ward bow she glinted around, head to the pack, and an opening allowed her to enter a little distance. This was gradually increased by stopping and starting until we were safe in the middle of it. Watching the compass and constantly taking soundings, we traced the edge of the pack, and in an hour or two made our escape into open water.

After the fog lifted we went again in search of the Lolita, and discovered her five or six miles below the Eskimo village. Dropping anchor at the edge of a sheet of firm shore-ice, we went across it to the wreck to see whether we could not get some pintles from it for our rudder. We found her rudder had been carried away, but procured some useful iron, blocks, tackle, spars, etc.; also, two barrels of oil which the natives had not yet appropriated. The transportation of these stores to the ship over ice, covered with sludge and full of dangerous holes, made a busy day for the sailors.

Back a hundred yards from the beach I found a few hints of the coming spring, though most of the ground is still covered with snow. The dwarf willow is beginning to put out its catkins, and a few buds of saxifrages, erigerons, and heathworts are beginning to swell. The bulk of the vegetation is composed of mosses and lichens. Half a mile from the wreck there is a deserted Eskimo village. All its inhabitants are said to have died of famine two winters ago. The traces of both local and general glaciation are particularly clear and telling on this island.

In the afternoon, the weather being calm and mild, we succeeded in mending and shipping the rudder, and the next morning we set out yet again for Plover Bay, where we now are, having arrived about midnight on the eleventh. The men have been busy sawing and blasting a sort of slip in the ice for the ship that she may be secure from drift ice and well situated for loading the coal that is piled on the shore opposite here. The coal belongs to the Russians. In loading, the coal was first stowed well forward in order to lift the stern high enough out of water to enable us to make the additional repairs required on the rudder, since we cannot find access to a beach smooth enough to lay her on.

The Indians here are very poor. They have offered nothing to trade. With a group of men and women that came to the ship a few mornings ago there was a half-breed girl about two years old. She had light-brown hair, regular European features, and was very fair and handsome. Her mother, a Chukchi, died in childbirth, and the natives killed her father. She is plump, red-cheeked, and in every way a picture of health. That in a Chukchi hut, nursed by a Chukchi mother-in-law, and on Chukchi food, a half-European girl can be so beautiful, well-behaved, happy, and healthy is very notable.

On the twelfth of June we had snow, rain, and sleet nearly all day. The view up the inlet was very striking – lofty mountains on both sides rising from the level of the water, and proclaiming in telling characters the story of the inlet's creation by glaciers that have but lately vanished. Most of the slopes and precipices seemed particularly dreary, not only on account of the absence of trees but of vegetation of any kind in any appreciable amount. No bits of shelf gardens were to be seen, though not wholly wanting when we came to climb, for I discovered some lovely garden spots with a tellima and anemone in full bloom. [The vegetation was] very dwarfed, and sparse, and scattered. No green meadow-hollows. The rock was fast disintegrating, and all the mountains appeared in general views like piles of loose stones dumped from the clouds. Plover Bay* takes its name from HMS *Plover*, which passed the winter of 1848–49 here while on a cruise in search of Franklin. It is a glacial fiord, which in the height of its walls is more Yosemite like than any I have yet seen in Siberia.

In the afternoon Dr. Rosse and I set out across the ice to the cliffs. We found a great many seal holes and cracks of a dangerous kind, and a good deal of water on top of the ice that made the walking very sloppy. There were dog-sled tracks trending up and down the inlet. The ice is broken along the shore by the rise and fall of the tides, but we made out to cross on some large cakes wedged together. Just before we reached the edge of rocks, in scanning the ruinous, crumbling face of the cliffs that here are between two and three

* Also known as Providence Bay

thousand feet high, I noticed an outstanding buttress harder and more compact in cleavage than the rest, and very obviously grooved, polished, and scratched by the main vanished glacier that once filled all the fiord. Up to this point we climbed, and found several other spots of the old glacial surface not yet weathered off. This is the first I have seen of this kind of glacial traces.

On the thirteenth the whaler *Thomas Pope** arrived here and anchored to the ice near us. Getting everything in trim for the return voyage, having already taken all the oil she can carry. All the fleet are doing well this year, or, as the natives express it, they are getting a "big grease."

[According to brief entries in Muir's journal the fourteenth, fifteenth, and sixteenth of June were spent aboard the Corwin, writing personal letters and several communications to the *San Francisco Bulletin*. From Captain Hooper's report of the cruise of the Corwin, the following interesting record of events during the interval is extracted:

On the fourteenth we worked all day, drawing coal on the sleds, assisted by the natives and two sleds with three dogs each, but the rapidly melting ice made it very tedious. On the fifteenth we continued work, although the softness of the ice compelled us to reduce the loads to half their former size. About four in the afternoon a slight roll of the vessel was perceptible, indicating a swell coming in from the outside. At the same time a slight undulating motion of the ice was observed. This was followed by crack in the ice running in every direction, and we had barely time to take in our ice anchors, call our men on board, and take the Thomas Pope in tow before the ice was all broken and in motion and rapidly drifting toward the mouth of the bay. At first it looked as if we might have to go to sea to avoid it. The wind by this time was blowing fresh from the northeast with a thick snow-storm, and, judging from the roll coming into the bay, a heavy sea must be running. Added to this was the fact of the sea being filled with large fields of heavy drift ice, making the prospect anything but a pleasing one. After lying off outside the ice for an hour or two and just when it seemed as if our only hope was in putting to sea, Captain Millard reported from the masthead that the whole body of ice had started offshore, and that if we could get in through it we could find good anchorage in clear water. Although the ice was pitching and rolling badly, it was well broken up, and we determined to make the attempt, and succeeded better than I had anticipated, and about midnight we came out into clear water, and anchored near the shore in twelve fathoms, the Thomas Pope coming to just outside of us in twenty fathoms.

Muir's journal continues with the following record under date of June 17th:]

Half-clear in the morning, foggy in the afternoon. Left Plover Bay at six in the morning with Thomas Pope in tow. Left her at the mouth of the bay. It was barred with rather heavy ice, which was heaving in curious commotion

---

* Captain M.V.B. Millard

from a heavy swell. We gave and received three cheers in parting. Have had a very pleasant time with Captains Millard and Kelly. Very telling views of the sculpture of the mountains along the Bay, at its head, and at the mouth, where the land-ice flowed into the one grand glacier that filled Bering Strait and Sea. The fronting cliffs of the sea glacier seem to be hardly more weathered than those of Plover Bay and adjacent fiords.

ST. MICHAEL, ALASKA, June 20th, 1881.   Sunshine now in the Far North, sunshine all the long nightless days! ripe and mellow and hazy, like that which feeds the fruits and vines! We came into it two days ago when we were approaching this old-fashioned Russian trading post near the mouth of the Yukon River. How sweet and kindly and reviving it is after so long a burial beneath dark sleety storm clouds! For a whole month before the beginning of this bright time, it snowed every day more or less, perhaps only for an hour or two, or all the twenty-four hours; not one day on which snow did not fall either in wet, sleety blasts, making sludge on the deck and rigging and afterward freezing fast, or in dry crystals, blowing away as fast as it fell. I have never before seen so cloudy a month, weather so strangely bewildering and depressing. It was all one stormy day, broken here and there by dim gleams of sunlight, but never so dark at midnight that we could not read ordinary print.

The general effect of this confusing interblending of the hours of day and night, of the quick succession of howling gales that we encountered, and of dull black clouds dragging their ragged, drooping edges over the waves, was very depressing, and when, at length, we found ourselves free beneath a broad, high sky full of exhilarating light, we seemed to have emerged from some gloomy, icy cave. How garish and blinding the light seemed to us then, and how bright the lily-spangles that flashed on the glassy water! With what rapture we gazed into the crimson and gold of the midnight sunsets!

While we were yet fifty miles from land a small grey finch came aboard and flew about the rigging while we watched its movements and listened to its suggestive notes as if we had never seen a finch since the days of our merry truant rambles along the hedgerows. A few hours later a burly, dozing bumblebee came droning around the pilot-house, seeming to bring with him all the warm, summery gardens we had ever seen.

The fourth of June was the most beautiful of the days we spent in the Arctic Ocean. The water was smooth, reflecting a tranquil, pearl-grey sky with spots of pure azure near the zenith and a belt of white around the horizon that shone with a bright, satiny lustre, trying to the eyes like clear sunshine. Some seven whale-ships were in sight, becalmed with their canvas spread. Chukchi hunters in pursuit of seals were gliding about in light skin-covered canoes, and gulls, auks, eider ducks, and other water birds in

*   The *San Francisco Bulletin*, in its issue of July 13th, 1881, noted the arrival in port of the whale bark *Thomas Pope* with a series of letters from John Muir.

countless multitudes skimmed the glassy level, while in the background of this Arctic picture the Siberian coast, white as snow could make it, was seen sweeping back in fine, fluent, undulating lines to a chain of mountains, the tops of which were veiled in the shining sky. A few snow crystals were shaken down from a black cloud towards midnight, but most of the day was one of deep peace, in which God's love was manifest as in a countenance.

The average temperature for most of the month commencing May twentieth has been but little above the freezing point, the maximum about 45° F. Today the temperature in the shade at noon is 65°, the highest since leaving San Francisco. The temperature of the water in Bering Sea and Strait, and as far as we have gone in the Arctic, has been about from 29° to 35°. But as soon as we approached within fifty miles of the mouths of the Yukon, the temperature changed suddenly to 42°.

The mirage effects we have witnessed on the cruise thus far are as striking as any I ever saw on the hot American desert. Islands and headlands seemed to float in the air, distorted into the most unreal, fantastic forms imaginable, while the individual mountains of a chain along the coast appeared to dance at times up and down with a rhythmic motion, in the tremulous refracting atmosphere. On the northeast side of Norton Sound I saw two peaks, each with a flat, black table on top, looming suddenly up and sinking again alternately, like boys playing see-saw on a plank.

The trading post of St. Michael was established by the Russians in 1833. It is built of drift timber derived from the Yukon, and situated on a low bluff of lava on the island of St. Michael, about sixty-five miles northeast of the northmost of the Yukon mouths. The fort is composed of a square of log buildings and palisades, with outlying bastions pierced for small cannon and musketry, while outside the fort there are a few small buildings and a Greek church, reinforced during the early part of the summer with groups of tents belonging to the Indians and the traders. The fort is now occupied by the employees of the Alaska Commercial Company. This is the headquarters of the fur traders of northern and central Alaska.

The Western Fur and Trading Company has a main station on the side of the bay about three miles from here, and the two companies, being in close competition, have brought on a condition of the fur business that is bitterly bewailed by the sub traders located along the Yukon and its numerous tributaries. Not only have the splendid profits of the good old times diminished nearly to zero, say they, but the big prices paid for skins have spoiled the Indians, making them insolent, lazy, and dangerous, without conferring any substantial benefit upon them. Since they can now procure all the traders' supplies they need for fewer skins than formerly, they hunt less, and spend their idle hours in gambling and quarreling.

The furs and skins of every kind derived annually from the Yukon and Kuskoquim regions, and shipped from here, are said to be worth from eighty thousand to one hundred thousand dollars. The trade goods are brought to this point from San Francisco by the rival companies in June, and delivered to their agents, by whom they are distributed to their traders and taken up the rivers to the different stations in the interior in boats towed most of the way by small stern-wheel steamers. Then, during the winter, the furs are collected and brought to this point and carried to San Francisco by the vessels that bring the goods for the next season's trade.

On the nineteenth instant the steamer belonging to the Western Fur and Trading Company arrived from a station fifteen hundred miles up the river, towing three large boats laden with Indians and traders, together with the last year's collection of furs. After they had begun to set up their tents and unload the furs, we went over to the storerooms of the Company to look at the busy throng. They formed a strange, wild picture on the rocky beach; the squaws pitching the tents and cutting armfuls of dry grass to lay on the ground as a lining for fur carpets; the children with wild, staring eyes gazing at us, or, heedless of all the stir, playing with the dogs; groups of dandy warriors, arrayed in all the colours of the rainbow, grim, and cruel, and coldly dignified; and a busy train coming and going between the warehouse and the boats, storing the big bundles of shaggy bearskins, black and brown, marten, mink, fox, beaver, otter, lynx, moose, wolf, and wolverine, many of them with claws spread and hair on end, as if still fighting for life. They were vividly suggestive of the far wilderness whence they came – its mountains and valleys, its broad grassy plains and far-reaching rivers, its forests and its bogs.

The Indians seemed to me the wildest animals of all. The traders were not at all wild, save in dress, but rather gentle and subdued in manners and aspect, like half-paid village ministers. They held us in a long interesting conversation, and gave us many valuable facts concerning the heart of the Yukon country. Some Indians on the beach were basking in the yellow, mellow sun. Herring and salmon were hanging upon frames or lying on the rocks – a lazy abundance of food that discouraged thought of the future.

The shores here are crowded with immense shoals of herring, and the Indians are lazily catching just enough to eat. Those we had for dinner are not nearly so good as those I ate last year at Cross Sound. The Yukon salmon, however, are now in excellent condition, and are the largest by far that I have seen. Yet the Yukon Indians suffer severely at times from famine, though they might dry enough in less than a week to last a year.

We are making a short stay here to take on provisions, and intend to go northward again tomorrow to meet the search party that we landed near Koliuchin Island. Another delightful Sunday – nearly cloudless and with lily-spangles on the bay. The temperature was 65° F. in the shade at noon. The birds are nesting and the plants are rapidly coming into bloom .

CHAPTER EIGHT

Return of the Search Party

STEAMER CORWIN, NEAR THE MOUTH OF METCHIGME BAY, ON THE WEST SIDE OF BERING STRAIT, June 27th, 1881. After leaving St. Michael, on the evening of the twenty-first, we crossed Bering Sea to Plover Bay to fill our coal-bunkers from a pile belonging to His Majesty, the Czar of Russia.

On the twenty-third we were sailing along the north side of St. Lawrence Island against a heavy wind. There was a rough sea and a clear sky, save on the island. I had a tolerably clear view of the most prominent portion of the island near the middle. It is here composed of lava, reddish in colour and dotted with craters and cones, most of which seem recent, though a slight amount of glaciation of a local kind is visible. About three in the afternoon we came to anchor off the northwest end of the island opposite the village. A few natives came aboard at eight o'clock.

The next day we got under way at four in the morning, going east along the south side of St. Lawrence Island. The norther again was blowing as hard as ever. We discovered an Eskimo village, but the natives were mostly dead. Coming to anchor there at six in the evening, we went ashore and met a few Eskimos who, though less demonstrative, seemed quite as glad to see us as those on the northwest end of the island. The village, as we examined it through our glasses, seemed so still and desolate, we began to fear that, like some of the villages on the north side of the island, not a soul was left alive in it, until here and there a native was discovered on the brow of the hill where the summer houses are.

After we had landed from the life-boat, two men and a boy came running down to meet us and took us up to the two inhabited houses. They all gathered about us from scattered points of observation, and when we asked where all the people were to whom the other houses belonged, they smiled and said, "All mucky." "All gone." "Dead?" "Yes, dead!" We then inquired where the dead people were. They pointed back of the houses and led us to eight corpses lying on the rocky ground. They smiled at the ghastly spectacle of the grinning skulls and bleached bones appearing through the brown, shrunken skin.

Being detained on the twenty-fifth by the norther which was still blowing, we went ashore after breakfast, and had a long walk through graves, back to noble views of the island, telling the grandeur of its glaciation by the northern ice-sheets. Weighed anchor and steered for Plover Bay shortly after nine in the evening, and arrived there early on the morning of the twenty-sixth. While the ship was being coaled, I climbed the east wall of the fiord three or four miles above the mouth, where it is about twenty-two hundred feet above the level of the sea, and, as the day was clear, I obtained capital views of the mountains on both sides and around the head of the fiord among the numerous ice-fountains which, during the glacial winter, poured their tribute through this magnificent channel into Bering Sea.

When the glacier that formed what is now called Plover Bay was in its prime, it was about thirty miles long and from five to six miles in width at the widest portion of the trunk, and about two thousand feet deep. It then had at least five main tributaries which, as the trunk melted towards the close of the ice period, became independent glaciers, and these again were melted into perhaps seventy-five or more small residual glaciers from less than a mile to several miles in length, all of which, as far as I could see, have at length vanished, though some wasting remnants may still linger in 'the highest and best-protected fountains above the head of the fiord. I had a fine glissade down the valley of a tributary glacier whose terminal moraines show the same gradual death as those of the Sierra. The mountains hereabouts, in the forms of the peaks, ridges, lake-basins, bits of meadow, and in sculpture and aspects in general, are like those of the High Sierra of California where the rock is least resisting.

Snow still lingers in drift patches and streaks and avalanche heaps down to the sea-level, while there is but little depth of solid snow on the highest peaks and ridges, so that, there being no warm, sunny base of gentle slopes and foothills, no varying belts of climate, this region as a whole seems to consist of only the storm beaten tops of mountains shorn off from their warm, well-planted bases. Still there are spots here and there, where the snow is melted that are already cheered with about ten species of plants in full bloom: anemones, buttercups, primulas, several species of draba, purple heathworts, phlox, and potentilla, making charming alpine gardens, but too small and thinly planted to show at a distance of more than a few yards, while trees are wholly wanting.

On our way north today we stopped a few minutes opposite a small native settlement, six or eight miles to the northeast of the mouth of Metchigme Bay, in search of Omniscot, the rich reindeer owner, whom we had met further up the coast two weeks ago, and who had then promised to have a lot of deerskins ready for us if we would call at his village.

Some of the natives, coming off to the steamer to trade, informed us that Omniscot lived some distance up the bay that we had just passed, and one of them, who speaks a little English, inquired why we had not brought back Omniscot's son. He told us that he was his cousin and that his mother was crying about him last night, fearing that he would never come back.

We informed him that his cousin was crazy and had tried to kill himself, but that he was now at Plover Bay with one of his friends and would probably be home soon. This young Omniscot, whom we had taken aboard at St. Lawrence Bay, thinking that he might be useful as an interpreter, is a son of the reindeer man and belongs to the Chukchi tribe. We soon came to see that we had a troublesome passenger, for the expression of his eyes, and the nervous dread he manifested of all the natives wherever we chanced to stop, indicated some form of insanity. He would come to the door of the cabin to warn the Captain against the people of every village that we were approaching as likely to kill us, and then he would hide himself below deck or climb for greater safety into the rigging.

On the twenty-fifth, when we were lying at anchor off St Lawrence Island, he offered his rifle, which he greatly prized, to one of the officers, saying that inasmuch as he would soon die he would not need it. He also sent word to the Captain that he would soon be "mucky," but came to the cabin door shortly afterward, with nothing unusual apparent in his face or behaviour, and began a discussion concerning the region back of St. Michael as a location for a flock of reindeer. He thought they would do well there, he' said, and that his father would give him some young ones to make a beginning, which he could take over in some schooner, and that they would get plenty of good moss to eat on the tundra, and multiply fast until they become a big herd like his father's, so big that nobody could count them.

In three or four hours after this he threw himself overboard, but was picked up and brought on deck. Some of the sailors stripped off his wet furs, and then the discovery was made that before throwing himself into the sea the poor fellow had stabbed himself in the left lung. The surgeon dressed his wound and gave as his opinion that it would prove fatal. He was doing well, however, when we left him, and is likely to recover. The Plover Bay natives, in commenting on the affair, remarked that the St. Lawrence people were a bad, quarrelsome set, and always kept themselves in some sort of trouble.

Having procured a guide from among the natives that came aboard here, we attempted to reach Omniscot's village, but found the bay full of ice, and were compelled to go on without our winter supply of deerskins, hoping, however, to be able to get them on the east coast.

There is quite a large Chukchi settlement near the mouth of the bay, on the north side. Seven large canoe-loads of the population came aboard, making quite a stir on our little ship. They are the worst-looking lot of Siberian natives that I have yet seen, though there are some fine, tall, manly fellows amongst them. Mr Nelson, a naturalist, and zealous collector for the Smithsonian Institution, who joined us at St. Michael, photographed a group of the most villainous of the men, and two of the women whose arms were elaborately tattooed up to their shoulders. Their faces were a curious study while they were trying to keep still under circumstances so extraordinary.

The glaciation of the coast here is recorded in very telling characters, the movement of the ice having been in a nearly south southwest direction.

There is also a considerable deposit of irregularly stratified sand and gravel along this part of the coast. For fifteen or twenty miles it rises in crumbling bluffs fifty feet high, and makes a flat, gently sloping margin, from one hundred yards to several miles in width, in front of the mountains. The bay, moreover, is nearly closed by a bar, probably of the same material. The weather is delightful, clear sunshine, only a few fleecy wisps of cloud in the west, and the water still as a mill-pond.

STEAMER CORWIN, June 28th. Anchored an hour or two this forenoon at the west Diomede, and landed a party to make observations on the currents and temperature of the water that sets through Bering Strait. Then proceeded on our way direct to Tapkan to seek our search party. The fine weather that we have enjoyed since the day before our arrival at St. Michael ended in the old, dark, gloomy clouds and drizzling fog on reaching the Diomedes, though the coast above East Cape has until now been in sight most of the time up to a height of about a thousand feet.

The glaciation, after the melting of the ice-sheet, has been light, sculpturing the mountains into shallow, short valleys and round ridges, mostly broad-backed. The valleys, for the most part, are not cut down to the sea. The shore seems to have been cut off by the glacier sheet that occupied the sea, after it was too shallow to flow over the angle of land formed by East Cape. This overflow is well marked, fifteen to twenty-five miles northwest of the Cape, in the trends of the ridges and valleys as far back as I could see, that is, about twenty-five miles from the shore. The north wind is, and has been, blowing for twenty-four hours, and we fear that we will soon meet with the drifting ice from the main polar pack.

STEAMER CORWIN, OFF THE CHUKCHI VILLAGE OF TAPKAN, NEAR CAPE SERDZEKAMEN, SIBERIA, June 29th, 1881. We arrived here about eight this morning to meet the search party that we landed about a month ago, near Koliuchin Island. They had been waiting for us nearly two weeks. We were unable to land on account of the stormy weather, but after waiting about two hours we saw them making their way out to the edge of the drift ice, which extended about three miles from shore, and after a good deal of difficulty they reached the steamer in safety. The air was grey with falling snow, and the north wind was blowing hard, dashing heavy swells, with wild, tumultuous uproar, against jagged, tumbling ice blocks that formed the edge of the pack. The life-boat was lowered and pulled to the edge of the pack and a line was thrown from it to the most advanced of the party, who was balancing himself among the heaving bergs. This line was made fast to a light skin boat that the party had pushed out over the ice from the shore, and, getting into it, they soon managed to get themselves fairly launched and free from the tossing, wave-dashed ice which momentarily threatened to engulf them.

Mr. Herring, the officer in charge, reported that they had proceeded along the coast as far as Cape Wankarem and had been so fortunate as to accomplish the main objects of their mission, namely, to determine the value of the stories prevalent among the natives to the southward of here concerning the lost whalers Vigilant and Mount Wollaston; to ascertain whether any of the crews of the missing vessels had landed on the Siberian coast to the south eastward of Cape Yakan; and in case any party should land there in the future, to bespeak in their behalf the aid and goodwill of the natives.

At the Chukchi village at Cape Onman they were told that at the village of Oncarima, near Cape Wankarem, they would find three men who could tell them all about the broken ship, for they had seen the wreck and been aboard of her, and had brought off many things that they had found on the deck and in the cabin. This news caused them to hurry on, and when they arrived at the village, and had bestowed the customary presents of tobacco and coffee, Mr. Herring stated the object of his visit.

Three natives then came forward and stated through the interpreter that last year, when they were out hunting seals on the ice, about five miles from the land, near the little island which they call Konkarpo, at the time of year when the new ice begins to grow in the sea, and when the sun does not rise, they saw a big ship without masts in the ice-pack, which they reached without difficulty and climbed on deck. The masts, they said, had been chopped down, and there was a pair of horns on the end of the jib-boom, indicating the position of them on a sketch of a ship. The hold, they said, was full of water so that they could not go down into it to see anything, but they broke a way into the cabin and found four dead men, who had been dead a long time. Three of them were lying in bunks, and one on the floor. They also got into the galley and found a number of articles which they brought away; also, some from the cabin and other parts of the ship.

While they were busy looking for things which they fancied, and considered worth carrying away, one of the three called out to his companions that the wind was blowing offshore, and that they must make haste for the land as the ice was beginning to move, which caused them to hurry from the wreck with what articles they could conveniently carry without being delayed. Next day they went as far out towards the spot where they had left the vessel as the state of the ice would allow, hoping to procure something else. But they found that she had drifted out of sight, and as the wind had been blowing from the southwest, they supposed that she had drifted in a northeasterly direction. They had looked for this ship many times after her first disappearance, but never saw her again.

After they had finished their story, Mr. Herring requested them to show him all the things that they had brought from the wreck, telling them that he would give them tobacco for some of them that he might want to show to his friends. Thereupon they brought forward the following articles, which were carefully examined by our party in hopes of being able to identify the vessel:

A pair of marine glasses
A pair of silver-mounted spectacles in a tin case (the lenses
    showing that they had belonged to an aged person)
A jack-knife
A carving-knife
A butcher's chopping-knife
Two table-knives, the handle of one of them marked V
A meat saw
A soup ladle
A stew pan
A tin colander
A hand lamp
A square tin lantern painted green
A draw-knife
An adze
Two carpenter's saws
A chisel
A file
A brace and bit
A tack hammer
A pump-handle
A shovel
A bullet-mould
A truss
A bottle of some sort of medicine
A sailor's ditty bag, with thread
A razor
A linen jumper
Two small coins
Two coils of Manila rope
Three whale spades
One harpoon

The harpoon and whale spades are marked "B.K.," and will no doubt serve to identify the owners. Not a single private name was found on any of the articles; nor did the natives produce any books or papers of any sort, though they said that they saw books in the cabin. A number of the articles enumerated above were purchased by Mr. Herring and are now on board the Corwin, namely, the marine glasses, spectacles, harpoon, and table-knives.

The fate, then, of one of the two missing ships is discovered beyond a doubt, though a portion of the crew may possibly be alive. If the statement as to the deer horns on the jib-boom is to be relied on, it is the Vigilant, as she is said to be the only vessel in the fleet that had deer horns on her jib-boom.

A party of Chukchi traders, also, were met here, being on their way to East Cape with reindeer skins. They stated that no vessel had been seen anywhere along the coast to the northwest of Wanhrem as far as Cape Yakan except one, a three-masted steamer, the Vega, two years ago; that if any ships had been seen they certainly should have heard about it. The place where the Vega wintered,[1] fifteen or twenty miles to the northwest of Cape Serdzekamen, is well known to nearly all the natives living within a hundred miles of it.

The Jeannette was last seen by the natives off Cape Serdzekamen two years ago, probably just before she went north into the ice. A party of walrus hunters went aboard of her. They described her as a three-masted steamer, with plenty of coal and dogs on deck. When Wrangell Land was pointed out on a chart to the natives at Camp Wankarem, they shook their heads and said that they knew nothing of land in that direction. But one old man told them that long ago he had heard something about a party of men who had come from some far unknown land to the north, over the ice.

According to Lieutenant Reynolds, nine Chukchi settlements were passed on the coast between Tapkan and Oncarima, namely, Naskan, Undrillan, Illwinoop, Youngilla,[2] Illoiuk, Koliuchin, Unatapkan, Onman, and Enelpan. The largest of these is Koliuchin, with twenty-seven houses and about three hundred people.

The natives, everywhere along the route travelled, treated the party with great kindness, giving them food for their dog-teams and answering the questions put to them with good-natured patience. At Koliuchin one of the chief men of the village invited them to dinner and greatly surprised them by giving them good tea served in handsome China cups, which he said he had bought from the Russians.

[1] Pittle Keg   [2] Iintlin

CHAPTER NINE

Villages of the Dead

STEAMER CORWIN, EAST CAPE, SIBERIA, July 1st, 1881. After getting our search party on board at Tapkan, we found it impossible, under the conditions of ice and water that prevailed, to land our Chukchi dog-driver, who lives there, and who had come off with the party to get his pay. He was in excellent spirits, however, and told the Captain that since he had received a gun and a liberal supply of ammunition he did not care where he was put ashore – Cape Serdzekamen, East Cape, or any point along the shore or edge of the ice-pack would answer, as he could kill plenty of birds and seals, and get home any time. The dogs and sledges were left in his care at Tapkan, to be in readiness in case they should be required next winter.

Speeding southward under steam and sail we reached East Cape yesterday at seven in the morning. By this time the wind was blowing what seamen call a "living gale," whitening the sea, and filling up the air with blinding scud. We found good anchorage, however, back of the high portion of the Cape, opposite a large settlement of Chukchis. East Cape is a very bold bluff of granite about two thousand feet high, which evidently has been over swept from the northwest. I eagerly waited to get off and to climb high enough to make sure of the trends of the ridges and grooves, and to seek scratches, bossed surfaces, etc. But the howling, shrieking norther blew all day, and had not abated at eleven o'clock last night.

This morning Mr. Nelson and I went ashore to see what we could learn. The village here, through which we passed on our way up the mountain-side, consists of about fifty huts, built on a small, rocky, terminal moraine, and so deeply sunk in the face of the hill that the entire village makes scarcely more show at a distance of a few hundred yards than a group of marmot burrows. The lower portion of the walls is built of moraine boulders, the upper portion and the curving beehive roof of driftwood and the ribs of whales, framed together and covered with walrus hide or dirt.

During the winter the huts are entered by a low tunnel, so as to exclude the cold air as much as possible. The floor is simply the natural dirt mixed into a dark hairy paste, with much that is not at all natural. Fires are made occasionally in the middle of the floor to cook the small portion of their food that is not eaten raw. Ivory-headed spears, arrows, seal nets, bags of oil, rags of seal or walrus meat, and strips of whale blubber and skin, lie on shelves or hang confusedly from the roof, while puppies and nursing mother-dogs and children may be seen scattered here and there, or curled snugly in the pots and eating-troughs, after they have licked them clean, making a kind of squalor that is picturesque and daring beyond conception.

In all of the huts, however, there are from one to three or four luxurious bedrooms. The walls, ceiling, and floor are of soft reindeer skins, and [each polog has] a trough filled with oil for heat and light. After hunting all day on the ice, making long, rough, stormy journeys, the Chukchi hunter, muffled and hungry, comes into his burrow, eats his fill of oil and seal or walrus meat, then strips himself naked and lies down in his closed fur nest, his polog, in glorious ease, to smoke and sleep.

I was anxious to reach the top of the cape peninsula to learn surely whether it had been over-swept by an ice-sheet, and if so from what direction, and to study its glacial conditions in general and the character of the rocks. I therefore hastened to make the most of my opportunity, and pushed on through the village towards the lowest part of the divide between the north and south sides followed by a crowd of curious boys, who good-naturedly assisted me whenever I stopped to gather the flowers that I found in bloom. The banks of a stream coming from a high basin filled with snow was quite richly flowered with anemones, buttercups, potentillas. drabas, primulas, and many species of dwarf willows, up to a height of about a thousand feet above the level of the sea; beyond this, spring had hardly made any impression, while nearly a thousand feet of the highest summits were still covered with deep snow.

Mr. Nelson soon left me in pursuit of a bird, and in crossing a rocky ridge to come up with me again, he came upon a lot of other game, which seemed to interest him still more, namely, dead natives scattered about on the rough stones at one of the cemeteries belonging to the village. The bodies of the dead, together with whatever articles belonged to them, are simply laid on the surface of the ground, so that a cemetery is a good field for collectors. A lot of ivory spears, arrows, dishes of various kinds, and a stone hammer, formed the least ghastly of his spoils. Leaving Mr. Nelson alone in his glory, I pushed on to the top of the divide, then followed it westward to the highest summit on the peninsula, whence I obtained the views I was in search of.

The dividing ridge all along the high eastern portion of the peninsula is rounded from nearly north to south. The curves on the north begin almost at the waters' edge, while the south side is quite precipitous along the shore. There is also a telling series of parallel grooves and ridges trending north and south across the peninsula. The highest point is about twenty-five hundred feet above the sea, and the mountainous portion has been nearly eroded from the continent and made an island like the two Diomedes, the wide gap of low ground connecting it with the high mainland being only a few feet above tide-water. In this low portion there is here and there a rounded upswelling of more resisting rock, with trends, all telling the same story of a vast over sweeping ice flood from the north.

I also had a clear view of the coast mountains for a hundred miles or thereabouts, all of which are tellingly glaciated in harmony with the above generalisation. Most of the rock is granite with cleavage planes that cause it to weather rapidly into flat blocks. One conical black hill, fifteen hundred feet high, is volcanic rock, close-grained and dense like some kinds of iron ore. I saw an Arctic owl, a big snowy fellow, fitting his place; also, snow-buntings and linnets. When the natives saw Mr. Nelson returning without me they said that he had killed me, not being aware of the fact that he understood their language.

On my way down to the shore I crossed another of the village cemeteries on a very rough and steep slope of weathered granite, several hundred feet above the village and to the westward of it. Whole skeletons or single bones and skulls lay here and there, wedged into chance positions among the stones, weathering and falling to pieces like the ivory-pointed spears, arrows, etc., mixed with them. The mountain that they were lying on is crumbling also – dust to dust. Some of the corpses have had stones piled on them, and their goods on top of all; others were laid on the rough rocks with a row of big stones on the lower side to keep them from rolling down.

The damp, lower portion of the wild north wind, as it was deflected up and over the slopes and frosty summit of the peninsula, has given birth to a remarkably beautiful covering of white ice crystals on the windward sides of exposed boulders, and in some places on the snow. The crystals resemble white feathers in their aggregate forms, but are firm and icy in structure, and as evenly and gracefully imbricated on each other over the rough faces of the rock as are the feathers on the breast of a bird. The effect is marvellously beautiful and interesting as seen on those castellated rock piles, so frequently found on bleak summits. The points of the feathers grow to windward, and indicate by their curves all the varying directions pursued by the interrupted wind as it glints and reverberates about the innumerable angles of the rock fronts. Thus the rocks, where the exposure to storms is greatest, and where only ruin seems to be the object, are all the more lavishly clothed upon with beauty – beauty that grows with and depends upon the violence of the gale. In like manner do men find themselves enriched by storms that seem only big with ruin, both in the physical and the moral worlds.

We weighed anchor and got away at two o'clock in the afternoon and reached the West Diomede Island village at half-past four. Here we took aboard the boatswain and Mr. Nelson's man, whom we had left to make observations on the currents, tides, etc. He was to have been assisted by the natives, but the rough weather prevented work. About half-past five we left the Diomede for Marcus Bay in order to land Joe, the Chukchi. The sea is smooth now, at a quarter of an hour before midnight, and there is a lovely orange-and-gold sunset. The gulls are still on the wing.

STEAMER CORWIN, July 2nd. Clear, calm, sunful; the coast of Asia is seen to excellent advantage; crowds of glacial peaks, ice-fountains and fiords far in reaching. The snow on them is melting fast. About noon* twelve canoes from a large village twenty miles north of Marcus Bay came off to trade. The schooners that came to this region to trade were perhaps afraid to touch here. Consequently the Corwin was the first vessel with trade goods that they have seen this year, and the business in bone and ivory went on with hearty vigour. A hundred or more Chukchis were aboard at once, making a stir equal to that of a country fair. One of them spoke a little whaler English, three quarters of which was profanity and nearly one quarter slang. He asked the Captain why he did not like him; [and intimated that] if he should come ashore to his house he, the Indian, would show him by his treatment that he liked him very much.

We are now, at five in the afternoon, approaching Marcus Bay, where Joe lives, for the purpose of taking him home. For his month's work and his team of five dogs he has been paid a box of hard bread, ten sacks of flour, some calico, a rifle, and a considerable quantity of ammunition. Although this is doubtless five times more than he expected, he does not show any excitement or rise of spirits, but only a stoical composure, which seems so Arctic and immovable that I doubt whether he would move a muscle of his face if he were presented with the whole ship's cargo and the ship itself thrown in.

STEAMER CORWIN, ST. LAWRENCE ISLAND, ALASKA, July 3rd, 1881. St. Lawrence Island, the largest in Bering Sea, is situated at a distance of about one hundred and twenty miles off the mouths of the Yukon, and forty-five miles from the nearest point on the coast of Siberia. It is about a hundred miles in length from east to west and fifteen miles in average width; a dreary, cheerless-looking mass of black lava, dotted with volcanoes, covered with snow, without a single tree, and rigidly bound in ocean ice for more than half the year.

Inasmuch as it lies broadside wise to the way pursued by the great ice-sheet that once filled Bering Sea, it is traversed by numerous valleys and ridges and low gaps, some of which have been worn down nearly to the sea-level. Had the glaciation to which it has been subjected been carried on much longer, then, instead of this one large island, we should have had several smaller ones. Nearly all of the volcanic cones with which the central portion of the island is in great part covered are post-glacial in age and present well-formed craters but little weathered as yet.

All the surface of the low grounds, in the glacial gaps, as well as the flat table-lands is covered with wet, spongy tundra of mosses and lichens, with patches of blooming heathworts and dwarf willows, and grasses and sedges,

* Opposite Cape Chaplin.

diversified here and there by drier spots, planted with larkspurs, saxifrages, daisies, primulas, anemones, ferns, etc. These form gardens with a luxuriance and brightness of colour little to be hoped for in so cold and dreary-looking a region.

Three years ago there were about fifteen hundred inhabitants on the island, chiefly Eskimos, living in ten villages located around the shores, and subsisting on the seals, walruses, whales, and water birds that abound here. Now there are only about five hundred people, most of them in one village on the northwest end of the island, nearly two thirds of the population having died of starvation during the winter of 1878–79. In seven of the villages not a single soul was left alive. In the largest village at the northwest end of the island, which suffered least, two hundred out of six hundred died. In the one at the southwest end only fifteen out of about two hundred survived. There are a few survivors also at one of the villages on the east end of the island.

After landing our interpreter at Marcus Bay we steered for St. Michael, and in passing along the north side of this island we stopped an hour or so this morning at one of the smallest of the dead villages. Mr. Nelson went ashore and obtained a lot of skulls and specimens of one sort and another for the Smithsonian Institution. Twenty-five skeletons were seen.

A few miles farther on we anchored before a larger village, situated about halfway between the east and west ends of the island which I visited in company with Mr. Nelson, the Captain, and the Surgeon. We found twelve desolate huts close to the beach with about two hundred skeletons in them or strewn about on the rocks and rubbish heaps within a few yards of the doors. The scene was indescribably ghastly and desolate, though laid in a country purified by frost as by fire. Gulls, plovers, and ducks were swimming and flying about in happy life, the pure salt sea was dashing white against the shore, the blooming tundra swept back to the snow-clad volcanoes, and the wide azure sky bent kindly over all – nature intensely fresh and sweet, the village lying in the foulest and most glaring death. The shrunken bodies, with rotting furs on them, or white, bleaching skeletons, picked bare by the crows, were lying mixed with kitchen-midden rubbish where they had been cast out by surviving relatives while they yet had strength to carry them .

In the huts those who had been the last to perish were found in bed, lying evenly side by side, beneath their rotting deerskins. A grinning skull might be seen looking out here and there, and a pile of skeletons in a corner, laid there no doubt when no one was left strong enough to carry them through the narrow underground passage to the door. Thirty were found in one house, about half of them piled like fire-wood in a corner, the other half in bed, seeming as if they had met their fate with tranquil apathy. Evidently these people did not suffer from cold, however rigorous the winter may have been, as some of the huts had in them piles of deerskins that had not been in use. Nor, although their survivors and neighbours all say that hunger was the sole cause of their death, could they have battled with famine to the bitter end, because a considerable amount of walrus rawhide and skins of other animals was found in the huts. These would have sustained life at least a week or two longer.

The facts all tend to show that the winter of 1878–79 was, from whatever cause, one of great scarcity, and as these people never lay up any considerable supply of food from one season to another, they began to perish. The first to succumb were carried out of the huts to the ordinary ground for the dead, about half a mile from the village. Then, as the survivors became weaker, they carried the dead a shorter distance, and made no effort to mark their positions or to lay their effects beside them, as they customarily do. At length the bodies were only dragged to the doors of the huts, or laid in a corner, and the last survivors lay down in despair without making any struggle to prolong their wretched lives by eating the last scraps of skin.

Mr. Nelson went into this Golgotha with hearty enthusiasm, gathering the fine white harvest of skulls spread before him, and throwing them in heaps like a boy gathering pumpkins. He brought nearly a hundred on board, which will be shipped with specimens of bone armour, weapons, utensils, etc., on the Alaska Commercial Company's steamer St. Paul.

We also landed at the village on the southwest corner of the island and interviewed the fifteen survivors. When we inquired where the other people of the village were, one of the group, who speaks a few words of English, answered with a happy, heedless smile, "All mucky." "All gone!" "Dead?" "Yes, dead, all dead!" Then he led us a few yards back of his hut and pointed to twelve or fourteen skeletons lying on the brown grass, repeating in almost a merry tone of voice, "Dead, yes, all dead, all mucky, all gone!"

About two hundred perished here, and unless some aid be extended by our government which claims these people, in a few years at most every soul of them will have vanished from the face of the earth; for, even where alcohol is left out of the count, the few articles of food, clothing, guns, etc., furnished by the traders, exert a degrading influence, making them less self-reliant, and less skilful as hunters. They seem easily susceptible of civilization, and well deserve the attention of our government.

CHAPTER TEN

Glimpses of Alaskan Tundra

ST. MICHAEL, ALASKA, July 8th, 1881. The Corwin arrived here on the Fourth, and, in honour of the day; made some noise with her cannon in concert with those belonging to the fort, to the steamer St. Paul, and to the post of the Western Fur and Trading Company across the bay. We have taken on a supply of coal and provisions for nine months, in case we should by any accident be caught in the ice north of Bering Strait before calling here again in the fall.

We hope to get away from here this evening for the Arctic, intending to cruise along the Alaskan coast beyond Point Barrow spending some time about Kotzebue Sound in order to look after revenue interests, and to make, perhaps, some explorations on the lower courses of the Inland[1] and Buckland Rivers, and on the Colville,[2] of which nearly nothing is yet known to geographers. The coast will also be carefully searched for traces of the Jeannette and missing whalers in case any portion of their crews have come over the ice last winter. Perhaps a month will be spent thus, when an attempt will be made to reach Wrangell Land, where the Jeannette probably spent her first winter. And since the Corwin has already passed Cape Serdzekamen twice this season, we have sanguine hopes of success under so favourable a condition of the ice.

Arctic explorations are exciting much interest among the natives here. Last evening the shamans called up the spirits supposed to be familiar with polar matters. The latter informed them that not only was the Jeannette forever lost in the ice of the Far North with all her crew, but also that the Corwin would never more be seen after leaving St. Michael this time, information which caused our interpreter to leave us, nor have we as yet been able to procure another in his place. The Jeannette took two men from here.[3]

This is the busy time of the year at St. Michael, when the traders come with their furs from stations far up the Yukon and return with next year's supply of goods. Those of the Western Fur and Trading Company left for

[1] Now called Naotak River.

[2] The upper reaches of the Colville and Buckland Rivers, according to the Geographical Survey map of 1915, are still unexplored. The former empties into the Arctic Ocean, the latter into Eschscholtz Bay.

[3] These are two native Alaskan hunters Alexey and Aneguin. The former was among those who perished with De Long on the delta of the Lena River.

the upper Yukon yesterday, and those connected with the Alaska Commercial Company will follow as soon as the new steamboat, which they are putting together here can be got ready.

The party of prospectors which left San Francisco this spring in a schooner, to seek a mountain of solid silver, reported to have been seen some distance up a river that flows into Golofnin Bay on the north side of Norton Sound, about one hundred miles from here, has arrived, and is now up the river prospecting. From what I can learn, they will not find the mountain to be solid silver, but some far commoner mineral. Gold is said to have been discovered by Mr. Harker on the Tanana River – bar diggings that would pay about twelve dollars per day. There will probably be a rush to the new mines ere long, though news of this kind is kept back as long as possible by the fur companies.

The weather is delightful, temperature about 60° F in the shade, and the vegetation is growing with marvellous rapidity. The grass already is about two feet high about the shores of the bay, making a bright green surface, not at all broken as far as can be seen from the steamer. Almost any number of cattle would find excellent pasturage here for three or four months in the year.

During our last visit Dr. Rosse and I crossed the tundra to a prominent hill about seven miles to the southward from the redoubt. We found the hill to be a well-formed volcanic cone with a crater a hundred yards in diameter and about twenty feet deep, from the rim of which I counted upwards of forty others within a distance of thirty or forty miles. This old volcano is said by the medicine men to be the entrance to the spirit world for their tribe, and the rumbling sounds heard occasionally are supposed to be caused by the spirits when they are conducting in a dead Indian. The last eruption was of ashes and pumice cinders, which are strewn plentifully around the rim of the crater and down the sides of the cone.

Our walk was very fatiguing, as we sank deep in spongy moss at every step, and staggered awkwardly on the tops of tussocks of grass and sedge, which bent and let our feet down between them. It was very delightful, however, and crowded with rare beauty.

We saw a great number of birds, most of which were busy about their nests; there were ptarmigan, snipes, curlews, sandpipers, song sparrows, titmice, loons, many species of ducks, and the Emperor goose. The ptarmigan is a magnificent bird, about the size of the dusky grouse of the Sierra. They are quite abundant here, flying up with a vigorous whirr of wings and a loud, hearty, cackling "kek-kek-kep" every few yards all the way across the tundra. The cocks frequently took up a position on some slight eminence to observe us. They seemed happily in place out on the wide moor, with abundance of berries to eat through the summer, spring, and fall, and willows and alder buds for winter. Then they are pure white, and warmly feathered down to the ends of their toes. The sandpipers had fine feeding-grounds about the shallow pools. The grey moor is a fine place for curlews, too, and snipe.

The plants in bloom were primula, andromeda, dicentra, mertensia, veratrum, ledum, saxifrage, empetrum, cranberry, draba of several species, lupine, stellaria, silene, polemonium, buckbean, bryanthus, several sedges, a liliaceous plant new to me, five species of willow, dwarf birch, alder, and a purple pedicularis, the showiest of them all. The primula and a bryanthus-like heathwort were the most beautiful.

The tundra is composed of a close sponge of mosses about a foot deep, with lichens growing on top of the mosses, and a thin growth of grasses and sedges and most of the flowering plants mentioned above, with others not then in bloom. The moss rests upon a stratum of solid ice, and the ice on black vesicular lava, ridges of which rise here and there above the spongy mantle of moss, and afford ground for plants that like a dry soil. There are hollows, too, beneath the general level along which grow tall aspidiums, grasses, sedges, larkspurs, alders, and willows – the alders five or six inches in diameter and from eight to ten feet high, the largest timber I have seen since leaving California.

Visits from Indians in kayaks. At full speed they can run about seven miles an hour for a short distance. The salmon, that is, the best red-fleshed species, are about finishing their run up the river now. A very fat one, weighing about fifty pounds, was bought from an Indian for a little hardtack. After enough had been cut from it for one meal, it was lost overboard by dropping from its head while suspended by it. Specimens of a hundred pounds or more are said to be caught at times. Mr. Nelson saw dried specimens six feet long.

[STEAMER CORWIN, EN ROUTE TO THE ARCTIC OCEAN.] July 9th. Left St. Michael, having on board provisions for nine months, and about one hundred tons of coal. Decks heavily piled. A weird red sunset; land miraged into most grotesque forms. Heavy smoke from the burning tundra southwest from St. Michael. The season's cruise seems now to be just beginning.

July 10th. Arrived this morning, about seven o'clock, in Golofnin Bay, and dropped anchor. There is a heavy sea and a stiff south wind, with clouds veiling the summits down to a thousand feet from sea level. I was put ashore on the right side of the bay after breakfast at a small Indian village of two huts made of driftwood. They were full of dried herring. Inhabitants not at home, but saw a few at another village farther up the bay. All the huts are strictly conical and of driftwood. A few Indians came off in canoes, very fine ones, of a slightly different pattern from any others I have seen. There is a round hole through the front end to facilitate lifting. I had a long walk and returned to the ship at three in the afternoon.

The principal fact I discovered is a heavy deposit of glacial drift about fifty feet high, facing several miles of coast. It is coarsely stratified and water-worn – the material of a terminal moraine, levelled by water flowing from a broad glacier, while separated from the sea by a low, draggled flat, and then eaten into bluffs by the sea waves. It is now overgrown with alders, willows, and a good crop of sedges and grasses, bright with flowers.* Found the small blue violet rather common. White spiraea, in flower, is abundant in damp places about alder groves where the tundra mosses are not too thick. The cranberries, huckleberries, and rubus will soon be ripe. The purple-flowered rubus is only in bloom now.

The driftwood is spruce and cottonwood. The rock, containing mica, slate, and a good deal of quartz, seems favourable for gold. The life-boat, rigged with sails, has been sent to board the prospectors' schooner anchored farther up the bay. Seven men are aboard, and seven are off prospecting. They are reported to have found promising galena assaying high values per ton. They mean to visit the quicksilver mines on the Kuskoquim. The rocks on the opposite side of the bay exhibit clear traces of glacial sculpture.

July 11th. Sailed this morning from the anchorage in Golofnin Bay, and reached Sledge Island at nine in the evening. The natives are mostly away on the mainland. The island seems to be of granite and to have been over-swept [by glaciers]. Obtained a pretty good view of the mountains at the head of Golofnin Bay. They seem to be from four to five thousand feet high.

July 12th. Reached King Island this morning about seven o'clock, and left at half-past ten. Reached Cape Prince of Wales about three in the afternoon and anchored. Left at six in the evening. Clear, bright day; water, pale green. Had a fine view of the Diomedes, Fairway Rock, King Island, Cape Prince of Wales, and the lofty mountains towards the head of the river that enters Golofnin Bay, all from one point of view. The King Island natives were away on the mainland, all save a few old or crippled men, and women and children.

Their town, of all that I have seen, is the most remarkably situated, on the face of a steep slope, almost a cliff, and presents a very strange appearance. Some fifty stone huts, scarcely visible at a short distance, like those of the Arizona cliff-dwellers, rise like heaps of stones among heaps of stones. These are the winter huts, and are entered by tunnels. The summer huts, large square boxes on stilts, are of skin, stretched over large poles of driftwood. There is no way of landing save amid a mass of great wave-beaten boulders. In stormy times the King Islanders' excellent canoes have to be pitched off into the sea when a wave is about to recede. Two are tied together for safety in rough weather. These pairs live in any sea. A few grey-headed old pairs came off with some odds and ends to trade.

* See "Botanical Notes," p.000

Mr. Nelson and I went ashore to obtain photographs and sketches and to bargain for specimens of ivory carvings, etc. A busy trade developed on the roof of a house, the only level ground. Groups of merry boys went skipping nimbly from rock to rock, and busily guided us over the safest places. They showed us where between the huge boulders it was best to attempt a landing, which was difficult. Though the sea was nearly calm, a slight swell made a heavy surf. One hut rose above another like a village on Yosemite walls. The whole island is precipitous, so much so that it seems accessible only to murres, etc., which flock here in countless multitudes to breed.

In the afternoon, at Cape Prince of Wales, we lay opposite a large village whose inhabitants have a bad character. They started a fight while trading on board of a schooner. Many of them were killed, and they have since been distrusted not only on account of their known bad character, but also because of the law of blood revenge which obtains universally among these natives. They are noted traders and go far in their large skin boats which carry sails. While we were here a canoe, met by our search party, arrived from East Cape – a party of Chukchi traders, bringing deerskins from Cape Yakan ..They are in every way much better-looking men than the natives of this side, being taller, better-formed, and more cordial in manner. They at once recognised our Third Lieutenant Reynolds, whom they had met at Tapkan. Fog at night; going under sail only.

July 13th. Lovely day, nearly cloudless. Average temperature of 50° F. At half-past five in the afternoon we fell in with a trading schooner[1] opposite an Indian village.[2] One of the boats came alongside the Corwin and traded a few articles. Nothing contraband was found, though rifles probably had been sold during the first part of her cruise. These vessels, as well as whalers, carry more or less whiskey and rifles in order to obtain ivory, whalebone, and furs. They go from coast to coast and among islands, and thus pick up valuable cargoes. The natives cannot understand why the Corwin interferes with trade in repeating rifles and whiskey. They consider it all a matter of rivalry and superior strength. No wonder, since our government does nothing for them. Common rifles would be better for them, partly on account of the difficulty of obtaining supplies of cartridges, and partly because repeating rifles tempt them to destroy large amounts of game which they do not need. The reindeer has in this manner been well-nigh exterminated within the last few years.

July 14th A hot, sunny day. Came to anchor this morning at the head of Kotzebue Sound opposite the mouth of the Kiwalik River. Between eight and nine o'clock this morning Lieutenant Reynolds, with six seamen, took Mr. Nelson and me up the river in one of the boats. We reached a point

---

[1] The O.S.Fowler.   [2] Near Cape Espenberg.

about eight miles from the mouth of the estuary near the head of the delta. Since the bay is shoal off the estuary, the ship was anchored about four miles from the mouth. We, therefore, had a journey of about twenty-four miles altogether. We first landed at the mouth of the estuary and walked a mile or two along a bar shoved up by the waves and the ice. Here we found one native hut in good repair. The inhabitants were away, but the trodden grass showed that they had not been gone very long. This is the time of the year when the grand gathering of the clans for trade takes place at Cape Blossom, and they probably had gone there. The floor of the hut was about ten feet in diameter, [and the hut itself] was made of a frame of driftwood covered with sod, and was entered by a narrow tunnel two feet high and eighteen inches wide. We saw traces of a great many houses, showing that quite a large village was at one time located here. In some only a few decaying timbers were to be seen, in others all the timbers had vanished and only the excavation remained. Some six miles farther up the stream I noticed other ruins, indicating that many natives once lived here, though now their number has dwindled to one family.

The delta is about five miles wide and about eight miles long. It is covered with a grassy, flowery, sedgy vegetation, with pools, lagoons, and branches of the river here and there. It is a lonely place, and a favourite resort of ducks, geese, and other water birds which come here to breed and to moult. We saw swans[1] with their young; eider ducks, also, were seen with their young, and some were found on their eggs, which are green and about the size of hens' eggs. Their nests were among the grass on the margin of a lagoon and were made with a handful of down from their breasts. These as well as other ducks, which had their young with them, could not be made to fly, though we came within three or four yards of them in a narrow pool. When I threw sticks at the flock they would only dive. They were very graceful, and took good care of their children. We could easily have killed them all.

The wild geese which we saw also had young – a dozen families altogether.[2] They are moulting now and cannot fly. We chased a large flock in the estuary. When they saw us coming, they made frantic efforts to keep ahead of the boat. When we overtook them, they dived and scattered, coming up here and there, often close to the boat, and always trying to keep themselves concealed by laying their necks along the water and sinking their bodies and lying perfectly still; or, if they were well away from the boat and fancied themselves unseen, they swam in this sunken, outstretched condition and were soon lost to view, if there was the least wind-ripple on the water. Saw three plovers, the godwit from the Siberian side, and many finches and

---

[1] Whistling swans (*Olor columbianus*).

[2] Mr E. W. Nelson reported the geese observed here as belonging to two species, the American white-fronted goose (*Anser albifrons gambeli*) and the white-cheeked goose (*Bernicla canadensis leucoparia*).

gulls. On a small islet in the middle of a pond we found one nest of the burgomaster gull. They tried to drive us away by swooping down upon us. I noticed also the robber gull and several others. Butterflies were quite abundant among the blooming meadow vegetation. I noticed six or more species. The vegetation is like that of Cape Prince of Wales and Norton Sound. Found one red poppy, one wintergreen, allium, saxifrages, primulas, lupines, pedicularis, and peas, quite abundant. This region is noted for its fossil ivory. Found only a fragment of a tusk and a few bones. The deposit whence they were derived is probably above the point reached by us. The gravel is composed of quartz, mica, slate, and lava. There are many lava cones and ridges on both sides of the estuary.

CHAPTER ELEVEN

Caribou and a Native Fair

JULY 15th. Rainy and cold; cleared at seven in the evening. Left the head of Kotzebue Sound this morning at seven-thirty, for Cape Blossom, where the natives assemble from near and far to trade, but only one poor family was left. We went ashore and found them engaged in fishing for salmon with a net which was pushed out from the shore by a long pole sixty feet in length, made of three tied together. The Indians had gone fifteen or twenty miles up the coast, near Cape Krusenstern. Their tents were to be seen, looking like Oakland across the bay from San Francisco, so numerous they seemed. A small schooner, the Fowler, was at anchor there trading. Soon half a dozen canoes came alongside of us, and offered to trade, but asked big prices. The Captain obtained only two wolfskins, a deerskin, and a few muskrats, and bunches of sinew. [The Corwin then proceeded to Hotham Inlet and came to anchor about two miles from the native village called Sheshalek, inhabited by Kobuk and Noatak River Eskimos.]

July 16th. A fresh breeze from the north, but the day is tolerably clear. A swell is breaking into whitecaps here and there. A busy day with the Indians, trading for a winter supply of deerskins. We obtained over a hundred altogether at the rate of about a dollar each for summer skins, and half as much for those taken in winter. With what we have already picked up here and there, and with the parkas we have collected, this will be amply sufficient. Reindeer are killed in immense numbers inland from here. All are wild; no domesticated herds are found on the American continent, though the natives have illustrations enough of their value on the opposite shores of Bering Sea. These Indians prefer herds that require no care, though they are not always to be found when wanted. Some of the wild herds that exist up the Inland River are said, by the Indians, to be so large as to require more than a day in passing.

The number of these animals, considering the multitude of their enemies, is truly wonderful. The large grey wolves kill many during the winter, and when the snow is deep, large flocks are slaughtered by the Indians, whether they need them or not. They make it a rule to kill every animal that comes within reach, without a thought of future scarcity, fearing, as some say, that, should they refuse to kill as opportunity offers, though it be at a time when food is no object, then the deer-spirit would be offended at the refusal of his gifts and would not send any deer when they are in want. Probably, however, they are moved simply by an instinctive love of killing on which their existence depends, and these wholesale slaughters are to be regarded as only too much of a good thing. Formerly there were large herds about St. Michael, but since the introduction of repeating rifles they have wholly vanished. Hundreds were surrounded in passes among the hills, were killed and left lying where they fell, not even the hides being taken. Often a band of moose or reindeer is overtaken in deep snow, when they are easily killed with clubs by Indians on snowshoes, who will simply cut out their tongues, and leave the rest to be eaten by wolves.

The reindeer is found in the Arctic and subarctic regions of both Asia and America, and, in either the wild or the domestic state, supplies to the natives an abundance of food and warm clothing, thus rendering these intensely cold regions inhabitable. I believe it is only in Lapland and Siberia that the reindeer is domesticated. They are never sold alive by the Chukchis on account of a superstitious notion that to do so would surely bring bad luck by incensing the spirit of the deer. A hundred can be bought, after they are killed, for less than one alive. Certain ceremonies must also be observed before killing.

Out on the frozen tundra great care is required, both by day and by night, to keep them from being scattered and torn by wolves. A reindeer weighs from three to four hundred pounds. The winter skins are heavier, the hair being long and tipped with white, giving them a hoary appearance, especially on the back; but the hair is easily broken and pulled out, a fact which renders them much less durable when used for bedding, tents, or clothing than those taken in summer, when the hair is short, and dark blue, almost black. Reindeer hides are easily tanned; those tanned in Siberia are dyed a rich reddish-brown on the inside with alder bark. The domestic reindeer skins are considered better than those of the wild animals. Wrangell[1] has described the herds as affording a grand sight.

At this point[2] the Indians from the interior, and from many miles up and down the coast, assemble once a year in July to trade with each other, with

---

[1]   Admiral Baron Ferdinand Petrovich von Wrangell, Polar explorer and Russian Govenor, Adminis-trator of the Russian-American colonies, 1829–1836.

[2]   The head of Kotzebue Sound.

parties of Chukchis who come from Siberia in umiaks, and with the few schooners that bring goods from San Francisco and from the Sandwich Islands. After trading they indulge in games of wrestling, playing ball, gambling, dancing, and drinking whiskey, if they can get it. Then they break up their camps and go to their widely scattered homes, some a month's journey or more up the Inland and down the Colville Rivers. They now have about one hundred and forty tents set in a row along the beach, their light kayaks in front of the tents in a neat row, each with paddles and spears that belong to it, and in front of these a row of large skin umiaks. They are a mixed, jolly multitude, wearing different ornaments, superb fur clothes, or shabby foreign articles; one sees long hair, short hair, or closely shaven; here is headgear of hats, caps, or cowls, and folk who go bareheaded; labrets, too, of every conceivable size, colour, and material – glass, stone, beads, ivory, brass. They show good taste and ingenuity in the manufacture of pipes, weapons, knick-knacks of a domestic kind, utensils, ornaments, boats, etc.

Though savage and sensual, they are by no means dull or apathetic like the sensual savages of civilization, who live only to eat and indulge the senses, for these Eskimos, without newspapers or telegraphs, know all that is going on within hundreds of miles, and are keen questioners and alive to everything that goes on before them. They dearly like to gossip. One tried to buy some of the cabin boy's hair, on account of its curious whiteness; another, who has red hair, is followed and commented on with ludicrous interest.

The shores hereabouts are comparatively low, the hills, back a few miles from shore, rolling and of moderate height, and mountains are to be seen beyond.

July 17th. The northerly wind still prevails; cloudy all day, but dry. Left the Eskimo "Long Branch" at four o'clock in the morning and sailed to Cape Thompson, where we mean to look into the condition of the Eskimos and inquire whether they have obtained whiskey from any of the traders, contrary to law. The coast is rather low. Mountains are visible thirty miles back; low hills between.

July 18th. Numerous snow squalls. Came to anchor at five this morning in the lee of Point Hope. Norther blowing. Remained all day in company with the Sea Breeze.* A few of the natives came offshore – good-natured fellows. A negro, who wintered here last season, was well used by them, for he was given the best of what they had. He had lost an axe overboard, so the story goes, and deserted on account of trouble he had over the matter with the second officer of the brig Hidalgo. He was taken on board again this spring.

We landed and walked through the village. Found a fine gravel beach, beautifully flowered beyond the reach of the waves. Most of the natives seem to be away – at the summer gathering, perhaps. The graveyard is of

* A whaling bark.

great extent and very conspicuous from the custom of surrounding the graves with poles.

July 19th. Cold, stiff, north wind; clear. Left our anchorage at five o'clock this morning and proceeded north, but found the gale too strong to make much headway and, therefore, turned back and anchored at Cape Thompson, thirty miles south of Point Hope. Watering ship all day; the wind is blowing hard. Going north again since seven o'clock this evening. Wind moderating slightly.

I went ashore this forenoon and, after passing a few minutes interviewing a group of vagabond natives from Point Hope who were camped here to gather eggs, kill murres, and loaf, I pushed on up the hillside, whose sheer scarped face forms the Cape. I found it five hundred and fifty feet high, composed of calcareous slates, much bent and contorted, and a considerable portion was fossiliferous. Where hills of this rock have steep slopes, and so much drainage and wash that soil is not allowed to form, nor the usual moss mantle to grow, they bleach white and present a remarkably desolate aspect in the distance. Such hills are common back of Kotzebue Sound. These barren slopes, however, alternate with remarkably fertile valleys, where flowers of fifty or more species bloom in rich profusion, making masses of white, purple, and blue. Sometimes this occurs on a comparatively thin soil where the leaves do not veil the rocky ground; but at the bottom of the valleys there usually is a green ground below the bloom.

The slopes over which I passed in today's walk are planted chiefly with sweet fern – Dryas – with its yellowish-white flowers. A purple silene is also very abundant, making beautiful bosses of colour. Phlox is present in dwarfed masses, only the stems and leaves being dwarfed, not the flowers. Anemones occur in fine patches, and buttercups, and several species of daisies and lupines. Dodecatheon I met here for the first time this season. Dwarf willows are abundant. There was one fern and one heathwort along a stream side. I saw no true tundra here, its absence, no doubt, being due to the free drainage of the surface. The winds from the north are violent here, as evidenced by the immense snow-drifts still unmelted along the shore where we landed, and also back in the hollows where they feed the stream at which we got water for the ship. They probably will last all summer. This circumstance, of course, leaves the hill slopes all the barer and dryer.

The trends of two main ridges, of which I obtained approximate measurements, probably coincide with the direction of the movement of the ice. There is a small wasted moraine in the lower part of the stream valley, extending to the shore. Partial after-glaciation has been light, and on rocks of this sort has left only very faint traces.

July 20th. Last night we again anchored on the south side of Point Hope, the norther still blowing hard. About noon today it began to abate, and we again pushed off northward. Now, at eight o'clock in the evening, we are approaching Cape Lisburne, a bold bluff of grey stratified rocks about fifteen hundred feet high. All along the coast, from the neighbourhood of Cape Prince of Wales, the peculiar grey colour of the rocks, and the forms into which they are weathered and glaciated, indicate one continuous formation, partially described yesterday. Magnificent sections are exposed between the north side of Point Hope and Cape Lisburne. The age of the formation I do not as yet certainly know. The existence of coal veins here and there in connection with conglomerates, and the few fossils, would tend to identify it as Carboniferous, though some of the sections show a wide vertical range. Probably a considerable amount of the formation is older. The few fossils I have seen point to the Carboniferous, or older formations.

Between eleven and twelve o'clock this forenoon several white whales were seen near the shore, showing their white backs above the water when they rose to breathe, so white at a little distance that they might easily have been mistaken for breaking waves. We saw the Indians shoot and kill one, and went ashore to have a good look at this Beluga. It proved to be a small one, only about seven feet long, and of a pale grey ashen colour, probably a young specimen. In general form it is like a whale, but more slender. The head is narrow and rather high in the forehead. The eyes are very small, about five eighths of an inch in diameter. The ears are hardly visible, would scarcely admit a common lead pencil. The blow-hole, as in the true whales, is about an inch in diameter. The forefeet, the only limbs, are in the form of short flippers, and the tail, which is large, is formed by an expansion of the thick skin. They are more nearly related to the dolphins than to the whales – the dolphins, porpoises, and grampuses forming one of the divisions of the three *Cetacea delphinoidea*.

While we were ashore looking at this specimen, a much larger one came along parallel with the shore-line and not more than twenty or thirty yards from it. The natives were on the watch and shot it through the body when it rose to blow. Instead of making out to sea when wounded, it kept its course alongshore and the natives followed excitedly, ready to get another shot. They kept it in sight while it was ten or twelve feet under water, which they were enabled to do on account of its whiteness. Eight or ten men jumped into a canoe and followed it, one standing in the bow with a spear. After swimming about half a mile and receiving four or more bullets from Henry and Winchester rifles, it began to struggle and die. The boat came up, an Eskimo drove in a spear, and the whale was taken in tow and brought back to where the first was killed, the crew, meanwhile, singing in triumph. Then a rolling hitch was made, and a dozen willing hands landed the animal, a female. She measured about twelve feet in length and nine in circumference. They at once began to eat the tail and back fin raw, cutting off blocks of it and giving it to the children, not because they were hungry, but because they regarded it as so very palatable. Then a fire was built of driftwood. Looking back from the ship, only two red spots were visible on the beach – and a group of fifty feasting Eskimos! Probably not a bit of the Belugas, except a little of the blubber, will be left by night.

The attitudes of the riflemen, legs spread, rifle to shoulder, and eyes vividly on the alert, as they watched the animal's appearance above water, were very striking. These animals are quite abundant hereabouts, and used to be killed with spears that had heads made of stone or ivory. Whales were killed in the same manner. A much larger number of right whales is killed by the natives about the shores of Bering Sea and along the polar shores than is supposed. Almost every village gets from one to five every season. Then comes a joyful time. The bone belongs to the boat's crew that strikes the whale, the carcass to all the village.

A mountain slope just to the northeast of Cape Lisburne is so covered at the top with slender, spirey columns of rock, that I at first glance took them for trees. A slight dusting of snow has lately whitened the peaks. To the south of the Cape twelve or fifteen miles two small valleys, cut nearly to the level of the sea, exhibit terminal and lateral moraines. After-glaciation has been light. The higher mountains do not approach the coast nearly. No deep fiords like those of the west coast.

CHAPTER TWELVE

Zigzags among the Polar Pack

JULY 21st. Rainy this forenoon, clear at night. Wind blowing hard from the southeast and raising a heavy swell. Reached Icy Cape about noon and found to our disappointment that, notwithstanding the openness of the season, further advance northeastward was barred by the ice. After the sky began to clear, and the rain to cease falling, we observed an ice-blink stretching all around the northern horizon for several hours before we sighted the ice, a peculiar brown and yellow band within a few degrees of the horizon. There was a dark belt beneath it, which indicated water beyond the ice.

We then turned westward, tracing the loose edge of the pack until eight in the evening, when we turned to the east again, intending to await the further movements of the ice for a few days, and especially a change of wind to blow it offshore. There is a coal vein between here and Cape Lisburne which we will visit and mine as much coal as possible, in case the weather permits. But as there is no shelter thereabouts, we may not be able to obtain any and in that case will be compelled to go to Plover Bay for our next supply.

About fifteen miles southwest of Icy Cape there is quite a large settlement of Eskimos on the low, sandy, storm-swept shore [Ututok?]. Cool and breezy must be their lives, and they can have but little inducement to look up, or time to spend in contemplation. Theirs is one constant struggle for food, interrupted by sleep and by a few common quarrels. In winter they hibernate in noisome underground dens. In summer they come out to take breath in small conical tents, made of white drill, when they can get it. They waved a piece of cloth on the end of a pole as we passed, inviting us to stop and trade with them. From Cape Lisburne up the coast to Point Barrow there is usually a two-knot current, but the wind and the ice have completely stopped the flow at present. The sun is above the horizon at midnight.

July 22nd. A dull, leaden day; dark fog and rain until about four in the afternoon; rained but a small fraction of an inch. About noon we once more sighted the ice-pack. The heavy swell of the sea is rapidly subsiding and the wind is veering to the northeast. We hope it will move the ice offshore and allow us to round Point Barrow. The pack is close and impenetrable, though made up of far smaller blocks than usual, owing, no doubt, to the mildness of last winter, and to the chafing and pounding of a succession of gales that have been driving over it at intervals all the spring. We pushed into it through the loose outer fringe, but soon turned back when we found that it stretched all around from the shore. By retreating we avoided the danger of getting fixed in it and carried away. Nearly all the vessels that have been lost in the Arctic have been caught hereabouts.

The approach to the ice was signalised by the appearance of walruses, seals, and ducks. The walrus is very abundant here, and when whales are scarce the whalers hunt and kill great numbers of them for their ivory and oil. They are found on cakes of ice in hundreds, and if a party of riflemen can get near, by creeping up behind some hummock, and kill the one on guard, the rest seem to be heedless of noise after the first shot, and wait until nearly all are killed. But if the first be only wounded, and plunges into the water, the whole ''pod'' is likely to follow. Came to anchor at half past ten this evening, a little to the south of Icy Cape.

July 23rd. Clear and calm. Weighed anchor at eight in the morning and ran close inshore, anchored, and landed with instruments to make exact measurements for latitude and longitude, and to observe the dip. I also went ashore to see the vegetation, and Nelson to seek birds and look for Eskimo specimens. Found only four plants in bloom – saxifrage, willow, artemisia, and draba. This is the bleakest and barest spot of all. Well named Icy Cape . A low bar of sand and shingle shoved up by the ice that is crowded against the shore every year. Inside this bar, which is only a hundred yards wide, there is a stretch of water several miles wide; then low gravelly coast. Sedges and grasses, dwarfed and frost-bitten, constitute the bulk of the flora.

We noticed traces of Eskimo encampments. There was blubber in abundance from a dead whale that had been cast up on the shore. They had plenty of food when they left. But before this they must have been hungry, for we found remains of dogs that they had been eating; also foxes' bones, picked clean. Found a dead walrus on the beach beyond the wreck of the whale.

At one in the afternoon we weighed anchor and turned north, crossing inside of Blossom Shoals, which are successive ridges pushed up by the ice, and extending ten or twelve miles offshore. In a few hours we reached the limit of open water. The ice extended out from the shore, leaving no way. Turned again to the south. Sighted the bark Northern Light [a whaler] and made up to her. She showed grandly with her white canvas on the dark water, now nearly calm. Ice just ahead as we accompanied her northward while the Captain visited her. The sun is low in the northwest at nine o'clock. A lovely evening, bracing, cool, with a light breeze blowing over the polar pack. The ice is marvellously distorted and miraged; thousands of blocks seem suspended in the air; some even poised on slender black poles and pinnacles; a bridge of ice with innumerable piers, the ice and water wavering with quick, glancing motion. At midnight the sun is still above the horizon about two diameters; purple to west and east, gradually fading to dark slate colour in the south with a few banks of cloud. A bar of gold in the path of the sun lay on the water and across the pack, the large blocks in the line [of vision] burning like huge coals of fire.

A little schooner* has a boat out in the edge of the pack killing walruses, while she is lying a little to east of the sun. A puff of smoke now and then, a dull report, and a huge animal rears and falls – another, and another, as they lie on the ice without showing any alarm, waiting to be killed, like cattle lying in a barnyard! Nearer, we hear the roar, lion-like, mixed with hoarse grunts, from hundreds like black bundles on the white ice. A small red flag is planted near the pile of slain. Then the three men pull off to their schooner, as it is now midnight and time for the other watch to go to work.

These magnificent animals are often killed for their tusks, like buffaloes for their tongues, ostriches for their feathers, or for mere sport and exercise. In nothing does man, with his grand notions of heaven and charity, show his innate, low bred, wild animalism more clearly than in his treatment of his brother beasts. From the shepherd with his lambs to the red-handed hunter, it is the same; no recognition of rights – only murder in one form or another.

July 24th. A lovely morning, sunful, calm, clear; a broad swath of silver spangles in the path of the sun; ice-blink to the north; a pale sky to the east and around to the south and west; blue above, not deep blue; several ships in sight. Sabbath bells are all that is required to make a Sabbath of the day. Ran inshore opposite the Eskimo village; about a hundred came off. Good-natured as usual. A few biscuits and a little coaxing from the sailors made them sing and dance. The Eskimo women laughed as heartily at the curious and extravagant gestures of the men as any of the sailors did. They were anxious to know what was the real object of the Corwin's cruise, and when the steam whaler Belvedere hove in sight they inquired whether she had big guns and was the same kind of ship. Our interpreter explained as well as he could.

In the afternoon we had the Sea Breeze, the Sappho, the Northern Light, and the schooner about us. The steam whaler had only six whales. He had struck ten, taken four, and found two dead. Last year he took twenty-seven. The whales were in windrows then; at one time twenty-five were so near that no gaps between them were so wide but that a man could strike on either side. They were more abundant last year on the American coast; this year, on the Asiatic. They are always more abundant in spring and fall than during the summer.

Had a graphic account, from Captain Owen, of the loss of the thirty-three ships of the whaling fleet near Point Barrow in 1874. Caution inculcated by such experiences. Anchored this evening near the Belvedere and four other vessels. The schooner people complain that this is a bad year for "walrusing"; ice too thin; after killing a few the hot blood so weakens the ice that in their struggles they break it and then fall in and sink.

---

* The R. B. Handy, Captain Winants.

July 25th. Steamed northward again, intending, after reaching the ice, to make an effort to go to Point Barrow with the steam launch, and the lifeboat in tow, to seek the Daniel Webster, and offer aid if necessary. [This whaler is] now shut in about Point Belcher. We found, however, that the ice was shoved close inshore south of Icy Cape, and extended in a dense pack from there to the southwest, leaving no boat channel even. This plan was therefore abandoned with great reluctance, and we again moved southward, intending to coal, if the weather allowed, near Cape Lisburne. Calm, lovely night; slight breeze; going slowly under sail alone.

July 26th. Lovely day; gentle breeze. Eight vessels in sight this morning. The Belvedere got under sail and is proceeding southward with us. Mirages in wonderful variety; ships pulled up and to either side, out of all recognition; the coast, with snow patches as gaps, pulled up and stratified; the snow looking like arched openings in a dark bridge above the waters. About nine-thirty we noticed a rare effect just beneath the sun – a faint, black, indefinite, cloud-like bar extended along the horizon, and immediately beyond this dark bar there was a strip of bright, keenly defined colours like a showy spectrum, containing nearly all the colours of the rainbow.

July 27th. A lovely day, bright and calm and warm. Coaling ship from a vein in a sandstone cliff twenty miles northeast of Cape Lisburne. In company with the Belvedere. Seeking fossils. Discovered only two species of plants. Coal abundant. Mined, took out and brought on board fifteen tons today. The Belvedere also is coaling and taking on water. Three Eskimo canoes came from the south this evening and camped at the stream which flows into the sea on the north side of the coal bluff. The dogs followed the canoe alongshore. After camping they came alongside, but not before their repeated signs of peace, consisting of throwing up hands and shouting "Tima," were answered by the officer of the deck. This custom seems to be dying out, also that of embracing and nose-rubbing.

July 28th. Lovely, tranquil day, all sunshine. Taking coal until half-past four in the afternoon. Then sailed toward Herald Island. I spent the forenoon along the face of the shore cliffs, seeking fossils. Discovered only four, all plants. Went three miles westward. Heavy snowbank, leaning back in the shadow most of the distance, almost changing to ice; very deep and of several years formation – not less than forty feet in many places. The cliffs or bluffs are from two hundred to nearly four hundred feet high, composed of sandstone, coal, and conglomerate, the latter predominating. Great thickness of sediments; a mile or more visible on upturned edges, which give a furrowed surface by unequal weathering. Some good bituminous coal; burns well. Veins forty feet thick, more or less interrupted by clayey or sandy strata. Fossils not abundant.

While I was scratching the rocks for some light on the history of their formation, eight canoe loads of Eskimos with all their goods, tents, children, etc., passed close along the shore, going toward Icy Cape; all except one were drawn by dogs – from three to five to each canoe – attached by a long string of walrus hide, and driven by a woman, or half-grown girl, or boy "Ooch, ooch, ooch," they said, while urging them along. They dragged the canoe with perhaps two tons altogether at two and one half miles per hour. When they came to a sheer bluff the dogs swam and the drivers got into the canoe until the beach again admitted of tracking. The canoe that had no dogs was paddled and rowed by both men and women. One woman, pulling an oar on the starboard bow, was naked to the waist. They came from Point Hope, and arrived last evening at a camping-ground on the edge of a stream opposite the Corwin's anchorage. This morning they had eight tents and all the food, canoes, arms, dogs, babies, and rubbish that belong to a village. The encampment looked like a settled village that had grown up by enchantment. Only one was left after ten in the morning, the occupants busying themselves caching blubber of walrus. In the sunshine some of the children enjoyed the luxury of running about naked.

Eleven-thirty; a calm evening. The sun has just set, its disk curiously distorted by refraction and light diminished by vaporous haze, so that it could be looked at, a glorious orb of crimson and gold with a crisp surface. . . . Horizontal layers of colour, piled on each other evenly, made the whole look like cheeses of different sizes laid neatly one on top of the other. Sketched the various phases. It set as a flat crimson cake of dull red. No cloud; only haze, dark at the horizon, purple higher, and then yellow.

July 29th. Calm, lovely, sunny day. Thermometer standing at 50° F. in the shade; warm in the sun; the water smooth with streaks; ruffled, like an alpine lake; mostly glassy, stirred with irregular breaths of air. Ice visible about noon, near "Post-Office Point."* Fine-grained, hazy, luminous mist about the horizon. A few gulls and ducks. Sun barely dipped beneath the horizon. Curiously modelled by refraction; bars dividing in sections always horizontal. Ducks flying at midnight.

July 30th. Another glassy, calm day, all sunshine from midnight to midnight. Kotzebue's gull, the kittiwake, about the ship; no seals or walrus. Herald Island came in sight about one o'clock. At a distance of eight to ten miles we reached the ice, but made our way through it, as it was mostly light and had openings here and there. But we suffered some hard bumps; pushed slowly and got close alongside, much to the satisfaction of the crew.

* Said to be a point north of Bering Strait in the Arctic Ocean where, for some reason the drift of oceanic currents is not strong. Whalers and other vessels customarily went there to exchange mail and news.

CHAPTER THIRTEEN

First Ascent of Herald Island

STEAMER CORWIN, OFF HERALD ISLAND, ARCTIC OCEAN, July 31st, 1881. We left Herald Island this morning at three o'clock, after landing upon it and exploring it pretty thoroughly from end to end. On the morning of the twenty-fifth we were steaming along the coast a few miles to the south of Icy Cape, intending to make an effort to reach Point Barrow in order to give aid to the whaleship Daniel Webster, which we learned was beset in the ice thereabouts and was in great danger of being lost.

We found, however, that the pack extended solidly from Icy Cape to the southward and pressed so hard against the shore that we saw it would be impossible to proceed even with the steam launch. We therefore turned back with great reluctance and came to anchor near Cape Lisburne, where we mined and took on about thirty tons of coal. About half-past four in the afternoon, July twenty-eighth, we hoisted anchor and sailed toward Herald Island, intending to make a general survey of the edge of the great polar ice-pack about Wrangell Land, hardly hoping to be able to effect a landing so early in the season.

On the evening of the thirtieth we reached Herald Island, having been favoured with delightful weather all the way, the ocean being calm and glassy as a mountain lake, the surface stirred gently here and there with irregular breaths of air that could hardly be called winds, and the whole of this day from midnight to midnight was all sunshine, contrasting marvellously with the dark, icy stormdays we had experienced so short a time ago.

Herald Island came in sight at one o'clock in the afternoon, and when we reached the edge of the pack it was still about ten miles distant. We made our way through it, however, without great difficulty, as the ice was mostly light and had openings of clear water here and there, though in some close-packed fields the Corwin was pretty roughly bumped, and had to steam her best to force a passage. At ten o'clock in the evening we came to anchor in the midst of huge cakes and blocks about sixty-five feet thick within two or three hundred yards of the shore.

After so many futile efforts had been made last year to reach this little ice-bound island, everybody seemed wildly eager to run ashore and climb to the summit of its sheer granite cliffs. At first a party of eight jumped from the bowsprit chains and ran across the narrow belt of margin ice and madly began to climb up an excessively steep gully, which came to an end in an inaccessible slope a few hundred feet above the water. Those ahead loosened and sent down a train of granite boulders, which shot over the heads of those below in a far more dangerous manner than any of the party seemed to appreciate. Fortunately, nobody was hurt, and all made out to get down in safety.*

While this remarkable piece of mountaineering and Arctic exploration was in progress, a light skin-covered boat was dragged over the ice and launched on a strip of water that stretched in front of an accessible ravine, the bed of an ancient glacier, which I felt assured would conduct by an easy grade to the summit of the island. The slope of this ravine for the first hundred feet or so was very steep, but inasmuch as it was full of firm, icy snow, it was easily ascended by cutting steps in the face of it with an axe that I had brought from the ship for the purpose. Beyond this there was not the slightest difficulty in our way, the glacier having graded a fine, broad road.

---

*   Captain Hooper's report of the incident and of Muir's skilful ascent of the island adds some interesting details:

Muir, who is an experienced mountaineer, came over the ice with an axe in his hand, and, reaching the island a few hundred feet farther north, opposite a bank of frozen snow and ice a hundred feet high, standing at an angle of 50°, he deliberately commenced cutting steps and ascending the ice cliff the top of which he soon reached without apparent difficulty, and from there the top of the Island was reached by a gradual ascent neither difficult nor dangerous.

While approaching the island, by a careful examination with the glass, Muir's practised eye had easily selected the most suitable place for making the ascent. The place selected by the others or rather the place upon which they stumbled, – for the attempt to ascend was made on the first point reached – was a small, steep ravine about two hundred feet deep. The jagged nature of its steep sides made climbing possible, and from the sea-level the top of this ravine appeared to these ambitious but inexperienced mountain-climbers to be the top of the island. After several narrow escapes from falling rocks they succeeded in gaining the top of the ravine, when they discovered that the ascent was hardly begun. Above them was a plain surface of nearly a thousand feet in height and so steep that the loose, disintegrating rock with which it was covered gave way on the slightest touch and came thundering to the bottom. Some of the more ambitious were still anxious to keep on, notwithstanding the difficulty and danger, and I found it necessary to interpose my authority to prevent this useless risk of life and limb. A retreat was ordered, and with a good deal of difficulty accomplished. The descent had to be made one at a time, the upper ones remaining quiet until those below were out of danger. Fortunately, all succeeded in reaching the bottom in safety. In the meantime Muir and several others had reached the top of the island and were already searching for cairns or other signs of white men. Although the search was kept up until half-past two in the morning, nothing was found.

C. F Hooper's Report of the *Cruise of the U.S. Revenue Steamer Thomas Corwin in the Arctic Ocean*, 1881, p.52.

Kellett, who discovered this island in 1849, and landed on it under unfavourable circumstances, described it as "an inaccessible rock." In general the sides are, indeed, extremely sheer and precipitous all around, though skilled mountaineers would find many gullies and slopes by which they might reach the summit. I first pushed on to the head of the glacier valley, and thence along the backbone of the island to the highest point, which I found to be about twelve hundred feet above the level of the sea. This point is about a mile and a half from the northwest end, and four and a half from the northeast end, thus making the island about six miles in length. It has been cut nearly in two by the glacial action it has undergone, the width at the lowest portion being about half a mile, and the average width about two miles.

The entire island is a mass of granite, with the exception of a patch of metamorphic slate near the centre, and no doubt owes its existence, with so considerable a height, to the superior resistance this granite offered to the degrading action of the northern ice-sheet, traces of which are here plainly shown, as well as on the shores of Siberia and Alaska and down through Bering Strait southward beyond Vancouver Island. Traces of the subsequent partial glaciation to which it has been subjected are also manifested in glacial valleys of considerable depth as compared with the size of the island. I noticed four of these, besides many marginal glacial grooves around the sides. One side remnant [of a glacier] with feeble action still exists near the middle of the island. I also noted several scored and polished patches on the hardest and most enduring of the outswelling rock-bosses. This little island, standing as it does alone out in the Polar Sea, is a fine glacial monument.

The midnight hour I spent alone on the highest summit – one of the most impressive hours of my life. The deepest silence seemed to press down on all the vast, immeasurable, virgin landscape. The sun near the horizon reddened the edges of belted cloud-bars near the base of the sky, and the jagged ice-boulders crowded together over the frozen ocean stretching indefinitely northward, while perhaps a hundred miles of that mysterious Wrangell Land was seen blue in the northwest – a wavering line of hill and dale over the white and blue ice-prairie! Pale grey mountains loomed beyond, well calculated to fix the eye of a mountaineer. But it was to the far north that I ever found myself turning, to where the ice met the sky. I would fain have watched here all the strange night, but was compelled to remember the charge given me by the Captain, to make haste and return to the ship as soon as I should find it possible, as there was ten miles of shifting, drifting ice between us and the open sea.

I therefore began the return journey about one o'clock this morning, after taking the compass bearings of the principal points within sight on Wrangell Land, and making a hasty collection of the flowering plants on my way. I found one species of poppy quite showy, and making considerable masses of colour on the sloping uplands, three or four species of saxifrage, one silene, a draba, dwarf willow, stellaria, two golden compositae, two sedges, one grass, and a veronica, together with a considerable number of mosses and lichens, some of them quite showy and so abundant as to furnish most of the colour over the grey granite.

Innumerable gulls and murres breed on the steep cliffs, the latter most abundant. They kept up a constant din of domestic notes. Some of them are sitting on their eggs, others have young, and it seems astonishing that either eggs or the young can find a resting-place on cliffs so severely precipitous. The nurseries formed a lively picture – the parents coming and going with food or to seek it, thousands in rows standing on narrow ledges like bottles on a grocer's shelves, the feeding of the little ones, the multitude of wings, etc.

Foxes were seen by Mr. Nelson* near the top of the northeast end of the island, and after we had all returned to the ship and were getting under way, the Captain discovered a polar bear swimming deliberately toward the ship between some floating blocks within a few yards of us. After he had approached within about a dozen yards the Captain shot at him, when he turned and made haste to get away, not diving, however, but swimming fast, and keeping his head turned to watch the ship, until at length he received a ball in the neck and stained the blue water with his blood. He was a noble-looking animal and of enormous strength, living bravely and warm amid eternal ice.

We looked carefully everywhere for traces of the crew of the Jeannette along the shore, as well as on the prominent headlands and cliffs about the summit, without discovering the faintest sign of their ever having touched the island.

We have been steaming along the edge of the pack all day after reaching open water, with Wrangell Land constantly in sight; but we find that the ice has been sheering us off farther and farther from it toward the west and south. The margin of the main pack has a jagged saw-tooth outline, the teeth being from two to ten miles or more in length, and their points reaching about forty miles from the shore of Wrangell Land. Our chances, however, of reaching this mysterious country some time this year seem good at present, as the ice is melting fast and is much lighter than usual, and its wind and current movements, after it breaks up, will be closely watched for an available opening.

* In an article in the *National Geographic Magazine* (November 1916, p.425) – "The Larger North American Mammals" – Mr. E. W. Nelson has given the following account of this incident:
The summer of 1881, when we landed from the Corwin on Herald Island, northwest of Bering Straits, we found many white foxes living in burrows under large scattered rocks on the plateau summit. They had never seen men before and our presence excited their most intense interest and curiosity. One and sometimes two of them followed closely at my heels wherever I went, and when I stopped to make notes or look about, sat down and watched me with absurd gravity. Now and then one at a distance would mount a rock to get a better view of the stranger.
On returning to the ship, I remembered that my notebook had been left on a large rock over a fox den, on the island, and at once went back for it. I had been gone only a short time, but no trace of the book could be found on or about the rock, and it was evident that the owner of the den had confiscated it. Several other foxes sat about viewing my search with interest and when I left followed me to the edge of the island. A nearly grown young one kept on the Corwin was extraordinarily intelligent, inquisitive, and mischievous, and afforded all of us much amusement and occasional exasperation.

CHAPTER FOURTEEN

Approaching a Mysterious Land

STEAMER CORWIN, OFF POINT BARROW, August 16th, 1881. We left Herald Island at three o'clock in the morning of July 31st. The clear water seen by me from the top of the island is called "the Hole" by whalers. I am told that it is remarkably constant in its appearance and position from year to year. What combination of currents, coast-lines, winds, etc., is the cause of it is not yet known. Neither is the Post-Office Point of ice understood.

On the day after leaving Herald Island the fine weather we had been enjoying for a week began to vanish, heavy cloud-piles grew about the horizon, and reeking fogs over the ice. We kept on around the serrated edge of the pack, and were glad to find a wide opening trending to the northwest, that is, toward the southmost point of Wrangell Land. Up we steamed, excited with bright hopes of effecting a landing and searching the shores for traces of the Jeannette. In the afternoon, while yet our way was tolerably clear, and after the land had been long in sight, we were enveloped in fog, and hove to, instead of attempting to grope a course through the drift ice and running the danger of getting the ship embayed. A few seals, gulls, and walruses were observed.

Next day, August 2nd, the fog lifted early in the morning, when we got under way and pushed hopefully onward once more, with the mountains and blue foothills of the long-lost land in full view, until noon, making our way easily through the drift ice, dodging to right and left past the large masses, some of which were a mile or more in length. Then the fog began to settle again over all the wild landscape; the barometer was falling, and the wind began to blow with indications of a stiff breeze that would probably press the ice toward the shore. Under these conditions we dared not venture farther, but loath to turn back we made fast to an ice-floe and waited developments. The fog partially cleared again, which induced us to make another short push ahead, but our hopes were again and again baffled by darkness and close-packed ice, and we were at length compelled to seek the open water once more, and await a general calm and clearance.

A piece of wood twenty-seven inches long, cut with a sharp axe, was picked up in the morning within, perhaps, twenty-five miles of Wrangell Land. It was evident, by its length and by the way it was split and cut, that it was intended for firewood. It seemed clearly to be the work of white men, possibly of some of the Jeannette's crew. But the grand excitement of the day, apart from the untrodden shore we were seeking, was caused by three polar bears, magnificent fellows, fat and hearty, rejoicing in their strength out here in the bosom of the icy wilderness.

When discovered they were regarding us attentively from a large cake of ice, each on a hummock commanding a good view of the ship, an object they no doubt saw for the first time in their lives. One of them was perched on top of a pile of blocks, the topmost of which was a pedestal square and level as if built up for an outlook. He sat erect and, as he was nearly the colour of the ice, was not noticed until we were quite near. They watched, motionless, for some time, throwing forward their long necks and black tipped noses as if trying to catch and pass judgment on the scent of the big, smoking, black monster that was approaching them.

When we were within about fifty yards of them, they started, walked a step or two, and turned to gaze again as the strange object came nearer. Then they showed fear and began to lumber along over and across the wavelike rough hills and dales of the ice, afraid, perhaps for the first time in their lives. For polar bears are the master existences of these frozen regions, the walruses being no match for them. First they broke into a lumbering trot; then, into a panicky, wallopy gallop, with fewer and fewer halts to look back, until they reached the far side of the ice-field and plunged into the water with a splash that sent the spray ten feet into the air. Then they swam, making all haste toward a larger floe. If they could have gained it they would have made good their retreat. But the steamer gave chase at the rate of seven knots an hour, headed them off, and all were shot without the least chance of escape, and without their being able to offer the slightest resistance.

The first one overtaken was killed instantly at the second shot, which passed through the brain. The other two were fired at by five fun-, fur-, and fame-seekers, with heavy breech-loading rifles, about forty times ere they were killed. From four to six bullets passed through their necks and shoulders before the last through the brain put an end to their agony. The brain is small and not easily penetrated, except from the side of the head, while their bodies may be shot through and through a score of times, apparently, without disabling them for fighting or swimming. When a bullet went through the neck, they would simply shake their heads without making any sort of outcry, the effect being simply to hasten their flight. The same was true of most other wounds. But occasionally, when struck in the spine, or shoulder, the pain would make them roar, and groan, and turn to examine the spot, or to snap at the wound as if seeking an enemy. They would dive occasionally, and swim under water a few yards. But, being out of breath, they were always compelled to come up in a minute or so. They had no chance whatever for their lives, and the whole affair was as safe and easy a butchery as shooting cows in a barnyard from the roof of the barn. It was prolonged, bloody agony, as clumsily and heartlessly inflicted as it could well be, except in the case of the first, which never knew what hurt him.

The Eskimos hunt and kill them for food, going out to meet them on the ice with spears and dogs. This is merely one savage living on another. But how civilized people, seeking for heavens and angels and millenniums, and the reign of universal peace and love, can enjoy this red, brutal amusement, is not so easily accounted for. Such soft, fuzzy, sentimental aspirations, and the frame of mind that can reap giggling, jolly pleasure from the blood and agony and death of these fine animals, with their human-like groans, are too devilish for anything but hell. Of all the animals man is at once the worst and the best.

Two of the bears were hoisted on board, the other was neglected until it could not be found. Then came the vulgar business of skinning and throwing the mangled carcasses back into the clean blue water among the ice. The skins were stretched on frames to be dried and taken home to show angelic sweethearts the evidence of pluck and daring.

The Indians sometimes adorn their belts with the claws of bears and place their skulls about the graves of the men who killed them. I have seen as many as eighteen set about the skeleton of an Eskimo hunter, making for his bones an oval enclosure like a frame of shells set around a grave. The strength of the polar bear is in proportion to the massiveness of his limbs. The view of their limb muscles, swelling in braided bosses, could not fail to awaken admiration as they lay exposed on the deck. Such is the strength of the large bears, which are nine to ten feet long, that they can stand on the edge of an ice-floe and drag up out of the water a walrus weighing more than a thousand pounds.

The feet of the larger one measured nine and a half inches across behind the toes. They have long hair on the soles and around the sides of the feet for warmth in the dreary solitudes which they inhabit. When standing, the claws are not visible; the whole foot seems to be a large mop of hair spreading all around. The expression of the eye is rather mild and dog like in the shape of the muzzle and the droop of the lips, and only the teeth would suggest his character as a killer.

The third of August was spent in groping anxiously landward again through fog and ice until about six in the evening, when we reached the heavy, unbroken edge of the coast ice, at a distance of about twenty-five miles from the nearest point of land, and all hope of advancing farther was now at an end. We, therefore, turned away, determined to bide our time, hoping that warm winds and waves would at length melt and smash the heavy fields alongshore some time before the setting-in of winter. Nor were we altogether without hope of finding open water leading around the west shore of Wrangell Land. We soon found, however, that the pack stretched continuously across to Cape North on the Siberian coast, thus promptly forbidding all efforts in that direction.

The bottom of the ocean in that region is very level. Soundings made every hour for three days* varied scarcely more than five fathoms, and for half a day not one fathom. We saw several small fishes among the ice at our nearest point to lee; also seals, both saddleback and hair. Just as we were turning we discovered a bear observing us from a large field of ice. He kept coming nearer a few steps and then halting to catch the smell of the ship. We did not attempt to kill him, however, as the advantage we had was not great enough. We could not chase him here with the steamer.

On the morning of the fourth we discovered a ship's foreyard with bits of rope stile attached to it in such a way as to show that it had been carried away while the sail was bent. It seemed to have been ground in the ice for a winter or two, and probably belonged to one of the missing whalers.

After cruising along the Siberian coast for a few days, and calling at the Cape Wankarem village to procure as many as possible of the articles taken by the natives from the wreck of one of the lost whalers, we found ourselves once more on the edge of Wrangell ice, and again in dense fog on the morning of the ninth of August. A huge white bear came swimming through the drizzle and gloom and black heaving waves toward the ship as we lay at anchor, guided doubtless by scent. He was greeted by a volley of rifle balls, no one of which injured him, however, and fortunately he could not be pursued.

The fog lasted in dismal thickness until one o'clock on the morning of the eleventh, when we once more saw the hills and dales of Wrangell Land hopefully near. We discovered a lead that enabled us to approach within perhaps fifteen miles of the nearest portion of the coast. At times we thought ourselves much nearer, when the light, falling favourably, would bring out many of the smaller features, such as the subordinate ridges on the faces of the mountains and hills, the small dimpling hollows with their different shades of colour, furrows that seemed the channels of small streams, and the peculiar rounded outlines due to glacial action. Then pushing eagerly through the huge drifting masses toward the nearest cape, judging by the distinctness of its features, it would suddenly seem to retreat again into the blue distance, and some other point catching the sunlight would be seen rising grandly across the jagged, hummocky ice-plain, relieved against the blue shadowy portions to right and left as a background.

It was not long, however, after tracing one lead after another, and coming always to a standstill with the ship's prow against ice of enormous thickness, before we were forced to the conclusion that all efforts made hereabouts would now be vain. The ice did not seem to have been broken or moved in any way for years. We turned, therefore, and made our way back to open

---

* In an average depth of twenty-five fathoms.

water with difficulty and steamed along the edge of the pack to the northeastward. After a few hours' run we found the ice more promising, for it showed traces of having been well crushed and pounded, enabling us to bear gradually in toward the land through a wedge-shaped lead about twenty miles in length.

At half-past five in the afternoon we were again brought to a standstill against heavy ice, but this time within about five miles of the shore. We now felt pretty sure that we would be able to make a landing, and the questions that we wanted to put to this land of mystery came thronging to mind. This being, perhaps, the most likely place to find traces of the Jeannette expedition, in case any portion of this island was reached, would we find such traces? Has the country any human inhabitants? Would we find reindeer or musk oxen? What birds shall we find? What plants, rocks, streams, etc?

We intended to walk the five miles of ice, dragging a light skin-covered boat with us to cross any open spot that we might come to; but ere we could set off, the fog began to settle gloomily down over the land and we determined to wait until the next morning, and in the meantime steam back out of the narrow, ice-jammed throat of the lead a few miles to a safer position, in case the ice should close upon us. Just as we turned from our nearest point of approach, we fired a cannon to stir the echoes among the hills and give notice of our presence in case anybody was near to listen.

The next morning, steaming ahead once more to the end of our water-lane, we were rejoiced to find that though there were now about eight or ten miles of ice separating us from the shore, it was less firmly packed, and our little vessel made a way through it without difficulty, until we were within two miles of the shore, when we found the craggy blocks extremely hard and wedged closely. But a patch of open water near the beach, now plainly in sight, tempted us to continue the struggle, and with the throttle wide open the barrier was forced. By ten o'clock in the morning the Corwin was riding an anchor less than a cable's length from a dry, gravel bar, stretching in front of the mouth of a river. The long battle we had fought with the ice was now fairly won, and neither the engine nor the hull of the ship seemed to have suffered any appreciable damage from the terrible shocks and strains they had undergone.

CHAPTER FIFTEEN

The Land of the White Bear

STEAMER CORWIN, WRANGELL LAND, August 12th, 1881. A notable addition was made to the national domain when Captain Calvin L. Hooper landed on Wrangell Land [August 12th, 1881] and took formal possession of it in the name of the United States. We landed near the southeast cape, at the mouth of a river, in latitude 71° 4', longitude 177° 40' 30" W. The extent of the new territory thus acquired is not definitely known, nor is likely to be for many a century, or until some considerable change has taken place in the polar climate, rendering the new land more attractive and more accessible. For at present even its southmost portion is almost constantly beset with ice of a kind that renders it all but inaccessible during both the winter and summer, while to the northward it extends far into the frozen ocean.

Going inland, along the left bank of the river, we found it much larger than it at first appeared to be. There was no snow left on the lowlands or any of the hills or mountains in sight, excepting the remnants of heavy drifts; nevertheless, it was still about seventy five yards wide, twelve feet deep, and was flowing on with a clear, stately current, at a speed of about three miles an hour. While the snow is melting it must be at least two hundred yards wide and twenty feet deep, and its sources must lie well back in the interior of the island.

Not the slightest trace, however, could we find along the river, along the shore, or on the bluff to the northeastward of the Jeannette party, or of any human inhabitant. A land more severely solitary could hardly be found anywhere on the face of the globe.

The beach was well tracked by polar bears, but none of the party could discover any sign of reindeer or musk oxen, though the country seems to abound in the kind of food they require. A single fox track was observed, and some burrows of a species of spermophile;[1] also a number of birds,[2]

---

[1]   E.W. Nelson, in *Mammals of Northern Alaska* (1886), identified this spermophile as *Spermophilus empetra empetra* (Pallas), and remarks, "upon the hill where we planted our flag on Wrangell Island were many of their burrows."

[2]   The following birds were observed by Mr. Nelson on Wrangell Land and Herald Island: Snow Bunting, Snowy Owl, Pacific Golden Plover, Pectoral Sandpiper, Red Phalarope, some kind of wild goose (perhaps Black Brant), King Eider Duck, Red-faced Cormorant, Ivory Gull, Pacific Kittiwake, Glaucous Gull, Glaucous-winged Gull, Ross's Gull, Sabine's Gull, Pomarine Jaeger, Long-tailed Jaeger, Rodgers's Fulmar, Horned Puffin, Crested Auk, Black Guillemot, Pigeon Guillemot, Thick-billed Guillemot, and a dead specimen of the Crested Shrike. This list is made from E.W. Nelson's *Birds of Bering Sea and the Arctic Ocean*, published with Muir's botanical observations in Treasury Department Document No. 429 (1883).

and about twenty species of plants [see Botanical Notes], most of them in bloom. The rock is clay slate, which weathers smoothly, and is covered with a sparse growth of mosses, lichens, and flowering plants, not unlike that of the adjacent coasts of Siberia and Alaska.

Some small fragments of knowledge concerning this mysterious country have been in existence for nearly a century, mostly, however, of so vague and foggy a character as to be scarce at all available as geography, while up to the time of Captain Hooper's visit no explorer so far as known had set foot on it. In the year 1820 Lieutenant Wrangell was ordered by Alexander, Emperor of Russia, to proceed from the mouth of the Kolyma as far as Cape Schelagskoj, and from thence in a northerly direction over the ice with sledges drawn by dogs, to ascertain whether an inhabited country existed in that quarter, as asserted by the Chukchis and others.

But the land in question was far from being generally known even by tradition among the Chukchis inhabiting the Siberian coast nearest to it. Wrangell seems to have found only one person during his long search for this land that had heard or could tell him anything concerning it. This man, an intelligent chief or head of a family, drew with charcoal a correct sketch of Cape Schelagskoj, Aratuan Island, and another to the east of the Cape, and then assured Wrangell in the most positive manner that there was no other island along the coast. When asked whether there was any other land to the north beyond the visible horizon, he seemed to reflect a little, and then said that, between Cape Schelagskoj and Cape North, there was a part of the coast where, from some cliffs near the mouth of a river, one might on a clear summer day descry snow-covered mountains at a great distance to the north, but that in winter it was impossible to see so far. He said also that formerly herds of reindeer sometimes came across the ice, probably from thence, but that they had been frightened back by hunters and wolves. He claimed to have himself once seen a herd returning to the north in this way in April, and followed them in a sledge drawn by two deer for a whole day until the roughness of the ice forced him to turn back. His opinion was that these distant mountains he had seen were not on an island, but on an extensive land similar to his own country.

He had been told by his father that a Chukchi elder had once gone there with a few followers in large boats, but what they found there, or whether they ever returned, he did not know. Still he maintained that the distant land was inhabited, and adduced as proof of it that some years ago a dead whale was found at Aratuan Island pierced by spears pointed with slate; and as his people did not use such weapons he supposed that the whale must have been killed by the people of the northland.

After spending three winters Baron Wrangell wrote concerning this country: "Our return to Nishne Kolymsk closed the series of attempts made by us to discover a northern land, which though not seen by us, may nevertheless exist, and be attainable under a combination of very favourable circumstances, the principal of which would be a long, cold, and stormless winter, and a late spring. If another attempt should be made, it would be advisable to leave the coast about Cape Yakan, which all the native accounts concur in representing as the nearest point to the supposed northern region."

STEAMER CORWIN, OFF POINT BARROW, ALASKA, August 17th, 1881. The Corwin made a very short stay at Wrangell Land, partly because of the condition of the ice, which threatened to shut us in; and partly because it seemed improbable that a prolonged search in the region about our landing-point could in any way advance the main objects of the expedition. A considerable stretch of the bluff coast where we landed was scanned closely as we approached. Captain Hooper, Mr. Nelson, and myself examined a mile or two of the left bank of the river, a gently sloping hillside back from the river, and a stretch of smooth beach at its mouth. Meanwhile a party of officers, after erecting a cairn, depositing records in it, and setting the flag on the edge of the bluff fronting the ocean, went northeastward along the brow of the shore-bluff to a prominent headland a distance of three or four miles, searching carefully for traces of the Jeannette explorers, and of any native inhabitants that might chance to be in the country; then all were hurriedly recalled, and we forced our way back through ten miles of heavy drifting ice to open water.

On the shore we found the skeleton of a large bowhead whale, an oak barrel stave, a piece of a boat mast about seven feet long and four inches in diameter, a double kayak paddle with both blades broken, and a small quantity of driftwood. Every bit of flotsam was much scoured and abraded, showing that the articles had long been exposed to the action of waves and ice.

Back on the hills and along the river-bank the tracks of geese, marmots, foxes, and bears were seen, but no trace whatever of human beings, though the mouth of a river would above all others be the place to find them if the country were inhabited or had been visited by Europeans within a decade or two. Not a stick of the driftwood seemed to have been turned over or stirred in any way, though, from the steepness of the slate bluffs for miles along the coast, and the heavy snowbanks drifted over them, this low, open portion of the shore is about the only place in the neighbourhood where driftwood could come to rest on a beach and be easily accessible to natives or others while travelling along the coast either on the ice or on land, and where they would also find a good campground and water.

A few yards back from high-water mark there is a low pile of broken slate, with level ground about it, where any traveller passing this way would naturally choose to camp. But the surface of the slate is covered with grey, brown, and yellow rock-lichens of slow growth, showing that not one of these stones had been moved for many a year. Again, neither the low nor the high ground in this vicinity is at all mantled with spongy tundra mosses and lichens like most of the Arctic shores over which a man might walk without leaving a footprint. On the contrary, it is mostly bare, presenting a soft clay soil, derived from the disintegration of slates, the scanty dwarf vegetation – saxifrages, drabas, potentillas, carices, etc. – occurring in small tufts at intervals of a yard or so, with bare ground between them, smooth and mellow and plastic, with gentle drainage, admirably adapted for the reception and preservation of footprints. Had any person walked on this ground any time in summer when the snow was gone, and where the drainage slopes are not too steep, his track would remain legible to the dullest observer for years.

We concluded, therefore, that this part of the country was not inhabited. Nor should the absence of inhabitants be wondered at, notwithstanding they might be derived from the Siberian coast at long intervals in accordance with the traditions bearing on the question among the Chukchis, or even from the coast of Alaska about Point Barrow or Cape Lisburne. For, though small parties of Eskimos or Chukchis might reach the land on floes detached from the pack while they chanced to be out hunting seals, or in boats driven by stormwinds or otherwise, such parties would probably seek to get back to their old homes again, or would die of famine. The seal and walrus, the two animals on which the natives of the Arctic shores chiefly depend for subsistence, are not to any great extent available, inasmuch as the ice seldom or never leaves the south Wrangell shores, and journeys twenty or thirty miles long would have to be made over rough ice to reach them.

Reindeer and musk oxen may exist in some other portions of the country, but if they occur in such numbers as would be required for the support of any considerable population the tracks of at least some few stragglers should have been seen hereabouts. Migratory water birds are no doubt abundant during the breeding and moulting season, producing sufficient food to last through a few of the summer months, and there are plenty of white bears, huge animals weighing from ten to twenty hundred pounds. Most of them, however, roam far out from land on the rugged edge of the ice-pack among the seals and walruses, and even under the most advantageous circumstances polar bears are poor cattle to depend on for a living. They certainly do not seem to have been fed upon lately to any marked extent, for we found them everywhere in abundance along the edge of the ice, and they appeared to be very fat and prosperous, and very much at home, as if the country had belonged to them always. They are the unrivalled master-existences of this ice-bound solitude, and Wrangell Land may well be called the Land of the White Bear.

Commander De Long, in a letter to his wife, written at sea, August 17th, 1879, said that he proposed to proceed north by the way of the east coast of Wrangell Land, touching at Herald Island, where he would build a cairn and leave records; that if he reached Wrangell Land from there he would leave records on the east coast under a series of cairns twenty-five miles apart. In a precious letter, dated July 17th, 1879, he said:

In the event of disaster to the ship, we shall retreat upon the Siberian settlements, or to those of the natives around East Cape, and wait for a chance to get back to our depot at St. Michael. If a ship comes up merely for tidings of us, let her look for them on the east side of Wrangell Land and on Herald Island. If I find that we are being carried east against our efforts to get north, I shall try to push through into the Atlantic by way of the east coast of Greenland, if we are far enough north; and if we are far south, then by way of Melville Bay and Lancaster Sound.

While evidently pursuing this plan, he was seen by the whaler Sea Breeze on the second of September, 1879, about fifty miles south of Herald Island, entering a lead in heavy ice, which probably closed in upon his vessel and carried him past Herald Island. The search we made over Herald Island shows pretty clearly that he did not succeed in landing there, for if a cairn had been built on any conspicuous point we could not have failed to see it, as we travelled over it all in good bright weather. Nor would the failure of this part of his plan be unlikely when it is considered that he was fifty miles from the island so late in the season as September, and when heavy ice a hundred feet thick was already about him, and packed around the island. Neither does it seem at all probable from what we have seen this summer that he could have been successful in reaching Wrangell Land so late in the season under so many adverse circumstances of weather and ice. That he did not build a cairn or leave any trace of his presence within a few miles of our landing point does not prove by any means that he did not reach Wrangell Land at all, or that cairns with records may not exist elsewhere to the northward or westward. But the point where we landed being the easternmost point of the lower portion of Wrangell Land, it would seem from his plans as well as from known conditions of the ice to be of all others the likeliest place to find traces of the expedition.

In the case of the loss of his vessel and his reaching the land farther up the coast, he would be likely, in following his plan of retreat, to travel southward past this east point where the ice is more broken and extends a shorter distance offshore than elsewhere – conditions that seem applicable to the last two years at least, judging by what we have observed. Even should he not have built a cairn on so prominent and comparatively accessible a point, likely to be discovered by relief vessels, he could hardly have been able to pass without leaving some sign on the bank of the river, whether he made efforts to mark his presence or not. In case the explorers passed their first winter on Wrangell Land, they might either try to cross over the ice to Siberia toward spring from some point to the westward of our landing, or in case they reached the easternmost cape, near the south extreme of the land, about midsummer, they would probably find it the most favourable point of departure in making their way to the Siberian coast with sleds over the shore pack, and thence in boats. But as no trace of the explorers appears here, and no tidings have been obtained concerning them from the Chukchis, this, with all the evidence discovered thus far, goes to show that the Jeannette expedition either did not reach Wrangell Land at all, or did not make any extended stay upon it.

Notwithstanding the improbability of finding the expedition, the Corwin would gladly have been fast to a stranded berg, for a few days at least, during the fine August weather we were enjoying at the time, in order to send out exploring and search parties along the coast fifty or sixty miles in opposite directions, and back into the mountains, to learn something about the topography, geology; and natural history of the country, and to determine as surely as possible whether the missing explorers had touched this portion of the coast. But in so doing we should have risked being shut in, losing the vessel, and thus making still another party to be searched for. Besides, we might then be prevented from making other landings farther north in case the ice should leave the shores in that direction, and from extending relief to other vessels that might stand in need of it among the ice of this dangerous sea.

The floe outside our anchorage was drifting along shore to the northeast with a powerful current at a speed of fifty miles a day, the majestic movement being made strikingly manifest by large bergs that were aground in water sixty feet deep, standing like islands, while the main mass of the pack went grating past them. With so much motion in the ice, the open lane and the strip of loose blocks and cakes through which we had forced our way in coming in was liable to close at any time, making escape impossible, at least until some chance change in the winds and currents might result in setting us free.

As it was, we escaped with difficulty after both engine and hull had been severely tested, the lane by which we entered having almost vanished, and the point where we reached open water was several miles to the northward of our ingoing track. Had our retreat been cut off, we would not, perhaps, have suffered greatly for a year or thereabouts, inasmuch as we had nine months provisions aboard, which, with what game we might chance to kill in the nature of seals, bears, and walruses, could easily have been made to last considerably longer. We also had plenty of reindeer clothing and pologs, bought with a view to spending a winter in the Arctic, in case it should be necessary to do so. Everything could have been landed under favourable auspices, and preparations could have been made in the way of building shelters and storehouses. Then we would have had a fine long opportunity to explore this grand wilderness in its untouched freshness during the remaining months of summer and all the winter, while the vessel might possibly have escaped being smashed if laid up at the mouth of the river, and by a hairbreadth chance have been gotten out next summer.

Perhaps the ice does not leave the shore free more than once in ten years. The small quantity of driftwood on the beach would seem to indicate open water at times, but it might have been brought in by shifting, tumbling ice, after being held fast and gradually worked inshore after years of change in its position among the shifting floes, without the occurrence of any perfectly free channel of communication with the open part of the ocean. Our plan of retreat would have been similar to that proposed by Commander DeLong, that is, to the coast of Siberia. The loss of the vessel, however, and any work and hardship that might follow would not have been allowed to weigh against any reasonable hope of finding the lost explorers and carrying relief to them. But it was decided that more could be done, in all probability towards carrying out the objects of the expedition by keeping the Corwin free. Only about half of the workdays of the summer were spent as yet, the weather was mild, the ice melting, and we had good hopes of finding open water reaching well inshore farther north, through which some other portion of the coast might be found accessible where the danger of being permanently beset would be less, and from whence extended land journeys might be made. Our efforts, however, to get northward along the eastern shore of Wrangell Land have, thus far, been unavailing.

CHAPTER SIXTEEN

Tragedies of the Whaling Fleet

STEAMER CORWIN, OFF POINT BARROW, August 18th, 1881. Finding it impossible to get northward through the ice anywhere near the east side of Wrangell Land, it was decided that we should cross to the American coast to make another effort to reach Point Barrow in order to learn the fate of the whale-ship Daniel Webster, which, as I have stated in a former letter, was beset in the ice there and to offer assistance in case it should be required.

On the fifteenth, near Icy Cape, we spoke with one of the whalers from whom we learned that the Daniel Webster was crushed and sunk, that about half the crew had made their way down the coast to near Icy Cape, where they found the Coral and were taken on board, and that the others were still at Point Barrow or scattered along the shore, unless picked up by some of the fleet that were going north in search of them as fast as the state of the ice would allow.

Captain Owen of the bark Belvedere had sent a letter to them by one of the natives, directing them to build large driftwood fires on the beach to indicate their positions, and assuring them that relief was near. We had hoped that, though beset in the heavy, drifting pack and carried northward helpless and rigid as a fly in amber, some change in the wind and current might set them free. But in discussing the question with an experienced whaler who had lost the first ship that he was master of at the same place and in the same way, he said that he had given her up for lost as soon as she was known to be embayed.

On receiving this news we started for Point Barrow and found the way clear, the pack having been blown offshore a few miles, and a heavy current was sweeping to the northward. Tuesday, the sixteenth, was calm and foggy at times; large masses of beautiful ice, blue and green and white, of every conceivable form, like the bergs derived from glaciers, were drifting with the riverlike current or lying aground – the remnants of the grand pack that so lately held possession of all the sea hereabouts.

When we were passing Point Belcher and Sunarnara [Sinaru?] we learned from the natives that the ice was offshore as far as Point Barrow and beyond, that several whale-ships were already there, and that all the men from the broken ship had been taken on board. For some time the fog was so dense and the huge bergs so abundant we were compelled to lie to and drift with the current; but shortly after noon the sun came out, making a dazzling show among the ice and silvery water. Then the conical huts of the Eskimo village on Point Barrow came in sight, and rounding the Point we found ourselves in the midst of a fleet of whalers, from whom we received the good news that, as we had been told by the natives, all the missing members of the wrecked crew had been picked up and were now distributed among the different vessels. A few of them have been permanently added to the crews of the rescuing ships lying here, and nine have been received on board of the Corwin.

The strip of water sometimes found between Icy Cape and Point Barrow is perhaps the most dangerous whaling ground yet discovered. The ice is of tremendous thickness, a hundred feet or more, and its movements are extremely variable from season to season, and almost from day to day. It seldom leaves this part of the coast very far, some years not at all, and it is always liable to be driven close inshore by a few hours or days of strong wind blowing from any point of the compass around from north to southwest. When, as frequently happens, there is a margin of fixed ice along the shore the position of ships is most dangerous, for when the pack comes in and catches vessels in this ice-bound lane while trying to beat southward against wind and current, it closes upon them and crushes them as between huge crunching jaws. Should there be no fixed ice, then vessels may simply be shoved ashore.

It is not long since the first whale-ship passed Bering Strait, and yet no less than forty-seven have been crushed hereabouts, or pushed ashore, or embayed and swept away northward to nobody knows where, while many others have had narrow escapes.

Thirty-three were caught and lost in this way here at one time, thirteen the following season, and one last July, while two others barely made their escape the same day just as the fatal ice-jaws closed behind them. This last victim, the Daniel Webster, left New Bedford in November, 1880, passed through Bering Strait on the tenth of June, and was caught in the pack on July 3rd. It seems from the account furnished us by the first mate that she was following up a lead of open water about five miles wide, between the main ocean pack and a strip of shore-ice, fancying that two other ships that she had been following the day previous were still ahead, and on whose movements the Captain, who had no experience here, this being his first voyage, was to some extent depending. These two leaders however, had turned and fled during the night without being observed, while the Daniel Webster kept on northward, until within sight of the end of the water-lane, when she turned and attempted to beat her way back. But wind and current were against her, the huge ice-walls came steadily nearer, and at length closed on the doomed vessel, carrying her away as if she were a mere bit of drift timber. About an hour later she was crushed, and sank to her upper deck in about twenty minutes. Then she fell over on her beam ends against the ice and soon vanished in the icy wilderness.

The Point Barrow Eskimos, keenly familiar with the actions of the winds and currents on the movements of the ice, watched the struggling ship, and came aboard before the ice had yet closed upon her, like wolves scenting their prey from afar. Many a wreck had they enjoyed here, and now, sure of yet another, they ran about the ship examining every movable article, and narrowly scanning the rigging and sails with reference to carrying away as much as possible, such as the sails, lead pipe for bullets, hard bread, sugar, tobacco, etc., in case they should have but a short time to work.

She filled so quickly after being crushed that the crew saved but little more than the clothes they were wearing. Some hard bread, beef, and other stores were hastily thrown over upon the ice, and one boat was secured. As soon as she was given up, the Eskimos climbed into the rigging, and dexterously cut away and secured all the sails, which they value highly for making sails for their large travelling canoes and for covers for their summer huts. Then they secured as much lead as possible and anything they could lay hands on, acting promptly and showing the completeness of the apprenticeship they had served.

The ship was then about five miles from the Eskimo village, and the natives were allowed to assist in carrying everything that had been saved. Under the circumstances, in getting over the five miles of ice with such riches, they, like white men, reasoned themselves into the belief that everything belonged to them, even the chronometers and sextants. Accordingly, at the village a general division was made in so masterly a manner that by the time the officers and crew reached the place their goods had vanished into a hundred-odd dens and holes; and when, hungry, they asked for some of their own biscuits, the natives complacently offered to sell them at the rate of so much tobacco apiece. Even the chronometers had been divided, it is said, after being taken apart, the wheels and bits of shining metal being regarded as fine jewellery for the young women and children to wear. A keg of rum, that the officers feared might fall into the Eskimos' hands and cause trouble by making them drunk, was thrown heavily over on the ice with the intention of smashing it, but it was not broken by the fall. One of the Eskimos picked up the prize, to him more precious than its weight in gold, and sped away over the slippery crags and hollow of the ice with admirable speed, vainly pursued by the first mate, and at the village it disappeared as far beyond recovery as if it had been poured into a hot sand bank. As wreckers, traders, and drinkers these sturdy Eskimos are making rapid progress, notwithstanding the fortunate disadvantages they labour under, as compared with their white brethren, dwelling in so severe a climate on the confines of the frozen sea.

The entire crew numbered twenty-eight men. All except the second mate and two of the sailors started down the coast afoot, after waiting some time for the ice to drift offshore far enough to allow some of the other ships to come to their relief, or at least far enough to leave a passage for their boat. At the river Cogrua* ten of the party turned back, weary and hungry and discouraged, to Cape Smyth, to pick up a living of oil and seal meat until relieved, rather than face the danger of fording the river and enduring yet greater hardships. The others pushed forward. Directed by one of the natives, they went up the bank of the river about twenty miles from its mouth, to where it is much narrower. Here they forded without danger, carrying their clothes on their heads to keep them dry.

Both parties seem to have suffered considerably from hunger as well as from cold and fatigue. The seal and oil meals, which the natives of the different villages they passed good-naturedly allowed them to share, but ill-supplied the place of their old-fashioned, rough, and regular rations. They speak of having been reduced to the strait of eating roots and leaves of the few dwarf plants found along their way. At Point Belcher they were so fortunate as to find a travelling party of natives, who, after their shaman had duly consulted the spirits, supposed to be influential and wise concerning the affairs of this rough region, and reported favourably, agreed to take the party in their canoe southward to seek the whaling fleet, the pack having by this time commenced to leave the shore. By this means the wanderers reached the bark Coral in four days, at a cost of two rifles and some tobacco.

The others were kindly received by the Cape Smyth people and entertained until the ice left the shore. One of the three left at Point Barrow, it seems, wandered southward alone and lost himself with fright and hunger. He was without food for five days, save what he could pick up from the sparse, sedgy vegetation, and was nearly dead when discovered by a relief party from one of the ships. The natives, he said, refused to allow him to enter their huts because his eyes were wild and he would soon be crazy. Fortunately, all are now cared for.

* Kugrua, a river tributary to the Arctic Ocean at the Seahorse Islands, a little east of Point Belcher. According to John Murdoch, Kug'ru is the Eskimo name of the Whistling Swan.

Newly discovered whaling grounds, like gold mines, are soon overcrowded and worked out, the whales being either killed or driven away. But whales worth four or five thousand dollars apiece are so intensely attractive and interesting that the grand game has been hunted in the face of a thousand dangers over nearly all the seas and oceans on the face of the globe. According to Alexander Starbuck, in his history of the American whale fishery, there belonged, in the year 1846, to the various ports of the United States six hundred and seventy-eight ships and barks, thirty-five brigs, and twenty-two schooners that were hunting whales. In 1843 the first bowhead whales taken in the North Pacific were captured on the coast of Kamchatka, and in 1848 the first whale-ship passed Bering Strait. This was the bark Superior, Captain Royce. A full cargo was easily obtained, because of the abundance and tameness of the whales.

The news, like a gold discovery, spread rapidly, and within the next three years two hundred and fifty ships had obtained cargoes of oil and bone here. This is, therefore, a comparatively new hunting ground. Nevertheless it is being rapidly exhausted. The precious bowheads are no longer seen in ''long winrows,'' as described by an old whale man familiar with the region. This year only twenty vessels are engaged in the business.

In 1871 thirty-three vessels were caught in one flock off Point Belcher and crushed or shoved ashore. One of them is said to have been ''crushed to atoms,'' the officers and crew escaping over the ice, saving scarcely anything but their lives. In a few days after the sixth of August most of the fleet was north of Blossom Shoals, and worked northeast as far as Wainwright Inlet. Here the ships either anchored or made fast to the ice, which was very heavy and densely packed. On August 11th a sudden change of wind drove the ice inshore, catching a large number of boats that were out in pursuit of whales, and forcing the ships to work inshore in the lee of the ground ice.

On the thirteenth of August the incoming pack grounded, leaving only a narrow strip of water, in which the fleet was imprisoned more and more narrowly until the twenty fifth, when a strong northeast gale drove the ice a few miles offshore, and whale catching went on briskly without fear of another imprisonment. But on the twenty-ninth a southwest wind again drove the ice inshore, and once more shut in the doomed fleet. The thirty-three vessels were scattered along the coast for twenty miles, more and more rigidly beset until the fourteenth of September, when they were abandoned – that is, those not already crushed.

The following protest, throwing a vivid light upon the subject. was written on the twelfth of September, and signed by all the captains before abandoning their vessels:

POINT BELCHER, ARCTIC OCEAN. September 12th, 1871

Know all men by these presents, that we, the under-signed, masters of whale-ships now lying at Point Belcher, after holding a meeting concerning our dreadful situation, have all come to the conclusion that our ships cannot be got out this year, and there being no harbours that we can get our vessels into, and not having provisions enough to feed our crews to exceed three months, and being in a barren country, where there is neither food nor fuel to be obtained, we feel ourselves under the painful necessity of abandoning our vessels, and trying to work our way south with our boats, and, if possible, get on board of ships that are south of the ice. We do not think it would be prudent to leave a single soul to look after our vessels, as the first westerly gale will crowd the ice ashore, and either crush the ships or drive them high upon the beach. Three of the fleet have already been crushed, and two are now lying hove out, which have been crushed by the ice and are leaking badly. We have now five wrecked crews distributed among us, we have barely room to swing at anchor between the ice-pack and the beach, and we are lying in three fathoms of water. Should we be cast on the beach it would be at least eleven months before we could look for assistance, and in all probability nine out of ten would die of starvation or scurvy before the opening of spring.

All the officers and crews – twelve hundred and nineteen souls – reached the seven relief vessels that lay waiting their arrival outside the ice, and were distributed among them, these seven being the remnant of the fleet that passed through Bering Strait in the spring. The next summer only five of the thirty-three were seen, one of them comparatively uninjured. All the rest had been smashed, sunk, burned, or carried away in the pack.

Five years later, in 1876, the fleet consisted of twenty ships and barks, and of this number thirteen were embayed in the pack, twenty or thirty miles off Point Barrow. After waiting and hoping for the coming of a liberating gale as long as they dared, the masters decided that it was necessary to abandon their vessels. Out of three hundred and fifty-three persons, fifty-three remained with the ships, hoping to get them free in the spring; but not one of the ships, or of those who stayed on them, was ever seen again. The three hundred who left their vessels, after enduring great hardships, succeeded in making good their escape to the rest of the fleet waiting outside the pack – all save three or four who perished by the way.

There are now twelve whale-ships about Point Barrow in sight from the Corwin, and all that would be necessary to shut them in is a gale from the southwest. Still the great love of action, and the great love of money, compel the risk here and elsewhere over and over again. The Corwin is now about to go southward to coal, at the mine twenty miles east of Cape Lisburne; or, in case the weather should be too rough to land at the mine, which is on a bare, exposed portion of the coast, to Plover Bay. Then we will return to the Arctic prepared to make other efforts to get on the south and east shores of Wrangell Land.

CHAPTER SEVENTEEN

Meeting the Point Barrow Expedition

STEAMER CORWIN, PLOVER BAY, SIBERIA, August 15th, 1881. We left icy, gloomy Point Barrow on the afternoon of the eighteenth, with fine Arctic weather, which held out good hopes that we would be able to lie two days at the mine twenty miles east of Cape Lisburne, in order to take out and get on board a sufficient quantity of coal to last the Corwin the remainder of the season in the Arctic. But by the time we got down the coast near the mine the weather was rough, with a heavy sea sending stormy breakers against the exposed coal bluff, rendering it impossible to land and work. And as there is no shelter whatever for a vessel anywhere in the vicinity, and no likelihood from any indications that the weather would improve, it was decided that we should proceed at once to Plover Bay, our next nearest coaling point.

This Arctic mine, the nearest to the North Pole, as far as I know, of any yet discovered on the American continent, produces coal of excellent quality in great abundance and easily worked. There are five principal veins, from two to ten feet thick, fully exposed on the face of a bluff about two hundred feet high, excepting some of the lower sections that are covered with icy snowbanks. The latter are derived from drift that comes from the wind-swept hills, and does not melt till late in the summer, or not at all. The lower exposed portions of all the veins are beaten and worn by the sea waves. There can scarcely be any doubt, from what I have seen of the formation in which it occurs, that this is a true carboniferous coal, and superior to the great bulk of the tertiary and cretaceous coal found on this side the continent farther south. The Corwin coaled here twice last summer, and again this summer, July 27th and 28th. So also did the steam whale-ship Belvedere. During calm weather the crew of the Corwin can dig out and put in sacks, and bring off in boats, about thirty tons per day.

On the twenty-first we passed through Bering Strait in a dense fog without sighting either of the Diomede Islands, which even in weather clear elsewhere are almost constantly enveloped in fog, causing no little anxiety to the navigator, inasmuch as they stand directly in the middle of the narrow part of the strait. A third islet called Fairway Rock, together with the uncertain flow of the currents hereabouts, renders the danger all the greater. The larger Diomede is about six miles long, the other half as large, and

Fairway Rock still smaller. All three are simply residual masses of granite brought into relief by glacial action before the strait was in existence. These rocks rise above the general level because of their superior strength considered with reference to the resistance they offered to glacial degradation.

Approaching the islands in thick weather, the first intimation the navigator has of his being near them, and of the direction in which they bear, is either from the winds which gurgle and reverberate in passing over them, or from the birds – auks, murres, and gulls – which dwell on the rocks in myriads, and come and go several miles into the adjacent waters to feed. To persons acquainted with their habits it is not difficult to determine whether their flight is directed homewards or away from home. Thus the natives who dwell on these gloomy, dripping rocks and visit the shores of the adjacent continents in their frail skin-covered canoes are directed. But how the birds themselves find their way, flying in arrow-like courses to their nests, when every direction seems to us the same, is truly marvellous.

On cloudy nights it is dark now at midnight. The sun sets before eight o'clock, but because it sinks only a few degrees below the horizon, the twilight lasts nearly all night. In a week or two, however, we shall have seven or eight hours of real night, for, of course, the transition from constant day to day and night is very rapid in these high latitudes. This new order of things will be delightful. A few days ago we saw two stars in the twilight, which to us was an exceedingly interesting event after two months of starless day. The glories of the midnight sun in this mysterious polar world are truly enchanting, but not nearly so much so as the glories of the midday sun in lower latitudes, succeeded by the glories of the night, the deep sky of stars and the grateful change and repose they bring.

After passing through the Strait we had two grey, howling days, with head winds. rain, and thick fog, through which the Corwin beat her way, or was held lying to, heaving and rolling somewhere between St. Lawrence Island and Indian Point, as near as could be made out at the time by dead reckoning, and guessing the speed of the northerly current. Lying to in a gale, enveloped in old fogs,* and with little sea-room, and variable currents, is anything but pleasant, to say nothing of the tedious discomforts caused by the movements of the vessel, the unceasing see-saw, creaking, pitching, and complaining. At such times only the gulls, those light-winged rovers of the sea, appear to be patient and comfortable as they gracefully drift and glide over the wild-tossing waves, or circle on easy wing about the ship, veering deftly from side to side, and wavering up and down through the grey, sleety gloom.

On the morning of the twenty-fourth, when the fog lifted, we found ourselves far north of our supposed position; the flow of the current to the northward during the two preceding days having been nearly eighty miles. We arrived here at five in the afternoon.

---

* Fogs that have lasted a long time and prevented the taking of observations for the position of the ship

Entering the harbour, we discovered the schooner Golden Fleece lying at anchor, and shortly afterward a party from her came aboard the Corwin, which proved to be Lieutenant Ray[1] and his company of Signal Service officers on their way to establish a station at Point Barrow – ten persons in all.[2] Mr. Ray seems to be the right man for the place. He hopes to be able to get his buildings up and everything put in order before the coming on of winter, making a home in that stern wilderness for three years.

Point Barrow is a low, barren spit putting out into the ice ocean, and, before the discovery of Wrangell Land, the northernmost point of the territory of the United States. For many years it was believed to be the northern extremity of the American continent. But the extreme point of the peninsula of Boothia proves to be a few miles farther north than this. At first sight it would seem a gloomy time to look forward to – three years in so remote and so severely desolate and forbidding a region, generally regarded as the topmost frost-killed end of creation!

But, amid all the disadvantages of position, these men have much in their lot for which they might well be envied by people dwelling in softer climates. There is the freshness of their field of research in natural history, the immense number of summer birds that visit this region to molt and rear their young; the fine opportunities they will have to study the habits of the reindeer on the tundras, and the magnificent polar bear among the ice – the master animal of the north. Then there is the chance to study the little-known western Eskimos, who have a village[3] on the point, numbering about two hundred persons.[4]

Advantage, too, I am told, will be taken of the opportunity offered to explore the Colville and Inland Rivers, both of them large streams, the one flowing into the [Arctic] Ocean about one hundred and thirty miles to the east of Point Barrow, the other into Bering Sea through Hotham Inlet and Kotzebue Sound. They are almost entirely unexplored. Some of their upper branches must approach each other, as the Eskimos ascend the Colville and, making a portage, descend the Inland River to Hotham Inlet every year to trade, or at the portage meet natives from the other river and trade there. The exploration of these rivers is a very interesting piece of work, and Mr. Ray tells me that he intends to make an effort to accomplish it at the earliest opportunity. Furthermore, he is ambitious to achieve something in the way of new discoveries out in the Polar Ocean to the northward of his station.

[1] P.H. Ray.

[2] This was the International Polar Expedition to Point Barrow, Alaska. The report of the valuable series of scientific observations and explorations made from 1881 to 1883 at the Point Barrow Station was published as House Executive Document No. 44, of the forty-eighth Congress. Among the members of the party were John Murdoch and Middleton Smith.

[3] Nuwuk.

[4] An admirable study of these Eskimos was, indeed, made by John Murdoch, a member of the party, and published in House Executive Document No. 44 (1885), and in the Ninth Annual Report of the Bureau of Ethnology(1892).

From the fact that a current sets northward past Herald Island, and keeps a long lane reaching far beyond Herald Island open every summer, while the ice remains jammed only a few miles off Point Barrow and Cape Yakan, Siberia, and some years does not leave the shores at all, it would seem that there is a land lying to the east of Wrangell Land, making a strait up which the northerly current flows, while the unknown land prevents any great movement in the ice immediately to the north of the American continent, as Wrangell Land [stays] the ice opposite Cape Yakán and the coast in its vicinity. Again, migratory birds in large flocks have been seen flying north from Point Barrow in the spring, and returning in the fall. Besides, certain vague reports, which may have their foundation in fact, have been in circulation to the effect that land in this direction has been actually seen by a whaler, who was well offshore to the northeastward from Point Barrow, in an exceptionally open season.

With the experience that he will gain among the ice at Point Barrow, and the resources at command in the way of good assistants, skilled native travellers, with good dogs and sleds, etc., Mr. Ray may possibly be able to cross over the ice to this land, if land there be. In any case, whatever journeys may be made, over the ice or over the land, in summer or in winter, some new facts will surely be gained well worth the pains, for no portion of the world is so barren as not to yield a rich and precious harvest of divine truth.

Nor will these men be likely to suffer greatly. The winter cold when skilfully met in soft hair and fur, is not hard to bear, while in summer it is so warm that the Eskimo children run about naked. The piling up of the ice on the shore in winter and spring must make a magnificent border for a home; and the auroral curtains and the deep starry nights, lasting for weeks, must be glorious.

The Corwin towed the Golden Fleece to sea this morning, and we hope to finish coaling, etc., in a day or two, and set out once more to the shores of Wrangell Land.

CHAPTER EIGHTEEN

A Siberian Reindeer Herd

STEAMER CORWIN, PLOVER BAY, SIBERIA, August 26th, 1881. This morning a party from the ship went to the head of the bay under the guidance of a pair of Chukchis to see a herd of reindeer that they told us was there. The distance, we found, is about eighteen miles from the lower harbour, where the Corwin is at anchor. The day was fine and we enjoyed the sail very much, skimming rapidly along in the steam launch over smooth water, past the huge ice-sculptured headlands and mountains that formed the walls, and the deep canyons and valleys between them that swept back to clusters of glacial fountains. The naturalist made desperate efforts now and then to obtain specimens of rare auks, petrels, ducks, etc., which were flying and swimming about us in great abundance, making lively pictures of happy, exuberant life.

The rocks bounding the bay, though beautiful in their combinations and collocations of curves and peaks, inflowing and touching delicately, and rising in bold, picturesque groups, are, nevertheless, intensely desolate-looking for want of trees, shrubs, or vegetation dense enough to give colour in telling quantities visible at a distance. Even the valleys opening back from the water here and there are mostly bare as seen at the distance of a mile or two, and have only faint tinges of green derived from dwarf willows, sedges, and heathworts that creep low among the stones. Yet here, in the larger valleys adjacent, where the main tributary glaciers came into the Plover Bay trunk, and in other valleys to the northeastward, large herds of reindeer, wild as well as tame, find sustenance, together with a few wild sheep and bears.

On the terminal moraine of the ancient glacier that formed the first main tributary of the Plover Bay glacier, some four miles from the extreme head of the bay, we noticed two small skin-covered huts, which our guides informed us belonged to the reindeer people we were seeking, and that we should certainly find them at home, because their herd was only a little one and found plenty of weeds and moss to eat in the valleys behind their huts without going far away, as the people had to do who owned big herds. At two days' distance, they said, where the valleys are wide and green, with plenty to eat, there is a big herd belonging to one of their friends, so big that they cover all the ground thereabouts; but the herd we were to see was only a little one, and the owner was not a rich man.

As we approached the shore, a hundred yards or so from the huts, a young man came running to meet us, bounding over the moraine boulders, with easy strength as if his limbs had been trained on the mountains for many a year, until running had become a pleasant indulgence. He was presently joined by three others, who gazed and smiled curiously at the steam launch and at our party, wondering suspiciously, when the interpreter had told our object, why we should come so far and seem so eager to see their deer. Our guides, who, of course, understood their prejudices and superstitions, told them that we wanted a big, fat deer to eat, and that we would pay them well for it – tobacco, lead, powder, caps, shot, calico, knives, etc., told off in tempting order. But they said they had none to sell, and it required half an hour of cautious negotiation to get them over their suspicious alarms, and [to induce them to] consent to sell the carcass of one, provided we would leave the skin, which they said they wanted to keep for winter garments.

Then two young men, fine, strapping, elastic fellows, threw off their upper parkas, tied their handsomely embroidered moccasins firmly across the instep and around the ankle, poised their long Russian spears, which they said they always carried in case they should meet a bear or wolf, and away they sped after the herd up a long, wide glacier valley along the bank of a stream, bounding lightly from rock to rock in easy poise, and across soft bits of tundra and rough sedgy meadows with long, heaving, undulating strides. Their gait, as far as we could see, was steadily maintained and was admirably lithe and strong and graceful. Their small feet and ankles and round tapered shanks showed to fine advantage in their tight-fitting leggings and moccasins as they went speeding over the ground like trained racers glorying in their strength. We watched them through field-glasses until they were about three miles away, during which time they did not appear to slacken their pace a single moment. They were gone about three hours, so that the herd must have been at least six or seven miles from the huts.

In the meantime we ate luncheon and strolled about the neighbourhood looking at the plants, at the views down the bay, and at the interior of the huts, etc. We chatted with the Chukchis about their herd, about the wild sheep on the mountains, the wild reindeer, bears, and wolves. We found that the family consisted of father, mother, a grown daughter, and the boys that were after the deer. The old folks were evidently contented and happy in their safe retreat among the hills, with a sure support from their precious herd. And they were proud of their red-cheeked girl and two strapping boys, as well they might be; for they seemed as healthy and rosy and robust a group of children as ever gladdened the heart of Chukchi parents. The boys appeared to be part owners of everything about the house, as well as of the deer, for in looking through the huts we saw a few curious odds and ends that we offered to purchase, but were told, in most cases, that they could not sell them until the boys came back.

Their huts are like all we have seen belonging to the Chukchis as far north and west as we have been – a balloon frame of long poles hewn on two sides so that they might be bent outward, the points coming together not in the middle, but a little to one side away from the direction of the prevailing wind, which gives them a curious hump-backed appearance. This frame is covered with skin of the walrus, if it can be had; if not, then with sealskin or deerskin. No great pains are taken to keep them rain-proof, so that in wet weather they are oftentimes damp or muddy. But there is not much rain in the Arctic regions, and the deerskin pologs, or drawing rooms inside, are kept perfectly dry and snug, whatever the state of the main outer tent may chance to be.

The two huts at this place are smaller and more leaky and dilapidated than is common. The covering is composed of different kinds of skin, perhaps a thousand pieces sewed together, some of them with the hair on, the whole appearing as one colossal patchwork, as if made up of small scraps. The head of the family seemed to be ? little ashamed of them, for he explained with the air of a man making an apology, that he did not construct them; they formerly belonged to some one else, and that soon after he came to take possession one of them was torn open by a hungry bear that went in and frightened his wife and daughter and stole some grease.

The Chukchis seem to be a good-natured, lively, chatty, brave, and polite people, fond of a joke, and, as far as I have seen, fair in their dealings as any people, savage or civilized. They are not savage by any means, however, but steady, industrious workers, looking well ahead, providing for the future, and consequently seldom in want, save when at long intervals disease or other calamities overtake their herds, or exceptionally severe seasons prevent their obtaining the ordinary supplies of seals, fish, whales, walruses, bears, etc., on which the sedentary Chukchis chiefly depend. The sedentary and reindeer Chukchis are the same people, and are said to differ in a marked degree, both in physical characteristics and in language, from the neighbouring tribes, as they certainly do from the Eskimos. Many of them have light complexions, hooked or aquiline noses, tall, sinewy, well-knit frames, small feet and hands, and are not, especially the men, so thick-set, short-necked, or flat-faced as the Eskimos.

After we had watched impatiently for some time, the reindeer came in sight, about a hundred and fifty of them, driven gently without any of that noisy shouting and worrying that are heard in driving the domestic animals in civilized countries. We left the huts and went up the stream bank about three quarters of a mile to meet them, led by the owner and his wife and daughter, who carried a knife and tin cup and vessels to save the blood and the entrails – which stirred a train of grim associations that greatly marred the beauty of the picture.

I was afraid from what I knew of the habits of sheep, cattle, and horses that a sight of strangers would stampede the herd when we met. But of this, as it proved, there was not the slightest danger; for of all the familiar, tame animals man has gathered about him, the reindeer is the tamest. They can hardly be said to be domesticated, since they are not shut in around the huts, or put under shelter either winter or summer. On they came, while we gazed eagerly at the novel sight – a thicket of antlers, big and little, old and young, led by the strongest, holding their heads low most of the time, as if conscious of the fact that they were carrying very big, branching horns. A straggler fell behind now and then to cull a choice mouthful of willow or dainty, grey lichen, then made haste to join the herd again.

They waded across the creek and came straight toward us, up the sloping bank where we were waiting, nearer, nearer, until we could see their eyes, their smooth, round limbs, the velvct on their horns, until within five or six yards of us, the drivers saying scarce a word, and the owner in front looking at them as they came up without making any call or movement to attract them. After giving us the benefit of their magnificent eyes and sweet breath they began to feed off, back up the valley. Thereupon the boys, who had been loitering on the stream-side to catch a salmon trout or two, went round them and drove them back to us. Then the deer stopped feeding and began to chew the cud and to lie down, with eyes partly closed and dreamy-looking, as if profoundly comfortable, we strangers causing them not the slightest alarm though standing nearly within touching distance of them. Cows in a barnyard, milked and petted every day, are not so gentle. Yet these beautiful animals are allowed to feed at will, without herding to any great extent. They seem as smooth and clean and glossy as if they were wild. Taming does not seem to have injured them in any way. I saw no mark of man upon them.

They are not so large as I had been led to suppose, nor so rough and bony and angular. The largest would not much exceed three or four hundred pounds in weight. They are, at this time of year, smooth, trim, delicately moulded animals, very fat, and apparently short-winded, for they were breathing hard when they came up, like oxen that had been working on a hot day. The horns of the largest males are about four feet long, rising with a backward curve, and then forward, and dividing into three or four points, and with a number of short palmated branches putting forward and downward from the base over the animal's forehead. Those of the female are very slender and elegant in curve, more so than any horns I have seen. This species of deer is said to be the only one in which the female has horns. The fawns, also, have horns already, six inches to a foot long, with a few blunt, knobby branches beginning to sprout. All are now in the velvet, some of which is beginning to peel off and hang in loose shreds about the heads of some of them, producing a very singular appearance, as if they had been fighting a rag-bag.

The so-called velvet is a close, soft, downy fur, black in colour, and very fine and silky, about three eighths or half an inch long, with a few hairs nearly an inch in length rising stiffly here and there over the general plushy surface. All the branches of their horns are covered, giving an exceedingly rich and beautiful effect. The eyes are large, and in expression confiding and gentle. The head, contrary to my preconceived notions derived from engravings, is, on the whole, delicately formed, the muzzle long and straight, blunt and cowlike. The neck is thin, tapering but little, rather deep, and held, while standing at ease, sloping down a little, and the large males have long hair on the under side. The body is round, almost cylindrical – the belly not at all bloated or bent out like that of a cow. The legs are stout, but not clumsy, and taper finely into the muscles of the shoulders and hips. The feet are very broad and spreading, making a track about as large as a cow's. This enables the animal to walk over boggy tundras in summer and over snow in winter.

In colour they vary almost as much in some specimens as do cattle and horses, showing white, brown, black, and grey at the same time. The prevailing colour is nearly black in summer, brownish-white in winter. The colours of the tame animals are not so constant as those of the wild. The hair is, when full grown, very heavy, with fine wool at the bottom, thus making a warm covering sufficient to enable the animal to resist the keenest frosts of the Arctic winter without any shelter beyond the lee side of a rock or hill.

After walking through the midst of the herd, the boys selected a rather small specimen to be killed. One caught it by the hind leg, just as sheep are caught, and dragged it backward out of the herd; then the other boy took it by the horns and led it away a few yards from the herd, no notice being taken of its struggles by its companions, nor was any tendency to take fright observed, such as would, under the circumstances, have been shown by any of the common domestic animals. The mother alone looked after it eagerly, and further manifested her concern and affection by uttering a low, grunting sound, and by trying to follow it.

After it was slain they laid it on its side. One of the women brought forward a branch of willow about a foot long, with the green leaves on it, and put it under the animal's head. Then she threw four or five handfuls of the blood, from the knife wound back of the shoulder, out over the ground to the southward, making me get out of the way, as if this direction were the only proper one. Next she took a cupful of water and poured a little on its mouth and tail and on the wound. While this ceremony was being performed all the family looked serious, but as soon as it was over they began to laugh and chat as before. The herd, during the time of the killing and dressing, were tranquilly chewing their cud, not noticing even the smell of the blood, which makes cattle so frantic.

One of our party was anxious to procure a young one alive to take home with him, but they would not sell one alive at any price. When we inquired the reason they said that if they should part with one, all the rest of the herd would die, and the same thing would happen if they were to part with the head of one. This they excitedly declared was true, for they had seen it proved many times though white men did not understand it and always laughed about it. When we indicated a very large buck and inquired why they did not kill that big one, and let the little ones grow, they replied that that big fellow was strong, and knew how to pull a sled, and could run fast over the snow that would come by-and-by, and they needed him too much to kill him.

I have never before seen half so interesting a company of tame animals. In some parts of Siberia reindeer herds numbering many thousands may be seen together. In these frozen regions they supply every want of their owners as no other animal could possibly do – food, warm clothing, coverings for their tents, bedding, rapid transportation, and, to some extent, fuel. They are not nearly so numerous in the immediate vicinity of the bay as they once were, a fact attributed to the sale of several live specimens to whalers.

CHAPTER NINETEEN

Turned Back by Storms and Ice

STEAMER CORWIN, ARCTIC OCEAN, BETWEEN HERALD SHOALS AND POINT HOPE, September 3rd, 1881. On the morning of August 27th, having taken on board a full supply of coal and water, and put the ship in as good condition as possible, we left Plover Bay and turned once more toward Wrangell Land.

In passing Marcus Bay, a short distance up the coast from Plover Bay, the Captain wished to make a landing to give some instructions to our Chukchi interpreter and dog-driver, who lives here, concerning the dogs and sleds that were left at Tapkan. The weather was too thick, however, to allow this, and the ship was put on her course for the western Diomede Island, where we arrived against a stiff head wind and through thick fog, shortly after noon on the twenty-eighth. We lay at anchor for a few hours, while the wind from the Arctic came dashing and swirling over the island in squally gusts.

In the meantime, while waiting to see whether the wind would moderate before we proceeded through the strait, we went ashore and greatly enjoyed a stroll through the streets and house of the curious village here. It is built on the bald, rugged side of the island, where the slope is almost cliff-like in steepness and rockiness. The winter houses are wood-lined burrows underground, entered by a tunnel, and warm and snug like the nest of a field mouse beneath a sod, though terribly thick and rancid as to the air contained in them. The summer houses are square skin boxes above ground, and set on long stilt poles. Neither the one nor the other look in the least like houses or huts of any sort. But those made of skin are the queerest human nests conceivable. They are simply light, square frames made of drift poles gathered on the beach, and covered with walrus hide that has been carefully dressed and stretched tightly on the frame like the head of a drum. The skin is of a yellow colour, and quite translucent, so that when in one feels as if one were inside a huge blown bladder, the light sifting in through the skin at the top and all around, yellow as a sunset. The entire establishment is window, one pane for the roof, which is also the ceiling, and one for each of the four sides, without cross sash-bars to mar the brave simplicity of it all.

Most of the inhabitants, of whom there are perhaps a hundred, had just returned from a long voyage in their canoes to Cape Prince of Wales, Kotzebue Sound, and other points on the American coast, for purposes of trade, bringing back ivory and furs to sell to the Chukchis of Siberia, who in turn will carry these articles by a roundabout way nearly a thousand miles to the Russian trading post, and return with goods to trade back to the Diomede merchants, through whose hands they will pass to the Cape Prince of Wales natives, and from these to several others up the Inland River, down the Colville, to Point Barrow and eastward as far as the mouth of the Mackenzie River.

The Diomede merchants are true middlemen, and their village a half-way house of commerce between northeastern Asia and America. The extent of the dealings of these people, usually regarded as savages, is truly surprising. And that they can keep warm and make a living on this bleak, fog-smothered, storm-beaten rock, and have time to beget, feed, and train children, and give them a good Eskimo education; that they teach them to shoot the bow, to make and throw the bird spears, to make and use those marvellous kayaks, to kill seals, bears, and walrus, to hunt the whale, capture the different kinds of fishes, manufacture different sorts of leather, dress skins and make them into clothing, besides teaching them to carry on trade, to make fire by rubbing two pieces of wood together, and to build the strange houses – that they can do all this, and still have time to be sociable, to dance, sing, gossip, and discuss ghosts, spirits, and all the nerve-racking marvels of the shaman world, shows how truly wild, and brave, and capable a people these island Eskimos are.

The wind having moderated, we got away from the box-and-burrow village and through the Strait before dark; then we steered for the south end of Wrangell Land, and after a speedy and uneventful voyage came in sight of the highest of the coast mountains, on the thirtieth at noon. Thus far we had not seen the ice, and, inasmuch as nineteen summer days had passed over it since our last visit, we hoped that it might have been melted considerably and broken up by the winds, so as to admit of a way being forced through it at some point up to the land, or so near it that we might get ashore by crossing over the coast ice, dragging our light skin boat after us in case we should come to lanes of open water.

In this, however, we were disappointed; for when three and a half hours later we came up to the edge of the pack it was found to all appearances unchanged. It still extended about twenty miles offshore; it trended as far as we could see in the same direction as was observed before, and it seemed as heavy and unbroken as ever, offering no encouragement for efforts in this direction. We therefore sailed along the edge of the pack to the eastward to see what might be accomplished towards our first landing place. We gazed at the long stretch of wilderness which spread invitingly before us, and which we were so eager to explore – the rounded, glaciated bosses and foothills, the mountains, with their ice-sculptured features of hollows and ridges and long withdrawing valleys, which in former visits we had sketched, and scanned so attentively through field-glasses, and which now began to wear a familiar look. The sky was overcast, the land seemed almost black in the gloomy light, and a heavy swell began to be felt coming in from the northeast. Towards night, when we were not far from our old landing near the easternmost extremity of the land, the Corwin was hove to, waiting for the morning before attempting to seek a way in. But the next day, August 31st, was stormy. The wind from the northeast blew hard inshore, therefore it was not considered safe to approach too near.

At eight o'clock we were in sight of the ice opposite the northeast cape, and it seemed to be farther off the land than at our first visit, and no opening appeared, though the weather was so dim and rough that nothing could be definitely determined. Generally, however, the ice was now drifting against the east side of Wrangell Land, and coming southward to so great an extent that our chances of effecting another landing began to be less promising.

When we were within twenty miles of Herald Island we hove to, waiting better weather before entering narrow lanes and bays in the pack when so heavy a sea was running. The sky was dismal all the afternoon – toward night, dull, lurid purple – and the wind was blowing a gale. The ice-breaker, made of heavy boiler iron, was broken by the pounding of the waves, and had to be cut away, which is unfortunate at this particular time.

September 1st was a howling storm-day, through which we lay to, swashing and rolling wildly among white waves, and drifting southeastward twenty or thirty miles a day. The next day there was no abatement in the force of the gale up to two o'clock in the afternoon. A heavy sea, streaked with foam, was running parallel to the direction of the wind, while the air was filled with snow, adding to the wintry aspect of the day. While we were still holding on, hoping the storm would subside from hour to hour, one of the rudder chains parted.

This made Captain Hooper decide that in view of the condition of the ship, and the ice, and the weather, the risk attending further efforts this year to search the shores of Wrangell Land should not be incurred, more especially since the position and drift of the ice held out but little promise of allowing another landing to be made, or of a sufficiently near approach to enable us to add appreciably to the knowledge already acquired. Accordingly, after the rudder was mended as securely as possible, the good Corwin, excused from further ice duty, was turned away from the war and headed for the American coast at Point Hope.

Had the ship been in good condition, the battle would probably have been waged a few more weeks along the edge of the ice barrier, watching the appearance of any vulnerable point of attack, whatever the result might have been. Now it seems we are homeward bound. We intend to stop at Kotzebue Sound, St. Michael, St. Paul, and Unalaska to make necessary repairs, take on coal, etc., and we may reach San Francisco by the middle of October.

We have not met the Rodgers. We learned from the natives at Plover Bay that she had called there and left seven days before our arrival. That was August 17th. We suppose she went to St. Michael from there to coal and take on provisions, which would probably require a week. If so, we may have passed the Strait ahead of her. But in case she had already been at St. Michael, then, in following out her instructions, she could trace the Siberian coast for some distance, making inquiries among the Chukchis, where she may possibly be at present. Or, if this part of the work of the expedition had been completed before the coming on of the gale, she may be sheltering about Herald Island or some point on the coast of Wrangell Land.*

CHAPTER TWENTY

Homeward Bound

STEAMER CORWIN, UNALASKA, October 4th, 1881. On the home voyage, all the hard Arctic work done, the Corwin stopped a week at the head of Kotzebue Sound, near Chamisso Island, to seek a fresh supply of water and make some needful repairs and observations, during which time I had a capital opportunity to examine the curious and interesting ice formations of the shores of Eschscholtz Bay. I found ice in some form or other, exposed at intervals of from a mile to a few yards, on the tide-washed front of the shore bluffs on both sides of the bay, a distance of about fifty miles. But it is only the most conspicuous mass, forming a bluff, at Elephant Point, on the south side of the bay, that seems to have been observed hitherto, or attracted much attention.

This Elephant Point, so called from the fossil elephant tusks found here, is a bluff of solid ice, one hundred and forty feet high, covered on the top

---

* Muir's supposition proved to be correct. The U.S.S. Rodgers, Lieutenant R. M. Berry commanding, reached Wrangell Land, August 25th, and found shelter the next day in a snug little harbour on the southeastern coast of the island. There the Rodgers remained until September 13th, while two search parties explored the shores of the island for traces of the Jeannette expedition.

with a foot or two of ordinary tundra vegetation, and with tall grass on the terraces and shelving portions of the front, wherever the slope is sufficiently gentle for soil to find rest. It is a rigid fossil fragment of a glacier leaning back against the north side of a hill, mostly in shadow, and covered lightly with glacial detritus from the hill slope above it, over which the tundra vegetation has gradually been extended, and which eventually formed a thick felt-like protection against waste during the summer. Thus it has lasted until now, wasting only on the exposed face fronting the bay, which is being constantly undermined, the soil and vegetation on top being precipitated over the raw, melting ice front and washed away by the tide. Were it not that its base is swept by tide currents, the accumulation of tundra moss and peat would finally re-bury the front and check further waste. As it is, the formation will not last much longer – probably not more than a thousand or fifteen hundred years. Its present age is perhaps more than this.

When one walks along the base of the formation – which is about a mile or so in length – making one's way over piles of rotten humus and through sloppy bog mud of the consistence of watery porridge, mixed with bones of elephants, buffaloes, musk oxen etc., the ice so closely resembles the wasting snout of a glacier with its jagged projecting ridges, ledges, and small, dripping, tinkling rills, that it is not easy to realise that it is not one in ordinary action.

Mingled with the true glacier ice we notice masses of dirty stratified ice, made up of clean layers alternating with layers of mud and sand, and mingled with bits of humus and sphagnum, and of leaves and stems of the various plants that grow on the tundra above. This dirty ice of peculiar stratification never blends into the glacier ice, but is simply frozen upon it, filling cavities or spreading over slopes here and there. It is formed by the freezing of films of clear and dirty water from the broken edge of the tundra, a process going on every spring and autumn, when frosts and thaws succeed each other night and morning, cloudy days and sunny days. This, of course, is of comparatively recent age, even the oldest of it.

A striking result of the shaking up and airing and draining of the tundra soil is seen on the face of the ice slopes and terraces. When the undermined tundra material rolls down upon those portions of the ice front where it can come to rest, it is well buffeted and shaken, and frequently lies upside down as if turned with a plough. Here it is well drained through resting on melting ice, and though not more than a foot or two in thickness, it produces a remarkably close and tall growth of grass, four to six feet high, and as lush and broad-leaved as may be found in any farmer's field. Cut for hay it would make about four or five tons per acre.

Only a few other plants that would be called weeds are found growing among the grass, mostly senecio and artemisia, both tall and exuberant, showing the effects of this curious system of cultivation on this strange soil. The vegetation on top of the bluff is the most beautiful that I have yet seen, not rank and cultivated looking like that on the face slopes, but showing the finest and most delicate beauty of wildness, in forms, combinations, and colours of leaf, stalk, and fruit. There were red and yellow dwarf birch, arbutus, willow, and purple huckleberry, with lovely greys of sedges and lichens. The neutral tints of the lichens are intensely beautiful.

I found the shore-bluff towards the mouth of the Buckland River from forty to sixty feet high, with a regular slope of about thirty degrees. It was covered with willows and alders, some of them five or six feet high, and long grass; also patches of ice here and there, but no large masses. The soil is a fine blue clay at bottom, with water-worn quartz, pebbles and sand above it, like that of the opposite side of the estuary, and evidently brought down by the river floods when the ice of the glaciers that occupied this river basin and that of the Kuuk* was melting.

The ice that I found here and on the opposite side of the bay, especially where the tundra is low and flat, let us say forty or fifty feet above the sea, and covered with pools and strips of water, is not glacier ice, but ice derived from water freezing in pools and veins and hollows, overgrown with mosses, lichens, etc., and afterwards exposed as fossil ice on the shore face of the tundra where it is being wasted by the action of the sea. The tundra has been cracked in every direction, and in looking over its surface, slight depressions, or some difference in the vegetation, indicate the location and extent of the fissures. When these are traced forward to the edge of the shore-bluff, a cross-section of ice is seen from two to four or five feet wide. The larger sections are simply the exposed sides of those ice veins that chance to trend in a direction parallel to the face of the bluff. Besides these I found several other kinds of ice, differing in origin from the foregoing, but which can hardly be described in a mere letter, however interesting to the geologist.

At St. Michael we found a party of wrecked prospectors from Golofnin Bay, who were anxiously awaiting the arrival of the Corwin, as she would be the last vessel leaving for California this year. This proved to be the Oakland party mentioned in a previous letter. With genuine Yankee enterprise [these men] had pushed their way into the far wilderness beyond the Yukon to seek for silver. Specimens of bright, exciting ore, assaying a hundred and fifty dollars to the ton, had been exhibited in Oakland, brought from a mine said to be located near tide water at Golofnin Bay, Alaska, and so easily worked that large ships could be loaded with the precious ore about as readily as with common ballast. Thereupon a company, called the Alaska Mining Company, was organised, the schooner W. F. March chartered, and with the necessary supplies a party of ten sailed from San Francisco on May 5th, 1881, for Golofnin Bay, to explore this mine in particular, and the region in general, and then to return, this fall, with a cargo of ore.

They arrived in Golofnin Bay on June 18th, lost their vessel in a gale on the north side of the bay on August 15th, and arrived in twenty one days at St. Michael in canoes and a boat that was saved from the wreck. They found the mine as rich as represented, but far less accessible. It is said to be

* A river tributary to Eschscholtz Bay from the east. It was called Kuuk on British Admiralty charts of the early eighties, but is now known as the Mungoark River.

about thirty miles from tide water. All feel confident that they have a valuable mine. Two or three of the party were away at the time of the disaster, prospecting for cinnabar on the Kuskoquim, and are left behind to pass the winter as best they may at some of the trading stations.

Our two weeks' stay at Unalaska has been pleasant and restful after the long cruise – about fourteen thousand miles altogether up to this point. The hill slopes and mountains look richly green and foodful, and the views about the harbour, at the close and beginning of storms, when clouds are wreathing the alpine summits, are very beautiful.

The huts of the Aleuts here are very picturesque at this time of the year. The grass grows tall over the sides and the roof, waving in the wind, and making a fine fringe about the windows and the door. When the church bell rings on Sunday and the good calico-covered people plod sedately forth to worship, and the cows on the hillside moo blandly, and the sun shines over the green slopes, then the scene is like a bit of New England or old Scotland. But later in the day, when the fiery kvass is drunk, and the accordians and concertinas and cheap music boxes are in full blast, then the noise and unseemly clang attending drunkenness is not at all like a Scotch sabbath.

Most of the Aleuts have an admixture of Russian blood. Many of them dance well. Three balls were given during our stay here, that is to say, American balls with native women. The Aleuts have their own dances in their small huts.

A few days ago I made an excursion to the top of a well-formed volcanic cone at the mouth of a picturesque glacial fiord, about eight miles from here. This mountain, about two thousand feet high, commands a magnificent view of the mountains of Unalaska, Akutan, and adjacent islands. Akutan* still emits black smoke and cinders at times, and thunders loud enough to be heard at Unalaska.

The noblest of them all was Makushin, about nine thousand feet high and laden with glaciers, a grand sight, far surpassing what I had been led to expect. There is a spot on its summit which is said to smoke, probably mostly steam and vapour from the infiltration of water into the heated cavities of the old volcano. The extreme summit of Makushin was wrapped in white clouds, and from beneath these the glaciers were seen descending impressively into the sunshine to within a thousand or fifteen hundred feet of sea-level. This fine mountain, glittering in its showy mail of snow and ice, together with a hundred other peaks dipping into the blue sky, and every one of them telling the work of ice or fire in their forms and sculpture – these, and the sparkling sea, and long inreaching fiords, are a noble picture to add to the thousand others which have enriched our lives this summer in the great Northland.

---

* The highest mountain of Akutan Island. The United States Coast and Geodetic survey Chart No. 8860 gives its altitude as forty-one hundred feet.

APPENDIX I

The Glaciation of the Arctic and Sub-Arctic Regions Visited During the Cruise

The monuments of the glaciation of the regions about Bering Sea and the northern shores of Siberia and Alaska are in general much broken and obscured on account of the intensity of the action of the agents of destruction in these low, moist regions, together with the perishable character of the rocks of which most of the monuments consist. Lofty headlands, once covered with clear glacial inscriptions, have been undermined and cast down in loose, draggled taluses, while others, in a dim, ruinous condition, with most of their surface records effaced, are rapidly giving way to the weather. The moraines, also, and the grooved, scratched, and polished surfaces are much blurred and wasted, while glaciated areas of great extent are not open to observation at all, being covered by the shallow waters of Bering Sea and the Arctic Ocean, and buried beneath sediments and coarse detritus which has been weathered from the higher grounds, or deposited by the ice itself when it was being melted and withdrawn towards the close of the main glacial period. But amid this general waste and obscurity a few legible fragments, favourably situated here and there, have escaped destruction – patches of polished and striated surfaces in a fair state of preservation, with moraines of local glaciers that have not been exposed to the heavier forms of water or avalanche action. And had these fading vestiges perished altogether, yet would not the observer be left without a sure guide, for there are other monuments of ice action in all glaciated regions that are almost indestructible, enduring for tens of thousands of years after those simpler traces that we have been considering have vanished. These are the material of moraines, though scattered, washed, crumbled, and reformed over and over again; and the sculpture and configuration of the landscape in general, canyons, valleys, mountains, ridges, *roches moutonnées* with forms and correlations specifically glacial. These, also, it is true, suffer incessant waste, being constantly written upon by other agents; yet, because the glacial characters are formed on so colossal a scale of magnitude, they continue to stand out free and clear through every after inscription whether of the torrent, the avalanche, or universal eroding atmosphere; opening grand and comprehensive views of the vanished ice, and the geographical and topographical changes effected by its action in the form of local and distinct glaciers. River-like, they flowed from the mountains to the sea, and, as a broad, undulating mantle, crawled over all the landscape through unnumbered centuries; crushed and ground and spread soil-beds; fashioned the features of mountain and plain; extended the domain of the sea; separated continents; dotted new coasts with islands, fringed them with deep inreaching fiords, and impressed their peculiar style of sculpture on all the regions over which they passed.

A general exploration of the mountain ranges of the Pacific Coast shows that there are about sixty-five small residual glaciers on the Sierra Nevada of California, between latitude 36° 30' and 39°, distributed singly or in small groups on the north sides of the highest peak at an elevation of about eleven to twelve thousand feet above the level of the sea, representatives of the grand glaciers that once covered all the range. More than two thirds of these lie between latitude 37° and 38°, and form the highest sources of the San Joaquin, Tuolumne, Merced, and Owens Rivers.

Mount Shasta, near the northern boundary of California, has a few shrinking glacier remnants, the largest about three miles in length. We find that, to the north of California, groups of active glaciers still exist on all the highest mountains – Mounts Jefferson, Adams, Saint Helens, Hood, Rainier, Baker, and others. Of these Mount Rainier is the highest and iciest. Its summit is fairly capped with ice, and eight glaciers, from seven to fifteen miles long, radiate from it as a centre and form the sources of the principal streams. The lowest descends to about thirty-five hundred feet above sea level, pouring a stream opaque with glacial mud into the head of Puget Sound.

On through British Columbia and southeastern Alaska the broad sustained mountain chain extending along the coast is generally glacier bearing. The upper branches of nearly every one of the main canyons are occupied by glaciers, which gradually increase in size and descend lower until the lofty region between Mount Fairweather and Mount St. Elias is reached, where a considerable number discharge into the waters of the ocean.

This is the region of greatest glacial abundance on the continent. To the northward from here the glaciers gradually diminish in size and depth and melt at higher levels until the latitude of about 62° is reached, beyond which few, if any, glaciers remain in existence, the ground being comparatively low and the annual snowfall light.

Between latitude 56° and 60° there are probably more than five thousand glaciers, great and small, hundreds of the largest size, descending through the forests nearly to the level of the sea, though, as far as I know after a pretty thorough exploration of the region, not more than twenty-five discharge into the sea.

All the long, high-walled fiords into which these great glaciers of the first class flow are of course crowded with icebergs of every conceivable form, which are detached at intervals of a few minutes. But these are small as compared with those of Greenland, and only a few escape from the intricate labyrinth of channels, with which this portion of the coast is fringed, into the open sea. Nearly all of them are washed and drifted back and forth in the fiords by wind and tide until finally melted by sunshine and the copious warm rains of summer.

The southmost of the glaciers that reach the sea occupies a narrow fiord about twenty, miles to the northwest of the mouth of the Stikine River, in latitude 56°

50'. It is called "Hutli"[1] by the natives, from the noise made by the icebergs in rising and falling from the inflowing glacier. About one degree farther north there are four of these complete glaciers at the heads of branches of Holkham Bay, at the head of Taku Inlet one, and at the head and around the sides of a bay[2] trending in a general northerly direction from Cross Sound, first explored by myself in 1879, there are no less than five of these complete glaciers reaching tide-water, the largest of which, the Muir, is of colossal size, having upwards of two hundred tributaries and a width of trunk below the confluence of the main tributaries of three to twenty-five miles. Between the west side of this icy bay and the ocean all the ground, high and low, with the exception of the summits of the mountain peaks, is covered by a mantle of ice from one to three thousand feet thick, which discharges to the east and west through many distinct mouths.

This ice-sheet, together with the multitude of distinct glaciers that load the lofty mountains of the coast, evidently once formed part of one grand, continuous ice-sheet that flowed over all the region hereabouts, extending southward as far as the Straits of Juan de Fuca, for all the islands of the Alexander Archipelago, great and small, as well as the headlands and promontories of the mainland, are seen to have forms of greatest strength with reference to the action of a vast press of oversweeping ice, and their surfaces have a smooth, rounded, over-rubbed appearance, generally free from angles. The canals, channels, straits, passages, sounds, etc., between the islands – a marvellous labyrinth – manifest in their forms and trends and general characteristics the same subordination to the grinding action of a continuous ice-sheet, and they differ from the islands, as to their origin, only in being portions of the general pre-glacial margin of the continent, more deeply eroded, and, therefore, covered with the ocean waters, which flowed into them as the ice was melted out of them.

That the dominion of the sea is being extended over the land by the wearing away of its shores is well known. But in these northern regions the coast rocks have been so short a time exposed to wave-action that they are about little wasted as yet, the extension of the sea affected by its own action in post-glacial time in this region being probably less than the millionth part of that affected by glacial action during the last glacial period.

Traces of the ancient glaciers made during the period of greater extension abound on the California Sierra as far south as latitude 36°. Even the most evanescent of them, the polished surfaces, are still found, in a marvellously perfect state of preservation, on the upper half of the middle portion of the range. They occur in irregular patches, some of which are several acres in extent, and, though they have been subjected to the weather with all its storms for thousands of years, their mechanical excellence is such that they reflect the sunbeams like glass, and attract the attention of every observer.

---

[1] Now known as Le Conte Glacier; also the Bay into which it discharges. Both were named in 1887 by Lieutenant-Commander Charles M. Thomas, U.S.N., presumably in the honour of Joseph Le Conte, the well-known California geologist. "Hutli" is the Tlingit Indian name for the mythical bird that produces thunder by flapping its wings. The word therefore means "The Thunderer."

[2] Now known as Glacier Bay.

The most perfect of these shining pavements lie at an elevation of about seven to eight thousand feet above the level of the sea, where the rock is close-grained, siliceous granite. Small fading patches may be found at from three to five thousand feet elevation on the driest and most enduring portions of vertical walls, where there is protection from the drip and friction of water; also, on compact swelling bosses partially protected by a covering of boulders.

On the north half of the Sierra the striated and polished surfaces are rarely found, not only because this portion of the chain is lower, but on account of the surface rocks being chiefly porous lavas subject to rapid waste. The moraines, also, though well preserved on the south half of the range, seem to be nearly wanting over a considerable portion of the north half, but the material of which they were composed is found in abundance, scattered and disintegrated, until its glacial origin is not obvious to the unskilled observer.

A similar blurred condition of the superficial records obtains throughout most of Oregon, Washington, British Columbia, and Alaska, due in great part to the action of excessive moisture. Even in southeastern Alaska, where the most extensive glaciers still exist, the more evanescent of the traces of their former greater extension, though comparatively recent, are more obscure than those of the ancient glaciers of California, where the climate is drier and the rocks more resisting. We are prepared, therefore, to find the finer lines of the glacial record dim or obliterated altogether in the Arctic regions, where the ground is mostly low and the action of frost and moisture specially destructive.

The Aleutian chain of islands sweeps westward in a regular curse, about a thousand miles long, from the Alaska Peninsula toward Kamchatka, nearly uniting the American and Asiatic continents. A very short geological time ago, just before the coming on of the glacial winter, the union of the two continents was probably complete. The entire chain appears to be simply a degraded portion of the North Pacific pre-glacial coast mountains, with its foot-hills and lowest portions of the connecting ridges between the peaks a few feet under water, the submerged ridges forming the passes between the islands as they exist today, while the broad plain to the north of the chain is now covered by the shallow waters of Bering Sea.

Now the evidence seems everywhere complete that this segregating degradation has been effected almost wholly by glacial action. Yet, strange to say, it is held by most observers who have made brief visits to different portions of the chain that each island is a distinct volcanic upheaval, but little changed since the period of emergence from the sea, an impression made no doubt by the volcanic character of most of the rocks, ancient and recent, of which they are composed, and by the many extinct or feebly active volcanoes occurring here and there along the summits of the highest masses. But, on the contrary, all the evidence we have seen goes to show that the amount of glacial denudation these rocks have undergone is very great, so great that, with the exception of the recent craters, almost every existing feature is distinctly glacial. The comparatively featureless pre-glacial rocks have been heavily sculptured and fashioned into the endless variety they now present of peak and ridge, valley and fiord and clustering islets, harmoniously correlated in accordance with glacial law.

On Mount Makushin,* whose summit reaches an elevation of about nine thousand feet above the sea, several small glaciers still exist, while others yet smaller may be hidden in the basins of other mountains not yet explored. The summit of Makushin, at the time my observations were made, was capped with heavy clouds, and from beneath these the glaciers were seen descending imposingly into the open sunshine to within a thousand or fifteen hundred feet of the sea level, the largest perhaps about six miles in length. After the clouds cleared away the summit was seen to be heavily capped with ice, leaving only the crumbling edges of the dividing ridges and subordinate peaks free. The lower slopes of the mountain and the wide valleys proceeding from the glaciers present testimony of every kind to show that these glaciers now lingering on the summit once flowed directly into the sea. The adjacent mountains, though now mostly free from ice, are covered with glacial markings, extending over all the low grounds about their bases and the shores of the fiords, and over many of the rocks now under water. But besides this evidence of recent local glacial abundance, we find traces of far grander glacial conditions on the heavily abraded rocks along the shores of the passes separating the islands, and also in the low wide valleys extending in a direction parallel with the passes across the islands, indicating the movement of a vast ice-sheet from the north over the ground now covered by Bering Sea.

The amount of degradation this island region has undergone is only partially manifested by the crumbling, sharpened condition of the ridges and peaks, the abraded surfaces that have been overswept, and by the extent of the valleys and fiords, and the gaps between the mountains and islands.

That these valleys, fiords, forges, and gaps, great and small, like those of the Sierra, are not a result of local subsidences and upheavals, but of the removal of the material that once filled them, is shown by the broken condition and the similarity of the physical structure and composition of their contiguous sides, just as the correspondence between the tiers of masonry on either side of a broken gap in a wall shows that the missing blocks required to fill it up have been removed.

The chief agents of erosion and transportation are water and ice, each being regarded as the more influential by different observers, though the phenomena to which they give rise are widely different. All geologists recognise the fact that glaciers wear away the rocks over which they move, but great vagueness prevails as to the size of the fragments of erosion, and the way they are detached and removed; and if possible still greater vagueness prevails as to the forms and characteristic in general of the mountains, hills, rocks, valleys, etc., resulting from this erosion.

Towards the end of summer, when the snow is melted from the lower portions of the glaciers, particles of dust and sand may be seen scattered over their surfaces, together with angular masses of rocks, derived from the shattered storm-beaten cliffs above their fountains. The separation of these masses, which vary greatly in size, is due only in part to the action of the glacier, though they are all

* Muir probably adopted current estimates of the altitude of this volcano. Gannett's Altitudes in Alaska (1900) gives the elevation as 5474 feet, and the United States Coast and Geodetic Survey Map, No. 8860 (1916), as 5691 feet.

transported on its surface like floating drift on a river, and deposited together in moraines. The winds supply a portion of the sand and dust, some of the larger fragments are set free by the action of frost, rains, and general weathering agents, considerable quantities are swept down in avalanches of snow where the inclination of the slopes is favourable to their action, and shaken down by earthquake shocks, while the glacier itself plays an important part in the production of these superficial effects by undermining the cliffs from whence the fragments fall.

But in all moraines boulders and small dust particles may be recognised that have not been thus derived from the weathered cliffs and dividing ridges projecting above the glaciers, but from the rocks past which and over which the glaciers flow. The streams which drain glaciers are always turbid with finely ground mud particles worn off the bed-rocks by a sliding motion, accompanied by great pressure, giving rise to polished surfaces, and keeping up a waste that never for a moment ceases while the glacier exists; and besides these small particles boulders are found that may be traced to their origin in the bottoms or sides of the channels. Accordingly, an abrupt transition is discovered from the polished and plain portions of the channels to the more or less angular and fractured portions, showing that glaciers degrade the rocks over which they pass in at least two different ways, by grinding them into mud, and by crushing, breaking, and splitting them into a coarse detritus of chips and boulders, the forms and sizes of which are in great part determined by the divisional planes the rocks possess, and the intensity and direction of application of the force brought to bear on them. The quantity of this coarser material remaining in the channels along the lines of dispersal, and the probable rate of movement of the glaciers that quarried and transported it, form data from which some approximation to the rate of this method of degradation may be reached.

The amount of influence exerted on the Aleutian region by running water in its various forms, and by the winds, avalanches, and the atmosphere in degrading and fashioning the surface subsequent to the melting of the ice, is as yet scarcely more appreciable than it is in the upper middle portion of the Sierra; for, besides being much feebler in their action, the time during which the region has been exposed to their influence is comparatively short.

On the other hand, the quantity of material quarried and carried away by the force of ice, in the process of bringing the region into its present condition, can hardly be overestimated; for, with the exception of the recent volcanic cones, almost every noticeable feature, great and small, has evidently been ground down into the form of greatest strength in relation to the stress of oversweeping floods of ice. And that these present features are not the pre-glacial features merely smoothed and polished and otherwise superficially altered, but an entirely new set sculptured from a surface comparatively featureless, is manifested by the relationship existing between the spaces that separate them and the glacier fountains. The greater the valley or hollow of any sort, the greater the snow-collecting basin above it whence flowed the ice that created it, not a fiord or valley being found here or on any portion of the Pacific coast that does not conduct to fountains of vanished or residual glaciers corresponding with it in size and position as cause and effect.

And, furthermore, that the courses of the present valleys were not determined by the streams of water now occupying them, nor by preglacial streams, but by the glaciers of the last or of some former glacial period, is shown by the fact that the directions of the trends of all these valleys, however variable, are resultants of the forces of the main trunk glaciers that filled them and their inflowing tributary glaciers, the wriggling fortuitous trends of valleys formed by the action of water being essentially different from those formed by ice; and therefore not liable to be confounded with them. Neither can we suppose pre-existing fissures or local subsidences to have exercised any primary determining influence, there being no conceivable coincidence between the trends of fissures and subsidences and the specific trends of ice-created valleys and basins in general, nor between the position and direction of extension of these hypothetical fissures, subsidences, and foldings and the positions of ice-fountains.

The Pribilof Islands, St. Paul, St. George, Walrus, and Otter, appear in general views from the sea as mere storm-beaten remnants of a once continuous land, wasted into bluffs around their shores by the action of the waves, all their upper surfaces being planed down by a heavy over-sweeping ice-sheet, slightly roughened here and there with low ridges and hillocks that alternate with shallow valleys. None of their features, as far as I could discover without opportunity for close observation, showed any trace of local glaciation or of volcanic action subsequent to the period of universal glaciation.

St. Lawrence Island, the largest in Bering Sea, is situated at a distance of about one hundred and twenty miles off the mouths of the Yukon, and forty miles from the nearest point on the coast of Siberia. It is about a hundred miles long from east to west, fifteen miles in average width, and is chiefly composed of various kinds of granite, slate, and lava .

The highest portion along the middle is diversified with groups of volcanic cones, some of which are of considerable size and clearly post-glacial in age, presenting well-defined craters and regular slopes down to the base, though I saw no evidence of their having poured forth extensive streams of molten lava over the adjacent rocks since the close of the glacial period; for, with the exception of the ground occupied by the cones, all the surface is marked with glacial inscriptions of the most telling kind – moraines, erratic boulders, *roches moutonnées*, in great abundance and variety as to size, and alternating ridges and valleys with wide U-shaped cross-sections, and with nearly parallel trends across the island in a general north to south direction, some of them extending from shore to shore, and all showing subordination to the grinding, furrowing action of a broad oversweeping ice-sheet.

Some of the widest gap-like valleys have been eroded nearly to the level of the sea, indicating that if the ice action had gone on much longer the present single island would have been eroded into a group of small ones; or the entire mass of the island would have been degraded beneath the sea level, obliterating it from the landscape to be in part restored perhaps by the antagonistic elevating volcanic action. The action of local glaciers has been comparatively light hereabouts, not enough greatly to obscure or interrupt the overmastering effects of the ice-sheet, though they have given marked character to the sculpture of some of the higher portions of the island.

The two Diomede Islands and Fairway Rock are mostly residual masses of granite brought into relief and separated from one another and from the general mass of the continent, by the action of ice in removing the missing material, while the islands remain because of superior resistance offered to the universal degrading force. That they are remnants of a once continuous land now separated by Bering Strait is indicated by the relative condition of the sides of the islands and of the contiguous shoulders of the continents, East Cape and Cape Prince of Wales, while the general configuration of the islands shows that they have been subjected to a glaciation of the most comprehensive kind, leaving them as *roches moutonnées* on a grand scale.

I discovered traces of local glaciation on the largest of the three, but the effects produced by this cause are comparatively slight, while the action of excessive moisture in the form of almost constant fogs and rains throughout the summer months, combined with frost and thaw, has effected a considerable amount of denudation, manifested by groups of crumbling pinnacles occurring here and there on the summits.

Sledge, King, and Herald Islands are evidently of similar origin, displaying the same glacial traces, and varying chiefly in the amount of post-glacial waste they have suffered, and in the consequent degree of clearness of the testimony they present. During our visit to Herald Island an exceptionally favourable opportunity offered as to the time of year, state of the weather, etc., for observation.

Kellett, who first discovered this island and landed on it under adverse circumstances, describes it as an inaccessible rock. The sides are indeed precipitous in the main, but mountaineers would find many slopes and gullies by which the summit could be easily attained. We landed on the southwest side, opposite the mouth of a small valley, the bed of a vanished glacier. A short gully which conducts from the water's edge to the mouth of the valley proper is very steep, and at the time of our visit was blocked with compacted snow, in which steps had to be cut, but beyond this no difficulty was encountered, the ice having graded a fine broad way to the summit. Thence following the highest ground nearly to the northwestern extremity, we obtained views of most of the surface. The highest point is about twelve hundred feet above the sea, about a mile and a half from the northwest end of the island, and four and a half miles from the southeast. This makes the island about six miles long, the average width being about two miles.

Near the middle of the island there is a low gap, where the width is only about half a mile, and the height of the summit of this portion of the water-shed between the two sides is only about two hundred and fifty feet. The entire island as far as seen is a mass of granite, with the exception of a patch of metamorphic slates near the middle, which no doubt owes its existence, with so considerable a height, to the superior resistance it offered to the degrading action of ice, traces of which are presented in the general *moutonnée* form of the island, and in the smooth parallel ridges and valleys trending north and south. These evidently have not been determined as to size, form, position, or the direction of their trends by subsidences, upheavals, foldings, or any structural peculiarity of the rocks in which they have been eroded, but simply by the mechanical force of an oversweeping ice-sheet.

The effects of local glaciers are seen in short valleys of considerable depth as compared with the area from which their fountain snows were derived. We noticed four of these valleys that had been occupied by residual glaciers; and on the hardest and most enduring of the upswelling rock bosses several patches of the ancient scored and polished surface were discovered, still in a good state of preservation. That these local glaciers have but recently vanished is indicated by the raw appearance of the surface of their beds, while one small glacier remnant occupying a sheltered hollow and possessing a well-characterised terminal moraine seems to be still feebly active in the last stage of decadence. This small granite island, standing solitary in the Polar Ocean, we regard as one of the most interesting and significant of the monuments of geographical change effected by general glaciation.

Our stay on Wrangell Land was too short to admit of more than a hasty examination of a few square miles of surface near the eastern extremity. The rock here is a close-grained clay slate, cleaving freely into thin flakes, with occasional compact metamorphic masses rising above the general surface or forming cliffs along the shore. The soil about the banks of a river of considerable size, that enters the ocean here, has evidently been derived in the main from the underlying slates, indicating a rapid weathering of the surface. A few small deposits of moraine material were discovered containing travelled boulders of quartz and granite, no doubt from the mountains in which the river takes its rise, while the valley now occupied by the river manifests its glacial origin in its form and trends, the small portion in the middle eroded by the river itself being clearly distinguished by its abrupt angular sides, which contrast sharply with the glacial outlines.

In general views obtained in sailing along its southern coast the phenomena presented seemed essentially the same as have been described elsewhere – hills, valleys, and sculptured peaks, testifying in all their main trends and contours to the action of ice. A range of mountains of moderate height extends from one extremity of the island to the other, a distance of about sixty-five miles, the highest point as measured by Lieutenant Berry being twenty-five hundred feet above the sea.

All the coast region of Siberia that came under our observation, from the Gulf of Anadir to North Cape, presents traces in great abundance and variety of universal as well as local glaciation. Between Plover and St. Lawrence Bays, where the mountains attain their greatest elevation and where local glaciation has been heaviest, the coast is lacerated with deep fiords, on the lofty granite walls of which the glacial records are in many places well preserved, and offer evidence that could hardly be overlooked by the most careless observer.

Our first general views of this region were obtained on June 7th, when it was yet winter, and the landscape was covered with snow down to the water's edge. After several days of storm the clouds lifted, exposing the heavily abraded fronts of outstanding cliffs; then the smooth overswept ridges and slopes at the base of the mountains came in sight, and one angular peak after another, until a continuous range forty to fifty miles long could be seen from one standpoint. Many of the peaks are fluted with the narrow channels of avalanches, and hollowed with névé amphitheatres of great beauty of form, while long withdrawing fiords and valleys may be traced back into the recesses of the highest groups, once the beds of glaciers that flowed in imposing ranks to the sea.

Plover Bay, which I examined in detail, may be taken as a good representative of the fiords of this portion of the coast. The walls rise to an average height of about two thousand feet, and present a severely desolate and bedraggled appearance, owing to the crumbling condition of the rocks, which in most places are being rapidly disintegrated, loading the slopes with loose, shifting detritus whenever the angle is low enough to allow it to come to rest. When examined closely, however, this loose material is found to be of no great depth. The solid rock comes to the surface in many places, and on the most enduring portions rounded glaciated surfaces are still found grooved, scratched, and polished in small patches from the sea-level up to a height of a thousand feet or more.

Large taluses with their bases under the water occur on both sides of the fiord in front of the side canyons that partially separate the main mountain masses that form the walls. These taluses are composed in great part of moraine material, brought down by avalanches of snow from the terminal moraines of small vanished glaciers that lay at a height of from one to five thousand feet, in recesses where the snow accumulated from the surrounding slopes, and where sheltered from the direct action of the sun the glaciers lingered longest. These recent moraines are formed of several concentric masses shoved together, showing that the glaciers to which they belonged melted and receded gradually with slight fluctuations of level and rate of decadence, in accordance with conditions of snow-fall, temperature, etc., like those of lower latitudes.

When the main central glacier that filled this fiord was in its prime as a distinct glacier it measured about thirty miles in length and from five to six miles in width, and was from two to three thousand feet in depth. It then had at least five main tributaries, which, as the trunk melted, became independent glaciers; and, again, as the trunks of these main tributaries melted, their smaller tributaries, numbering about seventy-five, and from less than a mile to several miles in length, became separate glaciers and lingered probably for centuries in the high, cool fountains. These also, as far as we have seen, have vanished, though possibly some wasting remnant may still exist in the highest and best-protected recesses about the head of the fiord.

Along the coast, a distance of fifteen or twenty miles to the eastward and southward of the mouth of Metchigme Bay, interesting deposits occur of roughly stratified glacial detritus in the form of sand, gravel and boulders. They rise from the shore in raw, wave-washed bluffs about forty feet high and extend to the base of the mountains as a gently inclined plain, with a width in some places of two or three miles. Similar morainal deposits were also observed on the American coast at Golofnin Bay, Kotzebue Sound, Cape Prince of Wales, and elsewhere. At Cape Prince of Wales the formation rises in successive well-defined terraces.

The peninsula, the extremity of which forms East Cape, trends nearly in an easterly direction from the mainland, and consequently occupies a telling position with reference to ice moving from the northward. I was therefore eager to examine it to see what testimony it might have to offer. We landed during favourable weather on the south side at a small Eskimo village built on a rough moraine, and pushed on direct to the summit of the watershed, from which good general views of nearly all the surface of the peninsula were obtained.

The dividing ridge along the high eastern portion is traversed by a telling series of parallel grooves and small valleys trending north and south approximately, the curves on the north commencing nearly at the water's edge, while the south side is more or less precipitous. The culminating point of the elevated eastern portion of the peninsula is about twenty-five hundred feet high, and has been cut from the mainland and added as another island to the Diomede group, the wide gap of low ground connecting it with the adjacent mountainous portion of the mainland being only a few feet above tide-water. Out in the midst of this low, flat region smooth upswelling *roches moutonnées* were discovered here and there like groups of small islands, with trends and contours emphatically glacial, all telling the action of a universal abrading ice-sheet moving southward.

Hence along the coast to Cape North, which is the limit of our observations in this direction, the same class of ice phenomena was discovered – moraine material, washed and reformed, *moutonnée* masses of the harder rocks standing like islands in the low, mossy tundra, and travelled boulders and pebbles lying stranded on the summits of rocky headlands

These enduring monuments are particularly abundant and significant in the neighbourhood of Cape Wankarem, where the granite is more compact and resisting than is commonly found in the Arctic regions we have visited, and consequently has longer retained the more evanescent of the glacial markings. Cape Wankarem is a narrow, flat-topped, residual mass of this enduring granite, on the summit of which two patches of the original polished surface were discovered that still retains the fine striae and many erratic boulders of slate, quartz, and various kinds of lava, which, from the configuration and geographical position of the cape with reference to the surrounding region, could not have been brought to their present resting-places by any local glacier.

Cape Serdzakamen is another of these residual island masses, brought into relief by general glacial denudation, manifesting its origin in every feature, and corroborating the testimony given at Cape Wankarem and elsewhere in the most emphatic manner.

All the sections of the tundra seen either on the Siberian or Alaskan coast lead towards the conclusion that the ground is glacial, reformed under the action of running water derived in broad, shallow currents from the melting, receding edge of the ice-sheet, and also in some measure from ice left on the high lands after the main ice-sheet had been withdrawn; for these low, flat deposits differ in no particular of form or composition that we have been able to detect from those still in process of formation in front of the large receding glaciers of southeastern Alaska. On many of the so-called "mud-flats" extending from the snouts of glaciers that have receded a few miles from the shore, mosses and lichens and other kinds of tundra vegetation are being gradually acquired, and when thus clothed these patches of tundra are not to be distinguished from the extensive deposits about the shores of the Arctic regions.

The phenomena observed on the American coast from St. Michael to Point Barrow differ in no essential particular from those which have been described on the opposite shores of Siberia. Moraines more or less wasted, and re-formations of moraine material, smooth overswept ridges with glacial trends and the corresponding valleys, *roches moutonnées*, and the fountain amphitheatres of local glaciers were observed almost everywhere on the mountainous portions of the coast, though in general more deeply weathered, owing mainly to the occurrence of less resisting rocks, limestones, sandstones, porous lavas, etc.

A number of well-characterised moraines so situated with reference to topographical conditions as to have escaped destructive washing were noticed near Cape Lisburne, and moraine deposits of great extent at Kotzebue Sound and Golofnin Bay, of which many fine sections were exposed. At the latter locality, judging from the comparatively fresh appearance of the rock surfaces and deposits around the head of the bay, and the height and extent of the ice-fountains, the glacier that discharged here was probably the last to vanish from the American shore of Bering Sea.

As to the thickness attained by the ice-sheet over the regions that we have been examining during the period of greatest glacial development, we have seen that it passed heavily over the islands of Bering Sea and the adjacent mountains on either side, especially at East Cape and Cape Prince of Wales, at a height of twenty-five hundred feet or more above the bottom of Bering Sea and Strait, the average depth of water here being about a hundred and fifty feet. And though the lowest portion of the land beneath the ice may have been degraded to a considerable depth subsequent to the time when these highest portions were left bare, on the other hand the level of the ice must have been considerably higher than the summits over which it passed, inasmuch as they give evidence of having been heavily abraded. It appears, therefore, that the thickness of the general northern ice-sheet throughout a considerable portion of its history was not less than twenty-five hundred feet, and probably more, over the northern portion of the region now covered by Bering Sea and part of the Arctic Ocean

In view of this colossal ice-flood grinding on throughout the hundreds of thousands of years of the glacial period, the excavation of the shallow basins of Bering Sea and Strait and the Arctic Ocean must be taken as only a small part of the erosion effected; for so shallow are these waters, were the tallest sequoias planted on the bottom where soundings have been made, their tops would rise in most places a hundred feet or more above the surface. The Plover Bay glacier, as we have shown, eroded the granite in the formation of its channel to a depth of not less than two thousand feet, and the amount of erosion effected by the ice-sheet was probably much greater.

It appears, therefore, in summing up the results of our observations along the North Pacific and Arctic coasts:

1. That the southernmost glacier lies on the Sierra near latitude 36°; the northernmost, with perhaps a few exceptions, near 62°.

2. That the region of greatest glaciation lies between 56° and 61°, where the mountains are highest and the snowfall greatest.

3. That an ice-sheet flowed from the Arctic regions, from beyond the end of the continent, pursuing a general southerly direction, and discharged into the Pacific Ocean south of the Aleutian Islands.

4. That of this continuous ice-sheet, extending from the Arctic Ocean beyond the northern extremity of the continent, the glaciers, great and small, now existing are the remnants.

5. That the basins of Bering Sea and Strait and of the adjacent portion of the Arctic Ocean are simply those portions of the bed of the ice-sheet which were eroded to a moderate depth beneath the level of the sea, and over which the ocean waters were gradually extended as the ice-sheet was withdrawn, thus separating the continents of Asia and America, at the close of the glacial period.

We are now better prepared to read the changes that have taken place on the Sierra, and fortunately, as we have already seen, nowhere is the glacial record clearer.

APPENDIX II

Botanical Notes

INTRODUCTORY

The plants named in the following notes were collected at many localities on the coasts of Alaska and Siberia, and on St. Lawrence, Wrangell, and Herald Islands, between about latitude 54° and 71° N., longitude 161° and 178° W., in the course of short excursions, some of them less than an hour in length. Inasmuch as the flora of the arctic and subarctic regions is nearly the same everywhere, the discovery of many species new to science was not to be expected. The collection, however, will no doubt be valuable for comparison with the plants of other regions. In general the physiognomy of the vegetation of the polar regions resembles that of the alpine valleys of the temperate zones; so much so that the botanist on the coast of Arctic Siberia or America might readily fancy himself on the Sierra Nevada at a height of ten to twelve thousand feet above the sea.

There is no line of perpetual snow on any portion of the Arctic regions known to explorers. The snow disappears every summer, not only from the low, sandy shores and boggy tundras, but also from the tops of the mountains, and all the upper slopes and valleys with the exception of small patches of drifts and avalanche-heaps hardly noticeable in general views. But though nowhere excessively deep or permanent, the snow mantle is universal during winter, and the plants are solidly frozen and buried for nearly three fourths of the year. In this condition they enjoy a sleep and rest about as profound as death, from which they awake in the months of June and July in vigorous health, and speedily reach a far higher development of leaf and flower and fruit than is generally supposed. On the drier banks and hills about Kotzebue Sound, Cape Thompson, and Cape Lisburne, many species show but little climatic repression, and during the long summer days grow tall enough to wave in the wind, and unfold flowers in as rich profusion and as highly coloured as may be found in regions lying a thousand miles farther south.

UNALASKA

To the botanist approaching any portion of the Aleutian chain of islands from the southward during the winter or spring months, the view is severely desolate and forbidding. The snow comes down to the water's edge in solid white, interrupted only by dark, outstanding bluffs with faces too steep for snow to lie on, and by the backs of rounded rocks and long, rugged reefs beaten and overswept by heavy breakers rolling in from the Pacific, while throughout nearly every month of the year the higher mountains are wrapped in gloomy, dripping storm-clouds.

Nevertheless, vegetation here is remarkably close and luxuriant, and crowded with showy bloom, covering almost every foot of the ground up to a height of about a thousand feet above the sea – the harsh trachytic rocks, and even the cindery bases of the craters, as well as the moraines and rough soil-beds outspread on the low portions of the short, narrow valleys.

On the twentieth of May we found the showy *Geum glaciale* already in flower, also an arctostaphylos and draba, on a slope facing the south, near the harbour of Unalaska. The willows, too, were then beginning to put forth their catkins, while a multitude of green points were springing up in sheltered spots wherever the snow had vanished. At a height of four or five hundred feet, however, winter was still unbroken, with scarce a memory of the rich bloom of summer.

During a few short excursions along the shores of Unalaska Harbour, and on two of the adjacent mountains, towards the end of May and the beginning of October, we saw about fifty species of flowering plants empetrum, vaccinium, bryanthus, pyrola, arctostaphylos, ledum, cassiope, lupinus, geranium, epilobium, silene, draba, and saxifraga, being the most telling and characteristic of the genera represented. *Empetrum nigrum*, a bryanthus, and three species of vaccinium make a grand display when in flower, and show their massed colours at a considerable distance.

Almost the entire surface of the valleys and hills and lower slopes of the mountains is covered with a dense, spongy plush of lichens and mosses similar to that which covers the tundras of the Arctic regions, making a rich green mantle on which the showy, flowering plants are strikingly relieved, though these grow far more luxuriantly on the banks of the streams where the drainage is less interrupted. Here also the ferns, of which I saw three species, are taller and more abundant, some of them arching their broad, delicate fronds over one's shoulders, while in similar situations the tallest of the five grasses that were seen reaches a height of nearly six feet, and forms a growth close enough for the farmer's scythe.

Not a single tree has been seen on any of the islands of the chain west of Kodiak, excepting a few spruces brought from Sitka and planted at Unalaska by the Russians about fifty years ago. They are still alive in a dwarfed condition, having made scarce any appreciable growths since they were planted. These facts are the more remarkable, since in southeastern Alaska, lying both to the north and south of here, and on the many islands of the Alexander Archipelago, as well as on the mainland, forests of beautiful conifers flourish exuberantly and attain noble dimensions, while the climatic conditions generally do not appear to differ greatly from those that obtain on these treeless islands.

Wherever cattle have been introduced they have prospered and grown fat on the abundance of rich nutritious pasturage to be found almost everywhere in the deep, withdrawing valleys and on the green slopes of the hills and mountains, but the wetness of the summer months will always prevent the making of hay in any considerable quantities.

The agricultural possibilities of these islands seem also to be very limited. The hardier of the cereals – rye, barley, and oats – make a good vigorous growth, and head out, but seldom or never mature, on account of insufficient sunshine and overabundance of moisture in the form of long-continued, drizzling fogs and rains. Green crops, however, as potatoes, turnips, cabbages, beets, and most other common garden vegetables, thrive wherever the ground is thoroughly drained and has a southerly exposure.

ST. LAWRENCE ISLAND

St. Lawrence Island, as far as our observations extended, is mostly a dreary mass of granite and lava of various forms and colours, roughened with volcanic cones, covered with snow, and rigidly bound in ocean ice for half the year. Inasmuch as it lies broadside wise to the direction pursued by the great ice-sheet that recently filled Bering Sea, and its rocks offered unequal resistance to the denuding action of the ice, the island is traversed by numerous ridges and low, gap-like valleys all trending in the same general direction. Some of the lowest of these transverse valleys have been degraded nearly to the level of the sea, showing that if the glaciation to which the island has been subjected had been slightly greater, we should have found several islands here instead of one.

At the time of our first visit, May 28th, winter still had full possession, but eleven days later we found the dwarf willows, drabas, erigerons, and saxifrages pushing up their buds and leaves, on spots bare of snow, with wonderful rapidity. This was the beginning of spring at the northwest end of the island. On July 4th the flora seemed to have reached its highest development. The bottoms of the glacial valleys were in many places covered with tall grasses and carices evenly planted and forming meadows of considerable size, while the drier portions and the sloping grounds about them were enlivened with gay, highly coloured flowers from an inch to nearly two feet in height, such as *Aconitum Napellus*, L., var. *delphinifolium*, Ser., *Polemonium coeruleum*, L., *Papaver nudicaule*, L., *Draba alpina*, L., and *Silene acaulis*, L., in large, closely flowered tufts, as well as andromeda, ledum, linnaea, cassiope, and several species of vaccinium and saxifraga.

ST. MICHAEL

The region about St. Michael is a magnificent tundra, crowded with Arctic lichens and mosses, which here develop under most favourable conditions. In the spongy plush formed by the lower plants, in which one sinks almost knee-deep at every step, there is a sparse growth of grasses, carices, and rushes, tall enough to wave in the wind, while empetrum, the dwarf birch, and the various heathworts flourish here in all their beauty of bright leaves and flowers. The moss mantle for the most part rests on a stratum of ice that never melts to any great extent, and the ice on a bed rock of black vesicular lava. Ridges of the lava rise here and there above the general level in rough masses, affording ground for plants that like a drier soil. Numerous hollows and watercourses also occur on the general tundra, whose well-drained banks are decked with gay flowers in lavish abundance, and meadow patches of grasses shoulder-high, suggestive of regions much farther south.

The following plants and a few doubtful species not yet determined were collected here:

Aspidium fragrans, Sw.
Woodsia ilvensis, (L.), R. Br.
Eriophorum capitatum, Hos.
Carex vulgaris, (Fries), Willd., var. *alpina*.
Lloydia serotina, (Sweet), Reichenb.
Tofieldia coccinea, Richards.
Betula nana, L.
Alnus viridis, DC.
Polygonum alpinum, All.
Arenaria lateriflora, L.
Stellaria longipes, Goldie.
Silene acaulis, L.
Anemone narcissiflora, L.
Anemone parviflora, Michx.
Caltha palustris, L., var. *asarifolia*, Rothr.

Corydalis pauciflora.
Draba alpina, L.
Draba incana, L.
Eutrema arenicola, Richards.
Saxifraga nivalis, L.
Saxifraga hieracifolia, Waldst. & Kit.
Rubus Chamaemorus, L.
Rubus arcticus, L.
Potentilla nivea, L.
Dryas octopetala, L.
Oxytropis podocarpa, Gray.
Astragalus alpinus, L.
Astragalus frigidus, Gray, var. *littoralis*.
Lathyrus maritimus, Bigel.
Epilobium latifolium, L.
Cassiope tetragone, (D. Don.), Desv.

Andromeda polifolia, L.
Loiseleuria procumbens, Desv.
Vaccinium Vitis-Idæa, L.
Arctostaphylos alpina, Spreng.
Ledum palustre, L.
Diapensia lapponica, L.
Armeria vulgaris, Willd.
Primula borealis, Duby.
Polemonium cœruleum, L.
Mertensia paniculata, Desv.
Pedicularis sudetica, Willd.
Pedicularis euphrasioides, Stev.

Pedicularis Langsdorffi, Fisch., var. *lanata*, Gray.
Pinguicula villosa, L.
Linnæa borealis, Gronov.
Valeriana capitata, (Pall.), Willd .
Saussurea alpina, DC.
Nardosmia frigida, Hook.
Senecio frigidus, Less.
Senecio palustris, Hook.
Arnica angustifolia, Vahl.
Artemisia arctica, Bess.
Matricaria inodora, L.

GOLOFNIN BAY

The tundra flora on the west side of Golofnin Bay is remarkably close and luxuriant, covering almost every foot of the ground, the hills as well as the valleys, while the sandy beach and a bank of coarsely stratified moraine material a few yards back from the beach were blooming like a garden with *Lathyrus maritimus*, *Iris sibirica*, *Polemonium cœruleum*, etc., diversified with clumps and patches of *Elymus arenarius*, *Alnus viridis*, and *Abies alba*.

This is one of the few points on the east side of Bering Sea where trees closely approach the shore. The white spruce occurs here in small groves or thickets of well-developed, erect trees fifteen or twenty feet high, near the level of the sea, at a distance of about six or eight miles from the mouth of the bay, and gradually becomes irregular and dwarfed as it approaches the shore. Here a number of dead and dying specimens were observed, indicating that conditions of soil, climate, and relations to other plants were becoming more unfavourable, and causing the tree-line to recede from the coast.

The following collection was made here on July 10th:

Aspidium spinulosum, Sw.
Elymus arenarius, L.
Poa trivialis, L.
Carex vesicaria, L., var. *alpigena* Fries.
Lloydia serotina, (Sweet), Reichenb.
Iris sibirica, L.
Arenaria peploides, L.
Eutrema arenicola, Hook.
Spiræa betulifolia, Pall.
Rubus arcticus, L..

Epilobium latifolium, L,
Vaccinium Vitis-Idæa, L.
Trientalis europœa, L., var. *arctica*, Ledeb.
Gentiana glauca, Pall.
Polemonium cœruleum, L.
Pinguicula villosa, L.
Chrysanthemum arcticum, L.
Artemisia Tilesii, Ledeb.

KOTZEBUE SOUND

The flora of the region about the head of Kotzebue Sound is hardly less luxuriant and rich in species than that of other points, visited by the Corwin, lying several degrees farther south. Fine nutritious grasses suitable for the fattening of cattle, and from two to six feet high, are not of rare occurrence on meadows of considerable extent, and along streambanks wherever the stagnant waters of the tundra have been drained off, while in similar localities the most showy of the arctic plants bloom in all their freshness and beauty, manifesting no sign of frost, or unfavourable conditions of any kind whatever.

A striking result of the airing and draining of the boggy tundra soil is shown on the ice-bluffs around Eschscholtz Bay, where it has been undermined by the melting of the ice on which it rests. In falling down the face of the ice-wall it is well shaken and rolled before it again comes to rest on terraced or gently sloping portions of the wall. The original vegetation of the tundra is thus destroyed, and tall grasses spring up on the fresh, mellow ground as it accumulates from time to time, growing lush and rank, though in many places that we noted these new soil-beds are not more than a foot in depth, and lie on the solid ice.

At the time of our last visit to this interesting region, about the middle of September, the weather was still fine, suggesting the Indian summer of the Western States. The tundra glowed in the mellow sunshine with the colours of the ripe foliage of vaccinium, empetrum, arctostaphylos, and dwarf birch; red, purple, and yellow, in pure bright tones, while the berries, hardly less beautiful, were scattered everywhere as if they had been sown broadcast with a lavish hand, the whole blending harmoniously with the neutral tints of the furred bed of lichens and mosses on which the bright leaves and berries were painted.

On several points about the sound the white spruce occurs in small, compact groves within a few miles of the shore; and pyrola, which belongs to wooded regions, is abundant where no trees are now in sight, tending to show that areas of considerable extent, now treeless, were once forested.

The plants collected are:

Luzula hyperborea, R. Br.
Allium schoenoprasum, L.
Salix polaris, Wahlenb.
Polygonum viviparum, L.
Stellaria longipes, Goldie.
Cerastium alpinum, L., var.
  Behringianum, Regel.
Papaver nudicaule, L.
Saxifraga tricuspidata, Retz.
Potentilla anserina, L., var.
Potentilla biflora, Willd.
Potentilla fruticosa, L.
Lupinusarcticus, Watson.
Hedysarum boreale, Nutt.
Empetrum nigrum, L.
Pyrola rotundifolia, L., var. *pumila*,
  Hook.

Arctostaphylos alpina, Spreng.
Cassiope tetragone, (D. Don), Desv.
Ledum palustre, L.
Vaccinium Vitis-Idœa, L.
Vaccinium uliginosua, L., var.
  mucronata, Herder.
Armeria vulgaris, Willd, var. *arctica*,
  Cham.
Trientalis europœa, L. var. *arctica*,
  Ledeb.
Mertensia maritima, L. (S. F. Gray),
  Desv.
Castilleia pallida, Kunth.
Pedicularis sudetica, Willd.
Pedicularis verticillata, L.
Galium boreale, L.
Senecio palustris, Hook.

CAPE THOMPSON

The Cape Thompson flora is richer in species and individuals than that of any other point on the Arctic shores we have seen, owing no doubt mainly to the better drainage of the ground through the fissured frost-cracked limestone, which hereabouts is the principal rock.

Where the hill-slopes are steepest the rock frequently occurs in loose, angular masses, and is entirely bare of soil. but between these barren slopes there are valleys where the showiest of the arctic plants bloom in rich profusion and variety, forming brilliant masses of colour – purple, yellow, and blue – here certain species form beds of considerable size, almost to the exclusion of others.

The following list was obtained here on July 19th:

Cystopteris fragilis, (L.), Bernh.

Trisetum subspicatum, Beauv., var. *molle*, Gray.

Glyceria –

Festuca sativa (?) [*F. ovina*, L.?]

Carex rariflora, Wahlenb.

Carex vulgaris, Fries, var. *alpina*, (*C. rigida*, Good.)

Salix polaris, Wahlenb., and two other species undetermined.

Polygonum Bistorta, L.

Rumex crispus, L.

Cerastium alpinum, L., var. *Behringianum*, Regel.

Silene acaulis, L.

Arenaria verna,L., var.*rubella*, Hook.f.

Arenaria arctica, Stev.

Stellaria longipes, Goldie.

Anemone narcissiflora, L.

Anemone multifida, Poir.

Anemone parviflora, Michx.

Anemone parviflora, Michx., variety.

Ranunculus affinis, R. Br.

Caltha asarifolia, DC.

Papaver nudicaule, L.

Draba stellata, Jacq., var. *nivalis*, Regel.

Draba incana, L.

Cardamine pratensis, L.

Cheiranthus pygmaeus, Adams.

Pedicularis capitata, Adams

Geum glaciale, Fisch.

Nardosmia corymbosa, Hook.

Erigeron Muirii, Gray, n. sp.

Parrya nudicaulis, (Boiss.), Regel, var. *aspera*, Regel.

Boykinia Richardsoni, Gray.

Saxifraga tricuspidata, Retz.

Saxifraga cernua, L.

Saxifraga flagellaris, Willd.

Saxifraga davurica, Willd.

Saxifraga punctata, L.

Saxifraga nivalis, L.

Dryas octopetala, L.

Potentilla biflora, Willd.

Potentilla nivea, L.

Hedysarum boreale, Nutt.

Oxytropis podocarpa, Gray.

Epilobium latifolium, L.

Cassiope tetragone, (D. Don.), Desv.

Vaccinium uliginosum, L., var. *mucronata*, Herder.

Vaccinium Vitis-Idæa, L.

Dodecatheon Meadia, L., var. *frigidum*, Gray.

Androsace chamæjasme, Willd.

Phlox sibirica, L.

Polemonium humile, Willd.

Polemonium cæruleum, L.

Myosotis sylvatica, var. *alpestris*, Hoffm.

Eritrichium nanum, Schrad., var. arctioides.

Taraxacum palustre, DC.

Senecio frigidus, Less.

Artemisia glomerata, Ledeb.

Artemisia tomentosa[*tomentella*,Trautv.?]

CAPE PRINCE OF WALES
At Cape Prince of Wales we obtained:

Tofieldia coccinea, Richards.

Loiseleuria procumbens, Desv.

Andromeda polifolia, L. *forma arctica*.

Vaccinium Vitis-Idœa, L.

Armeria arctica, (Wallr.), Stev.

Androsace chamœjasme, Willd.

Taraxacum palustre, DC.

TWENTY MILES EAST OF CAPE LISBURNE

Lychnis apetala, L.

Anemone narcissiflora, L., var.

Draba hirta, L.

Saxifraga Eschscholtzii, Sternb.

Saxifraga flagellaris, Willd.

Chrysosplenium alternifolium, L.

Potentilla nivea, L.

Potentilla biflora, Willd.

Oxytropis campestris, DC.

Primula borealis, Duby.

Androsace chamaejasme, Willd.

Phlox sibirica, L.

Geum glaciale, Fisch.

Erigeron uniflorus, L.

Artemisia glomerata, Ledeb.

CAPE WANKAREM, SIBERIA
Near Cape Wankarem on August 7th and 8th, we collected:

Elymus arenarius, L.

Alopecurus alpinus, Sm.

Poa arctica, R. Br.

Calamagrostis deschampsioides, Trin.

Luzula hyperborea, R. Br.

Luzula spicata, (DC.), Desv.

Lychnis apetala, L.

Claytonia virginica, L.

Ranunculus pygmaeus, Wahlenb.

Chrysosplenium alternifolium, L.

Saxifraga cernua, L.

Saxifraga stellaris, L. var. *comosa*.

Saxifraga rivularis, L. var. *hyperborea*, Hook.

Polemonium cœruleurn, L.

Pedicularis Langsdorffi, Fisch.

Nardosmia frigidia, Hook.

Chrysanthemum arcticum, L.

Senecio frigidus, Less.

Artemisia vulgaris, var. *Tilesii*, Ledeb.

PLOVER BAY, SIBERIA
The mountains bounding the glacial fiord called Plover Bay, though beautiful in their combinations of curves and peaks as they are seen touching each other delicately and rising in bold, picturesque groups, are nevertheless severely desolate-looking from the absence of trees and large shrubs, and indeed of vegetation of any kind dense enough to give colour in telling quantities, or to soften the harsh rockiness of the steepest portions of the walls. Even the valleys opening back from the water here and there on either side are mostly bare as seen at a distance of a mile or two, and show only a faint tinge of green, derived from dwarf willows, heathworts, and sedges chiefly.

The most interesting of the plants found here are *Rhododendron kamtschaticum*, Pall., and the handsome blue-flowered *Saxifraga oppositifolia*, L., both of which are abundant. The following were collected on July 12th and August 26th:

Arenaria macrocarpa, Pursh.

Aconitum Napellus, L., var.
   delphinifolium, Ser.

Anemone narcissiflora, L.

Draba alpina, L.

Parrya Ermanni, Ledeb.

Saxiffraga oppositifolia, L.

Saxifraga punctata, L.

Saxifraga caespitosa, L.

Dryas octopetala, L.

Oxytropis podocarpa, Gray.

Rhododendron kamtschaticum, Pall.

Cassiope tetragona, (D. Don.), Desv.

Diapensia lapponica, L.

Gentiana glauca, Pall.

Geum glaciale, Fisch.

HERALD ISLAND

On Herald Island the common polar cryptogamous vegetation is well represented and developed. So also are the flowering plants, almost the entire surface of the island, with the exception of the sheer, crumbling bluffs along the shores, being quite tellingly dotted and tufted with characteristic species. The following list* was obtained:

Gymnandra Stelleri, Cham. &
   Schlecht.

Alopecurus alpinus, Sm.

Luzula hyperborea, R. Br.

Salix polaris, Wahlenb.

Stellaria longipes, Goldie, var.
   Edwardsii, T. & G.

Papaver nudicaule, L.

Draba alpina, L.

Saxifraga punctata, L.

Saxifraga serpyllifolia, Pursh.

Saxifraga sileniflora, (Hook.), Sternb.

Saxifraga bronchialis, L.

Saxifraga stellaris, L., var. *comosa*,
   Poir.

Saxifraga rivularis, L., var.
   hyperborea, Hook.

Saxifraga hieracifolia, Waldst. & Kit.

Potentilla frigida, Vill. ?

Senecio frigidus, Less.

WRANGELL LAND

Our stay on the one point of Wrangell Land that we touched was far too short to admit of making anything like as full a collection of the plants of so interesting a region as was desirable. We found the rock formation where we landed and for some distance along the coast to the eastward and westward to be a close-grained clay slate cleaving freely into thin flakes, with here and there a few compact, metamorphic masses that rise above the general surface. Where it is exposed along the shore bluffs and kept bare of vegetation and soil by the action of the ocean, ice, and heavy snow-drifts, the rock presents a surface about as black as coal, without even a moss or lichen to enliven its sombre gloom. But when this

---

* Berthold Seemann, botanist of H. M. S. Herald in 1849, reported the finding of eight plants on a width of thirty feet of shore, which, he says, "was the whole extent we had to walk over." The plants were the following. *Artemisia borealis, Cochleria fenestrata, Saxifraga lamentiniana, Poa arctica*, and another undetermined grass, *Hepatica*, a moss, and red lichen covering the rocks. [EDITOR]

dreary barrier is passed the surface features of the country in general are found to
be finely moulded and collocated, smooth valleys, wide as compared with their
depth, trending back from the shore to a range of mountains that appear blue in
the distance, and round-topped hills, with their side curves finely drawn, touching
and blending in beautiful groups, while scarce a single rock-pile is seen or sheer-
walled bluff to break the general smoothness.

The soil has evidently been derived mostly from the underlying slates, though
a few fragmentary wasting moraines were observed, containing travelled boulders
of quartz and granite which doubtless were brought from the mountains of the
interior by glaciers that have recently vanished – so recently that the outlines and
sculptured hollows and grooves of the mountains have not as yet suffered sufficient
post-glacial denudation to mar appreciably their glacial characters.

The banks of the river at the mouth of which we landed presented a striking
contrast as to vegetation to that of any other stream we had seen in the Arctic
regions. The tundra vegetation was not wholly absent, but the mosses and lichens
of which it is elsewhere composed are about as feebly developed as possible, and
instead of forming a continuous covering they occur in small separate tufts,
leaving the ground between them raw and bare as that of a newly ploughed field.
The phanerogamous plants, both on the lowest grounds and on the slopes and
hilltops as far as seen, were in the same severely repressed condition, and as
sparsely planted in tufts an inch or two in diameter, with from one to three feet
of naked soil between them. Some portions of the coast, however, farther south,
presented a greenish hue as seen from the ship at a distance of eight or ten miles,
owing no doubt to vegetation growing under less unfavourable conditions.

From an area of about half a square mile the following plants were collected:

Gymnandra Stelleri, Cham. & Schlecht.
Poa arctica, R. Br.
Aira caespitosa, L., var. *arctica*.
Alopecurus alpinus, Sm.
Luzula hyperborea, R. Br.
Stellaria longipes, Goldie, var.
    Edwardsii, T & G.
Cerastium alpinum, L.
Anemone parviflora, Michx.
Papaver nudicaule, L.
Cochlearia officinalis, L.
Saxifraga flagellaris, Willd.
Saxifraga stellaris, L., var. *comosa*, Poir.
Saxifraga sileniflora, (Hook.),
    Sternb.

Saxifraga hieracifolia, Waldst. &
    Kit.
Saxifraga rivularis, L., var.,
    hyperborea, Hook.
Saxifraga bronchialis, L.
Saxifraga serpyllifolia, Pursh.
Potentilla nivea, L.
Potentilla frigida, Vill.?*
Armeria macrocarpa, Pursh.
Armeria vulgaris, Willd.
Artemisia borealis, (Pall.), Willd.
Nardosmia frigida, Hook.
Saussurea monticola, Richards.
Draba alpina, L.

---

* "*Potentilla emarginata*, Pursh. A very dwarf form of this species from Wrangell Land was
inadvertently named *Potentilla frigida* in the list of Muir's collection." (Note by Asa Gray in House
Executive Document No. 44 (1881–1885), p. 191.) [EDITOR]

EDWARD HENRY HARRIMAN

Edward Henry Harriman

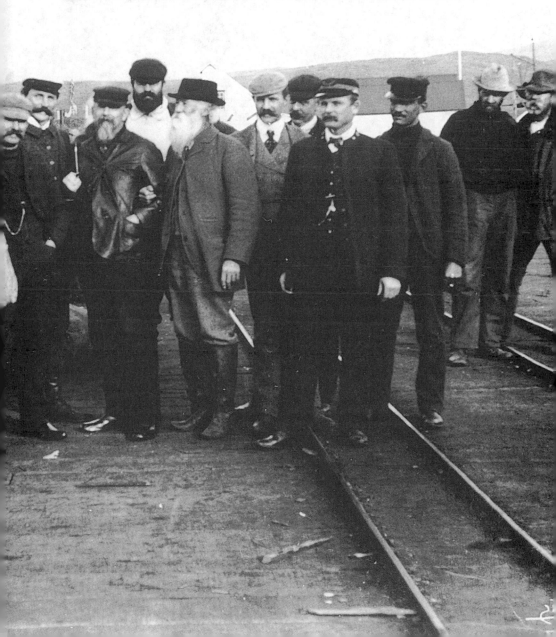

First published by Doubleday, Page and Company (New York, 1912)

Edward Henry Harriman

OF ALL THE GREAT BUILDERS – the famous doers of things in this busy world – none that I know of more ably and manfully did his appointed work than my friend Edward Henry Harriman. He was always ready and able. The greater his burdens, the more formidable the obstacles looming ahead of him, the greater was his enjoyment. He fairly revelled in heavy dynamical work and went about it naturally and unweariedly like glaciers making landscapes, cutting canyons through ridges, carrying off hills laying rails and bridges over lakes and rivers, mountains and plains, making the nation's ways straight and smooth and safe, bringing everybody nearer to one another. He seemed to regard the whole continent as his farm and all the people as partners, stirring millions of workers into useful action, ploughing, sowing, irrigating, mining, building cities and factories, farms and homes.

Nothing he had was allowed to lie idle. A great maker and harvester of crops of wealth, and of course a great spender, he used his income as seed for other crops of world-wealth in succession, sowing broadcast for present and future good, pouring back his gains again and again into new commonwealth currents to create new benefits, or to increase the fruitfulness of old ones after he himself had passed away. Fortunes grew along his railroads like natural fruit. Almost everything he touched sprang up into new forms, changing the face of the whole country.

In general appearance he was said to be undersized, but though I knew him well I never noticed anything either short or tall in his stature. His head made the rest of his body all but invisible. His magnificent brow, high and broad and finely finished, oftentimes called to mind well-known portraits of Napoleon. Every feature of his countenance manifested power, especially his wonderful eyes, deep and frank yet piercing, inspiring confidence, though likely at first sight to keep people at a distance.

When big business plans were growing in his head he looked severe, with scarce a trace of the loving kindness that, like hidden radium or the deep buried fires of ice-clad volcanoes, was ever glowing in his heart. Comparatively few have gained anything like adequate knowledge of the extent and warmth of his sympathies, but none who came nigh him could fail to feel his kindness, especially in his home, radiating a delightful, peaceful atmosphere, the finest domestic weather imaginable. His warm heart it was that endeared him to his friends, but in almost every way he was a man to admire – in apparent repose brooding his work plans, or in grand, overcoming, enthusiastic action shoving them forward, rejoicing and influencing all the country like climate; when silent in company, or at long intervals giving out something striking, saying the commonest things in unforgettable ways and making them seem uncommon in the new light flashed upon them; when severe and rigid as fate; or merry in friendly conversation, eye striking eye, thought clashing against thought, making wit sparkles fly.

I first heard of him in that year 1899, when my friend Dr. Merriam wrote that I was invited to join a scientific expedition to Alaska which Mr. Harriman was organising. Unwilling to accept the hospitality of a person of whom I knew little without seeing how something like compensation might be rendered, I requested particulars of the novel plan, and was informed that Mr. Harriman was a wealthy railroad man who had been advised by his physicians to rest from overwork; that he had decided to go to Alaska, and when he considered that the trip would be long, and would require a good sea-going steamer he thought it a pity to lose the opportunity to render a public service. He had therefore planned an expedition to be devoted to the interests of science, instead of a health and pleasure voyage for himself and family. Accordingly, as many scientific explorers as could be accommodated had been invited: about twenty five biologists, naturalists, ornithologists, geologists, artists, etc., with the necessary assistants for the preparation and care of specimens – making a rare company, assembled for work in a magnificent wilderness and under most favourable auspices.

While I still hesitated, a third letter was received, saying the time had come to decide, and explaining further that the expedition would not only go through the Alexander archipelago, stopping wherever we wished to work, but that Yakutat Bay, Prince William Sound, and probably Cook's Inlet would be explored; so I at last decided to go, leaving proud compensation to any chance opportunity that might offer.

I soon saw that Mr. Harriman was uncommon. He was taking a trip for rest, and at the same time managing his exploring guests as if we were a grateful, soothing, essential part of his rest-cure, though scientific explorers are not easily managed, and in large mixed lots are rather inflammable and explosive, especially when compressed on a ship. Nevertheless he kept us all in smooth working order, put us ashore wherever we liked, in all sorts of places – bays, coves, the mouths of streams, etc. – to suit the convenience of the different parties into which we naturally separated, dropping each with suitable provisions, taking us aboard again at given times, looking after everything to the minutest details; work enough to bring nervous prostration to ordinary mortals instead of rest.

All the Harriman family were aboard, together with Mr. and Mrs. Averell and their daughter Betty. Mrs. Harriman ably seconded her husband in making everything move harmoniously. The boys were very young, Roland only about two or three years of age. One of the telling sights that comes to mind as I write is Mr. Harriman keeping trot-step with little Roland while helping him to drag a toy canoe along the deck with a cotton string. The girls were so bright and eager to study the wonderful regions passed through that we were all proud to become their teachers.

We soon learned that Mr. Harriman was not only a wonderful manager of men, but that he was fearless. Nothing in his way could daunt him or abate one jot the vigour of his progress toward his aims, no matter what – going ashore through heavy breakers, sailing uncharted fiords, pursuing bears, etc. As we approached the head of one of the Prince William Sound fiords it seemed to be completely blocked by the front of a large glacier and an outreaching headland. The local pilot, turning to our Captain Doran, said: "Here, take your ship. I am not going to be responsible for her if she is to be run into every unsounded, uncharted channel and frog marsh." The captain slowed down, and in a few minutes stopped, after creeping forward to within half a mile or so of the front of the ice-wall.

Then Mr. Harriman asked me if I was satisfied with what I had seen and was ready to turn back, to which I replied: "Judging from the trends of this fiord and glacier there must be a corresponding fiord or glacier to the southward, and although the ship has probably gone as far as it is safe to go, I wish you would have a boat lowered and let me take a look around that headland into the hidden half of the landscape."

"We can perhaps run the ship there," he said, and immediately ordered the captain to "go ahead and try to pass between the ice-wall and headland." The passage was dangerously narrow and threatening, but gradually opened into a magnificent icy fiord about twelve miles long, stretching away to the southward. The water continuing deep, as the sounding line showed, Mr. Harriman quietly ordered the captain to go right ahead up the middle of the new fiord. "Full speed, sir?" inquired the captain. "Yes, full speed ahead." The sail up this majestic fiord in the evening sunshine, picturesquely varied glaciers coming successively to view, sweeping from high snowy fountains and discharging their thundering wave-raising icebergs, was, I think, the most exciting experience of the whole trip.

Near the head of the fiord I noticed a small cove where firewood could be procured and requested to be put ashore there to study the new wilderness while the ship, which had lost one of her propeller blades, was being repaired on a smooth beach near Cordova. Mr. Gannett, the topographer, and several others joined me, and we landed a little before midnight, secured the boat, hoisted blankets and provisions up a flat-topped bluff by rope and tackle, and encamped in a magnificent Cassiope garden on the margin of a forest of mountain hemlock. During the five days' absence of the steamer the fiord and the largest of the glaciers at the head of it were pretty thoroughly explored and mapped and worthily named for their discoverer, the Harriman Fiord and Harriman Glacier.

After this wonderful voyage I had occasional glimpses of Mr. Harriman when he came West, but a good many years passed before I felt that I was at all acquainted with him. He had been but little heard of, especially in the West, until the marvellous rebuilding of the Union and Southern Pacific railroads and their branch and extensions compelled attention and made him known to the world in general as the greatest railroad builder and manager of the age. But it was after dark years of anxiety and sorrow that I became intimately acquainted with him and discovered the greatness of his sympathies.

I saw him in the spring of 1903 in San Francisco just before he started back home, and only a few weeks later, when I was on my way to Europe and Asia, I visited him at the Hotel Netherland, New York, where he was recovering from a dangerous surgical operation. After cheery greetings he said he was getting well and would soon be up and at work. "You must have suffered terribly," I said. " Oh, never mind that; you know there is always more or less pain connected with surgery, but I made the quickest time across the continent that ever was made. I made it in less than three days from San Francisco to New York, and I didn't hurry the first day, either. Troubles seldom come singly. Now we are getting out of them all – strikes on the roads, scarlet fever in the family, etc. – and this evening for the first time since these troubles commenced we are going to dine together in my room. Join us and you will see all the family." But a prior engagement prevented, and I had to sail the next morning for Liverpool. Noticing I looked tired, he ordered a glass of milk for me and bade me remember there is such a thing as an electric cable, that he was president of two steamship companies, and when I got around to China and Japan, if I should happen to need anything, to let him know. And when I replied that I was already unconscionably deep in his debt, he said: "Oh, you can't keep accounts of that kind; pass them along anywhere whenever you get the chance."

Just as I was leaving St. Petersburg for the Crimea and the Caucasus I received a long letter from him, stating that it had occurred to him after I left that a letter to his agents in Japan and China might he of use to me. No heart could escape the influence of this sort of kindness from one overladen with so many great cares. That he should have thought of me at all under such crushing circumstances was an unmistakable token of affection, and brought more clearly to view his noble-hearted loyalty and depth of character, on which all sound friendship is founded.

He spent most of the summer of 1907 at his Pelican Bay Lodge on Klamath Lake, in southern Oregon. On his arrival in San Francisco, when he inquired: "You're going to the Lodge with us, are you not?"

I said, "Yes, I shall be very glad to pay my respects to Mrs. Harriman and the family and stay a few days, but I cannot afford to spend the summer there."

"Why?" he inquired.

"Because I am busy."

"What are you doing?"

"Writing a book."

"Well, you come up to the Lodge and I will show you how to write books. The trouble with you is you are too slow in your beginnings.

You plan and brood too much. Begin, begin, begin! Put forth what you wish to say in the first words that come to mind, just as you talk, until all that's to go into the book is got down. Then correct, transpose, add, strike out and change as much as you like. Hammer away at it until it suits you. Come on, and get something begun."

"So I went to the famous Lodge, intending to stay a few days or a week, but when I spoke of leaving, Mr. Harriman said I must stay and work, and directed his private secretary to follow me and put down everything I said. So I was fairly compelled to make a beginning in dictating to a stenographer, which proved rather awkward at first, but in a couple of months a sort of foundation for more than one volume was laid.

The Lodge was beautifully located at the head of Pelican Bay beside its famous crystal springs, the magnificent Klamath Lake in front of it, bordered with meadows and bounded in the distance by dark forested mountains and hills – a fine place for recreation and rest – air, water, and scenery reviving. The weather was mostly cool and bright, just right for soothing exercise, walks in the woods, and boating on the lake, which most of the time was mirror-like, reflecting the sky and the fringing meadows and forest-clad mountain shores.

On our return from boat excursions a beautiful picture was outspread before us about an hour before sundown, especially toward autumn, when the colours were ripening – the shining lake enlivened with leaping trout and flocks of waterfowl; the stream from the great springs like a river with broad brown and yellow meadows on either hand; and the dark forested mountains, changing to blue in the background, rising higher and higher, with Mt. Pitt, highest of all, pointing serenely heavenward through the midst of the sunset purple and gold.

But even here Mr. Harriman did not enjoy complete rest, for he called his lieutenants about him, and through them and a telegraph wire kept in touch with all his work and world affairs in general. Nevertheless we hoped for lasting benefits from the mountain air and water – nor were we altogether disappointed.

When at length we left the Lodge I accompanied him to Portland. At the stations along the road he was hailed by enthusiastic crowds, assembled to pay their respects, recognising the good he had done and was doing in developing the country and laying broad and deep the foundations of prosperity. A like enthusiasm marked his reception in Portland, and on the return trip a large body of Shriners on their way to Eugene stopped his train by taking possession of the track, climbed over the railing of his car, and literally took him by force and carried him away through the crowd on their shoulders, with cheers and hurrahs as straight from the heart as any I ever heard. The popular tide had turned, sweeping away hatred and most of the old hard railroad mistrust and suspicion. He was at last coming into his own after as hard a fair-play battle as man ever won.

In the last years of his life even the Southern Pacific, which had been almost universally disliked and regarded as a public enemy, became popular under his rule of never turning down any complaint whatever. He demanded that every case be taken up by the proper officers and tried, even if it should amount to nothing more than a discourteous answer to a question by an agent at some remote desert station. It was also recognised that no expense was being spared to improve the road not only as a carrier of goods but to make it safer for passengers. Every convenience, every precaution against accidents, was put in use at whatever cost.

The serene strength of his mind was manifested by being always equal to whatever might happen or to whatever he wished to do. None I ever knew faced the storm and stress of the world's affairs more calmly and resolutely, nor have I ever known another with such power of performance. He was quiet and reserved in manner, and to those who judged him only from news-paper reports or from meeting him in formal business matters he often seemed' unsympathetic, but never so to those who were permitted to see beneath the surface. His habit of silence was often remarked. No wonder he had little to say in society when he was carrying the affairs of a continent in his head. With a quick sense of plain right and wrong, and having no words to waste, he spoke with straight-ahead frankness. The same qualities seem inherent in all the family. "Good sense," "Perfectly natural," are phrases often repeated.

He said he was lucky, but his kind of luck was simply cause and effect. Always resourceful and self-reliant, full of initiative power, heart and mind worked together in turning out thorough and sincere work. And that he was far from being a man of one idea is plain from the wide range of public questions to which he turned his attention – education, public libraries, preservation of public parks, etc. The light that always follows good work never ceased to shine on all his ways, and showed him capable of being great in anything he liked. Flashing keenness of insight, quick decision, heroic strength and tenacity of purpose without shadow of turning enabled him to "make good," as he was so fond of saying, in all his undertakings. Overcoming so-called insurmountable obstacles, doing things judged impossible, were the tasks he liked best, such, for example, as damming the Colorado flood, filling in a way across the Great Salt Lake, tunnelling the Sierra above Truckee, and rushing all the vast resources at his command with incredible swiftness to the help of San Francisco after the great earthquake and fire.

With his network of roads he heaped benefits of every sort on all alike. Never before have the dry bones of railroad methods been so shaken into orderly effective life. His roads are his monuments, together with the life to which they gave rise, but however substantial, they are less enduring than the love of his friends.

No enterprise calculated to advance humanity failed to interest him, and few have been in touch with so many lives. He sympathised with his thousands of employees, paid good wages, and studied their welfare, but of course insisted on that strict discipline upon which safety and success in dangerous complicated work depend, making them feel his eyes; promptly weeding out incompetence; educating and encouraging the hopeful and strong. How else could so many wheels be kept on the tracks and rolled to their destination on time? But, however exacting, on none did he throw anything like so heavy a burden as the one he himself carried. It seemed too great for any human being.

On his inspection tours, especially in the West along his new roads, his coming was hailed with joy by all classes, and it was this steady development of general goodwill toward him that cheered his last years. Few fully realise the heroism with which in these last years, while struggling with oncoming illness, he continued to throw himself into his work; gaining new power as he went on his way; enriching himself by enriching others; and increasing the safety, comfort, and general well-being of millions of his fellow citizens as well as their wealth.

For money he never cared except as a tool like a locomotive or ship. Before I came to know him I thought like many others that money making might be one of the springs of his action. One evening when the Alaskan Expedition was at Kodiack the scientists, assembled on the forecastle awaiting the dinner bell, began to talk of the blessed ministry of wealth, especially in Mr. Harriman's case, now that some of it was being devoted to science. When these wealth laudations were sounding loudest I teasingly interrupted them, saying, "I don't think Mr. Harriman is very rich. He has not as much money as I have. I have all I want and Mr. Harriman has not." This saying somehow reached Mr. Harriman's ear and after dinner, seating himself beside me, he said: "I never cared for money except as power for work. I was always lucky and my friends and neighbours, observing my luck, brought their money to me to invest, and in this way I have come to handle large sums. What I most enjoy is the power of creation, getting into partnership with nature in doing good, helping to feed man and beast, and making everybody and everything a little better and happier."And this has proved true. He earned the means and inherited the courage to do and dare as his great head and heart directed.

He was flashing quick to see the best of things and the best of people. I never saw him bitter or stormily angry or unjust. None I ever knew had a greater capacity for kindness. He was a shrewd judge of character, had strong sense, broad humanity, and like underground irrigating streams did much in quiet, hidden ways for clubs, schools, churches, public parks, neglected children, etc., always ready to lend a hand.

To him I owe some of the most precious moments of my life. The memories of heart-to-heart talks that pleasant summer at Klamath Lake I shall always treasure with reverent affection, together with those of our last days at Pasadena, when, in the midst of his own crushing cares, he lavished whole-hearted sympathy and care on my sick child. I never knew a warmer heart. Our last meeting was in Los Angeles, at a public reception, where I was delighted with the good wishes and respect accorded him by the multitude that pressed around him to shake his hand. But when the meeting broke up, leaving him weary and pale, there fell a foreboding shadow that I could never shake off.

He will not be forgotten. Respect and admiration for his wonderful talents, and love for the greatness of his heart and service, are every day growing. And although scarce any one as yet is able to make anything like a fair estimate of his life and character, almost everybody comes at last to know a good man. His influence is touching everything, and he is coming to be recognised as one of the rare souls Heaven sends into the world once in centuries. When his work was finished his friends sang, "Well, done!" and soon or late the world must join in their "Well done!" song.

JOHN MUIR
AS OTHERS SAW HIM

John Muir
as others saw him

"John Muir – President of the Sierra Club," "John Muir as I Knew Him,"
"The Burial of John Muir," "Recollections of John Muir," "John Muir" ,
"John Muir and the Alaska Book," and "Muir's Love for Trees" (originally titled ''John Muir'') are
selected from appreciations that appeared after Muir's death in the
Sierra Club Bulletin, Vol. X, No.1, January 1916.

"To the Memory of John Muir"
was first published in the *Sierra Club Bulletin*, Vol. X, No.2, January 1917.

"Personal Recollections of John Muir"
was first published in the *Sierra Club Bulletin*, Vol. XIII, No.1, February 1928
reproduced by permission from the Sierra Club

"John Muir, Mountaineer"
was first published in the *Alpine Journal*, Vol. XCIX, 1994
reproduced by permission from the author.

CONTENTS

JOHN MUIR · MASTER OF ARTS · HARVARD UNIVERSITY

· JOHANNEM MVIR ·
LOCORVM INCOGNITORVM
EXPLORATOREM INSIGNEM · FLVMINVM
QVI SVNT IN ALASKA
SERRATISQVE MONTIBVS CONGLACIATORVM
STVDIOSVM · DILIGENTEM SILVARVM
ET RERAM AGRESTIVM
FERARAMQVE INDAGATORVM
ARTIVM MAGISTRVM

CAMBRIDGE MASSACHUSETTS   CHARLES WILLIAM ELIOT
JUNE 24 · A D 1896   PRESIDENT

PART ONE

John Muir – President of the Sierra Club

BY WILLIAM E COLBY

John Muir was the Sierra Club's first President and held that office for twenty-two years – until his death. The Sierra Club was organised in 1892 largely as a result of the widespread interest in California's wonderful mountain playgrounds, which had been aroused by his twenty years of preaching the necessity for their preservation before it should become too late. The Yosemite National Park had just been created as one result of his splendid work. While we could have this great leader of all true mountaineers and lovers of "pure wildness," it was unthinkable that anyone else should hold the office of President.

It was my good fortune to be Secretary of the Club for the last fifteen years of this period and I came to know this wonderful man as I have known few others. It is a priceless privilege to be in close contact with a man whose mind was as pure and whose ideals were as high as were John Muir's, and moreover, one who so thoroughly lived up to this ideal purity.

John Muir will never be fully appreciated by those whose minds are filled with money-getting and the sordid things of modern everyday life. To such Muir is an enigma – a fanatic – visionary and impractical. There is nothing in common to arouse sympathetic interest. That anyone should spend his whole life in ascertaining the fundamental truths of nature and glory in their discovery with a joy that would put to shame even the religious zealot is to many utterly incomprehensible. That a man should brave the storms and thread the pathless wilderness, exult in the earthquake's violence, rejoice in the icy blasts of the northern glaciers, and that he should do all this alone and unarmed, year in and year out, is a marvel that but few can understand. These solitary explorations were quite in contrast with the usual heavily equipped expeditions which undertake such work. John Muir loved and gloried in this sort of life and approached it with an enthusiasm and power of will that made hardships and those things which most human beings consider essentials, mere trifles by comparison. He was willing to subordinate everything in life to this work which he had set out to do supremely well, and it is little wonder that he attained his goal.

His latter days were so full of the rich experiences of these earlier years of devotion to his chosen work and he looked with such calm and serenity out upon the feverish haste and turmoil of those about him, engaged in making everything within reach "dollarable," that he seemed to be living in a world apart – a world created by his own wonderful spirit and efforts.

To those who thought him impractical and visionary, it is only necessary to point out his early skill as an inventor, which, if continued, would have made him world famous, or to his success as an orchardist, making his friends, the trees, bear as they had never been known to bear before or since. But these activities were chosen mainly because they seemed the duty of the hour and when finished were left for the nobler pursuits that lay nearest his heart.

His true position as a geologist will never be adequately recognised because his writings on his geological studies were so minimised by contrast with that greater field of beautiful literature in which he excelled. But anyone who has read his *Studies in the Sierra*, and who realises that his views on glaciation as bearing on the origin of Yosemite Valley were written at a time when geologists of great eminence were advancing other theories, and had no patience with any glacial theory, will appreciate that John Muir was no ordinary student of the physical laws of nature. I ran across the following extract from a little pamphlet on the Yosemite, published in 1872:*

There is and has been for two years past, living in the Valley, a gentleman of Scottish parentage, by name John Muir, who, Hugh Miller like, is studying the rocks in and around the Valley. He told me that he was trying to read the great book spread out before him. He is by himself pursuing a course of geological studies, and is making careful drawings of the different parts of the gorge. No doubt he is more thoroughly acquainted with this valley than anyone else. He has.been far up the Sierras where glaciers are now in action, ploughing deep depressions in the mountains. He has made a critical examination of the superincumbent rocks, and already has much material upon which to form a correct theory.

When we bear in mind the fact that at that time Muir had been in the Valley only a little over two years, and that his glacial theory of the origin of the Valley is now quite generally accepted, this prophecy is all the more striking.

John Muir himself can tell more fittingly than I am able to his relation to the Club and, therefore, the following extracts have been selected from some of his letters.

Martinez , January 15th, 1907

I herewith return the draft of a Club report on Kings River region with my hearty approval, excepting the first two pages of the MS., in which the Yosemite and Kings River regions are compared. Every possible aid and encouragement should be given by the Club for the preservation, road and trail-building etc., for the development of the magnificent Kings River region,

* *The Yosemite*, by John Erastus Lester, 1873 – prepared for and read before the Rhode Island Historical Society.

but unjust one-sided comparisons seeking to build up and glorify one region at the expense of lowering the other is useless work and should be left to real estate agents, promoters, rival hotel and stage owners, etc. Certainly the Club has nothing to do with such stuff, tremendous advantages, wealth and variety of mountain sculpture depending on greater depths and heights, etc., suggest boys with eyes to depth and height of butter and honey, seeing tremendous advantages in one slice of bread over another cut from the same loaf.

Have you seen the President's Proclamation of December 8th, 1906, creating the 'Petrified Forest National Monument' under the Act of Congress of June 8th, 1906? Contains 60,776.02 acres, and includes the Blue Jasper Forest Helen and I found. The large new forest to the north of Adamana is to be added to the above. Come up some Saturday night or Sunday and talk over matters.

Martinez, January 13th, 1908

Of course I heartily approve of the proposed vote of thanks to Mr. Kent, and suggest a slight change in the form of the resolution, as follows:

"*Resolved*: That the Sierra Club extend a hearty vote of thanks to Mr. William Kent in testimony of its appreciation of his noble gift to the Federal Government of the Redwood Canyon on Mount Tamalpais, with its magnificent primeval groves of *Sequoia sempervirens*, to be devoted as a public park and pleasure-ground to the people forever."

Los Angeles, California, January 16th, 1911

Thanks for your kind letter and the book which you forwarded.

I am now at work on the Kings River yosemites, and I would like to have the part of the Kings River region which ought to be added to the General Grant and Sequoia National parks definitely described, because I wish to recommend the preservation of the region in the Yosemite guidebook....

New York City, May 26th, 1911

I have just received a copy of *My First Summer in the Sierra*. It is dedicated "To The Sierra Club, Faithful Defender of the People's Playgrounds." Am stopping with the Harrimans. The above is my address until the first of July .

The American Alpine Club is arranging to give me a dinner, at which you may be sure there will be a lot of Hetch Hetchy work....

We may lose this particular fight, but truth and right must prevail at last. Anyhow we must be true to ourselves and the Lord.

Castle Rock, Garrisons on Hudson, N.Y. June 27th, 1911

I've just written to Mr. McFarland assuring him of my help in the Niagara fight and my eagerness to meet him. I had not in the least forgotten him or his magnificent work, but since coming here I've had so much Hetch Hetchy and book work to do, besides planning for S. America, and have also been tousled and tumbled hither thither, dinnered, honoured, etc., almost out of my wits, I could never set a day to see him. The society weather is now growing calm as the thermometer rises, and I hope to get a quiet week or two to see friends and finish my Yosemite book.

The American Alpine Club gave me a fine dinner, so did the Appalachian, and a great time at the Yale Commencement, getting honour for helping to save Hetch Hetchy. Glad you like the Sierra Club summer book. I'll get the publishers to send some. Remember me to Mrs. Colby and Parsons and your brave pair of young mountaineers. Good luck for your outing. Greet them all at your camp-fire with my warmest good wishes.

Para, Brazil, September 19th, 1911

I hope you all had a good time this summer, the usual Sierra Club luck. When I left New York August 12th, the Hetch Hetchy looked comparatively safe as far as I could see, but the wicked, whether down or up, are never to be trusted, so we must keep on watching, praying, fighting, overcoming evil with good as we are able.

I've had a glorious time up the Amazon. In about a week from above date, I hope to be on my way to Rio de Janeiro. Thence I intend going to Buenos Aires, sail up the Uruguay and La Plata, cross the Andes to Valparaiso and southward along the araucarian forests, etc. Then perhaps to South Africa to see its wonderful flora, etc.; may be home in the spring.

My kindest regards to Mrs. Colby and the great pair of boys and to the Parsons, and all the Club you see.

and from the steamer *Windkirk*, near Zanzibar, February 4th, 1912

I've had a great time in South America and South Africa. Indeed it now seems that on this pair of wild, hot continents I've enjoyed the most fruitful year of my life. Some happy California day I'll try to tell you about it. I'm now on my way from Beira to Mombasa after a grand trip to the Zambesi Baobab forests, Victoria Falls, and the magnificent glacial rock scenery of Southern Rhodesia. From Mombasa I intend to make a short trip into the Nyanza lake region, then home via Suez, Naples and New York, hoping to find you and all the Sierra Club and its friends and affairs hale and happy and prosperous.

Martinez, May 1st, 1912

I'll be down Friday and stop over for the Saturday meeting. If a few of the Club members wish very much to give me an informal dinner I'll not object, but my dress suit is in Los Angeles; have nothing but old clothes here, therefore the thing must be an informal sort of camp affair.

Hollywood, California, June 24th, 1912

I thank you very much for your kind wishes to give me a pleasant Kern River trip, and am very sorry that work has been so unmercifully piled upon me that I find it impossible to escape from it, so I must just stay and work.

I heartily congratulate you and all your merry mountaineers in the magnificent trip that lies before you. As you know, I have seen something of nearly all the mountain chains in the world, and have experienced their varied climates and attractions of forests and rivers, lakes and meadows, etc. In fact, I have seen a little of all the high places and low places of the continents, but no mountain range seems to me so kind, so beautiful, or so fine in its sculpture as the Sierra Nevada. If you were as free as the winds are, and the light, to choose a campground in any part of the globe, I could not direct you to a single place for your outing that, all things considered, is so attractive, so exhilarating and uplifting in every way as just the trip that you are now making. You are far happier than you know. Good luck to you all, and I shall hope to see you all on your return, boys and girls, with the sparkle and exhilaration of the mountains still in your eyes.

With love and countless fondly cherished memories. Ever faithfully yours,

JOHN MUIR.

Of course in all your camp-fire preaching and praying you will never forget Hetch Hetchy.

PART TWO

John Muir as I Knew Him*

BY ROBERT UNDERWOOD JOHNSON

Sometime, in the evolution of America, we shall throw off the two shackles that retard our progress as an artistic nation – philistinism and commercialism – and advance with freedom toward the love of beauty as a principle. Then it will not be enough that one shall love merely one kind of beauty, each worker his own art, or that art shall be separated from life as something too precious for use; men will search for beauty as scientists search for truth, knowing that while truth can make one free, it is beauty of some sort, as addressed to the eye, the ear, the mind, or the moral sense, that alone can give permanent happiness. When that apocalyptic day shall come, the world will look back to the time we live in and remember the voice of one crying in the wilderness and bless the name of John Muir. To some, beauty seems but an accident of creation: to Muir it was the very smile of God. He sung the glory of nature like another Psalmist, and, as a true artist, was unashamed of his emotions.

An instance of this is told of him as he stood with an acquaintance at one of the great viewpoints of the Yosemite Valley, and, filled with wonder and

---

* Read, in part, at a meeting of the American Academy of Arts and Letters in New York, Jan. 6th, 1916.

devotion, wept. His companion, more solid than most, could not understand his feeling, and was so thoughtless as to say so. "Mon," said Muir, with the Scotch dialect into which he often lapsed, "Can ye see unmoved the glory of the Almighty?" "Oh, it's very fine," was the reply, "but I do not wear my heart upon my sleeve." "Ah, my dear mon," said Muir, "in the face of such a scene as this, it's no time to be thinkin' o' where you wear your heart."

No astronomer was ever more devout. The love of nature was his religion, but it was not without a personal God, whom he thought as great in the decoration of a flower as in the launching of a glacier. The old Scotch training persisted through all his studies of causation, and the keynote of his philosophy was intelligent and benevolent design. His wonder grew with his wisdom. Writing for the first time to a young friend, he expressed the hope that she would "find that going to the mountains is going home, and that Christ's Sermon on the Mount is on every mount."

It was late in May, 1889, that I first met him. I had gone to San Francisco to organise the series of papers afterward published in the *Century Magazine* under the title of "The Goldhunters of California," and promptly upon my arrival he came to see me. It was at the Palace Hotel in San Francisco. I was dressing for dinner and was obliged to ask him to come up to my room. He was a long time in doing so and I feared he had lost his way. I can remember, as if it were yesterday, hearing him call down the corridor, "Johnson, Johnson! where are you? I can't get the hang of these artificial canyons," and before he had made any of the conventional greetings or inquiries, he added: "Up in the Sierra, all along the gorges, the glaciers have put up natural sign-posts, and you can't miss your way, but here – there's nothing to tell you where to go."

With all his Scotch wit and his democratic feeling, Muir bore himself with dignity in every company. He readily adjusted himself to any environment. In the High Sierra he was indeed a voice crying in the wilderness: moreover, he looked like John the Baptist as portrayed in bronze by Donatello and others of the Renaissance sculptors – spare of frame, hardy, keen of eye and visage, and on the march eager of movement. It was difficult for an untrained walker to keep up with him as he leaped from rock to rock as surely as a mountain goat, or skimmed the surface of the ground, a trick of easy locomotion learned from the Indians. If he ever became tired nobody knew it, and yet, though he delighted in badinage at the expense of the "tenderfoot," he was as sympathetic as a mother. I remember a scramble we had in the upper Tuolumne Canyon which afforded him great fun at my expense. The detritus of the wall of the gorge lay in a confused mass of rocks, varying in size from a market basket to a dwelling house, the interstices overgrown with a most deceptive shrub, the soft leaves of which concealed its iron trunk and branches. Across such a Dantean formation Muir went with certainty and alertness, while I fell and floundered like a bad swimmer, so that he had to give me many a helpful hand and cheering word, and when at last I was obliged to rest, Muir, before going on for an hour's exploration, sought out for me one of the most beautiful spots I had ever seen, where the rushing river, striking pot-holes in its granite bed, was thrown up into water wheels twenty feet high. When he returned to camp he showered me with little attentions and tucked me into my blankets with the tenderness that he gave to children and animals.

Another Scotch trait was his surface antipathies. He did not hate anything – not even his antagonists, the tree vandals – but spoke of those "misguided worldlings" in terms of pity; yet he had a wholesome contempt for the contemptible. His growl – he never had a bark – was worse than his bite. His pity was often expressed for the blindness of those who through unenlightened selfishness chose the lower utility of nature in place of the higher.

Many have praised the pleasures of solitude – few have known them as Muir knew them, roaming the High Sierra week after week with only bread and tea and sometimes berries for his sustenance, which he would have said were a satisfactory substitute for the "locusts and wild honey" of his prototype. His trips to Alaska were even more solitary and we should say forbidding – but not he, for no weather, no condition of wildness, no absence of animal life could make him lonely. He was a pioneer of nature, but also a pioneer of truth, and he needed no comrade. Many will recall his thrilling adventure on the Muir glacier, told in his story entitled *Stickeen*, named for his companion, the missionary's dog. I heard him tell it a dozen times – how the explorer and the little mongrel were caught on a peninsula of the glacier – and how they escaped. It is one of the finest studies of dogliness in all literature, and told in Muir's whimsical way, betrayed unconsciously the tenderness of his heart. Though never lonely, he was not at all a professional recluse: he loved companions and craved good talk, and was glad to have others with him on his tramps, but it was rare to find congenial friends who cared for the adventures in which he revelled. He was hungry for sympathy and found it in the visitors whom he piloted about and above the Yosemite Valley – Emerson, Sir Joseph Hooker, Torrey, and many others of an older day or of late years, including presidents Roosevelt and Taft.

Muir was clever at story-telling, and put into it both wit and sympathy, never failing to give, as a background, more delightful information about the mountains than a professor of geology would put into a chapter. With his one good eye – for the sight of the other had been impaired in his college days in Wisconsin by the stroke of a needle – he saw every scene, in detail and in mass. This his conversation visualised until his imagination kindled the imagination of his hearer.

Adventures are to the adventurous. Muir, never reckless, was fortunate in seeing nature in many a wonderful mood and aspect. Who that has read them can forget his wonderful descriptions of the windstorm in the Yuba which he outrode in a tree top, or of the avalanche in the Yosemite, or of the spring floods pouring in hundreds of streams over the rim of the Valley? And what unrecorded adventures he must have had as pioneer of peak and glacier in his study of the animal and vegetable life of the Sierra. Did any observer ever come nearer than he to recording the soul of nature? If "goodwill makes intelligence," as Emerson avers, Muir's love of his mountains amounted to divination. What others learned laboriously, he seemed to reach by instinct, and yet he was painstaking in the extreme, and jealous of the correctness of both his facts and his conclusions, defending them as a beast defends her young. In the Arctic, in the great forests of Asia, on the Amazon and in Africa at seventy-three, wherever he was, he incurred peril, not for "the game," but for some great emprise of science.

But Muir's public services were not merely scientific and literary. His countrymen owe him gratitude as the pioneer of our system of national parks. Before 1889 we had but one of any importance – the Yellowstone. Out of the fight which he led for the better care of the Yosemite by the State of California grew the demand for the extension of the system. To this many persons and organisations contributed, but Muir's writings and enthusiasm were the chief forces that inspired the movement. All the other torches were lighted from his. His disinterestedness was too obvious not to be recognised even by opponents. To a friend who in 1906 made an inquiry about a mine in California he wrote: "I don't know anything about the X mine or any other. Nor do I know any mine owners. All this $ geology is out of my line." It was in his name that the appeal was made for the creation of the Yosemite National Park in 1890, and for six years he was the leader of the movement for the retrocession by California of the Valley reservation, to be merged in the surrounding park, a result which, by the timely aid of Edward H. Harriman, was accomplished in 1905.

In 1896–7, when the Forestry Commission of the National Academy of Sciences, under the chairmanship of Professor Charles S. Sargent, of Harvard, was making investigations to determine what further reservations ought to be made in the form of national parks, Muir accompanied it over much of its route through the far west and the northwest, and gave it his assistance and counsel. March 27th, 1899, he wrote: "I've spent most of the winter on forest protection – at least I've done little beside writing about it." From its inception to its lamentable success in December, 1913, he fought every step of the scheme to grant to San Francisco for a water reservoir the famous Hetch Hetchy Valley, part of the Yosemite National Park, which, as I have said, had been created largely through his instumentality. In the last stages of the campaign his time was almost exclusively occupied with this contest. He opposed the project as unnecessary, as objectionable intrinsically, and as a dangerous precedent, and he was greatly cast down when it became a law. But he was also relieved. Writing to a friend, he said: "I'm glad the fight for the Tuolumne Yosemite is finished. It has lasted twelve years. Some compensating good must surely come from so great a loss. With the New

Year comes new work. I am now writing on Alaska. A fine change from faithless politics to crystal ice and snow." It is also to his credit that he first made known to the world the wonder and glory of the Big Trees; those that have been rescued from the saw of the sordid lumbermen owe their salvation primarily to his voice.

Muir's death, on Christmas Eve of 1914, though it occurred at the ripe age of seventy-six and though it closed a life of distinguished achievement, was yet untimely, for his work was by no means finished. For years I had been imploring him to devote himself to the completion of his record. The material for many contemplated volumes exists in his numerous notebooks, and though, I believe, these notes were to a great degree written *in extenso* rather than scrappily, and thus contain much available literary treasure, yet where is the one that could give them the roundness of presentation and the charm of style which are found in Muir's best literary work? One almost hesitates to use the word "great" of one who has just passed away, but I believe that history will give a very high place to the indomitable explorer who discovered the great glacier named for him, and whose life for eleven years in the High Sierra resulted in a body of writing of marked excellence, combining accurate and carefully co-ordinated scientific observation with poetic sensibility and expression. His chief books, *The Mountains of California*, *Our National Parks* and *The Yosemite*, are both delightful and convincing, and should be made supplemental reading for schools. When he rhapsodises it is because his subject calls for rhapsody, and not to cover up thinness of texture in his material. He is likely to remain the one historian of the Sierra; he imported into his view the imagination of the poet and the reverence of the worshipper.

Muir was not without wide and affectionate regard in his own state, but California was too near to him to appreciate fully his greatness as a prophet, or the service he did in trying to recall her to the gospel of beauty. She has, however, done him and herself honour in providing for a path in the High Sierra, from the Yosemite to Mount Whitney, to be called the John Muir Trail. William Kent, during Muir's life, paid him a rare tribute in giving to the nation a park of redwoods with the understanding that it should be named Muir Woods. But the nation owes him more. His work was not sectional but for the whole people, for he was the real father of the forest reservations of America. The National Government should create from the great wild Sierra forest reserve a national park, to include the Kings River Canyon, to be called by his name. This recognition would be, so to speak, an overt act, the naming of the Muir Glacier being automatic by his very discovery of it. It is most appropriate and fitting that a wild Sierra region should be named for him. There has been but one John Muir.

The best monument to him, however, would be a successful movement, even at this late day, to save the Hetch Hetchy Valley from appropriation for commercial purposes. His death was hastened by his grief at this unbelievable calamity and I should be recreant to his memory if I did not call special attention to his crowning public service in endeavouring to prevent the disaster. The Government owes him penance at his tomb.

In conclusion, John Muir was not a "dreamer", but a practical man, a faithful citizen, a scientific observer, a writer of enduring power, with vision, poetry, courage in a contest, a heart of gold, and a spirit pure and fine.

PART THREE

Recollections of John Muir

BY CHARLES KEELER

My earliest recollections of John Muir date back some twenty-odd years, to those golden days in William Keith's rather dingy but glorious studio on Montgomery Street, when Muir would drop in from his Martinez retreat for a chat with his old painter friend. The two Scotchmen, who had camped together in Sierra wilds in summer outings, and cracked jokes at one another's expense in the studio or at one of the little French restaurants where they lunched during winter visits, were big elemental natures, both of them. The child-heart each had treasured in his own peculiar way. They were Willie and Johnnie in their bantering sallies.

Both were deeply religious natures, but emancipated from formalism and tradition. Both were students and lovers of nature, but where Keith saw colour and atmosphere, poetry and romance, in mountain and vale, tree and sky, Muir's eyes were fixed on the ever-changing processes of immutable law.

Those who knew Keith's work best realised that it fell into two groups – a comparatively hard, literal portrayal of the facts of landscape, and a free, impassioned outburst of impressionistic depicting of nature's moods. In his own heart he scorned the former and frankly gloried in the latter. His naturalistic sketches in colour were either studies of underlying fact or potboilers for the uninitiated who were not up to his dream rhapsodies.

Muir was at heart a seer. But for him the wonder and glory of nature lay not in its romance of atmosphere and its appeal to human emotions. He saw in it rather the embodiment of divine law, and in a picture looked for a naturalistic portrayal rather than an impressionistic interpretation. So it was that he failed to appreciate his artist friend's finest work. With his dry Scotch humour he loved to twit him in good-natured raillery. Both in the old Montgomery Street studio, and later in the larger Pine Street rooms, I have spent many a happy hour with these two great souls, looking at the pictures and listening to Muir's talk.

As his keen grey eye ranged over the pictures stacked in piles all over the place, he would fall upon a big careful objective study of a Sierra landscape.

"Now there's a real picture, Willie," he would exclaim. "Why don't you paint more like that?"

With a look of defiance the big shaggy-haired painter would draw from the stack a mystical dream of live-oaks, with a green and gold sunset sky, and stand it up on an easel with an impatient wave of his hand.

"What are you trying to make of that? You've stood it upside down, haven't you?" Muir would sally with a mischievous twinkle.

And Keith would finally give it up with:

"There's no use trying to show you pictures, Johnnie."

But in spite of these little pleasantries, which revealed a fundamentally different approach to nature, the two men had a life-long admiration and friendship for one another.

Never have I met another man of such singleness of mind in his devotion to nature as Muir. He lived and moved and had his being as a devotee. He was naturally a recluse, but if he could get a listener, whether of high or low degree, he would talk by the hour of his beloved mistress. It was the passion of his life, the awakening of the dull and circumscribed soul of the average man or woman to the ineffable splendour of the great out-of-doors.

During the memorable two months of the Harriman Expedition to Alaska, Muir and I were room-mates. He had the tender kindliness of a father. Of himself he took little heed, but no zealous missionary ever went abroad to spread the gospel with his fervour in communicating a love of nature. And with him a love of nature meant an understanding of her laws. He has told me that he found it necessary, in getting people to listen, to tell them stories such as his immortal tale of Stickeen, but the real hope in his heart was to awaken their interest so they would want to go to nature themselves and to delve into the mysteries of her ways.

Our stateroom was filled with "brush" – pine and spruce boughs, with cones or blossoms, and other trophies gathered on shore rambles. "Look at that little muggins of a fir cone," he would say to me, lovingly stroking the latest accession with which he littered the room, to the despair of the steward who tried to keep it in order.

That other great child-soul of nature, John Burroughs, was with us in Alaska, and the coming together of these two men was an event in American life. Burroughs is naively human, Muir intensely aloof. But Muir's aloofness was never cold or hard. It was the result of his almost fanatical absorption in the thrilling play of nature.

We dubbed him "Ice Chief" in Alaska, because of his enthusiasm for the great ice sculptor of the Glacial Age who had carved out the mountains in their present form. In those far northern wilds he was in his element, for with glaciers thundering their bergs into the inlets and sweeping majestically down through rugged mountain defiles, it was easy for him to show how all the carving of the mountains of the West was the work of their Titan graving tools. He would not hear of earthquake faults as a factor even in the shaping of the Yosemite.

It was all the work of the ice, although he had himself witnessed a great avalanche there as the result of an earthquake, and loved to tell about rushing up on the great mass of granite when the blocks were still hot from crashing down the mountain.

To have explored with Muir the great glacier which bears his name, to have wandered with him in Yosemite and the Kings River Canyon, is to have come, through his enthusiasm and vision, a little nearer the hidden mysteries of nature. Every tree and flower, every bird and stone was to him the outward token of an invisible world in process of making. He sauntered over the mountains in his blue jeans overalls, claiming kinship with the rocks and growing things and gathering them all to his heart.

Nor can I forget the simple kindly welcome at his Martinez home, the strolls about his broad acres of fruit and vine, and the evening talks, prolonged far into the night, in his study, littered with the trophies of a lifetime of communion with the great outdoors in many lands. In the autumn, boxes of grapes would come to prove that Muir was not so absorbed in his studies as to forget his friends, and on his visits to Berkeley, shining gold pieces would be slipped almost shyly into the children's hands.

Here was a real man, one who would get lost on the city streets, but could find his way through any unmapped wilderness; one who had the outward bearing of an unsophisticated farmer but was at home with the most polished man of the world. Devoid of all shams and affectations, sincere to the very roots of his being, his deadly earnestness was saved by that touch of Scotch humour and that deep tenderness and sympathy which shone through his being, despite the habitual absorption in impersonal matters. And that Muir was able to fight, those who know with what zeal and single-minded devotion to a cause he carried on his campaign to save the Hetch Hetchy Valley, can testify. Recluse and devotee of nature though he was, he could come out among men and with unflinching courage, untiring energy and rare practical sense, work to save his beloved trees and mountains from being despoiled.

Others may praise him for his keen eye, his grasp of nature's laws, his enthusiasm as an explorer, his grace and charm of literary style, but for me he was a personality that defies analysis – a great soul, a genuine friend, and I am grateful to share, with all who touched his life closely, in the consciousness that we are better and closer to the great primal things because we knew and loved him.

PART FOUR

John Muir

BY HENRY FAIRFIELD OSBORN

I believe that John Muir's name is destined to be immortal through his writings on mountains, forests, rivers, meadows, and the sentiment of the animal and plant life they contain. I do not believe anyone else has ever lived with just the same sentiment toward trees and flowers and the works of nature in general as that which John Muir manifested in his life, his conversations and his writings.

In the splendid journey which I had the privilege of taking with him to Alaska in 1896 I first became aware of his passionate love of nature in all its forms and his reverence for it as the direct handiwork of the Creator. He retained from his early religious training under his father this belief, which is so strongly expressed in the Old Testament, that all the works of nature are directly the work of God. In this sense I have never known anyone whose nature philosophy was more thoroughly theistic; at the same time he was a thorough-going evolutionist, and always delighted in my own evolutionary studies which I described to him from time to time in the course of our journeyings and conversations.

It was in Alaska that he quoted the lines from Goethe's *Wilhelm Meister* which inspired all his travels:

> Keep not standing fixed and rooted,
>   Briskly venture, briskly roam;
> Head and hand, where'er thou foot it,
>   And stout heart are still at home
> In each land the sun doth visit
>   We are gay what 'er betide
> To give room for wandering is it
>   That the world was made so wide.

Another sentiment of his regarding trees and flowers always impressed me: that was his attributing to them a personality, an individuality such as we associate with certain human beings and animals, but rarely with plants. To him a tree was something not only to be loved, but to be respected and revered. I well remember his intense indignation over the proposal by his friend Charles S. Sargent to substitute the name *Magnolia foetida* for *Magnolia grandiflora* on the grounds of priority. He quoted Sargent as saying, "After all, 'what's in a name?' " and himself as replying, "There is everything in the name; why inflict upon a beautiful and defenceless plant for all time the stigma of such a name as *Magnolia foetida*? You yourself would not like to have your own name changed from Charles S. Sargent to 'the malodorous Sargent.' "

John Muir's incomparable literary style did not come to him easily, but as the result of the most intense effort. I observed his methods of writing in connection with two of his books upon which he was engaged during the years 1911 and 1912. He came to our home on the Hudson in June, 1911, after the Yale Commencement, where he had received the degree of LL.D. on June 21st. He brought with him his new silken hood, in which he said he had looked very grand in the Commencement parade. On Friday, June 21st, he was established in Woodsome Lodge [now John Muir Lodge], a log cabin on a secluded mountain height, to complete his volume on the Yosemite. Daily he rose at 4:30 o'clock, and after a simple cup of coffee laboured incessantly on his two books, *The Yosemite* and *Boyhood and Youth*. It was very interesting to watch how difficult it was for him. In my diary of the time I find the following notes:

> Knowing his beautiful and easy style it is very interesting to learn how difficult it is for him; he groans over his labours, he writes and rewrites and interpolates. He loves the simplest English language and admires most of all Carlyle, Emerson and Thoreau. He is a very firm believer in Thoreau and starts my reading deeply of this author. He also loves his Bible and is constantly quoting it, as well as Milton and Burns. In his attitude toward nature, as well as in his special gifts and abilities, Muir shares many qualities with Thoreau. First among these is his mechanical ability, his fondness for the handling of tools; second, his close identification with nature; third, his interpretation of the religious spirit of nature; fourth, his happiness in solitude with nature; fifth, his lack of sympathy with crowds of people; sixth, his intense love of animals.

Thoreau's quiet residence at Walden is to be contrasted with Muir's world-wide journeyings from Scotland to Wisconsin; his penniless journey down the Mississippi to Louisiana, Florida, across Panama and northward into California in its early grandeur; his establishment of the sawmill, showing again his mechanical ability, as a means of livelihood in the Yosemite; his climbs in the High Sierra and discovery of still living glaciers; his eagerness to see the largest glaciers of Alaska and his several journeys and sojourns there; his wandering all over the great western and eastern forests of the United States; his visits to special forests in Europe; his world tour, without preconceived plan, including the wondrous forests of Africa, Australia, New Zealand and Asia. Finally, his very last great journey.

When starting out on this South American journey, from which I among other friends tried to dissuade him, he often quoted the phrase, "I never turn back." Although he greatly desired to have a comrade on this journey, and often urged me to accompany him, he finally was compelled to start out alone, quoting Milton: "I have chosen the lonely way."

On July 26th I said "goodbye" to this very dear friend, leaving him to work on his books and prepare for the long journey to South America, especially to see the forests of Araucaria. I know that at this time he had little intention of going on to Africa. It was impulse which led him from the east coast of South America to take a long northward journey in order to catch a steamer for the Cape of Good Hope.

He remained at Garrison for more than two months, writing his *Boyhood and Youth* and *The Yosemite*, and I have just decided to erect a tablet at the log cabin where this work was done and to name it John Muir Lodge.

Among the personal characteristics which stand out like crystal in the minds and hearts of his friends were his hatred of shams and his scorn of the conventions of life, his boldness and fearlessness of attack, well illustrated in his assault on the despoilers of the Hetch Hetchy Valley of the Yosemite, whom he loved to characterise as "thieves and robbers." It was a great privilege to be associated with him in this campaign. But certainly his chief characteristic was his intimate converse with nature and passionate love of its beauties; also I believe his marvellous insight into the creative powers of nature, closely interwoven with his deep religious sentiments and beliefs.

There were published in the *New York Evening Mail* some verses by Charles L. Edson with which I would close this all too brief tribute:

John o' the mountains, wonderful John,
Is past the summit and travelling on;
The turn of the trail on the mountain side,
A smile and "Hail!" where the glaciers slide,
A streak of red where the condors ride,
And John is over the Great Divide.

John o' the mountains camps today
On a level spot by the Milky Way;
And God is telling him how He rolled
The smoking earth from the iron mold,
And hammered the mountains till they were cold,
And planted the Redwood trees of old.

And John o' the mountains says. "I knew,
And I wanted to grapple the hand o' you;
And now we're sure to be friends and chums
And camp together till chaos comes."

PART FIVE

John Muir and the Alaska Book

BY MARION RANDALL PARSONS

In November, 1912, not long after his return from his last long journey across South America and Africa, Mr. Muir came to Berkeley to begin work on his Alaska notes. For a month he worked at my home with a stenographer, getting an exact transcription of the journals. The travel-worn, weather-stained little books carried on those memorable exploring trips of nearly forty years before were crammed with sketches and voluminous notes, jotted down perhaps in the canoe, or around the campfire, but oftenest in the solitudes of the great glaciers in whose study he cheerfully underwent so much cold and hunger and hardship.

It was most amusing to watch Mr. Muir at work. His intense interest in his subject led him to make many a long digression as his notes brought this or that incident to mind. Time meant nothing to him. Household machinery might stop, food grow cold on the table, and the business members of the family miss their morning trains while Mr. Muir pursued the tranquil course of his subject to the end. And so for an hour or more he might discourse while the stenographer sat with her hands folded. Her stolidity and indifference exasperated him beyond measure. To have no curiosity about the "terrestrial manifestations of God," above all to have no interest in glaciers, was to him both incomprehensible and sinful.

Once started on a task Mr. Muir was a tireless worker. The book in hand might have lain fallow for thirty years, but when it began to take form and substance he was all afire with eagerness to see it finished. Long evenings he spent poring over the notebooks or drawing from them the texts of the monologues he delighted in. His mind, indeed, dwelt with such complete absorption on his work that his conversation nearly always indicated its trend. His speech had all the beauty of phrase, the force and vigour of style of his written word, but with an added spell of fire and enthusiasm and glowing vitality that made it an inspiration and never-ending delight. Many a page of this Alaska book is for me a living record of our fireside hours of companionship.

Not until many months later, however, did I have any close acquaintance with *Travels in Alaska*. After working on it only a short time, Mr. Muir laid the book aside to take an active part in the fight for Hetch Hetchy. A few weeks after the final defeat a severe illness, from whose effects he never fully recovered, again interrupted the book. In his weakened condition the mere sifting out of the enormous mass of material was a task almost beyond his strength. Finding him one day utterly discouraged over it, I offered to go to him a day or two each week to help him until he could find the secretary to his mind. The arrangement proved unexpectedly happy and congenial to us both, and lasted until within a week of his death.

No one unacquainted with Mr. Muir's habits of work and living could appreciate the difficulty, nor, indeed, the humorous nature of the task. He was living alone in the dismantled old home, unused save for his study and sleeping porch. He went to his daughter's home for his meals, but neither she nor anyone else was allowed to touch the study, overflowing as it was with books and papers. Confusion was no word for the state of the manuscripts. He had been collecting material for over thirty years. In the interval that had elapsed since he began real work on it the two typewritten copies of the journals had become mixed, and in some cases both had been revised. Material from certain parts of the journals, moreover, had been used in newspaper letters and again in magazine articles, so as many as five different versions of some passages were in existence. Even had they been collected together and in order, to read and compare and reject would have been sufficiently hard but fresh versions were constantly coming to light, or in my absence Mr. Muir would unearth a copy of some version already disposed of. He was in the habit of making notes on anything that came to hand – an opened envelope, a paper bag, the margin of a newspaper. No scrap of manuscript could ever be destroyed, and I could devise no system of putting the rejected material aside that served to keep him from "discovering" it at some later date. Finally I took to hiding copied and rejected sheets alike inside a great roll of papers conspicuously tied with red ribbons and labelled in huge capitals "Copied!" and little by little the orange-box full of manuscript and the piles of scattered notes littering desk and table were reduced to a single working copy.

By seven o'clock each morning Mr. Muir had breakfasted and was ready for the day's work, usually lasting, with but the interruption of an hour at lunch and dinner and another at mail time, until ten at night. Composition was always slow and laborious for him. "This business of writing books," he would often say, "is a long, tiresome, endless job." To read his easy, flowing, forceful sentences, as rich in imagery and simple in diction as Bible English, no one would dream what infinite pains had been taken in their creation. Each sentence, each phrase, each word, underwent his critical scrutiny, not once but twenty times before he was satisfied to let it stand. His rare critical faculty was unimpaired to the end. So too was the freshness and vigour of his whole outlook on life. No trace of pessimism or despondency, even in the defeat of his most deeply cherished hopes, ever darkened his beautiful philosophy, and only in the intense physical fatigue brought on by his long working hours was there any hint of failing powers.

Mr. Muir himself, however, seemed to know that the end was near. Very touching were his attempts to rehabilitate the old house, whose forlorn emptiness and desolation were never allowed to weigh upon his own serene spirit, to put it in readiness for whomsoever should next live there. During the latter months of his life he often expressed the conviction that he would never live to write another book. His plan had long been to have his books tell the story of his life and travels, and in the early days of our work together he would often speak of the volumes of this wanderer's autobiography that he hoped yet to complete. But he was curiously untroubled about leaving his work unfinished. To a most unusual degree he seemed to feel that his had been a glorious life, wholly worthwhile. "Oh, I have had a *bully* life!" he said once. "I have done what I set out to do." And again: "To get these glorious works of God into yourself – that's the great thing; not to write about them." That nature's beauty had a deep and lasting influence on character was one of his most earnest beliefs. No impassable gulf between things material and spiritual ever existed for him, and scientific study only served to deepen his natural reverence and faith. Throughout this book, as through all the others, rings his triumphant belief in the harmony and unity of our universe, its imperishable beauty, its divine conception, "reflecting the plans of God."

It was a rare privilege to work with him day by day, a man of the most original thought, of the very highest ideals, of simplicity and truth and kindliness unsurpassed. He gave of his best in conversation. His genial, whimsical humour, his acute appraisal of character and motives, his wide knowledge of literature and intimate friendship with many of the leading men of his time, made him a wonderful companion. The memory of our long hours together will always remain a delight and an inspiration, for they brought me not only increased love and reverence for a beautiful spirit, but a new conception of the spiritual significance of the great world of nature he loved so well.

The work on this book was the chief pleasure and recreation of Mr. Muir's last days, for through it he lived again many of the most glorious experiences of his life. Always I shall remember the glow that would light his face whenever he paused in his work to tell in stirring words the story of some particularly inspiring day. Many years ago, after watching a sunrise in Glacier Bay, he wrote: "We turned and sailed away, joining the outgoing bergs ... feeling that, whatever the future might have in store, the treasures we had gained this glorious morning would enrich our lives forever." How true this was, how vital a part of his life these treasures of memory were, no one who met him could fail to know. For him neither time nor age had power to dim the glory of that icy land, after the Sierra Nevada, the best loved of all his wilderness homes.

PART SIX

Muir's Love for Trees

BY CHARLES SPRAGUE SARGENT

Few men whom I have known loved trees as deeply and intelligently as John Muir. The love of trees was born in him, I am sure, and had abundant nourishment during his wanderings over the Sierra, where for months at a time he lived among the largest and some of the most beautiful trees of the world. No one has studied the Sierra trees as living beings more deeply and continuously than Muir, and no one in writing about them has brought them so close to other lovers of nature.

Muir and I travelled through many forests, and saw together all the trees of western North America, from Alaska to Arizona. We wandered together through the great forests which cover the southern Appalachian Mountains, and through the tropical forests of southern Florida. Together we saw the forests of southern Russia and the Caucasus and those of eastern Siberia, but in all these wanderings Muir's heart never strayed very far from the California Sierra. He loved the Sierra trees the best, and in other lands his thoughts always returned to the great sequoia, the sugar pine, among all trees best loved by him; the incense cedar, the yellow pine, the Douglas spruce, and the other trees which make the forests of California the most wonderful coniferous forests of the world. With these he was always comparing all minor growths, and when he could not return to the Sierra his greatest happiness was in talking of them and in discussing the Sierra trees.

PART SEVEN

To the Memory of John Muir

BY C. HART MERRIAM

John Muir was doubtless more widely known and more generally loved than any other Californian. He was a famous wanderer, and left a trail that is well worth following. It leads to the mountains and forests, to health and happiness, and to a better appreciation of nature. While he loved the mountains and everything in them, his chief interests centred about the dynamic forces that shaped their features and the vegetation that clothed their slopes.

But, of all the objects in nature, trees appealed to him most strongly. These he knew as no other man has known them. They were ever-present in his mind and formed an inexhaustible theme of conversation. On his walks and in his study he delighted to talk of their individual peculiarities, and with his pencil he would make rough but characteristic sketches showing the dominant distinctive features of each species. He knew the dates of flowering and the differences of the sexes, and could tell offhand the time required by the several pines for maturing their cones. In nearly every case he could recognise a tree at a distance by its general habit, and when specimens were shown him he could identify them at a glance by the branches, flowers, fruit, or bark.

To gratify his love of forests and increase his knowledge of them he travelled far, studying not only those of the Pacific Coast from Alaska and British Columbia to southern California, those of the Rocky Mountains from Montana to Arizona, those of the Eastern states in both the northern and southern Alleghanies and in the pine barrens and everglades of Florida, but also traversing Russia, Siberia, and India, visiting Australia, New Zealand, and the Philippines, and late in life even journeying to South America to see for himself the great tropical forests of the Amazon and the remarkable Araucaria of western Patagonia. Has any other human eye seen so many and diverse types of arboreous vegetation, or any other mind learned so much of the great forests of the world?

One often hears Muir spoken of as an authority on the animal life of the mountains. This is an error. For while he liked to see birds and mammals in the wilderness and about his camps, he rarely troubled himself to learn their proper names and relationships. Now and then a particular species impressed itself sufficiently upon his attention to appear in his writings, and in a few instances to form the subject of a special article or chapter. His accounts of the water-ouzel and Sierra red squirrel – which latter he confused with the Douglas squirrel of the coast – are real contributions to natural history, abounding in original observations, full of sympathy, and charmingly told. But for scientific study of the great army of small birds and mammals he cared little. Plants, on the other hand, were always dear to him; he knew the names of hundreds of species and could tell at what altitude and in what situation each was likely to be found.

He had a strong mechanical bent, was fond of machinery, quick to grasp principles of mechanics, and was familiar with the various applications of power. He loved to study the forces of nature, and was one of the first to recognise the part played by ice in sculpting mountains, canyons, and valleys.

In 1870 or 1871 Muir took my father to Clouds Rest, from which lofty outlook he pointed with enthusiasm and conviction to the several channels through which deep rivers of ice had found their way before uniting to form the glacier that had ploughed out and shaped Yosemite Valley. And later, when travelling together in the upper Tuolumne and Mokelumne regions, he often surprised me by the extent of his knowledge of the depth of the former glaciers and the details of ice action in those parts. It is a pity that his early studies of the ancient glaciers of the Sierra were not recorded in permanent form, but a matter of congratulation that his observations of those of Alaska have finally been published.[*]

Muir was a great talker, but not a loud talker. And although he usually monopolised the conversation, he was listened to with attention and often with delight. Like most men who have spent much of their lives in the mountains, he was an independent thinker and had well-digested opinions on a surprisingly large number of topics. He was argumentative by nature, and his Scotch blood showed in the persistence and tenacity with which he upheld his point of view. On the other hand, he was rarely aggressive or disagreeable. In fact, he was one of the most charming companions I have ever known. In addition to a kindly and generous nature, he possessed a keen sense of humour and was something of a tease. When walking the deck of the steamer on the Harriman Alaska Expedition, his most constant companion was the eminent geographer, the late Henry Gannett. Speaking of their friendship, he explained that when he first saw Gannett he was impressed by what he called the ''preternatural solemnity'' of his expression. This, he asserted, with a merry look in his eye, had convinced him that Gannett, like himself, was fond of humour, and he was not long in learning

[*] See *On the Glaciation of the Arctic and Sub-Arctic Regions visited by the United States Steamer "Corwin" in the year of 1881.* In U.S. Senate documents, 48th Congress, 1st Session. Vol. 8, No. 204, pp. 135–147; *Notes on the Pacific Coast Glaciers* in Harriman Alaska Expedition Vol. 1, pp.119–135, 1901. Also in this volume – p.699.

that Gannett, though not a Scotchman, also loved an argument. The result was that the two were always happy together.

Muir abhorred politics, and once, when speaking of a man whom he regarded as having fallen from grace, remarked, "this playing at politics saps the very foundations of righteousness."

As a woodsman he was peculiar, combining an unusual knowledge of forest and mountain with a remarkably slender fund of what is commonly called woodcraft. For, in spite of his having spent a large part of his life in the wilderness, he knew less about camping than almost any man I have ever camped with. He could choose a sheltered spot for the night, was an adept in building a small fire in a safe place, and could make an excellent cup of coffee in his tin cup. But of the art and conveniences of camping as ordinarily understood he was as innocent as a child. His earlier trips in the mountains had been made afoot. He had carried no bed or blanket, and in the way of food only bread and tea, so that his main concern was in finding a protected place, usually a hollow beside a log, where he could spend the night with a minimum of discomfort from the cold. The heat of a small fire, requiring frequent replenishment, served instead of the usual sleeping-bag or blankets.

In after years his visits to the mountains were made with others who looked after the camping. I shall never forget the equipment he brought on his first trip with me into the High Sierra. It was in the late fall, when we were likely to meet a snow-storm at any time. And in fact two such storms overtook us – one in Mokelumne Pass, the other in Mono Pass. Our route lay in the high mountains from Lake Tahoe to Bloody Canyon. The outfit he brought consisted of the clothes he wore and a small leather grip containing a clean shirt, a change of underclothing, and some extra socks. In spite of the lateness of the season, the high altitude, the icy nights, the almost certainty of snowstorms – in spite of all these, he carried not so much as a single blanket!

In reply to my inquiry as to the whereabouts of his bed, he replied that he had tramped the mountains for years, but had never carried one. I was amazed, but the condition confronting us permitted no compromise. I told him, therefore, that, although he had frequently slept on the ground without covering in summer when many years younger, he was too old to do so now, particularly at this late season of the year. I told him also that I had a good sleeping-bag, just big enough for one, with no extra blankets for two, and, further, that it was out of the question for me to set out on such a trip with a companion who had no bed. Recognising the justice of my argument, he compromised by asking "Where can I buy a bed in the mountains?" This problem was soon solved and the trip was carried out as had been planned. It may be added that, although my ground-canvas was a large one and did duty for us both, as we slept close together, yet the severity of the weather was such that he suffered nearly every night from cold. He made no complaint, but was always up and had a small fire burning and coffee brewing before full daylight. The incident is mentioned merely to emphasise a peculiarity of his character – that he rarely made any provision beforehand for his own comfort.

Another marked peculiarity for a woodsman was that he never carried a gun or killed game either for sport or meat, preferring to eat dry bread.

He was a light eater and never seemed really hungry. Even when tired after a long tramp or arduous horseback ride, he would rather talk than eat, and, as many who have camped with him know, he often had to be urged to eat in order that the camp-dishes might be packed to move on. And more than once his companions at the table have quietly taken what was on his plate while he, without noticing what had been done, kept right on talking. I remember an occasion when a plate of fried trout was set before him. It was well in the afternoon, and he had had nothing to eat since a six-o'clock breakfast; he had walked many miles and was tired. Nevertheless, he talked continuously of the forest and mountains through which he had gone, and was utterly oblivious to the fact that his plate was filled and emptied three 'times by his neighbours, while all he had taken was a piece of bread and a cup of coffee. I finally told him that it was time to go, and that if he would stop and eat I would do the talking for a few minutes until he had finished.

Muir was a worker. He felt that he had a task to perform and little time for idling. When in the wilderness he was continually making observations and recording them in his journals. These were usually, sometimes lavishly, illustrated by sketches that served to explain or emphasise the text. When at home he was busy looking after his fruit ranch or engaged in writing, and, as the years went by, the latter occupation consumed most of his time. While he did much writing, as shown by his books and manuscripts, he never did it easily or with pleasure, but from a sense of duty. More than once he spoke to me of the difference in this respect between John Burroughs and himself. Burroughs, he said, never would write except when the mood was on him; then he wrote rapidly, and sent his manuscript to the press with little or no revision, while he (Muir) made it his business to write every day, whether in the mood or not. To him writing was laborious, if not irksome, and much time was spent in smoothing, balancing, paragraphing, and arranging it for the press. He possessed a surprising amount of literary acumen, and usually cut out and trimmed down much that he had written, saying it was a serious error to dwell too long on one detail, that the reader wearied of a single theme, and should be led along by frequent changes. He had never used a stenographer until a few years before his death. When visiting the late E. H. Harriman at his Pelican Bay camp on Klamath Lake, Mr. Harriman had urged him to dictate an outline of his life. This he finally consented to attempt, dictating to one of Mr. Harriman's stenographers. The result formed the basis of his autobiography, since published.

While Muir was a man of marked individuality and pronounced tastes, and while at one period of his life he was much alone, he nevertheless prized congenial companionship and numbered among his friends men eminent in constructive enterprise as well as in art, literature, and science. His most intimate friends perhaps, outside his own family, were the educator John Swett and the painter William Keith. Keith, like himself, was a Scotchman, and the two were great cronies. To hear them spar in their native dialect was a real treat.

How much Muir's life work was influenced by his family it would be hard to say. His wife, who died a few years before he did, was a woman of more than ordinary character and ability. For years she relieved him of most of the cares of the home ranch at Martinez and a thousand and one little things that would have worried him or interrupted his work. She was a clever and noble woman, but so retiring that she was known to only a few. He owed much also to the sympathetic loyalty of his two daughters, Helen and Wanda, who, like their mother, were devoted to him and the work he was doing.

Muir's influence has been a strong factor in the development of our national parks and forests and in their utilisation as camping and recreation grounds, while to the people who could not go his writings have brought from the trees and mountains an inspiration and message of happiness.

PART EIGHT

Personal Recollections of John Muir*

BY SAMUEL MERRILL

Before giving a brief outline of Muir's life and my personal recollections of him, I will speak of an incident which occurred in Giant Forest, Sequoia National Park, as related to me by Judge Stephens, recently presiding judge of the Superior Court of Los Angeles County. About twenty years ago, Judge Stephens and John Muir were visitors in the park at the same time, but were strangers to each other. When Judge Stephens approached the office desk at the lodge in Giant Forest to register his name, he saw the name of John Muir on the line above, and in the column marked residence, Mr. Muir had written "The World." Judge Stephens wrote "Albert Lee Stephens – The Universe" on the line below, and then seated himself at a table in the dining-room. He observed a smile on the face of the desk clerk as she read what had been written on the hotel register, and noticed that she slipped over to Mr. Muir's table to whisper something in his ear. Mr. Muir

---

*   A camp-fire talk at Moraine Lake, July 17th, 1927

left the table and examined the register, and, going to the table where Judge Stephens was seated, introduced himself and insisted that the Judge join his party to see the wonders of the park. Judge Stephens declares that this day spent in the company of the great naturalist proved to be one of the most enjoyable in his life.

As many of you know, John Muir came to this country from Scotland when he was a lad of eleven years. His father settled on a piece of wild land in central Wisconsin. Muir received the usual education afforded by the country schools of those days, which was very limited. He educated himself, however, by reading all the books in his father's home and in the homes of neighbours for miles around. With very little financial assistance from his father, he succeeded by his own efforts in putting himself through the University of Wisconsin, at Madison. While in college he became greatly interested in the science of botany, and on leaving the university he made many extensive trips to nearby states and to Canada to study the flora of these regions. In order to carry on these explorations, he secured work from time to time, and in this way he came to Indianapolis in 1866, when he was twenty-eight years old. He found employment in a wagon factory. There he received a serious injury to one of his eyes. While adjusting a belt, a sharp tool slipped in his hand and pierced his eye, causing temporary blindness in both eyes.

It was at this time that John Muir became known to our family. Professor Butler, of Madison, Wisconsin, one of Muir's teachers at the university, hearing of the accident, wrote to my aunt, Miss Catherine Merrill, asking her to do what she could for the young man. Miss Merrill took charge of the case, employing the best oculist in Indianapolis. It was necessary for Muir to remain in a dark room for many weeks. During this enforced imprisonment, Miss Merrill and her sisters, Mrs. Moores and Mrs. Graydon, gave much of their time in reading to him and in keeping his room supplied with flowers; while my cousin, Katherine Merrill Graydon, to whom I am much indebted for material in this sketch, recalls to this day the wonderful stories he used to tell her. This story-telling ability, in later life, culminated in that classic dog story, *Stickeen*.

When Muir recovered from the injury to his eyes, he made a short excursion on foot to Danville, Illinois, accompanied by one of my cousins, Merrill Moores, a boy of eleven years of age. Five years later this same lad spent six months with Muir in Yosemite Valley, and in later years served his native city of Indianapolis and his country eight years in Congress. While in Congress he asked to be assigned to the committee which considered national park matters, in order that he might advance the causes to which Muir had dedicated his life.

Returning from Danville, Illinois, to Indianapolis, Muir stored the herbarium and notes of his first botanical trips in the attic of my aunt, Mrs. Moores, where they remained for more than a half-century until brought to light and examined by Muir's biographer, Dr. Badè. Saying goodbye to his

Indianapolis friends, Muir set out on that famous thousand-mile hike through the South to Florida. It was his intention to continue the journey to South America, but a fever, contracted in the South, caused him to change his mind and his destination to California.

Arriving in San Francisco by water in the spring of 1868, he lost no time in getting out of the city, headed for Yosemite Valley on foot; not that he had any aversion to San Francisco, but, as he puts it, "I cared not to spend time in a city when I could be in the open and see God making a world." Muir describes his tramp to Yosemite in these words:

> It was one of those perfectly pure, rich, ripe days of California sun gold, where distant views seem as close as near ones, and I have always thanked the Lord that I came here before the dust and smoke of civilization had dimmed the sky and before the wild bloom had vanished from the plain. Descending the Pacheco Pass, I waded out into the marvellous bloom of the San Joaquin, when it was in its prime. It was all one sea of golden and purple bloom, so deep and dense that in walking through it you would press more than a hundred blooms at every step. In this flower-bed five hundred miles long, I used to camp by just lying down wherever night overtook me, as if I had sunk beneath the waters of a lake, the radiant heads of compositae touching each other, ray to ray, shone above me like the thickest star clusters of the sky, and in the morning I sometimes found plants that were new, looking me in the face, so that my botanical studies would begin before I was up.

For the next ten years Muir buried himself in the Yosemite Valley and the High Sierra, living much of the time absolutely alone, in close communion with nature, studying the flowers, trees, and rocks of this region, not that he loved man the less but nature more, as Byron expresses it. During these years Muir gathered the material that later appeared in book and periodical form bringing him fame as an author and making him the foremost defender of the beautiful regions of the state which later became national parks.

Muir's life in the Sierra was interrupted by an eastern trip to his old home and to Indianapolis. Muir consented to give a talk on the mountains and big trees of California at my father's home before a number of invited guests. Although I was only a boy like my young friend Glen Dawson, Muir's visit and talk at our home made a deep impression upon me. I am sure that we all, both grown-up people and children, realised that John Muir was a great man – unlike any man we had ever known before. His language was simple and easily understood by a child, and yet had a charm for the most highly educated.

Years passed before I saw John Muir again. During the years which had elapsed, he had carried on extensive explorations on the Pacific Coast and in Alaska. On my return to California from India, in 1892, I made a pilgrimage to John Muir's ranch near Martinez.

Muir had only recently returned from an expedition to Alaska, and, though but fifty-four years of age at this time, he showed by the lines in his face and his general appearance that he had endured and suffered great hardships and privations. He was glad, however, to make the sacrifice that these trips entailed and did not complain, and referred to it once in this way, saying, "I have made a tramp of myself; I have gone hungry and cold; I have left bloody trails on sharp ice peaks to see the wonders of earth."

In spite of the deep lines in his face, Mr. Muir's personal appearance was most attractive. He was above the average in height, slender, lithe, and active as an Indian. His eyes were as clear and blue as California skies; his head was well shaped and covered with curly brown hair. He was modest in telling of his adventures – adventures which must have tried the soul of the bravest man. No woman could have been more tender than he, particularly to animals. He even went so far as to express regret for having killed a rattlesnake, saying that he hoped the Lord would forgive him for taking the life of a creature loved only by its Maker.

The family at this time consisted of Mr. and Mrs. Muir and their two young daughters, Wanda and Helen. Occasionally at the table were his brother David and wife, who lived on the upper part of the ranch, or friends from San Francisco, Oakland, or Berkeley.

Muir's study, or den, was on the second floor, in the front of the house. He was allowed to have his own way in this particular room and no one dared to put it in order. It was so full of his books, manuscripts, and sketches that it was difficult to find a chair unoccupied. Muir appreciated the best in art, as was evidenced by the pictures on the walls. I particularly recall a fine painting by William Keith on the wall to the right as one entered the study. Mr. Muir showed me many sketches of his recent Alaskan trip, and I realised that he was no mean artist himself. In fact, Muir was very versatile, a man learned in more than one branch of science, particularly in botany and geology, pre-eminent in his specialty of glaciers, a naturalist, a poet who wrote no verse, a great prose writer, a wonderful conversationalist, a natural-born story-teller, a successful farmer and fruit-grower, and an inventor of considerable ability.

Like Dr. Samuel Johnson, John Muir never appeared to better advantage than in conversation, but unfortunately he did not have a Boswell to preserve his sayings for posterity. It was a rare privilege to be included in a group in which Muir was a member. As one friend, in describing Muir's descriptive powers, puts it, "Our foreheads felt the wind and rain." Years ago it was my good fortune to be a visitor in the House of Commons, before Gladstone had retired to private life. An interesting debate was going on. Balfour had spoken on the bill – there was a pause – then the venerable figure of England's great Prime Minister, William E. Gladstone, rose in his place – immediately there was a dead silence. Then on every side of me I heard, "Hush! The old man is going to speak." So it was at Muir's table; whenever the great man was willing to talk, we were all glad to be quiet and listen.

Muir was even more delightful and entertaining in the out-of-doors than he was about the dining-table or in his study. I soon discovered that one must be accurate in statement of facts. One day I told Mr. Muir that I was thankful to be in California, to escape the thunder and lightning storms of India, and I described one particular storm in Calcutta where nearly a foot of water fell in one night and one could lie in bed and view the statues to British soldiers and statesmen on the Maidan by flashes of lightning. He replied, ''Then you have never been in the High Sierra, if you think that we have no electrical storms in California.'' Mr. Muir gave a graphic description of a violent electrical storm which he experienced in the High Sierra when a terrific bolt of lightning struck a lofty pine in front of him, splitting it from top to bottom and throwing out the pieces like spokes of a wagon-wheel.

At another time, while walking with Muir in his cherry orchard, I ventured the remark that all the cherries are alike on these trees and are Royal Anne cherries. ''No, I would not say that. True, they are known commercially as Royal Anne cherries, but in reality the cherries on no two trees in the orchard are alike. They all differ to some extent in size, colour, texture, shape, and flavour, as you will discover when you examine them closely.''

While a party of us were walking over the ranch one day with Muir, some one called his attention to a vigorous young oak tree in the vineyard which was robbing the grapevines near it of necessary nourishment. The vines were sickly in appearance and bearing poorly. Muir stood looking at the tree and vines for a few moments and then said, ''As a farmer, I think that I would be justified in removing this tree.'' Knowing Muir's love of trees, we were all just a little shocked to hear him say this. It proved to us all, however, that Muir was eminently sane in these matters and by no means fanatical in his love of the beautiful in nature. I may add for the benefit of all tree-lovers that, so far as I know, Mr. Muir never carried out his threat of digging out that offending oak tree.

The poetry in Muir's soul constantly expressed itself in his writings and conversation. My cousin, Katherine Merrill Graydon, spent several months on Mr. Muir's ranch teaching his children, Wanda and Helen. Later she secured a position in the Oakland High School, living at the home of Professor McChesney, principal of the school. While planning a party one day, she decided to surprise her guests with some of the delicious peaches from the Muir ranch. She wrote to Mr. Muir for the peaches. The peaches came, but with them a note from Mr. Muir in which he said, ''Why, Katherine, you might as well have asked me to send you a box of dewdrops as to send you a box of peaches and expect them to arrive in the same condition that you had them on the ranch.''

In speaking of India, I told Mr. Muir of the great banyan tree in the botanical gardens of Calcutta, under the boughs of which a regiment of soldiers could assemble without crowding, of the mango and jackfruit trees, of the deodar and teak wood – of the hundreds of varieties of orchids shown every winter in the annual flower show in Calcutta. I asked Mr. Muir if he had ever seen any orchids on his travels up and down the coast. "Yes," he replied; "I met two very rare and beautiful species of orchids in the wilds of British Columbia." I asked him to tell me their names. Mr. Muir answered, "Hush! we won't mention their names, for so rare were they, so delicate, so fragile, and so altogether lovely, that even to pronounce their names might frighten them away."

I am sure that you will pardon me for being proud of the fact that I was a member of Mr. Muir's household when the Sierra Club was born. I recall the day in the summer of 1892 when Mr. Muir returned from San Francisco and announced to us all at the supper table that the Sierra Club had been organised and that he had been chosen its first president. I had never seen Mr. Muir so animated and happy before.

According to the testimony of Lincoln himself, he admits that the happiest day in his life was not, as one might think, when he was elected to Congress, or became President of the United States, or signed the emancipation proclamation, or when he brought the Civil War to a successful conclusion, but, on the contrary, it dated back to the Black Hawk War, when Illinois was on our western frontier. The settlers had gathered together from far and near to take steps to protect their homes from attack by the Indians. The question of a leader came up, and, without a word being said or a vote being taken, the sturdy pioneers formed in a circle about the tall form of the future war President, and Lincoln realised that he had been elected captain.

I know not how the election of John Muir as President of the Sierra Club was conducted, but doubtless it was quite as informal and unanimous as that of Lincoln as captain of his company. As in Lincoln's case, it was not Muir's success as an author, or the honours that were conferred upon him in this country and abroad, that gave him the keenest pleasure, but the happiest day in his life, I venture to say, was the day in San Francisco in the summer of 1892, when he found himself the centre of a devoted and loyal group of citizens who organised themselves into the Sierra Club and made him President.

Up to that time, Muir had been waging a continuous war against selfish commercial interests which would exploit and destroy the forests and beautiful regions of our state and nation, fighting in his early years in the state, almost alone, with his back to the wall – yes, with his back against the granite walls of the Sierra which he loved so well. Is it any wonder, then, that Muir saw in the Sierra Club, the crystallisation of the dreams and labour of a lifetime, an organisation which would carry on the good work for generations yet to come? But an organisation is only what its members make it. Our great leader, after a long life of public service and self-sacrifice, has fallen, like some giant *Sequoia sempervirens* which has gone down before the storm. But, as there springs up around the base of the redwood a circle of vigorous young trees to take its place, so, my friends and fellow members, it devolves upon us to close in and fill up the breach in our ranks caused by the loss of our gallant leader. As we are gathered here about the campfire under the stars and beneath the shadow of these lofty lodgepole pines, let us here and now resolve to be more worthy disciples of this inspiring man.

PART NINE

John Muir, Mountaineer

BY SIR EDWARD PECK

One hundred years ago, in 1894, a book entitled *The Mountains of California* by John Muir was published in the United States. It was a collection of articles which had appeared in American monthly magazines over the previous sixteen years, captivating their mountaineering, and wider, audience. A contemporary reviewer wrote: "We have here nature pure and unadulterated . . . sixteen chapters, each a gem of landscape and animal painting." The writer did not exaggerate; like John Muir's earliest diaries (published as *My First Summer in the Sierra* in 1911), the articles do indeed reflect with vivid freshness Muir's devotion to his beloved Sierra Nevada.

But who was John Muir – this Scotsman who has only recently been recognised in the land of his birth but who has long been a household name in the United States? Perhaps he is best known internationally for his part in inspiring the Californian and Yosemite enthusiasts who, on June 4th, 1892, founded the Sierra Club, of which John Muir became the first President. Though its original remit was limited to the mountain regions of the Pacific Coast, the Sierra Club became America's leading environmental group, with a declared aim "to explore, enjoy and preserve the nation's forests, waters, wildlife and wilderness."

Although John Muir is often thought of exclusively as a conservationist, his interests were, in fact, uniquely wide-ranging. This remarkable Scotsman can be assessed, successively and sometimes simultaneously, as farmhand, inventor, shepherd, sawmill manager, mountain guide, geologist, glaciologist, ornithologist, philosopher, friend of Presidents, founder of the Sierra Club, advocate of the U.S. National Parks concept. But he was, above all, a man whose delight in mountains was all-embracing, and I propose here to consider John Muir primarily as a mountaineer.

Brought up in Dunbar until the age of eleven, when his stern God-fearing father emigrated to the plains of Wisconsin, John Muir did not set eyes on anything resembling a mountain until, in the course of a thousand-mile trek from Canada to Louisiana in 1866–67, he crossed the Unaka hills of the Cumberland range on the Tennessee border. Arriving in San Francisco in 1868, he made for the Sierra Nevada – the 'Range of Light' as he later called it – for his first enthralling visit to Yosemite. The following year (1869) he was fortunate in being engaged as a sheep-herder by one Pat Delaney. Impressed by the intellectual qualities of the young Scot, who had already made a name for himself at Wisconsin University with his inventive gadgets, Delaney agreed that, once Muir had helped the regular shepherd bring the sheep up to the Tuolumne Meadows for the summer grazing, he would be free to roam this wonderful area. His diaries record his early joy and enthusiasm for the mountains. When, in later years, he suffered ill-health or depression in the plains, a trip to the mountains never failed to restore his health and peace of mind. Once, vexed with himself after a minor fall, he addressed his feet severely: "That's what you get by intercourse with stupid town stairs and dead pavements." (One sympathises.) [1]

YOSEMITE

It was during this period that Muir acquired his close knowledge of the upper Tuolumne area and tested his steadiness of head and foot by climbing down the stream that leads to the Upper Yosemite Fall. At the "brink of the tremendous cliff," he took off shoes and stockings, working his way cautiously down "alongside the rushing flood, keeping feet and hands pressed firmly on the polished rock." Beyond the obvious lip of the fall, he found an "irregular flake of rock" which offered a view into the "heart of the snowy, chanting throng of comet-like streamers, into which the body of the fall soon separates." The telling sentence, "I concluded not to venture farther but did nevertheless" betrays the mountaineer's perennial need to 'feed the rat' of excitement. Muir's diary for that day (July 15th) sagely concludes: "Hereafter I'll try to keep from such extravagant, nerve-straining places." [2] But of course he did not and his subsequent solo exploits not only led to a number of close calls but also inspired some fine mountain writing.

The Yosemite valley enthralled Muir for the next five years, working as manager of a sawmill owned by the first innkeeper in the Valley and acting as mountain guide to early tourists, he acquired a deep knowledge of, and feeling for, the plants and birds of Yosemite, the scenery and mountains and the effect of glacial action. He had little patience with young ladies with unsuitable footwear and clothing, or the "blank, fleshly apathy of the ordinary tourist." [3] However, Mrs Jeanne Carr, a friend in San Francisco who knew Muir from his Wisconsin days, sent him a succession of distinguished Americans, including the geologist Joseph LeConte and the great Emerson himself.

While camping in the Upper Tuolumne in 1872, Muir broke away from his companions on a solo mountaineering venture to Mt. Ritter. This involved another close call in high, unexplored mountain country. Frustrated on one face of the mountain, where he found himself in "danger of being shed off like avalanching snow," he crossed the divide into "one of the most exciting pieces of pure wilderness that I ever discovered in all my mountaineering. There loomed the majestic mass of Mount Ritter." There follows a splendid description of the forbidding face, which he surveyed for a possible route. Climbing up into a "wilderness of crumbling spires and battlements", Muir found himself in the sort of situation familiar to many of us: "Having passed several dangerous spots, I dared not think of descending." Higher up, halfway up a cliff with minuscule holds, "I was suddenly brought to a dead stop with arms outspread," Muir recalled. "My doom appeared fixed. I must fall." But "the other self, bygone experience, instinct, or Guardian Angel, call it what you will, came forward and assumed control." His trembling muscles became firm again and, having regained strength, courage and morale, he overcame the bad step and made the first ascent of Mt. Ritter (13,157ft/4010m). Muir's vivid account of that incident, followed by the description of the view south along the range past the Minarets towards Mt. Whitney, belongs to the finest tradition of mountaineering literature.[4] The crest of the Sierra Nevada, along which he was looking to Mt. Whitney (14,494ft /4418m), is now closely followed by the John Muir Trail.

Muir's ascent of Mt. Whitney in October 1873 was made within two months of the four previous parties. It was memorable because, having run out of food while heading for the 'false' Mt. Whitney, Muir returned to Independence (a good deal further away than the present base of Lone Pine) and was back to climb by a difficult route to the summit two days later. "For climbers," he commented, "there is a canyon which comes down from the north shoulder of the Whitney Peak. Well-seasoned limbs will enjoy the climb of 9000 feet required for this direct route, but soft, succulent people should go the mule way."[5]

In his writings on Yosemite, Muir repeatedly referred to 'glaciers' and to the glacial action which formed the domes and canyons of the Yosemite area. Though he counted sixty-five glaciers in his day, many are now no more than névé. But Muir correctly read the signs, noting the striations, moraines and erosion caused by the passage of huge glaciers. His application to Yosemite of the theory of glacial erosion, in which he was supported by the American geologist Joseph LeConte, brought Muir into conflict with the traditional geologists, in particular the prestigious Josiah D.Whitney, who headed the Geological Survey of California in the 1860s. Whitney maintained that the Yosemite gorge had been created by earthquake or volcanic action causing the bottom of the valley floor to 'drop out'. The observations of the brash young Scot, branded as those of an 'ignoramus' and 'sheep herder', were later thoroughly vindicated by the detailed surveys of the French geologist François Matthes.

Among Muir's many climbs in Yosemite was his ascent of Half Dome, 8836ft/2698m, (or, as Muir called it, 'South Dome'), that dramatic, shorn-away dome that has become Yosemite's trade mark. In 1872 the Yosemite trail-builder John Conway had tried, with the help of his sons who "climbed smooth rocks like lizards", to forge by rope, hammer and spikes a way up the east shoulder of the Dome which, as Muir described it, "rises in a graceful curve a few degrees too steep for unaided climbing, besides being defended by overleaning ends of the concentric dome layers of the granite."[1] They failed, but, three years later in 1875, Anderson, the valley blacksmith, forged a set of eye-bolts and drilled his way to the top. Shortly afterwards Muir, though "apprehensive of the slipperiness of the rope and the rock", made his ascent in a "snow-muffled condition"[6] after a November storm. Though disappointed by the flatness of the view, he expressed the hope that no one should implement Anderson's plan to make Half Dome accessible to litter-leaving tourists and to charge for his *via ferrata*. Soon afterwards the latter was partially swept away in a winter snowstorm.

There was a sequel which (though it diverges from the Muir theme) should amuse members of the Alpine Club. In the summer of 1884 a fire was seen on the summit of Half Dome. Fearing a possible accident, a rescue party set out – needlessly, since the two climbers, Alden Sampson (a painter from New York) and Phimister Proctor (a sculptor from Colorado) managed to descend unaided. While making a horseback trip through the area, they had learnt from Galen Clark (the grand old man of Yosemite) that he was waiting for "some member of the English Alpine Club to come over and have the goodness to replace the rope." The pair resolved that "no foreigner will do that job till we have had a try at it." Their method of ascent was to cast a thin, frayed 'picket rope', cowboy fashion, from spike to spike. When the spikes gave out, they roped down to return the following day to complete the climb; this involved standing for over an hour on a two-inch pin while trying to lasso the pin above. Proctor's sketch of himself precariously balanced on one toe above an arch of granite belongs to the collection of Alpine comic horrors.[7]

In his early years in Yosemite John Muir's climbing techniques were scarcely less primitive. Climbing alone, he usually scorned any use of the rope, took a minimal amount of food, and relied on a comfortable pine tree for a bivouac; he seems reluctantly to have admitted that a few hobnails in his boots would help. At the same time, Muir was developing his mountain philosophy and recording in his journals magnificent descriptions of mountain scenery and close observations of trees, birds and animals, in particular his favourites – the Water Ouzel (or Dipper) and the fearless and inquisitive Douglas squirrel. His articles on glacial action, published in *Overland Monthly* 1874–75, were collected as *Studies in the Sierra*.

Muir was naturally driven to expand his mountain experience beyond Yosemite. His first visit to Mt. Shasta (14,162ft / 4317m), the semi-active volcano in North California, was in November 1874, when he enjoyed magnificent views over the clouds while snugly tucked up through successive

Phimister Proctor on Half Dome in 1884 drawn by him from memory in 1945.

storms in his camp on the tree-line. He returned in April 1875 with Jerome Fay, an experienced mountaineer. On the summit ridge a tremendous thunderstorm blew up, followed by a heavy snowstorm. Seeking refuge in the sludge of the hissing and spitting fumaroles, they passed the night broiled on one side and frozen on the other. Stumbling down the next morning, they met their rescue party and were escorted down, not without Muir suffering some permanent physical damage. "A Perilous Night on Shasta's Summit" makes exciting reading as another of Muir's close calls.[8]

Muir's passion for the study of glaciers could not be satisfied among the denuded glaciers of the Sierra Nevada. He wanted to see glaciers on the grand scale and spent three summer seasons – 1879, 1880 and 1890 – on the Pacific coast of the Alaska 'Panhandle', exploring, among others, the glacier that was to bear his name. On the way north, he made the ascent (probably the seventh) of Mount Rainier (14,408ft./4392m.) by the Nisqually and Cowlitz glacier route, which has now become the normal way up this "ice-crowned king of the northwest." Muir was accompanied by a veteran local guide and five ambitious young climbers. He did not find the ascent particularly difficult, though when the crevassed ice became too steep "every one of the party took off his shoes, drove stout steel caulks about half an inch long into them, having brought tools along for the purpose and not having made use of them until now so that the points might not get dulled on the rocks ere the smooth dangerous ice was reached." [9] They also carried 100ft of rope and one axe. The night was spent on a narrow ridge, at a spot now marked as 'Camp Muir' at 10,000ft, somewhat below Gibraltar Rock. All were in "light marching order, save one who pluckily determined to carry his camera to the summit."

ALASKA

On arriving in Alaska, Muir enjoyed the friendship of Samuel Hall Young, the missionary at Fort Wrangell. Their first expedition together, in July 1879, was up the Stickeen (now Stikine) river in the good ship Cassiar with a party of elderly clerics.[10] Muir and Young played truant to climb Glenora Peak. Young was scrambling well and keeping up with Muir until, a few feet below the summit, he slipped above a thousand-foot drop, dislocating both his shoulders (weakened from a previous accident), and was left with his toes scrabbling in slaty grit. With great skill and strength, at one point grabbing Young's shirt collar in his teeth, Muir hauled him to the summit, thereby missing the spectacular sunset he had promised himself. He reset one of Young's shoulders on the spot and escorted him painfully and slowly back to the Cassiar, to endure the reproaches of the clerical party for having gone on a wild-goose chase. [11]

On his return down the Stikine river, Muir made solo surveys of two of the considerable glaciers flowing down into the Stikine gorge – the so-called Dirt Glacier and the Big Stikeen Glacier. After struggling through dense forest and sliding moraine he was thrilled to make his first direct contact with a really extensive glacier – kettle-holes, rumbling stream, crevasses and all – and to stand inside an ice-cave to study the debris accumulated under the ice.[12]

Meanwhile, Hall Young, nothing daunted by his accident, invited Muir to join him on a canoe trip in October 1879 to the glaciers of the Lynn Canal and the Fairweather Range north of Icy Strait. This was intended primarily as a missionary trip to the Tlingit, Chilcat and Hootsenou Indians, some of whom were inclined to Christian virtues, while others preferred the delights of Bacchus (thereby originating the word 'hooch'). The Stickeen Indians, already Christian converts, were reluctant to set off north so late in the year, but Young's missionary zeal, and Muir's eagerness to see even greater glaciers, carried the day. The party sailed up Chatham Strait and, after refuelling at a wooded island in Icy Strait, ventured into what the Indians called Sit-a-kay, (or 'icy bay'). This is Glacier Bay, now accessible to tourist cruise ships for over fifty miles inland. Vancouver, in his careful charting of this coast in 1794, had failed to note this entrance which was entirely filled with ice. Only eighty-five years later, Muir's party navigated twenty-five or more miles of sea before reaching the snout of what was to be known as Muir Glacier. It has since retreated as far again towards the Canadian border. As a result of the advancing winter and the somewhat fearful Indian crew who could not understand why Muir should wish to visit these icy mountains, Muir and Young only spent five days (24th–29th October) in the area on this first visit. This was enough to allow Muir to name the James Geikie and Hugh Miller glaciers, after the Scots geologists of his day, and to climb as high as he could up the sides of the fjord. Through gaps in the mist and rain he obtained views over the huge glaciated expanse of mountains to the west – the Fairweather Range round Mount Crillon.

On their way down the east shore of Glacier Bay, dotted with icebergs, the party obtained the "first broad view of the glacier afterwards to be named the Muir.... The spacious prairie-like glacier with its many tributaries extending far back into the snowy recesses of its fountains made a magnificent display of its wealth and I was strongly tempted to go and explore it at all hazards. But winter had come and the freezing of the fjords was an unsurmountable obstacle."[13]

Back in California, Muir married Louise Strentzel in April 1880, but by October of that year he was already anxious to renew acquaintance with the huge glaciers around Fort Wrangell. On their second expedition, Muir and Young set out on August 10th up Frederick Sound where they first explored by canoe the SE branch, or Endicott Arm, where Muir described the 3500–4000ft "granite walls of the very wildest, surpassing in some ways those of Yosemite." He named the head glacier 'Young Glacier' after his friend, though later geographers have rechristened it 'Dawes'. In the northeast branch, or Tracy arm, they found "stupendous walls of grey granite crowded with bergs from shore to shore with domes as lofty and as perfect in form as those of the California valley," and, at the head, "a deeply and desperately hidden glacier."[14]

Returning to Frederick Sound, they headed west along Icy Strait to Cross Sound and made a base in Taylor Bay, west of the entrance to Glacier Bay and in front of the immense moraine-strewn Taylor Glacier. Muir could not resist a solo expedition on this glacier, setting out on a cold and cloudy day, accompanied by his faithful little dog Stickeen. Moving up the east side of the glacier, he found it easy work crossing the narrow crevasses; he then decided to cross to the west side, enjoying the "lovely colour and music [of the glacier rills] as they glided and swirled in their blue crystal channels and potholes . . . ." Starting back across the glacier at 5 p.m. towards camp about fifteen miles away, he struck a maze of deep and wide crevasses, involving cutting steps across slivers of ice bridges. He flattened these knife-edges to allow Stickeen to follow, but to escape from one particular ice island was only possible "over the very worst of these sliver bridges ... extending in a low, drooping curve like a loose rope." This involved some tricky step-cutting and a lot of coaxing of the little dog, but eventually both reached camp, too tired to sleep and with nightmares about their "dreadful ice bridge in the shadow of death."[15]

Muir was able to persuade the Indian captain, reluctant to endanger his craft close to the calving bergs, to go round into Glacier Bay and let him land near the edge of the Muir Glacier and to camp there for a night or two. On climbing 2500ft up the hill behind, he was able to enjoy in fine weather the splendid sight of Mts Fairweather, La Pérouse and Crillon, and also to study his eponymous glacier. He compared it to a "broad undulating prairie streaked with medial moraines and gashed with crevasses," comprising seven main tributary glaciers from ten to twenty miles long. He boldly claimed that the area "drained by this one grand glacier can hardly be less than seven or eight hundred square miles, and probably contains as much ice as all the eleven hundred Swiss glaciers combined." He observed that "the thundering ice-wall, while comfortably accessible, is also the most strikingly interesting portion of the glacier."[16] In the past 110 years the glacier has continued its retreat up Muir Inlet, and the frontal ice-wall is still magnificent.

Muir was not to return to *his* glacier for another ten years and by the time of his third visit, in 1890, tourist ship excursions were already plying to view this spectacular area. Leaving San Francisco on June 14th, he was able to set up his little base camp on the moraine at the snout of the Muir Glacier by June 23rd. His one-room cabin is now no more than an overgrown heap of stones and the glacier snout is twenty-five miles further inland. Muir's exploratory excursions were largely on his own, and his delight in the glacier and its surroundings shines vividly out of the pages of his diary.[17] The climax was his memorable sled trip up the glacier to survey the seven tributary glaciers he had noted in 1880. He hauled his sled over hummocky ice, crossing "many narrow nerve-trying, ice-sliver bridges, balancing astride and cautiously shoving the sled ahead of me with tremendous chasms on either side." He enjoyed a long spell of fine weather which brought the unexpected discomfort of snow-blindness.[18] This extensive exploration of the Muir Glacier was rounded off by an adventurous canoe trip to the Hugh Miller Inlet. Muir's canoe was nearly nipped between two converging bergs. However, to his intense delight, he enjoyed several splendid displays of *aurora borealis*.[19]

Muir paid two visits to the Arctic. The first was in 1881 when he was invited to join the US naval vessel *Corwin* in the search for the US expedition ship *Jeannette*, which had been caught in the Arctic ice north of the Bering Strait and was drifting across the East Siberian Sea. The Corwin's search did not succeed, as the Jeannette was crushed in the ice in June 1881; some of her crew reached the Siberian mainland near the mouth of the River

Lena. The Corwin voyage, however, did enable Muir to make the first ascent, on July 31st, of Herald Island (now known in Russian as Ostrov Gerald), east of Wrangell Island and some 450 miles northwest of the Bering Straits. The impetuous crew (no mountaineers, they) were anxious to get ashore on the steep-sided island, pronounced inaccessible by its discoverer, Kellett, in 1849. They rushed up a steep gully, dislodging rocks on themselves. Muir, as Captain Hooper reported, came over, axe in hand, and ''with the practised eye of an experienced mountaineer, selected a steep bank of frozen snow and ice at an angle of 50°, deliberately commenced cutting steps and ascended the ice-cliff.'' Muir found an easy way to the top and spent the arctic midnight on the summit where he observed signs of glacial striation, proving that the hard granite of this ''fine glacial monument'' had resisted the pressure of the northern ice sheet.[15]

Muir's final visit to Alaska and the Arctic was in much plushier circumstances, when his conservation activities had made him a national figure. Invited, along with twenty-five leading American scientists, to join Edward H. Harriman's 1899 Alaska expedition in the railroad king's own steamer, Muir was able to point out and explain the Alaskan glaciers he knew so well.

LATER LIFE

Muir had spent most of the years from 1881 to 1889 rearing a family, managing his father-in-law's California fruit farm and starting some of his writing projects, based on his vividly written diaries. It was during this period that he began to take a keen interest in the conservation of wild areas. With others, he founded the Sierra Club in 1892 – the first and leading mountain club of the United States – and took an active part in the National Parks debate. This was another fascinating aspect of Muir's life, which there is no space to describe here save for one highlight. This was a four-day private visit to the Yosemite valley which President Theodore Roosevelt agreed to make alone with Muir (without the usual journalists and others associated with Presidential tours). They visited Glacier Point and camped below the Bridal Veil fall. Muir convinced the President of the need for conservation of the natural beauties of the U.S., especially its trees and mountains, by a policy of Federal National Parks. Would that mountain diplomacy could nowadays be conducted on such intimate terms with a Head of State!

In his later years, Muir, having achieved fame and a modicum of wealth, travelled to Scotland and the Alps in 1893 and to the foot of the Himalaya in 1902. Though tempted by the Alps, he achieved nothing higher than a view of the Matterhorn from the Gornergrat. In 1911, aged 73, he visited South America and went high in the Andes in search of the monkey-puzzle tree. He travelled thence to Southern and to East Africa where, though he did not see the Ruwenzori, he may have sighted the equatorial snows of Kilimanjaro or Mount Kenya.

Revered as a national figure in the U.S.A., John Muir received scant recognition in his native Scotland or, indeed, in Britain until the foundation of the John Muir Trust in 1982 by a distinguished group of Muir enthusiasts. The Trust has acquired three fine mountain wilderness properties in Scotland in his memory. The first covers Li and Coire Dhorcaill, on the north side of Ladhar Bheinn on Knoydart peninsula; the second is at Torrin, on the southwest coast of Skye, including part of the east slope of the Black Cuillin; and the third, acquired in 1993, is the remote and desolately beautiful Sandwood Bay, on the northwest coast of Scotland twelve miles south of Cape Wrath, with its prominent sea-stack Am Buachaille and tales of a haunting mermaid.

John Muir died in his California home on December 24th, 1914, much venerated as the "patriarch of American lovers of mountains" and, as James Bryce wrote at the time, "one who had not only a passion for the splendours of nature, but a wonderful power of interpreting her to men."

REFERENCES

1   Letter to Jeanne Carr, presented as 'A Geologist's Winter Walk', Chapter 2 of *Steep Trails*.*
2   From Chapter 5 of *My First Summer in the Sierra.* *
3   Letter to Jeanne Carr, quoted in Margaret P. Sanborn's *Yosemite, its Discovery, its Wonders and its People*, p.116 (Random House, New York, 1981).
4   'A Near View of the High Sierra', Chapter 4 in *The Mountains of California.**
5   Quoted in Francis P.Farquhar's *History of the Sierra Nevada* (University of California Press, Berkeley and Los Angeles, 1965).
6   'The South Dome', Chapter 10 in *The Yosemite.**
7   *History of the Sierra Nevada* pp 192–194.
8   From 'Mount Shasta', Muir's fourth chapter in *Picturesque California*, reprinted in *Steep Trails*.*
9   From 'Washington and Puget Sound', Muir's fifth chapter in *Picturesque California* and reprinted in *Steep Trails*.*
10   Two accounts: Samuel Hall Young's *Alaska Days with John Muir* (pp.631–636 in this book); 'The Stickeen River', Chapter 4 in *Travels in Alaska.* *
11   'Glenora Peak', Chapter 7 in *Travels in Alaska.* *
12   'Exploration of the Stickeen Glaciers', Chapter 8 in *Travels in Alaska.* *
13   'The Discovery of Glacier Bay', Chapter 10 in *Travels in Alaska* *.
14   'Sum Dum Bay', Chapter 14 in *Travels in Alaska.* *
15   'From Taku to Taylor Bay', Chapter 15 from *Travels in Alaska.* *
16   'Glacier Bay', Chapter 16 in *Travels in Alaska.* *
17   'In Camp at Glacier Bay', Chapter 17 in *Travels in Alaska.* *
18   'My Sled Trip on the Muir Glacier', Chapter 18 in *Travels in Alaska.* *
19   'Auroras', Chapter 19 in *Travels in Alaska.* *
20   'First Ascent of Herald Island', Chapter 13 from *The Cruise of the Corwin* (pp. 792–795 in this book).

*   These books by John Muir, or compiled from his writings, are collected in *John Muir – The Eight Wilderness-Discovery Books* (Diadem, 1992).

DESCENT FROM INSPIRATION POINT.

INDEX

for THE LIFE AND LETTERS OF JOHN MUIR

Abridged from the first edition; with selected references from the rest of the omnibus.

(Italicised text is used for the additional page references and book titles, poems, newspapers, magazines and ships names. Magazine and journal articles etc. are shown within inverted commas.)